The Leibniz–Caroline–Clarke
Correspondence

The Leibniz–Caroline–Clarke Correspondence

Edited and Translated by
GREGORY BROWN

OXFORD
UNIVERSITY PRESS

Great Clarendon Street, Oxford, OX2 6DP,
United Kingdom

Oxford University Press is a department of the University of Oxford.
It furthers the University's objective of excellence in research, scholarship,
and education by publishing worldwide. Oxford is a registered trade mark of
Oxford University Press in the UK and in certain other countries

© Gregory Brown 2023

The moral rights of the author have been asserted

All rights reserved. No part of this publication may be reproduced, stored in
a retrieval system, or transmitted, in any form or by any means, without the
prior permission in writing of Oxford University Press, or as expressly permitted
by law, by licence or under terms agreed with the appropriate reprographics
rights organization. Enquiries concerning reproduction outside the scope of the
above should be sent to the Rights Department, Oxford University Press, at the
address above

You must not circulate this work in any other form
and you must impose this same condition on any acquirer

Published in the United States of America by Oxford University Press
198 Madison Avenue, New York, NY 10016, United States of America

British Library Cataloguing in Publication Data
Data available

Library of Congress Control Number: 2022950600

ISBN 978–0–19–287092–6

Printed and bound in the UK by
Clays Ltd, Elcograf S.p.A.

Links to third party websites are provided by Oxford in good faith and
for information only. Oxford disclaims any responsibility for the materials
contained in any third party website referenced in this work.

J'espère que S. A. R. ne nous aura point abandonnés entièrement pour les Anglois, ni voulu diminuer ses bontés pour nous par le partage. Comme le soleil ne luit pas moins à chacun, pour luire à plusieurs. V. E. qui nous appartient aura soin de nous à cet égard, et j'espère que vous voudrez, madame, me protéger en particulier contre les mauvais effets de l'absence, que je n'ai que trop de sujet de craindre.

    —Leibniz's letter to Johanne Sophie of 29 January 1715 (document 63)

Vous estes ferme et constante dans les choses grandes et importantes, mais je dois craindre, madame, que vous ne le soyez pas également dans les petites, comme doit être à votre garde tout ce qui a rapport à moi, et particulièrement la version de la Théodicée.

    —Leibniz's letter to Caroline of 28 April 1716 (document 113)

Mais d'où vient que vous me soupçonnez de n'être la même pour vous?

    —Caroline's letter to Leibniz of 5 May 1716 (document 115)

[…] V. A. Royale a paru un peu chancelante, non pas dans sa bonne volonté à mon égard, mais peut-être dans sa bonne opinion de moi et de mes opinions, surtout depuis qu'il semble que la version de la Théodicée demeure en arrière.

    —Leibniz's letter to Caroline of 12 May 1716 (document 117a)

Vous me trouverez malgré vos soupçons toujours la même.

    —Sign-off, Caroline's letter to Leibniz of 15 May 1716 (document 119)

Je chercherai avec empressement les occasions à vous marquer que je suis toujours la même.

    —Sign-off, Caroline's letter to Leibniz of 26 June 1716 (document 128)

[…] et vous me trouverez toujours la même.

    —Sign-off, Caroline's letter to Leibniz of
6 October 1716 (document 151)

[…] et je serais toujours la même pour vous.

    —Sign-off, Caroline's letter to Leibniz of
29 October 1716 (document 156)

Vous me trouverez comme toujours la même personne qui vous estime infiniment.

    —Sign-off, Caroline's last letter to Leibniz,
4 November 1716 (document 158)

Hence these tears.

    —A. Rupert Hall, *Philosophers at War*, p. 9

Contents

Acknowledgements	xvii
List of Abbreviations	xix
Preface	xxiii
Introduction	xxxv

1710–1712

1. *Essais de Théodicée sur la Bonté de Dieu, la Liberté de l'Homme et l'Origine du Mal: Discours de la Conformité de la Foy avec la Raison* §§ 18–19 (1710)   2

2. Leibniz to Nicolaas Hartsoeker (10 February 1711)   5

3. Isaac Newton's Unpublished Draft Letter to the Editor of the *Memoirs of Literature* (1712)   17

1714

4. Andreas Gottlieb von Bernstorff to Leibniz (3 March 1714)   25

5. John Chamberlayne to Leibniz (10 March 1714)   27

6. Leibniz to Andreas Gottlieb von Bernstorff (21 March 1714)   29

7. Leibniz to John Chamberlayne (21 April 1714)   29

8. Isaac Newton to John Chamberlayne (22 May 1714)   35

9. John Chamberlayne to Isaac Newton (31 May 1714)   37

10. Leibniz to Sophie of the Palatinate, Dowager Electress of Braunschweig-Lüneburg (24 May 1714)   39

11. Leibniz to Caroline of Brandenburg-Ansbach, Electoral Princess of Braunschweig-Lüneburg (24 May 1714)   45

12. Queen Anne to Sophie of the Palatinate, Dowager Electress of Braunschweig-Lüneburg (30 May 1714)   49

13. Queen Anne to Georg Ludwig, Elector of Braunschweig-Lüneburg (30 May 1714)   49

14. Queen Anne to Georg August, Electoral Prince of Braunschweig-Lüneburg (30 May 1714)   51

viii CONTENTS

15. Caroline of Brandenburg-Ansbach, Electoral Princess of
Braunschweig-Lüneburg, to Leibniz (7 June 1714)   53

16. Johanne Sophie, Gräfin (Countess) zu Schaumburg-Lippe,
to Baroness Mary Cowper (12 June 1714)   57

17. Benedictus Andreas Caspar de Nomis to Leibniz (13 June 1714)   61

18. Leibniz to Caroline of Brandenburg-Ansbach, Electoral
Princess of Braunschweig-Lüneburg (16 June 1714)   67

19. Leibniz to Caroline of Brandenburg-Ansbach, Electoral
Princess of Braunschweig-Lüneburg (7 July 1714)   73

20. John Chamberlayne to Leibniz (11 July 1714)   77

21. Johanne Sophie, Gräfin (Countess) zu Schaumburg-Lippe,
to Louise, Raugravine Palatine (12 July 1714)   79

22. Caroline of Brandenburg-Ansbach, Electoral Princess of
Braunschweig-Lüneburg, to Baroness Mary Cowper
(13 July 1714)   87

23a. John Chamberlayne to Leibniz (7 August 1714)   91

23b. Enclosure: Extract from the Journal of the Royal Society
(20 May 1714)   91

23c. Enclosure: Copy of a letter from John Keill to John
Chamberlayne (20 July 1714)   93

24. Benedictus Andreas Caspar de Nomis to Leibniz (19 August 1714)   93

25. Leibniz to Andreas Gottlieb von Bernstorff (22 August 1714)   97

26. Philipp Ludwig Wenzel von Sinzendorff to Johann Caspar
von Bothmer (4 September 1716)   99

27. Philipp Ludwig Wenzel von Sinzendorff to Friedrich Wilhelm
von Görtz (4 September 1714)   99

28. Philipp Ludwig Wenzel von Sinzendorff to Leibniz
(8 September 1714)   101

29. Leibniz to the Dowager Empress Wilhelmine Amalie of
Braunschweig-Lüneburg (16 September 1714)   101

30. Leibniz to Charlotte Elisabeth von Klenk (16 September 1714)   105

31. Leibniz to Georg August, Prince of Wales (17 September 1714)   107

32. Leibniz to Andreas Gottlieb von Bernstorff (20 September 1714)   109

33. Leibniz to Ernst Friedrich von Windischgrätz (20 September 1714)   113

34. Leibniz to Philipp Ludwig Wenzel von Sinzendorff (20 September 1714)   119

35. Leibniz to Claude Alexandre de Bonneval (21 September 1714)   121

CONTENTS ix

36. Leibniz to Johann Matthias von der Schulenburg
(30 September 1714) — 125

37. Leibniz to Eléonore Desmiers d'Olbreuse, Dowager
Duchess of Celle (3 October 1714) — 127

38. Leibniz to Caroline of Brandenburg-Ansbach, Princess of
Wales (3 October 1714) — 129

39. Claude Alexandre de Bonneval to Leibniz (6 October 1714) — 135

40. Leibniz to Johann Matthias von der Schulenburg (7 October 1714) — 139

41. Leibniz to Johann Matthias von der Schulenburg
(12 October 1714) — 141

42. Leibniz to Andreas Gottlieb von Bernstorff (14 October 1714) — 143

43. Johann Matthias von der Schulenburg to Leibniz (15 October 1714) — 147

44. Leibniz to Charlotte Elisabeth von Klenk (16 October 1714) — 147

45. Leibniz to Claude Alexandre de Bonneval (Beginning of
November 1714) — 151

46. Andreas Gottlieb von Bernstorff to Leibniz (1 November 1714) — 163

47. Andreas Gottlieb von Bernstorff to Leibniz (24 November 1714) — 165

48. Leibniz to Johann Matthias von der Schulenburg (3 December 1714) — 167

49. Leibniz to Andreas Gottlieb von Bernstorff (8 December 1714) — 169

50. Leibniz to Caroline of Brandenburg-Ansbach, Princess of
Wales (8 December 1714) — 175

51. Leibniz to Caroline of Brandenburg-Ansbach, Princess of Wales
(18 December 1714) — 179

52. Caroline of Brandenburg-Ansbach, Princess of Wales, to Leibniz
(28 December 1714) — 185

53. Leibniz to Andreas Gottlieb von Bernstorff (28 December 1714) — 187

54. Leibniz to Johanne Sophie, Gräfin (Countess) zu
Schaumburg-Lippe (28 December 1714) — 187

55. Leibniz to Friedrich Wilhelm von Görtz (28 December 1714) — 189

1715

56. Isaac Newton: *An Account of the Book entitled* Commercium Epistolicum
Collinii & aliorum, De Analysi promota; *published by order of the
Royal-Society, in relation to the Dispute between Mr.* Leibnitz *and
Dr. Keill, about the Right of Invention of the Method of* Fluxions, *by some
call'd* the Differential Method (February 1715) — 195

57.	Some Remarks by Leibniz on Roberval, Descartes, and Newton (1715?)	201
58.	Leibniz to Caroline of Brandenburg-Ansbach, Princess of Wales (Beginning of January 1715)	201
59.	Nicolas Rémond to Leibniz (9 January 1715)	205
60.	Caroline of Brandenburg-Ansbach, Princess of Wales, to Leibniz (16 January 1715)	207
61.	Leibniz to Nicolas Rémond (27 January 1715)	207
62.	Leibniz to Caroline of Brandenburg-Ansbach, Princess of Wales (29 January 1715)	209
63.	Leibniz to Johanne Sophie, Gräfin (Countess) zu Schaumburg-Lippe (29 January 1715)	211
64.	Caroline of Brandenburg-Ansbach, Princess of Wales, to Leibniz (12 February 1715)	213
65.	George Smalridge, Bishop of Bristol, to Caroline of Brandenburg-Ansbach, Princess of Wales (15 March 1715)	215
66.	Leibniz to Andreas Gottlieb von Bernstorff (15 March 1715)	221
67a.	Leibniz to Caroline of Brandenburg-Ansbach, Princess of Wales (29 March 1715)	225
67b.	Enclosure: Leibniz to Caroline of Brandenburg-Ansbach, Princess of Wales (29 March 1715)	227
68.	Nicolas Rémond to Leibniz (1 April 1715)	231
69.	Andreas Gottlieb von Bernstorff to Leibniz (5 April 1715)	231
70.	Leibniz to Johann Bernoulli (9 April 1715)	233
71.	Henriette Charlotte von Pöllnitz to Leibniz (c.10 May 1715)	235
72.	Leibniz to Caroline of Brandenburg-Ansbach, Princess of Wales (10 May 1715)	237
73.	Leibniz to Charlotte Elisabeth von Klenk (28 June 1715)	243
74.	Leibniz to Dowager Empress Wilhelmine Amalie of Braunschweig-Lüneburg (28 June 1715)	245
75.	Charlotte Elisabeth von Klenk to Leibniz (6 July 1715)	249
76.	Leibniz to Caroline of Brandenburg-Ansbach, Princess of Wales (3 August 1715)	253
77.	Leibniz to Louis Bourguet (5 August 1715)	255
78.	Caroline of Brandenburg-Ansbach, Princess of Wales, to Leibniz (13 September 1715)	265

CONTENTS xi

79a. Nicolas Rémond to Leibniz (18 October 1715) — 269

79b. Enclosure: Extracts from letters of Antonio Schinella Conti to Nicolas Rémond Concerning Newton (30 June, 12 July, and 30 August 1715) — 269

79c. Enclosure: Antonio Schinella Conti to Leibniz (April 1715) — 275

80. Leibniz to Caroline of Brandenburg-Ansbach, Princess of Wales (21 October 1715) — 279

81. Leibniz to Johanne Sophie, Gräfin (Countess) zu Schaumburg-Lippe (21 October 1715) — 285

82. Leibniz to Caroline of Brandenburg-Ansbach, Princess of Wales (not sent) (late October to mid-to-late December 1715) — 289

83. Charlotte Elisabeth von Klenk to Leibniz (13 November 1715) — 293

84. Caroline of Brandenburg-Ansbach, Princess of Wales, to Leibniz (14 November 1715) — 297

85. Leibniz to Caroline of Brandenburg-Ansbach, Princess of Wales (Late November 1715) — 303

86. Leibniz's First Paper (Late November 1715) — 317

87. Leibniz to Johann Bernoulli (December 1715) — 319

88a. Leibniz to Nicolas Rémond (6 December 1715) — 321

88b. Enclosure: Leibniz to Antonio Schinella Conti (6 December 1715) — 323

88c. Leibniz to Nicolas Rémond (early December 1715) — 331

89. Caroline of Brandenburg-Ansbach, Princess of Wales, to Leibniz (6 December 1715) — 333

90. First Reply of Samuel Clarke (*c.*6 December 1715) — 339

91. Leibniz to Caroline of Brandenburg-Ansbach, Princess of Wales (Mid-to-late December 1715) — 343

92. Leibniz's Second Paper (Mid-to-late December 1715) — 355

93. Leibniz to William Winde (23 December 1715) — 361

94. Leibniz to Christian Wolff (23 December 1715) — 367

1716

95. Caroline of Brandenburg-Ansbach, Princess of Wales, to Leibniz (10 January 1716) — 373

96. Second Reply of Samuel Clarke (*c.*10 January 1716) — 379

97. Leibniz to Caroline of Brandenburg-Ansbach, Princess of Wales (*c.*14 January 1714) — 385

xii CONTENTS

98. Leibniz to Louis Bourguet (24 February 1716) — 399

99. Leibniz to Caroline of Brandenburg-Ansbach, Princess of Wales (25 February 1716) — 407

100. Leibniz's Third Paper (*c*.25 February 1716) — 409

101a. Isaac Newton to Antonio Schinella Conti (*c*.8 March 1716) — 417

101b. Isaac Newton to Antonio Schinella Conti (*c*.8 March 1716) — 419

101c. Isaac Newton to Antonio Schinella Conti (*c*.8 March 1716) — 421

101d. Isaac Newton to Antonio Schinella Conti (*c*.8 March 1716) — 429

101e. Isaac Newton to Antonio Schinella Conti (*c*.8 March 1716 — 433

101f. Isaac Newton to Antonio Schinella Conti (*c*.8 March 1716) — 435

101g. Isaac Newton to Antonio Schinella Conti (17 March 1716) — 437

102. Nicolas Rémond to Leibniz (15 March 1716) — 445

103. Louis Bourguet to Leibniz (16 March 1716) — 445

104. Antonio Schinella Conti to Leibniz (26 March 1716) — 453

105. Leibniz to Nicolas Rémond (27 March 1716) — 457

106. Louis Bourguet to Leibniz (31 March 1716) — 461

107. Leibniz to Louis Bourguet (3 April 1716) — 463

108. Leibniz to Antonio Schinella Conti (9 April 1716) — 469

109. Leibniz to Nicolas Rémond (9 April 1716) — 491

110. Leibniz to Johann Bernoulli (13 April 1716) — 493

111. Leibniz to Caroline of Brandenburg-Ansbach, Princess of Wales (14 April 1716) — 495

112. Leibniz to Louis Bourguet (20 April 1716) — 499

113. Leibniz to Caroline of Brandenburg-Ansbach, Princess of Wales (28 April 1716) — 501

114. Leibniz to Johann Caspar von Bothmer (28 April 1716) — 503

115. Caroline of Brandenburg-Ansbach, Princess of Wales, to Leibniz (5 May 1716) — 513

116. Johann Caspar von Bothmer to Leibniz (5 May 1716) — 519

117a. Leibniz to Caroline of Brandenburg-Ansbach, Princess of Wales (12 May 1716) — 521

117b. Leibniz to Caroline of Brandenburg-Ansbach, Princess of Wales (P.S.) (12 May 1716) — 529

118.	Louis Bourguet to Leibniz (15 May 1716)	531
119.	Caroline of Brandenburg-Ansbach, Princess of Wales, to Leibniz (15 May 1716)	535
120.	Third Reply of Samuel Clarke (*c*.15 May 1716)	539
121.	Johann Bernoulli to Leibniz (20 May 1716)	545
122.	Caroline of Brandenburg-Ansbach, Princess of Wales, to Leibniz (26 May 1716)	549
123.	Johann Caspar von Bothmer to Leibniz (29 May 1716)	555
124.	Leibniz to Caroline of Brandenburg-Ansbach, Princess of Wales (2 June 1716)	557
125a.	Leibniz's Fourth Paper (*c*.2 June 1716)	563
125b.	Leibniz's Proposed Additions to his Fourth Paper (*c*.2 June 1716)	573
126.	Leibniz to John Arnold (5 June 1716)	577
127.	Leibniz to Johann Bernoulli (7 June 1716)	579
128.	Caroline of Brandenburg-Ansbach, Princess of Wales, to Leibniz (26 June 1716)	583
129.	Fourth Reply of Samuel Clarke (*c*.26 June 1716)	591
130.	Leibniz to Henriette Charlotte von Pöllnitz (30 June 1716)	605
131.	Leibniz to Louis Bourguet (2 July 1716)	607
132.	Johann Caspar von Bothmer to Leibniz (10 July 1716)	609
133.	Johann Bernoulli to Leibniz (14 July 1716)	611
134.	Pierre Des Maizeaux to Philipp Heinrich Zollmann (14 July 1716)	613
135.	Leibniz to Caroline of Brandenburg-Ansbach, Princess of Wales (31 July 1716)	613
136.	Leibniz to Robert Erskine (Areskin) (3 August 1716)	623
137.	Johann Caspar von Bothmer to Leibniz (11 August 1716)	625
138.	Leibniz to Nicolas Rémond (15 August 1716)	627
139.	Leibniz to Caroline of Brandenburg-Ansbach, Princess of Wales (18 August 1716)	629
140a.	First Draft of Leibniz's Fifth Paper (*c*.18 August 1716)	633
140b.	Leibniz's Fifth Paper (*c*.18 August 1716)	661
141.	Leibniz to Pierre Des Maizeaux (21 August 1716)	715

xiv CONTENTS

142. Caroline of Brandenburg-Ansbach, Princess of Wales, to Leibniz
(1 September 1716) — 719

143. Caroline of Brandenburg-Ansbach, Princess of Wales, to Leibniz
(8 September 1716) — 725

144. Leibniz to Caroline of Brandenburg-Ansbach, Princess of Wales
(11 September 1716) — 727

145. Leibniz to Dowager Empress Wilhelmine Amalie of Braunschweig-
Lüneburg (20 September 1716) — 733

146. Leibniz to Charlotte Elisabeth von Klenk (20 September 1716) — 739

147. Leibniz to George Cheyne (25 September 1716) — 739

148. Charlotte Elisabeth von Klenk to Leibniz (30 September 1716) — 741

149. Leibniz to Caroline of Brandenburg-Ansbach, Princess of Wales
(End of September to mid-October 1716) — 743

150. Nicolas Rémond to Leibniz (2 October 1716) — 749

151. Caroline of Brandenburg-Ansbach, Princess of Wales, to Leibniz
(6 October 1716) — 751

152. Caroline of Brandenburg-Ansbach, Princess of Wales, to Leibniz
(9 October 1716) — 753

153. Leibniz to Nicolas Rémond (19 October 1716) — 757

154. Leibniz to Johann Bernoulli (23 October 1716) — 759

155. Johann Caspar von Bothmer to Leibniz (27 October 1716) — 761

156. Caroline of Brandenburg-Ansbach, Princess of Wales, to Leibniz
(29 October 1716) — 763

157. Fifth Reply of Samuel Clarke (*c.* 29 October 1716) — 763

158. Caroline of Ansbach, Princess of Wales, to Leibniz
(4 November 1716) — 801

159. Johann Bernoulli to Leibniz (11 November 1716) — 803

160. Antonio Schinella Conti to Isaac Newton (10 December 1716) — 805

161. A Note by Isaac Newton Concerning his Dispute with Leibniz
(after 10 December 1716) — 809

1717–1718

162. Dedication and Advertisement to the Reader, Clarke's 1717
edition of the Correspondence (1717) — 813

163. Clarke's Appendix to his 1717 edition of the Correspondence (1717) — 819

CONTENTS XV

164. Isaac Newton to Pierre Des Maizeaux (*c.*August 1718)   835

165. Isaac Newton to Pierre Des Maizeaux (*c.*August 1718)   837

Starred References   839
Bibliography   873
Name Index   879
Subject Index   888

Acknowledgements

I would like to thank the staff at the Gottfried Wilhelm Leibniz Bibliothek in Hanover—especially Anja Fleck and Anke Hölzer—to whom I am grateful for helping me locate and secure copies of a number of the documents included in this volume. Thanks go as well to the many other librarians and archivists from across Europe and England who provided me with copies of documents for this volume. But above all I wish to express my thanks and deep gratitude to Dr Nora Gädeke, Wissenschaftliche Mitarbeiterin with the Leibniz-Archiv and Schriftführerin of the Gottfried Wilhelm Leibniz Gesellschaft, who was tireless in providing me with helpful suggestions about textual matters, and without whose generous help I would have been unable to secure copies of a number of important documents for this volume that were held by some of the noble families of the former German aristocracy.

List of Abbreviations

A	Leibniz, G. W. *Sämtliche Schriften und Briefe*. Edited by the Academy of Sciences of Berlin. Series I–VIII. Darmstadt, Leipzig, Berlin: 1923 ff. Cited by series, volume, and page.
AAK	*Briefe von Christian Wolff aus den Jahren 1719–1753. Ein Beitrag zur Geschicte der Kaiserlichen Akademie der Wissenschaften zu St. Petersburg.* Edited by Arist Aristovich Kunik (Ernst Eduard Kunik). St Petersburg: Eggers (and Leipzig: Leopold Voss) in Commission der Kaiserlichen Akademie der Wissenschaften.
AG	*G. W. Leibniz: Philosophical Essays*. Edited and translated by R. Ariew and D. Garber. Indianapolis: Hackett, 1989.
AT	*Oeuvres de Descartes*. Edited by Charles Adam and Paul Tannery. 11 vols. Paris: Vrin, 1974–1989.
Bodemann-BR	*Der Briefwechsel des Gottfried Wilhelm Leibniz in der Königlichen Bibliothek zu Hannover*. Edited by Eduard Bodemann. Hanover, 1889. Reprint, Hildesheim: Olms, 1966.
Bodemann-HS	*Die Leibniz-Handschriften der Königlichen öffentlichen Bibliothek zu Hannover*. Edited by Eduard Bodemann. Hanover and Leipzig, 1895. Reprint, Hildesheim: Olms, 1966.
CHH	*The History of Parliament: the House of Commons 1690-1715. Edited by Eveline Cruickshanks, Stuart Handley, and David W. Hayton. 5 vols. Cambridge: Cambridge University Press, 2002. Cited by volume and page.*
Dutens	Leibniz, G. W. *Opera omini, nunc primum collecta, in classes distributa, praefationibus et indicibus exornata*. Edited by Ludovici Dutens. 6 vols. Geneva: De Tournes, 1768; reprint Hildesheim Georg Olms, 1989. Cited by volume and page.
Erdmann	Leibniz, G. W. *Opera philosophica quae extant Latina Gallica Germanica omnia*. Edited by J. E. Erdmann. Berlin, 1839–1840.
FC	*Oeuvres de Leibniz*. Edited by Louis-Alexandre Foucher de Careil. 7 vols. Paris: Firmin Dido frères, fils et Cie, 1861–1875.
FXF	*Biographie Universelle, ou Dictionnaire Historique des Hommes qui se sont fait un Nom par leur Génie, leurs Talens, leurs Vertus, leurs Erreurs ou leurs Crimes. Tome Troisième. 13 vols. Edited by François-Xavier Feller* and François Marie Pérennès. Paris: Gauthier Frères et Cie. Paris: Gauthier, 1833–1838. Cited by volume and page.
GB	*Der Briefwechsel von Gottfried Wilhelm Leibniz mit Mathematikern.* Edited by C. I. Gerhardt. Berlin: Mayer & Müller, 1899.
GLW	*Briefwechsel zwischen Leibniz und Christiaan Wolff*. Edited by C. I. Gerhardt. Halle: H. W. Schmidt, 1860.

xx   LIST OF ABBREVIATIONS

GM   *Leibnizens mathematische Schriften.* Edited by C. I. Gerhardt. 7 vols. Berlin – Halle: A. Asher - H. W. Schmidt, 1849–1863. Cited by volume and page.

GP   *Die philosophischen Schriften von Gottfried Wilhelm Leibniz.* 7 vols. Berlin, 1875–1890. Cited by volume and page.

H   *Theodicy: Essays on the Goodness of God, the Freedom of Man, and the Origin of Evil.* Translated by E. M. Huggard. LaSalle, IL.: Open Court, 1985.

HALS   Hertfordshire Archives and Local Studies (Hertford, England).

HC   *The Encyclopædia Britannica.* Edited by Hugh Chisholm. 11th edn. 28 vols. Cambridge: Cambridge University Press, 1910. Cited by volume and page.

HGA   *The Leibniz-Clarke Correspondence.* Edited with introduction and notes by H. G. Alexander. New York: Manchester University Press, 1956.

JGHF   *Commercii epistolici typis nondum vulgati selecta specimina.* Edited by Johann Georg Heinrich Feder. Hannover: Gebrüder Hahn, 1805.

JHC   *Journals of the House of Commons.* Reprinted by order of the House of Commons, 1803. Cited by volume and page.

JK   *Neue Beiträge zum Briefwechsel zwischen D. E. Jablonsky und G. W. Leibniz.* Edited by J. Kvacala. Jurjew (Dorpat): C. Mattiesen, 1899.

Kemble   *State Papers and Correspondence Illustrative of the Social and Political State of Europe from the Revolution to the Accession of the House of Hanover.* Edited by John M. Kemble. London: John W. Parker and Son, 1857.

Klopp   *Die Werke von Leibniz Erste Reihe. Historisch-politische und staatswissenschaftliche Schriften.* Edited by Onno Klopp. 11 vols. Hannover, 1864–84. Reprint, New York: Georg Olms Verlag, 1973.

L   *Gottfried Wilhelm Leibniz: Philosophical papers and letters.* Edited and translated by Leroy E. Loemker. 2nd edn. Dordrecht and Boston: Reidel, 1969.

LBr   Leibniz-Briefwechsel. Hanover, Gottfried Wilhelm Leibniz Bibliothek-Niedersächsische Landesbibliothek.

LDB   *The Leibniz-Des Bosses Correspondence.* Translated by Brandon Look and Donald Rutherford. New Haven, CT: Yale University Press, 2007.

LH   Leibniz-Handshriften. Hanover, Gottfried Wilhelm Leibniz Bibliothek-Niedersächsische Landesbibliothek.

MJM   *G. W. Leibniz: Dissertation on Predestination and Grace.* Translated and edited by Michael J. Murray. New Haven, CT: Yale University Press, 2011.

NC   *The Correspondence of Isaac Newton.* 7 vols. Edited by H. W. Turnbull, J. F. Scott, A. Rupert Hall, and Laura Tilling New York: Cambridge University Press, 1959–1977.

OB   *Lahonton, Œuvres complètes.* Edited by Réal Ouellet and Alaine Beaulieu. Montreal: Les Presses de l'Université de Montréal, 1990.

Pertz   *Gesammelte Werke. Aus den Handschriften der Königlichen Bibliothek zu Hannover.* Edited by Georg Heinrich Pertz. 4 vols. Hannover: Hahnschen Hof-Buchhandlung, 1843–1847. Reprint, Hilesheim: Georg Olms, 1966. Cited by volume and page.

R   *Leibniz. Political Writings.* Translated and edited by Patrick Riley. 2nd edn. New York: Cambridge University Press, 1988.

RB   *G. W. Leibniz. New Essays on Human Understanding.* Translated and edited by Peter Remnant and Jonathan Bennett. New York: Cambridge University Press, 1996.

LIST OF ABBREVIATIONS   xxi

SHS   *Œuvres Complètes de Christiaan Huygens*, published by La Société Hollandaise des Sciences. 22 vols. La Haye: Martinus Nijhoff, 1888–1950. Cited by volume and page.

SMJ   *The New Schaff-Herzog Encyclopedia of Religious Knowledge*. 13 vols. Edited by Samuel Macauley Jackson, George William Gilmore, Clarence Augustine Beckwith, Henry King Carrol, James Francis Driscoll, James Frederic McCurdy, Henry Sylvester Nash, and Albert Henry Newman. New York: Funk and Wagnalls, 1908–1914.

Preface

The documents gathered in this volume cut a winding path through the tumultuous final thirty-three months of Leibniz's life, from March 1714 to his death on 14 November 1716. The disputes with Newton and his followers over the discovery of the calculus and, later, over the issues in natural philosophy and theology that came to dominate Leibniz's correspondence with Samuel Clarke*, certainly loom large in the story of these years. But as the title of this volume is intended to convey, the letters exchanged between Leibniz and Caroline* of Brandenburg-Ansbach, Electoral Princess of Braunschweig-Lüneburg and later Princess of Wales, also figure prominently in their telling, and I have included their complete extant correspondence from 1714 to 1716. These letters are of particular interest inasmuch as they provide valuable insights into how and why Leibniz's correspondence with Clarke arose, and why it developed as it did, with Caroline in the role of influential go-between—whence the title, *The Leibniz–Caroline–Clarke Correspondence*. But there is more; for these letters provide a window into the evolving personal relationship between Leibniz and Caroline. Much of the early correspondence between them after Caroline's arrival in England is filled with thoughtful and engaging exchanges about philosophy, literature, and politics, about people Caroline was meeting in England, about those known by Leibniz far and wide, about the new royal family in England, headed by George I (Georg Ludwig* of Braunschweig-Lüneburg), as well as gossip about affairs of state in both Great Britain and Europe at large. Beyond the interest they hold for Leibniz scholars in particular, many of these exchanges may also be of interest to historians of early eighteenth-century Great Britain and Europe, and especially to those interested in the period immediately preceding and following the Hanoverian succession to the throne of Great Britain. But even quite early on in their correspondence Leibniz seemed to sense a threat to his relationship with Caroline, and a worrisome paranoia began to creep into some of his letters to her, letters in which he expressed concerns about her continuing allegiance to him now that she had been installed in England amongst his rivals. As the correspondence progressed, Leibniz's paranoia only deepened; but it was nevertheless prophetic of a tragic truth to come. For the letters exchanged between Leibniz and Caroline document the rather sad story of the slow but steady erosion of Caroline's loyalty to Leibniz after she departed from Hanover on 12 October 1714 and landed in England at Margate in Kent on 22 October as the new Princess of Wales and future Queen of England. In 1727 the Scottish poet James Thomson penned *A Poem Sacred to the Memory of Sir Isaac Newton*, calling him 'our philosophic sun', and it was by force of the political and cultural mass of

xxiv PREFACE

this sun that Caroline was eventually, and inexorably, drawn into its orbit, and away from Leibniz.

As I have already intimated, not every word of the letters exchanged between Leibniz and Caroline recorded in this volume speaks directly to Leibniz's correspondence with Clarke and his dispute with Newton; but even when the words tack wide of those topics, they are not, for all that, lacking in interest to Leibniz scholars and historians of the period. The same may be said of the letters that Leibniz exchanged with other correspondents during this final period of his life, many of which are also included in this volume. For while most of them touch more or less directly on the dispute with Newton and the correspondence with Clarke, I judged that all of them record something of philosophical or historical value and thus contribute something of interest to the final chapters of the fascinating and complex story of Leibniz's life and career. The title of this volume should be understood in this light; and thus while the correspondence between Leibniz and Clarke, on the one hand, and that between Leibniz and Caroline, on the other, occupy centre stage in this project, they do not fall exclusively within its purview, a purview that encompasses a much broader perspective on the swirl of events that engulfed Leibniz during the last few months of his life.

All the documents gathered in this volume are arranged chronologically according to the dates on which they were either composed or transmitted. And so although Clarke published his edition of the correspondence between himself and Leibniz in 1717, I have arranged Clarke's papers chronologically according to the dates of the letters by which they were transmitted by Princess Caroline to Leibniz; similarly, I have arranged Leibniz's papers chronologically according to the dates of the letters by which he transmitted them to Caroline for delivery to Clarke. However, the Dedication and Advertisement to the Reader with which Clarke prefaced his edition of the correspondence, as well as the list of passages from Leibniz's works that he appended to that edition, are here reproduced in the section for the year 1717. In order to give the reader some idea of the sweep of the documents included in this volume, I have summarized a few highlights below.

March to September 1714 (documents 4–36)

The documents from March to September 1714 (documents 4–36) are from the period leading up to the death of Queen Anne on 12 August 1714, the consequent ascension to the throne of Great Britain by Elector Georg Ludwig, Leibniz's employer in Hanover, and Leibniz's hurried, and harried, departure from the imperial court in Vienna, where he had also been employed as a member of the imperial aulic council*, and his arrival in Hanover on 14 September. There are revealing letters exchanged between Leibniz and John Chamberlayne* concerning the calculus priority dispute with Newton (documents 5, 7, 20, 23a) and between Chamberlayne and Newton on the same subject (documents 8 and 9).

The letters exchanged between Leibniz and Caroline prior to the death of Queen Anne are valuable for what they reveal about the electoral family's anxiety during the so-called succession crisis (see Caroline's distraught letter to Leibniz of 7 June (document 15)), precipitated by the letters that Queen Anne had written on 30 May to the Dowager Electress Sophie* of the Palatinate (document 12), to her son, the Elector and future King of England Georg Ludwig (document 13), and to the elector's son, the Electoral Prince Georg August* (document 14). Among the other notable documents from this period is a poignant letter from Johanne Sophie*, Gräfin (Countess) zu Schaumburg-Lippe, of 12 July 1714 to Louise, Raugravine Palatine (document 21) recounting the collapse and death of the Dowager Electress Sophie, Leibniz's close friend and patroness in Hanover. Sophie had fallen ill while strolling in the gardens of Herrenhausen* with Caroline and Johanne Sophie; Sophie died there, in their arms, on 8 June 1716, just a day after Caroline had written her distraught letter to Leibniz. Johanne Sophie had written a shorter account of the ordeal in a letter of 12 June 1714 to Lady Mary Cowper* (document 16), who would eventually become one of Caroline's English ladies-in-waiting after her arrival in England as Princess of Wales some five months after Sophie's death. Caroline also sent a short account of the event to Lady Cowper on 13 July 1714 (document 22). There is also a moving letter of 7 July 1714 that Leibniz wrote to Caroline after hearing of the Dowager Electress Sophie's death (document 19). On 17 September Leibniz wrote a pleading letter of excuse (gout and plague) and pardon to the new Prince of Wales Georg August for not having returned to Hanover sooner, before the departure of the prince and his father the king (document 31; see also his letter to Minister Andreas Gottlieb Bernstorff* of 20 September (document 32), his letter to Minister Friedrich Wilhelm Görtz* of 28 December (document 55), and his letter to Caroline from the end of November 1715 (document 85)). On 20 September, three weeks before Caroline's departure for England, Leibniz wrote to the President of the Imperial Aulic Council, Ernst Friedrich Windischgrätz (document 33): 'I am preparing to go to England with Madame the Royal Princess, who has the kindness to desire it. I have reasons for not yet revealing any of it to others, but I think that it is my duty to inform Your Excellency of it in order that you may judge if I could be useful there for the service of the emperor.' And on 21 September Leibniz wrote to the Imperial General Claude Alexandre de Bonneval* in Vienna: 'If I were in a state to obey Her Royal Highness, I would go with her to England' (document 35). In letters to Johann Matthias von der Schulenburg* over the next three weeks (documents 36, 40, 41), he suggested more definitely that he intended to go to England soon.

October 1714 to the Middle of November 1715 (documents 37–83)

The documents from October 1714 to the middle of November 1715 are from the period immediately preceding Caroline's departure for England on 12 October

xxvi   PREFACE

1714 and leading up to the beginning of Leibniz's correspondence with Clarke. On 14 October 1714 Leibniz wrote to Minister Bernstorff (document 42) warning him of a rescript that was prepared by a minister of the King of Prussia to be sent to King George I of Great Britain suggesting that the Anglican religion, headed by George I, is different from the evangelical (Lutheran) religion of George I and the Hanoverian electorate. Leibniz suggested to Bernstorff that something should be said against the view that the king's religion is different from that of Anglican religion of Great Britain (see also the P.S. to his letter to Bernstorff of 8 December (document 49)). This signaled the beginning of several attempts by Leibniz to reconcile the Reformed and Evangelical churches through the mediation of the Church of England, a scheme in which he would soon attempt to enlist Caroline's support (documents 97, 111, 113, 117a, and 124). In the P.S. to the last of these documents, a letter of 2 June 1716, Leibniz, having been frustrated by the responses of Caroline (documents 115 and 122) and that of the king, which Caroline had reported to Leibniz in her letter of 26 May 1716 (document 122), finally gave up his attempt to reunite the Protestant churches, saying: 'I have done my duty, and the conscience of each will determine his own' (p. 561).

The documents from this period include an extraordinary and amusing letter from the beginning of November 1714 that Leibniz wrote to the Imperial General Claude Alexandre de Bonneval (document 45), answering the latter's equally extraordinary and amusing letter of 6 October (document 39), in which Bonneval related that Prince Eugène* of Savoy had suggested that since Leibniz was not going to England he should come to Vienna, a bit of information that Leibniz did not fail to share with Caroline in his letter to her from around 8 December 1714 (document 50, see also his unsent and undated draft letter to Caroline from late October to mid-to-late December 1715 (document 82)); then Bonneval described how the prince guards the copy of the *Principes de la nature et de la grâce, fondés en raison* that Leibniz had prepared for him, and how the prince forces Bonneval to kiss it, but without allowing him to copy it. Bonneval presents a rather bawdy analogy to illustrate how Leibniz might recompense him by giving him an even more expansive summary of his system than the one he prepared for the prince. Among other things in his response, Leibniz writes that he could still go to England before the end of the year, expresses his approval of and expands upon Bonneval's bawdy analogy, and implores Bonneval to apply himself to having Emperor Karl VI* issue a rescript to the Regency of Austria ordering them to grant Leibniz's requests and to follow his directions in the matter of the proposed Imperial Society of Sciences*.[1]

---

[1] As early as his letter of 20 September 1714 to Ernst Friedrich Windischgrätz (document 33, p. 113) and his letter of the same date to Philipp Ludwig Wenzel von Sinzendorff* (document 34, p. 119), Leibniz had expressed his intention and desire to return to Vienna. His reason for wanting to return to Vienna as soon as possible was to oversee the founding and administration of the proposed Imperial Society of Sciences*. In his letter to Bonneval of 21 September 1714 he also spoke of returning to Vienna, but mentioned being delayed in that by 'certain occupations', by which he meant his work on his history of the House of Braunschweig-Lüneburg, his so-called *Annales imperii occidentis Brunsvicenses**

PREFACE   xxvii

On 1 November 1714, Minister Bernstorff, having been informed that Leibniz was planning to leave for England, strongly advised him to remain in Hanover and to focus his attention on his history of the House of Braunschweig-Lüneburg, his so-called *Annales imperii occidentis Brunsvicenses** (document 46) (see also the letter from Nicolas Rémond* to Leibniz of 9 January 1715 (document 59)). Leibniz subsequently wrote to Schulenburg on 3 December (document 48) to inform him that he had changed his mind about going to England because of 'a touch of gout' (see also his letter to Rémond of 27 January 1715 (document 61)). In his response to Bernstorff of 8 December 1714 (document 49), Leibniz informed the minister of his progress on his history and then broached a topic that would surface periodically in his correspondence until nearly the end of his life, namely his desire to be appointed historiographer of Great Britain (see his letter to Bernstorff of 15 March 1715 (document 66); his letter to Caroline from *c.*8 December 1714 (document 50), of 18 December 1714 (document 51), of 29 March 1715 (document 67a), of 10 May 1715 (document 72), of 21 October 1715 (document 80); Caroline's letters to Leibniz of 28 December 1714 (document 52), of 16 January 1715 (document 60), of 13 September 1715 (document 78); the letters of 11 August 1716 and 27 October 1716 to Leibniz from Minister Johann Caspar Bothmer* (documents 137 and 155, respectively)). In the letter of 10 May 1715 (document 72) Leibniz revealed to Caroline for the first time his long struggle with Newton over the discovery of the calculus and suggested that if the king made him historiographer of Great Britain it would make him an equal of Newton and do honour to Hanover and Germany.

Leibniz's letter to Johanne Sophie of 29 January 1715 (document 63) is remarkable for its rather panicked worry about Caroline's loyalties drifting from him to the English, something he solicits the help of Johanne Sophie to prevent by appealing to her own Germanic loyalties. Leibniz's worry on this head, which was eventually shown not to be unjustified, surfaced again in his letter to Caroline of 21 October 1715 (document 80), this time in connection with her not having found a translator for his *Theodicy*, but blaming his suspicions on the wavering loyalties of Antonio Schinella Conti*. It surfaced yet again in his letter to Caroline of 28 April 1716 (document 113), this time tied to her failure to respond to his letters soliciting her help in his project to reunite the Protestant churches, but hinting once more at her need to deliver on the proposed translation of the *Theodicy* in order to alleviate his worry.

(document 35, p. 121). Leibniz also expressed his intent and desire to return to Vienna as soon as his historical work was completed in letters to the Dowager Empress Wilhelmine Amalie* of 28 June 1715 (document 74, p. 245) and 20 September 1716 (document 145, p. 735) and to her first lady-in-waiting, Charlotte Elisabeth von Klenk*, also of 28 June 1715 (document 73, p. 243) and 20 September 1716 (document 146, p. 739). See also Klenk's letters to Leibniz of 6 July 1715 (document 75, p. 249), of 13 November 1715 (document 83, p. 293), and of 30 September 1716 (document 148, p. 741). Some of these letters also concern Leibniz's worry about the news he had received that his wages for his service as aulic councilor had been cancelled.

xxviii PREFACE

In a letter apparently lost, but written in the third week of March 1715, Caroline transmitted to Leibniz a letter of 15 March written to her by the Bishop of Bristol (document 65), George Smalridge. As part of a plan to produce an English translation of Leibniz's *Theodicy*, Caroline had solicited his thoughts about a copy of the *Theodicy* that she had sent to him for evaluation. In his letter to Caroline of 29 March 1715 (document 67a), Leibniz acknowledged receipt of Smalridge's letter and defended his work against Smalridge's charge that the *Theodicy* was obscure, going so far as to enclose a separate paper of three folio pages (document 67b) in response to the objections that Smalridge had raised in his letter. Significantly, in the footnote to his letter to Caroline, Leibniz proposed Michel de la Roche* as a suitable translator for the *Theodicy*. Although aborted after Leibniz's death on 14 November 1716, the *Theodicy* translation project was an ongoing topic in several of the letters exchanged between Leibniz and Caroline following Leibniz's letter to Caroline of 29 March 1715 (see Leibniz's letters to Caroline of 21 October 1715 (document 80), from the end of November 1715 (document 85), of 28 April 1716 (document 113), of 12 May 1716 (document 117a), of 2 June 1716 (document 124), of 31 July 1716 (document 135), of 18 August 1716 (document 139), of 11 September 1716 (document 144) and Caroline's letters to Leibniz of 14 November 1715 (document 84), of 6 December 1715 (document 89), of 10 January 1716 (document 95), of 26 June 1716 (document 128), of 1 September 1716 (document 142); see also Leibniz's letter to Rémond of 6 December 1715 (document 88a), the letter of Pierre Des Maizeaux* of 14 July 1716 to Philip Heinrich Zollman* (document 134), and Leibniz's letter to Pierre Des Maizeaux of 21 August 1716 (document 141)).

Because of their philosophical significance I have included four letters from Leibniz to Louis Bourguet* (documents 77, 98, 112, and 131) and three letters from Bourguet to Leibniz (documents 103, 106, and 118). All but one of the letters in this group were written in 1716. That one letter was Leibniz's letter to Bourguet of 5 August 1715 (document 77), which was written in response to a letter from Bourguet in which Bourguet had apparently expressed his shock at the derogative remarks that Roger Cotes* had made in the preface to the second edition of Newton's *Principia* about those who, like Descartes* and Leibniz, rejected a non-mechanical, primitive force of gravity and instead explained the motion of the planets in terms of material vortices. Leibniz used the occasion to argue, not only against the notion of gravity that Cotes had defended in his preface, namely that it is essential to matter, but also against the void, which Leibniz argued the Newtonians had to accept because the mutual attraction of all the parts of matter could produce no change if there were a plenum. But beyond criticisms of the Newtonians and remarks about Clarke, the letters between Bourguet and Leibniz reproduced here involve two other significant discussions—one revolving around the generation of animals in light of the discoveries of the microscopist Antonie van Leeuwenhoek, and the other concerning whether the universe had a beginning in time, under either the hypothesis that the universe is always equally perfect or

the hypothesis that it always grows in perfection. This discussion, which also involves an interesting exchange on the nature of infinities and infinite series, has some relevance to the Leibniz-Clarke correspondence since the question of whether or not the world is eternal does come up there (see section 15 of their fourth papers and sections 55–63 and 73–75 of their fifth papers).

In her letter to Leibniz of 13 September 1715 (document 78), and despite her confession that she 'did not like [John Locke's] philosophy at all' (p. 265), Caroline praised the civility and the arguments of both Locke and Edward Stillingfleet in their famous exchange on the subject of substance. In his response of 21 October 1715 (document 80), published here for the first time, Leibniz conceded that Locke put up a tolerably good defense against Stillingfleet, but then added that 'Mr. Locke undermines the great truths of natural religion.' He went on to say that he 'had hoped that my *Theodicy* would be found a bit more sound in England, if one day it were read in English, and that it would furnish some better principles' (document 80, p. 279), and he lamented the fact that Caroline had not yet found anyone suitable to translate it into English.

In a letter of 18 October 1715 (document 79a), Nicolas Rémond transmitted to Leibniz a letter that Antonio Schinella Conti (the Abbé Conti) had left with him for Leibniz before Conti departed Paris for England (document 79c), as well as *some articles extracted from his letters that concern Mr. Newton*' (for which, see document 79b).

End of November 1715 to 14 November 1716 (documents 84–159)

These documents cover the entire period of Leibniz's correspondence with Clarke. One of the more important documents from this time period, and here published for the first time in its entirety, is the letter that Leibniz wrote to Caroline at the end of November 1715 (document 85), which includes the famous passage that initiated the correspondence with Clarke and which Clarke published as Leibniz's first paper in his 1717 edition of the correspondence (document 86). As in his letter to Caroline of 21 October 1715 mentioned in the previous section, Leibniz accuses Locke of undermining natural religion, but here he also indicts English philosophy in general, saying that 'natural religion itself declines precipitously there' (document 85, p. 313), and singles out Newton by name for having contributed greatly to this decline. In a letter dated December 1715 (document 87), Leibniz notified Johann Bernoulli* that the Newtonians were now attacking his philosophy and proceeded with his own attack on Newton's philosophy, in which he included some of the criticisms he had raised in his earlier letter to Caroline. He also mentioned the letter from Conti that Rémond had transmitted to him (document 79c) and stated that he was replying to it. His reply of 6 December 1715 (document 88b) included the important P.S. in which Leibniz begins with a brief defense against the charges made by Newton's followers that he had plagiarized Newton's calculus and

xxx PREFACE

ends with a lengthy and significant criticism of Newton's philosophy. Newton wrote several draft replies to this P.S. (documents 101a–101f) and a final version (document 101g) that he sent to Conti dated 6 March 171 $\frac{5}{6}$ (OS), that is, 17 March 1716 (NS). Conti transmitted Newton's reply in his letter to Leibniz of 26 March 1716 (document 104), a letter in which he asked for Leibniz's response to Newton's reply and notified Leibniz that the king wanted him (i.e., Conti) 'to inform him of everything that has passed between Mr. Newton and you' (see also Rémond's letter to Leibniz of 15 March 1716 (document 102)). Leibniz responded to Newton's reply in a letter to Conti of 9 April 1716 (document 108).

Since I shall deal in detail with the pertinent content of the letters exchanged between Leibniz and Caroline during this period in the first half of the introduction below, I will here merely list the letters with which Leibniz transmitted his papers for Clarke and those with which Caroline transmitted Clarke's replies: Caroline transmitted Clarke's First Reply (document 90) in her letter to Leibniz of 6 December 1715 (document 89), Clarke's Second Reply (document 96) in her letter to Leibniz of 10 January 1716 (document 95), Clarke's Third Reply (document 120) in her letter to Leibniz of 15 May 1716 (document 119), Clarke's Fourth Reply (document 129) in her letter to Leibniz of 26 June 1716 (document 128), and Clarke's Fifth Reply (document 157) in a letter written on 29 October (document 156), just fifteen days before Leibniz's death on 14 November. Leibniz transmitted his Second Paper for Clarke (document 92) in his letter to Caroline of December 1715 (document 91), his Third Paper (document 100) in his letter to Caroline of 25 February 1716 (document 99), his Fourth Paper (document 125a) in his letter to Caroline of 2 June 1716 (document 124), and the first half of his Fifth Paper (document 140b) in his letter to Caroline of 18 August 1716 (document 139), the second half being sent either without a cover letter or along with a letter that has been lost.

In addition to the letters exchanged between Leibniz and Caroline, the documents from this period include a number of letters describing his disputes with Newton and Clarke that Leibniz wrote to various of his correspondents, as well as some of their replies: Among them are Leibniz's letters to William Winde* and Christian Wolff* of 23 December 1715 (documents 93 and 94, respectively), to John Arnold of 5 June 1716 (document 126), to Robert Erskine of 3 August 1716 (document 136), to Pierre Des Maizeaux* of 21 August 1716 (document 141), to George Cheyne* of 25 September 1716 (document 147), the exchanges between Leibniz and Johann Bernoulli (documents 87, 110, 121, 127, 133, 154, 159), between Leibniz and Conti (documents 88b (which is a response to Conti's letter from April 1715 (document 79c)), 104, 108), between Leibniz and Louis Bourguet (documents 98, 103, 106, 112, 118, 131), between Leibniz and Nicolas Rémond (documents 102, 105, 109, 138, 150, 153), between Leibniz and Johann Caspar von Bothmer (documents 114, 116, 123, 132).

PREFACE xxxi

Additional Documents

Because of their pertinence to the quarrels between Leibniz, Newton, and their respective followers concerning natural philosophy and natural religion, I have included three documents that predate those mentioned in the previous paragraphs. Document 1 contains articles 18 and 19 of the *Discours de la Conformité de la Foy avec la Raison*, which was published in Leibniz's *Essais de Theodicée sur la Bonté of Dieu, la Liberté de l'Home et l'Origine du Mal* (1710). These two articles concern the dispute between some of the Reformed Protestants—in particular, as Leibniz says, 'those who follow Zwingli rather than Calvin on this matter'—and Evangelicals (that is, Lutherans) on the matter of the sacrament of the Eucharist. In article 19, by way of defending the Lutheran doctrine of real participation, Leibniz draws an analogy between that doctrine and the doctrine of 'operation at a distance [that] has just been rehabilitated in England by the excellent Mr. Newton'. But he makes clear that he, in contrast to Newton, does not believe that such remote action of bodies can be natural because it 'surpasses the forces of nature'. This represents the earliest public criticism that Leibniz made of the Newtonian doctrine of gravitation, and five years later he repeats this line of argument, which involves a comparison between the Eucharist and Newtonian gravitation, in his letter to Caroline of 10 May 1715 (document 72). Document 2 is a long letter of 10 February 1711 from Leibniz to the Dutch mathematician and physicist Nicolaas Hartsoeker in which Leibniz not only severely criticized the Newtonian doctrine of gravity, but also the doctrine of atoms and the void, which the Newtonians had adopted in conjunction with the doctrine of universal gravitation. The original French version of this letter reproduced in this volume was published in the *Mémoires pour l'Histoire des Sciences & des beaux-Arts* (aka, *Memoires de Trévoux*) for March 1712; the English translation reproduced in this volume was published in the *Memoirs of Literature* of London for 5 May 1712 (OS); the letter was later published again in the original French in the Amsterdam edition of the *Journal des Sçavans* for December 1712. Roger Cotes*, the editor of the second edition of Newton's *Principia*, drew Newton's attention to the English version that was published in *Memoirs of Literature*, and Newton prepared a lengthy draft reply intended for the editor of that journal (document 3).

I have also included some documents that postdate Leibniz's death. In addition to the Dedication and Advertisement to the Reader with which Clarke prefaced his edition of the correspondence and the list of passages from Leibniz's works that he appended to that edition, there is a letter that Conti wrote to Newton from Hanover on 10 December 1716 (document 160) in which he notified Newton of Leibniz's death. Document 161 is an excerpt from a private note summarizing his dispute with Leibniz that Newton composed sometime after Leibniz's death. Documents 164 and 165 are excerpts from draft letters that Newton wrote in response to Des

xxxii PREFACE

Maizeaux's request for comments on the proofs for volume II of the first edition of Des Maizeaux's *Recueil* (Des Maizeaux 1720).

Manuscripts, Transcriptions, and Documents

Nearly all the transcriptions included in this volume are those I have made based on copies of original manuscripts. The very few exceptions involve manuscripts that are presumed lost, and the corresponding transcriptions that are recorded in this volume are ones that have been previously published, as indicated in the notes. I have endeavored to follow best practice for transcribing original-language manuscripts, and I have therefore made every effort to record as accurately as possible the words written in those manuscripts, even when the grammar, spelling, capitalization, accentuation, or punctuation is not in accord with contemporary proper usage. I have also tried to preserve the layout of the original manuscripts. Where necessary, I have provided notes to the transcriptions to explain how I have interpreted problematic wording or spellings. This was often necessary in the case of the letters written by Caroline; for, due to her unsettled childhood,[2] her formal education was often neglected, and she was largely self-taught. Consequently, having been deprived of the kind of formal education in languages that was the norm at the time for children, especially female children, of the aristocracy, Caroline's French grammar and spelling are quite aberrant. Even in her maturity, Caroline never gained a solid mastery of written French, which she tended to spell phonetically, a practice made worse by the fact that the French phones were being filtered through the ears of someone whose native tongue was German. This resulted in Caroline's often substituting d's for t's, c's for g's, p's for b's, and a's for e's. These and many other instances of her idiosyncratic variations on French spelling can be found in her letters to Leibniz transcribed in this volume. But best practice has not always been followed by previous editors. For example, in his 1884 edition of Leibniz's correspondence with Caroline (Klopp XI), Onno Klopp simply put what he took to be Caroline's words into the proper French of his day, without explanation, sometimes just omitting, without notice, words that he could not decipher, or sometimes actually inventing words, again without notice, to fill in for those words he could not decipher. This served to mask the many errors and omissions that plague the transcriptions in his edition and of which readers cannot be aware without examining the original manuscripts, which is not easy to do and should scarcely be necessary if an edition is properly prepared. (In the notes for this edition I have flagged the errors and omissions to be found in the transcriptions of previous editors, which I hope will be helpful for those who have hitherto relied on those previous transcriptions.) Best practice for transcribing original-language manuscripts is doubly important for an edition like the present one in which the transcription is

---

[2] See the entry for Caroline in the starred references.

accompanied by an English translation. For readers can have no basis for judging whether the editor's interpretations of the original text, and hence whether the editor's translations of those texts, are trustworthy if the original manuscripts have not been transcribed as accurately as possible in the first place. This constitutes one reason an accurate transcription of original-language manuscripts is important. But in the case of Caroline's writing in particular, it is also valuable because it serves to tell part of the story of Caroline's life by reflecting the effects of the educational deprivations of her youth.

Dating

NS designates New Style; OS designates Old Style. Unless otherwise indicated, all dates in this volume are given in New Style, that is, according to the Gregorian calendar, although I will sometimes specifically indicate that a date is New Style in order to avoid possible ambiguity. The New Style dates for the time period covered in this volume are eleven days later than the corresponding Old Style dates. New Style dates came into use in the German Protestant states in February 1700; Old Style dating, according to the Julian calendar, was in use in Great Britain until 1752, and until then the new year in Great Britain officially began on 25 March.

Critical Apparatus

In the edited documents, I use single vertical bars to enclose text struck in the original documents, but which I thought was significant enough to include in the transcriptions and translations: | *struck text* |.

Text struck within struck text is enclosed within angled brackets: | *stuck text < text struck within struck text > struck text* |.

I use asterisks (*) to flag elements that are described in the starred references gathered at the end of the volume. Also, and unless otherwise indicated, square brackets enclose text added by the editor—that is, [*text added by the editor*]. The reader should be careful to distinguish these usages from Clarke's usage, in his 1717 edition of his correspondence with Leibniz, reproduced below, of *double* vertical bars (||) as well as asterisks (*) and daggers (†) to mark footnotes and sidebar notes.

Introduction

1. The Leibniz-Caroline Correspondence: 1714–1716

The correspondence between Leibniz and Newton's apologist, Samuel Clarke*, can be, and often has been, viewed as the culmination of the priority dispute that arose between Leibniz and Newton over the discovery of the calculus.[1] Newton's discovery of his method of fluxions in 1665/66 had preceded by some ten years Leibniz's discovery of his differential calculus in 1675; but Leibniz was the first to publish his results, in the *Acta Eruditorum* of 1684. Even after that it took some considerable time for the priority dispute to flare; but then, in 1710, it began to burn red hot in the wake of *John Keill's accusation, in an article published in the *Philosophical Transactions* of the Royal Society of London, that Newton's 'most highly celebrated arithmetic of fluxions, which without any doubt Mr. Newton first invented, […] was later published by Mr. Leibniz in *Acta Eruditorum* with a different name and form of notation'.[2] Leibniz responded to Keill's charge by lodging a complaint in a letter of 4 March 1711 to the Secretary of the Royal Society, Hans Sloane*. Keill responded in turn with a paper that he sent to Sloane for Leibniz in May 1711. This prompted a second reply from Leibniz, written to Sloane on 29 December 1711, in which he complained of Keill's 'empty and unjust braying' (NC VI 208). All this eventually led to the formation of a committee of the Royal Society—whose president at the time was, coincidentally, Isaac Newton—to examine the dispute between Keill and Leibniz. The committee issued a report on 24 April (5 May NS) 1712, drafted by Newton himself, that fairly concluded that Newton was the first discoverer of the calculus, but unjustly found Leibniz guilty of concealing his knowledge of the prior achievements of Newton. Toward the end of the year, this report was published with documentation under the title, *Commercium*

---

[1] The first part of the introduction is a significantly expanded and corrected version of my article, '[…] et je serai tousjours la même pour vous': Personal, Political, and Philosophical Dimensions of the Leibniz-Caroline Correspondence', in Lodge 2004, pp. 262–92, reprinted with permission. The second part of the introduction is taken from my article, 'The Correspondence with Clarke', in Lodge and Strickland 2020, pp. 228–49, reprinted with permission.

All translations are mine. All dates are New Style (NS) unless otherwise indicated. In the following discussion, I use 'Lz' or 'Cl', followed by a Roman numeral and an Arabic numeral, to refer, respectively, to a specific paper and section by Leibniz or Clarke in their correspondence. Thus 'Lz.I.1-4' would refer to the first four sections of Leibniz's First Paper, and 'Cl.II.1' would refer to the first section of Clarke's Second Reply.

[2] Keill 1708, p. 185. Although Keill's article was published in the *Philosophical Transactions* for 1708, that volume did not appear until 1710.

xxxvi INTRODUCTION

*Epistolicum**. In a letter to John Chamberlayne* of 21 April 1714, Leibniz recounted the history of the dispute with Keill up to and including the publication of the *Commercium Epistolicum*, complaining that the committee issuing the report had 'delivered a verdict in the matter, only *one party having been heard*, in a manner whose nullity is obvious' (document 7, p. 31). In the years following the publication of the report, Keill continued to stir the pot by publishing criticisms of Leibniz and goading Newton on to continue the fight, which he did, even long after Leibniz's death. But all of that having been said, it is important to understand the particular circumstances that triggered the correspondence between Leibniz and Clarke and why it never so much as touched in passing on the calculus priority dispute, but rather remained focused on philosophical issues, especially those having to do with natural religion.

In 1710, the very year that Keill's article appeared accusing him of plagiarism, Leibniz published his *Essais de Théodicée sur la Bonté de Dieu, la Liberté de l'Homme et l'Origine du Mal*. To the front end of that work Leibniz had attached a preliminary tract, the *Discours de la Conformité de la Foy avec la Raison*, and there, in §19 (document 1), he expressed publicly for the first time his disagreement with what he took to be Newton's acceptance of distant action between bodies. The following year, in a letter of 10 February 1711 to the Dutch natural philosopher Nicolas Hartsoeker (document 2), which was published in the *Mémoires pour l'Histoire des Sciences & des beaux-Arts* (aka the *Mémoires de Trévoux*) (March 1712), in the *Memoirs of Literature* (5 May 1712 OS), and in the Amsterdam edition of the *Journal des sçavans* (December 1712), Leibniz was even more pointed in his attack on those who held that gravity was due to some non-mechanical cause, which he suggested implied either a return to occult qualities or an appeal to miracles. There he had also criticized the Newtonian doctrine of atoms and the void, but the full airing of Leibniz's complaints against Newtonian natural philosophy and its implications for natural religion awaited his correspondence with Clarke; and then the letters from both parties were intended as much for the eyes of the recently installed Princess of Wales, Caroline* of Brandenburg-Ansbach, as they were for the eyes of their opponent. Circumstances had made Caroline the mediator between Leibniz and Clarke, and thus the correspondence between Caroline and Leibniz stands as a critically important source of information for understanding how and why the correspondence between Leibniz and Clarke arose and developed as it did; it also provides valuable insights into the personal, political, and philosophical issues that occupied Leibniz during the last two years of his life, especially the struggle against Newton and his followers that had been precipitated by the priority dispute concerning the discovery of the calculus. After briefly describing the events that set the stage for Leibniz's correspondence with Caroline after her arrival in England, I discuss its evolution in three phases: (1) Caroline's first year in England (December 1714–November 1715), (2) the beginning of the correspondence with Clarke (November 1715–January 1716), (3) from Caroline's apostasy to Leibniz's death (January 1716–November 1716).

INTRODUCTION   xxxvii

1.1 Setting the Stage

1.1.1 Leibniz in Vienna

At the beginning of August 1714 Leibniz was residing in Vienna. He had been there for more than a year and a half, moonlighting at the court of Emperor Karl VI*, where, with the reluctant permission of his employer, Elector Georg Ludwig* of Braunschweig-Lüneburg (Hanover), he had recently been appointed a member of the imperial aulic council*. Six months prior to this, on 3 March, Georg Ludwig's minister Andreas Gottlieb Bernstorff* had written to Leibniz on behalf of the elector to enquire when Leibniz intended to return to Hanover (document 4). Leibniz replied in a letter of 21 March (document 6) that he had been suffering from arthritis and that he thought he should delay his departure until May, when the weather would be better and he had had the chance to take the waters at Baden to treat his ailments. His reasons for delay, however, went far beyond these concerns with his health. For Leibniz had been intent upon the establishment of an Imperial Society of Sciences* in Vienna ever since the emperor had agreed to the project at the beginning of his stay in January 1713.[3] Leibniz was especially keen on the project because the Society (later Academy) of Sciences that he had helped to found in Berlin in 1700 had been languishing.[4] In replying to Bernstorff, however, Leibniz noted that 'I have not employed the time badly, since I have had the convenience of frequenting the library of the emperor and browsing the historical manuscripts' (document 6, p. 29). Leibniz here alludes, of course, to his work on the history of the House of Braunschweig-Lüneburg, his *Annales imperii occidentis Brunsvicenses**, which he had begun many years ago while in the service of Georg Ludwig's father, Ernst August*. Georg Ludwig was becoming increasingly obsessed with the completion of this project, and Leibniz realized that his time away from Hanover had to be justified to some extent in the service of the elector.

By the Act of Settlement* of 1701 the English parliament had made 'the most excellent Princess Sophia [Sophie* of the Palatinate] Electress and Dutchess Dowager of Hannover' and 'the Heirs of Her Body being Protestants' successors to

---

[3] For an outline of Leibniz's plans for the Imperial Society of Sciences, see his letter to the Dowager Empress Wilhelmine Amalie of 28 June 1715 (document 74, pp. 247, 249).

[4] The Berlin Society of Sciences grew out of a proposal made by Sophie Charlotte*, daughter of Sophie of the Palatinate, sister of Georg Ludwig of Brandenburg-Lüneburg, and Electress of Brandenburg (from 1688) and later first Queen in Prussia (1701). This proposal was for the construction of an observatory in Berlin, and when Leibniz heard of it, he wrote to the then electress to suggest that an academy of sciences, like those in Paris and London, be established in conjunction with the proposed observatory (see Klopp VIII 48–50). Undoubtedly with encouragement from his wife Sophie Charlotte, the Elector of Brandenburg, Friedrich III*, issued a Stiftungsbrief for both the observatory and the Society of Sciences on 19 March 1700 (see Klopp X 325–8). Leibniz was officially proclaimed president of the Society on 12 July (see Klopp X 328–30). However, in an act of singular ingratitude at the end of the year 1715, the Society first reduced, and then cancelled altogether, the small sum that had been allotted to Leibniz to cover his expenses for travel and correspondence (see the letters exchanged between Leibniz and the Director of the Society, Baron von Printzen, Klopp X 458–64). This effectively ended Leibniz's work on behalf of the Berlin Society of Sciences.

xxxviii   INTRODUCTION

the throne in England;[5] and the regnant Queen Anne had even taken the step, in 1706, of not only bestowing the Garter on Sophie's grandson and Caroline's spouse, the Electoral Prince Georg August*, but also of creating him Duke of Cambridge. But while he was still in Vienna, Leibniz received a distraught letter of 7 June from Caroline (document 18) reflecting the electoral family's anxiety during the so-called succession crisis, precipitated by the rather harsh letters that Queen Anne had sent on 29 May to the Dowager Electress Sophie (document 12), to her son, the Elector and future King of England Georg Ludwig (document 13), and to the elector's son and future Prince of Wales, the aforementioned Electoral Prince Georg August (document 14). Having heard rumours that Georg August might be intending to make an appearance in England with the blessing of Sophie, Queen Anne had sent those 'haughty letters'[6] to warn the electoral family that she would not permit Georg August to set foot in England as long as she was still alive, despite the fact that his status as Duke of Cambridge should have entitled him to take his seat in the House of Lords. But a greater grief was imminent; for in a letter to Leibniz of 13 June (document 17), Benedictus Andreas Caspar de Nomis* notified Leibniz of the death of the Dowager Electress Sophie, who, on 8 June, just a day after Caroline had written her distraught letter to Leibniz, had collapsed and died in the arms of Caroline and Johanne Sophie*, Gräfin (Countess) zu Schaumburg-Lippe while they were strolling in the gardens of the summer palace at Herrenhausen*.[7]

1.1.2 The Death of Queen Anne and the Hanoverian Succession: Leibniz Caught Between Hanover (England) and Vienna

Scarcely more than two months after Sophie's death there came news of the death, on 12 August 1714, of Queen Anne of England.[8] Since Sophie had preceded Anne in death, her eldest son, the Elector Georg Ludwig, was now the heir apparent. Given that, Leibniz knew he could no longer delay his departure from Vienna. He arrived back in Hanover on 14 September, but by then the king had already departed for England with the electoral prince in tow; Leibniz had missed them by three days. He hurriedly sent letters of explanation and apology to a number of the

---

[5] Leibniz himself had worked hard to establish this succession for the House of Braunschweig-Lüneburg. Sophie of the Palatinate qualified in the light of her Protestant credentials and her descent from James I through his daughter, Elizabeth Stuart, who was the wife of the Elector Palatine, Friedrich V, the ill-starred 'Winter King' of Bohemia.

[6] As Leibniz referred to them in his letter to Caroline of 16 June (document 18, p. 67).

[7] For a detailed account of Sophie's death, see the poignant letter of 12 July 1714 from Johanne Sophie, Gräfin (Countess) zu Schaumburg-Lippe, to Raugravine Palatine Louise (document 21). See also Johanne Sophie's letter of 12 June and Caroline's letter of 13 July to Lady Mary Cowper (documents 16 and 22, respectively). For Leibniz's reaction, see his letter to Caroline of 7 July (document 19, p. 73).

[8] Leibniz was notified of Queen Anne's death in a letter of 19 August from Benedictus Andreas Caspar de Nomis (document 24, p. 93).

INTRODUCTION xxxix

king's party, including Bernstorff[9] and the electoral prince.[10] Electoral Princess Caroline, however, was still in Hanover when Leibniz arrived—presumably to prepare herself and her children for the move to England. She would not depart until 12 October, and what she proposed doing in the month between surprised even Leibniz. Writing to the Imperial General Claude Alexandre de Bonneval* in Vienna a week after his arrival in Hanover, Leibniz described the situation in the following terms:

> I came here to apply myself during this winter to some labors that can free me from certain occupations[11] that could delay a bit my return to Vienna. But I am at present distracted from them here as I was at Vienna since the royal princess has wanted me to stay at the country estate [Herrenhausen], where she will be until her departure for England. I am very pleased to enjoy once more, as long as I can, the good graces of a princess so accomplished and so spiritual, who even wants to go over with me again (would you believe it?) the *Theodicy*, which she has read more than once. I seem to hear you, sir, accusing me of vanity, but I intend what I have just said to be praise of the princess and not of my work. For even if it be misguided, it is still a great thing that such a princess, surrounded by everything that can dissipate the spirit, gives so much attention to matters as elevated as those treated in my work.
>
> [document 35, p. 121]

From one perspective, I suppose, it might seem surprising that in the midst of the rush of changes that were overtaking her, Caroline should have wanted to take time to read through the *Theodicy* once more with Leibniz. But from another perspective, it seems a perfectly natural thing for her to want to do—I think it was precisely because she was 'surrounded', as Leibniz put it, 'by everything that can dissipate the spirit', that she sought solace once more in a book and in a friend that had seen her through so many difficult times in the past.[12] As I will argue later, it is likely that it was during Leibniz's stay with Caroline at Herrenhausen, as they discussed the *Theodicy* and awaited her departure for England, that they began to think about the prospect of having the *Theodicy* translated into English.

Before he had departed from Vienna, Leibniz had commissioned the Court Chancellor to Emperor Karl VI, Count Philipp Ludwig Wenzel von Sinzendorff*, to send letters to him in Hanover, addressed to the Hanoverian ministers Johann Caspar von Bothmer* and Friedrich Wilhelm Görtz*, expressing the emperor's

---

[9] See Leibniz's letters to Bernstorff of 22 August and 20 September (documents 25 and 32, respectively).

[10] See Leibniz's letter to Georg August of 17 September (document 31).

[11] Leibniz alludes here to his ongoing project of writing a history of the House of Braunschweig-Lüneburg, the *Annales imperii occidentis Brunsvicenses**.

[12] For more on this point, see Brown 2016a, especially pp. 51–4.

xl   INTRODUCTION

regret at Leibniz's departure and his and Sinzendorff's wish for Leibniz's swift return to Vienna. Leibniz's plan was to pass these letters on to the ministers as soon as he arrived back in Hanover. In his letter to Bothmer of 4 September 1714, Sinzendorff wrote this:

> The journey of Mr. Leibniz, who wishes to follow his king to England, is too favourable an occasion for me not to pay you my respects and to express the joy I take in your having been present at the happy change that has just taken place in the kingdom. Your good intentions are, of course, well known to the emperor, who is persuaded that general affairs will be favourably influenced by your good counsels. His Majesty has viewed the parting of Mr. Leibniz with regret; he desires to see his return soon.
>
> [document 26, p. 99]

And in his letter to Görtz of the same date, this:

> The departure of Mr. Leibniz, who is travelling to your court, has been too favourable an occasion for me not to assure you of my respects and express to you the interest I take in the advantageous change that has just taken place in England in favour of the king, your master. My intentions have long since been known to you. I had the occasion to renew our friendship in Frankfort. I hope that your kind regards will continue and that you will be persuaded of the esteem and veneration that I have for you. The emperor very reluctantly allowed Mr. Leibniz to leave. I appreciate him enormously and desire his return.
>
> [document 27, pp. 99, 101]

The letter that Leibniz commissioned Sinzendorff to write to Bothmer seems to suggest that Leibniz was intending to follow the new king to England, but both letters seem to urge the ministers to facilitate Leibniz's quick return to Vienna. Sinzendorff did not send Leibniz the letters he had written for Bothmer and Görtz immediately, but forwarded them to him in a letter written to Leibniz on 8 September 1714:

> You see that I am a man of my word. Here are the two letters that you requested. I believe that they will find you still in Hanover and that you will not go to England. Just in case, however, I am sending you the letter for Mr. Bothmer, which you can send to him if you do not have occasion to deliver it yourself.
>
> [document 28, p. 101]

Significantly, Sinzendorff expressed his belief that Leibniz 'will not go to England', but added that he was sending him the letter for Bothmer 'just in case', for Bothmer had long been stationed in London and was already there as Plenipotentiary

INTRODUCTION   xli

Minister when Queen Anne died on 12 August. Sinzendorff's belief that Leibniz would not go to England suggests, perhaps, that it was in fact the purpose of the letters he had written for Bothmer and Görtz to forestall Leibniz's having to go to England by stressing both his and the emperor's desire for Leibniz to return to Vienna.

In a letter written to the Dowager Empress Wilhelmine Amalie* on 16 September, just four days after his arrival in Hanover, Leibniz wrote:

> If I had had some letter to carry to the king or to one of his ministers, I would have been able to meet with him before his departure, and even now, if I left immediately, I could still join him in Holland. I would have done it if I had found here the letter that Count von Sinzendorff had promised for Baron von Görtz, our president of finances, who is accompanying the king; but it appears that he changed his mind. I console myself about that with the freedom that it allows me to do everything at my convenience.
>
> [document 29, p. 103]

And in a letter of the same date to Wilhelmine Amalie's first lady-in-waiting, Charlotte Elisabeth von Klenk*, he wrote:

> The king left Tuesday afternoon. If I had wanted to follow him immediately, I could doubtless have still met with him in Holland. For the wind is not favourable enough to go to sea. But I have no reason to rush so much, and my health is worth more to me than other concerns, so I took care of it while traveling.
>
> [document 30, p. 105]

In the letter to Klenk, Leibniz suggests that if he had wanted to follow him immediately, he could still have met with the king in Holland, and in his letter to Amalie he says he would have gone to join the king in Holland had he found the letter that he had commissioned Sinzendorff to write. In both letters he also suggests that he was quite happy not to have had to rush to meet the king in Holland, on the one hand because of 'the freedom that it allows me to do everything at my convenience', and on the other because it avoided his having to risk his health on such a hasty journey,[13] none of which, of course, suggests that he had foreclosed the possibility of a trip to England at some later date, when his health and his convenience permitted it. His letter to the dowager empress also reveals that he had not yet received the

---

[13] In his letter to Andreas Gottlieb von Bernstorff of 20 September (document 32, p. 109) Leibniz also excused his decision not to join the king in Holland because of concerns about his health, saying: 'As I have traveled like an old man, I only arrived here last Friday, the king having already departed on Tuesday. I thought that if I had taken the stagecoach straightaway in order to follow His Majesty, I could have done harm to my health, and perhaps uselessly, since I imagine that this monarch will be only too occupied in Holland.'

xlii INTRODUCTION

letters that Sinzendorff was supposed to send him. But four days later, on
20 September, he wrote to Sinzendorff to acknowledge receipt, two days earlier, of
the letters Sinzendorff had written for Bothmer and Görtz:

> Not seeing any reason to hurry too much, I have travelled like an old man, and
> I arrived here only last Friday. I had the honour of receiving the day before yester-
> day, that is Tuesday, the letters of Your Excellency, for which I thank you most
> humbly. Those which are for the two ministers of the King of Great Britain are
> very advantageous for me, and although they contain nothing that obliges me to
> hasten my journey to the king, whom I could have joined in Holland had it been
> necessary, they will serve to expedite my return to Vienna.
>
> [document 34, p. 119]

It seems clear from these remarks that the purpose of the letters that Leibniz had
commissioned Sinzendorff to write for Görtz and Bothmer was at least to facilitate
Leibniz's expeditious return to Vienna. Leibniz ended his letter to Sinzendorff by
saying that 'if Your Excellency has some order for me, I would be delighted to be
able to carry it out, either here or in England' (document 34, p. 119), which again
suggests that he had not foreclosed the possibility of a trip to England, but also
suggests that he was nevertheless glad to have the letters he had commissioned
from Sinzendorff to grease the wheels for a quick return to Vienna, whether from
England or from Hanover.

Leibniz wrote another letter on 20 September, this one to the President of the
Imperial Aulic Council, Ernst Friedrich Windischgrätz, saying: 'I am preparing to go
to England with Madame the Royal Princess, who has the kindness to desire it. I have
reasons for not yet revealing any of it to others, but I think that it is my duty to inform
Your Excellency of it in order that you may judge if I could be useful there for the
service of the emperor' (document 33, p. 115). This suggests that Leibniz had finally
made up his mind to go to England because Caroline had requested that he accompany her there. But the waters are muddied by what Leibniz added in his letter to
Windischgrätz. Alluding to the letters he had requested from Sinzendorff, he wrote:

> If I had been given a letter in Vienna, or had found one here to some minister of
> the king, such as I was led to expect, which would have put me in a position to say
> something, I could have returned to Vienna first without now going to England,
> and I could have provided some particular details about the views of the King of
> Great Britain. But there must have been a change of mind in regard to such a let-
> ter. Thus I will be in Vienna only after having been in England.
>
> [pp. 115, 117]

Here Leibniz says that if the letters for Görtz and Bothmer that he had commissioned Sinzendorff to write had arrived in Hanover, he 'could have returned to

INTRODUCTION xliii

Vienna first without now going to England', which suggests that the purpose of those letters was in fact to enable him to *avoid* going to England altogether and to return to Vienna forthwith. But we have seen that in his letter to Sinzendorff, written on the same day as this letter to Windischgrätz, Leibniz stated that he had received the letters he had commissioned Sinzendorff to write two days before this letter to Windischgrätz was written, contrary to Leibniz's claim that 'there must have been a change of mind in regard to such a letter'. But the passage may well have been revised in the final version of the letter sent to Windischgrätz to make it consistent with Leibniz's having already received the letters from Sinzendorff written for Bothmer and Görtz.[14] In any event, it seems that the letter to Windischgrätz supports the view that Leibniz would have preferred to return to Vienna rather than go to England but was moved, at least initially, to opt for England primarily because of Caroline's request that he accompany her. In any event, too, the letter suggests that Leibniz planned to return to Vienna after going to England with Caroline. And the aforementioned letter to Sinzendorff of 20 September reveals perhaps the most important consideration that was pulling Leibniz in the direction of Vienna. For after telling Sinzendorff that the letters Leibniz had commissioned him write to Görtz and Bothmer 'will serve to expedite my return to Vienna', he went on to ask Sinzendorff 'to preserve me in the good graces of the emperor to foster in the meantime the business of the Society Sciences,[15] since I hope that Mr. Schlick has expedited the rescript that I had requested,[16] and on favourable terms' (document 34, p. 119). The establishment of the Imperial Society of Sciences, of which the emperor had named Leibniz the president in an official proclamation issued on 14 August 1713, was a central concern of Leibniz during the last year of his life and undoubtedly the principal reason behind his desire to hasten his return to Vienna.

On 21 September, the day after he had written his letters to Sinzendorff and Windischgrätz, Leibniz wrote a letter to Bonneval in Vienna, saying 'If I were in a state to obey Her Royal Highness, I would go with her to England [...]' (document 35, p. 121). What is to be made of this hypothetical? It seems at least to suggest that Leibniz was somewhat less certain about going to England than he had been the day before, when he had written rather decisively in his letter to Windischgrätz that he was preparing to accompany Caroline to England at her request. His reference to his 'state' could suggest that concerns about his health were the cause of his

---

[14] The draft letter had originally been dated '16 de Sept. 1714', but Leibniz crossed out the '16' and wrote '20' above it. So the letter was apparently composed, or at least begun, on 16 September and then postdated to the 20th. So it would not be unreasonable to think that the passage in question was later revised in order to make it consistent with Leibniz's having received on the 18th the letters that Sinzendorff had sent him for Bothmer and Görtz.

[15] That is, the proposed Imperial Society of Sciences*.

[16] Concerning this rescript, see Leibniz's letter to Bonneval of November 1714 (document 45, pp. 157, 159).

xliv INTRODUCTION

uncertainty, something of which he had already made mention in his letter to Charlotte Elisabeth von Klenk of 16 September.

Just nine days after his letter to Bonneval, on 30 September, Leibniz wrote to Johann Matthias von der Schulenburg*, saying:

> I must tell you in confidence, sir, that my intention is to go to England shortly; I would like to have the honour of speaking with you beforehand. Madame the Princess approves the reasons I have for not going with her. I am thinking of going to Calais, since at present the roads are free.
>
> [...]
>
> I am pretending that I intend to go from here to the Leipzig fair, and I will depart for Hildesheim on or about Saturday. But from there I am thinking of going towards the Netherlands by the stagecoach that goes to Wesel. If you were in the neighborhood, sir, I would like to see you beforehand. You will learn my news at Hildesheim, in the place where the postal station of Brandenburg is located; it used to be at Steuerwald near the town.
>
> [document 36, p. 125]

The reasons Leibniz mentions here as those that Caroline approved for his not going to England with her might have been those that concerned his health, but he is still clearly determined to go to England, perhaps, as he suggests, by way of Calais. Leibniz had planned a devious route, intending to take the stagecoach south from Hanover to Hildesheim as a ruse to make those in Hanover believe he was indeed going to the Leipzig fair. But as he says, from Hildesheim he was thinking of heading west, towards the Netherlands, and eventually making his way to Calais, where he apparently intended to board a ship bound for England. It is clear that Leibniz wished to keep his travel plans hidden from the eyes of officials in Hanover, who would undoubtedly have made his movements known to the court in London.

Seven days later, on Sunday 7 October, Leibniz wrote to Schulenburg again, and again affirmed his intention to go to England sometime after Caroline's departure:

> Although my plan is to go to England, nevertheless, since I do not want to go in the retinue of the Royal Princess (although she did me the favour of letting me know that she would be very pleased by it), I am taking a trip to Braunschweig beforehand. I hope to be there Tuesday or Wednesday, and then I will decide on the route. If I could see you there, sir, I would be delighted.
>
> [document 40, p. 139]

Five days later, on 12 October, the very day that Caroline had departed Herrenhausen for England, Leibniz wrote yet again to Schulenburg:

Now that Madame the Princess of Wales has left, I will also leave tomorrow or the day after, at the latest; and after visiting Braunschweig, I will take a trip to Helmstedt, and from there I will give myself the honour of paying you a visit. Perhaps I will also have the benefit of finding your sister still there, whom I should have wished to be able to accompany. But I was not yet ready to leave, and I wanted to wait for the departure of Madame the Princess of Wales.

[document 41, pp. 141, 143]

In replying to Leibniz on 15 October, Schulenburg wrote this:

As soon as I was informed of your decision and of your trip to England, and that for this purpose you would be in Hildesheim on a certain determined day, I gave myself the honour of writing to you, and I sent this letter by courier to Steuerwald, where I would have traveled myself if I had not had a small trip to take, which I could not avoid. On my return, my letter for you, sir, was returned here, and by what you had done me the honour of writing to me, I learned at the same time that your trip to England was postponed for some time, that you would first go to Braunschweig and to Helmstedt in order to come here. I beseech you not to change your mind. My sister will be here until next Thursday. She will be very glad to see you here, as will my brother. We all entreat you to visit here as soon as it will be possible to do so, and we expect you late Tuesday or Wednesday near midday . I postpone the rest until I have the honour of seeing and embracing you […].

[document 43, p. 147]

Leibniz did finally make the trip and meet with Schulenburg, for in his letter to Leibniz of 31 October 1714, Schulenburg wrote that 'after having thanked you for the honour of your visit, which was as pleasant as it was useful, I would only wish that it had been longer and that I had the good fortune to be with you, sir, more often and longer; nothing would make me happier' (LBr. 840 Bl. 294r). And though his journey, just a day or two after Caroline's departure, first to Braunschweig and then to Helmstedt, and finally to Emden, Saxony-Anhalt, to meet Schulenburg, would probably have been less demanding than a trip to England, it does seem to weaken the case for thinking that Leibniz's reasons for not wanting to accompany Caroline to England had to do exclusively with concerns about his health. Although it is unclear whether a letter based on it was ever sent to, or received by, Caroline, there is an interesting draft letter that Leibniz wrote for Caroline around 8 December[17] in which he mentioned his recent trip through Saxony:

---

[17] On the question of whether a letter based on this draft was ever sent to, or received by, Caroline, see note 1 to document 50, p. 177.

xlvi INTRODUCTION

I have been greatly distressed by the departure of Your Royal Highness, which at first made Hanover unbearable for me, and in order to recover myself I had to take a trip to Saxony, which was also necessary for some domestic interests. I returned before the winter months. An attack of gout hindered my journey, but it passed along the way.

[document 50, p. 175]

So perhaps among Leibniz's reasons for not wanting to accompany Caroline to England was his desire to first take care of what he here calls 'domestic interests'. And although he does mention that he had experienced a brief bout of gout during his journey, that would not have affected his earlier decision to put off going to England with Caroline. Indeed, in an earlier letter to Bonneval at the beginning of November, even after his recent trip through Saxony, Leibniz revealed that he was still thinking about going to England in the very near future, and again by way of Calais: 'Now I must tell you, sir, that I could indeed still go to England this year, and perhaps soon. If I go there, I will travel to Calais, because the sea is going to become very stormy, and I do not fancy being driven to Norway, or running against some rock of the Orkneys' (document 45, p. 153). But on the other hand, Leibniz told Nicolas Rémond* early the next year, on 27 January 1715, that the 'distrust I had of my health prevented me from accompanying Madame the Princess of Wales. The gout has indeed since seized me [...]' (document 61, p. 207). This, then, would tend to support my earlier suggestion that when Leibniz told Bonneval, in his letter to him of 21 September, that 'If I were in a state to obey Her Royal Highness, I would go with her to England [...]', his uncertainty may have had to do with concerns about his health.

Leibniz's on-again, off-again decision to accompany Caroline to England is something of an enigma. Let us concede that concerns about his health might have been a factor, but it does not seem plausible to suppose that that by itself was decisive, given that upon Caroline's departure for England he left on a trip through Saxony, and given that after his return from that trip he was still actively planning on going to England soon, by way of Calais. One does not have to search far to find a much more decisive reason for Leibniz's vacillation. For Leibniz surely knew that Caroline's wish that he accompany her to England was of no consequence, since Caroline was not his employer. His employer was Georg Ludwig, now King of England, and the king seemed to have little interest in anything Leibniz was doing that did not touch on Leibniz's history of the House of Braunschweig-Lüneburg, his so-called *Annales imperii occidentis Brunsvicenses*; and now the king was especially roused against Leibniz because of the latter's long absence in Vienna.[18] Under

---

[18] Upon his return to Hanover from Vienna, Caroline informed Leibniz that Georg Ludwig had said of him that 'he comes only when I have become king', but in his letter to the Electoral Prince Georg August of 17 September 1714, Leibniz expressed the hope that the king was speaking merely in jest (document 31, p. 107).

INTRODUCTION   xlvii

the circumstances, to set off for England, with or without Caroline, while not having been granted the king's permission to do so, would have been an extraordinary violation of protocol, one that would no doubt have enraged the king further. So perhaps it came as no surprise to Leibniz that in a letter of 1 November 1714, Minister Bernstorff, having been informed that Leibniz was planning to leave for England, strongly advised him to remain in Hanover and focus his attention on his history of the House of Braunschweig-Lüneburg:

> I have postponed my response to yours because we have been informed that you are going to set off on a journey to this country, and there are even already some letters here addressed to you. You do well, sir, to remain in Hanover and resume your work there. You would not be better able to pay your respects to the king, nor better able to make amends for past absences, than by presenting to His Majesty when he comes to Hanover a good part of the works for which he has been waiting a long time.[19]

About a month later, on 3 December, Leibniz wrote again to Johann Matthias von der Schulenburg:

> A touch of gout has made me change my mind [about going to England]. It is an effect of the approach of winter. However, the pain has been tolerable. And upon arriving here from Saxony, I am nearly free of it. It is amusing that it has been reported here that I had left for England, and even that I had wanted to go to Calais. That may have come from what I had said here before I left, that if I wanted to go to England, I would go to Calais rather than from Holland.
>
> [document 48, p. 167]

Bernstorff's warning seems a more likely cause of Leibniz's change of mind than the 'touch of gout' he mentioned to Schulenburg; and it is somewhat ironic that Leibniz seems to dismiss the rumours that he had left for England and that he had wanted to go to Calais as 'amusing', since we have seen that in his letter to Schulenburg of 30 September 1714 and in his letter to Bonneval from the beginning of November 1714 he had expressed his desire to do precisely that.

In sum, we have seen that there is a fair amount of evidence that Leibniz wanted to make an appearance in England at some point, but there is also substantial

---

[19] Document 46, p. 163. It is worth noting that in his letter to Leibniz of 9 January 1715, Nicolas Rémond wrote:

> Everyone here supposed that you had arrived in England with the Princess of Wales; word had been sent from Hanover; they had written from London, and there were even some people to whom you have never written, to whom you never write, who had received your letters dated from Windsor.
>
> [document 59, p. 205]

xlviii INTRODUCTION

evidence that he did not wish to remain there for long. The letters that he had commissioned Sinzendorff to write to Bothmer and Görtz were intended to expedite his return to Vienna, or perhaps even to obviate the need of his having to go to England at all. We recall that in the letter to Windischgrätz, Leibniz had explained that he was planning to go to England with Caroline at her request, but he also mentioned that the emperor would probably be sending a lord to England for the embassy and said that 'if he arrived there while I was in England, I would do my utmost to be at his service', adding that 'if I return from England sooner, as could well be the case, I would try to make things ready [...]' (document 33, p. 115). So we need to address two questions: first, what reason could Leibniz have had for wanting to make an appearance in England, and second, why would Leibniz have wanted, were he to have gone to England, to return from there as soon as possible?

Although no direct evidence can be adduced to support an answer to the first question, I think a plausible, educated guess might emerge if we ask ourselves what Leibniz would have had to gain from making an appearance in London, even if he had no intention of staying. For I think there is one obvious and important advantage that Leibniz could have hoped to gain from such an appearance, namely, a demonstration to the English public at large, but especially to Newton and his followers, who had been accusing Leibniz of having plagiarized his infinitesimal calculus from Newton, that he still had standing within the Hanoverian court, now become the Court of Great Britain as well, and thus blunt, or even put an end to, the attacks that the Newtonians were launching against him. Moreover, I think a plausible answer to the second question will emerge from an answer to two further questions: first, what would Leibniz have had to gain from remaining in England, had it been possible for him to do so, and what would he have had to gain from returning to Hanover? As to the first of these questions, I think the answer is, 'not much'. It might be thought that England held out the promise of at least one thing that Leibniz could not resist, namely, the chance to act on a big stage with the great figures of science and philosophy and to participate directly in the activities of the Royal Society of London, of which he had been a member since 1673. By any standard, Hanover was in comparison with London an intellectual backwater.[20] But any hopes Leibniz might have had to find intellectual camaraderie in England had long since fallen victim to the priority dispute that had erupted between himself and Newton concerning the discovery of the calculus, a dispute that had already

---

[20] Indeed, in March of 1696 Leibniz had complained of his plight in Hanover to his English correspondent, Thomas Burnett. 'All that bothers me', he wrote,

is that I am not in a great city like Paris or London, which are full of learned men from whom one can benefit and even be helped. For there are many things that one cannot do by oneself. But here one finds scarcely anyone with whom to talk; or rather, in this region a courtier is not supposed to speak of learned matters, and without the electress [Sophie] they would be spoken of even less.
[GP III 175]

INTRODUCTION xlix

expanded to include serious matters of natural religion and natural philosophy:[21] he would have been an unwanted stranger in a strange land, a nemesis of Newton, the president of the Royal Society of London and England's greatest cultural and intellectual hero, who had directed the Society's sanctioning of Leibniz in 1712 through the publication of the *Commercium Epistolicum*.

As far as what Leibniz had to gain from returning to Hanover, we know from his letters to friends in Vienna that his plan was to finish his history of the House of Braunschweig-Lüneburg as quickly as possible in order to satisfy the king and then head back to Vienna,[22] where he held the prestigious position of imperial aulic councilor[23] and where he was deeply committed to the establishment of the proposed Imperial Society of Sciences, of which the emperor had already named him to be president once it was established. And although, as I have mentioned, Hanover was a relative intellectual backwater, Hanover was not Vienna, nor Vienna Hanover; and now that Leibniz had established himself in Vienna and had the prospect of creating and governing an Imperial Society of Sciences that could draw upon talent from across the Holy Roman Empire and Europe at large, the threat of intellectual isolation was no longer so pressing. If, then, I were allowed to hazard a

---

[21] Leibniz's earliest criticism of Newton's doctrine of gravity came in articles 18 and 19 of the *Discours de la Conformité de la Foy avec la Raison* (document 1), which was published in Leibniz's *Essais de Theodicée sur la Bonté de Dieu, la Liberté de l'Homme et l'Origine du Mal* (1710). These two articles concerned the dispute between some of the Reformed Protestants—in particular, as Leibniz says, 'those who follow Zwingli rather than Calvin on this matter' (p. 3)—and Evangelicals (that is, Lutherans) on the matter of the sacrament of the Eucharist. In article 19, by way of defending the Lutheran doctrine of real participation, Leibniz draws an analogy between that doctrine and the doctrine of 'operation at a distance [that] has just been rehabilitated in England by the excellent Mr. Newton' (p. 5). But he makes clear that he, in contrast to Newton, does not believe that such remote action of bodies can be natural because it 'surpasses the forces of nature' (ibid.). This represents the earliest public criticism that Leibniz made of the Newtonian doctrine of gravitation, and five years later he repeated this line of argument, which involves a comparison between the Eucharist and Newtonian gravitation, in his letter to Caroline of 10 May 1715 (document 72, pp. 237, 239). On 10 February of the following year, Leibniz wrote a long letter to the Dutch mathematician and physicist Nicolaas Hartsoeker* (document 2) in which he severely criticized not only the Newtonian doctrine of gravity, but also the doctrine of atoms and the void, which the Newtonians had adopted in conjunction with the doctrine of universal gravitation. The original French version of this letter reproduced in this volume was published in the *Mémoires pour l'Histoire des Sciences & des beaux-Arts* (aka, *Memoires de Trévoux*) for March 1712; the English translation reproduced in this volume was published in the *Memoirs of Literature* of London for 5 May 1712 (OS); the letter was later published again in the original French in the Amsterdam edition of the *Journal des Sçavans* for December 1712. Roger Cotes, the editor of the second edition of Newton's *Principia*, drew Newton's attention to the English version that was published in *Memoirs of Literature*, and Newton wrote a lengthy draft reply intended for the editor of that journal (document 3).

[22] See his letter to Bonneval of 21 September 1714 (document 35, p. 121) and his letters to the Dowager Empress Wilhelmine Amalie of 28 June 1715 (document 74, p. 245) and 20 September 1716 (document 145, p. 735) and to her first lady-in-waiting, Charlotte Elisabeth von Klenk, also of 28 June 1715 (document 73, p. 243) and 20 September 1716 (document 146, p. 739).

[23] As already noted, and with the support of Duke Anton Ulrich* of Brunswick-Wolfenbüttel, the grandfather of the regnant Empress Elisabeth Christine* of Braunschweig-Wolfenbüttel, Leibniz had been made aulic councilor, to which office the emperor had attached for Leibniz the special right of audience that was generally reserved only for the imperial ministers (see the postscript to Leibniz's letter to the Electress Sophie, 29 November 1713 (Klopp IX 414)).

1 INTRODUCTION

guess, it would be that Leibniz planned to return to Vienna as soon as he had completed his history in order to enlist the greatest scientists and philosophers of continental Europe in the proposed Imperial Society of Sciences,[24] an institution that would function as a counterweight to Newton's Royal Society of London, and then to spend whatever years remained to him in leading it in an intellectual war against Newton and his followers—something that would not have been possible were he stationed in England, where Newton himself was the reigning intellectual power.

Leibniz had many powerful and influential friends in Vienna that he knew would welcome him there—among them were the Regnant Empress Elisabeth Christine* of Braunschweig-Wolfenbüttel, granddaughter of Leibniz's employer in Wolfenbüttel, Duke Anton Ulrich*; the Dowager Empress Wilhelmine Amalie* of Braunschweig-Lüneburg, daughter of Duke Johann Friedrich*, Leibniz's first employer in Hanover; the dowager empress's first lady-in-waiting, Charlotte Elisabeth von Klenk*; the Imperial Chamberlain Theobald Schöttel; the Imperial Court Chancellor Count Philipp Ludwig Wenzel von Sinzendorff*; the President of the Imperial Aulic Council Ernst Friedrich Windischgrätz; the Imperial General Claude Alexandre de Bonneval*; and the Imperial Field Marshal and President of the Imperial War Council Prince Eugène* of Savoy. When he wrote to him on 6 October 1714, Bonneval informed Leibniz that 'Prince Eugène [...] assures you of all his friendship and asks me to tell you that since you are not going to England, you should really come to Vienna' (document 39, p. 135). In his draft letter to Caroline of 8 December 1714, Leibniz did not fail to mention that 'Count Bonneval tells me that Prince Eugène asks why, not having gone to England, I do not return

---

[24] Leibniz had, in fact, already begun to enlist members in the proposed Imperial Society of Sciences. In his letter of 20 September 1716 to the Dowager Empress Wilhelmine Amalie (document 145), Leibniz began by reminding the dowager empress of the regnant emperor's commitment to the establishment of the Imperial Society of Sciences and then explained that it was for that reason that he was working hard to quickly complete his 'history of the Western Empire, form the beginning of Charlemagne to the end of Henry the Saint'. He added that he was also preparing to be able to return to Vienna once the King of Great Britain, who at the time was visiting his Hanoverian electorate, had gone back to England. He then turned to the immediate purpose of his writing: 'And while I am thinking about all these things, I have suddenly been sent word that my wages, established by a decree of His Imperial Majesty, are to be cancelled.' Leibniz was particularly concerned that this cancellation of his wages would undermine the efforts he had already made to establish the Imperial Society of Sciences by having begun to enroll members:

But if the news that has just been given to me were true, it would be a blow that would greatly upset me; and beyond the disgrace of being degraded, so to speak, which I would not have suffered if I had never been received, I am hindered in the course of my good intentions in a very obvious way. For based on the spoken and written declarations of His Majesty, I began to enroll people of singular merit, and those who would not have even asked for any pledge in order to be members of the Imperial Society of Sciences when the actual founding would be accomplished. But now this cancellation would undermine all my influence.

[document 145, p. 737]

INTRODUCTION   li

to Vienna, where it is maintained that I ought not be uncomfortable' (document 50, p. 175).[25]

1.1.3 The Dispute with the Newtonians

On 10 March 1714 (27 February OS), John Chamberlayne*—one of only a very few Englishmen and members of the Royal Society still friendly towards Leibniz—stepped into the increasingly bitter war of words between Newtonians and Leibnizians over the discovery of the calculus and sought peace. In a letter to Leibniz of that date, he wrote:

> I have been inform'd of the Differences Fatal to Learning between two of the greatest Philosophers & Mathematicians of Europe, I need not say I mean Sr. Isaac Newton and Mr. Leibnitz, one the Glory of Germany the other of Great Britain [...] [I]t would be very Glorious to me, as well as Advantageous to the common Wealth of Learning, if I could bring such an Affair to a happy end, I humbly offer my Poor Mediation [...].
>
> [document 5, p. 27]

Leibniz responded to Chamberlayne on 21 April (document 7) and protested the findings of the *Commercium Epistolicum*. This was the notorious report of the Royal Society—written by the Society's then president, Isaac Newton himself, and rubber-stamped by a select committee of his supporters—which upheld John Keill's charge that Leibniz had plagiarized the calculus from Newton.[26] Chamberlayne showed Leibniz's letter to Newton in the hopes of initiating a private reconciliation, but Newton had other plans and intended to place Leibniz's

---

[25] In her recent intellectual biography of Leibniz, Maria Rosa Antognazza has written:

It must have been some consolation [to Leibniz] that his prestigious admirers in Vienna desired his return to the Imperial city. Indeed, notwithstanding his desire to move to London, he kept other options open, above all the possibility of returning to Vienna.

[Antognazza 2009, p. 523]

But this seems to get matters precisely the wrong way round. Leibniz was not keeping the possibility of returning to Vienna open as some backup plan in case he were unable to realize some supposed desire and preference to take up residence in London. On the contrary, and as I have argued, every indication is that although Leibniz may have initially wanted to leave open the possibility of making a brief appearance in England after he had decided to decline Caroline's request for him to accompany her, he was clearly not interested in making a permanent move to England; his clear intention and desire was to return to Vienna as soon as possible in order to tend to the proposed Imperial Society of Sciences and, as I have speculated, to wage intellectual war against Newton and his followers.

[26] In a paper he wrote in 1708, and which appeared in the *Philosophical Transactions* in 1710, Keill accused Leibniz, not only of stealing Newton's method of fluxions, but also of deliberately trying to cover up his thievery by changing 'the name and symbolism'. See Hall 1980, p. 145.

lii   INTRODUCTION

letter before the Royal Society.[27] And so on 31 May (20 May OS) Chamberlayne wrote to Newton and reminded him of some impending political realities:

> I am very sorry I can't wait on you this Afternoon when you are to consider of the Letter from Mr Leibnitz to me, concerning you, which Letter I did not intend to have expos'd to anybody's view, but your own, because I am not sure it wil be agreable to the writer, but since you have desired it, & to shew my Respect to you [...] I am content you should make what use you please thereof, only submitting it as a matter of Prudence how far you, in your private Capacity, may think it is adviseable to keep some Measures with a Gentleman that is in the Highest Esteem at the Court of Hanover.
>
> [document 9, pp. 37, 39]

Chamberlayne's admirable attempt to reconcile Leibniz and Newton—including the political warning he sounded here scarcely two and a half months before the death of Queen Anne and the succession of the House of Hanover—would prove to be of no avail. When he finally responded to Leibniz on 11 July, Chamberlayne reported that 'our Society has been prevail'd upon to vote that what you writ was Insufficient, & that it was not fit for them to concern themselves any further in that Affair &c, as will more fully appear by the Resolution enter'd into their Books of which I shal shortly send you a Copy [...]' (document 20, p. 79). Leibniz replied on 25 August, already nearly two weeks after the death of Queen Anne, threatening to retaliate by publishing his own *Commercium Epistolicum* concerning the calculus affair (NC VI 173; cf. his letter to Christian Wolff* at GLW, 161). So even as the wheels of the succession had begun to turn, Leibniz recognized that it was a foul wind indeed that was blowing his way from England. But by then the dispute between Leibniz and Newton had become even more bitter, having already begun, as I noted earlier, to encompass the serious issues concerning natural religion and natural philosophy that would eventually come to dominate Leibniz's correspondence with Newton's ally, Samuel Clarke. But it is worth remarking that at the time the Court of Hanover, and now of Great Britain as well, apparently knew little or nothing of the dark, corrosive conflict that had engulfed Leibniz, Newton, and their respective allies. The court, including Caroline, was still none the wiser when Caroline left Leibniz behind in Hanover and departed for England on 12 October. All of that, of course, would soon change. But Chamberlayne seemed certain about where the future political advantage would lie when the facts became known, as

---

[27] Newton translated Leibniz's letter from the original French (see NC VI 105-6), and as the following letter from Chamberlayne suggests, the letter was to be considered at the meeting of the Royal Society on 31 May 1714 NS. Later, in his letter to Leibniz of 7 August 1714 (27 July 1714 OS) (document 23a), Chamberlayne enclosed an abstract from the *Journal of the Royal Society* for 31 May (20 May OS), stating that Leibniz's letter was read at the meeting of that date but 'was not judged proper' (see document 23b, p. 91).

INTRODUCTION   liii

they inevitably would; and Leibniz also seems to have thought that such advantage as there might be could eventually be turned to his account. In retrospect it can be seen that thus far each man mistook much; but given the circumstances at the time, even Leibniz must have realized that setting sail under Caroline's banner, and without the permission of the king, to storm Newton's bulwarks on England's shores, would have been a hazardous and unpleasant manoeuvre, as much for Caroline as for himself. These may indeed have been among the reasons, alluded to in his letter of 30 September to Schulenburg, that Leibniz gave and Caroline approved for his not going with her to England. And so, I think, he thought better of it; and perhaps chastened by Bernstorff's warning in his letter to him of 1 November 1714, Leibniz ultimately chose to remain in Hanover, where he could discreetly cultivate his garden in Vienna in the hope that he would soon be able to reap its bounty.

1.2. The Correspondence: Phase One: the Princess Goes to London

1.2.1 Leibniz Requests an Appointment as Historiographer of Great Britain
It will be useful for expository purposes to divide the correspondence that transpired between Leibniz and Caroline after her departure for England into three distinct phases. In the first of these I place the letters roughly covering Caroline's first year in England—up to, but not including, her letter to Leibniz of 14 November 1715 (document 84)—which takes us nearly to the beginning of the controversy with Clarke. Leibniz composed an undated draft letter to Caroline that was probably written around 8 December 1714. Although it is unclear, as previously noted,[28] whether a letter based on this draft was ever actually sent to, or received by, Caroline, it does provide useful information. Leibniz began by telling her that he had been greatly upset by her departure, and then, as noted earlier, he mentioned that Count Bonneval had written from Vienna to say that 'Prince Eugène asks why, not having gone to England, I do not return to Vienna, where it is maintained that I ought not be uncomfortable.' But he then expressed his intention to spend the winter working on his history of the House of Braunschweig-Lüneburg, and this led him to propose that the king make him an historiographer of Great Britain, concerning which, he said, he had written to Minister Bernstorff (document 50, p. 175).

Ten days later, on 18 December 1714, Leibniz did write a letter to Caroline that she received and to which she responded. Leibniz was moved to write his letter in order to solicit Caroline's help in countering some intrigues against him at the Hanoverian court. 'There are some malicious individuals', he wrote,

who have suggested to the king that I neglected his service entirely, and a postscript on the subject reached the ministers here, which they have communicated

---

[28] See note 17 above.

liv   INTRODUCTION

to me and which seems to reduce to naught everything I have done to this point.[29] And as nothing can discourage me more than to see my labors disregarded, I wanted to make an effort to try to disabuse His Majesty and to merit his good graces. But I thought that nothing could contribute more to it than the intervention of Your Royal Highness.

[document 51, p. 179]

He then added some rather extensive political remarks concerning the relation between the king and Whigs, on the one hand, and between the king and Tories, on the other. But in the P.S. to his letter, Leibniz broached the topic of his hoped-for appointment to the position of historiographer:

The true means of encouraging me and treating me as I claim to have merited would be to give me now a pension of historiographer of England, since this post has sometimes been given to foreigners and admits more than one. I ask to be assured of it, but I do not ask to be in possession of it until after this winter, when I will have satisfied my written promise to Mr. Bernstorff, to whom I put this proposition before having received the postscript.

[p. 183]

The 'written promise' to Bernstorff that Leibniz mentions here was made in his letter to Bernstorff of 8 December (document 49, p. 169), written after he had already received the latter's letter advising him to stay in Hanover and work on his history. In response, Leibniz explained that he intended to complete one volume of his history that winter and gave a sketch of the material that it would cover. When he then stated his proposal for the position of historiographer, he argued specifically, even if somewhat speciously, that 'the act of Parliament that seemed to deny offices to foreigners [i.e., the Act of Settlement] only concerns offices that require naturalization' (p. 171).[30]

Onno Klopp cited the letter to Bernstorff requesting the position of historiographer of Great Britain in support of his claim that Leibniz was vacillating between Hanover (that is to say, England) and Vienna (Klopp XI xxiii). Maria Rosa Antognazza has taken a more decisive position in her recent intellectual biography of Leibniz, suggesting that it was in fact Leibniz's 'wish to follow the new king, George I, to London and serve as historiographer of Great Britain' (Antognazza 2009, p. 521). However, there is no indication in these letters, nor in any of the

---

[29]   See also Leibniz's letter to Görtz of 28 December 1714 (document 55, p. 191).

[30]   The relevant section of the Act of Settlement states that 'no person born out of the Kingdoms of England, Scotland, or Ireland, or the dominions thereunto belonging (although he be naturalized or made a denizen, except such as are born of English parents) shall be capable to be of the Privy Council, or a member of either House of Parliament, or to enjoy any office or place of trust, either civil or military, or to have any grant of lands, tenements or hereditaments from the Crown, to himself or to any other or others in trust for him.'

other letters that Leibniz wrote to Caroline and Bernstorff about this matter,[31] that Leibniz actually wanted to go to England, or that he thought it would be necessary for him to do so in order to receive such an appointment. Indeed, even when Caroline expressly stated her wish that Leibniz should come to England, as she would do on more than one occasion in her later letters, Leibniz simply ignored the suggestion or put it off. This is not to say, of course, that he did not want the position of historiographer. For I think it is likely that Leibniz thought he could moonlight as an historiographer of Great Britain even while operating out of Vienna as an imperial aulic councilor and president of the proposed Imperial Society of Sciences. After all, he had already been working both sides of the Hanover-Vienna street for some time, and there was no reason why he should not have wanted to exploit any third lane that might open up and permit him access to an additional pension from Great Britain. But as we shall see, beyond the promise of another pension there was an even more important goal that Leibniz seems to have had in mind when he made his proposal—one having quite specifically to do with his quarrel with Newton.

1.2.2 Leibniz's Suspicions and His Increasingly Bitter Dispute with the Newtonians

Caroline responded to Leibniz's letter of 18 December 1714 in a letter of 28 December 1714. It was a short response. After acknowledging receipt of Leibniz's letter, she turned immediately to the matter of his desire to be appointed historiographer: 'You are right to believe', she wrote,

> that it will always give me pleasure to oblige you and show you signs of my esteem. But it seems to me that it would be a mistake to take the king's time, and invite a refusal, to ask him for a new position for you before having made it clear to him that it is wrong to charge you with having so little advanced a history on which you have been working for so many years. When you shall have pushed this work as far as you hope to do this winter, it will be better justified to take on your behalf the step that you desire.
>
> [document 52, p. 185]

She then ended by curtly dismissing his political remarks about Whigs and Tories, saying: 'The space of a letter does not allow for discussion concerning the Whigs and Tories. It is safer to rely on those who, having seen matters up close, are more able to assess them.'

---

[31] See his letter to Bernstorff of 15 March 1715 (document 66, p. 223), his letter to Caroline of 18 December 1714 (document 51, pp. 181, 183), of 29 March 1715 (document 67a, p. 225), of 10 May 1715 (document 72, p. 237), and of 21 October 1715 (document 80, p. 279).

lvi INTRODUCTION

Leibniz wrote to Caroline again at the beginning of January in order, he said, 'to beg your pardon for the previous one' (document 58, p. 203); he then proceeded to lavish her with thanks and praise. Caroline responded to Leibniz on 16 January 1715,[32] explaining that 'I am sending the letter that Mr. Bernstorff gave me to respond to you, and that is the reason that I have not responded sooner to your two letters';[33] she added that 'if you are willing, sir, to take the trouble to apply yourself to the history of the family, I doubt that you can lack for what you want' (document 60, p. 207). To judge from Leibniz's reply of 29 January 1715—a letter simply dripping with paranoia—his foray into political commentary in his letter to Caroline of 18 December (document 51) seems to have been the subject of the letter from Bernstorff that Caroline had included with her own. 'It appears', he wrote,

> that Your Royal Highness wanted to take pleasure in honouring me with a letter in which everything was mysterious and almost strange, and it seems that she wanted to present me with an enigma for exercising the mind. [...] The response of others placed in there instead of that of Your Royal Highness prevents me from distinguishing her sentiments, which are laws for me, from those of others. I do not understand to what purpose the inserted response speaks to me about Whigs and Tories in a reproachful manner, since I do not believe that I have given reason to think that I have found fault with what is being done. [...] In it they will also have me remain in complete uncertainty about what I hoped for.[34] It is up to Your Royal Highness to leave me in these doubts or to extricate me from them to some extent.
>
> [document 62, p. 209]

The very same day he voiced his concerns in a letter to Johanne Sophie*, Gräfin (Countess) zu Schaumburg-Lippe, one of Caroline's German ladies-in-waiting:

> I hope that Her Royal Highness has not abandoned us entirely for the English, nor has wished to diminish her kindnesses by division, as the sun does not shine less on each in order to shine on several. Your Excellency, who belongs to us,[35] will take care of us in this regard, and I hope that you will seek, madame, to protect me

---

[32] In a previous article (Brown 2004, p. 268) I claimed that this letter was the first one that Leibniz had received from Caroline after her move to England. However, it may actually have been the second such letter. The first may have been the letter of 28 December 1714 (document 52) quoted above. But see note 33 below.

[33] This suggests that Caroline may not have sent her letter to Leibniz of 28 December after all, but was rather delayed by Bernstorff, after she had shown him Leibniz's letter to her of 18 December, so that he could write a response to Leibniz's political remarks and have them sent along with her letter to Leibniz of 16 January.

[34] Leibniz is referring to his request to be made a historiographer of Great Britain.

[35] Leibniz was here appealing to Johanne Sophie's sense of national solidarity in order to persuade her to help keep him in Caroline's thoughts, lest she forget him in favour of her new English subjects. This letter, written just three months after Caroline's arrival in England, demonstrates the extent to which Leibniz was preoccupied with the thought of losing Caroline's loyalty. This worry would become

INTRODUCTION lvii

in particular against the ill effects of absence, which I have only too much reason to fear.

[document 63, p. 211]

Caroline was nonplussed at Leibniz's suspicions, and in her next letter, of 12 February 1715, she sought to reassure him:

I do not know of what enigma you mean to speak, sir, in the letter that you have written to me. I sent you the letter that Mr. Bernstorff gave me to send to you. I added to it with my own hands, and you apparently did not notice that I was all but assured that if you apply yourself this winter to the history of the family, which the king takes very much to heart, I expect that you may then be able to obtain what you desire from the king. It seems to me that that is certain enough. I would like to be able to contribute to it, since I believe that I do my duty when I can do something to support a man of your merit.

[document 64, p. 213]

Bernstorff wrote to Leibniz on 5 April with the same message: no chance for the position of historiographer until the king sees progress on the history of the House of Braunschweig-Lüneburg (see document 69, p. 231).

Then, on 10 May, Leibniz received a letter from Henriette Charlotte von Pöllnitz* with news from Caroline:

I just received a letter from Her Royal Highness the Princess of Wales; she writes me these words:

I am reading the books of Locke; the one on the understanding appears fine to me, but as ignorant as I am I would think that there would be something to say in response, and I believe that Mr. Leibniz will be of my opinion. Please tell him that I will not respond to him until the king grants the position that he desires.

[document 71, p. 235]

When Leibniz then wrote to Caroline that same day, on 10 May (document 72), he had some reason to be upset and concerned. For his dispute with the Newtonians had been growing ever more bitter. In the summer of 1714 John Keill* had published a nasty reply to Leibniz in the *Journal Literaire* of the Hague, accusing him of, among other things, incompetence in the handling of second-order derivatives in one of his published treatises.[36] Keill's 'Answer' had been communicated to Leibniz by Christian Wolff in a letter of 3 October 1714, and Wolff had urged

---

a recurring theme, and a source of great tension, in Leibniz's later letters to Caroline, as she slipped slowly, but ineluctably, from his grasp into the hands of his Newtonian opponents in England.

[36] This was the *Tentamen de motuum coelestium causis* (*Essay on the Causes of the Heavenly Motions*), which had been published in the *Acta eruditorum* in 1689. For a discussion of Keill's charge, see Hall 1980, pp. 207–11.

lviii INTRODUCTION

Leibniz to make some reply (GLW, 160). Wolff wrote to Leibniz again in February 1715, urging him once more to reply to Keill (see GLW, 162). When Leibniz finally replied in a letter of 2 April 1715, he declared that 'I cannot bring myself to respond to that crude man Keill' (GLW, 162). A month later Wolff was still pressing Leibniz for a reply to Keill (see GLW, 164–5), and on 18 May Leibniz responded with a harshness of language that only Keill seems ever to have been able to provoke in him:

> Since Keill writes like a yokel, I do not wish to dispute with such a man [...]. Sometimes I think of beating the man back, with actual things, not words.
>
> [GLW, 168]

In his letter to Caroline of 10 May, Leibniz had written to Caroline to acknowledge the message she had sent him through Pöllnitz; but perhaps as a result of the latest provocation from Keill, he had then steered directly to the business of informing Caroline, apparently for the first time, of his dispute with Newton. With Caroline now behind enemy lines in England, Leibniz apparently felt it was not prudent to keep his peace any longer. Speaking of his hoped-for appointment to the position of historiographer, he wrote:

> It is true that what makes me aspire to the office in question is largely the point of honour. I should not want to yield any of it to a certain antagonist that the English have placed before me. Your Royal Highness will perhaps know that it is Chevalier Newton, who has a pension from the king, because he is superintendent of the mint. When the Court of Hanover was not on such good terms with that of England during the reign of the last ministry, some believed that it was a good time for them to attack me and to dispute the honour of a mathematical invention that has been attributed to me since 1684.[37]
>
> [document 72, p. 237]

Leibniz went on to point out that a French journalist had written that the dispute between himself and Newton had taken on the flavour of an international confrontation between England and Germany, and Leibniz suggested that the attack on him was primarily due to 'some rigid men, not very favourable to the cause of Hanover, at Cambridge (whence Newton came to London) as well as Oxford (where his seconds are found)'. This was obviously an attempt, certainly unfair, to associate Newton with anti-Hanoverian factions within England and to place the dispute in terms that might appeal to Caroline's sense of national pride. 'I dare say', Leibniz wrote,

---

[37] Leibniz had published a brief, but rather obscure outline of his differential calculus in the *Acta eruditorum* for October 1684, pp. 467–73, entitled *Nova methodus pro maximis et minimis, itemque tangentibus, quae nec fractas, irrationals quantitates moratum, et singular pro illis calculi genus.*

that if the king made me at least the equal of Mr. Newton in all respects (as one of his older servants may expect), then in these circumstances it would be to do honour to Hanover and to Germany in my person. And the position of historian, in which I claim to have distinguished myself, furnishes a fine occasion for it.

[document 72, p. 237]

He told Caroline that he had not had time to respond to the Newtonians, saying that 'I prefer to satisfy the king by producing my annals' and adding that 'His Majesty will be better able to refute them than I by treating me as the equal of Chevalier Newton, which will assuredly sting these gentlemen, hardly friendly to Hanover'. Newton 'is my rival', he declared, 'enough said' (p. 239). But Leibniz could not have adopted a more unpromising strategy. The last thing the Hanoverians could afford to do at the beginning of their reign was to present the appearance of split loyalties between England and Hanover. Caroline herself could scarcely have been expected to sympathize with Leibniz's motivations. She had gone to England—never to return to Germany—determined one day to become England's queen. There is no doubt she wanted Leibniz to obtain the office he desired, and it is clear that she worked hard to obtain it for him. But she could not have desired it for him on his own terms—as a reproach to Newton, the greatest light of the realm that was now her own. For such terms were politically impossible. Thus even as she worked for Leibniz's promotion, she strove with increasing fervour to reconcile him with Newton.

1.2.3 Cultivating His Garden in Vienna

Caroline held her peace for more than four months, but when she finally broke silence in a letter of 13 September 1715 she had bad news concerning the position Leibniz sought. '[T]he king', she wrote, 'gave me this response: "He must first show me that he can write histories; I hear he is diligent"' (document 78, p. 265). But as the king was planning to return to Hanover the following summer, Caroline expressed her belief that the matter would then be resolved in Leibniz's favour. In the meantime, Leibniz had not neglected Vienna. On 28 June he had written a long letter to the Dowager Empress Wilhelmine Amalie describing in detail his plans for the Imperial Society of Sciences and suggesting a scheme for its funding. But he also described his historical work and its importance for establishing the rights of the empire. Significantly, he now referred to the work not simply as a history of the House of Braunschweig, but as 'the annals of the empire and of Braunschweig' (document 74, p. 245), and he told the dowager empress that 'As I hope with the aid of God to ensure that this work be put in a state to be published this year, I plan to return to Vienna next year' (p. 245). Of interest in connection with this is an undated draft letter, intended for Caroline, that Leibniz appears to have written sometime between the end of October and mid-to-late December. It is marked by Leibniz as unsent, but in it he wrote that 'the king was advised that I would soon go to Vienna, and thereupon the council ordered me in a forbidding

lx INTRODUCTION

manner to do what I should have done well enough without its order'. He was dismayed that the king might believe he would behave in such a dishonourable way. 'It is true', he conceded,

> that I would not be unwelcome in Vienna, and perhaps someone who learned that imagined that I would run there immediately. But I prefer my duty even to my interests, and I want the king and the public to be satisfied above all. If this false report served as a pretext to delay longer the payment of my arrearages,[38] I would not know what to say about it. Can it be imagined that I would run away after having received them? And can I be suspected of such base acts? I do not believe the king is capable of attributing them to me.
>
> [document 82, p. 291]

While there is thus little reason to doubt that Leibniz intended to do his 'duty' and complete what he had promised to write on the history during the winter, there is also little reason to doubt that he intended thereupon to return to Vienna, where, he subtly suggested, his 'interests' lay.

1.3. The Correspondence: Phase Two: The Beginning of the Dispute with Clarke

1.3.1 The *Theodicy* Translation Project and Leibniz's Indictment of English Philosophy

Although Leibniz did not send the letter protesting the suspicions about his supposed designs on Vienna, he had sent Caroline a letter dated 21 October 1715 (document 80), a letter that he had mentioned in the unsent draft and in which he had thanked Caroline for remembering him and for speaking to the king on his behalf about his request for the position of historiographer of Great Britain. In her response of 14 November 1715, Caroline began by asking, 'How do you come to believe, sir, that I am able to forget a man such as yourself?'[39] She added that 'even the whole world would remind me of him'. She then turned quickly to an apparently new topic:

> I have spoken again today with the Bishop of Lincoln[40] concerning the translation of your *Theodicy*. He assures me that there is no one capable of that but Doctor Clarke, some of whose books I sent you [...].
>
> [document 84, p. 297]

---

[38] The king did not want to pay Leibniz for any more than three of the months that he had spent in Vienna. On the matter of Leibniz's arrearages, see Leibniz's letter to Bernstorff of 20 September 1714 (document 32) and to Görtz of 28 December 1714 (document 55).

[39] I had previously thought that Caroline was referring here to something that Leibniz had said in a letter that had been lost (see Brown 2004, p. 272), but I now understand that she was responding to Leibniz's letter of 21 October 1715.

[40] That is, William Wake*.

INTRODUCTION   lxi

She broached this topic again in her letter of 10 January 1716, saying that William Wake*, who had since become the Archbishop of Canterbury, 'spoke to me today about your admirable *Theodicy*, and immediately after his installation is done we will think about having it translated' (document 95, pp. 373, 375). But these were by no means the first mentions of the *Theodicy* translation project in the letters that were exchanged between Leibniz and Caroline after her arrival in England. Indeed the first mention of the project in the extant correspondence occurs in a letter that Leibniz had written to Caroline on 29 March 1715 (document 67a), scarcely more than five months after Caroline had landed at Margate, Kent on 22 October 1714. The letter from Caroline that Leibniz was answering is apparently lost,[41] but from Leibniz's reply we know that it concerned, at least in part, feelers that Caroline had sent out to the Bishop of Bristol, George Smalridge, concerning Leibniz's *Theodicy*. For Leibniz begins his letter by thanking Caroline for sending him the letter that the bishop had written to her concerning his *Theodicy*. The bishop had found the *Theodicy* obscure (see document 65, pp. 215, 217), and Leibniz replied, a bit defensively, and as if it were a compliment, or at least an adequate response, by pointing out that 'it does not appear that my book is thought to be obscure in France, or more obscure than the books of Father Malebranche and others that are quite in fashion'. 'When the Paris edition [...] is sold out', he continued, 'they are thinking of publishing another edition of it there with some additions. I would then explain the Latin and Greek citations, and if a genuine obscurity is pointed out to me, I will try to clarify it' (document 67a, p. 225). Leibniz was sufficiently stung by the bishop's remarks to have included with his letter a separate three-page response in folio (document 67b) that focused exclusively on the bishop's charge of obscurity.[42]

That Caroline's letter and her contact with the Bishop of Bristol was concerned with a project to have the *Theodicy* translated into English is made clear enough in the P.S. that Leibniz appended to his own letter. 'For translating my book into English', he wrote,

I believe that Mr. [Michel] de la Roche* would be suitable. He is a refugee clergyman who has published a kind of journal in English entitled *Memoirs of Literature*. It is true that I would prefer that an Anglican theologian undertake the translation.

[document 67a, p. 225]

---

[41] There are only three extant letters from Caroline to Leibniz after her arrival in England and dated prior to Leibniz's letter of 29 March 1715. None of them mentions the *Theodicy* translation project.

[42] The irony here is that in his letter to Caroline, Smalridge noted that 'My Lady Nottingham, when she first mention'd this Book to Me from Your Royall Highness, told Me that you complain'd of the Obscurity of it' (document 65, p. 215). So it may well be that Smalridge's accusation of obscurity was, wittingly or unwittingly, encouraged by Caroline's remark to Lady Nottingham, which the latter had conveyed to Smalridge and which Smalridge then mentioned in his letter. It must have come as a shock to Leibniz to read Smalridge's letter and learn that Caroline herself had complained of the obscurity of the *Theodicy*, which is perhaps why he replied a bit defensively and was moved to prepare the three-page response to the bishop's criticisms, which was certainly intended for Caroline and not for the bishop.

lxii INTRODUCTION

It is noteworthy that Leibniz reveals no hint here of having been previously unaware of the fact that Caroline was engaged in an attempt to have the *Theodicy* translated into English. Moreover, it appears that Caroline had wondered about who might make a suitable translator and had perhaps previously been aware of Leibniz's preference for a translator who was an Anglican theologian. All of this strongly suggests that the project was actually discussed before Caroline left Germany for England, and there seems no more likely time for that conversation to have taken place than during that month-long stay at Herrenhausen, when Leibniz and Caroline were reading through the *Theodicy* together before her departure for England. It would in fact have been extremely odd if the idea hadn't come up under the circumstances. For one thing, nearly two and a half years earlier, in a letter of 18 October 1712 to his Scottish correspondent Thomas Burnett, Leibniz had already floated the idea of having the *Theodicy* translated into English, in this case to disabuse some Anglican theologians of their mistaken views about the Lutheran doctrine of the Eucharist:

[A young German theologian] has told me that some from your Anglican Church have objected to him that we have an impanation and consubstantiation, which would be scarcely better than the transubstantiation of the Papists; but he referred them to my book [i.e., the *Theodicy*] and to the Memoirs of Literature [in which Michel de la Roche had favourably reviewed the *Theodicy*]. I believe that this indictment of our party, which is now being made, comes from the evil intention of those who favour the Papists and the Pretender and who would like to make us appear odious. This is why it would perhaps be good if my book were translated into English. I have not yet learned of the Bishop of Salisbury's opinion of my book, but I have learned that of the Archbishop of York, who having read at least the Latin piece placed at the end, much approves it.[43]

Given that, what could have been more natural under the circumstances than for Leibniz to suggest to Caroline that it might be edifying for the Anglican theologians to have an English translation of the *Theodicy* available to them and for Caroline to agree and think approvingly of having her favourite book, by her very close friend, translated into the language of her new realm, a language that she had been studying in preparation for her role as part of the royal family of England. But now there may well have been more on Leibniz's mind than simply instructing the Anglican theologians on the subtleties of his own take on the Lutheran doctrine of the Eucharist.[44] For it is quite conceivable that now, at Herrenhausen, Leibniz had

---

[43] GP III 323-4. I am grateful to Lloyd Strickland for drawing my attention to this passage.

[44] For a brief discussion of Leibniz's theory of the Eucharistic dogma of real participation as immediate operation, see articles 18 and 19 of the *Discours de la Conformité de la Foy avec la Raison* (document 1), which was published in Leibniz's *Essais de Théodicée sur la Bonté de Dieu, la Liberté de l'Home et l'Origine du Mal* (1710). See also his letter to Caroline of 10 May 1715 (document 72, pp. 237, 239).

already begun thinking about how the translation project might eventually be turned to his account in his ongoing conflict with the Newtonians; and now, in the person of the new Princess of Wales, there was an apparently willing instrument of stature to make the execution of that idea possible.

There is further evidence from the letter that the Bishop of Bristol wrote to Caroline, and which she forwarded to Leibniz, that Caroline was already prepared to act on the *Theodicy* translation project when she disembarked at Margate. The bishop's letter (document 65) is dated 4 March 1715 (that is, 15 March 1715 NS), and in it he notes that Caroline had personally delivered a copy of the *Theodicy* into his hands while he was in London and had requested that he report his thoughts concerning the book to her. But he tells Caroline that after his return to Oxford, he 'was taken with first a great heaviness, and afterwards an Acute pain in my Head, which hath for some Weeks indispos'd Me for writing, & which is not Yet quite remov'd, tho^{h} I thank God it is in great Measure abated' (p. 215). Assuming that by 'some Weeks', the bishop meant that he had been 'indispos'd [...] for writing' for at least a month, and allowing for the time he spent in London before returning to Oxford, and for the time in travelling from London to Oxford, and for the time it took him, as he says, to 'peruse & consider [the *Theodicy*] with the best Attention & closest Application I could' and compose his letter to Caroline, it seems that Caroline could not have placed the *Theodicy* in the bishop's hands much later than the beginning of February 1715, that is, scarcely more than three months after her arrival in England. Given how much of her initial time in England would have been given over to ceremonies of state (Georg Ludwig's coronation took place on 31 October) and establishing her household, Caroline's presentation of the *Theodicy* to the Bishop of Bristol must have taken place at her earliest possible convenience.

We have seen that in her letter to Leibniz of 14 November 1715, Caroline had written that the Bishop of Lincoln 'assures me that there is no one capable of [translating the *Theodicy*] but Doctor Clarke' (document 84, p. 297). As previously noted, this letter was written in response to Leibniz's letter of 21 October, which was itself written in response to Caroline's letter of 13 September (document 78), a letter in which Caroline had reported her appreciation of the letters exchanged between John Locke and the Bishop of Worcester, Edward Stillingfleet (p. 265). Leibniz had replied that Locke 'defends himself there nicely enough' (document 80, p. 279). But then, in a remark that anticipated the criticism he would level against English philosophy in the passage from his letter to Caroline from the end of November (document 85)[45] that Clarke would later publish as Leibniz's First Paper in his 1717 edition of their correspondence (document 86), Leibniz added: 'Mr. Locke undermines the great truths of natural religion; Mr. Stillingfleet perceived all the bad

---

[45] This letter (document 85) is here published for the first time in its entirety. In a previous article (Brown 2004, p. 273) I had mistakenly written that this letter had been lost, but I was subsequently able to locate it in the Stadtarchiv Hannover.

lxiv INTRODUCTION

consequences of it, but the other had the skill to parry the blows and get the last laugh.' Leibniz continued:

> I had hoped that my *Theodicy* would be found a bit more sound in England, if one day it were read in English, and that it would furnish some better principles. But I see that Your Royal Highness, who had made me hope by being willing to consider it, has not yet found anyone suited to carrying it out. If it is still her intention, and if she made it known, I believe that not one of the better English writers would refuse her.[46]

[p. 279]

It was to this remark that Caroline was responding in her letter to Leibniz of 14 November when she reported that the Bishop of Lincoln had assured her that Clarke was the best man for the job of translating the *Theodicy*, and it was undoubtedly because Leibniz had already informed her, in his letter of 10 May 1715, of his dispute with Newton over the discovery of the calculus that Caroline added, ominously, that 'this same man [Clarke] is an intimate friend of Chevalier Newton, and I do not believe that the matter is in very good hands' (document 84, p. 297).[47]

In his letter of 10 May, Leibniz had not only informed Caroline of his dispute with Newton over the discovery of the calculus, but had also gone on to argue that 'the philosophy of Mr. Newton [...] is a bit extraordinary', citing Newton's notion of gravity as a case in point:

> He claims that a body attracts another at whatever distance it may be and that a grain of sand on the earth exerts an attractive force as far as upon the sun, without any medium or means. After that will these sectarians wish to deny that by the omnipotence of God we can share in the body and blood of Jesus Christ without any impediment of distance? It is a good way to embarrass them, the men who,

---

[46] It is significant that Leibniz included these remarks about Caroline's not having found a suitable translator for the *Theodicy* in his response to her letter of 13 September (document 78), the letter with which she had broken her self-imposed four-month silence. For in that letter Caroline had said nothing about not having found a suitable translator. So barring the possibility that there is some other candidate letter that has been lost, the only letter that Caroline had written to Leibniz prior to her letter of 13 September that could be a candidate for the one that Leibniz was commenting on here would be the one, apparently lost, with which she had transmitted George Smalridge's letter to her of 15 March 1715 (NS), the letter in which Smalridge had given his assessment of the *Theodicy*. If that is correct, then it would appear that Caroline had already been in search of a translator before she transmitted Smalridge's letter to Leibniz and had perhaps reported in her cover letter to Leibniz that at that point she had still been unable to find one that was suitable. This tends, I think, to support my earlier speculation that Caroline had already been intent on finding a suitable translator for the *Theodicy* when she disembarked at Margate, Kent on 22 October 1714 and that this translation project had been discussed with Leibniz while they were reading through the *Theodicy* together during their month-long stay at Herrenhausen before Caroline's departure for England. It was perhaps during this same time at Herrenhausen that Caroline had made Leibniz 'hope', as he says here, 'by being willing to consider it.'

[47] See also her letter to Leibniz of 6 December 1715 (document 89, p. 335).

INTRODUCTION lxv

from an animus against the House of Hanover, now free themselves more than ever to speak against our religion of the confession of Augsburg, as if our Eucharistic reality were absurd.

[document 72, pp. 237, 239]

Leibniz never did raise the issue of the Eucharist in the exchanges with Clarke,[48] but the passage in this letter comparing the Lutheran doctrine of the Eucharist and the Newtonian doctrine of gravitation clearly alluded to—and was probably intended to remind Caroline of—the similar discussion in section 19 of the *Discours de la Conformité de la Foy avec la Raison* that prefaced the *Theodicy*.[49] At any rate, Leibniz seems to have decided early on that the best way to make his case to Caroline against the Newtonians was to turn the issue to philosophy—to natural religion in particular—and away from mathematics—something that he had already done to some extent in his published writings[50] and to an even larger extent in his private papers and correspondence. So finally, in late November 1715, came the aforementioned letter to Caroline. In response to Caroline's reservations about Clarke's suitability as a translator of the *Theodicy*, Leibniz wrote:

Since your Royal Highness wants my *Theodicy* to be translated into English, that is as good as done. And I would deem Mr. Clarke (if he wanted to be charged with it and if he had sufficient mastery of French for this) an honourable enough man, friend though he might be of my adversary, to acquit himself of it properly.

But facing the reality of the situation he continued by admitting that Clarke

will apparently [...] not think about it, and the Bishop of Lincoln (it seems) will not make himself think about it without an express order. If the need arose there would be no lack of men who would acquit themselves of it very well. I dare say

---

[48] Perhaps he did not raise the issue of the Eucharist with Clarke because in his letter to Caroline of 14 January 1716 (document 97, p. 385), he solicited Caroline's aid in a scheme to unite the Protestant churches—in which the disagreement among the churches on the issue of the Eucharist would eventually have to be addressed—and he wanted his own participation in it to be kept a secret.

[49] See note 21 above.

[50] In addition to what he had said about gravity in Section 19 of the Preliminary Dissertation of the *Theodicy*, and as mentioned in note 21 above, Leibniz disparaged the Newtonian concept of gravity in the letter of 10 February 1711 to the Dutch philosopher Nicolaus Hartsoeker. In the letter, Leibniz wrote:

[T]he Ancients and the Moderns, who own that Gravity is an *occult Quality*, are in the right, if they mean by it, that there is a certain Mechanism unknown to them, whereby all Bodies tend towards the Center of the Earth. But if they mean that the Thing is performed without any Mechanism, by a simple *primitive Quality*, or by a Law of God, who produces that Effect without using any intelligible Means; it is an unreasonable occult Quality, and so very occult, that 'tis impossible it should ever be clear, tho an Angel or God himself, should undertake to explain it.

[document 2, p. 11]

lxvi INTRODUCTION

that they would need a bit of it in England. For natural religion itself declines precipitously there.

[document 85, p. 313]

The last sentence quoted is the first sentence of the extract that would be published by Clarke as 'Mr. Leibniz's First Paper'[51] in his 1717 edition of the correspondence (document 86); what follows is Leibniz's bill of particulars against English philoso-phy (p. 313):

Many make souls out to be corporeal, and others make God himself out to be corporeal. Mr. Locke and his followers at least question whether or not souls are material and naturally perishable. Mr. Newton says that space is the organ that God uses to perceive things. But if he has need of some means of perceiving them, then they are not entirely dependent on him and were not produced by him. Mr. Newton and his followers also have a very strange view concerning the work of God. According to them God needs to wind up his watch from time to time, otherwise it would cease to operate. He has not had enough insight to make a perpetual motion. This machine of God is even so imperfect that he is forced to clean it from time to time by an extraordinary concourse, and even to repair it like a watchmaker who will be all the worse a master as he is more often forced to touch it up and make repairs to it. On my view, the same force and vigor always remains, and it only passes from matter to matter, following the laws of nature and the beautiful pre-established order. And when God works miracles, I maintain that it is not in order to support the needs of nature, but those of grace. Otherwise one would have a very base idea of the wisdom and power of God.[52]

With that the stage was set for the correspondence with Clarke. Leibniz knew that Caroline was not in a position to adjudicate his calculus priority dispute with Newton. On the other hand, he knew that she was keenly interested in both natural religion and his *Theodicy*; so naturally enough Leibniz sought to turn Caroline's attention to what he argued were the deleterious effects on natural religion of English philosophy in general, and of Newtonian philosophy in particular. Thus in a letter to Christian Wolff of 23 December 1715, dispatched shortly after he had sent off his Second Paper for Clarke (document 92), Leibniz wrote that 'it is wel-come that my adversary touches on a matter that is not resolved by mathematical

---

[51] However, in the draft letter Leibniz had written 'Car la religion naturelle meme y degenère extremement' (document 85, p. 312), whereas the sentence in the extract published by Clarke reads *'Il semble que la Rél, igion Naturelle* même *s'affoiblit extremement'* (document 86, p. 316). Thus the letter that was actually received by Caroline, and from which the extract was presumably taken, may have differed to some extent from the draft.

[52] This passage was the one that Caroline showed Clarke and which consequently sparked the corre-spondence between Clarke and Leibniz. The original letter in which this passage appears is here pub-lished in its entirety for the first time as document 85.

considerations, but about which the princess herself is easily able to form a judgment' (document 94, p. 367)—even though, of course, it was Leibniz himself who had steered the discussion in the direction of natural theology and away from mathematics. And by the time he was writing his Third Paper for Clarke (document 100), Leibniz had already set the main parameters of the debate. Noting that he had never disagreed with Clarke's view that 'God's Conservation is an actual Preservation and Continuation of the Beings, Powers, Orders, Dispositions, and Motions of all Things',[53] Leibniz went on to point out that

> Our Dispute consists in many other things. The Question is, whether God does not act in the most *regular* and most *perfect* manner? Whether his Machine is liable to *Disorders*, which he is obliged to mend by extraordinary Means? Whether the Will of God can act *without Reason*? Whether Space is an *absolute Being*? Also concerning the Nature of *Miracles*; and many such Things, which make a wide difference between us.
>
> [Lz.III.16/document 100, p. 415]

Thus everything was cast in terms of issues that Caroline could be expected to understand and care about—about natural religion and, in particular, about issues that in Leibniz's mind bore on the perfection of God. Even the question about the nature of space was no exception to this, since Leibniz argued that it was ultimately bound up with a question about God's perfection, viz., whether God could act without reason and hence without wisdom.

1.3.2 Caroline's Allegiance to Leibniz and Her Dispute with Clarke

Caroline responded to Leibniz's late-November letter in a letter to Leibniz of 6 December 1715. Caroline's letter was everything that Leibniz could have hoped for. After pronouncing herself absolutely satisfied with the case that Leibniz had made for the payment of his arrearages and telling him that the king also seemed satisfied, she announced that 'we are thinking very seriously of having your *Theodicy* translated, but we are seeking a good translator'. But now, after having spoken with Clarke and having shown him Leibniz's indictment of English philosophy, she firmly declared that 'he is too much of the opinion of Sir Isaac Newton, and I am myself engaged in dispute with him'. Clarke, she said,

> gilds the pill and does not want to admit absolutely that Mr. Newton holds the views that you attribute to him. But in fact you will see from this paper joined

---

[53] Although Clarke disagreed with Leibniz's later claim that 'God knows things, because he produces them continually' (Lz.IV.30/document 125a, p. 569), arguing instead that 'God discerns things [...]. Not by *producing them continually*; (For he *rests* from his work of *Creation* :) but by being *continually* omnipresent to every thing which he *created at the Beginning*' (Cl.IV.30/document 129, p. 599).

lxviii INTRODUCTION

herewith[54] that it comes to the same thing. I can only ever believe that which is suitable to the perfection of God. I find it much more perfect in your view than in that of Mr. Newton, in which God must actually always be present in order to mend the machine because he could not do it from the beginning. Neither Dr. Clarke nor Newton wants to profess to be of Mr. Locke's sect, but I neither can nor want to be of theirs.

[document 89, p. 335]

When he had formulated his indictment of English philosophy in his late-November letter to Caroline, Leibniz had intentionally invoked the authority of his *Theodicy*, a book that he well knew was close to Caroline's heart. When he later informed Johann Bernoulli of his ongoing dispute with Clarke on 7 June 1716, he somewhat disingenuously suggested that 'I had casually written to the Most Serene Royal Princess of Wales,[55] who due to her excellent nature is not unconcerned with these matters, that philosophy, or rather natural theology, is degenerating somewhat among the English' (document 127, p. 579). But the attack on the English philosophers seems to have been anything but 'casual'. Earlier, in his aforementioned letter to Christian Wolff of 23 December 1715, Leibniz had written that the Newtonians

have […] attacked even my philosophical principles, to induce me all the more to respond. But there, too, they will bite on something hard. The Most Serene Princess of Wales, who read my *Theodicy* with an attentive mind, and was delighted with it, recently disputed in favour of it with a certain Englishman of ecclesiastical order who has access to the court [Samuel Clarke], as she herself has pointed out to me.[56] She disapproves what Newton and his followers assert, that God needs to correct and revitalize his machine from time to time.

[document 94, p. 367]

Of course it was Leibniz himself who had disputed with the English philosophers in favour of the *Theodicy* in his late-November letter to Caroline, and Caroline had merely followed his lead. But one would scarcely know this from what Leibniz told Wolff. As we have seen, at the end of his letter to Wolff, Leibniz slyly declared that 'it is welcome that my adversary touches on a matter that is not resolved by mathematical considerations, but about which the princess herself is easily able to form a judgment'—even though, again, it was Leibniz himself who had steered the debate in the direction of natural theology and away from mathematics. His reasons for wanting to do so are not far to seek. It was no depreciation of Caroline that Leibniz implied that she could not fathom the details of the mathematical debate. In his letter to Leibniz of 5 May 1716,

---

[54] Here Caroline is referring to Clarke's First Reply (document 90).

[55] See Leibniz's letter to Caroline from the end of November 1715 (document 85, p. 313).

[56] See Caroline's letter to Leibniz of 6 December 1715 (document 89, p. 335).

INTRODUCTION   lxix

Minister Bothmer would decry Leibniz's calculus dispute with Newton on the grounds that it 'upsets you and diverts you from occupations to which you devote yourself for his [the king's] service, for the benefit of the public, and for your own glory, which will certainly be much greater and more immortalized by your history than by a dispute concerning a matter about which, among a thousand persons, scarcely a single one understands anything' (document 116, p. 519). Shortsighted it certainly was, but there was more than a little truth in Bothmer's observation. If Leibniz wanted to elicit Caroline's sympathy in his dispute with Newton, he had to frame the debate in terms she could appreciate and in terms that would appear favourable to his own position. Given Caroline's interest in philosophy and natural religion and her devotion to the *Theodicy*, Leibniz's decision was a no-brainer.

1.3.3 Leibniz's Response to Clarke, the Abbé Conti, and Caroline's Continuing Loyalty

Leibniz sent his Second Paper for Clarke (document 92) in a letter to Caroline from mid-to-late December 1715. In his letter Leibniz dismissed Clarke's response as a paper 'done as well as it can be for supporting a feeble cause' (document 91, p. 345) and then proceeded, to his later regret, to introduce the princess to a man of his acquaintance then in England:

> There is now a noble Venetian in England named Abbé Conti,[57] who applies himself earnestly to the investigation of fine things. When he was in France, he testified to being firmly on my side, and he wrote me a nice letter[58] in which, among other things, he makes known that he has marked well the beauty of the system I establish, above all in relation to souls. I do not know whether my antagonists from London will have since won him over a bit. He will be right to be accommodating in order to profit better from their conversation. However, I hope that the Abbé Conti will preserve some place for me. I would like him to have the honour of being known by Your Royal Highness, and I have since advised him to try to obtain it, if he has not yet done so.
>
> [document 91, p. 347]

In his absence, Leibniz knew he needed allies in England to prosecute his case, but the fact that he nominated the Abbé Conti for the position—someone he already suspected of being somewhat irregular in his affections[59]—is an indication of the paucity of candidates.

In her letter of 10 January 1716, with which she enclosed Clarke's Second Reply, Caroline volunteered that 'I do not know if the bias I have for your merit makes me

---

[57] That is, Antonio Schinella Conti*.
[58] That is, Conti's letter to Leibniz of April 1715 (document 79c).
[59] See Leibniz's letter to Nicholas Rémond of 6 December 1715 (document 88a, p. 321).

lxx INTRODUCTION

partial, but I find any reply to be rather words, without their being able to be called replies.' So far, so good for Leibniz. Caroline was still on his team and willing to share intelligence about the enemy: 'you are not mistaken about the author of the responses', she confided, 'they are not written without the advice of Chevalier Newton, whom I would like to reconcile with you' (document 95, p. 373). By then the Abbé Conti had introduced himself to Caroline, who thanked Leibniz for his acquaintance and notified him that she and the Abbé had set themselves up as mediators between himself and Newton. But on the philosophical issue that mattered most to her, Caroline made it clear that she was not going to be a neutral observer:

> I was unable to prevent myself from saying to Doctor Clarke that your opinion appeared to me the most suitable to the perfection of God, and that all philosophy that sought to alienate me from it appeared to me to be imperfect, since on my view it was done or ought to be sought in order to sooth us and to strengthen us against ourselves and from everything that assails us from outside, and I do not believe it could have this effect if it taught us the imperfection of God. He spoke to me a very long time in order to convert me to his view, and he did not succeed.
>
> [ibid.]

If this were not enough to convince Leibniz that his *Theodicy* strategy was working, Caroline ended by noting that her friend William Wake had just been elevated to the Archbishopric of Canterbury and that he had talked with her that day about 'your admirable *Theodicy*'. She added that 'immediately after his installation is done we will think about having it translated' and then ended on this splendid note:

> I am quite proud to agree with this great man, who finds that the more this book is reread the more it is found incomparable. The fondness I have for this book reminds me of the Bishop of Spiga [Agostino Steffani*], who said that he loved being admired in music by the greatest ignoramuses. I expect that you must feel the same way; so you ought to be very glad to be admired by as great an ignoramus as I, but the truth moves the ignorant and the most wise alike, and that is what I took the liberty of telling the late electress, who claimed not to be able to understand it [i.e., the *Theodicy*].
>
> [p. 375]

1.4. The Correspondence: Phase Three: Caroline's Apostasy and the End of the Affair

1.4.1 Leibniz's Suspicions and the Newtonian Blitz to Convert Caroline

Leibniz drafted a response to Caroline's letter on 25 February 1716 and sent it along with his Third Paper for Clarke (document 100). He thanked Caroline for her wish to reconcile him with Newton and suggested that there was a real possibility for

INTRODUCTION   lxxi

this since all the noise had been made, not by Newton (although he had 'connived' in it), but by 'a certain man who is not considered to be among the better governed'—by which, of course, he meant John Keill (document 99, p. 407). Earlier, around 14 January 1716, Leibniz had written a long letter (document 97)[60] in which he attempted to enlist Caroline's help in his scheme to unite the Reformed (i.e., Calvinist) churches of Brandenburg with the Evangelical (i.e., Lutheran) churches of Hanover through the mediation of the Anglican church in England. In a letter to Caroline of 28 April,[61] Leibniz wrote to remind her of his January letter, to which Caroline had not responded. This lack of response worried him:

> I hope to learn the thoughts of Your Royal Highness about it [i.e., the scheme to unite the Protestant churches], and I thought there was only something of this nature that could refresh her memory with regard to me. You are firm and constant in great and important matters, but I have to fear, madame, that you may not be equally so in small matters, since everything that relates to me must be in your care, and especially the translation of the *Theodicy*. It seems that Mr. Clarke thought he noticed something of this nature, which could have given him the audacity to publish a tract against me, apparently connected with our correspondence, which has had the honour of passing through the hands of Your Royal Highness. It would be wrong if he published it without her permission; however, I want at least to see this tract in order to evaluate it.
>
> [document 113, p. 501]

In Caroline's reply of 5 May there was unfortunate news concerning the Abbé Conti: he 'has taken the trouble to lose some of the papers that you wanted me to entrust to him'. But there were also some reassurances:

> how is it that you suspect me of not being the same for you? I believe that being steadfast for friends is one of the points of our duty, and I appeal to the king on account of it. Doctor Clarke has published nothing of what has passed between you and him, and what you probably heard about are some letters that he and a Scottish clergyman wrote some time ago.
>
> [document 115, p. 513]

Despite this, the rest of Caroline's letter could scarcely have encouraged Leibniz. In her letter of 10 January 1716 (document 95), she had told him that Clarke had

---

[60] In a previous article I mistakenly suggested that this undated letter had been written between the beginning of March and the middle of April (see Brown 2004, p. 277).

[61] In a previous article I had mistakenly suggested that this letter had been lost (see Brown 2004, p. 277).

lxxii INTRODUCTION

gotten nowhere in attempting to convert her; but now, four months later, all that had changed:

> Last Saturday I had the Abbé Conti and Clarke with me from six until ten o'clock. I very much wanted you to support me; their knowledge and Clarke's clear manner of reasoning nearly made me a convert to the void.
>
> [p. 513]

She noted that she had 'seen the letter that Chevalier Newton sent you through Conti'[62] and reported that Newton

> claims that everything he put in there are matters of fact. I impatiently await your response. Conti, at least between us, does not find any knowledge in France and says that the whole thing consists in dispute about religion. He considers you the greatest man, and Sir Isaac Newton is thought to be infinitely knowledgeable here. I am grieved to see that persons of such great knowledge as you and Newton are not reconciled. The public would profit immeasurably if it could be done. But great men are in that like women, who never relinquish their lovers but with the utmost chagrin and extreme mortification, and that is where you are lodged, gentlemen, on account of your opinions.
>
> [ibid.]

Caroline ended her letter with another plea for reconciliation, but added a most portentous postscript:

> The day after tomorrow we will see the experiments of Chevalier Newton. The king has provided a room for Desaguliers.[63] I wish for you there, as well as for Saturday, when Chevalier Newton, the Abbé Conti, and Clarke will be with me.
>
> [p. 515]

Ten days later, on 15 May, Caroline wrote again in order to send Clarke's Third Reply (document 120), which, she reported, 'has fortunately been recovered'. In a spirit of liberality, she advised Leibniz to 'Drop your serious dispute and prove to us

---

[62] This was Newton's response of 17 March 1715 (document 101g) to the postscript that Leibniz had appended to his letter of 6 December 1715 to Conti (document 88b) and that Conti had then transmitted to Newton in an attempt to open a dialog between the two. Leibniz responded to Newton's letter in his letter to Conti of 9 April 1716 (document 108).

[63] John Theophilus Desaguliers (1683–1744) was the son of a Huguenot minister. He was just two years of age when his father fled with him to England to escape persecution after Louis XIV revoked the Edict of Nantes in 1685. He was educated at Christ Church, Oxford, and became a fellow of the Royal Society in 1714. He succeeded Francis Hauksbee as 'Curator and Operator of Experiments' for the Society, and in that capacity he often assisted Newton with his experiments. See Gjertsen 1986, pp. 168–9.

the plenum, and let the chevalier [i.e., Newton] and Clarke prove the void on their side'; but she ended on a note that seemed to suggest that the Newtonians had already won her over, or nearly so:

> Tomorrow we will see the experiments about colours, and one that I have seen for the void has nearly converted me. It is up to you, sir, to bring me back into the right path, and I am expecting it by the response that you will make to Mr. Clarke.
>
> [document 119, p. 537]

And in a somewhat unconvincing attempt to assuage Leibniz's fears, she ended by saying that 'despite your suspicions, you will find me always the same'.

1.4.2 Caroline Begins to Turn

These last two letters from Caroline mark a watershed in her correspondence with Leibniz, and it is ironic that in the second of them she signed off by writing that 'despite your suspicions, you will find me always the same'. In one sense, I suppose, she *was* the same: she still regarded herself as Leibniz's friend and still continued to promote him to the king. But in another sense, of course, nearly everything had changed. No longer in these letters, nor in any of the others she would later write to Leibniz, do we find her defending Leibniz's position as more consonant with divine perfection than that of Clarke and Newton; and now she was on the verge of accepting the doctrine of atoms and the void, which she knew that Leibniz opposed. At best, she was now neutral: 'prove to us the plenum', she told Leibniz, 'and let the chevalier and Clarke prove the void on their side'. We know from these letters that the Newtonians were in the process of applying a full-court press to win Caroline over to their side. She was the only one in the Hanoverian court who cared much about philosophy, who knew enough about it to have been able to express her favour for Leibniz's views, and last, but not least, of course, she was the future Queen of England. The Newtonians realized that for political reasons they had to win her to their side. Leibniz must have realized it too, which may account for his increasing paranoia. As time wore on, the sheer weight of words, of personalities, and of experimental dramatics could not have failed to have had something of their intended effects on Caroline. And Clarke was not without persuasive arguments. In his Second Reply, he had responded to Leibniz's charge that on the Newtonian view the world is imperfect and requires occasional, miraculous repairs. '[T]he *Wisdom of God* consists', he argued,

> in framing *Originally* the *perfect* and *complete idea* of a Work, which *begun and continues*, according to that Original perfect idea, by the *Continual Uninterrupted Exercise* of his *Power* and *Government*.

lxxiv INTRODUCTION

8. The word *Correction*, or *Amendment*, is to be understood, not with regard to *God*, but to *Us* only. The present Frame of the Solar System (for instance,) according to the present Laws of Motion, will in time *fall into Confusion*; and perhaps, after That, will be *amended* or put into a *new form*. But this Amendment is only *relative*, with regard to *Our Conceptions*. In reality, and with regard to *God*; the present *Frame*, and the consequent *Disorder*, and the following *Renovation*, are all equally parts of the Design framed in Gods original perfect idea.

[Cl.II.6 & 7–8/document 96, p. 381]

Clarke's argument was fair enough, and it is one I think he may have prosecuted to good effect in his long discussions with Caroline. The world, Clarke concedes, will eventually want a reformation 'according to the present Laws of Motion'; but those 'present Laws of Motion' reflect only our still imperfect understanding of the laws by which God rules the world—laws which, if perfectly understood, would be seen to encompass even a reformation of the world.[64] This was enough to deflect Leibniz's criticism that the Newtonian view implies an imperfect creation and hence an imperfect creator. The account of miracles implicit in this passage, and later made explicit in section 17 of Clarke's Third Reply (document 120), was, of course, one that Newton himself had embraced.[65] But in section 17 of his Third Paper (document 100), Leibniz had written that '*Divines* will not grant the Author's position against me; viz. that there is no difference, with respect to *God*, between *Natural* and *Supernatural*: And it will be still less approved by most *Philosophers*'. Leibniz had always sought to accommodate his philosophical views, as much as possible, to the demands of theology, and he often cited the authority of divines against Clarke in their correspondence.[66] But Clarke and Newton were theological radicals, often hostile to conventional theological views.[67] And Clarke's response to

---

[64] For an enlightening discussion of the Newtonian view of miracles, see Dobbs 1992, pp. 230–43; cf. Harrison 1995.

[65] In the P.S. to his letter to Conti of 6 December 1715, Leibniz had charged that on Newton's view 'gravity must be a scholastic occult quality or else the effect of a miracle' (document 88b, p. 325). Newton responded to Leibniz's P.S. in his letter to Conti of 17 March 1716 (NS) (document 101g), but in one of the drafts for that letter he had written this:

For Miracles are so called not because they are the works of God but because they happen seldom & for that reason create wonder. If they should happen constantly according to certaine laws imprest upon the nature of things, they would be no longer wonders or miracles but might be considered in Philosophy as a part of the Phenomena of Nature notwithstanding that the cause of their causes might be unknown to us.

[document 101f, p. 435; see also documents 101c, p. 425, 101d, p. 429, 101e, p. 433]

[66] See Bertoloni Meli 1999, pp. 484–5.

[67] While the degree of Newton's theological heterodoxy has been debated, most modern scholars would not dispute that his views were extremely unconventional. Richard Westfall is typical of many who view Newton as having been an adherent of the heretical doctrine of Arianism from an early age until his death: 'Pious he undoubtedly was', Westfall argues, 'but his piety had been stained indelibly by the touch of cold philosophy. It is impossible to wash the Arianism out of his religious views' (Westfall 1980, p. 826). A somewhat less radical interpretation of Newton's heterodoxy has recently been suggested by Pfizenmaier 1997. Unlike Newton, who kept his theological views from the public eye, Clarke

INTRODUCTION lxxv

Leibniz in section 17 of his Third Reply does seem to get it exactly right: 'The Question', he wrote, 'is not *what* it is that *Divines* or *Philosophers* usually allow or not allow; but *what Reasons* Men alledge for their Opinions'. This response, I think, likely appealed to Caroline, who was certainly an independent thinker, with an unconventional streak of her own when it came to theological matters.

1.4.3 Leibniz's Attack on Atomism and the Void and Caroline's Collusion with Newton

On 12 May 1716 Leibniz wrote to 'beg pardon of Your Royal Highness if I feared some coolness', which he blamed on the behaviour of the Abbé Conti:

> It is a bit irregular toward me, and I made him aware of it with a response[68] as harsh as his letter,[69] but that scarcely matters. He does not appear to have any fixed principles and resembles the chameleon, which is said to take the colour of the things that it touches. When he returns to France, he will return from the void to the plenum.
>
> [document 117a, p. 521]

And speaking of the void, Leibniz declared that 'Since the void has been preached to Your Royal Highness, I am putting my view about it in a separate paper' (p. 523), which he attached as a P.S. (document 117b). He was still suspicious of Caroline and wrote that he was 'amazed that she has still found some time for me', given that 'Madame the Duchess of Orléans [Elisabeth Charlotte* of the Palatinate] has done me the honour of telling me that Your Royal Highness writes two substantial letters to her every week'. But then, still nursing his suspicions, he added: 'That consoles me about the fact that Your Royal Highness has seemed a little wavering, not in her good will toward me, but perhaps in her good opinion of me and my views, above all since it seems the translation of the *Theodicy* remains in arrears' (ibid.). From here on in the correspondence, Caroline's handling of the *Theodicy* translation would be treated by Leibniz as a measure of her loyalty to him.

In her letter of 26 May 1716, Caroline responded to Leibniz's apology for having feared some coolness on her part by declaring, 'You are right to beg my pardon, sir, for having suspected me of not being the same for you; your merit would always obligate me to it.' After defending Conti's efforts at mediation and urging Leibniz 'to employ your time more usefully than in disputing with each other', Caroline gave an enthusiastic report of the experiments with which the Newtonians had regaled

---

was widely accused in his own day of being an adherent of Arianism. He was removed from his position as a chaplain to Queen Anne as the result of the controversy aroused by his book, *The Scripture Doctrine of the Trinity* (1712).

[68] See Leibniz's letter to Conti of 9 April 1716 (document 108).

[69] That is, Conti's letter to Leibniz of 26 March 1716 (document 104).

lxxvi   INTRODUCTION

her; there was no indication that Leibniz's P.S. against the void had had any appreciable effect on her views. 'I am in on the experiments', she gushed, 'and I am more and more charmed by colours. I cannot help being a bit biased in favour of the void' (document 122, p. 549). Caroline did eventually mention the paper against the void that Leibniz had sent in his last letter, but only to joke that 'I have given it to the king so that he never leaves any [void] in your purse' (ibid.).[70] But the king was not the only one to whom Caroline gave Leibniz's P.S. on the void. For, as Richard Westfall has noted:

> Among Newton's papers is a copy in his own hand of the insulting passage on atoms and void printed as a postscript to Leibniz's fourth letter. At the bottom Newton wrote, 'Received of ye Princess May 7th 1716, & copied May 8.' Though attached to Leibniz's letter of 2 June in the published correspondence, this passage was a postscript to Leibniz's letter of 12 May (that is, 1 May in the Julian calendar); the princess must have dispatched it as soon as it arrived.
>
> [Westfall 1980, p. 778]

Westfall observes that 'at the least, Newton's copy of it indicates his active interest in the correspondence' between Clarke and Leibniz (Westfall 1980, pp. 778–9). To be sure. But what is even more significant for our purposes is that it indicates Caroline's now active engagement with Newton on the matters discussed in the correspondence—at least those in which she took a particular interest. Given her evident delight with the experiments she had witnessed Newton perform to demonstrate the existence of the void, and given her consequent attraction to the Newtonian doctrine, it may well be that, in a fine reversal of loyalties, she was now seeking

---

[70] Here Caroline is making a joking reference to the arrearages that Leibniz was hoping to get from the king: she showed the king his paper on the void 'so that he never leaves any in your purse.' (For Leibniz's own use of this joke, see his letter to Henriette Charlotte von Pöllnitz of 30 June 1715, document 130, p. 605.) At any rate, the king was thus being kept well informed about Leibniz's dispute with Newton, and to that point it is significant Leibniz had added to his letter to Minister Bothmer of 28 April 1716 a P.S. concerning his dispute with Newton (document 114, pp. 505 ff.). In his letter to Leibniz of 29 May 1716, Bothmer thanked Leibniz 'for the information that you have given me by means of your P.S. about the state of your dispute with Chevalier Newton.' He went on to note that 'I have informed the king about the content of your P.S., in order to show him that you have not offended Mr. Newton [...]' (document 123, p. 555). Later, in a letter of 10 July, Bothmer told Leibniz:

> I have shown your P.S. to some of Mr. Newton's friends, who seemed very satisfied with it, but I do not know yet what he himself says about it. At the same time I have made it known that this does not serve the king well to divert you with such cavils from the important works for the glory of his family that occupy you.
>
> [document 132, p. 609]

Further evidence of the king's knowledge of Leibniz's dispute with Newton is found in Conti's letter to Leibniz of 26 March 1716: 'His Majesty has wanted me to inform him of everything that has happened between M. Newton and you. I have done my best, and I would wish that it was with success for both' (document 104, p. 455).

INTRODUCTION lxxvii

Newton's help in answering Leibniz as she had initially sought Leibniz's help in answering Clarke.

Thus Leibniz may not have been far wrong when he worried that Caroline might be 'a little wavering, not in her good will toward me, but perhaps in her good opinion of me and my views'. Still, Caroline ended her letter by addressing Leibniz's worry about her finding time for him: 'There now', she wrote, 'a long letter that will show you that I always have time to remember my friends' (document 122, p. 549).

1.4.4 Leibniz's Continuing Suspicions and the *Theodicy* Translation Project

When Leibniz responded on 2 June 1716 to send his Fourth Paper for Clarke (document 125a), he was clearly unhappy. He complained that Clarke had failed to understand his principle of sufficient reason, a failure that had led Clarke to suppose, in the first section of his Second Reply (document 96, p. 379), that 'this *sufficient Reason* is oft-times no other, than the *mere Will* of God'. Leibniz reminded Caroline that he had refuted this 'error of vague indifference' in the *Theodicy*, an error, he noted, that 'is also the source of [the idea of] the void and atoms'. The experiments concerning the void with which Caroline had been so enthralled were dismissed as demonstrating nothing, since they 'exclude only a gross matter'. The *Theodicy* strategy, by which Leibniz first brought Caroline around to his side in the battle against Newton, was now redeployed against the void:

> I would not have touched upon this matter of the void if I had not found that the notion of the void derogates from the perfections of God, as do nearly all the other philosophical views that are contrary to mine. For mine are nearly all bound up with the great principle of the supreme reason and perfection of God. So I do not fear that Your Royal Highness will easily abandon what she will have had the leisure to understand thoroughly: her penetration and her zeal for the glory of God are my sureties.
>
> [document 124, p. 557]

He angrily rejected Caroline's suggestions that he had mistreated Conti: 'I could not fail', he wrote, 'to respond harshly to a letter as harsh as his;[71] but there is nothing which ought to offend him. He is in control of esteeming and favouring who appears good to him' (p. 559). Seizing this moment to raise further doubts about Caroline's loyalty to him, he wrote:

> If Your Serene Highness herself had less esteem for my views than before, I would be displeased by it, but I would not have any reason to complain about it. It is enough that she retains her kindness for me, and she has given great and real

[71] See above, notes 68 and 69.

lxxviii INTRODUCTION

proofs of it. What I ought to believe about the continuation of her esteem can be become known by what happens in relation to the translation of the *Theodicy*.

[p. 559]

In her letter to Leibniz of 26 June 1716 with which she enclosed Clarke's Fourth Reply (document 129), Caroline reacted sharply to the comments in Leibniz's previous letter: 'You will permit me, in spite of what I found a bit harsh against me in your letter, to be displeased to see men of your merit quarreling out of vanity, which you should destroy by the excellence of your arguments.' Her anger drove her so far as to ask, 'What does it matter whether you or Chevalier Newton discovered the calculus?' Her response to Leibniz's attempt to leverage the translation of the *Theodicy* was not encouraging: 'You understand', she wrote,

> that the translation of the *Theodicy* is extremely difficult at the moment, and I hope to find someone who will not corrupt it by his translation. The Archbishop [of Canterbury, William Wake] admires it, but he is not entirely in agreement with you. With your permission I will reread it in the presence of Mr. *Conti* and Doctor Clarke.
>
> [document 128, p. 583]

At the end of her letter, Caroline mentioned the impending trip of the king back to Hanover, and surprisingly, perhaps, informed Leibniz that the king 'has a lot of favour for you and [...] is upset when a person is not completely in agreement with your opinion'. She wrote that she hoped 'that perhaps there will soon be something here to bring you closer to this island', and closed once more with a variation on her now standard line of reassurance: 'I will eagerly seek opportunities to show you that I am always the same' (p. 585).

Leibniz responded on Friday 31 July, explaining that he had been forced to defer his response to Clarke's Fourth Reply and reporting that the king had arrived in Hanover the previous Sunday. His preoccupation with the quarrel between himself and Newton and Clarke showed not only in his attempt at the beginning of the letter to vindicate his reply to Newton's letter to Conti, but also in his report that 'I had the honour of dining with His Majesty the day after [his arrival], and he seemed cheerful, to the point of reproaching me for appearing somewhat less so than in the past.'[72] Again pressuring Caroline concerning the *Theodicy*, he told her that 'it will be applauded by the English to the extent that Your Royal Highness will be satisfied with it'. (document 135, p. 615). Given the Royal Society's refusal to satisfy his demand for redress against the Newtonians, Leibniz had clearly come to regard Caroline's public approval of the *Theodicy* as perhaps his only means of vindication

---

[72] The king may have guessed at the source of Leibniz's despondency, since Leibniz reports in his next letter, two and a half weeks later, that 'the king has joked more than once about my dispute with Mr. Newton' (document 139, p. 631).

INTRODUCTION lxxix

in his fight against Newton. Realizing both his need for defenders in England and their near extinction after the defection of Conti, Leibniz responded to Caroline's request for permission to reread the *Theodicy* in the presence of Conti and Clarke by attempting to recruit at least some neutral observers:

> You are a competent judge, madame, and as Abbé Conti and Doctor Clarke will read it before you, that is to say, indict it before your tribunal, it would be desirable for me also to have an advocate at that time, who was inclined to defend my cause. I could not nominate anyone in London, unless, perhaps, Mr. Des Maizeaux[73] or Mr. Coste,[74] although perhaps they are at best only neutral.
>
> [p. 615]

To retreat for a moment to 7 June 1716—being five days after he had sent his Fourth Paper to Caroline—Leibniz wrote to Johann Bernoulli to inform him of the nature of his on-going exchange with Clarke. This letter ended with one of those enigmatic statements that could nag a suspicious mind into doubts about Leibniz's sincerity: 'Perhaps', he wrote,

> our confrontation [...] will still be continued a bit longer, and I shall see how the matter turns out. For confrontations of this sort, because they are in philosophy, are mere sport to me.
>
> [document 127, p. 581]

Writing to Caroline two months later, on 18 August, in order to dispatch the first installment of his Fifth Paper for Clarke (document 140b), Leibniz now made it clear that he was growing weary of the game:

> This response is very expansive because I wanted to explain matters thoroughly and see from that whether there is hope of making Mr. Clarke listen to reason. For if he falls into repetitions, there will be nothing to do with him, and it will be necessary to try to end civilly.[75]
>
> [document 139, p. 629]

He informed Caroline that he had been in touch with Des Maizeaux about a translator for the *Theodicy* and reported that both a good translator and a bookseller willing to print it had been found. But 'they want', he wrote, 'to be permitted to

---

[73] That is, Pierre Des Maizeaux*.   [74] That is, Pierre Coste*.

[75] When Leibniz wrote to Des Maizeaux 3 days later, he reaffirmed his intention to end the affair sooner rather than later: 'I hope that you have received what has passed between Mr. Clarke and me, up to and including his fourth paper [that is, Clarke's Fourth Reply (document 129)], to which I am responding more extensively than to the others in order to clarify the matter thoroughly and come to the end of the dispute' (document 141, p. 715).

lxxx INTRODUCTION

dedicate the book to Your Royal Highness and to indicate on the title page that the translation was made by her order', which latter request, he suggested, 'would be to honour the book too much, though it were a hundred times better than it is' (document 139, p. 631). Still, as Clarke later observed in his own dedication to Caroline of his 1717 edition of the correspondence with Leibniz, 'the late learned Mr. *Leibnitz* well understood, how great an Honour and Reputation it would be to him, to have his Arguments approved by a Person of Your Royal Highnesses Character' (document 162, p. 813); and so, indeed, Leibniz continued:

> But I believe that Your Royal Highness will indeed permit it to be dedicated to her and permit it to be indicated in the dedication that Your Royal Highness wanted this book to be translated, since that is the truth, and it will be of great import for advancing a defense of religion and sound piety.
>
> [document 139, p. 631]

On 1 September Caroline wrote to acknowledge the receipt of Leibniz's Fifth Paper for Clarke, and she had news concerning the translation of the *Theodicy*:

> I have seen a man who told me that he would translate your incomparable *Theodicy* and would dedicate it to me, which I have accepted with much pleasure. I believe that Mr. Clarke will respond to it. So much the better, since the truth cannot be examined thoroughly enough.
>
> [document 142, pp. 719, 721]

Caroline explained that she had read Leibniz's responses to Clarke with pleasure: 'I do not know what he will be able to say in response to them', she wrote, but then confessed that 'he is a man of the greatest vivacity and of an eloquence that is to me incomparable'. There is a studied neutrality in all of this: Caroline expressed her hope 'that the king will bring you to this country', but it was so that she might have 'the pleasure of hearing you [i.e., Leibniz and Clarke] speaking together' (p. 721). A week later, on 8 September, Caroline wrote very briefly to Leibniz to remind him that Conti had lost many of his papers and to renew her request for replacements (document 143, p. 725).

1.4.5 The End of the Affair

In a letter to Des Maizeaux of 21 August 1716, Leibniz had expressed the hope that 'there are a lot of people in England who [...] will not approve of [...] that necessity in which the followers of Newton find themselves on account of denying the great principle of the need for a sufficient reason, by which I beat them into ruin' (document 141, pp. 715, 717). Three weeks later, on 11 September 1716, Leibniz sent his penultimate letter to Caroline, thanking her 'for the permission she has

given to dedicate the translation of the *Theodicy* to her and to speak in the dedication of the approval that she has given to this project'; but at the end of the letter he again turned to what he saw as the sticking point between himself and Clarke:

> If he continues to dispute the great principle *that nothing happens without there being a sufficient reason why it happens and why thus rather than otherwise,* and if he still claims that something can happen by a *Mere Will of God,* without any motive, a view completely refuted in the *Theodicy,* and again in my last paper,[76] it will be necessary to abandon him to his opinion, or rather to his obstinacy. For it is hard to believe that he is not moved by it in the depths of his soul; but I do not believe that the public will let him off the hook.
>
> [document 144, p. 731]

Similarly, in his final draft letter to Caroline, undated but written sometime between the end of September and mid-October, he told Caroline that if Clarke 'does not grant me entirely this great accepted axiom [...] I will not be able to refrain from doubting his sincerity, and if he grants it, farewell the philosophy of Mr. Newton' (document 149, p. 747). However, in his letter of 11 September he had added that 'I still hope for the best, above all because everything takes place under the eyes of Your Royal Highness, whom it is not easy to deceive' (document 144, p. 731). But if Caroline accepted Leibniz's version of the principle of sufficient reason as against Clarke's voluntarism, there is no indication of it in her final four letters, all of which are extremely brief and assiduously avoid mention of the matters at issue between Leibniz and Clarke. In the undated letter Leibniz also reported that he was working very hard on his history, and perhaps thinking of Caroline's hope, expressed in her letter of 1 September, that 'the king will bring you to this country' (document 142, p. 721), he wistfully explained his situation:

> I do not hope to go so soon to England. Nothing could tempt me to go there more than the kindnesses of Your Royal Highness; but as I do not hope to go there soon, I do not know if I could hope to go there later. For there is not much later to hope for in me.
>
> [document 149, p. 747]

In her pre-ante-penultimate letter to Leibniz of 6 October,[77] Caroline informed him that 'I have given Dr. Clarke your papers, and he is making me a collection of everything.' As for the *Theodicy,* she wrote that 'I have not yet seen the translation of your incomparable book. I have accepted as a great honour that it is to be

---

[76] That is, Leibniz's Fifth Paper, document 140b.

[77] In a previous article (Brown 2004, p. 287) I mistakenly followed Klopp's erroneous dating of this letter as 26 September 1716 (NS) (see Klopp XI 197).

lxxxii   INTRODUCTION

dedicated to me.' In what must have been a final disappointment for Leibniz, she added that the 'response [by Clarke] will also be dedicated to me' (document 151, p. 751). Clarke was no fool, and when he learned that Leibniz had arranged to have a translation of the *Theodicy* dedicated to Caroline, he apparently committed himself forthwith to writing a reply and then, determined to match Leibniz dedication for dedication, secured Caroline's imprimatur for his anticipated rebuttal. Tit for tat—and that was that for Leibniz's plan to secure his vindication against the Newtonians through Caroline's endorsement of the translation of the *Theodicy*. When Leibniz died, the project of translating the *Theodicy* died with him, and it is ironic that what translation there came to be of it was at the hands of Clarke himself, who provided translations of leading passages from the *Theodicy* in an appendix to his polemical 1717 edition of the correspondence with Leibniz (document 163)—dedicated, of course, to Caroline. But it is really no surprise that Caroline had accepted Clarke's earlier proposal to dedicate his planned rebuttal of the *Theodicy* to her. For over the previous five months—ever since the Newtonians had charmed her with their experiments on colours and the void and had launched their propaganda blitz to win her over to their side—Caroline had increasingly assumed in her letters to Leibniz the stance of a disinterested observer, no longer the advocate for his cause, as surely she had been at the beginning of her acquaintance with Clarke. Some particulars are worth recalling. In her letter to Leibniz of 15 May 1716 she had told Leibniz to 'prove to us the plenum, and let the chevalier [Newton] and Clarke prove the void on their side'; she and her ladies, she said, would play the part of witnesses to the dispute, like so many characters in a play by Molière.[78] Later, in her letter of 4 November, and less facetiously, she had said that she 'would gladly play the part of the College of Sorbonne, provided that [she] had the pleasure of talking with you [...] and of being, although very ignorant, witness to your disputes with Mr. Clarke'.[79] She had confessed her ignorance more than once and had become Socratic. The dispute between Clarke and Leibniz had, I think, taught her that philosophical debate rarely issues in a clear-cut victor and that it has, by its nature, to remain forever deeply ambiguous. When she discovered herself a patroness of philosophy and the arts, she seems to have realized that her role was not to declare a winner, but to secure and protect a civil forum, and then let the chips fall where they may. Her retreat into neutrality undoubtedly stung Leibniz, but it was, I think, all to her credit. It must have been a final and bitter irony to Leibniz that Caroline ended her letter to him of 6 October by saying that 'I should want you to be able to be acquainted with Mr. Clarke' and suggesting that 'you would certainly like him'. She told him that 'I hope to see you here with the king', and ended with her usual assurance that 'you will find me always the same' (document 151, p. 751).

---

[78] Document 119, p. 537. Concerning the reference to the play by Molière, see ibid. note 24.
[79] Document 158, p. 801. Concerning the reference to the College of Sorbonne, see p. 803 note 18.

INTRODUCTION   lxxxiii

Just three days later, on 9 October, Caroline wrote her ante-penultimate letter to Leibniz[80] at the behest of Clarke, who wished to have Leibniz's assurance that if he should decide to print their papers, he would do so in the language in which they were written. She reported the pleasure she had taken in her conversation with Clarke that day and ended with another expression of hope that Leibniz might join the two of them in England: 'I very much wish to see you together, and I hope that you will choose me when you desire to see each other to talk one-on-one. I shall always forever be your friend' (document 152, p. 755).

On 29 October, just sixteen days before Leibniz's death, Caroline wrote her penultimate letter to Leibniz, with which she enclosed Clarke's Fifth Reply; it was a thin, four-sentence affair, flatly non-committal on the dispute that had occupied them for so long:

> I send with these few lines, sir, the response of Doctor Clarke. I hope you may find it at least pleasant if not sound. I have made the acquaintance of a man who admires you a lot, who is the archbishop of Dublin, Doctor King.[81] I will respond to your letters the next post, and I shall always be the same for you.
>
> [document 156, p. 763]

On 4 November, just ten days before his death, Caroline wrote her ultimate letter to Leibniz, answering the ultimate, undated letter that Leibniz had written to her sometime between the end of September and mid-October 1716. She expressed her regrets about his skepticism concerning his prospects for ever going to England, whether sooner or later:

> I am displeased to see that you postpone your trip here for so long. You could work on the history in London as in Hanover, and your friends could have the pleasure of enjoying your conversation. I would represent with pleasure the College of Sorbonne, provided that I had the pleasure of speaking to you here, and of being, although very ignorant, witness to your disputes with Mr. Clarke. You will find me, as always, the same person who esteems you infinitely.
>
> [document 158, p. 801]

Leibniz never responded to these last four letters from Caroline, but on 20 September, shortly before he wrote his last letter to Caroline, Leibniz had been busy writing to Vienna—to the Dowager Empress Wilhelmine Amalie (document 145) and to her lady-in-waiting Charlotte Elisabeth von Klenk (document 146). He was seeking assurance from both of them that his salary as imperial aulic councilor

---

[80] In a previous article (Brown 2004, p. 286) I mistakenly followed Klopp's erroneous dating of this letter as 19 September 1716 (NS) (Klopp XI 191).

[81] William King (1650–1729) was the Archbishop of Dublin from 1703 to 1729. In 1702 he published *De Origine Mali*, which Leibniz critically discussed in an appendix to his *Theodicy* of 1710.

lxxxiv INTRODUCTION

was not being suspended, as rumour had reached him that it was, and he offered both of them his own assurance that he was planning to return to Vienna the following year—'when the King of Great Britain will have crossed over the sea again', as he put it in the letter to the dowager empress (document 145, p. 735). This is not to say, of course, that Leibniz had abandoned his desire for the office of historiographer of Great Britain, although it does suggest, as I argued earlier, that Leibniz did not desire that office as a passport to England, but primarily as a means to establish his position vis-à-vis Newton. Five weeks later, on 27 October, Georg Ludwig's Hanoverian minister Bothmer sent Leibniz an optimistic note from London:

> I observe with much pleasure, by the honour of your letter of the 9th of this month, the assiduity with which you continue to labor on your illustrious work. I do not doubt that Messrs. Bernstorff and Stanhope[82] are in return applying themselves effectively to deliver to you, on the return of the king from Göhrde*, the position you desire here of historiographer of His Majesty. Everyone will readily agree that no one deserves a more just title than you, not only for your knowledge, but more particularly still for the work about which I have just spoken.[83]

Onno Klopp has argued that 'the repeated indications of the Princess of Wales, as well as this letter of minister Bothmer, show that the appointment of Leibniz to the position of historiographer of the king was a matter already resolved, whose realization was only delayed because the king himself was in Ghörde' (Klopp XI xxxv). There is no doubt, as Klopp has also noted, that 'the letters of the Princess of Wales to Leibniz, as well as his own concerning his re-encounter with [the king], have verified that in the case of the latter every ill feeling about the long absence of Leibniz in Vienna had been extinguished and that the princess passionately desired him to be in England' (Klopp XI xxxvii). Still, and even so, it seems hard not to think that Klopp's optimistic assessment of Leibniz's prospects for appointment underestimates, or perhaps even ignores, the political realities under which Georg Ludwig had to labor at this very early stage in his reign. Not only was there the matter of the Act of Settlement, which forbad grant of British offices to foreigners— a prohibition that the king had assiduously respected[84]—but there was also, and perhaps more importantly, the matter of Newton. We have seen that in his letter to Caroline of 10 May 1715, Leibniz predicted that his appointment would 'sting', as he expressed it, Newton and his supporters (document 72, p. 239), as surely it would have; but then this very fact would likely have led Georg Ludwig's English ministers to advise strongly against the appointment, given that Newton was the ornament of England and that Leibniz had been portrayed as his mortal enemy. Georg Ludwig

---

[82] That is, James Stanhope*.

[83] Document 155, p. 761. See also Bothmer's letter to Leibniz of 11 August 1716 (document 137, p. 627).

[84] See Hatton 1978, p. 156.

INTRODUCTION lxxxv

could scarcely afford to alienate such an important constituency when the legitimacy of his own nascent reign was still so much in doubt.[85] Nearly four years after Leibniz's death, but still obsessed, Newton wrote to Abraham de Moivre early in 1720 and exalted in the power he had exerted to frustrate the designs of Leibniz's friends, including, presumably, Caroline and Conti: 'When the Court of Hanover came to London', he wrote, '[Leibniz's] friends endeavoured to reconcile us in order to bring him over to London, but they could not get me to yield' (NC VII 83).

Caroline had ended her letter to Leibniz of 9 October 1716 by assuring him that she would 'always forever be your friend' (document 152, p. 755), and the other three of the final four letters she had written to Leibniz had ended with her assurance that she would always be the same for him. But really too much had transpired in Caroline's life since Hanover for it to be true in any unequivocal sense that she was still the same for Leibniz. Proximity and politics had from the beginning given Clarke and the Newtonians a decided edge in their competition for Caroline's favour; and Clarke himself, as Caroline often intimated, was not without his charms. Indeed, he soon became, and would so remain until his death, Caroline's closest advisor on matters philosophical and theological. At the time of her last writing to Leibniz, her erstwhile comrade in mediation, the chameleon Abbé Conti, was making his way to Germany, on a mission to meet with Leibniz. But he arrived too late, and he wrote to Newton on 10 December to report that 'Mr. Leibniz is dead, and the dispute is finished' (document 160, p. 805). I have found no record of how Caroline reacted to this news, but there appear to have been no memorials. In the event, Caroline had precious little time to mourn for Leibniz, since she would very soon have more immediate tears to shed. For on 20 November (NS), just sixteen days after having written her last letter to Leibniz, and almost certainly before she had even received the news that Leibniz had died six days earlier, Caroline gave birth to a stillborn son.[86] When Newton died some eleven years later—three months before Caroline became queen—he was, of course, buried as a national hero in Westminster Abbey, and the court, that is to say, Caroline, offered Clarke Newton's old position as master of the mint, although he promptly refused it. When Clarke himself died two years later, Caroline had then been already nearly two years on the throne in England. She had never returned to Germany, nor ever would. By then, both Hanover and Leibniz were perhaps fond, but certainly distant memories.

---

[85] The previous year had seen the Jacobite Rebellion of 1715—an attempt to place the Pretender, James Francis Edward Stuart,* on the throne in England—and there always remained the threat that Stuart sympathizers would attempt to undo the Hanoverian succession, which they regarded as illegitimate.

[86] In his letter to Leibniz of 27 October 1716, Bothmer had notified Leibniz that 'Madame the Princess of Wales had alarmed us last week concerning her delivery, being frightened by a fairly perilous forward fall that the Princess Caroline suffered, without, however, doing herself any harm' (document 155, 761). This fall may well have been a contributing factor in the stillbirth of Caroline's son.

lxxxvi INTRODUCTION

2. The Leibniz–Clarke Correspondence

2.1 Principle of Sufficient Reason, Identity of Indiscernibles, God's Choice, Space and Time

In response to Leibniz's initial charge against the English philosophers in his late-November letter to Caroline (document 85), Clarke conceded that there were indeed some in England, as elsewhere, who had contributed to the decline of natural religion; but for that he blamed 'the false Philosophy of the *Materialists*, to which *the Mathematick Principles of Philosophy* are the most distinctly repugnant', because those Newtonian principles 'prove Matter, or Body, to be the smallest and most inconsiderable Part of the Universe' (Cl.I.1/document 90, p. 339). Leibniz responded by suggesting that the appeal to mathematical principles was to no effect, since the materialists themselves, in allowing that only bodies exist, accept only mathematical principles. Mathematics is governed by the principle of contradiction, but for natural philosophy, natural religion, and metaphysics more generally, a different principle is needed, namely '*the Principle of a sufficient Reason* [hereafter, PSR], *viz.* that nothing happens without a *Reason* why it should be *so*, rather than *otherwise*'. For 'by that single Principle [...] one may demonstrate the Being of a *God*, and all the other Parts of *Metaphsicks* or *Natural Theology*; and even, in some Measure, those Principles of *Natural Philosophy*, that are independent upon *Mathematicks*: I mean, the *Dynamick* Principles, or the *Principles of Force*' (Lz.II.1/document 92, p. 355; see also Lz.IV.5/document 125a, p. 563, Lz.V.18–20,125–130/document 140b, pp. 667, 711, 713).

2.2 God's Will and Absolute Space

Clarke agreed with the PSR, but interpreted it more narrowly than Leibniz, as the doctrine that 'where there is *no Cause*, there can be *no Effect*' (Cl.II.1/document 96, p. 379), and argued that the mere will of God could be a sufficient reason. He then manufactured an ill-fated example—that it would have made no difference, *ceteris paribus*, if God had created the material world in one part of space rather than another. Hence the reason for creating it here rather than there was God's mere will, and to suppose otherwise would introduce fatalism and destroy God's freedom. To Clarke's point about God's mere will, Leibniz responded that '*A mere Will* without any Motive, is a Fiction, not only contrary to God's Perfection, but also chimerical and contradictory; inconsistent with the Definition of the *Will*, and sufficiently confuted in my *Theodicæa*' (Lz.IV.2/document 125a, p. 563; see also Lz.III.7/document 100, p. 411); and to the point about fatality Leibniz argued that God's power of choosing is based upon reason and wisdom and that it is only 'a *Blind Fatality* or *Necessity*, void of All Wisdom and Choice, which we ought to

avoid' (Lz.III.8/document 100, p. 413; see also Lz.V.4–19/document 140b, pp. 661, 663, 665, 667). For Caroline's sake he pressed home the theological point:

> A Will without Reason, would be the *Chance* of the *Epicureans*. A God, who should act by such a Will, would be a God only in Name. The cause of these Errors proceeds from want of care to avoid what derogates from the Divine Perfections.
> [Lz.IV.18/document 125a, p. 567; see also Lz.V.70/document 140b, p. 691]

Over the course of the remaining correspondence, Clarke's example about God's creating here rather than there by a sheer act of will led to Leibniz's formulating a number of arguments against the Newtonian notion of absolute space, one of which he also applied against absolute time. As might be expected given the context of Clarke's remarks, all of these arguments maintained that the existence of absolute space was inconsistent with the PSR because it would imply an imperfection in God, that he has acted without reason and hence without wisdom.[87]

2.2.1 First Argument against Absolute Space

In his initial response to Clarke's example, Leibniz argued that space is uniform and one point of space does not differ from any other; so if space were absolute, there would be no sufficient reason for God, while keeping the order relation among bodies unchanged, to have placed them in space in one way rather than another— for example 'by changing *East* into *West*'. He added that on his own view, 'Space is nothing else, but That *Order* or *Relation*; and is nothing at all without Bodies, but the Possibility of placing them' (Lz.III.5/document 100, p. 411),[88] so the two

---

[87] In his extensive treatment of Leibniz's arguments in the correspondence with Clarke, Edward Khamara ignores the arguments in which Leibniz appeals to the PSR and God's wisdom and reformulates them as arguments based on the Principle of the Identity of Indiscernibles (hereafter, PII) alone. He suggests that arguments based on the PII alone are actually stronger than those that appeal to the PSR and that the PSR arguments 'rely on a theological version of that principle' that 'strictly speaking [...] has no bearing whatever on the theory under attack [that is, the absolute theory of space and time], which is theologically neutral' (Khamara 2006, p. 6). I suspect that the reason Khamara thinks the arguments based on the PII alone are stronger than those based on the PSR is precisely because the latter involve theological assumptions, so his two reasons for preferring PII-based arguments are not actually independent of one another. However, while it may be true, as Khamara maintains, that from a certain perspective the Newtonians' 'beliefs about how God is related to absolute space and absolute time [...] constitute a separable theological superstructure' (ibid.), it is nonetheless an anachronistic perspective from which to view the debate between Leibniz and Clarke, because those beliefs were certainly not separable for them. Thus they cannot be ignored, as Khamara does, if one wants to engage in a serious attempt to understand the nature of the debate between Leibniz and the Newtonians. To ignore the theological dimensions of Leibniz's arguments against absolute space and time would be, among other things, to miss their central dialectical point, which, like most of his other arguments in the correspondence with Clarke, was to reveal to the mediator Caroline what Leibniz took to be the theologically rebarbative features of Newtonian natural philosophy and hence prevent her from falling in with his English adversaries.

[88] See also Lz.V.104/document 140b, p. 703. Leibniz elaborates his relational theory of space at Lz.V.47/document 140b, pp. 677, 679, 681. Space, he says, 'can only be an Ideal Thing; containing a

lxxxviii INTRODUCTION

supposed states that are imagined to be the result of switching are not two at all, but being indiscernible, are one and the same. Consequently, God would not have been faced with a choice between two different, but indiscernible scenarios, and hence no violation of the PSR could have occurred. He argued similarly with respect to the case of time, against the supposition that God might have created the universe 'a Year sooner' than he did, concluding that 'Instants, consider'd without the Things, are Nothing at all; and that they consist only in the successive Order of Things: Which Order remaining the same, one of the two States, viz. that of a supposed Anticipation, would not at all differ nor could be discerned from, the other which Now is' (Lz.III.6/document 100, p. 411; see also Lz.IV.15/document 125a, p. 565 and Lz.V.55–8/document 140b, pp. 685, 687).

Clarke's response was question begging, simply assuming that one can speak intelligibly of different places in a homogenous space devoid of bodies, again asserting that God's will is 'to it self a sufficient reason of Acting in Any place, when All Places are Indifferent or Alike, and there [is] Good reason to Act in Some place', and adding finally that a similar response also holds good for Leibniz's argument against absolute time (Cl.III.5&6/document 120, p. 541). At Lz.IV.6/document 125a (p. 563), Leibniz responded with an argument against absolute space that some commentators have taken to be an argument that is independent of the prior one in Lz.III.5/document 100 (pp. 409, 411) because it does not appeal to the PSR, which the prior argument does, and does appeal to the Principle of the Identity of Indiscernibles (PII), which the prior argument does not. Note that in the prior argument at Lz.III.5/document 100, Leibniz only appeals to the PII when pointing out that on his own relational view of space, the two supposed states of the material universe would actually be indiscernible and hence not in fact distinct, which is precisely why Leibniz thought his view would avoid a violation of the PSR.[89] So the view that the two supposed states of the material universe would in fact be distinct is, as he says, only due to 'our Chimerical Supposition of the Reality of Space in it

certain Order, wherein the Mind conceives the Application of Relations' (p. 679). It is an abstraction constructed from our perception of relations between bodies. On the other hand, it is important to bear in mind that Leibniz thought that we do have an a priori, innate idea of space, which makes possible our a priori knowledge of the necessary propositions of geometry. And Leibniz also held that our awareness of innate ideas is triggered by experience (see, for example, the Preface and Book I, Chapter 1, § 5 of the New Essays). So when Leibniz says at the beginning of Lz.V.47/document 140b that 'I will here show, how Men come to form to themselves the Notion of Space' (p. 677), his subsequent discussion might reasonably be taken to be, as Anja Jauernig has suggested, 'part of an account of the original acquisition of the innate and, thus, a priori concept of space on the occasion of the perception of spatial relations between bodies', rather than 'a story about the empirical genesis of this concept' (Jauernig 2008, p. 60). In a similar vein, Vincenzo De Risi has argued that 'In some of his latest essays, where the connection between situational analysis and sensible perception is carried to its furthest extreme, Leibniz seems inclined to define space as a form of sensible perception (almost in Kantian terms) and even, to some extent, to posit a "transcendental" determination of space itself' (De Risi 2018, p. 256). For an elaboration of De Risi's interpretation, see De Risi 2007, especially chapters 3 and 4.

[89] Although Rodriguez-Pereyra recognizes this point about the argument at Lz.III.5/document 100, he nonetheless seems to think that the argument at Lz.IV.6/document 125a is independent of that argument (see Rodriguez-Pereyra 2014, pp. 162–5).

self' (Lz.III.5/document 100, p. 411). Similarly, in his response to Clarke at Lz.IV.6/ document 125a, Leibniz wrote:

> To suppose *two* things *indiscernible*, is to suppose the *same thing* under *two Names*. And therefore to suppose that the Universe could have had at first *another* position of *Time* and *Place*, than that which it actually had; and yet that all the Parts of the Universe should have had the same Situation among themselves, as that which they actually had; such a Supposition, I say, is an impossible *fiction*.
>
> [p. 563]

Given that Leibniz was here commenting on Clarke's response to his argument at Lz.III.5/ document 100, it seems to me that what he says is most reasonably taken to be simply a reiteration of what he had concluded there, namely, that *on his own relational view of space*, the two supposed states of the material universe would actually be indiscernible and hence not in fact distinct, which is precisely why the supposition that they would be distinct 'is an impossible fiction', or, as he put it in the argument at Lz.III.5/document 100, is something due to 'our *Chimerical* Supposition of the *Reality* of Space in it self'. Understood in this way, the argument at Lz.IV.6/document 125a is not independent of the argument at Lz.III.5/document 100 based on the PSR, since it presupposes it and merely repeats the conclusion that since space must be relational, the two supposed states of the material universe would in fact be one and the same.

This last point is reinforced, I think, by the fact that in the correspondence with Clarke, at Lz.IV.3/document 125a (p. 563) and Lz.V.21/document 140b (pp. 667, 669), Leibniz undertook to deduce that there are no indiscernible things in the world from the PSR on the grounds that the supposition of indiscernibles is inconsistent with God's wisdom; for that suggests that Leibniz would not have understood his appeal to the PII at Lz.IV.6/document 125a to be independent of the argument based on the PSR at Lz.III.5/document 100. While I do not have space here to discuss in detail Leibniz's argument for the PII based on the PSR,[90] it is important to note that it assumes as premise what Clarke consistently rejected in the correspondence, namely, that God must act for a reason. This has led Gonzalo Rodriguez-Pereyra to suggest that 'the argument has little dialectical force' (Rodriguez-Pereyra 2014, p. 112). But it must be remembered that Clarke was not the only party to the discussion. Caroline was a silent participant, and the fact that Leibniz knew that the argument would not be effective against Clarke makes it all

---

[90] For extended discussions of the argument, see Jauernig 2008, pp. 208–12 and Rodriguez-Pereyra 2014, pp. 104–14. Jauernig and Rodriguez-Pereyra disagree about how the argument should be reconstructed, and hence about how effective it is, although they agree that it is ineffective against Clarke inasmuch as it assumes that God must have a reason for acting. But that undoubtedly mattered little to Leibniz, who was addressing the point about God's wisdom and perfection primarily to Caroline. Given Leibniz's argumentative strategy, Clarke's rejection of the point could only help his case.

XC   INTRODUCTION

the more clear that it was an argument whose dialectical target was Caroline rather than Clarke and that its purpose was to alert her again to the fact, as Leibniz saw it, that the Newtonian position was inconsistent with God's perfection and, in particular, with his wisdom.

2.2.2 Second, Independent Argument against Absolute Space

Leibniz formulated another argument against absolute space in response to Clarke's suggestion that on Leibniz's view, God might 'remove in a straight Line the whole Material World Entire, with any swiftness whatsoever, yet it would still always remain in the *same Place*: And that nothing would receive any Shock upon the most sudden stopping of that Motion' (Cl.III.4/document 120, p. 541). Leibniz replied:

> To say that God can cause the whole Universe to *move forward* in a Right Line, or in any other Line, without making otherwise any Alteration in it; is another *Chimerical* Supposition. For, *two States indiscernible* from each other, are the *same* State; and consequently, 'tis a change without any change.
>
> [Lz.IV.13/document 125a, p. 565]

At first sight this again seems to be an argument based on the PII alone. But of course Leibniz realized that stated in this abbreviated form, the argument simply begs the question against Clarke, who had made it clear that on the Newtonian view the two states in question, even if indiscernible, would not be the same—since the one would be a state of motion in relation to absolute space whereas the other would not. So Leibniz added: 'Besides, there is neither *Rhime* nor *Reason* in it. But God does nothing without *Reason*; And tis *impossible* there should be any here' (p. ibid.). This addendum would make little sense if Leibniz was still assuming that space is relational, since it *assumes that there might be two indiscernible states*, and thence concludes that God could have no reason for choosing between them. So it seems Leibniz was arguing that *even if* one accepted absolute space, and hence denied that the two supposed states are the same, as he knew Clarke would, God could have no reason to produce one of the states rather than the other, and hence could produce neither, given that they are indiscernible. This is the argument against absolute space upon which the claim in the initial argument, that Clarke's supposition 'is another *Chimerical* Supposition', depends; it provides the reason why Leibniz thought that absolute space had to be rejected in favour of relational space.[91] As before, and because Leibniz also knew that Clarke would reject the view that God had to have a reason to act one way rather than another, I think it is

---

[91] Recall that in the argument at Lz.III.5/document 100, Leibniz's claim that ''tis impossible there should be a *Reason*, why God, preserving the same Situations of Bodies among themselves, should have placed them in Space after *one certain particular manner*, and not *otherwise*' was premised on the assumption that space is 'something in it self, besides the *Order of Bodies among themselves*' (p. 411).

obvious that this addendum was inserted for Caroline's sake rather than for Clarke's, in order to remind her that the Newtonians' commitment to absolute space committed them as well to a view that is inconsistent with the perfection of God. But then Leibniz immediately set forth a second addendum to the initial argument: 'Besides, it would be *agendo nihil agere*, as I have just now said, because of the Indiscernibility' (p. 565). Here Leibniz appears to be referring back to his initial argument, in which he assumed his own relational view of space, according to which the two states Clarke thought he could imagine would in fact be the same. Leibniz is thus asserting that the chimera of absolute space has led Clarke to imagine something that, in truth, would involve an absurdity: in truth 'it would be *agendo nihil agere*' because ''tis a change without any change'.[92] 'These are', he says, '*Idola Tribûs*, mere Chimeras, and superficial Imaginations. All this is only grounded upon the Supposition, that imaginary Space is real' (Lz.IV.14/document 125a. p. 565; see also Lz.V.29/document 140b, p. 671). Here indiscernibility can be seen to imply identity only once it is understood that the notion of absolute space is chimerical because it is inconsistent with God's wisdom.

In his Fourth Reply, Clarke argued that in order to be real, motion does not have to be perceived and that, moreover, if a man were shut up in the cabin of a ship that was moving uniformly, he might not perceive the motion, but he would certainly perceive the effects of deceleration were the ship suddenly stopped (Cl.IV.13/document 129, p. 595). Leibniz responded with what appears to be an appeal to a verifiability theory of truth:

> Motion does not indeed depend upon being *Observed*; but it does depend upon being *possible to be Observed*. There is no *Motion*, when there is no *Change that can be Observed*. And when there is no *Change that can be Observed*, there is *no Change at all*. The contrary Opinion is grounded upon the Supposition of a real absolute Space, which I have demonstratively confuted by the Principle of the *want of a sufficient Reason* of things.
>
> [Lz.V.52/document 140b, p. 685]

It is important to note that the ultimate basis of Leibniz's argument here is the PSR. Leibniz is suggesting that the only way one might imagine that the entire material universe is moving is by assuming 'a real absolute Space'. But that supposition, Leibniz reminds Clarke, has been refuted by the fact that God must have a sufficient reason for acting. Again, it is only once it has been understood that space is relative rather than absolute that one can understand that the impossibility of

---

[92] Recall that in the argument at Lz.III.5/document 100, after having stated the argument based on the PSR, Leibniz added that 'if Space is nothing else, but That *Order* or *Relation* […] then those two States […] would not at all differ from one another' and that '*Their Difference* therefore is only to be found in our *Chimerical* Supposition of the *Reality* of Space in it self' (p. 411; see also Lz.IV.16/document 125a, p. 567).

xcii INTRODUCTION

verifying a motion of the entire material universe implies there can be no such motion at all, because given that understanding an unverifiable motion of the entire material universe doesn't even make conceptual sense—it would again be 'a change without any change', and so Clarke's analogy with the man in the ship perceiving a shock upon the ship's suddenly stopping simply begs the question by assuming it makes sense to talk about an unperceivable motion of the entire material universe. On the other hand, Leibniz does not deny that there is a difference between a motion that is merely relative to other bodies and '*an absolute true motion of a Body*', that is, a motion 'the immediate Cause of [which] is in the Body'; and although it would not in general be observable which bodies were actually in motion, the relative change of position among bodies—which would imply the existence of true motion in at least some bodies—would be observable (Lz.V.53/ document 140b, p. 685).

2.2.3 Space: Substance or Attribute?

A final point about the debate concerning space is in order here. In his Third Paper, Leibniz charged the Newtonians with holding that '*Space* is a *real absolute Being*', which

> involves them in great Difficulties; For such a *Being* must needs be *Eternal* and *Infinite*. Hence Some have believed it to be *God himself*, or, one of his Attributes, his *Immensity*. But since Space consists of *Parts*, it is not a thing which can belong to God.
>
> [Lz.III.3/document 100, p. 409]

Leibniz was thus hanging the Newtonians on the horns of a dilemma, either one of which was theologically unacceptable. That God was identical with space was obviously heretical; and since it was widely regarded at the time that divisibility into parts was as an imperfection that belongs specifically to corporeal and perishable things, the view that space was an attribute of God clearly derogated from his perfection.

Clarke's reply to the first horn of the dilemma was confused and ultimately out of step with Newton's own view of the matter: '*Space* is not a *Being*, an eternal and infinite *Being*, but a *Property*, or a consequence of the Existence of a Being infinite and eternal. *Infinite Space*, is *Immensity*: But *Immensity* is *not God*: And therefore *Infinite Space*, is *not God*' (Cl.III.3/document 120, p. 539). The problem here is that while Newton had indeed maintained in *De Gravitatione* that space is not a substance, and hence not God because not 'absolute in itself', and had also maintained that space is rather 'an emanative effect of God'—or, as Clarke would have it, 'a consequence' of God's existence—he was also adamant that because there can be empty space where there are no bodies, space 'does not exist as an accident

inhering in some subject' (Newton 2014, p. 36). As to the second horn, Clarke asserted that neither space nor incorporeal substance has parts in the sense that bodies do, that is, as separable, and hence God's omnipresence in space does not imply that his substance is divided into separable parts (Cl.III.3/document 120, p. 541; Cl.IV.11 and 12/document 129, p. 595).

To the latter point, Leibniz argued that if infinite space has no parts and hence 'does not consist of *finite* Spaces', it would follow that all finite spaces could be removed and yet infinite space remain (Lz.IV.11/document 125a, p. 565). Moreover, Leibniz argued "tis sufficient that Space has parts, whether those parts be separable or not' (Lz.V.51/document 140b, p. 683). In response to the former claim, that space is a property of God, Leibniz simply asked, 'But *what Substance* will That *Bounded* empty Space be an Affection or Property of [. .]?' (Lz.IV.8/document 125a, p. 565). Clarke's response only made matters worse, since he again insisted that 'Space is not a *Substance*, but a *Property*' (Cl.IV.10/document 129, p. 593) and that 'void space' is an attribute of God (Cl.IV.9–10/document 129, ibid.). He confused matters again by reverting to Newton's own, and apparently quite different view, stating not that space is a property of God but that '*Space* and *Duration* [...] are *caused by*, and are *immediate and necessary Consequences of* His Existence.'[93] In his Fifth Paper, Leibniz proceeded to draw out a number of theologically troubling and bizarre consequences of Clarke's claim that space is an attribute or property of God (Lz.V.38–44/document 140b, pp. 675, 677) and raised a question about the very intelligibility of Clarke's proposal: 'if God is *in* Space, how can it be said that Space is *in* God, or that it is a Property of God? We have often heard, that a Property is in its Subject; but we never heard, that a Subject is in its Property' (Lz.V.45/document 140b, p. 677). Just three years after Clarke's publication of the correspondence with Leibniz, the swirl of confusion attending his discussion of the relation between space and time and God was revisited in the preface to Pierre Des Maizeaux's republication of the correspondence (1720):

M. Clarke has wished to warn his readers 'that when he speaks of *infinite Space* or *Immensity* and of *infinite Duration* or *Eternity* and gives them, by an inevitable imperfection of language, the name of Quality or Property of the immense or eternal Substance, he does not claim to take the term *quality* or *property* in the same sense that those who deal with logic and metaphysics take it when they apply them to matter; but that thereby he only means that *Space & Duration* are *Modes of existence* in all Beings & *infinite Modes*, & *Consequences* of the *existence* of the Substance that is really, necessarily, & substantially *omnipresent*, & *eternal*. This *Existence* is not a Substance, and it could not be attributed to any kind of *quality* or *property*; but it is the Substance itself, with all the *attributes*, all its *qualities*, & all

---

[93] Cl.IV.10/document 129, p. 593. Although it should be noted that Newton would probably not have agreed that space is a *causal* effect of God's existence. On this point, see Janiak 2015, p. 166.

xciv   INTRODUCTION

its *properties*, and *Place* and *Duration* are *Modes* of this existence, of such a nature that they could not be rejected without rejecting the Existence itself. When we speak of things that do not fall under our senses, it is difficult to speak of them without making use of figurative expressions.'

[Des Maizeaux 1720, vol. 1, pp. iv–v]

At some point after Clarke's publication of his correspondence with Leibniz, Newton must have insisted on clearing up the confusion himself; for as Alexandre Koyré and I. Bernard Cohen have shown, the words that Des Maizeaux here attributed to Clarke were actually crafted by Newton himself (see Koyré and Cohen 1962, p. 95).

2.3   Space as the Sensorium of God

As we have seen, the first item in Leibniz's bill of particulars against the English philosophers that was directed specifically against Newton was that he says 'that Space is an *Organ* which God makes use of to perceive Things by', so that 'it will follow, that they do not depend altogether upon him, nor were produced by him' (Lz.I.3/document 86, p. 317). The argument seems to be that if God required space as a sense organ to perceive things, then he could not have known things independently of their already existing in space and hence could not have intentionally created either space or things; nor could the continued existence of things in space depend on the intentional activity of a being whose knowledge of those things itself depends on their continued existence in space, which it must if space is God's organ for perceiving things. 'God is never determined by *external* things', Leibniz later explained, 'but always by what is *in himself*; that is, by his Knowledge of things, before any thing exists *without* himself' (Lz.IV.20/document 125a, p. 567).

Clarke responded to Leibniz's charge by denying that Newton ever said that space is an organ by which God perceives things, arguing instead that Newton maintains that

God sees *all Things*, by his immediate Presence to them: he being actually present to the *Things themselves* [...] as the Mind of Man is present to all the *Pictures of Things* formed in his Brain. [...]. And this *Similitude* is all that he means, when he supposes Infinite Space to be (*as it were*) the *Sensorium* of the Omnipresent Being.

[Cl.I.3/document 90, p. 339]

In his next paper, Leibniz insisted that he found, 'in express Words, in the *Appendix* to Sir *Isaac Newton's Opticks*, that *Space* is the *Sensorium* of *God*',[94] and he added

---

[94] In his Second Reply, Clarke himself insisted that 'Sir *Isaac Newton* does not say, that *Space* is the *Sensory*; but that it is, by way of Similitude only, *as it were* the Sensory, *&c.*' (Cl.II.3/document 96, p. 381). But for an intriguing discussion of what may have been the source of this dispute about what

that 'the Word *Sensorium* hath always signified the *Organ* of Sensation' (Lz.II.3/ document 92, p. 357). He also noted that 'More is requisite besides *bare presence*, to enable One thing to perceive what passes in another' (Lz.II.4, ibid.)—God perceives things not by 'His bare *Presence*, but also his *Operation*' (Lz.II.5, ibid.; see also Lz.V.85/document 140b, p. 695). Subsequently, the debate tended to degenerate into a dispute about the meaning of the term 'sensorium' (see Cl.II.3/document 96, p. 381; Lz.III.10/document 100, p. 413; Cl.III.10/document 120, p. 543; Lz.IV.24–28/document 125a, pp. 567, 569; Cl.IV.24–28/document 129, p. 597), although in his Fourth Paper Leibniz added that by taking space to be the sensorium of God, the Newtonians seem 'to make God the *Soul of the World*' (Lz.IV.27/ document 125a, p. 569). Ultimately, in his Fifth Paper, Leibniz suggested that whether you say 'Space is God's *Sensorium*' or 'only as *it* were his *Sensorium*', the 'latter seems to be as improper, and as little intelligible, as the former' (Lz.V.78/ document 140b, p. 693).

Although the debate about space and God's sensorium largely petered out into a dispute about the meaning of the term *sensorium*, it did give rise to some other, significant disputes—about how God is present to the world, about how God acts in the world, and about the nature of miracles—all of which were related to the second charge that Leibniz had lodged against the Newtonians in the bill of particulars that he had sent to Caroline.

2.4 God's Presence and Activity in the World, Miracles, and Gravity

2.4.1 God's Presence in the World

We recall that the second charge that Leibniz laid against the Newtonians in his First Paper was that they suppose that God made an imperfect world that requires miraculous fixing from time to time. More specifically, Leibniz argued that 'According to their Doctrine, God Almighty wants to *wind up* his Watch from Time to Time: Otherwise it would cease to move'; and he added that 'the Machine of God's making, is so imperfect, according to these Gentlemen; that he is obliged to *clean* it now and then by an extraordinary Concourse, and even to *mend* it, as a Clockmaker mends his Work' (Lz.I.4/document 86, p. 317). Here Leibniz was again referring to things that Newton had said in Query 23 of the 1706 Latin edition of his *Opticks*: first, that 'by reason of the tenacity of fluids, and the attrition of their parts, and the weakness of elasticity in solids, motion[95] is much more apt to be lost than got, and is always upon the decay' (Newton 2014, p. 183; cf. Lz.III.13/ document 100, p. 413; Lz.IV.38/document 125a, p. 571; Cl.III.13 and 14/document

---

Newton said in the 1706 Latin edition of the *Opticks* about space and God's sensorium, and one that seems to vindicate Leibniz's claim, see Koyré and Cohen 1961.

[95] That is, *quantity of motion* ($m|v|$), which Newton took to be the measure of the impulsive force of bodies and which is conserved in direct, perfectly elastic collisions only in reference frames in which the colliding bodies have equal quantities of motion.

xcvi INTRODUCTION

120, p. 543; Cl.IV.38/document 129, p. 601), and second, that in the solar system there are 'some inconsiderable irregularities [...] which may have risen from the mutual actions of comets and planets upon one another, and which will be apt to increase, till this system wants a reformation' (Newton 2014, pp. 185–6; see also Cl.II.8/document 96, p. 381). Recall that Leibniz's First Paper was actually an excerpt from a private letter to Caroline in which he was trying to convince her that English philosophers, and the Newtonians in particular, were subverting natural religion—the theme that then came to dominate the subsequent correspondence with Clarke. So in contrasting his own position with that of the Newtonians in his First Paper, Leibniz concluded:

> According to *My* Opinion, the *same* Force and Vigour remains always in the World, and only passes from one part of Matter to another, agreeably to the Laws of Nature, and the beautiful *pre-established* Order. And I hold, that when God works Miracles, he does not do it in order to supply the Wants of Nature, but those of *Grace*.[96] Whoever thinks otherwise, must needs have a very mean Notion of the Wisdom and Power of God.
>
> [Lz.I.4/document 86, pp. 317, 319]

And in his Second Paper, Leibniz concluded:

> If God is oblig'd to mend the Course of Nature from time to time, it must be done either *supernaturally*, or *naturally*. If it be done *supernaturally*, we must have recourse to *Miracles*, in order to explain Natural Things: Which is reducing a Hypothesis *ad absurdum*: For, every thing may easily be accounted for by *Miracles*. But if it be done *naturally*, then God will not be *Intelligentia Supramundana*: He will be comprehended under the Nature of Things; that is, He will be *the Soul of the World*.
>
> [Lz.II.12/document 92, p. 361; see also Lz.V.110–111/document 140b, p. 707]

To Leibniz's point about God's meddling in the workings of the world, Clarke argued that to suppose, as Leibniz did, that the world can go on without God's intervention, 'is the Notion of *Materialism* and *Fate*, and tends, (under pretence of making God a *Supra-Mundane Intelligence*,) to exclude *Providence* and *God's Government* in reality out of the World' (Cl.I.4/document 90, p. 341). But Leibniz replied that he did not say that the world could go on without God, who must, on his view, conserve the world in existence (Lz.II.9,11/document 92, p. 359; Lz.III.16/ document 100, p. 415), but rather that it did not need to be mended, since God's

---

[96] The original draft letter has 'Et quand Dieu fait des miracles je tiens que ce n'est pas pour soutenir les besoins de la nature, mais pour ceux de la grace' instead of 'Et je tiens, quand Dieu fait des Miracles, que ce n'est pas pour soutenir les besoins de la Nature, mais pour ceux de la Grace' (see document 85, p. 312).

wisdom had provided remedies in advance (Lz.II.8/document 92, p. 359; Lz.III.14/document 100, p. 413; see also Cl.III.13 and 14/document 120, p. 543; Lz.IV.39–40/document 125a, p. 571). This, as well as the dustup concerning Newton's claims about space and God's sensorium, led to a debate about how God is present to things in the world and how he knows them. Leibniz maintained that God is present to things by virtue of continually producing them, which is also how he knows them (Lz.II.5/document 92, p. 357; Lz.III.12/document 100, p. 413; Lz.IV.30,35/document 125a, p. 569; Lz.V.87/document 140b, p. 697). On the other hand, Clarke held that God knows things because he is immediately and substantially present to them in space; and because he supposed that nothing can act where it is not, he also held that God must be extended throughout space in order to act on things (Cl.II.4/document 96, p. 381; Cl.III.12,15/document 120, p. 543; Cl.IV.30/document 129, p. 599).[97]

2.5 Miracles and Gravity

The question concerning God's intervention in the world, and Leibniz's claim that miracles are wrought only to supply the needs of grace and not those of nature, also generated a debate about the nature of miracles themselves. Clarke had responded that the distinction between what is miraculous or supernatural, on the one hand, and what is natural, on the other, is nothing real with respect to God, but just a distinction of our reason, a distinction 'merely in *Our* Conceptions of things'; for everything that passes in the world is ultimately due to the power of God, and what happens regularly requires no less power than that which does not (Cl.II.12/document 96, p. 383). This provided Leibniz with a golden opportunity, not only to dispute Clarke's account of the miraculous by pointing out—doubtless again for Caroline's benefit—its divergence from theological orthodoxy, but also to bait Clarke on a topic that Leibniz had long since used as a bludgeon with which to beat Newton and his followers, namely, the cause of gravity:

> *Divines* will not grant the Author's position against me; *viz.* that there is no Difference, with respect to *God*, between *Natural* and *Supernatural*: And it will be still less approved by most *Philosophers*. There is a vast Difference between these two Things; but it plainly appears, it has not been duly consider'd. That which is *Supernatural*, exceeds *all the Powers of Creatures*. I shall give an Instance, which I have often made use of with good Success. If God would cause a Body to move free in the *Æther* round about a certain fixed Centre, without any other Creature acting upon it: I say, it could not be done without a *Miracle*; since it cannot be explained by the Nature of Bodies. For, a free Body does naturally recede from a Curve in the Tangent. And therefore I maintain, that the *Attraction* of Bodies,

---

[97] For more on this issue in relation to Newton, see Brown 2016b.

xcviii INTRODUCTION

properly so called, is a *Miraculous* Thing, since it cannot be explained by the Nature of Bodies.[98]

From a purely philosophical point of view, Clarke's reply, that 'The Question is not, *what* it is that *Divines* or *Philosophers* usually allow or not allow; but *what Reasons* Men alledge for their Opinions' (Cl.III.17/document 120, p. 545), was doubtless well taken. But from a strategic point of view, Leibniz's charge that the Newtonian view was theologically unorthodox was doubtless even more well taken given his interest in turning Caroline against his adversaries.

To address Leibniz's claim that it would involve a miracle if God caused a body to move in a curved path without any created thing acting on it, Clarke invoked a standard Newtonian view of miracles,[99] that they are simply unusual events, so that if the example Leibniz cited were usual, it would involve no miracle, whereas an unusual event would qualify as miraculous, whether the event in question was caused by God or by some created power (Cl.III.17/document 120, ibid.). In reply, Leibniz again suggested that Clarke had changed the ordinary sense of the term *miracle*, noting that 'The nature of a Miracle does not at all consist in *Usualness* or *Unusualness*; For then *Monsters* would be *Miracles*'; and he reiterated his point that bodies attracting one another at a distance, 'without any intermediate Means', or revolving about a centre without departing along the tangent when nothing hindered them, would be supernatural because inexplicable in terms of the nature of created things, that is, in terms of 'natural Forces' (Lz.IV.42–46)/document 125a, p. 571).

For his part, Clarke modified his position in light of Leibniz's point about monsters, now speaking of 'usual causes' rather than usual events:

> *Unusualness* is *necessarily* included in the Notion of a *Miracle*. […] Nevertheless, it does not follow that every thing which is *unusual*, is *therefore* a Miracle. For it may be only the irregular and more *rare* effect of usual Causes: Of which kind are *Eclipses, Monstrous Births, Madness in Men*, and innumerable things which the Vulgar call *Prodigies*.
>
> [Cl.IV.43/document 129, p. 601]

Clarke again addressed Leibniz's point about gravity, but now stressing in no uncertain terms that to suppose 'That *One Body* should *attract* another *without any* intermediate Means*, is indeed not a *Miracle*, but a *Contradiction*: For 'tis supposing something to *act* where it *is not*.'[100] But he added that 'the *Means* by which Two

---

[98] Lz.III.17/document 100, p. 415. For Leibniz's account of gravity, see Lz.V.35/document 140b, pp. 673, 675.

[99] For an extended discussion of the Newtonian view of miracles, see Dobbs 1992, pp. 230–43, and Harrison 1995.

[100] For more on Clarke's position with respect to action at a distance, see Brown 2016b.

Bodies attract each other, may be *invisible* and *intangible*, and of a different nature from *mechanism*; and yet, acting regularly and constantly, may well be called *natural* [...]' (Cl.IV.45/document 129, p. 603). Finally, and importantly, Clarke challenged Leibniz's apparent use of the expression 'natural Forces' to signify mechanical forces alone, something that Newton had long since rejected:[101]

> If the word *natural Forces*, means here *Mechanical*; then all *Animals*, and even *Men*, are as *mere Machines* as a *Clock*. But if the word does not mean, *mechanical Forces*; then *Gravitation* may be effected by *regular* and *natural* Powers, though they be *not Mechanical*.
>
> [Cl.IV.46/document 129, p. ibid.]

In his final paper, Leibniz again emphasized the heterodox nature of the Newtonian view of miracles, asserting that 'the *common* Opinion of *Divines*, ought not to be looked upon merely as *vulgar Opinion*. A Man should have *weighty Reasons*, before he ventures to contradict it [...]' (Lz.V.108/document 140b, p. 705). Addressing specifically the issue of gravity, Leibniz blasted the Newtonian rejection of mechanical explanations as involving either an appeal to miracles or a return to the discredited Scholastic doctrine of occult qualities, which 'bring us back again into the Kingdom of Darkness' (Lz.V.113/document 140b, p. 707). Leibniz argued that it is only in their beginning that the planetary motions and plant and animal bodies, including that of man, involve a miracle (namely, that of creation) and that thereafter in the physical world everything proceeds naturally, that is, mechanically.[102] Leibniz suggested that in rejecting mechanical explanations, the Newtonians had turned their backs on their own first president of the Royal Society, Robert Boyle, who 'made it his chief Business to inculcate, that every thing was done *mechanically* in natural Philosophy'; and thus, pursuing the dramatic theme of a return to the Kingdom of Darkness, Leibniz wrote:

> But it is Men's Misfortune to grow, at last, out of Conceit with Reason it self, and to be weary of Light. *Chimæra's* begin to appear again, and they are pleasing because they have something in them that is wonderful. What has happened in *Poetry*,

---

[101] Famously, in the General Scholium of the 1713 edition of the *Principia*, Newton had argued that mechanical explanations of gravity were incompatible with the observed motions of planets and comets (Newton 2014, pp. 109–10), a point he had made much earlier in a letter written to Leibniz in October 1693 (Newton 2014, pp. 143–4).

[102] Lz.V.115–16/document 140b, pp. 707, 709. See also Lz.IV.46/document 125a, p. 571. But Leibniz distinguished, of course, between bodies and immaterial souls, asserting that while 'All the natural forces of *Bodies*, are subject to *Mechanical Laws*; [...] all the natural powers of *Spirits*, are subject to *Moral Laws*' (Lz.V.124/document 140b, p. 711). The coordination of body and soul was accomplished by God's having created them in pre-established harmony (see Lz.IV.31/document 125a, p. 569; Lz.V.87,89–92,124/document 140b, pp. 697, 699, 711).

C   INTRODUCTION

happens also in the *Philosophical World*. People are grown weary of rational *Romances* [...] and they are become fond again of the *Tales of Fairies*.
[Lz.V.114/document 140b, p. 707]

In response to Clarke's concession that action at a distance would involve a contradiction, Leibniz wondered how that could be squared with the claim that bodies attract one another through empty space, pointing out that if this was done by God himself, then it would involve a miracle, and if done constantly by God, then a 'perpetual *Miracle*' (Lz.V.118,122/document 140b, p. 709). And if not by God, then by what?: 'perhaps some immaterial Substances, or some spiritual Rays, or some Accident without a Substance, or some kind of *Species Intentionalis*, or some other *I know not what*, the *Means* by which this is pretended to be performed?' (Lz.V.119/ document 140b, ibid.). Although Clarke's own views about the cause of gravity were among those at which Leibniz had guessed—namely, that it is done either by God himself or, more probably, by 'created intelligences' (Clarke 1738, vol. II, p. 697)—Clarke did not proffer his own theory in response to Leibniz's demand for an explanation; instead he retreated into that studied agnosticism about the cause of gravity that had been characteristic of Newton's own public pronouncements on the subject.[103]

2.6 Atoms and the Void

In his Second Paper, and in response to Clarke's assertion that Newton's mathematical principles are directly opposed to materialism because they alone 'prove Matter, or Body, to be the smallest and most inconsiderable Part of the Universe' (Cl.I.1/document 90, p. 339), the most considerable part being void space, Leibniz again pursued his overarching theme in asserting that the Newtonian position in fact detracts from the perfection of God, 'For, the *more* Matter there is, the *more* God has occasion to exercise his Wisdom and Power. Which is one Reason, among others, why I maintain that there is *no Vacuum* at all' (Lz.II.2/document 92, 357). Clarke attempted to deflect Leibniz's argument by suggesting that there are things other than matter, immaterial things, on which God can exercise his power and wisdom, so that space void of matter does not by itself imply that there exist fewer things upon which God may exercise his wisdom and power (LCl.II.2/document 96, p. 379). In response Leibniz began by asserting his own view that 'every created Substance is attended with Matter,'[104] but then argued that even granting that there

---

[103] See Cl.V.118–123/document 157, pp. 797, 799. For more on Clarke's own view in relation to Newton's, see Brown 2016b.

[104] See also Lz.V.61/document 140b, p. 689. Leibniz regarded (primitive) matter as the passive aspect of substance, which he identified with its confused perceptions (for example, see GP VII 322/L 365); only God is entirely active and hence free from confusion. And created monads, which were not extended on Leibniz's view, required at least a phenomenal body, since 'creatures freed from matter

should be some created things without matter, it would remain the case that '*More Matter* was consistent with those same Things; and consequently the said Objects will be still lessened' (Lz.III.9/document 100, p. 413).

Before Caroline transmitted Clarke's Third Reply in a letter to Leibniz of 15 May 1716 (document 119), she had sent a letter to Leibniz dated 5 May in which she reported that 'Last Saturday I had [...] Clarke with me from six until ten o'clock. I very much wanted you to support me; [...] Clarke's clear manner of reasoning nearly made me a convert to the void' (document 115, p. 513). This suddenly alerted Leibniz to the possibility that Caroline was beginning to soften in her allegiance to him, and consequently, in his letter to Caroline dated 12 May 1716, Leibniz wrote that 'Since the void has been preached to Your Royal Highness, I am putting my view of it in a separate paper. For this letter, it appears, is not intended to be seen elsewhere' (document 117a, p. 523). Thus Leibniz was apparently giving Caroline permission to share the separate P.S. with others, which she did, sending it post haste to Newton himself.[105]

In the P.S. Leibniz again emphasized what he took to be the theologically objectionable implications of the doctrine of atoms and void. In opposition to atomism, he expressed his view that matter is actually infinitely divided, so that any part of matter, however small, 'contains a world of new creatures, which the universe would lack if that corpuscle was an atom [...]'. Similarly, he argued that 'to admit a void in nature is ascribing to God a very imperfect production', since in any supposed empty space 'God could place some matter there without derogating in any way from all other things' (document 117b, p. 529).

Before his letter of 12 May could have reached Caroline, she had sent him Clarke's Third Reply, in which Clarke simply stated that God had created precisely the amount of matter that was '*most Convenient* for the *present Frame of Nature*, or the *Present State of Things* [...]' (Cl.III.9/document 120, p. 541). Caroline's letter reflected a growing impatience with the dispute; she admonished Leibniz to 'Drop your serious disputes and prove to us the plenum, and let the chevalier [Newton] and Clarke prove the void on their side'. But more worrisome still, she made reference to the experiments with which Newton was courting her allegiance: 'Tomorrow we will see the experiments about colours', she wrote, and even worse, she added that 'one that I have seen for the void has nearly converted me. It is up to you, sir, to bring me back to the right path, and I am expecting it by the response that you will make to Mr. Clarke' (document 119, p. 537). In his Fourth Paper Leibniz attempted to set Caroline on the right path by reiterating the argument from the P.S. based on the PSR, that there could be no reason to limit the quantity of matter and 'therefore such limitation can have no place' (Lz.IV.21/document 125a, p. 567). Moreover, as in the P.S., any constitution of things in which matter

---

would at the same time be detached from the universal connection, like deserters from the general order' (GP VI 546). For more on this last point, see Brown 2016c.

[105] See the quotation from Westfall in section 1.4.3 above, p. lxxvi.

cii INTRODUCTION

was limited could not be the most perfect, since 'something might always be added to it without derogating from the Perfection of those things which do already exist; and consequently something *must* always be added, in order to act according to the Principle of the Perfection of the divine Operations' (Lz.IV.22/document 125a, p. 567).

2.7. The End

In a letter dated 29 October 1716, just sixteen days before his death on 14 November, Caroline transmitted Clarke's Fifth Reply (document 157) to Leibniz. The cover letter consisted of four terse and wistful sentences, its brevity and tone betraying her weariness with the dispute:

> I send with these few lines, sir, the response of Doctor Clarke. I hope you may find it at least pleasant, if not sound. I have made the acquaintance of a man who admires you very much, the Archbishop of Dublin, doctor King.[106] I will respond to your letters the next post, and I will always be the same for you.
>
> [document 156, p. 763]

As the letter bearing Clarke's fifth and final reply was making its way to Hanover, Leibniz was dying. It could have reached him no sooner than a week before his passing, and his dying left him no time to reply, or even to reflect. Scarcely more than a year later Clarke published his Fifth Reply, along with the rest of the correspondence, dedicated to the Princess Caroline, without fear of any further contradiction from Leibniz.

---

[106] William King (1650–1729) was the Archbishop of Dublin from 1703 to 1729. In 1702 he published *De Origine Mali*, which Leibniz critically discussed in an appendix to his *Theodicy* of 1710.

1710–1712

Essais de Théodicée sur la Bonté de Dieu, la Liberté de l'Homme et l'Origine du Mal: Discours de la Conformité de la Foy avec la Raison §§ 18–19

18. Les deux partis Protestans sont assez d'accord entre eux, quand il s'agit de faire la guerre aux Sociniens: & comme la Philosophie de ces sectaires n'est pas des plus exactes, on a reussi le plus souvent à la battre en ruïne. Mais les mêmes Protestans se sont brouillés entre eux à l'occasion du Sacrement d'Eucharistie, lors qu'une partie de ceux qui s'appellent Reformez (c'est à dire ceux qui suivent en cela plûtôt Zwingle que Calvin) a paru reduire la participation du corps de Jesus-Christ, dans la Sainte Cene, à une simple representation de figure, en se servant de la maxime des Philosophes, qui porte qu'un corps ne peut être qu'en un seul lieu à la fois: au lieu que les *Evangeliques* (qui s'appellent ainsi dans un sens particulier, pour se distinguer des Reformés) étant plus atachés au sens literal, ont jugé avec Luther, que cette participation étoit réelle, & qu'il y avoit là un Mystere surnaturel. Ils rejettent, à la verité, le dogme de la Transubstantiation, qu'ils croyent peu fondé dans le Texte; & ils n'approuvent point non plus celui de la Consubstantiation ou de l'impanation, qu'on ne peut leur imputer que faute d'être bien informé de leur sentiment, puisqu'ils n'admettent point l'inclusion du corps de Jesus-Christ dans le pain, & ne demandent même aucune union de l'un avec l'autre: mais ils demandent au moins une concomitance, en sorte que ces deux substances soient reçuës toutes deux en même tems. Ils croyent que la signification ordinaire des paroles de Jesus-Christ dans une occasion aussi importante que celle où il s'agissoit d'exprimer ses dernieres volontés, doit être conservée; & pour maintenir que ce sens est exempt de toute absurdité qui nous en pourroit éloigner, ils soutiennent que la maxime Philosophique, qui borne l'existence & la participation des corps à un seul lieu, n'est qu'une suite du cours ordinaire de la nature. Ils ne detruisent pas, pour cela, la presence ordinaire du corps de nôtre Sauveur, telle qu'elle peut convenir au corps le plus glorifié. Ils n'ont point recours à je ne sai quelle diffusion d'Ubiquité, qui le dissiperoit & ne le laisseroit trouver nulle-part; & ils n'admettent pas non plus la Replication multipliée de quelques Scolastiques, comme si un même corps étoit en même tems assis ici & debout ailleurs. Enfin ils s'expliquent de telle sorte, qu'il semble à plusieurs que le sentiment de Calvin, autorisé par plusieurs confessions de foy des Eglises qui ont receu la doctrine de cet Auteur, lorsqu'il établit une participation de la substance, n'est pas si éloigné de la Confession d'Augsbourg, qu'on pourroit penser; & ne differe peut-être qu'en ce que pour cette participation il demande la veritable foy, outre la reception orale des Symboles, & exclut par consequent les indignes.

19. On voit par là que le dogme de la participation réelle et substantielle se peut soutenir (sans recourir aux opinions étranges de quelques Scolastiques) par une

1. *Essays on Theodicy, Concerning the Goodness of God, the Liberty of Man and the Origin of Evil: Discourse on the Conformity of Faith with Reason* §§ 18–19[1]

18. The two Protestant parties are sufficiently in accord when it comes to making war on the Socinians. And as the philosophy of these sectaries is not of the most exact, they have most often succeeded in beating it to ruin. But the same Protestants have fallen out with each other on the matter of the sacrament of the Eucharist, when some of those who are called Reformed (that is to say, those who follow Zwingli rather than Calvin on that matter) seemed to reduce the participation of the body of Jesus Christ in the Holy Communion to a mere figurative representation by availing themselves of the maxim of the philosophers that states that a body can only be in one place at a time. On the other hand, the *Evangelicals* (who call themselves thus in a particular sense, in order to distinguish themselves from the Reformed), who are more attached to the literal sense, have judged with Luther that this participation was real and that there was in that a supernatural mystery. They do indeed reject the dogma of transubstantiation, which they believe is textually unfounded; and neither do they approve that of consubstantiation or of impanation, which can only be imputed to them as a result of not being well informed about their view, since they do not admit the inclusion of the body of Jesus Christ in the bread and do not even require any union of the one with the other. But they require at least a concomitance, so that those two substances are both received at the same time. They believe that the ordinary sense of the words of Jesus Christ, on an occasion as important as that when it was a matter of expressing his last wishes, ought to be preserved. And in order to maintain that this sense is exempt from all absurdity that could alienate us from it, they hold that the philosophical maxim that limits the existence and participation of bodies to a single place is only a consequence of the ordinary course of nature. They do not on that account destroy the ordinary presence of the body of our Savior, such as can suit the most glorified body. They do not have recourse to I know not what diffusion of ubiquity, which would disperse it and would not allow it to be located anywhere; and neither do they admit the multiplied replication of some Scholastics, as if one and the same body were sitting here and standing elsewhere at the same time. They ultimately explain themselves in such a way that it seems to many that the view of Calvin, authorized by many confessions of faith by churches that received the doctrine of this author when he established a participation of the substance, is not so far from the Augsburg Confession as might be thought and perhaps differs only in this, that it demands true faith in addition to the oral reception of the symbols and consequently excludes the unworthy.

19. We thereby see that the dogma of real participation can be supported (without resorting to the strange opinions of some Scholastics) by an analogy, rightly

Analogie bien entenduë entre *l'operation immediate, & la presence*. Et comme plusieurs Philosophes ont jugé que, même dans l'ordre de la nature, un corps peut operer immediatement en distance, sur plusieurs corps éloignés, tout à la fois; ils croyent, à plus forte raison, que rien ne peut empêcher la toute-puissance divine de faire qu'un corps soit present à plusieurs corps ensemble; n'y ayant pas un grand trajet de l'operation immediate à la presence, & peut-être l'une dependant de l'autre. Il est vrai que, depuis quelque tems, les Philosophes modernes ont rejetté l'operation naturelle immediate d'un corps sur un autre corps éloigné, & j'avouë que je suis de leur sentiment. Cependant l'operation en distance vient d'être rehabilitée en Angleterre par l'excellent M. Newton, qui soûtient qu'il est de la nature des corps de s'attirer & de peser les uns sur les autres, à proportion de la masse d'un chacun & des rayons d'attraction qu'il reçoit: sur quoy le celebre M. Lock a déclaré en repondant à M. L'Evêque Stillingfleet, qu'aprés avoir vû le livre de M. Newton, il retracte ce qu'il avoit dit lui-même, suivant l'opinion des modernes, dans son Essai sur l'entendement, savoir qu'un corps ne peut operer immediatement sur un autre qu'en le touchant par sa superficie, & en le poussant par son mouvement: & il reconnoit que Dieu peut mettre des proprietés dans la matiere, qui la fassent operer dans l'éloignement. C'est ainsi que les *Théologiens* de la Confession d'Augsbourg soutiennent qu'il depend de Dieu, non seulement qu'un corps opere immediatement sur plusieurs autres éloignés entre eux ; mais qu'il existe même auprés d'eux, & en soit reçu d'une maniere dans laquelle les intervalles des lieux & les dimensions des espaces n'ayent point de part. Et quoique cet effet surpasse les forces de la nature, ils ne croyent point qu'on puisse faire voir qu'il surpasse la puissance de l'Auteur de la nature, à qui il est aisé d'abroger les loix qu'il a données, ou d'en dispenser comme bon lui semble; de la même maniere qu'il a pû faire nager le fer sur l'eau, & suspendre l'operation du feu sur le corps humain.

Leibniz to Nicolaas Hartsoeker

ARTICLE XL

LETTRES DE MONSIEUR
le Baron de Leibnits à Mr. Hartsoeker, avec les réponses de Mr. Hartsoeker

Monsieur de Leibnits, prié par Mr. Hartsoeker de lui dire son sentiment sur *les conjectures physiques* que le dernier a imprimées, envoya d'abord à Mr. Hartsoeker

understood, between *immediate operation* and *presence*. And as many philosophers have held that even in the order of nature a body can operate at a distance immediately on many remote bodies all at once, they believe all the more that nothing can impede the divine omnipotence from causing a body to be present to many bodies all at once, there being no great transition from immediate operation to presence, with the one perhaps depending on the other. It is true that for some time the modern philosophers have rejected the natural immediate operation of a body on another, remote body, and I confess that I am of their view. Meanwhile, operation at a distance has just been rehabilitated in England by the excellent Mr. Newton, who claims that it is of the nature of bodies to be attracted and to press on each other in proportion to the mass of each one and the rays of attraction that it receives. On account of this the celebrated Mr. Locke*, in responding to Bishop Stillingfleet, declared that after having seen the book of Mr. Newton, he retracts what he himself had said, following the opinion of the moderns, in his essay on the understanding, namely, that a body can operate immediately upon another only by touching it with its surface and by pushing it with its motion. And he confesses that God can place properties in matter that make it operate remotely. It is for this reason that the theologians of the Augsburg Confession hold that it depends on God, not only that a body may operate immediately upon many others remote from one another, but that it may even exist near them and be received by them in a manner in which the intervals of places and the dimensions of spaces have no part at all. And although this effect surpasses the forces of nature, they do not believe that it can be shown that it surpasses the power of the author of nature, for whom it is easy to abrogate the laws that he has laid down, or to dispense with them as it may seem good to him, in the same way that he was able to make iron float on water and suspend the operation of fire upon the human body.

[1] G. W. Leibniz, *Essais de Théodicé sur la Bonté de Dieu, la Liberté de L'Homme et L'Origine du Mal* (Amsterdam: Isaac Troyel, 1710), pp. 24–8.

2. Leibniz to Nicolaas Hartsoeker*[1]

[10 February 1711]

PHILOSOPHICAL LETTERS written by
M. LEIBNITZ *and* M. HARTSOEKER[2]

The following Letters have been publish'd by the Authors of the Memoirs of Trevoux. *Those Gentlemen have prefixed to them a short Preamble, which I shall insert here.*

'Mr. *Leibnitz*, being desired by M. *Hartsoeker* to give him his Opinion about the *Conjectures Physiques*, published by the latter, sent some Objections to M. *Hartsoeker*,

quelques objections, auxquelles ce Philosophe a répondu dans *ses Eclaircissemens*, sans nommer Mr. de Leibnits. La dispute n'a pas fini par l'impression des Eclaircissemens, elle est même devenuë plus vive. Mr. de Leibnits s'est trouvé insensiblement engagé à combattre les principes du système de son adversaire, c'est à dire, la parfaite liquidité d'un de ses élemens, & l'indivisibilité de l'autre. En lui soutenant que les atomes sont aussi impossibles qu'un liquide parfait, il lui a soutenu que la *cohesion* des parties d'un corps, qui en fait la dureté, avoit pour veritable cause la conformité des mouvemens qui poussent ces parties: selon lui, lorsque ces *mouvemens conspirans* sont toublez par quelque accident, les parties perdent leur union, & le corps devient liquide. Mr. Hartsoeker ne comprit pas d'abord ce que Mr. de Leibnits vouloit dire. La dispute en étoit là, quand Mr. de Leibnits envoya la premiere des lettres suivantes au Père Desbosses Jesuite demeurant à Cologne, pour la faire tenir à Monsieur Hartsoeker. Le père Desbosses, aujourd'hui Regent de Theologie à Paderborn, est depuis longtems ami intime du celebre Mr. de Leibnits. Beaucoup de sçavoir & de pénetration, jointes à toutes les vertus d'un ami Chrétien, qualitez que Mr. de Leibnits a reconnuës dans le Jesuite, ont lié entre eux cette étroite amitié, malgré la difference de Religion. Le Pere Desbosses a proposé à son illustre ami de rendre publique sa dispute avec Mr. Hartsoeker; nous en avons obtenu la permission de ce dernier, & c'est assûrément avoir rendu un grand service à ceux qui aiment à approfondir les principes de la Physique.

Lettre de Monsieur de Leibnits à Monsieur Hartsoeker

Monsieur

Vous parlez comme si vous n'entendiez pas ce que c'est que mouvemens conspirans, & vous demandez si ce que j'appelle de ce nom, ne seroit peut être pas la même chose que le repos. Mais je répons que non. Car le repos ne tend point à faire, ni à conserver, la liaison des parties qui reposent; & deux corps qui demeurent l'un auprès de l'autre, n'ont pour cela aucun effort à continuer de demeurer ensemble, soit qu'ils se touchent, ou qu'ils ne se touchent pas: mais lorsqu'il y a un mouvement conspirant dans leurs parties qui est troublé par la séparation, il faut de la force pour surmonter cet obstacle. Il n'est pas necessaire aussi que dans les mouvemens conspirans les parties ne changent point de distance: elles peuvent fort bien la changer, pourvû que ce changement spontané soit tout autre que le changement violent, qui feroit la séparation & qui troubleroit ces mouvemens; & les parties des corps résistent à la séparation, non pas parce qu'elles ont peu de tendance à se séparer, car en ce cas elles résisteroient encore, si elles étoient en repos absolument, contre ce que je soutiens; mais parce qu'elles ont un mouvement considerable qui doit être troublé par la séparation. Si ces parties tendent à la séparation d'elles mêmes, elles aident celui qui voudroit les séparer; mais quand elles n'aident point, il ne s'ensuit point qu'elles s'opposent, & il faut quelque raison positive pour cela.

which have been answered by that Philosopher in his *Eclaircissemens*, without naming M. *Leibnitz*. That Dispute, far from ending with the Impression of the *Eclaircissemens*, is grown warmer. M. *Leibnitz* found himself insensibly engaged to attack the Principles of his Adversary's System, *viz.* The perfect Liquidity of one of his Elements, and the Indivisibility of the other. He maintained against him, that Atoms are no less impossible than a perfect Liquid; and that the *Cohesion* of the Parts of a Body, wherein its Hardness consists, is occasioned by the Conformity of the Motions working upon those Parts. M. *Leibnitz* believes, that when those *conspiring Motions* are disturbed by some Accident, the Parts lose their Union, and the body becomes Liquid. M. *Hartsoeker* knew not at first what M. *Leibnitz* meant. The Dispute went thus far, when M. *Leibnitz* sent the first of the following Letters to Father *Desbosses* a Jesuit at *Cologne*, and desired him to get it delivered to M. *Hartsoeker*. Father *Desbosses*, who now teaches Divinity at *Paderborn*, has been a long time an intimate Friend of the Famous M. *Leibnitz*. His great Learning and Penetration, and his eminent Virtue have occasioned a strict Friendship between them, notwithstanding their being of different Religions. Father *Desbosses* proposed to his Illustrious Friend to publish his Dispute with M. *Hartsoeker*. The latter has given us leave to do it; and we think we have done a good Service to those, who love to dive into the Bottom of the Principles of Natural Philosophy.'

I

A Letter of M. Leibnitz to M. Hartsoeker.

You speak, Sir, as if you knew not what I mean by *conspiring Motions*; and you ask, whether what I call so, be not the same thing with Rest. I answer that it is not. For Rest does not tend to make or preserve the Cohesion of Parts that are at Rest; and tho the two Bodies remain one by another, they make no Effort to continue to remain together, whether they touch one another, or not: But when there is a *conspiring Motion* in their Parts, which is disturbed by a Separation, some Strength is requisite to overcome that Obstacle. Nor is it necessary, that in the *conspiring Motions* the Parts should not change their Distance. They may very well change it, provided that spontaneous Change be quite another Thing than a violent Change, which would occasion a Separation, and disturb those Motions: And the Parts of Bodies resist a Separation, not because they have a Tendency to be divided; for in such a Case they would resist still, if they were altogether at Rest, which is contrary to what I maintain; but because they have a considerable motion, which must be disturbed by a Separation. If those Parts tend to a Separation of themselves, they help any one who would separate them; but when they do not help him, it does not follow that they make an Opposition, and some positive Cause is requisite for that.

J'avouë qu'il faut de la force pour chasser un corps de sa place, ou pour le faire aller plus vîte qu'il ne feroit de lui-même; mais si le corps D, tend à chasser de sa place le corps C, la

```
            A
   ┌────────┬────────┐
   │        │        │
   │ B      │      C │
   │        │        │
   └────────┼────────┘
            │        │
            │   D    │
            │        │
            └────────┘
```

résistance du corps C, qui diminuë la vîtesse du corps D, ne contient rien dont on puisse inferer que le corps B, quoique rien ne tende à le chasser aussi, doit accompagner le corps C; soit que l'intervalle entre B & C, soit grand ou petit, ou tout à fait nul. Il faut donc pour produire cette liaison entre B & C, ou cet accompagnement, quelqu'autre raison que le repos, ou la situation de l'un auprès de l'autre, & comme cela doit venir du mécanisme, je ne le sçaurois trouver que dans le mouvement conspirant, commun à des parties des corps B & C, qui fait passer des parties de l'un dans l'autre par un espece de circulation, & doit être troublé par la séparation des corps.

Dire que les mouvemens conspirans sont des fictions, c'est dire en effet que tout mouvement est une fiction. Car comment voulez vous faire un mouvement, Monsieur, sans qu'il y ait quelque convenance entre les mouvemens des parties? Et la nature même des fluides agitez les porte aux mouvemens les plus accommodans. Vous dites, Monsieur, que vos atomes sont sans parties, & vous trouvez étrange que je suppose qu'on peut concevoir qu'un atome A, a deux parties B & C. Mais nêtes vous pas obligé d'avoüer qu'on peut concevoir qu'un atome D, va contre l'atome A, sans aller directement contre la partie B, & cela en telle sorte qu'il emporteroit C avec lui, & laisseroit B là, si par bonheur A nêtoit pas un atome, ou autrement un corps ferme? Il y a donc du fondement pour assigner des parties dans l'atome prétendu, & il faut maintenant assigner des causes de son atomité, pour ainsi dire, c'est à dire, pourquoi D ne peut pas emporter C avec lui, sans emporter B en même tems, & il faut que vous trouviez une bonne colle pour faire tenir une de ces parties à l'autre, si vous ne voulez recourir avec moi au mouvement conspirant.

Si vous n'alleguez que la volonté de Dieu pour cela, vous recourez à un miracle, & même à un miracle perpetuel: car la volonté de Dieu opere par miracle, toutes les fois qu'on ne sçauroit rendre raison de cette volonté & de son effet par la nature des objets. Par exemple, si quelqu'un disoit que c'est une volonté de Dieu qu'on planete aille circulairement dans son orbe, sans que rien cause & conserve son mouvement, je dis que ce sera un miracle perpetuel; car par la nature des choses, la planete en circulant, tend à s'éloigner de son orbe par la tangente, si rien ne l'empêche, & il faut que Dieu l'empêche perpetuellement, si quelque cause naturelle ne le fait. Il en est de même dans la supposition de vos atomes, car naturellement la masse C sera emportée par la masse D, sans que la masse B suive, s'il n'y a aucune raison qui s'oppose à cette séparation; & si vous ne cherchez cette raison que dans la volonté de Dieu, vous ne la trouverez que dans le miracle.

I own that some force is requisite to expel a Body from its Place, or to make it go faster than it would do of it self; but if the Body D tends to drive the Body C from its Place, the

Resistance of the Body C, which lessens the Swiftness of the Body D, has nothing in it, from whence it may be inferred that the Body B, tho nothing tends to drive it out, ought to accompany the Body C; whether the interval between B and C be great or small, or none at all. We must therefore suppose, in order to produce that Union between B and C, or their going along together, some other Reason than Rest, or the Situation of the one by the other; but because it ought to proceed from Mechanism, I can find it no where, but in the *conspiring Motion*, common to some Parts of the Bodies B and C, which conveys some Parts from the one into the other by a kind of Circulation, and which must be disturbed by the Separation of the Bodies.

To say that the conspiring Motions are a Fiction, is the same as to say that every Motion is a Fiction. For, Sir, how will you make a Motion, unless there be some Relation among the Motions of the Parts? The very Nature of Fluids in Agitation leads them to those Motions, that are most fitting. You say, your Atoms have no Parts; and you think it strange that I should suppose one may conceive that an Atom A has two Parts B and C. But are you not oblig'd to own, that one may conceive that an Atom D goes against the Atom A, without going directly against the Part B; and in such a manner that it would carry C along with it, and leave B, if A was not an Atom, or a solid Body? There is therefore some Reason to affirm that the pretended Atom is not without Parts. You must assign the Causes of its *Atomity*, if I may so speak, that is, why D cannot carry C along with it, without carrying B at the same time; and you must find a strong Glue to make one of those Parts stick to the other, if you are not willing to have recourse to the conspiring Motion.

If you alledge only the Will of God for it, you have recourse to a Miracle, and even to a perpetual Miracle; for the Will of God works through a Miracle, whenever we are not able to account for that Will and its Effect from the Nature of the Objects. For example, if any one should say, it is God's Will that a Planet should move round in its Orb, without any other Cause of its Motion; I maintain that it would be a perpetual Miracle: For, by the Nature of Things, the Planet going round tends to remove from its Orb through the Tangent, if nothing hinders it; and God must continually prevent it, if no natural Cause does it. The same ought to be said of your Atoms; for the Body C will be naturally carried away by the Body D, and the Body B will not follow, if nothing hinders such a Separation; and if you look out for the Reason of it in the Will of God, you must suppose a Miracle.

On peut dire dans un très-bon sens que tout est un miracle perpetuel, c'est à dire, digne d'admiration: mais il me semble que l'exemple de la planete, qui en circulant se conserve dans son orbe sans autre aide que celle de Dieu, comparée avec la planete retenuë dans son orbe par la matiere qui la pousse toûjours vers la soleil, fait bien sentir la difference qu'il y a entre les miracles naturels raisonnables, & entre les miracles proprement dits, ou surnaturels, ou plûtôt (quand ils n'ont point de lieu) entre une explication raisonnable, & entre les fictions où l'on a recours pour soutenir des opinions mal fondées. C'est ainsi que font ceux qui disent, après l'Aristarque de feu Mr. de Roberval, que c'est une loi de la nature que Dieu a donnée en créant les choses, que tous les corps doivent s'attirer les uns les autres. Car n'alleguant rien que cela pour obtenir un tel effet, & n'admettant rien que Dieu ait fait qui puisse montrer comment il obtient ce but, ils recourent au miracle, c'est à dire, au surnaturel, & à un surnaturel toûjours continué, quand il s'agît de trouver une cause naturelle.

Vous avez raison, Monsieur, de dire qu'on doit souvent reconnoître nôtre ignorance, & que cela vaut mieux que de se jetter dans le galimatias, pour vouloir rendre raison des choses, qu'on n'entend point. Mais autre chose est avouër qu'on n'entend la raison de quelque effet, & autre chose est assûrer qu'il y a quelque chose dont on ne peut rendre aucune raison; & c'est justement en cela qu'on peche contre les premiers principes du raisonnement, & c'est comme si quelqu'un avoit nié à Archimede l'axiome qu'il a employé dans son livre des Equiponderans, qu'une balance où tout est égal de part & d'autre demeure en équilibre, sous pretexte qu'on n'entend pas assez les chose, & que peutêtre la balance se change d'elle même sans en avoir aucun sujet.

Ainsi les Anciens & les Modernes, qui avoüent que la pesanteur est une *qualité occulte*, ont raison, s'ils entendent par là qu'il y a un certain mécanisme qui leur est inconnu, par lequel les corps sont poussez vers le centre de la terre. Mais si leur sentiment est que la chose se fait sans aucun mécanisme, par une simple *qualité primitive*, ou par une loi de Dieu, qui fait cet effet sans employer aucuns moyens intelligibles, c'est une qualité occulte déraisonnable, qui est tellement occulte, qu'il est impossible qu'elle puisse jamais devenir claire, quand même un Ange, pour ne pas dire Dieu même, la voudroit expliquer.

Il en est de même de la *dureté*. Si quelqu'un avouë que le mécanisme qui fait le fondement de la dureté lui est inconnu, il a raison; mais s'il veut que la dureté vienne de quelque autre chose que du mécanisme, & s'il a recours à une dureté primitive, comme font les défenseurs des atomes, il recourt à une qualité qui est tellement occulte, qu'elle ne sçauroit être renduë claire, c'est à dire, à quelque chose de déraisonnable, & qui peche contre les premiers principes du raisonnement par l'aveu qu'il renferme, qu'il arrive quelque chose de naturel dont il n'y a aucune raison naturelle.

C'est aussi en cela que pechent ceux qui introduisent une indifference d'équilibre, comme si jamais la volonté se déterminoit lorsque tout est égal de part & d'autre interieurement & exterieurement: ce cas n'arrive jamais, & il y a toûjours plus d'inclination d'une côté que de l'autre, & la volonté est toûjours inclinée par quelque raison, ou disposition, quoi qu'elle ne soit jamais necessitée par ces raisons; & j'ose

It may be said in a very good Sense, that every Thing is a continual Miracle, that is, Worthy of Admiration: but it seems to me that the Example of a Planet, which goes round, and preserves its Motion in its Orb without any other Help but that of God, being compared with a Planet kept in its Orb by the Matter, which constantly drives it towards the Sun, plainly shews what Difference there is between natural and rational Miracles, and those that are properly so call'd, or Supernatural; or rather between a reasonable Explication, and a Fiction invented to support an ill-grounded Opinion. Such is the Method of those who say, after Mr. *de Roberval's Aristarchus*, that all Bodies attract one another by a Law of Nature, which God made in the Beginning of Things. For alledging nothing else to obtain such an Effect, and admitting nothing that was made by God, whereby it may appear how he attains to that End, they have recourse to a Miracle, that is, to a supernatural thing, which continues for ever, when the Question is to find out a natural Cause.

You are in the right, Sir, when you say we ought frequently to acknowledge our Ignorance, and that it is a wiser Method than to run into Nonsense by pretending to Account for those Things which we do not understand. But, to own that we know not the Causes of some Effects, is a different thing from affirming that there are some Things, of which no Reason can be given; which is contrary to the first Principles of Reasoning: 'Tis just as if some body had denied the Axiom, which *Archimedes* made use of in his Book *de Æquiponderantibus, viz.* That a Ballance, when every thing is equal on both Sides, remains in an *Æquilibrium*; under Pretence that Things are not sufficiently understood, and that perhaps the Ballance undergoes some Alteration without any reason for it.

Thus the Ancients and the Moderns, who own that Gravity is an *occult Quality*, are in the right, if they mean by it, that there is a certain Mechanism unknown to them, whereby all Bodies tend towards the Center of the Earth. But if they mean that the Thing is performed without any Mechanism, by a simple *primitive Quality*, or by a Law of God, who produces that Effect without using any intelligible Means; it is an unreasonable occult Quality, and so very occult, that 'tis impossible it should ever be clear, tho an Angel, or God himself, should undertake to explain it.

The same ought to be said of *Hardness*. If any one acknowledges that the Mechanism, which occasions Hardness, is unknown to him, he is in the right; but if he pretends that Hardness proceeds from any other Cause than Mechanism, and if he has recourse to a primitive Hardness, as the Assertors of Atoms do, he recurs to a Quality that is so occult, that it can never be made clear; that is, to a Thing both unreasonable and contrary to the first Principles of Reasoning, since he owns that there are some Things natural, that have no natural Cause.

Those who are also guilty of the same Fault, who admit an Indifference of *Æquilibrium*, as if the Will could be determined, when all things are equal on both Sides both inwardly and outwardly. Such a Case never happens: There is always a greater Inclination on one Side than on the other; and the Will is always inclined by some Reason, or Disposition, without being necessitated: And I dare say, that many

dire qu'une grande partie des fautes qu'on fait dans le raisonnement, vient de ce qu'on n'observe pas bien ce grand principe, *que rien n'arrive dont il n'y ait une raison suffisante*: principe dont Mr. Descartes même, & quantité d'autres habiles gens, n'ont pas assez envisagé la force & les suites. Ce principe suffit lui seul pour détruire le vuide, les atomes, les qualitez occultes, & même le premier élement de Mr. Descartes, avec ses globes & quantité d'autres fictions.

Ainsi vous voyez bien, Monsieur, pourquoi Dieu ne pourroit point créer des atomes, c'est à dire, des corps durs par eux mêmes, des corps d'une dureté naturelle primitive, des corps d'une dureté invincible, & dont il n'y eut aucun raison, comme il ne sçauroit créer des planetes circulaires d'elles mêmes dans leurs orbes, sans qu'il y eut aucune raison qui les empêchât de s'éloigner par la tangente: car il faudra du moins que quelque miracle retienne la planete, ou empêche les parties du corps dur de se séparer, si quelque raison mécanique, ou intelligible, ne le fait pas. Quand on accorderoit les atomes, & quand on seroit éloigné d'admettre le vuide, on ne seroit point forcé pour cela de recourir à un premier élement, c'est à dire, à une matiere parfaitement fluide. Car pourquoi ne pourroit-on pas remplir l'espace d'un matiere qui eut des differens degrez de fluidité & de tenacité, comme je crois que c'est la nature de toute la matiere.

Je ne vois point aussi pourquoi il est necessaire que les corps durs reçoivent tout leur mouvement des corps fluides, & sur tout d'une masse parfaitement fluide, ou de vôtre premier élement. Car toute la matiere étant également susceptible de mouvement, & également incapable de le tirer d'elle-même, rien n'empêche la cause de son mouvement de le donner au plus ferme, aussi bien qu'au plus fluide. On pourroit même dire que le mouvement donné à peu de corps fermes, peut rendre raison du mouvement de beaucoup de corps fluides, & par conséquent qu'il est anterieur dans l'ordre. Car un corps ferme mis dans un fluide plein le met en mouvement tout entier, & produit une espece de circulation necessaire pour remplir le lieu, qui sans cela demeureroit vuide derriere le corps ferme; & cette circulation forme une espece de tourbillon, qui a quelque rapport à celui qu'on conçoit à l'entour de l'aimant. Il n'est pas permis de dire que l'univers est comme un animal plein de vie & intelligence: car on seroit porté à croire après cela que Dieu est l'ame de cet animal; au lieu que Dieu est *Intelligentia supramundana*, qui est la cause du monde, & si l'univers étoit sans bornes, il seroit un amas d'animaux & d'autres êtres; mais il ne pourroit être un animal.

Vôtre premier élement aussi n'est pas plus capable de vie & d'intelligence que toute autre masse, & ce corps n'étant point organique, il n'est point convenable qu'il ait de la perception, qui doit toûjours répondre aux actions des organes, si vous voulez que la nature agisse avec ordre & liaison.

Vôtre dites, Monsieur, qu'il est impossible que l'esprit humain pénetre comment il arrive qu'une substance ait de la vie & de la perception, & vous avez raison lorsqu'il s'agit du détail & du commencement des choses. Mais vous m'avoüerez peutêtre aussi qu'on s'explique plus intelligiblement dans mon système de l'Harmonie préétablie, en concevant que nos substances sont naturellement représentatives de ce que se fait dans la portion de matiere à laquelle elles sont unies.

Faults committed in arguing proceed from not duly observing this great Principle, *that nothing happens without a sufficient Reason for it.* A Principle, the Force and Consequences whereof have not been sufficiently considered by *Descartes*, and many other great Men. That Principle is sufficient to destroy the *Vacuum*, and the Atoms, and Occult Qualities of some Philosophers, and even the First Element of *Descartes*, with his Globes, and many other Fictions.

Thus, Sir, you see why God could not create Atoms, that is, Bodies hard by their own Nature, Bodies of a Primitive and insuperable Hardness not to be accounted for; as he could not create Planets that should move round of themselves, without any Cause that should prevent their removing through the Tangent: For a Miracle at least must keep the Planet in, and prevent the Separation of the Parts of the hard Body, if a Mechanical or intelligible Cause does not do it. Granting the Possibility of Atoms, and the Impossibility of a *Vacuum*, I don't see why we should be forced to have recourse to a First Element, that is, to a Matter altogether Fluid. Why may we not suppose the Space to be fill'd up with a Matter, that has different Degrees of Fluidity and Tenacity, as I believe it is the Nature of all Matter.

Nor do I see why hard Bodies should necessarily receive all their Motion from Fluid Bodies, especially from a Mass altogether Fluid, or from your First Element. For all Matter being equally susceptible of Motion, and equally uncapable of producing it in it self, the most solid Bodies may receive it, as well as those that are most Fluid. Nay, it might be said, that the Motion, communicated to some few hard Bodies, may serve to account for the Motion of many Fluid Bodies; and consequently that it is anterior in order. For a Solid Body, thrown into a Fluid, puts it into Motion, and produces a Kind of Circulation necessary to fill up the Place, which otherwise would remain empty behind the Solid Body; and that Circulation forms a Kind of Vortex, that has some Affinity with that, which we conceive round the Load-stone.

It ought not to be said, that the Universe is like an Animal endued with Life and Intelligence: For then one might be apt to believe, that God is the Soul of that Animal; whereas he is *Intelligentia Supramundana*, and the Cause of the World: And if the Universe was unlimited, it would be a Collection of Animals and other Beings; but it could not be a single Animal.

Your First Element is not more susceptible of Life and Intelligence than any other Bulk of Matter; and since it is not organized, it is not fit it should have any Perception, which must always answer the Actions of Organs, if you will have Nature to act orderly and coherently.

You say, Sir, that 'tis impossible for us to apprehend how a Substance comes to have Life and Perception; and you are in the Right, when the Question is about Particulars and the Beginnings of Things. But perhaps you will own, that the thing is more intelligible in my System of the *Pre-establish'd Harmony*, by conceiving that our Spiritual Substances do naturally represent what happens in that Part of Matter, to which they are united.

J'ai assez satisfait à ceux qui ont objecté, qu'après cela il n'y auroit plus de *liberté*; car Dieu sçachant ce que les esprits choisiront librement dans les tems, y a accommodé les corps par avance. Mr. Jaquelot, qui me fit une pareille objection de vive voix, fut satisfait de ma réponse, comme il a avoüé dans son livre contre Mr. Bayle; il l'a même éclaircie par une comparaison élegante. J'ai répondu aussi de la même maniere à l'objection de Dom Lami, & ma réponse est dans le Journal des Sçavans. Mr. Bernoulli, quand il étoit Professeur à Groningue, a soutenu des Theses où il a fort bien défendu mon sentiment de l'Harmonie préétablie.

Au reste les imperfections qui sont dans l'univers sont comme les dissonances dans une excellente piece de Musique, qui contribuent à la rendre plus parfaite, au jugement de ceux qui en sentent bien la liaison. Ainsi on ne peut point dire que Dieu en créant le monde en ait fait une machine imparfaite, & qui se developpe mal. Il est vrai qu'il y a des machines dans ce monde qui n'ont pas toûjours & d'abord toute la perfection dont elles sont capables.

Je vous rens graces, Monsieur, de vos bons souhaits sur le commencement de l'année, & je souhaite que vous puissiez encore contribuer long-tems à l'accroissement des Sciences, étant avec passion,

MONSIEUR,

Vôtre très-humble & très-

obéïssant serviteur

LEIBNITS.

Hannover ce 10. *Février*

I have sufficiently answered those, who objected to me that such a System was inconsistent with *Free-will*; for God knowing what Mens Minds would freely chuse in time, adapted their Bodies to it before hand. Mr. *Jaquelot*,[3] who raised such an Objection against me by Word of Mouth, was satisfied with my Answer, as he owned in his Book against Mr. [Pierre] *Bayle**: Nay, he has cleared it with an elegant Comparison. I have answered Father *Lami's* Objection in the same manner; and my Answer has been inserted in the *Journal des Scavans*.[4] When Mr. [Johann] *Bernoulli** was Professor at *Groningen*, he maintained some Theses, wherein he vindicated my Opinion concerning the *Pre-established Harmony*.

To conclude, the Imperfections observable in the Universe are like the Dissonances of an Excellent Piece of Musick, which contribute to render it more perfect, in the Opinion of the best Judges. And therefore it cannot be said, that when God created the World, he made an imperfect Machine. 'Tis true there are some Machines in this World, that have not always, and from the Beginning, all the Perfection that they are capable of.

I return you many Thanks, Sir, for your good Wishes about the Beginning of the New Year; and I wish you may long contribute to the Improvement of the Sciences, being with great Zeal,

SIR,

Your most Humble,
and most Obedient Servant,
LEIBNITZ.

Hanover,
Feb. 10.   1711.

---

[1] The original French version of Leibniz's letter of 10 February 1711 to Hartsoeker that is reproduced here was published in the *Mémoires pour l'Histoire des Sciences & des beaux-Arts* (aka the *Memoires de Trévoux*) for March 1712 (pp. 493–510). The English translation reproduced here was published in the *Memoirs of Literature* of London for 5 May 1712 OS (pp. 137–40). The letter was later published again in the original French in the Amsterdam edition of the *Journal des Sçavans* for December 1712 (pp. 603–15). The English version was previously published in Janiak 2014, pp. 144–9; the French version was previously published in GP III 516–21. For Newton's response in a draft letter to the editor of the *Memoirs of Literature*, see document 3.

[2] I have omitted Hartsoeker's response.

[3] That is, Isaac Jaquelot (1647–1708), the French-born Huguenot and later court chaplain to the French colony in Berlin. The book to which Leibniz refers below was Jaquelot's *Conformité de la foi avec la raison: ou défense de la religion, contre les principales difficultez répandues dans le Dictionaire historique et critique de Mr. Bayle* (Amsterdam, 1705).

[4] Leibniz refers here to the French Benedictine philosopher and theologian François Lamy (1637–1711) who, in the second edition of his book *De la Connoissance de soi-même* (1699), criticized Leibniz's 'Système nouveau', which had been published in the *Journal des savants* in 1695. Leibniz responded to Lamy's objections in an article written in 1704, but not published until 1709 in a supplement to the *Journal des savants*. See Woolhouse and Francks 1997, pp. 133–7.

3. Isaac Newton's Unpublished Draft Letter to the Editor of the *Memoirs of Literature*[1]

[After 5 May 1712 OS/16 May 1712 NS]

S^r

In your weekly paper dated May 5 1712 I meet wth two Letters, one by Mr Leibnitz to Mr Hartsoeker the other by Mr Hartsoeker to Mr Leibnitz in answer to ye former. And in the Letter of Mr Leibnitz I meet wth some things reflecting upon the English. I hope you will do them the justice to publish this vindication as you have printed the reflexion. He writes thus. It may be said in a very good sense that every thing is a continual Miracle, that is worthy of Admiration, but it seems to me that the example of a Planet wch goes round & preserves it[s] motion in its Orb without any other help but that of God, being compared wth a Planet kept in its Orb by y^t matter wch constantly drives it towards ye Sun, plainly shews what difference there is between natural & rational miracles & those that are properly so called or supernatural; or rather between a reasonable explication, & a fiction invented to support an ill grounded opinion. Such is the method of those who say, after Mr de Robervals Aristarchus[2], that all bodies attract one another by a law of nature wch God made in the beginning of things. For alledging nothing els to obtein such an effect & admitting nothing that was made by God whereby it may appear how he attains to that end, they have recourse to a miracle, that is, to a supernatural thing, wch continues for ever, when the Question is to find out a natural cause.[3] Thus far Mr Leibnits. I know not what just occasion there was for this reflexion in a discourse foreign to this matter but its plain that this was intended against some in England & I hope to make it as plain that it was undeserved. For The true state of the case is this. It has been proved by some that all bodies upon the surface of the earth gravitate towards the earth in proportion to ye quantity of matter in each of them: That the Moon tends towards the earth & all the Planets towards one another by the same law; & that by this tendency all their motions are performed. These things have been proved by mathematical demonstrations grounded upon experiments & the phænomena of nature: & Mr Leibnitz himself cannot deny that they have been proved. But he objects that because they alledge nothing else to obteine such an effect [he means a tendency of all bodies towards one another][4] besides a law of nature wch God made in the beginning of things & admitt nothing that was made by God (he means no vortices) whereby it may appear how God attains to that end, they have recourse to a Miracle, that is, to a supernatural thing wch continues for ever, when the question is to find out a natural cause. Because they do not explain gravity by a mechanical hypothesis, he charges them wth making it a supernatural thing, a miracle & a fiction invented to support an ill grounded opinion & compares their method of philosophy to that of Mr Robervals Aristarchus, wch is all one

3. NEWTON'S UNPUBLISHED DRAFT LETTER

3. NEWTON'S UNPUBLISHED DRAFT LETTER   19

as to call it Romantic. They shew that there is an universal gravity & that all the phenomena of the heavens are the effect of it & with ye cause of gravity they meddle not but leave it to be found out by them that can explain it whether mechanically or otherwise. And doth this deserve to be scouted with the language of a supernatural thing, a miracle, a fiction invented to support an ill grounded opinion, & a method of philosophy, after Mr Robervals Romance.

But Mr Leibnitz goes on. <u>The</u> Ancients & the Moderns who own that gravity is an occult Quality, are in the right, if they mean by it, that there is a certain Mechanism unknown to them whereby all bodies tend towards the center of the earth. But if they mean that the thing is performed without any mechanism by a simple primitive quality or by a law of God who produces that effect without using any intelligible means it is an unreasonable & occult Quality, & so very occult that it is impossible that it should ever be clear tho an Angel or God himself should undertake to explain it. The same ought to be said of hardness.[5] So then gravity & hardness must go for unreasonable occult qualities unless they can be explained mechanically. And why may not the same be said of the vis inertiæ & the extension the duration & mobility of bodies, & yet no man ever attempted to explain these qualities mechanically, or took them for miracles or supernatural things or fictions or occult qualities. They are the natural real reasonable manifest qualities of all bodies seated in them by the will of God from the beginning of the creation & per-fectly uncapable of being explained mechanically, & so may be the hardness of primitive particles of bodies. And therefore if any man should say that bodies attract one another by a power whose cause is unknown to us or by a power seated in the frame of nature by the will of God, or by a power seated in a substance in wch bodies move & flote without resistance & wch has therefore no vis inertiæ, but acts by other laws than those that are mechanical: I know not why he should be said to introduce miracles & occult qualities & fictions into ye world. For Mr Leibnitz him-self will scarce say that thinking is mechanical as it must be if to explain it otherwise be to make it a miracle an occult quality & a fiction.

But he goes on & tells us that God <u>could not create Planets that</u> should move round of themselves without any cause that should prevent their removing through the tangent. For a Miracle at least must keep <u>the Planet in</u>.[6] But certainly God could create Planets that should move round of themselves without any other cause than gravity that should prevent their removing through ye tangent. For gravity without a miracle may keep the Planets in. And to understand this wth out knowing the cause of gravity, is as good a progress in philosophy as to understand the frame of a clock & the dependance of ye wheels upon one another without knowing the cause of the gravity of the weight wch moves the machine is in the philosophy of clock-work, or the understanding the frame of the bones & muscles & their connection in the body of an animal & how the bones are moved by the contracting or dilating of

20   3. NEWTON'S UNPUBLISHED DRAFT LETTER

3. NEWTON'S UNPUBLISHED DRAFT LETTER   21

the muscles without knowing how the muscles are contracted or dilated by the power of ye mind, is [in] the philosophy of animal motion.

[1] University Library Cambridge Add. 3968(17), f. 257. Previously published in NC V 298–300 and Janiak 2014, pp. 150–2. It is not clear precisely when Newton composed this draft letter, but it was sometime after 5 May 1712 OS, when the translation of Leibniz's letter to Hartsoeker was published in the *Memoirs of Literature* (see document 2 above). In a letter that he wrote to Newton on 18 March 1712 OS (29 March 1712 NS) suggesting additions to be made in the second edition of Newton's *Principia*, Roger Cotes wrote:

> After this Specimen I think it will be proper to add some things by which Your Book may be cleared from some prejudices which have been industriously laid against it. As that it deserts Mechanical causes, is built upon Miracles & recurrs to Occult qualitys. That you may not think it unnecessary to answer such Objections You may be pleased to consult a Weekly paper call'd *Memoirs of Literature* sold by Ann Baldwin. In ye 18th Number of the Second Volume of those Papers, which was published May 5th 1712 You will find a very extraordinary Letter of Mr. Leibnitz to Mr. Hartsoeker which will confirm what I have said. I do not propose to mention Mr. Leibnitz's name, t'were better to neglect him; but the Object[ions] I think may very well be answered & even retorted upon the maintainers of Vortices. [NC V 392–3]

But since Newton did not acknowledge the information about Leibniz's published letter in his response to Cotes, it remains unclear whether he had previously seen Leibniz's letter and had already penned his draft letter to the editor of the *Memoirs of Literature* before receiving Cotes's letter or whether he read the published English translation of Leibniz's letter and penned his draft letter to the editor only after receiving the letter from Cotes.

[2] Gilles Personne de Roberval* published his *Aristarchi Samii de Mundi systemate, partibus et motibus ejusdem libellus* in Paris in 1644. As indicated by Newton's comment, Roberval supposed that there was a mutual attraction between all the parts of matter. See Koyré 1965, p. 59n2.

[3] Newton quotes from the English translation of Leibniz's letter to Hartsoeker that was published in the *Memoirs of Literature*, beginning with the words underlined above and ending with this sentence. See document 2 above, p. 11.

[4] The square brackets here and the words that are contained within them are Newton's own.

[5] Here, from the underlined 'The' to the end of this sentence, Newton again quotes from the English translation of Leibniz's letter to Hartsoeker. See document 2 above, p. 11.

[6] Here again, from the underlined 'could not create Planets that' to the end of this sentence, Newton quotes from the English translation of Leibniz's letter to Hartsoeker. See document 2 above, p. 13.

1714

Andreas Gottlieb von Bernstorff to Leibniz

Han. ce 3 de
Mars 14[2]

Monsieur

Msgr. l'Electeur vient de m'ordonner de vous demander de sa part, Monsieur, si vous ne songiés pas encor à votre retour. SA[el] commence a etre impatienter[3] ladessus, et je ne puis que vous conseiller en amy et serviteur, de la contenter sur ce point; nous ferons ce que nous pouvons pour que vous ayez sujet de l'etre aussy. Je suis Monsieur

votre

tresh. tresobéis.
serviteur
Bernstorff

4. Andreas Gottlieb von Bernstorff* to Leibniz[1]

Hanover

3 March 1714[2]

Sir

Monseigneur the Elector [Georg Ludwig* of Braunschweig-Lüneburg] has just ordered me to ask you on his behalf, sir, if you were still not thinking about your return. His Electoral Highness is becoming impatient[3] about this, and I can only advise you, as a friend and servant, to satisfy him on this point;[4] we will do what we can so that you will have reason to be satisfied as well. I am

sir

your

very humble very obedient

servant

Bernstorff

---

[1] LBr. 59 Bl. 96r–96v: letter as sent; 1.5 quarto sides in Bernstorff's hand. Previously published in Doebner 1881, p. 282, and Klopp XI 6–7.

[2] Doebner reads the date of this letter as 30 March 1714, confusing Bernstorff's 'd' with '0'; but Klopp reads it correctly as 3 March 1714. Only the latter date is consistent with the fact that Leibniz responded to this letter on 21 March 1714 (see document 6).

[3] Reading 'impatiente' for 'impatienter'.

[4] At the time of this writing, Leibniz had been on one of his many extended leaves from Hanover. He had spent most of September 1712 in Wolfenbüttel in the service of Duke Anton Ulrich*. Anton Ulrich had been in Frankfurt am Main for the coronation of Emperor Karl VI* on 22 December 1711, and the duke, whose granddaughter Elisabeth Christine* was married to the emperor, was able to elicit a promise from the newly crowned emperor to appoint Leibniz to the office of aulic councilor*. At the beginning of November, Leibniz was invited to meet with Czar Peter the Great* at Carlsbad. While Leibniz neglected to notify Hanover of his plans to meet with the czar, he did inform Duke Anton Ulrich, who then enlisted Leibniz to persuade the czar to join forces with Austria in its war against France (Antognazza 2009, p. 472). Leibniz accompanied the czar as far as Dresden, at which point he took his leave of the czar and travelled to Vienna in the hopes of meeting with the emperor. It later became clear that among his reasons for wanting to make the trip to Vienna was to lobby for the establishment of an Imperial Society of Sciences* and to follow up on the emperor's promise to appoint him aulic councilor. He met with the emperor for the first time around the middle of January 1713, and the Hanoverian ambassador to Vienna, Daniel Erasmi von Huldenberg, later recorded an audience he had on 22 February with the emperor's sister-in-law, the Dowager Empress Wilhelmine Amalie*, who was the daughter of the late Duke of Braunschweig-Lüneburg-Calenberg (Hanover) Johann Friedrich*, Leibniz's first employer in Hanover. Richard Doebner has written that Huldenberg reported that the emperor 'preserves the firm decision to take Leibniz into his service,' the emperor having stated that 'we are already well acquainted with each other and have even become good friends' (Doebner 1881, p. 217). Doebner also writes that according to Huldenberg, the empress dowager voiced her opinion that 'Leibniz could render good service to the elector even as aulic councilor' (ibid.), to which the ambassador responded as follows:

> However learned Leibniz might usually be in other matters, he is nevertheless fit for nothing less than being aulic councilor. He has no background for it. He has never reported transactions or made a decision, and he would certainly be very unsuccessful at it. His Majesty [the elector] would like to warn the emperor, otherwise it will be the same for him as for the elector; for by his genius he would want to do everything and therefore always find his pleasure in endless correspondences and travelling back and forth; he strives to satisfy his insatiable curiosity, but he would have either no talent or no desire to bring anything together and finish it. It would be regrettable that the

5. CHAMBERLAYNE TO LEIBNIZ

5. CHAMBERLAYNE TO LEIBNIZ 27

elector has to lose him and yet the emperor gain nothing useful from it. [The original German as quoted in ibid.; my translation]

Despite this, Leibniz received a document in April confirming his appointment as aulic councilor (Aiton 1985, p. 312). Still, Leibniz did not depart Vienna for Hanover until 3 September 1714, after hearing that Queen Anne had died on 12 August. As a consequence of the queen's death, Georg Ludwig had succeeded to the throne in England, and Leibniz rushed to return to Hanover. But by the time he arrived on 14 September, Georg Ludwig and his son Georg August* had already departed for England.

5. John Chamberlayne* to Leibniz[1]

Westminster
27 Febry 1714[2]

Most honored S^r.

I lately writ a long Letter, since when, I re^{ced} one from our com̂on [common] learned Friend D^r. [William] Wotton*, who not knowing that you understood our Language so well, writ to me in Latin with a design as I suppose that I should communicate a copy to you of it. I here have done, and entirely subscribe to what that great judge of Learning says concerning you &c.

I send this to you by M^r. Hasberg an Agent for the D. of Wolfenbuttel [Anton Ulrich*] and who has the Honor to Correspond with you; 'twas from him that I have been inform'd of the Differences Fatal to Learning between two of the greatest Philosophers & Mathematicians of Europe, I need not say I mean S^r. Isaac Newton and M^r. Leibnitz, one the Glory of Germany the other of Great Britain, and both of them Men that Honor me with their Friendship which I shall always Cultivate to the best of my Power, tho' I can never deserve it; now altho' I ought to say with the poet: Non nostrum est Tantas componere Lites,[3] yet as it would be very Glorious to me, as well as Advantagious to the common Wealth of Learning, if I could bring such an Affair to a happy end, I humbly offer my Poor Mediation, and shall esteem my self exceeding Happy if by this or any other Instance I can convince you with how great passion & Truth I am

Most Honored S^r.

Yo^r. obliged, Faithful
humble Servant
John Chamberlayne

---

[1] LBr. 149 Bl. 20r–20v. Letter as sent: two quarto sides in secretary's hand (signed in Chamberlayne's hand). Previously published (excerpt) in NC VI 71. For Leibniz's reply, see his letter to Chamberlayne of 21 April 1714 (document 7).

[2] That is, 10 March 1714 NS.

[3] 'It is not for us to settle such great disputes,' an adaptation of Virgil, Eclogues III, 108: Non nostrum inter vos tantas componere lites.

Leibniz to Andreas Gottlieb von Bernstorff

Vienne ce 21 de Mars 1714

Monsieur

La saison ayant eté fort rude juqu'icy, et des incommodités arthritiques etant encore recentes, quoyqu'elles m'ayent quitté graces à Dieu, j'ay crû que je devois attendre le mois de May pour voyager, de peur d'irriter et reveiller un mal assoupi; et que je ferois bien de me servir des bains de Bade, qui ne sont qu'à quatre lieues d'icy et sont particulierement recommandés pour ces sortes de maux. Si V. E. veut bien faire rapport de cela à Monseigneur l'Electeur S. A. E. a trop de bonte pour trouver mal que je menage ma santé à l'âge où je suis. Cependant je n'ay pas mal employé le temps, ayant eu la commodité d'etre tres souvent à la Bibliotheque de l'Empereur et d'en feuilleter les Manuscrits Historiques. Cependant je dois remercier V. E. de la bonté qu'Elle a de m'avertir de ce qui est de mes interests, et je me regleray là dessus, etant avec respect

Leibniz to John Chamberlayne

A M. Chamberlaine a West munster

Vienne ce 21
d'Avril 1714

Monsieur

Je vous suis obligé tant de la communication de la lettre de l'insigne M. Wotton, qui m'est plus favorable que je ne pouvois esperer, et que je vous supplie[3] de remercier de ses bons sentimens; que de votre offre obligeant de moyenner une bonne intelligence entre M. Newton et moy. Ce n'est pas moy qui l'aye interrompue. Un nommé M. Keil infera quelque chose contre moy dans une de vos Transactions Philosophicales. J'en fus fort surpris et j'en demanday reparation par une lettre à M. Sloane secretaire de la societé. M. Sloane m'envoya un discours de M. Keil, ou il justifioit son dire, d'une maniere qui attaquoit meme ma bonne foy. Je pris cela pour animosité particuliere de ce personnage; sans avoir la moindre soubçon, que la societé et même M. Newton y avoit part. et ne trouvant pas a propos d'entrer en dispute avec un homme mal instruit des affaires anterieures, et supposant d'ailleurs que

6. Leibniz to Andreas Gottlieb von Bernstorff[*1]

Vienna 21 March 1714

Sir

Because the season has thus far been very harsh, and because I have recently suffered again from some arthritic infirmities, although they have abated thanks to God, I thought that I should await the month of May in order to travel, for fear of irritating and awakening a dormant ailment, and that I would do well to avail myself of the baths at Baden, which are only ten miles from here and are particularly recommended for these kinds of maladies. If Your Excellency really wants to report this to Monseigneur the Elector [Georg Ludwig* of Braunschweig-Lüneburg], His Electoral Highness has too much kindness to consider it wrong that someone of my age looks after his health. Nevertheless, I have not employed the time badly, since I have had the convenience of frequenting the library of the emperor and browsing the historical manuscripts.[2] However, I must thank Your Excellency for the kindness that he has to advise me about what is in my interest, and I will conduct myself accordingly, being with respect,

Sir, of Your Excellency etc.

[1] LBr. 59 Bl. 97r. Draft: 0.5 quarto sides in Leibniz's hand. Previously published in Klopp XI 7. Answer to Bernstorff's letter of 3 March 1714 (document 4).

[2] Leibniz no doubt added this in order to assure the elector that he was employing his time well in the service of Hanover by browsing historical documents for use in his history of the House of Braunschweig-Lüneburg (Hanover), which he had come to call the *Annales imperii occidentis Brunsvicenses**.

7. Leibniz to John Chamberlayne[*1]

To Mr. Chamberlayne at Westminster

Vienna 21 April 1714[2]

Sir

I am obliged to you, both for sending the letter of the remarkable Mr. [William] Wotton*, who is more supportive of me than I could hope, and whom I pray[3] you thank for his kind sentiments, and for your kind offer to mediate an understanding between Mr. Newton and me. It is not I who broke it off. Someone named Mr. [John] Keill* inferred something against me in one of your *Philosophical Transactions*.[4] I was very surprised by it, and I demanded satisfaction in a letter to Mr. [Hans] Sloane*, Secretary of the [Royal] Society [of London]. Mr. Sloane sent me a discourse by Mr. Keill in which he justified his allegation in a way that impugned even my good faith.[5] I take that to be the personal animosity of this individual, without having the least suspicion that the Society, or even Mr. Newton, took part in it; and not finding it appropriate to enter into dispute with a man ill-informed of previous

30 7. LEIBNIZ TO CHAMBERLAYNE

M. Newton luy meme mieux informé de ce qui s'etoit passé, me feroit rendre justice; je continuay seulement a demander la satisfaction qui m'etoit due. Mais je ne say par quelle chicane et supercherie quelques uns firent en sorte qu'on prit la chose, comme si je plaidois devant la société, et me soûmettois à sa jurisdiction, a quoi je n'avois jamais pensé et selon la justice on devoit me faire savoir que la societé vouloit examiner le fond de l'affaire, et me donner lieu de declarer si je voulois y proposer mes raisons[6] et si je ne tenois aucun des juges pour suspect. Ainsi on n'y a prononcé, qu'una parte audita, d'une maniere dont la nullité est visible. Aussi ne crois-je pas que le jugement qu'on a porté, puisse etre pris pour un arret de la societé. Cependant M. Newton l'a fait publier dans le monde par un livre imprimé exprés pour me decrediter, et envoyé en Allemagne, en France et en Italie comme au nom de la societé. Ce jugement pretendu et cet affront fait sans sujet à un des plus anciens membres de la societé meme, et qui ne luy a point fait deshonneur, ne trouvera gueres d'approbateurs dans le monde et dans la societé même j'espere que tous les membres n'en conviendront pas. Des habiles François et Italiens et autres desapprouvent hautement ce procedé, et s'en etonnent, et on a la dessus leur lettres en main. Les preuves produites contre moy leur paroissent bien minces.

Pour moy, j'en avois tousjours usé le plus honnêtement du monde envers M. Newton, et quoyqu'il se trouve maintenant qu'il y a grand lieu de douter, s'il a sû mon invention avant qu'il l'a eue de moy,[9] j'avois parlé comme si de son chef, il avoit eu quelque chose de semblable à ma methode. Mais abusé par quelques flatteurs mal avisés, il s'est laissé porter à m'attaquer d'une manière tres sensible. Jugés maintenant, Monsieur, de quel coté doit venir[10] ce qui est necessaire pour faire cesser cette contestation.

Je n'ay pas encor vu le livre publié contre moy, estant a Vienne qui est l'extremité del Allemagne,[11] ou de tels livres sont portés bien tard et je n'ay point daigné le faire venir exprès[12] par la poste. Ainsi je n'ay pas encore pû faire une Apologie telle que l'affaire demande. Mais d'autres ont dejà eu soin de ma reputation. J'abhorre les disputes desobligeantes entre les gens de lettres, et je les ay tousjours evitées, mais apresent on a pris toutes les mesures possibles pour m'y engager. Si le mal pouvoit etre redressé, Monsieur, par votre entremise, à la quelle vous vous offrés si obligeament, j'en serois bien aise, et je vous en ay déja bien[13] de l'obligation par avance.

Vous rendrés, Monsieur un service considerable au public en faisant travailler à un dictionnaire de la Langue Biscayenne, qui est si ancienne, et dont la connoissance servira[14] à eclaircir les noms propres de beaucoup de lieux non seulement en Espagne, mais encore dans la France voisine. Car je voy qu'il y a des noms de rivieres des montagnes et des villes ou villages communs à l'Espagne et à la France meridionnale, ou je soubçonne que la langue[15] du temps de Cesar distinguée par luy meme de celle de la Gaule Celtique a eu quelque chose d'approchant de la Biscaienne. Et il sera[16] fort important d'examiner s'il n'y a pas dans le Hibernois

matters, and supposing moreover that Mr. Newton himself, better informed about what has taken place, did me justice, I continue only to demand the satisfaction that was due me. But I do not know by what chicanery and deceit some made sure that the matter was interpreted as if I pleaded before the Society and submitted myself to its jurisdiction, which I have never considered; and in fairness they ought to have informed me that the Society wanted to examine the affair thoroughly and given me the opportunity to state whether I wanted to offer my arguments to them[6] and whether I held any of the judges suspect. Thus they have delivered a verdict in the matter, only *one party having been heard*, in a manner whose nullity is obvious. And I do not believe that the ruling that they have delivered can be interpreted as a decision of the Society. However, Mr. Newton has had it published around the world in a book printed expressly to discredit me and sent to Germany, to France, and to Italy in the name of the Society.[7] This so-called ruling, and this affront given without cause to one of the earliest members of the Society itself,[8] who has not dishonoured it, will scarcely find any supporters in the world; and in the Society itself, I hope that none of the members will agree with it. Some able Frenchmen and Italians, and others, greatly disapprove of this proceeding and are astonished by it, and their letters on the subject are in hand. The evidence produced against me appears thin to them.

As for me, I had always treated Mr. Newton most honourably, and although it now turns out that there is good reason to doubt whether he knew my invention before he got it from me[9], I had spoken as if he had something similar to my method by his own initiative. But led astray by some ill-advised flatters, he has allowed himself to be persuaded to attack me in a very evident way. Now you judge, sir, from which side should that come[10] which is required to bring this dispute to an end.

I have not yet seen the book published against me, since I am in Vienna, which is at the furthest boundary of Germany,[11] where such books are brought very late, and I have not deigned to have it come express[12] by post. Thus I have not yet been able to vindicate myself in a way the matter requires. But others have already taken care of my reputation. I abhor ill-mannered disputes between men of letters, and I have always avoided them, but at present they have taken every possible measure to entangle me in it. If the mischief could be redressed, sir, by your intervention, which you so kindly offer, I would be very happy, and I am already much[13] beholden to you for it in advance.

You render a considerable service to the public, sir, by working on a dictionary of the Basque language, which is so ancient and the knowledge of which will serve[14] to clear up the proper names of many places, not only in Spain, but also in neighboring France. For I see that there are some common names of rivers, of mountains, and of towns or villages in Spain and southern France, where I suspect that the language[15] of the time of Caesar, distinguished by him from that of Celtic Gaul,

quelque chose du Biscayen. La langue Biscayenne meriteroit bien aussi que le reste de la Bible, c'est à dire le vieux testament y fut traduit; puisque vous m'apprenes, que le nouveau s'y trouve deja. J'ay quelque soubçon que Cades et Calis ou Calais sont a peu près le meme mot, et signifient la meme chose, c'est à dire un detroit. Ainsi une langue ancienne commune ou approchante pourroit[17] avoir eté repandue par la France et par l'Espagne.

7. LEIBNIZ TO CHAMBERLAYNE 33

had something much like Basque. And it will be[16] very important to examine whether there is not something of the Basque in Hebrew. The Basque language would also rightly merit that the rest of the Bible, that is to say the Old Testament, be translated into it, since you inform me that the New [Testament] has already been translated into it. I have some suspicion that *Cades* and *Calis*, or *Calais*, are nearly the same word and signify the same thing, that is to say, a channel. Thus the common, or similar, ancient language could[17] have been propagated by France and Spain.

[1] LBr. 149 Bl. 21r–22r. Draft: three quarto sides in Leibniz's hand. This is Leibniz's response to Chamberlayne's letter of 27 February 1714 (10 March 1714 NS), document 5. Previously published in Des Maizeaux 1720, vol. 2, pp. 116–20 and NC VI 103–4 (excerpt). Chamberlayne forwarded this letter to Newton, who took the time to write out an English translation of it (see NC VI 105–6).

[2] The letter published in Des Maizeaux 1720, vol. 2, pp. 116–20, is dated 28 April 1714. The copy of the letter held by the Royal Society (EL/L5/122) is also dated 28 April 1714.

[3] The version published by Des Maizeaux has 'prie' instead of 'supplie' (see Des Maizeaux 1720, vol. 2, 116).

[4] Leibniz is referring to Keill's paper, *Epistola ad Clarissimum Virum Edmundum Halleium Geometriae Professorem Savilianum, De legibus virium centripetarum*, which, although it was published in the *Philosophical Transactions* for 1708, did not appear until 1710. Toward the end of that paper, Keill clearly insinuated that Leibniz had plagiarized the calculus from Newton:

> All these things follow from the now most highly celebrated arithmetic of fluxions, which without any doubt Mr. Newton first invented, as will be easily established by anyone reading his letters published by Wallis. Nevertheless, the same arithmetic was later published by Mr. Leibniz in *Acta Eruditorum* with a different name and form of notation. [*Philosophical Transactions* 26 (1708), p. 185]

[5] Leibniz refers to a paper that Keill wrote in response to Leibniz, which Keill sent to Sloane, who in turn sent it on to Leibniz. See NC V 133–49.

[6] The version published by Des Maizeaux has 'si j'y voulois proposer mes raisons', instead of 'si je voulois y proposer mes raisons' (see Des Maizeaux 1720, vol. 2, p.117).

[7] Leibniz is referring to the *Commercium Epistolicum**.

[8] Leibniz had been elected a Fellow of the Royal Society in 1673.

[9] The version published by Des Maizeaux has 'avant que de l'avoir eue de moi' instead of 'avant qu'il l'a eue de moi' (see Des Maizeaux 1720, vol. 2, 118).

[10] The version published by Des Maizeaux has 'principalement' inserted after 'venir' (see Des Maizeaux 1720, vol. 2, p. 119).

[11] Reading 'de l'Allemagne' for 'del Allemagne'.

[12] The version published by Des Maizeaux has 'tout' inserted before 'exprès' (see Des Maizeaux 1720, vol. 2, p. 119).

[13] The version published by Des Maizeaux has 'beaucoup' instead of 'bien' (see Des Maizeaux 1720, vol. 2, p. 119).

[14] The version published by Des Maizeaux has 'serviroit' instead of 'servira' (see Des Maizeaux 1720, vol. 2, p. 119).

[15] The version published by Des Maizeaux has 'de Aquitains' inserted after 'la langue' (see Des Maizeaux 1720, vol. 2, p. 120).

[16] The version published by Des Maizeaux has 'aussi' inserted after 'sera' (see Des Maizeaux 1720, vol. 2, p. 120).

[17] The version published by Des Maizeaux has 'paroit' instead of 'pourroit' (see Des Maizeaux 1720, vol. 2, p. 120).

Isaac Newton to John Chamberlayne

Le 11. de Mai 1714. V. St.

Monsieur,

Je n'entends pas assez à fond la Langue Françoise, pour sentir toute la force des termes de la Lettre de Mr. *Leibniz*; mais je comprends qu'il croit que la Societé Royale & moi, ne lui avons pas rendu justice.

Ce que Mr. Fatio a écrit contre lui, il l'a fait sans que j'y aye eu la moindre part.

Il y a environ neuf ans que Mr. *Leibniz* attaqua ma réputation, en donnant à entendre que j'avois emprunté de lui la Méthode des Fluxions. Mr. *Keill* m'a défendu; & je n'ai rien su de ce que Mr. *Leibniz* avoit fait imprimer dans le Journal de Leipsic, jusqu'à l'arrivée de sa première Réponse à Mr. *Keill*, où il demandoit, en effet, que je rétractasse ce que j'avois publié.

Si vous pouvez me marquer quelque chose en quoi je lui aye fait tort, je tâcherai de lui donner satisfaction; mais je ne veux pas rétracter ce que je sai être véritable, & je crois que le Commité de la Societé Royale ne lui a fait aucun tort.

Je suis

Votre très-humble Serviteur

Is. Newton.

8. Isaac Newton to John Chamberlayne*[1]

11 May 1714.[2] V. St.

Sir,

I do not understand the French language thoroughly enough to feel the full force of the words of Mr. Leibniz's letter;[3] but I understand that he believes that the Royal Society and I have not done him justice.

What Mr. [Nicolas] Fatio [de Duillier]* has written against him was done without my having had the least part in it.[4]

It was about nine years ago that Mr. Leibniz attacked my reputation by suggesting that I had borrowed the method of fluxions from him.[5] Mr. [John] Keill* has defended me; and I knew nothing about what Mr. Leibniz had published in the Journal of Leipzig[6] until the arrival of his first response to Mr. Keill,[7] in which he did ask that I retract what I had published.[8]

If you can show me something by which I have wronged him, I will try to give him satisfaction; but I do not wish to retract what I know to be true, and I believe that the Committee of the Royal Society has not done him any wrong.[9]

I am

Your very humble servant

Is. Newton

---

[1] The French as published in Des Maizeaux 1720, vol. 2, pp. 121–2. My translation.

[2] That is, 22 May 1714 NS.

[3] Newton is referring to Leibniz's letter to Chamberlayne of 28 April 1714 (for the draft dated 21 April, see document 7). Chamberlayne had forwarded Leibniz's letter to Newton, who subsequently translated it into English (for Newton's translation, see NC VI 105–6). Newton then presented the letter at the meeting of the Royal Society that preceded that of 20 May 1714 (31 May 1714 NS). For the Society's response to Leibniz's letter, see the enclosure (document 23b) included in Chamberlayne's letter to Leibniz of 27 July 1714 (7 August 1714 NS) (document 23a). See also Chamberlayne's letter to Newton of 20 May 1714 (31 May 1714 NS), document 9.

[4] Leibniz refers to what Fatio had written on page 18 of his *Lineae brevissimi descensus investigation geometrica duplex* (London, 1699):

> [...] I recognize that Newton was the first and by many years the most senior inventor of the calculus, being driven thereto by the factual evidence on this point; as to whether Leibniz, its second inventor, borrowed anything from him, I prefer to let those judge who have seen Newton's letters and other manuscript papers, not myself. Neither the silence of the more modest Newton nor the eager zeal of Leibniz in ubiquitously attributing the invention of this calculus to himself will impose on any who perused those documents which I have myself examined. [The original Latin and this translation are given in NC V 98.]

[5] See *Acta Eruditorum*, January 1705, pp. 34–5.

[6] That is, the *Acta Eruditorum* of Leipzig.

[7] See *Commercium Epistolicum D.* Johannis Collins, *et aliorum de Analysi promota* (London: Pearson, 1712), pp. 109–10. This is a letter of 4 March 1711 from Leibniz to the then secretary of the Royal Society, Hans Sloane*. The original Latin and an English translation can be found in NC V 96–7.

[8] It is unclear to what Newton is referring when he says that in the letter to Sloane, Leibniz 'did ask that I retract what I had published'. There is a footnote to this comment in the letter that Pierre des Maizeau published in Des Maizeaux 1720, vol. 2, p. 122 that indicates that Newton is referring to what he

9. CHAMBERLAYNE TO NEWTON

had written 'in the introduction to the book *des Quadratures*' (that is, in the introduction to Newton's *Tractatus de Quadratura Cuvarum* (published 1704)). But Leibniz does not mention anything published by Newton in his letter to Sloane. Rather, he referred to what Keill had written toward the end of a paper (*Epistola ad Clarissimum Virum Edmundum Halleium Geometriae Professorem Savilianum, De legibus virium centripetarum*) that he had published in the *Philosophical Transactions*:

> All these things follow from the now most highly celebrated arithmetic of fluxions, which without any doubt Mr. Newton first invented, as will be easily established by anyone reading his letters published by Wallis. Nevertheless, the same arithmetic was later published by Mr. Leibniz in *Acta Eruditorum* with a different name and form of notation. [*Philosophical Transactions* 26 (1708, appeared 1710), p. 185]

In his letter of 4 March 1711 to Sloane, Leibniz wrote:

> Some time ago Nicholas Fatio de Duillier attacked me in a published paper for having attributed to myself another's discovery. I taught him to know better in the *Acta Eruditorum* of Leipzig, and you [English] yourselves disapproved of this [charge] as I learned from a letter written by the Secretary of your distinguished Society (that is, to the best of my recollection, by yourself). Newton himself, a truly excellent person, disapproved of this misplaced zeal of certain persons on behalf of your nation and himself, as I understand. And yet Mr. Keill in this very volume, in the [*Transactions* for] September and October 1708, page 185, has seen fit to renew this most impertinent accusation when he writes that I have published the arithmetic of fluxions invented by Newton, after altering the name and the style of notation. Whoever has read and believed this could not but suspect that I have given out another's discovery disguised by substitute names and symbolism. But no one knows better than Newton himself how false this is [...] However, although I do not take Mr. Keill to be a slanderer (for I think he is to be blamed rather for hastiness of judgement than for malice) yet I cannot but take that accusation which is injurious to myself as slander. For I think you yourself will judge it equitable that Mr. Keill should testify publicly that he did not mean to charge me with that which his words seem to imply, as though I had found out something invented by another person and claimed it as my own. In this way he may give satisfaction for his injury to me, and show that he had no intention of uttering a slander, and a curb will be put on other persons who might at some time give voice to other similar [charges]. [The original Latin and this translation are in NC V 96–7]

Keill responded to Leibniz's letter in a paper he sent to Sloane for Leibniz in May 1711. This prompted a second reply from Leibniz, written to Sloane on 18 December 1711, in which he complained of Keill's 'empty and unjust braying' (NC V 208).

[9] Newton here refers to the committee of the Royal Society that he himself chaired as president of the Society. This committee had been appointed to look into the charges that had been levelled against Leibniz by Keill, and which issued the report, drafted by Newton himself, known as the *Commercium Epistolicum**. This report, in which Keill was absolved of wrongdoing against Leibniz and in which Leibniz himself was found guilty of concealing his knowledge of the prior achievements of Newton (see Hall 1980, pp. 178–9), was published early in 1713.

9. John Chamberlayne* to Isaac Newton[1]

Petty France
20 May 1714[2]

Honored Sr

I am very sorry I can't wait on you this Afternoon when you are to consider of the Letter from Mr Leibnitz to me,[3] concerning you, which Letter I did not intend to have expos'd to any body's view, but your own, because I am not sure it wil be agreable to the writer, but since you have desired it, & to shew my Respect to you

Leibniz to Sophie of the Palatinate, Dowager Electress of Braunschweig-Lüneburg

Madame

V. A. E. aura receu la lettre que je me suis donné l'honneur de luy écrire, avec une inclose pour Madame la Raugrave et avec un mémoire d'un Ecossois de merite, qui espere de partir bientost d'icy.[2] Cependant j'ay eté frappé par les nouvelles d'Angleterre sur la demande de M. de Schuz; et il me semble de pouvoir juger par ce que V. A. E. a ecrit à la $M^{té}$ de l'Imperatrice Amalie, que cette demande Madame vous est due. Rien ne pouvoit étre fait plus à propos à mon avis; car elle est venue dans le temps que la Nation commence à ouvrir les yeux; et un grand nombre des principaux Toris, s'étant detachés du Ministere; il estoit tres important dans cette conjoncture de faire connoitre à la Nation, qu'on a de l'affection pour elle à Hanover, et qu'on prend soin de ses interests, d'autant que les mal intentionnés avoient taché de repandre cette croyance etrange, qu'on ne se soucie point à Hanover du Royaume de la Grande Bretagne, et qu'on a abandonné l'esperance de l'obtenir. J'ay écrit à un ami, qu'il faudroit que notre Cour fut bien Iroquoise si elle étoit dans de tels sentimens. Cependant cette opinion etant soutenue par notre inaction apparente, il estoit a propos de la refuter par une demarche reelle, telle que la demande d'un

(who ought to have no Enemy in the world, but such as are Enemys to Philosophy & Truth)[4] I am content you should make what use you please thereof, only submitting it as a matter of Prudence how far you, in your private Capacity, may think it adviseable to keep some Measures with a Gentleman that is in the Highest Esteem at the Court of Hanover &c and if I could be so Happy as to be Instrumental in begiñing a friendship between Two Men of very great Merit, it would be an exceeding great Pleasure to Hon[d] S[r]

your most Faithful Humble servant
John Chamberlayne

For the Honble
Sr Isaac Newton &c[5]

---

[1] King's College Library Cambridge Keynes MS. 141(c). One quarto side in Chamberlayne's hand. Previously published in NC VI 140.

[2] That is, 31 May 1714 NS.

[3] Chamberlayne is referring to Leibniz's letter of 28 April 1714 (for the draft dated 21 April, see document 7). Newton actually appears to have presented his translation of Leibniz's letter to the Royal Society during the meeting that preceded the 20th of May (31 May NS). See document 23b, which was enclosed in Chamberlayne's letter to Leibniz of 27 July 1714 (7 August 2014 NS), document 23a.

[4] I have inserted the right parenthesis, which was omitted by Chamberlayne.

[5] The last two lines are on the reverse side.

10. Leibniz to Sophie* of the Palatinate, Dowager Electress of Braunschweig-Lüneburg[1]

[Vienna, 24 May 1714]

Madame

Your Electoral Highness has probably received the letter that I was given the honour of writing her, with an enclosure for Madame the Raugravine [Palatine Louise*] and a memoire of a Scotsman of merit[John Ker*], who hopes to leave here soon.[2] However, I have been struck by the news from England concerning the request of Mr. Schütz;[3] and judging from what Your Electoral Highness has written to Her Majesty the [Dowager] Empress [Wilhelmine] Amalie*, it seems to me, Madame, that this request is due to you. In my opinion nothing more fitting could be done, since it has come at a time when the nation is beginning to open its eyes; and since a large number of prominent Tories have broken away from the ministry, it was very important at this juncture to make known to the nation that we in Hanover have affection for it and that we take care of its interests, especially as the ill-intentioned had tried to spread this outlandish belief around, that we do not care about the Kingdom of Great Britain in Hanover and that we have abandoned hope of obtaining it. I have written to a friend that our court would have to be truly Iroquoian if it felt that way.[4] However, since this opinion has been supported by our

Writ, faite au chancelier. Je presume que M. de Schuz a eu ordre de Mgr l'Electeur de la faire, mais s'il avoit agi sans ordre, je le comparerois à un general d'armée, qui auroit gagne une bataille sans avoir receu du chef l'ordre de combattre. Lors que le prince Eugene gagna celle de Zenta en Hongrie, le Conseil de guerre avoit projeté une lettre de reprimande de la part de l'Empereur, mais Leopold la biffa. En ce cas je trouve que M. de Schuz, prevenant son rappel par un promt depart, auroit delivre Mgr l'Electeur d'un embarras: car si S. A. E. eut voulu le rappeller cette espece de desaveu auroit fait un tres mauvais effect dans la nation et même dans le Monde.

La question est maintenant, si le Writ étant expedié, Mon^{sgr} le prince Electoral viendra prendre sa place. Ce n'est pas à moy de dire mon avis là dessus, quoyque V. A. E. aura peutetré sçû de l'Imperatrice Amalie, que le prince Eugene est fort de cet avis qu'il seroit bon de faire passer notre prince en Angleterre. Mais si Mon^{sgr} l'Electeur ne trouve pas encor à propos de consentir à ce trajet, peutetre pour ne point exposer dans ces conjonctures une personne aussi pretieuse que celle de S. A. S. Il importe que la Nation en attribue le retardement à la repugnance que le Ministere a témoigné, par cette étrange et mal fondée demarche de defendre la Cour à M. de Schuz, et qu'on ait soin d'eviter à Hannover tout ce qui peut faire croire qu'on n'est pas trop porté au voyage du prince. Notre Ecossoi qui est icy est persuadé de l'intention favorable de Mgr l'Electeur là dessus, et je n'ay garde de l'en faire douter. Il tient aussi pour certain, que si Mgr le prince Electoral venait, quand meme la Reine et le parlement n'établissoient[6] pas une Liste civile pour la succession, la ville de Londres, et les corporations y pourvoiroient abondamment par des donatifs. Au reste je me rapporte à ma precedente estant avec devotion

Madame de V. E. etc.

Vienne ce 24 de May 1714

A Sa Serenité Royale

Madame l'Electrice

à Hannover

10. LEIBNIZ TO SOPHIE OF THE PALATINATE 41

apparent inaction, it was fitting to refute it by an actual step, such as the request of a writ made to the chancellor. I presume that Mr. Schütz had orders from Monseigneur the Elector [Georg Ludwig* of Braunschweig-Lüneburg] to do it, but if he had acted without orders, I would compare him to a general of an army who had won a battle without having received the order to fight from the commander. When Prince Eugène* won the Battle of Zenta in Hungary,[5] the war council had prepared a letter of reprimand from the emperor, but Leopold [Emperor Leopold I, reigned 1658–1705] cancelled it. In this case I find that Mr. Schütz delivered Monseigneur the Elector from an embarrassment by preventing his recall by means of a prompt departure; for if His Electoral Highness had decided to recall him, this kind of disavowal would have had a very bad effect in the nation and even in the world.

The writ being dispatched, the question now is whether the electoral prince [Georg August* of Braunschweig-Lüneburg] will go to take his place [in the House of Lords]. It is not for me to state my opinion about that, although Your Electoral Highness will perhaps have known from the Empress Amalie that Prince Eugène* [of Savoy] is strongly of the opinion that it would be good to send our Prince to England. But if Monseigneur the Elector does not yet find it appropriate to consent to this journey, perhaps in order not to expose in these circumstances a person as precious as that of His Serene Highness, it is important that the nation attribute its delay to the aversion that the ministry has shown with this outlandish and ill-founded step of denying Mr. Schütz access to the court and that care is taken in Hanover to avoid anything that might give rise to the belief that we do not support the journey of the prince. Our Scotsman [John Ker*] who is here [in Vienna] is persuaded that Monseigneur the Elector is favorably disposed to it, and I am careful not to make him doubt it. He also takes it as certain that if Monseigneur the Electoral Prince went, the city of London and the corporations there would provide abundant donations, even if the queen [Anne of Great Britain] and parliament did not establish[6] a civil list for the succession. For the rest I refer to my previous [letter], being with devotion

   Madame, of Your Excellency etc.

Vienna this 24th of May 1714

   To Her Royal Serenity
    Madame the Electress
     in Hanover

---

[1] Niedersächsisches Landesarchiv-Hauptstaatsarchiv Hannover, Dep. 84 A 180 Bl. 653r–653v. Draft: 1.7 quarto sides in Leibniz's hand. Previously published in Klopp IX 448–50.

[2] This first sentence is omitted by Klopp (see Klopp IX 448).

[3] In 1706 Queen Anne had bestowed the Garter on the Electoral Prince Georg August and created him Duke of Cambridge, thus making him eligible for a seat in the House of Lords. On 23 April 1716 (NS), the Hanoverian envoy to England, Georg Wilhelm Sinold Schütz, angered by Queen Anne's refusal to issue a proclamation to apprehend her half-brother, the Catholic Pretender, James Francis Edward

42   10. LEIBNIZ TO SOPHIE OF THE PALATINATE

10. LEIBNIZ TO SOPHIE OF THE PALATINATE   43

Stuart*, visited her Lord Chancellor, Simon Harcourt, and requested a legal writ summoning the electoral prince to England to take his seat in parliament. He claimed to have done so on the orders of the Dowager Electress of Braunschweig-Lüneburg, Sophie* of the Palatinate, although she later claimed that she had only requested that Schütz ask why such a writ had not been issued. According to Schütz, Harcourt replied by saying that 'he would speak of it to the queen, not daring to give it me without her orders; but added, after being silent for some time, he did not recollect that a writ was demanded of him since he was in her Majesty's service… nor that any was sent beyond sea.' Schütz responded 'that, by delivering it to me, he did not send it out of the kingdom' (see Schütz's letter to John Robethon* of 24 April 1714 in MacPherson 1775, vol. 2, pp. 590–1; see also Gregg 2001, pp. 380–1). The queen's privy council could find no legal basis for denying the writ, so it was granted in the end; but Queen Anne, angered that Schütz had not consulted her personally on the matter, denied Schütz access to the court, as Leibniz notes below, and demanded that he be recalled to Hanover. Schütz left London on 1 May 1714 (Gregg 2001, p. 381).

Thomas Harley, a member of parliament and cousin of the Lord High Treasurer Robert Harley*, Earl of Oxford, arrived in Hanover on 24 April with orders from Oxford to oppose the Electoral Prince's trip to England. Although the Elector Georg Ludwig* resisted pressure to send the electoral prince to England without the queen's invitation, he was anxious to use the writ demand to secure concessions that would protect the Hanoverian succession. He and his mother, the Dowager Electress Sophie, in response to the queen's query, through Harley, as to 'what they wanted to be done for the greater security of the Protestant Succession established in their family', presented Harley with a memorial for the queen, 'desiring the Pretender's removal [from Lorraine]—A pension for the Princess Sophia—Leave to send a Prince of the Electoral family to Britain, and titles as Princes of the Blood to such of the protestant Princes of the family as have none' (MacPherson 1775, vol. 2, p. 608). After delays on Harley's part, Oxford finally received a copy of the memorial on 29 May. Before any other members of the government saw the memorial, Oxford sent letters to Hanover for the Elector Georg Ludwig, the Dowager Electress Sophie, and the Electoral Prince Georg August from himself and the queen (the queen's letters having been drafted by Oxford), informing them that no member of the electoral family was welcome in England while the queen lived. The letters arrived in Hanover on 5 June (see Gregg 2001, p. 384). For Caroline's reaction to the letters, see her letter to Leibniz of 7 June 1714, document 15. The letter from the queen to the Dowager Electress Sophie was published in Klopp IX 454–5 and translated in Boyer 1722, p. 699, MacPherson 1775, vol. 2, p. 621, and in Brown 1968, p. 413; it is translated below as document 12. The letters to the Elector Georg Ludwig and the Electoral Prince Georg August are translated in Brown 1968, pp. 413–15; they are translated below as documents 13 and document 14, respectively.

[4] Here Leibniz is probably referring to the fact that at the dawn of the eighteenth century, the Iroquois had decided to form alliances with both the French and the English in the New World, thus enabling them to remain neutral in the conflicts between those two colonial powers. During the War of the Spanish Succession* (1701–14), the Iroquois did maintain their neutrality between the French and the British, which may have prompted Leibniz's comparison between an imagined Hanover unconcerned with the interests of Great Britain and the Iroquois who refused to side with the British against the French during that conflict. This was probably intended to highlight the fact that, far from being neutral with respect to the interests of Great Britain, Hanover had fought on the side of Great Britain and the Holy Roman Empire against the French during the War of the Spanish Succession; indeed, the Elector Georg Ludwig* served as the Imperial Field Marshall in that conflict during the campaign of 1707 (see Hatton 1978, p. 102).

[5] The Battle of Zenta was fought on 11 September 1697 in present-day Serbia. It was a major battle in the Great Turkish War (1683–99) in which the Habsburg imperial forces, under the command of Prince Eugène* of Savoy, won a decisive victory over the Ottoman army.

[6] Klopp mistranscribes 'n'établissoient' as 'n'établiroient' (see Klopp IX 450).

Leibniz to Caroline of Brandenburg-Ansbach, Electoral Princess of Braunschweig-Lüneburg

Madame

Je n'ose pas me hazarder d'importuner V. A. S. par des lettres trop frequentes. Cependant la gazette m'ayant surpris agreablement en m'apprenant l'expedition du Writ pour que Mgr le prince Electoral put prendre seance au parlement de la Grande Bretagne, j'en ay voulu feliciter V. A . S. avec Mgr le prince. Car c'est un pas considerable, et rien ne pouvoit être fait plus à propos dans le Temps que les Toris commencent à ouvrir les yeux sur la mauvaise paix et sur l'intention du Ministere, et qu'on a taché de persuader a la Nation qu'à Hanover on regarde la Grande Bretagne avec un oeil indifferent. L'embarras du Ministere Anglois et sa mauvaise demarche de faire defendre la Cour à Mr. de Schuz, ont donné un relief à l'affaire et font voir qu'on les a touchés au vif. J'ay eu l'honneur d'apprendre de 1'Imperatrice Amalie que le prince Eugene de Savoye avoit dit à Sa Mté il y a plusieurs semaines, qu'il luy paroissoit bon de faire passer Mon^{sgr} le prince Electoral en Angleterre. Dieu veuille que cela se fasse bientost avec tout le succes possible, et que V. A. S. l'accompagne ou le suive de prés. des personnes bien informées qui sont du pays même sont persuadées qu'en cas que M^{sgr} le prince y passât, la ville de Londres et des compagnies ou corporations ne manqueroient pas de faire des donatifs, quand même la Reine et le parlement n'etabliroient rien. Mais si contre l'attente de la Nation et des gens bien intentionnés le trajet ne pouvoit pas encor se faire, et si l'on ne jugeoit pas encor à Hannover le passage de Monsg^{r} le prince Electoral seur et à propos, il faudroit avoir grand soin d'attribuer la cause de ce retardement à la repugnance que le Ministere Anglois a témoigne par un ressentiment si public & si mal fondé. Car en ce cas la Nation obligera en fin la Cour d'y consentir. Mais si la Cour pouvoit faire croire à la Nation, qu'il y a de la repugnance à [la] Cour d'Hanover meme, cela feroit un tres mauvais effect, und der letzte betrug würde arger seyn als der erste.[5] Suivant une gazette Mgr le prince Electoral étoit deja sur son depart. Mais je crois que j'auray encor l'honneur de faire la reverence à Vos Altesses S^{mes} à Hannover,[6] devant partir d 'icy avant la S. Jean et[8] cependant je suis avec devotion

Madame de V. A. S.

le tres humble & tres

Vienne ce 24 de May   obeissant serviteur
        1714

                    Leibniz

A Son Altesse Sme
Madame la princesse Electoral
        a Hanover etc.

11. Leibniz to Caroline* of Brandenburg-Ansbach, Electoral Princess of Braunschweig-Lüneburg[1]

[Vienna, 24 May 1714]

Madame

I don't dare risk annoying Your Serene Highness by writing too frequently. However, having been pleasantly surprised by the newspaper informing me of the dispatch of the writ so that Monseigneur the Electoral Prince [Georg August* of Braunschweig-Lüneburg] could take his seat in the Parliament of Great Britain,[2] I wanted to congratulate Your Serene Highness along with Monseigneur the Prince. For this is a significant step, and nothing could be more opportune at a time when the Tories are beginning to recognize the bad peace and the intention of the ministry,[3] and at a time when they have tried to persuade the nation that in Hanover, Great Britain is regarded with an indifferent eye. The embarrassment of the English ministry and its deplorable step of denying Mr. Schütz[4] access to court have highlighted the affair and shows that they have been cut to the quick. I have had the honour of learning from the[Dowager] Empress [Wilhelmine] Amalie* that Prince Eugène* of Savoy told Her Majesty several weeks ago that it seemed to him a good thing to send Monseigneur the Electoral Prince to England. May God grant that this be done soon with all possible success and that Your Serene Highness accompany him, or follow closely on his heels. Some well-informed persons who are from the country itself are persuaded that in case Monseigneur the Prince were to go there, the city of London and some companies or corporations would not fail to make donations, even if the queen [of Great Britain] and the parliament would establish nothing. But if, contrary to the expectation of the nation and well-intentioned people, the journey could not yet be undertaken, and if in Hanover they still did not think the passage of Monseigneur the Electoral Prince was certain and opportune, it would be necessary to take great care to attribute the cause of this delay to the aversion that the English ministry has displayed from a resentment so public and so ill founded. For in this case the nation will finally force the court to consent to it. But if the court could convince the nation that there is some aversion at the court of Hanover itself, that would bring about a bad result, 'and the final deceit would be worse than the first'.[5] According to a newspaper, the electoral prince was already about to depart. But I believe I will again have the honour of bowing to Your Most Serene Highnesses in Hanover,[6] since I must depart from here before St. John's Day [June 24], and[7] in the meanwhile I am with devotion

Madame, of Your Serene Highness

the very humble and very

Vienna this 24 of May   obedient servant

1714

Leibniz

To Her Most Serene Highness
Madame the Electoral Princess
in Hanover etc.

---

[1] Niedersächsisches Landesarchiv-Hauptstaatsarchiv Hannover, Dep. 84 A 180 Bl. 651r–651v. Draft: two quarto sides in Leibniz's hand. Previously published in Klopp IX 450–2. For Caroline's response, see her letter to Leibniz of 7 June 1716 (document 15).

[2] Concerning the events leading up to, and following upon, the issuing of this writ, see Leibniz's letter to the Dowager Electress Sophie of 24 May 1714 (document 10, p. 41 note 3).

[3] The bad peace to which Leibniz refers was the Treaty of Utrecht*, which ended the War of the Spanish Succession*. The ministry, headed at the time by Robert Harley*, the first Earl of Oxford, had been allowing Jacobite rebels to return to Britain, giving the impression that it opposed the Protestant Hanoverian succession in favour of the Catholic Pretender, James Francis Edward Stuart*. The Treaty of Utrecht had been engineered by Oxford and Henry St John*, the first Viscount Bolingbroke; and as Edward Gregg has observed, 'Oxford sponsored Jacobite propaganda because he knew full well that the Elector of Hanover [i.e., Georg Ludwig]—a staunch supporter of Habsburg interests—was alienated from the Tory ministers who had concluded the Treaty of Utrecht' (Gregg 2001, p. 364).

[4] That is, Georg Wilhelm Sinold Schütz, the Hanoverian envoy to England.

[5] Matthew 27:64.

[6] I have reconstructed this clause from Leibniz's text, which is quite unclear due to apparent deletions and insertions. Klopp provides this alternative reconstruction, 'Mais je crains d'avoir encor l'honneur de faire la reverence à Vos Altesses S^mes à Hanover' (Klpp IX 452), but I can make little sense of that in context.

[7] Klopp omits 'et' and begins a new sentence with 'Cependant' (see Klopp IX 452).

Queen Anne to Sophie of the Palatinate, Dowager Electress of Braunschweig-Lüneburg

Copy of a Letter from the Queen to the Princess Sophia.   May 19. 1714[2]

Depuis que le Droit de succeder a mes royaumes a été declaré appartenir à vous et à votre Maison, il y a toujours été des mecontens qui par de veües de leurs Interests particuliers sont entrées dans des mesures pour établir un Prince de votre sang dans mes Etats de mon vivant meme; jusques ici je n'ai pas crû que ce projet auroit pû aller si loin que de faire la moindre impression sur votre esprit, neanmoins comme je viens d'apprendre par les bruits publies qui sont semés avec beaucoup d'industrie, que votre Altesse Electorale tombe dans ce sentiment, Il est important par rapport a la Succession de votre maison que je vous dise qu'une telle demarche entraineroit infailliblement des suites tres dangereuses a cette Succession meme, qui n'est en seureté, qu'autant que le Prince qui porte actuellement la Couronne maintient son autorité, et ses Prerogatives. Il y a ici, tel est notre malheur, beaucoup d'esprits seditieux, ainsi je vous laisse a penser, quels tumultes ils pourroient exciter, s'ils avoient un pretexte a se mettre en mouvement. je suis donc persuadée, que vous ne consentirez pas, qu'on fasse la moindre chose, qui puisse troubler mon repos ou celui de mes sujets.

Ouvrez vous a moi avec la meme franchise que j'use envers vous et proposez tout ce que vous croirez pouvoir affermir la Succession. J'y donnerai les mains avez[3] zele, pourveu que cela ne deroge pas a ma dignité, que je suis resolüe de maintenir.

Queen Anne to Georg Ludwig, Elector of Braunschweig-Lüneburg

Copy of a Letter from the Queen to the Elector of Hanover   [May 19. 1714[2]]

Comme le bruit s'augmente que Mon Cousin le Prince Electoral a pris la resolution de passer ici pour s'établir de mon vivant dans mes Etats, je ne veux pas differer un seul moment de vouz en ecrire et vouz ouvrir ma pensée sur un sujet de cette importance: je vouz avouerai donc franchement que je ne sçaurois m'imaginer qu'un Prince qui a les lumieres et la penetration de votre Altesse Electorale puisse jamais preter les mains a un tel attentat, et que je vouz crois trop juste pour permettre qu'on donne aucune atteinte a ma Souveraineté que vouz ne voudriez pas qu'on donnât a la vôtre. Je suis fort persuadée que vouz ne souffririez pas la

12. Queen Anne to Sophie* of the Palatinate, Dowager Electress of Braunschweig-Lüneburg*[1]

Copy of a Letter from the Queen to the Princess Sophia.   May 19. 1714[2]

Since the right of succession to my kingdoms was declared to belong to you and your House [of Hanover], there have always been some malcontents who, in view of their private interests, have taken measures to establish a prince of your blood [Georg August* of Braunschweig-Lüneburg] in my estates even while I am alive. Until now I did not believe that this scheme could have gone so far as to make the least impression on your mind; but as I have lately learned from public rumors, which are spread with much diligence, that Your Electoral Highness agrees with this opinion, it is important in relation to the succession of your House that I tell you that such a proceeding would entail some very dangerous consequences for the succession itself, which is only secure so long as the prince who actually wears the crown maintains his authority and his prerogatives. There is here (such is our misfortune) many seditious minds, so I leave you to consider what tumults they could stir up if they had an excuse to move forward. I am thus persuaded that you will not allow the least thing to be done which may trouble my repose or that of my subjects.

Open up to me with the same frankness that I employ towards you and propose whatever you think may bolster the succession. I will work for it enthusiastically,[3] provided that it does not derogate from my dignity, which I am resolved to maintain.

[1] From a handwritten copy held by the British Library, London, B.M. Stowe MS 242, f. 134. Previously published, in significantly different form, in Klopp IX 454–5. A translation was published in Boyer 1722, p. 699 and in Brown 1968, p.413.

[2] That is, 30 May 1714 (NS).

[3] Reading 'avec' for 'avez'.

13. Queen Anne to Georg Ludwig*, Elector of Braunschweig-Lüneburg[1]

Copy of a Letter from the Queen to the Elector of Hanover   [May 19. 1714[2]]

As the rumour grows that my cousin the electoral prince [Georg August* of Braunschweig-Lüneburg] has resolved to come here in order to establish himself in my dominions while I am alive, I do not want to put off for a single moment writing to you about it and confiding my thoughts to you on a subject of this importance: I frankly admit, then, that I could not imagine that a prince who has the intelligence and penetration of Your Electoral Highness could ever lend his hands to such an outrage and that I believe you are too just to permit my sovereignty to suffer any infringement that you would not want yours to suffer. I am strongly persuaded that

moindre diminution de votre Autorité. Je ne suis pas moins delicate a cet égard et je suis determinée de m'opposer fortement a un projet si contraire a ma Royauté quelques funestes que les suites en puissent étre.

Votre Altesse Electorale est trop equitable pour ne pas vouloir me rendre les temoignages que j'ai donné en toutes occasions des preuves de mon desire que votre Maison pût succeder a mes Couronnes, ce que j'ai toujours recommandé a mes peuples comme l'appui le plus solide de leur Religion et de leurs loix. J'emploie tous mes soins a fin que rien n'efface ces impressions des cœurs de mes Sujets, mais il n'est pas possible qu'on deroge a la dignité et aux Prerogatives du Prince qui porte la Couronne, sans faire une plaie dangereuse aux droits des successeurs: ainsi je ne doute pas qu'avec votre Sagesse Ordinaire vouz n'empechiez qu'on ne fasse cette demarche, et que vouz ne me donniez occasion de vouz renouveller les assurances de l'amitié la plus sincere avec laquelle je suis _____

Queen Anne to Georg August, Electoral Prince
of Braunschweig-Lüneburg

Copy of a Letter from the Queen to the Electoral Prince of Hanover   May 19. 1714[2]

Un accident qui est arrivé dans la famille de my Lord Paget l'aiant empeché de partir aussi tôt qu'il avoit crû le faire, je ne puis pas tarder plus long temps sans vous faire scavoir ma pensées sur le dessein que vous avez formé de venir dans mes Etats; comme c'étoit a moi qu'on auroit dû premierement en faire l'ouverture, aussi me suis j'attendüe que vouz n'y auriez pas preté l'oreille, sans sçavoir auparavant mes sentimens là desùs. Neanmois ce que je dois a ma dignité l'amitié que j'ai pour vouz et pour la maison Electorale dont vouz éstés, et le veritable desir que j'ai qu'Elle puisse succeder a mes Royaumes, exigent de moi, que je vouz dise que rien ne sçau- roit étre plus dangereuse a la tranquillité de mes Etats, au Droit de la Succession dans votre Ligne, ni par consequent plus desagreable a moi dans cette conjoncture qu'une telle demarche.

14. QUEEN ANNE TO AUGUST, ELECTORAL PRINCE 51

you would not allow the least diminution of your authority. I am not less delicate in this regard, and I am determined to oppose vigorously a scheme so contrary to my royalty, however fatal the consequences may be.

Your Electoral Highness is too just not to bear witness that I have given on all occasions proofs of my desire that your House [of Hanover] might be able to succeed to my crowns, which I have always recommended to my people as the most solid support for their religion and their laws. I employ great care in order that nothing erases these impressions from the hearts of my subjects, but it is not possible to derogate from the dignity and the prerogatives of the prince who wears the crown without causing a dangerous wound to the rights of the successors; thus I do not doubt that with your usual wisdom you will prevent this step from being taken and will give me occasion to renew for you the assurances of the most sincere friendship with which I am _____

[1] From a handwritten copy held by the British Library, London, B.M. Stowe MS 242, f. 130. A translation was previously published in Brown 1968, pp. 413–14.

[2] That is, 30 May 1714 (NS).

14. Queen Anne to Georg August*, Electoral Prince of Braunschweig-Lüneburg[1]

Copy of a Letter from the Queen to the Electoral Prince of Hanover   May 19. 1714[2]

Since an accident that happened in the family of my Lord Paget[3] has hindered him from departing as soon as he had intended, I cannot put off any longer making known to you my thoughts concerning the plan that you have formed to enter my dominions; as it was to me that it would have been owed to make the overture in the first place, I likewise expected that you would not have lent your ear to it without first knowing my feelings about it. Nevertheless, what I owe my dignity, the friendship that I have for you and the Electoral House [of Hanover] to which you belong, and the true desire that I have that it may succeed to my kingdoms, requires me to tell you that nothing could be more dangerous to the tranquility of my dominions, to the right of succession in your line, or consequently more disagreeable to me in these circumstances than such an undertaking.

[1] From a handwritten copy held by the British Library, London, B.M. Stowe MS 242, f. 132. Previously translated in Boyer 1722, pp. 699–700 and in Brown 1968, pp. 414–15.

[2] That is, 30 May 1714 (NS).

[3] That is, Henry Paget (*c*.1663–1743), 8th Baron Paget, who was Captain of the Yeomen of the Guard and Lord Lieutenant of Staffordshire. He was the candidate that the Lord High Treasurer Oxford (Robert Harley*) supported to be special envoy to the Elector Georg Ludwig* of Braunschweig-Lüneburg. However, Paget was a supporter of the Protestant Succession, and he was reluctant to serve Oxford for fear of alienating Hanover. In the event, he refused to go on the mission unless Queen Anne created him an earl, which she would not do, and on 6 June 1714 (NS) she instead appointed her first cousin, the Earl of Clarendon (Gregg 2001, p. 385). After Georg Ludwig* ascended the throne of Great Britain, he rewarded Paget's loyalty by creating him 1st Earl of Uxbridge.

Caroline of Brandenburg-Ansbach, Electoral Princess of Braunschweig-Lüneburg, to Leibniz

Hanover le 7 Juin
1714[2]

Le seulle avantage que j'ay diray,[3] Monsieur, de toute les avantage qui adantoit[4] A M^r le P. E. e[s]t votre lettre que vous m[']avez écrit. M^r le P. E. vous a beaucoup d'oblication[5] de vous inderesser sy fortement pour luis[6] il auroit estte[7] a souhaiter que tout le monde eut heu les mes santiment.[8] Se n'est pas la feaute[9] de M^r le P: n'y de tout les honneste geans d'isy.[10] il a remuez ciel et tere,[11] et j'ean a'yèe parle moy même tres[12] fortement a M^r L'Electeur. nous avons estte deans la crisse jusqu'avant hier au[13] on a reçeu un Courie[14] de la Reine avec des lettres pour M^d L'E: et M^r L'E. et le P. E. qui sont d'un violances dingé[15] de Milord Bullinbrock, et par là le P. E. ces veu pres-que sans esperance daller prander sa seances celon ses droit[17]. Je ne scais ce que le monde peu[t] juger de la contevuite que nous avons denu isy.[19] Je ne regrede pas teans[20] la perte que peutestre nostre contevuite nous adirera[21] que d'avoir an[22] quelque manier apandoné linteres[23] de notre St Religion la liberdie d'uropé,[24] et tans de pravez et honeste amis an angeltere.[25] Je n'ay d'autre consolassion[26] que d'avoir veu humenent faire tout[27] au P: pour opdenir c'este[28] permission. M^d. L'E. ces joint a leuis, et ille veulle anvoiyer[29] leurs lettres de la R: qu'il on receu an angeltere.[30] M^r le P: m[']a chargé[e] de vous prier Monsieur d'assurer Mr le P: de Savois, de ces tres humble service,[31] et de le prier tres instamment de ne luis rien ynpuder an toutre ceste afaire qu'il savoit que M^r le P: la voit trouvez bon et apropo[33] il Ay a plus de deux anne que sy sa avoit despantu de luis,[34] il aurais desferais d'apore au santiment d'un sy grand home pour le quelle il avoit teans de venerassion, mais que tous avoit estte innudille.[35] Je ne trouver taure consolassion que destre per-suadée que la providance[36] fait tout pour notre bien, et votre prefaces sur la doeo-dyces, mest d'un grand secour.[37] enfin Monsieur jamais chacrin ne ma pareu sy vivez et insutenable come ce luis la.[38] Je crains pour la sante du P: E. et peutetre pour sa vié.[39] J'espere que votre retour restera fixees[40] a la St Jeans il n'y aura persone qui an sera plus a'yssez[41] que M^r le P: et moy, qui nous feron toujours vn plaisir[42] de vous marquer an toute les occasion que nous some de vos amies.[43]

Caroline

Mande moy[44] je vous prié ce que le P. Eugene vous a repondu et ce que l[']on dit a la cour de notre condevuite.[45]

15. Caroline* of Brandenburg-Ansbach, Electoral Princess of Braunschweig-Lüneburg, to Leibniz[1]

Hanover 7 June
1714[2]

The only benefit that I have derived,[3] sir, from all the benefits that awaited[4] the electoral prince [Georg August*, Electoral Prince of Braunschweig-Lüneburg], is your letter, which you have written to me. The electoral prince is much beholden[5] to you for concerning yourself so vigorously for him.[6] It would have been[7] hoped that everyone had felt the same.[8] It is not the fault[9] of the prince, nor of all the honourable men here.[10] He has moved heaven and earth,[11] and I myself have spoken very[12] emphatically about it with the elector [Georg Ludwig* of Braunschweig-Lüneburg]. We were in crisis until the day before yesterday when[13] we received a courier[14] from the queen [Anne of Great Britain] with some letters for the elector, the electress [the Dowager Electress of Braunschweig-Lüneburg, Sophie* of the Palatinate], and the electoral prince. These are of a violence worthy[15] of Milord Bolingbroke [Henry St John*],[16] and so the electoral prince is nearly without hope of going to assume his seat in accordance with his rights[17].[18] I do not know what the world may think of our conduct here.[19] I do not so much regret[20] the loss that our conduct may bring upon us[21] as to have in[22] some way abandoned the interests[23] of our holy religion, the liberty of Europe,[24] and so many brave and honourable friends in England.[25] I have no consolation[26] but to have seen the prince do everything humanly[27] [possible] in order to obtain this[28] permission. Madame the Electress has joined him, and she wants to send[29] the letters that they received from the queen to England.[30] The prince has charged me with asking you to assure the Prince of Savoy [Eugène*] of his very humble services[31] and to beseech him most urgently to impute nothing to him in this whole affair: that he knew that the prince had found it[32] fine and fitting[33] more than two years ago, that if it had depended on him,[34] he would have deferred from the beginning to the opinion of so great a man for whom he had so much veneration, but that everything had been to no avail.[35] I find no consolation but to believe that providence[36] does everything for our good, and your preface to the *Theodicy* is a great comfort to me.[37] Finally, sir, never has a sorrow seemed to me so violent and unbearable as this one.[38] I fear for the health of the electoral prince and perhaps for his life.[39] I hope that your return will remain fixed[40] on St. John's Day. No one will be more pleased by it[41] than the prince and I, who always take pleasure[42] in showing you on all occasions that we are among your friends.[43]

Caroline

Please do let me know[44] what Prince Eugène has replied and what is said at the court [in Vienna] about our conduct.[45]

15. CAROLINE OF BRANDENBURG-ANSBACH TO LEIBNIZ   55

[1] LBr. F 4 Bl. 30r-30v. Letter as sent: four quarto sides in Caroline's hand. Previously published in Klopp IX 452–3; Kemble 503–5. At the time this letter was written, Leibniz was in Vienna; it is Caroline's reply to Leibniz's letter of 24 May 1714 (document 11). Caroline wrote the present letter on the day before Leibniz's friend and patroness, the Dowager Electress of Braunschweig-Lüneburg, Sophie* of the Palatinate, collapsed and died in Caroline's arms in the gardens of Herrenhausen* (for an account of the event, see the letter of 12 June 1714 from Johanne Sophie*, Gräfin (Countess) of Schaumburg-Lippe, to Lady Mary Cowper* (document 16) and her letter of 12 July 14 to Louise* Raugravine Palatine (document 21), as well as Caroline's letter of 13 July 1714 to Lady Mary Cowper (document 22)). For Leibniz's response to the present letter, see his letter to Caroline of 16 June 1714 (document 18).

[2] '1714' is not in Caroline's hand.

[3] Reading 'tiré' for 'diray'.

[4] Reading 'tous les avantages qu'attendaient' for 'toute les avantage qui adantoit'.

[5] Reading 'd'obligation' for 'd'oblication'.

[6] Reading 'intéresser si fortement pour lui' for 'inderesser sy fortement pour luis'.

[7] Reading 'été' for 'estte'…

[8] Reading 'eût eu les mêmes sentiments' for 'eut heu les mes santiment'.

[9] Reading 'Ce n'est pas la faute' for 'Se n'est pas la feaute'.

[10] Reading 'tous les honnêtes gens d'ici' for 'tout les honneste geans d'isy'.

[11] Reading 'remué ciel et terre' for 'remeuez ciel et tere'.

[12] Reading 'j'en ai parlé moi-même très' for 'j'ean a'yée parle moy même tres'.

[13] Reading 'été dans la crise jusqu'avant hier où' for 'estte deans la crisse jusqu'à vant hier au'.

[14] Reading 'reçu un courrier' for 'reçeu un courie'.

[15] Reading 'd'une violence digne' for 'd'un violances dingé'.

[16] Henry St John*, First Viscount Bolingbroke, was a Tory politician and statesman, and, at the time of writing, Secretary of State for the Southern Department. But it had not been Bolingbroke's hand behind the letters that were sent to the members of the electoral family under the name of the queen, as Caroline and the rest of the family suspected; rather, it was Robert Harley*, Earl of Oxford, who had drafted the queen's letters (documents 12, 13, 14).

[17] Reading 's'est vu presque sans espérance d'aller prendre sa séance selon ses droits' for 'ces veu presque sans esperance daller prander sa seances celon ses droit'.

[18] In 1706 Queen Anne had bestowed the Garter on the Electoral Prince Georg August and created him Duke of Cambridge. Thus Caroline is asserting his right to take his seat as a member of the House of Lords.

[19] Reading 'conduite que nous avons tenue ici' for 'contevuite que nous avons denu isy'.

[20] Reading 'regrette pas tant' for 'regrede pas teans'.

[21] Reading 'peut-être nôtre conduite nous attirera' for 'peutestre nostre contevuite nous adirera'.

[22] Reading 'en' for 'an'.

[23] Reading 'manière abandonné l'intérêts' for 'manier apandoné linteres'.

[24] Reading 'liberté d'Europe' for 'liberdie d'uropé'.

[25] Reading 'tant de braves et honnêtes amis en Angleterre' for 'tans de pravez et honeste amis an angeltere'.

[26] Reading 'consolation' for 'consolassion'.

[27] Reading 'vu humainement faire tout' for 'veu humenent faire tout'.

[28] Reading 'obtenir cette' for 'opdenir c'este'.

[29] Reading 's'est jointe à lui et elle veut envoyer' for 'ces joint a leuis et ille veulle anvoiyer'.

[30] Reading 'de la R: qu'ils ont reçues en Angleterre' for 'de la R: qu'il on receu an angeltere'.

[31] Reading 'Savoie, de ses très humbles services' for 'Savois, de ces tres humble service'.

[32] That is, sending the electoral prince to England.

[33] Reading 'très instamment de ne lui rien imputer en toute cette affaire qu'il savait que M^r le P: l'avait trouvé bon et à propos' for 'tres instanment de ne luis rien ynpuder an toutre ceste afaire qu'il savoit que M^r le P: la voit trouvez bon et apropo'.

[34] Reading 'ans que si ça avoit dépendu de lui' for 'anne que sy sa avoit despantu de luis'.

[35] Reading 'déféré d'bord au sentiment d'un si grand homme pour lequel il avait tant de vénération, mais que tous avait été inutile' for 'desferais d'apore au santiment d'un sy grand home homme pour le quelle il avoit teans de venerassion, mais que tous avoit estte innudille'.

[36] Reading 'd'autre consolation que d'être persuadée que la providence' for 'taure consolassion que destre persuadée que la providance'.

56   16. SOPHIE, GRÄFIN ZU SCHAUMBURG-LIPPE, TO BARONESS COWPER

16. SOPHIE, GRÄFIN ZU SCHAUMBURG-LIPPE, TO BARONESS COWPER   57

[37] Reading 'préface sur la Théodicée m'est d'un grand secours' for 'prefaces sur la doeodyces, mest d'un grand secour'.

[38] Reading 'chagrin ne m'a paru si vif et insoutenable comme celui-là' for 'chacrin ne ma pareu sy vivez et insutenable cõme ce luis la'.

[39] Reading 'vie' for 'vié'.

[40] Reading 'fixé' for 'fixees'.

[41] Reading 'personne qui en sera plus aise' for 'persoñe qui an sera plus a'yssez'.

[42] Reading 'ferons toujours un plaisir' for 'feron toujours vn plaisir'.

[43] Reading 'en toutes les occasions que nous sommes de vos amis' for 'an toute les occasion que nous sõme de vos amies'.

[44] Reading 'Mandez-moi' for 'Mande moy'.

[45] Reading 'conduite' for 'condevuite'.

16. Johanne Sophie*, Gräfin (Countess) zu Schaumburg-Lippe, to Baroness Mary Cowper*[1]

Letter from the Countess of Buckenbourg wth an account of the Princess Sophia's Death.

Hannover June 12th [1714]

Mad[m]

I have lost last week my Dear & most belov'd Electrice,[2] a thunder stroke to my heart, for she was really all that made me & this Court easy, & w[ch] gave me any consolations in so many misfortunes that came upon me. Oh Dear Mad[m] what a dreadful chance was this to lose such a perfect good Princess on a sudden. Tho' I do not question but you have heard it already, since I was not able to write the very first post, yet must I give you some information of these particulars none can know better than my self since I had the misfortune to see her dye in my arms in the midst of the garden at Herenhausen before we cou'd give her any succour. Her R.H. had a little smack of the cholick last Thursday, but recover'd so well, y[t] she supp'd with the Elector the same night, & so was well the following Friday. When we came to wait upon her we did find her in a pretty good humour, she propos'd to walk to our Electoral Princess [Caroline of Brandenburg-Ansbach], who wou'd have dissuaded her but cou'd not prevent it. She walk'd very fast, entertaining us with that spirit she always had, & spoke upon English affairs wth lay very hard on her Heart, for the Queen's last letter[3] w[ch] was not thought as satisfactory as it cou'd have been expected, gave her a great mortification, & was really the mortal wound to this noble soul. When we came in the midst of the garden her R.H. begun to seem weary: The Princess ask'd her if she was ill, but her R.H. gave no other answer but touching her Breast she s[d] here—here it lyes—It began first to rain very hard & so every one retir'd, the Pss Electoral & I who were alone with her & M[r] Wind wou'd persuade her to go in one of those painted closets that were not far off, but our D[r] Electrice cou'd never reach it, she sunk down in our arms, saying only I am very

58 16. SOPHIE, GRÄFIN ZU SCHAUMBURG-LIPPE, TO BARONESS COWPER

16. SOPHIE, GRÄFIN ZU SCHAUMBURG-LIPPE, TO BARONESS COWPER 59

ill, pray give me your hand & hold me fast. So we did with all our forces sending soon away a footman[4] to fetch some hungary water & Gold Powder, she grew so heavy that it was impossible to prevent her sinking down to Earth. We lay'd her down very softly, & open'd her stays, & every thing that cou'd stop her Breath, but observing she was quite black in her face, & gave only an anguishing tone; in the same moment her Eyes were half broken, & a deadly pale colour overthrew her face. I took her upon my knee & observ'd she was no more to be succor'd, & that our exhortations cou'd not be heard, therefore did I beg the Princess and M[r]. Wind to join with me, & we recommended her soul to the misericordius Father in Heaven, to whom this dear Princess did always show a most hearty Love & confidence, repeating often that she did not question but God wou'd not have preserv'd her from Damnation having so many particular favours bestow'd upon her. The Elector [Georg Ludwig*, elector of Braunschweig-Lüneburg], Electoral Prince [Georg August* of Braunschweig-Lüneburg], & the rest of the family as well as all the Court came at last. Our Elector who cou'd never believe that she was Dead, gave orders to let her blood, & to bring her to Bed where above an hour she was handled and warm'd, but there was no help. It did please so God's Providence to stop the Glorious Course of this vertuous & great Princess in a moment, & deprive this Court of its delight. Her R.H. is generally regretted: Our Electoral Pr. And Princess, are in so great affliction that we are forc'd to let them blood, they know too well what they have lost & our Duke of Cambridge[5] will be now (I fear) disappointed, since the Queen & her Minister's letters prevented our designs.

Our Elector is going the other week to Py[r] [Pyrmont*] to drink the waters, & our Prince & Princess will do the same here. Our D[r] Electress was brought last Sunday night into this chappell where her body shall rest till every thing is prepar'd for the last Ceremony: Her R.H. did always shew an aversion to be embalm'd or shewn after her Death, therefore it was not convenient in this hot season to keep her longer in her room. Our Court will make a sad figure for every one will be in as black a mourning as one is full of sorrow. As mine will not give leave to say more, but pray Mad[m] Be sure that none can be more sincerely Y[rs] I am Mad[m]

Y[r]. most hum[ble] serv[t]

The Countess of Buckenbourg

[1] HALS D/EP F229 12–15. This is a copy of a letter from Johanne Sophie, Gräfin (Countess) zu Schaumburg-Lippe, to Baroness (later Countess) Mary Cowper made by Mary's daughter, Lady Sarah Cowper. For Johanne Sophie's letter to the Raugravine Palatine Louise* concerning the death of the Dowager Electress of Braunschweig-Lüneburg, Sophie* of the Palatinate, see document 21; for Caroline's letter to Mary Cowper concerning the death of the dowager electress, see document 22.

[2] The Dowager Electress Sophie died on Friday 8 June 1714 in the garden of Herrenhausen*.

[3] The reference is to Queen Anne's letter to the Dowager Electress Sophie of 19 May 1714 (29 May 1714 NS), for which see document 12.

[4] In her letter to the Raugravine Louise, Johanne Sophie identifies this footman as 'Chiarafan' (see document 21, p. 83).

[5] That is, Georg August. As a result of the *Act for the Naturalization of the Most Excellent Princess Sophia, Electress and Dowager of Hanover, and the Issue of her body*, which was enacted by the Parliament of England in 1705, Georg August became a naturalized citizen of England; in 1706 he was made a Knight of the Garter and created Duke and Marquess of Cambridge in the Peerage of England.

Benedictus Andreas Caspar de Nomis to Leibniz

H^r le 13 : de Juin 1714

Monsieur

Le Voiage que j'ay esté obligé de faire aux Terres de mon Beau Pere le General de Bothmer ou se trouvoit ma femme en danger de la Vie pour une fausse Couche qu'elle avoit eu le malheur de faire, m'a Monsieur empeché de vous remercier plus tost de l'honneur de la Vostre du 5e de May que j'ay trouvée à mon retour en cette Ville [...]

La mort inopinée de Madame Nostre Electrice arrivée Vendredi dernier dans le jardin de Herenhausen entre les bras de Mad^e la Princesse Electorale, et de Mad^e la Comtesse de Bucquebourg qui se promenoient avec Elle, m'a tellement surpris et consterné, que je n'ay pas l'esprit de songer à autre chose. [...]

Au reste la mort de nostre Electrice est attribüée au chagrin que les Affaires d'Engleterre[2] luy ont donné: Vous sçauréz sans doute comme les Amis de la Maison avoient conseillé de faire aller le P^{ce} El^l à Londres et qu'il[s] luy offroient jusqu'à $\frac{m}{400}$ livres Sterlines[3] par an, cette instance anima le jeune Schütz nostre Envoyé à demander le Uurit pour le d^t Prince comme duc de Cambridge, afin qu'il pût avoir seance dans le Parlement. Il s'adressa pour cela au Chancellier de la Couronne, qui en parla à la reyne, laquelle s'offensa que cette demande eut estée portée au Chancellier plustost qu'à elle, et depechà un Courier icy avec le Uurit accompagné des plaintes contre le Ministre, auquel Elle fit en mesme tems interdire la Cour: Celuy cy s'imaginant que cette defence portoit prejudice à son Caractère, prist la Poste et vint à Hannover, ou il est encore sans que le Maitre l'aye jamais voulu voir. La Cour a donc estée obligée de dissimuler et de deferer aux sentiments de la reyne qui, prenant courage sur nostre dissimulation, a depeché un autre Courier avec trois lettres, une pour Mad^e l'Electrice, et les deux autres pour Mg^{rs} l'Electeur et Prince Electoral, la premiere qu'on m'a expliquée portoit en substance, que S. M: ayant le malheur d'avoir des sujets factieux et turbulants,[8] elle reconnoissoit que ç'estoit à leur instigation que le P. El: souhaittoit de passer en Engleterre, mais qu'estant resolüe de gouverner son Peuple seule et en paix, Elle ne jugeoit pas à propos qu'il y allast, que la succession estoit assés bien establie pour qu'il ne nous en restast aucun doute, et qu'elle prioit S. A. E. de luy ouvrir son Coëur et luy dire sincerement ce qu'elle Reyne[9] pourroit faire en sa faveur, mais que si le Prince ou quelqu'autre pretendoit aller soulever ses sujets qu'elle se verroit contrainte de se servir des moyens que Dieu luy avoit donnés, pour conserver son Authorité, et le repos de ses Peuples, toutte la lettre estoit meslée de menaces et des promesses[10] concluant qu'il falloit se fier à Elle seulem^t: et ne pas ajouter foy aux discours des malins. Le contenu de la lettre à Mg^r l'Electeur n'est pas connu non plus que de l'autre au Prince Electoral; mais il y a qui soutie[n]nent que cette derniere ne contient que des menaces, et est conçeue en de[s] termes si hautains qu'un homme

17. Benedictus Andreas Caspar de Nomis* to Leibniz (excerpt)[1]

Hanover, 13 June 1714

Sir

The trip that I had to make to the lands of my father-in-law, General Bothmer, where my wife was in danger of her life from a miscarriage that she had had the misfortune of suffering, has prevented me, sir, from thanking you sooner for the honour of yours of the 5th of May, which I found on my return to this town [...]

The unexpected death of Madame our Electress [the Dowager Electress of Braunschweig-Lüneburg, Sophie* of the Palatinate] occurred last Friday [8 June 1714] in the garden of Herrenhausen* between the arms of Madame the Electoral Princess [Caroline* of Brandenburg-Ansbach, electoral princess of Braunschweig-Lüneburg] and Madame the Countess of Bückeburg [Johanne Sophie*, Gräfin (Countess) zu Schaumburg-Lippe], who were walking with her; this has so surprised and dismayed me that I think of nothing else. [...]

As for the rest, the death of our electress is attributed to the grief that the affairs of England[2] have given her. You must doubtless know how the friends of the House [of Hanover] had advised sending the electoral prince [Georg August* of Braunschweig-Lüneburg] to London and that they offered him up to $\frac{m}{400}$ pounds sterling[3] per annum; this request emboldened the young Schütz,[4] our envoy, to request the writ for the said prince as Duke of Cambridge,[5] so that he would be able to have a seat in parliament. He appealed to the chancellor of the crown [Lord Chancellor Simon Harcourt], who spoke about it with the queen [Anne of Great Britain]; she was offended that this request had been conveyed to the chancellor rather than to her, and she dispatched a courier here with the writ, accompanied by some complaints against the minister,[6] whom she at the same time denied access to the court.[7] Since he [Schütz] thought this prohibition impeached his character, he took the stagecoach and came to Hanover, where he still is, without the master ever wanting to see him. The court was therefore compelled to dissimulate and defer to the views of the queen, who, taking courage from our dissimulation, dispatched another courier with three letters, one for Madame the Electress, and the two others for Monseigneurs the Elector [Georg Ludwig* of Braunschweig-Lüneburg] and the electoral prince. The first, which was explained to me, says, in short, that Her Majesty, having the misfortune to have some seditious and unruly[8] subjects, recognized that it was at their instigation that the electoral prince wished to go to England, but that being resolved to govern her people alone and in peace, she did not consider it appropriate that he might go there; that the succession was sufficiently well established, so there did not remain any doubt about it for us, and that she bid Her Electoral Highness to open her heart to her and tell her sincerely what she the queen[9] could do in its favour; but that, if the prince, or someone else,

de nostre Calibre n'ecriroit pas à un Crocheteur, par ou l'on croyt qu'il n'y a aucun menagement, et qu'il faut s'attendre à de tres mechantes suites: Cette consideration, et la crainte de voir les Amis de la Maison sacrifiéz au ressentiment de la reyne et du Ministére, a tellement saisy Mad^e l'Electrice qu'Elle en a eu un' Apoplexie qui nous l'a ravye et dont nous sommes tous inconsolables: l'opinion la plus commune estoit que le Prince sans marchander allast en Engleterre, et que sur le lieu il demandast la seance dans le Parlem^t: ou un ainsi:[11] qu'aprez avoir reçeu le Uurit, il eut pris la Poste et se fut rendu préz de la reyne avant qu'elle eut le tems de se determiner, que la presence l'auroit empechée de se declarer de la sorte, et de nous faire le tort qu'elle nous prepare. Apresent ce' n'est plus [le] tems, et les Affaires ont tellem^t: changé de façe que sans un' espece de miracle je doute fort que nous montions sur le Trône: Cette revolution[12] obligerà peutestre nostre Cour, à s'attacher de plus en plus à celle de Vienne, pourveu que l'on veuille de ce' costé la y donner la main: On ne sçait pas encore si on envoyerà quelqu'un à Londres pour la notification de cette mort ou si l'on se contenterà de charger le Resident qu[']i[l] en donne part. S. A. E. irà la semaine prochaine à Pyrmont mais le jour n'en est pas fixé, parce que cela depend du düeil[13] qui n'est pas encore fait. Je ne vous dis rien de Bronsvich parce que je suppose que vous seréz bien informé que l'on n'y fait rien, et il y a apparence que l'on resterà dans l'inaction encor quelque tems: Je vous demande pardon de vous avoir envoyé avec ma longue lettre, et d'avoir tant tardé à Vous remercier de la Vostre de la quelle je vous suis fort obligé vous priant de la continuation, et de me croire avec une parfaitte Veneration et Reconnoissance

Monsieur

Vostre tres humble et
tres obeissant serviteur
Nota manus

P.S.

On nous fait esperer que S.M. l'Imperatrice Regnante soit grosse, je prie Dieu que celà soit, et le prie & vous asseure de tout mon Coëur pour la Consolation de la tres Auguste Maison et de toutte l'Europe aussi bien que de la mienne propre.

intended to go to stir up her subjects, she would find herself constrained to make use of the means that God had given her to conserve her authority and the peace of her peoples. The whole letter was mixed with threats and promises,[10] concluding that it was necessary to trust her alone and not give credit to the words of the malicious. The contents of the letter to Monseigneur the Elector is not known, any more than that of the other to the electoral prince; but there are those who maintain that the latter contains only threats and is expressed in terms so haughty that a man of our caliber would not write them to a porter, whereby it is believed that there is no discretion and that it is necessary to expect some bad consequences. This consideration, and the fear of seeing the friends of the House [of Hanover] sacrificed to the resentment of the queen and the ministry, so stunned Madame the Electress that she suffered an apoplexy from it, which has robbed us, and on account of which we are completely inconsolable. The most common view was that the prince might go to England without hesitating and demand the seat in parliament on the spot; or one like this:[11] if after having received the writ he had he taken the stagecoach and arrived near the queen before she had time to decide, his presence would have prevented her from declaring herself in that way and from doing us the harm that she is preparing for us. Now it is too late, and matters have so changed that, without a kind of miracle, I strongly doubt that we will mount the throne. This revolution[12] will perhaps compel our court to attach itself more and more to that of Vienna, provided that on this side they are willing to join forces with it. It is still not known whether they will send someone to London for the notification of this death, or whether they will be content charge the Resident with giving an account of it. His Electoral Highness will go to Pyrmont* next week, but the day for it is not determined, because that depends on the period of mourning,[13] which is not yet done. I say nothing to you about Braunschweig because I assume that you are probably well informed that they are doing nothing there, and it appears that they will remain idle for yet some time. Pardon me for having sent you my long letter and for having put off so long thanking you for yours, on account of which I am much obliged to you, requesting your continuation and to believe that I am with complete veneration and gratitude
sir

Your very humble and
very obedient servant
A known hand

P.S.

We are led to hope that her majesty the empress regnant [Elisabeth Christine* of Braunschweig-Wolfenbüttel] may be pregnant. I pray God it may be so, and I pray him and assure you of my whole heart for the consolation of the very August House and of all Europe, as well as my own.

17. DE NOMIS TO LEIBNIZ

17. DE NOMIS TO LEIBNIZ   65

[1] Gottfried Wilhelm Leibniz Bibliothek Ms 23, 1203 Bl. 138–140. Letter as sent: six quarto sides in Nomis's hand. Previously published in Klopp IX 481–3 (excerpt). Klopp mistakenly attributed the letter to Johann Mathias von der Schulenburg*, as does Maria Rosa Antognazza (see Antognazza 2009, p. 504).

[2] Reading 'Angleterre' for 'Engleterre'.

[3] Klopp mistranscribes '$\frac{m}{400}$ livres Sterlines' as ' m/40 livres Sterlines' (see Klopp IX 32). It is not altogether clear how to interpret Nomis's notation here, but my guess is that it represents 1400 pounds sterling, which in 1714 was the equivalent in purchasing power to somewhere between 250,000 and 300,000 pounds sterling in 2021.

[4] That is, Georg Wilhelm Sinold Schütz, the Hanoverian envoy to England. For more on this matter, see Leibniz's letter to the Dowager Electress Sophie of 24 May 1714 (document 10, p. 41 note 3).

[5] As a result of the *Act for the Naturalization of the Most Excellent Princess Sophia, Electress and Dowager of Hanover, and the Issue of her Body*, which was enacted by the Parliament of England in 1705, Georg August became a naturalized citizen of England; in 1706 he was made a Knight of the Garter and created Duke and Marquess of Cambridge in the Peerage of England.

[6] That is, the Hanoverian envoy to London, Georg Wilhelm Sinold Schütz.

[7] For some months prior to this, Schütz had been urging Hanover to demand a writ summoning the electoral prince to the House of Lords as Duke of Cambridge. He eventually received an equivocal letter from the Dowager Electress Sophie which he interpreted as an order to demand such a writ (although Sophie later claimed that she had only wanted Schütz to ask Queen Anne's Lord Chancellor Simon Harcourt why such a writ had not been issued). So on 23 April 1714 (NS), Schütz put the demand to Harcourt. The majority of the queen's cabinet agreed that there was no legal way to refuse issuance of the writ, so it was consequently granted, but immediately thereafter the queen refused Schütz access to court and demanded his recall. Schütz departed from London on 1 May. Resisting pressure from the Dowager Electress Sophie, the Electoral Princess Caroline, and Leibniz, the Elector Georg Ludwig* eventually decided not to allow his son to make the trip to England without the queen's permission. However, Georg Ludwig did use the occasion of the writ's issuance to seek further guarantees for the Hanoverian succession. On 18 May Sophie and Georg Ludwig presented a formal memorial to Thomas Harley, the British envoy to Hanover, setting out a number of requests to secure the Protestant succession. First 'their Electoral Highnesses take the liberty of representing to her Majesty the necessity of obliging the Pretender [James Francis Edward Stuart*] to remove to Italy, and the danger which may result from his staying longer in Lorrain, both to her Majesty's kingdoms and to her royal person, and the protestant succession.' The memorial insisted furthermore that 'it is necessary for the security of her royal person, and for that of her kingdoms, and of the protestant relation, to settle in Great Britain some one of the Electoral family', and it renewed a previous request that 'such a pension and establishment should be settled by an act of parliament on her Highness the Electress, as the nearest heir to the crown usually enjoy' (Macpherson 1775, p. 609). Finally, the dowager electress and the elector expressed their hope 'that her Majesty will be pleased to grant titles belonging to the princes of the blood of Great Britain, to such of the Protestant Princes of the Electoral family, as are not yet invested with them' (ibid., p. 610). Before the memorial had been presented to any other members of the British government, the queen's first lord of the treasury, Robert Harley*, Earl of Oxford, sent letters from himself and the queen (which he had drafted) to the dowager electress (see document 12), the elector (see document 13), and the electoral prince (see document 14).

[8] Reading 'turbulents' for 'turbulants'.

[9] Reading 'qu'elle la reine' for 'qu'elle reyne'.

[10] Reading 'de promesses' for 'des promesses'.

[11] Klopp omits 'un ainsi:' (see Klopp IX 483).

[12] Klopp mistranscribes 'revolution' as 'resolution' (see Klopp IX, 483).

[13] Reading 'deuil' for 'düeil'.

Leibniz to Caroline of Brandenburg-Ansbach, Electoral Princess of Braunschweig-Lüneburg

Madame

Je reçois aujourdhuy l'honneur de la lettre de V. A. S. et quoyque je n' aye pas encore pu executer ses ordres, je ne veux point differer de repondre, parce qu'il me semble que je ne dois pas tarder un moment de luy marquer que j'ay de grandes esperances non obstant tout ce qui s'est passé: J'envoyeray bien tot à V. A. S. un personnage qui servira à nous encourager, s'il falloit venir un jour aux voyes de fait. J'ay envoyé à Madame l'Electrice un memoire tres instructif qu'il a dressé, que Mad. l'Electrice a trouvé bon, et qui a encor eté applaudi par ceux à qui Elle l'a fait voir. Car Elle m'a fait l'honneur de repondre là dessus. Il est bon, puisque Monseigneur le prince Electoral ne peut point venir encor, d'en pouvoir rejetter la faute sur le Ministere Anglois, et cela vaut beaucoup mieux, que si la Reine s'etoit tenu en certain termes moyens,[3] et que nous eussions donné des marques de peu d'empressement, et c'est ce que j'ay craint plus que le reste. Le Ministere va combler la mesure de la maniere qu'il s'y prend.

Un confident du Grand Tresorier a ecrit à un de mes amis qui m'a communiqué l'extrait de la lettre. Il y a quelque maniere de menaces, qui veulent dire qu'on doit se donner des gardes de trop irriter la Reine, et de la pousser à des extremités. J'ay repondu à cet ami en des termes qu'il pourra envoyer à son correspondant ou je rends menaces pour menaces; car ces gens sont timides pendant qu'ils font les faux braves.

Je suis bien aise qu'on a fait écrire à la Reine des lettres hautaines. Il faudroit les publier, cela irritera la nation. Mais j'y trouve encor un autre bien: ces lettres irriteront Mon[sgr] l'Electeur, et rien ne sauroit venir plus à propos; comme aupres de ce president dont parle l'auteur des caracteres.

Ainsi, Madame, il faut se consoler de ce petit contretemps, et croire veritablement qu'il est pour le mieux, même par rapport à nous.

Je ne say si l'on n'a pris des mesures avec Messieurs les Etats en cas d'une equippée du pretendant. Si cela n'estoit pas, il y faudroit songer plus qu'à autre chose, et je crois que Monseigneur l'Electeur pourroit être le veritable Mediateur entre l'Empereur et Messieurs les Etats sur la barriere; y etant tant interessé car outre que le traité de Garantie y est lié, si ces deux puissances etoient d'accord, une alliance defensive entre eux pour la seureté des deux pays bas mettroit les Hollandois à couvert et en état de s'opposer aux protecteurs du pretendant sans rien apprehender.

Je parleray au premier jour à M[r] le prince Eugene conformement aux ordres de V. A. S Je parleray aussi à la Majesté de l'Imperatrice Amalie, qui s'y interesse fort. Je dirois même quelque chose de votre lettre, Madame, à l'Empereur même, si je

18. Leibniz to Caroline* of Brandenburg-Ansbach, Electoral Princess of Braunschweig-Lüneburg[1]

[Vienna, 16 June 1714]

Madame

Today I receive the honour of the letter from Your Serene Highness, and although I have not yet been able to carry out its orders, I do not want to put off responding, since it seems that I must not delay for a moment stating that I have great hopes, notwithstanding everything that has happened. I will soon send to Your Serene Highness a person who will serve to encourage us, if one day it were necessary to come to blows. I sent Madame the Electress [Sophie* of the Palatinate, Dowager Electress of Braunschweig-Lüneburg] a very instructive memoir that he drew up, which Madame the Electress found well done and which was again applauded by those to whom she showed it.[2] For she did me the honour of replying about this. Since Monseigneur the Electoral Prince [Georg August* of Braunschweig-Lüneburg] cannot yet go, it is useful to be able to put the blame for it on the English ministry, and that is much better than if the queen [Anne of Great Britain] had stuck to certain neutral terms,[3] and we had given signs of little enthusiasm, which is what I feared more than anything else. The ministry will fill the cup to the brim in the way it does it.

A confidant of the Lord High Treasurer [Robert Harley*, First Earl of Oxford] has written to one of my friends, who has sent me the extract of the letter. There are threats of a sort, which means that we must take care not to anger the queen too much and not to push her to extremes. I have responded to this friend in terms that he will be able to send to his correspondent, terms in which I return threats for threats; for these people are timid, while shamming bravery.

I am very glad that they have had the queen write haughty letters.[4] They should be published; this will anger the nation. But I find yet another good in it: these letters will anger Monseigneur the Elector [Georg Ludwig* of Braunschweig-Hannover], and nothing more fitting could come about, as with that president[5] of whom the author of the *Characters*[6] speaks.

Thus, madame, you must get over this small setback, and I truly believe that it is for the best, even with respect to us.

I do not know if they have taken measures with the States-General* in the event of an escapade by the Pretender [James Francis Edward Stuart*]. If that was not done, consideration would need to be given to it more than to anything else, and I believe that Monseigneur the Elector could be the true mediator between the emperor [Karl VI*] and the States-General* regarding the barrier;[7] I am interested in it so much because, quite apart from the fact that the Treaty of Guarantee[8] is tied to it, if these two powers were in agreement, a defensive alliance between them for

n'apprehendois de rendre deux grands personnages jaloux, une Imperatrice et un prince Electoral.

Votre grand coeur, Madame, qui symbolise tant avec celuy de son Serenissime Epous, aussi bien que vos esprits, me donne de tres grandes esperances. Reservés vous tous deux pour une meilleure occasion qui vous attend, et pensés cependant à écarter ce qui pourroit vous traverser. Pourveu qu'on empeche les mal intentionnés de faire venir le pretendant bien tôt, je crois qu'ils[11] ne pourroit[12] plus le faire dans la suite. Sur tout, Madame, conservés nous votre pretieuse sante, et celle de Monseigneur le prince Electoral; si par dessus cela vous pouvés nous donner une nouvelle colonne de la Maison nous serons tres satisfaits, et moy particulierement autant que qui que ce soit. Car on ne sauroit étre avec plus d'attachement que je le suis

Madame de V. A. S.

le tres sousmis et
tres obeissant serviteur

Vienne ce 16 Juin 1714

Leibniz

18. LEIBNIZ TO CAROLINE OF BRANDENBURG-ANSBACH   69

the security of the two low countries[9] would put the Dutch under cover and in a state to oppose the protectors of the Pretender without fearing anything.

I will speak with Monseigneur Prince Eugène* [of Savoy] at the first opportunity, in conformity with the orders of Your Electoral Highness. I will also speak with Her Majesty the [Dowager] Empress [Wilhelmine] Amalie*, who is very interested in it. I would even say something about your letter, madame, to the emperor himself, if I did not fear making two great persons jealous: an empress[10] and an electoral prince.

Your great heart, madame, which symbolizes so much, along with that of her most serene spouse, as well as your minds, give me some very great hopes. Reserve both for a better occasion which awaits you and meanwhile think of averting what could thwart you. Provided that the ill-intentioned are prevented from having the Pretender come soon, I don't believe that they[11] could[12] do it later. Above all, madame, conserve for us your precious health and that of Monseigneur the Electoral Prince; if beyond that you can give us a new pillar for the House [of Hanover], we will be very satisfied, and myself especially, as much as anyone. For no one could be more dedicated to it than I,

madame, of Your Serene Highness

the very submissive and
very obedient servant

Vienna this 16 June 1714

Leibniz

---

[1] Niedersächsisches Landesarchiv-Hauptstaatsarchiv Hannover, Dep. 84 A 180 Bl. 656–7. Letter as sent: four quarto sides in Leibniz's hand. Previously published in Klopp IX 455–7 (excerpt). This is Leibniz's response to Caroline's letter of 7 June 1714 (document 15).

[2] The person Leibniz is discussing here is the Scotsman, John Ker*. Leibniz makes reference to him and his memoir again in his letter to Caroline of 7 July 1714 (see document 19, pp. 73, 75).

[3] Reading 's'était tenue en certains termes moyens' for 's'etoit tenu en certain termes moyens.'

[4] Leibniz is referring to the letters that were sent to Sophie, the Elector Georg Ludwig, and the Electoral Prince Georg August by Queen Anne (see, respectively, documents 12, 13, and 14).

[5] The reference is to Nicolas Potier de Novion (1618–93) Premiere Président of the Parliament of Paris (1678–89).

[6] That is, Jean de La Bruyère (1645–96), whose *Caractères* appeared in 1688, appended to his translation of Theophrastus' *Ethical Characters* ('Ηθικοὶ χαρακτῆρες).

[7] Leibniz refers to the Barrier Treaties, and specifically to third of the Barrier Treaties. In the first of these, concluded between Great Britain and the States-General of the Republic of the Seven United Provinces of the Netherlands in 1709, the latter agreed to support the Hanoverian succession in England, while the former agreed to secure the right of the United Provinces to garrison troops in certain barrier places as protection against French aggression. The second treaty, again concluded between Great Britain and the States-General, reduced the number of barrier places that Great Britain agreed to secure for the United Provinces. The third treaty, concluded in 1715 between representatives of the Emperor and the States-General of the United Provinces, and mediated by William Cadogan, First Earl Cadogan and British ambassador to The Hague, secured an agreement with the emperor concerning the barrier for the United Provinces.

[8] That is, the Treaty of Guarantee for the Protestant Succession to the Crown of England made between Great Britain and the States General (1710).

18. LEIBNIZ TO CAROLINE OF BRANDENBURG-ANSBACH   71

[9] That is, the Austrian Netherlands, ceded to Austria from Spain under the Treaty of Utrecht*, and the Republic of the Seven United Provinces of the Netherlands.

[10] Here Leibniz would seem to be referring to the then-current empress, Elisabeth Christine* of Braunschweig-Wolfenbüttel, rather than the Dowager Empress Wilhelmine Amalie* of Braunschweig-Lüneburg. The reigning emperor was Karl VI, who was the second son of Emperor Leopold I. Before becoming emperor in 1711, Archduke Karl had declared himself King of Spain in 1700. The then so-called Karl III of Spain courted Caroline in 1704 in the hopes of marrying her (hence Leibniz's jesting reference to jealousy); but Caroline ultimately declined, not wishing to convert to Catholicism as a condition of the marriage. And although at the time Anton Ulrich, duke of Braunschweig-Wolfenbüttel and sometime employer of Leibniz, praised Caroline as a heroine of the Protestant cause, and, as Leibniz informed Caroline, wished to make her the heroine of one his romantic novels, he himself later converted to Catholicism and helped to arrange the marriage, in 1708, between his granddaughter, Elisabeth Christine, and the future Emperor Karl VI. In a letter of 28 December 1704, Caroline responded to Leibniz:

> I believe that the King of Spain [i.e., Karl III] no longer troubles himself about me. On the contrary, I am probably despised for not wanting to follow the good instructions of Mr. de St. Marie. Every post I receive letters from that good gentleman. I believe that his words contributed much to the discomfort that I felt during the three weeks, from which I am perfectly recovered. [...] I am very much obliged to Duke Anton Ulrich for wanting to pass me off as a heroine in his novel. You will see that with time they will show me on the stage with Mr. St. Marie, where I will defend myself marvelously. [Klopp IX 114]

The Mr. de St. Marie to whom Caroline refers was Father Ferdinand Orban (1655–1732), the Jesuit confessor (from 1705 to 1716) of the then Elector Palatine Johann Wilhelm (1658–1716), who was Karl's uncle on his mother's side. Orban had been commissioned to convert Caroline to Catholicism, and Caroline endured three weeks of his harangue at the palace Sophie Charlotte* in Lützenburg. In a letter of 21 October to her niece, the Raugravine Louise* of the Palatinate, the Dowager Electress Sophie wrote of Caroline's ordeal:

> I dare say that the dear Princess of Ansbach is assailed, and she is not at all resolved to do anything contrary to her conscience. But Father Orban has more understanding and can easily get the better of the stupid Lutheran priests (as they are described to me) such as those here. Had things gone according to my wish, the dear Princess would not have undergone the impeachment and would have been able to make our court happy [by marrying Sophie's grandson, Georg August* of Braunschweig-Lüneburg, which she eventually did less than a year later]. But it seems it has not pleased God to make me happy with her in this way; we at Hanover shall not find any one better. [K IX,107]

A few days later, she wrote again to the Raugravine Louise:

> Sometimes the dear Princess says 'Yes', and sometimes she says 'No'; sometimes she believes we [Protestants] have no priests, sometimes that Catholics are idolatrous and accursed; sometimes she says our religion may be the better. What the result will be [...] I still do not know. The dear princess, however, wishes to leave, so it must soon be either 'Yes' or 'No'. When Orban comes to be with her the Bible lies on the table, and they have a fine argument. Then the one who has studied more is victorious, and afterwards the dear princess weeps. [Klopp IX 108]

As for Anton Ulrich's proposal to make Caroline a heroine in one of his romantic novels, it is thought that Caroline was indeed the model for the heroine in his novel *Octavia*. Ironically, Anton Ulrich converted to Catholicism in 1709.

[11] Klopp mistranscribes 'ils' as 'il' (see Klopp IX 457).

[12] Reading 'pourroient' for 'pourroit'.

Leibniz to Caroline* of Brandenburg-Ansbach, Electoral Princess of Braunschweig-Lüneburg

A Madame   vienne ce 7
la princesse   de juillet 1714
Electoral

Madame.

La mort de Mad. l'Electrice m'a donne une grande emotion. Il me semble que je la vois expirer entre les bras de V. A. S. Sa mort a esté celle qu'elle a souhaitee. Ce n'est pas Elle, c'est Hannover, c'est l'Angleterre, c'est le monde, c'est moy qui y ont perdu. La lettre que V. A. S. m'a fait la grace de m'ecrire le jour avant la mort de Mad. l'Electrice m'a eté une grande consolation. Cependant si vous ne voulés pas Madame me recevoir comme un mauvais meuble que vous aves herité d'elle, vous me bannirés d'Hannover. Il faudroit que V. A. S. se fît donner ses recueils. Gargan en a beaucoup et puis Mlle. de Pelniz. Outre ce qui se trouvera dans son Cabinet, il faudroit supplier Madame d'Orleans de nous conserver ses lettres: tous ces reliques[5] ne sont rien au prix de sa personne. Mais ne pensons pas trop à sa mort, pensons plustost à sa vie heureuse et glorieuse. V. A. S. doit etre comme sa metempsychose.

Je n'ay point manqué de faire aupres de Mon[sgr] le prince Eugene le compliment dont Mon[sgr] le prince Electoral m'avoit charge. Le prince de Savoye s'en est tenu fort oblige, et m'a commis bien expressément de marquer son affection pour les interests de S. A. S. Il paroist qu'il juge[6] liés avec ceux de sa Mté imperiale. Il a eté bien aise d'apprendre plus distinctement, qu'il n'a pas tenu a Mon[sgr] le Prince Electoral, que le voyage ne s'est point fait. S. A. et d'autres Ministres icy ont cru que si Mon[sgr] y avoit pû passer d'abord, aussi tost que le Writ avoit eté expedié sans donner le loisir au Ministere Anglois de se reconnoistre, et de se gendarmer comme ils ont fait; leur oppositions auroient eté inutiles. Mais on reconnoist bien maintenant que de la maniere que l'affaire s'est passee, ce promt passage n'a point eté faisable.

Ce luy qui aura l'honneur de presenter cette lettre à V. A. S. est un Gentilhomme Escossois d'une famille considerable, c'est celle dont est le Duc de Roxbourg. Il est venu icy pour une proposition importante de la part de quelques particuliers Anglois. Comme il s'estoit adressé d'abord à moy, j'ay fait en sorte que l'affaire a eté traitée secretement avec l'Empereur même, sans que les instances y soyent entrées. Sa Majesté Imperiale en l'entendant a donné de grandes marques de son affection et de sa reconnoissance envers le bon parti Anglois qui l'avoit si fidelement assisté et a chargé ce gentilhomme de les en asseurer là ou il le seroit[8] apropos, et luy a donné un pourtrait enrichi de diamans, tout comme s'il avoit eté envoyé d'un souverain.

Or ce gentilhomme estant fort accredité dans son parti en Ecosse, qui est celuy des presbyteriens rigides, quoyqu'il soit tres modere luy même; j'avois envoyé à

19. Leibniz to Caroline* of Brandenburg-Ansbach, Electoral Princess of Braunschweig-Lüneburg[1]

To Madame
the Electoral
Princess

Vienna 7
July 1714

Madame

The death of Madame the Electress [the Dowager Electress of Braunschweig-Lüneburg, Sophie* of the Palatinate] has moved me deeply. I seem to see her expire in the arms of Your Serene Highness.[2] Her death was such as she desired. It is not she, it is Hanover, it is England, it is the world, it is I who have lost by it. The letter that Your Serene Highness did me the favor of writing the day before the death of the electress has been a great consolation to me.[3] However, madame, if you do not wish to receive me like bad furniture that you have inherited from her, you will banish me from Hanover. Your Serene Highness should be given her documents. Gargan[4] has a lot of them, and then Mademoiselle Pöllnitz [Henriette Charlotte von Pöllnitz*]. In addition to what will be found in her study, Madame d'Orléans [Elisabeth Charlotte* of the Palatinate, Duchess of Orléans] should be asked to preserve her letters for us. All these relics[5] are nothing at the price of her person. But let us not think too much about her death; rather let us think of her happy and glorious life. Your Serene Highness must be just like her reincarnation.

I did not fail to pay Monseigneur Prince Eugène* the compliment with which Monseigneur the Electoral Prince [Georg August* of Braunschweig-Lüneburg] had charged me. The Prince of Savoy was very gratified by it and commissioned me quite expressly to state his regard for the interests of His Serene Highness. It appears that he considers them[6] to be connected with those of His Imperial Majesty [Emperor Karl VI*]. He was very glad to learn more clearly that it was not the fault of the electoral prince that the trip was not made.[7] His Highness and some other ministers here thought that if the prince had initially been able to go as soon as the writ had been dispatched, without giving the English ministry the time to collect themselves and kick up a fuss as they have done, their opposition would have been futile. But it is now clearly recognized that in the way the affair transpired, this prompt departure was not feasible.

The person who will have the honour or presenting this letter to Your Serene Highness is a Scottish gentleman [John Ker*] from the eminent family of the Duke of Roxbrughe on behalf of an important proposition on the part of some English individuals. As it was addressed to me in the first place, I have seen to it that the matter was treated secretly with the emperor himself, without the requests having been included in it. While listening His Imperial Majesty gave some clear signs of his affection and gratitude towards the good English party, which has so loyally

Mad. l'Electrice un memoire, qu'il a dressé. Sa Serenité Royale le gouta fort et je crois qu'Elle l'a fait voir a M. de Bernsdorf. Il sera tres important, que V. A. S. Mon[sgr] le prince Electoral, et meme Mon[sgr] L'Electeur écoutent ce gentilhomme, et luy temoignent de la confiance. J'en ay écrit aussi à M. de Bernsdorf et à M. Robeton, mais je ne sais s'il les trouvera à Hannover ou en Cour. Il a eu grande part a la decouverte et à l'annihilation de la dernier invasion, quand le pretendant a voulu faire une descente en Ecosse. Il n'est nullement pour les Whigs de Cour, ny pour ceux qui voudroient perpetuer ces factions, mais pour ceux qui les voudroient abolir. Il est un des plus propres pour entretenir une bonne correspondance et pour prendre des mesures contre une nouvelle invasion. Il n'y a pas beaucoup de nos insulaires sur les quels on puisse faire grand fond sur tout parmy les gens de Cour. Mais dans celuy ci je crois avoir reconnu des marques d'une grande droiture et d'un grand et veritable zele pour la succession protestante.[10]

Un ami m'a donné a entendre (quoyqu'il soit hors d'Hannover) une bonne nouvelle par rapport à V.A.S. et à Mgr le prince Electoral. Dieu veuille qu'il en soit ainsi, et durablement. Rien ne vous peut arriver Madame ou je ne m'interesse de tout mon cœur. Vous ne saurés presque avoir la succession d'Angleterre plus à cœur que moy meme. Car je la considere comme l'unique moyen de sauver la religion reforgee, et la liberté publique. V. A S sait que Milord Midleton qui a eté secretaire d'Estat et premier ministre du Roy Jacques, et son fils sera bientost icy, ce sera sans doute comme un Envoyé du pretendant, quoyqu'il ne sera point reconnu pour tel. Le Comte de Ferrari qui est Maggiordomo du jeune prince de Lorraine, me dit qu'il est attendu tous les jours. Il aura quelque pretraille pour luy mais l'Empereur & son Ministere ont de tout autres sentimens. Un des plus grands points pour garantir la succession protestante seroit d'avancer l'accommodement entre l'Empereur & Messieurs les Etats. Il me semble que les bons offices de Mgr l'Electeur n'y pourroient pas moins contribuer que les mauvais offices de la France et du Ministere Anglois y nuisent. Si M. Robeton va en Hollande, comme quelcun m'a dit (pendant que M. Bothmar sera en Angleterre), il seroit a souhaiter qu'il fut chargé de faire de tels offices. J'ay deja dit qu'il me paroist bon de publier les lettres que la Reine a écrites et meme les reponses pour veu qu'elles soyent couchees d'une maniere propre à encourager les gens de bien. Car on gateroit beaucoup en repondant mollement. Je voudrois de pouvoir accompagner ce gentilhomme Ecossois, mais j'espere de le suivre bientost. Il me viennent quelques fois des choses dans l'esprit, dont je souhaiterois d'avoir l'honneur d'entretenir V. A. S. | et j'espere d'avoir bientost ce bonheur. |

Pour adjouter quelque chose de la Maison des Communes,[12] je vous diray Madame, que la fille que V.A.S. a renvoyée en Angleterre m'a ecrit d'Augsbourg, ou elle est allee avec son mari, marchand joaillier qu'elle a espousé depuis peu. Elle repassera en Angleterre l'automne qui vient. La pauvre fille etoit bien affligée de son renvoy jusqu'à me faire pitié. Je suis bien aise qu'elle a trouvé un homme qui l'a

19. LEIBNIZ TO CAROLINE OF BRANDENBURG-ANSBACH   75

assisted him, and charged this gentleman with assuring them of it, when it would be[8] appropriate, and gave him a portrait enriched with diamonds, just as if he had been an envoy of a sovereign.

Now since this gentleman is highly accredited in his party in Scotland (which is that of the rigid Presbyterians, although he is very moderate himself), I had sent Madame the Electress a memoire that he drew up.[9] Her Royal Serenity enjoyed it very much, and I believe that she showed it to Mr. Bernstorff.* It will be very important that Your Serene Highness, the Electoral Prince, and even Monseigneur the Elector [Georg Ludwig of Braunschweig-Lüneburg], listen to this gentleman and give him evidence of trust. I have also written to Mr. Bernstorff and Mr. [John] Robethon* about it, but I do not know whether he will find them in Hanover or at court. He had a large part in the discovery and destruction of the last invasion when the Pretender [James Francis Edward Stuart*] wanted to make a landing in Scotland. He is not in favor of the court Whigs, nor in favor of those who would want to perpetuate these factions, but in favor of those who would want to abolish them. He is one of the most suitable for maintaining a good correspondence and for taking some measures against a new invasion. There are not many of our island-ers upon whom we can reliably depend, especially among the courtiers. But in this one I believe I have recognized some signs of great integrity and true zeal for the Protestant succession.[10]

A friend has intimated to me (although he is outside of Hanover) good news in relation to Your Serene Highness and Monseigneur the Electoral Prince. May God grant that it is so, and lasting. Nothing can happen to you, madame, in which I do not take an interest with all my heart. You can scarcely have the succession of England more at heart than myself. For I consider it the only way of saving the reformed religion, and the public liberty. Your Serene Highness knows that Milord Middleton [Charles Middleton* (1650–1719)], who has been secretary of state and prime minister for King James, and his son will be here soon. He will no doubt come as an envoy of the Pretender, although he will not be recognized as such. The Count of Ferrari [Count Louis of Ferrari (1685–1733)], who is the butler of the young Prince of Lorraine [Léopold Clément Charles (1707–23)] tells me that he is expected any day. He will have some members of the priesthood on his side, but the emperor and his minister are of a completely different view. One of the more important matters for guaranteeing the Protestant succession would be to advance the accommodation between the emperor and the States-General*. It seems to me that the good offices of Monseigneur the Elector could not contribute less to it than the bad offices of France and the English ministry harm it. If Mr. Robethon goes to Holland, as someone has told me (while Mr. Bothmer* is in England), it is to be hoped that he will be charged with forming some such offices. I have already said[11] that it seems advantageous to me to publish the letters that the queen [Anne of Great Britain] has written, and even the responses, provided that they are

consolée mieux que je n'aurois pû faire. Elle est tousjours extremement zelée pour V. A. S. mais elle ne le sauroit etre autant que moy qui suis avec devotion Madame

couched in a way suitable for encouraging good people. For it would make matters worse to respond feebly. I would like to be able to accompany this Scottish gentleman, but I hope to follow him soon. Sometimes things come to mind about which I would wish to have the honour of speaking with Your Royal Highness | and I hope to have this good fortune soon |.

To add something about the House of Commons,[12] I will tell you, madame, that the young lady that Your Serene Highness sent away to England has written to me from Augsburg, where she has gone with her husband, a jewelry dealer whom she recently married. She will return to England next fall. The poor girl was very distressed by her dismissal, to the point of making me feel sorry. I am very happy that she has found a man who has consoled her better than I would be able to do. She is always extremely zealous for Your Serene Highness, but she cannot be so as much as I, who am with devotion

madame

---

[1] LBr. F 4 Bl. 32r–33v. Draft: 3.5 quarto sides in Leibniz's hand. Previously published in Klopp IX 462–5 (excerpt).

[2] The Dowager Electress Sophie died on Friday 8 June. Leibniz first learned of Sophie's death in a letter of 13 June 1714 from Benedictus Andreas Caspar de Nomis (see document 17). For the circumstances surrounding the death of the Dowager Electress, see also the letter of 12 July 1714 from Johanne Sophie*, Gräfin (Countess) of Schaumburg-Lippe to Raugravine Palatine Louise*, as well as her letter to Lady Mary Cowper* 12 June 1714 (respectively, documents 21 and 16). See also Caroline's letter to Lady Mary Cowper of 13 July 1714 (document 22).

[3] Leibniz is referring to Caroline's letter of 7 June 1714 (see document 15).

[4] Charles Nicolas Gargan was the secretary to the Dowager Electress Sophie.

[5] Reading 'toutes ces reliques' for 'tous ces reliques'.

[6] Reading 'qu'il les juge' for 'qu'il juge'.

[7] Leibniz refers to a proposed trip to England by the Electoral Prince Georg August for the purpose of taking his seat in the House of Lords as the Duke of Cambridge, for more on which see Nomis' letter to Leibniz of 13 June 1714 (document 17).

[8] Klopp mistranscribes 'il le seroit' as 'il le trouveroit' (see Klopp IX 463).

[9] See Leibniz's letter of 24 May 1714 to the Dowager Electress Sophie (document 10, p. 39).

[10] This paragraph is omitted by Klopp without notice (see Klopp IX 464).

[11] See Leibniz's letter to Caroline of 16 June 1714 (document 18).

[12] Here Leibniz seems to be using 'Maison des Communes' as a joking reference to commoners, i.e., those who are not members of the nobility, unlike those in the House of Lords.

---

20. John Chamberlayne* to Leibniz[1]

Westminster

Honored and dear Sr   30 June 1714[2]

I am asham'd I have been so long in acknowledging the great Favor of your last dated from Vieña 28 April 1714,[3] but the time that has been necessarily spent in comūnicating the same to Sr Isaac Newton,[4] & by him to the Royal Society (for I did presume your consent to shew it to all whom it concern'd, wil I hope justify my Delay) especially when I tel you that I waited for so good an opportunity of sending

Johanne Sophie, Gräfin (Countess) zu Schaumburg-Lippe, to Louise, Raugravine Palatine

Herrinhausen ce 12 Juillet
1714

Madame

Je me serois donnè L'honneur plustost de Repondre a vos deux cheres lettres, si nôtre voyage de Pyrmont, du quell nous ne somes de retour que depuis hier, ne m'en eut empechè. car Come savez[2] ma tres chere Raugrave[3] l'on n'a pas le tems de se reconnoitre dans ces endroits la, et si quelques chose[4] avoit put diminuër le Chagrein[5] que la grande perde[6] que nous venons de faire nous Cause, s'auroit[7] etè ce sejour, ou les eaux assoupissent tellement les Esprit[8] qu'on est presque come yvre, et ou la foule de toute sorte de gens vous empeche quelfois[9] de songer a autre chose qu'a ce qu'on a devant les yeux. Cependant Madame, come les yvrognes en s'eveillant ressentent de nouveaux[10] leur Chagreins plus que jamais, de même somes nous plongè[11] derechef dans nos afflictions, nous voyant dans un endroit ou nous etions accoutumès de voir tous le jours[12] nôtre Incomparable Electrice. Il me

my Answer above half the way to you by a very safe Conveyance, I mean by M^r [Charles] Whitworth [1675–1725, 1st Baron Whitworth] the Queen's Plenipotentiary to the Congress at Baden with whose Merit I suppose you are not unacquainted, especially if you knew him at the late Emperors Court &c. But I am very sorry to tel you S^r that my Negotiations have not met with the desired success, & that our Society has been prevail'd upon to vote that what you writ was Insufficient, & that it was not fit for them to concern themselves any further in that Affair &c, as will more fully appear by the Resolution enter'd into their Books of which I shal shortly send you a Copy, & in the meantime the inclos'd printed Pamphlet which Dr Keill* gave me last Thursday wil stay your stomach til you can hear further from   Hon^d S^r your most obliged humble servant

     John Chamberlayne

I have order'd my Dear Friend Mr Wilkins who superintends my collection &c at Amsterdam, to send you a specimen of ye L^ds Prayer in Chinese from the M.S. of the Famous Golius,[5] communicated to me by Mr Prof. Relandus of Utrecht.[6]

---

[1] LBr. 149 Bl. 14r–14v. Letter as sent: two quarto sides in Chamberlayne's hand. Previously published in NC VI 152–3 (excerpt).

[2] That is, 11 July 1714 NS.

[3] See Leibniz's draft letter to Chamberlayne of 21 April 1714, document 7.

[4] For Newton's response to Leibniz's letter, see Newton's letter to Chamberlayne of 11 May 1714 (30 April 1714 NS), document 8.

[5] Jacobus Golius (Jacob Gool) was a Dutch orientalist who was professor of oriental languages (from 1624) and mathematics (from 1629) at the University Leiden. When Descartes was at Leiden, Golius instructed him in mathematics.

[6] Hadrianus Relandus (Adriaan Reland) (1676–1718) was a Dutch cartographer, philologist, and orientalist, who was appointed professor of oriental languages at the University of Utrecht in 1701.

21. Johanne Sophie*, Gräfin (Countess) zu Schaumburg-Lippe, to Louise*, Raugravine Palatine (excerpt)[1]

Herrenhausen* 12 July
1714

    Madame

I would have given myself the honour of responding to your two dear letters sooner if our trip from Pyrmont,* from which we returned only yesterday, had not prevented me from doing so. For as you know,[2] my dearest Raugravine,[3] one does not have the time to know where one is in those places, and if something[4] had been able to lessen the grief[5] that the great loss[6] we have just suffered causes us, it would have[7] been this sojourn, where the waters dull the spirits[8] so much that one feels almost drunk, and where the crowd of all sorts of people sometimes[9] prevents you from thinking about anything but what is before your eyes. However, madame, as drunks awakening from their stupor feel their sorrows again[10] more than ever, we likewise plunged[11] ourselves once more into our afflictions upon looking around a place where we were accustomed to see our incomparable electress [Dowager

semble que tout le monde est mort pour moy, et je me vois tellement abandonnèe que je m'étonne moy mème co͞ment je puis resister a tant de Chagrein sans tomber malade, je languis et amaigris a veuë d'oeïll, enfin ma chere Raugrave il ny a que vous au monde Capable de juger Combien je souffre par ce que vous resentè[13] vous mème, vous me permettè[14] de vous entretenir de nôtre Comun malheur, ainsi je ne vous epargne point, puis que je trouve aussi de la Consolation dans un recit qui donne un nouveaux Cours a mes larmes. Vous avez seut[15] sans doute, tout ce qui s'est passè depuis vôtre depart, mais puis que vous m'ordonnè[16] de vous mander toutes les particularitès de la mort subite de nôtre tres chere Ellectrice, je vais vous obeyr et vous diray donc Madame, que le mème jour que vous partites qui êtoit un mercredy SAS se plaignit vers le soir d'un grand mal de tète, cependant elle fit deux tour[17] de jardin et soupa come a l'ordinaire, le lendemain a son reveill come elle avoit beaucoup suè, on tachoit de la persuader de garder le lit, mais elle n'en voulut rien faire, cependant quand elle êtoit a table elle se trouvoit si mal de sa colique d'estomach qu'il falloit la mettre au lit, nous la trouvàmes en cet Etàt vers les 6 heures du soir. J'eu[s] le bonheur de lui persuader de prendre deux lavemens de suite, qui la soulagerent tellement qu'elle se leva le mème soir pour souper avec Mong[r] l'Electeur. Le jour d'après qui êtoit le vendredy fatal, le 8me du mois passé, SAE se porta si bien, que non seulement elle dina en public, mais quand nous arrivames le soir vers l'heure de la promenade, elle temoignoit une grande envie de se promener, quoy que le tems etoit un peu Couvert, et menacoit de la pluye, elle Refusoit les porteurs, et marchoit come a l'ordinaire, parlant toûjours des affaires d'Angleterre avec Mad la princesse El[le], ces malheureuses Affaires lui tinrent fort au Coeur et la lettre de la Reine par la quelle SM Refusoit tout plat de ne vouloir avoir aucqu'un[18] de la Maison en Angleterre tant qu'elle vivroit, avoit tellement frappè nòtre bonne Ellectrice que jamais rien ne lui a etè plus sensible, aussi me disoit elle deux jours avant sa mort, cette affaire me rendra asseurement malade j'y succomberay, mais disoit elle, je fairois[19] imprimer cette gracieuse lettre pour faire voir a tout le monde que ce n'a pas etè par ma faute, si mes enfans perdent le trois Couronnes[20]. pardonnè[21] cette digression Madame, mais co͞me selon mon opinion c'est la la[22] malheureuse Cause Exterieure de la perde[23] irreparable que nous avons faite, je ne puis en omettre le Circonstances[24] après donc que Mad[e] l 'Ellectrice eut marchè quelque tems ainsi, s'entretenant avec Mad[e] la princesse Elect[le], et que je m'etois tenus[25] elloignée de quelque[s] pas par Respect SAE[le] se tourna vers moy, me donna sa main avec cette maniere obligente et grasieuse[26] d'ont elle étoit seule Capable, et poursuivoit ainsi son chemin entre Mad[e] la princesse E[le] et moy. elle discouroit de toute sorte de matiere entre autres de la beautè de Madame boush, qui se promenoit avec sa soeur a l'autre bout de l'allèe, et parloit avec cette vivacitè d'Esprit qui lui êtoit si naturele. quand nous etions au millieux[27] du jardin proche de ce[s] petits Cabinets peintes, et que nous eumës traversè l'allèe jusqu'a la premiere fontaine qui est vis a vis de la chambre de fr[le] pellnits, Mad l'Ellectrice Comenca a Chanceler et a marcher come si elle etoit fort lasse. Mad[e] la princesse qui s'en aperceut aussi bien que moy, lui demandoit si elle se portoit mal, mais elle

21. SOPHIE, GRÄFIN ZU SCHAUMBURG-LIPPE 81

Electress of Braunschweig-Lüneburg, Sophie* of the Palatinate] every day.[12] It seems that everyone is dead for me, and I am so forlorn that I am myself astonished how I am able to bear so much grief without falling ill; I am languishing and visibly wasting away. Finally, my dear Raugravine, you are the only one in the world capable of judging how much I am suffering, because you yourself feel the effects;[13] you permit[14] me to speak with you about our shared misfortune, so I will not spare you, since I also find some consolation in a report that gives new vent to my tears. You have no doubt been informed[15] of everything that has happened since your departure, but since you have directed me[16] to let you know all the details of the sudden death of our very dear electress, I am going to obey you, and therefore tell you, madame, that the very same day you departed, which was a Wednesday, Her Serene Highness complained towards evening of a bad headache. However, she made two laps[17] of the garden and dined as usual. As she had perspired a lot upon awakening the following day, we tried to persuade her to stay in bed, but she wanted nothing to do with it. However, when she was at table, she was so ill with her abdominal colic that it was necessary to put her to bed. We found her in this state at about six o'clock in the evening. I had the good fortune to persuade her to take two enemas in a row, which relieved her so much that she got up the very same evening in order to dine with Monseigneur the Elector [Georg Ludwig* of Braunschweig-Lüneburg]. The following day, which was the fatal Friday, the 8th of last month, Her Electoral Highness fared so well that not only did she dine in public, but when we arrived in the evening around the hour of the promenade, she expressed a strong desire to go for a walk, although the weather was a bit overcast and threatened rain. She refused the porters and walked as usual, speaking always of the affairs of England with Madame the Electoral Princess [Caroline* of Brandenburg-Ansbach]. These unhappy affairs concerned her greatly, and the letter of the queen [Anne of Great Britain], in which Her Majesty flatly refused to consent to having anyone[18] from the House [of Hanover] in England as long as she lived, had shocked our good electress so much that nothing had ever been more grievous to her. She also told me two days before her death, 'This affair will surely make me ill; I will be overcome by it.' 'But,' she said, 'I would have[19] this gracious letter published in order to show everyone that I am not to blame if my children lose the three crowns.'[20] Pardon[21] this digression, madame, but as that,[22] in my opinion, is the unfortunate exterior cause of the irreparable loss[23] that we have suffered, I cannot omit the circumstances.[24] Then after Madame the Electress had walked that way for some time, talking with Madame the Electoral Princess, and I had kept[25] myself a few steps away out of respect, Her Electoral Highness turned toward me, gave me her hand in that obliging and gracious[26] manner of which she alone was capable, and thus continued on her way between Madame the Electoral Princess and myself. She was chatting about all sorts of things, among others, of the beauty of Madame Boush, who was walking with her sister at the other end of the lane, and she spoke with that vivacity of spirit that was so natural to her. When we were in the middle[27] of the garden, near those small painted closets, and we had crossed the lane as far as

lui Repondit avec un grand soupir, montrant sur son estomach c'est icy, c'est icy. Je pris la libertè de lui proposer de vouloir se retirer dans un de ces Cabinets pour d'y reposer un peu, et pour la soulager en ouvrant un peut le laset[28], mais SAE nous montra que son Corps de jupe n'étoit point du tout serrè, et nous accorda la priere de vouloir se retirer dans son appartement, come en effect elle tachoit de faire. il Commençoit a pleuvoir bien fort ce qui fit deserter tout le monde, de sorte que Madam^e la princesse Ellectora^{le} et moy etions de toutes les Dames les seules qui avoient l'honneur d'assister cette Auguste princesse a sa derniere heure, qui arriva un moment après. car a peine pouvoit elle faire dix pas pour aller vers le Cabinet le plus proche que SAE nous dit Je me trouve tres mal, donne-moy[29] vôtre main. J'envoyois d'abord Chiarafan pour chercher du secours et de la poudre d'or. Mon^r [31] Campen Courut pour appeller les porteurs. Mon^r Wind, qui restoit seul avec nous, vouloit faire la même chose, mais je l'en empechois, voyant que Mad^e l'Ellectrice n'en pouvoit plus et qu'elle tomboit toute evanouïe entre nos bras. elle devint si pessante que nous etions obligès de la laisser aller doucement a terre, quand Mr Wind l'eut pris sous un bras. Je pris mon Couteau et lui ouvris le lasset[32] et tout ce qui pouvoit la serrer, mais quand je vins lui detacher ses Coiffes et sa steinkerken je m'aperceus qu'elle etoit toute noiratre et come elle fit un soupir avec un certain ton qui marquoit l'angoise de son Cœur je vis d'abord qu'elle se mouroit. Je me jettois[33]a terre et la pris sur mes genoux. Mad^e la princesse m'assistoit en tout cela et nous joignime[34] nos prieres pour recomender son ame a Dieux[35] Nous observame[36] un moment apres, qu'une paleur mortelle Couvroit son visage et quoy qu'elle ouvrit les yeux a demy ce n'étoit que pour nous laisser voir que leur lustre étoit eteint, et que cet Esprit qui les avoit si bien seut animer, avoit quittè son illustre demeure. Jugè Madame ce que nous devinme[37] nos Cris et nos larmes remplirent tout le jardin, et attirerent peu a peu toute la Cour. On nous apporta ce que nous avions demandè mais trop tard. Cependant on essaya tout. J'avois beau dire que nôtre chere Ellectrice n'étoit plus en Etat d'être secourue. On ne pouvoit se l'imaginer, et on étoit encore une heure après la tourmenter, pour la faire revenir. On lui tira du sang des bras et des pièz[38] il en sortit quelque goute. L'un se flatoit qu'elle avoit quelque reste de pouls, l'autre que sa Couleur se changeoit, qu'un miroir qu'on avoit tenu devant sa bouche avoit rendu temoignage, qu'il lui restoit un peu d'halaine[39]. enfin tout cela ne servoit que de faire voir Combien l'on souhaitoit de pouvoir conserver ses precieux jours. Mais la Providence l'avoit ordonè autrement et il avoit plut[40] a la sagesse divine d'arreter cette Auguste Carriere qui bien que longue avoit etè trop glorieuse pour en voir la fin, sans un sensible chagrein. Jamais il ne s'est veut[41] une mort plus douce ny plus heureuse, puis que cette Chere et bonne princesse n'en sentit point les atteintes, et etoit toujours dans une situation a pouvoir mourir tranquillement. Vôtre Resolution Madame quoy que tres Raisonable ne laisse pas que de me donner du Chagrein, car il m'est trop sensible de ne vous plus voir en cette Cour, ou tout les object[42] servent a me degoûter davantage de nôtre maniere de vivre depuis la mort de ma chere Ellectrice. Je Reve jour et nuit au moyens de me

the first fountain that is opposite the apartment of Fraulein Pöllnitz [Henriette Charlotte von Pöllnitz*], Madame the Electress began to stagger and walk as if she were very tired. Madame the Princess, who noticed it as well as I, asked her if she was feeling ill; but she replied with a deep sigh, pointing to her stomach: 'It is here, it is here.' I took the liberty of suggesting that she please retire to one of the closets in order to rest there a bit and to relieve her by loosening her staylace[28] a little, but Her Electoral Highness showed us that her stays did not squeeze at all, and she granted us the request that she please retire to her apartment, as she indeed tried to do. It began to rain very hard, which caused everyone to leave, so that Madame the Electoral Princess and I were, of all the ladies, the only ones who had the honour of assisting this august princess in her last hour, which arrived a moment later. For she was scarcely able to take ten steps toward the nearest closet before Her Electoral Highness said to us, 'I am very ill, give me[29] your hand.' I immediately sent Chiarafan[30] to seek help and gold powder. Mr.[21] Campen ran to call the porters. Mr. Wind, who alone stayed with us, wanted to do the same, but I prevented him, seeing that Madame the Electress was exhausted and was collapsing in a dead faint between our arms. She became so heavy that we had to let her fall gently to the ground when Mr. Wind had taken her under an arm. I took my knife and opened her staylace[32] and everything that could squeeze her, but when I went to undo her hair and her neckcloth, I noticed that she was quite blackish, and as she sighed with a certain tone that indicated the anguish of her heart, I saw at first sight that she was dying. I threw myself[33] on the ground and took her upon my knees. Madame the Princess assisted me in all that, and we joined together[34] our prayers to commend her soul to God.[35] A moment later we noticed[36] that a deathly pallor covered her face, and although her eyes were open halfway, this only allowed us to see that their luster was extinguished and that this spirit, which had known how to enliven them so well, had abandoned its illustrious abode. Consider, madame, what became of us.[37] Our cries and our tears filled the whole garden and drew in, little by little, the entire court. They brought us what we had requested, but too late. Nevertheless, they tried everything. I said in vain that our dear electress was beyond help. They could not comprehend it, and they were still an hour later tormenting her in order to revive her. They bled her from the arms and feet.[38] A few drops came out of them. One claimed that she had a pulse, another that her colour was changing, that a mirror they held in front of her mouth had provided evidence that a little breath[39] remained in her. In the end, all that only served to show how much they hoped to be able preserve her precious days. But Providence had decreed otherwise, and it had been pleasing[40] to the divine wisdom to bring to an end this august life, which, though long, had been too glorious for one to witness its end without acute grief. Never has there been[41] a gentler death, nor one more fortunate, since this dear and good princess did not feel its ravages, and she was always in a position to be able to die peacefully. Your resolution, to see you any longer in this court, where all objects[42] serve to disgust me more about our way of life since the death of my dear

tirer de cett galere les menaces,[43] réiterées de la Cour de viene et la necessitè d'eloigner peut etre dans peu mes fils d'icy m'y aidera a la fin. So muß mein unglück mir zu etwas dienen. Jay rendu les cheveux de feu nôtre Ellec^{tce} de tres glorieuse memoire, a nôtre princesse Ellectorl^e, qui m'a ordonè de vous en remercier de sa part. SAS vous en est sensiblement obligè, et vous asseure qu'elle aura soins des Eglises protestantes Reformèes, et les protegera autant qu'il sera en son pourvoir. Come SAS a temoignez,[44] elle mème a vos ministres qui ont ètè admis tout deux a l'audiance.[45] Je n'en puis plus ma tres chere Raugrave la tète me tourne car mon affliction a etè renouvellèe de tous les changement[s] que j[']ay trouvè[46] icy. Je loge près de vôtre appartement. Mad^e la princesse Ellec^e avec Mongr le prince logent dans l'orangerie vis a vis de f^{rl} pellnitz, et l'on mange dans la grande sa[l]le, ainsi on est tout depaisè. Cependant nôtre chere Ellectrice me manque par tout, et il n'y a point d'endroit icy ou jay veut cette Incomparable princesse qui ne r'ouvre[48] une playe qui n'est pas encore fermè.[49] Je finis ma chere Raugrave en vous Conjurant de vouloir me Conserver l'honneur de vôtre amitiè[50] et d'etre bien persuadè que je suis avec la tentresse[51] du monde la plus sincere et la plus parfaite

Madame,

vôtre tres humble
et tres obeissante serv~
La Comtesse de Buque
bourge

P S

[...]

21. SOPHIE, GRÄFIN ZU SCHAUMBURG-LIPPE   85

electress. I dream day and night of a way to extract myself from this nightmare of threats,[43] repeated by the court of Vienna, and the necessity of perhaps shortly sending my sons away from here will finally assist me in that. Thus must my misfortune be of some use to me. I have returned the hair of our late electress of most glorious memory to our electoral princess, who has ordered me to thank you on her behalf. Her Serene Highness is deeply grateful to you for it and assures you that she will take care of the reformed Protestant churches and protect them as far as it will be in her power. As Her Serene Highness has made known,[44] she even has your ministers, who have both been granted an audience.[45] I can take no more, my dearest Raugravine; my head is spinning, for my affliction has been revived by all the changes that I have found[46] here. I am staying near your apartment. Madame the Electoral Princess and Monseigneur the Prince are staying in the orangery,[47] across from Fraülein Pöllnitz, and we eat in the grand hall, so we are completely disoriented. But I miss our dear electress everywhere, and there is no place here where I have seen this incomparable princess that does not reopen[48] a wound that is still not closed.[49] I end, my dear Raugravine, by imploring you to please preserve for me the honour of your friendship[50] and to be entirely convinced that I am with the most sincere and complete affection[51] in the world,

madame,

your very humble
and very obedient servant,
the Countess of Bückeburg

P S

[...]

---

[1] Eight quarto sides in Johanne Sophie's hand. I wish to thank Countess Madeline Degenfeld for graciously supplying me with a copy of this letter from her family archive. Previously published in Klopp IX 457–62 (excerpt). I have omitted the postscript to the letter.

[2] Reading 'Comme vous savez' for 'Come savez'.

[3] Here and hereafter, reading 'Raugravine' for 'Raugrave'.

[4] Reading 'quelque chose' for 'quelques chose'.

[5] Reading 'chagrin' for 'Chagrein'.

[6] Here and hereafter, reading 'perte' for 'perde'.

[7] Reading 'ç'auroit' for 's'auroit'.

[8] Reading 'les Esprits' for 'les Esprit'.

[9] Reading 'quelquefois' for 'quelfois'.

[10] Reading 'de nouveau' for 'de nouveaux'.

[11] Reading 'plongés' for 'plongè'.

[12] Reading 'tous les jours' for 'tous le jours'.

[13] Reading 'ressentez' for 'resentè'.

[14] Reading 'permettez' for 'permettè'.

[15] Here and hereafter, reading 'su' for 'suet'.

Caroline* of Brandenburg-Ansbach, Electoral Princess of Braunschweig-Lüneburg to Baroness Mary Cowper

Letter to my Mother from the Princess Electoral of Hannover

Herenhausen le 13 Jul. [1714]

Madame

Je connois trop la part que vous prenez en tout ce qui regarde une famille pour laquelle milord et vous avez temoigné tant d'amitié et constance pour ne pas douter comme vous me l'avez marqué obligement que vous ressentirez avec nous la perte de la plus grande Princesse et de la meilleure mere de nos jours; C'etoit une malheur a la

22. CAROLINE OF BRANDENBURG-ANSBACH TO BARONESS COWPER   87

[16] Reading 'm'ordonnez' for 'm'ordonnè'.

[17] Reading 'tours' for 'tour'.

[18] Reading 'aucun' for 'aucqu'un'.

[19] Reading 'ferais' for 'fairois'.

[20] Reading 'las trois couronnnes' for 'le trois Couronnes'. The 'three crowns' were those of Great Britain, Ireland, and France. The French throne was first claimed by Edward III in 1340 and was subsequently claimed by all English sovereigns until the beginning of the nineteenth century.

[21] Reading 'pardonnez' for 'pardonnè'.

[22] Reading 'c'est là la' for 'c'est la la'.

[23] Reading 'perte' for 'perde'.

[24] Reading 'les circumstances' for 'le Circumstances'.

[25] Reading 'tenue' for 'tenus'.

[26] Reading 'obligeante et gracieuse' for 'obligente et grasieuse'.

[27] Reading 'milieu' for 'millieux'.

[28] Reading 'lacet' for 'laset'. Klopp mistranscribes 'laset' as 'corset' (see Klopp IX 460).

[29] I follow Klopp in reading 'donne-moy' as 'donnez-moy' (Klopp IX 460).

[30] In the letter that she sent to Mary Cowper* concerning the death of the dowager electress, Johanne Sophie reports 'sending soon away a footman to fetch some hungary water & Gold Powder' (see document 16, p. 59), so it would appear that 'Chiarafan' was the name of this footman.

[31] Klopp mistranscribes 'Mon' as 'Mad' (see Klopp IX 460).

[32] Reading 'lacet' for 'lasset'. Klopp mistranscribes 'lasset' as 'corset' (see Klopp IX 460).

[33] Klopp mistranscribes 'me jettois' as 'me jetay' (see Klopp IX 461).

[34] Reading 'joignîmes' for 'joignime'.

[35] Reading 'Dieu' for 'Dieux'.

[36] Reading 'observâmes' for 'observame'.

[37] Reading 'devînmes' for 'devinme'.

[38] Reading 'pieds' for 'pièz'.

[39] Reading 'haleine' for 'halaine'.

[40] Reading 'plu' for 'plut'.

[41] Reading 's'est vue' for s'est veut'.

[42] Reading 'tous les objets' for 'tout les object'.

[43] Reading 'cette galère des menaces' for 'cett galere les menaces'.

[44] Reading 'Comme SAS a témoigné' for 'Come SAS a temoignez'.

[45] Klopp omits the last six sentences without notice (see Klopp IX 461–2).

[46] Reading 'trouvés' for 'trouvè'.

[47] That is, the orangery at Herrenhausen.

[48] Reading 'rouvre' for 'r'ouvre'.

[49] Reading 'fermée' for 'fermè'.

[50] Klopp omits everything following 'amitiè' (Klopp IX 462).

[51] Reading 'tendresse' for 'tentresse'.

22. Caroline* of Brandenburg-Ansbach, Electoral Princess of Braunschweig-Lüneburg, to Baroness Mary Cowper*[1]

Letter to my Mother from the Princess Electoral of Hannover

Herrenhausen 13 July [1714]

Madame

I know too well the interest that you take in everything that regards a family for which milord[2] and you have shown so much friendship and loyalty to doubt, as you have kindly told me, that you feel with us the loss of the greatest princess [Dowager Electress of Brandenburg-Lüneburg, Sophie* of the Palatinate] and best mother of

verité qu'il auroit fallue[3] prevoir. La bonne santé, la netété de son Esprit, son humeur egal tout cela nous rassuroit, et a force de souhaiter nous croions feu S.A.E. immortelle. Cette bonne Princesse est mort aussi tranquillement qu'elle a vecu vertueusement. Vous pouvez croire Madame dans quelle abbatement cette perte m'a mise: S. A. E. et dans une parfaite santé se promenant avec moy et parlant avec beaucoup d'animosité et affliction sur de certaines lettres dont je crois Madame que vous auroit conoissance elle tombe morte entre mes bras, et il ne se trouva dans ce moment personne avec elle que la Countesse de Lippe un gentil-homme et moy. J'ay eu toutes les peines du monde a me remettre, et les Eaux de Pyrmont ont enfin fait cette effet. Je n'ay pas manqué de faire vos compliments a S. A. E. M[r] L'Electeur et a M[r] son fils le P. E. qui m'ont chargé de vous assurer Madame comme aussi milord de leurs tres parfaite reconnoissance, on est si persuadé de vous et de milord que rien ne vous pour[r]a changer pour une famille qui est tout de vos amis. Milord trouve icy jointe milles assurances de mon souvenir, vous me ferez plaisir de m'ecrire souvent, et de me donner de vos nouvelles qui me sont cheres, estant avec une tendre amitié Madame

votre tres affectionée amie

pour vous servir

Caroline

22. CAROLINE OF BRANDENBURG-ANSBACH TO BARONESS COWPER   89

our time. This was in truth a calamity that should have been[3] foreseen. The good health, the clarity of her mind, her even temper, all that reassured us, and by dint of wishing, we believed Her late Electoral Highness was immortal. This good princess died as peacefully as she lived virtuously. You can imagine, madame, into what despondency this loss has landed me: Her Electoral Highness, while both walking with me in perfect health and speaking with much animus and affliction about certain letters,[4] of which I believe, madame, you were aware, falls dead in my arms, and at that moment there was no one with her but the Countess of Lippe [Johanne Sophie*, Gräfin (Countess) zu Schaumburg-Lippe], a gentleman,[5] and I. I have had the utmost difficulty in recovering myself, and the waters of Pyrmont* have finally had this effect. I did not fail to pay your respects to His Electoral Highness the Elector [Georg Ludwig* of Braunschweig-Lüneburg] and his son, the electoral prince [Georg August* of Braunschweig-Lüneburg], who have entrusted me to assure you, madame, as well as milord, of their most complete gratitude; they are convinced that nothing will be able to change you and milord for a family that is entirely one of your friends. Milord may find here included a thousand assurances of my remembrance; you will please me by writing often and by passing on your news, which is dear to me, being with a loving friendship, madame,

your very affectionate friend

to serve you

Caroline

[1] HALS D/EP F229 16–17. Not previously published. This is a copy of a letter from the Electoral Princess Caroline to Baroness (later Countess) Mary Cowper made by Mary's daughter, Lady Sarah Cowper. Although it is short on details, I have included this letter here because it is the only surviving letter of which I am aware in which Caroline describes the circumstances surrounding the death of the Dowager Electress of Braunschweig-Lüneburg, Sophie* of the Palatinate, which occurred on Friday 8 June 1714 in the garden at Herrenhausen*. For a more expansive account of the details surrounding Sophie's death, see the letters of Johanne Sophie*, Gräfin (Countess) zu Schaumburg-Lippe, to Countess Mary Cowper and Raugravine Palatine Louise* (respectively, documents 16 and 21).

[2] That is, Mary's husband, William Cowper (1665–1723), who was appointed the first High Lord Chancellor of Great Britain under Queen Anne (1707), a position he resigned in 1710. After Georg Ludwig* of Braunschweig-Lüneburg succeeded to the throne as George I, he reappointed Cowper Lord High Chancellor in 1714.

[3] Reading 'il aurait fallu' for 'il auroit fallue'.

[4] That is, the letters from Queen Anne to the Dowager Electress Sophie, the Elector Georg Ludwig, and the Electoral Prince Georg August* (see, documents 12, 13, and 14, respectively).

[5] Identified in Johanne Sophie's letter of 12 July 1714 to Raugravine Palatine Louise* as a Mr. Wind (see document 21, p. 83).

90   23A. CHAMBERLAYNE TO LEIBNIZ

23a. John Chamberlayne* to Leibniz[1]

Petty France Westm[r]
27 July 1714[2]

Most Honor'd S[r]

I have already acknowledged the great honor of your Letter of the 28 April 1714 n. s. from Vienna,[3] but, as I told you then, I did not pretend to have Answer'd it fully til I had procur'd the Resolution of the R. Society about it, which I send you here inclos'd, together with a Copy of a Letter from D[r] Keill,[4] & a little book writ, by that gentleman relating to the Difference between S[r] Isaac Newton & you S[r], of which I am forced to say: <u>Non nostrum est Tantas Componere lites,</u>[5] & therefore humbly desiring you to accept of my Good will in that Affair, subscribe myself with utmost Passion & Truth

Honor'd S[r]

Your most Devoted Humble Servant

John Chamberlayne

[1] LBr. 149 Bl. 15r. Letter as sent: one quarto side in Chamberlayne's hand. Previously published in NC VI 158–9.

[2] That is, 7 August 1714 NS.

[3] For the draft of Leibniz's letter of 28 April 1714 (dated 21 April 1714), see document 7. For Chamberlayne's initial response to that letter, see document 20.

[4] For the resolution of the Royal Society, see document 23b; for the copy of Keill's letter, see document 23c.

[5] 'It is not for us to settle such great disputes,' an adaptation of Virgil, *Eclogues* III, 108: *Non nostrum inter vos tantas componere lites.*

23b. Extract from the Journal of the Royal Society[1]

Extract from the Journal of
the Royal Society

May 20th 1714.[2]

The Translation of Mons. Leibnitz' Letter to M[r]. Chamberlayne produced the last Meeting was read.[3]

It was not judged proper (since this Letter was not directed to them) for the Society to concern themselves therewith, nor were they desired so to do. But that if any person had any Material Objecon [Objection] to ye Commercium [Epistolicum]*, or to the Report of the Comēe [Committee], it might be considered at any time.

[1] LBr. 149 Bl. 27r. This extract was enclosed in Chamberlayne's letter to Leibniz of 27 July 1714 (7 August 1714 NS) (document 23a). Enclosure as sent: one octavo side in secretary's hand. Previously published in NC VI 159.

[2] That is, 31 May 1714 NS.

[3] For this translation, which was prepared by Newton himself, see NC VI 105–6. For my translation of the draft of Leibniz's letter, see document 7.

Benedictus Andreas Caspar de Nomis to Leibniz

Hᵣ le 19: d'Aoust 1714:

Monsieur

Quoy que Je n'aye pas reçeu Monsieur depuis quelque tems l'honneur de Vos lettres, et que celon le bruit commun vous deviéz estre en chemin pour nous venir trouver, Je ne veux pas laisser de vous ecrire ces deux mots pour vous donner la nouvelle de la mort de la reyne de la Grande Bretaigne arrivee le matin du 12 de cè Mois entre 7. et 8: heures: Le jour auparavant Elle avoit estée surprise d'un Accident qu'on ne Nomme pas Appoplexia mais qui la rendoit immobile et sans connoissence, on eut recours aux remedes et de là à quelque tems Elle reprist l'usage de la parole qu'Elle avoit perdüe, dans cette consternation. My Lord d'Oxwort ne laissa pas de se presenter pour luy remettre le Baton de Tresorier, que S. M. reçeut avec peine, et le donnà incontinent au düc de Shorusbery: Je dis avec peine parce qu'elle n'avoit pas la force de lever le Bras: Le Lendemain venü, le mal se redoubla et Elle rendit l'esprit entre les 7 et huit heures dü matin ainsi que J'ay eu l'honneur de Vous dire; On songea d'abord au quid agendum, on redoubla les Gardes par la Ville, et on assembla le Parlemᵗ qu'à pleines Voix ordonna qu'on proclameroit Nostre Le Sᵐᵉ Maistre pour Roy ce qui füt fait incontinent, avec des grandes acclamations de joye

23c. Copy of a letter from John Keill* to John Chamberlayne*[1]

Copy of a Letter from Dr Keill
to Mr Chamberlayne Dat. 20 July 1714[2]

I have sent you the Inclosed according to my Principles and find by it how much reason I had for what I before asserted. There were but 10 of them printed here but they are to be reprinted in Holland, and if Mr Leibniz makes any more Noise, I will stil give the world a greater knowledge of his Merits & Candor   I am

S^r

Your very humble Servt

John Keill

P.S.[3]

I am almost asham'd to send to the Honorable Mr Leibnitz the Copy of such a Harsh Letter, had I not thought it my Duty to hide nothing from him in this Affair &c.

J. C.

---

[1] LBr. 149 Bl. 27v–28r. This was enclosed in Chamberlayne's letter to Leibniz of 27 July (7 August NS) 1714 (document 23a). Enclosure as sent: one octavo side in secretary's hand and 0.5 octavo sides in Chamberlayne's hand.

[2] That is, 31 July 1714 NS.

[3] Chamberlayne added the P.S. to Keill's note in his own hand.

24. Benedictus Andreas Caspar de Nomis* to Leibniz[1]

Hanover the 19th of August 1714

Sir

Although I have not received the honour of your letters for some time, sir, and although according to the general rumor you must be on your way to visit us, I did not want to put off writing you this short note to give you the news of the death of the Queen of Great Britain, which occurred the morning of the 12th of this month between 7 and 8 o'clock. The day before she had been overtaken by a mishap that they do not call apoplexy, but which rendered her immobile and unconscious; they resorted to medicines, and sometime later she regained the ability to speak, which she had lost in that consternation. My Lord Oxford [Robert Harley*] did not fail to appear in order to return to her the staff of treasurer, which Her Majesty accepted with difficulty and gave it at once to the Duke of Shrewsbury: I say 'with difficulty' because she did not have the strength to lift her arm. When the next day arrived, the suffering intensified, and she gave up the ghost between 7 and 8 o'clock in the morning in the way I have had the honour of telling you. At first they thought about what to do; they increased the guards on the city and assembled the parliament, which gave a full-throated order that our most serene master would be proclaimed

de tout le Peuple, et l'aprèz diné[2] on comançà de prester le serment de fidelité entre les mains de Mr Baron de Bothmer Ministre Plenipotentier pour celá etc. On donna des ordres tres rigoureux dans tous les Ports de ne laisser debarquer qui que ce soit de Barques ou Vaisseaux Etrangers, et à l'Admiral d'equipper une flotte de 100: Vaisseaux de guerre pour aller Chercher leur Roy: Mr Kreggs füt deputé pour venir porter cette nouvelle à S. A. E. que 29. des Seigneurs les plus qualifiéz avoient signée avec des protestations d'obeissance et de respect les plus soumises, et on trouva parmy un si grand Peuple aprez tant des Contradictions qu'il n'y a pas un seul qui aye osé se declarer pour le Pretendant, au contraire ils declarent tous d'avoir estés[4] contraints de faire des fausses demarches pour plaire à la Reyne qui ne vouloit pas cette succession, mais qu'eux ont toujours eu le Coeur pour la Maison d'Hannover et qu'ils sont ravuys[5] d'estre delivréz de leurs Contrainte: My Lord Stradfort a d'abord ecrit icy pour reçevoir des ordres et des Instructions de son nouveau Maitre. Les autres Ministres en feront de mesme, et S. M. se prepare à partir dans dix ou douze jours au plus tard que la Flotte serà à la Rade de Hollande pour le prendre. Le Prince de Wallis accompagnerà S. M., et la Princesse son Epouse avec les Princesses ses filles les suyvront dans trois ou quatre semaines d'icy: Mr de Berenstorff et M^r le President sont nomméz pour passer avec S. M. in Engleterre, mais ils retourneront au Pais des ce'que[7] les Affaires seront dans le train qu'elles doivent estre et on croit que Mr de Berenstorff serà declaré Statthalter du Pais: Mg^r le duc Ernest a enuye[8] de passer aussi in Engleterre et il semble refuser les offres que le Roy luy fait du Gouvernement^t: de l'Electorat de sorte que nous allons rester dans l'affliction et dans un' affreuse solitude par la perte que nous ferons de tous nos Maitres à la reserve du Prince Fritz, que nous gardons pour gage de la sourveraineté: Voilà Monsieur des revolutions bien surprenantes, si elles estoient arrivées avant la signature de la paix de Rastatt, la France auroit tenu un'autre langage mais presentem^t Je crois que nous sommes trop avancéz pour pouvoir reculer. Il est vray que le Traitté de Commerce n'est pas encor signé et qu'il y a la paix avec l'Espagne à traitter, cependant Je ne sçay pas dans quelle intelligence on soit à present avec la Cour de Vienne, &. Je vous demande pardon de mon importunité, et quoy que Je ne doute point que vous n'en ayéz deja reçeu la nouvelle, Je ne puis pourtant laisser de vous mander ces particuliaritez, en Veue de vous marquer mon respect, et l'attachement avec lequel Je suis et seray toujours
Monsieur

Votre tres humble et tres obeiss^t
serviteur
Nomis

king [Georg Ludwig of Braunschweig-Lüneburg] which was done forthwith to shouts of joy from all the people; and after dinner,[2] they began to squeeze the oath of allegiance between the hands of Baron Bothmer,* Plenipotentiary Minister for that purpose, etc. Some very strict orders were given in all the ports not to allow anyone to disembark from foreign boats or vessels, and to the admiral to equip a flotilla of 100 vessels of war to go fetch their king. Mr. [James] Craggs[3] was appointed to come convey the news to His Electoral Highness that 29 of the most important lords had signed [the oath of allegiance] with the most submissive professions of obedience and respect, and among such great people, after so many disputes, not a single one was found who dared to declare himself in favor of the Pretender [James Francis Edward Stuart*]; on the contrary, they all claimed to have been[4] forced to take wrong steps in order to please the queen, who did not want this succession, but that their heart was always for the House of Hanover and that they are delighted[5] to be delivered from their constraint. My Lord Strafford[6] first wrote here in order to receive orders and instructions from his new master. The other ministers will do the same, and His Majesty is getting ready to leave in six or, at the latest, twelve days, when the flotilla will be at the Dutch harbor in order to pick him up. The Prince of Wales [Georg August* of Braunschweig-Lüneburg] will accompany His Majesty, and the princess his wife [Caroline* of Brandenburg-Ansbach], along with the princesses his daughters, will follow them in three or four weeks from now. Mr. Bernstorff* and the president [i.e., the Kammerpräsident Friedrich Wilhelm Görtz*] are appointed to go to England with His Majesty, but they will return to the country as soon as[7] matters are well arranged, and it is believed that Mr. Bernstorff will be declared governor of the country. Monseigneur Duke Ernst [Ernst August II*] is reluctant[8] to go to England, and he seems to reject the offers that the king has made to him of the government of the electorate, so that we will remain in distress and dire loneliness from the loss we will suffer of all our masters, except for Prince Fritz [Friedrich Ludwig*, of Braunschweig-Lüneburg], whom we retain for assurance of sovereignty. There, sir, some very surprising revolutions; if they had happened before the signing of the peace of Rastatt*, France would have changed its tune, but at present I believe that we are too far along to be able to turn back. It is true that the commercial treaty is not yet signed and that there is the peace with Spain to deal with, but I don't know in what collusion they may be at present with the court of Vienna, etc. I beg your pardon for my importunity, and although I do not doubt that you have already received news of it, I am nevertheless not able to omit informing you of these particulars, for the purpose of showing my respect for you and the affection with which I am, and will always be, sir,

your very humble and very obedient servant

Nomis

Leibniz to Andreas Gottlieb von Bernstorff

Monsieur

La nouvelle qui est arrivée icy par des courriers premierement de l'agonie et puis de la mort de la Reine de la Grande Bretagne avec la proclamation de Monseigneur l'Electeur notre maitre pour Roy m'oblige de supplier V. E. de me mettre aux pieds de Sa Majesté et de luy témoigner ma joye, qui m'est commune icy presque avec tout le monde, mais que j'ay avec bien de la raison en un plus haut degré. Cet evenement me fait hâter mon depart pour arriver au plutot aupres de sa personne. Car si je manquois de la trouver en deçà la mer, je serois au desespoir que le bonheur de l'Europe eût eté un malheur pour moy. Cette nouvelle ne guerira pas Middleton de sa maladie, qui luy est venue à ce qu'on dit parce que M. le vicechancellier de l'Empire et autres ministres avoient refusé tout plat d'entrer en matiere avec luy.

M. le prince Eugene partira lundi prochain à ce que M. le duc d'Arenberg et M. le comte de Wakebart viennent de me dire chez le comte de Bonneval ou j'ay disné. Le prince me disoit avanthier qu'il partiroit encore cette semaine, mais la grande nouvelle arrivée avanthier et hier l'a fait differer son depart de quelques jours. Je suis avec respect

Monsieur, de Votre Excellence

le treshumble et tres obéissant

serviteur

Leibniz.

Vienne ce mercredi 22 d'Aoust 1714.

[1] LBr. 697 Bl. 34r–35v. Draft: four folio sides in Nomis's hand. Not previously published.

[2] Reading 'dîner' for 'diné'.

[3] James Craggs the Younger (1686–1721) served, under George I (Georg Ludwig* of Braunschweig-Lüneburg), as Secretary at War (1717–18) and as Secretary of State for the Southern Department (1718–21).

[4] Reading 'd'avoir été' for 'd'avoir estés'.

[5] Reading 'ravis' for 'ravuys'.

[6] That is, Thomas Wentworth (1672–1739), 1st Earl of Strafford. He was First Lord of the Admiralty from 1712 to 1714 and served as one of the Lord Justices who represented George I (Georg Ludwig) prior to his arrival in England.

[7] Reading 'dès que' for 'des ce que'.

[8] Reading 'ennui' for 'enuye'.

25. Leibniz to Andreas Gottlieb von Bernstorff*[1]

[Vienna, 22 August 1714]

Sir

The news that arrived here by couriers, first of the agony and then of the death of the Queen of Great Britain, along with the proclamation of Monseigneur the Elector [Georg Ludwig* of Braunschweig-Lüneburg] our master as king,[2] obligates me to beseech Your Excellency to place me at the feet of His Majesty and bear him witness of my joy, which I share here with nearly everyone, but which I have, with good reason, to a higher degree. This event causes me to hasten my departure in order to arrive at his side as soon as possible. For if I failed to find him on this side of the sea, I would be in despair that the good fortune of Europe had been a misfortune for me. This news will not cure Middleton [Charles Middleton* (1650–1719)] of his illness, which began, according to what is said, because the Imperial Vice Chancellor of the Empire [Friedrich Karl von Schönborn (1674–1746)] and other ministers had flatly refused to negotiate with him.

Prince Eugène* [of Savoy] will depart next Monday according to what the Duke of Arenberg [Léopold Philippe* of Arenberg] and the Count of Wakebart just told me at the home of the Count Bonneval*, where I dined. The prince told me the day before yesterday that he would yet depart this week, but the great news arrived the day before yesterday, and yesterday it caused him to delay his departure a few days. I am with respect

sir, of Your Excellency

the very humble and very obedient

servant

Leibniz.

Vienna this Wednesday 22 August 1714.

[1] The original is presumably lost. Previously published in Doebner 1881, pp. 293–4.

[2] See Nomis's letter to Leibniz of 19 August 1714 (document 24).

Philipp Ludwig Wenzel von Sinzendorff to Johann Caspar von Bothmer

Monsieur

Le voiage de M^r de leibniz, qui veut suivre son Roy jusques en Angleterre, est une occasion trop favorable, pour ne vous pas assurer des mes respects, et de vous temoinger la joie que j'ay, que vous avez eté present a l'heureuse changement qui vient d'arriver dans le Roiaume. Vos bonnes intentions sont si fort connues a l'Empereur, qui se persuade que les affaires generales recevront des influences fort heureuses des vos bons conseils. Sa Majesté a vû partir avec regret Mr de Leibniz, elle souhaite de voir bientot son retour; pour moi Monsieur je vous prié de la continuation de l'honneur de Vôtre amitié, et je suis autant qu'on le sauroit etre

Monsieur

a vienne ce 4 de
9bre 1714

Votre tres humble
et tres obeissant serviteur
le comte de Sinzendorff

Philipp Ludwig Wenzel von Sinzendorff to Friedrich Wilhelm von Görtz

Monsieur

le depart de M^r de leibniz, qui se rend a vôtre cour, a eté une occasion trop favorable pour ne vous pas assurer des mes respects, et vous temoinger la part que je prend a l'avantageuse[2] changement qui vient d'arriver en Angleterre en faveur du Roy vôtre maître. mes intentions vous sont connues de longue main. j'ay eû occasion de renouveler notre amitié a Frankfort. je me flatte que vous continuerez vos bons sentiments, et que vous serez persuadé de l'estime, et de la veneration, que j'ay pour vôtre personne. l'Empereur a laissé partir Mr de Leibniz avec beaucoup de peine. je le goute extraordinairement, et souhaite son retour. je vous prie encore

26. Philipp Ludwig Wenzel von Sinzendorff* to Johann Caspar von Bothmer*[1]

[Vienna, 4 September 1714]

Sir

The journey of Mr. Leibniz, who wishes to follow his king [George I, Georg Ludwig* of Braunschweig-Lüneburg] to England, is too favourable an occasion for me not to pay you my respects and to express the joy I take in your having been present at the happy change that has just taken place in the kingdom. Your good intentions are, of course, well known to the emperor [Karl VI*], who is persuaded that general affairs will be favourably influenced by your good counsels. His Majesty has viewed the parting of Mr. Leibniz with regret; he desires to see his return soon. As for me, sir, I ask you for the continued honour of your friendship, and I am, as much as one could be,

sir,

	your very humble
in Vienna this 4	and very obedient servant
September 1714	the Count of Sinzendorff

[1] LBr. 867 Bl. 8. Letter as sent: two quarto sides in Sinzendorff's hand. Previously published in Klopp XI xx (excerpt). After hearing that Queen Anne had died on 12 August, and hence that the Elector Georg Ludwig* had succeeded to the throne of Great Britain, Leibniz hastened to depart Vienna in the hopes of arriving in Hanover before Georg Ludwig departed for England (see his letter to Bernstorff* of 22 August 1714, document 25). But by the time he arrived in Hanover on Friday 14 September, Georg Ludwig and his son Georg August* had already departed for England; he had missed them by three days. Before he took his leave of Vienna, however, Leibniz had asked Sinzendorff to send two letters to him at Hanover, one for Minister Bothmer, which is the present document, and the other for Minister Görtz* (see document 27). After sending these letters, Sinzendorff notified Leibniz in a letter of 8 September (see document 28).

27. Philipp Ludwig Wenzel von Sinzendorff* to Friedrich Wilhelm von Görtz*[1]

[Vienna, 4 September 1714]

Sir

The departure of Mr. Leibniz, who is travelling to your court, has been too favourable an occasion for me not to pay you my respects and express to you the interest I take in the advantageous[2] change that has just taken place in England in favour of the king [George I, Georg Ludwig* of Braunschweig-Lüneburg], your master. My intentions have long since been known to you. I had the occasion to

une fois, de me conserver l'honneur de vôtre amitie, et je suis avec toute la consideration du monde

de V. E.

a vienne ce 4 de 9bre
1714

le tres humble et
tres obeissant serviteur
comte de Sinzendorff

Philipp Ludwig Wenzel von Sinzendorff* to Leibniz[1]

a vienne ce 8 de 9bre
1714

Vous voiez, que je suis home [*sic*] de parole. Voicy, les deux lettres que vous avez demandé.[2] je crois, qu'elles vous trouveront encore a Hannover, et que vous n'irez pas en Angleterre. a tout hazard je vous envoie pourtant la lettre pour Mr de Bothmar, que vous pouvez luy envoier, si vous n'avez pas occasion de la rendre vous meme. conservez moy votre amitie et je suis tres parfaitement a vous

le comte de Sinzendorff

Leibniz to the Dowager Empress Wilhelmine Amalie of Braunschweig-Lüneburg

Madame

Je n'ay pû executer les ordres de V M imp aupres du Roy, parce ce qu'il etoit déja parti mais j'ay fait connoitre a Mad la princesse Royale, et à Mgr le duc Erneste Auguste, combien V. M. I. prend part à notre bonheur. Tous deux m'ont chargé de marquer leur[s] respects, et leur reconnoissance, et Mad. la princesse Royale témoigne particulierement son attachement et sa veneration. Elle espere de suivre

renew our friendship in Frankfort. I hope that your kind regards will continue and that you will be persuaded of the esteem and veneration that I have for you. The emperor [Karl VI*] very reluctantly allowed Mr. Leibniz to leave. I appreciate him enormously and desire his return. I ask you once more to preserve for me the honour of your friendship, and I am with all the respect in the world

of Your Excellency

the very humble and

in Vienna this 4 September
1714

very obedient servant
Count of Sinzendorff

[1] LBr. 867 Bl. 9r–9v. Letter as sent: two quarto sides in Sinzendorff's hand. Previously published in Klopp XI xx (excerpt). See note 1 in document 26.

[2] Reading 'avantageux' for 'avantageuse'.

28. Philipp Ludwig Wenzel von Sinzendorff* to Leibniz[1]

in Vienna this 8 of September
1714

You see that I am a man of my word. Here are the two letters that you requested[2]. I believe that they will find you still in Hanover and that you will not go to England. Just in case, however, I am sending you the letter for Mr. Bothmer*, which you can send to him if you do not have occasion to deliver it yourself.[3] Preserve your friendship for me and I am most perfectly yours

the Count of Sinzendorff

[1] LBr. 867 Bl. 10r. Letter as sent: one quarto side in Sinzendorff's hand. Previously published in Klopp XI xx. For Leibniz's response, see his letter to Sinzendorff of 20 September 1714 (document 34).

[2] Reading 'demandées' for 'demandé'. These were letters addressed to ministers Bothmer* and Görtz*, for which see, respectively, documents 26 and 27.

[3] Bothmer was already in London, where he was plenipotentiary minister (see Nomis's letter to Leibniz of 19 August 1714, document 24, p. 95).

29. Leibniz to the Dowager Empress Wilhelmine Amalie* of Braunschweig-Lüneburg [1]

[Hanover, 16 September 1714]

Madame

I have not been able to carry out the orders of Your Imperial Majesty with the king [George I, Georg Ludwig* of Braunschweig-Lüneburg], since he had already left [for England], but I have made known to Madame the Royal Princess [Caroline* of Brandenburg-Ansbach, Princess of Wales] and to Monseigneur Duke Ernst

bientôt quand l'Escadre Angloise reviendra. Mais Mgr le Duc a voulu rester icy, quoyque le Roy l'ait sollicité fortement de l'accompagner c'est ce qui m'a surprise.

Si j'avois eu quelque lettre à porter au Roy ou à quelcun de ses Ministres, j'aurois pû le trouver avant son depart, et même encore presentement, si je partois d'abord je le pourrois joindre en Hollande. Je l'aurois fait si j'avois trouvé icy la lettre que M. le Comte de Sinzendorf m'avoit promise pour M. le Baron de Goriz notre president des finances, qui accompagne le Roy; mais il paroist qu'on a changé de sentiment. Je m'en console par la liberté que cela me laisse de faire tout à mon aise.

Le Roy envoyera a Vienne une Ambassade Angloise assez solennelle. Et l'on s'imagine qu'encore celle de l'Empereur fera eclat car on a fort egard à la dignité dans les premieres Ambassades. On croit que le Roy repassera la mer l'été qui vient et qu'une bonne partie de ceux qui l'ont accompagné reviendront avec luy, et resteront icy.

Il seroit à souhaiter que Mgr le Duc Maximilien retournât dans ce pays cy, je crois qu'il y seroit bien mieux qu'à Vienne. Le Testament de Mad. l'Electrice a eté fait sans consulter des jurisconsultes, et les codicilles sont fort informes. Ainsi toute sa derniere volonté paroist douteuse.

On dit que le Roy de prusse y trouve le plus à redire. Tout est encore cacheté. Mais j'espere qu'on s'accommodera a l'amiable. Mgr le Duc Ernaste Auguste m'a dit qu'il est dans une entiere resignation à la volonté du Roy et Mgr le Duc Max paroissoit etre du meme sentiment. Ainsi tout depend maintenant de ce que les deux Rois trouvent bon. Je suis avec devotion de V. M. Imperiale.

à la Majesté de l'Imperatrice

Amalie

à Hannover ce 16 de Septembre

  1714   le tres sousmis et tres

              fidele serviteur

                Leibniz

29. LEIBNIZ TO THE WILHELMINE AMALIE   103

August [Ernst August II* of Braunschweig-Lüneburg] how much Your Imperial Majesty shares in our happiness. Both have entrusted me to express their respects and their gratitude, and Madame the Royal Princess in particular professes her affection and veneration. She hopes to follow [the king and her husband, Georg August*, to England] as soon as the English squadron returns. But Monseigneur the Duke wanted to remain here, although the king strongly urged him to accompany him, which surprised me.

If I had had some letter to carry to the king or to one of his ministers, I would have been able to meet with him before his departure, and even now, if I left immediately, I could still join him in Holland. I would have done it if I had found here the letter that Count von Sinzendorff* had promised for Baron von Görtz*, our president of finances, who is accompanying the king; but it appears that he changed his mind.[2] I console myself about that with the freedom that it allows me to do everything at my convenience.

The king will send a quite formal English embassy to Vienna. And we imagine that the one of the emperor [Karl VI*] will again make a splash, because dignity is highly regarded in first embassies. It is thought that the king will cross the sea again next summer and that a good number of those who have accompanied him will return with him and remain here.

It would be our wish that Monseigneur Duke Maximilian [Maximilian Wilhelm*of Braunschweig-Lüneburg] returned to this country; I believe that he would be much better off here than in Vienna. The testament of Madame the Electress [Dowager Electress of Braunschweig-Lüneburg, Sophie* of the Palatinate] was made without consulting the jurisconsults, and the codicils are very informal. Thus her entire last will appears doubtful.

It is said that the King of Prussia [Friedrich Wilhelm I*] takes the most exception to it. Everything is still sealed. But I hope they will come to terms amicably. Monseigneur Duke Ernst August told me that he is entirely resigned to the will of the king, and Monseigneur Duke Max appeared to be of the same sentiment. Thus everything now depends on what the two kings find proper. I am with devotion for Your Imperial Majesty
To the majesty of the Empress
Amalie
in Hanover this 16 September
    1714   the most submissive and most
                    faithful servant
                       Leibniz

---

[1] LBr. F 24 Bl. 20r. Draft: one folio side. Previously published, in Klopp XI 8–9.

[2] Before he took his leave of Vienna, Leibniz had asked Sinzendorff to send two letters to him at Hanover, one for Minister Bothmer*and the other for Minister Görtz*; both of these letters did eventually reach Leibniz at Hanover (documents 26 and 27). After sending these letters, Sinzendorff notified Leibniz in a letter of 8 September (document 28), to which Leibniz responded on 20 September (document 34).

Leibniz to Charlotte Elisabeth von Klenk

Hannover ce 16 Sept 1714

à Mlle de Klenck

Mademoiselle

Je m'acquite de la promesse que je vous ay donnée d'ecrire d'abord quoyque je n'aye encor veu que les personnes que j'ay recontrees hier à Herrnhausen, ou il ne reste plus que Mad. la princesse Royale et Mon^sgr le Duc Erneste Auguste. Ce dernier demeyrera[2] encor icy, mais Mad. la princesse Royale va suivre dans peu quoyque le temps pour cela ne soit pas encor fixé. Le Roy etoit parti Mardi matin. Si je l'avois voulu suivre d'abord je l'aurois encore trouvé en Hollande sans doute. Car le vent n'est pas asses favorable pour passer a mer. Mais je n'ay point de raison de tant courir, et ma santé me vaut mieux que les autres interests aussi l'ay je menagée en voyageant. Je me suis arreté un peu à Dresde, à Leipzig à Zeiz et à Wolfenbutel et graces à Dieu je me suis trouvé aussi bien en arrivant à Hannover que je l'etois en partant de vienne. Mons. de Huldenberg vous aura communiqué la liste de ceux qui accompagnent le Roy, mais on ne sait pas qui en restera en Angleterre, car on se flatte que le Roy repassera la mer l'eté qui vient, et alors on decidera qui devra fixer en Angleterre.

Il n'y a que Madame la Baronne de Goriz qui ait accompagné son epous, et Madame de Kielmanseck a suivi hier le sien, qu'elle croit attraper encor en deçà de la mer. J'ay rencontré en chemin deux Ministres publiques qui se seroient battus s'ils s'etoient rencontres eux memes, un etoit Mons. de Goriz de Holstein, qui ira (dit-on) jusqu'au Roy de suede, et l'autre etoit M. de Weiberg Ministre de Dannemarc qui retournoit à vienne. J'ay trouvé icy Mademoiselle de Pelniz, qui retient la pension que Madame l'Electrice luy donnoit. Je vous supplie de rendre la cyjointe a la Majesté de l'Imperatrice Amalie. Je suis avec respect

Mad^lle   votre

30. Leibniz to Charlotte Elisabeth von Klenk*[1]

Hanover this 16 September 1714

Mlle Klenk

Mademoiselle

I am fulfilling the promise that I gave to write to you at once, although I have still seen only the persons that I met yesterday at Herrenhausen*, where there remains no other than Madame the Royal Princess [Caroline* of Brandenburg-Ansbach, Princess of Wales] and Monseigneur Duke Ernst August [II]*. The latter will still remain[2] here, but Madame the Royal Princess will soon follow [her husband Georg August* and King Georg Ludwig* to England], although the time for that is not yet determined. The king left Tuesday afternoon.[3] If I had wanted to follow him immediately, I could doubtless have still met with him in Holland. For the wind is not favorable enough to go to sea. But I have no reason to rush so much, and my health is worth more to me than other concerns, so I took care of it while travelling. I stopped awhile at Dresden, at Leipzig, at Zeitz, and at Wolfenbüttel, and thanks to God I found myself as well upon arriving in Hanover as I was upon departing from Vienna. Mr. Huldenberg[4] probably sent you the list of those who are accompanying the king, but we do not know which of them will remain in England; for it is expected that the king will cross the sea again next summer, and then it will be decided who is to be established in England. There is only Madame the Baroness Görtz who accompanied her husband [Friedrich Wilhelm Görtz*], and yesterday Madame [Sophie Charlotte] Kielmansegg* followed hers, whom she thinks she will catch again short of the sea. On the way I encountered two public ministers who would have been fighting if they had met; one was Mr. Görtz of Holstein[5], who will go (it is said) all the way to the King of Sweden [Karl XII of Sweden], and the other was Mr. Weiberg, minister from Denmark, who was returning to Vienna.[6] I found Mademoiselle [Henriette Charlotte von] Pöllnitz* here; she retains the pension that Madame the Electress [Dowager Electress of Braunschweig–Luneburg, Sophie* of the Palatinate] gave her. Pray deliver the attachment to the Majesty of the [Dowager] Empress [Wilhelmine] Amalie*.

Mademoiselle your

---

[1] LBr. F 24 Bl. 20v. Draft: 0.7 folio pages in Leibniz's hand. Not previously published.

[2] Reading 'demeurera' for 'demeyrera'.

[3] That is, 11 September 1714.

[4] That is, Daniel Erasmi Huldenberg, the Hanoverian ambassador to Vienna.

[5] That is, Georg Heinrich Görtz, who was the cousin of Friedrich Wilhelm Görtz*. He did indeed enter the service of Karl XII of Sweden in 1714 and remained in his service until 1718.

[6] Leibniz alludes to the fact that Denmark was a member of the coalition, headed by Peter the Great* of Russia, fighting against Sweden in the Great Northern War (1700–21).

Leibniz to the Georg August, Prince of Wales

Hannover ce 17 de Sept. 1714
Monseigneur

A Sa Serenité Royale
Mon[sgr] le prince de Galles
prince Electoral de Bronsvic

A peine Votre Serenité Royale étoit partie avec le Roy, que je suis arrivé icy. Je n'ay pas osé courir apres, car quoyque j'eusse peut etre pû dire plusieurs particularités qui n'auroient pas eté desagreables, principalement sur la joye que l'Empereur et toutes les personnes imperiales avec les principaux Ministres de la Cour de vienne ont temoignée sur le grand evenement qui a tiré l'Europe d'affaires pour long temps, comme je l'espere, cela ne m'a pas paru assez important pour m'exposer d'avantage à un voyage de poste dans la saison qui commence à devenir rude; et j'ay pû supposer, qu'on en étoit informé d'ailleurs. Et quant à mes interests particuliers, j'ay crû que je me pouvois fier à la bonté et à la justice du Roy: quoyque j'aye eté surpris d'entendre de Madame la princesse Royale (qui m'a conservé ses bonnes graces, las quelles sont d'un si grand prix pour moy avec celles de Votre Serenité Royale) que Sa Mté a dit de moy: il ne vient que lors que je suis devenu Roy. J'espere pourtant qu'Elle l'aura dit en riant. Car Sa Mté aura eté informée de M. de Bernsdorf que je venois infailliblement avant l'hyvre comme je le luy avois écrit, et le grand evenement n'a fait qu'avancer mon voyage de quelques semaines. Sans cela je ne serois parti que lors que l'Empereur seroit allé à la diete de la Hongrie. J'etois sur le point de revenir au commencement de l'eté passé, j'avois deja envoyé mon bagage en Saxe, jusqu'aux habits, et je suivois lors qu'un ordre que je receu par M. de Bernsdorf sur l'affaire de Lauenbourg et que j'executay avec asses de succès, m'ar-reta et immediatement apres arriva la contagion et puis la goutte. Et ce delay m'en-gagea à des travaux à vienne pour l'Empereur dont j'ay eu toute la raison du monde de croire qu'on me doit savoir bon gré icy et c'est ainsi que le temps s'est passé. Outre que les Manuscrits de l'Empereur m'ont fourni de quoy embellir l'Histoire en plu-sieurs points. D'ailleurs il me semble que j'ay toujours donné toutes les preuves possibles de mon zele pour la gloire de la Serenissime et maintenant Royale mai-son. J'ay employé à son service la plus grande partie de ma vie, et si l'interest m'avoit eté plus cher que la reputation, j'aurois moins sujet d'etre content de mes succès. Ce que j'ay donné au monde pour faire connoitre sa grandeur et ses droits a eté applaudi; j'ay deterré avec bien de la peine sur l'antiquité de sa splendeur des choses inconnues, dont une bonne partie n'est pas encor publiée; et si j'ay cherché encor ailleurs et avec succes quelques avantages qui me paroissoient justes, l'honneur en rejaillissoit sur la Cour que j'ay servi tant d'années, et dont je n'ay jamais eu inten-tion de quitter entierement le service. La distinction que j'ay receue ailleurs, pou-voit justifier et faire applaudir davantage dans le monde les bontés que des grands princes et grandes princesses m'ont témoignées dans cette Maison, et contribuer à m'y faire encore rendre justice dans la suite avec plus d'étendue. Pendant que le

31. Leibniz to Georg August*, Prince of Wales[1]

Hanover this 17 of September 1714
Monseigneur

To His Royal Serenity
Monseigneur the Prince of Wales
Electoral Prince of Braunschweig

Your Royal Serenity had scarcely departed with the king [George I, Georg Ludwig* of Braunschweig-Lüneburg] when I arrived here.[2] I dared not run in pursuit, for although I might perhaps have been able to relate many particulars that would not have been disagreeable, chiefly about the joy that the emperor [Karl VI*] and all the imperial household, along with the principal ministers of the court of Vienna, have expressed concerning the great event that has extracted Europe from troubles for a long time, as I hope, that did not seem important enough to expose myself further to a trip by stagecoach in the season which is beginning to turn harsh; and for that matter, I could assume that you had been informed of it. And as concerns my particular interests, I believed that I could put my trust in the kindness and justice of the king, although I was surprised to learn from Madame the Royal Princess [Caroline* of Brandenburg-Ansbach, Princess of Wales] (who has preserved her good graces for me, which are of such great value to me, along with those of Your Royal Serenity) that His Majesty said of me: 'he comes only when I have become king.' But I hope that he said it while laughing. For His Majesty must have been informed by Mr. Bernstorff* that I would come without fail before winter, as I had written him, and the great event only moved my trip forward by a few weeks. Barring that, I would only have departed when the emperor would have gone to the diet of Hungary. I was on the point of returning at the beginning of last summer; I had already sent my baggage to Saxony, even my clothing, and I was following when an order that I received from Mr. Bernstorff concerning the Lauenburg affair, which I carried out successfully enough, stopped me, and immediately afterward the contagion arrived, and then the gout. And this delay committed me to some work in Vienna for the emperor, for which I have had every reason to believe that they ought to be grateful to me here, and it is in this way that the time has passed. Besides, the manuscripts of the emperor have furnished me with something to embellish the history[3] in several respects. Moreover, it seems to me that I have always given every possible proof of my zeal for the glory of the Most Serene and now Royal House. I have employed most of my life in its service, and if self-interest had been dearer to me than reputation, I would have less reason to be content with my success. What I have given to the world to make known its grandeur and its rights has been applauded; with much labor upon the antiquity of its splendor, I have unearthed things unknown, of which a good part is not yet published; and if I have yet sought elsewhere, with success, some advantages that appeared just to me, the honour reflected upon the court that I have served so many years and whose service I have never had the intention of entirely leaving. The distinction

public juge de tout ce que j'ay fait paroistre plus avantageusement que je n'avois osé me le promettre, j'espere que le Roy sera persuadé que mon interieur luy a tousjours été entierement devoué, que mon zele pour ce qui l'interesse a ete des plus ardens, que je n'ay pas eté le dernier a connoitre et a admirer les vertus qui le faisoient meriter les couronnes que la providence luy destinoit pour le bien general, comme je le feray voir un jour plus particulierement, et que personne a eté touché plus que moy de la grande revolution qui a donné pour ainsi dire le comble à nos souhaits. Les miens en particulier seroient de vivre encor assés et de garder assés de vigueur d'esprit, pour les transmettre dignement à la posterité. Vous y prenés part, Monseigneur, plus que personne, et c'est ce qui me donne la hardiesse de vous en tant parler; outre que je say que votre Generosité a tousjours paru envers un ancien serviteur dont vous connoissiés la bonne volonté. Je vous supplie de me la conserver dans l'eloignement comme de près, et faisant des vœux pour votre longue vie et parfait contentement, je suis avec devotion Monseigneur de Votre Serenité Royale

Leibniz to Andreas Gottlieb von Bernstorff

A Monsieur Bernsdorf   Hannover ce 20 de Septembre
Monsieur   1714

Comme j'ay voyagé en homme d'âge je ne suis arrivé icy que vendredi passé; le Roy estant déja parti mardi. J'ay jugé que si j'avois pris d'abord la poste pour suivre Sa Mté, j'aurois pû faire de tort à ma santé, et peutetre inutilement puisque je conçois que ce Monarque ne sera que trop occupée[2] en Hollande. V. E. l'est aussi sans doute. Cependant j'ay crû qu'il etoit de mon devoir de luy ecrire et de l'informer de mon retour. Je dois adjouter que j'ay appris de bonne part qu'on obligeroit extremement la Cour Imperiale, et à peu de frais si le Roy de la Grande Bretagne pouvoit abstenir[3] de reconnoitre le pretendu Roy de Sicile; comme Messieurs les Etats s'en sont abstenus jusqu'icy. Il semble que Sa Mté a des[4] grandes raisons pour cela. Il est vray que les traités que la Reine a faits sont pour la Royauté de ce Duc, mais le Roy a une raison particuliere tres forte pour ne point imiter[5] son

I have received elsewhere was able to justify and to have acclaimed around the world the kindnesses that some great princes and princesses have shown me in this House and to contribute to having me eventually do justice to it again to a greater extent. While the public judges everything I have published more favorably than I dared to expect, I hope that the king will be persuaded that inwardly I have always been entirely devoted to him, that my zeal for what concerns him has been among the most ardent, that I have not been the last to recognize and admire the virtues that made him merit the crowns that providence destined for him for the general good, as I will show more particularly one day, and that no one has been more touched than I by the great revolution that has given, so to speak, the zenith to our wishes. Mine in particular would be to live yet long enough and retain sufficient strength of mind to transmit them with dignity to posterity. You have shared in it, monseigneur, more than anyone, and this is what gives me the boldness to speak to you so much about it; besides, I know that your generosity has always appeared to an old servant with whose good will you are acquainted. Pray preserve it for me from afar as nearby; and offering prayers for your long life and perfect satisfaction, I am with devotion, monseigneur, for Your Royal Serenity

[1] LBr. F 10 Bl. 8r–8v. Draft: 1.2 folio sides in Leibniz's hand. Previously published in Klopp XI 9–11.

[2] After hearing of the death of Queen Anne and the consequent accession of Georg Ludwig* of Braunschweig-Lüneburg to the throne in England as George I, Leibniz hastened to return to Hanover from Vienna in the hopes of meeting with the king before he departed for England. However, Leibniz did not arrive in Hanover until 14 September, three days after the king and his son Georg August had left for England.

[3] Leibniz refers to the history of the House of Braunschweig-Lüneburg (Hanover), which he had come to refer to as the *Annales imperii occidentis Brunsvicenses*.

32. Leibniz to Andreas Gottlieb von Bernstorff*[1]

To Mr. Bernstorff   Hanover this 20 of September

Sir   1714

As I have travelled like an old man, I only arrived here last Friday [14 September 1714], the king [George I of Great Britain, Georg Ludwig* of Braunschweig-Lüneburg] having already departed on Tuesday [11 September 1714]. I thought that if I had taken the stagecoach straightaway in order to follow His Majesty, I could have done harm to my health, and perhaps uselessly, since I imagine that this monarch will be only too occupied[2] in Holland. Your Excellency is doubtless busy as well. However, I believed that it was my duty to write to you and inform you of my return. I should add that I have learned on good authority that the imperial court would be much obliged, and at little cost, if the King of Great Britain could refrain[3] from recognizing the pretended King of Sicily [Vittorio Amedeo Sebastiano*], as the States-General* have refrained from it up till now. It seems that

predecesseur. C'est que le Duc de Savoye avoit pris la liberté de protester contre la succession de la Grande Bretagne dans la maison d'Hannover, aussi tôt que le Roy Guillaume l'avoit etablie par Acte de parlement, et cette protestation avoit même eté signifiée en Angleterre. Il ne peut pas abolir une telle demarche éclatante par une simple dissimulation, et il ne suffiroit pas s'il vouloit maintenant reconnoitre Sa Mté, comme je ne doute point, qu'il ne soit disposé de faire: car des[6] telles reconnoissances se peuvent encor faire envers des Rois de facto, ou au moins sur le droit des quels on ne s'explique point. S'il etoit possible que l'Amiral Wishard pût encore venir à temps à la rade de Barcellonne, pour en sauver les habitans du massacre et de l'extermination[8] qui les menace, l'Empereur en seroit touché au vif, et extrement obligé. Je pourrois encore dire un jour quelques autres particularites de consequence sur l'harmonie et le concours de ces deux grands princes dont l'humeur[10] a beaucoup de rapport.

Nous nous flattons icy de l'heureux retour de Sa Mté l'eté qui vient. On prie déjà Dieu pour cela, avant que de luy avoir rendu graces sur l'heureux passage, dont nous attendons bien tost des nouvelles. Je souhaite que V. E. revienne en bonne santé le plustost que cela se pourra. Cependant je ne puis me dispenser de dire, que j'ay eté un peu surpris d'apprendre de M. Schild, qu'il n'a pas encor ordre de payer mes gages, echûs et avenir, ny de me rien faire donner pour le deuil, et que même l'on veut que les 50 écus que V. E. a fait donner à M. Ruhlman soyent mis sur mon compte. J'apprends même que les gages d'une demie année n'ont pas eté rendus au juif, et qu'il m'en demande de l'interest. Voilà des articles aux quels il semble que je ne me devois point attende[15] Mais j'espere qu'il y aura eu là dedans du mesentendu, et que V. E. avec M. le Baron de Goriz, à qui j'en ecris[16] aussi, le fera redresser. V. E. sait que j'etois prêt a partir de Vienne l'eté passé, et j'avois déja envoyé tout mon bagage en Saxe, lors que j'eus ordre de m'arrester un peu à cause de l'affaire de Lauenbourg. Je crois n'avoir pas mal executé les ordres, mais il survint la contagion et la goutte, et pendant ce delay l'Empereur me donna quelque occupation, dont on n'aura point sujet d'etre faché, et j'en avois ecrit. Cependant long temps avant le dernier changement, j'avois asseuré V. E. que je serois infalliblement icy avant l'hyver commence,[18] et je n'y ay point manqué. Je n'ay voulu faire aucune demarche qui pouvoit faire prejudice à[19] service d'un maitre si grand que j'ay eu si long temps l'honneur de servir avec affection et zele. Je ne devois pas me negliger entierement moy même, et pour donner une meilleure opinion de moy icy, il falloit montrer qu'on a encor quelque bonne opinion de moy ailleurs. Mais on peut bien croire que je serois faché qu'un travail de tant d'annees fut inutile. Au reste je suis avec respect Monsieur de V. E.

le tres humble & tres
obeissant serviteur
Leibniz

His Majesty has some[4] great reasons for that. It is true that the treaties that the queen [Anne of Great Britain] made are on behalf of the monarchy of this duke, but the king has a particular, very strong reason for not imitating[5] his predecessor. It is that the Duke of Savoy had taken the liberty to protest against the succession of Great Britain in the House of Hanover as soon as King William had established it by an act of parliament [the Act of Settlement*], and this protestation had even been made known in England. It is not possible to erase such a glaring step by a simple concealment, and it would not suffice if he now wished to recognize His Majesty, as I do not doubt that he is disposed to do; for such[6] recognitions can still be made respecting de facto kings, or at least we do not justify their right. If it were possible that Admiral Wishart[7] could yet go at once to the harbor of Barcelona in order to save the inhabitants from massacre and from the extermination[8] that threatens them,[9] the emperor [Karl VI*] would be touched to the quick by it and very much obliged. At some point I could cite yet some other particulars of consequence concerning the harmony and concurrence of these two great princes, whose temperaments[10] have much affinity.

Here we pride ourselves on the joyous return of His Majesty next summer.[11] We pray God for that already, before thanking him for the successful passage, news of which we are expecting soon. I hope that Your Excellency may return in good health as soon as that is possible. However, I cannot omit saying that I have been a bit surprised to learn from M. Schild that there has not yet been an order to pay my wages, in arrears and to come, nor to have anything given to me for the period of mourning[12], and that they even want the 50 écus that Your Excellency had given to M. Ruhlman[13] to be placed on my account. I even understand that a half-year's wages have not been paid to the moneylender and that he is demanding interest on it from me.[14] These are some things that it seems I ought not to expect.[15] But I hope that there has been some misunderstanding in this and that Your Excellency, along with Baron Görtz*, to whom I am also writing about it,[16] will straighten it out. Your Excellency knows that I was ready to depart from Vienna last summer, and I had already sent all my baggage to Saxony, when I was ordered to remain a bit on account of the Lauenburg affair. I believe I did not execute the orders badly, but the plague and the gout happened unexpectedly, and during this delay the emperor gave me some work with which there will be no reason to be displeased, and I have written about it. However, long before the last change,[17] I had assured Your Excellency that I would be here without fail before winter begins,[18] and I have not failed in that. I did not want to take any step which could prejudice the service[19] of so great a master whom I have had the honour of serving for so long with affection and zeal. I should not entirely neglect myself, and in order to bring about a better opinion of myself here, it was necessary to show that people still have some good opinion of me elsewhere. But you may well believe that I would be displeased if an

Leibniz to Ernst Friedrich von Windischgrätz

A Mons le comte de Windischgraz president du Conseil imperial Aulique
Monseigneur   Hannover ce | 16 | 20 de Sept. 1714[2]
L'Attachement particulier que je dois à V. E. me fait prendre la liberté de luy écrire
| un peu apres mon arrivée icy. Le Roy etoit déja parti, mais j'aurois pû le trouver
encor en Hollande, si j'avois receu la lettre qu'un Ministre de Sa Mté Imperiale
m'avoit promise pour M. le Baron de Göriz. | d'icy ou je suis arrivé un peu apres le
depart du Roy de la Grande Bretagne. Je n'ay trouve que Madame la pincesse Royale
(que les Anglois appellent Princesse de Galles), et Mgr le Duc Erneste Auguste qui

33. LEIBNIZ TO VON WINDISCHGRÄTZ 113

occupation of so many years were futile. Finally, I am with respect, sir, of Your Excellency

the very humble and very

obedient servant

Leibniz

---

[1] LBr. 59 Bl. 115r–115v. Draft: 1.2 folio sides in Leibniz's hand. Previously published in Klopp XI 12–14. For Bernstorff's response, see his letter to Leibniz of 1 November 1714 (document 46).

[2] Reading 'occupé' for 'occupée'.

[3] Reading 's'abstenir' as 'abstenir'.

[4] Reading 'de' for 'des'.

[5] Klopp mistranscribes 'pour ne point imiter' as 'pour n'imiter point'. (see Klopp XI 12).

[6] Reading 'de' for 'des'.

[7] That is, Admiral James Wishart (1659–1723), who at the time was British Commander-in-Chief of the Mediterranean.

[8] Klopp mistranscribes 'l'extermination' as 'l'intermination' (see Klopp XI 13).

[9] Leibniz was presumably unaware that the 'massacre' had already taken place nine days earlier, on 11 September, when the Catalonian defenders of Barcelona were overcome by forces loyal to Bourbon King Phillipe (Felipe) V* of Spain under the command of James Fitzjames*, 1st Duke of Berwick (1670–1734). This action ended the Siege of Barcelona* and was the last great battle of the War of the Spanish Succession*.

[10] Klopp mistranscribes 'l'humeur' as 'l'honneur' (see Klopp IX 13).

[11] Because of the threat of invasion by the Pretender James Francis Edward Stuart, Georg Ludwig was unable to return to his Hanoverian electorate in the summer of 1715. He did, however, return in the summer of 1716, and was still in the electorate when Leibniz died at Hanover on 14 November 1716.

[12] Leibniz is doubtless referring to the period of mourning for the Dowager Electress of Braunschweig-Lüneburg, Sophie* of the Palatinate, who had died on 8 June.

[13] In the letter he wrote to Görtz about this, Leibniz spells 'Ruhlman' with an umlaut, i.e. 'Rühlman,' and he explains that Rühlman 'had helped' him, although he does not explain in what way (see Leibniz's letter to Görtz of 20 September 1714, LBr. 59 Bl. 115v).

[14] In the letter he wrote to Görtz, Leibniz is clear that the 'half-year's wages' that he says are owed to the 'juif' (moneylender) are his own wages, which he had apparently borrowed against (see Leibniz's letter to Görtz of 20 September 1714, LBr. 59 Bl. 115v).

[15] Reading 'je ne devois point m'attendre' for 'je ne me devois point attende'.

[16] Klopp mistranscribes 'j'en cris' as 'j'ay écrit' (see Klopp XI 13).

[17] That is, the death of Queen Anne and the ascension of Georg Ludwig* of Braunschweig-Lüneburg to the British throne.

[18] Klopp's transcription omits 'commence' (see Klopp XI 14).

[19] Reading 'pouvait faire prejudice au' for 'pouvoit faire prejudice à.'

---

33. Leibniz to Ernst Friedrich von Windischgrätz[1]

To Monseigneur the Count of Windischgrätz president of the Imperial Aulic Council*
Monseigneur   Hanover | 16 | 20 September 1714[2]
The particular affection that I owe to Your Excellency causes me to take the liberty of writing to you | a little after my arrival here. The king [George I of Great Britain, Georg Ludwig* of Braunschweig-Lüneburg] had already departed, but I would still have been able to meet with him in Holland, if I had received the letter that a minister[3] of his Imperial Majesty [Karl VI*] had promised for Baron Görtz*. | from here, where I arrived shortly after the departure of the King of Great Britain.[4] I found

n'a pas encor pû se resoudre à aller en Angleterre, quoyque le Roy son frere l'ait solicité de l'accompagner. Mad. la pincesse Royale espere de suivre bien tost.

Autant que j'en puis juger partout ce qu'on me dit icy; le Roy persuadé des favorables intentions que Sa M. Imp. a tousjours eues pour luy (dont quelques uns l'ont voulu faire douter mal a propos) est parti dans la disposition la plus ferme du monde, de faire connoitre dans toutes les occasions que son elevation ne diminue en rien le zele pour le bien public pour celuy de l'Empire et pour la Tres Auguste maison d'Autriche, qu'il a marqué depuis tant d'années. Je me dispose à passer en Angleterre avec Mad. la princesse Royale, qui a la bonté de le desirer. J'ay des raisons pour n'en rien faire encor connoitre à d'autres, mais je trouve qu'il est de mon devoir d'en informer V. E. à fin qu'elle juge si je pourrois y etre utile pour le service de l'Empereur. La gloire de Sa Mté Imp., et la conservation de la grandeur et des droits de l'Empire, sont un des principaux objets de mes pensées. Je trouve que l'Empereur et le Roy de la Grande Bretagne symbolisent en beaucoup de belles qualités, mais particulierement en celle ou V. E. sert Sa Mté Imperiale, qui est l'amour de la justice, et je suis persuade que si cette harmonie est cultivée comme il faut ce sera le vray moyen de faire fleurir le bon ordre, de faire observer les constitutions de l'Empire, de garantir les petits de l'oppression des grands, et même de maintenir les droits de l'Empire, surtout en Italie, où ils ont eté si negligés, et si je l'ose dire, ignorés depuis long temps. J'ay envoyé à M. de Bernsdorf des raisons qui semblent devoir porter le Roy à ne point reconnoitre le pretendu Roy de Sicile; quoyque la Reine son predecesseur l'ait reconnu, & meme pour ainsi dire créé. J'ay appris qu'on a solicité le Roy de la Grande Bretagne de se relacher de cette ferme resolution de tenir la main autant qu'il depend de luy à l'execution de la justice dans l'Empire; et on l'a fait en luy proposant des veues d'utilité, et en tachant de l'aigrir sur certaines choses passées: mais on n'y a point reussi. J'espere qu'on continuera tousjours dans ce louable train. Sa Mte Britannique envoyera bien tôt une Ambassade solennelle à l'Empereur, et l'on parle comme si quel cun des principaux Lords y pourroit etre employé. Je ne doute point que l'Empereur n'y envoye aussi un Seigneur, qui fasse honneur à l'Ambassade. S'il y arrivoit pendant que je seray encor en Angleterre, je ferois mon possible pour le servir, mais si j'en reviens plutôt, comme cela se pourroit, je tacherois de preparer les choses, à mesure que je pourrois avoir des lumieres sur les intentions de la Cour Imperiale. | Si M. le Comte de Sinzendorf m'avoit envoyé la lettre qu'il m'avoit fait esperer | Si l'on m'avoit donné à Vienne ou fait trouver ici une lettre à quelque ministre du Roy telle qu'on m'avoit fait esperer, qui m'auroit mis en etat de dire quelque chose, j'aurois pû etre de retour à Vienne d'abord sans passer maintenant en Angleterre, et j'aurois pû apporter des particularités sur les sentimens du Roy de la Grande Bretagne. Mais il faut qu'on ait changé d'avis à l'egard d'une telle lettre.[6] Ainsi je ne seray à Vienne qu'apres avoir eté en Angleterre. Apparemment je n'y perdray rien en mon particulier. Mais je seray un peu moins utile au public, que j'aurois pû etre. Tout ce cy n'est que pour V. E. et pour l'Empereur meme si elle le juge à propos, et je la supplie de me conserver dans les bonnes graces de ce Monarque quand l'occasion s'en presentera.

only Madame the Royal Princess [Caroline* of Brandenburg-Ansbach], (whom the English call the Princess of Wales), and Monseigneur Duke Ernst August [Ernst August II* of Braunschweig-Lüneburg], who has still not been able to make up his mind to go to England, although his brother the king has asked him to accompany him. Madame the Royal Princess hopes to follow soon.

As far as I can judge, what I am told everywhere here, the king, persuaded of the favorable intentions that his Imperial Majesty has always had toward him (of which some have inappropriately wanted to make him doubt), has departed in the firmest possible frame of mind to demonstrate on all occasions that his elevation does not diminish at all the zeal for the public good, for that of the Empire, and for the very august House of Austria that he has shown for so many years. I am preparing to go to England with Madame the Royal Princess, who has the kindness to desire it. I have reasons for not yet revealing any of it to others, but I think that it is my duty to inform Your Excellency of it in order that you may judge if I could be useful there for the service of the emperor. The glory of His Imperial Majesty, and the preservation of the grandeur and rights of the empire, are one of the principal objects of my thoughts. I think that the emperor and the King of Great Britain agree in many fine qualities, but particularly in that in which Your Excellency serves His Imperial Majesty, which is the love of justice, and I am persuaded that if this harmony is cultivated as it should be, this will be the true means of making good order flourish, of enforcing the constitutions of the empire, of protecting common people from the oppression of the great, and even of maintaining the rights of the empire, above all in Italy, where they have been so neglected, and if I dare say, ignored for a long time. I have sent Mr. Bernstorff* some reasons that seem likely to incline the king not to recognize the pretended King of Sicily [Vittorio Amedeo Sebastiano*], although the queen his predecessor [Queen Anne] recognized him, and even, so to speak, created him.[5] I learned that the King of Great Britain has been asked to relax his firm resolution to enforce the execution of justice in the empire as far as it depends on him; and it has been done by offering him some prospects of profit and by trying to embitter him about certain past matters; but they have not succeeded in that. I hope they will always continue on this laudable course. His Britannic Majesty will soon send a formal embassy to the emperor, and people talk as if some of the principal lords could be engaged in it. I do not doubt that the emperor will also send a lord who will bring honour to the embassy. If he arrived there while I was in England, I would do my utmost to be at his service; but if I return from England sooner, as could well be the case, I would try to make things ready, as I could have some information about the intentions of the imperial court. | If Count Sinzendorff had sent me the letter that he had led me to expect | If I had been given a letter in Vienna, or had found one here to some minister of the king, such as I was led to expect, which would have put me in a position to say something, I could have returned to Vienna first without now going to England, and I could have provided some particular details about the views of the King of Great Britain. But there must

Estant avec respect   Monsgr de V. E. etc.
    P.S.

Mons. Schmid autres fois Conseiller d'un Comte de Leining[7], qui fera rendre cette lettre à V. E. a du savoir & du merite. Il s'est chargé de mes affaires particulieres, et je supplie V. E. de luy donner audience favorable au besoin.

33. LEIBNIZ TO VON WINDISCHGRÄTZ 117

have been a change of mind in regard to such a letter.[6] Thus I will be in Vienna only after having been in England. I will apparently not suffer any personal loss by it. But I will be a little less useful to the public than I could have been. All this is only for Your Excellency and for the emperor himself, if he deems it appropriate, and pray preserve me in the good graces of that monarch when the occasion presents itself.

With respect   Monseigneur of Your Excellency etc.

P.S.

Mr. Schmid, former councillor for a Count of Leiningen[7], who will deliver this letter to Your Excellency, is knowledgeable and meritorious. He has looked after my private affairs, and I pray Your Excellency to give him a favorable audience, if needs be.

---

[1] LBr. 1005 Bl. 10. Draft: one folio side in Leibniz's hand. Previously published (excerpt) in Klopp XI xxi and (excerpt) in Bodemann-BR 389–90.

[2] The draft had originally been dated '16 de Sept. 1714,' but Leibniz crossed out the '16' and wrote '20' above it. So the letter was apparently composed, or at least begun, on 16 September and then postdated to the 20th. This might explain why Leibniz inserts a complaint at the beginning of this draft letter, which he then deletes, about not having received a letter from one of the emperor's ministers (that is, Sinzendorff) for Minister Görtz* or Minister Bothmer*, as he had been promised, while at the same time thanking Sinzendorff in his letter to him of 20 September (see document 34) for having sent the letters that he had requested for both Minister Görtz* (document 27) and Minister Bothmer* (document 26), which he tells Sinzendorff that he received 'the day before yesterday,' that is, on 18 September. So it would appear that Leibniz received the letters from Sinzendorff two days after he had first begun to compose this draft to Windischgrätz; he apparently then postdated the letter to 20 September and deleted his complaint, made at the beginning of the draft, about not having received the letters from Sinzendorff in particular. But later in the draft the complaint is inserted again, and this was not deleted (see below, note 6).

[3] That is, Philipp Ludwig Wenzel von Sinzendorff. See documents 26 and 27.

[4] The king and his son Georg Ludwig*, the Prince of Wales, departed for England on 11 September; Leibniz arrived in Hanover from Vienna on 14 September.

[5] Leibniz here alludes to the fact that Anne was the ruling monarch in Great Britain when it became a signatory to the Treaty of Utrecht*, by whose terms Vittorio Amedeo Sebastiano was created the King of Sicily.

[6] Here Leibniz began by writing, and then deleting, 'If Count Sinzendorff had sent me the letter that he had led me to expect.' He then inserted in the margin, 'If I had been given a letter in Vienna or had found one here to some minister of the king, such as I was led to expect, which would have put me in a position to say something, I could have returned to Vienna first without now going to England [...].' This was followed in the body of the letter with: 'But there must have been a change of mind in regard to such a letter.' Perhaps all of this was revised in the final version of the letter sent to Windischgrätz in order to make it consistent with Leibniz's having received on the 18th the letters that Sinzendorff had written for Bothmer and Görtz.

[7] Reading 'Leiningen' for 'Leining'.

Leibniz to Philipp Ludwig Wenzel von Sinzendorff[*1]

A Monsieur le Comte de Sinzendorf Grand Chanelier de la Cour
Monseigneur

Ne voyant point de raison de me trop presser, j'ay voyagé en homme d'âge, et je
ne suis arrivé icy que vendredi passé. J'ay eu l'honneur de recevoir avanthier, c'est à
dire mardi, les lettres de V. E. dont je la remercie tres humblement. Celles qui sont
pour les deux Ministres du Roy de la Gr. Bretagne sont tres avantageuses pour moy,
et quoyqu'elles ne contiennent rien qui m'oblige de hater mon voyage vers le Roy,
que j'aurois pû joindre en Hollande au besoin elles serviront à presser mon retour à
Vienne. Et je supplie V. E. de me conserver dans les bonnes graces de l'Empereur de
favoriser cependant l'affaire de la Societé des Sciences, esperant que Mons. de
Schick aura expedié le Rescript que j'avois demandé, et en des termes favorables.
Écrivant une lettre de congratulation à Mgr le prince de Galles, j'ay envoyé à Sa
Serenité Royale un petit papier, qui contient quelques raisons qui semblent pouvoir
porter le Roy de la Grande Bretagne à ne point reconnoitre le pretendu Roy de
Sicile, quoyque la Reine l'ait reconnu et même crée pour ainsi dire. J'en ecriray aussi
à M. de Bernsdorf. Si V. E. m'ordonne quelque chose, je serois ravi de le pouvoir
executer, soit icy, ou en Angleterre; et je suis avec respect
Monseigneur de V. E.

le tres humble et tres obeissant

Hannover ce 20   serviteur
de Sept. 1714   Leibniz

34. Leibniz to Philipp Ludwig Wenzel von Sinzendorff[*][1]

To the Count of Sinzendorff, Grand Chancellor of the [Imperial] Court
Monseigneur

[20 September 1714]

Not seeing any reason to hurry too much, I have travelled like an old man, and I arrived here only last Friday [14 September]. I had the honour of receiving the day before yesterday, that is Tuesday, the letters of Your Excellency, for which I thank you most humbly.[2] Those which are for the two ministers of the King of Great Britain [George I, Georg Ludwig* of Braunschweig-Lüneburg] are very advantageous for me, and although they contain nothing that obliges me to hasten my journey to the king, whom I could have joined in Holland had it been necessary, they will serve to expedite my return to Vienna. And I beseech Your Excellency to preserve me in the good graces of the emperor to foster in the meantime the business of the Society of Sciences [the proposed Imperial Society of Sciences*], since I hope that Mr. Schick has expedited the rescript that I had requested,[3] and on favorable terms. In writing a letter of congratulation to the Prince of Wales [Georg August* of Braunschweig-Lüneburg], I have sent His Royal Serenity a small paper that contains some reasons that could lead the King of Great Britain not to recognize the pretended King of Sicily [Vittorio Amedeo Sebastiano*], although the queen [Anne of Great Britain] had recognized him and even created him[4], so to speak. I will write to Mr. Bernstorff* about this as well.[5] If Your Excellency has some order for me, I would be delighted to able to carry it out, either here or in England; and I am with respect

Monseigneur of Your Excellency

the very humble and very obedient

Hanover this 20   servant

September 1714   Leibniz

---

[1] LBr. 1005 Bl. 10v. Draft: 1 quarto side in Leibniz's hand. Previously published in Klopp XI xxi (excerpt). This is Leibniz's response to Sinzendorff's letter of 8 September (document 28).

[2] That is, the letters that Leibniz requested Sinzendorff to send to Hanover for ministers Bothmer* and Görtz* (see documents 26, 27, and 28).

[3] Concerning this rescript, see Leibniz's letter to Bonneval of November 1714 (document 45, pp. 157, 159).

[4] Leibniz here alludes to the fact that Queen Anne was the ruling monarch in Great Britain when it became a signatory to the Treaty of Utrecht*, by whose terms Vittorio Amedeo Sebastiano was created the King of Sicily.

[5] See Leibniz's letter to Bernstorff of 20 September 1714 (document 32).

Leibniz to Claude Alexandre de Bonneval

Monsieur

Puisque j'ay fait heureusement mon voyage de Vienne jusqu'à Hannover, en employant même la nuit quelques fois, je juge par plus forte raison, que vous vous devés bien porter, malgré votre voyage, jeune (en comparaison de moy) et vigoureux comme vous étes. Je seray pourtant ravi d'en etre certain et de changer ma foy en science. Je suis venu icy pour travailler pendant cet hyver à des ouvrages, qui me puissent debarasser de certains occupations capables de differer un peu mon retour à Vienne. Mais j'en suis a present distrait icy, comme à Vienne puisque Madame la princesse Royale a voulu me loger à la maison de plaisance ou elle sera jusqu'à son depart pour l'Angleterre; et je suis bien aise de jouir encore tant que je puis des bonnes graces d'une princesse si accomplie et si spirituelle; qui veut meme repasser avec moy (le croiriés vous) sur la Theodicée qu'elle a lûe plus d'une fois | avec attention |. Il me semble que je vous entends, Monsieur, m'accuser de vanité: mais je pretends que ce que je viens de dire est un eloge de la princesse, et non pas de mon ouvrage. Car quand il seroit mal fondé, c'est toujours beaucoup qu'une telle princesse environnée de tout ce qui peut dissiper l'esprit donne tant d'attention à des matieres aussi relevées que celles que mon ouvrage traite.

Si j'étois en etat d'obeir à Son Altesse Royale, je l'irois accompagner[3] jusqu'en Angleterre: et en ce cas, je souhaiterois de vous y voir, Monsieur, suivant ce que vous aviés fait esperer a Madame la Duchesse de Marlebourough. Je voudrois que Mons. le Duc d'Arenberg y fut aussi pour accomplir la prediction (qu'il me fit lors que j'eus l'honneur de luy souhaiter un heureux voyage dans votre maison,) que nous pourrions nous revoir en Angleterre. Je voudrois même qu'il y vint Ambassadeur de l'Empereur. Cela feroit honneur aux deux Monarques comme à luy et puisque le Roy espere de boire au mois de juin prochain les eaux de pirmont qui sont à une journée d'Hannover, cette Ambassade déclat ne pourroit manquer d'etre courte, et puis un autre Ambassadeur plus ordinaire pourroit prendre la place de notre Duc. Vous me trouverés plaisant de regler les Ambassades de l'Empereur: mais ne m'est il pas permis de dire ce que je souhaiterois, et de le dire à vous, Monsieur, à qui cela fournira de quoy faire rire Monseigneur le prince Eugene. Mais[4] j'espere que cela ne vous empechera pas de marquer ma devotion à S. A. S. et de contribuer à me conserver l'honneur [de] ses bonnes graces. Je ne say Monsieur ou cette lettre vous trouvera, et si vous serés encore dans le même endroit ou sont Monsieur le Duc d'Arenberg, et Messieurs les princes de Ligne. En ce cas, je vous supplie de leur marquer mes respects, et comme je m'imagine que vous serés tousjours en quelque commerce avec ce Duc, je vous supplie de les luy marquer quand même vous ne series plus ensemble. Je crois que l'homme de chambre de Monseigneur le prince de Savoye vous aura apporté un petit paquet de mon part,

35. Leibniz to Claude Alexandre de Bonneval*[1]

[21 September 1714]

Sir

Since I have successfully made my journey from Vienna to Hanover, by travelling sometimes even by night, I imagine with much greater reason that you must be faring well, despite your journey, young (in comparison with me) and vigorous as you are. I will be thoroughly delighted to be certain of it and to convert my faith into knowledge. I came here to apply myself during this winter to some labors that may be able to free me from certain occupations that could delay a bit my return to Vienna.[2] But I am currently distracted here, as I was in Vienna, since the Royal Princess [Caroline* of Brandenburg-Ansbach, Princess of Wales] has wanted me to stay at the country estate [Herrenhausen*] where she will be until her departure for England; and I am very glad to enjoy once more, as much as I can, the good graces of a princess so accomplished and so spiritual, who even wants to go back over with me (would you believe it) the *Theodicy*, which she has read more than once | with attention |. I seem to hear you, sir, accusing me of vanity. But I maintain that what I have just said is in praise of the princess, and not of my work. For while it may be ill founded, it is always becoming that such a princess, surrounded by everything that can dissipate the spirit, gives so much attention to matters as elevated as those with which my book is concerned.

If I were in a state to obey Her Royal Highness, I would go with her[3] to England; and in that case, I would hope to see you there, sir, in accordance with what you had made the Duchess of Marlborough [Sarah Churchill*] expect. I would want the Duke of Arenberg [Léopold Philippe* of Arenberg] to be there as well, in order to fulfill the prediction (which he made to me when I had the honour of wishing him a happy journey to your home) that we would be able to meet each other again in England. I would even want him to go there as the ambassador of the emperor [Karl VI*]. That would do honour to both monarchs and to him alike, and since next June the king expects to drink the waters of Pyrmont*, which are a day's journey from Hanover, this glamorous embassy could not fail to be short-lived, and then a different, more ordinary ambassador would be able take the place of our duke. You will think me ridiculous to arrange the ambassadors of the emperor; but I am not allowed to say what I would wish, and to say it to you, sir, will provide you with something to make Prince Eugène* laugh. But[4] I hope it will not prevent you from expressing my devotion to His Serene Highness and from helping to preserve for me the honour of his good graces. I do not know, sir, where this letter will find you, and if you will still be in the same location as the Duke of Arenberg and the Princes of Ligne. If you will be, pray pay them my respects, and as I imagine that

ou il y avoit quelque chose pour Monsieur Sully, qui m'avoit prié de le recommander à des amis à Paris.

On me mande de Hollande que M. de Chasteauneuf fait beaucoup de caresses aux gens qui appartiennent au Roy de la Grande Bretagne, qui avoient pris les devants.[7] Les autres Ministres, que la France a ailleurs, font a peu prés la même chose. Tout cela, joint à beaucoup d'autres circomstances, fait croire que la paix avec la France subsistera encor quelque temps, et que le pas de Calais pourra servir de communication entre l'Angleterre & nous. Je m'imagine aussi que la France ne fera point difficulté de remettre le commerce sur l'ancien pied. On est dans l'incertitude sur le siege de Barcellonne. Le Duc de Berwick n'écrira plus que les habitans de cette ville ne savent ny se defendre ny se rendre; pour peu qu'ils durent, j'espere que l'Amiral Wishard sera en estat de les sauver. Mais, pourquoy vous dire tant d'inutilités? Mon but a eté de vous marquer avec combien de zele; je suis

    Monsieur

votre tres humble & tres

obeissant serviteur

Hannover ce 21 de

Septembre 1714   Leibniz

    A Monsieur le Comte de Bonneval

    General au service de sa Mté Imperiale

    et Catholique

35. LEIBNIZ TO DE BONNEVAL 123

you will still be in some communication with this duke, pray pay them to him even though you should no longer be together. I believe that the chamberlain of the Prince of Savoy [Eugène*] has probably brought you a small package from me, in which there was something for Mr. Sully,[5] who had asked me to recommend him to some friends in Paris.

I received word from Holland that Mr. [Pierre-Antoine de Castagnéry (1647?–1728), marquis de] Châteauneuf[6] is stroking the advance men[7] of the King of Great Britain. The ministers that France has elsewhere are doing nearly the same thing. All that, along with many other circumstances, suggest that the peace with France will hold good for some time yet and that the Pas-de-Calais will be able to be used for communication between England and us. I also imagine that France will not cause trouble about restoring commerce on the previous footing. There is uncertainty about the Siege of Barcelona*. The Duke of Berwick [James Fitzjames*] will write nothing more than that the inhabitants of that town do not know whether to defend themselves or to surrender. If they hold out, I hope that Admiral Wishart will be able to save them.[8] But why tell you so many futilities? My aim has been to show you with how much enthusiasm I am

sir

your very humble and very
obedient servant

Hanover 21
September 1714   Leibniz

To Count Bonneval
General in the service of his Majesty Imperial
and Catholic

---

[1] LBr. 89 Bl. 7r–7v. Draft: two folio sides in Leibniz's hand. Previously published in JGHF 423–6; in Klopp XI 14–15 (excerpt); Kemble 497 (excerpt). For Bonneval's reply, see Bonneval's letter to Leibniz of 6 October (document 39).

[2] Leibniz is referring to his work on the history of the House of Braunschweig-Lüneburg, the *Annales imperii occidentis Brunsvicenses**.

[3] Feder mistranscribes 'je l'irois accompagner' as 'j'irois l'accompagner' (see JGHF 424).

[4] Feder omits 'Mais' and mistakenly begins a new paragraph here.

[5] In a letter to Nicole Rémond of 26 August 1714, Leibniz identifies Sully as an 'English watchmaker' (see GP III 624).

[6] At the time, the Marquis de Châteauneuf was the French Ambassador at The Hague.

[7] Feder mistranscribes 'les devants' as 'le devant' (see JGHF 426).

[8] See Leibniz's letter to Bernstorff* of 20 September 1714 (document 32), notes 7 and 9.

Leibniz to Johann Matthias von der Schulenburg

Monsieur

J'ay receu l'honneur de vos lettres qui me sont revenues de Vienne comme aussi celle que vous m'avés ecrite ayant sû mon retour. Cependant vous aurés receu la mienne envoyée a Mad. d'Oenhausen.

Je dois vous dire en confidence, Monsieur que mon intention est de passer dans peu en Angleterre, je souhaiterois d'avoir l'honneur de vous parler auparavant. Mad la princesse approuve les raisons que j'ay de ne point aller avec elle. Je pense de passer a Calais, puisqu'apresent les chemins sont libres. M. de Bernsdorf m'écrit du 27 de la Haye: nous nous embarquons. Ainsi le Roy sera passé et l'escadre Angloise reviendra bientôt. Ainsi Mad. la princesse Royale espere de partir dans dix jours ou environ. Elle attend pourtant encor des lettres de son Epous.

Les avis de Barcellonne sont tres variables. Il y a des nouvelles de Paris qui asseurent qu'on s'est logé sur le rempart d'autres de Suisse disent qu'on a levé le siege. Ce la paroist le plus souhaitable, mais je crains qu'on ne se flatte.

Je fais semblant, d'icy de vouloir aller a la foire de Leipzig, et je partiray pour Hildesheim samedi ou environ. Mais de là je pense d'aller vers les pays bas par la poste qui va à Wesel. Si vous eties dans le voisinage, Monsieur, je souhaiterois de vous voir auparavant. On apprendra de mes nouvelles à Hildesheim dans l'endroit ou est la poste de Brandebourg, c'estoit autres fois a Steyerwalde proche de la ville.   Je suis entierement

    Monsieur   de V. E.

Hannover ce   le tres humble

30 de Sept   et tres obeissant

   1714   serviteur

                                            Leibniz

36. Leibniz to Johann Matthias von der Schulenburg*[1]

[30 September 1714]

Sir

I received the honour of your letters which came back to me from Vienna, as well as the one you wrote to me after you learned of my return. However you probably received mine sent to Madame Oeynhausen.[2]

I must tell you in confidence, sir, that my intention is to go to England shortly; I would like to have the honour of speaking with you beforehand. Madame the Princess [Caroline* of Brandenburg-Ansbach, Princess of Wales] approves the reasons I have for not going with her. I am thinking of going to Calais, since at present the roads are free. Mr. Bernstorff* wrote to me on the 27th from The Hague: 'We are embarking.' So the king [George I, Georg Ludwig* of Braunschweig-Lüneburg] is probably gone, and the English squadron will return soon. Thus Madame the Royal Princess hopes to depart in ten days or so. However, she is still waiting for some letters from her spouse [Georg August* of Braunschweig-Lüneburg, Prince of Wales].

The opinions about Barcelona are quite diverse.[3] There is some news from Paris that assures that they are lodged on the rampart; some other news from Switzerland says that they have lifted the siege [Siege of Barcelona* (1713–1714)]. The latter seems the most desirable, but I fear that it is not expected.

I am pretending that I intend to go from here to the Leipzig fair, and I will depart for Hildesheim on or about Saturday. But from there I am thinking of going towards the Netherlands by the stagecoach that goes to Wesel.[4] If you were in the neighborhood, sir, I would like to see you beforehand. You will learn my news at Hildesheim, in the place where the postal station of Brandenburg is located; it used to be at Steuerwald near the town.

I am entirely,

sir,   of Your Excellency,

Hanover this
30 of September
1714

the very humble
and very obedient
servant

Leibniz

---

[1] Staatsbibliothek zu Berlin Bibliothek Savigny 38 Bl. 116r–117r. Letter as sent: three quarto sides in Leibniz's hand. Not previously published.

[2] That is, presumably, Sophie Juliane, born Freiin von der Schulenburg, wife of Rabe Christoph von Oeynhausen*.

[3] See Leibniz's letter to Bernstorff of 20 September 1714 (document 32, p. 111).

[4] It appears that Leibniz was intending to take the stagecoach south from Hanover to Hildesheim as a ruse to make those in Hanover believe he was indeed going to the Leipzig fair. But as he says, from Hildesheim he was thinking of heading west, towards the Netherlands, and eventually making his way to Calais, where he apparently intended to board a ship bound for England.

Leibniz to Eléonore Desmiers d'Olbreuse*, Dowager Duchess of Braunschweig-Lüneburg-Celle

Lettre à Madame la duchesse de Zell

Madame

Le grand service que V. A. S. a rendu à la serenissime Maison de Bronsvic dans une affaire dont nous goutons maintenant les fruits par la grace de Dieu, n'etant gueres connu du public, merite d'etre conservé dans la mémoire des hommes.

Vous futes, Madame, la premiere, ou plustôt la seule personne qui prit la liberté de parler au feu Roy de la Grande Bretagne, sur l'établissement de la succession des Royaumes Britanniques dans la personne de Madame l'Electrice et de sa posterité; lors que Sa Majesté vint à Zell apres la paix de Ryswick pour rendre visite à Monseigneur le Duc votre Epous. Et Vous le fites, Madame, sans qu'aucun de la Principauté ou du Ministere Vous en eût solicité; il est vray qu'il semble que vous avés prit ce que j'avois eu l'honneur de vous en dire, comme s'il venoit de plus haut. Il n'y a presque que moy parmi ceux qui ne sont pas dans le ministere, qui en soit informé à present: mais je n'en say pas toutes les circonstances, puisque je n'ay point été present à votre entretien avec le Roy; et je souhaiterois que V. A. S voulut bien nous faire la grace, d'en dire les particularités à Mad. la princesse Royale. Peut étre que sans l'ouverture que vous fites alors, Madame, L'affaire auroit encor trainé, ou seroit demeurée imparfaite; et la vie du Roy n'ayant pas duré beaucoup apres cette visite; on auroit eté bien loin de son compte, s'il eût fallu soliciter cet établissement sous le successeur.

La delicatesse de feu Monseigneur le Duc de Zell etoit grande par rapport à tout ce qui pouvoit embarrasser le feu Roy, et S. A. S. fut surprise, lors que Vous luy fites rapport, Madame, de la conversation que Vous aviés eue avec Sa Majesté, qui avoit pris le mieux du monde ce que V. A. S. luy avoit proposé | et s'etoit declaré la dessus aussi favorablement qu'on l'auroit pû esperer |. Le Roy qui regne heureusement a present, quand il vint alors à Zell, n'en fut pas moins étonné que Monseigneur le Duc: et Madame l'Electrice y etant aussi venue parler au Roy, sans oser toucher cette corde le moins du monde; fut toute emerveillée, et agreablement surprise quand ce Monarque (: apres la proposition que V. A. S. luy en avoit faite, mais dont Madame l'Electrice n'avoit point de connoissance alors :) luy parla de son propre mouvement du dessein qu'il avoit de la faire nommer expressément avec sa posterité dans un Acte de parlement. Ce qui fut execute et mis en perfection un peu avant la mort de ce Grand Prince. L'Acte passa dans le parlement d'Angleterre, et un Comte pair du Royaume vint l'apporter à Hannover de la part du Roy et de la Nation. Et ensuite la Princesse Sophie petite fille du Roy Jaques premier fut nommée avec ses descendans dans les sermens et dans les prières publiques; quoyqu'il y eut peutétre jusqu'à 30 personnes de la famille Royale, mais catholiques, qui la

37. Leibniz to Eléonore Desmiers d'Olbreuse*, Dowager Duchess of Braunschweig-Lüneburg-Celle[1]

[3 October 1714]

Letter to Madame the Duchess of Celle

Madame

Being scarcely recognized by the public, the great service that Your Serene Highness has rendered to the Most Serene House of Braunschweig, in an affair whose result we now enjoy by the grace of God, deserves to be preserved in the memory of men.

You, madame, were the first, or rather the only person who took the liberty of speaking to the late King of Great Britain [William III] about establishing the succession of the British kingdoms in the person of Madame the [Dowager] Electress [of Braunschweig-Lüneburg, Sophie* of the Palatinate] and her posterity, when His Majesty came to Celle after the Peace of Ryswick* in order to pay a visit to your husband, Monseigneur the Duke [Duke Georg Wilhelm* of Braunschweig-Lüneburg-Celle]. And you did it, madame, without anyone from the principality or from the ministry having approached you about it. It is true that it seems that you took what I had the honour of telling you about it as if it came from higher up.[2] There is scarcely anyone but myself among those not in the ministry who might be acquainted with it at present. But I do not know all the circumstances, since I was not present at your conversation with the king, and I would hope that Your Serene Highness might be willing to do us the favor of telling the particular details of it to Madame the Royal Princess [Caroline* of Brandenburg-Ansbach, Princess of Wales]. Perhaps without the overture that you made then, madame, the affaire would still have dragged on, or it would have remained incomplete; and since the life of the king did not last long after this visit, we would have been far from succeeding if it had been necessary to seek this settlement under his successor.

The late Monseigneur Duke of Celle was very tactful in connection with anything that could embarrass the late king, and His Serene Highness was surprised when you made your report to him, madame, of the conversation that you had had with His Majesty, who took what Your Serene Highness proposed to him extremely well | and declared himself about it as favorably as one could have hoped |. When the king who happily reigns at present [George I of Great Britain, Georg Ludwig* of Braunschweig-Lüneburg] arrived in Celle at that time, he was not any less astonished than Monseigneur the Duke. And Madame the Electress, who had also arrived there to speak with the king, without daring to touch on this point in the least, was completely amazed, and pleasantly surprised when this monarch (after the proposition that Your Serene Highness had made to him about it, but of which Madame the Electress had no knowledge at the time) spoke to her of his own

precedoient dans l'ordre lineal, et dont quelqu'une s'avisant de devenir protestante, luy auroit eté preferable sans cet Acte nouveau.

Ainsi la grande utilité des bons offices de V. A. S. est fort evidente, et le Ciel s'est maintenant declaré pour leur effect. Mais aussi c'est tout ce que je say, Madame, de vos demarches pour cette affaire, sur ce que Vous eûtes alors la bonte de me dire et que Madame l'Electrice me confirma. Il est à souhaiter que V. A. S. veuille suppléer par son recit à ce qui manque en cela à ma connoissance. | Sa posterité même luy en aura de l'obligation, et | Je suis avec devotion
Madame de V. A. S.

le tres humble et tres obéissant
serviteur

Herrnhausen ce 3 d'octobre
1714

Leibniz

Leibniz to the Caroline of Brandenburg-Ansbach, Princess of Wales

Lettre à Madame La Princesse de Galles
Madame

Puisque Votre Altesse Royale est curieuse de savoir à fond tout ce qui s'est passé par rapport à la Succession de la Grande Bretagne dans la Maison d'Hannover;

38. LEIBNIZ TO CAROLINE OF BRANDENBURG-ANSBACH 129

accord about the plan that he had for having her named expressly, along with her posterity, in an act of parliament [the Act of Settlement* of 1701]. This was carried out and completed a little before the death of this great prince. The act passed in the parliament of England, and a count peer of the kingdom[3] came to bring it to Hanover on behalf of the king and the nation. And then the Princess Sophie, granddaughter of King James I, was named along with her descendants in oaths and public prayers, although there were perhaps as many as thirty persons of the royal family, but Catholics, who preceded her in the lineal order; and any of them who decided to become Protestant would have been preferable to her without this new act.

Thus the great utility of the good offices of Your Serene Highness is very evident, and heaven has now declared itself for their effect. But then this is all I know, Madame, about your initiatives in this affair, about what you had the kindness to tell me at the time and which Madame the Electress confirmed to me. It is to be hoped that Your Serene Highness may choose through her account to make good what is lacking in that with which I am acquainted. | Her posterity itself will have some obligation to her on account of it, and | I am with devotion
Madame of Your Serene Highness

the very humble and very obedient
servant

Herrenhausen this 3 of October
1714   Leibniz

---

[1] Not previously published. There are two drafts of this letter held by the Haupstaatarchiv Hannover. Both are in Leibniz's hand. The second draft, Niedersächsisches Landesarchiv-Hauptstaatsarchiv Hannover 93, 487 Bl. 34r–35r, is transcribed here (1.5 sides on one quarto leaf and 0.5 sides on a second quarto leaf). The letter was written while Leibniz was staying at Herrenhausen* with Princess Caroline prior to her departure for England on 12 October 1714.

[2] In this sentence, which is not to be found in the first draft of the letter, Leibniz suggests that he was responsible for planting the idea that led the Duchess of Celle to nudge King William III in the direction of settling the succession of the British throne on the Electress Sophie and her descendants. He is much more direct in claiming credit in the letter he wrote to Caroline the same day (see Leibniz's letter to Caroline of 3 October 1714, document 38, p. 133).

[3] In a letter to Caroline, also written on 3 October, Leibniz identified this peer count as the 'Count of Macclesfield' (see document 38, ibid.) that is, the 3rd Earl of Macclesfield, Fitton Gerard (1663–1702).

38. Leibniz to Caroline* of Brandenburg-Ansbach, Princess of Wales[1]

[3 October 1714]

Letter to Madame the Princess of Wales
Madame

Since Your Royal Highness is curious to know in detail everything that has happened in relation to the succession of Great Britain in the House of Hanover, and

et comment par degrés l'affaire est venue à cette maturité, dont nous goutons maintenant les fruits par las grace de Dieu; j'ay voulu profiter de la presence de Madame la Duchesse de Zell, venue icy pour vous souhaiter, Madame, un heureuse voyage, et je luy ay voulu donner occasion de Vous raconter, comment Elle a été la premiere personne qui a pris la liberté d'en faire la proposition au feu Roy d'Angleterre, ce qu'Elle fit avec beaucoup de succés. Et pour en obtenir une Relation, j'ay écrit la Lettre cy jointe à S. A. S mais comme Elle est eloignée de tout ce qui pourroit avoir le moindre air de vanité; je ne l'ay pû porter à en faire le recit, qu'en luy representant, Madame, que cela Vous feroit plaisir. Elle m'a donc dicté ce qui s'est passé dans les conversations qu'Elle a eue la dessus. Et comme Elle en a dit autant à Votre Altesse Royal même, j'ay voulu mettre de tout par ecrit dans cette Lettre, que je me donne l'honneur de Vous ecrire, Madame, conformement à vos intentions; pour en conserver la mémoire.

Le feu Roy de la Grande Bretagne venant rendre visite à Monseigneur le duc de Zell, un peu apres la paix de Ryswick; je pris la liberté, etant à Zell un peu avant son arrivée, de dire à Madame la Duchesse de mon propre mouvement, mais par un motif de zele: qu'il étoit temps de parler à Sa Majesté sur l'etablissement de la Succession d'Angleterre dans la personne et posterité de Madame l'Electrice; que Madame la Duchesse en pouvoit mieux parler, et de meilleure grace que d'autres, et qu'en le faisant Elle obligeroit fort la Serenissime Maison. J'appuyay ce Conseil de plusieurs raisons et circomstances, qui determinerent S. A. S fort portée d'Elle meme à tout ce qui pouvoit faire plaisir à la Maison, à en faire ouverture au Roy. Car Elle croyoit apparemment que ce que je disois, venoit de la Cour d'Hannover. Elle luy en parla donc au Ghöeur, maison de chasse dans le pays de Lunebourg; et voicy maintenant ce que Mad. la Duchesse m'a dicté.

Sire (dit Elle) on m'a donné commission d'Hannover de proposer à V. M. de nommer Mad. L'Electrice et ses Descendans à la succession d'Angleterre, puisque Vous en avés exclus les Catholiques. Le Roy répondit: l'on n'a pas encore nommé personne à la succession d'Angleterre pour ne point des obliger M. de Savoye, qui estoit dans le parti. Madame la Duchesse repliqua: cette raison ne subsiste plus, Sire, puisqu'il l'a quitté; et si V. M. fait nommer Madame l'Electrice et ses descendans Elle s'acquerera la Maison d'Hannover, et l'attachera à Elle, comme M. le Duc. Le Roy fit connoitre qu'il étoit dans des dispositions favorables la dessus.

Apres cela, Madame la Duchesse dit: ne sera ce pas V. M. qui mariera le Duc de Glocester. Oui, dit le Roy, s'il vit assés pour cela, car il est bien delicat. Il est vray, que j'ay eté aussi bien delicat moy, et je vis encore. Et bien (repliqua Mad. la Duchesse) si V. M. le marie, n'aimeroit-Elle pas autant de procurer cet avantage à la Princesse d'Hannover, qu'à une autre. Mieux, mieux, dit le Roy, car Vous savés comme je suis pour M. le Duc. Mais je la voudrois bien voir. Sire, dit Mad. la Duchesse, quand V. M. à Son retour passera à Zell, on la fera venir. Ce qui fut ainsi, le Roy la vit à Zell, et la trouva fort à son gré.

how the affair gradually arrived at this completion, of which we now enjoy the fruits by the grace of God, I wanted to profit from the presence of the [Dowager] Duchess of Celle [Eléonore Desmiers d'Olbreuse*], who came here to wish you, madame, a happy journey, and give her the opportunity to relate to you how she was the first person who took the liberty to make a proposal about it to the late King of England [William III], which she did with much success. And in order to obtain an account of it, I wrote the attached letter[2] to Her Serene Highness, but as she is removed from everything that could have the least air of vanity, I have not been able to bring her to make a report about it by pointing out to her, madame, that it would please you. She has therefore dictated to me what happened in the conversations that she had about it. And since she has told so much to Your Royal Highness herself, I wanted to write everything down in this letter, which I have given myself the honour of writing to you, madame, in accordance with your intentions to preserve the memory of it.

When the late King of Great Britain came to pay a visit to Monseigneur the Duke of Celle [Georg Wilhelm*, Duke of Braunschweig-Lüneburg-Celle] a little after the Peace of Ryswick*, I, being at Celle shortly before his arrival, took the liberty, of my own accord but from a motive of zeal, to say to Madame the Duchess that it was time to speak to His Majesty about the establishment of the succession of England in the person and posterity of Madame the Electress [Dowager Electress of Braunschweig-Lüneburg, Sophie* of the Palatinate], that Madame the Duchess would be better able to speak about it, and with better grace than others, and that in doing so she would very much oblige the Most Serene House [of Hanover]. I supported this advice with many reasons and circumstances, which caused Her Serene Highness, who was strongly inclined by herself to everything that could please the House, to make an overture about it to the king. For she apparently believed that what I said came from the court of Hanover. She therefore spoke with him about it at Göhrde*, hunting lodge in the country of Lüneburg, and here now is what Madame the Duchess dictated to me.

'Sire' (she said) 'I have been given a commission from Hanover to propose that Your Majesty name Madame the Electress to the succession of England, since you have excluded Catholics.' The King responded: 'No one has yet been named to the succession of England in order not to displease M. de Savoy,[3] who was in the party. Madame the Duchess replied: 'This reason no longer applies, Sire, since he has left; and if Your Majesty has Madame the Electress and her descendants named, you will win for yourself the House of Hanover, and it will devote itself to you, like Monsieur the Duke.' The king announced that he was favorably disposed to it.

After that, Madame the Duchess said: 'Will it not be Your Majesty who will give the Duke of Gloucester[4] in marriage.' 'Yes,' said the king, 'if he lives long enough for that, because he is very frail. It is true that I myself have been frail as well, and I am still alive.' 'Well' (replied Madame the Duchess) 'if Your Majesty gives him in

Ensuite de cela Monseigneur le Duc dit à Mad. la Duchesse: Vous avés eu une longue conversation avec le Roy. Elle n'a pas roulé sur des bagatelles, repondit Mad. la Duchesse, et luy raconta ce qui s'etoit passé. Sur quoy Vous etes vous avisées, Madame, (luy repliqua Mgr. le Duc) de luy parler de ces choses. C'est M. de Leibniz, dit Elle, qui me l'a demandé. Pourquoy ne me l'avés Vous pas dit, repliqua Monseigr. le Duc. C'est (dit Elle) parce que Vous m'auriés defendu d'en parler, et je le voulois faire. Et bien, dit Mgr. la Duc, il faut rendre compte à M. l'Electeur de cette conversation. Sur quoy Mad. la Duchesse alla raconter à Monseigneur l'Electeur ce qui s'etoit passé qui dit là desus: Bon, le Roy croira, que c'est moy qui Vous ay fait dire ces choses: Mad. la Duchesse repliqua: je le crois aussi, moy, car c'est de chez vous qu'on est venu m'en parler.

Le Roy continua de s'expliquer favorablement sur cette importante matiere, et etant retourné en Angleterre, il prepara les choses pour faire regler la succession par Acte de Parlement. Et le Duc de Glocester fit faire un compliment à la Princesse d'Hannover, et dire qu'il esperoit de la voir en venant chasser avec le Roy dans le pays de Zell. Mais ce jeune Prince mourut un peu apres, et cela fit haster le reglement de la Succession et l'Acte fut porté à Hannover par le Comte de Maclesfield accompagné de quantité d'Anglois de distinction. Le Roy dit à la Princesse Anne, qu'il seroit a propos de faire venir le Prince Electoral. La Princesse repondit, qu'Elle etoit grosse. Cette grossesse ne se trouva point, mais le Roy ne vecut gueres apres cela, autrement il auroit fait venir le Prince.

C'est la substance de ce que Madame la Duchesse m'a fait la grace de me raconter. Je suis bien aise, puisque S. A. S. est maintenant icy, que Vous avés pû tout apprendre d'Elle-meme, Madame, et vous asseurer de la verité. Je suis avec devotion Madame de Votre Altesse Royale.

38. LEIBNIZ TO CAROLINE OF BRANDENBURG-ANSBACH   133

marriage, would he not like to procure this advantage for the Princess of Hanover[5] as much as for another.' 'Rather, rather,' said the king, 'because you know how I favor Monsieur the Duke. But I should very much like to see her.' 'Sire,' said Madame the Duchess, 'when Your Majesty goes to Celle on your return, she will be summoned.' This was done, and the king saw her at Celle, and he found her very much to his liking.

Afterwards Monseigneur the Duke said to Madame the Duchess: 'You had a long conversation with the king.' 'It did not turn upon trivial matters,' responded Madame the Duchess, and she told him what had happened. 'What possessed you, madame,' (replied Monseigneur the Duke) 'to speak with him about these matters.' 'It was Monsieur Leibniz,' she said, 'who asked me to do it.' 'Why didn't you tell me,' replied Monseigneur the Duke. 'It was' (she said) 'because you forbade me to speak about it, and I wanted to do it.' 'Well,' said Monseigneur the Duke, 'Monsieur the Elector [Georg Ludwig* of Braunschweig-Lüneburg] must be apprised of this conversation.' Whereupon Madame the Duchess went to relate what had happened to Monseigneur the Elector, who said thereupon: 'Good, the king will believe that it was I who made you say these things.' Madame the Duchess replied: 'I also believe it myself, because it is from your court that someone came to speak with me about it.'

The king continued to talk favorably about this important matter, and upon returning to England, he made preparations to have the succession regulated by act of parliament.[6] And the Duke of Gloucester had a compliment paid to the Princess of Hanover and let her know that he hoped to see her when he came to hunt with the king in the country of Celle. But this young prince died a short time after, which hastened the settlement of the succession, and the act was brought to Hanover by the Count of Macclesfield [Fitton Gerard (1663–1702), 3rd Earl of Macclesfield], accompanied by a large number of Englishmen of distinction. The king told Princess Anne that it would be appropriate to summon the electoral prince [Georg August* of Braunschweig-Lüneburg] [to England]. The Princess replied that she was pregnant. This pregnancy did not prove to be true, but the king did not live for long after that, otherwise he would have summoned the prince.

This is the substance of what Madame the Duchess did me the favor of telling me. I am very glad that since she is here now you have been able to learn everything from Her Most Serene Highness herself, madame, and be confident of the truth. I am with devotion, madame, of Your Royal Highness.

---

[1] Niedersächsisches Landesarchiv-Hauptstaatsarchiv Hannover 93, 487 Bl. 27r–29r. Fair copy: 4.2 folio sides in secretary's hand. Previously published in Klopp XI 15–17 (excerpt). The letter was written on 3 October 1714 while Leibniz was staying at Herrenhausen with Caroline before her departure for England on 12 October 1714.

[2] See Leibniz's letter to Eléonore Desmiers d'Olbreuse of 3 October 1714 (document 37).

[3] Presumably, Prince Eugène of Savoy*, who was Catholic.

[4] That is, Prince William, the only son of Princess Anne (later Queen Anne) of Great Britain and her husband, Prince Jørgen (George) of Denmark and Norway, to survive his infancy. Since William III had no offspring, Prince William (b. 1689), Duke of Gloucester, was expected to secure the

Claude Alexandre de Bonneval* to Leibniz

Monsieur   6. oct. 1714

J'ay receu la lettre que vous m'avés fait Lhonneur de m'écrire, je crois que vous ne douterés pas du sensible plaisir qu'elle m'a fait.

M. le prince Eugene n'a pas moins êté fasché que moy, de ne vous plus trouver a vienne nous souhaittons tous deux vôtre retour, revenés le plûtôt que vous pourrés. Les innovations que L'on va êtablir dans le reglement des finances semblent mettre S. M. I. plus au Large, ainsi quand vous reviendrés[2] vous trouverés des fonds pour L'academie, je pourrois presque vous Le cautioner.

Je ne suis point êtonné que Madame la princesse royale ait pris tant de gout a la Lecture de votre theodicée. Le portrait que l'on m'en a fait ne se dement point pas par la, je scais qu'aux agréements, & a la delicatesse de L'esprit de son sexe, elle a joint la solidité, & les lumieres des veritables philosophes, que sa curiosité sur tout ce qu['] il y a de beau, & de bon, ne permet pas a ceux qui ont L'honneur de L'approcher, ni aux biblioteques des scavants, d'avoir rien de caché pour elle qui soit digne dêtre sceu[3]; mais pourquoy refuser de suivre en angleterre, cette nouvelle Zenobie. Le famieux longin dont vous auriés renouvellé La memoire, ne trouva point un si beau naturel, ni un esprit aussi net dans sa reine des palmiriens. M. la duchesse de marlebouroug m'a decrit L'entrée de son epoux[6] en angleterre elle ne peut trop me marquer sa[7] joye de L'advenement du roy a la Couronne d'angleterre. Le petit duc d'aremberg est allé a paris, peut être ira til dela, a loudre; M. le prince Eugene qui a leu votre lettre vous asseure de toute son amitié, & me charge de vous dire que puisque vous n'allés pas en angleterre, vous devriés bien venir a vienne, il dit au surplus, que le roy est trop sage pour luy envoyer un ambassadeur Comme le duc d'aremberg, qu'un pareil ministre auroit mieux reussi du temps du roy guillaume; je vous laisse a juger si'il a raison. Nous nous sommes presque brouillés ensemble sur le refus qu'il m'a fait de me laisser copier L'abrege de vôtre sisteme. il le tient, Comme les prestres tiennent a naples, le sang de S^t genaro, c['] est a dire qu'il me la fait baiser, & puis la renferme dans sa cassette, je luy ay dit de ne point être si fier & que j'en aurois peut être un plus Complet, & que tel que[10] cette Contesse qui

Protestant succession to the throne in England. But Prince William was in ill health and died in 1700 at the age of 11.

⁵ The duchess was speaking of her granddaughter, Sophie Dorothea of Braunschweig-Lüneburg (1687–1757), later (from 1713) Queen consort in Prussia and Electress Consort of Brandenburg by her marriage to King Friedrich Wilhelm I* of Prussia (1688–1740). She was the only daughter of her mother, Sophie Dorothea* of Braunschweig-Lüneburg-Celle (1666–1726), and the Elector Georg Ludwig*, the future King George I of England. Georg Ludwig divorced the elder Sophie Dorothea in January of 1695, as a result of her affair with Philip Christoph von Königsmarck, who was assassinated in 1694 for his indiscretion.

⁶ This resulted in the Act of Settlement* of 1701.

39. Claude Alexandre de Bonneval* to Leibniz¹

Sir   6 October d1714

I have received the letter that you have done me the honour of writing to me; I believe that you will not doubt the considerable pleasure that it has given me.

Prince Eugène* has been no less displeased than I to find you no longer in Vienna. We both desire your return; come back as soon as you can. The innovations that are going to be established in the regulation of finances seem to enrich His Imperial Majesty [Emperor Karl VI*]. Thus when you return² you will find some funds for the academy [the proposed Imperial Society of Sciences*]; I could almost guarantee it.

I am not at all astonished that the royal princess [Caroline* of Brandenburg-Ansbach, Princess of Wales] has taken such a liking to reading your *Theodicy*. The description that has been given to me of her is not inconsistent with that. I know that to her sex's charms and delicacy of spirit she has joined the strength and insights of true philosophers, that her curiosity about everything fine and good does not allow those who have the honour to approach her, nor the libraries of scholars, to have anything worthy of knowing³ hidden from her. But why refuse to follow this new Zenobia⁴ to England; the famous Longinus,⁵ whose memory you would revive, did not find so natural a beauty, nor a spirit as pure, in his Queen of the Palmyrenes. The Duchess of Marlborough [Sarah Churchill*] has described the entrance of her spouse⁶ [John Churchill, Duke of Marlborough] in England; she cannot express to me enough her⁷ joy about the advancement of the king to the crown of England.

The young Duke of Arenberg [Léopold Philippe* of Arenberg] has gone to Paris; perhaps he will go from there to London. Prince Eugène, who has read your letter, assures you of all his friendship and asks me to tell you that since you are not going to England, you should really come to Vienna. Moreover, he says that the king [George I, Georg Ludwig* of Braunschweig-Lüneburg] is too wise to send him an ambassador like the Duke of Arenberg and that such a minister would have succeeded better in the time of King William [King William III of England]. I leave

etoit menacée par un Visconti que si elle ne luy remettoit plaisance, il feroit mourir ses deux enfants & qui luy montra pour reponce l[']entredeux de ses Cuisses de dessus les murailles, luy disant que telle chose qu[']elle luy faisoit voir en feroit d'autres[11], ainsi Monsieur tel dis je que la dite contesse acelli vous pouvés toujours reproduire le mesme sisteme, mesme plus ample que celuy qu'il m[']a refusé & reparer ainsi en me le donnant quand vous le jugerés a propos, ce que ses refus m'enlevent. il m'a repondu que je faisois une belle Comparaison d'un philosophe tel que vous; a une putain[12]. je luy ay dit que je vous le manderois & que je m'en rapportois a vous, & non a luy, puisque cette heroine, & non putain[13]; avoit fait une action qu'un philosophe ne desadvoueroit[14] pas; je vous en laisse le juge. Si la longeur[15] de ma lettre vous ennuye c'est a mon temperamment aidé de celuy de ma nation a qui vous devés vous en prendre, vous scavés que nous autres francois aimons a babiller. a l[']heure que je vous parle il me semble causer avec vous, je ne finirois jamais si je ne croyois vous derober des moments precieux que vous employerés mieux, & dont j'espere de profiter quelques jours, quand j'auray l'honneur de vous revoir. adieu, Conservés vous bien & me croyés plein d'estime, & de tendresse pour vous, ne m'oubliés pas, ecrivés moy a vos heures perdues, je vous feray reponce exactement.

L'imperatrice ira se faire couronner a presbourg incessament je resteray au fouxbourg en attendant son retour. Je suis tres parfaittement

Monsieur

Votre tres humble & tres obeissant serviteur

a vienne ce 6. 8bre   AL. Bonneval.

    1714

P. S. M. Sulli est allé a paris avec Le duc d'aramberg.

39. DE BONNEVAL TO LEIBNIZ   137

you to judge if he is right. We nearly had a falling out over his refusal to allow me to copy the summary of your system.[8] He keeps it as the priests keep the blood of Saint Gennaro at Naples,[9] that is to say, he has me kiss it and then shuts it up again in his strongbox. I told him not to be so proud, and that I would perhaps have a more complete one, and that just as[10] that countess who was threatened by a viscount, that if she did not give him pleasure, he would have her two infants killed, and who responded by showing him the space between her thighs from atop the walls, telling him that that which she showed to him she would show to others;[11] so I say sir, like the aforementioned Countess Acelli, you can always reproduce the same system, even more expansive than the one that he has refused me, and thus make amends by giving me, when you shall deem it fitting, that of which his refusals deprive me. He replied that I made a fine comparison of a philosopher like you to a whore.[12] I told him that I would write it to you and that I would refer it to you and not to him, since that heroine, and not a whore,[13] had taken an action that a philosopher would not disavow;[14] I leave it to you to judge. If the length[15] of my letter bores you, it is my temperament, aided by that of my nation, on which you ought to lay the blame; you know that we French love to babble. Now as I speak to you, it seems that I chatter with you; I would never finish if I did not believe that I rob you of precious moments that you will employ better and from which I hope to profit some day when I will have the honour of seeing you again. Goodbye, stay well, and believe that I am full of esteem and affection for you. Do not forget me, write me in your spare time; I will respond to you diligently.

The empress [Elisabeth Christine* of Braunschweig-Wolfenbüttel] will soon go to be crowned at Pressburg;[16] I will be staying in the faubourg while awaiting her return. I am quite entirely

sir

Your very humble and very obedient servant

in Vienna 6 October   AL. Bonneval.

     1714

P. S. Mr. Sully[17] has gone to Paris with the Duke of Arenberg.

---

[1] LBr. 89 Bl. 10r–13r. Letter as sent: 7.2 quarto sides in Bonneval's hand. Answer to Leibniz's letter to Bonneval of 21 September (see document 35). Previously published in JGHF 426–30; in Robinet 1954, p. 16 (excerpt).

[2] Feder mistranscribes 'reviendrés' as 'viendrez'.

[3] Reading 'd'être su' for 'd'être sceu'.

[4] Zenobia (d. c.275) was a third-century Queen of the Palmyrene Empire in Syria. In 269 she conquered Egypt, and later much of Asia Minor. She declared independence from Rome, but was defeated by the Roman Emperor Aurelian in 274 and taken captive to Rome.

[5] That is, Cassius Longinus (c.213–73 CE), a Hellenistic philosopher and literary critic. He studied at Alexandria and taught for many years in Athens. He later became, first the teacher, and later the chief counsellor of Queen Zenobia of Palmyra. He advised Zenobia to declare her independence from Rome, but this revolt was put down by the Roman Emperor Aurelian and Longinus was executed.

[6] Feder mistranscribes 'epoux' as 'mari' (see JGHF 427).

[7] Feder mistranscribes 'sa' as 'la'.

Leibniz to Johann Matthias von der Schulenburg

Monsieur

Quoyque mon dessein soit d'aller en Angleterre, neantmoins ne voulant point aller dans la suite de la princesse Royale, (: quoyqu'Elle m'eût fait la grace de me témoigner, qu'Elle en seroit bien aise :) je fais auparavant un tour à Bronsvic. J'espere d'y etre Mardi ou Mercredi, et là je me determineray sur la route. Si je vous y pouvois voir, Monsieur, j'en serois ravi. Ne sachant pas bien precisement ou vous estes je sçaurois vous adresser cette lettre assez directement, je tache pourtant de faire en sorte, qu'Elle vous soit rendue au plus tôt.

Madame la princesse Royale part vendredi prochain. Mesdames les princesses prendront les devants avec la Freule Gemming et partiront mardi, car elles iront à petites journées. Mons[gr] le Margrave d'Ansbach a esté en Hollande aupres du Roy.

40. LEIBNIZ TO VON DER SCHULENBURG   139

[8] Bonneval is referring to Leibniz's essay, *Principes de la nature et de la grâce, fondés en raison*, which Leibniz had prepared at the request of Prince Eugène.

[9] Saint Gennaro (Januarius) (d. *c.*305) was a bishop, now the patron saint of Naples, and is a martyr saint of the Roman Catholic Church. No contemporary accounts of his life exist, but later Christian sources maintain that he was martyred in the Diocletian persecution of 305. The supposed dried blood of Gennaro is kept in a sealed vial in a vault at the Cathedral of Naples. Several times a year, the vial is removed from the vault for a ritual in which the substance in the vial is said to liquefy miraculously:

> A dark mass that half fills a hermetically sealed four inch glass container, and is preserved in a double reliquary in the Naples cathedral as the blood of St. Januarius, liquefies 18 times during the year: (1) on the Saturday before the first Sunday in May and the eight following days; (2) on the feast of St. Januarius, and during the octave; and (3) on December 16. This phenomenon goes back to the fourteenth century when it was mentioned in the chronicle of an unknown Sicilian in 1389 (published by G. de Blasiis, Naples 1887), although tradition connects it with a certain Eusebia, who had allegedly collected the blood after the martyrdom and given the reliquary to the bishop of Naples on the Via Antoniana during the transfer of the body from Pozzuoli to the catacomb. The ceremony accompanying the liquefaction is performed by holding the reliquary close to the altar on which is located what is believed to be the martyr's head. While the people pray, often tumultuously, the priest turns the reliquary up and down in the full sight of the onlookers until the liquefaction takes place. He then announces, 'The miracle has happened,' and the *Te Deum* is chanted by the people and clergy. [Ryan 2003, p. 723]

[10] Feder mistranscribes '& que tel que' as 'comme' (see JGHF 428).

[11] Perhaps prudishness led Feder, or his publisher, to replace 'lentredeux de ses cuisses de dessus les murailles, luy disant que telle chose quelle luy faisoit voir en feroit d'autres' with 'de dessus les murailles—le moyen d'en avoir d'autres' (see JGHF 429).

[12] Feder replaces 'putain' with 'p...' (see JGHF 429).

[13] Feder replaces 'putain' with 'p...' (see JGHF 429).

[14] Feder mistranscribes 'desadvouerois' as 'désapprouveroit' (see JGHF 429).

[15] Reading 'longueur' for 'longeur'.

[16] At the time, a town in the Kingdom of Hungary. In 1536 it became the capital of Hungary and a part of the Habsburg Empire. It was often used as a coronation town by Habsburg royalty. It is now Bratislava, the capital of the Slovak Republic.

[17] See Leibniz's letter to Bonneval of 21 September 1714 (document 35, p. 123, note 5).

40. Leibniz to Johann Matthias von der Schulenburg*[1]

[7 October 1714]

Sir

Although my plan is to go to England, nevertheless, since I do not want to go in the retinue of the Royal Princess [Caroline* of Brandenburg-Ansbach, Princess of Wales] (although she did me the favor of letting me know that she would be very pleased by it), I am taking a trip to Braunschweig beforehand. I hope to be there Tuesday or Wednesday, and then I will decide on the route. If I could see you there, sir, I would be delighted. Not knowing precisely where you are, I was not able to address this letter directly enough; I will nonetheless try to ensure that it is delivered to you as soon as possible.

Madame the Royal Princess departs next Friday. Mesdames the Princesses will take the lead with Lady Gemming and will depart Tuesday, because they will go by short stages. Monseigneur the Margrave of Ansbach [Wilhelm Friedrich*] has

140   41. LEIBNIZ TO VON DER SCHULENBURG

Il est retrouné chez luy à la haste, mais il viendra trouver Madame la princesse Royale en Hollande, et je m'imagine qu'il passera la mer avec Elle.

On tient maintenant pour asseuré que le Roy de Suede va venir. Il passera par les terres Hereditaires de l'Empereur, et ira apparemment aux Deuxponts.

C'est dommage que Barcellonne n'a pû etre sauvée. Un peu plus de commerce et d'intelligence entre l'Empereur et le Roy de la Grande Bretagne auroit peutetre fait l'affaire. Mais le ceremoniel et le[3] quant à moy, gâtent bien des choses.

Les Hollandois fortifiés par la Grande Bretagne refusent maintenant de recevoir ce que les Espagnols ont voulu fourrer dans le Traité de commerce et les Anglois demandent la reforme des 3 Articles additionnels du leur. Mais je croy que les Espagnols plieront.

Si l'affaire de la Barriere peut être ajustée à l'amiable, tout ira bien. Le Roy a pris un bon parti, qui est de travailler par ses bons offices à un accommodement raisonnable entre l'Empereur et Mess. les Etats.

Il ne reste donc que l'affaire du Nord à regler: elle ne sera pas sans difficulté, mais tout depend du Czar, qui paroist porté à la moderation.

Je suis avec zeal
Monsieur de V. E.

le tres humble & tres
obéissant serviteur
Leibniz

Hannover ce 7 d'Octobre 1714

Leibniz to Johann Matthias von der Schulenburg

Monsieur

Madame la princesse Royale etant partie, je partiray aussi enfin demain ou apres demain au plus tard, et ayant eté à Bronsvic, je feray un tour à Helmstät, et dela je me donneray l'honneur de vous rendre visite. Peut etre auray j'aussi l'avantage d'y

been in Holland with the king [George I, Georg Ludwig* of Braunschweig-Lüneburg]. He returned home in a hurry, but he will meet Madame the Royal Princess in Holland, and I imagine that he will cross the sea with her.

It is now taken for granted that the King of Sweden is going to come. He will pass through the hereditary lands of the emperor [Karl VI*] and will apparently go to Zweibrücken.

It is a shame that Barcelona could not be saved.[2] A little more dealing and understanding between the emperor and the King of Great Britain would perhaps have done the trick. But the ceremonial and the,[3] so far as I am concerned, spoils many things.

The Dutch, strengthened by Great Britain, are now refusing to accept what the Spanish have wanted to stick into the commercial treaty, and the English are requesting the amendment of three additional articles from them. But I believe that the Spanish will yield.

If the matter of the barrier[4] can perhaps be settled amicably, everything will be fine. The king has made a good decision, which is to work through his good offices for a reasonable accommodation between the emperor and the States-General*.

There remains, then, only the matter of the North[5] to settle. It will not be without difficulty, but everything depends on the czar [Peter I the Great*], who appears inclined toward moderation.

I am enthusiastically,
sir, of Your Excellency

the very humble and very
obedient servant

Hanover 7 October 1714   Leibniz

---

[1] Staatsbibliothek zu Berlin Bibliothek Savigny 38 Bl. 120r–121r. Letter as sent: three quarto sides in Leibniz's hand. Not previously published.

[2] See Leibniz's letter to Bernstorff* of 20 September 1714 (document 32, p. 111).

[3] In this sentence Leibniz failed to insert any noun after the second 'le'; he clearly intended to mention something in addition to 'le ceremoniel' that is responsible for spoiling many things.

[4] See Leibniz's letter to Caroline of 16 June 1714 (document 18, p. 69 note 7).

[5] Leibniz is presumably referring to the ongoing Great Northern War (1700–21).

41. Leibniz to Johann Matthias von der Schulenburg*[1]

[12 October 1714]

Sir

Now that Madame the Princess of Wales [Caroline* of Brandenburg-Ansbach] has left, I will also leave tomorrow or the day after, at the latest; and after visiting Braunschweig, I will take a trip to Helmstedt, and from there I will give myself the honour of paying you a visit. Perhaps I will also have the benefit of finding your

trouver Mlle votre soeur encor, que j'aurois souhaité de pouvoir accompagner. Mais je nétois pas encor prét à partir, et je voulois attendre le depart de Madame la princesse de Galles. Je n'ay rien a adjouter presentement, si non, que je suis avec zele

Monsieur de Votre Excellence

le tres humble & tres obéissant

Hannover ce 12 d'Octobre 1714   serviteur   Leibniz

Leibniz to Andreas Gottlieb von Bernstorff

Bronsvic 14 d'Octobre   A son Excellence
         1714   Monsieur de Bernsdorf
Monsieur   premier Ministre d'Etat de
               Sa Mté Britannique Electeur
                   de Bronsvic
                     Londres

Je me donne l'honneur de temps en temps d'ecrire à V. E. quoyque je sache qu'elle a plus que jamais beaucoup de grandes affaires sur les bras. Mais je pense de le faire pour le service de notre Royal maitre, puisqu'il semble que V. E. ne trouve pas tout a fait mauvaise la liberté que je prends par le zele qui m'attache à Sa Mté. Une affaire qui vient de se passer à la diete de l'Empire, m'en donne maintenant l'occasion. Le Ministre du Roy de prusse sur un rescript de plainte du Roy son maitre de Berlin du 2 d'Octob. 1714 a proposé de sous mettre l'affaire des Ministres Evangeliques du palatinat, qui sont en contestation avec les Reformés sur leur[s] revenus, à l'arbitrage du Roy de la Grande Bretagne, il a communiqué l'extrait de ce rescript ou l'on allegue une raison dans la quelle je trouve quelque difficulté. Voicy les propres paroles du Rescript.

Sie (ihr konigl. Mt von Groß Britannien) seind wie bekand der <u>Lutherische</u> Religion zu gethan. Sie sind auch König von einem der <u>Reformierten Religion bekennenden Königreich</u> etc.

Je mets maintenant à part cet Epithete de <u>Lutherien</u>, qui n'est pas trop convenable, et que les Reformés et autres affectent de nous donner. Mais je remarqueray seulement qu'on y fait une opposition entre la religion de Sa Mté, et celle de son

sister still there, whom I should have wished to be able to accompany. But I was not yet ready to leave, and I wanted to wait for the departure of Madame the Princess of Wales. I have nothing to add at the moment, except that I am enthusiastically, sir, of Your Excellency

the very humble and very obedient

Hanover 12 October 1714   servant   Leibniz

---

[1] Staatsbibliothek zu Berlin Bibliothek Savigny 38 Bl. 119r. Letter as sent: one quarto side in Leibniz's hand. Not previously published. For Schulenburg's reply, see his letter to Leibniz of 15 October 1714 (document 43).

42. Leibniz to Andreas Gottlieb von Bernstorff*[1]

Braunschweig 14 October   To His Excellency
1714   Mr. Bernstorff
Sir   Prime Minister of State of
His Britannic Majesty, Elector
of Braunschweig
London

I give myself the honour from time to time of writing to Your Excellency, although I know that you have, more than ever, a lot of important matters on your hands. But I am thinking of doing it for the service of our royal master [King George I, Georg Ludwig* of Braunschweig-Lüneburg], since it seems that Your Excellency does not find entirely amiss the liberty that I take from the zeal that commits me to His Majesty. Something that has just transpired at the diet of the empire now gives me the occasion for it. The minister of the King [Friedrich Wilhelm I*] of Prussia, on account of a rescript of complaint from the king his master from Berlin of 2 October 1714, has proposed to submit the matter of the Evangelical[2] ministers of the Palatinate, who are in dispute with the Reformed [Calvinists] concerning their revenues, to the arbitration of the King of Great Britain. He has communicated the extract of this rescript in which a reason is put forward in which I find some difficulty. Here are the very words of the rescript:

'You (Your Royal Majesty of Great Britain) are, as is well known, devoted to the *Lutheran* religion. You are also king of a *kingdom committed to the Reformed religion*' etc.

Now I set aside this epithet of *Lutheran*, which is not very suitable and which the Reformed and others feign to give us.[3] But I will only remark that they there make a distinction between the religion of His Majesty and that of the kingdom of Great

Royaume de la Grande Bretagne; et l'on suppose que la Religion Anglicane est la meme avec celle des Reformés du palatinat. Mais l'un et l'autre point ne me paroist pas assez recevable. Car de la maniere que la Religion Anglicane est exposée dans la Liturgie et dans les 39 articles, et de la maniere que ces articles ont eté expliqués par M. l'Eveque de Salisbury dans son Commentaire approuvé par les Archeveques de Cantorbery Tillotson et Tennison, dont le dernier est encor en vie, une personne qui professe la Confession d'Augsbourg peut estre de l'Eglise Anglicane. Et tant du temps du Roy Edouard, que de celuy de la Reine Elisabet sa soeur, on a eu soin de ne point rompre avec nos Eglises d'Allemagne. Et on n'a point receu en Angleterre le Synode de Dordrecht qui est le livre symbolique des Reformés du palatinat. Et quoyque le Roy recommande la Tolerance, et retablisse en bonne partie les Whigs déplacés, et deplace des Torris qui leur ont succedé, ce n'est pas parce qu'ils sont Whigs ou Torris, mais parce que ce sont ces Whigs qui ont rendu de si grands services a la bonne cause, et que ces sont ces Torris qui luy ont causé un grand prejudice. Cela ne tire point a consequence pour d'autres Torris et Whigs, et ce n'est pas à dire que Sa Mté soit pour les presbyteriens ou reformés a la façon de Geneve, contre les Episcopaux qui symbolisent avec tant avec nos principles et dont nous pouvons signer les articles. Peut etre donc qu'il seroit a propos de faire insinuer quelque chose contre la pretendue difference entre la religion du Roy et du Royaume de la Grande Bretagne dont on s'est avisé de parler à Berlin, et contre la convenance entre la religion Anglicane et celle du palatinat. Une telle insinuation seroit peut etre fort au gre des Anglois. Mais V. E. qui est sur les lieux, et a des bonnes informations de tous cotés en jugera mieux. Une gazette sembloit dire que le Ministre de Savoye avoit eu audience du Roy quoyque avec peine, mais comme cela ne me paroissoit pas assez detaillé ny conformé à un mot que j'ay trouvé dans la lettre de V. E. j'en doute encore. Au reste je suis avec respect

Monsieur, de V. E. etc.

Leibniz

42. LEIBNIZ TO VON BERNSTORFF   145

Britain; and they suppose that the Anglican religion is the same as the Reformed of the Palatinate. But neither of these points seems quite acceptable to me. For from the manner in which the Anglican religion is presented in the liturgy and in the Thirty-Nine Articles,[4] and from the manner in which these articles have been explained by the Bishop of Salisbury [Gilbert Burnet (1643–1715)] in his commentary approved by the Archbishops of Canterbury [John] Tillotson* and [Thomas] Tenison,* of which the latter is still living, a person who professes the Confession of Augsburg can be of the Anglican church. And in the times of both King Edward [King Edward VI (1537–53)] and Queen Elizabeth [Queen Elizabeth I (1533–1603)] his sister, care was taken not to break with our German churches. And the Synod of Dordrecht, which is the emblematic book[5] of the Reformed of the Palatinate, has not been received in England. And although the king recommends tolerance, and restores in large part the displaced Whigs, and displaces some Tories who succeeded them, that is not because they are Whigs or Tories, but because it is those Whigs who rendered such great services to the good cause, and because these are those Tories who caused him a great harm. That does not have implications for any other Tories or Whigs, and it is not to say that His Majesty favors the Presbyterians or the Reformed after the fashion of Geneva against the Episcopalians, who agree so much with our principles and whose articles [of faith] we are able to endorse. Perhaps, then, it would be appropriate to suggest something against the pretended difference between the religion of the king and of the kingdom of Great Britain, of which they have ventured to speak in Berlin, and against the affinity between the Anglican religion and that of the Palatinate. Such a suggestion would perhaps be much to the liking of the English. But Your Excellency, who is on the spot and has good information from all sides, will judge better of it. A newspaper appeared to say that the minister of Savoy had had an audience with the king, although with reluctance, but as that did not appear sufficiently detailed to me, nor in accordance with a remark that I found in the letter of Your Excellency, I still doubt it. Finally, I am with respect,

sir, of Your Excellency etc.

Leibniz

[1] LBr. 59 Bl. 122r–122v. Draft: two quarto sides in Leibniz's hand. Not previously published.

[2] 'Evangelical' was Luther's, and Leibniz's, favoured term for Luther's reform movement. The term 'Lutheran' had been used by Luther's opponents, following the practice of naming a heresy after its founder.

[3] See note 2.

[4] The Thirty-Nine Articles of Religion were developed from the Forty-two Articles 'for the avoiding of controversy in opinions and the establishment of a godly concord in certain matters of religion,' which had been formulated by Archbishop Thomas Cranmer in 1553. These Articles were eliminated when Mary I became queen; but when Elizabeth I succeeded Mary to the throne in 1558, it was necessary to re-establish doctrinal articles for the Church of England. In 1563 the Canterbury Convocation of the Church of England revised the Forty-two Articles of Cranmer, and a final revision by convocation produced the Thirty-Nine Articles of Religion in 1571; this final version was approved by both convocation and Parliament. The purpose of the Thirty-Nine Articles was to define the doctrines of the Church of England in relation to Roman Catholicism and dissident Protestants.

[5] Leibniz is not referring to the Synod itself, but to 'The Decision of the Synod of Dort on the Five Main Points of Doctrine in Dispute in the Netherlands,' which published the results of the National Synod held in Dordrecht in 1618–19.

Johann Matthias von der Schulenburg* to Leibniz

Emden ce 15me d'

Monsieur Oct^{br} 1714

Des que j'ai eté informé de votre resolution et de votre voyage en Angleterre, et que pour cet effet vous vous trouveriez a Hildesheim a un certain jour marqué, je m'étois donné l'honneur de Vous ecrire, et j'avois envoyé cette lettre par un expret[2] a Steuervaldt, ou je me serois randu moy meme si je n'avois pas eu un petit voyage a faire, dont je n'ai seu me dispanser, a mon retour ma lettre pour Vous Monsieur, etoit ranvoyée ici, et j'apprennois en meme temp par celle que vous m'aviez fait l'honneur de m'ecrire que votre voyage d'Angleterre etoit differé de quelque temp que vous iriez auparavant a Bronsvig, et a Helmstedt pour venir ici, ne changez pas de santim[t] je vous en supplie, ma soeur sera ici jusqu'a jeudis[3] prochain. Elle sera bien aise de vous voir ici de meme que mon frere. Nous vous prions touts de vous randre ici le plustost que faire se pourra, et nous vous attandons pour le plus tard mardis ou mercredis a midis[4] prochain, je differe le reste jusqu'a l'honneur de vous voir et de vous embrasser et je suis avec au tant de sincertié que de passion Monsieur

votre tres humble
et tres obeiss[t]
serviteur
Schoulenbg

Leibniz to Charlotte Elisabeth von Klenk

A Mademoiselle de Klenck
Dame de la clef dor de l'Imperatrice Amalie
Vienne

Bronswic
ce 16
d'october
1714

Mademoiselle

J'espere que la lettre que je me suis donné l'honneur de vous écrire un peu apres mon arrivée icy, vous aura eté rendue, et que vous aures bien voulu me faire la faveur d'avoir soin de celle que j'avois écrite à la Majesté de l'Imperatrice Amaile.

43. Johann Matthias von der Schulenburg* to Leibniz[1]

Sir

Emden 15
October 1714

As soon as I was informed of your decision and of your trip to England, and that for this purpose you would be in Hildesheim on a certain determined day, I gave myself the honour of writing to you, and I sent this letter by courier[2] to Steuerwald, where I would have travelled myself if I had not had a small trip to take, which I could not avoid. On my return, my letter for you, sir, was returned here, and by what you had done me the honour of writing to me, I learned at the same time that your trip to England was postponed for some time, that you would first go to Braunschweig and to Helmstedt in order to come here. I beseech you not to change your mind. My sister will be here until next Thursday.[3] She will be very glad to see you here, as will my brother. We all entreat you to visit here as soon as it will be possible to do so, and we expect you late Tuesday or Wednesday near midday.[4] I postpone the rest until I have the honour of seeing and embracing you, and I am with as much sincerity as passion

sir

your very humble
and very obedient
servant
Schulenbg

---

[1] LBr. 840 Bl. 289–90. Letter as sent: three quarto sides in Schulenburg's hand. Not previously published. Reply to Leibniz's letter to Schulenburg of 12 October 1714 (document 41).

[2] Reading 'exprès' for 'expret.'

[3] Reading 'jeudi' for 'jeudis.'

[4] Reading 'mardi ou mercredi à midis' for 'mardis ou mercredis a midis'.

44. Leibniz to Charlotte Elisabeth von Klenk*[1]

To Mademoiselle Klenk
Lady of the golden key of the Empress Amalie*

Vienna

Braunschweig
16
October
1714

Mademoiselle

I hope that the letter that I gave myself the honour of writing you a little after my arrival here[2] has been delivered to you and that you will be willing to do me the favor of taking care of what I have written to the Majesty of the [Dowager] Empress [Wilhelmine] Amalie*.[3]

J'ay fait cependant ma Cour à Madame la princesse de Galles et son Altesse Royale est partie vendredi dernier. Il y a lieu de croire qu'elle trouvera en Hollande l'escadre Angloise retournée à l'embouchure de la Meuse et même il semble que le temps va se mettre expres au beau, et le vent à l'Est[4] pour favorise son passage: tant paroit-il que le Ciel prend part à l'établissement de la Maison d'Hannover sur le Trone d'Angleterre.

Pendant mon séjour à Herrnhausen, j'ay admire l'egalité de l'humeur[5] et la bonté et moderation que cette princesse conserve au milieu de cette grande prosperité. Madame la Duchesse douairiere de Zell, et Madame la Duchesse de Wolfenbutel sont venues à Herrenhausen luy souhaiter un heureux voyage.

Si Madame la Duchess de Bronsvic-Blankenbourg, Mere de la Majesté de l'imperatrice regnante avoit déjà été de retour nous l'aurions aussi vûe apparemment. M le Marcgrave d'Ansbach frere de S A R. est venu deux jours avant le depart, et accompagnera Madame la princesse de Galles. Peut-être irat-il avec Elle jusqu'en Angleterre.

Le Roy a eté receu des Hollandois comme leur liberateur. Et en effect le dernier Ministere Anglois s'entendoit avec les François et las Espagnols pour travailler à la ruine de la Hollande. Les Anglois ont sujet d'encherir sur les Hollandois, car ils étoient encor en plus grand danger.

Le Roy n'a eté que peu incommodé de la mer, mais le prince Royal bien d'avantage. Cela fera cet effect, que le Roy repassera plus aisement, comme nous espérons qu'il fera l'eté qui vient. Il est vray que les jeunes gens sont ordinairement plus incommodés de la mer, que les personnes plus avancées. Quand j'etois fort jeune j'avois de la peine à aller en carosse à reculons.

Mais je m'apperçois qu'il est temps de finir. Je vous supplie, Mademoiselle de contribuer à me conserver les bontés de la Majesté de l'Imperatrice, et de croire que je seray tousjours avec respect

Mademoiselle

> votre tres humble et tres
> obeissant serviteur
> Leibniz

P. S.

Je crois Mademoiselle de vous avoir dit un mot autresfois de M. Schmid Conseiller de M Comte de Leiningen demeurant à Vienne depuis plusiers annees, homme de savoir et de merite. Il a une tasse d'agate d'une façon fort extraordinaire. Une princesse de la Maison Royale de France grande patronne des gens de lettres, en avoit

I have meanwhile paid my court to Madame the Princess of Wales [Caroline* of Brandenburg-Ansbach], and her Royal Highness departed last Friday [12 October 1714]. There is reason to believe that she will find the English squadron in Holland, returned to the mouth of the Meuse, and it even seems that the weather is purposely going to turn out fine, and the east wind[4] in order to favor her passage; so much does it appear that heaven participates in the establishment of the House of Hanover on the throne of England.

During my stay at Herrenhausen*, I admired the evenness of temper[5] and kindness and moderation that this princess preserves in the midst of this great prosperity. Madame the Dowager Duchess of Celle [Eléonore Desmiers d'Olbreuse*] and Madame the Duchess of Wolfenbüttel [Elisabeth Sophie Marie of Schleswig-Holstein-Senderburg-Norburg][6] came to Herrenhausen to wish her a happy voyage.

If Madame the Duchess of Braunschweig-Blankenburg [Christine Louise of Oettingen],[7] mother of the majesty of the reigning empress [Elisabeth Christine* of Braunschweig-Wolfenbüttel], had already been back, we would obviously have seen her as well. The Margrave of Ansbach [Wilhelm Friedrich* of Brandenburg-Ansbach, brother of Her Royal Highness, arrived two days before her departure and will accompany Madame the Princess of Wales. Perhaps he will go with her as far as England.

The king [George I, Georg Ludwig* of Braunschweig-Lüneburg] has been received by the Dutch as their liberator. And indeed the last English ministry came to an agreement with the French and the Spanish to work for the downfall of Holland. The English had reason to one-up the Dutch because they were still at greater risk.

The king has been only a little indisposed by the sea, but the royal prince [Georg August* of Braunschweig-Lüneburg, Prince of Wales] much more. That will have the effect that the king will return more easily, as we hope that he will do next summer. It is true that young people are usually more indisposed by the sea than older persons. When I was very young, I found it difficult to travel in a coach facing the rear.

But I see that it is time to finish. I beseech you, Mademoiselle, to help preserve for me the kindnesses of the majesty of the empress and to believe that I will always be with respect

Mademoiselle

your very humble and very
obedient servant
Leibniz

P. S.

I believe, Mademoiselle, that I have previously mentioned to you Mr. Schmid, councillor of the Count of Leiningen residing in Vienna for many years, a man of wisdom and merit. He has an agate cup of quite an extraordinary form. A princess of the royal house of France, a great patron of men of letters, gave it to a famous

fait present il y a plus de 160 ans à un savant celebre du heritage du quel elle est parvenue a un ami de M. Schmid, qui est bien aise de la faire voir, et souhaite qu'elle soit vûe un jour de l'Imperatrice Amalie. Je vous supplie, Mad^lle, de me faire la grace de le favoriser dans son dessein.

Leibniz to Claude Alexandre de Bonneval

> A Monsieur le Comte de Bonneval
> General au service de sa
> Mté Imperiale & catholique
>
> > Vienne auff der land-
> > straß in des hofseilers
> > hauß

Monsieur

L'honneur et le plaisir de votre lettre m'est venu un peu tard, parce que j'ay eté obligé indispensablement de faire un tour à Zeiz, ou j'ay un artisan, que je fais travailler à une Machine Arithmetique d'une nouvelle espece. Elle doit faire les multiplications et les divisions de tres grand[s] nombres par des tours de roue, sans aucunes additions et substractions auxiliaires, sans qu'on ait besoin de chercher le quotient en divisant, et de telle sorte qu'un grand nombre soit aussitot multiplié qu'un petit, parce que le tout tourne à la fois. M. le duc de Saxe-Zeiz, frere de M. le Cardinal primat de Hungrie m'a fait l'honneur de me loger à la Cour. Il est asseurement le plus savant prince de l'Europe, en matiere d'Histoire, et sur tout par rapport à l'Histoire la plus utile, qui regarde les princes et Etats. Et quand un chancelier ou conseiller de quelque prince le vient trouver, ce Ministre est etonné de remarquer que S. A. S. sait par coeur tous les pactes de familles, branches, alliances, partages, acquisitions de la maison du prince mieux que son Ministre; elle étend même sa curiosité jusqu'à de moindres familles mais distinguées. Quand je vous ay

scholar more than 160 years ago, and it has found its way to a friend of Mr. Schmid, who is very happy to show it and wishes that it may be seen one day by the Empress Amalie. I beseech you, mademoiselle, to do me the favor of helping him in his plan.

[1] LBr. F 24 Bl. 38r–39r. Draft: two quarto sides in Leibniz's hand. Previously published in Klopp XI 17–19 (excerpt).
[2] See Leibniz's letter to Klenk of 16 September 1714, document 30.
[3] See Leibniz's letter to Wilhelmine Amalie of 16 September 1714, document 29.
[4] Reading 'de l'Est' for 'à l'Est'.
[5] Klopp mistranscribes 'l'humeur' as 'l'honneur' (see Klopp XI 18).
[6] In 1710 Elisabeth Sophie Marie (1683–1767) married August Wilhelm (1662–1731), third and eldest surviving son of Duke Anton Ulrich* of Braunschweig-Wolfenbüttel, who succeeded his father as duke upon the latter's death in March of 1714. She was August Wilhelm's third wife.
[7] In 1690 Christine Louise of Oettingen (1671–1747) married Ludwig Rudolf (1671–1735), the youngest son of Duke Anton Ulrich* of Braunschweig-Wolfenbüttel. In the same year, Anton Ulrich gave Ludwig Rudolf the county of Blankenburg am Harz, which became a principality of the Holy Roman Empire in 1707, after Ludwig Rudolf's daughter, Elisabeth Christine* had been betrothed to Archduke Karl of Austria, the future Emperor Karl VI*. In 1731 Ludwig Rudolf inherited Wolfenbüttel.

45. Leibniz to Claude Alexandre de Bonneval* (excerpt)[1]

[Beginning of November, 1714]
To Count Bonneval
General in the service of his
Imperial and Catholic Majesty

Vienna on the Land-
straße at the Hofseiler
house

Sir

The honour and the pleasure of your letter came to me a bit late, since I have been unavoidably forced to take a trip to Zeitz, where I have an artisan whom I am having work on a new kind of arithmetic machine. It is supposed to do multiplications and divisions of very large numbers by some turns of a wheel, without any supplementary additions and subtractions, without any need to seek the quotient by dividing, so that a great number may as soon be multiplied as a small one, because everything turns at once. The Duke of Saxe-Zeitz [Moritz Wilhelm (1664–1718)], the brother of the Cardinal Primate of Hungary [Christian August of Saxe-Zeitz (1666–1725)], has done me the honour of housing me at the court. He is assuredly the most learned prince of Europe in historical matters, and above all in relation to the most useful history, which concerns princes and states. And when a chancellor or counselor of some prince meets him, this minister is astonished to observe that His Serene Highness knows by heart all the pacts of families, branches, alliances, divisions, acquisitions of the house of the prince better than his

nommé, Monsieur, il a douté si vous n'esties pas des pays bas, ou les Comtes de Bouquoy prenoient le nom de Bonneval. Madame la Duchesse son Epouse est soeur du feu[2] Roy de prusse. Elle et M. le Duc m'ont fait la grace de me mener à leur[s] vendanges, avec les gentils hommes et demoiselles de la Cour, et j'ay pensé vendages[3] que M. l'Electeur de Baviere vient de faire en france en compagnie de quelques dames qui representoient des Pomonnes avec leur[s] paniers. Mais maintenant: adieu panier, vendages sont faites. S. A. E. retourne à regret (dit on) dans ses etats, quant a ses plaisirs personnels detaches de la grandeur. Mais il faut que l'homme cede au Heros. Voilà un preambule, sur les lieux ou je suis, qui ne vous interessera guere.

Maintenant je dois vous dire Monsieur, que je pourrois bien aller encor en Angleterre cette année et peut etre bientôt. Si j'y vay, je passeray à Calais, car la mer va devenir fort orageuse, et je n'ay point envie d'etre pousse en Norwegue, ou de heurter contre quelque rocher des orcades. Le Roy de la Grande Bretagne, et Mad. la princesse de Galles, ont eu chacun un ordre exprés du ciel enjoignant à Neptune de leur donner la plus favorable navigation du monde;

> parmy tant d'orages,
> et tant de naufrages
> Le ciel à leur tour
> fit briller un beau jour.

Mais moy, chetif mortel, je ne me saurois promettre le privilege des demi-dieux. Le plus seur sera d'aller terre à terre le plus qu'il me sera possible.

Peut etre y[4] verray je Monsieur le Duc d'Arenberg, à qui je n'ay garde de faire part des reflexions un peu malignes qui se trouvent dans votre lettre. Pour estre[6] jeune et beau garçon, est-on moins capable d'affaires? Au contraire

> gratior est pulcro veniens in corpore virtus.[7]

La sagesse la plus severe d'un Roy, ne l'oblige point de fermer les yeux aux agrémens exterieurs. Il y avoit hier aux vendanges un homme un peu simple, mais suspect de quelque non-conformisme. On l'avoit accusé de trop aimer trop la compagnie[8] de quelque jeune valet de pied. Pour s'excuser, il avoit dit que S. Jean avoit eté plus aimé que S. Pierre, par ce que le premier étoit plus jeune. Cette reponse tres imprudente and incongrüe pensa faire de mechantes affaires à ce pauvre homme. Un vieux Ministre d'Etat homme sage et grave qui étoit present à ce discours le voulut faire jetter par les fenestres. Et il s'est peu fallu qu'on ne l'ait mis en justice pour deux chefs, l'un de blaspheme, l'autre de desordre. Mais il est tousjours vray que la jeunesse et la beauté donnent du relief aux belles qualités, et les anges sont representés en beaux garçons. Les dialogues de Platon eloignent toutes les idées de dereglement et je crois que c'est la malice qui a inventé des Contes sur Alcibiade, pour noircir la

45. LEIBNIZ TO DE BONNEVAL 153

ministers. He even extends his curiosity to the least, but distinguished, families. When I named you, sir, he wondered if you were not from the Netherlands, where the Counts of Bouquoi took the name 'Bonneval.' Madame the Duchess his wife [Marie Amalie of Brandenburg-Schwedt (1670–1739)] is the sister of the late[2] King of Prussia [Friedrich I* of Prussia]. She and the duke did me the favor of conducting me to their grape harvest with the gentlemen and young ladies of the court, and I thought of grape harvests[3] that the Elector of Bavaria [Maximillian II Emanuel (1662–1726)] recently made in France in the company of some women who represented Pomonas with their baskets. But now, *goodbye basket, grape harvests are done.* His Electoral Highness is returning to his estates with regret (it is said) as regards his personal pleasures detached from grandeur. But the man must give way to the hero. There, a prelude to the place where I am, which will scarcely interest you.

Now I must tell you, sir, that I could indeed still go to England this year, and perhaps soon. If I go there, I will travel to Calais, because the sea is going to become very stormy, and I do not fancy being driven to Norway, or running against some rock of the Orkneys. The King of Great Britain [George I, Georg Ludwig* of Braunschweig-Lüneburg] and Madame the Princess of Wales [Caroline* of Brandenburg-Ansbach] have each had an express order from heaven commanding Neptune to give them the most favorable navigation possible:

> amidst so many storms
> and so many shipwrecks,
> heaven in their turn
> made a beautiful day shine

But I, wretched mortal, would not be able to expect the privilege of the demi-gods. The safest will be to go land to land, the most that will be possible for me.

Perhaps I will see the Duke of Arenberg [Léopold Philippe* of Arenberg] there,[4] with whom I am far from sharing the somewhat malicious remarks that are found in your letter.[5] Is he less competent for being[6] a young and handsome lad? On the contrary:

> *virtue is more dear when it appears in a beautiful body.*[7]

The strictest wisdom of a king does not oblige him to close his eyes to outward attractiveness. At the grape harvest yesterday there was a rather simple man, but suspect of some nonconformity. He was accused of loving too much the company[8] of some young footman. In order to excuse himself, he said that St. John had been loved more than St. Peter because the former was younger. This very imprudent and unseemly response nearly caused some nasty business for this poor man. An old minister of state, a wise and serious man who was present at this speech, wanted to have him thrown out through the windows. And they nearly had him brought to

reputation d'un homme aussi sage que Socrate. Un mechant auteur italien d'un livre intitulé Scuola d'Alcibiade, les a outrés.[9]

Si j'osois me meler de votre contestation avec le prince, je dirois que S. A. S. a eté un peu promte à donner un mauvais nom à cette dame, que vous luy aviés alleguée, qui montra sa fermeté par un endroit, qui en a ordinairement si peu. Il y a ce me semble plus de l'Heroine, que de la femme imprudente dans cette Action. Des Matrones de l'ancienne Grece firent quelque chose de semblable; voyant les troupes de leur parti ebranslées, et des jeunes soldats fuyans vers la ville, elles leur firent la meme decouverte du haut des murailles, et montrant officinam humani generis, il leur demanderent,[11] s'ils vouloient rentrer dans l'endroit d'ou ils etoient sortis. Ce reproche fit retourner les fuyards vers l'ennemi, et gagner la bataille. Ainsi

teterrima belli
Causa[12]

chez Horace, a eté cause quelques fois de la conservation de la patrie et cette cause a eu souvent part aux belles actions des anciens chevaliers. On ne croit pas que les modernes en soyent tout à fait exemts. Et un jour quelque faiseur de Roman ne croira pas choquer la vraisemblance en attribuant à cette cause toutes les belles actions de M. le prince qui comme un autre gand Cyrus passant sur le ventre des plus grandes armées de son temps est allé à Paris uniquement pour s'y montrer triomphant à quelque jeune beauté. Et on l'a appaisé et fait consentit à la paix [de] Rastat, en luy envoyant cette belle personne en posture suppliante pour sauver la France; comme on envoya la mere à Coriolan pour sauver Rome. Voilà ce que dira un jour quelque Roman du siecle prochain.

Au reste la comparaison d'un philosophe avec une dame charmante galante et complaisante, comme l'Electeur palatin Charles Louis appelloit celles que d'autres nommeroient comme les Stoiciens,

scapham scapham,[13]
Nommans[14] un chat un chat, et Rulet un frippon[15]

n'est pas tant choquante, qu'on pourroit penser d'abord. Il n'y a point de comparaison qui cloche en tout. Une femme facile, cherche le plaisir du corps, et le philosophe a pour but celuy des ames. Le celebre Hobbes Anglois grand philosophe à sa mode,[16] m'a fait un peu sousrire, par sa manière de dire, que les hommes negligent la philosophie, par ce qu'ils ignorent, combien elle donne de plaisir. Quantam voluptatem afferat validissimus animæ[18] cum mundo congressus.[17] Et peut etre n'est ce pas sans mystere, que Pythagore, philosophe amateur des expressions symboliques, a dit que les dieux luy ayant accordé le privilege d'avoir la memoire de ses metamorphoses passées, il se souvenoit que son ame avoit eté un jour dans le corps d'une Läis.

justice on two counts, blasphemy and disorderly conduct. But it is always true that youth and beauty enhance fine qualities, and the angels are depicted as handsome young men. The dialogues of Plato repudiate all ideas of debauchery, and I believe that this is the malice that has fabricated some tales about Alcibiades, in order to sully the reputation of a man as wise as Socrates. A wicked Italian author of a book entitled *The School of Alcibiades* has exaggerated them.[9]

If I dared involve myself in your dispute with the prince [Eugène* of Savoy], I would say that His Serene Highness has been a bit quick to give a bad name to this lady whom you had adduced for him, who showed her firmness through a place that ordinarily has so little of it.[10] It seems to me there is more of the heroine than of the imprudent woman in this action. Some matrons of ancient Greece did something similar; when they saw the troops of their side shaken and some young soldiers fleeing towards the village, they did the same uncovering to them from atop the ramparts, and while showing the manufactory of the human race, they asked them[11] if they wanted to go back into the place from which they had emerged. This reproach made the runaways turn back towards the enemy and win the battle. Thus

of war a most shameful

cause[12]

in Horace has sometimes been the cause of the preservation of the homeland, and this cause has often played a part in the fine actions of the ancient knights. We don't believe that the moderns are suddenly exempt from it. And one day some novelist will not believe the likelihood shocking when attributing to this cause all the fine actions of the prince, who, like another Cyrus the Great defeating the greatest armies of his time, went to Paris only in order to appear triumphant there to some young beauty. And they appeased him and made him consent to the peace of Rastatt* by sending him this beautiful person begging in order to save France, as they sent his mother to Coriolanus in order to save Rome. There is what some novel of the next century will one day say.

Besides, the comparison of a philosopher to a charming, courageous, and complacent lady, as the Elector Palatine Karl Ludwig* called those whom others would call, as the Stoics did,

a *scapha* a *scapha*,[13]
Let us call[14] a cat a cat, and Rolet a rogue[15]

is not as shocking as one might think at first. There is no comparison that is entirely wrong. An easy woman seeks pleasure of the body, and the philosopher has that of souls as his goal. The celebrated Hobbes*, great English philosopher after his fashion,[16] made me smile a little by his way of saying that men neglect philosophy because they are ignorant of how much pleasure it gives. *How much pleasure may*

Vous vous souviendrés, Monsieur que la meme abregé que j'ay eu l'honneur de presenter à S. A. S. a eté entre vos mains, et que vous l'aviés fait copier pour M. le duc d'Arenberg, qui le vouloit[21] envoyer au prince de Horne, si je ne me trompe. Mais pour faire un petit volume, j'y ay joint des reponses aux objections de M. Bayle, et d'autres habiles gens. Ces reponses sont imprimées excepté la derniere, et la plus ample par la quelle j'ay taché de satisfaire aux repliques de M. Bayle, qui sont dans la seconde edition de son dictionnaire. J'ay composé cela exprés à Vienne à fin que rien ne manquât en ce genre. Mais j'en ay gardé une copie, et quoyque M. le prince puisse etre comparé avec Alexandre, je ne saurois estre comparé avec Aristote, ainsi je ne crains point qu'il me reproche, ce que ce Roy reprocha à ce philosophe, lors qu'il avoit publié[22] ses livres Acroamatiques que le Roy vouloit garder pour soy; il est vray que la lettre d'Alexandre à Aristote, ou cela se lit[23] passe pour une piece supposée.

Au reste vous me rejouissés beaucoup, Monsieur, en me marquant les bontés de M. le prince et les grandes apparences de parvenir à un fonds pour une Societé Imperiale des Sciences, ou S. A. S peut contribuer aupres de l'Empereur et s'il le faut aupres des Etats des Pays autant et plus que personne. Ses sentimens genereux et ses lumieres l'y portent, et il m'a fait la grace de m'en asseurer un peu[25] avant son[26] depart. Je souhaiterois que l'affaire fut un peu avancée avant mon retour à Vienne à fin que je ne sois point obligé de recommencer alors. Car à l'âge ou je suis je dois chercher d'abreger le temps autant qu'il est possible,[27] et je crains que sans cela, il ne m'arrive ce qui arriva à Moyse, (pardonnés la comparaison) qui ne pût voir que de loin la terre de promission.

Une des demarches les plus necessaires sera peut etre l'Expedition d'un Rescript de l'Empereur à la regence d'Austriche resolu plusieurs semaines avant mon depart. Monsieur le Comte de Sinzendorf m'avoit promis positivement plus d'une fois de le faire depecher à la chancellerie de la Cour:[28] on crût même l'affaire faite. Mais quand je vins à M. le Referendaire de Schick, qu'elle regardoit, je trouvay qu'il n'y avoit rien de tel. Son Excellence me promit là dessus, qu'Elle le feroit ordonner dés le lendemain, puisque l'Empereur l'avoit commandé il y a long temps, mais la multitude des affaires plus pressantes aura fait oublier cette expedition. Je suis parti la dessus,[29] et elle est demeurée pendue au croc[30] quoyque j'en aye ecrit à S. E. Ainsi je vous supplie, Monsieur, de vous employer pour faire expedier ce Rescript. M. le Comte de Sinzendorf vous considere, et a beaucoup d'egard à vos recommendations, et peut étre que M. le prince Eugene voudra bien en dire ou faire dire un mot. C'est pour faire sortir l'affaire des bornes d'une simple idée, et la faire mettre sur le tapis. Il sembloit parce que S. A. S me dit un peu avant son depart que Sa Mté Imperiale l'avoit chargé de la favoriser et de la faire avancer. Le meilleur sera que ce Rescript soit conçû en termes tout a fait generaux, et que j'y sois pourtant marqué nommement, en vertu d'un autre decret deja expedié il y a prés de deux ans, ou l'Empereur me charge du soin de cette affaire.[31] Ainsi il suffira qu'il contienne[32] que Sa Mté Imperiale et Caltholique étant portée à fonder une Societé des Sciences

very vigorous intercourse[17] *with the world impart to the soul.*[18] And perhaps it is not without mystery that Pythagoras, philosopher lover of symbolic expressions, said that since the gods had accorded him the privilege of remembering his past metamorphoses, he remembered that his soul had once been in the body of a Lais.[19]

You will remember, sir, that the same summary that I had the honour of presenting to His Serene Highness[20] was in your hands and that you had it copied for the Duke of Arenberg, who wanted[21] to send it to the Prince of Horne, if I am not mistaken. But in order to make a small volume, I have joined to it some responses to the objections of Mr. [Pierre] Bayle and other able men. These responses are printed, except the last and most extensive, in which I have tried to answer the replies of Mr. Bayle that are in the second edition of his dictionary. I composed this expressly in Vienna in order that nothing along these lines was missing. But I have kept a copy of it, and although the prince can be compared with Alexander, I could not be compared with Aristotle; so I am not afraid that he will reproach me with what that king reproached this philosopher when he had published[22] his esoteric books, which the king wanted to keep for himself. It is true that the letter from Alexander to Aristotle in which that is read[23] is considered a spurious piece.[24]

Finally, you make me very happy, sir, by mentioning the services of the prince and the great prospects for attaining a fund for an Imperial Society of Sciences*, to which His Serene Highness can contribute with the emperor [Karl V*], and, if it is necessary, with the nation states, as much and more than anyone. His general feelings and his understanding lead him to it, and he has done me the favor of assuring me of it shortly[25] before his[26] departure. I would hope that progress might be made before my return to Vienna, so that I am not forced to start all over again at that time. For at my age, I must seek to shorten the time as much as possible;[27] and without that, I fear that what happened to Moses (forgive the comparison), who was able to see the promised land only from afar, may happen to me.

One of the most needed steps will perhaps be the dispatch of a rescript by the emperor to the Regency of Austria, resolved several weeks before my departure. Count Sinzendorff* had more than once positively promised me to have it sent to the chancellery of the court;[28] he even believed that the matter was done. But when I went to the Referendary Mr. Schick, whom it concerned, I found that there was no such thing. His Excellency thereupon promised that he would have it arranged the following day, since the emperor had ordered it a long time ago. But the crush of more pressing cases must have diverted attention from this dispatch. I departed thereupon,[29] and it has remained hung on the hook,[30] although I have written to His Excellency about it. So I beseech you, sir, to apply yourself to having this rescript issued. Count Sinzendorff esteems you and has much respect for your recommendations, and perhaps Prince Eugène will be willing to say, or have said, a word about it. It is for the sake of bringing the case out from the confines of a simple idea and having it placed on the table. It seemed from what His Serene Highness told me shortly before my departure that His Imperial Majesty had charged him

pour faire fleurir les Etudes et arts utiles, veut que Sa Regence d'Austriche écoute la dessus le Conseiller Imperial Aulique de Leibniz chargé particulierement du soin de cette affaire et luy accordant des Commissaires qu'il pourra desirer, fasse conferer par Eux avec luy et avec ceux qu'il pourra prendre pour assistans sur la manière d'etablir cette societé, et de trouver dans la capitale et dans les pays ce qui y pourroit etre requis et convenable, pour concerter quelque chose qui seroit rapporté à Sa Majesté avec les protocolles, et sous mis à son bon plaisir.[33]

Ces expressions ou d'autres equivalentes donneront quelque poids à mes representations aupres de la Regence. On ne pourra pas les rejetter facilement, on sera obligé d'entrer avec moy en discussion, on ne pourra pas me refuser des Commissaires que je jugeray propres à aider le dessein de Sa Mté, je pourray etre assisté à mon choix[34] par des personnes capables et informées des affaires du pays. On ne pourra pas faire un rapport à l'Empereur sans communication avec moy; et on sera obligé de joindre les protocolles de ce qui s'est passé à fin qu'ils supppleent à ce qui pourroit manquer à la Relation si quelque cabale la vouloit rendre desavantageuse. Car quoyque je n'espere point un tel resultat, on ne sauroit cependant trop prendre ses[35] precautions.[36] J'ay mis en Allemand dans un papier cyjoint le desir que je viens de marquer touchant le contenu du Rescript. On voudra[37] peut étre à la chancelerie donner un autre tour à la chose, mais si Sa Mté I. approuvoit cette forme, dont il ne faut pas se relacher aisement, on seroit quasi asseuré d'un bon succés. Et[38] je vous supplie en cas que vous me veuilliés honnorer d'avantage de vos lettres, de les envoyer à M. Schleger Agent de S. A. S. de Saxe-Zeiz à Vienne, pour étre adressées à M. de Munch Conseiller privé de ce prince à Zeiz. Et je suis avec zele

Monsieur etc.

[...]

45. LEIBNIZ TO DE BONNEVAL 159

with promoting it and having it moved forward. It will be best that this rescript is conceived in entirely general terms and that I am nevertheless noted particularly, in virtue of another decree already issued nearly two years ago, in which the emperor charged me with the care of this matter.[31] Thus it will suffice that it includes,[32] *that since His Imperial and Catholic Majesty is disposed to found a society of sciences for promoting useful studies and arts, he wants his Regency of Austria to listen on this subject to the Imperial Aulic Councilor* Leibniz, charged specifically with the care of this matter, and granting him any commissioners he may desire, to confer through them with him and with those whom he may choose for assistants about how to establish this society and to find in the capital city and in the lands what might be required and suitable for it, in order jointly to plan something that would be reported to His Majesty with protocols and submitted at his convenience.*[33]

These words, or other equivalent ones, will give some weight to my presentations to the Regency. They will not be able to reject them easily, they will be obliged to enter into discussion with me, and they will not be able to deny me any commissioners that I may judge suitable for supporting His Majesty's plan. I will be able to be assisted, at my choice,[34] by some capable persons who are informed about the affairs of the country. They will not be able to report to the emperor without communication with me, and they will be obliged to attach the protocols about what has happened so that they make up the deficiency in what could be missing in the report if some faction wanted to render it disadvantageous. For although I do not expect such a result, it would nevertheless not be too much to take these[35] precautions.[36] I have put in German, in an attachment, the desire that I have just expressed concerning the content of the rescript. They will[37] perhaps want to give it a different spin at the chancellery, but if His Imperial Majesty approved this form, of which he must not easily let go, we would be almost assured of success. And[38] in case you want to honour me further with your letters, I pray you send them to Mr. Schleger, Agent of His Serene Highness [Moritz Wilhelm (1664–1718)] of Saxe-Zeitz in Vienna, to be addressed to Mr. Munch, privy councilor of this prince at Zeitz. And I am enthusiastically,

sir etc.

[…]

---

[1] LBr. 89 Bl. 3r–4v. Draft: 3.5 quarto sides in Leibniz's hand. Previously published in JGHF 430–8 (excerpt). Answer to Bonneval's letter to Leibniz of 6 October (see document 39). I have omitted the postscript and the attachment in German, mentioned at the end of the letter, expressing Leibniz's desire concerning the content of the ruling from the emperor.

[2] Feder omits 'feu' (see JGFH, 431).

[3] Reading 'pensé aux vendages' for 'pensé vendages'.

[4] Feder omits 'y' (see JGHF 432).

[5] See Bonneval's letter to Leibniz of 6 October (document 39, p. 135).

[6] Feder mistranscribes 'Pour estre' as 'Peut-être' (see JGHF 432).

[7] A slight variation of Virgil, Aeneid 5, 344: *Gratior et pulcro veniens in corpore virtus.*

[8] Reading 'de aimer trop la compagnie' for 'de trop aimer trop la compagnie.'

160   45. LEIBNIZ TO DE BONNEVAL

45. LEIBNIZ TO DE BONNEVAL 161

[9] Feder replaces the entire passage, from 'Il y avoit hier aux vendanges' to the end of the paragraph, with a single sentence: 'La jeunesse et la beauté donnent du relief aux belles qualités, et les anges sont représentés en beaux garçons' (see JGHF 433).

[10] That is, her vulva. See Bonneval's letter to Leibniz of 6 October (document 39, p. 137).

[11] Reading 'elles leur demanderent' for 'il leur demanderent'.

[12] Horace, *Satires* I.3.107–8: *Nam fuit ante Helenam cunnus taeterrima belli causa* ('For before Helen's time, a cunt was a most shameful cause of war').

[13] The Latin term *scapha* is derived from the Greek σκάφη, which means, variously, a '*trough, tub, basin*, or *bowl*...; *kneading-trough* or *baker's tray*,' as well as a '*light boat, skiff*' (Liddell and Scott, *A Greek-English Lexicon*). When Leibniz refers to the Stoics calling a *scapha* a *scapha*, the meaning is the same as the English expression, 'calling a spade a spade,' meaning to speak frankly, to call something by its real name. So the meaning here is that those whom Karl Ludwig euphemistically called charming, courageous, and complacent ladies, others, like the Stoics, would have called whores, plain and simple. The English expression ultimately derives from an ancient Greek expression found in several sources, but which entered the language via a controversial translation of a Greek source into the Latin by Erasmus. In both his *Adagia* (II, iii, 5) and his *Apophthegmata* of 1531, Erasmus quotes a line from Menander Frag. 545K (which in the *Adagia* he mistakenly attributes to Aristophanes and which in the *Apophthegmata* he simply calls 'that celebrated proverb'):

τὰ σῦκα σῦκα, τὴν σκάφην σκάφην λέων.

Instead of using the Latin *scapham* to translate σκάφην, Erasmus used the Latin term *ligonem*, meaning hoe or mattock: *Ficus ficus, ligonem ligonem vocat*. Later English writers, based on Erasmus's Latin translation, translated *ligonem* as 'spade,' whence the expression, 'calling a spade a spade,' made its way into the English language. (For an exhaustive study of the source and history of the expression, see Mieder 2002.) In attributing frankness of speech to the Stoics, Leibniz was echoing what Cicero told his young friend, Papirius Paetus:

habes scholam Stoicam: ὁ σοφὸς εὐθυρρημονήσει. quam multa ex uno verbo tuo! te adversus me omnia audere gratum est ; ego servo et servabo (sic enim adsuevi) Platonis verecundiam. itaque tectis verbis ea ad te scripsi, quae apertissimis agunt Stoici ; sed illi etiam crepitus aiunt aeque liberos ac ructus esse oportere. [*Epistulae ad Familiares* 9.22.5]

There you have the Stoic lecture: the wise man will speak plainly. Many words from a single word of yours! It is pleasing that you venture anything in speaking to me. I preserve and will preserve (for so I am accustomed to do) Plato's modesty; accordingly, I have written to you in reserved language those things which the Stoics discuss in the most outspoken way: but they even say that farts should be just as unrestrained as belches. [my translation]

[14] Reading 'Nommons' for 'Nommans.'

[15] Feder omits 'Nommans un chat un chat, et Rolet un frippon' (see JGHF 434). Charles Rolet was an attorney in the Paris Parliament of roguish reputation. Convicted of fraud in 1681, he was fined and banished for nine years, although his banishment was later rescinded. He was lampooned by Nicolas Boileau-Despréaux (1636–1711) in his *Satire* I, 50–2:

Je suis rustique et fier, et j'ai l'âme grossière.
Je ne puis rien nommer, si ce n'est par son nom.
J'appelle un chat un chat, et Rolet un fripon.

That is,

I am rustic and proud, and I have a crude spirit.
I cannot name anything if it is not by its name.
I call a cat a cat and Rolet a rogue.

See Boileau-Despréaux 1821, vol. I, p. 81.

[16] Feder omits the appositive (see JGHF 434).

[17] I have intentionally translated the Latin 'congressus' here as 'intercourse,' in order to capture the double entendre that Leibniz clearly intended. 'Intercourse' in English can be used in the general sense of a 'coming together,' or of an 'interaction or engagement' with, as well as in the more specific sense of 'copulation'; and the same is true of the Latin word 'congressus'.

[18] Feder omits 'animæ' (see JGHF 434).

Andreas Gottlieb von Bernstorff to Leibniz[1]

à Londr. le
1 Nov. 14

Monsieur

J'ay remis ma reponse à la votre parce que l'on nous a mandé que vous alliés vous mettre en chemin pour ce pays cy, et on addressoit[2] même deja des lettres icy pour vous. Vous faites bien Monsieur de rester à Hann. et d'y reprendre vos travaux, vous ne sçauriés[3] mieux faire votre Cour au Roy, ny mieux raccommoder les absences passées, qu'en presentant a Sa Mté quand Elle viendra à Hann. une bonne partie des ouvrages qu'Elle attend depuis longtemps. J'espere Monsieur que vous n'y oublierés pas les chapitres dont nous avons parlé cy devant, sur tout celuy de migratione gentium. Mr. Eccard nous a promis de preparer plusieurs matieres utiles à vos desseins ainsy j'espere Monsieur que vous pourrés d'autant plustost achever l'ouvrage, à la satisfaction du maitre et à votre propre gloire. Je suis Monsieur votre

tresh. tresobéiss.
serviteur
B.

[19] 'Lais,' referring to Lais of Corinth (fl.425 BCE) and Lais of Hyccara (died c.340 BCE), two famous courtesans of ancient Greece.

[20] The summary to which Leibniz is referring here is the 'Principles of Nature and Grace, Based on Reason.'

[21] Feder mistranscribes 'vouloit' as 'voulut' (see JGHF 435).

[22] Feder mistranscribes 'avoit publié' as 'publia' (see JGHF 435).

[23] Feder mistranscribes 'lit' as 'dit'.

[24] For the supposed letter see Plutarch, *Life of Alexander* VII.

[25] Feder omits 'un peu' (see JGHF 436).

[26] Feder mistranscribes 'son' as 'mon' (see JGHF 436).

[27] Feder omits 'il est' (see JGHF, 436).

[28] Feder omits 'à la chancellerie de la Cour' (see JGHF 436).

[29] Feder omits 'Je suis parti la dessus' (see JGHF 437).

[30] That is, 'remained on the shelf'. Feder mistranscribes 'pendue' as 'cependant' (see JGHF 437).

[31] Feder omits this entire sentence (see JGHF 437).

[32] Feder replaces 'Ainsi il suffira qu'il contienne' with 'Il suffira que ce rescript contienne' (see JGHF, 437).

[33] Feder omits the last part of this long sentence, from 'sur la maniere' to the end (see JGHF 437).

[34] Feder omits 'à mon choix' (see JGHF 438).

[35] Reading 'ces' for 'ses'.

[36] Feder omits this sentence (see JGHF 438).

[37] Feder mistranscribes 'voudra' as 'voudroit' (see JGHF 438).

[38] Feder omits 'Et' (see JGHF 438).

46. Andreas Gottlieb von Bernstorff* to Leibniz[1]

London

1 November [17]14

Sir

I have postponed my response to yours because we have been informed that you are going to set off on a journey to this country, and there are even already some letters here addressed[2] to you. You do well, sir, to remain in Hanover and resume your work there. You would not be better able[3] to pay your respects to the king [George I, Georg Ludwig* of Braunschweig-Lüneburg], nor better able to make amends for past absences, than by presenting to His Majesty when he comes to Hanover a good part of the works for which he has been waiting a long time.[4] I hope, sir, that you will not omit the chapters about which we have previously spoken, and above all that concerning the migration of peoples. Mr. Eckhart[5] has promised to prepare for us many useful materials for your purposes; thus I hope, sir, that you will be able to complete the work so much the sooner, for the satisfaction of the master and for your own glory. I am, sir, your

very humble, very obedient

servant

B.

PS.

Il auroit eté à souhaiter Monsieur que l'on auroit pu sauver Barcellone mais le destin en a ordonné autrement. Le Roy n'a pas encor admis jusqu'icy l'Ambass. de Savoye ou de Sicile, cependant la recognition de Sa Royauté ne feroit pas toute l'affaire.

Le Roy envoit Mr. le General Stanhop son Secretaire d'Etat à Vienne pour communiquer ses pensées à Sa Mté Imp. Il mene avec luy Milord Cobham qui restera et residera à Vienne.

Andreas Gottlieb von Bernstorff* to Leibniz[1]

Londr. ce 24
Nov. [17]14

Monsieur

J'ay reçu par le derniere ord. la votre du 24 Oct[2]. Vous avés toute raison en ce que[3] vous dites in pͤo religionis[4], et nous sommes la dessus d'accord avec vous. L'Ambas. de Sicile n'a pas eu encor audience du Roy. Je vous prie Monsieur de me dire en quel etat vous avés trouvé les travaux et collectanea à Hann. et si vous croyés que l'on en pourra former[5] bientost un ouvrage que l'on puisse produire. Je suis

Monsieur

> votre
>
> tresh. tresobéis.
>
> serviteur
>
> B.

47. VON BERNSTORFF TO LEIBNIZ   165

P. S.

It would have been desirable, sir, that Barcelona could have been saved, but fate has ordained otherwise concerning it. Up until now the king has not accepted the ambassador of Savoy or of Sicily, but the recognition of his royalty[6] would not be the whole affair.

The king sent his secretary of state General Stanhope* to Vienna in order to communicate his thoughts to His Imperial Majesty [Karl VI*]. He is taking with him Milord Cobham,[7] who will remain and reside in Vienna.

---

[1] LBr. 59 Bl. 125r–126r and LBr. 59 Bl. 113r–113v (postscript). Letter as sent: 4.5 quarto sides in Bernstorff's hand, including postscript. Response to Leibniz's letter to Bernstorff of 20 September 1714 (document 32). Previously published in JGHF 231–2; Doebner 1881, pp. 295–6; Klopp XI 22 (excerpt). Klopp mistakenly takes the postscript of this letter to belong to Bernstorff's letter to Leibniz of 24 November 1714 (document 47).

[2] Feder mistranscribes 'addressoit' as 'adressa' (see JGHF 232).

[3] Feder (see JGHF 232) and Doebner (see Doebner 1881, p. 295) mistranscribe 'sçauriez' as 'sauriez'.

[4] The reference is to Leibniz's work on the history of the House of Braunschweig-Lüneburg (Hanover), his *Annales imperii occidentis Brunsvicenses*.

[5] Johann Georg Eckhart was Leibniz's Secretary at Hanover.

[6] That is, the royalty of George I (see Leibniz's letter to Bernstorff of 20 September 1714, document 32, p. 111).

[7] Field Marshall Richard Temple (1675–1749), 1st Viscount Cobham, was a soldier and Whig politician. In October 1714 George I created him Baron Cobham and appointed him ambassador to Vienna.

---

47. Andreas Gottlieb von Bernstorff* to Leibniz[1]

London 24
November 1714

Sir

I have received by the last mail yours of 24 October.[2] You are entirely right in what you say[3] regarding religion,[4] and we are in agreement with you on that. The Ambassador of Sicily has not yet had an audience with the king [George I, Georg Ludwig* of Braunschweig-Lüneburg]. I ask you, sir, in what state you have found the works and collections in Hanover and if you believe that a volume will soon be able to be made[5] about them that can be produced. I am

sir

your

very humble very obedient

servant

B.

---

[1] LBr. 59 Bl. 123r–123v. Letter as sent: 1.5 quarto sides in Bernstorff's hand. Previously published in Doebner 1881, p. 296, and Klopp XI 21. Reply to Leibniz's letter to Bernstorff of 14 October (document 42).

[2] Bernstorff mistakenly writes '24 Oct.' instead of '14 Oct.'

[3] Klopp mistranscribes 'Vous avés toute la raison en ce que' as 'Nous avons (parlé de) ce que' (see Klopp XI 21).

[4] 'pͨo' abbreviates the Latin 'puncto,' so 'in pͨo religionis' means 'in point of religion' or 'regarding religion.'

[5] Klopp mistranscribes 'former' as 'faire' (see Klopp XI 21).

Leibniz to Johann Matthias von der Schulenburg* (excerpt)

Monsieur

Un ressentiment de goutte m'a fait changer de sentiment. C'est l'effect des approches de l'hyver. Cependant le mal a eté tolerable. Et en arrivant icy de la Saxe, j'en suis presque quitte. Il est plaisant qu'on a debité icy que j'etois parti pour l'Angleterre, et même que j'avois voulois³ passer à Calais. Cela peut venir de ce que j'avois dit icy avant que de partir, que si je voulois aller en Angleterre, je passerois à Calais plustost que de la Hollande.

J'ay receu des lettres de Vienne qui me font esperer que l'Empereur mettra bien tôt ses finances en état de pourvoir fournir encor aux belles curiosités. Cela vient de bon lieu, puisque même M. le prince Eugene me fait savoir qu'il ne doute point du succés de la Societé des Sciences. Cependant avant que d'y revenir, je voudrois voir les affaires plus avancées.

On voit qu'en Angleterre le parti du Ministere disgracié tache d'inspirer aux peuples l'opinion que le Roy est tout à fait Whig. Ainsi son interest est sans doute de faire comprendre aux gens, qu'il fait une grand difference entre les Toris ordinaires et entre les creatures du dernier Ministere. Et j'espere qu'il sera de ce sentiment.

[…] Je suis avec zele

    Monsieur de V. E.

le tres humble & tres
obéissant serviteur
Leibniz

Hanover ce 3 de decembre
    1714

48. Leibniz to Johann Matthias von der Schulenburg* (excerpt)[1]

[Hanover, 3 December 1714]

Sir

A touch of gout has made me change my mind.[2] It is an effect of the approach of winter. However, the pain has been tolerable. And upon arriving here from Saxony, I am nearly free of it. It is amusing that it has been reported here that I had left for England, and even that I had wanted[3] to go to Calais.[4] That may have come from what I had said here before I left, that if I wanted to go to England, I would go to Calais rather than from Holland.[5]

I have received letters from Vienna[6] that make me hope that the emperor [Karl VI*] will soon put his finances in a state to be able to supply again fine curios. This comes from a good source, since even Prince Eugène* informs me that he has no doubts about the success of the Society of Sciences [the proposed Imperial Society of Sciences*]. However, before I return there I would like to see matters further along.

It is understood that in England the party of the disgraced ministry is trying to instill in the people the view that the king [George I, Georg Ludwig* of Braunschweig-Lüneburg] is entirely a Whig. Thus his interest is without doubt to make people understand that he makes a big distinction between ordinary Tories and the creatures of the last ministry. And I hope that he will be of this view. [...] I am enthusiastically,

  sir, of Your Excellency

the very humble and very
obedient servant

Hanover 3 December
  1714

              Leibniz

---

[1] Staatsbibliothek zu Berlin Bibliothek Savigny 38 Bl. 124r–125v; N. 32. Letter as sent: four octavo sides in Leibniz's hand. Not previously published.

[2] What Leibniz seems to have changed his mind about is his plan to go to England. In his letter to Schulenburg of 30 September (document 36, p. 125), he had written:

> I must tell you in confidence, sir, that my intention is to go to England shortly; I would hope to have the honor of speaking with you beforehand. [...] I am thinking of going to Calais, since at present the roads are free. [...]
>
> I am pretending that I intend to go from here to the Leipzig fair, and I will depart for Hildesheim on or about Saturday. But from there I am thinking of going towards the Netherlands by the stagecoach that goes to Wesel.

Thus it appears that Leibniz was intending to take the stagecoach south from Hanover to Hildesheim as a ruse to make those in Hanover believe he was indeed going to the Leipzig fair. But as he says, from Hildesheim he was thinking of heading west, towards the Netherlands, and eventually making his way to Calais, where he apparently intended to board a ship bound for England. But then a week later, in a letter of 7 October (document 40, p. 149), Leibniz again wrote to Schulenburg:

> Although my plan is to go to England, nevertheless, since I do not want to go in the retinue of the Royal Princess [i.e., Caroline* of Brandenburg-Ansbach, Princess of Wales] (although she did me the favor of letting me know that she would be very pleased by it), I am taking a trip to Braunschweig beforehand. I hope to be there Tuesday or Wednesday, and then I will decide on the route. If I could see you there, sir, I would be delighted.

Leibniz to Andreas Gottlieb von Bernstorff (excerpt)

A Mons. de Bernsdorf   Hanover 8 xbre 1714

Monsieur

J'a receu l'honneur de deux reponses de V. E. et je dois luy dire là dessus que je m'applique à achever pendant cet hyver un Tome de mes Annales. Il ira jusqu'à la fin de Henri second, vulgairement dit le Saint, c'est à dire jusqu'à l'extinction de la ligne des Empereurs de l'ancienne Maison de Bronsvic. Cet ouvrage comprendra aussi par consequent les origines de la presente maison de Brunsvic car Azon chef commun reconnu de cette maison et d'elle d'Este d'Italie a eté né avant la mort de cet Empereur Henri.

Apres cela la race de Wibeling est parvenue au trone de l'Empire, et ses contestations avec les papes où les Welfes et ceux d'Este avec nos Saxons sont entrés, remplira[5] depuis une bonne partie de l'Histoire de l'Empire, et de mon second Tome. Ainsi je puis dire que mes Annales de Bronsvic sont indispensablement en même temps des Annales de l'Empire.[6] Mon travail sera tel, que si Dieu disposoit de moy avant que je puisse finir le second Tome, le premier sera un ouvrage achevé en son genre sur nos antiquites et contiendra des decouvertes considerables pour la maison; puisqu'entre autres on y voit que les ancêtres en ligne directe masculine, ont esté Ducs et Marquis de la Toscane. Ce qui pourra aider la Maison d'Este à rentrer dans cet ancien patrimoine et en obtenir l'expectative apres l'extinction de la

Five days later, on 12 October, Leibniz sent yet another letter to Schulenburg (document 41, pp. 141, 143), writing:

> Now that Madame the Princess of Wales has left, I will also leave tomorrow or the day after, at the latest; and after visiting Braunschweig, I will take a trip to Helmstadt, and from there I will give myself the honor of paying you a visit. [...] I wanted to wait for the departure of Madame the Princess of Wales.

Leibniz did finally meet with Schulenburg, for in his letter to Leibniz of 31 October 1714, Schulenburg wrote that 'after having thanked you for the honor of your visit, which was as pleasant as it was useful, I would only wish that it had been longer and that I had the good fortune to be with you, sir, more often and longer; nothing would make me happier' (LBr. 840 Bl. 294r). So again, what Leibniz seems to have changed his mind about is his plan to go to England. This may have been due, at least in part, to Bernstorff's telling Leibniz, in his letter of 1 November, after having heard that Leibniz was planning to travel to England, that 'you do well, sir, to remain in Hanover and resume your work there' (document 46, p. 163).

   [3] Reading 'j'avois voulu' for j'avois voulois'.

   [4] Leibniz may be referring to, among other things, what Bernstorff* wrote to him in a letter of 1 November, namely, that 'we have been informed that you are going to set off on a journey to this country [that is, England]' (document 46, p. 163).

   [5] Thus Leibniz suggests that any talk of his going to England by way of Calais was merely a hypothetical, based on the assumption that he wanted to go there. But it is worth noting again that in his letter to Schulenburg of 30 September, Leibniz had written: 'I must tell you in confidence, sir, that my intention is to go to England shortly [...] I am thinking of going to Calais, since at present the roads are free' (document 36, p. 125).

   [6] For example, see Bonneval's letter to Leibniz of 6 October 1714 (document 39, p. 135).

49. Leibniz to Andreas Gottlieb von Bernstorff* (excerpt)[1]

To Mr. Bernstorff   Hanover 8 December 1714

    Sir

I have received the honour of two responses from Your Excellency, and about that I must tell you that during this winter I am applying myself to completing a volume of my Annals.[2] It will go up to the end of Henry II, commonly called the 'Saint,' that is to say, up to the extinction of the line of emperors of the ancient House of Braunschweig. Consequently, this work will also include the origins of the present House of Braunschweig, since Azzo,[3] acknowledged joint head of this house and of that of Este of Italy, was born before the death of this Emperor Henry.[4]

After that the line of Wibeling attained the throne of the empire, and its disputes with the popes, in which the Welfs and those from Este took part, along with our Saxons, will then fill[5] a good part of the history of the empire and of my second volume. Thus I can say that my Annals of Braunschweig are necessarily at the same time annals of the empire.[6] My work will be such that if God disposed of me before I was able to finish the second volume, the first will be a completed work in its genre concerning our antiquities and will contain some significant discoveries for the House [of Braunschweig-Lüneburg], since among other things it will there be seen that the ancestors in the direct male line have been dukes and marquis of Tuscany.

posterité du Grand Duc d'apresent: sur tout depuis qu'il y a non seulement des imperatrices de la Maison de Brunsvic dont l'une est tante des princes de Modene, mais qu'encore notre Maistre devenu Roy de la Grande Bretagne, peut appuyer efficacement de si justes esperances. Car outre les egards de[8] la Cour de Vienne aura pour luy par bien de raisons sa puissance maritime le fera considerer encor en Italie. J'en ay touché quelque chose aupres de la Majesté de l'imperatrice Amalie, qui en est ravie. Mais je n'ay pas encor trouvé a propos d'en dire quelque chose ailleurs. Ainsi je juge que V. E. trouvera a propos de menager la chose, cependant il paroist important que le Roy en soit instruit.

Quand le premier Tome des Annales sera fait j'acheveray plus commodement le preambule des antiquités naturelles du pays, et des migrations et origines des peuples, ou j'ay quelque chose de bon à dire.

Puisque maintenant un Electeur de Bronsvic est monté sur le Trone d'Angleterre, et puisqu'il y a eu autrefois une grande liaison entre les Rois d'Angleterre et les Ducs of Bronsvic je trouve à propos de faire entrer dans mes Annales quelque chose d'essentiel de l'Histoire d'Angleterre et qui viendra le plus a propos, et j'espere de donner un tel tour aux choses qu'on aura sujet d'en etre content. Cela viendra d'autant plus a propos que les Anglois sont une colonie des anciens Saxons, et que les eclaircissements sur les grands antiquités sont communs aux deux peuples. Et les Anglois savans en ces materieres sont contents de mes recherches là dessus, temoin ce qui a eté dit de mes remarques dans le petit livre de M. Wotton qui donne notice du grand ouvrage de M. Hikkes, intitulé Thesaurus antiquitatum septentrionalium, ou sur les anciennes langues du Nord.[10] Cela estant j'ose ouvrir à V. E. une pensée que j'ay qui est que Sa Mté me pourra accorder l'honneur et la pension d'un Historiographe de la Grande Bretagne. De tels honneurs & emolumens peuvent encor convenir à d'étrangers car il y a des exemples qu'un tel employ leur a ete accordé sans qu'ils ayent ete naturalisés. Or l'acte du parlement qui paroist refuser des charges a des étrangers ne regarde que les charges qui ont besoin de naturalisiation.

Les nouvelles écrites à la main, qu'on communique ordinairement aux Conseillers meme de la Cour me viennent trop tard, ainsi je supplie V. E. de faire savoir à M. Stamke qu'il est juste que je les puisse recevoir immediatement apres les Ministres d'Etat effectifs comme mon rang le porte en effect. Je n'espere pas d'avoir merité un peu trop de reserve, qui seroit un grand desagrément à un ancien serviteur et a qui son sejour à Hannover ne doit pas estre trop desagreable.

[...]

Je suis avec respect

Monsieur de V. E. etc.

A Monsieur de Bernsdorf
premier Ministre d'Etat d'Hannover
au service de la Mté de la Grande Bretagne

This can help the House of Este enter again into this ancient inheritance and obtain from it the reversion after the extinction of the posterity of the present grand duke [Cosimo III de' Medici (1642–1723)]—above all because there are not only some empresses from the House of Braunschweig, of which one is the aunt of the princes of Modena,[7] but also because our master [George I of Great Britain, Georg Ludwig* of Braunschweig-Lüneburg], having become King of Great Britain, can effectively support such just hopes. For besides the respect that[8] the court of Vienna will have for him for many reasons, his naval power will cause him to be respected in Italy as well. I have expressed something about it to the Majesty of the [Dowager] Empress [Wilhelmine] Amalie*, who is delighted with it. But I have not yet found it appropriate to say anything about it elsewhere. Thus I imagine that Your Excellency will find it appropriate to take care of the matter; however it seemed important that the king be informed of it.

When the first volume of the Annals is done, I will more easily complete the preamble concerning the natural antiquities of the county and the migrations and origins of the people, in which I have something fine to say.

Since an elector of Braunschweig has now ascended the throne of England, and since there was formerly a significant connection between the kings of England and the dukes of Braunschweig, I have found it appropriate to include in my Annals something essential about the history of England, which will come to be most appropriate, and I hope to give such a twist to things that people will have reason to be pleased. That will come to be all the more appropriate because the English are a colony of the ancient Saxons, and the elucidations concerning the great antiquities are common to both peoples. And the English scholars in these matters are pleased with my studies about this, as witnessed by what has been said of my remarks in the small book of Mr. [William] Wotton*, which gives a review of the great work of Mr. Hickes[9] entitled *Thesaurus atntiquitatum septentrionalium*, or on the ancient languages of the north.[10] That being so, I dare reveal to Your Excellency a thought that I have, which is that His Majesty may accord me the honour and the pension of an historiographer of Great Britain. Such honours and emoluments are still suitable for foreigners. For there are some examples of such a post having been accorded to them without their having been naturalized. Now the act of parliament that seemed to deny some offices to foreigners only concerns offices that require naturalization.[11]

The handwritten news, which is ordinarily communicated to the councilors of the court themselves, comes to me too late; so I beseech Your Excellency to inform Mr. Stamke that it is proper that I be able to receive them immediately after the actual ministers of state, as my rank in fact entitles me. I do not expect to have merited a little too much reserve, which would be a great inconvenience to an old servant whose stay in Hanover should not be made too disagreeable.

P. S.

Pusique le Roy a jugé (comme la chose est ainsi en effect) que l'Eglise Anglicane n'est point differente dans le fond avec les Eglises de la Confession d'Augsbourg, les quelles sont pourtant differentes de celles ou la doctrine & la discipline of Geneve est receue; il me semble qu'en cela le Roy a de quoy donner contentement aux bons Toris, et les faire cesser de craindre Geneve autant & plus que Rome.

Je ne say si V. E. a trouvé a son gré ce gentilhomme Ecossois que je luy avois adresse de Vienne. Les sentimens au moins qu'il fit paroistre, m'avoient contenté, et il me semble qu'il merite encor qu'on luy donne quelque accces, et qu'on luy sache quelque gré de sa bonne volonté qu'il fit paroistre dans un temps que nos affaires ne paroissoient pas fort avancées. Et peutestre qu'encore maintenant il ne seroit pas mal de l'ecouter quelquesfois. Il m'a ecrit, mais sans me demander que j'ecrive comme je fais.

49. LEIBNIZ TO VON BERNSTORFF   173

[...]
I am with respect,
sir, of Your Excellency etc.
    To Mr. Bernstorff
Prime Minister of the State of Hanover
in the service of the Majesty of Great Britain
    P. S.
Since the king has judged (as the matter is so in fact) that the Anglican church is basically no different from the churches of the confession of Augsburg,[12] which are nevertheless different from those in which the doctrine and discipline of Geneva are received,[13] it seems to me that in that the king has something to give satisfaction to the good Tories and make them stop fearing Geneva as much and more than Rome.

    I do not know if Your Excellency has found to his liking that Scottish gentleman [John Ker*] that I had sent from Vienna.[14] At least the sentiments he expressed had pleased me, and it seems to me that he still merits being given some access to you and shown some gratitude for his good will, which he showed at a time when our affairs did not appear very advanced. And perhaps even now it would not be amiss to listen to him on occasion. He has written to me, but without asking me to write as I do.

[1] LBr. 59 Bl. 127r–127v. Draft: two folio sides in Leibniz's hand. Previously published in JGHF 222–4 (excerpt) and Klopp XI 22–5 (excerpt). Response to Bernstorff's letters to Leibniz of 1 and 24 November (see documents 46 and 47 respectively).

[2] Leibniz is referring to his history of the House of Braunschweig-Lüneburg (Hanover), which he entitled *Annales imperii occidentis Brunsvicenses**.

[3] That is, Alberto Azzo II of Este (996–1097). Azzo married Kunigunde (Cuniza) von Altdorf (d. *c*.1055), daughter of Imiza of Luxembourg and Welf II (d. *c*.1030), Graf in Lechrain. After her son Welf III died without heir around 1055, Imiza found an heir in the son of her daughter Kunigunde and her husband Azzo II; this son continued the Welf line as Welf IV (d. *c*.1101), Duke of Bavaria.

[4] Emperor Henry II died in 1024.

[5] Reading 'rempliront' for 'remplira'.

[6] Feder omits the preceding two sentences (see JGHF 222).

[7] Charlotte Felicitas (1671–1710) was the sister of the Dowager Empress Wilhelmine Amalie*. She was married to Rinaldo III, Duke of Modena.

[8] Reading 'que' for 'de'.

[9] George Hickes (1642–1715) was an English theologian and scholar, noted especially for his work in linguistics and Anglo-Saxon languages. The full title of Hickes' book to which Leibniz refers is *Linguarum veterum septentrionalium thesaurus grammatico-criticus et archaeologicus.*

[10] Feder omits the previous two sentences (see JGHF 224).

[11] Leibniz is referring to the Act of Settlement* of 1701. The basis of Leibniz's interpretation of the act is unclear. The relevant section of the act reads as follows:

[...] no person born out of the kingdoms of England, Scotland or Ireland or the dominions thereunto belonging, although he be naturalized or made a denizen (except such as are born of English parents), shall be capable to be of the privy council or a member of either House or Parliament or to enjoy any office or place of trust either civil or military or to have any grant of lands, tenements or hereditaments from the Crown to himself or to any other or others in trust for him.

Leibniz to Caroline* of Brandenburg-Ansbach, Princess of Wales

Madame

Le depart de V. A. R. m'a donné bien du chagrin et m'a rendu Hanover insupportable d'abord; et pour me remettre j'ay eté obligé de faire un voyage en Saxe, qui aussi bien etoit nécessaire pour quelques interests domestiques. J'en suis revenu avant la mauvaise saison. Une attaque de goutte avoit borné ma course, mais elle s'est passée en chemin. La joye que l'heureuse arrivée de vtre Altesse Royale m'a donnée, avec toutes les belles suites de la revolution ont contribué à ma santé, et font mon present contentement pendant que je suis renfermé icy dans ma chambre pour travailler sans sortir presque et sans me soucier gueres des nouvelles que par rapport à V. A. R. et a tout ce qui luy est cher. Il est vray que je reçois quelques fois des nouvelles de Vienne. Mademoiselle de Klenk m'apprend la continuation de la joye que l'imperatrice Amalie a du bonheur de la Maison Royale; et le Comte de Bonneval me dit que M. le prince Eugene demande, pourquoy n'etant pas allé en Angleterre je ne reviens pas a Vienne, ou l'on pretend que je ne dois pas être mal. Mais je veux employer cet hyver à mettre le principal de mon travail dans un état, qu'apres cela je pourrois meme prendre congé pour aller dans l'autre monde, sans que notre Cour pourroit avoir sujet de se plaindre de moy. Si j'y puis survivre un peu, je verray combien mon zele sera remarqué. Je me flatte qu'au moins V. A. R et Monseigneur le prince de Galles ne le mepriseront pas. J'ay une pensée, dont le succés m'encourageroit beaucoup. Comme dans mon Histoire je suis obligé de toucher souvent à celle d'Angleterre, tant à cause des Antiquités saxonnes, puisque les Anglois ont esté une colonie des saxons, qu'à cause des anciennes liaisons de la Maison Royale d'Angleterre & celle de Henri le Lion; le Roy n'employeroit pas mal l'honneur et la pension d'Historiographe de la Grande Bretagne, s'il me l'accordoit. Ces sortes de charges se sont donnees encor à d'etrangers. Car il y en peut avoir plus d'un. J'en ay ecrit à M. de Bernsdorf. Si Vos Altesses Royales y etoient favorables; j'espererois de reussir. La parole qu'on m'en donnera me pourra suffire, pourveu qu'elle ait son effect; aussi tost que j'auray donné cette principale partie de mon ouvrage, dont j'ay écrit a M. de Bernsdorf, & que je pretends d'achever cet hyver.

J'ay eté bien aise de voir dans la Ceremonie du Couronnement, que le Roy a communié à l'Angloise. Je m'imagine même que sa Mté continuera et que ce ne sera pas seulement une conformité occasionnelle. Cette demarche devroit etre tres

[12] That is, what Leibniz and others called the 'Evangelical' churches in preference to 'Lutheran,' since the latter term had been coined by Luther's opponents.

[13] That is, the Reformed churches that followed the teachings of Calvin.

[14] See Leibniz's letter to Caroline of 7 July 1714 (document 19, pp. 73, 75).

50. Leibniz to Caroline* of Brandenburg-Ansbach, Princess of Wales[1]

[Hanover, *c*.8 December 1714]

Madame

I have been greatly distressed by the departure of Your Royal Highness,[2] which at first made Hanover unbearable for me, and in order to recover myself I had to take a trip to Saxony, which was also necessary for some domestic interests. I returned before the winter months. An attack of gout hindered my journey, but it passed along the way. The joy that the successful arrival of Your Royal Highness[3] has given me, along with all the fine consequences of the revolution, have contributed to my health and constitutes my present satisfaction while I am closed in my room in order to work, hardly ever leaving and scarcely troubling myself with news unless it relates to Your Royal Highness and to all that is dear to her. It is true that I sometimes receive news from Vienna. Mademoiselle Klenk* informs me of the continuing joy that the [Dowager] Empress [Wilhelmine] Amalie* takes in the good fortune of the Royal House [of Braunschweig-Lüneburg (Hanover)], and Count Bonneval* tells me that Prince Eugène*[of Savoy] asks why, not having gone to England, I do not return to Vienna,[4] where it is maintained that I ought not be uncomfortable. But I want to employ this winter in putting the principal part of my work in a state that after that I could even take my leave to go to the other world without our court being able to have reason to complain of me. If I am able to survive there a little while, I will see how my zeal will be noted. I hope that at least Your Royal Highness and the Prince of Wales [Georg August* of Braunschweig-Lüneburg] will not despise it. I have an idea whose success would encourage me a lot. Since in my history I am obliged to touch often on that of England—as much on account of the Saxon antiquities, because the English were a colony of the Saxons, as on account of the ancient connections between the Royal House of England and that of Henry the Lion—the king [George I, Georg Ludwig* of Braunschweig-Lüneburg] would not employ badly the honour and pension of historiographer of Great Britain if he accorded the office to me. These kinds of offices are still given to foreigners because there can be more than one of them. I have written to Mr. Bernstorff* about it.[5] If Your Royal Highnesses were in favor of it, I would hope to succeed. The promise of it will suffice for me, provided that it takes effect as soon as I will have produced this principal part of my work, about which I have written to Mr. Bernstorff, and which I intend to finish this winter.

agreable aux Toris, et la seroit peut etre si l'on la faisoit valoir comme il faut. Les Eglises de la Confession d'Augsbourg se pouvant mieux accommoder sans doute de la Liturgie Angloise que de la discipline genevoise, il me semble que le Clergé Anglican n'aura point sujet de craindre Geneve maintenant autant et plus que Rome. Le Roy me paroissoit autresfois assés content de l'Eglise Anglicane, et peu disposé a chagriner les Toris en general en faveur des Whigs. Je crois que sa Mté n'a point changé de sentiment, et qu'il n'y a que la faction du dernier Ministere, et nullement les autres Toris qu'Elle a voulu eloigner. Mais les bonnes intentions de sa majesté son[t] mal interprétées par le parti disgracié: mais j'espere que les provinces ne donneront pas dans le panneau et que la Cour aura l'adresse de faire ce que fit le ministere qui preceda le dernier.

50. LEIBNIZ TO CAROLINE OF BRANDENBURG-ANSBACH   177

I was very glad to see that the king spoke in English at the coronation ceremony. I even imagine that His Majesty will continue and that this this will not be just an occasional conformity. This initiative should have been very pleasing to the Tories, and it would perhaps be so if it were exploited as it should be. Since the churches of the Augsburg Confession[6] are doubtless able to accommodate themselves better to the English liturgy than to the discipline of Geneva,[7] it seems to me that the Anglican clergy will not now have reason to fear Geneva as much and more than Rome. The king previously appeared to me to be quite satisfied with the Anglican church, and little disposed to provoke the Tories at large to the benefit of the Whigs. I believe that His Majesty has not changed his view and that it is only the faction from the last ministry, and not the other Tories, that he has wanted to remove. But the good intentions of His Majesty are misinterpreted by the disgraced party; I hope that the provinces will not fall into the trap and that the court will have the skill to do what the ministry before the last did.[8]

---

[1] LBr. F 4 Bl. 34r. Draft: one folio side in Leibniz's hand. Previously published in Klopp XI 19–21. It is not clear that a letter based on this draft was actually sent to, or received by, Caroline. For in the first extant letter that Caroline wrote to Leibniz from England (document 52), she begins by acknowledging her receipt of his letter 'of $\frac{7}{18}$ of this month,' that is, Leibniz's letter to her of 18 December 1714 (document 51). I date the present draft to around 8 December because of the similarity of language between it and Leibniz's letter of that date to Bernstorff (document 49) on the matter of the relationship between the Anglican church and the churches of the Augsburg Confession. Similar too is the language that Leibniz uses in both this draft and in the letter to Bernstorff to request the position of historiographer of Great Britain. In the present draft Leibniz states that he has written to Bernstorff about this position, which seems to be a clear reference to his letter to Bernstorff of 8 December.

[2] Caroline departed from Hanover, bound for England, on 12 October 1714.

[3] Caroline landed at Margate, Kent on 22 October 1714 and arrived in London on 24 October 1714.

[4] See Bonneval's letter to Leibniz of 6 October 1714 (document 39, p. 135).

[5] See Leibniz's letter to Bernstorff of 8 December 1714 (document 49).

[6] That is, the Lutheran churches, or what Leibniz preferred to call the Evangelical churches.

[7] That is, the Calvinist churches, or what Leibniz often referred to as the Reformed churches.

[8] The 'ministry before the last' to which Leibniz refers was Queen Anne's first ministry, headed by Sidney Godolphin (1645–1712), 1st Baron Godolphin, who was Lord High Treasurer, and John Churchill (1650–1722), 1st Duke of Marlborough, who was Master-General of the Ordnance and Captain-General of the armies. Robert Harley* (1661–1724), who was a leader of the so-called 'Country Whigs,' was at the time Speaker of the House of Commons. He had been working closely with Godolphin and Marlborough for some time, and Marlborough had a hand in having him appointed Secretary of State for the Northern Department in 1704, by which time he had come to identify himself with the moderate Tories. The three of them worked in concert to establish a mixed ministry of moderate Whigs and Tories, until the Whigs became dominant in 1708. In 1710 the Tories assumed a dominant position that lasted until the queen's death on 12 August 1714 (NS) and the ascension of Georg Ludwig as George I.

Leibniz to Caroline* of Brandenburg-Ansbach, Princess of Wales

Madame

J'etois dans le dessein de me donner l'honneur d'écrire à V. A. Royale, pour ne point laisser passer l'année sans m'aquiter du devoir de mon zele et sans temoigner la joye que j'ay d'apprendre que V. A. R. est adorée en Angleterre lors qu'une raison nouvelle d'écrire est survenue, mais qui est desagreable, et qui m'oblige d'avoir recours à la grande bonté que V. A. R. m'a temoignée. Il y a des gens malicieux qui ont suggeré au Roy que je negligeois entierement son service, et là dessus il est venu un postscriptum aux Ministres qui sont icy et qui me l'ont communiqué, qui semble reduire à rien tout ce que j'ay fait jusqu'icy. Et comme rien ne me peut decourager davantage que de voir voir[3] mes peines méconnues, j'ay voulu faire un effort pour tacher de desabuser sa Majesté et pour meriter ses bonnes graces. Mais j'ay crû que rien n'y pouvoit plus contribuer que l'intervention de V. A. R. C'est pour quoy je prends la liberté Madame de vous adresser la lettre cy jointe et de supplier V. A. R. de la donner au Roy, ou plustost de la luy envoyer, avant qu'Elle luy en parle, a fin qu'il l'aye luë auparavant et soit deja informé de mes raisons. Je supplie aussi V. A. R. de la lire auparavant, pour l'être aussi, et pour les pouvoir appuyer. Je ne cede a personne du coté du zele pour la gloire de sa Mté, et je suis surpris qu'il n'en paroist pas assez informée. Mais il est juste qu'un serviteur zelé se voye au moins agreé, et ne voye point tout le contraire. C'est le moyen de travailler avec plus de plaisir et plus de succès.

J'ay touché en passant en un mot seulement, une occasion importante ou j'ay montré mon zele pour le service de sa Mté, dont Mad. la duchesse de Zell a informé V. A. R. Et j'en parle d'une maniere qui laisse au choix de V. A. R. de l'expliquer au Roy ou non. Il est vray qu'il me semble que cela ne viendroit pas maintenant mal apropos. Tout ce que V. A. R. jugera bon de faire en cette rencontre sera compté par moy pour une grace; car je connois egalement sa bonté, et ses lumieres.

Bien de gens s'imaginent que le Roy fait trop pour les Whigs, et trop peu pour les Toris. Mais persuadé de la prudence de sa Mté, et sachant d'ailleurs qu'il n'avoit aucune passion autres fois contre les Toris moderés; je suis persuadé que le Roy a eté obligé de faire les changemens qu'il a faites. Il estoit de la justice et de l'interest du public, de retablir les gens bien intentionnés ou attachés aux bien intentionnés du temps du precedent Ministere, que le dernier Ministere avoit deplacés. Comme la plus part des restitués ont eté des Whigs, et la plus part de ceux qui ont été obligés de leur faire place, ont été des mauvais Toris ou du moins attachés à eux; mais tousjours des Toris; de cela est venue que les Whigs ont eu maintenant beaucoup d'avantage, mais cela etoit inevitable; et ne prouve nullement que le Roy voudroit

51. Leibniz to Caroline* of Brandenburg-Ansbach, Princess of Wales[1]

[Hanover, 18 December 1714]

Madame

My intention was to give myself the honour of writing to Your Royal Highness in order not to allow the year to pass without fulfilling the duty of my zeal and expressing the joy I have in learning that Your Royal Highness is adored in England when there unexpectedly arose a new reason for writing, which is disagreeable, and which forces me to have recourse to the great kindness that Your Royal Highness has shown me. There are some malicious individuals who have suggested to the king [George I, Georg Ludwig* of Braunschweig-Lüneburg] that I neglected his service entirely, and a postscript on the subject reached the ministers here, which they have communicated to me and which seems to reduce to naught everything I have done to this point.[2] And as nothing can discourage me more than to see[3] my labors disregarded, I wanted to make an effort to try to disabuse His Majesty and to merit his good graces. But I thought that nothing could contribute more to it than the intervention of Your Royal Highness. That is why I am taking the liberty, Madame, to send you the enclosed letter[4] and to beseech Your Royal Highness to give it to the king, or rather to send it to him before you speak with him about it, so that he has read it before and is already acquainted with my reasons. I also beseech Your Royal Highness to read it before, in order to be acquainted with my reasons as well and to be able to support them. I yield to no one in zeal for the glory of His Majesty, and I am surprised that he does not appear sufficiently informed of it. But it is just that a zealous servant find himself at least approved and not witness the complete opposite. This is the means to working with more pleasure and success.

I have alluded [in the enclosed letter] with but a word in passing to an important occasion on which I demonstrated my zeal for the service of His Majesty, about which, Madame, the [Dowager] Duchess of Celle [Eléonore d'Olbreuse*] has informed Your Royal Highness.[5] And I speak of it in a manner which leaves to the discretion of Your Royal Highness to explain it to the king or not. It is true that it seems to me that it would not be inappropriate now. Anything Your Royal Highness will deem fitting to do in this meeting will be counted by me as a favor; for I am acquainted equally with her kindness and her wisdom.

Many people imagine that the king does too much for the Whigs and too little for the Tories. But as I am convinced of the prudence of His Majesty, and knowing moreover that he did not previously have any strong feelings against the moderate Tories, I am persuaded that the king has been compelled to make the changes that he has made. It was just and in the public interest to reestablish the well-intentioned individuals, or those attached to them at the time of the preceding ministry, that

generalement preferer un Whig à un Tory quand tout seroit egal. Je ne doute point que sa Mté ne fasse connoitre cela dans les occasions. Car il me semble d'ailleurs que les principes et les dogmes des Toris moderes tant en matiere de politique, que sur la Religion conviennent mieux avec ceux que le Roy me paroisoit avoir. Il seroit peutetre a propos de le faire mieux connoitre dans le temps que les Elections approchent. Un des moyens seroit d'exciter quelques savans à dedier au Roy quelques livres conformes aux sentimens des Toris moderés, et recompenser les auteurs d'une manière qui marque l'agrément de sa Mté. Si j'avois eté en Angleterre, j'aurois peutetre pû suggérer quelques bons expediens de cette nature, ou je puis peutetre mieux entrer que ceux qui ne sont pas tant que moy du metier des lettres. Mais considerant combien on a prevenu le Roy à mon egard, j'aime mieux le desabuser, et d'employer cet hyver à pousser mes travaux d'une maniere raisonnable. J'adjouteray encor, afin que V. A. R.[6] entende mieux la lettre au Roy, que j'ay decouverte que les anciens princes italiens indubitables auteurs des Maisons de Bronsvic et d'Este sont descendus en ligne directe masculine des Ducs de Toscane. Et que cela pourra contribuer à faire obtenir a la Maison d'Este et de Modene la survivance de la Toscane dans un temps qu'elle est Allié avec l'Empereur, et que la Maison de Bronsvic de plus est montée à un tel degré elevation et de puissance qu'elle peut meme appuyer les affaires d'italie. C'est encor un grand secret. L'imperatrice Amalie a fort applaudi à ce que j'en ay dit a sa Mté et le travail dont l'Empereur m'avoit chargé dernierement y convenoit beaucoup. Car j'ay montré par des preuves solides que Charles quint a donné la Toscane aux males seuls de la Maison de Medicis, et que c'est aux Empereurs d'en disposer encor.

Je supplie V. A. R de marquer aussi ma devotion a l'Altesse Royale de son Epous avec mes souhaits d'une heureuse nouvelle annee, qui egale en bonheur celle d'apresent. Si mes voeux sont exaucés V. A. R. y contribuera pour le moins autant que luy. On dit que le prince de Galles sera Grand Amiral d'Angleterre, rien ne paroist plus raisonnable, et je le souhaite pour bien des raisons. Au reste je suis avec devotion

Madame de V. A. R. etc.

P. S.

Je supplie V. A. R. de parler aussi à M. de Bernsdorf pour le faire concourir à mes veues aupres du Roy; mais il n'est pas necessaire de luy montrer mes lettres au Roy et a V. A. R. Le vray moyen de m'encourager et de me traiter comme je pretends de l'avoir merite, seroit maintenant me donner une pension d'Historiographe d'Angleterre, cette charge ayant eté donnée quelque fois à des etrangers et pouvant convenir à plus d'un. Je demande d'en etre seur mais je ne demande pas d'en jouir qu'apres cet hyver quand j'auray satisfait ma promesse écrite à M. Bernsdorf, à qui j'ay deja fait ouverture de cette proposition, avant que d'avoir receu le post scriptum. Aussi bien seray j'obligé de faire entrer dans mes Annales plusieurs points essentiels de l'histoire d'Angleterre. J'adjouteray seulement, a fin que V. A. R.[9]

51. LEIBNIZ TO CAROLINE OF BRANDENBURG-ANSBACH   181

the last ministry had removed. Since most of the reinstated have been Whigs, and most of those who have been compelled to make way for them have been the bad Tories, or at least attached to them, but always Tories, it has turned out that the Whigs have now had a great advantage; but that was inevitable and does not at all prove that the king would generally prefer a Whig to a Tory if everything would be equal. I do not doubt that when occasions present themselves, His Majesty makes that known. For besides, it seems to me that the principles and tenets of the moderate Tories, as much in political matters as on religion, agree better with those that the king appeared to me to have. It would perhaps be appropriate to make it better known when the elections are approaching. One of the ways would be to prompt some scholars to dedicate to the king some books that conformed to the views of the moderate Tories and to reward the authors in a way that shows the agreement of His Majesty. If I had been in England, I would perhaps have been able to suggest some good expedients of this nature, in which I am perhaps better able to be employed than those who do not have as much experience with the literati as I. But considering how the king has been prejudiced in my regard, I prefer to disabuse him and employ this winter to carry on with my labors in a reasonable way. I will only add, so that Your Royal Highness[6] may better understand the letter to the king, that I have discovered that the ancient Italian princes, unquestionable founders of the Houses of Braunschweig and of Este, are descended in a direct male line from the Dukes of Tuscany. And that will be able to contribute to securing for the House of Este and of Modena the survival of Tuscany at a time when it is allied with the emperor and when, moreover, the House of Braunschweig has ascended to such a degree of greatness and power that it can even support the affairs of Italy. It is still a big secret. The [Dowager] Empress [Wilhelmine] Amalie* has strongly approved what I have said about it to His Majesty, and the work with which the emperor [Karl VI*] had recently entrusted me was very much suited to it. For I have shown, by some solid proofs, that Karl the Fifth [Holy Roman Emperor from 1516 to 1556] gave Tuscany to the males alone of the House of Medici and that it is for the emperors to dispose of it again.

I beseech Your Royal Highness to express my devotion also to the Royal Highness of her spouse [Georg August* of Braunschweig-Lüneburg, Prince of Wales], along with my wishes for a happy new year that will equal in good fortune that of the present. If my prayers are granted, Your Royal Highness will contribute to it at least as much as he. It is said that the Prince of Wales will be Grand Admiral of England; nothing seems more reasonable, and I desire it for many reasons. Finally, I am with devotion

Madame of Your Royal Highness etc.

P.S.

I beseech Your Royal Highness to speak with Mr. Bernstorff* as well in order to have him promote my views to the king. But it is not necessary to show him my

182   51. LEIBNIZ TO CAROLINE OF BRANDENBURG-ANSBACH

51. LEIBNIZ TO CAROLINE OF BRANDENBURG-ANSBACH   183

letters to the king and Your Royal Highness. The true means of encouraging me and treating me as I claim to have merited would be to give me now a pension of historiographer of England, since this post has sometimes been given to foreigners and admits more than one. I ask to be assured of it, but I do not ask to be in possession of it until after this winter, when I will have satisfied my written promise to Mr. Bernstorff, to whom I put this proposition before having received the postscript.[7] The more so as I will have to include in my Annals[8] several essential points concerning the history of England. I will only add, so that Your Royal Highness[9]

---

[1] LBr. F 4, Bl. 89r–89v. Draft: 1.5 folio sides in Leibniz's hand. Previously published in Doebner 1881, pp. 304–7. The letter is not dated, but in her draft reply to this letter from Leibniz (document 52), Caroline notes that she 'received [...] your [i.e., Leibniz's] letter of $\frac{7}{18}$ of this month,' so it seems that the copy sent to Caroline was dated 18 December 1714 NS, which is, as indicated, 7 December 1714 OS. But there are two versions of Caroline's reply. One is a heavily edited draft that may have been dictated by Caroline to an attendant, since it is not in Caroline's hand. This draft is clearly dated 28 December, and, as noted above, it clearly gives '$\frac{7}{18}$ of this month' as the date of the letter based on this draft that Caroline indicates she received from Leibniz. The other version is a fair version in a secretary's highly stylized hand, which seems to be dated 29 December and seems to read '$\frac{7}{19}$ of this month' as the date given for the letter that Caroline reports having received from Leibniz. It is apparently on the basis of this fair copy, then, that Doebner assigned a date of 19 December to the present letter of Leibniz (Doebner 1881, p. 304). But this conflicts with the NS date given for Leibniz's letter in the draft of Caroline's letter, as well as with the fact that in December of 1714 there were only eleven days' difference between the OS date and the NS date. So the fact that the date given for Leibniz's letter in the edited draft of Caroline's letter gives the correct difference between OS and NS dating, namely, 7 December and 18 December, respectively, and the fair copy of Caroline's letter gives an incorrect difference between OS and NS dating, namely 7 December and 19 December, respectively, provides rather strong evidence for accepting the draft's date of 18 December NS as the correct date for the present letter from Leibniz to Caroline. My guess is that the fair copy of Caroline's letter was made the day after the heavily edited draft and that the copyist changed the date of Caroline's letter from 28 December to 29 December and then, perhaps by unconscious association, inadvertently also changed the NS date given for Leibniz's letter from 18 December to 19 December.

[2] Cf. Leibniz's letter to Görtz of 28 December 1714 (document 55, p. 191).

[3] Reading 'voir' for 'voir voir.'

[4] The enclosed letter (Niedersächsisches Landesarchiv-Hauptstaatsarchiv-Hannover 92, 77 Bl. 15–16) was addressed to the king and was dated 18 December 1714, which would seem to support the date I assigned to the present letter from Leibniz to Caroline in note 1 above. The enclosed letter to the king discussed the matter of the postscriptum that Leibniz mentions in the letter to Caroline; it also reminded the king of Leibniz's many years of loyal service to the House of Braunschweig-Lüneburg, emphasizing especially his work on the history of the House. A transcription of this letter to the king was published in Doebner 1881, pp. 301–4.

[5] On this, see Leibniz's letter to Eléonore d'Olbreuse of 3 October 1714 and his letter to Caroline of the same date (documents 37 and 38, respectively).

[6] Here in the margin, Leibniz picks up the sentence he began at the end of the postscript.

[7] See Leibniz's letter to Bernstorff of 8 December 1714 (document 49, p. 171).

[8] Here Leibniz refers to his history of the House of Braunschweig-Lüneburg, entitled *Annales imperii occidentis Brunsvicenses*.

[9] Here the P. S. breaks off. Leibniz apparently decided to include his final thoughts in the body of his letter. They were added in the margin, as indicated in note 6 above.

Caroline of Brandenburg-Ansbach,
Princess of Wales, to Leibniz

de la pcesse[2]   St. James le 28e Xbre 1714

J'ay recû, Monsieur, vostre lettre du $\frac{7}{18}$ de ce mois.[4] Vous avez raison de croire, que je me feray tousjours un plaisir de vous obliger, et de vous donner des marques de mon estime. Mais il me paroist, que ce seroit mal prendre son temps, et vouloir s'attirer un refus, que de demander au Roy pour vous une nouvelle charge d'historiographe, avant que de luy avoir fait comprendre que c'est à tort qu'on vous impute d'avoir si peu advancé[6] une histoire à laquelle vous travaillez depuis tant d'années. Quand vous aurez poussé cet ouvrage pendant cet hyver aussi loin que vous le faites esperer, on sera mieux fondé à faire en vostre faveur la demarche que vous desiréz.

L'espace d'une lettre ne permet pas d'entrer en discusion touchant les Whigs et les Toris. Le plus seur est, de s'en raporter à Ceux qui voyant les choses de pres sont plus à portée d'en juger. Le Prince vous remercie de vos bons souhaits. Luy et moy seront toujours fort disposez à vous faire plaisir.

A Monsieur[8]
de Leibnitz
      a Hannover

52. Caroline* of Brandenburg-Ansbach, Princess of Wales, to Leibniz[1]

from the princess[2]   St. James 28 December 1714[3]

I have received, sir, your letter of $\frac{7}{18}$ of this month.[4] You are right to believe that it will always give me pleasure to oblige you and show you signs of my esteem. But it seems to me that it would be a mistake to take the king's time,[5] and invite a refusal, to ask him for a new position for you before having made it clear to him that it is wrong to charge you with having so little advanced[6] a history[7] on which you have been working for so many years. When you shall have pushed this work as far as you hope to do this winter, it will be better justified to take on your behalf the step that you desire.

The space of a letter does not allow for discussion concerning the Whigs and Tories. It is safer to rely on those who, having seen matters up close, are more able to assess them. The prince [Georg August*, Prince of Wales] thanks you for your good wishes. He and I will always be willing to please you.

To Mr.[8]

Leibniz

in Hanover

---

[1] Niedersächsisches Landesarchiv-Hauptstaatsarchiv Hannover 92, 2095 Bl. 110r–111r. Draft: 2.2 octavo sides in an attendant's hand. Previously published in Doebner 1881, pp. 307–8. There is also a fair copy of this draft letter in a highly stylized secretary's hand (LBr. F 4 Bl. 90r). This responds to Leibniz's letter of 18 December 1714 (document 51).

[2] This is found only in the edited draft of the letter and not in the fair copy.

[3] 8 January 1715 (NS).

[4] The fair copy has ' $\frac{7}{19}$ de ce mois.' For my attempt at explaining the discrepancy between the date given for Leibniz's letter in this draft of Caroline's response and the one given in the fair copy of her response, see note 1 to document 51, p. 183.

[5] The king being George I of Great Britain (Georg Ludwig* of Braunschweig-Lüneburg).

[6] The fair copy has 'avancé' instead of 'advancé.'

[7] That is, Leibniz's history of the House of Braunschweig-Lüneburg (Hanover), which he had been commissioned to write in 1685, following his own suggestion, by Georg Ludwig's father, Ernst August*, and which he had come to refer to as *Annales imperii occidentis Brunsvicenses**.

[8] This and the following two lines are found in the edited draft of the letter and not in the fair copy.

Leibniz to Andreas Gottlieb von Bernstorff[*][1]

A Monsieur de Bernsdorf
Monsieur
Je ne dois point manquer de temoigner mon zele à V. E. en luy souhaitant une heureuse nouvelle annee, et priant Dieu de la combler de toute sorte de satisfactions avec son illustre famille, et sur tout de la conserver en parfaite santé. V. E. marque quelques parts que des lettres pour moy sont venues en Angleterre. Je ne say ce que c'est, mais oserois je supplier V. E. d'ordonner qu'on me les fasse tenir.

Au reste je me rapporte à mes precedentes, ne doutant point que ce que j'ay écrit ne suffise pour mon Apologie. J'espere que cela portera coup, et que par ce moyen je seray mieux en estat de satisfaire au public et à moy même.

Et je suis avec respect etc.

Leibniz to Johanne Sophie,
Gräfin (Countess) zu Schaumburg-Lippe

A Mad. la Comtesse de Bikebourg-Lippe & de Schaumbourg née de Hohenloh
Madame
Je ne laisseray point passer l'année sans marquer mes respects à V. E. pour me conserver l'honneur de vos bontés. Et comme les expressions des souhaits sont autorisés par le temps, je prie Dieu, Madame, de vous donner une heureuse nouvelle année, avec beaucoup d'autres et de vous y combler de toute sorte de satisfaction. Je vous supplie aussi de contribuer à me conserver les bonnes graces de S. A. R. Madame la princesse de Galles. Je ne doute point que le séjour de Londres ne vous soit tres agreable, car outre que vous savés la langue du pays, vous avés de quoy entretenir toute sorte d'esprits, politiques, savans, galans, vous estes faite à tout, Madame, et c'est un theatre qui merite que vous y brillies. V. E. sait qu'avec permission de Mad. la princesse de Galles j'ay envoyé en Angleterre avec les hardes

53. Leibniz to Andreas Gottlieb von Bernstorff*[1]

[28 December 1714]

To Mr. Bernstorff

Sir

I must not fail to express my zeal to Your Excellency by wishing you a happy new year and praying God to fill it with all kinds of enjoyment with your illustrious family, and above all to preserve them in perfect health. Your Excellency somewhere[2] points out that some letters for me have arrived in England. I do not know what it is, but dare I beseech Your Excellency to order that they be sent to me.

Finally, I refer to my previous letters, not doubting that what I have written suffices for my apology.[3] I hope that that will make a great impression and that by this means I will be better able to satisfy the public and myself.

And I am respectfully, etc.

[1] LBr. 59 Bl. 128r. Draft: 0.5 folio sides in Leibniz's hand. Not previously published. The letter is not dated, but it is written on the opposite side of a page containing a draft of a letter to Friedrich Wilhelm von Görtz* (see document 55) that is dated 28 December 1714, which makes it probable that this letter was composed on the same day, especially since both letters begin with wishes for the new year.

[2] Specifically, in Bernstorff's letter to Leibniz of 1 November (document 46, p. 163).

[3] Presumably his apology for not returning to Hanover before Georg Ludwig* of Braunschweig-Lüneburg left for England to ascend the throne as George I. For this apology, see Leibniz's letter to Bernstorff of 20 September (document 32).

54. Leibniz to Johanne Sophie*, Gräfin (Countess) zu Schaumburg-Lippe[1]

[28 December 1714]

To Madame the Countess of Bückeburg-Lippe and Schaumburg, née Hohenlohe

Madame

I will not let the year to pass without paying my respects to Your Excellency in order to preserve the honour of your kindnesses for me. And as expressions of wishes are sanctioned by the season, I pray God, Madame, to give you a happy new year, along with many others, and in them to fill you with every sort of satisfaction. I also beseech you to help preserve for me the good graces of Her Royal Highness the Princess of Wales [Caroline* of Brandenburg-Ansbach]. I do not doubt that the sojourn in London is very pleasant for you; for in addition to knowing the language of the country, you have something to entertain minds of every sort—political, learned, gallant—you do everything, Madame, and it is a theater that merits that you shine there. Your Excellency knows that with permission from Madame the

de S. A. R. Madame la princessse Royale & les votres certains balots de livres. Je ne doute point que le tout ne soit bien arrivé. Mais oserois-je bien vous supplier Madame d'ordonner qu'on les fasse rester en un lieu seur, jusqu'à ce que j'en puisse disposer. J'espere que le parlement nouveau sera au gré de sa Mté. Les Toris modérés doivent etre contents de ce qu'Elle a deplacé les créatures du dernier Ministere qui avoit si mal fait, et retabli celles du precedent qui avoit fait si bien. Cela ne tire point à consequence contre le Toris[2] en general, et il me semble d'avoir remarqué autres fois que le Roy n'avoit rien contre eux.

Leibniz to Friedrich Wilhelm von Görtz

Hanover
28 Xbr 1714

Monsieur

En souhaitant une heureuse nouvelle année à V. E. et priant Dieu de la combler de toute sorte de satisfaction avec son illustre famille, et sur tout de la conserver en parfaite santé, je dois la remercier en même temps de la peine qu'Elle a prise en ma faveur aupres du Roy. Je n'ay garde de vouloir contester avec un si grand prince: mais comme Sa Mté a trop d'affaires sur les bras, pour pouvoir tout approfondir d'abord, il est peutêtre permis de luy faire des remonstrances respectueuse. Sa Mté me veut accorder seulement trois mois pour les ordres qu'Elle m'avoit donnés de m'arrêter un peu a Vienne. Mais je ne pouvois partir apres cela sans risquer beaucoup parce que la contagion avoit fermé tous les passages, et parce qu'il falloit faire des quarantaines facheuses, ou l'on hazardoit sa santé plus qu'en demeurant. Car en plusieurs endroits ou l'on avoit assigné les quarantaines les habitans, malgré les ordres, ne vouloient point recevoir les voyageurs, et les logeoient plusieurs ensemble dans de mechans trous, ce qui étoit non seulement tres incommode, mais même dangereux, et faisoit cet effect, qu'en Saxe et en quelques autres endroits on ne vouloit point respecter les quarantaines faites dans le pays de l'Empereur, et qu'il falloit en faire deux. On me manda meme d'Hanover, que je ferois mieux de ne point venir alors. Ainsi je ne crois pas qu'on me puisse blamer de ne m'etre point exposé dans cette mauvaise conjoncture et d'avoir attendu la cessation de la contagion: mais apres cela je fus incommodé par[2] quelques semaines par la goutte; et je crois

Princess of Wales, I have sent certain parcels of books to England along with the clothing of Her Royal Highness, Madame the Princess of Wales, and with yours. I do not doubt that everything has arrived well. But dare I indeed beseech you, madame, to arrange for them be put in a safe place until I can dispose of them? I hope that the new Parliament will be to the liking of His Majesty [George I, Georg Ludwig* of Braunschweig-Lüneburg]. The moderate Tories ought to be pleased that he has removed the creatures of the last ministry, who had performed so badly, and re-established those of the preceding ministry, who had performed so well. This won't have any repercussions for the Tories[2] in general, and it seems to me that I previously pointed out that the king had nothing against them.

---

[1] LBr. 59 Bl. 128r. Draft: 0.5 folio sides in Leibniz's hand. Previously published in JGHF 227–8. Although this draft is not dated, the opposite side of the page on which it is written contains a draft of a letter to Friedrich Wilhelm von Görtz that is dated 28 December 1714 (see document 55), which makes it probable that the present draft was written on the same day, especially since both begin by expressing wishes for the new year.

[2] Reading 'les Toris' for 'le Toris'.

55. Leibniz to Friedrich Wilhelm von Görtz*[1]

Hanover

28 December 1714

Sir

In wishing a happy new year to Your Excellency and praying God to fill it with all kinds of satisfaction with your illustrious family, and above all to preserve you in perfect health, I must thank you at the same time for the effort that you have made on my behalf with the king [George I, Georg Ludwig* of Braunschweig-Lüneburg]. I have kept from wanting to dispute with such a great prince, but as His Majesty has too many matters on his hands to be able to examine thoroughly everything at once, it is perhaps permitted to make some respectful complaints to him. His Majesty wants to grant me only three months for the orders that he gave me to remain awhile in Vienna. But I could not leave after that without a lot of risk, because the contagion had closed all the crossings and because it required being in some unfortunate quarantines in which a person risked his health more than by staying put. For in many places where quarantines were assigned, the inhabitants, despite orders, did not want to receive travellers, and they lodged them, several together, in some miserable holes that were not only very uncomfortable, but even dangerous; and it had this effect, that in Saxony and some other places they did not want to respect the quarantines established in the countries of the emperor [Emperor Karl VI*], and it was necessary to do two of them [i.e., quarantines]. They even sent word to me from Hanover that I would do better not to come at that time. So I do not believe that I can be blamed for not having exposed myself in this

de ne pouvoir étre obligé à me justifier que sur quatre mois du dernier eté. Mais c'estoit alors que l'Empereur m'avoit chargé d'un travail dont je rendis compte au Roy d'abord, et qui ne devoit pas etre desagreable à Sa Mté. Je promis alors que je viendrois infalliblement au mois de Septembre et je n'y manquai pas. Si Sa Mté pouvoit entrer dans ce detail, pendant qu'Elle a tant de grandes affaires sur les bras je suis asseuré qu'Elle seroit contente de ma justification. Cependant ce ne sont pas tant mes arrerages qui me tiennent au coeur, que la mauvaise opinion que Sa Mté paroissoit avoir de mon travail, et qui se remarquoit dans un postscriptum que Messieurs les Ministres laissés icy m'ont communiqué, et qui m'a touché plus que je ne saurois dire, de voir que pendant que l'Europe me rend justice, on ne le fait pas ou j'aurois plus de droit de l'attendre. Ce qui ne peut venir que de sinistres informations que le Roy doit avoir receues, mais dont j'espere que Sa Mté commencera a étre desabusee. Je supplie V. E. de m'y favoriser dans les occasions, et je suis avec respect Monsieur de V. E. etc.

55. LEIBNIZ TO VON GÖRTZ 191

bad circumstance and for having awaited the passing of the contagion. But after that I was indisposed for[2] some weeks by the gout, and I believe that I can only be obliged to justify myself about four months of last summer. But it was at that time that the emperor charged me with a job, of which I gave at once an account to the king and which ought not to be disagreeable to His Majesty. I promised then that I would certainly come in the month of September, and I did not fail in that. If His Majesty could go into these particulars, while he has so many important matters on his hands, I am sure that he would be satisfied with my justification. However, I do not care as much about my arrearages as about the bad opinion that His Majesty appears to have of my work, which was noted in a postscript that the ministers left here have communicated to me and which has affected me more than I can say, to see that while Europe does me justice, it is not done where I would have the most right to expect it.[3] This can only be the result of sinister news that the king must have received, but of which I hope His Majesty will begin to be disabused. I beseech Your Excellency to help me when the occasion presents itself, and I am with respect, sir, of Your Excellency etc

[1] LBr. 59 Bl. 128v. Draft: one folio side in Leibniz's hand. Previously published in JGHF 225–7, and in Klopp XI 26–7. Feder and Klopp mistakenly identify this letter as being addressed to Bernstorff* rather than to Görtz (see, respectively, JGHF 225 and Klopp XI 26). Although the draft is not addressed explicitly to Görtz, but rather to an unnamed 'Monsieur,' it is fairly clear that it was not written to Bernstorff. For one thing, it is written on the opposite side of a page that contains a short draft letter addressed explicitly to Bernstorff in which Leibniz wishes him a happy new year. It is therefore highly unlikely that Leibniz would have written another letter to Bernstorff on the opposite side of the page that also began by wishing him a happy new year. Furthermore, the present letter contains a plea for payment of Leibniz's arrearages and an explanation for why Leibniz had remained so long in Vienna before returning to Hanover three days after the new king, George I (Georg Ludwig* of Braunschweig-Lüneburg), had left for England. It would make sense for Leibniz to plead to Görtz for payment of his arrearages since Görtz was the financial administrator at the court of Hanover. And, finally, in his letter to Bernstorff of 15 March 1715, Leibniz informed Bernstorff that 'I have written at length to Baron Görtz on the subject of the arrearages, and I have explained that when His Majesty ordered me to postpone my return until the spring of 1713, the contagion and the closure of the roads occurred unexpectedly, and the places where it was necessary to be quarantined were in such bad condition and filled with so many people that it was more dangerous to be exposed there than to remain in Vienna,' and that is pretty clearly a reference to the present letter to Görtz.

[2] Reading 'pour' for 'par'. Feder (see JGHF 226) and Klopp (see Klopp XI 26) omit 'par'.

[3] Cf. Leibniz's letter to Caroline of 18 December 1714 (document 51, p. 179).

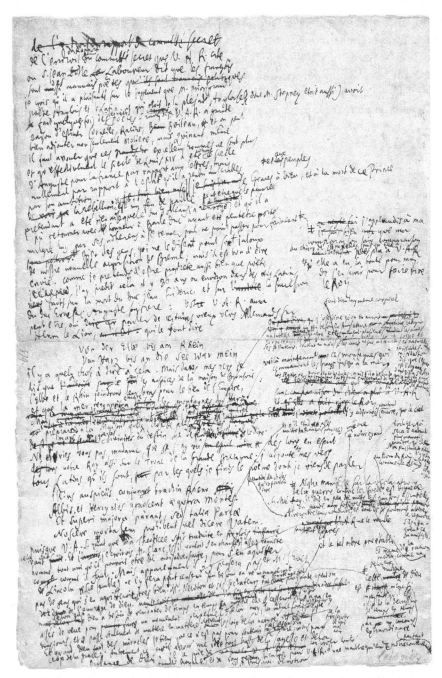

Figure 1. Stadtarchiv Hannover 4.AS.01.1400. Last page of Leibniz's draft letter to Caroline from late November 1715 (document 85), containing the famous passage that Caroline showed to Clarke (beginning mid-page, right-hand margin) and that consequently triggered the Leibniz-Clarke correspondence. Reproduced with permission of the Stadtarchiv Hannover.

1715

56. Isaac Newton: *An Account of the Book entitled* Commercium Epistolicum* Collinii & aliorum, De Analysi promota; *published by order of the* Royal-Society, *in relation to the Dispute between* Mr. Leibnitz *and Dr.* Keill, *about the Right of Invention of the Method of* Fluxions, *by some call'd* the Differential Method (excerpt)[1]

[...]

The Philosophy which Mr. *Newton* in his *Principles* and *Optiques* has pursued is Experimental; and it is not the Business of Experimental Philosophy to teach the Causes of things any further than they can be proved by Experiments. We are not to fill this Philosophy with Opinions which cannot be proved by Phænomena. In this Philosophy Hypotheses have no place, unless as Conjectures or Questions proposed to be examined by Experiments. For this Reason Mr. *Newton* in his Optiques distinguished those things which were made certain by Experiments from those things which remained uncertain, and which he therefore proposed in the End of his Optiques in the Form of Queries. For this Reason, in the Preface to his *Principles*, when he had mention'd the Motions of the Planets, Comets, Moon and Sea as deduced in this Book from Gravity, he added: *Utinam cætera Naturæ Phænomena ex Principiis Mechanicis eodem argumentandi genere derivare liceret. Nam multa me movent ut nonnihil suspicer ea omnia ex viribus quibusdam pendere posse, quibus corporum particulæ per causas nondum cognitas vel in se mutuo impelluntur & secundum figuras regulares cohærent, vel ab invicem fugantur & recedunt: quibus viribus ignotis Philosophi hactenus Naturam frustra tentarunt.*[2] And in the End of this Book in the second Edition, he said that for want of a sufficient Number of Experiments, he forbore to describe the Laws of the Actions of the Spirit or Agent by which this Attraction is performed. And for the same Reason he is silent about the Cause of Gravity, there occurring no Experiments or Phænomena by which he might prove what was the Cause thereof. And this he hath abundantly declared in his *Principles*, near the Beginning thereof, in these Words; *Virium causas & sedes Physicas jam non expendo.*[3] And a little after: *Voces Attractionis, Impulsus, vel Propensionis cujuscunque in centrum indifferenter & pro se mutuo promiscue usurpo, has Vires non Physice sed Mathematice tantum considerando. Unde caveat Lector ne per hujusmodi voces cogitet me speciem vel modum actionis, causamve aut rationem physicam alicubi definire, vel Centris (quæ sunt puncta Mathematica) vires verè & physicè tribuere, si forte aut Centra trahere aut vires Centorum esse dixero.*[4] And in the End of his Opticks: *Qua causa efficiente hæ attractiones* [sc. gravitas, visque magnetica & electrica][5] *peragantur, hic non inquiro. Quam ego Attractionem appello, fieri sane potest ut ea efficiatur impulsu vel alio aliquo modo nobis incognito. Hanc vocem Attractionis ita hic accipi velim ut in universum solummodo vim aliquam significare intelligatur qua corpora ad se mutuo tendant, cuicunque demum causæ attribuenda sit illa vis. Nam ex Phænomenis Naturæ illud nos prius edoctos*

56. NEWTON: *AN ACCOUNT OF THE BOOK ENTITLED* COMMERCIUM 197

oportet quænam corpora se invicem attrahant, & quænam sint leges & proprietates istius attractionis, quam in id inquirere par sit quanam efficiente causa peragatur attractio.[6] And a little after he mentions the same Attractions as Forces which by Phænomena appear to have a Being in Nature, tho' their Causes be not yet known; and distinguishes them from the occult Qualities which are supposed to flow from the specifick Forms of things. And in the Scholium at the End of his *Principles*, after he had mentioned the Properties of Gravity, he added: *Rationem vero harum Gravitatis proprietatum ex Phænomenis nondum potui deducere, & Hypotheses non fingo. Quicquid enim ex Phænomenis non deducitur Hypothesis vocanda est; & Hypotheses seu Metaphysicæ seu Physicæ, seu Qualitatum occultarum, seu Mechanicæ, in Philosophia experimentali locum non habent. —— satis est quod Gravitas revera existat & agat secundum leges à nobis expositas, & ad Corporum cœlestium & Maris nostri motus omnes sufficiat.*[7] And after all this, one would wonder that Mr. Newton should be reflected upon for not explaining the Causes of Gravity and other Attractions by Hypotheses; as if it were a Crime to content himself with Certainties and let Uncertainties alone. And yet the Editors of the *Acta Eruditorum, (a)* have told the World that Mr. *Newton* denies that the cause of Gravity is Mechanical, and that if the Spirit or Agent by which Electrical Attraction is performed, be not the *Ether* or *subtile Matter* of *Cartes*, it is less valuable than an Hypothesis, and perhaps may be the Hylarchic Principle of Dr. *Henry Moor*[8]: and Mr. *Leibnitz (b)* hath accused him of making Gravity a natural or essential Property of Bodies, and an occult Quality and Miracle. And by this sort of Railery they are perswading the *Germans* that Mr. *Newton* wants Judgment, and was not able to invent the Infinitesimal Method.

It must be allowed that these two Gentlemen differ very much in Philosophy. The one proceeds upon the Evidence arising from Experiments and Phænomena, and stops where such Evidence is wanting; the other is taken up with Hypotheses, and propounds them, not to be examined by Experiments, but to be believed without Examination. The one for want of Experiments to decide the Question, doth not affirm whether the Cause of Gravity be Mechanical or not Mechanical: the other that it is a perpetual Miracle if it be not Mechanical. The one (by way of Enquiry) attributes it to the Power of the Creator that the least Particles of Matter are hard: the other attributes the Hardness of Matter to conspiring Motions, and calls it a perpetual Miracle if the Cause of this Hardness be other than Mechanical. The one doth not affirm that animal Motion in Man is purely mechanical: the other teaches that it is purely mechanical, the Soul or Mind (according to the Hypothesis of an *Harmonia Præstabilita*) never acting upon the Body so as to alter or influence its Motions. The one teaches that God (the God in whom we live and move and have our Being) is Omnipresent; but not as a Soul of the World: the other that he is not the Soul of the World, but *INTELLIGENTIA SUPRAMUNDANA*, an Intelligence above the Bounds of the World; whence it seems to follow that he cannot do any thing within the Bounds of the World, unless by an incredible Miracle.

56. NEWTON: *AN ACCOUNT OF THE BOOK ENTITLED* COMMERCIUM   199

The one teaches that Philosophers are to argue from Phænomena and *Experiments* to the Causes thereof, and thence to the Causes of those Causes, and so on till we come to the first Cause: the other that all the Actions of the first Cause are Miracles, and all the Laws imprest on Nature by the Will of God are perpetual Miracles and occult Qualities, and therefore not to be considered in Philosophy. But must the constant and universal Laws of Nature, if derived from the Power of God or the Action of a Cause not yet known to us, be called Miracles and occult Qualities, that is to say, *Wonders* and *Absurdities*? Must all the Arguments for a God taken from the Phænomena of Nature be exploded by *new hard Names*? And must Experimental Philosophy be exploded as *miraculous* and *absurd*, because it asserts nothing more than can be proved by Experiments, and we cannot yet prove by Experiments that all the Phænomena in Nature can be solved by meer Mechanical Causes? Certainly these things deserve to be better considered.

[1] *Philosophical Transactions of the Royal Society* 29:342 (February 1715), pp. 173–224. The *Account* was published anonymously by Newton. In 1715 Newton had a French translation of the work published in the *Journal Literaire de la Haye*, under the title *Extrait du livre intitule Commercium epistolicum*, and a Latin version was included in the second edition of the *Commercium Epistolicum** (1722) under the title 'Recensio Libri Qui inscriptus est Commercium Epistolicum Collinii & aliorum de Analysi Promota...'

[2] 'If only we could derive the other phenomena of nature from mechanical principles by the same kind of reasoning! For many things lead me to have a suspicion that all phenomena may depend on certain forces by which the particles of bodies, by causes not yet known, either are impelled toward one another and cohere in regular figures, or are repelled from one another and recede. Since these forces are unknown, philosophers have hitherto made trial of nature in vain'. As translated in Newton 1999, pp. 382–3.

[3] '[...] I am not now considering the physical causes and sites of forces'. As translated in ibid., p. 407.

[4] '[...] I use interchangeably and indiscriminately words signifying attraction, impulse, or any sort of propensity toward a center, considering these forces not from a physical but only from a mathematical point of view. Therefore, let the reader beware of thinking that by words of this kind I am anywhere defining a species or mode of action or a physical cause or reason, or that I am attributing forces in a true and physical sense to centers (which are mathematical points) if I happen to say that centers attract or that centers have forces'. As translated in ibid., p. 408.

[5] The square brackets here are Newton's.

[6] '*What the* efficient *Cause of these Attractions is, I do not here inquire. What I call* Attraction, *may possibly be caused by some* Impulse, *or some other way unknown to us. I use the Word* Attraction, *only in general, to signify the Force by which Bodies tend towards each other; whatever be the Cause of that Force. For we must first learn from the Phænomena of Nature, what Bodies attract each other, and what are the Laws and Properties of that Attraction, before 'tis proper to inquire what the efficient Cause of Attraction is*'. As translated by Clarke in his Fifth Reply to Leibniz, document 157, p. 793n.

[7] 'I have not as yet been able to deduce from phenomena the reason for these properties of gravity, and I do not "feign" hypotheses. For whatever is not deduced from the phenomena must be called a hypothesis; and hypotheses, whether metaphysical or physical, or based on occult qualities, or mechanical, have no place in experimental philosophy. [...] it is enough that gravity really exists and acts according to the laws that that we have set forth and is sufficient to explain all the motions of the heavenly bodies and of our sea'. As translated in Newton 1999, p. 943.

[8] That is, Henry More (1614–1687), who was an English philosopher and one of the so-called Cambridge Platonists; he held that immaterial substances were extended in space. What Newton here refers to as More's 'Hylarchic Principle' was what More called the 'Spirit of Nature', which he conceived to be an extended, active spirit that was responsible for the non-mechanical activity found in the physical world.

Some Remarks by Leibniz on Roberval, Descartes, and Newton

Monsieur Roberval a supposé dans son Aristarque que chaque partie de la matiere dont l'univers est composée, a une certaine propriete, au moyen de la quelle elles se portent toutes les unes vers les autres et s'attirent reciproquement l'une l'autre. M. des Cartes tome 3 lettre 95 censurant cet Aristarque trouve cela tres absurde, et dit que pour concevoir cela, il faut supposer que chaque partie de l'univers est animée, et meme animée de plusieurs diverses ames, qui ne s'empechent point l'une l'autre, mais que meme ces ames soyent intelligentes et toutes divines, pour pouvoir connoistre ce qui se passe en des lieux fort eloignés d'elles sans en courier[4] qui les en avertisse et pour y exercer leur pouvoir.

Cette supposition de M. Roberval est justement celle de M. Newton et ce que M. des Cartes dit des ames dans chaque partie de l'univers est mon sentiment, mais il ne soit point de cette hypothese, et il n'est point vray qu'elles manquent de couriers pour etre averties de ce qui se fait dans l'univers.

M. Newton n'a pas bien conceu la chose, car tout etant plein il suivroit de son hypothese, que les attractions se compenseroit.[5] Mais il faut savoir que le Matiere grossiere ou d'un certain systeme, a les parties attirées Mutuellement par une matiere plus subtile, quoyque cette matiere plus subtile à nostre egard ne soit pas de la derniere subtilité, & qu'elle soit grossiere elle meme à proportion d'une autre Matiere plus fluide.

Leibniz to Caroline of Brandenburg-Ansbach, Princess of Wales

A V. A. R Madame la princesse de Galles
Madame
J'ay pris la liberté dernierement d'écrire une grande lettre à V. A. R. et j'espere qu'elle l'aura prise en bonne part. J'ay eu cette confiance en Sa bonté, dont Elle m'avoit donné des marques en tant d'occasions; et ayant satisfait à mon devoir, je me remets

57. Some Remarks by Leibniz on Roberval*, Descartes, and Newton[1]

[1715?]

In his *Aristarchus*,[2] Mr. [Giles Personne de] Roberval* has supposed that each part of matter of which the universe is composed has a certain property by means of which they are all moved towards each other and are reciprocally attracted to each other. In censuring this *Aristarchus*, volume 3 letter 95,[3] Mr. *Descartes* finds that quite absurd and says that in order to conceive it, it is necessary to suppose that each part of the universe is animated, and even animated with many different souls, which do not impede one another, but even that these souls are intelligent and wholly divine in order to be able to know what is happening in places very far from them without a messenger from those places[4] who notifies them about it, and in order to be able to exercise their power there.

This supposition of Mr. Roberval is precisely that of Mr. Newton, and what Mr. Descartes says about souls in each part of the universe is my view, but it is not from this hypothesis, and it is not true that they lack messengers in order to be notified about what is done in the universe.

Mr. Newton has not understood the matter well, for since everything is filled, it would follow from his hypothesis that the attractions would balance each other.[5] But it should be understood that the coarse matter, or the matter of a certain system, has mutually attracted parts due to a more subtle matter, although this more subtle matter is in our view not the least subtle and is itself coarse in relation to another, more fluid matter.

---

[1] LH 4, 1, 4K. Draft: two octavo sides in Leibniz's hand. Previously published in Bodemann-HS 57–8; Robinet 1991, pp. 43–4; Schüller 1991, pp. 220–1 (German translation).

[2] *Aristarchii Samii de Mundi systemate* (Paris: Bertier, 1644).

[3] That is, volume three, letter 95, of Clerselier's edition of Descartes' correspondence (1667). See AT IV 399.

[4] Reading 'd'elles sans un courier' for 'd'elles sans en courier'.

[5] Reading 'compenseroient' for 'compenseroit'.

58. Leibniz to Caroline* of Brandenburg-Ansbach, Princess of Wales[1]

[Beginning of January 1715]

To Your Royal Highness, Madame, the Princess of Wales

Madame

I recently took the liberty to write a long letter to Your Royal Highness,[2] and I hope that she will have taken it well. I had this trust in her kindness, of which she had given me signs on so many occasions; and having fulfilled my duty, I leave the

au reste à la providence. Cette lettre, Madame, est pour vous demander des excuses de la precedente qui me parut necessaire, et encore pour vous marquer l'ardeur de mes souhaits pour votre parfait bonheur dans l'annee que nous allons entrer, et dans un grand nombre d'autres, egalement heureuses. J'avoue que j'y suis un peu interessé: vous me tenes lieu, Madame, des Reines et des Electrices; mais mon zele n'est point mercenaire et quand je serois tousjoûrs privé de l'honneur de vous voir, ce que je n'espere pourtant pas, et quand je n'aurois point l'occasion de jouir de votre protection, ce que j'ay connu de vos excellentes perfections, me rendroit tousjours sensible a votre bonheur. Je ne doute point, Madame, que vous ne soyés d'un grand secours au Roy et au prince pour gagner les cœurs, et pour les tenir. On a besoin de cela en Angleterre autant qu'en lieu du monde.[4] Et ce qui rend vos conquestes durables, c'est que vous y travaillés naturellement et sans y penser. Vous savés même comment il faut mesurer les témoignages de bonté selon le merite des gens, et c'est ce qui les rend plus estimables. Je fais quelques fois ma cour à l'aimable prince qui nous est resté icy, et j'en suis charmé. Il semble qu'il vous a tousjours devant les yeux, Madame, et que vous le gouvernés merveilleusement, non obstant votre absence. Le monde vous en a bien de l'obligation, et moy qui m'interesse pour le public, suivant les maximes de ma Theodicée je prends part a la reconnoissance generale, quoyque je vous en doive des biens particulieres pour moy même, et je suis avec devotion

Madame de V. A. R. etc.

58. LEIBNIZ TO CAROLINE OF BRANDENBURG-ANSBACH   203

rest to providence. This letter, madame, is intended to beg your pardon for the previous one, which seemed to me to be necessary, and to show you again the ardor of my wishes for your perfect happiness in the year that we are entering, and in a large number of others equally happy. I confess that I am somewhat interested in it: for me, madame, you take the place of queens and electresses.[3] But my zeal is not mercenary, and even if I would always be deprived of the honour of seeing you, which I still do not expect, and even if I would not have the opportunity to enjoy your protection, which I have experienced due to your excellent perfections, it would always make me concerned for your happiness. I do not doubt, madame, that you are a great help to the king [George I, George Ludwig* of Braunschweig-Lüneburg] and to the prince [Georg August* of Braunschweig-Lüneburg, Prince of Wales] for winning hearts and keeping them. There is as much need of this in England as anywhere else in the world.[4] And what renders your conquests enduring is the fact that you work there naturally and without thinking about it. You even understand how the tokens of kindness must be measured out according to the merit of individuals, and that is what makes them more estimable. Sometimes I wait upon the amiable prince who was left here with us,[5] and I am charmed by him. It seems that he always has you before his eyes, madame, and that you govern him magnificently, despite your absence. The world is much beholden to you for it, and as for me who has concern for the public, following the maxims of my *Theodicy*, I take part in the general recognition, although I owe you some on account of particular benefits for myself. And I am with devotion

Madame of Your Royal Highness etc.

[1] LBr. F 4 Bl. 35r. Draft: one folio side in Leibniz's hand. Previously published in Klopp XI 30–1. At the top left of the manuscript the date January 1716 appears in square brackets with a '5' later added beneath the '6', thus:

    1716]
     5

These appear to be much later additions by an unknown editor, but a date of the beginning of January 1715 seems reasonable based on the wishes for happiness 'in the year which we are entering' that Leibniz expresses near the beginning of the draft letter.

[2] The reference seems to be to Leibniz's letter to Caroline of 18 December 1714 (document 51 above).

[3] Leibniz here alludes to his friend and patroness, the Dowager Electress of Braunschweig-Lüneburg, Sophie* of the Palatinate, who died on 8 June 1714, and her daughter, Sophie Charlotte*, Electress of Brandenburg and first Queen of Prussia, who was also a friend and follower of Leibniz, and who died tragically in 1705 at the age of 36. The loss of Sophie and her daughter Sophie Charlotte had been traumatic for both Leibniz and Caroline—for Caroline because she had been taken in by Sophie Charlotte at the court in Berlin when she was orphaned in 1696 at the age of 13, and because she had subsequently—in the same year that Sophie Charlotte died—married Sophie's grandson, Georg Ludwig*, and hence had known Sophie intimately for some nine years as a member of the electoral family in Hanover.

[4] Reading 'autant qu'en tout autre lieu du monde' for 'autant qu'en lieu du monde'.

[5] Leibniz refers here to Caroline's eldest son, Friedrich Ludwig* (1707–1751).

Nicolas Rémond to Leibniz (excerpt)

Remond

Monsieur   9 Janvier 1715

tout le monde vouloit ici que vous fussiez arrivé en Angleterre avec la princesse de Galles on l'avoit mandé d'Hanover; on l'avoit ecrit de Londres et il y avoit mesme des gens à qui vous n'avez jamais ecrit, a qui vous n'ecrivez jamais qui avoient receu de vos lettres dattées de Windsor. je le souhaitois fort dans l'esperance que bientost degouté de ce pays là vous seriez tenté de venir faire un tour ici ou la grande admiration qu'on a pour vous étousse l'envie naturelle aux hommes. mais je savois deja (car j'avois ecrit en Angleterre pour estre bien instruit) que vous n'attristiez point les Anglois par votre presence importune <u>uris enim fulgore tuo</u>[3] et la lettre que vous m'avez fait l'honneur de m'ecrire d'Hanover le 17 de Decembre m'a apprit[4] que vous comptiez de passer tout l'hyver dans votre cabinet. je souhaite que vous en sortiez sain, gaillard, et dispos <u>cum Zephyris et hirundine prima.</u>[5]

[...]

a Paris ce IX de Javier
1715

[...]

59. Nicolas Rémond* to Leibniz (excerpt)[1]

Rémond

Sir   9 January 1715
Everyone here supposed that you had arrived in England with the Princess of Wales [Caroline* of Brandenburg-Ansbach]; word had been sent from Hanover; they had written from London, and there were even some people to whom you have never written, to whom you never write, who had received your letters dated from Windsor.[2] I very much wished it were so, in the hope that, disgusted with that country by and by, you would be tempted to come make a journey here, where the great admiration that people have for you stifles the envy that is natural to men. But I already know (because I had written to England in order to be well informed) that you do not grieve the English with your troublesome presence, *for you inflame with your brilliance*,[3] and the letter that you did the honour of writing me from Hanover on 17 December [1714] informed[4] me that you intended to spend the winter in your study. I hope that you emerge in health, vigorous, and fit and well *with the Zephyr and the first swallow*.[5]
[...]

in Paris this 9th of January
1715

[...]

---

[1] LBr. 768 Bl. 28r–30v. Letter as sent: 6.25 quarto sides in Rémond's hand. Previously published in GP III 630–4. For Leibniz's response, see Leibniz's letter to Rémond of 27 January 1715 (document 61).

[2] In the P. S. to a letter written to Rémond on 26 August 1714 while he was still in Vienna, Leibniz had written:

> I hope to leave here soon, and I do not know if I will take a trip to England. If I am to receive the honour of your letters, they can always be addressed to Hanover. [GP III 625]

At the end of his letter to Leibniz of 12 October 1714, Rémond responded as follows:

> The news that you are going to England fills me with joy. Will you be so near France without being tempted to come here? I confess that I would prefer the honour of speaking with you sometime at the court of England. [GP III 630]

[3] Adapted from Horace, *Epistles* Book II.1.13: *Urit enim fulgore suo.*

[4] Reading 'appris' for 'apprit'.

[5] Horace, *Epistles* Book I.7.13.

Caroline of Brandenburg-Ansbach,
Princess of Wales, to Leibniz

St. James le $\frac{5}{16}$ Janv
1715

Je vous envoiyë[3] la lettre que Mr. Bernestorff m['] a donne pour vous reponder et c'est la raison pour quoy je ne vous ayée[4] pas repondu plus tost sur vos deu lettres. Je crois Monsieur que sy vous voule[z] bien vous donner la peñe de vous apliquer a listoir de la famille je toute que ce que vous souhaité vous puise manquer.[6] vous pouvez toujours conter que je ferais[7] tout ce qui depantera[8] de moy pour vous.

Caroline

Leibniz to Nicolas Rémond (excerpt)

Monsieur

A Monsieur Remond
du Conseil de S. A. R. Mgr
le Duc d'Orleans 27 Janvier
1715

Vos lettres marquent tousjours également votre bonté, et vos lumieres, je voudrois meriter les unes, et satisfaire aux autres. La défiance que j'avois de ma santé m'a empeché d'accompagner Mad. la princesse de Galles: en effect la goutte m'a pris depuis; elle n'est point fort doulo[u]reuse, mais elle m'empeche d'agir autrement que dans le cabinet ou je trouve tousjours le temps trop court, et par consequent je ne m'ennuye point. Ce qui est un bonheur dans le mal. [...] Et je suis avec zele et obligation

60. Caroline* of Brandenburg-Ansbach, Princess of Wales, to Leibniz[1]

St. James $\frac{5}{16}$ January

1715[2]

I am sending[3] the letter that Mr. Bernstorff* gave me to respond to you, and that is the reason that I have[4] not responded sooner to your two letters. If you are willing, sir, to take the trouble to apply yourself to the history of the family, I doubt that you can lack for what you want.[5,6] You can always be sure that I will do[7] everything for you that will depend[8] on me.

Caroline

[1] LBr. F 4 Bl. 36r. Letter as sent: one quarto side in Caroline's hand. This appears to be Caroline's response to Leibniz's letters of 18 December 1714 (document 51 above) and the beginning of January 1715 (document 58 above). Previously published in Klopp XI 32 and Echeverría 1989, p. 145 (Spanish translation).

[2] That is, 5 January 1715 OS and 16 January 1715 NS.

[3] Reading 'envoie' for 'anvoiyë'.

[4] Reading 'ai' for 'ayée'.

[5] Caroline is referring to Leibniz's history, the *Annales imperii occidentis Brunsvicenses**, and his request for the position of historiographer of Great Britain.

[6] Reading 'Si vous voulez bien, Monsieur, vous donner la peine de vous appliquer à l'histoire de la famille, je doute que ce que vous souhaitez vous puisse manquer' for 'Je crois Monsieur que sy vous voule bien vous donner la peñe de vous appliquer a listoir de la famille je toute que ce que vous souhaité vous puisse manquer'. Caroline began the sentence with 'Je crois' and then began the consequent of her conditional statement with an inappropriate 'je toute'. I have corrected this by reading 'Je crois' as 'Si' at the beginning of the sentence. Klopp mistranscribes the consequent of the conditional statement as 'tout ce que vous souhaitez, vous puisse arriver' (Klopp XI 32).

[7] Reading 'compter que je ferai' for 'conter que je ferais'.

[8] Reading 'dépendra' for 'depantera'.

61. Leibniz to Nicolas Rémond* (excerpt)[1]

Sir

To Mr. Rémond
of the Council of His Royal Highness Monseigneur
the Duke of Orleans 27 January
1715

Your letters always exhibit your kindness and your wisdom equally; I would wish to be deserving of the one and to satisfy the other. The distrust I had of my health prevented me from accompanying Madame the Princess of Wales [Caroline* of Brandenburg-Ansbach]. The gout has indeed since seized me; it is not very painful, but it prevents me from doing anything outside my office, where I always find the time too short, and consequently I am not bored. That is a joy within the pain.

Monsieur   votre etc.

[…]

Leibniz to Caroline of Brandenburg-Ansbach, Princess of Wales

Hanover 29 janvier 1715

Madame   A Mad. la princesse de Galles

Il paroist que V. A. R a voulu prendre plaisir de m'honnorer d'une lettre où tout fut mysterieux et comme etranger, et il semble qu'Elle a voulu me donner un enigme pour exercer l'esprit. D'abord le cachet fait en tête, est cause que je ne puis savoir par quelles mains la lettre a passé. La reponse d'autruy mise là dedans à la place de celle de V. A. R m'empeche de distinguer | ses sentimens de ceux d'autruy. Je suis obligé de douter si V. A. R. n'a pas abandonné à ceux qu'Elle a consultés tout ce que je n'avois écrit que pour Elle; | ses sentimens, | pour les quels je dois temoigner une preference. Je suis en peine de savoir ce qu'on a fait de ma lettre au Roy et si ce que je crus n'ecrire qu'à V. A. R. seule est allé plus loin et ce qu'on a fait demande du Roy | qui sont des loix pour moy, de ceux d'autruy. Je ne comprends pas a quel propos la response inserée me parle des Whigs et des Toris par une maniere de reproche, car je ne crois pas d'avoir donné sujet de juger que j'aye critiqué ce qu'on fait. Au contrarie je ne vois rien que je ne croye fait comme il faut. On y veut aussi que je demeure dans une parfaite incertitude sur ce que j'avois souhaité. Il depend de V. A. R. de me laisser dans ces doutes ou de m'en tirer en partie. Il n'y a qu'une chose dont je ne puis point douter c'est la genereuse bonté de V. A. R. estant avec devotion

62. LEIBNIZ TO CAROLINE OF BRANDENBURG-ANSBACH 209

[…]

And I am enthusiastically and with obligation,

       sir   your etc.

[…]

[1] LBr. 769 Bl. 31r–32v. Draft: four folio sides in Leibniz's hand. Previously published in GP III 634–40. Gerhardt mistakenly gives 11 February 1715 as the date of this letter (see GP III 639). This is Leibniz's response to Rémond's letter of 9 January 1715 (document 59).

62. Leibniz to Caroline* of Brandenburg-Ansbach, Princess of Wales[1]

Hanover 29 January 1715

Madame   To Madame the Princess of Wales

It appears that Your Royal Highness wanted to take pleasure in honouring me with a letter in which everything was mysterious and almost strange, and it seems that she wanted to present me with an enigma for exercising the mind. First, the seal at the top is the reason I am unable to know through whose hands the letter has passed. The response of others placed in there instead of that of Your Royal Highness prevents me from distinguishing | her sentiments from those of others. I am compelled to doubt whether Your Royal Highness has not handed over to those she has consulted everything that I had written only for her | her sentiments, | for which I must show a preference. I am at a loss to know what has been done with my letter to the king[2] and if what I thought I was writing only to Your Royal Highness alone has gone further and what has been requested from the king[3] | which are laws for me, from those of others. I do not understand to what purpose the inserted response speaks to me about Whigs and Tories in a reproachful manner, since I do not believe that I have given reason to think that I have found fault with what is being done. On the contrary, I see nothing that I believe is done improperly. In it they will also have me remain in complete uncertainty about what I hoped for.[4] It is up to Your Royal Highness to leave me in these doubts or to extricate me from them to some extent. There is only one thing about which I am not able to doubt, and that is the generous kindness of Your Royal Highness, being with devotion

[1] LBr. F 4 Bl. 92r. Draft: one folio side in Leibniz's hand. Previously published in Klopp XI 32–3; Echeverría 1989, p. 146 (Spanish translation). Reply to Caroline's letter of 16 January 1715 (document 60).

[2] That is, the letter to George I (Georg Ludwig* of Braunschweig-Lüneburg). See Leibniz's letter to Caroline 18 December 1714 (document 51).

[3] See Leibniz's letter to Caroline from c.18 December 1714 (document 50 above, p. 175) and Leibniz's letter to Caroline of 18 December 1714 (document 51 above, pp. 181, 183), in which he requests the position of historiographer of Great Britain.

[4] Leibniz is referring to his request to be made a historiographer of Great Britain.

Leibniz to Johanne Sophie, Gräfin (Countess) zu Schaumburg-Lippe

29 Janvier 1715   A Mad la Comtesse de Bükebourg
à Londres

Madame

La lettre que j'ay eu l'honneur de recevoir de la part de V. E. me rejouit, non seulement par las marques de Sa bien veueillance, mais aussi en me faisant comprendre la satisfaction qu'Elle goute aupres de la grande princesse, qui fait les delices de l'Angleterre ou plustost du genre humain. J'espere que S. A. R. ne nous aura point abandonnés entierement pour les Anglois, ni voulu diminuer ses bontés pour nous par le partage. Comme le soleil ne luit pas moins a chacun, pour luire à plusieurs. V. E. qui nous appartient aura soin de nous à cet egard, et j'espere que vous voudrés, Madame, me proteger en particulier contre les mauvais effects de l'absence, que je n'ay que trop de sujet de craindre.

Je suis rejoui d'apprendre que les bonnes intentions du Roy sont reconnues de plus en plus dans le general de la Nation. On peut s'appercevoir clairement que Sa M. n'est pas pour les Whigs ny contre les Toris, mais qu'elle est pour un bon ministere contre un mauvais. Je crois aussi que Sa Mté a pris une bonne resolution en ne voulant point qu'on gagne les Elections par des corruptions. J'espere que cela fera un grand effect dans les Elections mêmes. J'apprends que les Ecossois en grande partie voudroient rompre l'Union. Il est vray qu'il y ont eté fort leses, mais on pourroit les soulager par des temperamens. Nous esperons que les mesures prises entre le Roy de la Grande Bretagne et celuy de prusse empecheront que les desordres n'aillent plus loin dans le Nord de l'Allemagne, et que M. Landgrave de Cassel, qui est un prince sage, contribuera à des conseils moderés auprés du Roy de Suede, à fin que ce prince n'acheve pas de se perdre. On a d'autant plus de besoin de se précautionner que l'Empereur pourroit etre enveloppé dans une guerre avec les Turcs si la porte s'opiniastroit d'en vouloir au pays des Venitiens; mais j'espere qu'elle se contentera de quelque argent.

Je say que V. E. n'a point besoin de mes services, mais si j'etois capable de luy en rendre je le ferois de tout mon cœur. Pourveu que mes balots n'incommodent point. J'oseroit la supplier de les laisser encor un peu là ou ils sont, car je n'ay pas encor pû prendre des mesures pour en disposer.

63. Leibniz to Johanne Sophie*, Gräfin (Countess) zu Schaumburg-Lippe[1]

29 January 1715   To Madame the Countess of Bückeburg
in London

Madame

The letter that I have had the honour of receiving from Your Excellency delights me, not only by the signs of her kindness, but also by making me aware of the satisfaction that she feels in the service of the great princess [Caroline* of Brandenburg-Ansbach, Princess of Wales], who delights England, or rather the human race. I hope that Her Royal Highness has not abandoned us entirely for the English, nor has wished to diminish her kindnesses by division, as the sun does not shine less on each in order to shine on several. Your Excellency, who belongs to us,[2] will take care of us in this regard, and I hope that you will seek, madame, to protect me in particular against the ill effects of absence, which I have only too much reason to fear.

I am delighted to learn that the good intentions of the king [George I, Georg Ludwig* of Braunschweig-Lüneburg] are recognized more and more in the majority of the nation. They can clearly see that His Majesty is not in favour of the Whigs nor against the Tories, but that he is in favour of a good ministry as opposed to a bad one. I believe that His Majesty has made a good decision in not wanting to win the elections by corrupt means. I hope that that will have a significant effect in the elections themselves. I hear that the Scots, for the most part, would like to break the Union. It is true that they have been greatly hurt by it, but they could be relieved with some compromises. We hope that the measures taken between the King of Great Britain and that of Prussia [Friedrich Wilhelm I*] will prevent the disturbances from going further into the north of Germany, and that the Landgrave of Cassel [Karl I (1654–1730)], who is a wise prince, will contribute to some moderate counseling with the King of Sweden [Karl XII (1682–1718)], so that this prince does not end up going astray. There is all the more need to take precautions when the emperor could be entangled in a war with the Turks if the Porte should insist on wanting to declare war on the country of the Venetians; but I hope that he will be content with some money.

I know that Your Excellency has no need of my services, but if I were capable of rendering her some, I would do it wholeheartedly. Provided that my bundles are not an inconvenience, I would dare beseech her to leave them where they are yet a bit longer, for I have not yet been able to take measures to dispose of them.

Caroline of Brandenburg-Ansbach,
Princess of Wales, to Leibniz

St. James le $\frac{12}{1}$ Fev

1714

Je ne sçais de quelle Eniqumé vous voulez parler Monsieur par la lettre que vous m'avez écrit. Je vous a'yée anvoiyée[3] la lettre que Mr de Bernestorff m'avoit donne pour vous anvoiyer. J'y avois ajoutée de ma proper[4] mains et qu'aparament[5] vous n'avez pas remarqué que jestée persqué assuré[6] que sy vous vous apliquiée c'est hiver a listoire[7] de la famille que le Roy a fort a[u] coeur, je me fladerais que lon put optenir alors du Roy se que vous souhaité.[9] il me samble que sela[10] est assez gleré.[11] Je souhaiterais y pouvoir contripuer, croiyeant[12] faire mon devoir quand je puis faire quelque chose pour l[']establissement d'un home de votre merité.

Caroline

64. CAROLINE OF BRANDENBURG-ANSBACH TO LEIBNIZ   213

[1] LBr. F 4 Bl. 92r–92v. Draft: 0.7 quarto sides in Leibniz's hand. The beginning of this letter occupies the bottom half of LBr. F 4 Bl. 92r. Previously published in Klopp XI 33–4. The top half contains Leibniz's letter to Caroline of the same date (document 62)—a short letter that is simply dripping with paranoia, a fact that probably explains why, in this letter written immediately afterward to Johanne Sophie, Leibniz solicits her protection against being forgotten by Caroline.

[2] The Johanne Sophie was one of Caroline's German ladies-in-waiting, and Leibniz was appealing to her sense of national solidarity in order to persuade her to help keep him in Caroline's thoughts, lest she forget him in favour of her new English subjects. This letter, written just three months after Caroline's arrival in England, demonstrates the extent to which Leibniz was preoccupied with the thought of losing Caroline's loyalty. This worry would become a recurring theme, and a source of great tension, in Leibniz's later letters to Caroline, as she slipped slowly, but ineluctably, from his grasp into the hands of his Newtonian opponents in England.

64. Caroline of Brandenburg-Ansbach, Princess of Wales, to Leibniz[1]

St. James $\frac{12}{1}$ February

1714 [2]

I do not know of what enigma you mean to speak, sir, in the letter that you have written to me. I sent[3] you the letter that Mr. Bernstorff* gave me to send to you. I added to it with my own[4] hands, and you apparently[5] did not notice that I was all but assured[6] that if you apply yourself this winter to the history[7] of the family,[8] which the king [George I, Georg Ludwig* of Braunschweig-Lüneburg] takes very much to heart, I expect that you may then be able to obtain what you desire from the king.[9] It seems to me that that[10] is clear[11] enough. I would like to be able to contribute to it, since I believe[12] that I do my duty when I can do something to support a man of your merit.

Caroline

[1] LBr. F 4 Bl. 28r–28v. Letter as sent: 1.2 quarto sides in Caroline's hand. Previously published in Klopp XI 34–5. This is Caroline's reply to Leibniz's letter of 29 January 1715 (document 62).

[2] That is, 1 February 1714 OS in England, in which the legal year began on 25 March. So the corresponding NS date is 12 February 1715.

[3] Reading 'ai envoyé' for 'a'yée anvoiyée'.

[4] Reading 'ajouté de ma propre' for 'ajoutée de ma proper'.

[5] Reading 'apparemment' for 'aparament'.

[6] Reading 'j'étais presque assurée' for 'jestée persqué assuré'.

[7] Reading 'appliquiez cet hiver à l'histoire' for 'apliquiée c'est hiver a listoire'.

[8] Caroline is referring to Leibniz's history of the House of Braunschweig, *Annales imperii occidentis Brunsvicenses**.

[9] Reading 'me flatterais que l'on peut obtenir alors du Roy ce que vous souhaitez' for 'me fladerais que lon put optenir alors du Roy se que vous souhaité'.

[10] Reading 'semble que cela' for 'samble que sela'.

[11] Reading 'clair' for 'gleré'. Klopp mistranscribes 'gleré' as 'seur' (see Klopp XI 35).

[12] Reading 'contribuer, croyant' for 'contripuer, croiyeant'.

214   65. SMALRIDGE TO CAROLINE OF BRANDENBURG-ANSBACH

65. George Smalridge*, Bishop of Bristol, to Caroline of Brandenburg-Ansbach, Princess of Wales[1]

[4 March 1714 OS/15 March 1715 NS]

Madam,

The Book [Leibniz's *Théodicée*], which Your Royall Highness was pleas'd to put into my Hands, when I was in Town, I did, soon after my return to this place, peruse & consider with the best Attention & closest Application I could; and when I had gone through it, I did intend in Obedience to Your Highnesses commands to do my self the Honour of giving You my thoughts concerning It. But I was taken with first a great heaviness, and afterwards an Acute pain in my Head, which hath for some Weeks indispos'd Me for writing, & which is not Yet quite remov'd, tho[h] I thank God it is in great Measure abated. Were My Head never so clear, I should not hope to write any thing worthy of Your Highnesses View; as it is Now more than ordinarily weak and confus'd, I should be Unpardonable in presuming to trouble Your Highness with my crude thoughts, if it were not still more Inexcusable not to write at All, after Your Highness had condescended both to permit Me so to do, & to signifie, that You expected to have heard from Me.

My Lady Nottingham, when she first mention'd this Book to Me from Your Royall Highness, told Me that You complain'd of the Obscurity of it.[2] I cannot but think that there is great reason for that Complaint, for tho[h] it doth not become Me to measure the Extent of Your Highnesses Abilities by the common standard, Yet I believe I may, without too much presumption, say, that there is scarce any Other Person of Your sex, who can thoroughly understand all the parts of this Book.

The subject it self, of which the Learned Author treats, is very Nice & Intricate, such as hath puzled the Wisest and Ablest Heads in All Ages, & such as Those who have most maturely weigh'd & consider'd, have most readily acknowledg'd to be attended with great, if not Insuperable, Difficulties.

The Author in treating of this subject hath employ'd many school-Terms, & Metaphysicall Distinctions (such as <u>Absolute</u> and <u>Hypotheticall</u> Necessity; the Necessity of y[e] <u>Consequence</u>, & of the <u>Consequent</u>; the <u>Antecedent</u> & <u>Consequent</u> will of God; science of <u>Simple Intelligence</u>, of <u>Vision</u>, & a <u>Middle</u> science between these two; the <u>Physicall</u> & <u>Metaphysicall</u> Communication of the Soul with the Body; and the like) which Terms to Persons not vers'd in the peculiar Idiom & Language of the schools must of Necessity be, what even by some, who have been sufficiently skill'd in this sort of Learning, they have been declar'd to be, mere Jargon, empty words without any Meaning, and utterly Unintelligible.

The Author hath also inserted severall Citations from Greek & Latin Authors, which He hath not translated into the Language, in which He writes, & which therefore a Reader, who is not acquainted with Greek & Latin, can make Nothing

216   65. SMALRIDGE TO CAROLINE OF BRANDENBURG-ANSBACH

65. SMALRIDGE TO CAROLINE OF BRANDENBURG-ANSBACH   217

of, & You ought to Know, not merely for the sake of the Citations themselves, but also because without the Understanding of these, what goes before or follows after cannot be well Understood.

The Author doth in severall places illustrate what He delivers by Similitudes or Examples, taken from Mathematicks or Naturall Philosophy; which Resemblances, tho[h] to Persons skill'd in those sciences they may make the Matters treated of clearer, Yet to Others Unacquainted with those parts of Learning, or who have not searcht into y[e] depths of them, they must Necessarily render what is said rather more, than less, Obscure.

The Author doth in severall places allude to Books, which He had before publish'd, & which He supposes the Reader of this to be well Acquainted with; but it may happen that some Readers may have never seen, or never consider'd those former Discourses of His, & therefore may be the less prepar'd, & the less Able to understand what is advanc'd in this.

The Author hath in the prosecution of this subject made many, & sometimes very long Digressions, which tho[h] in themselves perhaps very Usefull & Instructive, Yet, as they are brought in here, do interrupt the thread of the Discourse, & thereby make it more difficult for the Reader to carry on the pursuit of the Principall subject in his thoughts.

For the Reasons w[ch] have been alleg'd, & for many others, w[ch] might be offer'd, this Book must to the Generality of Readers, at least in some parts of it, appear Difficult and Obscure.

But however, it is very Easie for any Intelligent Reader with the least Degree of Attention to discover in it many Excellent thoughts, a great compass of Knowledge & Learning, a close way of Reasoning, a solidity of Judgment, much Candour towards those from whom the Author differs, & against whom He writes, &, which must render it still more Valuable to all Serious & Devout Christians, a true spirit of Piety, an ardent Zeal for the glory of God, for the Vindicating his Attributes, for inspiring the Reader with a Love of Him, & for rectifying those false Notions of Reason or about Religion, which must have a very bad Influence upon Mens practise.

What this Author hath at large alleg'd to prove that the Permission of Evil, & even of sin, is consistent with the goodness, Wisdom, & Holiness of God, will, I believe, appear satisfactory to all Unprejudic'd and well-disposed Minds; but still there will be room for Cavils from those who are Irreligiously inclin'd; & even sober, and pious Persons, who are firmly persuaded of the Divine Attributes, may not be able fully & clearly to answer All the Objections which may be brought against them.

Your Royall Highness will find the Objection against the Goodness of God drawn from the Permission of Evil consider'd, and Answer'd by AB[p] [John] Tillotson* in the 3[d] sermon of the 7th Volume of the sermons publish'd after his Death.

218   65. SMALRIDGE TO CAROLINE OF BRANDENBURG-ANSBACH

65. SMALRIDGE TO CAROLINE OF BRANDENBURG-ANSBACH 219

The Answers given there by the Archbishop, & more at large by the Author of the Learned Book, which Your Royall Highness put into my Hands, appear to Me very solid; but were they less satisfactory than they are, I should not at all be stagger'd in my firm belief of ye Divine Wisdom & Goodness, tho^h I were not able to reconcile these with the sufferance of Evil.

For since it is Evident from Experience, that God doth permit Evil; & since it is Demonstrable by Reason & by Revelation, that God is Holy & Good, these Truths must be consistent One with the Other, whether I by my shallow reasoning can make out their Consistency or not.

The Attempt of Learned Men to reconcile the Appearances of Repugnancy between such undoubted Truths, as do seem to interfere with each Other, is extremely laudable; and the Reasons wch they have offer'd to prove ye permission of Evil & the Goodness of God to be fairly consistent, are much stronger than any wch are brought to prove them Repugnant; but still there may remain some difficulties not to be solv'd whilst We are in this state of Imperfection, but reserv'd, till We are translated to a state of greater Illumination.

In the mean-time it will become all humble, serious, & sober-minded Christians, rather to apply themselves to ye diligent & Conscientious practise of Known Duties, than to perplex their Minds with an over-curious search into hidden & mysterious Truths, as considering, that secret Things belong to the Lord our God; but that those things wch are reveal'd, belong to Us, that We may do all the words of the Law. That God would direct Your Royall Highness by his Holy Spirit in the true Knowledge of Him & of his Word; that He would confirm & strengthen You in all Goodness, & pour down upon Your Royall Person & Family the choisest of his blessings, is the earnest Prayer of,

Madam,

Your most Dutifull, most Obedient, &

most Obliged servant

Christ-Church, Oxford
Mar. 4th. 1714.^{3} George Bristol

---

[1] LH 4, 4, 1 Bl. 1r–6r. Letter as sent: 10.5 quarto sides in Smalridge's hand. Not previously published. Caroline sent this letter of Smalridge to Leibniz, and he responded to it in his letter to Caroline of 29 March 1715 (documents 67a and 67b).

[2] It is worth noting that Smalridge knew from Lady Nottingham that Caroline thought the *Theodicy* was obscure. That undoubtedly coloured Smalridge's own assessment of the work, and Caroline apparently left Leibniz in the dark about her own opinion concerning the obscurity of the *Theodicy*, contenting herself with sending Smalridge's assessment to Leibniz. In her diary entry of 19 November 1714 OS (30 November 1714 NS), Lady Mary Cowper* wrote:

> In the morning, whilst I was in Waiting, came in my Lady *Nottingham*. We had just before been talking of Dr. *Smaldridge*, Bishop of *Bristol*, who had been praised to the *Princess* [Caroline] as the greatest Saint upon Earth [...] When my Lady *Nottingham* came in, the *Princess* addressed herself to her, and said: 'We have been talking of Dr. *Smaldridge*.' Upon which the other launched out in his Praise; and says my Mistress: 'Here's Dr. *Clarke** shall be one of my Favourites; his Writings are the finest Things in the World.' Says the *Countess* [of Nottingham]: 'Yes, Madam, his first Writings;

Leibniz to Andreas Gottlieb von Bernstorff

Hanover ce
15 de Mars 1715

Monsieur

Je supplie V. E. de souffrir que j'insiste sur mes interests indispensables. J'avois esperé qu'à la chambre on recevroit ordre de payer mes arrerages, mais M. Schild n'en a receu que pour 3 mois depuis paques de l'an 1713. Je ne saurois croire que le dessein du Roy soit de me faire des retranchemens, pendant que j'aurois grand sujet d'esperer des graces: j'ay ecrit amplement à M. Le Baron de Goriz sur le sujet des arrerages, et j'ay fait voir que lors que Sa Mté me donna ordre de suspendre mon retour au printemps 1713, il survint la contagion et la cloture des passages, et les lieux ou il falloit faire la quarantaine étoient si mal accommodés, et remplis de tant de monde, qu'il étoit plus dangereux de s'y exposer que rester à Vienne. Ainsi tout le monde me conseilla de ne point voyager en ce temps là, et je crois même que ce fut l'avis de V. E. En 1714 la goutte, et puis une occupation à la quelle j'etois engagé par ordre de l'Empereur et dont j'informay V. E. m'empecherent de revenir avant le Septembre. Et ce travail étoit d'une telle nature que je crois qu'on a sujet de le compter pour un service considerable rendu[3] à la Maison. J'ay d'ailleurs bien employé mon temps à des recherches Historiques peu communes dans les Ms. de la Bibliotheque de l'Empereur, et en un mot, à bien estimer les choses, j'aurois sujet d'esperer autant que quique ce soit qu'on me payât meme le voyage. Tantum abest que j'en doive souffrir. Et de l'avoir fait sans ordre, cela ne me doit point nuire, car feu Mg^r l'Electeur et le Roy m'ont tousjours laissé la liberté de faire de tels voyages conformement à ce que je trouverois à propos pour mieux faire mes recherches.

but his last are tainted with Heresy.' And so she said an abundance upon that Subject; and in speaking of his Scripture Doctrine of the Trinity, that Part relating to *Athanasius's* Creed, which she called the test of Religion, she quoted Dr. *Smaldridge* as an Authority against Dr. Clarke. Mrs. *Clayton* was by, and said that Dr. *Smaldridge*, whatever he had said to the *Countess*, yet had said to her that every private Christian was not obliged to believe in every Part of the Athanasian Creed. Notwithstanding this, Lady *Nottingham* defended her Opinion of Dr. *Clarke's* being a Heretic as well as she could; and I said to her: 'Madam, I have read these Books, and I really see no Cause to accuse him of Heresy, which is a heavy Charge; but I suppose your Ladyship is better acquainted with them than I am. Since you can accuse him, pray quote a Passage out of his Books.' To which she answered, drawing herself up as if she had been afraid of Something: 'Not I, indeed. I dare not trust myself with the Reading such Books. I'll assure you I never looked into them.' 'What, Madam?' said I, 'Do you undertake to condemn Anybody as a Heretic, or to decide upon a Controversy, without knowing what it is they believe and maintain? I would not venture to do so for all the World.' This Dispute happening before the *Princess*, will hardly be a Step to making her Governess to the young *Princesses*, which she had asked to be; nor do I believe that Dr. *Smaldridge* will have Power to do so much Harm as he has done, or designs to do, for I am told for a Certainty that he and my Lord *Nottingham* are in the Hopes of the Tories, and that the one in the Church, and the other in the State, had undertaken to set all Things upon the right Foot, as they call it. [Cowper 1865, pp. 17–18]

[3] That is, 15 March 1715 (NS).

66. Leibniz to Andreas Gottlieb von Bernstorff[*][1]

Hanover

15 March 1715

Sir

I beseech Your Excellency to allow me to insist upon my essential interests. I had hoped that an order would be received in the chamber to pay my arrearages, but Mr. Schild has only received some for three months after Easter of the year 1713. I could not believe that the intention of the king [George I, Georg Ludwig* of Braunschweig-Lüneburg] is to dock me while I would have considerable reason to expect thanks. I have written at length to Baron Görtz* on the subject of the arrearages,[2] and I have explained that when His Majesty ordered me to postpone my return until the spring of 1713, the contagion and the closure of the roads occurred unexpectedly, and the places where it was necessary to be quarantined were in such bad condition and filled with so many people that it was more dangerous to be exposed there than to remain in Vienna. So everyone advised me not to travel at that time, and I even believe that this was the advice of Your Excellency. In 1714 the gout, and then a job on which I was engaged by order of the emperor [Karl VI*], and of which I informed Your Excellency, prevented me from returning before September. And this job was of such a nature that I believe there is reason to count it a significant service rendered[3] to the House [of Hanover]. Moreover, I have employed my time well in some unusual historical investigations into the manuscripts from the emperor's library, and, in a word, to appraise matters rightly, I would have reason to expect, as much as anyone, to be paid even for the travel, far from having to suffer for it. And to have done it without order should not be prejudicial

Je ne sçaurois me dispenser d'ecrire tout cela à V. E. car le terme de paques approche, et j'espere que M. Schild aura ordre de me payer en même temps les vieux termes et le nouveau. Sans quoy je me trouverois extremement embarrassé tant par rapport aux autres, qu'à l'egard de moy même.

Quoyque je sois si peu encouragé, je ne laisse pas de faire ce que je puis, même au-delà de ce qui paroist convenir à ma santé, qui est insultée de temps in temps par des maux arthritiques. Je me presse moy même pour depecher la partie la plus necessaire de mon travail; mais je serois bien attrappé, s'il étoit peu consideré, et les sujets de douter qu'on me donne ne laissent point de me faire du tort et même à mon travail.

Ma pretension tres juste va à un poste d'Historiographe d'Angleterre, qu'il est dans le pouvoir du Roy de donner à un Etranger, et on en a des exemples. Mais je ne pretends pas d'en recevoir les gages quoque courans de puis la concession du Roy que lors que j'auray achevé le second tome, qui finira avec les Empereurs de l'ancienne race de Bronsvic, c'est à dire avec Henry le Saint ou le boiteux. La Grande Bretagne ne peut manquer de s'interesser dans l'Histoire de la Maison de Bronsvic, qui est maintenant la Maison Royale. Et personne pourra trouver à redire à cette grace de Sa Mté pour plusieurs raisons. J'espere donc que V. E. m'obtiendra l'asseurance de ce que je viens de demander.

Comme j'ay besoin de l'eclaircissement de de quantité de Genealogies de grands familles qui entrent dans cette Histoire, mais qui ont eté fort mal menées par nos Historiens; j'ay crû que je ne pouvois meiux employer M. Eccard, que de l'y faire donner ces soins. Cela reussit assés bien. Il vient maintenant chez moy la plus part des jours deux fois, et comme il travaille sous mes yeux, je l'assiste dans les endroits difficiles, et je luy fournis mes collections. Le succés l'y fait prendre goust, on deterre bien de choses vulgairement inconnues, dont l'intelligence est necessaire pour une bonne Histoire. Autrement il y a quantité de faits, dont on ne sauroit rendre raison, quand on ne fait comment les familles ont eté liées, ce qui est fort obscur dans ces vieux temps.

Au reste je suis avec respect
Monsieur de V. E.

le tres humble & tres obeissant
serviteur
Leibniz

66. LEIBNIZ TO VON BERNSTORFF   223

to me, for the late elector [Ernst August* of Braunschweig-Lüneburg] and the king have always allowed me the liberty to make any trips in line with what I would find appropriate to advance my research.

I could not dispense with writing all this to Your Excellency because the Easter term is approaching, and I hope that Mr. Schild will have the order to pay me the old terms and the new at the same time. Otherwise I would find myself at a loss, both in relation to others and in regard to myself.

Although I am so little encouraged, I do not cease to do what I can, even beyond what appears conducive to my health, which is assaulted from time to time by severe arthritis. I push myself to dispatch the most essential part of my work, but I would be rather disappointed if it were little regarded, and the reasons I am given for doubting do not cease to harm me and even my work.

My very just pretension is for a position as historiographer of England, which is in the power of the king to grant to a foreigner, and there are examples of it. But I do not intend to receive the wages from it, although accruing after the concession of the king only when I will have finished the second volume,[4] which will end with the emperors of the ancient race of Braunschweig, that is to say, with Henry the Saint, or the Lame. Great Britain cannot fail to have an interest in the history of the House of Braunschweig, which is now the Royal House. And no one will be able to object to this favour of His Majesty for many reasons. I therefore hope that Your Excellency will obtain assurance for what I have just requested.

As I need to elucidate of a number of genealogies of great families that enter into this history, but which have been very badly carried out by our historians, I thought that I could not better employ Mr. Eckhart[5] than by having him attend to them. That is succeeding fairly well. Most days he now comes to my house two times, and as he works before my eyes, I assist him in the difficult places, and I furnish him with my collections. Success makes him take a liking to it; many things not commonly known are unearthed, whose understanding is necessary for a good history. Otherwise there are a number of facts that cannot be explained when it is not known how the families were connected, which is very obscure in those days of old.

For the rest, I am with respect,
sir, of Your Excellency

the very humble and very obedient

servant

Leibniz

---

[1] LBr. 59 Bl. 129r–129v. Draft: two folio sides in Leibniz's hand. Previously published in Doebner 1881, pp. 312–14. For Bernstorff's answer, see Bernstorff's letter to Leibniz of 5 April 1715 (document 69).

[2] See Leibniz's letter to Görtz of 28 December 1714 (document 55, pp. 189, 191).

[3] Doebner omits 'rendu' (see Doebner 1881, p. 312).

[4] That is, the second volume of his *Annales imperii occidentis Brunsvicenses**.

[5] That is, Johann Georg Eckhart, Leibniz's secretary.

Leibniz to Caroline of Brandenburg-Ansbach, Princess of Wales

Hannover 29 Mars 1715

A Son Altesse Royale
Mad. la princesse de
Galles

Madame

J'ay appris de Mlle de pelniz que V. A. R. se souvient gracieusement de moy, et je l'ay reconnu encore d'avantage par la lettre de M. l'Evêque de Bristol à V. A. R qu'elle a bien voulu me faire communiquer. Cela m'a donné bien de la joye. Je prends la liberté Madame, de vous envoyer le papier cyjointe là dessus. Il ne paroist pas qu'on trouve mon livre obscur en France ou plus obscur que les livres du p. Malebranche et d'autres qui sont assés à la mode. Quand l'Edition de paris qui est en 12° sera debitée on y pense d'en donner une autre avec des augmentations. Je ferois alors expliquer les citations latines ou Grecques. Et si l'on m'indique quelque veritable obscurité, je tacheray de l'éclaircir.

M. l'Abbé de S. pierre[4] qui est cousin Germain du Mareschal duc de Villars m'a envoyé son livre sur la paix perpetuelle qu'il medité d'etablir par un Tribunal ou les souverains plaideront comme à Wezlar. Il m'a demandé mon sentiment là-dessus. Comme il me paroissoit démembrer l'Empire par son nouveau projet, je l'ay prié dans ma reponse de ne point detacher de l'Empire ny le Duc de Savoye ny d'autres.

J'ay écrit à M. de Bernsdorf et a M. de Goriz pour les prier de me faire payer mes arrerages, & j'ay prié aussi M. de Bernsdorf de penser pour moy a la place d'Historiographe d'Angleterre, car elle a eté donnée plus d'une fois à l'estrangers. J'espere que la protection de V. A. R. le fera reussir. Il semble qu'Elle m'en donne quelque esperance dans sa derniere que j'ay eu l'honneur de recevoir de sa part. et je suis avec devotion

P. S. Pour traduire mon livre en Anglois je crois que M. de la Roche y seroit propre. C'est un Ministre Refugié qui a donné en Anglois une espece de journal intitulé Memoirs of Literature. Il est vray que j'aimerois mieux qu'un Theologien Anglican en entreprit la traduction.

67a. Leibniz to Caroline* of Brandenburg-Ansbach, Princess of Wales[1]

Hannover 29 March 1715

To Her Royal Highness
Madame the Princess of
Wales

Madame

I learned from Mademoiselle Pöllnitz [Henriette Charlotte von Pöllnitz*] that Your Royal Highness graciously remembers me, and I recognized it still more from the letter of the Bishop of Bristol[2] to Your Royal Highness that she has kindly transmitted to me. That has given me much joy. I take the liberty, madame, of sending you the enclosed paper about this subject.[3] It does not appear that my book is thought to be obscure in France, or more obscure than the books of Father [Nicolas] Malebranche* and others that are quite in fashion. When the Paris edition, which is in duodecimo, is sold out, they are there thinking of publishing another edition of it with some additions. I would then explain the Latin and Greek citations, and if a genuine obscurity is pointed out to me, I will try to clarify it.

The Abbé de Saint-Pierre,[4] who is first cousin of the Marshal Duke of Villars,[5] has sent me his book on the perpetual peace, which he plans to establish by a tribunal where the sovereigns would plead their cases as at Wetzlar.[6] He asked for my opinion of it. As he seemed to me to dismember the empire by his new project, I have asked him in my response not to detach either the Duke of Savoy or any others from the empire.

I have written to Mr. Bernstorff* and to Mr. Görtz* to ask them to have my arrearages paid, and I have also asked Mr. Bernstorff to think about the position of historiographer of England for me, since it has been given more than once to foreigners. I hope that the support of Your Royal Highness will make it succeed. It seems that she gives me some hope of it in her last letter, which I have had the honour of receiving from her.

P. S. For translating my book [i.e., the *Théodicée*] into English, I believe that Mr. [Michel] de la Roche* would be suitable. He is a refugee clergyman who has published a kind of journal in English entitled *Memoirs of Literature*. It is true that I would prefer that an Anglican theologian undertake the translation and I am with devotion

---

[1] LBr. F 4 Bl. 37r–37v. Draft: two octavo sides in Leibniz's hand. Previously published in Klopp XI 35–6.

[2] That is, George Smalridge (1662–1719), who was Bishop of Bristol from 1714 to 1719. For his letter to Caroline, see document 65 above.

[3] For the enclosure, see document 67b.

[4] That is, Charles-Irénée Castel (1658–1743), abbé de Satin-Pierre, a French political and economic theorist. He was one of the earliest proponents of an international organization for maintaining peace, to which Leibniz here refers. In 1693 he became the almoner to the Duchess of Orléans, Elisabeth Charlotte*, who was the daughter of the brother of Sophie* of the Palatinate, the Elector Palatine Karl Ludwig*. Saint-Pierre was elected to the French Academy in 1695.

[5] That is, Claude Louis Hector de Villars (1653–1734), Marshall of France from 1702; later General Marshal of France, from 1733.

[6] Wetzlar is a city in Hesse, Germany. In 1689 the high court of the empire, the Reichskammergericht, was moved from Speyer to Wetzlar.

Leibniz to Caroline of Brandenburg-Ansbach,
Princess of Wales

Le jugement que Mylord Evêque de Bristol fait de mon livre est tel que je n'en appelleray pas, si ce n'est peut etre à Mad. la pincesse de Galles, dans un seul article. C'est quand il semble en exaggerer un peu trop l'obscurité. Car S.A.R. ne l'a point trouvée si grande. Il est vray comme il dit fort bien, qu'il ne serait point raisonnable to mesure the extent of her Royal Highnesses abilities by the common standard.

Quant aux termes philosophiques; (comme par exemple dans les differentes especes et definitions du Mal, de la necessité, de la science de Dieu); il semble qu'on les explique assés nettement, et qu'apres cela, il est permis de les employer, car autrement on auroit besoin de trop de circumlocutions. Et il en est ainsi par tout ou l'on se sert des termes des Arts. On ne peut pas dire que ce sont des paroles vuides de sens, mere jargon, empty words car on en donne des definitions bien intelligibles. Et celuy que voudroit tousjours eviter les Termes des Arts, deviendroit plus obscur par ce qu'il deviendroit trop prolixe, et le lecteur se perdroit dans la multitude des paroles. C'est comme si au lieu de dire, deux, trois, quatre on y vouloit toujours substituer, un et un, un et un et un, un et un et un et un.

J'avoue que les endroits où je me sers de quelques notions physiques et mathematiques, et où je me rapporte à ce que j'en ay dit ailleurs, ne peuvent manquer d'etre obscurs à la plus part des Lecteurs: mais ils les peuvent passer sans s'en embarasser; et ils ont leur utilité pour ceux qui veulent approfondir la matiere extraordinairement, et qui font profession de s'attacher aux recherches. Car on a crû qu'ils y trouveroient quelques nouvelles lumieres. Tout ce qu'on pourroit trouver à dire la dessus seroit peut estre, qu'il auroit fallu distinguer ces endroits des autres, pour avertir les Lecteurs de les passer. Mais outre que ce n'est point l'usage; il n'y a peut etre point de tel endroit, ou l'on ne trouve quelque chose de clair et d'utile mêlé; et dans ce que y demeure difficile, le Lecteur attentif ne laissera[4] peutêtre d'entrevoir un certain clair-obscur qu'il ne sera point faché de considerer.

Je me sers par exemple de l'inertie de la matiere, pour expliquer par cette comparaison la nature privative du mal. Un Lecteur qui n'est point philosophe ny mathematicien trouvera cela difficile. Mais s'il voudra prendre la peine de mediter sur ce que je dis, il ne s'en repentira pas.

Quant à mes disgressions, peut etre ne sont elles pas assés longues pour faire perdre le fil du principal sujet, et il est aisé de le reprendre. D'autres m'en ont sû gré bien loin de s'en plaindre. Ils ont esté bien aises que j'aye égayé un peu la matiere.

Il y a une accusation ou je me reconnois guilty. C'est que je devois expliquer en François quelques citations Latines ou Greques.

67b. Leibniz to Caroline* of Brandenburg-Ansbach, Princess of Wales[1]

[Hanover 29 March 1715]

The judgement that My Lord the Bishop of Bristol has made of my book[2] is such that I will not appeal, except perhaps to Madame the Princess of Wales, in respect of only a single point, namely, when he seems to exaggerate its obscurity a bit too much. For Her Royal Highness has not found it so great.[3] It is true, as he very rightly says, that it would not be reasonable 'to measure the extent of her Royal Highnesses abilities by the common standard.'

As for philosophical terms (as, for example, in the different kinds and definitions of evil, of necessity, of divine knowledge), it seems that they are explained clearly enough, and after that they may be used, because otherwise one would need too many circumlocutions. And it is so everywhere that terms of art are employed. These words cannot be said to be devoid of sense, 'mere jargon', 'empty words', because they have been given some very intelligible definitions. And he who would seek always to avoid terms of art would become more obscure because he would become too prolix, and the reader would lose himself in the multitude of words. It is as if instead of saying two, three, four, a person always chose to replace them with one and one, one and one and one, one and one and one and one.

I admit that the places where I make use of some notions from physics and mathematics, and where I refer to what I have said elsewhere, cannot fail to be obscure to the majority of readers; but they can pass over them without troubling themselves with them, and they have their use for those who want to go further into the material and who profess to interest themselves in research. For I thought they would find some new insights there. All that one might be able come up with to say about that would perhaps be that those places should have been distinguished from the others, in order to warn the reader to pass them over. But besides the fact that it is not the custom, there is perhaps not any such place where one does not find something clear and useful mixed in; and in what remains difficult there, the attentive reader will perhaps allow himself[4] to catch a glimpse of a certain chiaroscuro that he will not be displeased to consider.

For example, I make use of the inertia of matter to explain by this comparison the privative nature of evil. A reader who is neither a philosopher nor a mathematician will find that difficult. But if he will take the trouble to think about what I am saying, he will not regret it.

As for my digressions, perhaps they are not long enough to lose the thread of the main subject, and it is easy to return to it. Far from complaining about them, others have been grateful to me for them. They were very glad that I enlivened the material a little.

Au reste mon livre a eté rapporté dans des journaux, dans un Latin et dans un Allemand de Leipzig, dans le journal de paris, et dans celuy de Trévoux, dans les Nouvelles de la Republique de lettres de Hollande, dans the Memoirs of literature de M. de la Roche à Londres; et pas un des journalistes m'a accusé d'obscurité | quoyqu'on reconnoisse que la matiere en elle-même est tres obscure |. Il y a même des journalistes qui m'ont loué d'avoir donné de la clarté à une matiere tres obscure. Et cela a fait que la livre a esté dernierement reimprimé à paris nonobstant que j'y parle en protestant.

Mais quand je reconnoistrois toute cette obscurité que M. l'Eveque de Bristol m'attribue, je ne laisserois pas d'estre plus que content de ce qu'il dit en faveur des endroits de mon livre qu'il trouve clairs; et qui en sont, comme j'espere, la plus grande partie.

Il semble qu['] il croit qu'il y a des objections que je n'ay pas encore resolues. J'ay taché de n'en point omettre et je seray tousjours obligé à ceux qui m'en fourniront de nouvelles. Mais il ne faut point compter pour des objections les plaintes qu'on fait ordinairement de l'obscurité de l'interieur des choses. Par exemple en reduisant en forme l'objection contre la permission du mal, et en y repondant, il est assés de faire voir que dieu peut avoir, et a même des raisons justes de la permettre; mais il n'est pas necessaire d'expliquer ces raisons en detail; et d'en exaggerer l'impenetrabilité n'est point faire une objection. Toute objection peut etre reduite en bonne forme, et pour donner une forme à cette objection pretendue, il faudroit debuter par cette fausse maxime: tout ce que je ne saurois connoitre, n'est point.

Je suis bien aise d'apprendre l'endroit où feu M. l'Archeveque de Canterbury Tillotson parle de la matiere que je traite, et j'en consulteray. Je me souviens d'avoir vû entre les mains de Madame l'Electrice un sermon de feu M. Sharp Archêvêque de York, prononcé (si je ne trompe) devant la Cour, et imprimé en pamphlet, qui me revenoit extremement. Mais il s'etoit perdu.

67B. ENCLOSURE: LEIBNIZ TO CAROLINE OF BRANDENBURG-ANSBACH   229

There is one accusation to which I plead *guilty*, namely, that I ought to explain in French some Latin or Greek citations.

Finally, my book has been reviewed in some journals, in a Latin one and in a German one of Leipzig [the *Acta eruditorum*], in the journal of Paris [*Journal des sçavans*], and in that of Trévoux [*Mémoires pour l'Histoire des Sciences & des beaux-Arts*, aka *Journal de Trévoux*], in the *Nouvelles de la république des lettres* of Holland, in the *Memoirs of Literature* of Mr. [Michel] de la Roche* in London; and not one of the journalists accused me of obscurity | although they recognize that the material itself is very obscure |. There are even some journalists who have praised me for having brought some clarity to a very obscure subject. And that has resulted in the book having been recently reprinted in Paris, notwithstanding my speaking in it as a Protestant.

But even if I acknowledged all this obscurity that the Bishop of Bristol attributes to me, I would not cease to be more than satisfied by what he says in favour of the parts of my book that he finds clear, which, I hope, constitute most of it.

It seems that he believes that there are some objections that I have not yet resolved. I have tried not to omit any, and I will always be grateful to those who furnish me with new ones. But the usual complaints that are made about the obscurity of the core of things must not be counted as objections. For example, in reducing to form the objection against the permission of evil, and in responding to it, it is enough to show that God can have, and even has some just reasons for, permitting it. But it is not necessary to explain these reasons in detail, and to exaggerate the inscrutability of it is not to formulate an objection. Every objection can be reduced to good form; and in order to give a form to this supposed objection, it would be necessary to begin with this false maxim: everything that I cannot understand is not the case.

I am very glad to learn the place where the late Archbishop of Canterbury [John] Tillotson* speaks about the subject I discuss, and I will consult it. I remember having seen in the hands of Madame the [Dowager] Electress [of Braunschweig-Lüneburg, Sophie* of the Palatinate] a sermon by the late Mr. [John] Sharp,[5] Archbishop of York, preached (if am not mistaken) before the court and printed in a *pamphlet*, which I liked very much. But it has been lost.

---

[1] LH 4, 4, 1 Bl. 7r–8r. Draft: three folio sides in Leibniz's hand. This is the enclosure that Leibniz sent with his letter to Caroline of 29 March 1715 (document 67a above). Not previously published.

[2] That is, the judgement of George Smalridge, for which see his letter to Caroline of 4 March 1715 (document 65).

[3] It seems odd that Leibniz should say this in light of the fact that in his letter to Caroline, Smalridge had noted that 'My Lady Nottingham, when she first mention'd this Book to Me from Your Royall Highness, told Me that you compalin'd of the Obscurity of it' (see document 65, p. 215). Leibniz was perhaps trying to put as good a face on this as possible by quoting what Smalridge immediately added, namely, that while he thought there was good reason for Caroline's complaint, he did not think it reasonable 'to measure the Extent of Your Highnesses Abilities by the common standard', thus perhaps suggesting that while the book was indeed obscure, it was not so obscure to be beyond the ken of Caroline. Indeed, in deference to Caroline Smalridge also added that 'I believe I may, without too much

Nicolas Rémond to Leibniz (excerpt)

Monsieur

Vous me ferez grand plaisir de me donner des nouvelles de vostre santé. La goutte est un mal douloureux, et je vous avoue que malgré mon respect pour les Stoiciens je ne puis pas croire que la douleur ne soit pas un mal. Je ne suis pas faché que cette incommodité que vous me dittes estre legere vous retienne dans vostre cabinet mais je le suis extremement de ce qu'elle vous a empesché d'accompagner Mad. la princesse de Galles en Angleterre. je me flattois que ce pays en estant si proche vous ne pourriez pas resister a tous nos empressements. tout ce qu'il y a ici d'hommes d'apres de ce nom[2] vous respectent et vous admirent quel ravissement en particulier pour moi et combien je cueillerois de fleurs pour en orner la teste du plus sage et plus eclairé des humains.

[...]

a Paris ce 1 d'Avril 1715

Votre tres humble et
Tres obeissant serviteur
Remond

Andreas Gottlieb von Bernstorff to Leibniz

Londr. ce
5 Avril

Monsieur

J'ay vu la votre du 15 de Mars. Je suis faché de ne vous pouvoir donner encor la reponse que vous desirez. L'opinion qu'a le Roy, qu'il ne verra jamais rien des ouvrages promis depuis si longtemps, y fait obstacle, et je ne croy pas que l'on y puisse attendre de changement, à moins que l'on le desabuse la dessus, et qu'il voye de ses yeux une partie de votre Historie;[2] apres quoy[3] vous pouvez tout esperer, et tous vos amis seront apres cela en etat de vous rendre service. Ce que vous

presumption, say, that there is scarce any Other Person of Your sex, who can thoroughly understand all the parts of this Book', thus implying that, despite its obscurity, the *Theodicy* was certainly not beyond the capacity of Caroline to understand. The misogyny here displayed is too obvious to require further comment.

⁴ Reading 'se laissera' for 'ne laissera'.
⁵ John Sharp (1645–1714), was Archbishop of York from 1691 to 1714.

68. Nicolas Rémond* to Leibniz (excerpt)[1]

[Paris, 1 April 1715]

Sir

You will please me greatly by giving me news of your health. Gout is a painful ailment, and I confess to you that despite my respect for the Stoics, I cannot believe that pain is not an evil. I am not upset that this discomfort, which you tell me is slight, keeps you in your study, but I am extremely so about the fact that it has prevented you from accompanying Madame the Princess of Wales [Caroline* of Brandenburg-Ansbach] to England. I hoped that since this country is so close to it, you would not be able to resist all our urgings. Here all real men[2] respect and admire you; what a delight in particular for me, and how many flowers I picked to adorn the head of the wisest and most enlightened of human beings.

[…]

Your very humble and

in Paris 1 April 1715

very obedient servant

Rémond

¹ LBr. 768 Bl. 33r–36v. Letter as sent: eight quarto sides in Rémond's hand. Previously published in GP III 640–44.
² Gerhardt mistranscribes 'ici d'hommes d'apres de ce nom' as 'ici d'hommes digne de ce nom' (see GP III 640).

69. Andreas Gottlieb von Bernstorff* to Leibniz[1]

London

5 April [1715]

Sir

I have seen yours of 15 March. I am sorry that I am still not able to give you the response that you desire. The view that the king [George I, Georg Ludwig* of Braunschweig-Lüneburg] has, that he will never see any of the works promised for so long, stands in the way of it, and I do not believe that you can expect any change unless he is disabused about that and sees with his eyes a part of your history;[2] then[3] you can expect everything, and after that all your friends will be in a position

proposez Monsieur, d'une recherche à Venise, Padoüe, Lucque, n'est pas à negliger,[4] mais le Roy ne croit pas, que ces Mess. voudront confier leurs archives aux ministres de Modene, desquels ils sont jaloux, plustost donneront ils accès à un allemand,[5] sur tout quand on feroit semblant, que la Maison de Modene n'y auroit nulle part, sur quoy je vous prie de me dire vos sentiments. Je suis

> Monseiur
> > votre
> tresh. Tresobeis.
> > Serviteur
> > Bernstorff

Leibniz to Johann Bernoulli (excerpt)

> Vir Celeberrime Fautor
> Honoratissime

[…]

Cum accepissem Newtonum mira quaedam de Deo dicere in Optices suae editione Latina, quam hactenus nondum videram, inspexi et risi <u>spatium esse sensorium Dei</u>; quasi Deus, a quo cuncta procedunt, sensorio opus habeat. Praeterea spatium nihil aliud est, quàm ordo coexistendi, ut tempus ordo mutationum

to render you service. What you propose, sir, concerning research in Venice, Padua, Lucca, should not be disregarded,[4] but the king does not believe that these gentlemen will entrust their archives to the ministers of Modena, of whom they are jealous; they will rather give access to a German,[5] especially when they pretend that the House of Modena would have no part in it, about which I beseech you to tell me your views. I am

sir

your

very humble very obedient

servant

Bernstorff

[1] LBr. 59 Bl. 99r–100v. Letter as sent: four quarto sides in Bernstorff's hand. Previously published in JGHF, 233 (excerpt); in Doebner 1881, p. 315; Klopp XI 36. Answer to Leibniz's letter to Bernstorff of 15 March 1715 (document 66 above).

[2] Feder mistranscribes 'de changement, à moins que l'on le desabuse la dessus, et qu'il voye de ses yeux une partie de votre lhistoire' as 'un changement avant que vous le contentiez là dessus, et qu'il voie de ses yeux une partie de votre histoire' (see JGHF 233); Doebner mistranscribes it as 'de changement, à moins que l'on le dira bien là dessus et qu'il voye de ses yeux une partie de votre historie' (see Doebner 1881, p. 315); Klopp simply omits 'que l'on le desabuse là desssus' without notice and mistranscribes the passage as 'du changement, à moins qu'il voye de ses yeux une partie de vostre Histoire' (see Klopp XI 36). Bernstorff is referring to Leibniz's history of the House of Braunschweig-Lüneburg, his so-called *Annales imperii occidentis Brunsvicenses**.

[3] Feder omits 'quoy' after 'apres' (see JGHF 233).

[4] Feder mistranscribes 'Ce que vous proposez Monsieur, d'une recherche à Venise, Padoue, Lucque, n'est pas à negliger' as 'Ce que vous proposez, Monsieur, d'une ressource à Vienne, *j'avoue qu'il* n'est pas à négliger' (see JGHF 233). Klopp simply omits 'd'une recherche à Venise, Padoue, Lucque' without notice and mistranscribes the entire passage as 'Ce que vous proposez, Monsieur, n'est pas à negliger' (see Klopp XI 36).

[5] Feder simply omits 'desquels ils sont jaloux' and mistranscribes 'le Roy ne croit pas, que ces Mess. voudront confier leurs archives aux ministres de Modene, desquels ils sont jaloux, plustost donneront ils accès à un allemand' as 'le Roi ne croit pas, que les Messieurs voudront confier leurs *intentions* aux Ministres de Modéne..... plutôt donneront ils accès à un allemande' (see JGHF, 233). Klopp also omits 'desquesl ils sont jaloux' and mistranscribes the passage as 'le Roy ne croit pas, que ces Mess. voudront confier leur armée aux ministres de Modène. Plustost donneront-ils accès à un Allemand' (see Klopp XI 36).

70. Leibniz to Johann Bernoulli (excerpt)[1]

[Hanover 9 April 1715]

Most Celebrated Sir

Most Honourable Supporter

[…]

When I had heard that Newton says certain astonishing things about God in the Latin edition of his *Opticks*, which at that point I had not yet seen, I looked into it and laughed: *that space is the sensorium of God*, as if God, from whom all things proceed, had need of a sensorium. Besides, space is nothing but the order of

generalis seu ordo existendi incompatibilium; unde spatium abstractum à rebus non magis est res vel substantia quàm tempus. Atque ita Metaphysica huic viro parum succedunt. Notavi etiam quaedam, unde apparet Dynamicen seu virium leges non esse ipsi penitus exploratas. Vacui demonstratio quam cum asseclis molitur, paralogistica est.
[…] Dabam Hanoverae 9 April 1715.
P. S
[…]

dedissimus
Godefridus Guilielmus
Leibnitius

Henriette Charlotte von Pöllnitz to Leibniz

Je vien de recevoir une lettre de SAR M^e la Princesse de Galle elle me mande ces mots Je lis les livres de loc seluy sur l[']entendement me paroit beau, mais toute jngnorente[2] que je suis je croirois qu'il y auroit quelque chose a repondre, et je crois que M^r leibenits sera de mon sentiment. Je vous prié de luy dire que je ne luy reponderais pas jusqu'a ce que le Roy m'accorde la charge qu'il souhaite.
Je vous souhaite M^r une parfaite santé pour vostre bien et ma satisfaction car je serois bien aise de jouir bien tost de vostre conversation.

coexisting, as time is the general order of changes, or the order of existing of incompatible things; whence space abstracted from things is no more a thing or substance than time, and so metaphysics is not successful enough for this man. And furthermore, I have observed certain things from which it appears that dynamics or the laws of forces are not thoroughly examined by him. The demonstration of a vacuum that he undertakes with his sycophants is a paralogism.

[…] Delivered at Hanover 9 April 1715

P. S.

[…]

most devoted
Gottfried Wilhelm
Leibniz

[1] Universitätsbibliothek Basel L Ia 19 fols. 316–17. Three quarto sides in secretary's hand. Previously published in GM III-2 938–9; Schüller 1991, p. 203 (excerpt in German translation).

71. Henriette Charlotte von Pöllnitz* to Leibniz[1]

[Hanover, c.10 May 1715]

I just received a letter from Her Royal Highness the Princess of Wales [Caroline* of Brandenburg-Ansbach]; she writes me these words:

> I am reading the books of Locke*; the one on the understanding appears fine to me, but as ignorant[2] as I am, I would think that there would be something to say in response, and I believe that Mr. Leibniz will be of my opinion. Please tell him that I will not respond to him until the king [George I, Georg Ludwig* of Braunschweig-Lüneburg] grants the position that he desires.[3]

I wish you, sir, perfect health, for your well-being and my satisfaction; for I would be very glad to enjoy your conversation before long.

[1] LBr. F 4 Bl. 77r. Letter as sent: 0.75 quarto sides in Pöllnitz's hand. Previously published in Klopp XI 37, and in Echeverría 1989, pp. 147–8 (Spanish translation). The letter is undated, but since both Pöllnitz and Leibniz were in Hanover at the time, so that her letter would have been delivered to Leibniz on or about the same day it had been written, her letter was probably written on or about the same day as Leibniz's letter to Caroline of 10 May 1715 (document 72), which begins with a reference to this letter from Pöllnitz.

[2] Reading 'ignorante' for 'jngnorente'.

[3] That is, the position of historiographer of Great Britain.

Leibniz to Caroline of Brandenburg-Ansbach, Princess of Wales

	A son Altesse Royal
Madame	Madame la princesse de Galles
	10 May 1715

Ce que V. A. R. m'a fait dire par Mlle de Pelniz peut passer pour une grace très insigne ou pour une menace tres grande. Car ce n'est qu'à condition qu'Elle obtienne du Roy la charge que je demande, qu'Elle me fait esperer de pouvoir revoir un jour ses pretieux caractères addressés à moy même. Mais je veux le tourner du coté de l'esperance.

Speranza
Speranza non lasciare in abandonno il cor.[4]

Elle est tousjours plus agréable que la crainte, et j'en remercie V. A. R. de tout mon coeur. Sa bonté me rendra le bien fait du Roy encore plus souhaitable, et me fera travailler plus ardemment pour le mériter.

Il est vray que ce qui me fait ambitionner le poste en question est en bonne partie le point d'honneur. Je ne voudrois ceder en rien à un certain Antagoniste que les Anglois m'ont mis en tête. V. A. R. saura peutétre que c'est le Chevalier Newton, qui a une pension du Roy, parce qu'il a l'inspection sur la Monneye. Lors que la Cour d'Hanover n'étoit pas trop bien avec celle d'Angleterre, pendant le regne du dernier Ministere, quelques uns crurent que le temps leur étoit favorable pour m'attaquer, et me disputer l'honneur d'une invention Mathematique[5] qu'on m'attribue depuis l'an 1684. Un journaliste Hollandois ou plus tost François écrivant en Hollande, dit là dessus, qu'il sembloit que ce n'étoit pas une querelle entre M. Newton et moy, mais entre l'Allemagne et l'Angleterre. Mais un savant homme m'écrivit d'Angleterre, que l'esprit de quelques Rigides, peu favorables au parti d'Hanover, tant à Cambridge (:d'où M. Newton est venu à Londres:) qu'à Oxford (:ou se trouvent ses seconds:) y avoit beaucoup de part. J'ose dire que si la Roy m'egaloit pour le moins à M. Newton à tous égards (comme un de ses plus anciens serviteurs le peut esperer),[7] que dans ces circonstances ce seroit faire honneur à Hanover et à Allemagne en ma personne. Et la qualité d'Historien, ou je pretends m'être distingué, en fournit une belle occasion.

Je n'ay pas eu le loisir de repondre à M. Newton et à ses seconds qui sont venus à la charge il y a un an ou environ: mais d'autres habiles gens, même en France et en Suisse l'ont fait pour moy. Il est vray que des amis me pressent d'examiner par moy même la philosophie de M. Newton, qui est un peu extraordinaire. Il pretend qu'un corps attire l'autre à quelque distance que ce soit, et qu'un grain de sable chez nous exerce une force attractive jusques sur le soleil, sans aucun milieu ny moyen. Apres

72. Leibniz to Caroline* of Brandenburg-Ansbach, Princess of Wales[1]

To her Royal Highness
Madame the Princess of Wales
10 May 1715

Madame

What Your Royal Highness has communicated through Mademoiselle Pöllnitz[2] can be taken as a very remarkable favour or a very great threat. For it is only on condition that she obtains from the king [George I, Georg Ludwig* of Braunschweig-Lüneburg] the position I request[3] that she gives me hope of being able to see again one day her precious handwriting addressed to me. But I want to view it from the side of hope.

Hope
Hope, leave not the heart abandoned.[4]

It is always more pleasing than fear, and I thank Your Royal Highness for it with all my heart. Her kindness will make the favour of the king even more desirable to me, and it will make me work more ardently in order to merit it.

It is true that what makes me aspire to the office in question is largely the point of honour. I should not want to yield any of it to a certain antagonist that the English have placed before me. Your Royal Highness will perhaps know that it is Chevalier Newton, who has a pension from the king, because he is superintendent of the mint. When the court of Hanover was not on such good terms with that of England during the reign of the last ministry, some believed that it was a good time for them to attack me and to dispute the honour of a mathematical[5] invention that has been attributed to me since 1684.[6] A Dutch journalist, or rather a Frenchman writing in Holland, says about it, that it did not appear to be a dispute between Mr. Newton and me, but between Germany and England. But a learned man wrote me from England that the mood of some rigid men, not very favourable to the cause of Hanover, at Cambridge (whence Newton came to London) as well as Oxford (where his seconds are found), had a large part in it. I dare say that if the king made me at least the equal of Mr. Newton in all respects (as one of his oldest servants may expect),[7] then in these circumstances it would be to do honour to Hanover and to Germany in my person. And the position of historian, in which I claim to have distinguished myself, furnishes a fine occasion for it.

I have not had the leisure to respond to Mr. Newton and his seconds, who went on the attack about a year ago, but other able men, in France as well as in Switzerland, have done it for me. It is true that some friends are urging me to examine on my own the philosophy of Mr. Newton, which is a bit extraordinary. He claims that a body attracts another at whatever distance it may be and that a grain of sand on the earth exerts an attractive force as far as upon the sun, without any

cela comment ces sectateurs voudront ils nier que par la toute puissance de Dieu nous pouvons avoir participation du corps et du sang de Jesus Christ sans aucun empechement des distances. C'est un bon moyen de les embarasser, des gens[8] qui par un[e] animosité[9] contre la Maison d'Hanover, s'emancipent maintenant plus que jamais de parler contre nostre Religion[10] de la confession d'Augsbourg,[11] comme si notre Realité Eucharistique étoit absurde. Pour moy je crois qu'il faut reserver une operation extraordinaire et miraculeuse en effect pour les mystères divins,[12] et ne les point faire entrer dans l'explication des choses naturelles. Ainsi mes Antagonistes me donnent assés de prise, mais je n'ay point le loisir maintenant de me servir de mes avantages; j'aime mieux de satisfaire au Roy en donnant mes Annales, et Sa Majesté pourra mieux refuter ces gens que moy, en me traitant à l'égal de M. le Chevalier Newton: ce qui piquera asseurément ces Messieurs peu amis d'Hanover. Mais quantité d'honnêtes et d'habiles gens en Angleterre en seront bien aises, et il y en a assés qui me font l'honneur de m'estimer. M. Newton est en effect un homme d'un tres grand merite, quoyqu'il n'en use pas bien à mon egard. Mais il est mon rival, c'est tout dire.[14] Je suis avec devotion

   Madame etc.

Hanover ce 10 de May
  1715
  P. S.

J'admire que V. A. R. paroist avoir deja trouvé le foible de M. Lock. Son livre sur l'entendement contient quelques bonnes choses, mais assés minces, et il y en a beaucoup qui n'ont aucune solidité. Je le trouve aussi un peu ennuyeux, et il s'en faut beaucoup qu'il aille au fond des choses. Ce sont souvent des subtilités, qui ne font qu'effleurer. Son amie, Madame Masham fille du celebre M. Cudworth, etoit ma correspondante. Elle mouroit un peu apres luy. Je trouvay bien du merite à cette Dame; mais M. Lock je trouva un peu moins philosophe que je n'avois crû. J'avois fait quelques <u>remarques</u> sur son livre. Il s'en facha, je ne l'ay appris que par un Recueil de ses posthumes, ou elles se trouvent inserées, et où il en parle avec mepris dans une lettre à un savant à Dublin nommé M. Molineux. Mais tout le monde n'est pas de son avis, et une personne capable d'en juger dit, que ce qu'il y a de meilleur dans ce Recueil sont mes objections. Son mepris venoit apparemment de ce que mes sentimens sont diametralement opposés aux siens sur des grands articles; et il ne me connoissoit pas assés ny mes raisons. Il paroist que selon luy tout est corporel, que la matiere est capable de penser, et choses semblables qui ruinent la religion. Ces Messiers s'imaginent qu'on ne sauroit avoir l'esprit fort ny solide, sans etre de leur sentiment.

Si V. A. R. jette les yeux sur la seconde Edition des Caracteristiques de Mylord Shafsbury, mort à Naples il y a deux ans ou environ, Elle y trouvera quelque chose de moy: au moins si l'on a suivi son intention, et si M. Coste a pû tenir parole, qui etoit son correspondent, et gouverneur (je crois) de son fils. Je fis quelques remarques sur l'ouvrage de ce Mylord qui est profond en effect, et dont il m'avoit fait

72. LEIBNIZ TO CAROLINE OF BRANDENBURG-ANSBACH 239

medium or means. After that will these sectarians wish to deny that by the omnipotence of God we can share in the body and blood of Jesus Christ without any impediment of distance? It is a good way to embarrass them, people[8] who, from an animus[9] against the House of Hanover, now free themselves more than ever to speak against our religion[10] of the confession of Augsburg,[11] as if our Eucharistic reality were absurd. For my part, I believe that an extraordinary and miraculous operation must in fact be reserved for the divine mysteries[12] and not introduced in the explanation of natural things. Thus my antagonists give me sufficient opportunity, but I do not now have the leisure to press home my advantage; I prefer to satisfy the king by producing my annals,[13] and His Majesty will be better able to refute these men than I by treating me as the equal of Chevalier Newton, which will assuredly sting these gentleman, hardly friends of Hanover. But a lot of honourable and able men in England would be very happy about it, and there are enough of them who do me the honour of esteeming me. Mr. Newton is indeed a man of very great merit, although he does not use it well in regard to me. But he is my rival; enough said.[14] I am with devotion
   Madame etc.
Hanover 10 May
  1715
  P. S.

I admire that Your Royal Highness appears to have already discovered the weakness of Mr. Locke*. His book on the understanding contains some good but rather trivial things, and there is much in it that it is not sound at all. I also find it a bit tedious, and it is far from going to the bottom of things. These are often subtleties that only skim the surface. His friend, Madame [Damaris Cudworth] Masham*, daughter of the celebrated Mr. [Ralph] Cudworth*, was my correspondent. She died a little after him. I find much merit in this woman; but Mr. Locke was a little less philosophical than I had thought. I had made some *remarks* about his book. He took offence at them; I only learned of it from a review of his posthumous works, in which they are inserted, and in which he speaks of them with scorn in a letter to a scholar in Dublin named Mr. [William] Molyneux.[15] But not everyone is of his opinion, and a person capable of judging it says that the best things in this review are my objections. His scorn apparently came from the fact that my views are diametrically opposed to his on some major points; and he did not sufficiently understand me or my reasons. It appears that according to him everything is corporeal, that matter is capable of thinking, and similar things that overthrow religion. These gentlemen imagine that it is impossible to have a strong and sound mind without being of their opinion.

If Your Royal Highness casts her eyes on the second edition of the *Characteristics* of Milord Shaftesbury, who died in Naples about two years ago, she will find there something by me, at least if his intention was followed, and if Mr.[Pierre] Coste*, who was his correspondent and, I believe, tutor of his son, was able to keep his word.[16] I made some remarks about the work of this milord, which is indeed

present par M. Coste. Il trouva mes remarques si à son gré (: quoiqu'il y en eût ou je n'etois pas de son sentiment :) qu'il voulut qu'elles fussent jointes à la seconde Edition de son ouvrage. Il etoit fils du celebre Chancelier Shafsbury. Je suis faché de sa mort, et je crois qu'il auroit contenté V. A. R. Il avoit été Locciste au commencement mais dans le progrés de ses meditations il s'etoit approché de mes sentimens sans les savoir. Je ne say si M. Coste a eu l'honneur d'etre remarqué de V. A. R. à Hanover. Il y avoit été avec un jeune Anglois. Il est François Reformé. C'est luy qui a traduit en François l'ouvrage de M. Locke.[18] Mais je crois que V. A. R. le lit en Anglois.

72. LEIBNIZ TO CAROLINE OF BRANDENBURG-ANSBACH 241

profound, of which he was made a present by Mr. Coste. He found my remarks so much to his liking (although there were some in which I was not of his opinion) that he wanted them to be added to the second edition of his work. He was the son of the celebrated Chancellor Shaftesbury.[17] I am sorry about his death, and I believe that he would have pleased Your Royal Highness. He had been a Lockean in the beginning, but in the development of his meditations he had come nearly to my views without knowing them. I do not know if Mr. Coste has had the honour of being noted by Your Royal Highness in Hanover. He was there with a young Englishman. He is French Reformed. It is he who translated into French the work of M. Locke.[18] But I believe that Your Royal Highness reads it in English.

[1] LBr. F 4 Bl. 38r–39r. Draft and fair copy: three quarto sides in Leibniz's hand. Bl. 38r and 38v are a revised version of the letter, apparently in Leibniz's hand, with corrections also in Leibniz's hand. Bl. 39r is a fair copy, in a secretary's hand, of the P. S. to the letter. An initial draft of this letter (LBr. F 4 Bl. 40r–40v) was published in Klopp XI 37–40. In the initial draft, the material in the P.S. of the fair copy was included within the body of the letter. For the most part there are only minor differences between the revised version transcribed here and the original draft. The revised version, along with the P.S. in the fair copy, were published in Kemble 528–31.

[2] That is, Henriette Charlotte von Pöllnitz*. See her letter to Leibniz of 10 May 1715 (document 71).

[3] That is, the position of historiographer of Great Britain.

[4] This line about hope does not appear in the initial draft.

[5] Kemble omits 'Mathematique' (see Kemble 529).

[6] Leibniz published a brief, but rather obscure outline of his differential calculus in the *Acta Eruditorum* for October 1684, pp. 467–73. It was entitled 'Nova Methodus pro Maximis et Minimis, itemque tangentibus, quae nec fractas, irrationals quantitates moratum, et singular pro illis calculi genus'. Johann Bernoulli and his brother Jacob were two of the most gifted early practitioners of Leibniz's differential calculus. Johann became Leibniz's staunch ally of in the priority dispute with the Newtonians. He wrote of his and his brother's encounter with Leibniz's calculus in his autobiography (as quoted in GM III-1 5n, my translation):

> After these beginnings, my brother and I fell, by an unforeseen accident, upon a small writing by Mr. Leibnitz inserted in the *Acta* of Leipzig of 1684, where in only 5 or 6 pages he presents a very sketchy idea of the differential calculus, which was an enigma rather than an explanation. But there was enough of it for us to fathom the whole secret in a few days; a lot of pieces we published afterwards upon the subject of the infinitely small are witness to that.

[7] This parenthetical addition is not found in the original draft.

[8] Klopp omits 'des gens' (see Klopp XI 38).

[9] Klopp has 'esprit' instead of 'animosité' (see Klopp XI 39); Kemble has 'esprit d'animosité' (see Kemble 529).

[10] In the original draft, this first part of the sentence reads: 'C'est un bon moyen de les embarrasser, qui par un esprit contraire à la Maison d'Hanover, s'emancipent maintenant plus que jamais de parler mal de nostre religion'.

[11] The phrase 'de la confession d'Augsbourg' is not found in the original draft.

[12] In the original draft this first part of the sentence reads: 'Pour moy, je crois qu'il faut reserver ces miracles pour les mysteres divins'.

[13] Leibniz here refers to his history of the house of Braunschweig, which he came to refer to as the *Annales imperii occidentis Brunsvicenses**.

[14] The last two sentences appear in the draft of the letter, but do not appear in the copy.

[15] That is, the Irish philosopher William Molyneux (1656–98).

[16] Leibniz's remarks were not published in the second edition of Shaftesbury's *Characteristics*. However, Coste sent Leibniz's remarks to Samuel Masson who published them under the title 'Eloge critique des Oeuvres de Milord Shaftsbury, par Mr. Leibnits, communiqué par Mr. Coste', *Histoire critique de la république des lettres* X (1715), pp. 306–27.

[17] He was actually the grandson, not the son, of Anthony Ashley Cooper (1621–83), 1st Earl of Shaftesbury (from 1672), Lord Chancellor from 1672–3.

[18] The original draft adds 'avec approbation de l'auteur'.

Leibniz to Charlotte Elisabeth von Klenk

à Mle de Klenck   Hanover ce 28

Madamoiselle   de Juin 1715

Je me donne quelque fois l'honneur de vous écrire, pour me conserver l'avantage de votre souvenir favorable, et pour vous supplier de me conserver les bontés gracieuses de Sa Majesté nostre incomparable Impeatrice à laquelle je vous supplie de presenter ma lettre.

Je suis fort occupé icy à mettre mon travail Historique en estat de paroitre à pres[2] quoy je fais compte je revenir[3] à Vienne l'année qui vient s'il plait à Dieu.

Nous esperons tousjours encore l'arrivee du Roy cette annee. Et il l'espere luy meme. Cependant des personnes bien informees en parlent comme d'un probleme.

J'ose supplier la Mté de l'Imperatrice de sonder un jour l'Empereur sur le chapitre de l'Academie des Sciences. C'est une affaire où je pense plus pour la bien public et pour la gloire de Sa Mté que pour mon interest propre. Je crois que M. Schmid vous aura donné un papier our[5] la Majeste de l'Imperatrice, qui sert à l'informer d'un projet qui me paroist raisonnable [c'est que l'Empereur employe[7] aux sciences, Bibliotheque, Cabinet de raretés, et antiquites, Belles curiosités, experiences, observations jardins de simples, Ecoles de chirurgie, mineraux et laboratoires, observatoires (toutes choses du ressort des sciences) l'impost du papier, qui luy est revenu en main depuis que le temps pour le quel il l'avoit engagé aux estats est expiré. Rien ne paroist plus à propos, plus utile & plus glorieux][8] mais je souhaiterois que Sa Mté contentât[9] de sonder l'Empereur là dessus sans s'en ouvrir à d'autres parce que je ne voudrois pas mettre un tel projet sur le tapis, avant que de savoir si l'Empereur y incline. Autrement je ne ferois que me prostituer par des propositions qui seroient rebutées. Je Vous supplier donc Mademoiselle de me procurer quelques lumieres la dessus.

Je suis avec respect

Mlle etc.

73. Leibniz to Charlotte Elisabeth von Klenk*[1]

To Mademoiselle Klenk   Hanover 28
Mademoiselle   June 1715
I have sometimes given myself the honour of writing to you in order to preserve
the benefit of your favourable remembrance and to ask you to preserve for me the
gracious kindness of Her Majesty, our incomparable empress [Dowager Empress
Wilhelmine Amalie* of Braunschweig-Lüneburg], to whom I ask you to show
my letter.

I am very much occupied here to put my historical work in a state to be published,
after[2] which I intend to return[3] to Vienna next year, if it please God.

We still yet expect the arrival of the king [George I of Great Britain, Georg
Ludwig of Braunschweig-Lüneburg] this year, and he expects it himself. However,
some well-informed persons are speaking of it as a problem.

I dare beseech the Majesty of the Empress[4] to sound out the emperor [Emperor
Karl VI*] on the topic of the Academy of Sciences [the proposed Imperial Society
of Sciences*]. This is a matter in which I think more for the public good and the
glory of His Majesty than for my own interest. I believe that Mr. Schmid must have
given you a paper for[5] the Majesty of the Empress, which serves to inform her of a
project that appears reasonable to me[6] [namely, that the emperor apply himself[7] to
the sciences, library, museum of rarities, and antiquities, fine curios, experiments,
observations, medicinal plant gardens, schools of surgery, minerals and laboratories, observatories (all things within the purview of the sciences) the paper tax,
which has come back to him since the period for which he had pledged it to the
states has expired. Nothing seems more fitting, more useful and more glorious],[8]
but I would like Her Majesty content herself[9] with sounding the emperor out about
it without talking about it with others, because I would not want to put such a project on the table before knowing whether the emperor is inclined to it. Otherwise
I would only prostitute myself for some proposals that would be rejected. Hence
I beseech you, mademoiselle, to procure some information about it for me.

          I am with respect
Mademoiselle etc.

---

[1] LH 13 Bl. 157r–157v. Draft: 1.2 quarto sides in Leibniz's hand. Not previously published. For Klenk's
reply, see document 75 below.

[2] Reading 'après' for 'à pres'.

[3] Reading 'de revenir' for 'je revenir'.

[4] Again, the reference would appear to be to the Dowager Empress Wilhelmine Amalie of Braunschweig-
Lüneburg rather than the reigning Empress Elisabeth Christine* of Braunschweig-Wolfenbüttel.

[5] Reading 'pour' for 'our'.

[6] The reference is presumably to Leibniz's letter of 28 June 1715 to the Dowager Empress Amalie
(document 74).

[7] Reading 's'emploie' for 'employe'.

[8] The square brackets are Leibniz's.

[9] Reading 'se contenât' for 'contentât'.

Leibniz to Dowager Empress Wilhelmine Amalie of Braunschweig-Lüneburg

A la Mté de l'Imperatrice
Amalie

Sacrée Mte

Les gracieuses bontés que V. M. Imp. a eues pour moy depuis long temps m'encouragent a luy donner des informations de ce qui me regarde par rapport au service. Je travaille avec succés a mettre bien tost en estat de paroistre un grand ouvrage. Ce sont des Annales de l'Empire et de Bronsvic depuis les commencemens de charlemagne jusqu'au dernier des Empereurs de l'ancienne race de Bronsvic. Car V. M. sait qu'apres la posterité de charlemagne éteinte en Allemagne, suivie par Conrad le premier, le septre fut entre le[s] main[s] de Henri l'oiseleur des trois Ottons et de Henri le saint, tous princes de l'ancienne Maison de Bronsvic. Cela va depuis l'an de notre seigneur 76[3]... jusqu'à 1025. Il y aura la race de Witikind, et il y entrera ce qui regarde la race de Witikind, et d'autres vieux princes saxons, les anciens Guelfes de la haute Allemagne et de la Baviere, et les anciens Guelfes et les anciens princes de Toscane et de Ligurie veritables ancestres de la Maison de Bronsvic moderne de sorte que ses origines seront comprises dans cet ouvrage que les Historiens de Bronsvic et d'Este ont ignoré en bonne partie jusqu'à moy.[4] Il y aura dans cet ouvrage quantité de decouvertes Historiques singulieres et aussi des remarques importantes sur les droits de l'Empire en Italie & ailleurs. Et les origines d'une bonne partie des familles souveraines d'aujourdhuy tombent dans cette periode & seront eclairees en passant. J'auray meme occasion de dire quelque chose de notable et non vulgaire sur celle de Habspourg. Ainsi j'ose dire que l'Allemagne n'a jamais encor vû tel ouvrage, dont elle en avoit pourtant grand besoin. Et en venir à bout il falloit ma patience et les annees que Dieu m'a accordées et les occasions que j'ay eues pour deterrer dans les Archives & vieux Manuscrits des choses peu connues. l'Histoire de temps qui suivent,[5] sera plus aisée à faire, et celuy qui voudra y penser apres moy, n'aura plus besoin de tant de meditations. J'espere que cela encouragera l'Empereur et d'autres princes a faire chercher encor davantage dans les Archives et monumens de l'antiquité, sur tout pour establir et delivrer de l'oubli les droits de l'Empire si negligés auparavant et si mal connus en bien des occasions sur tout par rapport à l'Italie.

Comme j'espere avec l'aide de Dieu, de faire en sorte cette annee, que cet ouvrage soit mis en estat de paroistre; je fais estat de revenir à vienne l'année qui vient. Mais comme je pense à bien employer le peu de temps qui me reste, je souhaiterois à ne le point perdre alors a soliciter et que deux choses fussent reglées avant mon retour, et l'affaire de mon ajuto et celle de l'Academie des Sciences. Quant à mon ajuto

74. Leibniz to Dowager Empress Wilhelmine Amalie*
of Braunschweig-Lüneburg[1]

[Hanover, 28 June 1715]

To the Majesty of the Empress
Amalie

Sacred Majesty

The gracious kindnesses that Your Imperial Majesty has shown me for a long time encourage me to give her some information about my service. I am working with success to put a great work in a state to be published before long. It consists in the annals of the empire and of Braunschweig,[2] from the dawn of Charlemagne to the last emperors of the ancient race of Braunschweig. For Your Majesty knows that after the extinction of the posterity of Charlemagne in Germany, followed by Conrad I, the scepter was in the hands of Henry the Fowler [Henry (Heinrich) I (876–936)], the three Ottos [Emperor Otto I (912–73), Emperor Otto II (955–83), and Otto III (980–1002)], and Henry the Saint [Henry (Heinrich) II (972–1024)], all princes of the old House of Braunschweig. That goes from the year of our lord 768[3] to 1025. There will be the race of Witikind, and it will include there what concerns the tribe of Witikind and other old Saxon princes, the ancient Welfs of Upper Germany and Bavaria, and the ancient Welfs and the ancient princes of Tuscany and Liguria, true ancestors of the modern House of Braunschweig, so that it will include its origins, which the historians of Braunschweig and Este before me[4] have ignored. In this work there will be a number of singular historical discoveries, as well as some important observations concerning the rights of the empire in Italy and elsewhere. And the origins of a large part of the contemporary sovereign families fall in this period and will be clarified in passing. I will even have occasion to say something of note and novel concerning that of Habsburg. So I dare say that Germany has never yet seen such a work, which it nevertheless needs badly. And it required my patience to accomplish it, as well as the years that God has accorded me and the occasions I have had to unearth some little known things in the archives and old manuscripts. The history of the times that follow[5] will be easier to do, and those who wish to think about them after me will no longer need so much reflection. I hope that this will encourage the emperor [Karl VI*] and other princes to have the archives and the monuments of antiquity searched still further, above all in order to establish and rescue from oblivion the rights of the empire, which were previously so neglected and in many cases so misunderstood, especially in relation to Italy.

As I hope with the aid of God to ensure that this work be put in a state to be published this year, I plan to return to Vienna next year. But as I am thinking about employing well the little time that remains to me, I should not want to waste it then

premierement le Comte de Windischgratz m'a dit que l'Empereur m'accorde encor d'autres 2000 florins outre ceux qui m'ont deja esté accordés. Mais l'expedition de cet ajuto a esté arrestee par mon depart, et par le changement des affaires de la Chambre des Finances. C'est donc ce que je solicite par un memoire que j'ay fait presenter à Sa Mté.

Mais quant au point de l'Academie des Sciences, comme il s'agit d'un Fond, je crois de pouvoir dire que celuy que je propose seroit en tous sens le plus convenable. Mais je n'ose le mettre sur le tapis et le soliciter dans les Formes avant que de savoir si l'Empereur incline à ce fond. Car Sa Mté peut avoir des considerations qui me sont inconnues et je me prostituerois si je m'ingerois autrement que selon ses inclinations. C'est pour cette raison que je souhaite avant tout d'apprendre le sentiment de Sa M. Imp. et Cath. là dessus. Je n'ose point de m'adresser auparavant pour cela a Mess. les Ministres, car aussi tost que je le feray, cela passera pour une demande de ma part, qu'on sera fort porté a rebuter. Ainsi sachant combien V. M. est affectionnée pour le bien public et la gloire de l'Empereur je voudrois bien supplier V. M. Imp. si je l'osois de sonder l'Empereur la dessus. Voicy ce que c'est. Un impost sur le papier est deja etabli. On l'avoit engagé aux Estats pour un certain temps. Ce temps est expiré, et il est revenu libre a l'Empereur. Or rien ne paroist plus naturel et plus plausible que d'appliquer cet impost aux sciences, arts, et tout ce qui y est lié. Comme seroient Bibliotheque, manuscrits et recherches Historiques, Cabinet d'antiquités et raretés de la nature et de l'art, belles curiosités et experiences, et decouvertes nouvelles dans les arts, medicine, chymie;[7] ecoles de Chirurgie, etablissement perpetuel pour le soin de la santé publique; cartes et descriptions des pays, recherches des minieres,[8] conduite [des] travaux publics pour arrester les eaux, et autres inconveniens, jardins de simples, menageries, observatoires, laboratoires et mille autres choses qui sont du ressort des sciences et arts, et pour les quelles la societé des sciences seroit comme un Conseil qui fourniroit des notices au Gouvernement. Votre Majesté voit l'etendue et l'importance de la chose, et combien l'Empereur en pourroit tirer de la satisfaction & du plaisir, et le public de l'utilité de sorte que l'impost sur le papier, tel qu['])i[l] est deja etabli, seroit la chose du monde la mieux employee si on l'y affectoit. Et entre les mains d'une telle societe, il serviroit encor à mettre en meilleure estat la manufacture et la commerce du papier, et encor à l'impression de bons livres dans le pays, et à y retablir la librairie, au lieu que l'argent ne fait que sortir du pays a l'egard des livres sans qu'il l'entre par leur moyen.[9] Et quand il n'y auroit que cela l'impost du papier entre les mains de cette societé seroit profitable au pays au lieu de luy etre a charge. L'Empereur n'a donc qu'a dire un mot efficacement. Il n'a qu'à dire à l'imitation de Dieu, la lumiere soit faite, et elle sera faite. Si son intention est seure, cela suffit pour qu'il fasse naistre quelque chose qui sera admirée de son temps, et memorable à la posterité. Et j'oserois de dire, que même au temps de guerre [on] ne la devroit point negliger. La guerre est le regne de la force, et par consequent des

to solicit and would hope that two things might be settled before my return, both the matter of my support and that of the Academy of Sciences [Imperial Society of Sciences*]. As regards my support, Count Windischgrätz[6] has told me that the emperor grants me yet another 2000 florins in addition to those I have already been granted. But the dispatch of this support has been delayed by my departure and by the change of affairs at the treasury. This is therefore what I am requesting in a memorandum that I have had presented to His Majesty.

But as regards the point about the Academy of Sciences, as it is a matter of a fund, I believe I am able to say that what I propose would in every sense be the most suitable. But I dare not put it on the table and request it formally before knowing if the emperor inclines to this fund; for His Majesty may have some considerations of which I am unaware, and I would prostitute myself if I interfered in a way contrary to his wishes. It is for this reason that I wish above all to learn the sentiment of His Imperial and Catholic Majesty about it. I do not dare first approach the ministers for that, for as soon as I do it, it will be considered a demand on my part, which they will be very much disposed to reject. So knowing how much affection Your Majesty has for the public good and the glory of the emperor, I should indeed wish to beseech Your Imperial Majesty, if I dared, to sound the emperor out about it. Here is my proposal. A tax is already imposed on paper. It had been pledged to the states for a certain period of time. This period has expired, and it is the emperor's free revenue. Now nothing would seem more natural and plausible than to give this tax to the sciences, the arts, and to everything connected with them—as would be a library, historical manuscripts and research, a museum of antiquities and rare objects of nature and of art, fine curios and experiments, and new discoveries in the arts, medicine, chemistry,[7] colleges of surgery, a permanent establishment for the care of the public health; maps and descriptions of countries, mining explorations,[8] management of public works to restrain the waters and other inconveniences, medicinal plant gardens, menageries, observatories, laboratories, and a thousand other things which are within the purview of the sciences and the arts, and for which the society of sciences would be like a council that would supply the government with records. Your Majesty sees the extent and importance of the matter, and how much satisfaction and pleasure the emperor would be able to draw from it, and the public from the utility, so that the paper tax, such as is already imposed, would be best employed if it were appropriated for it. And in the hands of such a society, it would again be used for putting in a better state the manufacture and commerce of paper, and again for the printing of good books in the country, and for reestablishing the book trade there, instead of which the money only goes out of the country with regard to books without entering it by their means.[9] And even if there was only that, the paper tax in the hands of this society would be profitable to the country instead of being a burden to it. The emperor has therefore only to say a word effectively. He only has to say, in imitation of God, let there be light,

mathematiques et mechaniques. Et on en tireroit des utilites encor alors de grandes utilites, qui bien loin de faire regretter l'employ de ce fond, en feroient voir[10] le grand usage quand ce ne seroit que par la conservation de quantité de personnes qui periront autrement[11] faute d'un bon establissement pour la chirurgie, et pour soin de la santé publique—sans parler des bestiaux et des machines de guerre. Mais je ferois tort aux grandes lumieres de V. M. si je m'etendois d'avantage sur l'utilité de ce dessein. Il ne s'agit que d'apprendre jusqu'à ou l'Empereur le goute.

Quoyque le Roy de Grande Bretagne espere luy meme venir cet Esté dans ses Etats de Allemagne, cela ne laisse pas d'etre un probleme a cause des grandes affaires qu'il a sur le bras. On a reconnu que Sa Mté fera bien de se faire souvent voir en public, sa bonne mine et ses manieres ont charmé le peuple, lors qu'il a fait dernierement une reveue.

Je suis avec la plus fidele devotion

Madame de Votre Sacrée Mté

le etc.

Charlotte Elisabeth von Klenk to Leibniz

de Schönbrunn le 6 de Juillet

Mon silence seroit impardonable Monsieur si je ne n[']avoit attendù a vous ecrire que j[']eusse quelque chose a vous dire sur vos interests dans ce pais cy. J[']ay parlez au Conte Schlik et au Conte de Sinzendorf qui tous deus croyent votre Presence

and it will be done. If his intention is unwavering, that suffices to create something which will be admired in his time and memorable to posterity. And I would dare say that even in times of war it should not be neglected. War is the reign of force, and consequently of mathematics and mechanics. And there would be some benefits drawn from it, even in that case some great benefits, which, far from making one regret the use of this fund, would show[10] the great benefit of it, though it would only be by conserving a number of persons who will otherwise[11] perish due to the lack of a good establishment for surgery and care of the public health—not to mention livestock and machines of war. But I would offend the great intelligence of Your Majesty if I dwell further on the benefit of this plan. It is only a matter of learning the extent to which the emperor approves of it.

Although the King of Great Britain [George I, Georg Ludwig* of Braunschweig-Lüneburg] himself expects to go to his German states this summer, it is nevertheless a problem on account of the great matters he has on his hands. It has been recognized that His Majesty will do well to make himself seen often in public; his fine bearing and his manners charmed the people when he recently did a review.

I am with the most loyal devotion
Madame of Your Sacred Majesty
the etc.

---

[1] LH 13 Bl. 157v–158v. Draft: 2.7 quarto sides in Leibniz's hand. The draft is undated, but it begins on the same page as the end of a draft letter to Amalie's lady-in-waiting, Charlotte Elisabeth von Klenk, that is dated 28 June 1715. Previously published in Klopp XI 41–5.

[2] That is, the work that Leibniz came to call the *Annales imperii occidentis Brunsvicenses**.

[3] Reading '768' for '76 . . '. 768 was the year Charlemagne came, after the death of his father Pippin the Younger, to share the Frankish throne with his brother Carloman.

[4] Klopp mistranscribes 'moy' as 'nous' (see Klopp XI 41).

[5] Klopp mistranscribes 'suivent' as 'suit' (see Klopp XI 42).

[6] Count Windischgrätz was the president of the Imperial Aulic Council*.

[7] Klopp mistranscribes 'chymie' as 'chymique' (see Klopp XI 43).

[8] Klopp omits 'recerces des minieres' (see Klopp XI 43).

[9] Klopp mistranscribes 'l'argent ne fait que sortir du pays a l'egard des livres sans qu'il l'entre par leur moyen' as 'l'argent ne fait que sortir du pays sans qu'il revienne' (see Klopp XI 44).

[10] Klopp mistranscribes 'Et on en tireroit des utilites encor alors de grandes utilites, qui bien loin de faire regretter l'employ de ce fond, en feroient voir le grand usage' as 'Et on en tireroit alors de grandes utilités, qui bien loin de faire regretter l'employ de ce fond, en feroient le grand usage' (see Klopp XI 44).

[11] Klopp mistranscribes 'autrement' as 'autrefois' (see Klopp XI 44).

75. Charlotte Elisabeth von Klenk* to Leibniz[1]

from Schönbrunn 6 of July [1715]

My silence would be unpardonable, sir, if I had not waited to write you that I had something to say to you about your interests in this country. I have spoken to Count [Leopold Anton Joseph von] *Schlick* [1663–1723] and to Count [Philipp Ludwig

nesseçaire pour presser l[’]execution du dessein pour l[’]acadmie, surtout par ce que J[’]ay Compris du premier de ses[2] Messieurs il pense tout de bon a y Contribuer de tous[3] ce qui dependra de luy et il m[’]a repetèz plusieurs fois que vous ferièz bien si vos affaires vous le permette de venir icy. SM limperatrice m[’]a aussy ordonnèz de vous dire qu[’]elle a plusieurs fois parlèz de ce que vous regarde mais qu[’]il luy semble, qu'aussy longtemps que le nouveau reglement des finances ne sera pas dans un meilleur estat on ne sauroit penser a un nouvel etablissement comme le seroit celuy d'un academie pour lequel il faudroit un fond Considerable. L[’]imperatrice souhaiterois aussy que vous luy envoyez une information de l[’]origine des Templiers. On a disputèz devant elle sur ce sujet et elle est persuadèz, que personne ne pour[r]a mieu[x] decider la dessus que vous. Je croy nesseçaire de vous advertir, mais entre nous, qu[’]il Court un bruit Comme si le Conte de Schlik vouloit se demettre de sa charge par le chagrin qu'on luy veut donner de faire le Conte Kinsky qui nestoit que que[5] vicechancelier de bohome[6] chancelier, Comme alors il auroit quásy la mesme authoritèz que luy et qu[’]il ne differoit que du titre cela ne sçauroit luy faire Plaisir mais l[’]on ne sçait pas encore positivement ce qui en sera. l[’]ambassadeur de france est arrivèz depuis deus Jour[7] mais il ne paroit pas encore en public. celuy qui doit al[l]er en france de la part de cette Cour n'est point nom̄ez[8] jusqu'a present. l[’]on parle du Conte d'harrach[9] qui autrefois a estèz en l[’]espagne. Vous verèz par la datte de ma lettre que nous sommes a la Campagne. Comme s'est[10] mon sejour favory je m[’]y porte a merveille et je souhaiteray d[’]y[11] avoir quelquefois votre Conversation pour qu[’]il ne manquá[12] rien aus[13] agrements que j'y trouve. Honorèz moy de vos nouvelles et me Croyez plus que personne

 Monsieur

   votre tres obeissante

   servante de Klenk

75. VON KLENK TO LEIBNIZ   251

Wenzel von] *Sinzendorff**, who both believe your presence is necessary in order to hasten the execution of the plan for the academy [the proposed Imperial Society of Sciences*], especially from what I have understood from the first of these[2] gentlemen. He is earnestly thinking about contributing everything[3] to it that will depend on him, and he has repeated to me many times that you would do well to come here if your circumstances permit. Her Majesty the Empress[4] has also ordered me to tell you that she has spoken many times about your concerns, but it seems to her that as long as the new regulation of finances is not in a better state, it would not be possible to think about a new establishment like an academy, for which a considerable fund would be needed. The empress should also like you to send her information about the origin of the Templars. This matter has been discussed in her presence, and she is persuaded that no one will be able to resolve it better than you. I believe it is necessary to warn you, but between us, a rumor is going around that Count Schlick supposedly wanted to resign his position from the grief that they want to cause him by making Count [Stephan Wilhelm] Kinsky [1679–1749] chancellor, who was only[5] vice chancellor of Bohemia,[6] since he [Kinsky] would then have almost the same authority as he [Schlick] and would differ only by title. It could not please him, but it is not yet positively known what will come of it. The ambassador of France arrived two days[7] ago, but he is not yet appearing in public. The one who should to go to France from this court has not yet been named.[8] They are talking about the Count of Harrach,[9] who was previously in Spain. You will see from the date of my letter that we are in the countryside. As this is[10] my favourite sojourn, I am doing wonderfully by it, and I wish sometimes to have your conversation here[11] so that it might lack[12] nothing in[13] the amenities that I find here. Honour me with your news and believe me more than anyone,

     sir,

        your very obedient
        servant Klenk

---

[1] LBr. F 24 Bl. 24r–25r. Letter as sent: 2.2 quarto sides in Klenk's hand. Previously published in Klopp XI 45–6.

[2] Reading 'ces' for 'ses'.

[3] Reading 'tout' for 'tous'.

[4] Klenk is presumably referring to her mistress, the Dowager Empress Wilhelmine Amalie* of Braunschweig-Lüneburg.

[5] Reading 'n'estoit que' for 'nestoit que que'.

[6] Reading 'Bohême' for 'bohome'.

[7] Reading 'deux jours' for 'deus Jour'.

[8] Reading 'nommé' for 'nomez'.

[9] Reading 'Comte d'Harrach' for 'Conte d'harrach'. Probably Aloys Thomas Raimund, Count Harrach (1669–1742), who served as imperial envoy to Spain from 1697 to 1700.

[10] Reading 'c'est' for 's'est'.

[11] Klopp omits 'dy' (see Klopp XI 46).

[12] Reading 'manquât' for 'manquá'.

[13] Reading 'aux' for 'aus'.

Leibniz to Caroline of Brandenburg-Ansbach, Princess of Wales

A la princesse de Galles
Hanover ce 3 d'Aoust
1715

Madame

pour mieux excuser la liberté que je prends de continuer d'ecrire a V.A. Royale j'accompagne ma lettre d'une grosse piece d'argent. Vous me dirés, Madame, que c'est porter de l'eau dans la Tamise, mais je pretends que la forme y vaut encore plus que la matiere. En un mot c'est une Medaille d'une grandeur extraordinaire. Je n'y ay point de part. Un Medialleur m'a esté recommandé d'Erfurt. Il a apporté son coin tout fait, on luy a permis icy d'en faire l'empreinte à la Monnaye. Il veut la presenter au Roy; et j'ay crû que V.A. Royale auroit bien la bonté de jetter l'oeil sur l'ouvrage pour en juger. Pour moy je ne dis rien sur le reste, mais il m'a paru que le visage du Roy n'est pas mal tiré.

Vous estes un juge souverain, Madame, et en medailles et en livres, et puisque Mlle de Pelniz m'a dit que vous aves achevé la lecture du Monsieur Lock, je seray ravi d'apprendre un jour votre jugement la dessus, car ses principes sont fort differens des miens; et ils sont plus populaires. Mais j'en parlé assés et là dessus et sur autres choses dans ma derniere que je me suis donné l'honneur d'écrire, et je suis avec devotion

Madame de V.A.R. etc.

76. Leibniz to Caroline* of Brandenburg-Ansbach, Princess of Wales[1]

To the princess of Wales
Hanover 3 August
1715

Madame

In order to better excuse the liberty that I am taking to continue to write to Your Royal Highness, I send with my letter a large piece of silver. You will tell me, Madame, that it is carrying water into the Thames,[2] but I maintain that the figure in it is even more valuable than the material. In a word, it is a medal of extraordinary size. I had no part in it. A medalist [Nicolaus Seeländer*] was recommended to me from Erfurt. He brought his die readymade; he was permitted here to make the imprint at the mint. He wants to present it to the king [George I, Georg Ludwig* of Braunschweig-Lüneburg], and I thought that Your Royal Highness would be kind enough to look the work over in order to pass judgement on it. For my part, I say nothing of the rest, but it seemed to me that the face of the king is not badly drawn.

You are a supreme judge, madame, both of medals and of books, and since Mademoiselle [Henriette Charlotte von] Pöllnitz* has told me that you have finished reading Mr. Locke*, I will be delighted to learn your judgement about that sometime, for his principles are very different from mine, and they are more popular.[3] But I have said enough, both about that and about other things in my last [letter][4] that I was given the honour of writing, and I am with devotion,

Madame, of Your Royal Highness etc.

---

[1] LBr. F 4 Bl. 41r: one quarto side in Leibniz's hand. Previously published by Eduard Bodemann in *Zeitschrift des Historischen Vereins für Niedersachsen*, 1890, pp. 170–1.

[2] That is, something pointless, unnecessary, or excessive. Compare the British saying, 'carrying coals to Newcastle'.

[3] Similarly, in the preface to the *New Essays Concerning Human Understanding*, Leibniz wrote:

Indeed, although the author of the *Essay* [i.e., Locke] says hundreds of fine things which I applaud, our systems are very different. His is closer to Aristotle and mine to Plato, although each of us parts company at many points from the teaching of both these ancient writers. He is more popular whereas I am sometimes forced to be a little more esoteric and abstract—which is no advantage for me, particularly when writing in a living language. [A.VI.vi.47–8/RB.47–8]

[4] Leibniz is apparently referring to his letter to Caroline of 10 May 1715 (document 72 above).

Leibniz to Louis Bourguet

Monsieur

Je suis bien aise, que mes réponses à vos objections sont venues inutilement, c'est à dire; que vous aviés trouvé vous même les réponses aux difficultés qui vous etoient venues sur ma Theodicée. Je seray ravi de voir un jour ce que vous avés ecrit à un ami, pour soutenir un principe de mon systeme, qui est, que de tous les Mondes possibles, Dieu a choisi le meilleur.

Il est bon sans doute de considerer les choses avec vous dans leur constitution primitive. C'est pourquoy j'ay dit quelque part dans ma Theodicée, qu'il n'auroit point été convenable, que les Anges, ou les hommes eussent été pecheurs d'abord. Cependant comme Dieu a egard non seulement à l'état present d'une chose, mais encore à toutes ses suites, il n'auroit point permis la cheute, si elle n'eut été enveloppée dans le meilleur des systemes possibles. On ne m'a demandé de Paris aucuns eclaircisemens particuliers, ny sur cela ny sur autre chose, mais on en a desiré seulement en general. Mais comme les tours des esprits sont fort differens, on ne sauroit gueres en donner de satisfaisans, qu'en sachant à quoy l'on s'arrête particulierement. Vous avés raison, Monsieur, de dire que notre globe devoit etre une espece de Paradis, et j'adjoute que si cela est, il pourroit bien encore le devenir, et avoir reculé pour mieux sauter. Il est fort raisonnable de juger que sans le mal moral il n'y auroit point eu de mal physique des Creatures raisonnables; le parallelisme des deux regnes, c'est à dire de celuy des Finales et de celuy des Efficientes, qui reviennent à celuy de la Nature et de la Grace, le paroit porter ainsi.

Je ne saurois rien dire sur le detail de la generation des Animaux. Tout ce que je crois pouvoir asseurer est, que l'ame de tout animal a preexisté, et a eté dans un corps organique, qui enfin par beaucoup de changemens, involutions et evolutions est devenu l'animal present. Votre conjecture, que tout animal seminal humain parviendra enfin à etre raisonnable, est ingenieuse, et pourrout etre vraye, cependant je ne vois point qu'elle soit necessaire. S'il y en avoit beaucoup qui demeuroient de^2 simples animaux, il n'y auroit point de mal. Je n'oserois asseurer que les animaux que M. Leewenhoek a rendu visibles dans les semences sont justement ceux que j'entends; mais aussi je n'osserois encore asseurer qu'ils ne le sont point; et j'attends avec impatience ce que M. Vallisnieri nous donnera pour les refuter. Et en attendant je n'en voudrois pas parler aussi decisivement que vous le faites, Monsieur, en disant que le sentiment de M. Leewenhoek est une fable des plus creuses. Mons. Hugens, qui etoit un homme des plus penetrans de son temps, n'en jugeoit pas ainsi. La prodigieuse quantité de ces animaux (qui sont votre premiere objection) ne s'y oppose en rien. On trouve une abondance semblable dans les semences de quelques plantes. Il y en a par exemple dont la graine consiste en une poussiere trés menüe. Je ne vois pas aussi, qu'il y ait de difficulté sur l'introduction dans l'oeuf de l'un de ces animaux à l'exclusion de l'autre, ce qui fait votre seconde objection, il s'en

77. Leibniz to Louis Bourguet*[1]

[5 August 1715]

Sir

I am very glad that my responses to your objections have arrived to no purpose, that is to say that you yourself had found the responses to the difficulties which occurred to you concerning my *Theodicy*. I will be delighted to see sometime what you have written to a friend in support of a principle of my system, which is that of all the possible worlds, God has chosen the best.

It is doubtless profitable to consider with you the first constitution of things. It is why I have said somewhere in my *Theodicy* that it would not have been fitting that angels or men had been sinners from the beginning. But as God has regard not only to the present state of a thing, but also to all its consequences, he would not have permitted the Fall if it had not been included in the best possible system. I have not been asked from Paris for any particular explanations of this or any other thing, but they have desired only some in general. But as there are very different turns of mind, it would scarcely be possible to give any satisfactory explanations but by knowing on what they are focused in particular. You are right, sir, to say that our globe had to be a kind of paradise, and I add that if this is true, it might well become so again, and it might have retreated in order to jump better. It is very reasonable to think that without moral evil there would not have been any physical evil for rational creatures. The parallelism of the two realms, that is to say, that of final and that of efficient [causes], which amount to that of nature [the latter] and of grace [the former], seems to bring it about in this way.

I could say nothing about the particulars of the generation of animals. All I believe I am able to assert is that the soul of every animal has pre-existed and has been in an organic body that has eventually, through a lot of changes, involutions, and evolution, become the present animal. Your conjecture, that every human seminal animal will eventually come to be reasonable, is ingenious and could be true. However I do not see that it is necessary. Had there been a lot of them that remained simple animals,[2] there would not have been any harm. I would dare not assert that the animals that Mr. Leeuwenhoek[3] has made visible in the sperm are precisely those that I intend. But I would also not yet dare to assert that they are not, and I impatiently await what Mr. Vallisneri[4] will present us to oppose them. And while waiting for it, I should not want to speak about it as decisively as you do, sir, in saying that the view of Mr. Leeuwenhoek is an empty fable. Mr. [Christiaan] Huygens,* who was a man of the greatest penetration in his time, did not deem it so. The prodigious quantity of these animals (which is your first objection) does not conflict with it in any way. A similar abundance is found in the seeds of some plants. There are some, for example, whose seed consists in a very minute dust. Neither do I see that there is any difficulty about the

introduit beaucoup apparement, puisqu'ils sont si petits, mais il y a apparemment dans un oeuf un seul endroit, et pour ainsi dire un <u>punctum saliens</u>, qui en peut recevoir avec effect. Et cela satisfait aussi à votre <u>troisieme objection</u>; qui est que leur petitesse extreme n'a point de proportion avec l'oeuf. C'est comme dans un fruit, qui est tres grand quelque fois, la partie seminale est tres petite et insensible. La <u>quatrieme</u> objection est, que l'oeuf et le foetus sont le même animal; mais cette proposition n'est point prouvée; il se pourroit que l'oeuf ne fût qu'un receptacle propre à donner l'accroissement et à aider à la transformation. La <u>cinquieme</u> objection est, que selon les Zoologues modernes et particulierement selon Mr. Vallisnieri ces animaux qui se trouvent dans les spermes doivent être des animaux de leur espece qui se propagent et se perpetuent tout comme il arrive aux autres animaux qui nous sont connus. C'est de quoy je demeure entierement d'accord: mais à mon avis, quand ces animaux seroient les vrais animaux seminaux, ils ne laisseroient pas d'etre une espece paricluiere de vivans, dont quelques individus seroient elevés à un plus haut degré par une transformation.

Cependant je n'oserois pas asseurer non plus que votre sentiment soit faux, qui va à soutenir que l'animal à transformer est deja dans l'oeuf, quand la conception se fait. Mais l'opinion qu'il y entre par la conception paroist plus vraysemblable. Ne decidons donc rien d'un ton trop affirmatif, et sur tout ne traitons point mal un homme comme M. Leewenhoek, à qui le public doit des graces, pour les peines qu'il a prises dans ses recherches. Il est tres permis de combattre son sentiment et je suis bien aise qu'on le fasse, mais il n'est point juste de le mépriser. Il y a une difficulté qui me paroist commune à toutes les Hypotheses, et sur la quelle je voudrois apprendre le sentiment de M. Vallisnieri pourquoy dans la copulation de quelques especes d'animaux un seul oeuf ordinairement est rendu fecond, et pourquoy les gemeaux y sont assés rares.

Vous avés raison, Monsieur, d'étre choqué des expressions peu polies de celuy qui a fait la preface de la seconde Edition de M. Newton et je m'etonne que M. Newton l'a laissé passer. Ils devoient parler avec plus de consideration de M. des Cartes, et avec plus de moderation de ses sectateurs. Pour ce qui est de moy, et de mes amis, qu'ils ont aussi eu en veüe, ils sont fachés que dans les Actes de Leipzig on a desaprouvé quoyque trés modestement leur pretendue vertu attractive, qui n'est qu'un renouvellement des chimeres deja bannies. Ils y commettent un Sophisme malin, pour se donner un air de raison, et pour nous mettre dans un tort apparent, comme si nous etions contre ceux qui supposent la pesanteur, sans en rendre raison. Ce n'est pas cela, mais nous desaprouvons la methode de ceux qui supposent comme les Scholastiques d'autres fois, des qualités déraisonnables, c'est à dire des qualités primitives, qui n'ont aucune raison naturelle, explicable par la nature du sujet à qui cette qualité doit convenir. Nous accordons et nous soutenons avec eux, et nous avons soutenu avant qu'ils l'ont fait publiquement, que les grands globes de notre système d'une certaine grandeur sont attractifs entre eux: mais comme nous soutenons que cela ne peut arriver que d'une maniere explicable, c'est à dire par une

introduction in the egg of one of these animals to the exclusion of another, which forms your second objection. It admits many of them, since they are so small, but in an egg there is apparently a single location, and a *starting point*, so to speak, that can receive any effectively. And that also answers your *third objection*, which is that their extreme smallness does not have any proportion with the egg. It is just as in a fruit, which is sometimes very large, the seminal part is very small or imperceptible. The *fourth* objection is that the egg and the fetus are the same animal. But this proposition is not proved; it could be that the egg was only a proper receptacle to provide growth and to aid the transformation. The *fifth* objection is that according to modern zoologists, and particularly according to Mr. Vallisneri, these animals that are found in sperm must be animals of their species that propagate and perpetuate themselves, just as it happens with other animals that are known to us. About this I agree entirely. But in my opinion, though these animals would be the true seminal animals, they would not stop being a particular species of living things, of which some individuals would be elevated to a higher degree by a transformation.

However I would not any more dare to assert that your view is false, which maintains that the animal to be transformed is already in the egg when conception takes place. But the opinion that it enters there through conception appears more likely. Let us therefore decide nothing in too affirmative a tone, and above all let us not treat badly a man such as Mr. Leeuwenhoek, to whom the public owes some thanks for the pains that he has taken in his research. It is very much permitted to oppose his view, and I am very glad that it is done, but it is not right to scorn it. There is a difficulty that seems common to all the hypotheses, and about which I would like to learn the view of Mr. Vallisnieri: Why in the copulation of some species of animals is a single egg ordinarily made fertile and why are twins rather rare?

You are right, sir, to be shocked by the rude remarks of the one responsible for the preface to the second edition of Mr. Newton,[5] and I am astonished that Mr. Newton let it pass. They ought to speak about Mr. Descartes with more respect and about his followers with greater moderation. As for me and my friends, whom they also had in mind, they are angry that in the Acts of Leipzig [the *Acta Eruditorum*] their alleged attractive virtue, which is only a revival of some previously banished chimeras, was disapproved, although very modestly. In that they commit a clever sophism in order to give themselves an air of reason and to put the apparent blame on us, as if we were against those who assume gravity without giving a reason for it. It is not that; but we disapprove of the method of those who, like the Scholastics in former times, assume irrational qualities, that is to say, primitive qualities, which have no natural basis, explicable by the nature of the subject to which this quality has to be suitable. We agree and maintain with them, and maintained before they made it public, that the great globes of our system, of a certain size, attract each other; but as we maintain that this can only happen in an intelligible way, that is to say, by an impulse of more subtle bodies, we cannot at all accept that attraction is a

impulsion des corps plus subtils, nous ne pouvons point admettre que l'attraction est une proprieté primitive essentielle à la matiere, comme ces Messieurs le pretendent. Et c'est cette opinion qui est fausse, et etablie par un jugement precipité, et ne sauroit etre prouvée par les phenomenes. Cette erreur a fait naitre cette autre erreur, qu'il faut qu'il y ait un vuide. Car ils voyent bien que leur pretendue attraction mutuelle de toutes les parties de la matiere seroit inutile, et sans aucun effect, si tout etoit plein. Je ne repondray point à des gens qui m'attaquent d'une maniere grossiere et desobligeante. Selon ces Auteurs, non seulement les substances nous sont entierement inconnues, comme vous le remarqués fort bien, Monsieur, mais même il est impossible à qui que ce soit de les connoitre, et Dieu même, si leur nature est telle qu'ils disent, n[']y connoitroit rien. Tout ce qu'ils peuvent dire à cela avec quelque espece de raison, sera que Dieu les fait agir ainsi par miracle, ou agit plus tost pour eux. Ainsi il faut revenir à la Philosophie Mosaique de Robertus Fluddus, que M. Gassendi a traité comme il faut dans un ouvrage exprés. Et comme M. Roberval avoit deja dit dans son Aristarque que les planetes s'attiroient (ce qu'il a peut etre entendu comme il faut) M. des Cartes le prenant dans le sens de nos nouveaux Philosophes, le raille fort bien dans une lettre au Pere Mersenne.

Vous m'obligerés, Monsieur, en m'indicant ou M. Clark, M. Ditton et quelques autres se servent du principe que j'ay mis en avant, que Dieu a choisi le meilleur plan possible. Je suis trop distrait pour pouvoir assez lire.

Nous ne saurions dire en quoy consiste la perception des plantes et nous ne concevons pas même bien celle des animaux: cependant il suffit qu'il y ait une varieté dans l'unité, pour qu'il y ait une perception; et il suffit qu'il y ait une tendence à des nouvelles perceptions pour qu'il y ait de l'appetit, selon le sens general que je donna à ces mots. M. Swammerdam a donné des observations, qui font voir que les insectes approchent des plantes du coté des organes de la respiration, et qu'il y a un certain ordre dans la nature qui descend des animaux aux plantes. Mais il y a peut etre ailleurs des étres entre deux.

Pour ce qui est de la succession, il est difficile de prouver qu'il y doit avoir eu un premier instant. Il est vray que les nombres ont un principe qui est l'unité, il est vray aussi que les composés se reduisent aux Monades, et qu'il y a une premiere Monade fondamentale; mais je ne vois point qu'il soit necessaire qu'il y ait un premier instant fondamental, car chaque instant est fondamental à l'egard de tous les autres qui le doivent suivre; et je ne vois point comment on puisse prouver qu'il y ait necessairement un instant primitif, et qu'il puisse etre prouvé par des raisons naturelles; il faudroit qu'il fut ou infiniment plus parfait que les autres, ou infiniment plus imparfait, et il ne me paroist point que l'un ou l'autre soit soutenable. On diroit par la même raison qu'il faudroit qu'il y eut une monade primitive parmy les creatures. Peut etre que tous les instans sont egalement parfaits, les perfections etant variablement distribuées dans les differentes parties de l'univers. Je ne saurois pourtant encore refuter demonstrativement celuy qui soutiendroit que tout l'univers croit tousjours en perfection à l'infini. Cependant il ne s'ensuivroit pas

primitive property essential to matter, as these gentlemen claim. And it is this opinion that is false and founded on a precipitous judgement and that cannot be proved by the phenomena. This error has given rise to this other error, that there must be a void. For they well understand that their alleged mutual attraction of all the parts of matter would be useless and without any effect if all were full. I will not respond to these people who attack me in a crude and disparaging manner. According to these authors, not only are substances entirely unknown to us, as you very well note, sir, but it is even impossible for anyone at all to know them, and even God himself could know nothing about them, if their nature is as they say. All they can say to this with any kind of sense would be that God makes them act in this way by a miracle, or rather acts for them. Thus it is necessary to return to the Mosaic philosophy of Robert Fludd*, with which Mr. [Pierre] Gassendi* has properly dealt in a work dedicated to it.[6] And as Mr. [Giles Personne de] Roberval* had already said in his *Aristarchus*[7] that the planets attract each other (which he had perhaps understood properly), Mr. Descartes, taking it in the sense of our new philosophers, ridicules it very nicely in a letter to Father[Marin] Mersenne*.[8]

You will oblige me, sir, by indicating where Mr. Clarke*, Mr. Ditton,[9] and some others make use of the principle that I have put forward, that God has chosen the best possible plan. I am too distracted to be able to read enough.

We cannot say in what the perception of plants consists, and we don't even entirely understand that of animals. However, it suffices that there be a variety in unity in order for there to be a perception; and it suffices that there be a tendency to new perceptions in order for there to be appetite, according to the general sense that I give these words. Mr. Swammerdam[10] has provided some observations that show that insects approach plants in respect of organs of respiration, and that there is a certain order in nature that descends from animals to plants. But there are perhaps other beings between two.

As for succession, it is difficult to prove that there must have been a first instant. It is true that numbers have an element, which is unity; it is also true that composites are reduced to monads, and that there is a first, fundamental monad. But I do not see that it is at all necessary that there be a first, fundamental instant; for each instant is fundamental with respect to all the others which must follow it, and I do not see how it can be proved that there is necessarily a primitive instant, and that it can be proved by natural reasons; it would have to be either infinitely more perfect than the others or infinitely more imperfect, and it does not seem to me that either is tenable. By the same argument one would think it would be necessary that there was a primitive monad among creatures. Perhaps all instants are equally perfect, perfections being variably distributed in different parts of the universe. Even so, I could still not demonstratively refute one who would maintain that the entire universe always increases in perfection to infinity. Nevertheless, it would not follow even from that that there was a first instant, the most imperfect of all, a chaos. For the asymptotes of the hyperbola show how the

même de cela, qu'il y a eu un premier instant, le plus imparfait de tous, un parfait chaos. Car les Asymptotes de l'Hyperbole font voir comment encore les diminutions peuvent aller à l'infini. Et s'il y avoit jamais eu un parfait chaos, il semble qu'il en resteroit tous jours une partie, et cependant je crois qu'il n'y en a qu'en apparence.[11]

Pour ce qui est de la succession, ou vous semblés juger, Monsieur, qu'il faut concevoir un premier instant fundamental, comme l'Unité est le fondement des Nombres, et comme le point est le fondement of l'Etendue. A cela je pourrois repondre, que l'instant est aussi la fondement du temps: mais comme il n'y a point de Point dans la Nature, qui soit fondamental à l'egard de tous les autres points, et pour ainsi dire le Siege de Dieu; de même je ne voy point qu'il soit necessarie de concevoir un instant principal. J'avoue cependant qu'il y a cette difference entre les instans et les points, qu'un point de l'univers n'a point l'avantage de priorité de nature sur l'autre; au lieu que l'instant precedent à[12] tousjours l'avantage de priorité non seulement de temps, mais encore de nature sur l'instant suivant. Mais il n'est point necessaire pour cela qu'il ait un premier instant. Il y a de la difference en cela entre l'Analyse des Necessaires, et l'Analyse des Contingens: L'Analyse des Necessaires qui est celle des Essences, allant <u>à naturâ posterioribus ad naturâ priora</u>, se termine dans les Notions primitives, et c'est ainsi que les Nombres se resolvent en Unités. Mais dans les Contingens ou Existences cette Analyse <u>à natura posterioribus ad priora natura</u> va à l'infini, sans qu'on puisse jamais la reduire à des Elemens primitifs. Ainsi l'Analogie des Nombres aux instans ne procede point icy. Il est vray que la Notion des Nombres est resoluble enfin dans la Notion de l'Unité qui n'est plus resoluble, et qu'on peut considerer comme le nombre primitif. Mais il ne s'ensuit point que les notions des differens instans se resolvent enfin dans un instant primitif. Cependant je n'ose point nier qu'il y ait eu un instant premier. On peut former deux Hypotheses, l'une que la Nature est tousjours egalement parfait, l'autre qu'elle croit toujours en perfection. Si elle est toûjours egalement parfait mais variablement, il est plus vraisemblable qu'il n'y ait point de commencement. Mais si elle croissoit tousjours en perfection (supposé qu'il ne soit point possible de luy donner toute la perfection tout à la fois) la chose se pourroit encore expliquer de deux façons, savoir par les ordonées de l'Hyperbole B, ou par celles du Triangle C. Suivant l'Hypothese de l'Hyperbole, il n'y auroit point de commencement, et les instans ou etats du Monde seroient crûs en perfection depuis toute l'eternité, mais suivant l'Hypothese du Triangle, il y auroit eu un commencement. L'Hypothese de la perfection egale seroit celle d'un Rectangle A. Je ne voy pas encore le moyen de faire voir demonstrativement ce qu'on doit choisir par la pure raison. Cependant quoyque suivant l'Hypothese de l'accroissement, l'etat du monde ne pourroit jamais etre parfait absolument, etant pris dans quelque instant que ce soit; neantmoins toute la suite actuelle ne laisseroit pas d'être la plus parfaite de toutes les suites possibles; pour

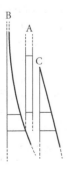

decrements can go to infinity. And if there had ever been a perfect chaos, it seems that there would always remain a part of it, and yet I believe that there is only an appearance of it.[11]

As for succession, in which you seem to think, sir, that a first fundamental instant must be conceived, as unity is the foundation of numbers and as the point is the foundation of extension. To that I could respond that the instant is also the foundation of time; but as there is not any point in nature that is fundamental with respect to all the other points and, so to speak, the seat of God, I likewise do not see that it is at all necessary to conceive a primary instant. But I admit that there is this difference between instants and points: a point of the universe does not have priority over any other, whereas the preceding instant always has[12] priority over the following instant, not only in time but also by nature. But it is not at all necessary for this that there be a first instant. There is some difference here between the analysis of necessary things and the analysis of contingent things. The analysis of necessary things, which is that of essences, proceeding *from what is posterior by nature to what is prior by nature*, terminates in primitive notions, and this is how numbers are resolved into unities. But in contingent things, or existing things, this analysis *from the posterior by nature to the prior by nature* goes to infinity, without it ever being possible to resolve it into primitive elements. Thus the analogy of numbers to instants cannot be carried out here. It is true that the notion of numbers is finally resolvable into the notion of unity, which is not further resolvable and can be considered the primitive number. But it does not at all follow that the notions of different instants resolve finally into a primitive instant. But I do not venture to deny that there was a first instant. Two hypotheses can be formed: one that nature is always equally perfect, the other that it always grows in perfection. If it is always equally perfect, but variably so, it is more likely that there wasn't any beginning. But if it always increased in perfection (assuming that it is not possible to give it all the perfection at once), the matter could still be explained in two ways, namely by the ordinates of the hyperbola B or by those of the triangle C. On the hypothesis of the hyperbola, there would be no beginning, and the instants or states of the world would have increased in perfection from eternity; but on the hypothesis of the triangle, there would be a beginning. The hypothesis of equal perfection would be that of a rectangle A. I do not yet see how to show demonstratively which should be chosen by pure reason. But although the state of the world would never be absolutely perfect at any moment whatever on the hypothesis of increase, the entire actual sequence would nevertheless not cease to be the most perfect of all possible series, because God always choses the best possible. When I said that *unity* is not further resolvable, I mean that it could not have any parts whose notion is more simple than it. Unity is divisible, but not resolvable, for fractions, which are the parts of unity, have notions less simple, because the whole numbers (less simple than unity) always enter into

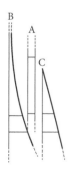

la raison que Dieu choisit tousjours le meilleur possible. Quand j'ay dit que l'Unité n'est plus resoluble, j'entends qu'elle ne sauroit avoir des parties dont la notion soit plus simple qu'elle. L'unité est divisible, mais elle n'est pas resoluble, car les fractions qui sont les parties de l'unité, ont des notions moins simples, parceque les nombres entiers (moins simples que l'unité) entrent tousjours dans les notions des fractions. Plusieurs qui ont philosophé en Mathematique sur le Point et sur l'Unité, se sont embrouillés faute de distinguer entre la Resolution en notions et la Division en parties. Les parties ne sont pas tousjours plus simples que le tout, quoyqu'elle soyent tousjours moindres que le tout.

Vous m'avés fort obligé, Monsieur, de me donnant la connoissance de M. Zendrini dont je pourray encore profiter quand vous ne serés plus à Venise. En me marquant le prix des livres, vous n'expliqués pas les nombres; je m'imagine que ce sont lire et soldi, mais en ce cas les livres paroissent bien chers, par exemple le Catalogue de la Bibliotheque du Cardinal Imperiale marqué de 40. Ayés las bonté, Monsieur, de m'en marquer la valeur à proportion de nos florins d'Allemagne, ou bien des ecus en espece dont un vaut deux de nos florins. Au reste vous aurés la bonté , Monsieur, de me marquer votre adresse quand vous partirés, et je suis avec zéle

Monsieur

> votre tres humble et tres
> obéissant serviteur

Hanover ce 5 d'Aout
1715

Leibniz[14]

77. LEIBNIZ TO BOURGUET   263

the notions of fractions. Many who have philosophized in mathematics concerning the point and unity become confused by failing to distinguish between resolution into notions and division into parts. The parts are not always more simple than the whole, although they are always less than the whole.

You have very much gratified me, sir, by informing me of Mr. Zendrini*, from whom I will still be able to benefit when you are no longer in Vienna. In telling me the price of the books, you did not explain the numbers. I imagine that these are lire and soldi, but in that case the books seem very expensive: for example, the Catalogue of Cardinal Imperiali's Library[13] marked at 40. Have the kindness, sir, to indicate the value in proportion to our German florins, or else to écus in kind, of which one is worth two of our florins. Finally, be so kind, sir, to tell me your address when you depart, and I am enthusiastically

sir

your very humble and very
obedient servant

Hanover 5 August
1715   Leibniz[14]

---

[1] Universiteitsbibliotheek Leiden Ms. 293 B Bl. 265r–268r. Letter as sent: seven quarto sides in secretary's hand. There is also a draft in Leibniz's hand and parts of an earlier fair copy (LH 1, 1, 3, 7 Bl. 1r–6v). Previously published in Dutens II-1 328–33; GP III 578–83; L 663–5 (excerpt).

[2] 'demeurassent' was crossed out and replaced with 'demeuroient de'. The draft has 'demeuroient tres' (LH 1, 1, 3, 7 Bl. 1r), and the earlier fair copy has 'demeureroient' (LH 1, 1, 3, 7 Bl. 3v).

[3] That is, the Dutch scientist Antonie van Leeuwenhoek (1632–1723), sometimes called the 'Father of Microbiology'.

[4] That is, the Italian medical scientist and naturalist, Antonio Vallisneri (1661–1730).

[5] That is, the second edition of Newton's *Philosophiae naturalis principia mathematica*; the preface was authored by Roger Cotes*.

[6] Namely, Gassendi's *Epistolica exercitatio in qua praecipua principia philosophiae Roberti Fluddi retegnuntor* (1630).

[7] *Aristarchii Samii de Mundi systemate* (Paris: Bertier, 1644).

[8] See Descartes's letter to Marin Mersenne of 20 April 1646 (AT IV 391–96).

[9] Humphry Ditton (1675–1715) was an English mathematician.

[10] That is, the Dutch biologist and microscopist Jan Swammerdam (1637–80).

[11] This paragraph, enclosed with vertical lines, was struck from the earlier fair copy (LH 1, 1, 3, 7 Bl. 5r–5v).

[12] Reading 'à' for 'à'.

[13] The reference is to the catalogue of the library of Cardinal Giuseppe Renato Imperiali (1651–1737) that was compiled by the librarian Giusto Fontanini (1666–1736) and published in Rome in 1711 under the title *Bibliothecæ Josephi Renati Imperialis Sanctæ Romanæ Ecclesiæ Diaconi Cardinalis Sancti Georgii Catalogus secundum auctorum cognomina ordine alphabetico dispositus, una cum altero Catalogo Scientiarum & artium.*

[14] The signoff, beginning with 'Monsieur' and ending with Leibniz's signature, are in Leibniz's own hand.

Caroline of Brandenburg-Ansbach,
Princess of Wales, to Leibniz

St. James le $\frac{13}{12}$ Semp 1715

la comtesse de buckenbourg m['Ja randu votre lettre.[3] l'home que vous avez recomande[4] n'a pas paru aupres de moy. Mr Bernestorff dité que c'est vn asiyet et non pas vne medalyé an celon.[5] il ya quelque jour sur lau, ou le Roy feu pressante a vn experiment.[6] l'occasion vien des plus apropo de parler pour vous Monsieur au Roy qui me dona c'este reponce,[7] ehr mus mir erst weissen das ehr historyen schreiben kann, ich höre ehr ist fleisig. Je ne toute pas qu'à l'arivez[8] du Roy dans l'Electorat vos afaire vint asouhait.[9] Je vous prié seulment de faire tout cequi despan de vous,[10] afin d'y forcer le Roy ale faire qui y parait pour tans fort anglin.[11] J'ay finy il ya lon tems loque.[12] Je vous avouè que je ne goudé nullement sa filosofié.[13] ce que je trouvez tres beau, c'est les dispudè avec L'Eveque Stilinflid, qui son d'une pollidée acompanyé de tres bone raison.[14] Je lie la tratuction d'homere[15] par Popé, qui e[s]t admirable, rien n'est plus beau que la prefacée et ces Essais,[16] avec les remarqué[s] sur chaque liver.[17] Je vous lanverais ala premier occation avec les sermon du docteur Thilontohn, archevequé.[18]

Caroline

78. Caroline* of Brandenburg-Ansbach, Princess of Wales, to Leibniz[1]

St. James le $\frac{13}{2}$ September 1715[2]

The Countess of Bückeburg [Johanne Sophie* Gräfin (Countess) zu Schaumburg-Lippe] delivered your letter to me.[3] The man whom you recommended[4] has not appeared to me. Mr. Bernstorff* says that at this length it is a dinner plate and not a medal.[5] There was a day on the water where the king [George I, Georg Ludwig* of Braunschweig-Lüneburg] was present at an experiment.[6] The occasion arose once again to speak on your behalf, sir, to the king, who gave me this response[7]: 'He must first show me that he can write histories; I hear he is diligent.' I do not doubt that on the arrival[8] of the king in the electorate your business will turn out as desired.[9] I only pray you do everything that depends on you[10] to compel the king to do it, which he nevertheless appears strongly inclined to do.[11] I finished Locke* a long time ago.[12] I confess that I did not like his philosophy at all.[13] What I found very fine are the debates with Bishop Stillingfleet, which are both civil and well-reasoned.[14] I am reading the translation of Homer[15] by [Alexander] Pope, which is admirable; nothing is finer than the preface and his essays,[16] with remarks on each book.[17] I will send it to you at the first opportunity, along with the sermons of doctor [John] Tillotson*, Archbishop[18] [of Canterbury].

Caroline

[1] LBr. F 4 Bl. 42r-43r. Letter as sent: two quarto sides in Caroline's hand. Previously published in Klopp XI 46–7 (excerpt), and in Echeverría 1989, pp. 151–2 (excerpt in Spanish translation). This is Caroline's reply to Leibniz's letter of 3 August 1715 (document 76). For Leibniz's response, see his letter to Caroline of 21 October 1715 (document 80).

[2] That is, 2 September OS and 13 September NS.

[3] The letter is presumably Leibniz's letter to Caroline of 3 August 1715 (document 76).

[4] Reading 'recommandé' for 'recomande'. The reference is to the medalist Nicolaus Seeländer*, whom Leibniz mentions in his letter to Caroline of 3 August 1715 (document 76, p. 253).

[5] Reading 'Mr. Bernstorff dit que c'est une assiette et non pas une médaille en ce long' for 'Mr Bernestorff dité que c'est vn asiyet et non pas vne medalyé an celon'. Klopp omits this sentence (see Klopp XI 46). The reference is to a large silver medal featuring the bust of King George I (Georg Ludwig* of Braunschweig-Lüneburg) that was struck by the medalist Nicolaus Seeländer*. See Leibniz's letter to Caroline of 3 August 1715 (document 76, p. 253).

[6] Reading 'Il y eut quelque jour sur l'eau où le Roy fut présent à un experiment' for 'il ya quelque jour sur lau ou le Roy feu pressante a vn experiment'. Klopp omits this sentence. The experiment to which Caroline refers was reported in the *Weekly Packet* (London) of 27 August–3 September 1715 as follows:

> On Monday [that is, 9 September 1715 (NS)] in the Evening his Majesty, with the Prince and Princess, went on the River, to see the Experiment of a new Engine for diving, invented by Col. Becker, and approv'd [by] the same. 'Twas observ'd the Person who went under Covert of the Engine, walk'd under Water 3 Quarters of an Hour, but by Reason of the low Tide, could then [not] go any farther than from Whitehall to Somerset-Stairs; but on the next [day?], upon a second

78. CAROLINE OF BRANDENBURG-ANSBACH TO LEIBNIZ   267

Tryal, he went much farther. So that those Persons who said, that this Diving Engine was an instrument only to pick Pockets with, have fail'd in their Conjectures.

The *Exeter Mercury; or, Weekly Intelligence of News* of 2 September 1715 reported the event in a column entitled 'London Intelligence', dated 30 August (OS):

Yesterday [that is, 9 September 1715 (NS)] in the Afternoon his Majesty (*Geo. I.*) the Prince and Princess &c. went to take the Air in their Barge; during which an Experiment was made of a Diving-Ingine of a new Invention in which a man walked at the Bottom of the River from Whitehall almost to Somerset House, being under water three Quarters of an Hour. This Ingine is said to be invented by one Major Becker and they say it's the best of the kind ever was heard of. It was made of Leather with Glass Eyes in such a manner as the use of this Hands and Feet were entirely preserved. For Conveniency of air a long Pipe was fixed from the Engine to a Vessel, and at the top of the Pipe was a Man planted, who by that Contrivance could discourse with the Diver the whole Time. [As quoted in Amery 1880, p. 495]

   [7] Reading 'L'occasion vint de plus à propos de parler pour vous, Monsieur, au Roy qui me donna cette réponse' for 'l'occasion vien des plus apropo de parler pour vous Monsieur au Roy qui me dona c'este reponce'. Klopp mistranscribes the clause as 'L'occasion m'est venue de parler pour vous, Monsieur, au Roy qui me donna cette réponse' (see Klopp XI 46).

   [8] Reading 'Je ne doute pas qu'à l'arrivée' for 'Je ne toute pas qu'à l'arivez'.

   [9] Reading 'votre affaire vient à souhait' for 'vos afaire vint asouhait'. The reference is to Leibniz's request to be appointed an historiographer of Great Britain. See Leibniz's letters to Caroline of December 1714, of 18 December 1714, and of 10 May 1715 (respectively, documents 50, 51, and 72).

   [10] Reading 'Je vous prié seulement de faire tout ce qui dépend de vous' for 'Je vous prié seulment de faire tout cequi despan de vous'.

   [11] Reading 'à le faire qui y parait pourtant fort enclin' for 'ale faire qui y parait pour tans fort anglin'.

   [12] Reading 'J'ay fini il y a longtemps Locke' for 'J'ay finy il ya lon tems loque'.

   [13] Reading 'goûtais nullement sa philosofie' for 'goudé nullement sa filosofié'.

   [14] Reading 'Ce que je trouvais très beau, ce sont les disputes avec L'Evêque Stillingfleet, qui sont d'une politesse accompagnée de très bonne raison' for 'Ce que je trouvez tres beau, c'est les dispudé avec L'Eveque Stilinflid, qui son d'une pollidée acompanyé de tres boñe raison'. The reference is to the long-winded published correspondence between the Bishop of Worcester Edward Stillingfleet (1635–99) and John Locke. The correspondence had been occasioned by Stillingfleet's *A Discourse in Vindication of the Trinity* (1696)—a book written in response to John Toland's *Christianity not Mysterious* (1696), but in which Stillingfleet had suggested that the kind of skepticism and impiety he found in Toland's work was something to which the views expressed in Locke's *Essay Concerning Human Understanding* could lead. This prompted Locke to respond with *A Letter to the Right Reverend Edward, Lord Bishop of Worcester* (1697), to which Stillingfleet replied with *The Bishop of Worcester's Answer to Mr. Locke's Letter* (1697), which prompted a second response from Locke in 1697, to which, in turn, Stillingfleet replied in 1698, prompting a third and final response from Locke in 1699, the year of Stillingfleet's death.

   [15] Reading 'Je lis la traduction d'Homère' for 'Je lie la tratuction d'homere'.

   [16] Reading 'la préface et ses Essais' for 'la prefacée et ces Essais'.

   [17] Reading 'livre' for 'liver'.

   [18] Reading 'l'enverrai à la première occasion avec les sermons du docteur Tillotson, archevêque' for 'lanverais ala premier occation avec les sermon du docteur Thilontohn, archeveque'.

Nicolas Rémond to Leibniz

Monsieur
[...]
Je vous envoie une lettre pour vous que Monsieur l'abbé Conti m'avoit laissée en partant pour l'Angleterre et j'y joins quelques articles extraits de ses lettres qui regardent M. Newton j'ai perdu ou je n'ai pu retrouver la derniere qui contenoit plus de choses sur les quelles j'aurois été fort aise d'avoir vos sentimens.
[...]
Je finis parceque je suis un peu las de copier mon abbé Conti qui me paroit dans l'enthousiasme, pour moi je serai comme Marot

> là me tiendrai ou a present me tiens.[3]

apres un trait si galant il ne me reste plus qu'a Vous assurer des sentimens de respect et d'admiration avec les quels je serai toute ma vie
 Monsieur

Votre tres humble et tres
obeissant serviteur

a Paris ce 18 d'octobre 1715

Remond

Extracts from letters of Antonio Schinella Conti to Nicolas Rémond Concerning Newton

30 Juin [1715]

Mr Newton ne parle de l'ame et du corps que par rapport aux phenomenes il proteste d'ignorer parfaitement la nature de ces deux etres. par corps il n'entend que ce qui est étendu, impenetrable pesant &tc. par ame ce qui pense, ce qui sent en nous &tc. il dit qu'il n'en scait pas davantage.[2]

79a. Nicolas Rémond* to Leibniz (excerpt)[1]

[18 October 1715]

Sir

[...]

I am sending you a *letter* that *the Abbé Conti** left for me when he departed for England, *and I enclose with it some articles extracted from his letters that concern Mr. Newton.*[2] I lost, or cannot find, the last, which contained many things about which I would have been very happy to have your opinions.

[...]

I am finishing because I am a little tired from copying my Abbé Conti, who seems enthusiastic; for my part, I will be like Marot

There I will stand where I am now standing.[3]

After so elegant a line, it only remains for me to assure you of the sentiments of respect and admiration with which I will be all my life,

sir

your very humble and very

obedient servant

in Paris this 18 October 1715

Rémond

---

[1] LBr. 768 Bl. 41r–41v, 54r. Letter as sent: three quarto sides in Rémond's hand. Previously published in GP III 651–2.

[2] For these articles, see document 79b below.

[3] From the poem *Du content en amours* by Clément Marot (1496–1544).

79b. Extracts from letters of Antonio Schinella Conti* to Nicolas Rémond* Concerning Newton[1]

30 JUNE [1715]

Mr. Newton talks about the soul and the body only in relation to phenomena; he professes to be perfectly ignorant of the nature of these two beings. By body he understands only what is extended, impenetrable, heavy, etc.; by soul what thinks, what senses in us, etc. He says that he knows nothing more about them.[2]

Le docteur Clark va plus loing[3]: il pretend qu'on ne sauroit prouver que l'ame soit quelque chose qui appartienne au corps et voicy son raisonnement: on demontre que tout corps est divisible; mais on scait par les phenomenes que la substance pensante est quelque chose d'indivisible. comme ces deux proprietez sont contradictoires, elles ne se sauroient trouver dans le mesme sujet; par consequent on ne peut prouver que le corps et l'ame soient la mesme chose. Je crois de ne me tromper pas en distant que cela ne prouve autre chose que l'existence de la force dans les corps: dans les corps il y a une force, et cette force n'est point les corps; par consequent elle a des propietez differentes des corps.

Mr Newton pretend de prouver par les phenomenes que l'espace est une propieté de la divinité: selon lui ou plustost selon ses disciples la pesanteur est produite par une cause qui n'est point mecanique: comme chaque partie de la matiere est pesante, on voit qu'il y a dans chaque partie quelque chose qui agit, et qui agit avec ordre et par consequent avec intelligence. comme cet estre est repandu dans toute la matiere, il est, selon lui, étendu: mais son etendue n'empesche point qu'il ne soit indivisible. l'espace ne se peut pas diviser; et croire que l'Espace est rien, c'est la plus grande folie du monde selon les Anglois. l'Espace n'a aucun changement comme les corps; et comme il contient les corps, qu'il est le lieu des corps, qu'il est eternel, qu'il est immense, il a bien plus de perfections que les corps. Si vous demandez ce qu'il y a dans les espaces vuides de matiere, les Newtonistes vous repondent, que comme l'espace est une propieté de la divinité, il y a tout ce qui accompagne la divinité.

Mr Newton croit que le system des corps qui est apresent et qu'on appele Le monde ne sera point eternel, mais qu'il aura des changemens. selon lui la terre diminue toujours et le peu de resistance qu'il y a dans les Espaces celestes change peu à peu le mouvement des Planetes. ll y a Newtonistes qui pretendent que les Cometes entrent quelquefois dans le soleil et qu'elles fournissent par la la lumiere qui sort du soleil par la lumiere: on croit ici qu'il s'ecoule toujours du soleil de petits corps qui font la lumiere.

ce qui semble beau dans le système de M. Newton c'est qu'il ne suppose rien et n'admet dans les choses que ce qu'il y voit; puis par sagacité il tire des consequences dont personne ne se seroit avisé. il ne decide point sur les principes; mais si vous lui accordez qu'il y a certaines loix que l'experience nous fait voir, il tire de là les plus belles propositions qu'on ait jamais veues.

12 DE JUILLET [1715]

on a publié dans les actes de la societé Royalle l'extrait du commerce epistolicum avec des remarques à la fin touchant la philosophie. on fait voir la difference qu'il y a entre la methode de Mr Newton et celle d Monsieur de Leibniz. on pretend que dans celle de M Newton il y a plus d'original et que tout ce que Monsieur de Leibniz a ajouté ne sont que des noms qui mal à propos introduisent des questions dans les

Doctor Clarke* goes further.[3] He claims that it cannot be proved that the soul is something that pertains to the body, and here is his reasoning: it is demonstrated that every body is divisible; but it is known from the phenomena that thinking substance is something indivisible. Since these two properties are contradictories, they cannot be found in the same subject; consequently, it cannot be proved that the body and the soul are the same thing. I don't believe I err in saying that it proves nothing but the existence of force in bodies: in bodies there is a force, and this force is not the bodies; consequently, it has some properties different from bodies.

Mr. Newton claims to prove from the phenomena that space is a property of the divinity. According to him, or rather according to his disciples, gravity is produced by a cause that is not mechanical: since each part of matter is heavy, it is understood that there is in each part something that acts, and that acts in an orderly fashion, and consequently with intelligence. Since this being is diffused in all matter, it is, according to him, extended: but its extension does not prevent it from being indivisible. Space cannot be divided; and to believe that space is nothing is the greatest folly in the world according to the English. Space does not undergo any change like bodies; and as it contains bodies, and is the place of bodies, and is eternal, and is immense, it has much more perfection than bodies. If you ask what there is in spaces void of matter, the Newtonians answer that since space is a property of the divinity, there is [there] everything that accompanies the divinity.

Mr. Newton believes that the system of bodies that now exists and is called the world will not be eternal but will undergo changes. According to him the earth always falls into decay, and the slight resistance that exists in the celestial spaces gradually changes the movement of the planets. There are some Newtonians who maintain that comets sometimes enter the sun and that they thereby supply the light that leaves the sun by the light. They believe here that some small bodies, which cause the light, always flow from the sun.

What seems fine in the system of Mr. Newton is that he doesn't assume anything and admits in things only what he sees in them. He then shrewdly derives consequences of which no one would have thought. He does not settle on principles, but if you grant him that there are certain laws that experience reveals to us, he derives from that the most beautiful propositions that have ever been seen.

12 July [1715]

The extract from the *Commercium Epistolicum** was published in the acts of the Royal Society with some remarks at the end concerning philosophy. They explain the difference between the method of Mr. Newton and that of Mr. Leibniz. They claim that in that of Mr. Newton there is more originality and that all that Mr. Leibniz has added is nothing but names that inappropriately introduce questions into mathematics. They then justify the physics of Mr. Newton. There is, they say, an

mathematiques. on justifie après la physique de M. Newton. il y a, dit on, une philosophie experimentale et un philosophie conjecturale. la premiere ne fait que tirer consequences des experiences qu'elle compare: la seconde fait des hypotheses et tache par là d'expliquer la cause des phenomenes. M. Newton ne s'est pas appliqué qu'à la philosophie experimentale; des phenomenes de la force, de la pesanteur, de la force electrique et de la force magnetique il tire des consequences, il ne se soucie point des causes: il ne decide pas si la cause de la pesanteur est mecanique ou non il n'en scait rien. c'est aux Carthesiens et aux Leibniziens de la demontrer s'ils peuvent. voila en peu de mots toute sa justification.

M.ᵣ Newton ne veut pas expliquer ce que c'est que cet esprit tres subtile dont il parle à la fin de ses principes il scait certainement qu'il est materiel il n'en cherche pas davantage il n'a pas assez d'experiences pour aller plus loing[5]; il est different de l'esprit ou du principe hylarchique. on fait apres un parallele entre la manière de philosopher de M. Newton et de Monsieur de Leibniz.

M.ᵣ Newton ne decide point sur la cause de la pensanteur, Monsieur Leibniz dit qu'elle est mecanique. l'un dit que les premieres parcelles de la matiere sont dures par les mouvements conspirants. M.ᵣ Newton n'ose affirmer que les motions de la machine animal soient mecaniques ou non, Monsieur de Leibniz donne ces mouvemens à l'harmonie preetablie. M.ᵣ N. dit que Dieu est <u>omnipresens</u>[6] mais qu'il n'est pas comme l'ame dans le corps. Monsieur de Leibniz appele Dieu <u>Intelligentia supra mundana</u> d'où il s'ensuit, dit on, que Dieu ne peut pas faire quelque chose dans les corps que par <u>miracle</u>. on le querelle fort sur le mot de <u>miracle</u>.

CE 30 D'AOUST [1715]

Je vais trois fois la semaine chez M.ᵣ Newton et quand je reviendrai à Paris, je vous assure que vous serez content de lui et de moi: vous ne pouvez pas croire combien il est scavant dans l'ancienne histoire et les reflexions justes et exactes qu'il fait sur les faits. il a beaucoup lu et beaucoup medité sur l'ecriture sainte mais il en parle avec une grande sagesse, bien du bon sens, en depouillant les expressions du allegorique et le reduisant a l'histoire. comme il scait beaucoup l'ancienne histoire des Egyptiens et des Pheniciens ou plustost qu'il a beaucoup medité sur ce que de ces peuples en disent Heradote, Diodore, Eusebe, Manethon &tc. il fait usage du caractere et du genie de ces peuples pour bien expliquer le sens de l'ecriture qui a été ecrite par des Orientaux c'est à dire par des gens qui parloient de la meme maniere.

Il croit qu'on ne peut pas prouver par l'ecriture que la matiere a été crée car le mot <u>créer</u> dans l'ecriture ne signifie que former. il pense que les Etoiles et ce que nous appelons le Ciel a été avant la formation de la terre qui etoit envelopée dans un grand abysme. Moyse, dit il, a ecrit l'histoire de la generation de la terre comme un homme qui etant dans les tenebres ecrivoit successivement ce qu'il voit paroitre. cependant M. Newton ne pense point qu'absolument on puisse dire que la matiere

experimental philosophy and a conjectural philosophy. The first only derives consequences from experiences that it compares. The second makes hypotheses and tries in this way to explain the cause of phenomena. Mr. Newton only applies himself to experimental philosophy; from the phenomena of force—of gravity, of electrical force, and of the magnetic force—he derives consequences; he is not concerned with the causes. He does not determine whether the cause of gravity is mechanical or not; he knows nothing about it. It is for the Cartesians and the Leibnizians to demonstrate it if they can. There in a few words is his entire justification.

Mr. Newton does not want to explain what that very subtle sprit is of which he speaks at the end of his *Principia*.[4] He knows certainly that it is material. He does not seek any more. He does not have enough experiments to go further[5]; it is different from the hylarchic principle. They then make a comparison between the manner of philosophizing of Mr. Newton and Mr. Leibniz.

Mr. Newton does not settle on the cause of gravity; Mr. Leibniz says that it is mechanical. The one [that is, Leibniz] says that the primary particles of matter are hard due to conspiring motions. Mr. Newton does not venture to affirm that the motions of the animal machine are mechanical or not; Mr. Leibniz attributes these motions to the pre-established harmony. Mr. Newton says that God is *omnipresent*[6] but that he is not like the soul in the body. Mr. Leibniz calls God *Intelligentia supramundana*, from which it follows, it is said, that God can only do something in bodies by a *miracle*. They dispute with him a great deal about the word *miracle*.

30 August [1715]

I go to Newton's place three times a week, and when I return to Paris, I assure you that you will be satisfied with him and with me. You cannot believe how learned he is in ancient history, and the apt and accurate remarks he makes about the facts. He has read a lot and thought a lot about the Holy Scriptures, but he speaks about them with great wisdom, plenty of good sense, in analyzing the allegoric expressions and reducing them to history. Because he knows a lot of the ancient history of the Egyptians and the Phoenicians, or rather because he has thought a lot about what Herodotus, Diodorus, Eusebius, Manetho etc. say about these peoples, he makes use of the character and genius of these peoples in order to explain clearly the sense of Scripture, which has been written by Orientals, that is, by people who spoke in the same way.

He does not believe it is possible to prove by Scripture that matter has been created because the word *to create* in Scripture does not mean *to form*. He believes that the stars and what we call heaven existed before the formation of the earth, which was enveloped in a great abyss. Moses, he says, wrote the history of the generation of the earth as a man who, being in the darkness, wrote successively what he saw. However, Mr. Newton does not think that it can be said absolutely that matter is

est eternelle ce qui est eternel est necessaire et parfait: or s'il y a un vuide la matiere n'est pas tout. c'est un raisonnement fort simple, mais bien fort.

Il croit qu'on peut fort bien demontrer par les phenomenes que Dieu existe mais il distingue la nature et Dieu. la nature n'a point de domaine ni de providence et elle n'agit point par des causes finales: Dieu au contraire a tout cela.

Antonio Schinella Conti to Leibniz

Je scay, Monsieur, qu'il n'est pas permis d'interrompre les Meditations des Grands Philosophes, ni de leur derober ces pretieux moments qu'ils employent à perfectionner les Sciences et les Arts, et à instruire les Hommes. Cependant une loi si respectable et si necessaire à l'utilité publique n'est point sans exception, et il me semble, qu'on est quelquefois en droit de la violer, lorsqu'il faut consulter ces grands Genies sur les disputes qu'on a.

Ce sont les reflexions, Monsieur, qui me donnent la liberté de m'adresser à vous dans la dispute, que j'ay avec le Sieur Nigrisoli, Medecin de Ferrare. Permettez moy de vous exposer nettement l'etat de la question.

Le Sieur Nigrisoli pretend, que la Generation des Animaux et des Plantes est l'effet d'une certaine Lumiere, qu'il appelle seminale. Vous scaurez, que Flud avec plusieurs Alchemistes, et plusieurs Medecins ont adoptè la meme hypothese. Elle est trop comode pour masquer la Nature sous des Noms eclatans.

79C. ENCLOSURE: CONTI TO LEIBNIZ   275

eternal; what is eternal is necessary and perfect. Now if there is a void, matter is not everything. This reasoning is very simple, but very strong.

He believes that it can be demonstrated very clearly from the phenomena that God exists, but he distinguishes between nature and God. Nature does not have any domain or providence, and it does not act by final causes: God, on the other hand, has all that.

[1] LBr. 768 Bl. 43r–44v, 42r. Letter as sent: four quarto sides in Rémond's hand. Previously published in GP III 653–6, Schüller 1991, 208–12 (German translation). Enclosed with Rémond's letter to Leibniz of 18 October 1715 (see document 79a).

[2] Gerhardt mistranscribes 'qu'il n'en scait pas davantage' as 'qu'il n'ensuit pas davantage' (see GP III 653).

[3] Reading 'loin' for 'loing'.

[4] The reference is to what Newton says in the final paragraph of the General Scholium that was added to the end of the second edition of the *Principia* (1713). There Newton wrote:

> A few things could now be added concerning a certain very subtle spirt pervading gross bodies and lying hidden in them; by its force and actions, the particles of bodies attract one another at very small distances and cohere when they become contiguous; and electrical [i.e., electrified] bodies act at greater distances, repelling as well as attracting neighboring corpuscles; and light is emitted, reflected, refracted, inflected, and heats bodies; and all sensation is excited, and the limbs of animals move at command of the will, namely, by the vibrations of this spirit being propagated through the solid fibers of the nerves from the external organs of the senses to the brain and from the brain to the muscles. But these things cannot be explained in a few words; furthermore, there is not a sufficient number of experiments to determine and demonstrate accurately the laws governing the actions of this spirit. [Newton 1999, pp. 943–4]

[5] Reading 'loin' for 'loing'.

[6] Reading 'omniprésent' for 'omnipresens'.

79c. Antonio Schinella Conti* to Leibniz[1] (excerpt)

[April 1715]

I know, sir, that it is not permitted to interrupt the meditations of great philosophers, nor steal those precious moments that they use to perfect the sciences and the arts and to instruct mankind. However, a law so respectable and so necessary for the public utility is not without exception, and it seems to me that one is sometimes entitled to violate it when it is necessary to consult these great geniuses about the disputes that one has.

These are the reflections, sir, that grant me the liberty to speak to you about the dispute that I have with Mr. Nigrisoli,[2] a physician from Ferrara. Permit me to explain clearly the state of the question.[3]

Mr. Nigrisoli claims that the generation of animals and plants is the effect of a certain light, which he calls seminal. You know that [Robert] Fludd* and many alchemists and physicians, have adopted the same hypothesis. It is too convenient to conceal nature under some glittering names.

276   79C. ENCLOSURE: CONTI TO LEIBNIZ

Il y a deux ans que ie me suis opposé à cette hpothese là. Je n'ay pû souffrir, qu'en Italie on preferat le système des Cablistes au Système Mécanique, que Galilee, Toricelli, Borelli nous ont tracé. Ma critique est dans la lettre, que i'ay ecrite au scavant Eveque d'Adria, et ie vous dirai en passant, que dans ma lettre i'ay parlé fort an long du Systeme de l'Harmonie preetablie. Ainsi i'ay eu l'honneur d'en parler le premier en Italie, ce qui a donné envie à plusieurs d'en avoir une connoisance plus exact.

[…]

M. Neuuton parle d'un certain esprit universel, et qui est repandu par toute la matiere. Si par cet esprit M. Newton entend la Nature plastique, il ne dit rien de clair, ni de nouveau mais je suis tenté de croire, que l'esprit, dont parle M. Neuuton dans sa derniere edition de son Livre, n'est que le Concours de Loix Naturelles, et que par consequent M. Neuuton a son ordinaire il dit la meme chose que vous, mais sous termes un peu obscurs.

[…]

Mais en voilà assez pour la premiere fois, que j'ay l'honneur de vous entretenir. Je vous prie de dire librement ce que vous pense[z] sur ma question, car je ferai imprimer votre lettre, si vous le permettez. Je parts demain pour Angleterre, et je ne manquerai pas d'y soutenir votre cause, comme j'ay fait a Paris. M. Remond et M. l'Abbé Fraguier en sont temoins. Ils m'ont chargé tous les deux de vous faire leurs compliments. Je suis avec tout le respect.

Votre tres-humble, et tres
obeissant serviteur
Conti

79C. ENCLOSURE: CONTI TO LEIBNIZ   277

It was two years ago that I set myself against this hypothesis. I could not stand that in Italy the Cabalist system was preferred to the mechanical system that Galileo, [Evangelista] Torricelli*, [Giovanni Alfonso] Borelli have laid out for us. My criticism is in the letter that I wrote to the to the learned Bishop of Adria, and I will tell you in passing that in my letter I spoke at great length about the system of the *preestablished harmony*. So I have had the honour of speaking the first about it in Italy, which has made many want to have a more precise understanding of it. [...]

Mr. Newton speaks of a certain universal spirit which is spread throughout matter.[4] If by this spirit Mr. Newton understands the plastic nature, he is saying nothing clear, nor new, but I am tempted to believe that the spirit of which Mr. Newton speaks in his last edition of his book is only the concurrence of natural laws and that consequently Mr. Newton ordinarily says the same thing as you, but in somewhat obscure terms.

[...]

But this is enough for the first time that I have the honour of conversing with you. Pray speak freely about what you think about my question because I will publish your letter if you permit it. I leave tomorrow for England, and I will not fail to support your cause there, as I have done in Paris. Mr. [Nicolas] Rémond* and the Abbé Fraguier[5] are witnesses of it. They have both charged me with paying you their compliments. I am with all respect.

Your very humble and very
obedient servant
Conti

---

[1] LBr. 173 Bl. 1r–4r. 6.5 quarto sides in Conti's hand. Previously published in GB 258–62; NC VI 215 (excerpt); Schüller 1991, 203–4 (excerpt in German translation). This letter was left for Leibniz in the care of Nicolas Rémond* in Paris before Conti departed for England; Rémond finally sent it to Leibniz enclosed with his letter of 18 October 1715 (see document 79a). Conti's letter is not dated, but there is reason to believe that it was written in April of 1715. In his *Memoirs of the Life, Writings, and Discoveries of Sir Isaac Newton*, David Brewster wrote that Conti went 'to England to observe the great solar eclipse of the 15th April 1715' (Brewster 1855, vol. 2, p. 431). Brewster was mistaken about the date of the eclipse, which actually occurred on 22 April 1715 (OS), that is, 3 May 1715 (NS); but if it is true, as is likely, that Conti departed for England before the solar eclipse, his letter to Leibniz would have had to have been written sometime in April of 1715. For Leibniz's response to the letter, see his letter to Conti of 6 December 1715 (document 88b).

[2] That is, Francesco Maria Nigrisoli (1648–1727). Nigrisoli had published a book entitled *Considerations Regarding the Generation of Living Thing, Particularly of Monsters* (*Considerazioni intorno alla generazione de' viventi, e particolarmente de' mostri* (Ferrara: Bernadino Barbieri, 1712)), to which Conti had responded in what was at the time Italy's premier intellectual journal, *Giornale de' letterati d'Italia*. In his response, Conti defended experimental and mechanistic philosophy.

[3] The 'state of the question' that Conti proceeds to describe concerns Nigrisoli's notion of 'lumiere seminale', which Conti discusses in relation to various concepts found in the works of other writers, including Leibniz and Newton.

[4] Here Conti alludes to something that Newton wrote at the end of the General Scholium that was added to the 1713 edition of the *Principia* (see document 79b, p. 275 note 4).

[5] That is, Claude-François Fraguier (1666–1728), French Jesuit, Latinist, Hellenist, and editor of the *Journal des savants*. He was elected to the Académie des inscriptions et belles-lettres in 1705.

Leibniz to Caroline of Brandenburg-Ansbach, Princess of Wales

A son Altesse Royale
et Madame la prince[sse] de Galles
[21 Octobre 1715]

Madame

V.A. Royale m'a extremement rejoui par les lignes qu'elle m'a fait l'honneur d'écrire en marquant qu'Elle s'est souvenue de moy, et même qu'Elle en a fait souvenir le Roy. Sa Mté a marqué par sa reponse qu'il est aussi spirituel qu'il est grand prince. Apparemment c'est par respect que le medailleur n'a pas osé se presenter à V.A.R. On avoit crû autres fois que les medailles ne pouvoient pas etre trop grandes. On estime les medaillons en cuivre mais pour les donner en or, cela iroit loin et c'est peutestre pour cela que celle qu'on a apportee a pû deplaire. J'ay veu à Vienne le Colonel Becker qui a donné au Roy le spectacle aquatique. Il y gouvernoit les pontons de l'Empereur, mais ne pouvant pas avoir ses arrerages, il quitta. Il me semble qu'il est du pays d'Hanover, et que son fils étoit dés lors au service du Roy. Son invention sera bonne encore pour la peche du corail mais il aimera mieux pecher de l'argent. Les Relations que j'ay vues n'ont point marqué à quelle profondeur il pretend pouvoir desendre.

Nous avons eté terriblement allarmés par les nouvelles d'Angleterre. Les premiers bruits parloient d'un incendie, et on ne savoit ce qui en etoit, nous etions egalement en peine pour toute la famille Royale, et par consequent V.A.R. y avoit une grande part: enfin nous avons sû, que ce n'a esté qu'un projet, mais un projet terrible et qui n'a pas eté trop loin de l'execution. Cela doit servir d'avertissement au Roy et à Votre Altesses Royales, de se precautionner d'avantage, et de ne pas trop compter sur la bonne foy de gens.

Comme V.A.R. a renvoyé ses femmes de chambre, il semble qu'elle soit servie maintenant par des Angloises. Dieu veuille qu'on ait bien choisi. V.A.R. me pardonnera cette échappade, qui ne vient que de mon zele.

J'ay les livres échangés entre M. l'Eveque de Worcester Stillingfleet et M. Locke. Le dernier s'y defend assés joliment. Mais dans le fond on n'y apprend pas grand chose. M. Locke affoiblit les grandes verités de la religion naturelle, M. Stillingfleet en sentoit toutes les mauvaises consequences, mais l'autre avoit l'adresse de parer les coups, et de mettre les rieurs de son coté. J'avois esperé que ma Theodicée seroit trouvée un peu plus solide en Angleterre, si elle étoit un jour lüe en Anglois, et qu'elle donneroit de meilleurs principes: mais je voy que V.A.R. qui m'avoit faite esperer d'y vouloir faire songer, n'a pas encore trouvé de gens propres à l'executer. Si c'est encore son dessein, et si elle le faisoit connoistre, je crois que pas une des meilleures plumes d'Angleterre la refuseroit. Il y a maintenant une espece de guerre civile en France sur le merite d'Homere. C'est une dispute bien inutile. Je suis bien aise que le Traducteur Anglois contente si bien V.A.R. Il est bon de connoitre un auteur que l'antiquité a rendu venerable, et au lieu de disputer de son merite, entrer par son moyen dans ces

80. Leibniz to Caroline* of Brandenburg-Ansbach, Princess of Wales[1]

To her Royal Highness
and Madame the Princess of Wales
[21 October 1715][2]

Madame

I was extremely delighted by the lines that Your Royal Highness has done me the honour of writing, indicating that she has remembered me and even that she has reminded the king [George I, Georg Ludwig* of Braunschweig-Lüneburg] about it. His Majesty has shown by his response[3] that he is a prince as witty as he is great. It is apparently out of respect that the medalist [Nicolaus Seeländer*] has not dared to present himself to Your Royal Highness. In former times, it was thought that medals could not be too big. Medallions in copper are esteemed. But to produce them in gold, that would go further, and it is perhaps for that reason that the one that was offered might have been displeasing.[4] I have seen in Vienna the Colonel Becker who presented the aquatic spectacle to the king. He managed the emperor's pontoons, but he resigned because he was unable to obtain his arrearages. I think he is from the region of Hanover and that ever since then his son was in the service of the king. His invention will also be good for fishing coral, but he will prefer fishing for money. The reports that I have seen have not indicated to what depth he claims to be able to descend.[5]

We were terribly alarmed by the news from England. The first rumors spoke of a fire, and we did not know what it was. We were also worried about the entire royal family, and consequently Your Royal Highness played a large part in it. Eventually we knew that it was only a plot, but a terrible plot, and one that was not too far from being executed. That must serve as a warning to the king and to Your Royal Highnesses to take further precautions, and not to count too much on the good faith of men.

Since Your Royal Highness has sent back her [German] ladies of the chamber, it appears that she is now attended by some English [ladies]. May God grant that they have been chosen well. Your Royal Highness will forgive me this slip, which comes only from my zeal.

I have the books exchanged between the Bishop of Worcester Stillingfleet and Mr. Locke*.[6] The latter defends himself there nicely enough. But at bottom, there is not much to learn there.

Mr. Locke undermines the great truths of natural religion; Mr. Stillingfleet perceived all the bad consequences of it, but the other had the skill to parry the blows and get the last laugh. I had hoped that my *Theodicy* would be found a bit more sound in England, if one day it were read in English, and that it would furnish some better principles. But I see that Your Royal Highness, who had made me hope by being willing to consider it, has not yet found anyone suited to carrying it out. If it is still her intention, and if she made it known, I believe that not one of the better English writers would refuse her. There is now a kind of civil war in France concerning the merit of Homer. It

vieux temps reculés; je voudrois qu'on dechifrât un peu mieux les voyages d'Ulysse. Quelques fabuleux qu'ils soyent, il semble pourtant qu'Homere a eu en veue des pays éloignés dont on parloit alors. Un Suedois nommé Rudbeck nous veut persuader, que l'Atlantique de platon, que les champs Elisées, que presque tous les dieux de l'antiquité ont eté en Suede; et s'imagine plaisamment, qu'Ulysse y a eté aussi. Il y a des gens qui ont crû, que <u>phoracia</u> étoit la Grand Bretagne. Car il est seur que les phoeniciens y navigeoient autres fois aussi bien que les Grecs. Lors que M. Addison (qui est un des meilleurs écrivains Anglois) m'envoya son voyage d'Italie enluminé par des passages des anciens; je luy fis remarquer par des textes de Claudianus et de Procopius qu'il semble qu'on a crû du temps de ces Auteurs que les ames alloient passer de notre continent dans les isles Britanniques; et peutetre que la Fable du purgatoire de S. Patrice en Irlande vient d'une fable plus ancienne. Mons. Addison avoit eté icy avec Myl. Halifax comme secretaire de l'Ambassade, et puis il estoit passé avec Mylord Warton en Irlande quand il y alla vice Roy. Ainsi il a tousjours passe pour un Whig zelé. On estime fort la Tragedie nommee <u>Caton</u>, et il y a une dispute de nation entre cette Tragedie et autre françoise de même nom. Ces disputes...[14]

M. Falaiseau que V.A.R. aura connu autres fois a Berlin, vint aussi icy avec Mylord Halifax. Madame l'Electrice le regala fort genereusement parcequ'il faisoit esprerer une correspondence reglée: mais il la rompit tout d'un coup, et je crois qu'il s'etoit brouillé avec ses patrons. Je voudrois bien savoir s'il est encor en vie.

Ayant écrit a Madame la duchesse douairiere d'Orleans une lettre de condoleance et de congratulation, elle m'a fait la grace de reponde d'une maniere tres belle et tres gracieuse.

Il semble que V.A.R. sera bien tôt en état d'ecrire en Anglois. C'est à quoy je n'arriveray jamais et il faut que je me contente à mon âge des langues que j'ay déja apprises. Si V.A.R. vouloit parler les langues de tous les peuples qui luy sont sujets, il faudroit qu'elle en apprit encore trois Européennes l'Esclavonne du pays de Lunebourg, la langue du pays de Galles (qui est des anciens Gaulois et encore des bas Bretons) et en fin la langue Hibernoise. Sans parler des langues Americaines, comme est celle des Algonquins dont M. de la Honton nous fredonnoit quelque chose. A Dieu ne plaise qu'on condamne V.A.R. a savoir toutes ces langues: à ce prix on renounceroit à la royauté. Mais la langue Angloise est assez belle pour meriter qu'on la sache a fond. Par bonheur la nouvelle acquisition du pays de Breme et de Verde n'apporte point de nouvelle Langue; car le platteutsch[16] en Lunebourg n'est gueres different de celuy de Breme. Cette acquisition fait bien des jaloux meme en Angleterre et en Hollande, mais il est fort naturel qu'un Electeur de Bronsvic aille jusqu'à la mer, et qu'il puisse dire comme Henry Lyon:

𝔙om 𝔥arʒ bis am die see war mein.

Son fils Henri Comte Palatin et Duc de Saxe avoit encore Stade. Mais je voy que je commence à babiller comme les vieillards, il est temps de finir, et je fuis avec devotion

80. LEIBNIZ TO CAROLINE OF BRANDENBURG-ANSBACH   281

is an entirely useless debate. I am very glad that Your Royal Highness is so well pleased with the English translator. It is good to know an author whom antiquity has rendered venerable, and instead of arguing about his merit to enter by his means into these old, remote times. I would like the voyages of Ulysses deciphered a little better. However fabulous they may be, it seems nevertheless that Homer had in view some remote countries that were discussed at that time. A Swede named Rudbeck[7] seeks to persuade us that the Atlantis of Plato, that the Elysian fields, that nearly all the gods of antiquity were in Sweden; and he amusingly imagines that Ulysses was also there. There are some people who have believed that *Phoracia*[8] was Great Britain. For it is certain that the Phoenicians sailed there in former times as well as the Greeks. When Mr. [Joseph] Addison* (who is one of the better English writers) sent me his Italian journey illuminated by passages from the ancients,[9] I pointed out to him, by means of some texts of Claudianus and Procopius, that it seems that at the time of these authors people believed that souls were going to pass from our continent into the British Iles and that it seems that perhaps Saint Patrick's fable of purgatory in Ireland comes from an older fable. As secretary of the embassy, Mr. Addison had been here with Milord Halifax,[10] and then he had gone to Ireland with Milord Wharton[11] when he [Wharton] went there as viceroy. Thus he has always been considered a zealous Whig. The tragedy named *Cato*[12] is esteemed very much, and there is a national dispute between this tragedy and a French one of the same name.[13] These disputes...[14]

Mr. [Pierre de] Falaiseau*, with whom Your Royal Highness must have formerly been acquainted in Berlin, also came here with Milord Halifax. Madame the Electress [Dowager Electress of Braunschweig-Lüneburg, Sophie of the Palatinate*] treated him very generously because he held out the promise of a regular correspondence. But he suddenly broke it off, and I believe that he was on bad terms with his patrons. I should very much like to know if he is still alive.

Since I wrote to Madame the Duchess of Orleans [Elisabeth Charlotte* of the Palatinate] a letter of condolence and congratulation, she did me the favour of responding in a very fine and gracious way.[15]

It seems that Your Royal Highness will soon be in a position to write in English. It is something I will never achieve, and at my age I must content myself with the languages that I have already learned. If Your Royal Highness wanted to speak the languages of all the peoples who are her subjects, she would still have to learn three European languages: the Slavonian of the country of Lüneburg, the language of the country of Wales (which is the language of the ancient Gauls and also of the people of Lower Brittany) and finally the Gaelic language. Not to speak of American languages, as is that of the Algonquians, of which M. [Louis-Armand de Lom d'Arce, Baron] de Lahontan* has hummed something for us. God forbid that Your Royal Highness be condemned to know all these languages: at this price one would renounce the royalty. But the English language is fine enough to merit knowing it thoroughly. Fortunately the new acquisition of the countries of Bremen* and Verden* does not bring a new language; for the Low German[16] in Lüneburg is scarcely different from that of Bremen. This acquisition makes quite a number of

Madame de Votre etc. Altesse Royale etc.

le tres humble

P.S.

Le complement que l'orateur de la Chambre des Communes a fait à Vos Altesses Royales m'a charmé, on peut dire encor en particulier, que le mariage de V.A.R. a porté bonheur a la famille, et que nostre cher Prince Royal a eu un instinct divin en le prevoyant.

80. LEIBNIZ TO CAROLINE OF BRANDENBURG-ANSBACH   283

people jealous, even in England and Holland, but it is very natural that an Elector of Brunswick go as far as the sea and say, like Henry the Lion:

From the Hartz to the sea, it was mine.

His son Henry Count Palatine and Duke of Saxony had Stade besides. But I see that I am beginning to babble like old men. It is time to finish, and I am with devotion, Madame, of Your etc. Royal Highness etc.

the very humble

P. S.

The compliment that the speaker of the House of Commons [Spencer Compton, 1st Earl of Wilmington] paid Your Royal Highness charmed me. Moreover, it can be said in particular that the marriage of Your Royal Highness has brought happiness to the family and that our dear royal prince [Georg August* of Braunschweig-Lüneburg] had a divine instinct in foreseeing it.

[1] Stadtarchiv Hannover 4.AS.01.1401. Draft: 2.5 folio sides in Leibniz's hand. This is Leibniz's reply to Caroline's letter of 13 September 1715 (see document 78). Not previously published. For Caroline's reply, see her letter to Leibniz of 14 November 1715 (document 84).

[2] The last page of this draft letter contains the beginning of a draft letter to Johanne Sophie*, Gräfin (Countess) zu Schaumburg-Lippe, the fair copy of which was sent to Johanne Sophie and was dated 21 October 1715 (see document 81). On this basis I also date the present letter to 21 October 1715.

[3] For the king's response to Leibniz's request to be historiographer of Great Britain, see Caroline's letter to Leibniz of 13 September 1715 (document 78, p. 265).

[4] For Leibniz's references to medallions, see his letter to Caroline of 3 August 1715 (document 76, p. 253).

[5] On Becker's invention, see Caroline's letter to Leibniz of 13 September 1715 (document 78, p. 265 note 6).

[6] The reference is to the long-winded published correspondence between the Bishop of Worcester Edward Stillingfleet (1635–99) and John Locke. See Caroline's letter to Leibniz of 13 September 1715 (document 78, p. 267 note 14).

[7] That is Olaus Rudbeck (1630–1702), a Swedish linguist and anatomist who was a professor of medicine at Uppsala University. Leibniz is referring to the various claims that Rudbeck attempted to defend in his four-volume book *Atlantica sive Manheim* (*Atland eller Manheim*) (1679–1700).

[8] That is, present-day Corfu Island.

[9] Leibniz refers here to Addison's *Remarks on Several Parts of Italy*, published in 1705.

[10] That is, Charles Montagu (1661–1715), Baron of Halifax from 1700. Later, upon the ascension of George I to the throne in England, he was made 1st Earl of Halifax (1714). In the summer of 1706 he led a delegation to Hanover for the purpose of delivering the 'Act for the Naturalization of the Most Excellent Princess Sophia, Electress and Duchess Dowager of Hanover, and the Issue of her Body' to the Dowager Electress and her son, Elector Georg Ludwig, as well as for investing the elector with the ensigns of the Order of the Garter. Joseph Addison*, who at the time was the undersecretary of state for the southern department, accompanied Halifax on this mission.

[11] That is, Thomas Wharton (1648–1715), 1st Marquess of Wharton. He served as Lord Lieutenant of Ireland from 1708 to 1710.

[12] That is, Addison's tragedy entitled *Cato, a Tragedy* (1712, first performed in April of 1713). The play is based on the last days of Marcus Porcius Cato Uticensis, a politician and statesman of the late Roman Republic known for his moral integrity.

[13] The French play by the same name is *Caton d'Utique: Tragédie* (1715) by Françoise-Michel-Chrétien Deschamps (1683–1747).

[14] Here the sentence breaks off; the following page begins: 'M. Falaiseau que'.

[15] The condolence was for the death of her brother-in-law, Louis XIV, who died on 1 September 1715; the congratulation was for the appointment of her son, Philippe II*, Duke of Orléans, as regent of France, in which capacity he served until Louis XV reached his maturity in 1723.

[16] Reading 'plattdeutsch' for 'platteutsch'.

Leibniz to Johanne Sophie, Gräfin (Countess) zu Schaumburg-Lippe

Madame

Votre Excellence est à la source des grandes affaires, et l'Empereur le Roy de la Grande Bretagne et le Regent de France composent maintenant le Triumvirat qui regle l'Europe. Le Roy de France estant mort aussi à propos que la Reine Anne; il semble que la providence a un soin particulier de notre Roy, et de sa famille. Le Roy le mérite par sa sagesse et par sa bonté, et le prince Royal marche sur ces[4] traces. On peut encore dire que la princesse Royale a porté bonheur dans la famille par sa pieté sans parler de ses autres belles qualités. Selon toutes les apparences l'Empereur sera obligé de declarer la guerre aux Turcs. M. le General Schulenbourg m'écrit de Vienne, qu'on y a fait un dernier effort pour l'eviter: en faisant de nouvelles propositions aux Turcs: mais comme ils tendent à la restitution, qu'il faudra faire aux Venitiens, on ne croit pas que l'orgueil Ottoman s'y accommode. L'Empereur presse fort de finir auparavant l'affaire de la Barriere, et il semble qu'on en viendra enfin à bout. La nouvelle acquisition du pays de Breme[6] fera bien des jaloux, même en Angleterre et en Hollande. Mais cette acquisition est tres naturelle, et il est convenable que l'issüe de nos rivieres ne soit pas entierement entre les mains d'autruy. On peut croire que la Cour de Vienne aimeroit mieux que l'affaire fût allée tout autrement: mais puisque l'affaire est faite, je crois qu'Elle la laissera aller son train. Je me souviens d'un temps ou nous étions assés prevenus, si je l'ose dire, pour aimer mieux de ne point avoir le pays de Breme, que de voir la Pomeranie entres les mains[8] du Roy de Prusse: mais le parti qu'on a pris maintenant me paroist plus raisonnable. Nous avons eté durant quelque temps à l'egard de la suede, comme ces grands chien[10] des pays bas (sans comparaison) qui vont querir la viande à la boucherie et la menent à la maison dans des traineaux. Ces chiens la defendent avec vigueur contre d'autres chiens. Mais on a remarqué que si les autres chiens étoient en trop grand nombre, et qu'il n'y eût pas moyen de la sauver; ces chiens gardiens en prenoient leur part. Nous avons fait assez d'efforts auparavant pour sauver le Roy de Suede; mais ce prince a eté intraitable, et il semble que maintenant les choses sont portés à l'extremité.

J'espere que la guerre d'Ecosse sera un feu de paille. La terrible conspiration d'Angleterre etoit plus dangereuse, mais elle a eté decouverte graces à Dieu, et le public raisonne diversement sur le comment. Je crois que ce qui est le plus sensible au Roy, est qu'il faudra ensanglanter la scene. Il est difficile de comprendre la manie de ces gens là, sur tout de ceux qui sont protestans. C'est beaucoup que le Roy Philippe a paru content de ce qu'on a fait en France sur la Regence. Et le Comte d['] oxford a eu raison d'alleguer cet evenement dans ses defenses.

81. Leibniz to Johanne Sophie*, Gräfin (Countess) zu Schaumburg-Lippe[1]

[21 October 1715]

Madame

Your Excellency is at the source of great affairs, and the emperor [Karl VI*], the King of Great Britain [George I, Georg Ludwig* of Braunschweig-Lüneburg], and the Regent of France [Philippe II* (1674–1723), Duke of Orléans] now form the triumvirate that rules Europe. The King of France[2] being dead as opportunely as Queen Anne,[3] it seems that providence has a particular care for our king and his family. The king deserves it for his wisdom, and for his goodness, and the royal prince [Georg August* of Braunschweig-Lüneburg)] follows in his[4] footsteps. And it can also be said that the royal princess [Caroline* of Brandenburg-Ansbach, Princess of Wales] has brought happiness into the family through her piety, not to mention her other fine qualities. From all appearances the emperor will be forced to declare war on the Turks. General [Johann Matthias von der] Schulenburg* writes me from Vienna that a final effort has been made there to avoid it, by making some new proposals to the Turks, but since they are directed towards the restitution which will have to be made to the Venetians, he does not believe that the arrogant Ottoman will agree to them. The emperor is pushing hard to finish the barrier affair[5] first, and it seems that we will finally come to the end of it. The new acquisition of the country of Bremen*[6] will make quite a number of people jealous, even in England and Holland. But this acquisition is very natural, and it is appropriate that the mouth of our rivers is not entirely in the hands of others.[7] You can believe that the court of Vienna would prefer that the affair had gone completely otherwise. But since the affair is done, I believe that they will let it run its course. I remember a time when we were prejudiced enough, if I dare say so, to prefer not having the country of Bremen to seeing Pomerania in the hands[8] of the King of Prussia;[9] but the course that has now been taken seems very reasonable to me. We have for some time been with regard to Sweden like those great dogs[10] of the low countries (beyond compare) which go in quest of the meat at the butcher shop and take it to the house in sleds.[11] These dogs defend it vigorously against other dogs. But it has been observed that if the other dogs were too great in number, and if there were no way to save it, those guardian dogs would take their share of it. We have previously made enough efforts to save the King of Sweden [Karl XII of Sweden (1682–1718)] but this prince has been intractable, and it seems that matters have been now brought the brink.

I hope that the Scottish war will be a flash in the pan.[12] The terrible English conspiracy was more dangerous, but thank God it was discovered, and there are

Le Roy se rend extremement considerable: Comme il est le chef des protestans, il semble que le veritable temps de les reunir soit venu. Car puisque Sa Mté trouve avec raison que la Religion Anglicane est compatible avec la religion Evangelique et puisqu'il est constant que les Theologiens Anglicans (excepté quelque peu d'outrés) regardent les autres Reformés comme des freres en Jesus Christ; le chemin paroist entierement applaudi; et je crois que si le feu Roy de Prusse vivoit encore, il y travailleroit.

La grande Medaille est plus extraordinaire sans doute par sa grandeur que par sa beauté. La plus part des medailles du Roy ne sont pas trop ressemblantes.[15]

On m'a envoyé un distique Latin sur la mort du Roy de France:

Papa, patres, mulier, Rex victus, Rex quoque fictus
    Vix alii lacrymas dant, Ludovice, tibi.

Oserois je supplier V. E. de souffrir encor mes paquets de livres parmy ses hardes?
Au reste je suis avec respect
Madame de Votre Excellence
À Hanover ce 21 d'octobre 1715   le tres humble et tres obeissant
                         serviteur   Leibniz

81. LEIBNIZ TO SOPHIE, GRÄFIN ZU SCHAUMBURG-LIPPE   287

differing views among the public about how it happened.[13] I believe that what is most evident to the king is that it will be necessary to bathe the scene in blood. It is difficult to comprehend the mania of the people there, above all of those who are Protestant. It is a great step that King Philippe [(Felipe) V* of Spain] has appeared satisfied with what has been done in France concerning the Regency, and the Earl of Oxford [Robert Harley*] was right to cite this fact in his defense.

The king becomes extremely important. Since he is the head of the Protestants, it seems that the right time to reunite them has arrived. For since His Majesty correctly believes that the Anglican religion is compatible with the Evangelical[14] religion, and since it is an established fact that the Anglican theologians (except a few of the immoderate ones) regard the other Protestants as brothers in Jesus Christ, the path appears entirely approved, and I believe that if the late King of Prussia [Friedrich I and III* of Prussia] were still alive, he would apply himself to it.

The great medal is without doubt more extraordinary on account of its size than on account of its beauty; most medals of the king are not very good likenesses.[15]

I was sent a Latin couplet concerning the death of the King of France:[16]

Pope, priests, wife, a vanquished king, a sham king too
   Others, Louis, scarcely shed tears for you.

Dare I ask Your Excellency to endure again my parcels of books among her clothes?

As for the rest, I am with respect,
Madame, of Your Excellency

In Hanover 21 October 1715   the very humble and very obedient
                                        servant   Leibniz

---

[1] Niedersächsisches Landesarchiv-Abteilung Bückeburg F1 A XXXV 9a 20. Letter as sent: 1.5 octavo sides in Leibniz's hand. A draft of this letter (1.2 folio sides in Leibniz's hand) is held by the Stadtarchiv Hannover (StadtAH 4.AS.01.1401). Not previously published.

[2] That is, Louis XIV, who died on 1 September 1715.

[3] Queen Anne died on 12 August 1714 (NS).

[4] The draft of the letter has 'ses' instead of 'ces', and here I follow the draft reading.

[5] On the matter of the Barrier Treaties, see Leibniz's letter to Caroline of 16 June 1714 (document 18, p. 69 note 7).

[6] In the draft Leibniz had written, 'La nouvelle acquisition du pays de Breme et de Verde'.

[7] The mouths of the Weser and the Elbe bordered the Duchy of Bremen on the west and east, respectively. Thus the acquisition of the Duchy of Bremen gave the Electorate of Braunschweig-Lüneburg (Hanover) access to the North Sea.

[8] Reading 'entre les mains' for 'entres les mains'.

[9] According to the treaties that the allies (Prussia, Hanover, Russia, Denmark) in the Great Northern War against Sweden concluded between April and October 1715, Hanover was to receive Bremen and Verden while Prussia was to receive 'Pomerania beyond the Peene river' (Hatton 1978, p. 186).

[10] Reading 'chiens' for 'chien'.

[11] Leibniz seems to be referring to the Bouvier des Flandres, a dog breed that was developed in Belgium to pull butchers' carts and herd cattle. In her reply to Leibniz's letter of 21 October 1715, Caroline mentions that she had read this letter of Leibniz to the Countess of Bückeburg (Johanne Sophie, Gräfin (Countess) zu Schaumberg-Lippe) and had related his comparison with 'the great dogs

Leibniz to Caroline of Brandenburg-Ansbach,
Princess of Wales

Madame   nicht abgangen[3]

Apres avoir eu l'honneur d'ecrire une longue lettre à V.A.R., je ne devrois point y revenir si tost; mais la bonté qu'Elle me temoigne fait que je l'informe d'une piece qu'on m'a jouée. On a donné avis au Roy que j'irois bien tot à Vienne. Et la dessus la Conseil m'a ordonné d'une maniere rebutante ce que j'aurois assez fait sans son ordonnance. Cela ne diminuera point mon assiduité, mais il diminue le plaisir avec le quel je travaille, qui a de l'influence sur le succés. Est il possible que le Roy me

82. LEIBNIZ TO CAROLINE OF BRANDENBURG-ANSBACH   289

of the low countries' to the king; she there refers to the dogs as the 'dogs of Brussels' (see Caroline's letter to Leibniz of 14 November 1715, document 84, p. 299).

[12] Leibniz is referring to the Jacobite Rebellion of 1715, aimed at deposing King George I in favour of The Old Pretender, James Francis Edward Stuart*. The rebellion had been largely subdued by the time James Francis Edward Stuart left France and landed in Scotland in December. Realizing that success of rebellion was vanishingly small, he returned to France in February 1716.

[13] After George I assumed the throne in England, Tory Jacobites conspired to organize armed rebellions against the new monarch.

[14] 'Evangelical' is Leibniz's preferred term for 'Lutheran'.

[15] After this sentence in the draft, Leibniz first wrote, and then struck, the following two sentences: 'Je n'apprends Rien de ce medailleur, quoyqu'il m'ait promis d'écrire. J'espère que V. E. aura bien la bonté de souffrir encore mes paquets de livres parmy ses hardes'. That is: 'I hear nothing from this medalist [that is, Nicolaus Seeländer*], although he promised to write to me. I hope that Your Excellency will have the kindness to allow again my parcels of books among her clothes'. On the matter of the 'great medal', see Leibniz's letter to Caroline of 3 August 1715 (document 76, p. 253), Caroline's letter to Leibniz of 13 September 1715 (document 78, p. 265), and Leibniz's letter to Caroline of 21 October 1715 (document 80, p. 279).

[16] Georg Heinrich Pertz published the couplet as a poem apparently written by Leibniz (Pertz IV 367), but as Leibniz makes clear here, the couplet was sent to him, not written by him. It is not entirely clear to whom 'Rex victus' and 'Rex fictus' are supposed to refer, but it is likely that 'Rex victus' refers to the aforementioned King Philippe V of Spain. When the throne of Spain became vacant in 1700, Louis XIV agreed to permit his grandson, Philippe, then Duke of Anjou, to ascend the throne in Spain. Since Philippe was in the line of succession to the throne of France, the other European powers were concerned that the kingdoms of Spain and France might eventually be united under a single Bourbon monarch in the person of Philippe or one of his descendants, thus upsetting the balance of power in Europe. This formed the pretext for the so-called War of the Spanish Succession* (1701–14), with France, Bavaria, and the Spanish loyal to Philippe, on the one side, and Austria, Great Britain, Holland, Portugal, Denmark, the Duchy of Savoy and the Spanish loyal to the Habsburg claimant to the Spanish throne, Archduke Karl (later Holy Roman Emperor Karl VI*), on the other. Hostilities between the allies (excluding Austria) and France were concluded with the treaty of Utrecht*. Although Philippe was allowed to remain king in Spain by the terms of this treaty, he was forced to renounce his and his descendants' claim to the throne of France, as well as forfeit significant portions of Spain's European empire, which were divided among the allies. Thus Philippe V was, in a clear sense, a vanquished king.

'Rex fictus', on the other hand, could refer to Louis XV, who was only five years old when his great-grandfather Louis XIV died on 1 September 1715. It might have been fitting to call him 'Rex fictus' since France was actually ruled for eight years by Louis XIV's nephew, Regent Philippe II*, Duke of Orléans, from 1715 to 1723, until Louis XV reached his majority. But perhaps it would have been even more fitting to call Phillipe II himself 'Rex fictus'; for while he was the power behind the throne during the Regency, he was not actually king.

82. Leibniz to Caroline* of Brandenburg-Ansbach, Princess of Wales[1]

[late October to mid-December 1715][2]

Madame   not sent[3]

After having had the honour of writing a long letter to Your Royal Highness, I should not return to it so soon; but the kindness that she shows me leads me to inform her of a trick that has been played against me. The king [George I, Georg Ludwig* of Braunschweig-Lüneburg] was advised that I would soon go to Vienna, and thereupon the council ordered me in a forbidding manner to do what I would

croye assez mal honneste homme pour contrevenir à des asseurances assés fortes, que je viens de donner, de vouloir achever avant toute la chose le travail que Sa Mté demande voir achevé? Et seroit ce même convenable aux interests d'un homme, qui compte encore beaucoup sur les bonnes graces de Sa Mté. Il est vray, que je ne serois point mal venu[5] à Vienne, et peutestre que quelcun qui l'a appris s'est imaginé que j'y courrois tout aussi tost. Mais je prefère mon devoir même à mes interests, et je veux que le Roy et le public soyent satisfaits avant toutes choses. Si ce faux rapport servoit de pretexte d'arreter plus long temps mes arrerages, je ne saurois qu'en dire. Est ce qu'on peut s'imaginer qu'apres les avoir receus je m'en irois? Et peut on me soubçonner de telles bassesses. Je crois que le Roy est incapable de me les attribuer. Ainsi j'espere d'apprendre un effect de ses bonnes graces par un acte de sa justice. Et sans ses bonnes graces il vaudroit mieux sans doute de plier bagage apres le travail achevé. Mais je ne crois point qu'un homme qui a servi si long temps avec tant de zele, et peutestre avec quelque succès, au moins dans l'opinion du monde, doive craindre qu'un prince aussi sage que le Roy ne luy rende point la justice que tant d'autres luy rendent, sans qu'il ait travaillé pour eux. Ainsi j'espere que Sa Mté en ordonnera bientost le payement, et ce sera une marque que les fausses impressions n'ont point prevalu. Ce rayon des bonnes graces de Sa Mté m'encouragera beaucoup, et V. A. R. m'en ayant fait pressentir quelque lueur, je luy en ay des obligations infinies, ne doutant point que l'effect ne s'ensuive.

C'est une chose etrange que M$_{gr}$ le Duc Maximilien se peut flatter de l'Eveché Osnabruc. Quand je luy dis un jour qu'il devoit suivre le Roy en Angleterre, et qu'entendant si bien la marine, il pourroit avoir la place de Grand Amiral comme le Duc de York, il me dit que l'Angleterre ne luy convenoit plus, et il m'en dit meme la raison. Et il faut avoir les visions du P. Wolf pour croire que la paix de Westfalie ne subsiste plus parceque d'autres Traités de paix luy ont derogé en certaines choses.

Nous esperons tout de bon de posseder le Roy cet eté, puisque la rebellion est aux abois. Mais je suis faché que nous ne pouvons pas nous flatter de posseder encor V. A. R. avec Monsgr le prince. Cependant je ne desespere point qu'elle ne puisse un jour nous venir rejouir.

Je crois qu'on commence a s'appercevoir, que le bruit[9] de la conspiration de la France de l'Espagne et des princes italiens sont presentement des chimeres. Si le feu Roy de France avoit eu de tels desseins, il n'auroit point fait la Paix de Rastat. Il semble qu'il a eu le pretendant en veue, et la paix avec l'Empereur etoit necessaire pour cela. Mais si la Reine Anne et le Roy de France avoient vecu, et si le pretendant avoit etabli[10] alors il auroit eté temps de retourner à l'Empereur. Dieu en a disposé tout autrement et on luy en doit rendre graces. La Cour de Vienne a bien reconnu aussi l'importance de la revolution d'Angleterre.

have done satisfactorily without its order. This will not diminish my assiduousness, but it diminishes the pleasure with which I work, which has some influence on its success. Is it possible that the king believes that I am a dishonest enough man to contravene some quite strong assurances, which I have just given, of wanting above all to finish the work that His Majesty asks to see finished?[4] And would it even be suitable to the interests of a man who still depends a lot on the good graces of His Majesty? It is true that I would not be unwelcome[5] in Vienna, and perhaps someone who learned that imagined that I would run there immediately. But I prefer my duty even to my interests, and I want the king and the public to be satisfied above all. If this false report served as a pretext to delay longer my arrearages, I would not know what to say about it. Can it be imagined that I would run away after having received them? And can I be suspected of such base acts? I do not believe the king is capable of attributing them to me. So I hope to learn of an effect of his good graces by an act of his justice. And without his good graces it would doubtless be better to pack up and go after the work is finished. But I do not believe that a man who has served so long with so much zeal, and perhaps with some success, at least in the opinion of the world, ought to fear that a prince as wise as the king may not render him the justice that so many others do without his having worked for them. So I hope that His Majesty will soon order the payment of them, and this will be an indication that the false impressions have not prevailed. This ray of His Majesty's good graces will encourage me a great deal, and since Your Royal Highness has given me a glimmer of it in advance,[6] I am infinitely indebted to her for it and do not at all doubt that the effect will follow.

It is a strange thing that Monseigneur Duke Maximilian [Maximilian Wilhelm* of Braunschweig-Lüneburg] can hope for the bishopric of Osnabrück. When I told him one day that he ought to follow the king to England and that, since he understands navel administration so well, he could have the position of Grand Admiral as the Duke of York, he told me that England no longer suited him, and he even told me the reason for it. One needs to have the visions of Father Wolf[7] to believe that the Peace of Westphalia* no longer holds good because some other peace treaties have departed from it in certain matters.[8]

We earnestly hope to have the king this summer, since the rebellion [in Scotland] is at bay. But I am sorry that we cannot hope to have again Your Royal Highness with Monseigneur the Prince [Georg August*, Prince of Wales]. However, I do not despair of her being able to come to rejoin us one day.

I believe that we are beginning to realize that the rumor[9] concerning the conspiracy of France, Spain, and the Italian princes are imaginary at present. If the late King of France [Louis XIV] had had some such plans, he would not have made the Peace of Rastatt*. It seems that he had the Pretender [James Francis Edward Stuart*] in mind, and the peace with the emperor [Karl VI*] was necessary for that reason. But if Queen Anne and the King of France had lived, and if the Pretender had been established,[10] then it would have been time to go back to the emperor.

Charlotte Elisabeth von Klenk to Leibniz

de Vienne le 13 de 9bre [1715]

Sa Majestèz l[']imperatrice ma ordonnèz Monsieur de vous ecrire qu'enfin SM l[']empereur luy a rendŭe une reponse decisive sur vostre sujet, il est entierement resolŭe a l[']etablissement d'une academie des sc[i]ences, et quoy qu'on naÿe pas encore trouvèz[2] les fonds nesseçaire pour ce dessein on y travaille, vostre presence y sera fort utile et on la souhaite; SM l[']imperatrice m[']a dit positivement que

God disposed of it in an entirely different way, and one ought to give thanks to him for it. The Court of Vienna has also rightly recognized the importance of the English revolution.

[1] LH 41, 9 Bl. 55r–55v: draft, two quarto sides in Leibniz's hand. Previously published in Klopp XI 47–9 and Echeverría 1989, pp. 52–3 (excerpt in Spanish translation).
[2] This undated draft of an unsent letter is very difficult to date with any precision. Given that it mentions 'le feu Roy de France', Louis XIV, who died on 1 September 1715, it is certain that it was written sometime after that date. However, there are three long letters that Leibniz wrote to Caroline after September 1715 that might fit Leibniz's reference, at the beginning of this draft, to a long letter he had recently written to Caroline, namely, his letter of 21 October (document 80), his letter of late November (document 85), and even his letter of mid-to-late December (document 91). Perhaps favouring the letter of late November is that it, and not the letter of 21 October, gives some of those 'quite strong assurances' that Leibniz says in the present draft that he has 'just given, of wanting above all to finish the work that His Majesty asks to see finished'. But perhaps favouring the letter of mid-to-late December is the fact that in the present draft letter Leibniz makes remarks dismissing Maximilian's chances of succeeding to the Prince-Bishopric of Osnabrück, remarks that look much like follow-ups to some remarks made in the letter of mid-to-late December. For in that latter letter (see p. 347), Leibniz mentions the death, on 4 December, of the Elector of Trier Karl Joseph and uses it as a pretext for again dismissing Maximilian Wilhelm's chances of succeeding to the Prince-Bishopric of Osnabrück; so it might be thought hard to explain why Leibniz was put in mind, in the present draft letter, of writing about Maximilian Wilhelm's chances of succeeding to that position unless he had already heard of Karl Joseph's death. Of course, neither of these considerations is decisive, which is why I have not ventured to assign a more precise date to this undated draft letter.
[3] This is written in Leibniz's hand.
[4] That is, the history of the House of Braunschweig-Lüneburg, Leibniz's *Annales imperii occidentis Brunsvicenses**.
[5] Klopp mistranscribes 'mal venu' as 'mal reçu' (see Klopp XI 47–8).
[6] See document 78, p. 265, and document 89, p. 333.
[7] Father Wolf was Maximilian Wilhelm's Jesuit confessor, who had converted him to Catholicism.
[8] A provision of the Peace of Westphalia (1648) held that the Prince-Bishopric of Osnabrück would alternate between Protestants and Catholics, with the Protestant bishops being chosen from the cadets of the House of Braunschweig-Lüneburg. At the time of Leibniz's letter, the Prince-Bishopric of Osnabrück was held by Karl Joseph of Lorraine, who was Catholic. Apparently Maximilian was of the opinion that the provisions of the Peace of Westphalia no longer held good and that he might therefore eventually receive the bishopric, even though, to the lasting chagrin of his mother Sophie, he had already converted to Catholicism. Karl Joseph was actually succeeded by Maximilian's youngest, Protestant brother Ernst August II*.
[9] Klopp mistranscribes 'le bruit' as 'les bruits' (see Klopp XI 49).
[10] Reading 'avait été établi' for 'avoit etabli'.

83. Charlotte Elisabeth von Klenk* to Leibniz[1]

from Vienna 13 November [1715]

Her Majesty the [Dowager] Empress [Wilhelmine Amalie* of Braunschweig-Lüneburg] has ordered me, sir, to write you that His Majesty the Emperor [Karl VI*] himself has finally rendered a decisive response concerning your case. He is entirely decided upon the establishment of an academy of sciences, and although the necessary funds for this project have not yet been found,[2] he is working on it.

vous venièz icy dés qu[']il vous sera possible. L[']empereur vous accorde les 2000 f d'augmentation mais il[s] ne sont pas encore assignèz SM l[']imperatrice fera tous son possible afin qu'on vous les assure d'une façon que vous en puissiez Jouir; mais avec tous cela elle ne repond de rien quoy qu[']elle s[']engage a soliciter pour a moÿ il me semble qu'a present il n[']y a plus a Hesiter et que si vous pouvèz quiter Hannovre de bonne grace vous ne Hazardèz rien a vous etablier icÿ apres les bontèz que SM l[']empereur marque pour vous. J[']ay reçue les[3] Gazette manuscripte que vous m[']avèz envoyèz mais nostre imperatrice n[']aime point des sortes de lectures. Tous ce prepare pour la guerre des Turcs dieu vueillent benir[4] les bonnes intentions de SM. La grossesse de l[']imperatrice regnante avance dieu mercy fort Heureusement on est en peine des affaires d'engleterre la Conspiration que l[']on a decouverte contre la personne du roy donne lieu de craindre qu[']il ne s'en trame de nouvelle[5]. Mr de Schoulenbourg est party d'icy pour venise fort Content de cette Cour qui l[']a aussy determinèz a prendre le Comandement de larmez[6] des venitiens on dit que le General voerner pourroit le suivre mais il me semble que son intention seroit plus tost de s[']engager au service de l[']empereur Mlle de Jörger que vous avèz connŭe a nostre Cour en est sortie pour estres[7] chanoinesse a Buchaŭ. elle est partie d[']icy il y a 15 Jour[8] pour se rendre au chapitre dans de Carosse de nostres imperatrices ressouvenèz vous que je n'ecrits[9] que pour vous et qu'ainsy Je vous mande toutes sortes de choses, comme a un amis avec le quel J'en use librement J'espere bien tost le bonheur de pouvoir vous dire moi mesme, que je suis

> Monsieur
>> votre tres obeissante
>> servante
>>> de Klenk

83. VON KLENK TO LEIBNIZ 295

Your presence will be very useful for it, and we hope for it. Her Majesty the Empress has told me positively that you may come here as soon it is possible for you. The emperor has accorded you the raise of 2000 florins, but they have not yet been allocated. Her Majesty the Empress will do her utmost in order that they are secured for you so that you will be able to benefit from them. But with all that she is not responsible, although she is committed to making a request. For my part, it seems to me that at present there is no need for you to hesitate and that if you can leave Hanover graciously, you risk nothing to establish yourself here after the kindness that His Majesty the Emperor shows you. I have received the[3] hand-written newspaper you sent me, but our empress does not like any kind of reading. Everyone is preparing for the war with the Turks; may God bless[4] the good intentions of His Majesty. The pregnancy of the reigning empress [Elisabeth Christine* of Braunschweig-Wolfenbüttel] is progressing, thank God, very happily. We are uneasy about the English affairs. The conspiracy that has been discovered against the king leads one to fear that it may be hatched again.[5] Mr. [Johann Matthias von der] Schulenburg* left from here for Venice very pleased with this court, which has also made him take command of the Venetian army.[6] It is said that General Voerner could follow him, but it seems to me that his intention would rather be to enlist in the service of the emperor. Mademoiselle Jörger, whom you were acquainted with at our court, has left it to be[7] a canoness at Buchau. She left fifteen days[8] ago in order to go to the chapter house in some coach of our empresses. Remember that I only write[9] for you and that I thus let you know all kinds of things, as to a friend with whom I deal freely. I hope soon to have the pleasure of being able to tell you myself that I am

sir

your very obedient

servant

Klenk

---

[1] LBr. F 24 Bl. 28r–29r. Letter as sent: three quarto sides in Klenk's hand. Not previously published.
[2] Reading 'quoiqu'on n'ait pas encore trouvé' for 'quoy qu'on naÿe pas encore trouvèz'.
[3] Reading 'le' for 'les'.
[4] Reading 'dieu veuille benir' for 'dieu vueillent benir'.
[5] Reading 's'en trame de nouveau' for 's'en trame de nouvelle'.
[6] Reading 'l'armée' for 'larmez'.
[7] Reading 'être' for 'estres'.
[8] Reading 'jours' for 'Jour'.
[9] Reading 'écris' for 'ecrits'.

Caroline of Brandenburg-Ansbach,
Princess of Wales, to Leibniz

St. James le $\frac{14}{3}$ 9ber 1715

Douvien que vous croié[3] Monsieur que je puise oubliyer vn home t'elle[4] que vous, et même toute la tere m'an ferais resouvenir.[5] J'espere que quand vous verais[6] le Roy, qu'il vous condantera,[7] et je ne toute[8] pas qu'il aura lieu de lesttre[9] de vous. Je n'ay point estte charmé de lexperimant du colonelle[10] Becker la chose selon moy ett impratiqu'able.[12] Hiër nous an avons veu[13] d'une autre espesse[14] qui n'a pas plus reusy.[15] c'estoit de pouvoir pruller vn véseau[16] de loin. Je ne scais dous vien le preuit que lon avoulu pruller[17] St James avec le Roy et toute sa familje.[18] J'avoue que je suis des incredullé.[19] Je vous ayée beaucoup d'oblication[20] des soins que vous me marqué[21] dans votre lettre. Je dois rander justice au femes et dames angloise qui sont alantour de moy, quelle me servée avec toute ladantion[22] du monde. J'ay parlais ancore aujourdehuis avec L'Eveque de lincolme pour la tratuction de votre theodice.[23] il ny a persone capable de sela[24] a ce qu'il m'assure que le docteur clerque, don je vous ayée anvoiyée des liver[25] par onhausen. ce même home et amié indimé du chevalié nuthon,[27] et je ne crois pas la chose en fort bone[28] mains. J'espere que la traedistion[29] de pope que je vous ayée ausy anvoiyée vous fera tout a fait descider pour le merité du bonhome[30] Homer. Je souhaiteray avec vous que lon peu deschifrere les voiages d'ulisee.[31] il y a des persones icy qui crois[32] que tous se liver et plus to vne moralle[33] que des voiages. il me samble que lamour de lapaterié du Sevedois luy a fait mestre les chans elicien an son peais.[35] il me samble que c'estois plus tost c'est androis ou il faisoit le saquerifice d'un bouque noire au anfer, apres quoy il vit les ame, et sy je ne me trompé samere.[37] Je n'ay pas veu adisson de quelque semaine.[38] sa tragity et tres belles[40] et caton luy même ne se plainderais[41] pas des santiment noble et dinge d'un home come luy[42] qu'il luy a done.[43] Je n'ay point veu la francoise. Falaiseau don vous voulée[45] savoir des nouvelles a ancore vne petite pansion[46] du duc de montécus. on ne parle pas avec trop d'avantage de luy. il n'a pas pareu icy de puis mon arivée[47] les raison de prouljerié[48] avec le feu Duc son bien faitteur[49] on estte causé par lamour,[50] que Falaiseau avee[51] pour la C. de santwitz et don le Duc aestte chalou.[52] Je vous anvois des ver[53] que Madame ma anvoiyé et qui doivée estter fort louée anfrance.[55] Je vous avoue mon mauvais gou quelle ne me plaise pas.[56] vous aurais remarqué dans le raport conter le dernier Minister[57] que le feu Ld. Boulinbrouck dit que les francois sont ausy mechant poétté[59] que les anglois politicien.[60] Je suis pour tant fort pour ceu de cornelle, Rasine, beaulau, Renié.[61] il sepeut que ne possetan pas sy bien[62] lalangue anglois que la francoise, jadmire plus seque j'antan.[63] Je vous dire vn mot[64] de nos nouvelles, qui sont que Mr le duc dorleans, a ranvoiyé le pretandan an lorene,[65] que les rebelle sur les frondier d'angueltere sesont proulyé,[66] que le general carbenter les adispercé, et qu'il va joinder le

84. Caroline* of Brandenburg-Ansbach, Princess of Wales, to Leibniz[1]

St. James $\frac{14}{3}$ November 1715[2]

How is it that you believe,[3] sir, that I am able to forget a man such[4] as yourself? And even the whole world would remind me of him.[5] I hope that when you see[6] the king [George I, Georg Ludwig* of Braunschweig-Lüneburg], he will satisfy you,[7] and I do not doubt[8] that he will have reason to be[9] satisfied with you. I was not charmed by the experiment of colonel[10] Becker;[11] in my opinion the thing is impractical.[12] Yesterday we saw[13] one of them of another sort[14] which was no more successful.[15] It was to be able to burn a ship[16] from afar. I don't know the origin of the rumor that someone tried to burn[17] St. James along with the king and all his family.[18] I confess that I am among the unbelievers.[19] I am much obliged to you[20] for the care you show[21] for me in your letter. I must do justice to the English maids and ladies around me, who serve me with all the attention[22] in the world. I have spoken again today with the Bishop of Lincoln [William Wake*] concerning the translation of your *Theodicy*.[23] He assures me that there is no one capable of that[24] but doctor Clarke*, some of whose books I sent you[25] by way of Oeynhausen.[26] This same man is an intimate friend of chevalier Newton,[27] and I do not believe that the matter is in very good[28] hands. I hope that the translation[29] of Pope that I have also sent you will cause you to decide entirely in favour of the merit of the good man[30] Homer. I wish along with you that the voyages of Ulysses could be deciphered.[31] There are some people here who believe[32] that the whole book is rather a moral philosophy[33] than [a book] about travels. It seems to me that the Swede's[34] love of the homeland made him place the Elysian Fields in his country.[35] It seems to me that it was rather this place where he [i.e., Ulysses] sacrificed a black buck[36] to the underworld, after which he saw the souls, and if I am not mistaken, his mother.[37] I have not seen [Joseph] Addison* for some weeks.[38] His tragedy[39] is very beautiful,[40] and Cato himself would not complain[41] about the noble and worthy sentiments of a man like him[42] [i.e., Addison], which he has given to him[43] [i.e., Cato]. I have not seen the French version.[44] [Pierre de] Falaiseau*, about whom you wish[45] to hear some news, still has a small pension[46] from the Duke of Montagu [John Montagu, 2nd Duke of Montagu (1690–1749)]. He is not spoken of very favourably. He has not appeared here since my arrival.[47] The reasons for the falling out[48] with his benefactor[49] the late duke [Ralph Montagu, 1st Duke of Montagu (1638–1709)] were caused by the love[50] which Falaiseau had[51] for the Countess of Sandwich, of whom the Duke was jealous.[52] I am sending you some verses[53] that Madame[54] sent me and which must be highly praised in France.[55] I confess to you my bad taste that I don't like them.[56] You probably noticed in the report against the last ministry[57] that the late Lord Bolingbroke[58] says that the French are as

duc dargeile pour finir lafaire.[67] les troup holandaise sont adandu atous moment le vean estant tres bon.[68] le peais[69] de Bremen et fort apropo,[70] et la comparaisson que vous avez fait dans la lettre de la C. de P. des chien de Prusselle et[72] selon moy, parfaite. elle a fait rire le Roy, a qui je l'ais dit. Jespere que vous aurais toujours sujest destre contand et je souhaite dy pouvoir contripuer.[73] Caroline

apres avoir leu le sonet vouterais vous lanvoiyer a[74] M^d pelnitz

84. CAROLINE OF BRANDENBURG-ANSBACH TO LEIBNIZ   299

bad poets[59] as the English are politicians.[60] Yet I very much favour those [verses] of Corneille [Pierre Corneille (1606–84)], Racine [Jean Racine (1639–99)], Boileau [Nicolas Boileau-Despréaux (1636–1711)], Régnier [Mathurin Régnier (1573–1613)].[61] It may be that because I do not have as much command[62] of English as I have of French, I admire more what I understand.[63] I will tell you a bit[64] of our news, which is that the Duke of Orléans [Philippe II*, Duke of Orléans] has sent the Pretender [James Francis Edward Stuart*] back to Lorraine,[65] that the rebels on the frontiers of England are in trouble,[66] that General Carpenter [George Carpenter, 1st Baron Carpenter of Killaghy (1657–1731)] has dispersed them, and that he is going to join the Duke of Argyle [John Campbell (1680–1743), 2nd Duke of Argyle] in order to bring the matter to an end.[67] The Dutch troops are expected at any moment since the wind is very favourable.[68] The country[69] of Bremen* is quite fitting,[70] and in my opinion the comparison that you made in the letter to the Countess of Bückeburg[71] with the dogs of Brussels is[72] perfect. It made the king, to whom I repeated it, laugh. I hope that you will always have reason to be satisfied, and I wish to be able to contribute to it.[73] Caroline

After you have read the sonnet, would you send it to[74] madame [Henriette Charlotte von] Pöllnitz*?

---

[1] LBr. F 4 Bl. 44r–46v. Letter as sent: six quarto sides in Caroline's hand. Previously published in Klopp XI 49–51; Kemble 531–3; Schüler 1991, p. 212 (excerpt in German translation); HGA 190 (excerpt in English translation). This is Caroline's response to Leibniz's letter of 21 October 1715 (document 80). For Leibniz's response to the present letter, see his letter to Caroline from the end of November 1715 (document 85).

[2] That is, 3 November 1715 OS and 14 November 1715 NS.

[3] Reading 'D'où vient que vous croyez' for 'Douvien que vous croié'.

[4] Reading 'puisse oublier un homme tel' for 'puise oubliyer vn homme t'elle'.

[5] Reading 'terre m'en ferait ressouvenir' for 'tere m'an ferais resouvenir'.

[6] Reading 'verrez' for 'verais'.

[7] Reading 'contentera' for 'condantera'.

[8] Reading 'doute' for 'toute'.

[9] Reading 'l'être' for 'lesttre'.

[10] Reading 'été charmée de l'expériment du colonel' for 'estte charmé de lexperimant du colonelle'.

[11] For Becker's experiment, see Caroline's letter to Leibniz of 13 September 1715 (document 78 above, p. 265 note 6).

[12] Reading 'moi est impraticable' for 'moy ett impratiqu'able'.

[13] Reading 'en avons vu' for 'an avons veu'. Kemble omits 'an' (see Kemble 531).

[14] Reading 'espèce' for 'espesse'.

[15] Reading 'réussi' for 'reusy'.

[16] Reading 'brûler un vaisseau' for 'pruller vn véseau'.

[17] Reading 'sais d'où vient le bruit que l'on a voulu brûler' for 'scais dous vien le preuit que lon avoulu pruller'. Kemble mistranscribes 'dous vien' as 'dons rien' (see Kemble 531).

[18] Reading 'famille' for 'familje'.

[19] Reading 'incrédules' for 'incredullé'.

[20] Reading 'ai beaucoup d'obligation' for 'ayée beaucoup d'oblication'.

[21] Reading 'marquez' for 'marqué'.

[22] Reading 'rendre justice aux femmes et dames anglaises qui sont à l'entour de moi quelles me servent avec toute l'attention' for 'rander justice au femes et dames angloise qui sont alantour de moy quelle me servée avec toute ladantion'.

84. CAROLINE OF BRANDENBURG-ANSBACH TO LEIBNIZ   301

[23] Reading 'J'ai parlé encore aujourd'hui avec l'Evêque de Lincoln pour la tratuction de votre *Theodicy*' for 'J'ay parlais ancore aujourdehuis avec L'Eveque de Lincolñe pour la tratuction de votre theodice'.

[24] Reading 'Il n'y a personne capable de cela' for 'il ny a persoñe capable de sela'.

[25] Reading 'dont je vous ai envoyée des livres' for 'don je vous ayée anvoiyée des liver'.

[26] This is almost certainly a reference to Rabe Christoph von Oeynhausen (1655–1748), who was the Oberstallmeister (stable master) and Kammerherr (Chamberlain) at the Hanoverian Court. His wife was Sophie Juliane (1668-1755), born Freiin von der Schulenburg, a sister of George I's mistress, Ehrengard Melusine von der Schulenburg* (known as Melusine von Schulenburg), and of Johann Matthias von der Schulenberg*. The youngest of the three daughters that were born to George I and Melusine, Margarethe Gertrud (b. 1701), was registered as the child of Oeynhausen and his wife Sophie Juliane. The other two daughters had been registered as the children of Magarethe Gertrud, another of Melusine's sisters. Although none of the three daughters of George I and Melusine were legitimized, they moved to England with Melusine when Georg Ludwig became King of England in 1714. See Hatton 1978, pp. 52, 406. It is probable that Oeynhausen had been on a visit to London and that Caroline had asked him to deliver Clarke's books to Leibniz when he returned to Germany.

[27] Reading 'homme est ami intime du chevalier Newton' for 'hoñe et amié indimé du chevalié nuthon'.

[28] Reading 'bonnes' for 'boñe'.

[29] Reading 'traduction' for 'traedistion'.

[30] Reading 'ai aussi envoyée vous fera tout à fait décider pour le mérite du bon homme' for 'ayée ausy anvoiyée vous fera tout a fait descider pour le merité du bonhoñe'.

[31] Reading 'l'on pût déchiffrer les voyages d'Ulysse' for 'lon peu deschifrere les voiages d'ulisee'.

[32] Reading 'personnes ici qui croient' for 'persoñes icy qui crois'.

[33] Reading 'tout ce livre est plutôt une morale' for 'tous se liver et plus to vne moralle'.

[34] The Swede mentioned here is Olaus Rudbeck (1630–1702). See Leibniz's letter to Caroline of 21 October 1715 (document 80, p. 283 note 7.

[35] Reading 'Il me semble que l'amour de la patrie du Suédois lui a fait mettre Les Champs Elysées en son pays' for 'il me semble que lamour de lapaterié du Sevedois luy a fait mestre les chans elicien an son peais'.

[36] That is, a black male goat. The term in Pope's translation is rather 'ram', which denotes a male sheep.

[37] Reading 'Il me semble que c'étais plutôt cet endroit où il faisait le sacrifice d'un bouc noire aux enfers, après quoi, il vit les âmes, et si je ne me trompe sa mère' for 'il me semble que c'estois plus tost c'est androis ou il faisoit le saquerifice d'un bouque noire au anfer, apres quoi, il vit les ame, et sy je ne me trompé samere'. Caroline is describing events depicted in Book 11 of the *Odyssey*. She speculates that what Homer refers to as 'the dusky nation of Cimmeria' (Pope's translation) was located in what is now the nation of Sweden.

[38] Reading 'quelques semaines' for 'quelque semaine'.

[39] Caroline refers to Joseph Addison's play, *Cato: A Tragedy*, written in 1712. The play is based on the last days of Marcus Porcius Cato Uticensis, a politician and statesman of the late Roman Republic known for his moral integrity.

[40] Reading 'Sa tragédie est très-belle' for 'sa tragity et tres belles'.

[41] Reading 'plaindrait' for 'plainderais'.

[42] Reading 'sentiments nobles et dignes d'un homme comme lui' for 'santiment noble et dinge d'un hoñe come luy'.

[43] Reading 'lui a donnés' for 'luy a doñe'.

[44] The French version, by Françoise-Michel-Chrétien Deschamps (1683–1747), was entitled *Caton d'Utique: Tragédie* (1715).

[45] Reading 'dont vous voulez' for 'don vous voulée'.

[46] Reading 'encore une petite pension' for 'ancore vne petite pansion'.

[47] Reading 'depuis mon arrivée' for 'de puis mon arivée'.

[48] Reading 'raisons de brouillerie' for 'raison de prouljerié'.

[49] Reading 'bien faiteur' for 'bien faitteur'.

[50] Reading 'ont été causées par l'amour' for 'on estte causé par lamour'.

[51] Reading 'avait' for 'avee'.

[52] Reading 'dont le Duc a été jaloux' for 'don le Duc aestte chalou'.

[53] Reading 'envoie des vers' for 'anvois des ver'.

Leibniz to Caroline of Brandenburg-Ansbach, Princess of Wales

Madame   Novembre 1715

J'ay eté charmé des marques de la bonté de V.A. Royale exprimées dans sa lettre, que j'ay eu l'honneur de recevoir. Rien ne sauroit me consoler d'avantage de la mort de Madame l'Electrice, et de la privation de l'aspect de V.A.R. et de celuy du Roy et

85. LEIBNIZ TO CAROLINE OF BRANDENBURG-ANSBACH   303

[54] That is, Elisabeth Charlotte* of the Palatinate, Duchess of Orléans.

[55] Reading 'm'a envoyés et qui doivent être fort loués en France' for 'ma anvoiyé et qui doivée estter fort louée anfrance'.

[56] Reading 'goût qu'ils ne me plaisent pas' for 'gou quelle plaise pas'.

[57] Reading 'Vous aurez remarqué dans le rapport contre le dernier Ministère' for 'Vous aurais remarqué dans le raport conter le dernier Minister'. Caroline refers to the report of the committee of secrecy that was appointed by the Whig-dominated Parliament in March 1715 to investigate the acts of the previous ministry, especially the negotiations leading up to the Treaty of Utrecht*, as well as possible Jacobite plots by Tory ministers (see Gregg 2001, p. 399).

[58] That is, Henry St John*, 1st Viscount Bolingbroke. In referring to Bolingbroke as the 'late Lord Bolingbroke', Caroline was not, of course, suggesting that Bolingbroke was deceased, but rather referring to the fact that he had lost his titles after having been attainted for treason in September 1715.

[59] Reading 'aussi méchants poètes' for 'ausy mechant poétté'.

[60] Reading 'politiciens' for 'politicien'. In *A Report from the Committee of Secrecy, Appointed by Order of the House of Commons to Examine Several Books and Papers laid before the House, relating to the late Negotiations of Peace and Commerce, &c.,* there is quoted this line from a letter that Bolingbroke wrote to Matthew Prior: 'For God's sake, dear *Matt*, hide the Nakedness of thy Country, and give the best turn thy fertile Brain will furnish thee with, to the Blunders of thy Countrymen, who are not much better Politicians than the *French* are Poets' (Walpole 1715, p. 47).

[61] Reading 'ceux de Corneille, Racine, Boileau, Reynier' for 'ceu de Cornelle, Rasine, Beaulau, Renié'.

[62] Klopp mistranscribes 'il sepeut que ne possetan pas sy bien' as 'peutestre parce que je ne possède pas si bien' (see Klopp XI 51).

[63] Reading 'Il se peut que ne possedant pas si bien la langue anglaise que la française, j'admire plus le que j'entends' for 'il sepeut que ne possetan pas sy bien lalangue anglois que la francoise, jadmire plus seque j'antan'.

[64] Reading 'dirai un mot' for 'dire vn mot'.

[65] Reading 'a renvoyé le prétendant en Lorraine' for 'a ranvoiyé le pretandan an lorene'.

[66] Reading 'rebelles sur les frontières d'Angleterre se sont brouillés' for 'rebelle sur les frondier d'angueltere sesont proulyé'.

[67] Reading 'Carpenter les a disperés, et qu'il van joindre le duc d'Dargyle pour finir l'affaire' for 'carbenter les adispercé, et qu'il va joinder le duc dargeile pour finir lafaire'.

[68] Reading 'troupes hollandaises sont attendues à tout moment le vent étant très bon' for 'troupe holandaise sont adandu atous moment le vean estant tres bon'.

[69] Reading 'pays' for 'peais'.

[70] Reading 'est fort à propos' for 'et fort apropo'.

[71] See Leibniz's letter of 21 October 1715 to Johanne Sophie*, Gräfin zu Schaumburg-Lippe, Countess of Bückeburg (document 81, p. 285).

[72] Reading 'des chiens de Brusselles est' for 'des chien de Prusselle et'.

[73] Reading 'J'espere que vous aurez toujours sujet d'être content et je souhaite d'y pouvoir contribuer' for 'Jespere que vous aurais toujours sujest destre contand et je souhaite dy pouvoir contripuer'.

[74] Reading 'apres avoir lu le sonnet voudriez-vous l'envoyer à' for 'apres avoir leu le sonet vouterais vous lanvoiyer a'.

85. Leibniz to Caroline* of Brandenburg-Ansbach, Princess of Wales[1]

Madame   November 1715

I was charmed by the signs of the kindness from Your Royal Highness expressed in her letter that I had the honour of receiving. Nothing could console me more concerning the death of Madame the [Dowager] Electress [of Braunschweig-Lüneburg, Sophie* of the Palatinate] and the privation of the sight of Your Royal

du prince. Nous avions esperé de jouir de la presence de Sa Mté cet automne, mais cela n'ayant pas eté possible, nous nous flattons tousjours d'avoir cet avantage l'année qui vient, et peutêtre pour l'eté tout entier, puisque le Parlement s'assemblera à son temps ordinaire en hyver. Si le Roy étoit venu, je crois, qu'il m'auroit fait la grace de faire payer plus d'un an et demi d'arrerages qui me sont dus, et dont le refus m'incommode extremement, pendant que je travaille presque au delà de mes forces, jour et nuit, et ne voy quasi personne pour contenter le Roy et moy meme, et finir mon travail. Si mon inclination à travailler et à ne point laisser un ouvrage imparfait

n'y remedioit, il est seur que cela me rebuteroit. Je ne l'attribue pas au Roy, mais au peu d'empressement de Messieurs les Ministres, qui me laissent languir. J'en ay écrit à M. de Bernsdorf et à M. de Goriz. Il y a long temps, ils m'ont donné des esperances, mais qui ont eté sans effect; et depuis quelques mois M. de Bernsdorf ne répond plus. Je l'attribue à la grandeur et multitude des affaires, mais aussi à un peu d'indifference pour un ancien serviteur. J'ay mandé à luy et à M. de Bernsdorf des raisons invincibles pour contenter le Roy. Sa Majesté m'a tousjours permit de faire des voyages comme je le trouverois

ne me soûtenoit il est seur que cela me decourageroit extremement, et me feroit penser à couler le temps plus agreablement comme il dependroit de moy de faire; mais je me fais un point d'honneur de satisfaire au Roy, à la Maison, au public et à moy même, et de produire tant de belles découverts Historiques sur les veritables origines de la maison, et quantité de matieres liées, qu'on ignoreroit sans moy. Feu Monseigneur l'Electeur et le Roy m'ont toujours permis de faire des voyages à mon gré pour faire des recherches. Estant allé aux bains de Carlsbard à la fin de l'automne 1711 j'etois assés avancé pour aller a Vienne, et jugeant qu'il etoit necessaire de voir encor une fois les Manuscrits de l'Empereur avant que de finir, j'y poussay, et j'informay M. de Bernsdorf de mon voyage pour qu'on me pût ordonner quelque chose au besoin. J'y arrivay vers la fin de l'année et j'employay tres bien l'hyver pour le service du Roy. Et le dernier voyage que j'ay fait a Vienne a eté tres bien employée pour ce but, car j'ay eté fort assisté à travailler sur les Manuscrits de l'Empereur | dont j'avois tres grand besoin avant que de finir mon ouvrage |. J'y arrivay au commencement de l'hyver. Au printemps de l'an 1712 mes affaires étoient faites, et j'en voulus partir. Je l'ecrivis à M. de Bernsdorf, qui m'ordonna de rester encore pour insinuer quelque chose à l'Empereur | dans une audience | ayant appris que j'aurois un accés assés particulier aupres de ce Monarque, ce que j'eus la commodité d'executer asses bien. Mais la dessus la goutte me prit, et par surcroist de malheur les chemins furent fermés cet eté là a cause de la peste qui éclata, et M. de Bernsdorf même me fit savoir que je ferois mieux de ne point venir alors. Je restay donc à Vienne cette année 1713, et une partie de l'année 1714 jusqu'à ce que les chemins furent ouverts. Ainsi je ne pouvois venir qu'au printemps 1714. Mais outre un peu indisposition de la goutte, la principale raison qui m'empecha de venir avant

Highness and that of the king [George I, Georg Ludwig* of Braunschweig-Lüneburg] and of the prince [Georg August* of Braunschweig-Lüneburg]. We had hoped to enjoy the presence of His Majesty this autumn, but since that was not possible, we still hope to have this honour next year, and perhaps for the entire summer, since the Parliament will assemble at its usual time in the winter. If the king had come, I believe that he would have done me the favour of having paid more than a year and a half of arrearages that are due me and whose denial greatly inconveniences me while I work nearly beyond my powers, day and night, and see almost no one in order to satisfy the king and myself and to finish my work [his *Annales imperii occidentis Brunsvicenses**]. If my inclination to work and not allow an imperfect work

did not a remedy it, it would certainly dishearten me. I do not attribute it to the king, but to a bit of eagerness on the part of the ministers, who let me languish. I have written to Mr. Bernstorff* and to Mr. Görtz*. They have given me some hopes for a long time, but they have been without effect; and for some months Mr. Bernstorff has no longer responded. I attribute it to the magnitude and multitude of affairs, but also to a bit of indifference toward an old servant. I have sent to him and to Mr. Bernstorff some irrefutable reasons to satisfy the king.[2] His Majesty always permitted me to make some trips as I would find it

did not sustain me it would certainly discourage me very much and make me think about passing the time more enjoyably, as would depend on me. But I make it a point of honour to satisfy the king, the House [of Braunschweig], the public, and myself, and to bring forth so many fine, historical discoveries about the true origins of the House [of Braunschweig] and a lot of related matters that would not be known were it not for me. The late elector [Ernst August* of Braunschweig-Lüneburg] and the king have always permitted me to take trips at my pleasure in order to do research. Having gone to the baths of Carlsbad at the end of autumn 1711, I was far enough along to go to Vienna, and judging that it was necessary to see the manuscripts of the emperor [Emperor Karl VI*] one more time before finishing, I went there, and I informed Mr. Bernstorff of my trip so that I could be given some order should the need arise. I arrived there towards the end of the year, and I employed the winter very well for the service of the king. And the last trip that I made to Vienna was very well employed for that purpose, for I have been greatly assisted by working on the manuscripts of the emperor | of which I have very great need before finishing my work |. I arrived there at the beginning of the winter. In the spring of the year 1712 my business was finished, and I wanted to leave. I wrote that to Mr. Bernstorff, who, having learned that I had a rather special access to this monarch, ordered me yet to stay in order to suggest something to the emperor | in an audience |, which I had the opportunity to execute pretty well. But thereupon the gout gripped me, and to make matters worse the roads were closed that summer on account of the plague that broke out, and Mr. Bernstorff himself informed me that I would do better not to come at that time. Therefore I remained

l'automne fut que je voulus achever un travail dont l'Empereur m'avoit chargé, et que j'avois eté bien aise d'accepter à cause de l'interest que la Maison d'Este qui est originairement la même avec celle de Bronsvic y peut prendre. Ce travail regardoit le droit de l'Empire sur la Toscane, que je monstray par des pieces incontestables qui manquoient à Vienne n'avoit eté donnée qu'aux males de la Maison de Medicis, et il paroist (entre nous, si j'ose parler ainsi à V.A. Royale) que cette province si l'on s'y prend bien apres leur extinction pourroit retourner à la Maison d'Este par concession de l'Empereur, maison dont les ancêtres (qui sont aussi ceux de la Maison de Bronsvic) l'ont possedée avant plusieurs siecles comme aussi nos Guelfes en particulier. Et cela paroist d'autant la plus raisonnable que la Maison d'Este puisqu'elle a si bien merité de l'Empire, et que la branche Italienne a eté la seule de toutes les puissances d'Italie qui ce soit declarée[3] dans la derniere guerre pour l'Empereur et en a terriblement souffert, et qu'avec cela elle est aussi si bien alliée maintenant avec la Maison d'Austriche par le mariage du Duc de Modene avec la soeur de l'imperatrice Amalie, fecond en males. Voilà ce qui m'a fait differer mon retour jusqà l'automne de l'an passé. Ainsi à toute rigueur on ne me pourroit contester que l'eté de cette année là, c'est à dire environ 3 mois de gages. Mais je crois que Sa Mté considerant ce que je viens de dire, bien loin de me retrancher quelque chose m'en saura gré; et y trouvera un nouveau motif de me faire de nouvelles graces. Or ayant maintenant fait partout une si grande emplette de Recherche, je travaille avec une assiduité, qui ne sera gueres limitee à finir l'ouvrage que j'en tire, et toutes les apparences sont que j'acheveray de fournir cette carriere l'annee qui vient, si Dieu m'accorde encor asses de vie et de santé pour cela comme j'ay sujet d'esperer. Je ne prendrois point la liberte d'entretenir V.A. Royale de ce detail, si Elle n'avoit la bonté de s'interesser pour moy auprés de Sa Mté, et s'il n'étoit necessaire par consequent de vous faire connoistre, Madame, toute la justice de ma cause. Apres ce <u>Factum</u>, je viens à la gracieuse lettre de V. A. R.

Je la remercie tres humblement des vers envoyés par Madame la Duchesse douairiere d'Orleans sur le triomphe de la grace combattue par les Jesuites. La Grace dans la bouche de ceux qui s'appellent disciples de S. Augustin, et que leur[s] adversaires appellent Jansenistes, est quelque chose d'un peu chimerique, revetu d'un beau nom. Ils s'imaginent, que lors que Dieu veut sauver quelcunes, il le fait par une maniere de miracle, et par l'influence d'une grace si efficace par elle même, que si le Ciel et la terre se liguoient à l'encontre leur opposition ne seroit rien: mais à quoy bon ce miraculeux effort, puisqu'il suffit que Dieu employe les voyes naturelles externes, de la naissance, de l'education, du temperament de l'instruction, et d'autres circonstances, jointes à une grace interieure suffisante; et pour quoy ne pourroit on point dire, que peut etre S. Augustin n'auroit point eté sauvé par la seule grace interne immediate que Dieu a mise dans son ame, si Ste Monique sa mere n'avoit point versé tant de larmes, s'il n'avoit point rencontré S. Abroise, etc. Il etoit decreté de la part de Dieu de sauver S. Augustin, mais il etoit decreté aussi de le

in Vienna that year of 1713, and a part of the year 1714, until the roads were opened. So I was only able to come in the spring of 1714. But beyond a little indisposition of the gout, the principal reason that prevented me from coming before the fall was that I wanted to complete a task with which the emperor had entrusted me, and which I had been very glad to accept because of the interest that the House of Este, which was originally of the same house as the House of Braunschweig, can take in it. This task concerned the right of the empire over Tuscany, which I showed by some incontestable documents, which were missing in Vienna, had been given only to the males of the House of Medici, and it appears (between us, if I dare speak in this manner to Your Royal Highness) that after their extinction this province could, if it were done correctly, be returned by concession of the emperor to the House of Este, a house whose ancestors (which are also those of the House of Braunschweig) possessed it many centuries before, including our Welfs in particular. And the House of Este seems all the more reasonable because it has so well deserved the recognition of the empire, and because the Italian branch [of the Welfs] was the only one of all the powers of Italy that declared itself[3] for the emperor in the last war, from which it suffered terribly, and because, on top of that, it is also now so well allied with the House of Austria through the marriage of the Duke of Modena with the sister of the [Dowager] Empress [Wilhelmine] Amalie,[4] a marriage teeming with males. That is what made me postpone my return until the autumn of last year. So strictly speaking, only the summer of that year, that is to say about 3 months of wages, could be disputed. But considering what I have just said, I believe that His Majesty, far from taking something from me, will be grateful to me for it, and he will find in it a new motive for doing me some new favours. Yet having now made everywhere such a large purchase of research, I am working with an assiduity that will scarcely be contained to finish the work that I am drawing from it, and in all probability I will complete it next year, if God still grants me enough life and health for that, as I have reason to hope. I would not take the liberty to speak with Your Royal Highness about these details if she did not have the kindness to involve herself for me with His Majesty, and if it were not therefore necessary to make you aware, madam, of the whole justice of my cause. After this *factum*, I come to the gracious letter of Your Royal Highness.

I thank her very humbly for the verses sent by Madame the Dowager Duchess of Orleans [Elisabeth Charlotte* of the Palatinate] concerning the triumph of grace combated by the Jesuits. Grace in the mouth of those who call themselves disciples of Saint Augustine, and whom their adversaries call Jansenists, is something a bit chimerical, dressed up with a pretty name. They imagine that when God desires to save some, he does it by a kind of miracle and by the influence of a grace so efficacious by itself that if heaven and earth conspired against it, their opposition would not matter. But what use is this miraculous effort, since it is suffices that God employs natural external means, of birth, of education, of temperament, of

sauver de cette maniere, et d'employer l'ordre des choses. J'ay touché ce point dans la Theodicée. La doctrine des Jesuites convient assés en cela avec la nôtre, ainsi ils pourroient avoir raison dans le fond, mais ils ne l'ont point dans leur procedé, en persecutant leur[s] adversaires.

Il est bon que l'invention de bruler un vaisseau de loin n'a point reussi. Il faudroit diminuer au lieu d'augmenter les manieres de nuire. J'aimerois mieux de voir reussi l'invention du Colonel Becker car elle donneroit un moyen de faire du bien, d'augmenter nos forces de recouvrer les tresors perdus. Il faudroit l'envoyer maintenant à Havane, puisqu'on dit que la Flotte d'argent de l'Amerique Espagnole a perdu par une tourmente plusieurs vaisseaux richement chargés.

Il semble que la lettre de V.A.R. dit que M. pope est pour le merite du bon homme Homere, j'en suis bien aise car nous penchons naturellement du coté des pauvres affligés. Le pauvre Homere est terriblement mal traité en France, et Mad. Dacier a grand besoin de secours. Il faudroit faire traduire au plus tot la preface de M. pope. En attendant je diray qu' Homere est venerable par son antiquité, et d'etre acharné à le poursuivre et à découvrir ses defauts, c'est imiter le denaturé Cham, qui s'attira la malediction de Noë son père. Je crois que la bon homme Noë ayant un peu bû de son vin nouveau, avoit fait des vers tout comme Homere, et que Cham son fils s'en moqua et en montra quelques petits defauts, comme La Motte, Terrasson et autres en montrent dans Homere, c'est cette nudite qu'il découvrit, et c'est ce qui le fit maudire. En effet Homere est le plus ancien auteur que nous ayons apres les Saints Ecrivains, et c'est pour cela qu'il importe de le dechiffrer.

C'est dommage que quelcun n'a pas mis en abregé et traduit les plaisantes pensés de Rudbeckius sur les champs Eliseens[12] en Suede. Elle est selon luy la patrie de tous les dieux de l'antiquité. V.A.R. a raison d'y chercher plus tot le sejour des ames damnées. Car il fait froid dans l'enfer, puisqu'il y aura 𝕳𝖊𝖚𝖑𝖊𝖓 𝖚𝖓𝖉 𝖅̈𝖆̈𝖍𝖓-𝖐𝖑𝖆𝖕𝖕𝖊𝖗𝖓. Mais les anciens ont planté le Royaume de pluton (comprenant tant les champs Elisiens que l'enfer,) au de là de la zone torride et de l'Equateur, vers le pole antarctique. Virgile le dit en termes expres.

Hic vertex nobis semper sublimis at illum
Sub pedibus Styx atra vides, manesque profundi[13]
𝖂𝖎𝖗 𝖘𝖊𝖍𝖊𝖓 𝖉𝖎𝖊𝖘𝖊𝖓 𝕻𝖔𝖑, 𝖉𝖊𝖗 𝖓𝖎𝖊𝖍𝖒𝖆𝖑𝖘 𝖚𝖓𝖙𝖊𝖗𝖌𝖊𝖍𝖊𝖙
𝕯𝖊𝖗 𝖆𝖓𝖉𝖊𝖗 𝖇𝖊𝖞 𝖉𝖊𝖒 𝕾𝖙𝖞𝖝 𝖚𝖓𝖉 𝕾𝖈𝖍𝖆𝖙𝖙𝖊𝖓-𝕷𝖊𝖚𝖙𝖊𝖓 𝖘𝖙𝖊𝖍𝖊𝖙

Je suis ravi que V.A.R. est si bien servie des dames Angloises, mais je ne m'en étonne pas, il faudroit qu'elles fussent aveugles ou stupides, pour ne point trouver le plus grand plaisir du monde dans le service d'une princesse environnée de tant de graces. Je n'ose rien adjouter de plus pour ne point choquer la modestie de V.A.R. Dieu veuille seulement qu'il n'y ait quelque monstre parmy tant d'honnêtes gens. Il est vray que V.A.R. peut apprivoiser jusqu'aux monstres.

J'apprends avec plaisir que V.A.R. approuve la Tragedie de M. Addison, dont j'estime et la personne et les ouvrages que j'ay vûs. Je n'ay point vû son Caton, non plus

85. LEIBNIZ TO CAROLINE OF BRANDENBURG-ANSBACH   309

instruction and other circumstances joined with a sufficient internal grace; and why could it not be said that perhaps Saint Augustine would not have been saved by the mere internal, immediate grace that God placed in his soul, if Saint Monique his mother had not shed so many tears, if he had not met Saint Ambrose, etc. God decreed that Saint Augustine be saved, but it was also decreed to save him in this way and by employing the order of things. I have touched on this point in the *Theodicy*. The doctrine of the Jesuits agrees well enough in that with ours, so they could be right all things considered, but they are not right in their conduct, in persecuting their adversaries.

It is good that the invention for burning a vessel from a distance did not succeed. The ways of doing harm need to be diminished rather than increased. I would rather see the invention of Colonel Becker succeed because it would provide a means of doing some good, by increasing our power to recover lost treasures.[5] It would now need to be sent to Havana, since it is said that the silver fleet from Spanish America has lost several richly loaded vessels in a storm.[6]

It seems that the letter of Your Royal Highness states that Mr. Pope is in favour of the merit of the good Homer. I am very pleased about that because we naturally incline toward the side of the poor afflicted. The poor Homer is terribly mistreated in France, and Madam Dacier[7] has great need of help. The preface of Mr. Pope needs to be translated as soon as possible. While waiting I will say that Homer is venerable on account of his antiquity, and to be relentless in persecuting him and discovering his faults is to imitate the perverted Ham, who brought upon himself the curse of his father Noah.[8] I believe that the good Noah, having drunk a bit of his new wine, had written some verses like Homer and that his son Ham made fun of them and pointed out some small faults in them, as La Motte,[9] Terrasson,[10] and others point some out in Homer. This is the nudity that he discovered, and it is what made him curse. Homer is in fact the most ancient author that we have after the sacred writers, and that is why it is important to decipher him.

It is a shame that no one has abridged and translated the pleasant thoughts of Rudbeck[11] about the Elysian Fields[12] in Sweden. According to him it is the homeland of all the gods of antiquity. Your Royal Highness is right to look there instead for the dwelling place of the souls of the damned. For it is cold in hell, since there will be wailing and chattering of teeth. But the ancients set the kingdom of Pluto (comprising both the Elysian Fields and hell) outside of the torrid zone and the equator, towards the Antarctic pole. Virgil says it explicitly.

This pole is always above us and the other
Under our feet sees black Styx and infernal shades[13]
We see this pole, which never sets
The other lies with the Styx and shadow-people

I am delighted that Your Royal Highness is so well served by the English ladies, but I am not surprised by it; they would have to be blind or stupid not to find the

que le Caton François. Je me souviens de l'endroit du Rapport du Committé secret que V.A.R. cite ou S. Jean le Laboureur dit que les françois sont | aussi mauvais poëtes aussi qu'ils sont mauvais politiques | des mauvais poëtes. Je crois qu'il a plaisanté sur le jugement que M. prior (grand poëte Anglois et le Latinist qui etois de la pleiade Angloise dont M. Stepney etoit aussi) avoit fait quelque fois des derniers poetes François. V.A.R. a grande raison d'estimer Corneille, Racine, Boileau, et on peut bien adjouter non seulement Moliere, mais Quinault même. Il faut avouer que ces excellens hommes ne sont plus, et qu'effectivement le siecle de Louis XIV a ete comme le siecle d'Auguste pour la france par rapport aux lettres, mais nullement par rapport à l'estat et aux peuples qu'il a rendu miserables par son ambition.

Graces à Dieu, et à la mort de ce Prince la rebellion d'Ecosse est un feu de paille. Peut etre que le pauvre pretendant a eté bien aise que le Duc d'orleans l'a renvoyé et qu'il a pû retourner avec honneur à Bar le Duc, ayant eté peutetre porté malgré luy par ses adherens à se remuer pour ne point passer pour faineant. J'applaudis à ma comparaison sans comparaison du chien de Bruxelles, puisqu'elle a plu à V.A.R. et qu'elle a eu la bonté pour moy de s'en servir pour faire rire le Roy. Bien des gens, qui ne le disent point sont jaloux de nostre nouvelle acquisition de Breme; mais il est bon d'etre envié. Comme je pretends d'estre prophète aussi bien que poète, j'ay predit cela il y [a] 36 ans ou environ dans des vers Latins faits sur la mort du Duc Jean Frideric, et sur la succession de Duc Ernest Auguste son frere: V.A.R. aura peut etre oui parler de certaines vieux vers Allemands sur Henri le Lion, qui le font dire

Von der Elbe bis am Rhein
Vom Harz bis an die See war mein

Il y a quelque chose à dire à cela. Mais dans mes vers je dis que sous les auspices de la maison de Bronsvic, l'Elbe et le Rhin joindront leur[s] bras pour le bien de l'Empire, et que la mer reconnoitra encore les montagnes du Harz. Voilà maintenant ces montagnes qui commandent les pays jusqu'à la mer. J'y adjoutois pourtant encore, que le Ciel prepraroit a la Maison quelque chose de plus grand mais que les divinités du destin me defendoient de le dire. Ne envies Vous pas Madame, que j'ay vû dés lors en esprit notre Roy assi[21] sur le Trone de la Grande Bretangne. J'adjoutes icy mes vers tous Latins qu'ils sont, par les quels je finis le poëme dont je viens de parler

Illius auspiciis conjunget brachia Rheno
Albis, et Hereynios agnoscent a'quora montes.
Et superi majora parant, sed talia Parcae
Noscere mortalem prohibent vel dicere Vatem.

Nostre manifeste sur la declaration de la guerre contre la suede, au nom du Roy comme Electeur, est digne de Sa Mté. Il dit en peu de mots les raisons essentielles et

greatest pleasure in the world in the service of a princess surrounded with so many charms. I dare add nothing more in order not to shock the modesty of Your Royal Highness. May God only grant that there not be some monster among so many honourable people. It is true that Your Royal Highness is able to tame even monsters.

I learn with pleasure that Your Royal Highness approves the tragedy of Mr. [Joseph] Addison*, of whom I esteem the person and the works that I have seen. I have not seen his Cato or the French Cato. I remember the place in the report of the secret committee that Your Royal Highness cites, where St John the Laborer[14] says that the French are | as bad poets as they are bad politicians | bad poets.[15] I believe that he was joking about the judgement that Mr. Prior[16] (great English poet and the Latinist who was a member of the English pleiad to which Mr. Stepney[17] also belonged) had sometimes made about the greatest French poets. Your Royal Highness is very right to esteem Corneille [Pierre Corneille (1606–84)], Racine [Jean Racine (1639–99)], Boileau [Nicolas Boileau-Despréaux (1636–1711)], and one can well add not only Molière,[18] but also Quinault [Philippe Quinault 1635–88]. It must be admitted that these excellent men are no longer and that the century of Louis XIV has actually been like the century of Augustus for France in relation to letters, but not at all in relation to the state and to the people, which he made miserable by his ambition.

Thanks be to God, and to the death of this prince,[19] the Scottish rebellion is a flash in the pan. Perhaps the poor Pretender [James Francis Edward Stuart*] has been very glad that the Duke of Orléans [Philippe I*, Duke or Orleans] sent him back and that he has been able to return with honour to Bar-le-Duc, having perhaps been inclined by his followers, despite himself, to move in order not to be taken for an idler. I applaud my comparison beyond compare with the dog of Brussels,[20] because it has pleased Your Royal Highness and because she has done me the kindness of using it to make the king laugh. Many people who don't admit it are jealous of our new acquisition of Bremen*; but it is good to be envied. As I claim to be a prophet as well as a poet, I predicted that about 36 years ago in some Latin verses written upon the death of Duke Johann Friedrich* and upon the succession of his brother Duke Ernst August*. Your Royal Highness has perhaps heard talk of certain old German verses about Henry the Lion that portray him as saying:

From the Elbe to the Rhine
From the Harz to the sea, it was mine

There is something to be said about that. But in my verses I say that under the auspices of the House of Braunschweig, the Elbe and the Rhine will join their arms for the good of the empire and that the sea will recognize the Harz Mountains. Now behold, these mountains that command the country as far as the sea. I added to it further, however, that Heaven would prepare something greater for the House but

312 85. LEIBNIZ TO CAROLINE OF BRANDENBURG-ANSBACH

on garde aux suedois quantité de choses qu'on pourroit dire contre leur conduite même à notre egard, et dont ils se pourront attirer le reproche s'ils attaquent ce Manifeste.

Puisque V.A.S. veut que ma Theodicée soit traduite en Anglois cela vaut fait. Et je croirois M. Clarc (s'il vouloit s'en charger, et s'il etoit assés maitre du François pour cela) assez honnête homme tout ami qu'il pourroit etre de mon adversaire, pour s'en aquitter comme il faut. Mais apparemment il n'y pensera pas, et M. l'Eveque de Lincoln (ce semble) ne l'y fera point penser sans un ordre exprés. Au besoin on ne manqueroit pas de gens qui s'en aquitteroient tres bien. J'ose dire qu'on en auroit un peu besoin en Angleterre. *La religion naturelle meme y degenère extremement. Plusieurs font les ames corporelles, et d'autres font Dieu luy meme corporel. M. Locke et ses sectateurs, doutent au moins si les ames ne sont materielles et naturellement perissables. M. Newton dit que l'espace est l'organe dont Dieu se sert pour sentir les choses. Mais s'il a besoin de quelque moyen pour las sentir, elles ne dependent donc point entierement de luy et ne sont point sa production. M. Newton et ses sectateurs ont encore une fort plaissante opinion de l'ouvrage de Dieu. Selon eux Dieu a besoin de remonter de temps en temps sa montre, autrement elle cesseroit d'agir. Il n'a pas eu assés de veue pour faire un mouvement perpetuel. Cette machine de Dieu est même si imparfaite qu'il est obligé de la decrasser de temps en temps par un concours extraordinaire et meme de la raccommoder, comme un horloger qui sera d'autant plus mauvais maitre, qu'il sera plus souvent obligé d'y retoucher et d'y corriger. Selon moy, la meme force et vigueur y subsiste tousjours, et passe seulement de matiere en matiere, suivant les loix de la nature, et le bel ordre preétabli. Et quand Dieu fait des miracles je tiens que ce n'est pas pour soutenir les besoins de la nature, mais pour ceux de la grace. Autrement ce seroit avoir une idée fort basse de la sagesse et de la puissance de Dieu.*[23]

Je le prie de conserver toute famille Royale, de la preserver de tout mal heur, et de nous rejouir bientost par V.A.R. d'une maniere que rendre notre contentement parfait. Et je suis avec devotion   Leibniz.[24]

that the divinities of fate forbade me from telling it. Do not be envious, madame, that from then on I saw in spirit our king seated[21] upon the throne of Great Britain. All Latin as they are, I add here the verses with which I end the poem of which I have just spoken.

Under its auspices the Elbe joins arms
With the Rhine, and the seas will recognize the Harz Mountains.
And the gods above prepare more, but such things The Fates
Prohibit a mortal to know or a prophet to tell.

Our manifesto on the declaration of war against Sweden, in the name of the king as elector, is worthy of His Majesty.[22] It states in a few words the essential reasons, and a lot of things are reserved for the Swedes that could be said against their conduct even toward us and for which they may draw reproach upon themselves if they attack this manifesto.

Since Your Royal Highness wants my *Theodicy* to be translated into English, that is as good as done. And I would deem Mr. Clarke* (if he wanted to be charged with it and if he had sufficient mastery of French for this) an honourable enough man, friend though he might be of my adversary, to acquit himself of it properly. But apparently he will not think about it, and the Bishop of Lincoln (it seems) will not make him think about it without an express order. If the need arises there would be no lack of men who would acquit themselves of it very well. I dare say that they would need a bit of it in England. *Natural religion itself declines precipitously there. Many make souls out to be corporeal, and others make God himself out to be corporeal. Mr. Locke* and his followers at least question whether or not souls are material and naturally perishable. Mr. Newton says that space is the organ which God uses to perceive things. But if he has need of some means of perceiving them, then they are not entirely dependent on him and were not produced by him. Mr. Newton and his followers also have a very strange view concerning the work of God. According to them God needs to wind up his watch from time to time, otherwise it would cease to operate. He has not had enough insight to make a perpetual motion. This machine of God is even so imperfect that he is forced to clean it from time to time by an extraordinary concourse, and even to repair it like a watchmaker who will be all the worse a master as he is more often forced to touch it up and make repairs to it. On my view, the same force and vigor always remains, and it only passes from matter to matter, following the laws of nature and the beautiful pre-established order. And when God works miracles, I maintain that it is not in order to support the needs of nature, but those of grace. Otherwise one would have a very base idea of the wisdom and power of God.*[23] I pray him to conserve the royal family, to preserve it from all evil, and to delight us soon through Your Royal Highness in a way that renders our satisfaction perfect. And I am with devotion, Leibniz.[24]

314   85. LEIBNIZ TO CAROLINE OF BRANDENBURG-ANSBACH

85. LEIBNIZ TO CAROLINE OF BRANDENBURG-ANSBACH   315

[1] Stadtarchiv Hannover 4.AS.01.1400. Draft: four folio sides in Leibniz's hand. Not previously published. Reply to Caroline's letter of 14 November 1715 (document 84). The letter is dated simply November 1715, but since it was a reply to Caroline's letter of 14 November, it was probably composed sometime during the last week of November.

[2] See Leibniz's letter to Görtz of 28 December 1714 (document 55, pp. 189, 191) and his letter to Bernstorff of 15 March 1715 (document 66, pp. 221, 223).

[3] Reading 'se soit déclarée' for 'ce soit declarée'.

[4] That is, Charlotte Felicitas of Braunschweig-Lüneburg (1671–1710), elder sister of the Dowager Empress Wilhelmine Amalie* of Braunschweig-Lüneburg.

[5] For Colonel Becker's invention for recovering treasure, see Caroline's letter to Leibniz of 13 September 1715 (document 78, p. 265 note 6).

[6] Leibniz is referring to the Spanish treasure fleet that had departed from Havana, Cuba on 24 July 1715. Seven days later, on 31 July 1715, all eleven ships of this fleet were lost in a hurricane near Cuba and present-day Florida.

[7] In 1711 Madame Anne le Fèvre Dacier (1647–1720) had published a French translation, with commentary, of Homer's *Iliad*. In his own translation and commentary, Pope acknowledged his use of Dacier's notes in the notes to his own version, which appeared in installments between 1715 and 1720.

[8] See Genesis 9:20–27.

[9] That is, Antoine Houdar de la Motte (1672–1731), a French writer and author of *Discours sur Homère* (1714).

[10] That is, Jean Terrasson (1670–1750), a French poet and author of *Dissertation critique sur l'Iliade de Homère* (1715).

[11] See Leibniz's letter to Caroline of 21 October 1715 (document 80, p. 283 note 7).

[12] Reading 'Elisiens' for 'Eliseens'.

[13] The verse is from Virgil's *Georgicon* I.242–3.

[14] That is, Henry Saint John*, Viscount Bolingbroke. Leibniz refers to him contemptuously as 'St John the Laborer' since after having been attainted for high treason and other high crimes and misdemeanors in September 1715, he had been stripped of his title in the peerage and demoted to the lowest social rank of common laborer, and so no longer had a right to the title 'Lord Bolingbroke'.

[15] In *A Report from the Committee of Secrecy, Appointed by Order of the House of Commons to Examine Several Books and Papers laid before the House, relating to the late Negotiations of Peace and Commerce, &c.*, there is quoted this line from a letter that Bolingbroke wrote to Matthew Prior: 'For God's sake, dear *Matt*, hide the Nakedness of thy Country, and give the best turn thy fertile Brain will furnish thee with, to the Blunders of thy Countrymen, who are not much better Politicians than the French are Poets' (Walpole 1715, p. 47). Here, in the deleted phrase, Leibniz began by mistakenly paraphrasing Bolingbroke as having said that the French were as bad poets as politicians, when in fact Bolingbroke was suggesting that his countrymen, the English, were about as bad as politicians as the French were as poets. Realizing his mistake, Leibniz struck the mistaken phrase and simply reported Bolingbroke as having said that the French were bad poets.

[16] That is, Matthew Prior (1664–1721), English poet, diplomat, and fellow of the Royal Society.

[17] That is, George Stepney (1663–1707), English poet, diplomat, fellow of the Royal Society, and sometime correspondent of Leibniz.

[18] Jean-Baptiste Poquelin (1622–73), French playwright and actor, used the stage name 'Molière'.

[19] Louis XIV had died on September 1, 1715.

[20] On this comparison, see Leibniz's letter to Johanne Sophie* Gräfin zu Schaumburg-Lippe, Countess of Bückeburg, of 21 October 1715 (document 81, p. 285) and Caroline's letter to Leibniz of 14 November 1715 (document 84, p. 299).

[21] Reading 'assis' for 'assi'.

[22] In his office as Elector of Hanover, King George I of Great Britain declared war on Sweden on 15 October 1715. He thereby joined a coalition against Sweden that included Denmark, Prussia, and Russia. George promised British naval support in the conflict with Sweden in exchange for a guaranteed return of Bremen* and Verden* to Hannover. Sweden had acquired the prince-bishoprics of Bremen and Verden in the Thirty Years' War, but they were reoccupied by Danish troops beginning in 1712. On the very day that George declared war on Sweden, Frederick IV, King of Denmark and Norway, handed Bremen and Verden over to the Elector of Hannover. See Hatton 1968, pp. 404–7 and Hatton 1978, pp. 184–8.

Leibniz's First Paper

Prémier Ecrit de Mr. LEIBNITZ.

Extract d'une Letter écrite au Mois
de *Novembre*, 1715.

1. *Il semble que la* Réligion Naturelle même *s'affoiblit[2] extremement. Plusieurs font
les* Ames *corporelles* ; *d'autres font* Dieu luy même *corporel*.

2. *M.* Locke, *& ses* Sectateurs, doutent au moins, *si les* Ames *ne sont* Materielles,
& naturellement perissables.

3. *M.* Newton *dit que l'*Espace *est* l'Organe, *dont Dieu se sert pour sentir les choses.
Mais s'il a besoin de quelque Moyen pour les sentir, elles ne dependent donc entierement de luy, & ne sont point sa production*.

4. *Monsieur* Newton, *& ses* Sectateurs, *ont encore une fort plaisante Opinion de
l'ouvrage de Dieu. Selon eux Dieu a besoin de* remonter *de temps en temps sa Montre :
Autrement elle cesseroit d'agir. Il n'a pas eu assez de veue, pour en faire un Mouvement
perpetuel. Cette Machine de Dieu est même si imparfaite selon eux, qu'il est obligé de
la* décrasser *de temps en temps par un concours extraordinaire, & même de la* raccommoder, *comme un* Horloger *son ouvrage[4] ; qui sera d'autant plus mauvais
Maistre, qu'il sera plus souvent obligé d'y retroucher & d'y corriger. Selon mon
Sentiment,[5] la* même Force *&* Vigueur *y subsiste toujours, & passe seulement de matiere en matiere, suivant les loix de la Nature, & le bel Ordre* préétabli. *Et je tiens,*

[23] This italicized passage (my italics) is the source of the excerpt that was eventually published by Clarke as Leibniz's first paper in the Leibniz-Clarke correspondence. The published excerpt differs in only minor ways from the passage that occurs in this letter (for the published excerpt, see document 86).

[24] The signature was added in pencil and is not in Leibniz's hand.

86. Leibniz's First Paper[1]

Mr. LEIBNITZ'S First *Paper.*

BEING

An Extract of a Letter Written in

November, 1715

1. *Natural Religion it self,* seems to decay[2] [*in England*] very much. Many will have Human *Souls* to be material : Others make *God himself* a corporeal Being.

2. Mr. *Locke*[3], and his Followers, are *uncertain* at least, whether the *Soul* be not *Material,* and naturally perishable.

3. Sir *Isaac Newton* says, that Space is an *Organ,* which God makes use of to perceive Things by. But if God stands in need of any *Organ* to perceive Things by, it will follow, that they do not depend altogether upon him, nor were produced by him.

4. Sir *Isaac Newton,* and his Followers, have also a very odd Opinion concerning the Work of God. According to their Doctrine, God Almighty *wind up* his Watch from Time to Time : Otherwise it would cease to move. He had not, it seems, sufficient Foresight to make it a perpetual Motion. Nay, the Machine of God's making, is so imperfect, according to these Gentlemen ; that he is obliged to *clean* it now and then by an extraordinary Concourse, and even to *mend* it, as a Clockmaker mends his Work ; Who must consequently be so much the more unskilful a Workman, as he is oftner obliged to mend his Work and to set it Right. According to *My* Opinion, the † *same* Force || and Vigour remains always in the World, and only passes from one part of Matter to another, agreeably to the Laws of Nature, and the beautiful

---

* *The Place Mr.* Leibnitz *here seems to allude to, is as follows.* Dum Cometae moventur in Orbibus valdè eccentricis, undiq ; & quoquoversum in omnes Cœli Parres ; utiq ; nullo modo fieri potuit, ut cæco fato tribuendum sit, quod Planatæ ub Irbubys cibcebtrucus nity cibsunuku ferantur eodem omnes ; exceptis nimirum irregularitatibus quibusdam vix notatu dignis, quæ ex mutuis Cometarum & Planetarum in se invicem actionibus oriri potuerint, quæq ; verisimile est fore ut longinquitate temporis majors usq ; evadant, donec hæcNaturæ Compages manum emendatricem tandem sit desideratura. *i. e. Whilst the Comets move in Orbs very eccentrical, with all variety of Directions towards every Part of the Heavens ; 'tis not possible it should have been caused by Blind Fate, that the Planets All move with one similar Direction in concentrick Orbs ; excepting only some very small irregularities, which may have arisen from the mutual Actions of the Planets and Comets one upon another ; and which 'tis probable will in length of time increase more and more, till the present System of Nature shall want to be anew put in Order by its Author.* Newtoni Optice, Quæst. ult. pag. 346.

† *See the* Note *on Dr.* Clarke's Fifth *Reply* §93–95.

|| *See* [. . .] *Mr.* Leibnitz's Fifth *Paper,* § 87, *and* 91.

87. LEIBNIZ TO BERNOULLI

quand Dieu fait des Miracles, que ce n'est pas pour soutenir les besoins de la Nature, mais pour ceux de la Grace.[6] En juger autrement,[7] ce seroit avoir une idée fort basse de la Sagesse & de la Puissance de Dieu.

Leibniz to Johann Bernoulli

Vir Nobilissime & Celeberrime
   Fautor Honoratissime

[...]

Dominus Abbas de Conti scripsit ad amicum Parisinum qui mihi significavit, Anglos longa recensione Commerii Epistolici in Transactionum aliqua suas contra me argutationes iterasse; atque inter alia etiam philosophiam meam impugnasse. De Analysi nostra dicunt, Newtonum originarium esse, nos tantum nomina adjecisse, eaque apta ad controversias in Mathesin introducendas. Philosophiam Newtoni esse mere experimentalem, meam conjecturalem. Sed ni fallor Harmonia præstabilita seu quale nos statuimus Commercium Animæ & Corporis res demonstrata est; demonstratum etiam ni fallor firmitatis seu nexus in corporibus originem non posse desumi nisi à motibus conspirantibus atomsque esse rem absurdam. At Newtonus minimè per sua experimenta demonstrat materiam ubique esse gravem, seu quamvis partem à quavis attrahi, aut vacuum dari, ut ipse quidem jactat. De Deo etiam miras fovet sententias, extensum esse, sensorium habere et vereor ne revera inclinet in sententiam Averrois et aliorum etiam Aristoteli tributam de Anima seu intellectu agente generali in corpore quovis pro ratione organorum operante. Illud etiam mihi planè absurdum videtur quod putat machinæ mundanæ motum ex se desiturum, nisi à Deo subinde rursus animaretur. Itaque miraculis opus habet, nec sine perpetuis miraculis suam attractionem explicare poterit.

87. LEIBNIZ TO BERNOULLI 319

pre-established Order. And I hold, that when God works Miracles, he does not do it in order to supply the Wants of Nature, but those of *Grace*. Whoever thinks otherwise, must needs have a very mean Notion of the Wisdom and Power of God.

[1] I here reproduce both the original French and the English translation of Leibniz's first paper that were published in Clarke's 1717 edition of the correspondence (Clarke 1717, pp. 3–7). This paper is actually an extract (with but minor differences) from a letter that Leibniz wrote to Caroline at the end of November 1715 (see document 85). There is a draft of the extract in Leibniz's hand that is entitled 'Extrait d'une letter écrite au mois de Novembre 1715' (LBr. 160 Bl. 2r–2v), as well as a copy of that draft in a secretary's hand (LBr. 160 Bl. 3r–3v). For Clarke's response, see document 90 below. The footnotes are Clarke's; the endnotes are mine. Square brackets in the text and what they contain are Clarke's.

[2] The original draft letter has 'degenère' instead of 's'affoiblit' (see document 85, p. 312).

[3] That is, John Locke*.

[4] 'son ouvrage' is not found in the original draft letter (see document 85, ibid.).

[5] The original draft letter has 'Selon moy' instead of 'Selon mon Sentiment' (see ibid.).

[6] The original draft letter has 'Et quand Dieu fait des miracles je tiens que ce n'est pas pour soutenir les besoins de la nature, mais pour ceux de la grace' instead of 'Et je tiens, quand Dieu fait des Miracles, que ce n'est pas pour soutenir les besoins de la Nature, mais pour ceux de la Grace' (see ibid.).

[7] The original draft letter has 'Autrement' instead of 'En juger autrement' (see ibid.).

87. Leibniz to Johann Bernoulli* (excerpt)[1]

Most Noble and Celebrated Sir
    Most Honourable Patron

[December 1715]

[...]

The Abbé [Antonio Schinella] Conti* has written to a Parisian friend [Nicolas Rémond*] who informed me that the English have renewed their quibbling against me with a long review of the *Commercium Epistolicum** in some one or another of the [*Philosophical*] *Transactions*;[2] and among other things, it has even attacked my philosophy. Concerning our analysis, they say that Newton was the originator, that we have merely added names, and that these were adapted for introducing controversies into mathematics; that the philosophy of Newton is purely experimental, while mine is conjectural. But unless I am mistaken, the pre-established harmony, or, as we hold, the correspondence of the soul and the body, is a demonstrated fact; and unless I am mistaken, it is also demonstrated that the source of the firmness or cohesion in bodies can only be derived from conspiring motions and that atoms are an absurdity. But Newton does not at all demonstrate by his experiments that matter is everywhere heavy, or that any part you please is attracted by any other part you please, or that there is a vacuum, as he himself in fact boasts. He also supports astonishing opinions about God, that he is extended, that he has a sensorium, and I fear in truth that he inclines to the opinion of Averroes and others, which is attributed even to Aristotle, concerning a soul or intellect acting universally on body in any place whatever, just as the operative principle of an organ. It also seems simply absurd to me that he assumes that the motion of the world-machine is going to cease of itself unless it is revived from time to time by God. Thus he has recourse to miracles, and he cannot explain his attraction without perpetual miracles.

Dm. Abbas Contius Parisiis discedens Epistolam ad me reliquit, quæ mihi nunc reddita est. Ipsi jam respondeo, et ut pulsum Anglorum Analystarum nonnihil tentemus rogo ut quasi suo proprio motu, aut amici rogatu problema hoc illis proponat. Invenire lineam BCD quæ ad angulos rectos secet omnes curvas determinati ordinis ejusdem generis; exempli causa omnes Hyperbolas ejusdem verticis et ejusdem centri AB, AC, AD, etc idque via generali. Ita videbimus quousque suis fluxionibus[5] profecerint.

[...]

Decembre 1715   deditissimus
                                                          G. G. Leibnitius

Leibniz to Nicolas Rémond (excerpt)

Hanover ce 6 de decembre 1715   A Monsieur Remond
                                                                à Paris

Monsieur

Comme je vous ay ecrit depuis peu par M. Hulin, compagnon de voyage du jeune M. pequet, cette lettre sera courte, mais l'inclose en recompense est assés longue et même double. Elle est écrite autant pour vous, Monsieur, que pour M. l'Abbé Conti, car vous m'avés temoigné de le desirer. [...]

Je suis pas faché que M. d'Abbé Conti se soit Anglisé un peu et pour un temps (pourveu qu'il soit le même pour ses amis); il reviendra à nous par rapport aux sentimens quand le charme des impressions presentes sera passé. En attendant, pendant qu'il donne dans le sens de ces Messieurs, il en profitera mieux. Cependant je luy envoye un petit preservatif à fin que la contagion n'opere trop fortement sur luy.

Et je suis avec zele

Monsieur   votre tres humble &
                                                 tres obeissant serviteur
                                                           Leibniz

When he departed from Paris the Abbé Conti left a letter for me,[3] which has now been delivered to me. I am replying to it now,[4] and in order that we may take in some measure the pulse of the English analysts, I am asking that he propose this problem to them, as if by his own initiative or at the request of a friend. To find the line BCD that cuts at right angles all the curves of a determinate order [and] of the same kind—for example, all hyperbolas AB, AC, AD, etc. with the same vertex and centre—and that by a general method. Thus shall we see how far they will have advanced with their fluxions.[5]

[...]

December 1715

most devoted
G. W. Leibniz

[1] Universitätsbibliothek Basel L I a 19 Bl. 320–1. 2.2 quarto sides in Leibniz's hand. Previously published in GM III-2 951–3; NC VI 260–2 (excerpt with English translation); Schüller 1991, pp. 221–2 (excerpt in German translation).

[2] That is, the *Philosophical Transactions* of the Royal Society of London.

[3] See Conti's letter to Leibniz of April 1715 (document 79c).

[4] For Leibniz's reply, see his letter to Conti of 6 December 1715 (document 88b).

[5] Newton's expression, corresponding to the derivative of a continuous function.

88a. Leibniz to Nicolas Rémond* (excerpt)[1]

Hanover 6 December 1715

To Mr. Rémond
in Paris

Sir

Since I have recently written to you by way of Mr. Hulin, travelling companion of the young Mr. Pequet, this letter will be short, but the enclosure,[2] in compensation, is rather long and even double. It is written as much for you, sir, as for l'Abbé [Antonio Schinella] Conti*, because you have expressed a desire for it. [...]

I am not displeased that Abbé Conti has become anglicized a bit and for a while (provided that he is the same for his friends). His sentiments will revert to us when the charm of present impressions wears off. In the meantime, while he falls into the opinion of these gentleman, he will benefit from them better. However, I have sent him a little antidote,[3] so that the infection does not affect him too strongly.

And I am enthusiastically,

sir,

your very humble and
very obedient servant
Leibniz

[1] LBr. 768 Bl. 49r–49v. Draft: 2 quarto sides in Leibniz's hand. Previously published in GP III 660–2.

[2] The enclosure is a letter addressed to Conti (see document 88b).

[3] The 'antidote' that Leibniz sent to Conti was a letter bearing the same date as the present letter to Rémond (see Leibniz's letter to Conti of 6 December 1715 (document 88b)).

Leibniz to Antonio Schinella Conti* (excerpt)

Hanover 6 Decembre 1715
A Monsieur
L'Abbé Conti
Noble Venitien
à Londres

On m'a dit tant de bien, Monsieur, de vostre penetration, et de vos nobles desseins pour la recherche de la verité, que l'honneur de votre lettre ne m'a pû etre que tres agreable; et je souhaiterois de vous y pouvoir aider. Monsieur Negrisoli doit etre homme de merite et de reputation, puisque vous avés pris la peine d'entrer en dispute avec luy. La lumiere seminale est un beau mot; mais dont on ne connoist point le sens. Je m'imagine que ces Messiers qui s'en servent, l'entendent dans un sens metaphorique. Que la lumiere leur signifie quelque matiere subtile douée de grandes perfections, comme la luimere paroist le plus parfait fluide qui nous soit connu. Ils logeront dans un corps si parfait un artifice assez grand pour former les animaux, mais cela n'explique rien, il faut qu'une matiere capable d'organiser soit organisée elle meme, mais un fluide tel que la lumiere ne dit pas cela. La lumiere prise dans ce sens metaphorique, dont je viens de parler conviendroit assez avec l'esprit de M. Newton. […]

Je suis avec zele
Monsieur
P. S.

Voilà, Monsieur, la lettre dont vous pourrés faire usage si vous jugés apropos. Je viens maintenant a ce qui nous regarde. Je suis ravi que vous estes en Angleterre, il y a de quoy profiter. Et il faut avouer qu'il y a là de tres habiles gens. Mais ils voudroient passer pour etre presque seuls inventeurs: et c'est en quoy apparemment ils ne reussiront pas. Il ne paroist point que M. Newton ait eu avant moy la caracteristique et l'Algorithme infinitesimal, suivant ce que M. Bernoulli a tres bien jugé, quoyqu'il luy auroit eté fort aisé d'y parvenir s'il s'en fut avisé. Comme il auroit esté fort aisé à Apollonius de parvenir à l'Analyse de Descartes sur les Courbes, s'il s'en etoit avisé. Ceux qui ont ecrit contre moy n'ayant pas fait difficulté d'attaquer ma candeur par des interpretations forcées et mal fondées; il[s] n'auront point le plaisir de me voir répondre à de petites raisons de gens qui en usent si mal, et qui d'ailleurs s'ecartent du fait. Il s'agit du Calcul des differences, et ils se jettent sur les Series, ou M. Newton m'a precedé sans difficulté; mais je trouvay enfin une Methode generale pour les Series, et après cela je n'avois plus besoin de recourir à ses extractions. Ils auroient mieux fait de donner les Lettres entieres comme M. Wallis a fait avec mon consentement, et il n'a pas eu la moindre dispute avec moy, comme ces gens là voudroient persuader au public. Mes adversaires n'ont publié du Commercium

88b. Leibniz to Antonio Schinella Conti* (excerpt)[1]

Hanover 6 December 1715

To Abbé Conti
Noble Venetian
London

I have been told so many good things, sir, about your penetration and your lofty plans for the search for truth that the honour of your letter could only be very pleasing to me, and I would hope to be able to help you in it. Mr. Nigrisoli[2] must be a man of merit and reputation, since you have taken the trouble to enter into dispute with him. The *seminal light* is a nice word, but its meaning is not known. I imagine that these gentlemen who make use of it understand it in a metaphorical sense, that light signifies for them some subtle matter endowed with great perfections, since light appears to be the most perfect fluid that is known to us. They place in so perfect a body a contrivance great enough to form animals, but that explains nothing. Matter capable of organizing must itself be organized, but a fluid such as light is not like that. Light taken in this metaphorical sense, of which I have just spoken, would be quite in accord with the spirit of Mr. Newton.[3] [...]
I am enthusiastically
  sir
  P. S.
There, sir, is the letter of which you can make use if you think it appropriate. I come now to what concerns us. I am glad that you are in England; there is something to gain. And it must be admitted that there are very able people there. But they would like to be considered almost sole inventers,[4] and in this they will obviously not succeed. It does not appear that Mr. Newton had the characteristic and the infinitesimal algorithm before me, following what Mr. [Johann] Bernoulli* has determined very well, although it would have been very easy for him to arrive at them if he had been informed of them, just as it would have been very easy for Apollonius to arrive at Descartes's analysis of curves if he had become aware of it. Since they have not scrupled to attack my candor by forced and ill-founded interpretations, those who have written against me will not have the pleasure to see me respond to any trifling arguments of people who use them so badly and who also stray from the facts. It is a matter of the calculus of differences, and they pounce on series, where Mr. Newton has preceded me without difficulty; but I found at last a general method for series, and after that I no longer needed to have recourse to his extractions. They would have done better to supply the complete letters, as Mr. [John] Wallis* did with my consent, and he has not had the slightest dispute with me, as these gentlemen would like to persuade the public. My adversaries have published from the *Commercium Epistolicum** of Mr. [John] Collins* only what

Epistolicum de M. Collins que ce qu'ils ont crû capable de recevoir leur mauvaises interpretations. Je fis connoissance avec M. Collins dans mon second voyage d'Angleterre, car au premier (qui dura tres peu, parceque j'estois venu avec un ministre public) je n'avois pas encore la moindre connoissance de la Geometrie avancée, et n'avois rien vû ny entendu du commerce de M. Collins avec Mss. Gregory et Newton, comme mes lettres exchangées avec M. Oldenbourg en ce temps là, et quelque temps après, feront assez voir. Ce n'est qu'en France que j'y suis entré, et M. Hugens m'en donna l'entrée. Mais à mon second voyage M. Collins me fit voir une partie de son Commerce et j'y remarquay que M. Newton avoua aussi son ignorance sur plusieurs choses, et dit entre autres qu'il n'avoit rien trouvé sur la dimension des Curvilignes clebres que la dimension de la Cissoide. Mais on a supprimé tout cela. Je suis faché qu'un aussi habile homme que M. Newton s'est attiré la censure des personnes intelligentes, en deferant trop aux suggestions de quelques flatteurs qui l'ont voulu brouiller avec moy. [[La Societé Royale ne m'a point fait connoitre qu'elle vouloit examiner l'affaire; ainsi je n'ay point eté oui, et si l'on m'avoit fait savoir les noms de ceux qu'on avoit nommés comme Commissaires j'aurois pû m'expliquer, si je recusois quelques uns, et si j'en desirois. C[']est pourquoy les formalités essentielles n'ayant point eté observées la Societé a declaré qu'elle ne pretend point d'avoir jugé definitvement entre M. Newton et moy.]][5]

Sa Philosophie me paroist un peu etrange, et je ne crois pas qu'elle puisse s'establir. Si tout corps est grave, il faut necessairement, quoyque disent ses defenseurs, et quelque emportement qu'ils temoignent, que la gravité soit une qualité occulte Scholastique, ou l'effect d'un miracle. J'ay fait voir autres fois à M. Bayle que tout ce qui n'est pas explicable par la nature des creatures est miraculeux. Il ne suffit pas de dire, Dieu a fait une telle loy de nature, donc la chose est naturelle. Il faut que la loy soit executable par les natures des creatures. Si Dieu donnoit cette loy par exemple à un corps libre, de tourner à l'entour d'un certain centre, il faudroit ou qu'il y joignit d'autres corps qui par leur impulsion l'obligeassent de rester tousjours dans son orbite circulaire, ou qu'il mit un ange a ses trousses; ou enfin il faudroit qu'il y concourut extraordinairement. Car le mobile[6] s'ecartera naturellement par la Tangente. Dieu agit continuellement sur les Creatures par la conservation de leurs natures, et cette conservation est une production continuelle de ce qui est perfection en elles. Il est <u>intelligentia supramundana</u>, parce qu'il n'est pas Ame du Monde, et n'a pas besoin de <u>sensorium</u>.

Je ne trouve pas le vuide demonstré par les raisons de M. Newton ou de ses sectateurs, non plus que la pretendue gravité universelle, ou que les Atomes. On ne peut donner dans le vuide et dans les Atomes, que par des vues trop bornées. M. Clark | (dans un livre que Mad. S. A. R. Mad la princesse de Galles m'a fait l'honneur de m'envoyer dernierement avec d'autres) | dispute contre le sentiment des Cartesiens qui croyent que Dieu ne sauroit destruire une partie de la matiere pour faire un vuide, mais je m'etonne qu'il ne voit point que si l'Espace est une substance differente de Dieu, la meme difficulté s'y trouve. Or de dire que Dieu est l'Espace, c'est luy

they have thought capable of accommodating their flawed interpretations. I made the acquaintance of Mr. Collins on my second trip to England, for on the first (which did not last long because I had come with a public minister) I did not yet have the slightest acquaintance with advanced geometry and had seen nothing nor heard of the correspondence of Mr. Collins with Messrs. [James] Gregory* and Newton, as the letters I exchanged with Mr. [Henry] Oldenburg* at that time, and some time later, will suffice to show. It was only in France that I entered into it, and Mr.[Christiaan] Huygens* introduced me to it. But on my second trip Mr. Collins showed me a part of his correspondence, and I noted that Mr. Newton had there also admitted his ignorance of many things, and he said among other things that he had discovered nothing about the dimension of notable curvilineals except the dimension of the cissoid. But they have omitted all that. I am sorry that such an able man as Mr. Newton has drawn the censure of intelligent persons by deferring too much to the suggestions of certain toadies who have wanted to set him at odds with me. [[The Royal Society did not inform me that it wanted to examine the matter; so I have not been heard, and if they had made known to me the names of those that have been appointed as commissioners, I would have been able to explain myself, if I objected to some, and if I desired some. This is why, the essential formalities not having been observed, the Society has declared that it does not claim to have judged definitively between Mr. Newton and me.]][5]

His philosophy appears a bit strange to me, and I do not believe it can be established. If every body is heavy, gravity must be an occult Scholastic quality or the effect of a miracle, whatever his defenders may say and whatever anger they may exhibit. I have previously shown Mr. [Pierre] Bayle* that everything that is not explicable by the nature of creatures is miraculous. It is does not suffice to say that God has made a certain law of nature, therefore the thing is natural. The law must be capable of being carried out by the natures of creatures. For example, if God gave this law to a free body, to turn around a certain centre, he would either have to join to it some other bodies that constrained it to remain in its circular orbit by their impulse, or place an angel at its heels, or, finally, concur in it extraordinarily. For the moving body[6] naturally moves off along the tangent. God acts continually upon creatures by the conservation of their natures, and this conservation is a continual production of the perfection in them. He is *intelligentia supramundana* because he is not the soul of the world and has no need of a *sensorium*.

I do not find the void demonstrated by the arguments of Mr. Newton or his followers, any more than the alleged universal gravity or atoms. It is possible to fall into the void and atoms only through very limited views. Mr. [Samuel] Clarke* | (in a book that Her Royal Highness Madame the Princess of Wales [Caroline* of Brandenburg-Ansbach] did me the honour of recently sending me along with some others) | disputes the view of the Cartesians who believe that God could not destroy a part of matter to make a void, but I am astonished that he does not see that if space is a substance different from God, the same difficulty arises. Now to say

donner des parties. L'Espace est quelque chose, mais comme le temps, l'un et l'autre est un ordre general des choses: l'espace est l'ordre des coexistences, et le temps est l'ordre des existences successives: Ce sont des choses veritables mais ideales, comme les Nombres.

La matiere même n'est pas une substance mais seulement Substantiatum, un Phenomene bien fondé et qui ne trompe point quand on y procede en raisonnant suivant les loix ideales de l'Arithmetique, de la Geometrie et de la Dynamique etc. Tout ce que j'avance en cela paroist demontré. Apropos de la Dynamique ou de la doctrine des forces, je m'etonne que M. Newton et ses sectateurs croyent que Dieu a si mal fait sa machine, que s'il n'y mettoit la main extraordinairement la montre cesseroit bien tôt d'aller. C'est avoir des idées bien étroites de la sagesse et de la puissance de Dieu.

J'appelle extraordinarie toute operation de Dieu, qui demande autre chose que la conservation des natures des creatures. Ainsi quoyque je croye la Metaphysique de ces Messierus là a narrow one et leur Mathematique asses arrivable [[c'est-à-dire, commune ou superficielle]][7] je ne laisse pas d'estimer extremement les meditations ϕysico-mathematiques de M. Newton, et vous obligeriés infiniment le public, Monsieur, si vous portiés cet habile homme à nous donner jusqu'à ses conjectures en physique. J'approuve fort sa methode de tirer des phenomenes ce qu'on en peut tirer sans rien supposer quand même ce ne seroit quelques fois que de tirer des consequences conjecturales. Cependant quand les data ne suffisent point il est permis (comme on fait quelques fois en déchifrant) d'imaginer des hypotheses, et si elles sont heureuses on s'y tient provisionnellement en attendant que des nouvelles experiences nous apportent nova data et ce que Bacon appelle Experimenta Crucis pour choisir entre les hypotheses. Comme j'apprends que certains Anglois ont mal representé ma philosophie dans leur[s] Transactions, je ne doute point qu'avec ce que je vous mande icy, Monsieur, je ne puisse estre justifié. Je suis fort pour la Philosophie experimentale, mais M. Newton s'en ecarte fort quand il pretend que toute la matiere est pesante (ou que chaque partie de la matiere en attire chaque autre partie) ce que les Experiences ne prouvent nullement, comme M. Hugens a deja fort bien jugé. La matiere gravifique ne sauroit avoir elle meme cette pesanteur dont elle est la cause. Et M. Newton n'apporte aucune experience ny raison suffisante pour le vuide et les Atomes ou pour l'attraction mutuelle generale. Et parcequ'on ne sait pas encor parfaitement et en detail comment se produit la gravité ou la force elastique, ou la magnetique etc. on n'a pas raison pour cela d'en faire des qualités occultes Scholastiques ou des miracles; mais on a encore moins raison de donner des bornes à la sagesse et à la puissance de Dieu, et de luy attribuer un sensorium et choses semblables. Au rest, je m'etonne que les sectateurs de M. Newton ne donnent rien qui marque que leur maistre leur a communiqué une bonne methode. J'ay eté plus heureux en disciples. C'est dommage que M. le Chevalier Wren de qui M. Newton et beaucoup d'autres ont appris quand il etoit jeune, n'a pas continué de

that God is space is to endow him with parts. Space is something, but like time. Each is a general order of things: space is the order of coexisting things and time is the order of successively existing things. These are true but ideal things, like numbers.

Matter itself is not a substance, but only *substantiated*, a well-founded phenomenon that does not deceive when one proceeds to reason about it following the ideal laws of arithmetic, geometry, and dynamics, etc. Everything I am advancing here appears demonstrated. Concerning dynamics, or the doctrine of forces, I am astonished that Mr. Newton and his followers believe that God has constructed his machine so poorly that if he did not act on it extraordinarily, the watch would soon cease to run. This is to have very narrow ideas about the wisdom and power of God.

I call 'extraordinary' every operation of God that requires something other than the conservation of the natures of creatures. So although I believe that the metaphysics of those gentlemen there is *a narrow one* and that their mathematics is quite *arrivable* [[that is to say, *common or superficial*]],[7] I do not cease to esteem highly the physico-mathematical reflections of Mr. Newton, and you would immensely gratify the public, sir, if you persuaded this able man to give us his latest conjectures in physics. I strongly approve his method of inferring from the phenomena what can be inferred from them without supposing anything, even if this would sometimes be only to infer some conjectural consequences. However, when the *data* are not sufficient, it is permitted (as is done in deciphering) to suppose some hypotheses; and if they are successful, they are held provisionally while awaiting new experiments, bringing us *new data* and what [Francis] Bacon* calls *experimenta crucis* for choosing between the hypotheses. As I hear that certain Englishmen have misrepresented my philosophy in their *Transactions*,[8] I do not doubt, sir, that I will be vindicated by what I am writing you here. I am strongly in favour of the experimental philosophy, but Mr. Newton strays from it very much when he claims that all matter is heavy (or that every part of matter attracts every other part), which experiments do not at all prove, as Mr. Huygens has already very well determined. Gravitational matter could not itself have this heaviness of which it is the cause, and Mr. Newton does not provide any experiment or sufficient reason for the void and atoms, or for mutual universal gravitation. And because it is not yet perfectly known and in detail how gravity or elastic or magnetic force etc. is produced, there is no reason on that account to make them Scholastic occult qualities or miracles. But there is even less reason to set limits to the wisdom and power of God and to attribute to him a *sensorium* and other similar things. Furthermore, I am astonished that Mr. Newton's followers produce nothing that indicates that their master has taught them a good method. I have been more fortunate in respect of disciples. It is a shame that Chevalier [Christopher] Wren*, from whom Mr. Newton and many others learned when he was young, has not continued to regale the public. I believe that he is still living. It would be good to make his acquaintance.

regaler le public. Je crois qu'il est encor en vie. Il seroit bon de faire connoissance avec luy. Dans le temps qu'il estoit jeune, on se seroit moqué en Angleterre de la nouvelle philosophie de quelques Anglois, et on l'auroit renvoyée à l'école.[9] Luy et M. Flamstead avec M. Newton sont presque le seul reste du siecle d'or d'Angleterre par rapport aux sciences. M. Whiston étoit en bon train. Mais un certain zele étrange l'a jetté d'un autre coté. Je plains le public de cette perte. Depuis quelque temps on s'y est trop jetté dans les <u>ghiribizzi</u> <u>politici</u>, ou dans les controverses Ecclesiastiques. Il y a un François en Angleterre, nommé M. Moyvre, dont j'estime les connoissances Mathematiques. Il y a sans doute d'autre habiles gens, mais qui ne font point de bruit, dont vous saures sans doute des nouvelles, Monsieur, et vous m'obligerés de m'en apprendre. Je serois bien aise d'apprendre comment on tire le ϕosϕore de toute sorte de corps; par exemple du miel, du seigle.

Vous avés raison, Monsieur, pour expliquer la nature du Beau, de joindre aux proportions la douceur ou la suavité, c'est à dire des raisons ϕysiques ou sensibles aux raisons mechaniques ou intelligibles. Cependent il est vray que les raisons physiques sont tousjours occultement Mechaniques, comme la Musique fait connoistre dans la quelle la suavité depend des proportions cachées aux sens, et découvertes par la raison. La nature en cachant aux ames les dernieres raisons, et en leur presentant des perceptions confuses, crée autant de nouveaux etres en apparence ou de nouvelles qualités, lesquelles comme disoit Democrite, subsistent <u>νόμῳ</u> animi, <u>non re</u>, mais qui sont un merveilleux ornement au monde. Ainsi vous avés excellement bien remarqué, Monsieur, que chez les Cartesiens il y a un vuide de formes ou de qualités, et que par les ames sans nombre et leur[s] differentes veues la nature a trouvé moyen de multiplier infiniment les qualités ou les resultats des raisons simples, c'est à dire les ornemens.[12]

When he was young, they would have scoffed in England at the new philosophy of some Englishmen, and they would have referred it to the school.[9] He and Mr. [John] Flamsteed*, along with Mr. Newton, are nearly the only ones remaining from the golden century of English science. Mr. Whiston was well on the way, but a certain strange enthusiasm has thrown him in another direction.[10] I pity the public for this loss. For some time there they have been thrown too much into political whims or ecclesiastical controversies. There is a Frenchman in England named Mr. Moivre,[11] whose knowledge of mathematics I admire. There are doubtless other able people, who do not make any noise, about which you doubtless know some news, sir, and you will gratify me by informing me about them. I would be very glad to learn how phosphorus is drawn from all sorts of bodies, for example, from honey, from rye.

You are right, sir, to explain the nature of beauty by adding sweetness or charm to proportions, that is to say, physical reasons, or sensibles, to mechanical reasons, or intelligibles. However it is true that physical reasons are always occultly mechanical, as is shown by music, in which charm depends on proportions hidden to the senses and discovered by reason. By hiding the ultimate reasons in minds, and by presenting them with confused perceptions of them, nature creates so many new beings in appearance or new qualities that, as Democritus said, exist *by the convention of minds, not in things,* but which are a wonderful embellishment to the world. Thus you have excellently well remarked, sir, that among the Cartesians there is a vacuum of forms or qualities and that from innumerable minds and their different views, nature has found a way to multiply infinitely the qualities or the effects of simple grounds, that is to say, ornaments.[12]

[1] LBr. 173 Bl. 5r–6v. Draft: four folio sides in Leibniz's hand. Previously published in Raphson 1715, pp. 97–9 (only an excerpt from the postscript); Des Maizeaux 1720, vol. 2, pp. 3–11 (only an excerpt from the postscript); GB 262–7; NC VI 250–5 (excerpt); HGA 184–6 (English translation of part of the postscript). This is Leibniz's reply to Conti's letter of April 1715 (see document 79c). For Newton's replies, see documents 101a–g. For Conti's reply, see his letter to Leibniz of 26 March 1716 (document 104).

[2] See note 2 to Conti's letter to Leibniz of April 1715 (document 79c, pp. 275, 277).

[3] That is, 'the very subtle spirit pervading gross bodies and lying hidden in them' that Newton mentions at the end of the General Scholium that was added to the 1713 edition of the *Principia* (see Newton 1999, pp. 943–4).

[4] That is, sole inventors of the infinitesimal calculus.

[5] The material I have placed within double square brackets does not appear in the version published in Des Maizeaux 1720, vol. 2 (see p. 5), nor in the version published in Raphson 1715 (see p. 98).

[6] The version published in Des Maizeaux 1720, vol. 2 (see p. 6) has 'il' instead of 'le mobile'.

[7] The words I have placed within double brackets are not found in the draft, but in the version published in Des Maizeau 1720 (see vol. 2, p. 8).

[8] That is, the *Philosophical Transactions* of the Royal Society of London.

[9] That is, the Scholastic philosophy. The version published in Des Maizeaux 1720, vol. 2 (see p.10) omits 'et on l'auroit renvoyée à l'école'.

[10] William Whiston (1667–1752) was an English theologian, historian, and mathematician, who, with the support of Newton, succeeded the latter to the Lucasian Chair of Mathematics at the University of Cambridge. But shortly after assuming that chair, he began publicly criticizing the Athanasian

Leibniz to Nicolas Rémond

A Monsieur Remond
Monsieur

Vous aurés receu mon [Traite]² latin de l'origene des François par M. Hullin et par la poste mes remarques sur le refutateur du P. de Malebranche, et enfin ma depeche tres ample à M. l'Abbé Conti, que je vous ay envoyée par le dernier courrier. Je trouve quelque chose que je vous supplie, d'y adjouter en la luy envoyant. (1) J'ay oblié de nommer deux habiles hommes que je crois être à Londres, et qui meritent d'etre connus et sont deux de mes amis: Monsieur Sloane, qui a un excellent Cabinet, et a exercé long temps la fonction de Secreté de la Societé Royale; et M. Woodward qui a fait de tres belles recherches sur les changements du globe de la terre. Peut etre que M. l'Abbé Conti a deja fait connoissance avec eux. (2) Madame la princesse de Galles me marque qu'elle seroit bien aise, que Ma Theodicée fut traduite en Anglois.⁴ Mais ceux à qui elle en a parlé y font naitre de la difficulté, et ont renvoyé la chose à des gens partiaux pour M. Newton. Il y en a sans doute assés d'autres capables d'une telle traduction: Je ne say si M. de la Roche François, qui a écrit autres fois des memoires de literature en Anglois, et qui a inseré une Recension de la Theodicée,⁵ écrit assés bien l'Anglois (au jugement des connoisseurs,) pour recourir à luy. En ce cas je crois qu'il seroit homme à s'en charger. Si non, je m'imagine qu'on en trouveroit assés d'autres. L'habile M. Wotton qui a ecrit autres fois en Anglois elegamment et savamment avec moderation sur les anciens et les modernes, et sur les progres de sciences, en seroit bien capable, si on l'y pouvoit porter. Car je say qu'il ne meprise pas mes sentimens. Mais enfin si quelques uns savoient qu'ils feroient plaisir à son Altesse Royale en faisant cette Traduction, je crois qu'ils seroient ravis de l'entreprendre. (3) Si M. l'Abbé Conti n'est pas encore connu de Mad. la princesse de Galles, et s'il desire cet honneur là; il suffiroit qu'il s'en rapportât à moy. Il pourroit etre introduit auprès d'Elle ou par l'entremise de M. Querini, son compatriote, ou par Madame la Comtesse de Lippe-Bikebourg, qui est une Comtesse de l'Empire, fort aimée de Mad. la princesse, car elle a bien du merite, et elle a aussi de la bonté pour moy. (4) On pourra adjouter quelque chose à mon grand post scriptum à M. l'Abbé Conti. Apres ces mots: ferant assez voir,

doctrine of the Trinity and denying the divinity of Christ, which in 1710 led to his being deprived of the chair and being banished from the university.

[11] That is, the mathematician Abraham de Moivre (1667–1754), who moved to London sometime in the mid-1680s.

[12] This last paragraph is omitted in the version published in Des Maizeaux 1720, vol. 2 (see p. 10).

88c. Leibniz to Nicolas Rémond*[1]

[Hanover c.6 December 1715]

To Mr. Rémond

Sir

You probably received my Latin [treatise][2] on the origins of the French people by way of Mr. Hullin and, by the post, my remarks on the refuter of Father [Nicolas] Malebranche*, and finally my very lengthy letter to l'Abbé [Antonio Schinella] Conti*, which I have sent to you by the same courier. I find something that I entreat you to add to it by sending it to you. (1) I forgot to mention two able men, who I believe are in London, who deserve to be recognized and are two of my friends: Mr. [Hans] Sloane*, who has an excellent practice and has for a long time performed the function of Secretary of the Royal Society, and Mr. Woodward,[3] who has made very fine investigations of changes in the terrestrial globe. Perhaps the Abbé Conti has already made their acquaintance. (2) The Princess of Wales [Caroline* of Brandenburg-Ansbach] tells me that she would be very happy if my *Theodicy* were translated into English.[4] But those to whom she has spoken there are raising trouble and have referred the matter to some individuals partial to Mr. Newton. There are without doubt enough others capable of a such a translation of it: I do not know if Mr. [Michel] de la Roche*, a Frenchman, who has previously written some literary essays in English, and who inserted a review of the *Theodicy*,[5] writes English well enough (in the judgement of connoisseurs) to have recourse to him. In this case I believe he would be a man to undertake it. If not, I imagine that enough others would be found for it. The able Mr. [William] Wotton*, who in the past has written elegantly and learnedly in English, with moderation, about the ancients and the moderns and about the progress of sciences, would be very capable of it, if he could be persuaded to do it. For I know that he does not slight my views. But finally, if some knew that they would please her Royal Highness by doing this translation, I believe that they would be delighted to undertake it. (3) If the Abbé Conti is not yet known by the Princess of Wales, and if he desires this honour, it would suffice that he referred it to me. He could be introduced to her, either through the mediation of his compatriot Mr Querini[6] or by the Countess of Lippe-Bückeburg [Johanne Sophie*, Gräfin (Countess) zu Schaumburg-Lippe], who is a countess of the empire, much beloved by the princess because she has much merit, and she also shows kindness to me. (4) Something could be added to my extensive postscript to

qui seront vers la fin de la premiere page de ce post scriptum,[7] ou gueres loin du commencement de la seconde, on peut adjouter: ce n'est qu'en France… Et a la fin du permier ¶ dans la seconde page, apres ces mots: brouiller avec moy, on peut adjouter: la Societé Royale ne m'a point…

Je suis avec zele etc.

Caroline of Brandenburg-Ansbach, Princess of Wales, to Leibniz

St. James le $\frac{16}{25}$ 9ber 1715

J'ay trouvez[3] Monsieur que tout ce que vous avez dit sur se que lon vous doit[4] de vos gages a Hanover, e[s]t sy juste et sy bien repressanté que jorais creu cater[5] la chose sy je n'avoit donné a lire au Roy votre lettre, qui an aparu contant et ma dit quelle estte fort vivé et bien écrit.[6] Je ne conte pas que vos afaire soit finy jus-que alarivez[7] de S. M. vous savez que je ne suis geure jesuvite.[8] il faut leur rander[9] justice puis-que ausy bien il lont rarement.[10] il me samble que ce qu'il croi de la graces, et plus rais-onable,[11] et plus convenable adieu.[12] J'espere que vous aurais les livers[13] que je vous ayée anvoiyée.[14] mandé moy[15] je vous prie ce que vous pances[16] sur les ouvrages du D. glerck, qui selon moy on[t] beaucoup de bon, bien que je ne lais trouvez[17] pas la deodiscée. Je suis faché que vos[18] douceur finise trop tost. il n[']y a rien qui puise excuser d'aimer a etter flader[19] que de l'estre d'un home com[m]e vous. J'aime les profete qui predisce tans de chose pour lagrantissement[20] de notre famille. per-metté moy, destre faché qu'vne home come vous ayéez ette[21] vn moment sans

89. CAROLINE OF BRANDENBURG-ANSBACH TO LEIBNIZ 333

l'Abbé Conti. After these words, *ferant assez voir*, which are towards the end of the first page of this postscript,[7] or close to the beginning of the second, you can add: *ce n'est qu'en France*... And at the end of the first paragraph on the second page, after these words, *brouiller avec moy*, you can add: *la Societé Royale ne m'a point*... I am enthusiastically, etc.

[1] LBr. 173 Bl. 5v. Draft: one folio side in Leibniz's hand. Previously published in Des Maizeaux 1720, vol 2, pp. 112–15; Dutens III 448–9; GB 267–8. This draft appears in the margin of a letter of 6 December 1715 for Conti (see document 88b above). But the internal evidence clearly suggests that it was written after the letter for Conti had been dispatched to Rémond (see document 88a).

[2] 'Traité' appears in the version published by Des Maizeaux, but it does not appear in the original draft.

[3] That is, the English naturalist and geologist, John Woodward (1665–1728). He was elected a fellow of the Royal Society in 1693. In 1695 he published *An Essay toward a Natural History of the Earth and Terrestrial Bodies, especially Minerals: As also of the Sea, Rivers, and Springs. With an Account of the Universal Deluge: And of the Effects that it had upon the Earth*. A second edition was published in 1702 and a third in 1723.

[4] In the version published by Des Maizeaux, this sentence reads as follows: 'Madame la Princesse de Galles me marque dans une Lettre que j'ai eu l'honneur de recevoir, qu'elle seroit bien aise que ma Theodicée fut traduite en Anglois' (see Des Maizeaux 1720, vol. 2, p. 113).

[5] This relative clause about the *Theodicy* is omitted in the version published by Des Maizeaux (see Des Maizeaux 1720, vol. 2, p. 113).

[6] Presumably, the Venetian Giacomo marchese de Querini, who had served as chamberlain at the court in Hanover, as well as construction supervisor and garden and palace manager at Herrenhausen*, where he would have been known to Caroline.

[7] Here and in the previous sentence the version published by Des Maizeaux has '*Apostille*' instead of 'post scriptum' (see Des Maizeaux 1720, vol. 2, p. 114).

89. Caroline* of Brandenburg-Ansbach, Princess of Wales, to Leibniz[1]

St. James $\frac{16}{25}$ November 1715[2]

I have found,[3] sir, that everything you have said about what is owed[4] to you from your wages at Hanover is so just and so well represented that I thought I would have spoiled[5] the matter if I had not given your letter to the king [George I, Georg Ludwig* of Braunschweig-Lüneburg] to read; he appeared satisfied with it and told me that it was very lively and well written.[6] I do not think that your business will be completed until the arrival[7] of His Majesty [in Hanover]. You know that I am hardly a Jesuit.[8] It is necessary to do[9] them justice because they rarely have it .[10] It seems to me that what they believe about grace is very reasonable[11] and very fitting for God.[12] I hope that you have the books[13] that I sent you.[14] Pray let me know[15] what you think[16] of the works of Dr. [Samuel] Clarke*, which are quite good in my view, although I do not find the *Theodicy* in them.[17] I am sorry that your[18] sweetness ends too soon. There is nothing that can excuse loving to be flattered[19] but to be flattered by a man like you. I love the prophet who predicts so many things for

savoir ce qu'il disoit. le Roy apareu ettre aissez que vous fuciée comtan[22] du manifeste. Nous panson for[23] serieusement a faire trad vuire votre deodicé,[24] mais nous
cheron vn bon tratucteur.[25] D. glerck e[s]t trop oposez a vos opinnion[26] pour le
faire sans conterdit.[27] il serait le plus proper[28] de tous. il e[s]t trop de l[']opinion de
Sr Eizack newton et je suis moy meme an disputé avec luy. J'implore votre secour. il
dore la pillule et ne veut avouer tout afait que Mr newton a'yée les santiment[29] que
vous luy donne. mes an efait vous verais par sepapié sy joint[30] que c[']est la même
chose. Je ne puis jamais croire, que ce qui et convenable a laperfection[31] de Dieu. Je
la trouvez[32] beaucoup plus parfait dans vos[33] opinon, que dans celle de M^r newton
ou effetivement Dieu doit esttre toujours presans pour raquemoder[34] la machine
par cequ'il ne la peu faire des le comancement.[35] D^r glerck ny newton ne se veulle[36]
dire de la secte de M^r locke, mais je ne puis ny ne veut esttre[37] de la leur. il[s] on[t]
vn autre nossion sur lame.[38] il disce[39] qu'il ne crois[40] pas, mais que Dieu peut
aneantir l[']ame come vous leverais ausy[41] icy.[42] J'ay tout vne autre opinion. Je crois
que Dieu les a fait imortelle[43] et je tire se la[44] de la St Écriture ou il dit qu'il fera
l'home selon son imagé. C'est imagé estte[45] surement l[']ame, puis-que notre pauver[46] corps tout parfait qu'on nous le veut faire acroire n'aurait peu esttére.[47] ainsy
c'est [l']amé et immortelle et selon l[']image de dieu. Je ne puis donc croire que dieu
ne la puise anneantire.[48] tout com[m]e il ne peut faire que ce que je tien[s] dans ma
main sois[49] plus grande qu'elle, ensy je crois lamême chose de lame. Je vous prie de
me tire vos santimens la de ceu.[50] J[']espere de n'ecrire pas a vne Eveque. Einsy je
vais plus loin et dis que je suis persuadé que c'est vne pardit[51] de c'estte[52] perfection
divine. Je crain que nous ne seron pas ta cord.[53] Je vous prie de reponder au papie et
de me monderer mes erreur,[54] que je quiterais avec beaucoup de plaisir et de defer-
ance pour vn home du merite du grand Monsieur L'Ebeniz.

Caroline

89. CAROLINE OF BRANDENBURG-ANSBACH TO LEIBNIZ   335

the aggrandizement[20] of our family. Permit me to be sorry that a man like you has gone[21] a moment without knowing what he said. The king seemed to be pleased that you were satisfied[22] with the manifesto. We are thinking very[23] seriously of having your *Theodicy* translated,[24] but we are seeking a good translator.[25] Dr. Clarke is too much opposed to your views[26] to do it without disagreeing.[27] He would be the most suitable[28] of all. He is too much of the opinion of Sir Isaac Newton, and I am myself in dispute with him. I implore your help. He gilds the pill and does not want to admit absolutely that Mr. Newton holds the views[29] that you attribute to him. But in fact you will see from this paper joined herewith[30] that it comes to the same thing. I can only ever believe that which is suitable to the perfection[31] of God. I find[32] it much more perfect in your[33] view than in that of Mr. Newton, in which God must actually always be present in order to mend[34] the machine because he could not do it from the beginning.[35] Neither Dr. Clarke nor Newton wants[36] to profess to be of Mr. Locke's* sect, but I neither can nor want to be[37] of theirs. They have a different notion of the soul.[38] They say[39] that they do not believe[40] but that God can destroy the soul, as you will also see[41] here.[42] I have a completely different opinion. I believe that God made them immortal,[43] and I infer that[44] from Holy Scripture, where he says that he will make man in his image. This image was[45] certainly the soul, since our poor[46] body could not have been,[47] however perfect one may wish to have us believe it is. So it is the soul, at once immortal and in the image of God. Thus I cannot believe that God can destroy[48] it. Just as he cannot make what I hold in my hand be[49] bigger than it, so I believe the same thing about the soul. Please tell me your views about this.[50] I do not expect to write to a bishop. So I go further and say I am persuaded that it is part[51] of this[52] divine perfection. I fear that we will not be in agreement.[53] Please respond to the paper and show me my errors,[54] which I would abandon with great pleasure and with great respect for a man of the merit of the great Mr. Leibniz.

Caroline

---

[1] LBr. F 4 Bl. 44r–46v. Letter as sent: six quarto sides in Caroline's hand. Previously published in Klopp XI 52–3; Kemble 533–4; Echeverría 1989, pp. 154–5 (excerpt in Spanish translation); Schüller 1991, 213–14 (excerpt in German translation); Robinet 1991, pp. 27–8 (excerpt); HGA 190 (excerpt in English translation). This is Caroline's reply to Leibniz's letter from the end of November 1715 (document 85), within which she enclosed Clarke's First Paper for Leibniz (see document 90). For Leibniz's reply, see his letter to Caroline from mid-to-late December 1715 (document 91).

[2] Caroline misdates the letter. The date should presumably be 6 December (NS)/25 November (OS) 1715.

[3] Reading 'trouvé' for 'trouvez'.

[4] Reading 'ce que l'on vous doit' for 'se que lon vous doit'.

[5] Reading 'j'aurais cru gâter' for 'jorais creu cater'.

[6] Reading 'en a parû content et m'a dit qu'elle était fort vive et bien écrite' for 'an aparu contant et ma dit quelle estte fort vivé et bien écrit'.

[7] Reading 'compte pas que votre affaire soit finie jusqu'à l'arrivée' for 'conte pas que vos afaire soit finy jus-que alarivez'. Klopp mistranscribes 'conte pas' as 'doute pas' (see Klopp XI 52).

[8] Reading 'guère jesuite' for 'geure jesuvite'.

[9] Reading 'rendre' for 'rander'.

89. CAROLINE OF BRANDENBURG-ANSBACH TO LEIBNIZ   337

[10] Reading 'puisque aussi bien ils l'ont rarement' for 'puis-que ausy bien il lont rarement'.

[11] Reading 'semble que ce qu'ils croient de la grâce, est plus raisonnable' for 'samble que cequ'il croi de la graces, et plus raisonable'.

[12] Reading 'à Dieu' for 'adieu'.

[13] Reading 'aurez les livres' for 'aurais les livers'.

[14] Reading 'ai envoyés' for 'ayée anvoiyée'.

[15] Reading 'Mandez-moi' for 'Mandé moy'.

[16] Reading 'pensez' for 'pances'.

[17] Reading 'les trouve' for 'lais trouvez'.

[18] Reading 'votre' for 'vos'.

[19] Reading 'à être flatté' for 'a etter flader'.

[20] Reading 'le profète qui prédit tant de choses pour l'agrandissement' for 'les profete qui predisce tans de chose pour lagrantissement'.

[21] Reading 'permettez-mois d'être fâchée qu'un homme comme vous ait été' for 'permetté moy destre faché qu'vne home come vous ayée ette'.

[22] Reading 'a paru être aise que vous fussiez content' for 'apareu ettre aissez que vous fuciée comtan'.

[23] Reading 'pensons fort' for 'panson for'.

[24] Reading 'traduire votre Theodicy' for 'trad vuire votre deodicé'.

[25] Reading 'cherchons un bon traducteur' for 'cheron vn bon tratucteur'.

[26] Reading 'opposé à vos opinions' for 'oposez a vos opinnion'.

[27] Reading 'contredit' for 'conterdit'.

[28] Reading 'propre' for 'proper'.

[29] Reading 'ait les sentiments' for 'a'yée les santiment'.

[30] Reading 'Mais en effet vous verais par ce papier ci-joint' for 'mes an efait vous verais par sepapié sy joint'. Here Caroline is referring to Clarke's First Paper for Leibniz (see document 90 below).

[31] Reading 'est convenable à la perfection' for 'et convenable a laperfection'.

[32] Reading 'trouve' for 'trouvez'.

[33] Reading 'votre' for 'vos'.

[34] Reading 'où effectivement Dieu doit être toujours présent pour raccommoder' for 'ou effetivement Dieu doit esttre toujours presans pour raquemoder'.

[35] Reading 'parcequ'il ne l'a pu faire dès le commencement' for 'par cequ'il ne la peu faire des le comancement'.

[36] Reading 'veulent' for 'veulle'.

[37] Reading 'être' for 'esttre'.

[38] Reading 'une autre notion sur l'âme' for 'vn autre nossion sur lame'.

[39] Reading 'Ils disent' for 'il disce'.

[40] Reading 'qu'ils ne croient' for 'qu'il ne crois'. Klopp omits 'qu'il ne crois pas' (see Klopp XI 53).

[41] Reading 'le verrez aussi' for 'leverais ausy'.

[42] In these last two sentences, Caroline could be referring to either Locke or to Newton and Clarke, or to all three. In his response to this letter (document 91, p. 345), Leibniz seems to write as though he thought Caroline was referring to all three, which is why I have interpreted her singular pronouns and verbs to be plural.

[43] Reading 'immortelles' for 'imortelle'.

[44] Reading 'cela' for 'se la'.

[45] Reading 'Cette image était' for 'C'est imagé estte'.

[46] Reading 'pauvre' for 'pauver'.

[47] Reading 'pu être' for 'peu esttére'.

[48] Reading 'anéantir' for 'anneantire'.

[49] Reading 'soit' for 'sois'.

[50] Reading 'dire vos sentiments là-dessus' for 'tire vos santimens la de ceu'.

[51] Reading 'partie' for 'pardit'.

[52] Reading 'cette' for 'c'estte'.

[53] Reading 'crains que nous ne serons pas d'accord' for 'crain que nous ne seron pas ta cord'.

[54] Reading 'répondre au papier et de me montrer mes erreurs' for 'reponder au papie et de me monderer mes erreur'.

First Reply of Samuel Clarke

Premiere Replique de Mr. CLARKE.

1. *Il est vrai, & c'est une chose déplorable, qu'il y a en Angleterre, aussi bien qu'en d'autres païs, des personnes, qui nient même la* Réligion Naturelle, *ou qui la corrompent extrémement. Mais, après le déreglement des moeurs, on doit attribuer cela principalement à la fausse Philosophie des* Materialistes, *qui est directement combatue par les* Principes Mathematiques de la Philosophie. *Il est vrai aussi, qu'il y a des personnes, qui font l'*Ame *materielle, &* Dieu *lui-même corporel ; mais ces gens-là se déclarent ouvertement contre les* Principes Mathematiques de la Philosophie, *qui sont les seuls Principes qui prouvent que la* Matiere *est la plus petite & la moins considerable Partie de l'Univers.*

2. *Il y a quelques endroits dans les Ecrits de Mr.* Locke, *qui pourroient faire soupçonner avec raison, qu'il doutoit de l'*Immaterialité *de l'*Ame *; mais il n'a été suivi en cela que par quelques* Materialistes, Ennemis *des* Principes Mathematiques de la Philosophie, *& qui n'approuvent presque rien dans les Ouvrages de Mr.* Locke *que ses Erreurs.*

3. *Mr. le Chevalier* Newton *ne dit pas, que l'*Espace *est l'*Organe, *dont Dieu se sert pour appercevoir les choses. Il ne dit pas non plus, que Dieu ait besoin d'aucun* moyen *pour les apercevoir. Au contraire, il dit que Dieu, étant* present par tout, *apperçoit les choses par sa presence immédiate, dans tout l'Espace où elles sont, sans l'intervention ou le secours d'aucun* Organe, *ou d'aucun* moyen. *Pour rendre cela plus intelligible, il l'éclaircit par une* Comparaison. *Il dit que comme l'Ame, étant immédiatement presente aux* Images, *qui se forment dans le Cerveau par le moyen des Organes des Sens, voit ces* Images, *comme si elles étoient les* choses mêmes *qu'elles representent ; de même, Dieu voit* tout *par sa presence immédiate, étant actuellement present aux cho-*ses mêmes, *à* toutes les *choses qui sont dans l'Univers, comme l'Ame est presente à* toutes les Images, *qui se forment dans le Cerveau. Mr.* Newton *considere le Cerveau & les Organes des Sens, comme le Moyen par lequel ces* Images *sont formées ; & non comme le Moyen par lequel l'Ame voit ou apperçoit ces Images, lors qu'elles sont ainsi formées. Et dans l'Univers, il ne considere pas les choses, comme si elles étoient des* Images *formées par un certain* Moyen *ou par des* Organes, *mais comme des choses réelles, que Dieu lui-même a formées, & qu'il voit dans tous les lieux où elles sont, sans l'intervention d'aucun* Moyen. *C'est tout ce que Mr.* Newton *a voulu dire par la* Comparaison, *dont il s'est servi, lors qu'il suppose que l'Espace infini* † *est,* (pour ainsi dire,) *le* Sensorium *de l'Etre qui est* present par tout.

---

† Voici le Passage dont il s'agit. *Annon Sensorium Animalium,* &c. i.e. C'est-à-dire[3] : Le *Sensorium* des Animaux n'est-il pas le Lieu, où la Substance qui apperçoit, est presente, & où les Images sensibles des chose sont portées par les Nerfs & le Cerveau, afin qu'elles y soient apperçues, comme étant presentes à la Substance qui apperçoit ? Et les Phénomenes de la Nature ne sont-ils pas voir, qu'il y a un Etre Incorporel, Vivant, Intelligent, Present par tout, qui, dans l'Espace infini, lequel est, *pour ainsi dire,* son *Sensorium* (ou le Lieu où il apperçoit,) voit & discerne de la manière la plus intime & la plus parfaite, les

90. First Reply of Samuel Clarke*[1]

Dr. CLARKE's *First Reply.*

1. That there are some in *England*, as well as in other Countries, who deny or very much corrupt even *Natural Religion it self*, is very true, and much to be lamented. But (next to the vitious Affections of Men) this is to be principally ascribed to the false Philosophy of the *Materialists*, to which *the Mathematick Principles of Philosophy* are the most distinctly repugnant. That Some make the *Souls of Men*, and Others even *God* himself to be a Corporeal Being ; is also very true : But those who do so, are the great Enemies of the *Mathematical Principles of Philosophy* ; which Principles, and which alone, prove Matter, or Body, to be the smallest and most inconsiderable Part of the Universe.

2. That Mr. *Locke*[2] *doubted* whether the *Soul* was *immaterial* or no, may justly be suspected from some Parts of his Writings : But herein he has been followed only by some *Materialists*, Enemies to the *Mathematical Principles of Philosophy* ; and who approve little or nothing in Mr. *Locke's* Writings, but his Errors.

3. Sir *Isaac Newton* doth not say, that Space is the *Organ* which God makes use of to perceive Things by ; nor that he has need of any *Medium* at all, whereby to perceive Things : But on the contrary, that he, being *Omnipresent*, perceives all Things by his immediate Presence to them, in all Space whereever they are, without the Intervention or Assistance of any *Organ* or *Medium* whatsoever. In order to make this more intelligible, he illustrates it by a *Similitude* : That as the Mind of Man, by its immediate Presence to the *Pictures* or *Images* of Things, form'd in the Brain by the means of the Organs of Sensation, sees those *Pictures* as if they were the Things themselves ; so God sees *all Things*, by his immediate Presence to them : he being actually present to the *Things themselves*, to all Things in the Universe ; as the Mind of Man is present to all the *Pictures of Things* formed in his Brain. Sir *Isaac Newton* considers the Brain and Organs of Sensation, as the Means *by which those Pictures are formed* ; but not as the Means *by which the Mind sees or perceives* those Pictures, when they are so formed. And in the Universe, he doth not consider Things as if they were Pictures, formed by certain *Means*, or *Organs* ; but as real Things, form'd by God himself, and seen by him in all Places whereever they are, without the Intervention of any *Medium* at all. And this *Similitude* is all that he means, when he supposes Infinite Space † to be (*as it were*) the *Sensorium* of the Omnipresent Being.

---

† *The Passage referred to, is as follows.* Annon Sensorium Animalium, est Locus cui Substantia sentiens adest, & in quem sensibiles rerum Species per nervos & cerebrum deferuntur, ut ibi præsentes à præsente sentiri possint? Atque——annon ex Phænomenis constat, esse Entem Incorporeum, Viventem, Intelligentem, Omnipræsentem, qui in Spatio infinito, *Tanquam* Sensorio suo, *Res Ipsas* intime cernat, penitusq ; perspiciat, totasq ; intra se præsens præsentes complectatur ; quarum quidem rerum, Id quod in Nobis sentit & cogitat, *Imagines tantum* ad se per *Organa* Sensuum delatas, in Sensoriolo suo percipit & contuetur? *i. e. Is not the Sensory of Animals, the Place where the Perceptive*

340 90. FIRST REPLY OF CLARKE

4. *Si, parmi les* Hommes, *un Ouvrier passe avec raison pour être d'autant plus habile, que la* Machine *qu'il a fait, continue plus long temps d'avoir un mouvement réglé, sans qu'elle ait besoin d'être retouchée ; c'est parce que l'habileté de tous les* Ouvriers Humains *ne consiste qu'à composer & à joindre certains pieces, qui ont un mouvement, dont les* Principes *sont tout-à-fait indépendans de l'Ouvrier ; comme les* Poids & les Ressorts, &c. *dont les forces ne sont pas* produites *par l'Ouvrier, qui ne fait que les ajuster & les joindre ensemble. Mais il en est tout autrement à l'égard de Dieu ; qui non seulement compose & arrange les choses, mais encore est l'Auteur de leurs Puissances* Primitives, *ou de leurs* Forces Mouvantes, *& les conserve perpetuellement : Et par conséquent, dire qu'il ne se fait rien sans sa* Providence *& son* Inspection, *ce n'est pas avilir son Ouvrage, mais plûtôt en faire connoitre la grandeur & l'excellence. L'idée de ceux qui soûtiennent, que le Monde est une grande Machine, qui se meut* sans que Dieu *y intervienne, comme une Horloge continue de se mouvoir sans le secours de l'Horloger ; cette idée, dis-je, introduit le* Materialisme *& la* Fatalité *; & sous prétexte de faire Dieu une* Intelligentia Supra-mundana, *elle tend effectivement à bannir du monde la* Providence *& le* Gouvernement de Dieu. *J'ajoute que par la même raison qu'un* Philosophe *peut s'imaginer, que tout se passe dans le Monde, depuis qu'il a été créé, sans que la Providence y ait aucune part ; il ne sera pas difficile à un* Pyrrhonien *de pousser ses raisonnements plus loin, & de supposer que les choses sont allées de toute éternité, comme elles vont presentement, sans qu'il soit nécessaire d'admettre une Création, ou un autre Auteur du Monde que ce que ces sortes de Raisonneurs appellent la* Nature très-Sage & Eternelle. *Si un* Roi *avoit un* Royaume, *où tout se passeroit, sans qu'il y intervint, & sans qu'il ordonnât de quelle maniere les choses se feroient ; ce ne seroit qu'un Royaume de nom par rapport à lui ; & il ne mériteroit pas d'avoir le* Titre de Roi ou de Gouverneur. *Et comme on pourroit soupçonner avec raison que ceux qui prétendent, que dans un Royaume les choses peuvent aller parfaitement bien, sans que le Roi s'en mêle : comme on pourroit, dis-je, soupçonner qu'ils ne seroient pas fâchez de se passer du Roi ; de même, on peut dire que ceux qui soûtiennent que l'Univers n'a pas besoin que Dieu le dirige & le gouverne continuellement, avancent une Doctrine qui tend à le bannir du Monde.*

---

choses mêmes ; & les comprend, comme étant entierement & immediatement presentes en lui ? Au lieu que la Substance, qui apperçoit & qui pense en *Nous*, n'apperçoit & ne contemple dans son petit *Sensorium*, que les *Images* de ces choses ; lesquelles *(Images)* y sont portèes par les *Organes* des Sens. *Newtoni* Optice, Quest. 20. *pag.* 315.

4. The Reason why, among *Men*, an Artificer is justly esteemed so much the more skilful, as the Machine[4] of his composing will continue longer to move regularly without any farther Interposition of the Workman ; is because the skill of all *Human* Artificers consists only in composing,[5] adjusting, or putting together certain Movements, the *Principles* of whose Motion are altogether independent upon the Artificer : Such as are *Weights* and *Springs*, and the like ; whose forces are not *made*, but only *adjusted*, by the Workman. But with regard to *God*, the Case is quite different ; because *He* not only composes or puts Things together, but is himself the Author and continual Preserver of their *Original Forces* or *moving Powers* : And consequently tis not a *diminution*, but the true *Glory* of his Workmanship, that *nothing* is done without his *continual Government* and *Inspection*. The Notion of the World's being a great *Machine*, going on *without the Interposition of God*, as a Clock continues to go without the Assistance of a Clockmaker ; is the Notion of *Materialism* and *Fate*, and tends, (under pretense of making God a *Supra-Mundane Intelligence*,) to exclude *Providence* and *God's Government* in reality out of the World. And by the same Reason that a *Philosopher* can represent all Things going on from the beginning of the Creation, *without* any Government or Interposition of Providence ; a *Sceptick* will easily Argue still farther Backwards, and suppose that Things have from Eternity gone on (as they do now) *without* any true Creation or Original Author at all, but only what such Arguers call *All-Wise and Eternal Nature*. If a *King* had a *Kingdom*, wherein all Things would continually go on *without* his Government or Interposition, or *without* his Attending to and Ordering what is done therein ; It would be to *him*, merely a *Nominal* Kingdom ; nor would he in reality deserve at all the Title of King or Governor. And as those Men, who pretend that in an Earthly Government Things may go on perfectly well *without* the *King himself* ordering or disposing of any Thing, may reasonably be suspected that they would like very well to set the King aside : So whosoever contends, that the Course of the World can go on *without* the Continual direction of *God*, the Supreme Governor ; his Doctrine does in Effect tend to Exclude God out of the World.

Substance is present, and To which the Sensible Images of Things are convey'd by the Nerves and Brain, that they may there be Perceived, as being Present to the Perceptive Substance? And do not the Phænomena of Nature show, that there is an Incorporeal, Living, Intelligent, Omnipresent Being, who in the Infinite Space, which is as it were His Sensorium (or Place of Perception,) sees and discerns, in the inmost and most Thorough Manner, the Very Things themselves, and comprehends them as being entirely and immediately Present within Himself ; Of which Things, the Perceptive and Thinking Substance that is in Us, perceives and views, in its Little Sensory, nothing but the Images, conveyed thither by the Organs of the Senses? Newtoni Optice, Quæst. 20. Pag. 315.

Leibniz to Caroline of Brandenburg-Ansbach, Princess of Wales

Madame

Recevant tout presentement l'honneur des ordres de V. A. Royale j'etois sur le point de commencer une Lettre pour la remercier treshumblement des livres que M. Oinhausin m'a apportés; et pour faire en meme temps mes souhaits de la nouvelle année, comme je les fais presentement, priant Dieu qu'il rende le contentement de V. A. R. parfait, qui sera aussi le nostre; et que cette même année soit le commencement d'un grand nombre d'autres, toutes egalement heureuses, dans une royaume tranquille et fleurissant; que Monseigneur le prince de Galles participe parfaitement à cette satisfaction, et que le Roy et toute la famille Royale rendent à V. A. R. toute le contentement qu'ils reçoivent de son bonheur.

Je viens d'écrire en Allemand à une lettre assés ample[3] à Madame qui apparemment à voulu[4] repondre aux miennes pour s'exercer dans la Langue Allemande. Elle loue le courage de V. A. R. elle trouve cependant qu'on seroit plus heureux à Hanover. J'ay répondu qu'à considerer les personnes par raport à elles mêmes seules et prises a part cela seroit vray; mais qu'en les considerant suivant leur vocation, il faut dire que le Roy pris en prince tel qu'il est, ne pouvoit et ne devoit faire que ce qu'il a fait. Un gentilhomme à son aise paroist aussi plus heureux sur sa terre, qu'aux armées et à la Cour, mais quand on considere que la noblesse n'a ses biens et honneurs que pour servir la patrie, il faut dire qu'il fait mal, et a des reproches a se faire, s'il prefere son repos à son devoir. J'ay adjouté que le Roy a montré que l'ambition ne le poussoit point, lors qu'il a attendu tranquillement ce que le destin (c'est à dire la providence) ordonneroit sans se donner des mouvemens prematurés pour monter sur le Trone; mais qu'aussi il auroit eu grand tort et auroit combattu contre la vocation divine, s'il avoit refusé une couronne qu'une grande nation luy offroit. D'autant que le parti Evangelique de l'Europe auroit eu grand sujet de le blamer comme s'il avoit negligé ce qui importoit au commun salut de l'Eglise protestante. Et qu'on ne doit point blamer les nations Evangeliques, si elles excluent les Rois Catholiques; puisque les Nations Catholiques leur en ont montré le chemin dans la

91. LEIBNIZ TO CAROLINE OF BRANDENBURG-ANSBACH 343

[1] English and French translation are from Clarke's edition of the correspondence (Clarke 1717, pp. 9–17). LBr. 160 Bl. 5r, 6r, 7r, 8r is the English original in Clarke's hand (four quarto sides). LH 1, 20 Bl. 385r–386r is a copy in a secretary's hand (three folio sides). This reply was sent to Leibniz by Caroline in her letter to him of 6 December 1715 (document 89). It is Clarke's reply to Leibniz's First Paper (document 86). The footnote is Clarke's; endnotes are mine. Clarke's references to the Appendix of his 1717 edition of the correspondence have been omitted.

[2] That is, John Locke*.
[3] The Errata of the 1717 edition of the correspondence deletes 'C'est à dire'.
[4] The original reads 'a Machine'.
[5] The original reads 'in the composing'.

91. Leibniz to Caroline* of Brandenburg-Ansbach, Princess of Wales[1]

[mid-to-late December 1715]

Madam

Having just now received the honour of the orders of Your Royal Highness, I was on the point of beginning a letter to thank her very humbly for the books that Mr. Oeynhausen[2] has brought me, and to make at the same time my wishes for the new year, as I do now, by praying to God that he may make complete the contentment of Your Royal Highness, which will also be ours, and that this year may be the beginning of a great number of others, every bit as happy, in a peaceful and flourishing kingdom; that Monseigneur the Prince of Wales [Georg August* of Braunschweig-Lüneburg] may share completely in this satisfaction, and that the king [Georg I, Georg Ludwig* of Braunschweig-Lüneburg] and the entire royal family may return to Your Royal Highness all the satisfaction that they receive from her happiness.

I have just written a rather long letter[3] in German to Madame [Elisabeth Charlotte*, Duchess of Orléans], who apparently wanted[4] to respond to my letters in order to practise her German. She extols the courage of Your Royal Highness, but she thinks that you would be happier in Hanover. I replied that to consider persons in relation to themselves alone and taken separately, that would be true, but that in considering them according to their vocation, it must be said that the king, taken for the prince he is, could only do, and had to do, what he has done. A gentleman at ease also appears happier on his estate than in the armies or at court, but when one considers that nobility has its property and honours only for serving the fatherland, it must be said that he acts badly and dishonours himself if he prefers his repose to his duty. I added that the king showed that ambition did not drive him, when he awaited peacefully what destiny (that is to say, providence) would ordain without making any premature moves to mount the throne, but also that it would have been a great mistake and would have opposed the divine calling if he had refused a crown that a great nation offered him; further, that the Evangelical party of Europe would have had great reason to blame him, as though he had neglected what concerned the common welfare of the Protestant church, and that

personne de Henry IV, qui a eté obligé de se ranger dans le parti de Rome pour regner en France. Mais je supplie V. A. R. de ne point toucher à tout cecy en écrivant à Madame, de peur qu'elle ne s'apperçoive et ne trouve peut-etre mauvais que j'en aye fait part à V. A. R.

L'Ecrit que V. A. Royale m'a envoyé est aussi bien fait qu'il se puisse pour soutenir une cause foible. Cependant, il me semble que M. Clark qui en paroist l'auteur se trouve quelques fois embarassé un peu; et je ne say si ma reponse cy jointe n'augmentera son embarras: on verra bien tôt s'il procede avec ingenuité, ou s'il est capable au moins de se degager des prejugés. Il témoigne grande envie de m'imposer quelque mauvais sentiment, mais en vain. Je n'ay point voulu le relever, pour ne point aigrir la dispute. Je souhaite que V. A. R. fasse garder des copies de ce qu'on luy donne, et de ce que j'envoye, pour en mieux juger.

J'ay parcouru les deux livres de M. Clarc ou du moins la plus grande partie, mais il faut que je les relise avec plus d'attention. Il dit souvent de tres bonnes choses; mais il demeure en beau chemin faute de poursuivre ou d'envisager assés mes principes. Il a raison de soutenir contre M. Dodwel et contre un Anonyme, que l'Ame est immaterielle à cause de son indivisibilité, et que tout ce qui est composé de parties, ne sauroit rien avoir en luy que ce qui est dans les parties. Ce la estant, je ne voy point comment il veut soutenir que l'Ame est étendue. Car par tout où il y a étendue il y a parties: à moins qu'on prenne le mot d'une manière inusitée.

La verité est et V. A. R. l'a soutenu dignement que Dieu a fait l'Ame immortelle, c'est à dire qu'Elle est immortelle naturellement; et ne sauroit etre aneantié[9] que par un miracle, comme Dieu pourroit aneantir tout l'univers créé. Mais ce seroit une chose inconvenable. Ces Messieurs qui abbaissent fort l'idée de Dieu, en font de même de celle de l'Ame. Il semble quasi que selon eux l'ame peut perir naturellement, c'est à dire par l'operation ordinaire de Dieu, qui a fort la mine selon eux d'estre l'Ame du monde; et quelcun de leur secte se pourroit persuader aisement, que selon l'idée de quelques anciens dont j'ay parlé dans mon discours sur la conformité de la raison et de la foy, les ames naissent quand la Machine est organisée, pour recevoir comme un jeu d'orgues le souffle general, et qu'elles perissent par la destruction des organes, le souffle general cessant d'y produire du sentiment; ainsi dans le fonde il n'y auroit qu'une seule ame durable, savoir celle du Monde. Je ne voudrois point leur imputer ce sentiment; mais tandis qu'ils ne nous donnent point des principes contraires à cette doctrine, la leur y peut mener. Selon moy c'est toute autre chose. Chaque Ame est une image ou representation vivante de l'univers créé selon son point de veue et ne sauroit plus perir que l'univers des creatures, et il y a des Ames par tout. Mais l'Ame raisonnable est quelque chose de plus, elle est même l'image de la divinité. C'est ce que dit aussi merveilleusement bien la Sainte Ecriture, et V. A. R. a excellem[m]ent bien appuyé là dessus, et c'est beaucoup qu'Elle peut soutenir seule la verité contre de si habiles gens. Toutes les Ames gardent leur substance et sont imperissables

91. LEIBNIZ TO CAROLINE OF BRANDENBURG-ANSBACH   345

the Evangelical nations ought not to be blamed if they exclude the Catholic kings, since the Catholic nations have shown them the way in the person of [King] Henri IV [of France], who was forced to side with the party of Rome in order to rule in France.[5] But I beg Your Royal Highness not to bring all this up in writing to Madame, for fear that she may notice and perhaps think it wrong that I informed Your Royal Highness about it.

The paper that Your Royal Highness sent me[6] is done as well as it can be for supporting a feeble cause. However, it seems to me that Mr. Clarke*, who appears to be the author, sometimes finds himself a bit embarrassed; and I do not know whether my enclosed response[7] will increase his embarrassment. We will soon see if he proceeds candidly, or if he is at least capable of freeing himself of prejudices. He exhibits a great desire to impose on me some bad opinion, but in vain. I have not wanted to take it up in order not to embitter the dispute. I hope that Your Royal Highness has copies kept of what is given to her, and of what I send, in order to judge them better.

I have perused the two books of Mr. Clarke, or at least the greatest part of them, but I must reread them with more attention. He often says some very good things, but he makes no progress for want of pursuing or sufficiently considering my principles. He is right to maintain, against Mr. Dodwell[8] and an anonym, that the soul is immaterial on account of its indivisibility, and that everything that is composed of parts could have nothing in it but what is in the parts. That being so, I do not see how he intends to maintain that the soul is extended; for wherever there is extension, there are parts, unless the word is being used in an unusual way.

The truth is, and Your Royal Highness has justly supported it, that God made the soul immortal, that is to say, that it is naturally immortal, and could be annihilated[9] only by a miracle, as God could annihilate the entire created universe.[10] But that would not be fitting. These gentlemen, who very much debase the idea of God, do some of it with that of the soul as well. It almost seems that according to them the soul can perish naturally, that is to say, by the ordinary operation of God, who on their view gives every appearance of being the soul of the world. And someone of their sect could easily have persuaded himself, according to the idea of some ancients of whom I have spoken in my discourse on the conformity of reason and faith,[11] that souls arise when the machine is organized, in order to receive, like an organ stop, the universal breath, and that they perish with the destruction of the organs, the universal breath ceasing to produce any sensation in them. Thus at bottom there would be only a single enduring soul, namely, that of the world. I would not want to impute this view to them, but as they don't provide us with any principles contrary to this doctrine, it can lead them into it. On my view, it is an entirely different matter. Each soul is an image or living representation of the created universe according to its point of view and could no more perish than the universe of creatures, and there are souls everywhere. But the rational soul is something more; it is even the image of the divinity. This is what the Holy Scriptures also say marvelously well, and Your Royal Highness has supported it extremely well with these words; it a great step that she is

même celles des bestes; mais les seules Ames raisonnables gardent encor leur personalité, c'est à dire la connoissance reflechie sur elle meme[12] de ce qu'elles sont ou la conscience. C'est ce qui les rend capables de recompense et de chastiment. Je voudrois que nos Messieurs s'expliquassent sur les bêtes, s'ils leur donnent des Ames ou non. Et si elles ont des ames (je veux dire immaterielles) on demande si elles perissent ou non; et (en cas qu'ils enseignent leur extinction) sur quoy ils batissent le privilege de l'ame humaine d'etre imperissable; si sur la nature ou seulement sur la grace, c'est à dire sur une operation extraordinaire de Dieu, qui en effect seroit le sentiment de Dodwel, et de quelques nouveaux mais mauvais philosophes. Ainsi il importeroit de savoir ce qu'il faut dire dans les principes de Mons. Newton. Pour moy je crois d'avoir expliqué distinctement en quoy consiste la difference entre les consecutions des bestes qui imitent la raison, et entre les raisonnemens de l'homme. Il semble que Messieurs les Antagonistes détruisent la veritable difference entre le Miracle et la Naturel, et que selon eux la nature de Dieu est d'agir tousjours par miracles dans les actions qui devroient etre les plus naturelles.

Il y a maintenant un Noble Venitien en Angleterre appellé l'Abbé Conti, qui s'applique fort à la recherche des belles choses. Quand il estoit en France, il témoignoit d'estre fort de mon parti, et il m'a écrit une belle Lettre, ou entre autres il fait connoistre d'avoir bien remarqué la beauté du systeme que j'etablis, sur tout par rapport aux Ames. Je ne say si Messieurs mes Antagonistes de Londres ne l'auront un peu seduit depuis. Il aura raison d'estre accommodant pour mieux profiter de leur conversation. Cependant j'espère que M. l'Abbé Conti me gardera quelque place. Je voudrois qu'il eût l'honneur d'etre connu de V.A.R. et je luy ay conseillé depuis de tacher de l'obtenir, s'il ne l'a pas encore acquis.

Voila un surcroist de bonheur pour la Maison du Roy dans la mort de l'Electeur de Treves. Ainsi l'Eveché d'osnabruc revient. Nous ne doutons point que Mgr le duc Ernest Auguste n'y doive succeder. On me mande de Vienne que le pere Wolf qui passe generalement pour un mauvais chicaneur, et qui perd tous les procès ou il engage le prince; pretend soutenir l'eligibilité de Mgr le duc Max. Mais c'est le pere Wolf même qui est cause en bonne partie de son in-eligibilité, puisqu'il l'a porté si avant sur la religion. J'espere que le Roy n'attendra pas son retour pour me consoler, car j'ay bien besoin de mes arrerages, et je ne voudrois pas etre renvoyé à ne les avoir qu'un peu avant ma mort. Le temps m'est pretieux, et je ne saurois m'en promettre encore beaucoup. Differer est à demy nier à mon egard. Je voudrois faire quelques dispositions pendant que je suis encor en etat de le faire, et j'ay fort besoin pour cela de cette somme qui me reste. Je presse Mess. les Ministres de representer mes besoins au Roy puisque la justice y est toute entiere. Et je supplie V. A. R. de continuer de me faire la grace d'y porter Sa Mté. Mess. les ministres me font entendre, que les bontés de V. A. R. pour moy ont fait un grand effect. Je suis etc.

able to support the truth on her own against such able people. All souls retain their substance and are imperishable, even those of beasts; but only rational souls also retain their personality, that is to say, knowledge reflected on itself[12] about what they are, or consciousness. This is what makes them capable of reward and punishment. I would like our gentlemen to explain themselves concerning beasts, whether they endow them with souls or not. And if they have souls (I mean immaterial souls), we may ask whether or not they perish, and (in case they teach their extinction) upon what do they establish the privilege of the human soul of being imperishable, whether upon nature or only upon grace, that is to say, upon an extraordinary operation of God, which would in fact be the view of Dodwell, and of some new but bad philosophers. So it would be important to know what must be said according to the principles of Mr. Newton. For my part, I believe that I have explained distinctly the difference between the consecutions of the beasts, which imitate reason, and human reasoning. It seems that the antagonists destroy the true difference between the miracle and the natural and that according to them the nature of God is always to act by miracles in operations that should be the most natural.

There is now a noble Venetian in England named Abbé [Antonio Schinella] Conti* who applies himself earnestly to the investigation of fine things. When he was in France, he testified to being very much on my side, and he wrote me a nice letter[13] in which, among other things, he makes known that he has marked well the beauty of the system I establish, above all in relation to souls. I do not know whether my antagonists from London will have since won him over a bit. He will be right to be accommodating in order to profit better from their conversation. However, I hope that the Abbé Conti will preserve some place for me. I would like him to have the honour of being known by Your Royal Highness, and I have since advised him to try to obtain it, if he has not yet done so.[14]

There is an increase of good fortune for the House of the king in the death of the Elector of Trier [Karl Joseph of Lorraine (d. 4 December 1715)]. The Bishopric of Osnabrück returns. We do not doubt that Monseigneur Duke Ernst August ought to succeed to it.[15] I am informed from Vienna that Father Wolf, who is generally considered to be a malicious pettifogger, and who loses all the proceedings in which he engages the prince, intends to support the eligibility of Monseigneur Duke Max. But it is father Wolf himself who is in large part the cause of his ineligibility, since he has carried him so far in religion.[16] I hope that the king will not wait for his return in order to console me, because I am in great need of my arrearages, and I should not want to be put off to having them only a little before my death. Time is precious to me, and I could not look forward to yet a lot of it. In my case, to defer is to deny by half. I would like to make some arrangements while I am still in a state to do so, and for that reason I am in great need of this sum that remains to me. I am urging the ministers to represent my needs to the king, since they are entirely just, and I implore Your Royal Highness to continue doing me the favour of directing His Majesty to them. The ministers inform me that the Your Royal Highness's favours for me have had a great effect. I am etc.

P. S.[17]

La Cour imperial est fort touchée de la mort de l'Electeur de Treves. On a dit que l'Empereur avoit destiné au prince joseph François[19] de Lorraine l'ainée des princesses josephines, et quelques uns sont allés jusqu'à croire, que la petite verole ayant enlevé ce jeune prince: (: qui me paroissoit fort raisonnable :) l'Empereur avoit jeté les yeux sur l'Electeur de Treves luy même, et qu'on seroit peutetre venu (apres avoir pris les mesures sur la succession dans l'Electorat, à le desecclesiastiquer: mais j'ay eu de la peine à y adjouter foy. Maintenant on a debité en Hollande que l'Empereur destinoit au Duc de Lorraine le Gouvernement general des pays bas Austrichiens et les Hollandois en estoient d'autant plus jaloux, qu'ils ne savoient pas encor la mort de L'Electeur de Treves, dont les deux Evéchés ne relevoient pas peu la grandeur de la Maison de Lorraine. Pour moy je doute un peu de toutes ces nouvelles. Quand j'estois à Vienne, quelques un[21] disoient que l'Empereur donneroit ce Gouvernement a sa soeur ainée et on croit qu'elle en seroit fort capable. Depuis tout le monde le a donné au prince Eugene. L'Empereur est un prince dont il n'est pas aisé de penetrer les sentimens. Je crois que l'Empereur ne le donneroit point au prince Eugene, et que le prince ne le recevroit point si cette grande charge l'obligeoit de resider. Si j'étois du conseil secret de l'Empereur je luy conseillerois d'accorder au Roy la possesion du pays de Hadelen, qui aussi bien luy est dûe, et d'étendre l'Electorat, jusqu'à la branche de Wolfenbutel, à fin que toute la Maison de Bronsvic soit Electorale comme les autres maisons. Ce qui n'est point dû à la Maison. Mais il seroit pourtant de la dignité de l'Empereur de marquer cette consideration pour la ligne dont est son epouse etc.

P. S.[25]

J'espere que Votre Altesse Royale permettra gracieusement que j'adjoute encor quelques mots. Je la remercie tres humblement de la bonté qu'Elle a eue de faire valoir ma lettre ma lettre auprés du Roy. J'espere que le Roy n'attendra point son retour pour me consoler. Car j'ay bien besoin de mes arrerages, et je ne voudrois pas étre renvoyé à les avoir un peu avant ma mort. Le temps m'est pretieux, et je ne saurois m'en promettre encore beaucoup. Differer c'est à demi nier à mon egard et dans ma situation. Je voudrois faire quelques dispositions pendant que je suis encor en état de le faire. Et j'ay fort besoin pour cela de cette somme qui me reste.

Je presse Mess. les ministres de representer mes besoins au Roy, puisque la justice y est toute entiere et je supplie V.A. Royale de continuer de me faire la grace d'y porter Sa Mté dans l'occasion. Mess. les Ministres me font entendre que les bontés de V.A.R. pour moy ont fait un grand effect.

Apres avoir écrit cecy, je viens de recevoir une lettre de M. de Bernsdorf, où il me marque qu'il semble que le Roy accordera mes arrerages aussi tost qu'on pourra l'asseurer que le premier Tome est achevé. Or c'est une chose seure, qu'il l'est. On

91. LEIBNIZ TO CAROLINE OF BRANDENBURG-ANSBACH   349

P.S.[17]

The imperial court is very moved by the death of the Elector of Trier. They say that the emperor [Emperor Karl VI*] had intended the eldest of the Josephine Princesses [Maria Josepha][18] for Prince François Joseph of Lorraine,[19] and some have gone so far as to believe that since smallpox took this young prince (which seemed very reasonable to me), the emperor had cast his eyes on the Elector of Trier himself and that perhaps he would have come (after taking the measures concerning the succession in the electorate) to laicize him. But I have had trouble lending it credence. Now in Holland they have been spouting that the emperor intended the general government of the Austrian Netherlands for the Duke of Lorraine,[20] and the Dutch were all the more envious of it when they were not yet aware of the death of the Elector of Trier, whose two bishoprics much enhanced the grandeur of the House of Lorraine. For my part, I am a little doubtful of all of this news. When I was in Vienna, some[21] said that the emperor would give this government to his eldest sister, and it is thought that she would be very capable of it. Since then everyone has given it to Prince Eugène* [of Savoy]. The emperor is a prince whose sentiments are not easy to penetrate. I do not believe that the emperor would give it to Prince Eugène, nor that the prince would accept it if this great office would force him to reside there. If I were [a member] of the emperor's secret council, I would advise him to grant the king possession of the country of Hadeln,[22] which is owed to him as well, and to extend the electorate as far as Wolfenbüttel, so that the entire House of Braunschweig may be electoral like the other houses.[23] This is not owed to the House, but it would nevertheless be of the dignity of the emperor to show this consideration for his spouse's lineage.[24]

P.S.[25]

I hope that Your Royal Highness will graciously permit me to add yet some words. I thank her very humbly for the kindness that she has had to turn my letter to account with the king. I hope that the king will not wait for his return to console me. For I am in great need of my arrearages, and I would not want to be put off to having them a little before my death. Time is precious to me, and I could not look forward to yet a lot more of it. In my case, to defer is to deny by half. I would like to make some arrangements while I am still in the state to do so. And for that reason I am in great need of this sum that remains to me.

I am urging the ministers to represent my needs to the king, since they are entirely just, and I implore Your Royal Highness to continue doing me the favour of directing His Majesty to them when the opportunity arises. The ministers inform me that the favours Your Royal Highness has shown me have had a great effect.

After having written this, I just received a letter from Mr. Bernstorff*, in which he indicates that it seems the king will grant my arrearages as soon as he can be assured that the first volume[26] is completed. But it is a certainty that it is completed. It could be published forthwith, but I would be very pleased to complete the second

pourroit le faire imprimer dés à cette heure; mais on seroit bien aise d'achever aussi le second. Car le soin de l'impression causera beaucoup de distraction. Je prends la liberté d'ecrire celà à V. A. Royale, à fin qu'Elle n'aye point besoin d'en parler de nouveau au Roy, jusqu'à ce qu'on sache, si ce qu'on vient de dire aura quelque effect: ainsi Elle gardera la continuation de ses bontés pour une occasion ou l'on aura plus de sujet d'y avoir recours; puisque le premier coup a déjà produit un si bon effect.

91. LEIBNIZ TO CAROLINE OF BRANDENBURG-ANSBACH   351

as well. For care of the printing will cause a lot of distraction. I take the liberty to write that to Your Royal Highness so that she will not need to speak to the king about it again, as far one can tell, if what I just said will have some effect. Thus she will reserve the continuation of her favours for an occasion when there will be more reason to have recourse to them, since the first stroke has already produced such a good result.

[1] LBr. F 4 Bl. 48r–48v. Draft: two folio sides in Leibniz's hand. Previously published in Klopp XI 58–65; Schüller 1991, pp. 214–17 (excerpt in German translation); HGA 190–2 (excerpt in English translation). This is Leibniz's reply to Caroline's letter of 6 December 1715 (document 89). It is not dated, but since the letter mentions the death of Elector of Trier, Charles Joseph of Lorraine, who died on 4 December 1715, it had to have been written after that date. Caroline's response to the present letter (see document 95), with which she enclosed Clarke's Second Reply (document 96), is dated 10 January 1716 (NS). Given the time for mail to pass between London and Hanover, and the time for Caroline to pass Leibniz's second paper along to Clarke, and for Clarke to prepare his second reply and return it to Caroline, Leibniz's letter could not have been sent much later than the third week of December 1715.

[2] This is almost certainly a reference to Rabe Christoph von Oeynhausen. See Caroline's letter of Leibniz of 14 November 1715 (document 84 above, p. 301 note 26).

[3] Reading 'une lettre assés ample' for 'à une lettre assés ample'.

[4] Reading 'a voulu' for 'à voulu'.

[5] Here Leibniz reports that he told Elisabeth Charlotte, who had converted to Catholicism prior to her marriage, in 1671, to Philippe I*, Duke or Orleans, that the Evangelical nations, like England, should not be blamed for excluding Catholics from becoming king, since Henri IV had been forced to convert to Catholicism before he could reign in France.

[6] That is, Clarke's First Reply. See document 90.

[7] That is, Leibniz's Second Paper. See document 92.

[8] Henry Dodwell (1641–1711) was an English scholar and theologian. In 1689 he published anonymously a tract entitled *Concerning the Case of Taking the New Oath of Fealty and Allegiance*, which argued against taking an oath of allegiance to William and Mary. As a result, he lost his chair in history at Oxford. He subsequently became a leader in the nonjuring movement. His reputation later suffered from his defense of the doctrine that the soul is naturally mortal and that immortality can only be obtained by being baptized at the hands of the regularly ordained clergy.

[9] Reading 'anéantie' for 'aneantié'.

[10] Here Leibniz gently corrects Caroline by suggesting only that the soul cannot be destroyed *naturally*, whereas Caroline herself had suggested that even God could not destroy the soul (see her letter to Leibniz of 6 December 1715 (document 89, p. 335)).

[11] That is, the *Discours de la conformité de la foy avec la raison*, published at the beginning of the *Theodicée*.

[12] Klopp mistranscribes 'sur elle-même' as 'sur elles-memes' (see Klopp XI 62).

[13] That is, Conti's letter to Leibniz of April 1715 (document 79c).

[14] As time went on, Leibniz came to regret his introduction of Conti, suspecting him of not simply being accommodating to the Newtonians, but of actually changing his allegiances after arriving in England and of colluding with the Newtonians. See Leibniz's letters to Caroline of 28 April 1716 (document 113, p. 501), 12 May 1716 (document 117a, p. 521), 2 June 1716 (document 124, pp. 557, 559), and from the end of September to mid-October 1716 (document 149, p. 1745).

[15] The Treaty of Westphalia* (1648) stipulated that the Prince-Bishopric of Osnabrück should alternate between Lutheran princes from the House of Braunschweig-Lüneburg and Catholic princes. The Elector of Trier that Leibniz mentions was Charles Joseph of Lorraine, Elector-Archbishop of Trier from 1711 to 1715, whose death meant that the bishopric would revert to a prince of the House of Braunschweig-Lüneburg, the first such prince having been the Elector Ernst August*, late husband of the late Electress Sophie* of the Palatinate. The Ernst August Leibniz mentions here, Ernst August II*, was the youngest son of the Elector Ernst August and the Electress Sophie and was officially installed as Prince-Bishop of Osnabrück on 2 March 1716.

[16] The 'Duke Max' to whom Leibniz refers was Maximilian Wilhelm* (1666–1726), the third surviving son of the Duke (later Elector) Ernst August* of Braunschweig-Lüneburg and the Duchess (later

352   91. LEIBNIZ TO CAROLINE OF BRANDENBURG-ANSBACH

91. LEIBNIZ TO CAROLINE OF BRANDENBURG-ANSBACH   353

Electress) of Braunschweig-Lüneburg, Sophie* of the Palatinate. When the present letter was written, he was the second eldest surviving son, George I being the eldest, and he apparently had been induced to believe that he should be next in line for the Prince-Bishopric of Osnabrück. But Maximilian had been converted to Catholicism by his Jesuit Confessor, the 'Father Wolf' mentioned by Leibniz, and hence was not eligible for succession on the terms of the Treaty of Westphalia. Sophie developed a fierce hatred for the Jesuits, whom she blamed not only for Maximilian's conversion but also for keeping him away from Hanover. Maximilian died in Vienna. See Hatton 1978, pp. 71–2, 405.

[17] This first P. S. is written in the right-hand margin of the first page of the letter (LBr. F 4 Bl. 48r).

[18] Maria Josepha (1699–1757) was the eldest daughter of Karl VI's deceased brother, Emperor Joseph I (1678–1711), and the Dowager Empress Wilhelmine Amalie* of Braunschweig-Lüneburg, who was herself the eldest daughter of Leibniz's first employer at Hanover, Duke Johann Friedrich*. In 1734 she was crowned Queen consort of Poland by marriage to King August III (1696–1763).

[19] Reading 'François Joseph' for 'joseph François'. François Joseph de Lorraine (1670–75) was the only son of Louis Joseph de Lorraine (1650–71), Duke of Guise, and Elisabeth Marguerite d'Orléans (1646–96). When his father died in 1671, François Joseph became the seventh and last duke of Guise.

[20] At the time, this would have been Leopold Joseph Charles Dominique Agapet Hyacinthe (1679–1729), son of Charles Leopold Nicolas Sixte, Duke Charles V of Lorraine.

[21] Reading 'quelquesuns' for 'quelques un'.

[22] Hadeln was a small territory in northern Germany, near the mouth of the river Elbe. The emperor eventually ceded Hadeln to Hanover in 1731, during the reign of George I's son, Georg August* of Braunschweig-Lüneburg (George II) (see Hatton 1978, p. 79).

[23] Under Duke Ernst August, the duchy of Braunschweig-Lüneburg-Calenberg (Hanover), had been elevated to the status of electorate in 1692, although it was not recognized by the electoral college of the Imperial Diet until 1708 (Hatton 1978, p. 399). When Duke Georg Wilhelm* of Braunschweig-Lüneburg-Grubenhagen (Celle) died in 1705, the duchy of Celle was united with the Electorate of Hanover under the rule of Ernst August's son, the Elector Georg Ludwig* (later George I of England). The electorate of Braunschweig-Lüneburg (Hanover) was the junior branch of the House of Braunschweig, the senior branch being Braunschweig-Wolfenbüttel. Leibniz was suggesting that the emperor should give the duchy of Braunschweig-Wolfenbüttel to Hanover so that the House of Braunschweig could finally be united to form a single electoral house.

[24] In 1704, the then Archduke Karl of Austria was seeking the hand of Caroline* of Brandenburg-Ansbach, the future Princess of Wales and Queen Consort of England (by her marriage, in 1705, to Georg Ludwig's son, Georg August*, the future George II of England). But as marriage to the Hapsburg prince would have required her conversion to Catholicism, Caroline eventually declined. In Protestant circles Caroline's decision was regarded as heroic. Leibniz himself sent her news of Hanover's praise and told her that Anton Ulrich*, duke of the senior branch of the House of Braunschweig (Braunschweig-Wolfenbüttel), was so impressed that he wanted to make her the heroine of one of his romantic novels (Caroline is thought to have been the model for the heroine in Anton Ulrich's novel *Octavia*). But in January 1710, Anton Ulrich converted to Catholicism and later helped to arrange the marriage between Karl VI and his own granddaughter, Elisabeth Christine*, in 1711 (it was in part through the influence of Anton Ulrich that Leibniz later secured the position of imperial privy counselor in 1713). (See Brown 2004b, pp. 82–5.) So Leibniz was proposing that the emperor would be doing his wife's lineage (the House of Braunschweig-Wolfenbüttel) honour by making Braunschweig-Wolfenbüttel a part of the Hanoverian electorate.

[25] This second P.S. is found on 1.5 octavo sides in Leibniz's hand (LBr. F 4 Bl. 21r–21v). Parts of it match what Leibniz wrote at the end of his letter, just before the first P.S. above. Klopp includes the whole of this P.S. within the body of the letter (see Klopp XI 63–4).

[26] Here Leibniz refers to the first volume of his history of the House of Braunschweig, the *Annales imperii occidentis Brunsvicenses**.

Leibniz's Second Paper

Sécond Ecrit de Mr. Leibnitz

ou

Réplique au prémier Ecrit Anglois.

1. On *a raison de dire dans le Papier donné à* Madame la Princesse de Galles, *& que son Altesse Royale m'a fait la grace de m'envoyer ;*[2] *qu'après les passions vitieuses,* les Principes des Materialistes *contribuent beaucoup à entretenir l'impieté. Mais je ne crois pas qu'on ait sujet d'adjouter, que* les Principes Mathematiques de la Philosophie sont opposés à ceux des Materialistes. *Au contraire, ils sont les mêmes ; excepté que les* Materialistes, *à l'Exemple de* Demoncrite, *d'*Epicure, *& de* Hobbes, *se bornent aux seuls Principes* Mathematiques, *& n'admettent que des corps ; & que les* Mathematiciens Chrétiens *admettent encore des Substances immaterielles. Ainsi ce ne sont pas les* Principes Mathematiques, *(selon le sens ordinaire de ce terme,) mais les Principes* Metaphysiques, *qu'il faut opposer à ceux des* Materialistes. Pythagore, Platon, *& en partie* Aristote, *en ont eu quelque connoissance ; mais je pretends les avoir établis Demonstrativement, quoi qu'exposés populairement, dans ma* Theodicée. *Le grand Fondement des* Mathematiques, *est* le Principe de la Contradiction, ou de l'Identité, *c'est à dire, qu'une Enontiation ne* sauroit etre vraye & fausse *en même temps ; & qu'ainsi* A *est* A, *& ne sauroit étre* non A. *Et ce seul Principe suffit pour demonstrer toute l'Arithmetique & toute la Geometrie, c'est à dire tous les Principes* Mathematiques. *Mais pour passer de la* Mathematique *à la* Physique, *il faut encore un autre Principe, comme j'ay remarqué dans ma* Theodicée ; *c'est le* Principe de la Raison suffisant ; *c'est que rien n'arrive, sans qu'il y ait une* Raison *pourquoy cela soit ainsi plustot qu'autrement. C'est pourqouy* Archimede *en voulant passer de la* Mathematique *à la* Physique *dans son Livre* de l'Equilibre, *a été obligé d'employer un cas particulier du Grand Principe de la Raison suffisante. Il prend pour accordé, que s'il y a une* Ballance *où tout soit de même de part & d'autre, & si l'on suspend aussi des poids égaux de part & d'autre aux deux Extremités de cette Ballance, le tout demeurera en repos. C'est parce qu'il n'y a aucune Raison pourquoy un coté descende plustot que l'autre. Or par ce principe seul, savoir, qu'il faut qu'il y ait une* Raison suffisante, *pourquoy les choses sont plustost ainsi qu'autrement, se demonstre la* Divinité, *& tout le reste de la* Metaphysique, *ou de la* Theologie Naturelle ; *& même en quelque façon les* Principes Physiques *independans de la* Mathematique, *c'est à dire les Principes* Dynamiques *ou de* la Force.

2. *On passe à dire que selon les* Principes Mathematiques, *c'est à dire selon la* Philosophie *de* M. Newton, *(car les* Principes Mathematiques *n'y decident rien,)* la Matiere est la partie la moins considerable de l'Univers. C'est qu'il admet, outre la Matiere, *un* Espace vuide ; *& que, selon luy,* la Matiere *n'occupe qu'une très petite partie de* l'Espace. *Mais* Democrite *&* Epicure *ont soutenu la même chose, excepté qu'ils differoient en cela de* M. Newton *du plus au moins ; & que peut être selon eux il*

92. Leibniz's Second Paper[1]

Mr. LEIBNITZ'S *Second Paper.*
BEING
An Answer to Dr. CLARKE'S *First Reply*

1. It is rightly observed in the Paper delivered to the *Princess of Wales*, which Her *Royal Highness* has been pleased to communicate to me,[2] that, next to Corruption of Manners, *the Principles of the Materialists* do very much contribute to keep up Impiety. But I believe the Author had no reason to add, that *the Mathematical Principles of Philosophy are opposite of those of the Materialists.* On the contrary, they are the same ; only with this difference, that the *Materialists*, in imitation of *Democritus, Epicurus,* and *Hobbes*[3], confine themselves altogether to *Mathematical* Principles, and admit only *Bodies* ; whereas the *Christian Mathematicians* admit also Immaterial Substances. Wherefore, not *Mathematical* Principles (according to the usual sense of that Word) but *Metaphysical* Principles ought to be opposed to those of the *Materialists. Pythagoras, Plato,* and *Aristotle* in some measure, had a Knowledge of these Principles ; but I pretend to have established them demonstratively in my *Theodicæa*, though I have done it in a popular manner. The great Foundation of *Mathematicks,* is *the principle of Contradiction, or Identity*, that is, that a Proposition cannot be *true and false* at the same time ; and that therefore A is A, and cannot be *not A*. This single Principle is sufficient to demonstrate every part of Arithmetick and Geometry, that is, all *Mathematical* Principles. But in order to proceed from *Mathematicks* to *Natural Philosophy*, another Principle is requisite, as I have observed in my *Theodicæa* : I mean, *the Principle of a sufficient Reason, viz.* that nothing happens without a *Reason* why it should be *so*, rather than *otherwise*. And therefore *Archimedes* being to proceed from *Mathematicks* to *Natural Philosophy*, in his Book *De Æquilibrio*, was obliged to make use of a particular Case of the great Principle of *a sufficient Reason.* He takes it for granted, that if there be a *Balance*, in which every thing is alike on both Sides, and if equal Weights are hung on the two ends of that Balance, the whole will be at rest. 'Tis because no *Reason* can be given, why one side should weigh down, rather than the other. Now, by that single Principle, *viz.* that *there ought to be a sufficient Reason why Things should be so, and not otherwise,* one may demonstrate the Being of a *God*, and all the other Parts of *Metaphsicks* or *Natural Theology* ; and even, in some Measure, those Principles of *Natural Philosophy*, that are independent upon *Mathematicks* : I mean, the *Dynamick* Principles, or the *Principles of Force.*

2. The Author proceeds, and says, that according to the *Mathematical Principles,* that is, according to Sir *Isaac Newton's Philosophy,* (for *Mathematical Principles* determine nothing in the present Case,) *Matter is the most inconsiderable part of the Universe.* The reason is, because he admits *empty Space*, besides *Matter* ; and because, according to *his* Notions, *Matter* fills up only a very small part of *Space.*

y avoit plus de Matiere dans la monde, que selon M. Newton : *En quoy je crois qu'ils étoient preferables ; Car* plus *il y a de la Matiere, plus y a-t-il de l'occasion à Dieu d'exercer sa sagesse & sa puissance ; & c'est pour cela, entre autres Raisons, que je tiens qu'il n'y a point de vuide du tout.*

3. *Il se trouve expressement dans l'*Appendice de l'Optique *de* M. Newton ; *que l'*Espace est le Sensorium de Dieu. *Or le mot* Sensorium *a toujours signifié l'*Organe de la Sensation. *Permis à luy & à ses amis de s'expliquer maintenant tout autrement. Je ne m'y oppose pas.*

4. *On suppose que la* presence de l'Ame *suffit pour qu'elle s'apperçoive de ce qui se passe dans le cerveau. Mais c'est justement ce que le Pere* Mallebranche *& toute l'Ecole Cartesienne nie, & a raison de nier. Il faut toute autre chose que la seule* presence, *pour qu'une chose represente ce qui se passe dans l'autre. Il faut pour cela quelque communication explicable ; quelque manière d'*influence. L'*Espace selon* M. Newton, *est intimement* present *au corps qu'il contient, & qui est commensuré avec luy ; s'en-suit il pour cela que l'*Espace s'apperçoive *de ce qui se passe dans le corps, & qu'il s'en* souvienne *après que le corps en sera sorti? Outre que l'Ame estant* indivisible, *sa* presence *immediate qu'on pourroit s'imaginer dans le corps, ne seroit que dans* un Point. *Comment donc s'appercevroit elle de ce qui se fait hors de ce Point? Je pretends d'étre le premier qui ait montré,* comment l'ame s'apperçoit de ce qui se passe dans *le corps.*

5. *La Raison pourquoy Dieu s'apperçoit de tout, n'est pas sa simple* presence, *mais encore son* Operation ; *c'est parce qu'il conserve les choses par une action qui* produit continuellement *ce qu'il y a de bonté & de perfection en elles. Mais les* ames n'ayant point d'*influence immediate sur les* corps, *ny les* corps sur les *ames ; leur correspond-ence mutuelle ne sauroit étre expliquée par la* Presence.

6. *La veritable raison qui fait louër principalement une Machine, est plustost prise de l'effect de la Machine, que de sa Cause. On ne s'informe pas tant de la* Puissance *du* Machiniste, *que de son* Artifice. *Ainsi la raison qu'on allegue pour louër la Machine de Dieu, de ce qu'il l'a faite* toute entiere, *sans avoir emprunté de la Matiere de dehors, n'est point suffisante. C'est un petit detour, où l'on a été forcé de recourir. Et la raison qui rend Dieu preferable à un autre Machiniste, n'est pas seulement parce qu'il fait le tout, au lieu que l'Artisan a besoin de chercher sa Matiere. Cette* preference viendroit seulement *de la* Puissance. *Mais il y a une autre raison de l'excellence de Dieu, qui vient encore de la* Sagesse. *C'est que sa Machine dure aussi* plus long temps, *& va* plus juste, *que celle de quelque autre Machiniste que ce soit. Celuy qui achete la Montre, ne se soucie point si l'*Ouvrier *l'a faite toute entiere, ou s'il en a fait faire les pieces par d'*autres Ouvriers, *& les a seulement ajustees ; pourveu qu'elle aille comme il faut. Et si l'*Ouvrier *avoit receu de Dieu le don jusqu'à créer la Matiere des roües, on n'en seroit point content, s'il n'avoit receu aussi le don de les bien ajuster. Et de même, celuy qui voudra étre content de l'ouvrage de Dieu, ne le sera point par la seule raison qu'on nous allegue.*

But *Democritus* and *Epicurus* maintained the same Thing : They differ'd from Sir *Isaac Newton*, only as to the *Quantity* of Matter ; and perhaps they believed there was *more* Matter in the World, than Sir *Isaac Newton* will allow : Wherein I think their Opinion ought to be preferred ; For, the *more* Matter there is, the *more* God has occasion to exercise his Wisdom and Power. Which is one Reason, among others, why I maintain that there is *no Vacuum* at all.

3. I find, in ‖ express Words, in the *Appendix* to Sir *Isaac Newton's Opticks*, that *Space* is the *Sensorium* of *God*.[4] But the Word *Sensorium* hath always signified the *Organ* of Sensation. He, and his Friends, may *now*, if they think fit, explain themselves quite otherwise : I shall not be against it.

‖ *See the Note*, in *Dr. Clarke's First Reply*, § 3.

4. The Author supposes that the *presence* of the Soul is sufficient to make it perceive what passes in the Brain. But this is the very Thing which Father *Mallebranche*[5], and all the *Cartesians* deny ; and they *rightly* deny it. More is requisite besides *bare presence*, to enable One thing to perceive what passes in another. Some Communication, that may be explained ; some sort of *influence*, is requisite for this purpose. *Space*, according to Sir *Isaac Newton*, is intimately present to the Body contained in it, and commensurate with it. Does it follow from thence, that Space *perceives* what passes in a Body ; and *remembers* it, when That Body is gone away? Besides, the Soul being *indivisible*, it's immediate *presence*, which may be imagined in the Body, would only be in *one Point*. How then could it perceive what happens *out of* that Point? I pretend to be the first, who has shown *how* the Soul perceives what passes in the Body.

5. The Reason why God perceives every thing, is not His bare *Presence*, but also his *Operation*. 'Tis because he preserves Things by an Action, which *continually produces* whatever is good and perfect in them. But the *Soul* having no immediate *Influence* over the *Body*, nor the *Body* over the *Soul* ; their mutual Correspondence cannot be explained by their being *present* to each other.

6. The true and principal Reason why we commend a Machine, is rather grounded upon the *Effects* of the Machine, than upon its *Cause*. We don't enquire so much about the *Power* of the Artist, as we do about his *Skill* in his Workmanship. And therefore the Reason alledged by the Author for extolling the Machine of God's making, grounded upon his having *made it entirely*, without wanting any Materials to make it of ; That Reason, I say, is not sufficient. 'Tis a mere Shift the Author has been forced to have recourse to : And the Reason why God exceeds any other Artist, is *not only* because he makes the *Whole*, whereas all other Artists must have Matter to work upon. This Excellency in God, would be *only* on the account of *Power*. But God's Excellency arises also from *another* Cause, *viz. Wisdom* : whereby his Machine *lasts longer*, and moves *more regularly*, than those of any other Artist whatsoever. He who buys a Watch, does not mind whether the *Workman* made every Part of it *himself*, or whether he got the several Parts made by *Others*, and did only put them together ; provided the Watch goes right. And if the Workman had received from God even the Gift of *creating* the Matter of the Wheels ; yet the Buyer

358   92. LEIBNIZ'S SECOND PAPER

7. *Ainsi il faut que l'artifice de Dieu, ne soit point inferieur à celuy d'un Ouvrier ; il faut même qu'il aille infiniment au delà.* La simple Production de tout, *marqueroit bien la* Puissance *de Dieu ; mais elle ne marqueroit point assez sa* Sagesse. *Ceux qui soutiendront le contraire, tomberont justement dans le defaut de* Materialistes & *de* Spinoza, *dont ils protestent de s'éloigner : Ils reconnoitroient de la* Puissance, *mais non pas assez de* Sagesse *dans le Principe des choses.*

8. *Je ne dis point que le Monde corporel est une Machine ou Montre qui va* sans *l'interposition de Dieu, & je presse assés que les Creatures ont besoin de son* influence *continuelle : Mais je soutiens que c'est une Montre qui va sans avoir besoin de sa* Correction : *Autrement il faudroit dire que Dieu se ravise. Dieu a tout prevû, il a remedié à tout par* avance : *Il y a dans ses ouvrages une harmonie, une beauté* dejà préétablie.

9. *Ce Sentiment n'exclut point la* Providence *ou le Gouvernement de Dieu : Au contraire, cela le rend* parfait. *Une veritable* Providence *de Dieu, demande une* parfait Prevoyance : *Mais de plus elle demande aussi, non seulement qu'il ait tout* preveu, *mais aussi qu'il ait* pourveu *à tout par des remedes convenables* préordonnés : *Autrement il manquera ou de* Sagesse *pour le* prevoir, *ou de* Puissance *pour y pourvoir. Il resemblera à un Dieu* Socinien, *qui vit du jour à la journée, comme disoit* M. Jurieu. *Il est vray que Dieu, selon les Sociniens, manque même de* prevoir *les inconveniens ; au lieu que, selon ces Messieurs qui l'obligent à se corriger, il manque d'y* pourvoir. *Mais il me semble que c'est encore un* manquement *bien grand ; il faudroit qu'il manquât de* Pouvoir, *ou de* bonne Volonté.

10. *Je ne crois point qu'on me puisse reprendre avec raison, d'avoir dit que Dieu est* Intelligentia supramundana. *Diront-ils qu'il est* Intelligentia Mundana, *c'est à dire qu'il est l'Ame du Monde?*[7] *J'espere que non. Cependant ils feront bien de se gareder d'y donner sans y penser.*

11. *La Comparaison d'un Roy, où tout iroit sans qu'il s'en melât,*[8] *ne vient point à propos ; puisque Dieu conserve tousjours les choses, & qu'elles ne sauroient subsister sans lui : Ainsi son Royaume n'est point* nominal. *C'est justement comme si l'on disoit, qu'un Roy qui auroit si bien fait élever ses Sujets, & les maintiendroit si bien dans leur capacité & bonne volonté, par le soin qu'il auroit pris de leur subsistence,*[9] *qu'il n'auroit point besoin de les redresser ; seroit seulement un Roy de nom.*

12. *Enfin, si Dieu est obligé de corriger les choses naturelles de temps en temps, il faut que cela se fasse ou* surnaturellement *ou* naturellement. *Si cela se fait* surnaturellement, *il faut recourir au Miracle pour expliquer les choses naturelles ; ce qui est en effect une reduction d'un hypothese* ad absurdum. *Car avec les Miracles, on peut rendre raison de tout sans peine. Mais si cela se fait* naturellement, *Dieu ne sera point* Intelligentia supramundana ; *il sera compris sous la nature des choses, c'est à dire il sera l'Ame du Monde.*

of the Watch would not be satisfied, unless the Workman had also received the Gift of *putting them well together.* In like manner, he who will be pleased with *God's* Workmanship, cannot be so, without some *other* Reason than that which the Author has here alleged.

7. Thus the *Skill* of *God* must not be inferior to that of a Workman ; nay, it must go infinitely beyond it. The bare *Production* of every thing, would indeed show the *Power* of God ; but it would not sufficiently show his *Wisdom.* They who maintain the contrary, will fall exactly into the Error of the *Materialists*, and of *Spinoza*, from whom they profess to differ. They would, in such case, acknowledge *Power*, but not sufficient *Wisdom*, in the Principle or Cause of all Things.

8. I do not say, the Material World is a Machine, or Watch, that goes *without* God's *Interposition* ; and I have sufficiently insisted, that the Creation wants to be continually influenc'd by its *Creator.* But I maintain it to be a Watch, that goes *without* wanting to be *Mended* by him : Otherwise we must say, that God *bethinks himself again.* No ; God has *foreseen* every thing ; He has provided a Remedy for every thing *before-hand* ; There is in his Works a Harmony, a Beauty, already *pre-established.*

9. This sentiment does not exclude God's *Providence*, or his *Government* of the World : On the contrary, it makes it *perfect.* A true *Providence* of God, requires a perfect *Foresight.* But then it requires moreover, not only that he should have *fore-seen* every thing ; but also that he should have *provided* for every thing *before-hand*, with proper Remedies : Otherwise, he must want either *Wisdom* to *foresee* Things, or *Power* to *provide* against them. He will be like the God of the *Socinians*, who *lives only from day to day*, as Mr. *Jurieu*[6] says. Indeed God, according to the *Socinians*, does not so much as *foresee* Inconveniences ; whereas, the Gentlemen I am arguing with, who put him upon *Mending* his Work, say only, that he *does not provide against* them. But this seems to me to be still a very great *Imperfection.* According to This Doctrine, God must want either *Power*, or *Good Will.*

10. I don't think I can be rightly blamed, for saying that God is *Intelligentia Supramundana.* Will they say, that he is *Intelligentia Mundana* ; that is, the *Soul of the World?* I hope not. However, they will do well to take care, not to fall into that Notion unawares.

11. The Comparison of a King, under whose Reign every thing should go on without his Interposition, is by no means to the present Purpose ; since God preserves every thing continually, and nothing can subsist without him. His Kingdom therefore is not a *Nominal* one. 'Tis just as if one should say, that a King, who should originally have taken care to have his Subjects so well educated, and should, by his Care in providing for their Subsistence, preserve them so well in their Fitness for their several Stations, and in their good Affection towards him, as that he should have no Occasion ever to be amending any thing amongst them ; would be only a *Nominal* King.

Leibniz to William Winde

Je n'ay point voulu laisser passer l'année, sans me donner l'honneur de vous ecrire et de vous souhaiter la suivante heureuse avec beaucoup d'autres toutes pleines de contentement. Ce que vous me dites Monsieur, des amis qui seroient bien aises de me voir en Angleterre, est obligeant: mais mon âge, et quelques circonstances, dont les principales sont mes occupations icy et à Vienne, ou l'on m'a fait Conseiller Imperial Aulique, ne me donnent pas grande esperance que je puisse avoir un jour la satisfaction de revoir ce beau Royaume ou il y a tant d'excellens hommes. Il y a quelques uns maintenant qui me font la guerre à outrance. Mais outre qu'encore personne hors des isles Britanniques est entré dans leur sentiments, et que même de tres habiles gens se sont declarés contre eux, et que je say que dans la Societé Royale même plusieurs ne sont pas contents du procedé dont on en a usé à mon egard; cette guerre ne m'empeche point de dormir. Et comme M. Newton n'a point parlé luy même, et a seulement detaché certains enfans perdus; je n'ay pas crû necessaire de me mettre en frais pour leur repondre, et je me suis remis au jugement du public; mais des amis ont pris mon parti, sans que je les en eusse prié. Je souhaiterois de trouver quelque ami à Londres qui me fit l'honneur de m'informer de temps

93. LEIBNIZ TO WINDE   361

12. To conclude. If God is oblig'd to mend the Course of Nature from time to time, it must be done either *supernaturally*, or *naturally*. If it be done *supernaturally*, we must have recourse to *Miracles*, in order to explain Natural Things : Which is reducing a Hypothesis *ad absurdum* : For, every thing may easily be accounted for by *Miracles*. But if it be done *naturally*, then God will not be *Intelligentia Supramundana* : He will be comprehended under the Nature of Things ; that is, He will be *the Soul of the World*.

[1] Original French and English translation are from Clarke's edition of the correspondence (Clarke 1717, pp. 18–35). LBr. 160 Bl. 74r–75r is the original draft: 2.7 folio sides in Leibniz's hand. LBr. 160 Bl. 9r–12r and LH 1, 20 Bl. 387r–388v are fair copies in secretaries' hands. Leibniz enclosed this paper with his letter to Caroline of mid-December 1715 (document 91). It answers Clarke's First Reply (document 90). Clarke's references to the Appendix of his 1717 edition of the correspondence have been omitted.

[2] The phrase '*dans le Papier donné à* Madame la Princesse de Galles, *& que son Altesse Royale m'a fait la grace de m'envoyer*' is crossed out in the original draft and is omitted in the two fair copies mentioned in note 1.

[3] That is, Thomas Hobbes*.

[4] On this point, see Koyré and Cohen 1961.

[5] That is, Nicolas Malebranche*.

[6] That is, the French Protestant leader and Anglican priest, Paul Jurieu (1637–1713).

[7] In the original draft and in the two fair copies mentioned in note 1 above, this sentence reads: 'Ceux qui le desaprouvent, diront ils qu'il est *Intelligentia Mundana*, c'est à dire qu'il est l'Ame du Monde?'

[8] In the original draft and in the two fair copies mentioned in note 1 above, this phrase reads: 'chez qui tout iroit sans qu'il s'en melât'.

[9] In the original draft, the phrase '*& les maintiendroit si bien dans leur capacité & bonne volonté, par le soin qu'il auroit pris de leur subsistence*' is omitted.

93. Leibniz to William Winde* (excerpt)[1]

[23 December 1715]

I did not want to let the year pass without giving myself the honour of writing to you and wishing you a happy new year, along with many others, all filled with contentment. What you tell me, sir, about friends who would be very glad to see me in England, is gratifying; but my age and a few circumstances, of which the principle ones are my occupations here[2] and in Vienna, where I have been made an Imperial Aulic Councilor*, do not give me great hope that I will be able one day to have the pleasure of seeing once more that beautiful kingdom, where there are so many excellent men. There are now some who are waging all-out war against me. But apart from that, still no one outside the British Isles has sided with them, and even some very able men have declared themselves against them, and I know that even several in the Royal Society are not happy with the process that has been employed in my case.[3] This war has not prevented me from sleeping. And as Mr. Newton has not spoken himself, and has only unleashed certain *enfants perdus*, I have not thought it necessary to trouble myself in order to respond to them, and I have left it up to the judgement of the public; but some friends have taken my side without my having asked them. I would hope to find some friend in London who might do me

en temps de ce qui s'y passe dans la Republique des Lettres. Car il s'y fait tousjours quelque chose de bon, malgré les desordres publics; lesquels, comme j'espere, ne dureront pas trop long tems. Si le Pretendant fut venu avant les deux échecs receus par les rebelles, je crois qu'il auroit fait plus d'impression. Maintenant je crois que son parti sera fort découragé. Le meilleur est qu'il n'y a point de secours à esperer pour luy de dehors; à moins que le Pape n'arme à Civita-Vecchia en sa faveur. Le Roy de Suede seroit plus à portée, et il ne manqeroit pas de bonne volonté, mais le pauvre Roy traité maintenant ou fait traiter d'autres pour luy, pour se sauver de Stralsund. Pour achever de ruiner la Suede, les Alliés ne peuvent mieux faire que de l'y renvoyer. Je m'imagine que M. Scot sera maintenant retourné en Angleterre. Je l'ay bien crû Tory, mais jamais Jacobite, ainsi j'espere que ceux qui l'ont noirci, luy auront fait tort. Je suis tousjours porté à presumer le meilleur des gens, jusqu'à ce que je sois asseuré du contraire. J'espere la même chose de Mylord Lexington et de Mylord Peterbourg; quoyque je ne m'étonne point si le gouvernement se défie un peu d'eux. Ils ont un peu trop favorisé la mechante paix.

Je suis faché pour l'amour des belles lettres que Monsieur Prior est allé si avant dans ces matieres. Et de l'autre côté je suis bien aise pour les belles lettres, que Monsieur Addison est dans le bon chemin. Je voudrois bien savoit quel employ il a maintenant. Je ne say ce que peut faire maintenant M. Falaiseau s'il paroist à Londres, ou s'il est encore dans quelque province. Mad. l'Electrice le regala fort genereusement, mais aussi tost qu'il eût ce regal, il nous planta là. Que fait maintenant M. le Chevalier Fountaine, et notre pauvre M. Thomas Bournet de Kemney, pour lequel je crains que les rebelles d'Ecosse ne l'ayent enveloppé; soit qu'ils l'ayent pris prisonnier, ou qu'ils luy ayent mis un mousquet sur le dos malgré luy. Je serois bien aise aussi de savoir le destin d'autres Anglois ou Ecossois qui ont été à Hanover et ont esté un peu connus. Par exemple de M. Murray le Gouverneur de Wolfenbutel, et de ses fils, dont l'ainé faisoit deja l'homme d'importance pour les affaires, et le second qui a été page de Mad. l'Electrice sera apparemment aussi en Angleterre. Car s'il estoit en Ecosse, je n'en aurois pas bonne opinion à moins qu'il ne fut dans nos trouppes. Il me semble que M. Worstley l'Arabe, qui étoit venu à Hanover avec Myl. Rivers ne doit pas etre mal en Cour, puisqu'on l'a envoyé à Lisbonne, si je ne me trompe. Je crois que M. King le Heraut est mort. Il avoit fait des calculs fort jolis sur la Political-Arithmetic que je voudrois n'estre point perdus. Enfin, vous voyés, Monsieur, que je vous parle comme si j'avois l'honneur de vous entretenir de vive voix, je vous supplie de le prendre en bonne part, et de me repondre de même, et de satisfaire à ma curiosité, autant que vous le jugerés apropos. J'aurois presque oublie un des principaux, Sir Rowland Gwyn, Roland ou Heros, mais en même temps, martyr de la succession. Où est il maintentant? at-on trouvé quelque moyen de le soulager? Je ne say qui m'avoit dit que le Roy luy accordoit le privilege de faire battre quelque petite monnoye. Mais c'est de quoy je doute un peu. C'est dommage que

the honour of informing me from time to time about what is happening there in the Republic of Letters. For something good is always done there, despite the public disorder, which, as I hope, will not last too long. If the Pretender [James Francis Edward Stuart*] had come before the two defeats suffered by the rebels, I believe that he would have made more of an impression. Now I believe that his party will be very discouraged. The best is that there is not any aid to expect for him from the outside, unless the Pope arms Civitavecchia[4] on his behalf. The King of Sweden [Karl XII (1682–1718)] would be more inclined, but the poor king is now negotiating, or is having others negotiate for him, in order to save Stralsund. In order to finish off Sweden, the Allies[5] cannot do better than to send him back there. I imagine that Mr. Scot will now be returned to England. I have indeed believed him to be a Tory, but never a Jacobite, so I hope that those who have blackened him will have wronged him. I am always inclined to assume the best of men, until I am assured of the contrary. I hope the same for my Lord Lexington [Robert Sutton, 2nd Baron Lexington (1662–1723)] and my Lord Peterborough [Charles Mordaunt, 3rd Earl of Peterborough (1658–1735)], although I will not be surprised if the government distrusts them a bit. They have promoted the bad peace [i.e., Treaty of Utrecht*] a bit too much.

I am sorry for the love of belles-lettres that Mr. [Matthew] Prior [1664–1721] has gotten so far in these matters. And on the other hand, I am very happy for the belles-lettres that Mr. [Joseph] Addison* is on the right track. I should indeed like to know what position he has now. I do not know what Mr. [Pierre de] Falaiseau* can do now, whether he appears in London or is still in some province. Madam the Electress [the Dowager Electress of Braunschweig-Lüneburg, Sophie* of the Palatinate] regaled him very generously, but as soon as he had this treat, he left us in the lurch. What is Chevalier Fontaine[6] doing now, and our poor Thomas Burnett of Kemney,[7] whom I fear the rebels of Scotland have surrounded; it may be that they have taken him prisoner, or that they have placed a musket on his back despite himself. I would also be very happy to know the fate of other Englishmen or Scotsmen who have been in Hanover and were not well known. For example, about Mr. Murray the Governor of Wolfenbüttel[8] and his sons, the elder of whom was already the important businessman, and the second, who was a page of the electress, will apparently also be in England. For if he were in Scotland, I would not have a good opinion of him unless he were among our troops. It seems that Mr. [Henry] Worsley the Arab, who had come to Hanover with my Lord Rivers, must not be out of favour since he has been sent to Lisbon, if I am not mistaken.[9] I believe that Mr. [Gregory] King the Herald[10] is dead. He had made some very nice calculations concerning *Political Arithmetic* that I would not wish to be lost.[11] Finally, you see, sir, that I am speaking to you as if I had the honour of conversing with you in person; I beg you to take it well and respond likewise and satisfy my curiosity so far as you deem it appropriate. I would have nearly forgotten one of the principals,

notre bon Docteur Hutton est mort. Tout Tory qu'il estoit, il me paroissoit bien intentionné. Voila une lettre remplie de bien de questions: mais il vous est aisé d'y satisfaire; autrement je n'aurois garde de vous donner de la peine. Je vous supplie de faire tenir la cyjointe à Mons. Stebbing, et je suis avec zele; Monsieur

Hanover le 23 de Xbre 1715

à M. Winde

P. S. Ayes la bonté Monsieur,   à Londres
de m'apprendre l'employ ou
titre de M. Stebbing.

93. LEIBNIZ TO WINDE

Sir Rowland Gwynne,[12] Roland or hero,[13] but at the same time, martyr of the succession. Where is he now? Have they found some way to assist him? I do not know who had told me that the king accorded him the privilege of minting some small change. But I doubt this a bit. It is a pity that our good Doctor [John] Hutton[14] is dead. Tory that he was, he seemed to me well intentioned. Here is a letter full of many questions. But it is easy for you to answer them; otherwise I would have been far from bothering you. I ask you to send the attachment to Mr. Stebbing,[15] and I am enthusiastically, sir

Hanover 23 December 1715

To Mr. Winde

P. S. Have the kindness sir,   in London
to tell me the occupation or
title of Mr. Stebbing

---

[1] LBr. 1001 Bl. 1r–2r. Copy of letter as sent: 2.5 quarto sides in a secretary's hand. Not previously published.

[2] His occupation in Hanover was primarily his work on his history of the House of Braunschweig, his *Annales imperii occidentis Brunsvicenses**.

[3] Leibniz is referring to a committee, handpicked by the then president of the Royal Society, Isaac Newton, to adjudicate the calculus priority dispute between himself and Newton. Predictably, the committee found in favour of Newton and issued its report on 24 April 1712 (5 May 1712 NS), which was published early in 1713 under the title *Commercium Epistolicum**.

[4] Civitavecchia is an Italian coastal town northwest of Rome that at the time was under papal control.

[5] That is, the Allies in the Great Northern War against Sweden (1700–21).

[6] That is, Sir Andrew Fontaine (1676–1753). He was a member of the English delegation that went to Hanover in 1701 to deliver the Act of Succession* to the Elector Georg Ludwig* of Braunschweig-Lüneburg. He and Leibniz carried on a fitful correspondence between 1701 and 1714.

[7] Thomas Burnett (1654–1729) of Kemney (Kemnay), Scotland, was a jurist who conducted a wide correspondence on political philosophy and theology, including an extensive correspondence with Leibniz and the Electress Sophie between 1695 and 1715.

[8] That is, Anthony Murray, who was Vize-Obermeister (Vice-schoolmaster) at the Ritterakademie (knight academy) in Wolfenbüttel from 1710 to 1712.

[9] Henry Worsley (1672–1740) was MP for Newtown (1705–15) and later envoy to the King of Spain (1708) and to Portugal (1713–22); he was governor of Barbados from 1721 to 1731. In August–October 1710, Richard Savage (1654–1712), 4th Earl Rivers, was in Hanover on a special mission to reassure the Electress Sophie and her son the Elector Georg Ludwig of Braunschweig-Lüneburg that the new ministry in Great Britain remained committed to the protestant succession. He returned to Hanover in October and November 1711, now with Worsley in tow, on a special mission to discuss terms of peace in the War of the Spanish Succession* (see Hattendorf 2008). It is not entirely clear why Leibniz refers to Worsley as 'l'Arabe', but in the patois of seventeenth-century French, 'Arabe' was often used as a slur, meaning 'greedy person' or 'miser', and Worsley seems to have had a reputation for being rather avaricious. If that is what Leibniz meant to be suggesting by calling Worsley 'l'Arabe', it may have been because Worsley had refused to accept a permanent diplomatic post at the court in Hanover because he regarded the pay for such a post to be insufficient (see CHH V 920).

[10] Gregory King (1648–1712) was a surveyor and mapmaker, who was the Lancaster Herald of Arms in Ordinary from 1688 until his death in 1712.

[11] Here Leibniz is probably referring to some of the calculations that King had made in his unpublished manuscript, *Natural and Political Observations and Conclusions upon the State and Condition of England*. This work was eventually published in 1802 as appendix to George Chalmers's book, *Estimate of the Comparative Strength of Great Britain*.

Leibniz to Christian Wolff

[...]

Isti homines aliòs ferre non possunt. Urit eos quod responsione ipsos non dignor. Itaque crambem commercii in Transactionibus recoxerunt et versionem transactionis inseri curarant Diario Hagiensi literario. Et quo magis me ad respondendum permoverent etiam mea principia Philosophica ibidem aggressi sunt; ut audio. Sed ibi quoque dentem solido illident. Serenissima Princeps Walliæ quæ Theodiceam meam legit cum attentione animi, eaque delectata est, nuper pro ea cum quodam Anglo Ecclesiatici ordinis, accessum in aula habente disputavit, ut Ipsa mihi significat. Improbat illa, quod Newtonus cum suis vult, Deum subinde opus habere correctione suæ mahinæ et reanimatione. Meam sententiam qua omnia ex præstabilito bene procedunt nec opus est correctione, sed tantum sustentatione Divina, magis perfectionibus Dei congruere putat. Ille dedit Serenitati Suæ Regiæ schedam Anglico sermone a se conscriptam, qua Newtoni sententiam tueri conatur, meamque impugnare; libenter mihi imputaret Divinam gubernationem tolli, si omnia per se bene procedant, sed non considerat Divinam gubernationem circa naturalià in ipsa sustentatione consistere, nec debere eam sumi ἀνθρωποπαθῶς. Respondi nuperrimè et responsionem meam ad Principem misi. Videbimus an ille sit replicaturus. Gratum est quod materiam antagonista attigit, quæ non resolvitur in considerationes Mathematicas, sed de qua ipsa Princeps facilè judicium ferre potest. Vale et fave. Dabam Hanoveræ 23. Decembre 1715.

P.S.

Felicia festa precor.

[12] Rowland Gwynne (1658–1726) was a Welsh Whig politician who was knighted by Charles II in 1680. He was elected a Fellow of the Royal Society in 1681. He was a supporter of the Hanoverian succession to the British crown, and in August of 1714 he accompanied Georg Ludwig* on his journey to England to ascend the British throne as George I.

[13] Apparently a reference to Roland (d. 778), the Frankish military leader under Charlemagne, who was immortalized in the eleventh-century epic poem *La Chanson de Roland*.

[14] Presumably, Dr. John Hutton (d. 1712), who was appointed court physician to King William III of England in 1689. He was elected a Fellow of the Royal Society in 1697.

[15] Perhaps the English churchman Henry Stebbing (1687–1763).

94. Leibniz to Christian Wolff* (excerpt)[1]

[23 December 1715]

[...]

These men [the Newtonians] cannot tolerate others. It galls them that I do not consider them worthy of a response. Therefore they have served up a rehash of the correspondence in the *Transactions* and have taken care that a version has been inserted in the *Journal Literaire de la Haye*.[2] And, as I hear, they have in the same place attacked even my philosophical principles, to induce me all the more to respond. But there, too, they will bite on something hard. The Most Serene Princess of Wales [Caroline* of Brandenburg-Ansbach], who read my *Theodicy* with an attentive mind and was delighted with it, recently disputed in favour of it with a certain Englishman of ecclesiastical order who has access to the court [Samuel Clarke*], as she herself has pointed out to me.[3] She disapproves what Newton and his followers assert, that God needs to correct and revitalize his machine from time to time. She thinks that my view, according to which everything proceeds properly from what is and has no need of correction, but only of divine maintenance, is more in agreement with the perfections of God. He [Clarke] has given Her Royal Serenity a paper written by himself in English,[4] in which he attempts to defend the view of Newton and attack mine. He has willingly charged me with holding that divine governance is done away with if all things proceed properly by themselves, but he does not consider that divine governance, as concerns natural things in themselves, consists in maintenance, and it ought not be assumed anthropopathically. I have very recently responded and have sent my response[5] to the princess. We shall see whether he is going to respond. It is welcome that my adversary touches on a matter that is not resolved by mathematical considerations, but about which the princess herself is easily able to form a judgement. Farewell and be well disposed. Delivered at Hanover, 23 December 1715.

P.S.

I wish you a prosperous holiday

368   94. LEIBNIZ TO WOLFF

¹ LBr. 1010 Bl. 183r–183v. Letter as sent: 2 quarto sides in secretary's hand. Previously published in GLW 179–81; GP VII 348 (excerpt); Dutens II-1 105 (excerpt); NC VI 257–9 (excerpt, original Latin and English translation); Schüller 1991, pp. 222–3 (excerpt in German translation); HGA 188 (excerpt in English translation).

² Leibniz is referring to '*An Account of the Book entitled* Commercium Epistolicum Collinii & aliorum, De Analysi promota; *published by order of the* Royal-Society, *in relation to the Dispute between Mr.* Leibnitz *and Dr.* Keill, *about the Right of Invention of the Method of* Fluxions, *by some call'd* the Differential Method'. The *Account* was published anonymously by Newton in the *Philosophical Transactions* 29:342 (February 1715), pp. 173–224, and he had a French translation of the work published in the *Journal Literaire de la Haye* 7 (1715), pp. 114–58 and 344–65, under the title *Extrait du livre intitule Commercium epistolicum*; a Latin version was included in the second edition of the *Commercium Epistolicum** (1722), pp. 1–50, under the title *Recensio libri qui inscriptis est Commercium epistolicum*. For an excerpt from the *Account* published in the *Philosophical Transactions*, see document 56.

³ See Caroline's letter to Leibniz of 6 December 1715 (document 89, p. 335).

⁴ Clarke's First Reply (see document 90).

⁵ Leibniz's Second Paper (see document 92).

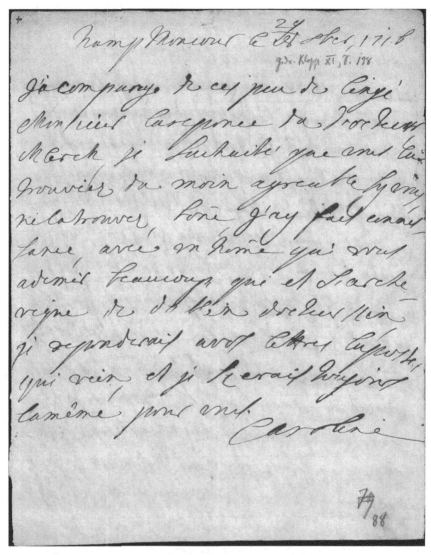

Figure 2. Gottfried Wilhelm Leibniz Bibliothek-Niedersächsische Landesbibliothek LBr. F 4 [175] 88r. Caroline's letter to Leibniz of 29 October 1716 (document 156), with which she transmitted Clarke's Fifth Reply for Leibniz. Reproduced with permission of the Gottfried Wilhelm Leibniz Bibliothek-Niedersächsische Landesbibliothek.

1716

Caroline of Brandenburg-Ansbach, Princess of Wales, to Leibniz

St James le $\frac{10}{30}$ December[2] 1715

J'ay eu vn sy grand R[h]ume que je n'ay peu vous reponder[4] Monsieur. Je suis bien[5] que mes livers on etté agreablement receu[6] de vous. Vous trouverais dans D: Thilonson[7] beaucoup de rapors[8] avec vos opinions, que vous nous avez sy admirablement marqu[é]e[s] dans votre deodisce. J[']espere que vos souhaits seron exsaucée, et qu'a lavenir nous n'andanteron plus parller de repellion dans c'est ille.[9] Madame, ne s'est pas contandé[10] de vous dire ces santimens[11] elle me les a écrité[12] avec la même franchise, an dissan mille bien[13] du feu duc dormont, ce qui ma porté de luy anvoiyer an francois[14] le Raporte de la comitée segrette[15] ou elle trouvera le caractere de c'est honest home,[16] avec les santiment[17] de Mr Torcy sur la renonciassion du Roy d'Espanye a la courone de France.[18] J'espere qu[']elle le fera lire a M^r le Regent. Je l'ay doñe au comte de Salmour[19] pour le luy rander.[20,21] Je vous ranvois vne reponce a votre papié[22] je conservez[23] avec tout le soins[25] du monde les reponce de codée[24] et d'autre. Je ne scais sy la prevantion[26] que j'ay pour votre merité me rand parcialle,[27] mais je trouvez tout replique, plus tos des môs[28] sans qu'on les puis[s]e nom[m]er des replique[s] vous ne vous ette[29] point trompé a lodeur des reponce,[30] elle[s] ne sont pas écrit[es] sans la vie[31] du chev. neuthon, que je vous derais racomodé[32] avec vous. Je ne scais sy[33] vous y voulez consantir,[34] mais l'abée condy et moy nous nous avons erigée an médyateurs,[35] et il serais a plainder que deu ausy grands homes que vous et luy feusiée des vny pour des mesandantus.[36] Je vous remercy de la connaissance de l'abée qui as-ceque londit ettres savans.[38] c[']es[t] de quoy je ne puis juger, mais je luy trouvez de l'Espris[39] et vn grande Estime pour vous. Je n'ay peu manpécher[40] de dire au docteur glerch que votre opinion me paraissait la plus convenable ala[41] perfection de dieu, et que toute philosophie qui m'an voulet Eloinger,[42] me paressoit[43] imparfait puisque selon moy elle estté fait ou devoit estre recherché[44] pour nous tranquilliser, et fortifier conter[45] nous même et de[46] tout ce qui nous hurdé hor'de[47] nous, que je ne croiet pas quelle pouroit faire c'est effait[48] sy elle nous monderait[49] l'imperfection de dieu il ma fort lon tems parlle[50] pour me faire de son opinion, et il ya perdu son ladin.[51] Je vous prie dy reponder.[52] vous saurais que mon bon amis[53] L'Eveque de Lincolme et Archevèque de canterbury, cequi ma estte vn sansible[54] plaisir, non seulment par raport aluy,[55] mais davoir vn home de son merité ala detté de nos Eglise protestande[56] il ma parlle aujour-dehuy de votre admirable deodisee et d'apor apres que[57] son installassion sera fait nous panseron alafaire[58] traduire. Je suis toute glorieuse d'avoir les même santiment avec se[59] grand home, qui trouvez que plus on rélié seliver plus on le trouvez imcomparable.[60] Le gout, que j'ay pour se liver me

95. Caroline* of Brandenburg-Ansbach, Princess of Wales, to Leibniz[1]

Saint James, $\frac{10}{30}$ December[2] 1715[3]

I have had such a bad cold that I have not been able to respond,[4] sir. I am very glad[5] that my books have been pleasantly received[6] by you. You will find in Dr. Tillotson[7] much affinity[8] with your views, which you have so admirably stated for us in your *Theodicy*. I hope that your wishes will be granted and that in the future we will hear no more talk of rebellion on this island.[9] Madame [Elisabeth Charlotte* of the Palatinate, Duchess of Orléans] is not content[10] to tell you her opinions.[11] She has written[12] them to me with the same frankness in saying a thousand good things[13] about the late Duke of Ormonde, which has led me to send her, in French,[14] the report of the committee of secrecy,[15] in which she will discover the character of this honourable man,[16] along with the opinions[17] of Mr. Torcy [the French diplomat, Jean-Baptiste Colbert, marquis de Torcy (1665–1746)] concerning the King of Spain's renunciation of the crown of France.[18] I hope that she will have it read to Monseigneur the Regent [Philippe II*, Duke of Orléans]. I gave it to the Count of Salmour[19] to deliver[20] it to her.[21] I am sending back to you a response to your paper.[22] I will preserve[23] the responses on both sides[24] with all the care[25] in the world. I do not know if the bias[26] I have for your merit makes me partial,[27] but I find any reply to be rather words,[28] without their being able to be called replies. You are[29] not mistaken about the author of the responses;[30] they are not written without the advice[31] of Chevalier Newton, whom I would like to reconcile[32] with you. I do not know[33] if you will consent[34] to it, but Abbé [Antonio Schinella] Conti*, and I have set ourselves up as mediators,[35] and it would be a pity if two men as great as you and he were divided by misunderstandings.[36] I thank you for the acquaintance of the Abbé,[37] who is, so they say, very learned.[38] This is something about which I am not able to judge, but I think that he is witty[39] and that he has a great respect for you. I was unable to prevent myself[40] from saying to Doctor [Samuel] Clarke* that your opinion appeared to me the most suitable to the[41] perfection of God, and that all philosophy that sought to alienate[42] me from it appeared[43] to me to be imperfect, since on my view it was done or ought to be sought[44] in order to sooth us and to strengthen us against[45] ourselves and from[46] everything that assails us from outside,[47] since I do not believe it could have this effect[48] if it taught[49] us the imperfection of God. He spoke to me a very long time[50] in order to convert me to his view, and he did not succeed.[51] Please respond to it.[52] You must know that my good friend[53] the Bishop of Lincoln [William Wake*] is Archbishop of Canterbury, which has been a palpable[54] pleasure for me, not just in relation to him,[55] but to have a man of his merit at the head of our Protestant church.[56] He spoke to me today about

fait souvenir de L'Evèque de Spica,[61] qui dissoit aimé estter ademiré[62] dans la musique[63] par les plus grand ingoran.[64] Je me fladee que vous aurais le même santiment,[65] ensy vous devez ettre tres condans destre ademirer[66] par vne ausy grande ingorante que moy, mais la verité frapée les ingoran come les plus savan, et c'es[67] ce que j'ay prie la liberdée[68] de dire a feu M^d L'Electrice, qui pretandes ne le pouvoir andantre.[69] Je crois que [l']on donnera quelque order ahañover pour votre argeans[70] du moins j'y fais de mon mieux et le ferais toujours ou il sagira[71] de vous faire plaisir.

Caroline

95. CAROLINE OF BRANDENBURG-ANSBACH TO LEIBNIZ 375

your admirable *Theodicy*, and immediately after[57] his installation is done we will think about having it[58] translated. I am quite proud to agree with this[59] great man, who finds that the more this book is reread the more it is found incomparable.[60] The fondness I have for this book reminds me of the Bishop of Spiga[61] [Agostino Steffani*], who said that he loved being admired[62] in music[63] by the greatest ignoramuses.[64] I expect that you must feel the same way;[65] so you ought to be very glad to be admired[66] by as great an ignoramus as I, but the truth moves the ignorant and the most wise alike, and that is[67] what I took the liberty[68] of telling the late electress [Dowager Electress of Braunschweig-Lüneburg, Sophie* of the Palatinate], who claimed not to be able to understand it[69] [i.e., the *Theodicy*]. I believe that some order will be given at Hanover for your money;[70] at least I am doing my best and will always do it when it is a matter[71] of pleasing you.

Caroline

[1] LBr. F 4 Bl. 49r–51v. Letter as sent: six quarto sides in Caroline's hand. Previously published in Kemble 534–6; Klopp XI 71–3; Schüler 1991, pp. 223–4 (excerpt in German translation); HGA 193 (excerpt in English translation). Reply to Leibniz's letter of mid-December 1715 (document 91). For Leibniz's reply to the present letter, see the extract from his letter to Caroline of 25 February 1716 (document 99).

[2] Reading 'Decembre' for 'December'.

[3] That is, 30 December 1715 (OS)/10 January 1716 (NS).

[4] Reading 'pu vous répondre' for 'peu vous reponder'.

[5] Reading 'bien aise' for 'bien'.

[6] Reading 'livres ont été agréablement reçus' for 'livers on etté agreablement receu'.

[7] Reading 'trouverez dans Dr. Tillotson' for 'trouverais dans D: Thilonson'. The reference is to John Tillotson*.

[8] Reading 'rapport' for 'rapors'.

[9] Reading 'souhaits seront exaucés, et qu'à l'avenir nous n'entendrons plus parler de rébellion dans cette île' for 'souhait seron exsaucée, et qu'a lavenir nous n'andanteron plus parller de repellion dans c'est ille'.

[10] Reading 'contentée' for 'contandé'.

[11] Reading 'ses sentiments' for 'ces santimens'.

[12] Reading 'écrites' for 'écrité'.

[13] Reading 'en disant mille biens' for 'an dissan mille bien'.

[14] Reading 'm'a portée de lui envoyer en François' for 'ma porté de luy anvoiyer an francois'.

[15] Reading 'le rapport de la comité secret' for 'le Raporte de la comitée segrette'. Klopp mistranscribes this as simply 'un autre rapport' (see Klopp XI 71). Caroline is referring to the report of the committee of secrecy that was appointed by the Whig-dominated Parliament in March 1715 to investigate the acts of the previous ministry, especially the negotiations leading up to the Treaty of Utrecht*, as well as possible Jacobite plots by Tory ministers (Gregg 2001, p. 399).

[16] Reading 'caractère de cet honnête homme' for 'caractere de c'est honest home'. Caroline is being sarcastic when she refers to the 2nd Duke of Ormonde (James Butler, 1665–1745) as 'this honourable man', since Ormonde was impeached for 'high treason and other high crimes and misdemeanours' by the House of Commons in June of 1715. He consequently fled to France in August, whereupon the Parliament passed an act of attainder confiscating his titles and estates. He later took part in the First Jacobite Rebellion of 1715. Caroline refers to him as 'the late Duke of Ormonde', not because he was deceased, but rather to indicate that his title of 'Duke of Ormonde' had been abolished in the Peerage of England by the 1715 act of attainder.

[17] Reading 'sentiments' for 'santiment'.

95. CAROLINE OF BRANDENBURG-ANSBACH TO LEIBNIZ 377

[18] Reading 'renonciation du Roy d'Espagne à la couronne de France' for 'renonciassion du Roy d'Espanye a la courone de France'. Caroline is referring to Philippe V* of Spain (1683–1746), who renounced his claim to the French throne in 1712 in order to retain the throne of Spain.

[19] Reading 'donné au comte de Salmour' for 'doñe au com̃te de Salmour'. At the time, the Count of Slamour was Joseph Anton Gabaleon von Wackerbarth-Salmour (1685–1761).

[20] Reading 'rendre' for 'rander'.

[21] Klopp omits this sentence (Klopp XI 71).

[22] Reading 'renvoie une réponse à votre papier' for 'ranvois vne reponce a votre papié'. The 'response' is Clarke's Second Reply (document 96), and the 'paper' is Leibniz's Second Paper (document 92).

[23] Reading 'conserverai' for 'conservez'.

[24] Reading 'réponses de côté' for 'reponce de codé'.

[25] Reading 'soin' for 'soins'.

[26] Reading 'sais si la prévention' for 'scais sy la prevantion'.

[27] Reading 'mérite me rend partiale' for 'merité me rand parcialle'.

[28] Reading 'trouve toute replique plutôt des mots' for 'trouvez tout replique plus tos des môs'.

[29] Reading 'êtes' for 'ette'.

[30] Reading 'à l'auteur des réponses' for 'a lodeur des reponce'.

[31] Reading 'l'avis' for 'la vie'.

[32] Reading 'voudrais raccommoder' for 'vous derais racomodé'.

[33] Reading 'sais si' for 'scais sy'.

[34] Reading 'consentir' for 'consantir'.

[35] Reading 'sommes érigés en médiateurs' for 'avons erigée an médyateurs'.

[36] Reading 'il serait à plaindre que deux aussi grands hommes fussent désunis pour des mésentendus' for 'il serais a plainder que deu ausy grands hom̃es que vous et luy feusiée des vny pour des mesandantus'.

[37] As time went on, Leibniz came to regret his introduction of Conti, suspecting him of not changing his allegiances after arriving in England and of colluding with the Newtonians. See Leibniz's letters to Caroline of 28 April 1716 (document 113, p. 501), 12 May 1716 (document 117a, p. 521), 2 June 1716 (document 124, pp. 557, 559), and from the end of September to mid-October 1716 (document 149, p. 745).

[38] Reading 'à ce que l'on dit est très savant' for 'as-ceque londit et tres savans'.

[39] Reading 'trouve de l'esprit' for 'trouvez de l'Espris'.

[40] Reading 'pu m'empêcher' for 'peu manpécher'.

[41] Reading 'à la' for 'ala'.

[42] Reading 'm'en voulait éloigner' for 'm'an voulet Eloinger'.

[43] Reading 'paraissait' for 'paressoit'.

[44] Reading 'étoit fait ou devait être recherchée' for 'estté fait ou devoit estre recherché'.

[45] Reading 'contre' for 'conter'.

[46] Klopp omits 'de' (see Klopp XI 72).

[47] Reading 'heurte hors de' for 'hurdé hor'de'.

[48] Reading 'croyais pas qu'elle pourrait faire cet effect' for 'croiet pas quelle pouroit faire c'est effait'.

[49] Reading 'montrait' for 'monderait'.

[50] Reading 'm'a fort longtemps parlé' for 'ma fort lon tems parlle'.

[51] Reading 'il y a perdu son latin' for 'il ya perdu son ladin'. Literally: 'he wasted his Latin'.

[52] Reading 'd'y répondre' for 'dy reponder'.

[53] Reading 'ami' for 'amis'.

[54] Reading 'ce qui m'a été un sensible' for 'cequi ma estte vn sansible'.

[55] Reading 'par rapport à lui' for 'par raport aluy'.

[56] Reading 'mérite à la tête de notre Eglise protestante' for 'merité ala detté de nos Eglise protestande'.

[57] Reading 'd'abord après que' for 'd'apor apres que'. Klopp omits 'd'apor' (see Klopp XI 72).

[58] Reading 'installation sera faite nous penserons à la faire' for 'installassion sera fait nous panseron alafaire'.

[59] Reading 'mêmes sentiments avec ce' for 'même santiment avec se'.

[60] Reading 'trouve que plus on relit ce livre plus on le trouve incomparable' for 'trouvez que plus on rélié seliver plus on le trouvez imcomparable'.

[61] Klopp transcribes 'de L'Evêque de Spica' as 'd'un autre Evêque' (Klopp XI 72).

[62] Reading 'disait aimer être admiré' for 'dissoit aimé estter ademiré'.

[63] Klopp omits 'dans la musique' without notice (see Klopp XI 72).

Second Reply of Samuel Clarke

Séconde Replique de Mr. CLARKE.

1. *Lors que j'ai dit que les* Principes Mathematiques de la Philosophie *sont contraires à ceux des* Materialistes, *j'ai voulu dire, qu'au lieu que les* Materialistes *supposent que la Structure de l'Univers peut avoir été produite par les Seuls Principes* Mechaniques, *de la* Matiere & *du* Mouvement, *de la* Nécessité & *de la* Fatalité ; *les* Principes Mathématiques de la Philosophie *font voir au contraire, que l'Etat des choses* [*la* Constitution *du* Soleil & des Planetes] *n'a pu être produit que par une Cause intelligente & libre. A l'égard du* mot de Mathematique *ou de* Metaphysique, *on peut appeler, si on le juge à propos, les Principes* Mathematiques, *des Principes* Metaphysiques, *selon que les Consequences* Metaphysiques *naissent démonstrativement des Principes* Mathematiques.   *Il est vrais que rien n'existe, sans une* Raison suffisante ; & *que rien n'existe d'une certaine manière, plûtôt que d'une autre, sans qu'il y ait aussi une Raison suffisante pour cela ; & par conséquent, lors qu'il n'y a aucune cause, il ne peut y avoir auncun Effet. Mais cette* Raison suffisante, *est souvent la* simple Volonté *de Dieu. Par exemple ; si l'on considere pourquoi* une certaine Portion ou Systeme de Matiere a été créée *dans* un certain *lieu* ; & *une autre dans* un autre certain *lieu, puisque* tout lieu *etant absolument indifferent à* toute Matiere, *c'eut été précisément la même chose* vice versa, *supposé que les deux Portions de* Matiere [*ou leurs* Particules,] *soient semblables* ; *si, dis-je, l'on considere cela, on n'en peut alleguer d'autre raison, que la* simple Volonté de Dieu. Et si cette Volonté ne *pouvoit jamais agir, sans être prédeterminée par quelque cause, comme une* Balance *ne sçauroit se mouvoir, sans le poids qui la fait pencher ; Dieu n'auroit pas la liberté de* choisir ; & *ce seroit introduire la* Fatalité.

2. *Plusieurs anciens Philosophes* Grecs, *qui avoient emprunté leur Philosophie des* Pheniciens, & *dont la doctrine fut corrompue par* Epicure, *admettoient en général la* Matiere & *le* Vuide. *Mais ils ne sçurent pas se servir de ces Principes, pour expliquer les* Phénomenes de la Nature *par le moyen des Mathematiques. Quelque* petite *que soit la* Quantité *de la* Matiere, Dieu *ne manque pas de Sujets, sur lesquels il puisse exercer sa sagesse & sa puissance ; car il y a d'*autres choses, *outre la* Matiere, *qui sont*

64 Reading 'grands ignorants' for 'grand ingoran'.

65 Reading 'flatte que vous aurez le même sentiment' for 'fladee que vous aurais le même santiment'.

66 Reading 'ainsi vous devez être très content d'être admiré' for 'ensy vous devez ettre tres condans destre ademirer'.

67 Reading 'frappe les ignorants comme les plus savants, et c'est' for 'frapée les ingoran comme les plus savan, et c'es'.

68 Reading 'pris la liberté' for 'prie la liberdée'.

69 Reading 'prétendait ne le pouvoir entendre' for 'pretandes ne le pouvoir andantre'.

70 Reading 'ordre à Hannover pour votre argent' for 'order ahañover pour votre argeans'.

71 Reading 'ferai toujours où il s'agira' for 'ferais toujours ou il sagira'.

96. Second Reply of Samuel Clarke*[1]

Dr. CLARKE's Second Reply.

1. When I said that the *Mathematical Principles of Philosophy* are opposite to those of the *Materialists* ; the Meaning was, that whereas the *Materialists* suppose the Frame of Nature to be such as could have arisen from mere *Mechanical* Principles of *Matter* and *Motion*, of *Necessity* and *Fate* ; the *Mathematical Principles of Philosophy* show on the contrary, that the State of Things [the *Constitution* of the *Sun and Planets*] is such as could not arise from any thing but an *Intelligent* and *Free Cause*. As to the Propriety of the *Name* ; so far as *Metaphysical* Consequences follow demonstratively from *Mathematical* Principles, so far the *Mathematical* Principles may (if it be thought fit) be called *Metaphysical* Principles.

'Tis very true, that nothing *is*, without a sufficient *Reason why* it *is*, and why it is *thus* rather than *otherwise*. And therefore, where there is *no Cause*, there can be *no Effect*. But this *sufficient Reason* is oft-times no other, than the *mere Will* of God. For instance ; Why *This* particular System of Matter, should be created in *one* particular Place, and *That* in *another* particular Place ; when, (*all Place* being absolutely indifferent to *all Matter*,) it would have been exactly the same thing *vice versa*, supposing the two *Systems* [or the *Particles*] of Matter to be *alike* ; there can be *no other Reason*, but the *mere Will* of God. Which if it could in No Case act without a predetermining Cause, any more than a *Balance* can move without a preponderating Weight ; this would tend to take away all Power of *Chusing*, and to introduce *Fatality*.

2. Many Ancient *Greeks*, who had their Philosophy from the *Phœnicians*, and whose Philosophy was corrupted by *Epicurus*, held indeed in general *Matter* and *Vacuum* ; but they knew not how to apply those Principles by *Mathematicks*, to the Explication of the *Phænomena of Nature*. How *Small* soever the *Quantity* of Matter be, God has not at all the less Subject to exercise his Wisdom and Power upon : For, *Other* Things, as well as *Matter*, are equally Subjects, on which God exercises his Power and Wisdom. By the same Argument it might just as well have been proved,

380 96. SECOND REPLY OF CLARKE

également des Sujets, sur lesquels Dieu exerce sa puissance & sa sagesse. On auroit pu prouver par la même raison, que les Hommes, *ou toute autre Espece de Creatures, doivent être* infinis en nombre, *afin que Dieu ne manque pas de Sujets pour exercer sa Puissance & sa Sagesse.*

3. *Le Mot de* Sensorium *ne signifie pas proprement l'*Organe, *mais le* Lieu *de la* Sensation. *L'*Oéil, *l'*Oreille, &c. *sont des* Organes ; *mais ce ne sont pas des* Sensoria. *D'ailleurs, Mr. le Chevalier* Newton * *ne dit pas, que l'*Espace *est un* Sensorium ; *mais qu'il est, (par voye de Comparaison,) pour ainsi dire le* Sensorium, &c.

4. *On n'a jamais supposé que la Presence de l'Ame suffit pour la Perception : On a dit seulement que cette Presence est nécessaire afin que l'Ame apperçoive. Si l'Ame n'étoit pas presente aux Images des Choses, qui sont apperçues, elle ne pourroit pas les apercevoir : Mais sa Presence ne suffit pas, à moins qu'elle ne soit aussi une* Substance vivante. *Les Substances* inanimées, *quoique presentes, n'apperçoivent rien : Et une Substance vivante n'est capable de Perception, que dans le Lieu où elle est presente ; soit aux choses mêmes, comme Dieu est present à tout l'Univers ; soit aux* Images *des choses, comme l'Ame leur est presente dans son* Sensorium. *Il est impossible qu'une chose* agisse, *ou que quelque Sujet* agisse *sur elle, dans un lieu où elle n'est pas.*   Quoique l'Ame soit indivisible, *il ne s'ensuit pas qu'elle n'est presente que* dans un seul Point. *L'*Espace, *fini ou infini, est absolument indivisible, même par la pensée ; car on ne peut s'imaginer que ses parties se separent l'une de l'autre, sans s'imaginer qu'elles † sortent, pour ainsi dire, hors d'elles mêmes ; & cependant l'Espace n'est pas un* simple Point.

5. *Dieu n'apperçoit pas les chose par sa simple* Presence, *ni parce qu'il agit sur elles ; mais parce qu'il est, non seulement* present par tout, *mais encore un* Etre Vivant & Intelligent. *On doit dire la même chose d'l'Ame, dans sa petite Sphere. Ce n'est point par sa simple* Presence, *mais parce qu'elle est une Substance* vivante, *qu'elle appersoit les* Images *auxquelles elle est presente, & qu'elle ne ssauroit apercevoir sans leur être presente.*

6 & 7. *Il est vrai, que l'Excellence de l'Ouvrage de Dieu ne consiste pas seulement en ce que cet Ouvrage fait voir la* Puissance *de son Auteur, mais encore en ce qu'il montre sa* Sagesse. *Mais Dieu ne fait pas paroitre cette* Sagesse, *en rendant la Nature capable de se mouvoir sans lui, comme un Horloger fait mouvoir une Horloge. Cela est impossible, puis qu'il n'y a point de Forces dans la Nature, qui soient indépendantes de Dieu, comme les Forces des Poids & des Ressorts sont indépendantes des hommes. La Sagesse de Dieu consiste donc en ce qu'il a formé dès le commencement une Idée parfaite & complete d'un Ouvrage, qui a commencé & qui subsiste toûjours, conformément à cette Idée, par l'exercice perpetuel de la puissance & du Govern'ment de son Auteur.*

8. *Le mot de* Correction, *ou de* Réforme, *ne doit pas être entendu par rapport à* Dieu ; *mais uniquement par rapport à Nous. L'Etat present du système* Solaire, *(par exemple,) selon les Loix du mouvement qui sont maintenant, établies, tombera un jour ‡ en confusion ; & ensuite il sera peut-être redressé, ou bien il recevra une*

---

* Voïez la Note dans ma prémiére Réplique, § 3.

† Ut partium Temporis Ordo est immutabilis, sic etiam Ordo partium *Spatij.* Moveantur hæ de locis suis, & movebuntur (ut ita dicam) *de Seipsis. Newton. Princip. Schol. Ad Defin.* 8.

‡ Voïez la Note sur le *prémier Ecrit de Mr. Leibnitz,* § 4.

96. SECOND REPLY OF CLARKE 381

that *Men*, or any other particular Species of Beings, must be *infinite in Number*, least God should want Subjects, on which to exercise his Power and Wisdom.

3. The Word *Sensory* does not properly signify the *Organ*, but the *Place* of Sensation. The Word *Sensory* does not properly signify the *Organ*, but the *Place* of Sensation. The *Eye*, the *Ear*, &c. are *Organs*, but not *Sensoria*. Besides, Sir *Isaac Newton* * does not say, that *Space* is the *Sensory* ; but that it is, by way of Similitude only, *as it were* the Sensory, *&c*.

4. It was never supposed, that the *Presence* of the Soul was *sufficient*, but only that it is *necessary* in order to Perception. *Without being present* to the Images of the Things perceived, it could not possibly perceive them : But *being present* is not *sufficient*, without it be also a *Living Substance*. Any *inanimate* Substance, tho' *present*, perceives nothing : And a *Living* Substance can only *there* perceive, where it is *present* either to the *Things themselves*, (as the Omnipresent God is to the whole Universe ;) or to the *Images* of Things, (as the Soul of Man is in its proper Sensory.) Nothing can any more *Act*, or *be Acted upon*, where it is not present ; than it can *Be*, where it is not. The Soul's being *Indivisible*, does not prove it to be present *only in a mere Point. Space*, finite or infinite, is *absolutely indivisible*, even so much as in *Thought* ; (To imagine its Parts moved from each other, is to imagine them † moved *out of themselves* ;) and yet *Space* is *not a mere Point*.

5. *God* perceives Things, not indeed by his simple *Presence* to them, nor yet by his *Operation* upon them, but by his being a *Living* and *Intelligent*, as well as an *Omnipresent* Substance. The *Soul* likewise, (within its narrow Sphere,) not by its simple *Presence*, but by its being a *Living* Substance, perceives the *Images* to which it is *present* ; and which, *without being present* to them, it could not perceive.

6 & 7. 'Tis very true, that the Excellency of *God*'s Workmanship does not consist in its showing the *Power* only, but in its showing the *Wisdom also* of its Author. But then this *Wisdom of God* appears, not in making Nature (as an Artificer makes a Clock) capable of going on *Without him* : (For that's *impossible* ; there being *no Powers* of Nature *independent* upon *God*, as the *Powers* of *Weights* and *Springs* are *independent* upon *Men* :) But the *Wisdom of God* consists, in framing *Originally* the *perfect* and *complete Idea* of a Work, which *begun and continues*, according to that Original perfect Idea, by the *Continual Uninterrupted Exercise* of his *Power* and *Government*.

8. The Word *Correction*, or *Amendment*, is to be understood, not with regard to *God*, but to *Us* only. The present Frame of the Solar System (for instance,) according to the present Laws of Motion, will in time ‡ *fall into Confusion* ; and perhaps, after *That*, will be *amended* or put into a *new Form*. But this Amendment is only *relative*, with regard to *Our Conceptions*. In reality, and with regard to *God* ; the present *Frame*, and the consequent *Disorder*, and the following *Renovation*, are *all* equally parts of the Design framed in Gods Original perfect Idea. 'Tis in the Frame of the

---

* *See the* Note *in my First Reply*, § 3.

† Ut partium Temporis Ordo est immutabilis, sic etiam Ordo partium *Spatij*. Moveantur hæ de locis suis, & movebuntur (ut ita dicam) *de Seipsis. Newton. Princip. Schol. Ad Defin.* 8.

‡ *See the* Note *on Mr.* Leibnitz's *First* Paper. § 4.

382   96. SECOND REPLY OF CLARKE

nouvelle forme. Mais ce changement n'est que relatif, *par rapport à notre manière de concevoir les choses.* L'Etat prsent *du Monde, le* desordre *où il tombera, & le* Rénouvellement *dont ce desordre seera suivi, entrent également dans le dessien que Dieu a formé. Il en est de la Formation du Monde, comme de celle du Corps Humain : La Sagesse de Dieu ne consiste pas à les rendre éternels, mais à les faire durer aussi long temps qu'il le juge à propos.*

9. *La Sagesse & la* || *Préscience de Dieu ne consistent pas à préparer des remedes par avance, qui gueriront d'eux-mêmes les desordres de la Nature. Car, à proprement parler, il n'arrive aucun desordre dans le Monde, par rapport à Dieu ; & par conséquent, il n'y a point de Remedes, il n'y a point même de Forces naturelles, qui puissent agir d'elles mêmes, comme les* Poids *& les* Ressorts *agissent d'eux-mêmes par rapport aux hommes. Mais la Sagesse & la Préscience de Dieu consistent, comme on l'a dit ci-dessus, à former dès le commencement un dessein, que sa puissance met continuellement en execution.*

10. *Dieu n'est point une* Intelligentia Mundana, *ni une* Intelligentia Supramundana, *mais une Intelligence qui est* par tout, *dans le Monde, & hors du Monde. Il est* en tout, par tout, & par dessus tout.

11. *Quand on dit que Dieu* conserve *les choses ; si l'on veut dire par là, qu'il agit actuellement sur elles, & qu'il les gouverne, en continuant & en continuant leurs Etres, leurs Forces, leurs Arrangemens, & leurs Mouvemens ; c'est precisément ce que je soûtiens. Mais si l'on veut dire simplement, que Dieu en* conservant *les choses ressemble à un Roi, qui crééroit des Sujets, lesquels seroient capables d'agir, sans qu'il eut aucune part à ce qui se passeroit parmi eux ; si c'est-là, dis-je, ce que l'on veut dire, Dieu sera un* véritable Createur, *mais il n'aura que le* Titre de Gouverneur.

12. *Le raisonnement que l'on trouve ici, suppose que tout ce que Dieu fait, est* Surnaturel *ou* Miraculeux ; *& par conséquent, il tend à exclure Dieu du Gouvernement actuel du Monde. Mais il est certain que le* Naturel *& le* Surnaturel *ne different en rien l'un de l'autre par rapport à Dieu : Ce sont que des Distinctions, selon nôtre maniere de concevoir les choses. Donner un mouvement réglé au Soleil (ou à la Terre,) c'est une chose que nous appellons* Naturelle : *Arrêter ce mouvement pendant un jour, c'est une chose* Surnaturelle *selon nos idées. Mais la derniere de ces deux choses n'est pas l'effet d'une plus grande puissance que l'autre ; & par rapport à Dieu, elles sont toutes deux egalement* Naturelles *ou* Surnaturelles. *Quoique Dieu soit* present *dans tout l'Univers, il ne s'ensuit point qu'il soit* * *l'Ame du Monde. L'Ame humaine*

|| Voïez mes Discours sur l'Existence de Dieu, la Verité de la Réligion Naturelle, &c. Part I. Pag. 106. quatriéme Edition.

* *Deus omnia regit, &c.* Dieu gouverne tout, non comme une *Ame du Monde,* mais comme le *Seigneur de l'Univers.* Le mot de *Dieu* est Rélatif : Il emporte une idée de Rélation à des *Serviteurs* ; & la *Divinité* de Dieu, est sa *Domination,* qui ne ressemble pas à celle de l'Ame sur *son propre corps,* mais à celle d'un *Seigneur* ou d'un *Maitre sur ses Serviteurs.* _____ Tout Subsiste & se meut en Dieu ; mais sans aucune passion mutuelle. Dieu n'est en aucune maniere affecté par le mouvement des corps ; & le mouvement des corps n'est point interrompu par la presence de Dieu. ___ Dieu n'a ni Corps, ni figure corporelle : c'est pourquoi on ne ssauroit le voir, l'entendre, ni le toucher ; & il ne doit être adoré sous la ressemblance d'aucune chose corporelle. Nous avons des Idées de ses *Attributs ;* mais les *Substances* des

World, as in the Frame of Mans *Body* : The *Wisdom of God* does not consist, in making the *present Frame* of Either of them *Eternal*, but to last *so long* as *he thought fit*.

9. The *Wisdom* and || *Foresight* of God, do not consist in *providing originally Remedies*, which shall *of themselves* cure the Disorders of Nature. For in Truth and Strictness, with regard to God, there are *No Disorders*, and consequently *no Remedies*, and indeed *no Powers* of Nature *at all*, that can do any Thing *of themselves*, (as *Weights* and *Springs* Work *of themselves* with regard to *Men* :) But the *Wisdom and Foresight* of God, consist (as has been said) in *contriving* at *once*, what his *Power and Government* is *Continually* putting in actual Execution.

10. God is neither a *Mundane* Intelligence, nor a *Supra-Mundane* Intelligence ; but an *Omnipresent* Intelligence, both *In* and *Without* the World. He is *In* all, and *Through* all, as well as *Above* all.

11. If God's *conserving* all Things, means his *actual Operation and Government*, in preserving and continuing the Beings, Powers, Orders, Dispositions and Motions of all Things ; this is *all that is contended for*. But if his *conserving* Things, means no more than a King's creating such Subjects, as shall be able to act well enough without his intermeddling or Ordering any thing amongst them ever after ; This is making him indeed a *real Creator*, but a *Governour only Nominal*.

12. The Argument in this Paragraph supposes, that whatsoever *God* does, is *Supernatural* or *Miraculous* ; and consequently it tends to exclude *All Operation* of *God* in the *Governing and Ordering* of the *Natural* World. But the Truth is ; *Natural* and *Supernatural* are nothing at all different with regard to *God*, but distinctions merely in *Our* Conceptions of things. To cause the *Sun* [or *Earth*] to *move* regularly, is a thing we call *Natural* : To *stop* its Motion for a Day, we call *Supernatural* : But the *One* is the Effect of *no greater Power*, than the *Other* ; nor is the *One*, with respect to *God*, more or less *Natural* or *Supernatural* than the *other*. God's being *present In* or *To* the World, does not make him to be the * *Soul of the World*. A *Soul*,

---

|| *See my Sermons preach'd at Mr.* Boyles *Lecture.* Part I. Page 106. Fourth Edition.

* Hic [*Deus*] omnia regit, non ut *Anima Mundi*, sed ut universorum *Dominus*. _____ Deus est vox relativa, & ad *Servos* refertur ; & *Deitas* est Dominatio Dei, non in *corpus proprium*, sed in *Servos*. _____ In ipso continentur & moventur universa, sed absq; mutuâ *passione*. Deus nihil patitur ex corporum Motibus ; illa nullam sentiunt resistentiam ex Omnipræsentiâ Dei. _____ Corpore omni & figurâ corporeâ prorsus destituitur ; ideoq; videri non potest, nec audiri, nec tangi, nec sub species rei alicujus corporei coli debet. Ideas habemus *Attributorum* ejus ; sed quid sit rei alicujus *Substantia*, minimè cognoscimus. _____ Intimas [*corporum*] Substantias nullo Sensu, nulla actione reflexâ cognoscimus, & multò minus Ideam habemus Substantiæ Dei. Hunc cognoscimus solummodò per Proprietates suas & Attributa, & per sapientissimas & optimas rerum structuras, & causas finales ; veneramur autem & colimus ob dominium. Deus enim sine Dominio, Providentia, & Causis Finalibus, nihil aliud est quàm Fatum & Natura. i.e. *God Governs all Things, not as a* Soul *of the World, but as the* Lord *of the Universe.* _____ God, *is a relative Word, carrying in it the notion of Relation to* Servants. *And the* Godhead *of God, is his* Dominion : *A Dominion, not like that of a* Soul *over its own Body, but that of a* Lord *over his* Servants. _____ *In Him all Things subsist and move, but without a mutual affecting of each other,* [such as is between Soul and Body.] *God is no way affected by the Motions of Bodies ; and the Motion of Bodies meets with no Obstruction from the Omnipresence of God.* _____ *He is altogether without Body or Bodily Shape ; and therefore can neither be Seen, nor Heard, nor Felt ; nor ought to be worshipped under the similitude of any Corporeal Thing. We have Ideas of his* Attributes ; *but what the* Substance *of any Thing is,*

est une partie d'un Composé, *dont le Corps est l'autre partie* ; *& ces deux parties agissent mutuellement l'une sur l'autre, comme étant les parties d'un même Tout. Mais Dieu est dans le Monde, non comme une* partie *de l'Univers, mais comme un* Gouverneur : *Il agit sur tout, & rien n'agit sur lui.* Il n'est pas loin de chacun de nous ; car en lui nous (& *toutes les choses qui existent*) avons la vie, le mouvement, & l'être.

Leibniz to Caroline of Brandenburg-Ansbach,
Princess of Wales

Madame

Apres avoir eu l'honneur depuis peu d'ecrire une longue lettre à V. A. R. je ne devrois pas y revenir si tost, si la lettre d'un ami de Berlin ne m'avoit donné occasion de penser à une chose importante aux les'Eglises protestante[3] en General; ou il me paroist que V. A. Royale, pourroit estre un organe choisi par la providence pour la faire reussir. Afin d'entrer en matiere il faut vous raconter, Madame, ce qui s'est passé déja la dessus autres fois.[4] Feu Monsieur de Spanheim passant un jour par Hanover eût ordre du Roy son maitre de sonder notre Roy, alors Electeur, s'il n'y avoit moyen de venir à une meilleure intelligence entre les deux Eglises protestantes, dont les Theologiens de Brandebourg et de Bronsvic, etant constamment les plus moderés de l'Empire pourroient jetter les premiers fondemens. Cela fut agreé, Monsieur l'Eveque Ursinus et M. Jablonski furent nommés d'un cote, et Monsieur l'Abbé Molanus de l'autre qui voulut que j'y fusse joint ce que Mon^sgr l'Electeur trouva bon. On vint à des conferences de vive voix et a des communications par ou

---

Etres, sans aucune exception, nous sont entierement inconnues. _____ Nous ne sçaurions même connoitre les *Substances* des *Corps* ni par quelqu'un de nos *Sens*, ni par quelque *Acte réflechi de notre Esprit.* La *Substance de Dieu* nous est encore moins connue. Nous ne le connoissons que par ses *proprietez* & ses *Attributs*, par son *excellente* & *très-Sage disposition des choses*, & par les *Causes Finales* : Et nous l'adorons, & le servons, à cause de sa *Domination.* Car un *Dieu* sans *Domination*, sans *Providence*, & sans *Causes Finales*, n'est autre chose que le *Destin* & la *Nature. Newtoni Principia, Scholium generale sub finem.*

97. LEIBNIZ TO CAROLINE OF BRANDENBURG-ANSBACH   385

is *part* of a *Compound*, whereof *Body* is the *Other* part ; and they *mutually Affect* each other, as *parts* of the *same whole*. But *God* is *present* to the *World*, not as a *Part*, but as a *Governor*; Acting upon all Things, himself acted upon by nothing. *He is not far from every one of Us, for in him We* (and all Things) *live and move and have our Beings*.

[1] English and French translation are from Clarke's edition of the correspondence (Clarke 1717, pp. 36–53). LBr. 160 Bl. 13r, 14r, 15r, 16r, 17r, 18r is the original in Clarke's hand. There is also a copy in a secretary's hand (LH 1, 20 Bl. 389r–390v). This is Clarke's reply to Leibniz's Second Paper (document 92); it was transmitted to Leibniz along with Caroline's letter to him of 10 January 1716 (document 95). All footnotes are Clarke's; the endnote is mine. Clarke's references to the Appendix of his 1717 edition of the correspondence have been omitted.

97. Leibniz to Caroline* of Brandenburg-Ansbach, Princess of Wales[1]

[*c*.14 January 1716]

Madame

After recently having had the honour of writing a long letter to Your Royal Highness,[2] I would not have had to come back to it again so soon if the letter from a friend in Berlin had not given me occasion to think about a matter important to the Protestant[3] churches in general, a matter in which it seems to me that Your Royal Highness could be an instrument chosen by providence in order to make it succeed. In order to enter into the matter, it is necessary to relate to you, madame, what has already transpired in former times[4] on that head. The late Mr. [Ezechiel] Spanheim*, passing one day through Hanover, had orders from his master the king [Friedrich I and III*] to sound out our king [George I, Georg Ludwig* of Braunschweig-Lüneburg], then elector, on whether there was not a way to come to a better understanding between the two protestant churches,[5] of which the theologians of Brandenburg and Braunschweig, being always the most moderate of the empire, could lay the first foundations. That was agreed; the Bishop [Benjamin] Ursinus* and Mr. [Daniel Ernst] Jablonski* were named on one side, and on the other the Abbot [Gerhard Wolter] Molanus*, who wanted me to be added to it, which the elector found appropriate. Some face-to-face meetings took place and some communications, through which we made not a little progress, and I believe

*we know not at all.*_____ *The very* Substances themselves, *even of* Bodies, *we cannot come at the knowledge of, either by any of our* Senses, *or by any* reflex Act of the Mind : *much less have we any Idea of the* Substance of God. *Him we know, only by his* Properties *and* Attributes, *and by his most* Wise *and* Excellent Disposition *of* Things, *and by* Final Causes : *And we adore and worship him, upon account of his* Dominion. *For a* God *without* Dominion, *without* Providence *and* Final Causes, *is nothing but* Fate *and* Nature. *Newtoni Principia, Scholium generale sub finem.*

l'on n'avança pas peu: et je crois que l'affaire seroit allé[6] loin; si le Roy de prusse avoit ete constant dans les mesure prises et les avoit poursuivi sur un meme pied. Mais il etoit fort sujet à changer. Il se degoûta d'une affaire qui ne pouvoit point courir la poste, et il se laissa entraîner par les projets des pietistes, et particulierement du docteur Winkler de Magdebourg avec son Arcanum Regium. Ces gens encourageoient le Roy a faire des changemens chez luy au prejudice de nos Eglises en vertu de sa souveraine puissance ce qui étoit directement contraire à ce qu'on avoit concerté savoir que les Eglises de Brandebourg et de Bronsvic viendroient à des declarations procurées par le commun accord des deux souverains. Ainsi la negotiation fut suspendue par un silence mutuel; et le Roy de prusse cependant reconnut que l'avis des pietistes ne serviroit qu'à de nouvelles aigreurs, de sorte que tout demeura en suspens. Il pensa un jour à introduire dans le Brandebourg l'usage des Eglises Anglicanes. Mais ce ne fut aussi qu'une pensée passagere.

Maintenant que l'Electeur de Bronsvic devenu Roy de la Grande Bretagne est entré dans l'Eglise Anglicane sans avoir changé de religion, comme Sa Mté declare avec raison dans les occasions; il s'ensuit qu'Elle juge que l'Eglise Anglicane et la notre ne different point de Religion, mais seulement de Rite, c'est à dire dans les ceremonies et dans des dogmes non essentiels des docteurs dont l'Eglise n'exige point la creance dans ses membres et je ne doute point que V. A. Royale ne soit dans le même sentiment. Mais de l'autre coté l'Eglise Anglicane soutient de n'avoir pas une autre religion que celle qu'ont les Eglises Reformees du pays de Brandebourg: puis qu'aussi bien les unes et les autres ne s'attachent point au Synode de Dordrecht | dont l'Angleterre n'a point receu les decisions |. Or deux choses etant une meme chose avec une troisieme sont un entre Elles. La Religion des Eglises de Bronsvic est la meme avec l'Anglicane. La Religion des Eglises Reformees de Brandebourg est aussi la même avec l'Anglicane. Donc la Religion des Eglises Evangeliques de Bronsvic et Reformees de Bronsvic[11] est aussi la même, sans que la diversité des Rites, et des dogmes doctoresques le puisse empecher.

Il s'agit maintenant de faire en sorte que cela soit bien compris des peuples, et mis en jour par des declarations des souverains concertées par les Theologiens. Et il semble qu'il faudroit reprendre le fil de la negotiation commencée, et non encore rompue entre les Theologiens de Brandebourg et de Bronsvic, sous l'autorité des deux Rois d'autant plus aisément que les deputés vivent encore de part et l'autre et d'y joindre des Theologiens de l'Eglise Anglicane comme mediateurs puisque cette Eglise fait[12] le lien et qu'elle est ce tiers, lequel estant un avec chacun des deux partis, fait qu'ils sont un entre eux. Le Roy de prusse y est peutetre autant et plus propre que son predecesseur. Car quoyqu'il prenne peutetre moins feu d'abord sur des choses de cette nature; en echange je crois qu'il sera plus attaché à des mesures prises et pourra faire conduire une affaire jusqu'au bout.

that the matter would have gone[6] a long way if the King of Prussia had been stead-fast in the measures taken and had pursued them on an equal footing. But he was highly subject to change. He took a dislike to an matter that could not proceed quickly, and he allowed himself to be carried away by the projects of the Pietists, and particularly of Doctor Winckler of Magdeburg with his *Arcanum Regium*.[7] These people encouraged the king to make some changes in his realm to the preju-dice of our churches in virtue of his sovereign power, which was directly contrary to what had been jointly planned, namely that the churches of Brandenburg and Braunschweig would arrive at some declarations procured by the mutual agree-ment of the two sovereigns. So the negotiation was suspended in a mutual silence,[8] and meanwhile the King of Prussia recognized that the advice of the Pietists would only conduce to some new animosities, so everything remained in suspense. One day he thought about introducing in Brandenburg the practices of the English Anglicans. But this was also only a passing thought.

Now that the Elector of Braunschweig, having become King of Great Britain, has joined the Anglican church without having changed his religion, as His Majesty rightly declares when the opportunity presents itself, it follows that he thinks that the Anglican church and ours do not differ in respect of religion, but only in respect of rite, that is to say, in respect of ceremonies and some non-essential dogmas of the doctors, belief in which the church does not require of its members, and I do not doubt that Your Royal Highness is of the same opinion. But on the other hand, the Anglican church maintains that it does not have a religion different from that of the Reformed churches of the country of Brandenburg, since in any case neither adheres to the Synod of Dordrecht[9] | whose decisions England has not accepted |. Now two things being one and the same thing with a third, are one with each other, the religion of the churches of Braunschweig[10] is the same as the Anglican. The religion of the Reformed churches of Brandenburg [i.e., Calvinism] is also the same as the Anglican. Therefore, the religion of the Evangelical churches of Braunschweig and the Reformed of Brandenburg[11] are also the same, without the diversity of rites and doctoral dogmas preventing it.

It is now a matter of ensuring that it is fully understood by the people and brought up to date by some declarations of the sovereigns, jointly prepared by the theologians. And it seems that the thread of the negotiation begun, and not yet broken, between the theologians of Brandenburg and Braunschweig, needs to be taken up again under the authority of the two kings, all the more easily as the dele-gates on both sides are still living, and to add to them some theologians from the Anglican church as mediators, since this church forms[12] the link and is this third party, which being one with each of the two parties, makes them one with each other. The King of Prussia [Friedrich Wilhelm I*] is perhaps as much and more suitable for it than his predecessor. For although he may perhaps be initially less enthused about things of this nature, I believe that in exchange he will be more

Il s'agit presentement de faire entrer nostre Roy dans la Resumtion de cette affaire, et il faut que cela se tente avec toute la delicatesse imaginable, et sur tout il faut qu'il ne paroisse point que j'y ay la moindre part. Le vray moyen pour cela seroit que des Grands hommes de l'Eglise Anglicane en parlassent à Sa Mté, et la priassent d'interposer son autorité pour faire cesser ou pour diminuer au moins le grand schisme des Eglises protestantes, qui leur a causé tant de maux, et qui les a mise autresfois à deux doigts de leur perte dans l'Empire. Et pour y mieux porter Sa Mté ils pourroient alleguer pour exemple, ou comme les Anglois disent pour precedent ce que l'Eglise Anglicane commença de faire du temps de Charles premier. Le primat et autres prelats de l'Eglise Anglicane d'alors envoyerent tout exprés en Allemagne un savant Theologien de leur Eglise nomme Johannes Duraeus qui eut des instructions des prelats et des recommendations de la Cour. Mais les rebellions qui commencerent un peu apres en Ecosse et en Angleterre firent tomber un projet si salutaire. Or il est à noter que l'affaire fut entreprise alors par des Eveques et Theologiens qu'on appelleroit Toris aujourdhuy; et qu'ainsi en cas que l'Archeveque de Cantorbery et quelques autres prelats entrassent dans cette negotiation; ceux du parti contraire n'auroient point de raison de s'y opposer, et en tout cas pourroient étre convaincus par leur predecesseurs. Et peut etre pourroit on y faire entrer quelques prelats qui passent pour Toris, comme par exemple l'Eveque de Londres.

La grande question est maintenant avec qui V. A. Royale en pourroit parler en secret, pour faire mettre en mouvement l'Archeveque de Cantorbery. Car si ce prelat si venerable par son âge et par sa dignité, en parloit au Roy et luy recommendoit cette affaire sans qu'on en sut ailleurs le sujet de son audience, je ne doute point que le Roy n'agreât son zele et l'autorisât à en conferer en secret avec quelque peu d'autres prelats et Theologiens bien intentionnés, pour prendre des mesures, et choisir quelque Theologien comme secretaire de leur congregation, propre à entrer en communication par lettre avec nostre Abbé de Loccum. Apres quoy les choses estant un peu preparees on pourroit envoyer icy; et meme la communication par ecrit etant commencee avant la fin de l'hyver, quelque Theologien choisi pourroit venir icy avec le Roy sans faire semblant de rien.

Je doute qu'il soit apropos d'en parler à M. l'Eveque de Lincoln, car il est grand aumonier du Roy. Il faut un homme moins eleve dejà en dignite, mais en passe d'avancer, doué de beaucoup de zele, de moderation et de capacité. Il faudroit aussi qu'il fut estimé et bien venu de l'Archeveque, et propre à etre l'entremetteur entre V. A. Royale et ce primat. En cas que V. A. R. fut embarrassee sur le choix je pourrois peutetre luy proposer quelque sujet. A moins que V. A. R n'ait occasion de s'entretenir Elle meme avec M. l'Archeveque. C'est tout ce que je puis dire pour le present. Rien ne siera mieux a V. A. R.: sa pieté et sa prudence vont du pair et sa dignite leur donne de l'efficace. Et il y a lieu d'esperer que la Benediction divine n'y

wedded to any measures taken and will be able to have an affair carried out to the end.

It is now a matter of having our king take part in the resumption of this affair, and this must be attempted with all the delicacy imaginable; and above all it must not appear that I have the least part in it. The true means for that would be for some great men of the Anglican church to speak to His Majesty about it and ask him to interpose his authority in order to put a stop to, or at least diminish, the great schism of the Protestant churches, which has caused them so many difficulties and which previously brought them to the brink of ruin in the empire. And in order to more readily persuade His Majesty, they could cite for example, or, as the English say, *for precedent*, what the Anglican church began to do in the time of Charles I.[13] For this very purpose the primate and other prelates of the Anglican church of that time sent to Germany a learned theologian of their church named *John Dury**, who had some instructions from the prelates and some recommendations from the court.[14] But the rebellions that began a little later in Scotland and England brought an end to this very salutary project. Now it is to be noted that the affair was undertaken at that time by some bishops and theologians who would now be called Tories, and so if the Archbishop of Canterbury[15] and some other prelates entered into this negotiation, those of the opposition party would not have any reason to oppose it and in any case could be convinced by their predecessors. And perhaps some prelates who are considered Tories, for example the Bishop of London [John Robinson (1650–1723)], could be made to take part in it.

The main question now is with whom could Your Royal Highness speak about it in secret, in order to have the Archbishop of Canterbury set in motion. For if this prelate, so venerable by his age and dignity, spoke to the king about it and recommended this matter to him without the subject of this audience being known elsewhere, I do not doubt that the king would approve his zeal and authorize him to confer in secret with a few other well-intentioned prelates and theologians in order to take some measures and select some theologian as secretary of their congregation suited to enter into communication by letter with our Abbot of Loccum [Molanus]. After which, matters being somewhat prepared, some chosen theologian could be sent here, and even, if communication in writing began before the end of the winter, could come here surreptitiously with the king.

I doubt that it is appropriate to speak about it with the Bishop of Lincoln,[16] since he is High Almoner of the king. It requires a man not already so elevated in dignity, but on the verge of advancing, endowed with a lot of zeal, moderation, and ability. He would also have to be esteemed and welcomed by the archbishop and suited to being a mediator between Your Royal Highness and this primate. In the event Your Royal Highness were at a loss as to the choice, I could perhaps propose some subject to her, unless Your Royal Highness has occasion to undertake it herself with the archbishop. This is all I can say for the time being. Nothing will better suit Your

manquera point. Pour moi, je serois ravi de voir encore quelque fruit de mes travaux passés; et au reste ne doutant point que V. A. R. ne ménage l'affaire comme il faut

je suis avec devotion

Madame de V. A. Royal etc.

Je n'aurois rien a adjouter à une longue lettre que j'ay pris la liberté d'ecrire à V. A. Royale sur un sujet de quelque consequence, si la gazette ne m'avoit appris la mort de l'Archeveque de Cantorbery, et la nomination que le Roy a faite de M. l'Evêque de Lincoln pour remplir ce grand poste. Cela doit faire changer les mesures à l'egard des personnes; et je crois que si V. A. Royale veut prendre l'affaire en main, il faut qu'Elle en parle elle meme au nouveau primat, mais sans faire paroistre que j'y aye la moindre part le zele et les lumieres de V. A. Royale y suffisent.

Theodicée

p. 25

Comme le nouveau primat est d'un âge, comme je crois a se pouvoir promettre d'achever l'ouvrage s'il le commence, je crois qu'il en sera d'autant plus disposé.

Il sera bon qu'il paroisse que l'affaire vient entierement des Anglois, et elle en sera mieux receue du Roy et de la Nation. Mais je crois que le secret sera tousjours bon au commencement.

97. LEIBNIZ TO CAROLINE OF BRANDENBURG-ANSBACH 391

Royal Highness: her piety is on a par with her prudence, and her dignity gives them some efficacy. And there is reason to hope that the divine benediction will not be lacking in it. As for me, I would be delighted to see once more some fruit from my past labors; and to conclude, not doubting that Your Royal Highness will arrange matters properly,

I am with devotion,

Madame, of Your Royal Highness etc.

I would have nothing to add to a long letter that I have taken the liberty to write to Your Royal Highness concerning a subject of some consequence if the newspaper had not informed me of the death of the Archbishop of Canterbury and the king's nomination of the Bishop of Lincoln to fill this important post. That has to alter the arrangements with respect to persons, and I believe that if Your Royal Highness wishes to take the matter in hand, she must speak with the new primate about it herself, but without making it appear that I have the least part in it. The zeal and wisdom of Your Royal Highness are sufficient for it.

Theodicy
p. 25[17]

As the new primate is of an age, as I believe, to be able to commit himself to completing the work if he begins it, I believe that he will be all the more disposed to it.

It will be advantageous that the matter appears to originate entirely with the English, and the king and the nation will receive it more readily from them. But I believe that secrecy will always be advantageous in the beginning.

---

[1] LBr. F 4 Bl. 93r–95r. Draft: body of letter is 3.5 folio pages in Leibniz's hand; P. S. to letter is 0.7 quarto sides in Leibniz's hand. Previously published in Klopp XI 85–90; Kemble 541–5. For Caroline's reply, see her letter to Leibniz of 5 May 1716 (document 115). The draft is undated, but I think it can be approximately dated in light of Leibniz's letter of 14 January 1716 to Daniel Ernst Jablonski*, who was the chaplain at the Berlin court of Friedrich Wilhelm I*, King of Prussia. That letter appears to be a response to Jablonski's letter to Leibniz of 11 January 1716 (NS), which I believe to be the letter 'from a friend in Berlin' that Leibniz mentions at the beginning of the present letter to Caroline. For in his letter of 14 January 1716 (NS) to Jablonski, Leibniz proposes taking up again their previous efforts to unite the Protestant churches, the history of which efforts he briefly outlines at the beginning of the present letter to Caroline. In that letter to Jablonski, Leibniz also makes note of the fact that all the participants in the original project are still living, as he does as well in the present letter to Caroline. In both letters he also indicates that he thinks that the fact that King George I did not believe he had changed religions when he became a member of the Anglican church is something that should be seized upon and used in the service of the reunion project. Finally, in his letter to Jablonski Leibniz wrote that 'I see an excellent way to bring the matter up with the king to some extent' (Kvacala 1899, p. 132), by which I think he clearly meant the scheme that he lays out in the present letter to Caroline. Given that it was Jablonski's letter of 11 January 1716 that inspired Leibniz's response of 14 January 1716, and given the similarity of subject matter in the letters to Jablonski and Caroline, it seems reasonable to think that it was Jablonski's letter of 11 January 1716 that was the letter 'from a friend in Berlin' that Leibniz says also inspired the writing of the present letter to Caroline. Thus it seems reasonable to conclude that the present letter to Caroline was not written earlier than 14 January 1716. But it seems just as certain that it was not written later than the third week of January. For in her letter of 10 January 1716 (NS) to Leibniz Caroline writes that 'you must know that my good friend the Bishop of Lincoln is Archbishop of Canterbury' (see document 95, p. 373). But in the post script to the present letter to Caroline, Leibniz writes that he had just learned

97. LEIBNIZ TO CAROLINE OF BRANDENBURG-ANSBACH 393

from the newspaper that the Bishop of Lincoln had been nominated to replace the previous Archbishop of Canterbury, Thomas Tension, who died on 25 December 1716 (NS), so it seems clear that he had not yet received Caroline's letter of 10 January. Given the usual time of about two weeks for letters to be delivered between London and Hanover, Leibniz would probably have received Caroline's letter around 24 January, give or take a few days, so it seems reasonable to conclude that the present letter to Caroline was not written later than the beginning of the third week of January, and was most likely written on the same day that Leibniz replied to Jablonski's letter, namely 14 January.

² This probably refers to the long letter that Leibniz wrote to Caroline in mid- to late December 1715 (document 91).

³ Reading 'aux Eglises protestantes' for 'aux les'Eglises protestante'.

⁴ Klopp omits 'autres fois' from the end of this sentence without notice (see Klopp XI 85).

⁵ That is, that of the Lutherans, which Leibniz often referred to as the 'Evangelical', and that of the Calvinists, which Leibniz often referred to as the 'Reformed'.

⁶ Reading 'allée' for 'allé'.

⁷ At the time of the affair, Johann Joseph Winckler (1670–1722) was a deacon of Magdeburg Cathedral. In 1703 he published *Arcanum Regium*, his plan for the union of the Reformed (Calvinist) and Evangelical (Lutheran) churches, which proposed putting the Lutheran churches under the control of the King of Prussia.

⁸ The affair that Leibniz describes here is summarized in Gruhauer 1846, pp. 231–6, and in Antognazza 2009, pp. 398–402. Daniel Ernst Jablonski*, chaplain to the court of Friedrich I and III* in Berlin, composed an anonymous treatise designed to prepare the way for the unification of the Lutheran and Reformed (Calvinist) churches under the title, *Kurtze Vorstellung der Einigheit und des Unterscheides, im Glauben beyder Evangelischen so genandten Lutherischen und Reformirten Kirchen: woraus zugleich erhellet, daß sothaner Untersheid den Grund Christ[lichen] Glaubens keinesweges anfechte*, or '*A Short Exposition of the Unity and Difference in Faith of the Two Evangelical Churches (Commonly Called Lutheran and Reformed) Which Also Makes Clear that Such Difference in No Way Disturbs the Foundation of Christian Faith*' (as translated in Antognazza 2009, p. 399). Spanheim delivered this treatise to Hanover on 24 December 1697, which is presumably the day to which Leibniz was referring when he wrote of Spanheim 'passing one day through Hanover'. (Since Friedrich did not become king in Prussia until 1701, Leibniz should perhaps have noted that Friedrich was then only Elector of Brandenburg, as he indicated that Georg Ludwig was only Elector of Hanover at the time. He may have chosen not to do this, however, since Friedrich did become king before the affair ended in 1703.) Leibniz worked with Molanus to compose a reply to Jablonski's treatise, which was completed a little more than a year later and sent to Berlin under the title, *Unvorgreiffliches Bedencken über eine Schrift genandt Kurtze Vorstellung*, or *Impartial Reflections concerning a Paper entitled Short Exposition*. Despite the efforts of Jablonski and Leibniz, the other Lutheran and Reformed participants could not reach agreement. The Prussian King Friedrich I and III* became impatient with the pace of progress, and toward the end of 1702 he ordered his Evangelical (Lutheran) Bishop Ursinus to convene a *Collegium Irenicum* in Berlin, with Jablonski and the theologian Samuel Strimesius (1684–1744) representing the Reformed churches and Johann Joseph Winckler, Pietist deacon of the cathedral at Magdeburg, and Berlin provost Franz Julius Lütke (1650–1712) representing the Lutheran churches. Leibniz mentions Winckler's *Arcanum Regium*, which was published in Frankfort in 1703, before the discussions of the *Collegium* had even gotten underway. In this work, Winckler defended a plan to make union compulsory through a declaration of the Prussian King, a proposal that led to violent disputes when the conference began. A second round of disputes erupted when Lütke printed a criticism of the way the *Collegium* had been organized. Shortly thereafter, as Leibniz reports, 'the negotiation was suspended in mutual silence'.

Even before Jablonski's initiative, Leibniz had attempted to enlist the aid of James Cresset (1655–1710), the British Envoy Extraordinary to Hanover, to get the English king involved in the cause of Protestant reunion. In his letter to Cresset of 6 November 1697, Leibniz recalled England's past involvement in the reunion project. In particular, as in the present letter to Caroline, he mentioned one of John Dury's trips to Germany, not the one he alludes to below, which took place during Dury's tour of the continent between 1635 and 1641, but rather the one that Dury made in 1654 as a diplomat for Oliver Cromwell. He told Cresset that Dury 'took great pains to confer with those of the Augsburg Confession; but the affair still did not die except for the fact that the name of Cromwell was odious' (A I xiv 692). He went on to declare:

97. LEIBNIZ TO CAROLINE OF BRANDENBURG-ANSBACH   395

Now it is an entirely different matter. Some able men authorized in some fashion by the king [that is, King William III] could now act with the aid of God under some better auspices and with an entirely different outcome. But it certainly requires some talents in order to succeed. It requires a good understanding, not only of the doctrines, but also of the facts and circumstances. I would claim to be able to give some good information about that one day, if I have the good fortune to see the matter put on the table. [ibid.]

On 15 January 1698, Cresset wrote an encouraging letter to Leibniz, saying that 'as regards the project in question, I must tell you that your good intentions are already known by the Archbishop of Canterbury [Thomas Tenison*], the Bishop of Salisbury [Gilbert Burnet (1643–1715)], and by His Majesty himself: the two prelates show signs of great satisfaction with such a plan' (A.I.xv.198). Knowing that King William III was planning to visit Celle in the autumn of 1698, Leibniz presented Cresset with a letter shortly before the king's arrival in which he outlined the political and religious dangers facing the Protestant churches in light of the concord shown between France and the Catholic princes of Germany during the negotiations for the Treaty of Ryswick*. He again made reference to Dury's trips to Germany. He called upon the British monarch to join forces with the Elector of Brandenburg to support the cause of Protestant union, and in the process he briefly outlined the negotiations that had commenced as a result of Jablonski's anonymous treatise. While at Celle he planted seeds that led the Duchess of Celle, Eléonore Desmiers d'Olbreuse*, to speak to William III in favour of establishing 'the succession of England in the person and posterity of Madam the Electress' Sophie (see document 37 above).

In a letter of 8 January 1699 to the Bishop of Salisbury, Gilbert Burnet, Leibniz broached the topic of Protestant reunion, again mentioning Dury's early involvement, but reporting as well on the negotiations lately begun in Berlin and on William III's recent trip to Celle (see A.I.xvi.431–5). Burnet responded on 27 February 1699, encouraging the moderate and accommodating approach of the Church of England in dealing with doctrinal controversies; he specifically explained how the dispute over the Eucharist and the doctrine of election and predestination had been resolved in England (see A.I.xvi.595). When Burnet's *Exposition of the Thirty-Nine Articles of the Church of England* appeared that same year, Leibniz undertook to compose an extensive commentary on it, which he only completed in 1705 (see MJM). But before it could be published, 'the deterioration of the relationship between Hanover and Brandenburg in 1706 caused the manuscript to be shelved, together with the whole idea of inter-Protestant church unity' (Antognazza 2009, p. 404). But after his master George I had ascended the throne in England, Leibniz clearly thought that the time had come once more to enlist Great Britain and the Church of England in the cause of Protestant reunion; and Providence, he thought, might have provided an agent for this in the person of Caroline, Princess of Wales. But his plans for reunion would soon be frustrated for one last time (see documents 111, 113, 115, and 117a).

⁹ The Synod of Dordrecht was a national council of the Dutch Reformed churches held in Dordrecht in 1618–1619. The purpose of the Synod was to resolve a controversy that had arisen in the Dutch churches as a result of certain objections to Calvinist doctrine that had been raised by the so-called Remonstrants, who were followers of the Dutch theologian Jacobus Arminius (Jakob Hermanszoon, 1560–1609). The Synod attracted delegates representing Reformed groups from across continental Europe, as well as delegates from the Church of England and the Church of Scotland. The synod ultimately rejected the views of the Remonstrants, and a document explaining the decision was issued under the title *Judicium Synodi Nationalis Reformatarum Ecclesiarum Belgicarum, habitae Dordrechti, Anno 1618. & 1619. de Quinque Doctrinæ* Capitibus *in Ecclesiis Belgicis Controversis* (that is, *The Decision of the National Synod of the Reformed Belgic Churches, held in Dordrecht in the year 1618 and 1619, on the Five Main Points of Doctrine in Dispute in the Belgic Churches*). In this document, the 'five main points of doctrine in dispute' were answered with the doctrines of *total depravity, unconditional election, limited atonement, irresistible grace,* and the *perseverance of the saints.*

¹⁰ Namely, Lutheranism, or, as Leibniz would prefer, the religion of the Evangelical churches.

¹¹ Reading 'Brandenbourg' for 'Bronsvic'.

¹² Klopp mistranscribes 'fait' as 'estant' (see Klopp XI 87).

¹³ Charles I (1600–1649) was the second son of James VI and I of England and was King of England, Scotland, and Ireland from 27 March 1625 (6 April 1625 NS) until his execution on 30 January 1649 (9 February 1649 NS).

¹⁴ Leibniz is here referring to the travels that Dury undertook on the continent between 1635 and 1641 to further the cause of the unification of the Protestant churches.

97. LEIBNIZ TO CAROLINE OF BRANDENBURG-ANSBACH   397

[15] Leibniz is referring to Thomas Tenison*, who was Archbishop of Canterbury from December 1694 until his death on 25 December 1715 (NS). But before he sent the letter, he learned that Tenison had died, as he makes clear in the P.S.

[16] Leibniz was referring to William Wake*, but, as Leibniz notes in the P.S., at the time of writing William Wake had been nominated to be Archbishop of Canterbury, an office for which he was confirmed on 27 January 1716 (NS).

[17] This reference to the *Theodicy* is in Leibniz's hand. Page 25 is identical in both the first edition (1710) and second edition (1712) of the *Theodicy*. It contains a significant portion of section 18 of the Preliminary Dissertation on the Conformity of Faith with Reason (for which, see document 1), in which Leibniz is discussing the disagreement between a certain faction of Reformed Protestants (those that follow Zwingli rather than Calvin) and the Evangelical Protestants (Lutherans) on the matter of the sacrament of the Eucharist; it was this disagreement that led to the schism between the Protestant parties. He suggests that the followers of Zwingli

> seemed to reduce the participation of the body of Jesus Christ in the Holy Communion to a mere figurative representation, making use of the maxim of philosophers that states that a body can only be in one place at a time.

On the other hand, he argues that

> the *Evangelicals* (who call themselves thus in a particular sense, in order to distinguish themselves from the Reformed), who are more attached to the literal sense, have judged with Luther that this participation was real and that there was in that a supernatural mystery. They do indeed reject the dogma of transubstantiation, which they believe is textually unfounded; and neither do they approve that of consubstantiation or of impanation, which can only be imputed to them as a result of not being well informed about their view, since they do not admit the inclusion of the body of Jesus Christ in the bread and do not even require any union of the one with the other. But they require at least a concomitance, so that these two substances are both received at the same time. They believe that the ordinary sense of the words of Jesus Christ, on an occasion as important as that when it was a matter of expressing his last wishes, ought to be preserved. And in order to maintain that this sense is exempt from all absurdity that could alienate us from it, they hold that the philosophical maxim that limits the existence and the participation of bodies at a single place is only a consequence of the ordinary course of nature. They do not on that account destroy the ordinary presence of the body of our Savior, such as can suit the most glorified body. They do not have recourse to I know not what diffusion of ubiquity, which would disperse it and would not allow it to be found anywhere; and neither do they admit the multiplied replication of some Scholastics, as if one and the same body were sitting here and standing elsewhere at the same time. They ultimately explain themselves in such a way that it seems to many that the view of Calvin, authorized by many confessions of faith by the churches that received the doctrine of this author when he established a participation of the substance, is not so far from the Augsburg Confession as might be thought and perhaps differs only in this, that it demands true faith in addition to the oral reception of the symbols and consequently excludes the unworthy. [document 1, p. 3]

The fact that Leibniz includes in his draft letter to Caroline a marginal reference to this discussion in the *Theodicy* helps to explain his meaning when he asserts that 'the religion of the Evangelical churches of Braunschweig and the Reformed of Brandenburg are … the same, without the diversity of rites and doctoral dogmas preventing it'. It is clear that he believed that the differences in doctoral dogmas concerning the interpretation of the Eucharist were not enough to make a genuine difference of faith; for as the passage from section 18 of the Preliminary Dissertation on the Conformity of Faith with Reason makes clear, he did not believe that the differences concerning the interpretation of the Eucharist were as far apart 'as might be thought'. It was this that gave Leibniz the hope of healing the schism between Lutheranism and Calvinism through the mediation of the Anglican Church.

Leibniz to Louis Bourguet (excerpt)

Monsieur

[...]

Pour venir à la matiere de votre premiere lettre, la suite des choses est tousjours contingeante, et un état ne suit point necessairement d'un autre état precedent, soit qu'il y ait commencement ou non. La connexion de deux états est une consecution naturelle, mais non pas necessaire; comme il est naturelle à l'arbre de porter des fruits, quoyqu'il puisse arriver par certaines raisons qu'il n'en porte point. L'unité est une partie du nombre, car il y a proportion entre le nombre et l'unité comprisé dans le nombre, mais l'instant n'est pas une partie du temps, aussi n'ont ils point de proportion entre eux. Il est très vray que la notion de l'éternité en Dieu est toute differente de celle du temps, car elle consiste dans la necessité, et celle du temps dans la contingeance. Mais il ne s'en suit point si on ne trouve d'autres moyens, que la contingeance a un commencement.

Je viens à votre seconde lettre, et je vous diray Monsieur, que lorque je parle de la raison de la rareté des jameaux[4] dans certaines especes, je n'en demande pas la cause finale, mais la cause efficiante. Car la connoissance de cette raison, serviroit à mieux connoitre la generation. En écrivant cette seconde lettre, vous avés fort bien medité sur la principale matiere de la premiere. Les huit propositions que vous y mettés d'abord, peuvent passer, excepté peutétre la derniere, où il est dit (1) que tous les etres bornés ne peuvent repondre à la foy, qu'à un nombre limité de rapports, si limité vous est autant que fini; Car je crois que ces etres bornés sont tousjours infinis en nombre et il ne faut pas (2) mettre <u>inter postulata</u> ce qui est en question, savoir que leur aggregé ne peut point recevoir d'abord toute la perfection qui luy peut convenir. Cette collection peut avoir toute sa perfection, quoyque les choses singulieres qui la composent puissent augmenter et diminuer en perfection. Vous dites Monsieur qu'on ne sauroit jamais produire un rapport total, auquel il soit impossible d'en ajouter d'autres. Mais un rapport d'un état de l'univers ne reçoit jamais aucune addition sans qu'il ait en même temps une subtraction ou diminution pour passer dans un autre état . Le changement des ordonnées dans le rectangle est tousjours tel que la posterieure garde les traces de l'anterieure, et il ne suit point que cela importe une augmentation de perfection; car s'il reste quelque chose de l'état precedent, quelque chose aussi n'en reste point. Quoyque l'univers fût tousjours également parfait, il ne sera jamais souverainement parfait; car il change tousjours et gagne de nouvelles perfections quoiqu'il en perde d'anciennes. Pour ce qui est de l'hypothese de l'hyperbole, il ne s'en suit pas non plus que ce qui n'a point de commencement subsiste necessairement, car il peut tousjours avoir été produit voluntairement par l'Etre souverain. Ainsi il n'est

98. Leibniz to Louis Bourguet* (excerpt)[1]

[24 February 1716]

Sir

[...]

To come to the subject of your first letter,[2] the series of things is always contingent, and one state does not follow necessarily from another, preceding state, whether or not there is a beginning. The connection of two states is a natural succession, but not necessary, just as it is natural for a tree to bear fruit, although it may happen for certain reasons that it does not bear. Unity is a part of number, for there is proportion between number and the unity included in the number; but the instant is not a part of time, so they do not have any proportion between them. It is very true that the notion of eternity in God is completely different from that of time, for it consists in necessity, and that of time in contingency. But it does not follow, if some other ways are found, that contingency has a beginning.

I come to your second letter,[3] and I will tell you, sir, that when I speak of the reason for the rarity of twins[4] in certain species, I am not demanding the final cause of it, but the efficient cause. For knowledge of this reason would serve to understand generation better. In writing this second letter, you have reflected very well about the principal subject of the first. The eight propositions that you have placed there first can go through, except perhaps the last, where it is said (1) that all the bounded beings can answer at the same time to only a limited number of relations, if limited amounts to finite for you. For I believe that these bounded beings are always infinite in number and it is not necessary (2) to place among the postulates what is in question, namely whether their aggregate cannot receive from the outset all the perfection that may be suitable for it. This collection can have all its perfection, although the individual things that compose it can increase and decrease in perfection. You say, sir, that a total relation could never be produced to which it is impossible to add others. But a relation of a state of the universe never receives any addition without there being at the same time a subtraction or diminution in order to pass to another state. The change of ordinates in the rectangle is always such that the later preserves traces of the former, and it does not follow that it signifies an increase of perfection; for if there remains something of the preceding state, something of it also does not remain. Even if the universe might always be equally perfect, it will never be supremely perfect, for it always changes and gains new perfections, although it loses some old ones. As for the hypothesis of the hyperbola, it does not any more follow that what does not have any beginning exists necessarily, for it can always have been produced voluntarily by the sovereign being. So it is not so easy to decide

pas si aisé de decider entre les trois hypotheses, et il faut encore beaucoup de meditation pour en venir à bout.

Nous sommes icy dans une espece de solitude depuis que nostre cour est allée en Angleterre, ainsi je ne connois point d'occasion de procurer quelque employ à Mons. Malplac; Berlin seroit plûtôt son fait. Si vous passés à Geneve, Monsieur, ayés la bonté de faire mes recommendations aupres de Monsieur Turretin, à qui j'espere que ma derniere lettre aura été rendue l'année passée. Il y a à Lausanne un savant homme qui a donné un bel ouvrage sur le beau, et fait connoitre qu'il a de bonnes entrées. Il y a là un autre qui a commenté sur Puffendorf du droit de nature, et m'a fait un procés sur la manière avec la quelle je parle en passant dans la Theodicée de son Auteur, lequel soûtient que les verités morales dependent de la volonté de Dieu, doctrine qui m'a tousjours parû extremement déraisonnable, et j'ay dit la-dessus, que Mons. Puffendorf ne devoit pas étre conté sur cette matiere. La-dessus ce Professeur de Lausanne s'est faché contre moy, et dit que le sentiment de son Auteur paroitra tousjours plus raisonnable que mon Harmonie préetablie. Mais je crois de pouvoir bien dire aussi, que son jugement ne doit pas etre conté non plus sur cette matiere.

Au reste je vous supplie Monsieur, d'une faveur, elle demande une petite depense, mais je la rendrai ponctuellement. Il y a dans ce voisinage d'icy des Seigneurs et Dames, qui prennent grand plaisir à nourrir de vers à foy ayant des jardins où il y a quantité de meuriers blancs. Ils desireroient quelques onces de bonne graine, des vers qui fussent de bonne race et bien conservés, car ils ont été trompés quelques fois par celles qu'on leur a envoyé. Vous m'obligeriés beaucoup Monsieur, si par un amy seur vous me pouviés procurer quatre onces de telles graines, et me la faire envoyer directement par la poste bien envelopée et bien munie. Si les graines ont été sur du papier on les gate aisement en les voulant detacher, au lieu qu'elles se detachent plus aisement, si elles ont été sur de la laine; il est bon aussi que la graine soit prise de papillons dont les cocons ont été beaux et grands. Je m'imagine qu'une bonne graine de cette nature pourra venir du Milanois, mais vous jugerés mieux Monsieur, de l'endroit le plus convenable. Il faudroit que cela me fut envoyé avant que le temps devient chaud, de peur que la graine ne devienne vivante en chemin.

Le livre de Mons. Herman a paru. Il flatte un peu trop certains Anglois, mais ces gens n'en sont pas plus traitables pour cela et voudroient passer pour les seul[s] capables de faire quelque chose de bon sur ces matieres. Mons. Newton croit que la force de l'univers va en diminuant, comme celle d'une montre, et a besoin d'être retablie par une action particuliere de Dieu, au lieu que je soutiens que Dieu a fait les choses d'abord en sorte que la force ne sauroit se perdre. Ainsi sa Dynamique est bien differente de la mienne, et ne convient pas à mon avis avec la perfection des operations Divines. Un auteur nommé Mons. Clark Chapelain du Roy est entré en dispute avec moy la dessus par lettres, à l'occasion de ce que j'en avois ecrit à Madame la Princesse de Galles. Et Son Altesse Royale qui a lû ma Theodicée avec

between the three hypotheses, and a lot of reflection is still necessary in order to accomplish it.[5]

Here we are in a kind of solitude since our court has gone to England, so I do not have any opportunity to obtain employment for Mr. Malplac. Berlin would rather be what suits him. If you go over to Geneva, sir, be kind enough to make my recommendations to Mr. [François] Turrettini,[6] to whom I hope that my last letter was delivered last year. There is at Lausanne a learned man who has published a fine work concerning beauty, and it reveals that he has some good insights.[7] There is another man[8] there who has commented on [Samuel] Pufendorf* concerning the right of nature and has made accusations against me about the manner in which I speak in passing in the *Theodicy* about his author, who maintains that moral truths depend on the will of God, a doctrine that has always seemed extremely unreasonable to me, and on this topic I have said that Mr. Pufendorf should not be taken into account on this matter.[9] Thereupon this professor from Lausanne got angry with me and said that the view of his author will always appear more reasonable than my preestablished harmony.[10] But I believe I can also rightly say that his judgment should not be taken into account on this matter either.

Finally, I beg a favour of you, sir; it requires a small expense, but I will repay it promptly. There are around here lords and ladies who take great pleasure in keeping silkworms, since they have gardens in which there is an abundance of white mulberries. They would like a few ounces of good egg from worms that were from good stock and well maintained, for they have been tricked a few times by the ones that have been sent to them. You will gratify me a lot, sir , if by means of a reliable friend you can procure for me four ounces of such eggs and have it sent directly to me by post, well wrapped and supplied. If the eggs have been on paper, they may be easily damaged in trying to detach them, instead of coming off more easily if they have been on wool. It is also beneficial if the egg is taken from butterflies whose cocoons have been nice and large. I imagine that a good egg of this nature may come from Milan, but you will judge better, sir, of the most fitting place. It must be sent to me before the weather turns hot, for fear that the egg may come alive in transit.

The book by Mr.[Jakob] Hermann* has appeared. He flatters a little too much certain Englishmen, but these people are not more tractable on account of that and would like to be considered the only ones capable of doing something worthwhile in these matters.[11] Mr. Newton believes that the force of the universe keeps decreasing, like that of a watch, and needs to be replenished by a special action of God, whereas I maintain that God has made things from the beginning in such a way that force could not be lost. Thus his dynamics is very different from mine and in my opinion is not in agreement with the perfection of the divine operations. On

attention, a temoigné que mon sentiment luy paroissoit plus convenable. Vous aurés la bonté, Monsieur, de me marquer comment je dois adresser mes lettres pour vous. Celles que vous me voulés faire l'honneur de m'envoyer, pourroient etre recommandées à Monsr Schroek Agent de Sa Maj^{té} le Roy de la Grande Bretagne, Electeur de Bronsvic à Augsbourg. Mais la graine me devroit étre envoyée tout simplement par la post.

Je suis avec zele

Monsieur

votre tres humble et

tres obéissant serviteur

Hanover ce 24 de

Fevrier 1716

Leibniz

98. LEIBNIZ TO BOURGUET 403

the occasion of what I had written to Madame the Princess of Wales [Caroline* of Brandenburg-Ansbach],[12] an author named Mr. [Samuel] Clarke*, chaplain of the king [George I, Georg Ludwig* of Braunschweig-Lüneburg], entered into a dispute with me about it in correspondence. And her Royal Highness, who has read my *Theodicy* with attention, has testified that my view seems more fitting. You will have the kindness, sir, to indicate how I should address my letters to you. Those that you want to do me the honour of sending to me could be sent in care of Mr. Schroek, agent of His Majesty the King of Great Britain, Elector of Braunschweig, at Augsburg, but the seed should be sent to me simply by the post.

I am enthusiastically

sir

> your very humble and
> very obedient servant

Hanover 24
 February 1716

> Leibniz

---

[1] Leiden Universiteitsbibliotheek Ms. 293 B, Bl. 221r–223v. Letter as sent: body of letter is 5.5 quarto sides in a secretary's hand; closing salutation, date, and signature in Leibniz's hand. Previously published in: GP III 588–91, Schüller 1991, p. 239 (excerpt in German translation); Robinet 1992, p. 61 (excerpt). For Bourguet's response, see his letter to Leibniz of 16 March 1716 (document 103).

[2] The reference is to Bourguet's letter to Leibniz of 6 October 1715, a relevant excerpt from which can be found at GP III 583–6.

[3] The reference is to Bourguet's letter to Leibniz of 7 February 1716, an excerpt from which can be found at GP III 587–8.

[4] Reading 'gemeaux' for 'jameaux'.

[5] For the three hypotheses that Leibniz discusses in this paragraph, see his letter to Bourguet of 5 August 1715 (document 77).

[6] That is, the Reformed scholastic theologian François Turrettini (1623–1687).

[7] Leibniz is referring to the *Traité du beau* that was published in 1714 by the Swiss theologian and philosopher Jean-Pierre de Crousaz (1663–1750).

[8] That is, the French jurist and Huguenot refugee Jean Barbeyrac (1674–1744).

[9] It is in *Theodicy* 182 that Leibniz wrote in passing about Pufendorf:

182. Mr. [Pierre] Bayle* has put a specific chapter in his *Continuation des Pensées diverses* (it is chap. 152) in which he shows *that the Christian Doctors teach that there are some things that are just antecedently to the decrees of God* [see Bayle 1705, p. 767]. Some theologians of the Confession of Augsburg have reprimanded a few Reformed who have appeared to be of a different view, and they have considered this error as if it were a consequence of the absolute decree, the doctrine of which seems to exempt the will of God from any kind of reason, *ubi stat pro ratione voluntas*. But as I have remarked more than once above, Calvin himself recognized that the decrees of God are in accordance with justice and wisdom, although the reasons that could show this conformity in detail are unknown to us. So according to him the rules of goodness and justice are anterior to the decrees of God. Mr. Bayle, in the same place, cites a passage from the celebrated Mr. Turrettini, who distinguishes divine natural laws and divine positive laws. Moral laws are of the first kind and ceremonial laws are of the second kind. Mr. Samuel Desmarets [1599–1673], famed theologian previously at Groningen, and Mr. Strimesius [that is, the German Reformed theologian Samuel Strimesius (1684–1744)], who is still at Frankfurt an der Oder, have taught the same thing. I believe that it is the view most received even among the Reformed; Thomas Aquinas and all the Thomists have been of the same view, along with the majority of Scholastics and theologians of the Roman church. The casuists are also of that view;

98. LEIBNIZ TO BOURGUET   405

I count Grotius among the most eminent of them, and he has been followed in that by his commentators. Mr. Pufendorf has appeared to be of a different opinion, which he sought to maintain against the censures of some theologians, but he should not be taken into account, and he has not gone far enough into matters of this sort. He cries out formidably against the absolute decree in his *Fecialis divinus* [see Pufendorf, 1695, pp. 242–8], and yet he approves what is worse in the views of the defenders of this decree, and without which this decree (as other Reformed explain it) becomes tolerable. Aristotle was very orthodox on the subject of justice, and the School has followed him. It distinguishes, as do Cicero and the jurisconsults, between perpetual right, which binds everyone and everywhere, and positive right, which is only for certain times and certain peoples. I previously read with pleasure the Euthyphro of Plato, who has Socrates maintain the truth on this matter, and Mr. Bayle has noted the same passage. [my translation]

[10] In the Avertissement to the second edition of his French translation of Pufendorf's *De jure naturae et gentium*, Barbeyrac wrote:

Those who, in speaking of this work [of Pufendorf], have been pleased to refer a lot to theologians who examine the same matters in the treatises concerning human actions, laws, right and justice, those [as becomes clear below, the reference here is specifically to Leibniz's discussion in *Theodicy* 182], I say, will hardly persuade anyone who does not have an interest in maintaining the reputation of the Scholastics and the casuists. Moreover, they have not understood the intention of Mr. Pufendorf, since they reprimand him for the fact that, while he often cites the secular authors, the canons of the church, the Fathers, the canonists etc. are not found in his books, as if he had to trouble himself with all that, being Protestant, and while explaining the natural right common to all men, of whatever religion and of whatever sect they may be! I add that there is an absence of method throughout the whole work [here Barbeyrac is referring to the whole of Leibniz's *Theodicy*], which consists in confusing matters and in passing from one subject to a totally different one, as if they had some connection. The reader will decide whether this criticism is well founded. As for me, I do not believe I am obliged to waste any time and paper to prove something about which everyone can quickly inform themselves with their own eyes. I say just as much about the haughtiness and contempt with which he has just spoken about Mr. Pufendorf on the occasion of his thoughts about the basis of justice and injustice [here Barbeyrac adds a note referring to page 349 of the *Essais sur la Bonté de Dieu &c.*, that is, to the page containing the passage quoted above from *Theodicy* 182 in which Leibniz mentions Pufendorf in passing] 'He should not be taken into account', says he, and 'he has not gone far enough into matters of this sort'. That is easy to say, but if it were worth the trouble, it would not be difficult to show that the one who speaks in this way does not even understand the thought of my author. I am, at any rate, much mistaken if all those who will examine it do not find it infinitely more reasonable than the entire system of the preestablished harmony. [Pufendorf 1712, vol 1, p. xii; my translation]

[11] Hermann's book, *Phoronomia, sive de Viribus et Motibus corporum solidorum et fluidorum libri duo* (1716), was a treatise on theoretical mechanics that Leibniz reviewed in the *Acta eruditorum* of January 1716. Although Hermann had dedicated the book to him, Leibniz was a bit perturbed by a particular stanza of the Latin poem that had been written by Hermann's friend, Nicolaus Westerman, and had been printed after the preface to the book:

> NEWTONUS hospes divitis insulæ,
> Sed nil habentis se magis aureum,
> Hac primus ivit, Tuque forte
> Nil populis dederis secundum.

That is,

> Newton, sojourner in a wealthy isle,
> But possessing nothing more golden than he,
> Was first to go this way, and you, perhaps,
> Have given the people nothing inferior.

In a letter to Hermann of 17 September 1715, Leibniz wrote:

Leibniz to Caroline of Brandenburg-Ansbach, Princess of Wales

Extract de ma letter a Mad. la princess
de Galles le 25 Fevrier 1716.

V. A. Royale marque de la bonte pour moy, et de la charité pour d'autres en voulant me raccommoder avec M. Newton. Je crois effectivement que ce raccommod[em]ent se peut faire parce qu'il n'a pas encor voulu paroistre luy meme publiquement contre moy: mais un certain homme qui ne passe pas pour être des mieux reglés luy a voulu complaire là dedans, et a fait tout ce bruit, en quoy M. Newton et d'autres | membres de la Societé | ont connivé et il a osé même employer[2] le nom de la Societé. Si ces Messieurs s'estoient contentés de soutenir que M. Newton a inventé le premier le Calcul dont il s'agit, quoyqu'il n'en ait donné aucun connoissance à personne, n'y aucun indice; je ne m'en soucierois pas, car cela se pourroit. Mais il semble qu'ils sont allés jusqu'a attaquer ma bonne foy, comme si [je] l'avois appris de luy, et l'avois dissimulé. Il seroit donc necessaire pour me rendre justice qu'on declare de la part de la Societé qu'on n'a point voulu

99. LEIBNIZ TO CAROLINE OF BRANDENBURG-ANSBACH   407

I have not been able to refrain from looking through your work, although with the greatest haste and as we are accustomed to read history books or romances. The demonstrations certainly cannot be evaluated now, especially the somewhat longer ones, although I am not judging the work. The prefixed verses are elegant, but because they say:

> Newton, sojourner in a wealthy isle,
> Was first to go this way,

I do not know whether it can be said without injury to so many others. [GM IV 398]

For his part, Hermann attempted to defend his friend in a letter to Leibniz of 22 November 1715:

First of all, I am truly grateful that my little work *Phoronomia* has been regarded favourably and that you have been willing to share with me the things that have come to your mind in reading it. However, I am sorry for this one thing, regarding the little verse by a friend about Newton, that it has been received in a sense as if it were injurious to many excellent men, which was far from the intent of the poet. For by the aforementioned little verse he did not mean to indicate anything other than that Newton first assembled into a kind of system and shared with the public both his own reflections about matters investigated in his own *Principia* as well as the discoveries of others advanced by themselves, with the honour of discovery preserved, which belongs to their authors with regard to the particular proofs treated in Newton's book, such as are of the rules of motion in the collision of bodies, of the theory of centrifugal forces, of the isochronism of falling weights, of proportions between the times of motions and the areas of the orbits described by the planets, and other things. [GM IV 403]

Not entirely satisfied, Leibniz responded in a letter to Hermann of 3 December 1715: 'I find very little fault with the verses of your friend, of a poet, as is clear, properly taught. But I know well the custom of the Germans, who (against which Tacitus, among the Greeks, asserts something) admire only the views of others' (GM IV 409).

¹² See document 85, p. 312.

99. Leibniz to Caroline* of Brandenburg-Ansbach, Princess of Wales[1]

Extract from my letter to the Princess
of Wales 25 February 1716

Your Royal Highness shows some kindness for me, and some charity for others, by wishing to reconcile me with Mr. Newton. I in fact believe that this reconciliation is possible because he himself has not yet wanted to appear publicly against me. But a certain man [John Keill*], who is not considered to be among the better governed, has wanted to try to please him in this matter, and has made all this noise in which Mr. Newton and some others | members of the Society | have connived, and he has dared even to use[2] the name of the Society.[3] If these gentlemen were content to maintain that Mr. Newton had invented the first calculus, which is what it is about, even though he did not give anyone any knowledge of it, nor any indication to anyone, I would not be concerned about it, for that could be true. But it seems that they have gone so far as to attack my good faith, as if I had learned it from him and had concealed it. To do me justice, then, it would be necessary for someone to

revoquer en doute ma candeur, et qu'on ne donnera point de permission de le faire.

Leibniz's Third Paper

Troisième Ecrit de Mr. Leibnitz,

ou

Réponse au Sécond Ecrit Anglois.

1. *Selon la maniere de parler ordinaire*, les Principes Mathematiques *sont ceux qui consistent dans les* Mathematiques pures, *comme Nombres, Figures, Arithmetique, Geometrie. Mais* les Principes Metaphysiques *regardent des* notions plus generales, *comme la Cause & l'Effect.*

2. *On m'accorde ce* Principe *important*, que rien n'arrive sans qu'il y ait une raison suffisante, pourquoy il en soit plûtôt ainsi qu'autrement. *Mais on me l'accorde* en paroles, *& on me le refuse* en Effect. *Ce qui fait voir qu'on n'en a pas bien compris toute la force. Et pour cela on se sert d'une instance qui tombe justement dans une de mes demonstrations contre l'*Espace réel absolu, *Idole de quelques Anglois Modernes. Je dis*, Idole, *non pas dans un sens Theologique, mais Philosophique ; comme le Chancelier Bacon disoit autres fois, qu'il y a* Idola Tribûs, Idola Specûs.

3. *Ces Messieurs soutiennent donc, que l'*Espace *est un* Etre réel absolu ; *mais cela les mene à de grandes difficultés. Car il paroist que cet* Etre *doit être* eternel & infini. *C'est pourquoy il y en a qui ont crû que c'estoit* Dieu lui même, *ou bien son Attribut, son Immensité. Mais comme il a des* parties, *ce n'est pas une chose qui puisse convenir à Dieu.*

4. *Pour moy, j'ay marqué plus d'une fois, que je tenois l'*Espace *pour quelque chose de* purement relatif, *comme le* Temps ; *pour un* Ordre des Coexistences, *comme le* Temps *est un* Ordre des Successions. *Car l'*Espace *marque en termes de possibilité*, un Ordre *des choses qui existent en même temps, en tant qu'elles existent* ensemble ; *sans entrer dans leur manieres d'exister*[3] *: Et lors qu'on voit plusieurs choses* ensemble, *on s'apperçoit de* cet Ordre des choses entre elles.

5. *Pour refuter l'imagination de ceux qui prennent l'*Espace *pour un* Substance, *ou du moins pour quelque* Etre absolu ; *j'ay plusieurs Demonstrations. Mais je ne*

declare on behalf of the Society that they did not intend to call my honesty into question and that they will not give permission to do so.

[1] LBr. F 4 Bl. 52r–52v. 1.2 quarto sides in Leibniz's hand. This an extract from Leibniz's reply to Caroline's letter of 10 January 1716 (document 95). Previously published in Klopp XI 78–9; Robinet 1991, p. 51; Schüller 1991, p. 224 (excerpt in German translation); HGA 193 (excerpt in English translation). Leibniz enclosed his Third Paper for Samuel Clarke* (document 100) with the letter from which this excerpt was taken.

[2] For 'il a osé même employer', Klopp has 'aussi même employé' (Klopp IX 78), and Robinet has 'il a esté meme employé' (Robinet 1991, p. 51).

[3] That is, the Royal Society of London, of which Newton was then president.

100. Leibniz's Third Paper[1]

Mr. LEIBNITZ's *Third Paper.*

BEING

An Answer to Dr. CLARKE's *Second Reply*

1. According to the usual way of Speaking, *Mathematical* Principles concern only *mere Mathematicks*, viz. Numbers, Figures, Arithmetick, Geometry. But *Metaphysical* Principles concern *more general Notions*, such as Cause and Effect.

2. The Author grants me this important *Principle* ; that *Nothing happens without a sufficient reason, why it should be So, rather than otherwise.* But he grants it only in *Words*, and *in reality* denies it. Which shows that he does not fully perceive the Strength of it. And therefore he makes use of an Instance, which exactly falls in with one of my Demonstrations against *real absolute Space*, which is an *Idol* of some Modern *Englishmen*. I call it an *Idol*, not in a Theological Sense, but in a Philosophical one ; As Chancellor *Bacon*[2] says, that there are *Idola Tribûs, Idola Specûs.*

3. These Gentlemen maintain therefore, that *Space* is a *real absolute Being.* But this involves them in great Difficulties ; For such a *Being* must needs be *Eternal* and *Infinite.* Hence Some have believed it to be *God himself,* or, one of his Attributes, his *Immensity.* But since Space consists of *Parts*, it is not a thing which can belong to God.

4. As for my Own Opinion, I have said more than once, that I hold *Space* to be something *merely relative*, as *Time* is ; that I hold it to be an *Order of Coexistences*, as *Time* is an *Order of Successions.* For *Space* denotes, in Terms of Possibility, *an Order of Things which exist as the same time, considered as existing *together* ; without enquiring into their Manner of Existing.[3] And when many Things are seen *together*, one perceives *That Order of Things among themselves.*

5. I have many Demonstrations, to confute the Fancy of Those who take *Space* to be a *Substance*, or at least an absolute *Being.* But I shall only use, at the present, one Demonstration, which the Author here gives me Occasion to insist upon.

veux me servir à present, que de celle dont on me fournit icy l'occasion. Je dis donc, que si l'Espace étoit un Etre absolu, il arriveroit quelque chose dont il seroit impossible qu'il y eut une raison suffisante ; ce qui est contre notre Axiome. Voicy comment je le prouve. L'Espace est quelque chose d'uniforme absolument ; & sans les chose y placées, un point de l'Espace ne differe absolument en rien d'un autre point de l'Espace. Or il suit de cela (supposé que l'Espace soit quelque chose en lui même outre l'ordre des corps entre eux,) qu'il est impossible qu'il y ait une raison, pourquoy Dieu, gardant les mêmes situations des corps entre eux, ait placé[4] les corps dans l'Espace ainsi & non pas autrement ; & pourquoy tout n'a pas été pris[5] à rebours, (par exemple,) par un Echange de l'Orient & de l'Occident. Mais si l'Espace n'est autre chose que cet Ordre ou Rapport, & n'est rien du tout sans les corps, que la possibilité d'en mettre ; ces deux Etats, l'un tel qu'il est, l'autre supposé à rebours, ne differeroient point ente eux. Leur Difference ne se trouve donc, que[6] dans notre Supposition chimerique, de la realité de l'Espace en lui même. Mais dans la verité, l'un seroit justement la même chose que l'autre, comme ils sont absolument indiscernables ; & par consequent, il n'y a pas lieu de demander la raison de la preference de l'un à l'autre.

6.   Il en est de même du Temps. Supposé que quelqu'un demande pourquoy Dieu n'a pas tout créé un An plûtôt ; & que ce meme personnage veuille inferer de là, que Dieu a fait quelque chose dont il n'est pas possible qu'il y ait une raison pourquoy il l'a fait ainsi plûtôt qu'autrement ; On lui repondroit que son illation seroit vraye, si le temps étoit quelque chose hors des choses temporelles ; Car il seroit impossible qu'il y eut des raisons pourquoy les choses eussent été appliquées plûtôt à de tels instans, qu'à d'autres, leur succession demeurant la même. Mais cela même prouve que les instans hors des choses ne sont rien, & qu'ils ne consistent que dans leur ordre successif ; lequel demeurant le meme, l'un des deux Etats, comme celuy de l'anticipation imaginée, ne differeroit en rien, & ne sauroit étre discerné de l'autre qui est maintenant.

7.   On voit par tout ce que je viens de dire, que mon Axiome n'a pas été bien pris ; & qu'en semblant l'accorder, on le refuse. Il est vray, dit on, qu'il n'y a rien sans une raison suffisante pourquoy il est, & pourquoy il est ainsi plûtôt qu'autrement : Mais on adjoute, que cette raison suffisante est souvent la simple [ou mere][7] Volonté de Dieu : Comme lors qu'on demande pourquoy la Matiere n'a pas été placée autrement dans l'Espace ; les mêmes situations entre les corps demeurant gardées. Mais c'est justement soutenir que Dieu veut quelque chose, sans qu'il y ait aucune raison suffisante de sa Volonté ; contre l'Axiome, ou la Regle generale de tout ce qui arrive. C'est retomber dans l'Indifference vague ; que j'ay amplement refutée, & que j'ay montrée chimerique absolument, même dans les Creatures ; & contraire à la Sagesse de Dieu, comme s'il pouvoit operer sans agir par raison.

I say then, that if *Space* was an absolute *Being*, there would Something happen, for which it would be impossible there should be a *sufficient Reason*. Which is against my Axiom. And I prove it thus. *Space* is Something absolutely *Uniform* ; and, without the Things placed in it, *One Point* of Space does not absolutely differ in any respect whatsoever from *Another Point* of Space. Now from hence it follows, (supposing Space to be Something in it self, besides the *Order of Bodies among themselves*,) that 'tis impossible there should be a *Reason*, why God, preserving the same Situations of Bodies among themselves, should have placed them in Space after *one certain particular manner*, and not *otherwise* ; why every thing was not placed the *quite contrary way*, for instance, by changing *East* into *West*. But if Space is nothing else, but That *Order* or *Relation* ; and is nothing at all without Bodies, but the Possibility of placing them ; then those two States, the *one* such as it now is, the *other* supposed to be the quite contrary way, would not at all differ from one another. *Their Difference* therefore is only to be found in our *Chimerical* Supposition of the *Reality* of Space in it self. But in truth the *one* would exactly be the same thing as the *other*, they being absolutely *indiscernible* ; and consequently there is no room to enquire after a Reason of the Preference of the one to the other.

6. The Case is the same with respect to *Time*. Supposing any one should ask, why God did not create every thing *a Year sooner* ; and the same Person should infer from thence, that God has done something, concerning which 'tis *not possible* there should be a *Reason*, why he did it *so*, and not *otherwise* : The Answer is, That his Inference would be right, if *Time* was any thing distinct from Things existing in Time. For it would be *impossible* there should be any *Reason*, why Things should be applied to such *particular Instants*, rather than to *others*, their Succession continuing the same. But then the same Argument proves, that *Instants*, consider'd without the Things, are *Nothing at all* ; and that they consist only in the successive *Order* of Things : Which Order remaining the same, *one* of the two States, *viz.* that of a supposed Anticipation, would not at all differ, nor could be discerned from, the *other* which Now is.

7. It appears from what I have said, that my Axiom has not yet been well understood ; and that the Author denies it, tho' he seems to grant it. 'Tis true, says he, *that there is nothing without a sufficient Reason why it Is, and why it is Thus, rather than otherwise*: But he adds, that *This sufficient Reason*, is often *the simple or mere Will of God*: As, when it is asked why Matter was not placed *otherwhere* in Space ; the same Situations of Bodies among themselves being preserved. But this is plainly maintaining, that God *Wills* Something, without any *sufficient Reason* for his Will : Against the Axiom, or the general Rule of whatever happens. This is falling back into the *loose Indifference*, which I have confuted at large, and showed to be absolutely *chimerical* even in Creatures, and contrary to the Wisdom of God, as if he could operate without acting by Reason.

8. *On m'objecte qu'en n'admettant point cette* simple [& mere][7] Volonté, *ce seroit ôter à Dieu le pouvoir de* choisir, & *tomber dans la* Fatalité. *Mais c'est tout le contraire : On soutient en Dieu le pouvoir de choisir, puisqu'on le fonde sur la* raison du choix *conforme à sa Sagesse. Et ce n'est pas cette* Fatalité (*qui n'est autre chose que l'ordre le plus sage de la Providence,*[8]) *mais une* Fatalité ou Necessité brute, *qu'il faut eviter ; où il n'y a ny Sagesse, ny Choix.*

9. *J'avois remarqué, qu'en diminuant la* Quantité de la Matiere, *on diminue la quantité des* Objets *où Dieu peut exercer sa Bonté. On me repond, qu'au lieu de la Matiere, il y a d'autres choses*[9] *dans le vuide, où il ne laisse pas de l'exercer. Soit. Quoique je n'en demeure point d'accord ; car je tiens que toute Substance créée est accompagnée de Matiere. Mais soit, dis-je ; je reponds, que plus de Matiere étoit compatible avec ces mêmes choses ; & par consequent, c'est tousjours diminuer le dit Objet. L'instance d'un plus grand nombre d'Hommes ou d'Animaux, ne convient point ; car ils ôteroient la Place à d'autres choses.*

10. *Il sera difficile de nous faire accroire, que dans l'usage ordinaire,* Sensorium *ne signifie pas l'Organe de la Sensation. Voicy les paroles de* Rudolphus Goclenius, *dans son* Dictionarium Philosophicum, *v.* Sensiterium : Barbarum Scholasticorum, *dit il*, qui interdum sunt Simiæ Græcorum. Hi dicunt Ἀισθητήριον. Ex quo illi fecerunt *Sensiterium, pro* Sensorio, id est, Organo Sensationis.

11. *La* simple Presence *d'une Substance, même animée, ne suffit pas pour la* Perception. *Un aveugle, & même un distrait, ne voit point. Il faut expliquer comment l'Ame s'apperçoit de ce qui est hors d'elle.*

12. *Dieu n'est pas present aux choses par* Situation, *mais par* Essence ; *sa Presence se manifeste par son* Operation immediate. *La Presence de l'*Ame *est tout d'une autre nature. Dire qu'elle est diffuse par le corps, c'est la rendre étendue & divisible ; dire qu'elle est toute entiere en chaque partie de quelque corps, c'est la rendre divisible d'elle même. L'attacher à* un Point, *la repandre par* plusieurs Points, *tout cela ne sont qu'expressions abusives,* Idola Tribûs.

13. *Si la* Force active *se perdoit dans l'Univers par les Loix naturelles que Dieu y a établies, en sorte qu'il eut besoin d'une* nouvelle Impression *pour restituer cette force, comme un Ouvrier qui remedie à l'imperfection de sa Machine ; le desordre n'auroit pas seulement lieu à l'égard de* nous, *mais à l'égard de* Dieu *lui même. Il pouvoit le prevenir, & prendre mieux ses mesures, pour éviter un tel inconvenient : Aussi l'a-t-il fait en effect.*

14. *Quand j'ay dit que Dieu a opposé à de tels desordres des remedes par avance, je ne dis point que Dieu laisse venir les desordres,*[10] *& puis les remedes ; mais qu'il a trouvé moyen par avance d'empecher les desordres d'arriver.*

15. *On s'applique inutilement à critiquer mon* Expression, *que Dieu est* Intelligentia Supramundana. *Disant qu'il est au dessus du* Monde, *ce n'est pas nier qu'il est dans le* Monde.

100. LEIBNIZ'S THIRD PAPER 413

8. The Author objects against me, that if we don't admit this *simple and mere Will*, we take away from God the Power of *Chusing*, and bring in Fatality. But the quite contrary is true. I maintain that God has the Power of *Chusing*, since I ground That Power upon the *Reason of a Choice* agreeable to his Wisdom. And 'tis not *This Fatality*, (which is only the wisest Order of Providence) but a *Blind Fatality* or *Necessity*, void of All Wisdom and Choice, which we ought to avoid.

9. I had observed, that by lessening the *Quantity of Matter*, the Quantity of Objects, upon which God may exercise his Goodness, will be lessen'd. The Author answers, that instead of *Matter*, there are other things in the Void Space, on which God may exercise his Goodness. Be it so : Tho' I don't grant it ; for I hold that every created Substance is attended with Matter. However, let it be so : I answer, that *More Matter* was consistent with those same Things ; and consequently the said Objects will be still lessened. The Instance of a greater Number of *Men*, or *Animals*, is not to the purpose ; for They would *fill up* Place, in Exclusion of other Things.

10. It will be difficult to make me believe, that *Sensorium* does not, in its *Usual* Meaning, signify an *Organ* of Sensation. See the Words of *Rudolphus Goclenius*, in his *Dictionarium Philosophicum* ; v. Sensiterium. *Barbarum Scholasticorum*, says he, *qui interdum sunt Simiæ Græcorum. Hi dicunt* Ἀισθητήριον. *Ex quo illi fecerunt* Sensiterium, *pro* Sensorio, *id est, Organo Sensationis*.

11. The *mere Presence* of a Substance, even an animated one, is not sufficient for Perception. A blind Man, and even a Man whose Thoughts are wandering, does not *See*. The Author must explain, how the Soul perceives what is *without* it self.

12. God is not present to Things by *Situation*, but by *Essence* : His Presence is manifested by his immediate *Operation*. The Presence of the *Soul*, is quite of another Nature. To say that it is diffused all over the Body, is to make it extended and divisible. To say it is, the Whole of it, in every Part of the Body, is to make it divided from it self. To fix it to a *Point*, to diffuse it all over *many Points*, are only abusive Expressions, *Idola Tribûs*.

13. If *active Force* should *diminish* in the Universe, by the Natural Laws which God has established ; so that there should be need for him to give a *new Impression* in order to restore That Force, like an Artist's Mending the Imperfections of his Machine ; the Disorder would not only be with respect to *Us*, but also with respect to *God himself*. He *might have* prevented it, and taken better Measures to avoid such an Inconvenience : And therefore, indeed, he has *actually* done it.

14. When I said that God has provided Remedies before-hand against such Disorders, I did not say that God suffers Disorders to happen, and then finds Remedies for them ; but that he has found a way before-hand to prevent any Disorders happening.

15. The Author strives in vain to criticize my Expression, that God is *Intelligentia Supramundana*. To say that God is Above the World, is not denying that he is In the World.

16. *Je n'ay jamais donné sujet de douter que la Conservation de Dieu est un Preservation & Continuation actuelle des Etres, Pouvoirs, Ordres, Dispositions & Motions ; & je crois l'avoir peutetre mieux expliqué que beaucoup d'autres. Mais dit on ;* This is All that I contended for ; *C'est en cela que consiste toute la Dispute. A cela je reponds,* Serviteur tres humble. *Nostre Dispute consiste en bien d'autres choses. La Question est, Si Dieu n'agit pas le plus* Regulierement, *& le plus* Parfaitement? *Si sa Machine est capable de tomber dans des Desordres, qu'il est obligé de redresser par des voyes extraordinaires? Si la Volonté de Dieu est capable d'agir sans Raison? Si l'Espace est un* Etre absolu? *Sur la Natue du* Miracle;[11] *& quantité de Questions semblables, qui font une grande Separation.*

17. *Les* Theologiens *ne demeureront point d'accord de la These qu'on avance contre moy, qu'il n'y a point de difference par rapport à* Dieu, *entre le* naturel *& le* surnaturel. *La plus part des* Philosophes *l'approuveront encore moins. Il y a une difference infinie ; mais il paroist bien qu'on ne l'a pas bien considerée. Le* surnaturel *surpasse* toutes les forces des Creatures. *Il faut venir à un* Exemple[12] : *en voicy un, que j'ay souvent employé avec Succés. Si Dieu vouloit faire en sorte qu'un corps libre se promenât dans l'Ether en round à l'entour d'un certain Centre fixe, sans que quelque autre Creature agisse sur lui ; Je dis que cela ne se peut que par* Miracle, *n'étant pas explicable par les natures des corps. Car un corps libre s'écarte naturellement de la ligne courbe par la tangente. C'est ainsi que je soutiens que l'attraction proprement dite des corps, est une chose* miraculeuse, *ne pouvant pas étre expliquée par leur Nature.*

100. LEIBNIZ'S THIRD PAPER   415

16. I never gave any Occasion to doubt, but that God's Conservation is an actual Preservation and Continuation of the Beings, Powers, Orders, Dispositions, and Motions of all Things : And I think I have perhaps explained it better than many Others. But, says the Author, *This is all that I contended for*. To this I answer ; *Your Humble Servant for That, Sir*. Our Dispute consists in many other Things. The Question is, Whether God does not act in the most *regular* and most *perfect* Manner ? Whether his Machine is liable to *Disorders*, which he is obliged to mend by extraordinary Means ? Whether the Will of God can act *without Reason* ? Whether Space is an *absolute Being* ? Also concerning the Nature of *Miracles* ; and many such Things, which make a wide difference between us.

17. *Divines* will not grant the Author's position against me ; *viz.* that there is no Difference, with respect to *God*, between *Natural* and *Supernatural* : And it will be still less approved by most *Philosophers*. There is a vast Difference between these two Things ; but it plainly appears, it has not been duly consider'd. That which is *Supernatural*, exceeds *all the Powers of Creatures*. I shall give an Instance, which I have often made use of with good Success. If God would cause a Body to move free in the *Æther* round about a certain fixed Centre, without any other Creature acting upon it : I say, it could not be done without a *Miracle* ; since it cannot be explained by the Nature of Bodies. For, a free Body does naturally recede from a Curve in the Tangent. And therefore I maintain, that * the *Attraction* of Bodies, properly so called, is a *Miraculous* Thing, since it cannot be explained by the Nature of Bodies.

---

* *See* [...] *the* Note *on Dr.* Clarke's Fifth Reply, N°. 113.

[1] Original French and English translation are from Clarke's edition of the correspondence (Clarke 1717, pp. 54–71). LBr. 160 76r–77v is the original draft (four folio sides in Leibniz's hand). LBr. 160 Bl. 19r–22r (6.5 quarto sides) and LH I, 20 Bl. 391r–392v (four folio sides) are fair copies in secretaries' hands. Leibniz enclosed this paper with his letter to Caroline of 25 February 1716 (document 99): at the head of the original draft, Leibniz had written 'Duplique Envoyée à mad. la princesse de Galles 25 Februar 1716'. It answers Clarke's Second Reply (document 96). The footnote is Clarke's; the endnotes are mine. Clarke's references to the Appendix of his 1717 edition of the correspondence have been omitted.

[2] That is, Francis Bacon*.

[3] Clarke omits here the word 'particulieres' that Leibniz had inserted after 'd'exister' in the fair copy of his reply. So the phrase in question should read 'dans leur manieres d'exister particulieres', that is, 'into their particular manner of existing'.

[4] The original draft and the fair copies have 'a placé' instead of 'ait placé'.

[5] The original draft and the fair copies have 'mis' instead of 'pris'.

[6] The original draft and the fair copies have 'se trouve que' instead of 'se trouve donc, que'.

[7] Square brackets here are Clarke's.

[8] The original draft and the fair copies have 'l'ordre du plus sage ou de providence' instead of 'l'ordre du plus sage de la Providence'.

416   101A. NEWTON TO CONTI

[9] The original draft and the fair copies have 'il y a autres choses' instead of 'il y a d'autres choses'.

[10] The original draft and the fair copies have 'venir ces desordres' instead of 'venir les desordres'.

[11] The original draft and the fair copies have 'Si la volonté de Dieu est capable d'agir sans raison, si l'espace est un être absolu, en quoy consiste la nature du miracle' instead of 'Si la Volonté de Dieu est capable d'agir sans Raison? Si l'Espace est un Etre absolu? Sur la Nature du Miracle'.

[12] The original draft and the fair copies have '[…] un exemple. Et en voicy […]' instead of '[…] un Exemple: en voicy […]'.

101a. Isaac Newton to Antonio Schinella Conti* (excerpt)[1]

[c.8 March 1716 (NS)][2]

Sr

[…]

You know that the Commercium Epistolicum* conteins the ancient Letters & Papers preserved in the Archives & Letter Books of the R. S. & Library of Mr [John] Collins* relating to the dispute between Mr Leibnitz & Dr [John] Keill* and that they were collected & published by a Committee appointed by the R. Society for that purpose; & Mr Leibnitz has hitherto avoided returning an Answer to the same; for the Book is matter of fact & uncapable of an Answer. For avoiding an answer he pretended that he had not seen this Book nor had leasure to examin it, but had desired an Eminent Mathematician[3] to examin it. And the Answer of the Mathematician or pretended Mathematician was inserted into a defamatory Libel & published in Germany without the name of the author or publisher or City where it was published.[4] And I have since seen some Letters written since by Mr Leibnitz in all wch he excused himself from returning an Answer. And the Postscript which you shewed me is of the same kind.[5] For He tells you in it that the English shall not have the pleasure of seing him return an Answer to their slender reasonings as he calls them, & he falls upon my Philosophy, wch is nothing at all to the Question & in squabbling about it corrupts the significations of words calling those things miracles wch happen constantly & those things occult qualities wch are not occult & at the same time he has sent a Mathematical Probleme to be solved by the English Mathematicians wch is as little the purpose & contends for Hypotheses in opposition to Propositions proved from experiments & observations & experiments by the argument of Induction, & ascribes opinions to me which are not mine.

[…]

Hitherto he avoided returning an answer to the Commercium Epistolicum by pretending that he had not seen it being at Vienna. And he still escapes answering it, telling you that the English shall not have the pleasure to see him answer to their slender reasonings as he calls them & by endeavouring to engage me in

101B. NEWTON TO CONTI 419

disputes about Philosophy & about solving of Problems which are nothing to the Question.

I do not contend about skill in Mathematicks having left off that study 20 years ago & look upon solving of Problems a very unfit method to decide who was the best Mathematician or invented any thing above 40 years ago. And as to Philosophy it is as little to the purpose. He colludes in the significations of words he takes words in new significations peculiar to himself, prefers Hypotheses to Arguments of Induction taken from Phenomena accuses me of opinions that are not mine & instead of proposing Questions to be examined by experiments before they are admitted into Philosophy, he would have Hypotheses admitted & believed before they are examined. But all this is nothing to the Commercium Epistolicum.

He complains of the Committee

[...]

---

[1] Draft in Newton's hand. Cambridge University Library Add 3968, 38, ff. 560r–561v. Previously published in Koyré and Cohen 1962, p. 107 (excerpt). For the final version of the letter, see Newton's letter to Conti of 17 March 1716 (NS), document 101g.

[2] This dating is based on the fact that a draft that is virtually identical to the final version of Newton's letter (see note 1 of document 101g, p. 443) was dated 26 February 171 $\frac{5}{6}$ (OS), that is, 8 March 1716 (NS).

[3] As it turned out, this 'Eminent Mathematician' was Johann Bernoulli*.

[4] This publication was the so-called *Charta Volans* (see NC VI 15–21), which was penned by Leibniz himself. See note 3 to document 117a, pp. 525, 527.

[5] See the P.S. to Leibniz's letter to Conti of 6 December 1715 (document 88b, pp. 323, 325, 327, 329).

101b. Isaac Newton to Antonio Schinella Conti* (excerpt)[1]

[*c*.8 March 1716 (NS)][2]

Sr

You know that the Commercium Epistolicum* conteins the ancient Letters & Papers preserved in the Archives & Letter Books of the Royal Society & Library of M^r [John] Collins* relating to the dispute between Mr Leibnitz & D^r [John] Keill*, & that they were collected & published by a numerous Committee of Gentlemen of several nations appointed by the Royal Society for that purpose. Mr Leibnitz hath hitherto avoided returning an Answer to the same: for the book is matter of fact & uncapable of an Answer. To avoid answering it he pretended the first year that he had not seen this book nor had leasure to examin it, but had desired an eminent Mathematician[3] to examin it. And the Answer of the Mathematician (or pretended Mathematician) dated 7 June 1713 [NS], was inserted into a defamatory Letter dated 29 July [NS] following & published in Germany without the name of the Author or Printer or city where it was printed.[4] And the whole has been since

420   101C. NEWTON TO CONTI

101C. NEWTON TO CONTI   421

translated into French & inserted into another abusive Letter (of the same Author as I suspect) & answered by Dr Keill in July 1714 & no answer is yet given to the Doctor.

Hitherto Mr Leibnitz avoided returning an Answer to the Commercium Epistolicum by pretending that he had not seen it. And now he avoids it by telling you that the English shall not have the pleasure to see him return an answer to their slender reasonings (as he calls them) & by endeavouring to engage me in disputes about Philosophy & about solving of Problems both which are nothing to the Question.[5]

As to Philosophy, he colludes in the signif[ic]ations of words, preferrs Hypotheses to arguments of Induction from experiments, accuses me of opinions wch are not mine, & instead of proposing Questions to be examined by experiments before they are admitted into Philosophy he proposes Hypotheses to be admitted & believed before they are examined. But all this is nothing to the Commercium Epistolicum.

He complains of the Committee of the Royall Society [...]

---

[1] Draft in Newton's hand. Cambridge University Library Add 3968, 38, ff. 562r–562v. Previously Koyré and Cohen 1962, pp. 107–8 (excerpt). For the final version of the letter, see Newton's letter to Conti of 17 March 1716 (NS), document 101g.

[2] This dating is based on the fact that a draft that is virtually identical to the final version of Newton's letter (see note 1 of document 101g, p. 443) was dated 26 February 171$\frac{5}{6}$ (OS), that is, 8 March 1716 (NS).

[3] As it turned out, this 'eminent Mathematician' was Johann Bernoulli*.

[4] This publication was the so-called *Charta Volans* (see NC VI 15–21), which was penned by Leibniz himself. See note 3 to document 117a, pp. 525, 527.

[5] See the P.S. to Leibniz's letter to Conti of 6 December 1715 (document 88b, pp. 323, 325, 327, 329).

101c. Isaac Newton to Antonio Schinella Conti*[1]

[*c.*8 March 1716 (NS)][2]

Sr

The more I consider the Postscript of Mr Liebnitz the less I think it deserves an answer. For it is nothing but a piece of railery from the beginning to the end. He saith that the English would be the solle Inventors & another man may say that they will be so if Mr Leibnitz would let them keep their inventions. He saith that it doth not appear that I had the infinitesimal Characteristick & Analysis before him, but he is to prove that he had it before me. he has accused me of plagiary before the R. S. & by the laws of all nations he is guilty of calumny if he doth not prove his accusation. He appeals from the judgment of the Committee of the R. S. to the judgment of M. [Johann] Bernoulli*. But M. Bernoulli claims a share wth Mr Leibnitz in the infinitesimal Method, & D^r [John] Wallis* above 20 years ago gave

422   101C. NEWTON TO CONTI

a contrary judgment & D^r [John] Keill* hath showed that Mr Bernoulli hath erred. He said that it was easy for me to have found the Method before him if it had been notified to me: & Dr Wallis said above 20 years ago that I expressed it to Mr Leibnitz in the year1676. He said that the Committee of the R. Society have attacked his candor by misinterpretations, that he will not answer their little reasons: but they that read the Papers printed by their Committee wth their observations upon them will find that the whole is matter of fact which admits of no answer. He complains that in falling upon series they go from the fact, but the Question is whether Mr Leibnitz or I be guilty of Plagiary & what they say about series is very apposite to decide that Question. He insists upon his own candor & endeavours to suppose him self a witness in his own case and they speak to the credit of the witness. On the other hand he himself is guilty of what he complains of in others. For he goes from the fact both when he falls foul upon my philosophy, & when he sends Mathematical Problems to try who was the best Mathematician 45 or 50 years ago when he knew nothing of Geometry. He saith that I invented series before him but at length he found a general method after wch he had no further need of my extractions. But this general method is mine. It is mentioned in my Letters of 13 June & 24 Octob. 1676. He complains that the Committee of the R. S. did not print the Letters entire as Dr Wallis did with his consent: but it would have been impertinent to print what did not relate to the matter in hand. He saith that when he came to London the second time (wch was in Octob. 1676) he saw in the hands of M^r [John] Collins* a part of his Commerce with me & [James] Gregory*, & there he observed that I acknowledged my ignorance in many things, & particularly that I said that I had found nothing about the demonstration of the celebrated Curvi-linears besides that of the Cissoid: & that the Committee had supprest all this. He alledges this as an instance that they had acted partially in omitting things which made against me. But he ignores them. For you will find this printed in the Commercium Epistolicum* pag 74, & I am not ashamed of it. It is in my Letter of 24 Ocob. 1676 & therefore he saw that Letter in the hands of Mr Collins before he left London. And he might at the same time see my Analysis wch D^r [Isaac] Barrow* in the year 1669 communicated to Mr Collins, & in wch my method of moments & fluxions was described.

After this he falls foul upon my philosophy, that is upon the Philosophy of the ancient Phenicians & Greeks as if they had introduced miracles & occult qualities. & | tells you that <all the actions of God are miracles> <they introduced miracles & occult qualities & that all the actions of God are miracles> he has proved to M^r [Pierre] Bayle* that [all the actions of God are miracles or wonders even tho they happen constantly or by reason of their happening constantly create no wonder, that is, he has proved that the word Miracles signifies constant events wch create no wonder]³ | tells you that he has proved to Mr Bayle that the word Miracles signifies not only wonders but also constant events, such as by reason of their constancy create no wonder. He tells you also that God cannot be in the world without

424 101C. NEWTON TO CONTI

animating the world tho a mans soul according to his Philosophy doth not animate his body. He accuses me as if I said that God had a sensorium in a literal sense. He pretends that all places not filled with tangible bodies may be filled with an intangible corporeal fluid, that its the fault of ye workman & not of the Watch that it will at length cease, & that it would be God's fault if the world should ever want an amendment. He commends Exp[erim]entall Philo[so]phy & yet adheres to such Hypotheses as can never be proved by experiments & brings his hypotheses as arguments against things proved from experiments by the argum^t of Induction & thereby endeavours to overthrow that Philosophy, & to set up in its room a heap of precarious Hypotheses wch are nothing better than a Romance.

But I beg leave to acquaint you that its almost 40 years since I left of writing Letters about Mathematicks & Philosophy & twenty years since I left of those studies. And therefore I cannot now suffer my self to be engaged in disputes of this kind; especially since they are nothing to the Question in hand about the infinitesimal method. For understanding the Question more fully I must referr you to the Commercium Epistolicum it self & to the Account given of it in the Phil. Transactions & the Answer of Dr Keill to the Libel published in Germany & Holland against the Committee of the R. S.[4]

He accuses me & by consequence the ancient Phenicians & Greeks as if they had introduced miracles & the occult qualities of the Schoolmen into Philosophy. And to make this appear he tells us that he has proved to Mr Bayle that the word Miracles, that is wonders, includes the laws imprest by God upon nature tho by their constant acting they create no wonder, & that the words occult qualities signify qualities wch are not occult but whose causes be occult tho qualities be very manifest. He saith that God must be Intelligentia supramundana because if he were in the world he would be the soul of the world that is he would animate he world, & yet according to his Philosophy of an Harmonia præstabilita the soul of a man doth not animate his body. He accuses me as if I affirmed that God hath a Sensorium in a litteral sense. He saith that I have not demonstrated a vacuum nor universal gravity nor Atoms. But he denyes Conclusions without shewing the fault of the Premisses, & means that the Argument of Induction from Experiments upon wch the Experimental Philosophy is grounded is not a good one. For I never attempted to demonstrate any thing universally in natural Philosophy by any stronger argument then that of Induction from Experiments, And as for Atomes I never attempted to demonstrate them by this Argument, but put them amongst a set of Quæres. He saith that Space is the order of coexistences & time the order of successive existences: I suppose he means that space is the order of coexistences in space & time the order of successive existences in time, or that space is space in space & time is time in time. He insinuates that it is the fault of the workman & not of the materials that a Watch will at length cease to go & in like manner that it would be Gods fault if the world should ever decay & want an amendment. And by the same way of arguing a man may say that it would be Gods fault if matter do not think. He

426   101C. NEWTON TO CONTI

101C. NEWTON TO CONTI 427

applauds Experimental Philosophy but recom[m]ends Hypotheses to be admitted into Philosophy in order to be examined by experiments: whereas he should propose not Hypotheses to be admitted but Questions to be examined & decided by experiments-

He complains that in falling upon series they go from the fact: & yet he himself goes from the fact both in falling foul upon Philosophy & in sending a Problem to try who was the best Mathematician 45 or 50 years ago at wch time he understood nothing of Geometry[.] The Question is about Mr Leibnitz's candor & mine & if he claimed our series as invented by himself & afterwards wrote to M^r [Henry] Oldenburg* to procure & send to him the method of inventing it; if he received from London a series invented by Mr Gregory & afterwards published it as his own: the world by these instances may judge of his candor in being silent 20 years ago when Dr Wallis told him that I had in my Letters in the year 1676 explained to him the method of fluxions found by me ten years before or above & now pretending that he was the first inventor. He saith that I invented series before him

---

experiments before they are admitted into Philosophy. And whilst he applauds experimental Philosophy & cries out against miracles, he introduces an Hypothesis of an Harmonia præstabilita w^{ch} [is contrary to the daily experience of all Mankind &]^5 cannot be true without an incredible miracle, & which is contrary to the daily experience of all mankind. For all men find & experience that they can move their bodies by their wills & that they see & hear & feel by means of their bodies. [He is of opinion that space void of all tangible body may be full of a corporeal intangible fluid whereas the Ancients believed that all things intangible were incorporeal. I understand tangibility not in a mathematical but in a physical sense, such a tangibility as by some resistance can affects the sense of touching.]^6 He glories in the number of disciples, but you know that he has spent his life in making them by a general correspondence, whilst I leave truth to shift for it self. For its almost 40 years since I left of all correspondence about Math & Philos. & about 20 since I left of these studies. And for that reason I hope you will pardon me if I am averse from being engaged in disputes of this kind.

He sends you also Mathematical Problems to be solved by the English Mathematicians. And all this is nothing else than an arrangement to avoid proving his accusations against me & returning a fair answer to the matter of fact wch has been published by order of the R. Society. If he pleases to return such answer, I desire that he will be constant to himself & continue to acknowledge what he acknowledged above 15 years ago, & not contradict what he did not contradict in those days, or else to forbear boasting of his candor. By his Letter of [29 May 1675 (NS)] he acknowledged the receipt of Mr Oldenburgs Letter of [15 April 1675 (OS)] & expect that he continue to acknowledge it still. By his letter of [12 May 1676 (NS)] he acknowledged that he [had] not then the method of finding a series for that arc whose sine was given, & I expect that he acknowledg it still.

Dr. Wallis died in October 1703, the last of the old men who knew what had passed between Mr Leibnitz & me by means of Mr Oldenburg. And afterwards I was accused in the Acta Eruditorum & before the R. Society as a plagiary who had taken the method from Mr Leibnitz. And when the R. Society caused the ancient Letters & papers extant in their Archives & Letter Books & in the Library of Mr Collins to be published, all wch are unanswerable matters of fact; instead of answering the same in a fair manner & proving his accusation of plagiary against me, a defamatory Libel dated 29 July 1713[7] was published against me in Germany without the name of the Author or publisher or City where it was published, & dispersed over Germany France & Italy, & the Libel it self represents that Mr Leibnitz set it on foot. And instead of proving his accusation he goes on to write defamatory & wrangling Letters.

In the Latter part of his Postscript he falls foul upon my Philosophy as if I (& by consequence the ancient Phenicians & Greeks) introduced Miracles & occult qualities. And to make this appear he gives the name of miracles or wonders to the Laws imprest by God upon nature tho by their constant working they create no wonder, & that of occult qualities to qualities wch are not occult but whose causes are occult tho the qualities themselves be very manifest.

¹ Draft in Newton's hand. Cambridge University Library Add 3968, 38, ff. 571r–572v. Previously published in Koyré and Cohen 1962, pp. 109–112 (excerpt). For the final version of the letter, see Newton's letter to Conti of 17 March 1716 (NS), document 101g.

² This dating is based on the fact that a draft that it is virtually identical to the final version of Newton's letter (see note 1 of document 101g, p. 443) was dated 26 February 171$\frac{5}{6}$ (OS), that is, 8 March 1716 (NS).

³ The square brackets here are Newton's.

⁴ The reference is to the so-called *Charta Volans* (see NC VI 15–21), which was penned by Leibniz himself. See note 3 to document 117a, pp. 525, 527.

⁵ The square brackets here are Newton's.

⁶ The square brackets here are Newton's.

⁷ See note 4 above.

101d. Isaac Newton to Antonio Schinella Conti* (excerpt)[1]

[*c*.8 March 1716 (NS)][2]

In the second part of his Postscript he tells you that if all bodies be heavy gravity must be a scholastick occult quality & a miracle notwithstanding that it may be supposed to act constantly by a certain law imprest by God upon the nature of things; that is to say it must be a miracle tho it be no miracle. For Miracles are so called because they happen seldome & for that reason create wonder. All qualities are occult whose causes are not known, & Mr Leibnitz has not yet told us the cause of Gravity. But a Scholastck occult quality is that whose cause in our opinion cannot be found out because it was unknown to Aristotle, & no body can go beyond

him. Mr Newton holds no such opinion, but leaves it to | Mr Leibnitz | every man to find out the cause of gravity if he can.

But Mr Leibnitz insinuates that gravity must be caused by the action or impulse of some bodies or subtle matter & the matter wch causes gravity cannot gravitate it self. He goes upon the Hypothesis of the materialists viz that all the phænomena in nature are caused by mere matter & motion & man himself is a mere machine. His body is not actuated by any mind but moves by mere mechanism. And his zeale for this precarious hypothesis makes him rail at Mr Newton's universal gravity. He denys none of Mr Newton's experiments. He denys not the Third Rule of Philosophy. And yet from the Experim^ts & that Rule universal gravity necessarily follows. But he denys the conclusion. And indeed he has a very good faculty at denying conclusions. That Third Rule is the Rule of Induction. And without it no Proposition can become general in Naturall Philosophy. Without it we cannot affirm that all bodies are impenetrable. And the argument by Induction for universal gravity is as strong as the argument for universal impenetrability. Yet Arguments from Induction are not Demonstrations. They are only to take place till some experimental exception can be found. And if Mr Leibnitz out of zeale for the Hypothesis of the Materialists will except his subtile matter, the Exception will do Mr Newton's Philosophy no harm. And by the same liberty any body also may except the Impenetrability of the particles of his subtile matter.

He saith that God is Intelligentia Supramunda because he is not the soul of the world & has no need of a sensorium: as if the soul of a man would be the soul of the pictures of visible objects made in the sensoriū[m] if it were in the place where they are made, or as if any man (except the Anth[r]opomorphites ever feigned that God had a Sensorium in a litteral sense. But what he means by banishing God out of the world wants an explication. Doth he mean that God is beyond all space: a being that's nusquà. And is he angry at Mr Newton for saying that God is every where & that he is not far from every one of us: for in him we live & move & have our being.

He saith that he is astonished that Mr Newton believes that God hath made the world so ill that like a watch it would at length cease to go without the extraordinary hand of God; & that this is to have very narrō[w] Ideas of Gods wisdom & power. And by the same Argument any man may affirm that God was able to endow matter wth an active & self moving principle, & enable it to think, & therefore has done it because he is wise & good, & that God created the world from all Eternity & made it a being absolutely perfect because he was able to do so & that to deny all this is to have narrow ideas of Gods power & wisdome & goodness.

He commends experimental Philosophy, but adds that when experiments are wanting, it is allowed to imagin Hypotheses, & expect till new experiments shall determine which of them are true & upon this account thinks his philosophy may be justified. But he should consider that Hypotheses are nothing more than imaginations, conjectures, & suspicions & ought not to be proposed as Truths or Opinions nor admitted into Philosophy as such until they are verified & established

432   101E. NEWTON TO CONTI

by experiments. And if you consider his Philosophy you will find that it consists generally in such Hypotheses as can never be established by experiments: Such as are That God is intelligentia supramundana, that the bodies of animals are moved not by the mind or will of the animal but mechanically by an Harmonia præstabilita that all the Phænomena in Nature are purely mechanical. That the world is so perfect that it can last for ever without running into disorder, that the Planets revolve in Vortices, That God has never intermedled with the frame of things since the first creation.

It's not impossible but that an exception may be found in time. But a mere hypothesis or supposition of an exception is no exception. The exception ou[gh]t to be experimental. The meaning of Conclusions made by Induction is that they are to be looked upon as general till some real exception appeare. And in this sense gravity is to be looked upon as universal. To make an exception upon a mere Hypothesis is to feign an exception. It is to reject the argument from Induction & turn Philosophy into a heap of Hypotheses, which are no better than a chimerical Romance.

[1] Draft in Newton's hand. Cambridge University Library Add 3968, 38, ff. 436r–436v. Previously published in Koyré and Cohen 1962, pp. 113–15. For the final version of the letter, see Newton's letter to Conti of 17 March 1716 (NS), document 101g.

[2] This dating is based on the fact that a draft that is virtually identical to the final version of Newton's letter (see note 1 of document 101g, p. 443) was dated 26 February $171\frac{5}{6}$ (OS), that is, 8 March 1716 (NS).

101e. Isaac Newton to Antonio Schinella Conti*[1]

[*c*.8 March 1716 (NS)][2]

What he saith about Philosophy is foreign to the Question & therefore I shall be very short upon it. He denys conclusions without telling the fault of the premises. His arguments against me are founded upon metaphysical and precarious hypotheses & therefore do not affect me; for I meddle only with experimental Philosophy. He changes the signification of the words Miracles & Occult qualities that he may use them in railing at universal gravity. For Miracles are so called not because they are the actions of God but because they happen seldom & by happening seldom create wonder. If they happened constantly they would not be wonders. And occult qualities are denied not because their causes are unknown, but because the Schoolmen believed that those things wch were unknown to their Master Aristotel [*sic*], could never be known. He insinuates that I ascribe to God a sensorium in a literal sense, wch is a fiction. He presents that God must be Intelligentia Supramundana least he should be the soul of the world & by the same way of reasonings man may prove that the soul of a man is not in his head least it should be the soul of the Images of Objects formed in the sensorium. He represents that God has made this world so perfect that it can last eternally without needing any

434 101F. NEWTON TO CONTI

amendment because God was able to make it so, & by the same way of arguing a man may prove that matter can think. He pleads for Hypothetical Philosophy because there may happen experiments to decide which of the Hypotheses are true, & yet almost all his Philosophy consists in Metaphysical Hypotheses such as never were [and] never can be decided by experiments, & one of them (that of the Harmonia præstabilita) is contrary to the daily experience of all mankind. For every man finds in himself a power of moving his body by his will | And if he is happy in disciples (as he boasts) it is because he has spent all his life in corresponding with men of all nations for propagating his opinions whilst I have rested and left truth to shift for it self. | Hypotheses may be prop[o]unded by way of Questions to be examined by experiments: but when they are pro[po]unded as Opinions to be believed without examination, they turn Philosophy into a Romance. He boasts of the number of his disciples, that is of his having spent all his life in keeping a correspondence with men of all nations to make disciples whilst I keep no such correspondence but leave truth to shift for it self.

[1] Draft in Newton's hand. Cambridge University Library Add 3968, 38, f. 587v. Previously published in Koyré and Cohen 1962, pp. 74–5. For the final version of the letter, see Newton's letter to Conti of 17 March 1716 (NS), document 101g.

[2] This dating is based on the fact that a draft that is virtually identical to the final version of Newton's letter (see note 1 of document 101g, p. 443) was dated 26 February 171$\frac{5}{6}$ (OS), that is, 8 March 1716 (NS).

101f. Isaac Newton to Antonio Schinella Conti*[1]

[*c.*8 March 1716 (NS)][2]

| Philosophy is not to meddle |

For miracles are so called not because they are the works of God but because they happen seldom & for that reason create wonder. If they should happen constantly, according to certaine laws imprest upon the nature of things, they would be no longer wonders or Miracles but might be considered in Philosophy as a part of the Phenomena of Nature | [notwithstanding their being the effects of <Gods> the laws impressed upon Nature by the powers of God][3] | notwithstanding that the cause of their causes might be unknown to us. And occult qualities have been exploded not because their causes are unknown to us but because by giving this name to the specific qualities of things, a stop has been put to all enquiry into the causes of those qualities as if they could not be known because the great Philosopher Aristotel [*sic*] was not able to find them out. But Mr Leibnitz alters & enlarges the signification of these words Miracles and occult Qualities that he may make use of them in exploding (I do not say confuting) the | argument for the Being of a God taken from the Phenomena of Nature | Philosophy of Mr. Newton so far as it relates

436   101G. NEWTON TO CONTI

to the argument for proving a Deity from the Phenomena of nature. And at the same time he is propound

But its said that hypotheses may in time meet with an Experimentum Crucis & < then desend to be considered in Philosophy > when Hypotheses meet with Experimenta Crucis they will cease to be Hypotheses & desend & Mr Leibnitz proposes Hypotheses for that end. I answer that when his Hypotheses that God is Intelligentia supramundana, that there is an Harmonia præstabilita[,] that all motion (even in man himself) is purely mechanical, that God has created the world so perfect that it never can fall into disorder or need to be amended, that all the Phænomena in nature are purely mechanical, that matter is endued with a self moving power

ing Hypotheses (not Quæres to be examined by experiments but præcarious | suppositions or | opinions to [be] believed without any proof) which turn Philosophy into a Romance][4]

---

[1] Draft in Newton's hand. Lehigh University Special Collections, MS 731v. Previously published in Hall and Hall 1961, pp. 583–4. Hall and Hall have suggested that this draft was intended for Samuel Clarke* (see ibid., p. 584), but I agree with Koyré and Cohen that 'it seems [...] much more likely that this document is a portion of one of the numerous drafts of Newton's letter to the Abbe Conti' (Koyré and Cohen 1962, p. 78); the letter itself (document 101g) was dated 25 Feb. 171$\frac{5}{6}$ (that is, 8 March 1716 (NS)).

[2] This dating is based on the fact that a draft that is virtually identical to the final version of Newton's letter (see note 1 of document 101g, p. 443) was dated 26 February 171$\frac{5}{6}$ (OS), that is, 8 March 1716 (NS).

[3] The square brackets here are Newton's.

[4] The square bracket after 'Romance' is Newton's.

101g. Isaac Newton to Antonio Schinella Conti*[1]

6 March 171$\frac{5}{6}$[2]

S^r

You know that the Commercium Epistolicum* conteins the ancient Letters & Papers preserved in the Archives & Letter-books of the Royal Society & Library of M^r [John] Collins* relating to the dispute between Mr Leibnitz & D^r [John] Keill* & that they were collected & published by a numerous Committee of Gentlemen of several nations appointed by the R. Society for that purpose. Mr Leibnitz hath hitherto avoided returning an Answer to ye same: for the Book is matter of fact & uncapable of an answer. To avoid answering it, he pretended the first year that he had not seen this book nor had leasure to examin it, but had desired an eminent Mathematician[3] to examin it. And the Answer of the Mathematician (or pretended Mathematician) dated 7 June 1713 [NS] was inserted into a defamatory Letter dated 29 July [NS] following & published in Germany without the name of the Author or Printer or City where it was printed.[4] And the whole has been since translated into French & inserted into another abusive Letter (of the same Author,

438 101G. NEWTON TO CONTI

as I suspect) & answered by Dr Keill in July 1714 & no answer is yet given to the Doctor.

Hitherto Mr Leibnitz avoided returning an Answer to the Commercium Epistolicum* by pretending that he had not seen it: & now he avoids it by telling you that the English shall not have the pleasure to see him return an Answer to their slender reasonings (as he calls them) & by endeavouring to engage me in disputes about Philosophy & about solving of Problems; both which are nothing to the Question.[5]

As to Philosophy he colludes in the significations of words, calling those things miracles wch create no wonder, & those things occult qualities whose causes are occult tho the qualities themselves be manifest, & those things the souls of man wch do not animate their bodies. His Harmonia præstabilita is miraculous & contradicts the daily experience of all mankind, every man finding in himself a power of seeing with his eyes & moveing his body by his will. He prefers Hypotheses to arguments of Induction drawn from experiments, & accuses me of opinions wch are not mine, & instead of proposing Questions to be examined by experiments before they are admitted into Philosophy, he proposes Hypotheses to be believed & admitted before they are examined. But all this is nothing the Commercium Epistolicum.

He complains of the Committee of the Royall Society as if they had acted partially in omitting what made against me. But he fails in proving the accusation. For he instances in a Paragraph concerning my ignorance, pretending that they omitted it, & yet you will find it in the Commercium Epistolicum, pag. 74, lin. 10, 11, & I am not ashamed of it. He said that he saw this Paragraph in the hands of Mr Collins when he was in London the second time, that is, in October 1676. It is in my Letter of 24 Octob. 1676, & therefore he then saw that Letter. And in that & some other Letters writ before that time, I described my method of fluxions. And in the same Letter I described also two general methods of series, one of wch is now claimed from me by Mr Leibnitz.

I believe you will think it reasonable that Mr Leibnitz be constant to himself & still acknowledge what he acknowledged about 15 years ago, & still forbear to contradict what he forbore to contradict in those days.

In his Letter of 20 May 1675 he acknowledged the receipt of a Letter from M^r [Henry] Oldenburg* dated 15 Apr. 1675 with several converging series conteined therein. And I expect from him that he still acknowledge the receipt thereof. Many Gentlemen of Italy, France & Germany (you your self being one of them) have seen the original Letters & the entries thereof in the old Letter books of the Royal Society, & the series of [James] Gregory* in the Letter of 15 Apr. 1675, & in Gregories original Letter dated 15 Feb. 1671.

In a Letter dated 12 May (seen by that same Gentleman) he acknowledged that he then wanted the method for finding a Series for the Arc whose sine was given & by consequence that he wanted it when he wrote his Letter of 24 Octob. 1674. And I expect that he still acknowledge it.

440   101G. NEWTON TO CONTI

In the Acta Eruditorum for May 1700, in answer to M^r [Nicolas] Fatio [de Duillier]* who had said that I was the oldest Inventor by many years,[6] Mr Leibnitz acknowledged that no body so far as he knew had the method of fluxions or differences before me & him, & that no body before me had proved by a specimen made publick that he had it. Here he allowed that I had the Method before it was published or communicated by him to any body in Germany, & that the Principia Philosophiæ were a proof that I had it, & the first specimen made publick of applying it to the difficulter Problems. And I expect that he still continues to make the same acknowledgement. At that time he did not deny what Mr Fatio affirmed, & nothing but want of candor can make him unconstant to himself.

In a Letter to me dated 7 March 1693 & now in the custody of the Royal Society, he wrote, Mirifice ampliaveras Geometriam tuis seriebus, sed edito Princip[i]orum opere ostendisti patere tibi quæ Analysi receptæ non subsunt. Conatus sum ego quoque notis commodis adhibitis quæ differentias et summas exhibent, Geometriam illam quam transcendentem appello Analysi quodammodo subjicere, nec res male processit &c.[7] And what he then acknowledged he ought still to acknowledge.

In his Letter of 21 June 1677 writ in answer to mine of 24 Octob. 1676 wherein I had described my method partly in plane words & partly in cyphers, he said that he agreed with me that the method of Tangents of Slusius was not yet made perfect, & then set down a differential method of tangents published by D^r [Isaac] Barrow* in the year 1670 & disguised it by a new notation pretending it was his own, & shewed how it might be improved so as to perform those things wch I had ascribed to my method & concluded from thence that mine differed not much from his, especially since it facilitated Quadratures. And in the Acta Eruditorum for October 1684, in publishing the elements of his method, he added that it extended to the difficulter Problems which without this method or another like it, could not be managed so easily. He understood therefore in those days that in the year 1676 when I wrote my said Letter I had a method wch did the same things with the method which he calls differential, & he ought still to acknowledge it; Especially now the sentences in cyphers are deciphered, & other things in that Letter relating to this method are fully explained & the Compendium mentioned therein is made publick.

In his Letter of 27 Aug. 1676 he represented that he did not believe that my methods were so general as I had described them in my Letter of 13 June preceding & affirmed that there were many Problems so difficult that they did not depend upon equations nor Quadratures, such as (among many others) were the Inverse Problemes of Tangents. And by these words he acknowledged that he had not then found the reduction of Problems to differential equations. And what he then acknowledged he acknowledged again in the Acta eruditorum for April 1691, pag. 178, & ought in candor to acknowledge still.

D^r [John] Wallis* in the Preface to the two first Volumes of his works published in April 1695, wrote that I in my two Letters written in the year 1676 had explained

to Mr Leibnitz the Method (called by me the method of fluxions & by him the differential method) invented by me ten years before or above (that is, in the year 1666 or before;) & in the Letters which followed between them, Mr Leibnitz had notice of the Paragraph & did not then contradict it nor find any fault with it. And I expect that he still forbear to contradict it.

But he has lately attaqued me with an accusation wch amounts to plagiary: if he goes on to accuse me, it lies upon him by the laws of all nations to prove his accusation on pain of being accounted guilty of calumny. He hath hitherto written Letters to his Correspondents full of affirmations complaints & reflexions without proving any thing. But he is the Aggressor & it lies upon him to prove his charge.

I forbear to descend further into particulars. You have them in the Commercium Epistolicum & the Abstract[8] thereof, to both of which I refer you. I am
 Sr

Yo^r most humble

& most obedient Servant

Is. Newton.

[1] Forschungsbibliothek Gotha A 448–449 Bl. 5–6. 2.2 folio sides in Newton's hand: letter as sent. Not previously published. A virtually identical draft in Newton's hand (Cambridge University Library Add 3968, 38, ff. 564r–565r), dated (in old style) at 'Leicester Fields, London. 26 Feb. 171 $\frac{5}{6}$' (that is, 8 March 1716 NS) was previously published in Raphson 1715, pp. 100–3; in Koyré & Cohen 1962, p. 108 (excerpt); in NC VI 285–90; in HGA 186–7 (excerpt). This is Newton's response to the P. S. that Leibniz appended to his letter to Conti of 6 December 1715 (document 88b). For Leibniz's response, see his letter to Conti of 9 April 1716 (document 108).

[2] That is, 17 March 1716 (NS).

[3] As it turned out, this 'eminent Mathematician' was Johann Bernoulli*.

[4] This publication was the so-called *Charta Volans* (see NC VI 15–21), which was penned by Leibniz himself. See note 3 to document 117a, pp. 525, 527.

[5] See the P.S. to Leibniz's letter to Conti of 6 December 1715 (document 88b, pp. 323, 325, 327, 329).

[6] Newton here refers to an infamous passage from Fatio's *Lineæ brevissimi descensus investigatio geometrica duplex* (1699) in which Fatio fairly asserted that Newton was first inventor of the calculus, but then slyly and unfairly insinuated that Leibniz had plagiarized Newton's work:

> [...] I recognize that Newton was the first and by many years the most senior inventor of the calculus, being driven thereto by the factual evidence on this point; as to whether Leibniz, its second inventor, borrowed anything from him, I prefer to let those judge who have seen Newton's letters and other manuscript papers, not myself. Neither the silence of the more modest Newton nor the eager zeal of Leibniz in ubiquitously attributing the invention of this calculus to himself will impose on any who have perused those documents which I myself have examined. [As quoted in Hall 1980, pp. 106–7]

[7] 'You had enlarged geometry wonderfully with your series, but with the published work of the *Principia* you have shown that things that are not subject to the received analysis are accessible to you. I also have tried to subject that geometry that I call transcendental to analysis in a certain way, with convenient notations having been employed that exhibit differences and sums, and the matter has not turned out badly' etc.

[8] On this, see Conti's letter to Leibniz of 26 March 1716 (document 104), p. 457 note 5.

Nicolas Rémond to Leibniz (excerpt)

Monsieur

[…]

M. l'abbé Conti est tous les jours plus charmé de l'Angleterre et plus amoureux de Mr Newton il a eu l'honneur de souper avec le Roy d'Angleterre et aux propos de table il paroit bien que ce grand Prince a vecu avec Monsieur de Leibniz Sa Majesté Britannique voulut savoir de lui l'historique de vostre dispute avec Mr Newton je lui ecris sur tout cela comme je dois c'est a dire suivant ce que[2] je dois a la verité et a mon attachement declaré pour vous, car vous devez compter, Monsieur, d'avoir en moi un admirateur tres sincere et un ami tres fidele.

[…]

Monsieur

a Paris ce 15 de Mars 1716   Votre tres humble et tres
obeissant serviteur
Remond

Louis Bourguet to Leibniz (excerpt)

Monsieur,

Il y a huit jours que j'ai receu la belle lettre qu'il vous a plû m'écrire. Le landemain j'écrivis à un ami à Milan pour votre commission des graines des vers à soye: l'avertissant, que s'il croyoit la saison trop avancée, il ne les envoyat point, de peur qu'elles ne devins[s]ent vivantes en chemin. J'espere d'apprendre dans peu ce qu'il en sera, souhaitant que la commission soit faite comme il faut.

Je vous remercie bien humblement Monsieur, des belles choses, que vous avez daigné me dire sur mes deux lettres. Je n'ai pretendu ôter la contingeance aux éta[t]s du Monde, en leur donnant le titre de suite necessaire de quelque autre état precedent: ainsi necessaire, n'est ici, que ce que vous nommez naturel. Ce n'étoit que pour opposer un état donné qui seroit une suite naturelle d'un autre état semblable, à celui qui n'auroit été précédé que d'un état de pure possibilité, ou qui n'auroit été que dans l'idée de l'Etre qui l'auroit rendu actual. Je tombe d'accord que l'unité par

102. Nicolas Rémond* to Leibniz (excerpt)[1]

[15 March 1716]

Sir

[…]

The Abbé [Antonio Schinella] Conti* is every day more charmed by England and more smitten with Mr. Newton. He has had the honour of dining with the King of England [George I, Georg Ludwig* of Braunschweig-Lüneburg], and from the table talk it indeed appeared that this great prince has spent time with Mr. Leibniz. His British Majesty wanted to know from him the history of your dispute with Mr. Newton. I am writing him about all this as I must, that is to say, according to what[2] I owe to the truth and to the devotion I have declared for you, because you ought to count, sir, on having in me a very sincere admirer and very loyal friend.

[…]

Sir

<table>
<tr><td>in Paris 15 March 1716</td><td>Your very humble and very
obedient servant
Rémond</td></tr>
</table>

---

[1] LBr. 768 Bl. 60r–62r. Letter as sent: five quarto sides in Rémond's hand. Previously published in GP III 670–2; Schüller 1991, pp. 238–9 (excerpt in German translation). For Leibniz's reply, see his letter to Rémond of 27 March 1716 (document 105).

[2] Gerhardt mistranscribes 'ce que' as 'ce qui'. See GP III 672.

103. Louis Bourguet* to Leibniz (excerpt)[1]

[16 March 1716]

Sir

Eight days ago I received the nice letter that it pleased you to write me. The next day I wrote to a friend in Milan in behalf of your commission about silkworm eggs, warning him that he should not send them if he believed the season was too advanced for fear that they might come alive along the way. I hope to learn shortly what will happen, hoping that the commission is carried out properly.

I thank you very humbly, sir, for fine things that you have deigned to tell me about my two letters. I did not intend to remove contingency from the states of the world by giving them the title of necessary consequence of some other preceding state. So necessary here is only what you call natural. It was only for opposing a given state that would be a natural consequence of another similar state to one that would have been preceded only by a state of pure possibility, or that would only have been in the idea of the Being who would have made it actual. I agree that the unity in

rap[p]ort au nombre, differe de l'instant par rap[p]ort au tems: Le nombre étant une repetition de l'unité; au lieu que l'instant n'est qu'une partie assignable dans le tems, sans que celui-ci soit une repetition de celui-là. Je m'étois trompé en confondant deux choses differentes sous une même notion.

Je vous demande pardon Monsieur, la connoissance de la cause éfficiente de la rareté des gemeaux dans certaines especes d'animaux, ne peut point servir à mieux connoître la generation: C'est à dire, si c'est dans le sperme des Mâles, ou dans les Oeufs des femelles, qu'il faut chercher la base du developement de l'animal futur déja préformé dans l'un, ou dans l'autre de ces sujets. L'on peut indiquer quatre sources generales de la cause éfficiente de l'infecondité des oeufs: les dispositions vicieuses du Mâle; celles de la femelle; le tems plus ou moins convenable à la copulation; & enfin les mouvemens qui regnent dans l'action même. Mais ce n'est pas ici le lieu pour m'etendre sur cette matiere quoique très curieuse.

Je vien[s] aux huit propositions de ma seconde lettre, que vous avez eu la bonté d'approuver, excepté peut-être la derniere. Et la difficulté que vous faites Monsieur, de l'admettre, ne vient que, de ce que je ne me suis pas assés expliqué, de quelle manière je pren[ds] la perfection des êtres Créez. Je convien[s] que les êtres en question sont toûjours infinis en nombre, & que leur agregé peut recevoir d'abord toute la perfection qui lui convient dans cet état donné; mais il ne s'ensuit pas qu'il puisse recevoir d'abord toutes les perfections dont il est capable dans une suite infinie d'états consequens; et c'est là ce que j'ai voulû dire dans ma huitieme proposition. Les êtres bornez sont semblables à ces <u>Series</u> ou suites infinies dont la somme est égale à un nombre fini & determiné: Les Creatures, les Animaux, les Globes, en un mot, tous les êtres, dont la collection fait ce que nous appellons l'Univers, sont de cette nature: Et quelqu'infinis qu'ils soient en nombre, leur perfection ou le resultat de leur accord, qui en est comme la somme, ne sauroit jamais être, ni devenir veritablement infinie.

L'on peut considerer l'univers ou la Collection des êtres créez de deux manieres: La premiére en égard à leur nombre actuel, dont il n'est point de dernier terme, comme je l'ai dit dans ma premiére proposition: La seconde par rapport au developpement des Singuliers qui la composent. au premier égard l'on peut dire, que cette collection a toute la perfection qui lui convient actuellement: Mais l'on ne peut pas le dire au second, qu'en abusant des termes; puis que le développement de chaque singulier, s'étend dans toute l'éternité future. Le contraste apparent qu'on aperçoit entre la progression infinie du nombre des creatures, & celle de leur développement continuël, vient des differentes manieres dont l'Etre Suprême borne, tout ce qui existe hors de lui. Sa substance unique & absoluë, qui ne peut souffrir aucun repetition d'elle-même, borne toutes les repetitions possibles des substances qui admettent le nombre; Et sa maniere d'exister qui n'est point sujette au moindre changement, borne toutes les variations dont les substances numeriques sont capables. L'un se rapporte à l'idée necessaire des essences; l'autre à l'operation libre & volontaire de la

relation to number differs from the instant in relation to time, since number is a repetition of unity, whereas the instant is only an assignable part of time, without the latter being a repetition of the former. I erred by confounding two different things under the same notion.

I beg your pardon, sir, the knowledge of the efficient cause of the rarity of twins in certain species of animals cannot serve to understand generation better, that is to say, if it is only in the sperm of males or in the eggs of females that one must seek the basis of the development of the already preformed future animal in one or the other of those subjects. Four general sources of the efficient cause of infertility of eggs can be pointed out: the vicious dispositions of the male, those of the female, the time more or less suitable for copulation, and finally the movements that prevail in the action itself. But this is not the place to elaborate on this matter, though very curious.

I come to the eight propositions of my second letter, which you have had the kindness to approve, except, perhaps, the last.[2] And the difficulty that you make, sir, for accepting it comes only from the fact that I did not sufficiently explain myself about how I conceive the perfection of created beings. I agree that the beings in question are always infinite in number, & that their aggregate is able to receive at first all the perfection that suits it in this given state; but it does not follow that it can receive at first all the perfections of which it is capable in an infinite succession of consequent states, and that is what I meant in my eighth proposition. Bounded beings are similar to those infinite *series* or successions whose sum is equal to a finite and determinate number. Creatures, animals, celestial spheres, in a word, all beings whose collection forms what we call the universe, are of this nature. And however infinite they may be in number, their perfection, or the result of their concurrence, which is like the sum of them, could never be, or become, truly infinite.

The universe, or the collection of created beings, can be considered in two ways. The first in regard to their actual number, of which it is not some last term, as I said in my first proposition.[3] The second in relation to the development of individuals that compose it. In the first regard it can be said that this collection has all the perfection that actually suits it. But it cannot be said in regard to the second but by abusing terms, since the development of each individual extends into the entire future eternity. The apparent contrast that is perceived between the infinite progression of the number of creatures and that of their continual development comes from different ways by which the supreme being limits everything that exists outside him. His unique and absolute substance, which can admit no repetition of itself, limits all the possible repetitions of substances that admit of number, and his manner of existing, which is not subject to the least change, limits all the variations of which the numeric substances are capable. The one is related to the necessary idea of essences, the other to the free and voluntary operation of the wisdom, which acts necessarily for an end. This brings us directly to the consideration of the necessary and the contingent.

Sagesse, qui agit necessairement pour une fin. Ceci nous méne droit à la consideration des necessaires & des contingeants.

L'éternité de Dieu, dites vous Monsieur, est la seule chose necessaire, & le tems est proprement ce en quoi consiste la contingeance. Si l'on regarde l'entendement Divin, qu'on ne sauroit concevoir sans la sagesse, comme la Region des veritez éternelles, (comme il l'est en éffet) où tout se trouve necessairement rangé suivant son essence, ne pourra-t-on pas dire, que tout est d'une égale necessité, puis que l'idée de l'homme ou de quelqu'autre être que ce soit, ne sauroit être changée, non plus que celle de la proportion de deux nombres égaux? L'on auroit beau repondre, que l'idée de cette derniere verité, est fondée sur une necessité aveugle & geometrique, au lieu que l'autre vient d'une necessité de convenence qui rapporte à la sagesse; Car la Sagesse de Dieu est aussi immuable que son Entendement. La notion de la necessité, ne se rapporte point à ces deux sortes de veritez pour en confondre la nature; mais pour montrer qu'elles sont d'une égale éternité, sans qu'on puisse dire, que par une abstraction Metaphysique, que les unes précedent les autres d'une priorité d'ordre, comme l'entendement précede la sagesse. Quel lieu donc peut-il rester à la contingeance, si les productions de la Sagesse sont coéternelles avec elle? La Sapience éternelle de Dieu, ne précedera l'existence des Creatures que d'une simple priorité d'ordre, & comme elle n'est ni ne sauroit être contingente, ses émanations ne le sauroient être non plus. L'on ne pourra plus reporter les Creatures à aucun état de pure possibilité, puis que toûjours elles auront existé par la même necessité que fait subsister la Sagesse, de qui elles tirent leur origine. Ce qui est contraire aux propositions quatriéme & cinquiéme de ma lettre.

Pour chercher donc en quoi consiste la contingeance, il faut necessairement admettre, qu'il est une infinité de Mondes possibles, qui n['']ont jamais existé, et qui n'existeront point; ce qui suppose comme je l'ai dit dans ma precedente que le Monde actuel doit être aussi rap[p]orté anterieurem^t à son existence parmi le nombre des possibles. Secondement il faut admettre une éternité en Dieu, qui précéde non seulement en ordre, mais aussi d'existence, l'être des Creatures. En troisiéme lieu il faut admettre dans la volonté de Dieu, une maniere d'agir, que nous ne connoissons bien, que par analogie, dans les productions de l'art humain, où l'on voit que l'idée de l'ouvrage précéde toûjours l'ouvrage même: En sorte que les productions de la volonté de Dieu quoi qu'éternelle, different essentiellement des émanations interieures que les Chrétiens admettent dans la Divinité. En quatriéme lieu enfin, il faut reconnoitre; que tous les êtres qui existent hors de Dieu, sont necessairément limitez, quelque nombreux qu'ils puissent être. En éffet, c'est Dieu luimême qui est le principe ou le commencement des Creatures, comme il est le premier moteur, & la premiere unité, où tout se rapporte, comme à un centre commun, au delà de qui il est impossible d'aller, pas même par la pensée. Et comme ce sont la sagesse, & la volonté de Dieu qui bornent les Creatures; et que c'est dans l'institution libre de leurs limites, que consiste leur commencement & leur

The eternity of God, say you, sir, is the only necessary thing, and time is properly that in which contingency consists. If we consider the understanding of God, which could not be conceived without wisdom, as the region of eternal truths (as it is in fact), in which everything is necessarily ordered according to its essence, could we not say that everything is equally necessary, since the idea of man, or of whatever other being it may be, could not be changed, any more than that of the proportion of two equal numbers? It would be in vain to respond that the idea of this last truth is based on a blind and geometric necessity, whereas the other comes from a necessity of fittingness, which refers to wisdom; for the wisdom of God is as immutable as his understanding. The notion of necessity does not refer to those two sorts of truth in order to confuse their nature, but to show that they are equally eternal, without it being possible to say, by a metaphysical abstraction, that the ones precede the others by a priority of order, as the understanding precedes wisdom. What place then remains for contingency, if the productions of wisdom are coeternal with it? The wisdom of God will precede the existence of creatures only by a simple priority of order, and as it is not, nor could be, contingent, its emanations could not be either. It will no longer be possible to refer creatures to any state of pure possibility, since they will always exist by the same necessity that brings into existence the wisdom from which they derive their origin, which is contrary to propositions four and five of my letter.[4]

In order to seek, then, in what contingency consists, it must be admitted that there is an infinity of possible worlds, which never existed and will not exist, which assumes, as I have said in my previous [letter], that the actual world must also be placed, prior to its existence, among the number of possibles. Secondly, it is necessary to accept an eternity in God that precedes, not only in order, but also by existence, the being of creatures. In the third place, it is necessary to admit in the will of God a way of acting that we understand aright only by analogy in the productions of human art, in which we see that the idea of the work always precedes the work itself, so that the productions of the will of God, although eternal, differ essentially from the inner emanations that Christians admit in the divinity. Finally, in the fourth place, it must be recognized that all the beings that exist outside of God are necessarily limited, however numerous they may be. In fact, it is God himself who is the principle or the beginning of creatures, since he is the first mover and the first unity, to which everything relates, as to a common centre, beyond which it is impossible to go, not even in thought. And as it is the wisdom and the will of God that limits creatures, and as it is in the free institution of their limits that their beginning and their contingency consist, it cannot be said that they are produced from all eternity, since they would have, and would not have any beginning, which is contradictory. For however so far one may go back into the past eternity, the limits of bounded beings; they will never change their nature and will not be able to reach eternity itself, which will entirely limit them always in every way.

contingeance: l'on ne peut pas dire qu'elles sont produites de toute éternité, parce qu'elle sauroient, & n'auroient point de commencement; ce qui est contradictoire. Car pour si fort que l'on recule dans l'éternité anterieure, les limites des êtres bornez; jamais ils ne changeront de nature, et ne pourront atteindre jusqu'à l'éternité elle même, qui toute entiere, les bornera toûjours de toutes manieres.

Il s'ensuit ce semble, de tout ce que je vien[s] de dire, que l'Hypothese de l'Hyperbole ne peut avoir lieu. Si l'Univers gagnoit de nouvelles perfections qui fussent absolument égales à celles qu'il perdroit; il seroit vrai de dire qu'il n'augmenteroit jamais en perfection. Mais la nature des singulieres qui composent la collection qu'on appelle l'Univers, autant qu'elle nous est connuë, & qu'analogiquement elle nous exprime ce qui se passe dans celle des choses qui sont moins à nôtre portée; la connoissance dis-je de leur nature, ne nous permet pas d'admettre l'Hypothese du Rectangle. Car les changemens de leurs rapports vont en augmentant par leur developpement: Et si l'on ne peut appercevoir d'une manière également senssible [*sic*] cette augmentation de perfection dans certaines parties; c'est qu'il leur faut une long periode de tems pour cela, pendant lequel leur état paroît toûjours le même quoi qu'il ne se soit pas. Si les parties changent en augmentant de perfection, leur suite ou leur collection, qui n'est autre chose, que le resultat de leurs accords; doit aussi suivre l'état de leurs positions soit dans la diminution, soit dans l'égalité, ou l'augmentation de leur perfection. Ainsi il semble toûjours que l'Hypothese du Triangle soit la plus convenable.

La creation du Monde est un Mystere, S. Paul dit aux Ebreux Chap: XI: <u>Que par la Foy, nous entendons que les siecles ont été ordonnez par la Parole ou la Verbe de Dieu, en sorte que les choses qui se voyent, n'ont point été de choses qui apparussent.</u> Ce qui insinuë la possibilité du Monde anterieure à son existence, & son être ideal dans l'Entendement Divin, avant sa production ou sa constitution actuelle par la Sagesse ou le Verbe. Et bien que ce soit un objet de la foy, selon l'Apôtre; je croi[s] que la lumiere de la raison, bien loin d'en renverser la verité, doit plûtot nous fournir des argumens pour l'établir, & c'est ce que j'ai taché de faire par mes foibles éfforts, en attendant qu'aidé par vos sages conseils, & guidé par vos lumieres, je puisse venir à bout d'un si beau dessein.

Si je va[i]s à Geneve, je ne manquerai pas de voir Mr. Turretin, & de luis demander s'il a receu Vôtre lettre. J'ai lû avec plaisir le Traité du Jean; et j'ai aussi remarqué que l'auteur medite asses bien. Pour ce qui est de l'autre Professeur, j'observai dès que je vis la derniere edition de sa version de Pufendorf, qu'il vous taxoit dans la preface, & j'en écrivis mon sentiment à une jeune demoiselle pleine d'esprit, qui reside à Neufchatel; & qui a commerce de lettre avec le Traducteur. Elle me repondit fort agreablement, qu'il se pouvoit que ce savant, ne connoissoit pas toute la beauté du systéme de l'harmonie préetablie, parce qu'un homme ne pouvoit pas tout savoir. Je suis bien-aise que le livre de Mr Herman ait vû le jour. J'atten[ds] encore de ses

103. BOURGUET TO LEIBNIZ   451

It seems to follow from everything I have just said, that the hypothesis of the hyperbola cannot obtain. If the universe gained new perfections that were absolutely equal to those that it would lose, it would be true to say that it would never increase in perfection. But the nature of the individuals that compose the collection that we call the universe, so far as it is known to us, and that analogically expresses to us what happens in the things that are less within our reach, the knowledge, I say, of their nature does not allow us to admit the hypothesis of the rectangle. For the changes of their proportions keep on increasing by their development, and if this increase of perfection in certain parts cannot be perceived in an equally obvious way, it is because for them a long period of time is necessary for that, during which their state appears always the same, although it is not. If the parts change by increasing perfection, their succession, or their collection, which is nothing but the result of their concurrences, must also follow the state of their situations, either in the decrease, or in the equality, or the increase of their perfection. So it always seems that the hypothesis of the triangle is the most suitable.

The creation of the world is a mystery, Saint Paul tells the Hebrews Chapter XI [verse 3]: *that by faith we understand that the ages have been ordered by the word of God, so that the things that are seen were not made from things that were manifest,* which suggests the possibility of the world prior to its existence and its being ideal in the divine understanding before its production or its actual constitution by wisdom or the word. And although this is an object of faith, according to the Apostle, I believe that the light of reason, far from overturning the truth, must rather supply us with arguments to establish it, and this is what I have tried to do by my feeble efforts while waiting, so that aided by your sage advice and guided by your wisdom, I may be able to succeed in such a fine plan.

If I go to Geneva, I will not fail to see Mr. [François] Turrettin[i][5] and to ask him if he received your letter. I have read with pleasure the *Traité* of Jean,[6] and I have also noted that the Author meditates quite well. As for the other professor,[7] as soon as I saw the latest edition of his translation of Pufendorf*, I observed that he accused you in the preface,[8] and I wrote my view of it to a witty young lady who resides in Neufchâtel and has a correspondence with the translator. She responded to me very pleasantly that it was possible that this scholar did not know all the beauty of the system of the preestablished harmony, since a man could not know everything. I am glad that Mr. [Jakob] Hermann's* book has appeared.[9] I still look for his letters, and I pine to see the book itself. The English author about whom you speak to me [i.e., Samuel Clarke*], sir, is an able man and a good philosopher. But I observe with much pleasure that her Royal Highness the Princess of Wales [Caroline* of Brandenburg-Ansbach] approves and prefers your dynamics to that of Mr. Newton, which certainly presents a much meaner idea of the power of God than yours. This princess must have a great mind and good discernment. Mr. Ostervald, zealous pastor at Neufchâtel, wrote me that he was informed from England that she there attracted

lettres, & je languis de voir l'ouvrage même. L'auteur Anglois dont vous me parlez Monsieur, est habile homme & bon Philosophe. Je voi[s] pourtant avec bien du plaisir que Son Altesse Royalle Madame la Princesse de Galles, approuve et préfere vôtre Dynamique à celle de Mr. Newton, qui assurement donne une bien moindre idée de la puissance de Dieu, que la vôtre. Il faut que cette Princesse ait un grand esprit & un bon discernement. Mr Ostervald Pasteur zêlé à Neufchatel, m'écrivoit qu'on lui mandoit d'Angleterre, qu'Elle y attiroit l'ap[p]laudissement du public, & que sa charité pour nos pauvres Refugiez la rendoit extremement recommendable. Ce que vous m'en dites, doit necessairement augmenter la haute estime que tout le monde a conçu pour une Princesse si accomplie. Dieu veuille la conserver, et le Roy, & le Prince avec toute la famille Royalle pour l'Eglise, & pour le bonheur de leur Peuple.

[…] Je souhaiterois de savoir si Vous ne pensez pas Monsieur, a mettre en ordre les definitions que vous avez preparées, & si enfin vôtre dynamique verra le jour. Je prie Dieu pour vôtre conservation, et finissant je demeure avec bien du respect

Monsieur

Morges le 16: Mars 1716.

T. S. V. P.

Votre tres-humble et tres obeissant
serviteur
Louis Bourguet

P. S. [...]

Antonio Schinella Conti to Leibniz

J'ay differe jusqu'a cette heure de repondre a vos lettres,[2] parce que j'ay voulu accompagner ma Reponse de celle, qu'on vient de faire a votre P. S.

the applause of the public and that her charity for our poor refugees made her highly commendable. What you tell me about her must necessarily increase the high esteem that everyone has expressed for such an accomplished princess. May God preserve her, and the king [George I, Georg Ludwig* of Braunschweig-Lüneburg], and the prince [Georg August* of Braunschweig-Lüneburg, Prince of Wales], along with the entire royal family for the sake of the church and the happiness of their people.

[…] I would like to know if you are not thinking, sir, about putting in order the definitions that you have prepared and if your dynamics will finally appear. I pray God for your perseveration and in ending I remain with much respect

> sir

Morges 16 March 1716.   your very humble and very obedient

          Please turn the page   servant

                         Louis Bourguet

P. S. […]

---

[1] LBr. 103 Bl. 47r–50v. Letter as sent: eight quarto sides in Bourguet's hand. Not previously published. This is a response to Leibniz's letter to Bourguet of 24 February 1716 (see document 98). For Leibniz's reply, see Leibniz's letter to Bourguet of 3 April 1716 (document 107).

[2] The last of the eight propositions that Bourguet proposed in his letter to Leibniz of 7 February 1716 states: 'All bounded beings can answer at once to only a limited number of relations [rapports], which prevents them from being able to receive at first all the perfection possible' (GP III 588).

[3] The first of the eight propositions that Bourguet proposed in his letter to Leibniz of 7 February 1716 states: 'The universe is a collection of different beings, all limited, of which the number has no last term' (GP III 587).

[4] The fourth proposition in Bourguet's letter to Leibniz of 7 February 1716 states: 'Suppose a complete change of relations without any connection; the result is another being. Apply this change to a given succession of beings; the result is a new universe. And it is the idea of all these changes and of all these combinations in an infinity of given successions that forms in the divine understanding the knowledge of all possibles' (GP III 587). The fifth proposition states: 'The possibility of all these successions, or of all these worlds, proves that the wisdom of God made a choice and necessarily implies that the actual world was among the number of possibles before having received existence' (GP III 587).

[5] That is, the Reformed scholastic theologian François Turrettini (1623–1687).

[6] See Leibniz's letter to Bourguet of 24 February 1716, p. 403 note 7.

[7] That is, the French jurist and Huguenot refugee Jean Barbeyrac (1674–1744).

[8] That is, the Avertissement to the second edition of Barbeyrac's French translation (Le Droit de la Nature et des Gens (Amsterdam: Pierre de Coup, 1712), p. xii)) of Pufendorf's De jure naturae et gentium. See Leibniz's letter to Bourguet of 24 February 1716, document 98, p. 405 note 10.

[9] Concerning Jakob Hermann's book, see Leibniz's letter to Bourguet of 24 February 1716, document 98, pp. 405, 407 note 11.

104. Antonio Schinella Conti* to Leibniz[1] (excerpt)

[26 March 1716 (NS)]

I have put off responding to your letters[2] till now because I wanted to send my response along with that which has just been made to your P. S.[3]

Je n'entrerai dans aucun detail a l'egard de la dispute, que vous avez avec M. Keill, ou plutost avec M. Newton. Je ne puis dire historiquement[4] ce que j'ai vû, et ce que j'ay lû, et ce qu'il me manque encore de voir et de lire.

J'ay lû avec beaucoup d'attention, et sans la moindre prevention le Commercium Epistolicum, et le petit Livre, qui en contient l'Extrait.[5] J'ay vû a la Societé Royal les Papiers originaux des Lettres du Com̅ercium vne petite Lettre ecrite de votre main a M. Newton; l'ancien manuscrit, que M. Newton envoya au Docteur Barow, et que M. Jones a publié depuis peu.[6]

De tout cela j'en infere, que si on ote a la dispute toutes les digressions etrangeres il ne s'agit, que de chercher, si Mr. Newton avoit la methode[7] des Fluxions, ou infinitesimal avant vous; ou si vous l'avez eu avant lui. Vous l'avez publié le premier; il est vrai, mais il semble, que[8] vous avez avoué aussi, que Mr. Newton en avoit laissé entrevoir beaucoup dans les lettres, qu'il a ecrit a M. Oldenburg, et aux autres. On prouve cela fort au long dans le Com̅ercium, et dans son extrait. Quelles sont vos Reponses? Voila ce qui manque encor au Public pour juger exactement de l'affaire.

Vos amis attendent votre reponse avec impatience,[10] et il leurs[11] semble, que vous ne scauriez vous dispenser de repondre si non a M. Keill, du moins a M. Newton luy meme, qui vous fait un defy en termes expres, com̅e vous verrez dans sa lettre.

Je voudrois vous voir en bonne intelligence. Le public ne profite guere des[13] vos disputes,[14] et il perd sans ressource pour bien de siecles[15] toutes les lumieres, que ces memes disputes luy derobent.

Sa Majesté a voulu, que je l'informasse de tout ce qui s'est passé entre M. Newton, et vous. Je l'ay fait de mon mieux, et je voudrois, que ce fut avec succes pour l'un, et pour l'autre.

[...]

Je vous parlerai une autre fois de la Philosophie de Mr. Newton. Il faut convenir auparavant de la methode de Philosopher, et distinguer avec beaucoup de soin la philosophie de M. Newton, des consequences, que plusieurs en tirent fort mal a propos. On luy attribue bien des choses, que il n'admet pas, com[m]e il a fait voir aux Francois, qui etoit venus a Londre[s] a l'occasion de la grande eclipse.[16]

[...]

Je suis avec tout le respect.

Londre[s] ce 15 de Marz 171 $\frac{5}{6}$ [17]   Monsieur

Votre tres humble, et tres
obeissent serviteur[18]

Conti

I will not go into any detail as regards the dispute that you have with Mr [John]. Keill*, or rather with Mr. Newton. I can only state historically[4] what I have seen, and what I have read, and what I yet stand in need of seeing and reading.

I have read with great attention, and without the least prejudice, the *Commercium Epistolicum*, and the small book which contains the extract.[5] I have seen at the Royal Society the originals of the letters of the *Commercium*; a small letter written in your hand to Mr. Newton; the old manuscript that Mr. Newton sent to Doctor [Isaac] Barrow* and which Mr. [Willaim] Jones* has recently published.[6]

From all that I infer that if all the irrelevant digressions are removed from the dispute, it is only a matter of investigating whether Mr. Newton had the method[7] of fluxions, or infinitesimal method, before you, or you had it before him. It is true that you published first, but it seems that[8] you have also admitted that Mr. Newton had allowed you to look at a lot of it in the letters that he wrote to Mr. [Henry] Oldenburg* and others.[9] That is proved at great length in the *Commercium* and its extract. What are your replies? That is what is still lacking to the public in order to judge the matter aright.

Your friends impatiently await your response,[10] and it seems to them[11] that you cannot avoid responding, if not to Mr. Keill, at least to Mr. Newton himself, who challenges you in express terms, as you will see in his letter.[12]

I would like to see you on good terms. The public scarcely profits from[13] your disputes,[14] and it irretrievably loses for many centuries[15] all the knowledge that these same disputes steal from it.

His Majesty [King George I, Georg Ludwig* of Braunschweig-Lüneburg] has wanted me to inform him of everything that has happened between Mr. Newton and you. I have done my best, and I would wish that it was with success for both. [...]

I will speak to you again about the philosophy of Mr. Newton. One must first agree on the method of philosophizing and distinguish very carefully the philosophy of Mr. Newton from the consequences that many improperly draw from it. Many things are attributed to him that he does not accept, as he revealed to the Frenchmen who had come to London on the occasion of the great eclipse.[16] [...]

I am with all the respect.

London 15 March 171$\frac{5}{6}$ [17]   Sir

your very humble, and very
obedient servant[18]

Conti

---

[1] Forschungsbibliothek Gotha A 448–449 Bl. 3–4. Letter as sent: 2.5 quarto sides in Conti's hand. Previously published in the *Philosophical Transactions* 30, no. 359 (1719), pp. 923–5; Des Maizeaux 1720, vol. 2, pp. 12–15; GB 269–70 (taken from Des Maizeaux); Dutens III 449–51; NC VI 295–6 (excerpt from Des Maizeaux); Schüller 1991, pp. 239–40 (excerpt in German translation); Robinet

Leibniz to Nicolas Rémond

Hanover ce 27 de Mars 1716.

Monsieur

[…]

Mes petits maux sont fort tolerables & même sans douleur, quand je me tiens en repos. Ils ne m'ont point empêché de faire un tour à Brunswick, pour souhaiter un heureux voyage à Madame la Duchesse, Mere de l'Imperatrice regnante, qui va

1991, p. 62 (excerpt). The version published by Des Maizeaux follows the version published in the *Philosophical Transactions* rather than the letter that Conti actually sent to Leibniz. This is Conti's response to Leibniz's letter of 6 December 1715 (document 88b). For Leibniz's reply, see his letter to Conti of 9 April 1716 (document 108).

[2] The version published by Des Maizeaux has 'votre Lettre' instead of 'vos lettres' (see Des Maizeaux 1720, vol. 2, p. 12).

[3] The response to Leibniz's P.S. that Conti refers to here is the one made by Newton in his letter to Conti of 17 March 1716 (NS) (see document 101g).

[4] I follow Des Maizeaux in reading 'Je ne puis dire qu'historiquement' for 'Je ne puis dire historiquement'.

[5] Des Maizeaux adds this note: 'This is a work of 38 pages in octavo, entitled *Extract du Livre intitulé:* Commercium Epistolicum Collinii & aliorum de Analysi promota, *published by order of the Royal Society on the occasion of the dispute raised between Mr. Leibniz and Dr. Keill on the right of invention to the method of fluxions, which some call the* differential method. It has been included in volume VII of the *Journal Literaire*' (Des Maizeaux 1720, vol. 2, pp. 12–13).

[6] Des Maizeaux adds this note: 'This manuscript, entitled de Analysi per Æquationes infinitas, was published in 1711 by Mr. Jones, in the collection entitled *Analysis per Quantitatum Series, Fluxiones, ac Differentias: cum enumeratione Linearum tertii ordinis: in 4*' (Des Maizeaux 1720, vol. 2, p. 13).

[7] Conti had first written 'Calcul', but then crossed it out and wrote 'methode' above it. The version published by Maizeaux has 'Calcul' instead of 'methode'.

[8] The version published by Des Maizeaux omits 'il semble, que' (see Des Maizeaux 1720, vol. 2, p. 13).

[9] On this point, see Hall 1980, pp. 46–69.

[10] The version published by Des Maizeaux has 'avec beaucoup d'impatience' for 'avec impatience' (see Des Maizeaux 1720, vol. 2, p. 14).

[11] Reading 'leur' for 'leurs'.

[12] That is, Newton's letter to Conti of 6 March 1716 (i.e., of 17 March 1716 NS; see document 101g).

[13] Reading 'de' for 'des'.

[14] The version published by Des Maizeaux has 'des Disputes' instead of 'des vos disputes' (see Des Maizeaux 1720, vol. 2, p. 14).

[15] Reading 'des siecles' for 'de siecles'.

[16] The version published by Des Maizeaux has : 'On attribuë à ce grand homme bien des choses qu'il n'admet pas ; comme il l'a fait voir à ces Messiers François qui vinrent à Londres, à l'occasion de la grande Eclipse' (see Des Maizeaux 1720, vol. 2, p. 15) for 'On luy attribue bien des choses, que il n'admet pas, come il a fait voir aux François, qui etoit venus a Londre, a l'occasion de la grande eclipse'. The reference here is to the solar eclipse of 3 May 1715 (NS).

[17] That is, 26 March 1716 (NS). The following paragraph was appended to the version of the letter published in the *Philosophical Transactions*:

N.B. *Mr. l'Abbé Conti spent some Hours also in looking over the old Letters and Letter Books kept in the Archives of the* Royal Society, *to see if he could find any thing which made either for Mr. Leibnitz, or against Mr. Newton, and had been omitted in the* Commercium Epistolicum Collinii & aliorum: *but could find nothing of that kind.*

[18] The Version published by Des Maizeaux has 'Je suis avec tout le respect possible, Monsieur, vôtre &c' (see Des Maizeaux 1720, vol. 2, p. 15) for 'Je suis avec tout le respect. Monsieur Votre tres humble, et tres obeissent serviteur'.

105. Leibniz to Nicolas Rémond* (excerpt)[1]

Hanover 27 March 1716

Sir

[...]

My little ailments are very tolerable and even without pain when I rest. They have not prevented me from taking a trip to Braunschweig in order to wish a happy journey to the Duchess [Christine Luise of Öttingen (1671–1747), Duchess of

trouver sa fille pour assister à l'acouchement. Et ces maux, s'ils ne deviennent point plus grands, ne m'empêcheront point dans la suite de faire de plus grands voyages. Mais à présent je travaille à achever mes Annales qui sont presque de trois siècles de l'Empire d'Occident, & même des plus ténébreux. Je rectifie quantité de points même sur l'Histoire de France. L'Ouvrage sera en état d'être imprimé avant la fin de cette année. J'ai eu des moyens de lever presque toutes les difficultez Chronologiques. Après cela, si Dieu me laisse quelque tems de reste, ce sera pour pousser quelques méditations, & pour les pousser jusqu'à la démonstration.

M. Clarke, Chapelain du Roi de la Grande-Bretagne, attaché à M. Newton, dispute avec moi pour son Maître, & Madame la Princesse de Galles a la bonté de prendre connoissance de notre Dispute. Je lui ai envoyé derniérement une démonstration que l'Espace, qui est *idolum tribus* de plusieurs, comme parle *Verulamius*, n'est plus une Substance, ni un Etre absolu, mais un ordre comme le Tems. C'est pour cela que les Anciens ont eu raison d'appeller l'Espace hors du monde, c'est-à-dire l'Espace sans le Corps, imaginaire. Je crois que M. l'Abbé Conti prend connoissance de notre Dispute & en a communication, quoiqu'il ne me dise plus rien après ce que vous m'avez envoyé de sa part. Jusqu'ici on n'a pas bien vû les conséquences de ce grand principe que *rien n'arrive san s une Raison suffisante*; & il s'ensuit entre autres, que l'Espace n'est pas un Etre.

Je suis fort content que M. l'Abbé Conti estime M. Newton, & en profite: & comme il ne me connoît guères, je ne serois point surpris s'il panchoit[4] plus de son côté. Mais je serois fâché qu'il eût fait quelque chose à mon égard, où j'aurois eu sujet de ne me point attendre. [...]

Je trouve fort raisonnable que la Sorbonne soit pour la superiorité des Conciles, & pour les Libertez Gallicanes; mais je ne voudrois pas qu'on prit trop le parti de la prétenduë grace efficace par elle-même ; & d'autres sentimens outrez des Disciples de S. Augustin. Je crois d'avoir développé & distingué ces choses dans ma *Théodicée*, & je voudrois savoir ce qu'en jugent les Théologiens qui ne font pas trop pour outrer les matiéres. Il faut que je sois un peu plus libre pour achever tout-à-fait mon Discours sur la Théologie naturelle Chinoise. Je vous demande pardon, Monsieur, d'écrire si peu lisiblement, la poste presse, & je suis avec zèle, Votre, &c.

P. S. Oserois-je vous charger de ma Lettre pour son Altesse Royale Madame.

Braunschweig-Wolfenbüttel], mother of the reigning empress [Elisabeth Christine* of Braunschweig-Wolfenbüttel], who is going to meet her daughter in order to help with the delivery of her baby. And these ailments, if they do not become worse, will not prevent me from eventually taking some very extensive trips. But at present I am working to complete my Annals,[2] which are about almost three centuries of the Western Empire, and even of the most obscure. I correct a number of points, even about the history of France. The work will be in a state to be printed before the end of this year. I have some ways of removing nearly all the chronological difficulties. After that, if God allows me some spare time, it will be to pursue some reflections and pursue them to the point of demonstration.

Mr. [Samuel] Clarke*, Chaplain of the King of Great Britain [George I, Georg Ludwig* of Braunschweig-Lüneburg], attached to Mr. Newton, disputes with me for his master, and the Princess of Wales [Caroline* of Brandenburg-Ansbach] has the kindness to take note of our dispute. I recently sent him a demonstration that space, which is the *idolum tribus* of many, as Verulam [i.e., Francis Bacon*] says, is neither a substance, nor an absolute being, but an order, like time. That is why the ancients had been right to call space outside the world, that is to say space without body, imaginary. I believe that the Abbé [Antonio Schinella] Conti* takes note of our dispute and has communication about it, although he may tell me nothing more after what you sent me from him.[3] Up to this point he has not appreciated the consequences of the great principle that *nothing happens without a sufficient reason*; and it follows, among other things, that space is not a being.

I am very pleased that Abbé Conti esteems Mr. Newton and benefits from him. And as he scarcely knows me, I would not be surprised if he leaned[4] more to his side; but I would be angry if he had done something in regard to me that I would not have had reason to expect. [...]

I find it very reasonable that the Sorbonne is in favour of the superiority of the Councils and the Gallican Liberties;[5] but I should not want them to take too far the side of the supposed unaided efficacious grace and other excessive views of the disciples of St. Augustine. I believe I have elucidated and distinguished these things in my *Theodicy*, and I would like to know what the theologians who do not do too much to exaggerate the matters think of it. I must be a bit more free to finish entirely my Discourse on the Natural Theology of the Chinese. I beg pardon, sir, for writing so illegibly; the post presses, and I am enthusiastically, your, etc.

P.S. Dare I entrust you with my letter for her Royal Highness Madame [Elisabeth Charlotte* of the Palatinate, Duchess of Orléans].

---

[1] This letter and its draft have apparently been lost. Here I rely on the version published in Des Maizeaux 1720, vol. 2, pp. 346–51. It is Leibniz's reply to Rémond's letter to Leibniz of 15 March 1716 (document 102). Previously published in Dutens V 30–2; GP III 673–5; Schüller 1991, p. 240 (excerpt in German translation); Robinet 1991, pp. 61–2 (excerpt).

[2] That is, Leibniz's *Annales imperii occidentis Brunsvicenses**.

[3] See documents 79a–c above.

[4] Reading 'penchait' for 'panchoit'.

[5] That is, the liberties of the Catholic Church in France.

Louis Bourguet to Leibniz (excerpt)

Monsieur,

Je suis fort mortifié, que je n'aye pû effectuer par le moyen du seul amis & correspondant que j'aye a Milan, la comission des graines de vers à soye. Vous verrez par l'enclose que j'ai receu depuis peu comme il n'a pas tenu à moi, que vous n'ayez été servi. Une autre année il faudra donner la com[m]ission à meilleur[e] heure s'il plait à Dieu. Mais s'il n'importoit pas que ce fussent des graines de Bologne, peut être me seroit-il plus facile d'en obtenir de là, y ayant un plus grand nombre de connoissances. [...] Je vous prie tres-humblement me pardonner la liberté que je pren[ds] de vous adresser l'encolse pour Mr Herman. Il y a bien environ un an que je suis sans aucune de ses lettres; ce qui me mît en peine m'imaginant qu'ap[p]aremment, il n'aura pas eu mes lettres, ou bien que ses grandes occupations l'ont empeché de me repondre. J'ai un desir extréme de voir son ouvrage, et je souhaiterois qu'enfin vous voulussiez permettre que Vôtre Dynamique vit le jour. Après quoi je doute que la doctrine de Mrs. les Anglois puisse long tems subsister. Déja Mr. le Comte Riccati a trouvé que Mr. Newton s'étoit mepris dans son hypothese des Cours des Planetes, qui surement decrivent des Ellipses d'une espece particuliere, ce qui demonte tout à fait le sentiment de cet habile homme. Je croi[s] que le Comte donnera quelque jour des essais sur cette matiere; au moins c'est ce que j'en ai pû recueillir des discours de Monsieur Zendrini. Ce Monsieur Clark, dont vous me parliez Monsieur dans vôtre derniere, est le même qui a aussi employé vôtre Principe que Dieu choisit toujours le meilleur, et cela dans un ouvrage qu'il a composé sur la Religion. Il me souvient d'avoir lû l'extrait d'un ouvrage Philosophique, d'un autre auteur Anglois, qui semble avoir percé jusques à la notion des substances. Il dit quelque part que l'objet de la vüe est different de celui du Toucher. J'en suis persuadé de même que lui. Enfin j'ose esperer que les Philosophes ouvriront les yeus,[6] et reconnoitront, malgré l'erreur & l'ignorance, qu'il faut recourir a la source de toutes les notions, & principalem^t à celles de la substance, comme vous l'avez très-heureusement, et très-sagement pratiqué. Alors nous verrons une infinité de decouvertes nouvelles, utiles et agreables; Et l'on trouvera quelque fondement solidé sur quoi s'appuyer dans l'Etude de la Philosophie. Je fai[s] toujours des voeux très sinceres pour vôtre conservation, & pour vôtre prosperité, et suis avec beaucoup de respect.

Monsieur

Morges le 31: Mars 1716.

Vôtre-tres-humble etres[7]
obeissant serviteur
Louis Bourguet

106. Louis Bourguet* to Leibniz (excerpt)[1]

[31 March 1716]

Sir

I am very mortified that I have not been able to carry out the commission of silk-worm eggs by means of the only friend and correspondent that I have in Milan. You will see from the enclosure that I recently received how it is not my fault that you have not been served. Another year it will be necessary to give the commission at a better time if it please God. But if it doesn't matter that they are eggs from Bologna, perhaps it would be easier for me to obtain some from there, since I have a greater number of acquaintances there. [...] I beseech you very humbly to pardon me the liberty that I take to send you the enclosure for Mr. [Jakob] Hermann*. It has been about a year that I have been without any of his letters, which troubled me, since I imagine that he apparently must not have received my letters, or else that his great occupations have prevented him from responding to me. I have an extreme desire to see his work,[2] and I would like to request that you might finally want to allow your dynamics to appear, after which I doubt that the doctrine of the English could survive for long. Count Riccati[3] has found that Mr. Newton was mistaken in his hypothesis concerning the orbits of the planets, which certainly describe ellipses of a special kind, which undoes completely the view of that able man. I believe that the count will eventually present some essays on this subject, at least that is what I am able to gather from the lectures of Mr. [Bernadino] Zendrini*. This Mr. [Samuel] Clarke* of whom you spoke in your last letter,[4] sir, is the same one who has also employed your principle that God always chooses the best, and that in a work that he has composed on religion. I remember having read the extract from a philosophical work by another English author who seems to have penetrated to the very notion of substances. He says somewhere that the object of sight is different from that of touch.[5] I am convinced of it just as he is. Finally, I dare hope that philosophers will open their eyes[6] and recognize, despite their error and ignorance, that it is necessary to have recourse to the source of all notions, and principally to those of substance, as you have very happily and very wisely practised. Then we will see an infinity of useful and pleasing new discoveries; and we will find some solid foundation upon which to rely in the study of philosophy. I always offer up some very sincere prayers for your preservation and your prosperity, and I am with much respect.

Sir

Morges 31 March 1716.

your very humble and very[7]
obedient servant
Louis Bourguet

Leibniz to Louis Bourguet

Monsieur

Je viens de recevoir l'honneur de votre lettre, et je vous remercie d'abord de la bonté que vous avés eue de donner ordre[2] à un ami pour des graines des vers à soye: il est encore temps sans doute de les envoyer durant le mois d'Avril et même au commencement du may car dans les Alpes et en Allemagne les chaleurs ne viennent pas si tost. En tout cas il vaut mieux le hazarder. Je souhaite que les graines soyent de bonne race. En mettant le papier dans une petite boiste[3] de fer blanc je crois que les graines demeureront plus fraiches.

A l'egard de la comparison entre l'instant et l'unité, j'adjoute encor, que l'unité est une partie du nombre plus grand que l'unité; mais que l'instant n'est pas à proprement parler une partie du temps. Car dans le style au moins des Mathematiciens le tout et la partie doivent etre homogenes.

Quant à la grande question s'il est possible de demontrer par raison quelle hypothese, savoir du rectangle, du triangle ou de l'hyperbole est preferable dans la constitution de l'Univers, je crois qu'il faudroit s'attacher à un raisonnement rigoureux en bonne forme. Car comme en Metaphysique on n'a pas l'avantage des Mathematiciens de pouvoir fixer les idees par des figures; il faut que la rigueur du raisonnement y supplée, la quelle ne peut gueres être obtenue en ces matieres, qu'en observant la forme logique. C'est ce que j'ay observé plus d'une fois; et j'ay remarqué que M. des Cartes et Spinosa s'ecartant de la rigueur de la forme dans leur pretendues demonstrations Metaphysiques, sont tombés dans des paralogismes. Ainsi je vous prie, Monsieur, de penser, comment vous pourries reduire vos raisonnemens là dessus à une forme due, car je n'en voy pas encore le moyen. Sans cela il y aura tousjours des remarques et des repliques à faire, sans qu'on sache si l'un est bien avancé ou non.

107. LEIBNIZ TO BOURGUET   463

[1] LBr. 103 Bl. 44r–45r. Letter as sent: three quarto sides in Bourguet's hand. Previously published in Schüller 1991, p. 241 (excerpt in German translation); Robinet 1991, p. 61 (excerpt).

[2] That is, Hermann's book, *Phoronomia, sive de Viribus et Motibus corporum solidorum et fluidorum libri duo* (1716), concerning which see Leibniz's letter to Bourguet of 24 February 1716, document 98, pp. 405, 407 note 11.

[3] That is, the Venetian mathematician Jacopo Francesco Riccati (1676–1754).

[4] See Leibniz's letter to Bourguet of 24 February 1716 (document 98, p. 403).

[5] Here Bourguet seems to be referring to George Berkeley's *An Essay towards a New Theory of Vision* (1709), although Berkeley was, of course, Irish and not English. Later, in his letter to Leibniz of 15 May 1716, Bourguet had recovered his memory: 'The Englishman who seemed to catch a glimpse of something about substance is Mr. Berkeley, Scottish if I am not mistaken. But he entangles himself in occasional causes' (document 118, p. 533)

[6] Reading 'yeux' for 'yeus'.

[7] Reading 'et très-' for 'etres-'.

107. Leibniz to Louis Bourguet*[1]

[3 April 1716]

Sir

I have just received the honour of your letter, and I thank you first of all for the kindness that you have had to give instruction[2] to a friend for some silkworm eggs. There is doubtless still time to send them during the month of April, and even at the beginning of May, for in the Alps and in Germany, the hot season does not arrive so soon. In any case, it is better to risk it. I hope that the eggs are from good stock. By placing the paper in a small tin box,[3] I believe that the eggs will remain very cool.

As regards the comparison between the instant and unity, I again add that unity is a part of any number greater than unity, but the instant is not, properly speaking, a part of time. For in the style at least of mathematicians, the whole and the part must be homogeneous.

As for the great question whether it is possible to demonstrate by reason which hypothesis, namely of the rectangle, of the triangle, or of the hyperbola is preferable in the constitution of the universe,[4] I believe that it would be necessary to adhere to a rigorous argument in good form. For since in metaphysics one does not have the advantage of mathematicians to be able to fix ideas by figures, rigor of the argument must make up for it, which can only be obtained in these matters by observing logical form. I have observed this more than once, and I have noticed that Descartes and Spinoza, by deviating from rigor of form in their supposed metaphysical demonstrations, have fallen into paralogisms. So I pray you, sir, think how can you reduce your arguments about this to a due form, for I do not yet see the way. Without that there will always be some remarks and replies to make, without knowing whether or not one [of the hypotheses] is better.

Vous avés raison, Monsieur, de dire que de ce que les Etres finis sont infinis en nombre, il ne s'ensuit point que leur système doit recevoir d'abord toute la perfection dont il est capable. Car si cette consequence étoit bonne, l'Hypothese du Rectangle seroit demontrée.

Je crois aussi que le resultat en est veritablement infini, et ne doit pas etre comparé à une suite infinie de nombres, dont la somme est finie. Mais un infini pour parler selon notre portee est plus grand qu'un autre par exemple la somme de cette series $\frac{1}{1}+\frac{1}{2}+\frac{1}{3}+\frac{1}{4}+\frac{1}{5}+$ etc. à l'infini, est infini, et surpasse tout nombre assignable; mais cependant la somme de cette autre series $\frac{1}{1}+\frac{1}{1}+\frac{1}{1}+\frac{1}{1}+\frac{1}{1}$ etc. à la infini, est infiniment plus grande que la percedente. Ainsi la perfection du system toute infinie qu'elle seroit, ne seroit pas pour cela la plus grande possible; mais y approcheroit tousjours.

Les idées ou essences sont toutes foundées sur une necessité independante de la sagesse, de la convenance et du choix. Mais les Existences en dependent.

Quand même le rectangle auroit lieu, il n'y auroit point de production de la sagesse coëternelle avec elle, car ses productions changement tousjours. Une production necessaire ne doit point etre sujette au changement.

Chaque estat de l'univers est tousjours limité en perfection, quand même le precedent seroit egal en perfection au suivant car tous deux ensemble enveloppent plus de perfection, que l'un seul. C'est aussi pour cela que le changement est à propos, afin qu'il y ait plus d'especes ou formes de perfection, quand même elle[s] seroient egales en degré. Encor en Dieu l'idée de l'ouvrage precede tousjours l'ouvrage, l'estat present des choses etoit tousjours preconnu.

Vous avés raison, Monsieur, de juger que Mad. la princesse de Galles doit avoir une elevation d'esprit admirable, puisque elle entre si avant dans des matieres si sublimes. Je vous diray pour le confirmer, qu'elle a lû la Theodicée plus d'une fois, et avec goust; et qu'elle s'est moquée de ceux qui l'avoient voulu detourner de cette lecture sous pretexte, que les choses etoient trop abstraites.

Le professeur de Lausanne n'estoit pas oblige de connoitre mon Harmonie préetablie, mais n'y entendant rien, il pouvoit se dispenser de la mépriser. Le meilleur est que son jugement là dessus ne sera point mis en ligne de compte, non plus que celuy de M. pufendorf sur la question si la moralité depend de la volonté de Dieu. Il s'est mis un peu trop en colere, voyant que je ne faisois pas un asses grand cas de son Auteur sur cette matiere de la force de la moralité.

Au reste je suis avec passion
Monsieur

votre tres humble et
tres obëissant serviteur
Leibniz

À Hanover ce 3 d'Avril
1716

P. S. La nouvelle du massacre des Jesuites à la chine a ete fausse, le Monarque de la Chine s'est reconcilié avec son heritier. Le Roy de portugal solicite pour les Jesuites

You are right, sir, to say that from the fact that finite beings are infinite in number, it does not follow that their system must receive at first all the perfection of which it is capable. For if this conclusion were correct, the hypothesis of the rectangle would be demonstrated.

I also believe that the result is truly infinite and must not be compared to an infinite sequence of numbers whose sum is finite.[5] But one infinity, to speak according to our capacity, is greater than another; for example, the sum of this series $\frac{1}{1}+\frac{1}{2}+\frac{1}{3}+\frac{1}{4}+\frac{1}{5}+$ etc. to infinity is infinite and surpasses every assignable number; but nevertheless the sum of this other series $\frac{1}{1}+\frac{1}{1}+\frac{1}{1}+\frac{1}{1}+\frac{1}{1}$ etc. to infinity is infinitely greater than the preceding one. Thus the perfection of the system, however infinite it may be, would not be the greatest possible on account of that, but would always approach it.[6]

Ideas or essences are all founded on a necessity independent of wisdom, of fitness, and choice. But existing things are dependent on them.

Even if the rectangle would have obtained, there would not have been any production of the wisdom coeternal with it [i.e., the wisdom], for its productions always change. A necessary production must not be subject to change.[7]

Each state of the universe is always limited in perfection, even if the preceding state were equal in perfection to the following state; for both together involve more perfection than the one alone. It is also for this reason that change is fitting, in order that there be more kinds or forms of perfection, even if they would be equal in degree. Yet in God the idea of the work always precedes the work; the present state of things was always known in advance.

You are right, sir, to judge that the Princess of Wales [Caroline* of Brandenburg-Ansbach] must have an admirable elevation of mind because she goes so far into such sublime matters. In order to confirm that, I will tell you that she has read the *Theodicy* more than once, with approval, and that she scoffs at those who had wanted to put this reading aside on the pretext that the matters were too abstract.[8]

The professor from Lausanne[9] was not obligated to be acquainted with my preestablished harmony, but since he understands nothing about it, he could excuse himself from scorning it. The best thing is that his judgment about it will not be taken into consideration any more than that of Mr. [Samuel] Pufendorf* on the question of whether morality depends on the will of God. He got a little too angry, seeing that I did not make much of a case about his author on this matter of the force of morality.

To conclude, I am passionately

sir

Hanover 3 April
1716

your very humble and
very obedient servant
Leibniz

P. S. The news of the massacre of Jesuits in China was false. The monarch of China has reconciled with his heir. The King of Portugal [João (John) V of Portugal

en Cour de Rome, et ne veut point qu'on publie à Macao la constitution du pape contre les Rites chinois. Les moscovites continuent tousjours leur[s] Caravanes pour aller à la Chine. Il y a à Pekin un temple de la religion Greque.[10]

M. Hobbes a déja eu la pensée que la Lune tournoit à l'entour de son axe. Il faut joindre les raisonnment[s] aux observations. M. Flamstead grand observateur Anglois m'a fait savoir, qu'il n'est pas encore d'accord avec M. Newton en bien des choses. Si le mouvement de la Lune étoit assés connu, nous aurions déja les longitudes en mer.

107. LEIBNIZ TO BOURGUET 467

(1689–1750)] appeals for the Jesuits in the Court of Rome and does not want the Papal Constitution against the Chinese rites to be published in Macao. The Muscovites still go on with their caravans to China. There is in Peking a temple of the Greek[10] religion.

Mr. [Thomas] Hobbes* already had the idea that the moon turned on its axis. It is necessary to join reasonings to observations. Mr. [John] Flamsteed*, the great English observer, has let me know that he is still not in agreement with Mr. Newton on a lot of things. If the movement of the moon were well enough known, we would already have longitudes at sea.

[1] Leiden Universiteitsbibliotheek Ms. 293 B, Bl. 269r–270v. Letter as sent: four quarto sides in Leibniz's hand. Previously published in Dutens II-1 335–7; Erdmann 743–4; GP III 591–3. This is Leibniz's response to Bourguet's letter of 16 March 1716 (document 103). For Bourguet's reply, see his letter to Leibniz of 15 May 1716 (document 118).

[2] Gerhardt mistranscribes 'ordre' as 'pour moy' (see GP III 591).

[3] Gerhardt mistranscribes 'boiste' as 'boete' (see GP III 591).

[4] Concerning these different hypotheses, see Leibniz's letter to Bourguet of 5 August 1715 (document 77).

[5] In his letter to Leibniz of 16 March 1716, Bourguet had written: 'Bounded beings are similar to those infinite *series* or successions whose sum is equal to a finite and determinate number. Creatures, animals, celestial spheres, in a word, all beings whose collections forms what we call the universe, are of this nature. And however infinite they may be in number, their perfection, or the result of their concurrence, which is like the sum of them, could never be, or become truly infinite' (document 103 p. 447).

[6] In suggesting that while the sum of the series '$\frac{1}{1}+\frac{1}{2}+\frac{1}{3}+\frac{1}{4}+\frac{1}{5}+$ etc. to infinity is infinite and surpasses every assignable number', it is nevertheless the case that 'the sum of this other series $\frac{1}{1}+\frac{1}{1}+\frac{1}{1}+\frac{1}{1}+\frac{1}{1}$ etc. to infinity is infinitely greater than the preceding one', Leibniz seems to be thinking that because the partial sums of the latter series become unboundedly greater than the partial sums of the former series as the summations proceed, it is reasonable to think that 'the latter series is infinitely greater than the preceding one'. And in suggesting that 'the perfection of the system, however infinite it may be, would not be the greatest possible on account of that', he seems to be thinking that for any given divergent infinite series, S_1, there exists some other divergent infinite series, S_2, whose partial sums become unboundedly greater than the partial sums of S_1 as the summations proceed; and thus in the sense he intends, S_2 would be 'infinitely greater' than S_1. But it is harder to see what he could mean by suggesting that any given divergent infinite series 'would always approach' 'the greatest possible'. For 'the greatest possible' divergent infinite series makes no sense by Leibniz's own reckoning, since by his own reckoning there is, for any given divergent infinite series, another that would be 'infinitely greater'. Perhaps, then, he simply means, to revert to my previous example, that however great a particular partial sum of the series S_2 may be, there is a particular partial sum of the series S_1 that surpasses it, and, in that sense, S_1 'would always approach' S_2. But still, and speaking strictly on Leibniz's own terms, there could not literally be a 'greatest possible' divergent infinite series. And even if by 'the greatest possible' perfection Leibniz means 'infinite perfection', it would still make little sense to suggest of any divergent infinite series that it could 'approach' the 'greatest possible', i.e. infinity, since no matter how great a particular partial sum of such a series might be, there would still remain a divergent infinite series following it.

[7] In his letter to Bourguet of 24 February 1716, Leibniz had argued that 'the notion of eternity in God is completely different from that of time, for it consists in necessity, and that of time in contingency. But it is does not follow, if some other ways are found, that contingency has a beginning' (document 98, p. 399).

[8] Leibniz seems to have in mind what Caroline wrote in her letter to him of 10 January 1716, namely: 'the truth moves the ignorant and the most wise alike, and that is what I took the liberty of telling the late Electress [of Braunschweig-Lüneburg, Sophie* of the Palatinate], who claimed not to be able to understand it [i.e., the *Theodicy*]' (document 95, p. 375).

[9] That is, the French jurist and Huguenot refugee Jean Barbeyrac (1674–1744).

[10] Reading 'Grecque' for 'Greque'.

Leibniz to Antonio Schinella Conti (excerpt)

A Monsieur L'Abbé Conti   Hannover

     Noble Venitien   ce 9 d'Avril

        London   1716

      Monsieur

C'est sans doute pour l'amour de la verité que vous vous etes chargé d'une espece de cartel de la part | de M. Newton | de M. N. Je n'ay point voulu entrer en lice avec des enfans perdus, qu'il avoit detachés contre moy, soit qu'on entende celuy qui a fait l'accusateur sur le fondement du commercium Epistolicum, soit qu'on regarde la preface pleine d'aigreur qu'un autre a mise devant la nouvelle edition de ses principes. Mais puisqu'il veut bien paroitre luy même, je seray bien aise de luy donner satisfaction.

Je fus surpris au commencement de cette dispute d'apprendre qu'on m'accusoit d'etre l'aggresseur. Car je ne me souvenois pas d'avoir parlé de M. | Newton | N. que d'une maniere fort obligeante. Mais je vis depuis qu'on abusoit pour cela d'un passage des Actes de Leipzig du Janvier 1705. ou il y a ces mots: <u>Pro diferentiis L…tianis, D. N…nus adhibet, semperque adhibuit Fluxiones;</u>[2] ou l'Auteur des remarques sur le Commercium Epistolicum dit pag. 108. <u>Sensus verborum est quod N…nus Fluxiones differentiis L…tianis substituit.</u>[3] Mais c'est une interpretation maligne d'un homme qui cherchoit noise. Il semble que l'auteur des paroles inserées[4] dans les Actes de Leipzig a voulu y obvier tout expres par ces mots: <u>adhibet semperque adhibuit</u>; pour insinuer que ce n'est pas apres la veue de mes differences, mais deja auparavant, qu'il s'est servi des fluxions. Et je defie qui que ce soit de donner un autre but raisonnable à ces paroles <u>semperque adhibuit</u>. Au lieu qu'on se sert du mot <u>substituit</u> en parlant de ce que le pere Fabri a fait[5] apres Cavallieri. D'ou il faut conclure, ou que M. | Newton | N. s'est laissé tromper par un homme qui a empoisonné ces paroles des Actes, qu'on supposoit n'avoir pas eté publiées sans ma connoissance, et s'est imaginé qu'on l'accusoit d'etre plagiaire; ou bien qu'il a eté bien aise de trouver un pretexte de s'attribuer ou faire attribuer privativement[7] l'invention du nouveau Calcul (depuis qu'il en remarquoit le succés, et le bruit qu'il faisoit dans le Monde) contre ses connoissances contraires avouées dans son livre des principes, p. 253 de la premiere edition. Si l'on avoit fait connoitre qu'on trouvoit quelque difficulté ou sujet de plainte dans les paroles des Actes de Leipzig, je suis assuré que ces Messieurs qui ont part à ces Actes auroient donné un plein contentement, mais il semble qu'on cherchoit un pretexte de rupture.

Je n'ay pas eu connoissance du <u>numerous committee of gentlemen of several nations</u>[9] <u>relating to the dispute car on ne m'en a donné aucune part</u>. Et je ne say pas encor presentement les noms de tous ces commissaires, et particulierement de ceux qui ne sont pas des Isles Britanniques. Je ne crois pas qu'ils approuvement tout ce qui a eté mis dans l'ouvrage publié contre moy.

108. Leibniz to Antonio Schinella Conti* (excerpt)[1]

To Abbé Conti   Hanover
    Noble Venitian   9 April
      London   1716
       Sir

It is without doubt due to love of the truth that you have taken care of a kind of challenge on the part of Mr. Newton. I have not wanted to enter into a dispute with some *enfants perdus* whom he had unleashed against me, whether you listen to the one [John Keill*] who has played the accuser on the basis of the *Commercium Epistolicum**, or you look at the acerbic preface that another [Roger Cotes*] has placed at the front the new edition of his *Principia*. But since he is willing to make an appearance himself, I will be very happy to give him satisfaction.

I was surprised at the beginning of this dispute to learn that I was accused of being the aggressor. For I do not recall having spoken of Mr. Newton but in a most courteous manner. But I since saw that instead of that they made ill use of a passage from the *Acts* of Leipzig [the *Acta Eruditorum*] of January 1705, where there are these words: *Pro differentiis L…tianis, D. N…nus adhibet, semperque adhibuit Fluxiones;*[2] where the author of some remarks on the *Commercium Epistolicum* says, page 108 *Sensus verborum est quod N…nus Fluxiones differentiis L…tianis substituit.*[3] But it is a malicious interpretation by a man who picked a quarrel. It seems that the author of the words inserted[4] in the Acts of Leipzig wanted expressly to prevent it with these words, *adhibet semperque adhibuit*, in order to suggest that it was not after the inspection of my differences, but already before that he made use of fluxions. And I defy anyone to give a different reasonable purpose to these words, *semperque adhibuit*. Rather the word *substituit* is employed in speaking of what Father Fabri did[5] following Cavalieri.[6] Whence it is necessary to conclude, either that Mr. Newton has allowed himself be misled by a man who has poisoned these words from the *Acta Eruditorum*, which he assumed were not published without my knowledge, and has imagined that they have accused him of being a plagiarist; or else that he was delighted to find a pretext for claiming for himself, or for having assigned exclusively[7] to himself, the invention of the new calculus (since he noted its success and the talk that it caused in the world) against his contrary knowledge confessed in his book of principles, p. 235 of the first edition.[8] If it had been made known that some difficulty or subject for complaint in the words of the *Acta* of Leipzig had been found, I am certain that these gentlemen who are involved in these *Acta* would have given full satisfaction, but it seems that he sought a pretext for a falling out.

I have not had information about the *numerous committee of gentlemen of several nations*[9] *relating to the dispute because they have not given me any hand in it.* And at present I still do not know the names of all those commissioners, and

108. LEIBNIZ TO CONTI

Il est aisé à croire que j'ay eté quelque temps à Vienne, avant que d'avoir vû le Commercium Epistolicum deja publié, quoyque j'en eusse des nouvelles. Ainsi un ami sachant cela, aussi zelé pour moy que les seconds à | M. Newton | M. N le peuvent etre pour luy a publié un papier, que M. Newton appelle diffamatoire (defamatory lettre). Mais cette piece n'estant pas plus forte que ce qu'on a publié contre moy, | M. Newton | M. N n'a pas droit de s'en plaindre. Si l'on n'a pas marqué l'auteur ny le lieu de l'impression du papier; on connoit assés le nom et le lieu de l'auteur de la lettre y inserée d'un excellent Mathematicien, que j'avois prié de dire son sentiment sur le commercium, et cela suffit. | M. Newton] M. N (dont les partisans ont marqué qu'il ne leur etoit point inconnu) l'appelle un Mathematicien ou pretendu Mathematicien et apres avoir fait inutilement des efforts pour le gagner il le meprise contre l'opinion publique qui le met entre ceux du premier rang et contre l'evidence des choses verfiées par ses decouvertes.

Lors que j'eus enfin le Commercium Epistolicum, je vis qu'on s'y écartoit entierement du but, et que les lettres qu'on publioit ne contenoient pas un mot qui pût[11] faire revoquer en doute mon invention du Calcul des differences dont il s'agissoit. Au lieu de cela je remarquay qu'on se jettoit sur les series ou l'on accorde l'avantage | à M. Newton | à M. N et que les remarques contenoient des glosses mal tournées, pour tacher de me decrier par de[s] soubçons sans fondement, quelques fois ridicules et quelques fois forgées[12] contre la conscience de quelques uns de ceux qui en étoient les auteurs ou approbateurs.

Pour repondre donc de point en point à l'ouvrage publie contre moy, il falloit un autre ouvrage, aussi grand pour le moins que celuy là; il falloit entrer dans un grand detail de quantité de minuties passées il y a 30 à 40 ans dont je ne souvenois gueres. Il me falloit chercher mes vieilles lettres dont plusieurs se sont perdues, outre que le plus souvent je n'ay point gardé les minutes des miennes, et les autres sont ensevelies dans un grand tas de papiers, qui je ne pouvois debrouiller qu'avec du temps et de la patience. Mais je n'en avois gueres le loisir, étant chargé presentement d'occupations d'une toute autre nature.

De plus je remarquay que dans la publication du Commercium Epistolicum on a supprimé des endroits qui pouvoient être au desavantage de M. Newton; au lieu qu'on n'y a rien omis de ce qu'on croyoit pouvoir tourner contre moy par des glosses forcées. Comme je n'ay pas daigné de lire le Commercium Epistolicum avec beaucoup d'attention, je me suis trompé dans l'exemple que j'ay cité n'ayant pas pris garde, ou ayant oublié qu'il s'y trouvoit. Mais j'en citeray un autre. | M. Newton | M. N. avouoit dans une de ses lettres à M. Collins qu'il ne pouvoit point venir a bout des sections secondes (ou segmens seconds) des spheroides ou corps semblables, mais on n'a point inseré ce passage dans le Commercium Epistolicum. Il auroit eté plus sincere par rapport à la dispute, et plus utile au public, de donner le Commerce literaire de M. Collins tout entier, là ou il contenoit quelque chose qui meritoit d'etre sû,[15] Et particulierement de ne point tronquer les lettres. Car il y en a peu parmy mes papiers, ou dont il me reste des minutes.

particularly of those who are not from the British Isles. I do not believe that they approve everything that has been placed in the work published against me.

It is easy to believe that I was in Vienna for some time before having seen the *Commercium Epistolicum*, although I had some news of it. So a friend, knowing that, as zealous for me as Mr. Newton's seconds can be for him, published a paper that Mr. Newton calls defamatory (*defamatory letter*). But since this document[10] is no stronger than what they have published against me, Mr. Newton has no right to complain of it. If he did not note either the author or the place of printing of the paper, he knew well enough the name and place of the author of the letter inserted there from an excellent mathematician [namely, Johann Bernoulli*] whom I had asked to express his view of the *Commercium*, and that is sufficient. Mr. Newton (the partisans of whom have indicated that he was not unknown to them) calls him a mathematician, or a pretended mathematician, and after having futilely made some efforts to win him over, he scorns him, contrary to public opinion, which places him among those of the first rank, and contrary to the evidence of things confirmed by his discoveries.

When I finally got the *Commercium Epistolicum*, I saw that in it they completely strayed from the purpose and that the letters that they published did not contain a word that could[11] cast doubt on my invention of the calculus of differences, which was in question. Instead of that I noted that they pounced on series, where they give the advantage to Mr. Newton, and that the remarks contained some poorly turned criticisms, to try to slander me with unfounded suspicions, sometimes ridiculous and sometimes fabricated[12] contrary to the conscience of some of those who were their authors or approvers.

To respond point by point to the work published against me, another work, at least as large as that one, was necessary; it was necessary to go into great detail about many past minutiae, 30 to 40 years ago, that I scarcely remember. I had to search my old letters, many of which are lost; besides, in most cases I did not keep the drafts of mine, and the others are buried in a large pile of papers that I could disentangle only with time and patience. But I scarcely had the leisure, being presently charged with occupations of an entirely different nature.[13]

Furthermore, I noticed that in the publication of the *Commercium Epistolicum* they suppressed some points that could to the disadvantage of Mr. Newton; whereas they did not omit anything they believed could be turned against me by some contrived criticisms. Since I have not deigned to read the *Commercium Epistolicum* with much attention, I was mistaken in the example I cited,[14] because I was not careful, or because I forgot that it was there. But I will cite another one. In one of his letters to Mr. [John] Collins*, Mr. Newton admitted that he could not manage second sections (or second segments) of spheroids or similar bodies, but they have not inserted this passage in the *Commercium Epistolicum*. It would have been more honest in relation to the dispute, and more useful to the public, to present the entire literary correspondence of Mr. Collins, where it contained something

472 108. LEIBNIZ TO CONTI

Ainsi tout consideré, voyant tant de marques de malignité et de chicane, je crûs indigne de moy d'entrer en discussion avec de[s] gens, qui en usoient si mal. Je voyois qu'en les refutant on auroit de la peine à eviter des reproches et des expressions fortes, telles que meritoit leur procedé; et je n'avois point envie de donner ce spectacle au public, ayant dessein de mieux employer mon temps qui me doit etre pretieux et meprisant assez le jugement de ceux qui sur un tel ouvrage voudroient prononcer contre moy; d'autant que la Societé Royale même ne l'a point voulu faire; comme je l'ay appris par un extrait de ses Registres.

Je ne crois point d'avoir dit, (comme M. Newton me l'impute) que les Anglois n'auroient point le plaisir de me voir repondre à des raisonnemens si minces[16] car je ne crois point que tous les Anglois fassent leur cause de celle de M. Newton. Il y en a de trop habiles et de trop honnêtes pour epouser les passions de quelques uns de ses adherens.

Apres cela, il m'accuse d'avoir voulu faire diversion, en combattant sa philosophie, et en voulant l'engager dans des problemes. Mais quant à la philosophie, j'ay donné publiquement quelque chose de mes principes sans attaquer les siens; si ce n'est que par occasion j'en ay parlé dans des lettres particulieres depuis qu'on m'en a donné sujet. Et pour ce qui est des problemes je n'ay gardé d'en proposer à M. Newton, car je ne voudrois pas m'y engager quand on en proposeroit à moy. Nous pouvons nous en dispenser à l'âge ou nous sommes mais nous avons des amis qui y peuvent suppleer à notre defaut.

Je ne veux point entrer ici dans le detail de ce que M. | Newton | N dit un peu aigrement contre ma philosophie ou[17] pour la sienne ce n'en est point le lieu. J'appelle miracle tout evenement qui ne peut etre arrivé que par la puissance du createur, sa raison n'estant pas dans la nature des creatures. Et quand on veut neanmois l'attribuer aux qualités ou forces des creatures, alors j'appelle cette qualité une qualité occulte à la Scholastique, c'est à dire qu'il est impossible de rendre manifeste telle que seroit une pesanteur primitive: car les [sic] qualites occultes qui ne sont point chimeriques, sont celles dont nous ignorons la cause mais dont nous ne l'excluons point. Et j'appelle l'ame de l'homme cette substance simple, qui s'appercoit de ce qui se passe dans le corps humain, et dont les appetits ou volontés sont suivis par les efforts du corps. Je ne prefere point les Hypotheses aux arguments tirées[18] de l'induction des experiences. Mais quelques fois on fait passer pour inductions generales ce qui ne consiste qu'en observations particulieres; et quelquefois on veut faire passer pour une Hypothese ce qui est demonstratif. L'idée que M. N donne icy de mon harmonie préetablie n'est pas celle qu'en ont quantité d'habiles gens hors de l'Angleterre, et quelquesuns en Angleterre et je ne crois pas que vous meme, Monsieur en ayés eu une semblable, ou l'ayés maintenant, à moins que d'etre bien changé.

Je n'ay jamais nié qu'à mon second voyage en Angleterre j'aye vû quelques lettres de M. Newton et autres chez M. Collins. Mais je n'en ay jamais vû ou M. | Newton |

that deserved to be known,[15] and particularly not to truncate the letters. For there are few of them among my papers, or of which I still have some drafts.

So everything considered, seeing so many signs of malignancy and chicanery, I believed it unworthy of me to enter into discussion with people who used it so badly. I saw that by refuting them I would have difficulty avoiding reproaches and strong words, such as their conduct deserved; and I did not fancy presenting this spectacle to the public, since I intend to better employ my time, which has to be precious to me, and since I am quite contemptuous of the judgment of those who wanted to declare against me on the basis of such a work, all the more so because the Royal Society itself did not want to do that, as I learned from an extract of its records.

I do not believe I said (as Mr. Newton imputes to me) *that the English would not have the pleasure of seeing me respond to such slight arguments.*[16] For I do not believe that all Englishmen make their cause with that of Mr. Newton. There are some too able and honest to embrace the passions of a few of his followers.

After that, he accuses me of having wanted to cause a diversion by opposing his philosophy and by wanting to engage him in some problems. But as for his philosophy, I have presented publicly some of my principles without attacking his; if only occasionally, I have spoken about it in some particular letters, since I was given reason to do so. And as for problems, I have refrained from proposing any to M. Newton, for I should not want to get involved in them were some proposed to me. We can dispense with them at our age, but we have friends who can make up for our absence.

I do not want to enter into detail about what Mr. Newton says, a bit acrimoniously, against my philosophy or[17] in favour of his; this is not the place. I call a *miracle* any event that can have occurred only through the power of the creator, its reason not being in the nature of creatures. And when somebody chooses nevertheless to attribute it to the qualities or forces of creatures, I then call this quality an *occult quality in the scholastic sense,* meaning it is impossible to make clear, such as would be a primitive gravity. For occult qualities that are not chimerical are those whose cause we don't know but do not rule out. And I call *the soul of man* that simple substance that is aware of what happens in the human body and whose appetites or wills are followed by the efforts of bodies. I do not prefer hypotheses to arguments drawn[18] by induction from experiments. But sometimes people pass off as general inductions what consists only in particular observations, and sometimes they want to pass off as an hypothesis what is demonstrative. The idea that Mr. Newton presents here of my preestablished harmony is not the one a number of able individuals outside of England, and some in England, have of it, and I do not believe that you yourself, sir, have had, or now have, a similar idea of it, unless by being completely changed.

I have never denied that on my second trip to England[19] I saw some letters of Mr. Newton and others at the home of Mr. Collins. But I have never seen where

N ait expliqué sa Methode de des Fluxions, et je n'en trouve point dans le Commercium Epistolicum.

Je n'ay pas vû non plus qu'il y[20] ait expliqué la Methode des series que je m'attribue, je crois qu'il veut parler de celle ou je prends une series arbitraire je l'ay fait avant mon second retour en Angleterre. Je ne nie pourtant pas que M. | Newton | N n'eût pû l'avoir aussi et ce n'est pas même une invention fort difficile.

M. Newton veut que j'avoue et que j'accorde ce que j'ay avoué ou accordé il y a 15 ans. On devroit en attendre de luy autant.[21] Car il y a maintenant deux fois quinze ans que dans la premiere edition de ses principes p. 253–254 il m'accorde l'invention du Calcul des Differences; independement de la sienne. Et depuis il s'est avisé je ne say comment, de faire soutenir le contraire.

Il est bon de savoir qu'à mon premier voyage d'Angleterre au commencement de l'an 1673[23]. Je n'avois pas la moindre connoissance des series infinies telles que M. Mercator venoit de donner ny d'autres matieres de la Geometrie avancée par les dernieres methodes. Je n'etois pas même assés verse dans l'Analyse de des Cartes. Je ne traitois les Mathematiques que comme un parergon, et je ne savois queres que la Geometrie practique vulgaire, quoyque j'eusse vû par hazard la Geometrie des indivisibles de Cavallerius, et un livre du Pere Leotaud ou il donnoit les quadratures des lunules, et figures semblables, ce qui m'avoit donné quelque curiosité.[25] Mais je me divertissois plus tôt aux proprietés des Nombres, à quoy le petit traité que j'avois publié presque petit garçon de l'art des combinaisons en 1666, m'avoit donné occasion. Et ayant observé des lors l'usage des differences pour les sommes, je l'appliquay a des suites des nombres. On voit bien par mes premieres lettres echangees avec M. Oldenbourg, que je n'etois gueres allé plus avant. Aussi n'avois je point alors la connoissance de M. Collins; quoyqu'on ait feint malicieusement le contraire.

Ce fut peu a peu que M. Hugens me fit entrer en ces matieres quand je le practiquois à paris et cela joint au traité de M. Mercator (que j'avois rapporté avec moy d'Angleterre parce que M. pell m'en avoit parlé) me fit trouver environ vers la fin de l'an 1673 ma quadrature Arithmetique du Cercle qui fut fort approuvée par M. Hugens et dont je parlay à M. Oldenbourg dans une lettre de l'an 1674. Alors ny M. Hugens ny moy nous ne savions rien des series de M. | Newton | N ny de M. Gregory. Ainsi je crûs etre le premier qui eût donne la valeur du cercle par une suite de nombres rationaux. Et M. Hugens le crût aussi. J'en ecrivis sur ce ton là a M. Oldenbourg qui me repondit qu'on avoit déja de telles series en Angleterre. Et l'on voit par ma lettre du 15 Juillet de 1674, et par la reponse de M. Oldenbourg du 8 decemb. de la meme annee que je n'en devois avoir aucune connoissance alors. Autrement M. Oldenbourg n'auroit point manqué de me le faire sentir si luy ou M. Collins m'en eussent communiqué quelque chose auparavant.[27] Ce ne fut donc qu'alors que j'en appris quelque chose. Mais je ne savois pas alors les extractions des racines des equations par des series, ny les regressions, ou l'extraction d'une equation infinie. J'etois encore un peu neuf en ces matieres. Mais je trouvay pourtant

Mr. Newton has explained his method of fluxions, and I don't find it in the *Commercium Epistolicum.*

Neither have I seen that he has there[20] explained the method of series that I claim for myself; I believe he means to speak of the one in which I assume an arbitrary series; I did it before my second return trip to England. But I do not deny that Mr. Newton could have had it as well, and it is not even a very difficult discovery.

Mr. Newton wants me to admit and grant what I admitted or granted 15 years ago. The same ought to be expected from him.[21] For it is now two times fifteen years ago, in the first edition of his *Principia* pp. 253–254, that he granted me the discovery of the calculus of differences independently of his.[22] And since then he has somehow taken it into his head to maintain the contrary.

It is good to know that on my first trip to England at the beginning of 1673[23] I did not have the least knowledge of the sort of infinite series that Mr. [Nicholas] Mercator[24] had just produced, nor of other matters of advanced geometry by the latest methods. I was not even sufficiently versed in the analysis of Descartes. I treated mathematics only as a parergon, and I scarcely knew the practical common geometry, although I had by chance seen the geometry of indivisibles of Cavalieri and a book by Father [Vincent] Léotaud in which he presented the quadratures of lunules and other similar figures, which aroused my curiosity.[25] But I instead amused myself with the properties of numbers, to which the small treatise on the art of combinations that I had published when I was all but a small boy in 1666 had given me occasion. And having observed since then the use of differences for sums, I applied it to some sequences of numbers. You clearly see from my first letters exchanged with Mr. [Henry]Oldenburg* that I had scarcely gone further. I also did not then have the acquaintance of Mr. Collins, although they have maliciously feigned the contrary.

It was little by little that Mr. [Christiaan] Huygens* had me enter into these matters when I kept company with him in Paris; and that, along with the treatise of Mr. Mercator (which I had brought back with me from England because Mr. [John] Pell[26] had spoken to me about it), made me find for myself, around the end of 1673, my arithmetic quadrature of the circle, which was highly approved by Mr. Huygens and about which I spoke to Mr. Oldenburg in a letter of 1674. At that time neither Mr. Huygens nor I knew anything about the series of Mr. Newton or Mr. [James] Gregory*, so I thought I was the first who had given the value of the circle by a series of rational numbers, and Mr. Huygens thought so too. I wrote about it like that to Mr. Oldenburg, who replied that they already had such series in England. And you can see from my letter of 15 July 1674, and from the reply of Mr. Oldenburg of 8 December of the same year, that I must not have had any knowledge of it at that time. Otherwise Mr. Oldenburg would not have failed to make me aware of it, if he or Mr. Collins had communicated something about it to me previously.[27] It was therefore only at that time that I learned something about it. But at that time I did not know the extractions of roots of equations by series, nor the regressions, or the

bien tost ma Methode generale par des series arbitraires; et j'entray enfin dans mon Calcul des Differences ou les observations que j'avois faites encor fort jeune sur les differences des suites des nombres contribuerent à m'ouvrir les yeux. Car ce n'est pas les Fluxions des Lignes, mais par les differences des Nombres que j'y suis venu, en considerant en fin que ces differences appliquées aux grandeurs qui croissent continuellement, evanouissent en comparaison des grandeurs differentes au lieu qu'elles subsistent dans les suites des nombres. Et je croy que cette voye est la plus analytique. Le Calcul Geometrique des differences qui est le même que celuy des fluxions, n'estant qu'un cas special du Calcul Analytique des differences en general; et ce cas special[28] devient plus commode par les evanouissemens.

Monsieur | Newton | N. allegue par apres les passages ou j'accorde qu'il a eu un calcul approchant de mon calcul des differences. Mais il pourra bien se souvenir qu'il m'en a accordé autant. Et s'il luy est permis de se rectracter; pourquoy ne me sera[-]t-il point permis d'en faire autant? sur tout apres les verisimilitudes que M. Bernoulli a remarquées. J'ay eu[29] une si grande opinion de la candeur de M. Newton que je l'ay crû sur sa parole. Mais le voyant conniver à des accusations dont la fausseté luy est connue; il estoit naturel que je commençasse de douter.

Je ne puis avouer ny desavouer aujourd'huy d'avoir écrit ou receu des lettres écrites il y a plus de 40 ans, telles qu'on les a publiées, je suis obligé de m'en rapporter à ce qui se trouve dans les papiers qu'on cite. Mais je ne remarque rien contre moy dans celles que M. N. allegue du 15 Avril et 20 May 1675, et du 24 d'Octobre 1676. si non dans les faussetés du glossateur. Je crois que c'etoit purement par distraction dans un sejour comme celuy de paris, ou je m'occupois à bien d'autres choses encore qu'aux mathematiques, et par l'eloingnement que j'avois des calculs dont je craignois la longueur, que j'ay demandé quelque fois à M. Oldenbourg la demonstration ou la Methode d'arriver à certains choses, ou j'aurois bien pû arriver moy meme. Par exemple, je crois d'avoir déja eu au 12 de May 1676 ma methode d'une series arbitraire, qui m'auroit pû mener a des series dont j'y demande la raison. Car ayant consulté mon vieux traité de la quadrature Arithmetique acheve quelque temps avant ma sortie de France, je me sers de la series arbitraire. Cependant les series marquées dans cette lettre sont une chose dont je consens d'etre redevable à d'autres. Et je crois de ne les avoir pas même connues en 1674.

N'entendant pas bien ce que M. N allegue des actes de Leipzig du May 1700[30] j'y ay regardé, et je trouve, qu'il n'en a pas bien pris la sens. Il n'y est point parlé de l'invention du nouveau Calcul des Differences, mais d'un artifice particulier de Maximis et Minimis, qui en[31] est independent et dont je m'étois avisé bien du temps avant que M. Bernoulli eut proposé son probleme du la plus courte descente mais dont je jugeois que M. N. se devoit etre avisé aussi lors qu'il avoit donné la figure de son vaisseau dans ses principes. Ainsi j'ay voulu dire qu'il a fait connoistre publiquement avant moy, qu'il possedoit cet artifice ce que je ne pouvois pas dire du Calcul des Differences et des fluxions puisque j'en avois fait voir l'utilité publiquement avant la publication de ce livre. Cet artifice particuliere de Maximis et Minimis n'est

extraction of an infinite equation. I was still a bit inexperienced in these matters. But I nevertheless soon found my general method by arbitrary series; and I finally entered into my calculus of differences, where the observations that I had made. still very young, about the differences of sequences of numbers helped to open my eyes. For it is not by the fluxions of lines, but by the differences of numbers that I arrived at it, by finally considering that these differences, applied to magnitudes that continually increase, vanish in comparison to other magnitudes instead of remaining in the series of numbers. And I believe that this approach is the most analytic, since the geometric calculus of differences, which is the same as that of fluxions, is only a special case of the analytic calculus of differences in general; and this special case[28] becomes easier with the cancelling out.

Mr. Newton cites thereafter the passages in which I grant that he has had a calculus something like my calculus of differences. But he will be able to remember well that he has granted as much to me. And if he is permitted to recant, why shall I not be permitted to do as much, especially after the similarities that Mr. [Johann] Bernoulli* has noted? I have had[29] such a high opinion of Mr. Newton's candor that I have taken his word. But seeing him connive in accusations whose falsity is known to him, it was natural that I began to doubt.

Today I can neither avow nor disavow having written or received letters written more than forty years ago, such as have been published [in the *Commercium Epistolicum*]; I am forced to rely on what is found in the papers that they cite. But I do not notice anything against me in those that Mr. Newton cites from 15 April and 20 May 1675, and from 24 October 1676, except in the falsehoods of the commentator. I believe that it was purely by inattention, during a stay like the one in Paris, where I was still occupied with a lot of things other than mathematics, and by the aversion I had to some calculations whose length I feared, that I sometimes asked Mr. Oldenburg for the demonstration or the method of arriving at certain things at which I would have been quite able to arrive myself. For example, I believe that on 12 May 1676 I already had my method of an arbitrary series, which had been able to lead me to some series whose ratio I requested from him. For having consulted my old treatise on arithmetic quadrature, completed sometime prior to my leaving France, I made use of the arbitrary series. However, I agree that the series indicated in this letter are due to others, and I don't believe I even knew of them in 1674.

Since I do not entirely understand what Mr. Newton alleges about the *Acts* of Leipzig of May 1700,[30] I have looked at it, and I find that he has not taken the sense of it aright. It does not apeak of the invention of the new calculus of differences, but of a particular artifice concerning *maxima* and *minima* that is independent of it[31] and of which I became aware well before Mr. Bernoulli had proposed his problem about the shortest descent,[32] but of which I thought that Mr. Newton must also have become aware when he had presented the shape of his ship in his *Principia*.[33] So I meant that he had made it known publicly before me that he possessed this artifice, which I could not say of the calculus of differences and fluxions, since I had

478   108. LEIBNIZ TO CONTI

point necessaire quand il s'agit simplement d'une grandeur (car alors la methode de M. Fermat perfectionée par les nouveaux calculs suffit) mais quand il s'agit de toute une figure qui doit faire le mieux un effect demandé, il faut autre chose.

M. | Newton | N hazarde icy de faire une accusation mais qui va tomber sur luy même. Il pretend que ce que j'ay écrit pour luy à M. Oldenbourg en 1677 est un deguisement de la Methode de M. Barrow. Mais comme M. Newton avoue dans la page 253 et 254 de la premiere edition de ses principes me ipsi (tunc) methodum communicasse à methodo ipsius vix abludentem præterquam in verborum et notarum formulis;[35] il s'ensuivra que sa Methode aussi n'est qu'un deguisement de celle de M. Barrow.

Je croy que luy et moy nous serons aisément quittes de cette accusation. Car une infinité de gens liront le livre de M. Barrow sans y trouver notre calcul. Il est vray que feu M. Tschirnhaus, qui s'apperçut un peu tard de l'avantage de ce Calcul, pretendoit qu'on pouvoit arriver à tout cela par les methodes de M. Barrow. Comme l'Abbé Catelan François pretendit que même l'Analyse de des Cartes suffisoit pour toutes ces choses. Mais il estoit plus aise de le dire que de le montrer.

Cependant si quelcun a profité de M. Barrow, ce sera plus tost M. Newton, qui a étudié sous luy, que moy, qui (autant que je m'en puis souvenir[37]) n'ay vu les livres de M. Barrow qu'à mon second voyage d'Angleterre; et ne les ay jamais lûs avec beaucoup[38] d'attention; parce qu'en voyant le livre je m'apperçus que par la consideration du Triangle characteristique dont les cotés sont les elemens de l'abscisse de l'ordonnee et de la Courbe semblable à quelque triangle assignable, j'étois venu comme en me jouant aux quadratures, surfaces et solides, dont M. Barrow avoit rempli un chapitre des plus considerables de ses leçons. Outre que je ne suis venu à mon Calcul des Differences dans la Geometrie, qu'apres en avoir vû l'usage (mais moins considerable) dans les nombres comme mes premieres lettres dans le Commercium Epistolicum le peuvent insinuer. Il se peut que M. Barrow en ait plus seu qu'il n'a dit dans son livre[39] et qu'il ait donné des lumieres à M. Newton que nous ne savons pas. Et si j'étois semblable à certains temeraires, je pourrois asseurer sur de simples soubçons sans autre fondement, que le Calcul des Fluxions de M. Newton, quel qu'il puisse étre, luy a eté enseigné par M. Barrow.

On peut bien juger que lors que j'ay parlé en 1676 des problemes qui ne dependoient, ny des Equations ny des quadratures, j'ay voulu parler des Equations telles qu'on connoissoit alors dans le monde. C'est à dire des Equations de l'Analyse ordinaire. Et on le peut juger de ce que j'adjoute les Quadratures comme quelque chose de plus que ces equations. Mais les Equations Differentielles vont au delà meme des quadratures et l'on voit bien que j'entendois meme parler des problemes qui vont à ces sortes d'equations inconnues alors au public. Cette objection se trouvoit déja dans les remarques au Commercium; mais je n'avois point crû que M. | Newton | N. estoit capable de l'employer.

Je juge par un endroit de ma lettre du 27 d'Aoust 1676 (pag. 65. du Commercium Epistolicum) que je devois déja avoir alors l'ouverture du Calcul des Differences,

shown the usefulness of it publicly before the publication of that book. This particular artifice concerning maxima and minima is not necessary when it is simply a
matter of a magnitude (for then the method of Mr. Fermat,[34] perfected by the new
calculi, is sufficient), but when it is a matter of an entire figure that has to make the
best a required result, something else is needed.

Mr. Newton dares to make an accusation here, but one which will fall upon himself. He claims that what I wrote for him to Mr. Oldenburg in 1677 is a disguise of
the method of Mr. [Isaac] Barrow*. But since Mr. Newton admits on pages 253 and
254 of the first edition of his *Principia* that *I myself (then) communicated a method
scarcely different from his own method except in the form of words and notations*,[35] it
will follow that his method is also only a disguise of that of Mr. Barrow.

I believe that he and I will be easily cleared of this accusation. For a host of people will read Mr. Barrow's book without finding our calculus in it. It is true that the
late Mr. Tschirnhaus*, who perceived a bit late the advantage of this calculus,
claimed that it would be possible to arrive at all that by the methods of Mr. Barrow,
just as the Frenchman Abbé Catelan[36] claimed that even the analysis of Descartes
sufficed for all these things. But it was easier to say it than to prove it.

However, if anyone has profited from Mr. Barrow it will be Mr. Newton, who
studied under him, rather than I, who (as far as I can recall[37]) only saw the books of
Mr. Barrow on my second trip to England and never read them with much[38] attention because when I saw the book, I noticed that through consideration of the characteristic triangle, whose sides are the elements of the abscissa, of the ordinate, and
of the curve, similar to some assignable triangle, I had easily arrived at quadratures,
surfaces, and solids, about which Mr. Barrow had filled up a very considerable
chapter of his lectures. Besides, I arrived at my calculus of differences in geometry
only after seeing its use (but less considerable) in numbers, as my first letters in the
Commercium Epistolicum may suggest. It may be that Mr. Barrow knew more
about it than he said in his book[39] and that he gave some insights to Mr. Newton
that we do not know. And if I were like certain reckless individuals, I could assert
on the basis of some simple conjectures, without other basis, that Mr. Newton's
calculus of fluxions, whatever it may be, was taught to him by Mr. Barrow.

People may indeed think that when I spoke in 1676 about problems that
depended neither on equations nor on quadratures, I intended to speak about
equations such as were then widely known, that is, equations of ordinary analysis.
And people may belief it from the fact that I add quadratures as something more
than these equations. But differential equations go beyond even quadratures, and
it is clear that I even intended to speak about problems that go to these kinds of
equations, which were not then publicly known. This objection is already found in
the notes to the *Commercium*, but I had not thought that Mr. Newton was capable
of using it.

I judge from a passage in my letter of 27 August 1676 (p. 65 of the *Commercium
Epistolicum*) that I must have then already had the beginning of the calculus

car j'y dis que j'avoir[40] resolu d'abord par une certaine Analyse (*Certa Analysi solvi*) le probleme de M. Beaune proposé à M. Descartes. Cette[42] Analyse n'etoit que cela. On le peut resoudre sans cela, et je crois que M. Hugens et M. Barrow l'auroient donné au besoin, comme beaucoup d'autres choses, mais selon ma maniere de noter ce n'est qu'un jeu. [...]

Je ne saurois dire aujourdhuy si j'ay remarqué le passage de M. Wallis, ou il dit que M. Newton savoit déja la methode des fluxions en 1666. Mais quand je l'aurois remarqué je l'aurois laissé passer apparemment, etant fort porté alors à croire M. Newton sur sa parole. Mais son procedé m'a forcé d'etre plus circonspect à cet egard.

M. | Newton | N dit que je l'ay accusé d'etre plagiaire. Mais ou est ce que je l'ay fait? Ce sont ses adherens qui ont paru intenter cette accusation contre moy. Et il y a connivé. Je ne say pas s'il adopte entierement ce qu'ils ont publié. Mais je conviens avec lui que la malice de celuy qui intente une telle accusation sans la prouver le rend coupable de calomnie.

Il finit sa lettre en m'accusant d'etre l'Aggresseur, et j'ay commence celle cy, en prouvant le contraire. Il sera fort aisé de vuider ce point preliminaire. Il y a eu du mesentendu, mais ce n'est pas ma faute. Au reste, je suis avec zele

A M. l'Abbé Conti

P. S.   Hanover

Monsieur   ce 9 d'Avril

1716

Vous avés donné, Monsieur, la solution d'un problem que les partisans de M. Newton n'avoient point trouvée jusqu'icy. Car vous aves trouvé la moyen de me faire reponde en m'envoyant une lettre de M. Newton luy même. Apres cela vous n'avies point besoin de me faire des exhortations la dessus. Si la question avoit eté seulement le quel de nous deux de M. | N. | Newton ou de moy a trouvé le premier le calcul en question; je ne m'en mettrois point en peine. Aussi est il difficile de decider ce que l'un ou l'autre peut avoir gardé *in petto*, et combien long temps. Mais un adherent de M. Newton a pretendu que je l'avois appris de lui; et depuis il a paru plus probable à quelques autres et meme à M. Bernoulli que la manire de calculer que | M. N. | M. Newton a publiée dans les œuvres de M. Wallis a été fabriquee à l'imitation de mon Calcul des Differences déja publié.

Il n'y pas la moindre trace ny ombre du Calcul des Differences ou fluxions dans toutes les anciennes lettres de M. Newton que j'ay vües, excepté dans celle qu'il a écrite le 24 d'Octobre 1676 ou il n'en a parlé que par enigme (Commerce p. 86). Et la solution de cet Enigme qu'il n'a donnée que dix ans apres; dit quelque chose mais elle ne dit pas tout ce qu'on pourroit demander. Cependant, prevenu pour M. Newton, j'ay eu autres fois la condescendance d'en parler comme si elle disoit presque tout. Et c'est apres moy que d'autres en ont parlé de meme. Mon honneteté

of differences, for I say there that by a certain analysis (*certa analysis solvi*), I solved[40] at first sight the problem that Mr. [Florimond de] Beaune proposed to Mr. Descartes.[41] This[42] analysis was only that. It is possible to solve it without that, and I believe that Mr. Huygens and Mr. Barrow would have provided it if needed, like many other things; but according to my way of making notes, it is only amusement. [...]

I could not say today whether I noticed the passage from Mr.[John] Wallis* in which he says that Mr. Newton already knew the method of fluxions in 1666. But if I had noticed it, I probably would have let it pass, since I was then strongly inclined to take Mr. Newton at his word. But his latest behavior has forced me to be more circumspect in this regard.

Mr. Newton says that I have accused him of being a plagiarist. But where have I done it? It is his supporters who seemed to bring this accusation against me, and he has connived in it. I do not know if he entirely endorses what they have published, but I agree with him that the malice of the one who makes such an accusation without proving it makes him guilty of calumny.

He finishes his letter by accusing me of being the aggressor, and I have begun this one by proving the contrary. It will be very easy to make an end of this initial point. There has been some misunderstanding, but it is not my fault. To conclude, I am enthusiastically

To l'Abbé Conti

P. S.		Hanover
Sir		9 April
		1716

You, sir, have provided the solution to a problem that Mr. Newton's supporters had not found up until now. For you have found the way to have me respond by sending me a letter from Mr. Newton himself. After that you do not need to exhort me about it. If the question had only been which of the two of us, Mr. Newton or I, first discovered the calculus in question, I would not trouble myself with it. It is also difficult to tell what either one may have kept secret and for how long. But a follower of Mr. Newton [John Keill*] has claimed that I took it from him, and since then it has seemed more probable to some others, and even to Mr. Bernoulli, that the manner of calculating that Mr. Newton published in the works of Mr. Wallis was fabricated in imitation of my previously published calculus of differences.

There is not the least trace or shadow of the calculus of differences or fluxions in all the old letters of Mr. Newton that I have seen, except in the one he wrote on 24 October 1676, in which he spoke of it only by riddle (*Commerce*, p. 86). And the solution of this riddle that he only provided ten years after says something, but it does not say everything that that could be asked.[43] However, biased in favour of Mr. Newton, I previously had the deference to speak of it as if it said nearly

a été mal reconnue. Vous me dites, Monsieur, que M. Jones a publié une de mes lettres à M. Newton, ayés la bonté de m'apprendre où.[44]

[…]

Je m'étonne, Monsieur, que vous dites qu'avant que de parler de la philosophie de M. Newton il faut covenir de la Methode de ϕilosofer. Est ce qu'il y a une autre Logique à Londres qu'à Hanover? Quand on raisonne en bonne forme sur des faites bien averés, ou sur des Axiomes indubitables, on ne manque pas d'avoir raison. Si les sentimens de M. Newton sont meilleurs qu'on n'a dit, tant mieux. Je seray tousjours bien aise de luy rendre justice, | soit qu'il m'en rende ou non |

Je vois bien que vous n'aves pas encor eu le loisir, Monsieur de toucher à rien de tout ce que j'avois eu l'honneur de vous écrire excepté ce qui regarde M. Newton. J'avois souhaité d'apprendre quelques nouvelles de M. Wren et de quelques autres excellens hommes. Mais je ne puis vous les demander qu'en grace. Et chacun est le maitre des graces qu'il veut faire. Cependant si vous en apprenés quelque chose, ou quelques autres particularités de doctrine, que vous voudriés bien me communiquer comme vous me le faites esperer, je vous supplie de ne me point remettre jusqu'au retour[45] de M. le Baron de Discau en Angleterre pour m'en faire part; puisque tous les ordinaires me peuvent apporter l'honneur de vos ordres. Et vous voyés que je n'attends pas le retour de M. Diskau de pologne pour vous repondre.

Je crois de vous avoir dit, Monsieur, que le regne de charles II (au mois dans sa permiere moitié) me paroissoit le siecle d'or des Sciences en Angleterre. Il semble que je vous ay paru comme ce vieillard d'Horace, laudator temporis acti,[47] et que vous avés voulu me redresser là dessus, en disant que les sciences et les Arts fleurissent a present à Londres plus que jamais. Vous m'obligerés fort si vous me le faites connoistre, car j'en seray ravi. Mais des gens plus informés que moy m'ont avoué que depuis quelque temps on s'étoit trop attaché a i ghiribizzi della politica, et aux controverses de religion. Je voudrois voir revivre un Prince Robert dans les les Mechaniques, un chevalier Boyle dans la Chymie, un M. Hook dans les observations de microscope, un M. Sydenham ou M. Lyster dans celles de la Medicine, un M. Ray dans la Botanique; & ainsi des autres. Et quand M. Wren, M. Newton, M. Flamstead, M. Halley, M. Sloane, M. Woodward et M. Wotton ne seront plus, je ne say si les gens qui paroissent à present les pourront remplacer. Il semble que presque tous les adherens de M. Newton ne sont apresent que des copistes,[55] et que les plus aigres le sont le plus. Mais quand les presentes passions qui divisent la nation seront appaisées, j'espere que les esprits encouragés par le Roy et par le prince (pour ne rien dire de la princesse) reprendront leur ancien lustre.

J'ay peur que ma lettre precedente sur le systeme de M. Nigresoli, vous aura donné aussi peu de contentement que le systeme meme; puisque vous n'en dites rien d'avantage. Mais j'ai tousjours voulu vous Marquer mon zele.

Vous voyes, que le P.S. est pour vous, Monsieur, et la lettre est plustôt pour M. Newton à l'exemple de celle qu'il vous a écrite.

108. LEIBNIZ TO CONTI 483

everything. And following me, others have spoken of it in the same way. My honesty has been poorly recognized. You say, sir, that Mr. [William] Jones* has published one of my letters to Mr. Newton; have the kindness to let me know where.[44] [...]

I am astonished, sir, that you say that before speaking of the philosophy of Mr. Newton, it is necessary to agree on the method of philosophizing. Is there a different logic in London than in Hannover? When a person reasons in good form on the basis of well-established facts, or on the basis of indubitable axioms, he cannot fail to be right. If the views of Mr. Newton are better than they have said, so much the better. I will always be very glad to do him justice, | whether or not he does it to me |

I clearly see, sir, that you have not yet had the leisure to touch on anything about all that I have had the honour of writing you beyond what concerns Mr. Newton. I had hoped to learn some news about Mr. [Christopher] Wren* and about some other excellent men. But I can only ask you for it as a favour. And each person is the master of the favours he wants to do. However, if you learn something, or some other peculiarities of doctrine that you would be willing to communicate to me, as you have made me hope, I beseech you not to delay sharing it with me until the return[45] of Baron de Discau to England, since every post can bring me the honour of your orders. And you understand that I am not waiting for the return of Mr. Discau from Poland to respond to you.[46]

I believe I have told you, sir, that the reign of Charles II (at least in his first half) seemed to me to be the golden century of the sciences in England. It seems that I appeared to you to be like that old man of Horace, *praiser of times past,*[47] and that you wanted to reprimand me about that by saying that the sciences and the arts presently flourish in London more than ever. I will be very grateful if you make that known to me, because I will be delighted by it. But some people, better informed than I, have admitted that for some time people were too focused on political whims and religious controversies. I would like to see a Prince Rupert[48] come alive again in mechanics, a Sir Robert Boyle* in chemistry, a Mr. [Robert] Hooke[49] in microscopic observations, a Mr [Thomas] Sydenham[50] or Mr. [Martin] Lister[51] in those of medicine, a Mr. [John] Ray[52] in botany, and so of others. And when Mr. Wren, Mr. Newton, Mr. [John] Flamsteed*, Mr. [Edmond] Halley,[53] Mr. Hans Sloane*, Mr.[John] Woodward[54] and Mr. [William] Wotton* will be no more, I do not know if the people who are now making their appearance will be able to replace them. It seems that nearly all the followers of Mr. Newton are now only copyists[55] and that the most bitter are the most so. But when the current passions that divide the nation are calmed, I hope that the intellects, encouraged by the king [George I, Georg Ludwig* of Braunschweig-Lüneburg] and by the prince [Georg August* of Braunschweig-Lüneburg, Prince of Wales] (to say nothing of the princess [Caroline* of Brandenburg-Ansbach, Princess of Wales]) will regain their old luster.

484   108. LEIBNIZ TO CONTI

108. LEIBNIZ TO CONTI   485

I fear that my previous letter[56] concerning the system of Mr. Nigrisoli[57] must have given you as little satisfaction as the system itself, since you say nothing further about it. But I have always wanted to give you signs of my enthusiasm.

You understand that the postscript is for you, sir, and the letter is rather for Mr. Newton, like the one he has written to you.[58]

[1] Forschungsbibliothek Gotha A 448–449 Bl. 14r–18v. Draft: eight folio sides in Leibniz's hand. Previously published in (Newton's 1717 or 1718 reissued version of) Raphson 1715, pp. 103–11; Des Maizeaux 1720, vol. 2, pp. 48–66; NC VI 304–12; HGA 187–8 (excerpt in English translation). This is Leibniz's answer to Conti's letter to Leibniz of 26 March 1716 (NS) (document 104), in which he had included Newton's response (see Newton's letter to Conti of 17 March 1716 (NS), document 101g) to the P.S. that Leibniz had appended to his letter to Conti of 6 December 1715 (document 88b, pp. 323, 3235, 327, 329).

[2] That is: 'Instead of the Leibnizian differences, Mr. Newton employs, and has always employed, fluxions' (*Acta Eruditorum*, January 1705, p. 35). This is a quotation from the anonymous review by Leibniz of the two mathematical treatises that Newton appended to the first edition of his *Opticks* (1704), namely, *Tractatus de Quadratura Curvarum* and *Enumeratio Linearum Tertii Ordinis*.

[3] That is, 'The sense of the words is that Newton substituted fluxions for the Leibnizian differences.' This is a quotation from a note on p. 108 of the *Commercium Epistolicum*.

[4] Raphson 1715, p. 103, and NC VI 305 have 'inseré' instead of 'inserées'.

[5] Raphson 1715, p. 104, and NC VI 305 have 'avoit fait' instead of 'a fait'.

[6] In his *Synopsis geometrica* (1669), the Jesuit theologian Honoré Fabri (1608–88) rewrote the method of indivisibles employed by the Italian mathematician Bonaventura Francesco Cavalieri (1598–1647) in terms of flowing quantities (*fluxus*). As a result, he was widely regarded as having plagiarized his method from Cavalieri by merely changing the terms in which the method was expressed. Consequently, Newton read Leibniz's remarks here as suggesting that Leibniz had his method of differentials before Newton's method of fluxions, just as Cavalieri had his method of indivisibles before Fabri's method in terms of *fluxus*. And thus in the *Commercium Epistolicum*, as Leibniz notes, Newton had argued that 'the sense of the words [that Leibniz had written in his anonymous review in the *Acta Eruditorum* of 1705] is that Newton substituted fluxions for the Leibnizian differences'. But in the present passage, Leibniz pleads innocent of accusing Newton of plagiarism by pointing out that the author of the review used the word *substituit* only when speaking of what Fabri had done in relation to Cavalieri and not in relation to what Newton had done in relation to himself. For his part, Newton was not convinced, and at the beginning of some rather expansive remarks on what Leibniz wrote in this letter, he blasted Leibniz's plea of innocence:

> Mr. *Leibnitz* by his letter of the 29th of *December* 1711 [to the then Secretary of the Royal Society Hans Sloane] justified the Passage in the *Acta Eruditorum* for *January* 1705. *Pag.* 34, and 35. and thereby made it his own, and now endeavours in vain to excuse it, pretending that the Words *adhibet semperque adhibuit* are maliciously interpreted by the Word *substituit*. But in the Interpretation which he would put upon the Place, he omits the Words *igitur* and *quemadmodum*, the first of which makes the Words, *semperque adhibuit*, a Consequence of what went before, and the latter makes them equipollent to *substituit*; neither of which can be true in the Sense which Mr. *Leibnitz* endeavours now to put upon the Words. He has therefore accused me. [NC VI 341]

[7] Raphson 1715, p. 104 and NC VI 305 have 'privément' instead of 'privativement'.

[8] That is, the Scholium to Book 2, Proposition 7, Theorem V of the first edition of Newton's *Principia mathematica*, which reads as follows:

> In correspondence which I carried on ten years ago with the very able geometer G. W. Leibniz, I indicated that I was in possession of a method of determining maxima and minima, drawing tangents, and performing similar operations, and that the method worked for surd as well as rational terms. I concealed this method under an anagram comprising this sentence: 'Given an equation involving any number of fluent quantities, to find the fluxions, and vice versa.' The distinguished gentleman wrote back that he too had come upon a method of this kind, and he communicated his method, which hardly differed from mine except in the forms of words and notations. The foundation of both methods is contained in this lemma. [Newton 1999, p. 649n]

486   108. LEIBNIZ TO CONTI

108. LEIBNIZ TO CONTI 487

[9] The italicized words to this point are quoted from Newton's letter to Conti of 6 March 1716 (NS) (see document 101g).

[10] This document was the so-called *Charta Volans* (see NC VI 15–21), which was penned by Leibniz himself (see note 3 in document 117a, pp. 525, 527). The 'friend' with whom Leibniz entrusted its printing and distribution was Christian Wolff*; see Wolff's letter to Leibniz of 11 December 1713 (GLW 154) and Johann Bernoulli's letter to Leibniz of 23 May 1714 (NC VI 131, 133).

[11] Raphson 1715, p. 104, and NC VI 306 have 'peut' instead of 'pût'.

[12] Reading 'forgés' for 'forgées'.

[13] Here Leibniz presumably refers to his work on the history of the House of Hanover, his *Annales imperii occidentis Brunsvicenses*.

[14] That is, the example he cited in the P. S. to his letter to Conti of 6 December 1715 (see document 88b, p. 325).

[15] Raphson 1715, p. 105, and NC VI 306 have 'lû' instead of 'sû'.

[16] Des Maizeaux 1720, vol. 2, p. 54, has '*les Anglois n'auroient point le Plaisir de me voir repondre à leurs petites raisons*' instead of '*les Anglois n'auroient point le plaisir de me voir repondre à des raisonnemens si minces*' (for Newton's exact wording in English, see his letter to Conti of 17 March 1716 (NS) (document 101g, p. 616)). What Leibniz actually wrote in his letter to Conti of 6 December 1715 was 'Il[s] n'auront point le plaisir de me voir répondre à de petites raisons de gens qui en usent si mal […]' (see document 88b, p. 322), where 'Il[s]' refers, not to 'the English' in general, as Newton had written, but to 'ceux qui ont ecrit contre moy'.

[17] Raphson 1715, p. 106, and NC VI 307 have 'car' instead of 'ou'.

[18] Reading 'tirés' for 'tirées'.

[19] After accepting a position as counselor and librarian to the court of Johann Friedrich* of Braunschweig-Lüneburg at the beginning of 1676, Leibniz began a leisurely journey from Paris to Hanover. It took him first to London, where he arrived on 15 October, and where he stayed until his departure on 29 October, and then to Holland, where he spent nearly a month before continuing his journey to Hanover, where he arrived sometime around mid-December. Leibniz had first visited London from the end of January to the end of February 1673.

[20] Raphson 1715, p. 106, and NC VI 307 have 'ne pas vû' for 'n'ay pas vû' and omit 'y' after 'qu'il'.

[21] The Des Maizeaux 1720, vol. 2, p. 56, Raphson 1715, p. 106, and NC VI 308 all insert 'ou autrement' before 'On devroit'.

[22] See note 8 above.

[23] Des Maizeaux 1720, vol. 2, p. 57, Raphson 1715, p. 107, and NC VI 308 all have 'en 1673' instead of 'au commencement de l'an 1673'.

[24] That is, the German mathematician and astronomer Nicholas Mercator (originally Nikolaus Kauffman) (c.1620–1687), who lived and taught mathematics in London from 1658 to 1682. He was elected a Fellow of the Royal Society in 1666. He designed and constructed the fountains at Versailles, for which he never received payment. He died in Paris.

[25] Des Maizeaux 1720, vol. 2, p. 57, has 'et je ne savois guere que la Geometrie des indivisibles de Cavallieri, & un Livre de Pere Leotaud' instead of 'et je ne savois queres que la Geometrie practique vulgaire, quoyque j'eusse vû par hazard la Geometrie des indivisibles de Cavallerius, et un livre du Père Leotaud'. Leibniz here refers to a book by the French Jesuit mathematician Vincent Léotaud (1595–1672), entitled *Examen circuli quadraturæ* (1654).

[26] John Pell (1611–1685) was a British mathematician.

[27] Raphson 1715, p. 107, and NC VI 308 omit 'auparavant', as well as the following sentence.

[28] Raphson 1715, p. 108, and NC VI 309 omit 'du Calcul Analytique des differences en general; et ce cas special'.

[29] Raphson 1715, p. 108, and NC VI 309 omit 'eu'.

[30] Des Maizeaux 1720, vol. 2, p. 61, has 'mois de May 1700' instead of 'May 1700'.

[31] NC VI 309 omits 'en'.

[32] That is, the brachistochrone problem, which Johann Bernoulli posed in the *Acta Eruditorum* in June 1696. Only five solutions were submitted: by Newton, Leibniz, Johann Bernoulli, Johann's brother Jacob, Ehrenfried Walther von Tschirnhaus, and the French mathematician Guillaume François Antonie, Marquis de l'Hôpital (1661–1704).

[33] The reference here is to the Scholium to Book 2, Section 7, Proposition 39, Theorem 28 (see Newton 1999, p. 729–30).

[34] That is, the French mathematician Pierre de Fermat (1607–1665).

488   108. LEIBNIZ TO CONTI

[35] Here Leibniz paraphrases what Newton wrote in the Scholium to Book 2, Proposition 7 Lemma 2, of the first edition of the *Principia*, namely: '[…] rescripsit Vir Clarissimus se quoque; in ejusmodi methodum incidisse, & methodum suam communicavit a mea vix abludentem præterquam in verborum & notarum formulis'. For the complete translation of this Scholium, see note 8 above.

[36] That is, Abbé François Catelan, (fl. *c*.1700), French mathematician and zealous defender of Cartesian mechanics.

[37] Des Maizeaux 1720, vol. 2, p. 63, Raphson 1715, p. 109, and NC VI 310 all have 'autant que je puis m'en souvenir' rather than 'autant que je m'en puis souvenir'.

[38] Des Maizeaux 1720, vol. 2, p. 63, Raphson 1715, p. 109, and NC VI 310 all omit 'beaucoup'.

[39] Des Maizeaux 1720, vol. 2, p. 63, has 'qu'il n'en a dit dans son livre' instead of 'qu'il n'a dit dans son livre'.

[40] Raphson 1715, p. 110, and NC VI 311 have 'j'ay dit d'avoir' instead of 'j'y dis que j'avoir'.

[41] Florimond de Beaune (1601–1652) was a French mathematician who proposed a number of mathematical problems to Descartes, as well as providing *Notes brèves* to Descartes's *La Géométrie*, which were published in 1649 as part of the first Latin edition of that work. The eponymous problem that Leibniz refers to here is famous for posing the problem of inverse tangents, that is, the problem of determining a curve from a property of its tangent. For a discussion of this problem and Descartes's proposed solution, see AT II 520–2.

[42] Raphson 1715, p. 110, and NC VI 311 insert 'si' before 'Cette'.

[43] In his letter of 24 October 1676 (OS) for Leibniz, Newton included an anagram, which he later decoded in the Scholium to Book 2, Proposition 7 Lemma 2, of the first edition of the *Principia* (see quotation in note 8 above).

[44] In the version published by Des Maizeaux, the editor added this note: 'Mr. Leibniz here confuses Mr. Newton's treatise *de Analysi* &c, published by Mr. *Jones*, with the letter of Mr. *Leibniz* to Mr. *Newton* written in 1693. See above, p. 13' (Des Maizeaux 1720, vol. 2, p. 68n2). Concerning Mr. Jones and his publication, see Conti's letter to Leibniz of 26 March (NS), document 104, p. 457 note 6.

[45] Des Maizeaux 1720, vol. 2, p. 69, has 'jusqu'à l'arrivée' instead of 'jusqu'au retour'.

[46] Leibniz is indicating that he does not want the Duke of Discau to act as a letter courier between Conti and himself, since that would cause a delay in his receiving news from Conti.

[47] Horace, *Ars poetica*, line 173.

[48] That is, Prince Rupert of the Rhine (1619–1682), who was an older brother of Leibniz's late friend and patron Sophie* of the Palatinate. He was made Duke of Cumberland and Earl of Holderness by his uncle, King Charles I of England. He became the Royalist commander during the English Civil War and, after his retirement in later life from his command of the Royal Navy, he devoted much of his time to scientific research and invention, especially of military technology. He was one of the founding members of the Royal Society of London, which was officially established by royal charter in 1662 under the patronage of his first cousin, King Charles II.

[49] Robert Hooke (1635–1703) was English natural philosopher, founding member of the Royal Society, and author of *Micrographia* (1665), an influential, pioneering work in microscopy.

[50] Thomas Sydenham (1624–1689) was an English physician who came to be known as 'the English Hippocrates' and was the author of the influential *Observationes Medicae* (1676), which became a standard medical textbook for two hundred years.

[51] Martin Lister (1639–1712) was an English naturalist and physician. He was elected a Fellow of the Royal Society in 1671 and vice-president of the Royal Society in 1685. He became court physician to Queen Anne in 1702.

[52] John Ray (1627–1705) was an English naturalist who was elected a Fellow of the Royal Society in 1667. His magnum opus, *Historia plantarum species*, was issued in three volumes, published, respectively, in 1686, 1688, and 1704.

[53] Edmond Halley (1656–1742) was an English astronomer, physicist, and mathematician who was elected a Fellow of the Royal Society in 1678; his ground-breaking catalog of southern stars, *Catalogus Stellarum Australium*, was published early in the following year. He was appointed the Savilian Professor of Geometry at Oxford in 1704, and in 1720, following the death of John Flamsteed*, he became the second Astronomer Royal in Britain.

[54] John Woodward (1665–1728) was an English naturalist and geologist who was elected a Fellow of the Royal Society in 1693. The first edition of his *Essay toward a Natural History of the Earth and Terrestrial Bodies* was published in 1695.

[55] Des Maizeaux 1720, vol. 2, p. 71, omits 'des' before 'copistes'.

Leibniz to Nicolas Rémond (excerpt)

A M Remond
à Paris

Hanover ce 9 d'Avril
1716

Monsieur

Je prends la liberté de vous envoyer les pieces d'un procés nouveau ou renouvellé puisque vous avés la bonté de vous interesser pour moy. M. l'Abbé Conti qui avoit fait des demarches de mediateur m'a envoyé maintenant un cartel de defy de la part de M. Newton. Je reponds à la lettre de l'un et de l'autre; à M. Newton dans la lettre à M. l'Abbé et à M. l'Abbé dans le post scriptum,[3] et je suis bien aise, Monsieur, que vous et vos amis, et particulierement M l'Abbé Varignon, et d'autres personnes de l'Academie Royale des sciences à qui il en voudra faire part en soyent informés. Je vous supplie de garder la copie des lettres de M. l'Abbé et de M. Newton, et d'envoyer ma response à Monsieur l'Abbé. Vous voyés bien, Monsieur[,] pourquoy j'ay voulu me servir de la voye de la France, au lieu de repondre directement d'icy. Si vous croyes, Monsieur, que cette response vaille la peine qu'on en garde aussi une copie; cela depend de votre jugement. Mais je ne voudrois pas qu'on en imprimât rien sans mon consentement. Je ne fais point d'autres reflexions sur ces lettres; on en sera assez sans moy.

J'ay pris la liberté de vous dire dernierement, Monsieur que je souhaiterois que l'Academie Royale des inscriptions vist mon discours de origine Francorum, et que je voudrois que cela se fist avant qu'on en parlat dans les Memoires de Trevoux. Je laisse la disposition de cela à vos bontés.

Il y a déja du temps, Monsieur, que je vous ay envoyé mon sentiment sur le livre fait contre le P. Malebranche peut etre que les Reverends peres Jesuites aussi bien que les amis de ce père ne seront point fachés de le voir. Ce que j'ay crû conforme à la verité m'a fait prendre le parti du milieu.

[...]

Au reste, je me rapporte à ma precedente, & je suis avec zele, Monsieur, Votre &c.[5] P. S. Je vous envoye la Lettre à M. l'Abbé Conti *sub sigillo volante*, & il n'est point necessaire que vous la fermiez. Je veux bien qu'on sache que vous l'avez vûë, Monsieur, & que je suis bien aise que vous en soyez informé.

56 That is, Leibniz's letter to Conti of 6 December 1715 (document 88b).
57 See note 2 to Conti's letter to Leibniz of April 1715 (document 79c, p. 277).
58 That is, Newton's letter to Conti of 17 March 1716 (NS) (document 101g).

109. Leibniz to Nicolas Rémond* (excerpt)[1]

To Mr. Rémond   Hanover 9 April
            in Paris   1716
    Sir

I am taking the liberty of sending you the documents from a new or renewed proceeding, since you have the kindness to take an interest in me. The Abbé [Antonio Schinella] Conti*, who has taken some mediatory steps, has now sent me a challenge from Mr. Newton.[2] I am responding to the letter of both, to Mr. Newton in the letter to the Abbé and to the Abbé in the postscript,[3] and I am very glad, sir, that you and your friends, and in particular the Abbé Varignon[4] and some other members of the Royal Academy of Sciences with whom he will want to share it, are informed of it. I beseech you to keep the copy of the letters of the Abbé and Mr. Newton and to send my response to the Abbé [Conti]. You clearly see, sir, why I have wanted to make use of the French route instead of responding directly from here. If you believe, sir, that it is also worthwhile to keep a copy of this response, that is up to you. But I would not want any of it printed without my consent. I do not make any other remarks about these letters; they will be enough without me.

I have recently taken the liberty to tell you, sir, that I would like the Royal Academy of Inscriptions to see my discourse *On the Origin of the Franks*, and that I would like that to be done before it is discussed in the *Memoires de Trévoux*. I leave the arrangement for that to your kindness.

It's been a while, sir, since I sent you my opinion of the book written against Father [Nicolas] Malebranche*. Perhaps the reverend Jesuit fathers, as well as the friends of this father, will not be displeased to see it. What I believed conforms to the truth made me take the middle position.

[…]

For the rest, I refer to my previous letter, and I am enthusiastically, sir, your etc.[5]
P. S. I am sending you the letter to Abbé Conti under open seal, and it is not necessary that you seal it. I certainly want people to know that you have seen it, sir, and that I am very glad that you are acquainted with it.

---

1 Forschungsbibliothek Gotha A 448–449 Bl. 19. Draft: 1 folio side in Leibniz's hand. Previously published in Des Maizeaux 1720, vol. 2, pp. 72–4; Dutens III 473–4; GB 284–5; Schüler 1991, p. 241 (excerpt in German translation); Robinet 1991, p. 63 (excerpt).
2 See Conti's letter to Leibniz of 26 March 1716 (NS) (document 104).
3 GB 284–5 and Des Maizeaux 1720, p. 72, both have 'la Lettre de l'un et de l'autre par la Lettre et par l'Apostille ci-jointes: c'est-à-dire à M. Newton dans la Lettre et à M. l'Abbé dans l'Apostille' instead of

Leibniz to Johann Bernoulli

Vir Noblissime & Celeberrime
Fautor Honoratissime

Opportunè literas Tuas accipio, renovata jam lite Anglicana. Newtonus ipse cum videret mihi Keilium indignum responsione haberi, in arenam descendit, literis ad Dn. Abbatem Contium scriptis, qui ad me misit. Ego respondi, et versionem Anglicæ Newtoni Epistolæ cum responsione mea ad Dn. Remondum misi Parisios Abbati Contio transmittendam, et amicis Parisinis ostendendam. Ex Gallia Tibi omnia communicabuntur: miraberis tam levibus argumentis actum. Potissimum est, me aliquoties ipsi inventum concessisse, ergo nunc salvo candore negare non posse. Respondeo, me tantam de ipsius candore tunc opinionem habuisse, ut quidvis affirmanti facile crediderim: nunc dum accusationi contra me connivet imò accedit quam falsam novit, dubitare de ejus sinceritate coactum. Epistolam quam Tuam esse scit, ait à Mathematico, vel Mathematicum affectante scriptam (par un Mathematicien ou pretendu Mathematicien) quasi merita Tua ignoret. Totam chartam cui Tua Epistola inserta est, vocat diffamatoriam, quasi magis famam lædat quam addita Commercio Epistolico. Dn. Arnoldus mihi scripsit, Keilium in novo quodam Transactionum loco contendere Te quoque ignorare Calculum differentialem, sed homo indignus est cui respondeatur.

[...]

Quod superset vale et fave. Dabam Hanoveræ13. Aprilis 1716.

Dedissimus

Hanoveræ 13 April
1716

Godefridus Guilielmus
Leibnitius[9]

110. LEIBNIZ TO BERNOULLI   493

'la lettre de l'un et de l'autre; à M. Newton dans la lettre à M. l'Abbé et à M. l'Abbé dans le post scriptum'. For the letter and the postscript, see Leibniz's letter to Conti of 9 April 1716 (document 108).

[4] That is, the French mathematician Pierre Varignon (1664–1722).

[5] This sentence and the following postscript are not included in the draft manuscript; they are, however, found in the version published by Gerhardt (GB 285) and by Des Maizeaux (Des Maizeaux 1720, vol. 2, p. 74). Here I follow the version published by Des Maizeaux.

110. Leibniz to Johann Bernoulli* (excerpt)[1]

Most Noble and Celebrated Sir
Most Honourable Supporter

[13 April 1716]

I receive your letter opportunely since the English dispute has already been renewed. Newton himself, when he saw that I regarded [John] Keill* unworthy of a response, has descended into the arena, since a letter had been written to the Abbé [Antonio Schinella] Conti*, which he has sent to me.[2] I have responded[3] and have sent a translation of Newton's English letter, with my response, to Mr. [Nicolas] Rémond* in Paris,[4] to be transmitted to the Abbé Conti and shown to his Paris friends. Everything will be communicated to you from France; you will be astonished at the employment of such trifling arguments. The principal one is that I have granted discovery to him several times, therefore I cannot now deny it without violation of integrity. I respond that I then had such a high opinion of his integrity that I would have readily believed anything he had asserted. Now that he connives at the accusation against me, or rather assents to what he has known to be false, I have been forced to doubt his sincerity,. He says that the letter, which he knows to be yours, has been written by a mathematician or a pretended mathematician (*par un Mathematicien ou pretendu Mathematicien*[5]), as if he were unacquainted with your merit. He calls defamatory the entire document in which your letter is inserted,[6] as if it would harm a reputation more than what has been added to the *Commercium Epistolicum**. Mr. [John] Arnold[7] has written me that Keill, in some new passage in the *Transactions*,[8] maintains that you are also ignorant of the differential calculus, but the man is unworthy to be answered.

[...]

To conclude, farewell and be well disposed. Delivered at Hanover 13 April 1716.

most devoted

Hanover 13 April   Gottfried Wilhelm
1716   Leibniz[9]

---

[1] Forschungsbibliothek Gotha A 448–449 Bl. 324–325. 2.2 quarto sides in a secretary's hand. There is also draft of the letter in Leibniz's hand (Forschungsbibliothek Gotha A 448–449 Bl. 63–64). Previously published in GM III-2 959–60 (excerpt) and NC VI 318–21 (excerpt with English translation). For Bernoulli's response, see his letter to Leibniz of 20 May 1716 (document 121).

Leibniz to Caroline of Brandenburg-Ansbach, Princess of Wales

A Madame la princesse de Galles   Hanover
                              Londres   14 de Avril 1716

Madame

Je souhaite que toute autre chose plus tost que l'incommodité de V. A. Royale m'ait privé de ces[2] ordres excepté cette espece d'incommodité, qu'ait un acheminement à la joye publique. Je crois que M. Clarke n'aura rien d'apparent à repondre à ma demonstration contre Espace Reel, que son maitre avoit appellé le sensorium de Dieu, ou l'organe de son sentiment comme si Dieu avoit besoin d'organes.

Mais il importe d'avantage d'apprendre si V. A. Royale a receu il y a longtemps deux de mes lettres sur l'affaire de la Reunion des protestans et ce qu'Elle en pense. Et maintenant pour faire juger à V. A. Royale qu'il semble que la providence s'en mele, je dois adjouter icy l'extrait d'une lettre que j'ay receu de M Jablonski Concionateur Aulique du Roy de prusse, depuis que j'avois eu l'honneur d'écrite de cette matiere à V. A. R.

Die an dem Christloblichsten Werk annoch geschefftige providenz hat mir unverhofft eine angenehme materi zu schreiben dargeben. Da nehmlich am jungsten etc.

Ainsi V. A. R peut juger combien il importe que quelque Eveque capable, considerable et bien intentionné de l'Eglise Anglicane parle au Roy de cette matiere, et encourage Sa Mté à en communiquer avec le Roy de prusse. Il paroist a propos que cet Eveque ne sache point presentement que je m'en mêle: et il n'est peutestre pas même necessaire que cet Eveque parle à Sa Mté de V. A. R. Mais comme Sa Mté bien informée sera peutestre bien aisé d'amener avec Elle quelque Theologien capable de la servir dans ce dessein; il sera bon alors qu'il s'adresse a M. Molanus et a moy, pour estre pleinement informé des choses passées. Je ne say si le present

111. LEIBNIZ TO CAROLINE OF BRANDENBURG-ANSBACH   495

[2] See Newton's letter to Conti of 17 March 1716 (document 101g).

[3] For Leibniz's response, see his letter to Conti of 9 April 1716 (document 108).

[4] See Leibniz's letter to Rémond of 9 April 1716 (document 109).

[5] Here Leibniz translates into French Newton's expression, 'or pretended Mathematician' (see Newton's letter to Conti of 17 March 1716 (NS), document 101g, p. 437).

[6] That is, the so-called *Charta Volans* (see NC VI 15–21 and note 3 in document 117a, pp. 525, 527).

[7] John Arnold was a physician from Devonshire and practicing at Exeter. He received his M.D. degree from Padua in 1715. In 1720 he was admitted Extra-Licentiate of the Royal College of Physicians of London. For the letter Leibniz says he received from Arnold, see NC VI 274–6. For Leibniz's letter to him of 5 June 1716, see document 126.

[8] That is, the *Philosophical Transactions* of the Royal Society; but see NC VI 276 note 14.

[9] The last three lines, beginning with 'Dedissimus', are in Leibniz's hand.

111. Leibniz to Caroline* of Brandenburg-Ansbach,
Princess of Wales[1]

To Madame the Princess of Wales   Hanover
                          London   14 April 1716

Madame

I hope that something other than the inconvenience of Your Royal Highness has deprived me of her[2] orders, except that kind of inconvenience that has a way to achieve public happiness. I don't believe that Mr. [Samuel] Clarke* will have anything probable to reply to my demonstration against real space, which his master had called the sensorium of God, or the organ of his sensation, as if God needed organs.

But it is more important to learn whether Your Royal Highness received, quite some time ago, two of my letters regarding the matter of the reunion of the Protestants[3] and what she thinks about it. And now, in order to have Your Royal Highness conclude that it seems that providence has a hand in it, I must add here an excerpt from a letter that I received from Mr. [Daniel Ernst] Jablonski*, Court Chaplain of the King of Prussia [Friedrich Wilhelm I*] since I had the honour of writing about this matter to Your Royal Highness.

'Providence, which is still active in the most commendable work for Christians, has unexpectedly given me something pleasing to write. For namely last etc.'[4]

So Your Royal Highness can imagine how important it is that some capable, eminent, and well-intentioned bishop of the Anglican church speak with the king [George I, Georg Ludwig* of Braunschweig-Lüneburg] about this matter and encourage His Majesty to communicate with the King of Prussia about it. It seems appropriate that this bishop not know at present that I have a hand in it, and perhaps it is not even necessary that this bishop speak to His Majesty about Your Royal

Grand Aumonier du Roy, le Docteur Nicolson, n'est pas celuy qui a écrit autres fois quelque chose sur ces matières. Ce seroit tant mieux. Quoyque le Roy de prusse qui regne apresent, n'entre pas si aisement que feu son pere dans telles matières il est plus constant dans ce qu'il entreprend.

En attendant les ordres et sentimens de V. A. R. je suis avec devotion

111. LEIBNIZ TO CAROLINE OF BRANDENBURG-ANSBACH   497

Highness. But as well informed His Majesty will perhaps be very glad to bring in some capable theologian to serve him in this plan; it will then be advisable that he [i.e., the theologian] be directed to Mr. [Gerhard Wolter] Molanus* and me in order to be fully informed about some previous matters. I don't know if the present Lord High Almoner of the King, Doctor [William] Nicolson*, is the one who has formerly written about these matters. That would be all the better. Although the present King of Prussia does not enter into such matters as readily as his late father [Friedrich* I and III of Prussia], he is more constant in what he undertakes.

While awaiting the orders and opinions of Your Royal Highness, I am with devotion

---

[1] LBr. F 4 Bl. 53r–53v. Draft: two quarto sides in Leibniz's hand. Previously published in Schüller 1991, p. 243 (excerpt, German translation).

[2] Reading 'ses' for 'ces'.

[3] The first of the letters that Leibniz mentions is LBr. F4 Bl. 93r–95r (see document 97), which was probably written on, or shortly after, 14 January 1716. The second letter may have been Leibniz's letter to Caroline of 25 February 1716; but only an extract of that letter, made by Leibniz, survives (see document 99), and in that extract there is no mention of the reunion project.

[4] This is Leibniz's paraphrase of something that Jablonski had written in his letter to Leibniz of 22 February 1716. Jablonski's letter itself was a response to a letter that Leibniz had written to him on 14 January 1716. In his letter to Jablonski, as in the first of his letters to Caroline mentioned in note 3 above, Leibniz observed that 'His Royal Majesty in Great Britain has himself clearly declared that he does not think that he has changed his religion by entering into the English church', and then went on to remark that 'it would be a great blindness if we of the Evangelical party did not make use of that' (JK 132). He also told Jablonski that he saw 'an excellent way to bring the matter up to some extent with the king' (ibid.), by which he no doubt meant the plan he had laid out in the first of his letters to Caroline mentioned in note 3 above. But he insisted that the initiative had to come from the King of Prussia, and he urged Jablonski to brief the King of Prussia about the reunion project, which had originally been pursued, although without ultimate success, by the king's father, Friedrich I and III*. In his reply, Jablonski told Leibniz that he 'lamented the limited prospects for successful continuation of this important work with each other, especially since it was insinuated [in Leibniz's letter] that the initial motive for the resumption of the former plan might be given from here, for which there was little hope' (JK 133). But then Jablonski added the remark that led Leibniz to propose his plan to Caroline in the first of the letters mentioned in note 3 above and that Leibniz paraphrased in part in the present letter to Caroline:

> And I was certainly quite concerned about what I should reply to Your Excellency had not the Providence that is still active in this work [later] unexpectedly provided me with something pleasing; for namely last February 9 (on which day His Royal Majesty received communion at Charlottenburg) the king, when I probably expected it least of all, gave me occasion for a private and rather long discussion, which for the most part turned upon the union. His Royal Majesty began to speak about it unexpectedly of his own accord and testified to an extraordinary ardor for this cause. Admittedly the ideas that he himself has formed of it did not yet appear to be fully mature; but because he is a person of quite extraordinary penetration, he will very soon reach the root of the matter if the proposals should come to pass. Then at the end of this kind of discussion I testified that God wished to bid His Majesty to be willing to support this heroic and truly royal project and give his blessing to it; I also testified that I would on the very least command always make known my humble thoughts about it, orally or in writing. The king said: 'in writing and orally'. Although a fine door has now been opened for me as a result of this, I still do not foresee that anything fruitful can be done in this matter until his Majesty the King of Great Britain will have arrived in Germany, since then both majesties will without doubt speak with one another, and in that way the foundation for future transactions can then be laid. This is also the opinion of the Bishop [Benjamin Ursinus*], who was extremely pleased about the pre-established event at Charlottenburg and thought he noticed a footprint of Providence in it. [JK 133–4]

Leibniz to Louis Bourguet (excerpt)

Monsieur

Je viens de recevoir l'honneur de votre lettre, avec l'incluse pour M. Herman, que je luy enverray d'abord. Il me semble qu'on flatte un peu trop M. Newton et les Anglois dans son livre. Au reste il y a de fort bonnes choses.

Si vos amis de Milan n'ont pas trouvé apropos déja d'envoyer de la graine à Augsbourg, il ne sera plus temps apparement de le faire. Cependant je vous suis obligé, Monsieur de vos soins.

La deviation des planetes de la Ligne Elliptique ne peut venir apparemment que de l'operation des planetes entre elles, ou de la resistance du milieu. Pour en juger, il faudroit joindre les observations avec le Calcul. Le plus utile seroit de regler le cours de la Lune, apres avoir bien reglé celuy de la Terre. M. Flamstead pretend que M. Newton n'a pas assés employé les observations. M. Zendrini ne m'a rien marqué du dessein de M. le Comte Rizzati sur les planetes. Je souhaite qu'il joigne les observations aux raisonnemens.

M. Clarke ne m'a point donné grande satisfaction. Il n'a pas bien compris la force de cette Maxime, que rien n'arrive sans une raison suffisante pour le determiner.

Je ne me souviens pas de cet autre Anglois qui doit avoir parlé de la substance.

Je ne saurois penser à ma Dynamique ny à matieres de ϕhilosophie ou de Mathématique, avant que d'avoir eté débarrassé de mon présent travail Historique.

Au reste je suis avec zele

Monsieur

votre tres humble
et tres obëissant
serviteur
Leibniz

Hanover ce 20
d'Avril 1716

As is reflected in these remarks of Jablonski, Leibniz had informed him that 'here we are of the opinion that our king [Georg Ludwig of Braunschweig-Lüneburg, George I of England] will come over this year' (JK 132), which he did in fact. George I visited his Hanoverian electorate for six months from the summer of 1716 to January 1717. But the following passage from a letter that Leibniz wrote to Caroline sometime between the end of September and the beginning of October 1716 suggests that George I and the King of Prussia failed to meet: 'There are still some people who imagine that he [that is, the King of Prussia] could visit the king [i.e., George I], who is to be found so near to his estates; but it appears very doubtful, and there are people close to this prince who do not press him to confer with the King of Great Britain' (document 149, p. 745). Leibniz's final plan for the reunion of the Protestant churches was thus ruined.

112. Leibniz to Louis Bourguet* (excerpt)[1]

[20 April 1716]

Sir

I have just received the honour of your letter with the enclosure for Mr. [Jakob] Hermann*, which I will send to him straightway. It seems that he flatters Mr. Newton and the English a bit too much in his book.[2] Otherwise there are some very good things.

If your friends from Milan have not already found it appropriate to send some [silkworm] egg to Augsburg, there will apparently be no time left to do it. However I am grateful to you, sir, for your solicitude.

The deviation of the planets from the elliptical path can apparently only arise from the operation of the planets among themselves, or from the resistance of the medium. To determine it, it would be necessary to join observations with the calculus. The most useful thing would be to determine the lunar orbit, after having rightly determined that of the earth. Mr. [John] Flamsteed* claims that Mr. Newton has not employed observations enough. Mr. [Bernardino] Zendrini* has not told me anything about the intention of Count Riccati[3] concerning the planets. I hope that he joins observations with reasonings.

Mr. [Samuel] Clarke* has not given me much satisfaction. He has not entirely understood the force of this maxim, that nothing happens without a sufficient reason for determining it.

I do not remember this other Englishman who has supposedly spoken about substance.[4]

I can't think about my dynamics, or about philosophical or mathematical matters, until I have been freed from my present historical work.[5]

To conclude, I am enthusiastically

sir

Hanover 20
April 1716

your very humble
and very obedient
servant
Leibniz

Leibniz to Caroline of Brandenburg-Ansbach, Princess of Wales

A Madame la princesse de
Galles

Hanover ce
28 d'Avril
1716

Madame

J'ay pris la liberté depuis peu d'écrire à V. A. Royale pour luy renouveller le souvenir de deux de mes Lettres precedentes, et celle de M. Jablonski de Berlin, dont je viens de luy envoyér l'extrait en meme temps, m'en a donné l'occasion. J'espere d'apprendre les penses de V. A. Royale là dessus, et j'ay crû qu'il n'y avoit qu'une chose de cette nature, qui pût renouveller son souvenir à mon egard. Vous est[es]³ ferme et constante dans les choses grandes et importantes, mais je dois craindre Madame, que vous ne le soyés pas egalement dans les petites, comme doit étre à son⁴ garde tout ce qui a rapport à moy, et particulierement la version de la Theodicée. Il semble que M. Clarke ait crû s'appercevoir de quelque chose de cette nature, qui luy aura donné la hardiesse, de publier une brochure contre moy tirée apparemenent de notre commerce qui a eu l'honneur de passer par les moins de V. A. Royale; et il auroit tort s'il l'avoit publié sans Sa permission: cependant je souhaite de voir au moins cette brochure, pour en juger.

L'Abbé Conti, s'etant peutétre apperçu aussi de quelque changement apparent dans V. A. Royale a passé de la qualité de mediateur, à celle de confident de mon adversaire et s'est changé d'un cartel de M. Newton. Je n'attendois que cela ne voulant point entrer en dispute avec certaines gens qui parloient pour luy, et il aura ma reponse, que je fais passer par les mains d'un ami à Paris, à fin que des connoisseurs qui y sont, en puissent prendre connoissance. | Car ce cartel ne me donne gueres de peine, et si je puis avoir assés de loisir, je me fais fort de tenir tête à M. Newton et à tous ses adherens, car je ne manque point d'assistens. |

L'Abbé Conti a dit aussi que M. l'Envoyé de Modene se plaignoit de moy de se que⁸ je retenois mal apropos [un] Manuscrit qu'on m'avoit envoyé de Modene. Comme cela est mal fondé, et que le MS. m'a eté envoyé pour l'examiner, à quoy il falloit du temps; je me suis plaint de cela à Monseigneur le Duc de Modene, et son Altesse S^{me} m'a repondu, qu'elle desapprouvoit ces plaintes, et en feroit écrire à son

113. LEIBNIZ TO CAROLINE OF BRANDENBURG-ANSBACH 501

¹ Leiden Universiteitsbibliotheek Ms. 293 B, Bl. 271r–272r. Letter as sent: 3 octavo sides in Leibniz's hand. Previously published in Dutens VI-1 220; GP III 594; Schüller 1991, p. 243 (excerpt in German translation); Robinet 1991, p. 61 (excerpt). Response to Bourguet's letter of 31 March 1716 (document 106).

² On this, see Leibniz's letter to Bourguet of 24 February 1716 (document 98, p. 582 note 11).
³ That is, the Venetian mathematician Jacopo Francesco Riccati (1676–1754).
⁴ On this, see Bourguet's letter to Leibniz of 31 March 1716 (document 106, p. 649 note 5).
⁵ That is, his work on the *Annales imperii occidentis Brunsvicenses**.

113. Leibniz to Caroline* of Brandenburg-Ansbach, Princess of Wales[1]

To Madame the Princess of
Wales

Hanover this
28 of April
1716

Madame

I recently took the liberty of writing to Your Royal Highness to refresh her memory about two of my previous letters, and that of Mr. [Daniel Ernst] Jablonski from Berlin, of which I have just sent her an excerpt at the same time, gave me occasion to do it.[2] I hope to learn the thoughts of Your Royal Highness about it, and I thought there was only something of this nature that could refresh her memory with regard to me. You are[3] firm and constant in great and important matters, but I have to fear, madame, that you may not be equally so in small matters, since everything that relates to me must be in your care,[4] and especially the translation of the *Theodicy*. It seems that Mr. [Samuel] Clarke* thought he noticed something of this nature, which could have given him the audacity to publish a pamphlet against me, apparently connected with our correspondence,[5] which has had the honour of passing through the hands of Your Royal Highness. It would be wrong if he published it without her permission; however, I wish at least to see this pamphlet in order to evaluate it.

The Abbé [Antonio Schinella] Conti*, having perhaps also noticed some apparent change in Your Royal Highness, has passed from the position of mediator to that of confidant of my adversary and has been converted by a challenge from Mr. Newton.[6] I waited only for that, since I did not want to enter into dispute with certain people who spoke for him, and he will have my response,[7] which I have sent in care of a friend in Paris [Nicolas Rémond*], so that some connoisseurs who are there can peruse it. | For this challenge scarcely troubles me, and if I am able to have enough leisure, I am determined to stand up to M. Newton and all his followers, for I do not lack assistants. |

The Abbé Conti has also said that the envoy from Modena complained that[8] I inappropriately retained the manuscript that had been sent to me from Modena. Since that is ill founded, and the manuscript was sent to me in order to examine it,

114. LEIBNIZ TO VON BOTHMER

Ministre. Je laisse juger à V. A. Royale si ceux qui donnent creance à telles faussetés qu'on invente contre moy, observent les regles de l'equité, et si je m'en dois mettre en peine.

Je me fais fort, si j'ay du loisir, de tenir teste à M. Newton et à tous ses adherens, soit en mathematique soit en philosophie, car je ne manque point d'assistans. Sa philosophie semble faire Dieu ame du Monde, et luy donner des organes, et des imperfections. Et quant aux Mathematiques, nous verrons par le moyen de qui on viendra le mieux à bout de questions difficiles. J'en parle à V. A. Royale comme si Elle prenoit encore quelque part à ce qui me regarde. Je suis bien aise de m'en flatter, estant avec devotion Madame de V. A. R.

Leibniz to Johann Caspar von Bothmer

Monsieur

Pendant que V. E. me mande fort obligeamment que je ne me dois point laisser de tourner de mes travaux Historiques par la dispute avec M. Newton; des personnes de consideration de notre Cour, et qui ont l'honneur d'etre distinguees du Roy; et qui d'ailleurs me témoignent de sa bonté, m'envoyent une espece de cartel de la part de M. Newton, et me font presser d'y repondre, comme si elles s'imaginoient que je n'aurois gueres de quoy; elles me font même le tort de me faire conseiller quasi de ceder, ce qui seroit fort beau et fort digne du pays qui a donné le Roy aux Anglois sur tout puisqu'on me fait savoir tout exprés que Sa Mté a pris conoissance de l'affaire. J'ay fait repondre qu'Hanover tout petit qu'il est, ne cede point à Londres tout

which takes time, I have complained about it to Monseigneur the Duke of Modena [Rinaldo d'Este (1655–1737)], and His Most Serene Highness has replied that he disapproved of these complaints and would write to his minister about it. I leave it to Your Royal Highness to determine whether those who give credence to such falsehoods that are contrived against me observe the rules of equity and whether I should trouble myself about them.

If I have some leisure, I am determined to stand up to M. Newton and all his supporters, whether in mathematics or in philosophy, for I do not lack assistants. His philosophy seems to make God soul of the world and to give him organs and imperfections. And as to mathematics, we will see by whose means we will best deal with difficult problems. I am speaking to Your Royal Highness about it as if she still took some part in my affairs. I am very glad to pride myself on it, being with devotion, madame, of Your Royal Highness

[1] Forschungsbibliothek Gotha A 448–449 Bl. 30r–30v. Draft: 1.5 folio sides in Leibniz's hand. Not previously published. For Caroline's response, see her letter to Leibniz of 5 May 1716 (document 115).

[2] See Leibniz's letter to Caroline of 14 April 1716 (document 111).

[3] Leibniz had originally begun the sentence with 'V. A. Royale', but he crossed it out and wrote 'Vous' instead, without changing the verb from 'est' to 'êtes'.

[4] Reading 'votre' for 'son'. See previous note.

[5] Leibniz had apparently received notice of this from one of his English correspondents, Dr. John Arnold, as suggested in Leibniz's letter to Arnold of 5 June 1716 (document 126, p. 577). In her letter to Leibniz of 5 May (document 115, p. 513), Caroline denied that Clarke had published anything about his correspondence with Leibniz. But Leibniz reiterated his accusation in his letter to Caroline of 12 May (document 117a, p. 523), saying specifically 'that in a printed paper Mr. Clarke has touched on my view about space'. Finally, in her letter to Leibniz of 26 May (document 122, p. 549), Caroline replied, in apparent exasperation, that 'I have already told you about the situation concerning Doctor Clarke in one of my letters.' But in his letter to Arnold of 5 June, Leibniz persisted in seeking information about the pamphlet that Clarke had supposedly published concerning his correspondence with Leibniz.

[6] See Newton's letter to Conti of 17 March 1716 (NS), document 101g.

[7] See Leibniz's letter to Conti of 9 April 1716, document 108.

[8] Reading 'de ce que' for 'de se que'.

114. Leibniz to Johann Caspar von Bothmer*[1]

[Hanover, 28 April 1716[2]]

Sir

While Your Excellency writes me very obligingly that I ought not allow myself to turn from my historical work[3] by the dispute with Mr. Newton, some esteemed individuals of our court, who have the honour to be honoured by the king [George I, Georg Ludwig* of Braunschweig-Lüneburg], and who moreover testify to me of his kindness, are sending me a kind of challenge from Mr. Newton and are pressing me to respond to it, as if they imagined that I would have scarcely anything [to say].[4] They even wronged me by advising me almost to concede, which would be very nice and very worthy of the country which has given the king to the English,

504   114. LEIBNIZ TO VON BOTHMER

grand qu'il est, ny en affection pour le Roy, ny en Geometrie ny même en philosophie. Et si j'ay du loisir, je me fait fort de tenir tete à M. Newton, et à tous ses adherens, car je ne manque pas assistans aussi. Sa philosophie semble faire Dieu Ame du monde, et luy donner des organes et des imperfections; ses partisans desapprouvent que j'appelle Dieu Intelligentiam Supramundanam, c'est l'Antipode de ma Thodicée. Et quant à la Geometrie, nous verrons par le moyen de qui on viendra mieux à bout de questions difficiles comme de celle que M. Bernoulli a proposée il y a long temps avant cette dispute; et qu'on a renouvellée à cette occasion. C'est une espece de pierre de touche.

J'ay repondu à la lettre de M. Newton et j'ay fait passer ma reponse par les mains d'un ami à paris, a fin que des connoiseurs qui y sont en prennent connoissance. Comme M. Newton est l'aggresseur, c'est à luy qu'on s'en doit prendre. Je ne puis étre indifferent lors qu'il s'agit de conserver ma reputation. Si s'agissoit de le quel a sçû la chose le premier in petto (car on ne peut nier que je l'aye produit le premier) je ne m'en mettrois en peine, ny même si la question estoit le quel de nous deux est le plus habile dans la matiere dont il s'agit; mais ses adherens ont osé avancer que j'avois excroqué mon invention de luy; et mes amis pensent entrevoir, que c'est luy plus tost qui a profité en cela de mes decouvertes. Le moyen conforme à la justice de faire cesser ces aigreurs est d'imposer silence aux accusations prejudiciables, à moins qu'on les ait justifiées devant des juges intelligens et impartiaux. Autrement on sera entrainé dans de grands details qui m'occuperont plus que je ne voudrois: mais ce n'est pas ma faute. V. E jugera bien de ce qu'il faut, et saura les moyens d'y contribuer.

> Je suis entierement
> > Monsieur de V. E. etc.
> P.S.

Je suis bien obligé à V. E. de ce qu'elle paroist desapprouver les chicanes que certaines Anglois me font. Je veux croire que les personnes qui s'en sont mêlées, qui ont informeé le Roy de mon procés avec M. Newton, et qui m'ont envoyé son cartel l'ont fait par un zele de la verité. Et comme on est allâ jusqu'a m'accusé de mauvais tours, je n'ay pû m'empecher de me defendre, et de monstrer des apparences qu'il faudroit plus tost tourner la medaille, et que c'est à moy de me pleindre.

personnes m'ont suscité. Mais puis je m'empecher de repondre, quand on n'attaque pas seulement ma science mais aussi ma bonne foy et ma reputation? Je fis connoitre en 1676 par une lettre écrite au secretaire de la société Royale d'Angleterre, que j'avois trouvé un nouveau calcul Mathematique. Je ne le publiay qu'en 1684, et il fit grand bruit parmy les connoiseurs, et fut bien tôt introduit par tout et appliqué utilement à cent questions difficiles. M. Newton publia un livre en 1686. ou il marqua qu'il avoit donné il y a long temps quelque chose de cette nature par enigme, mais qu'il n'expliqua qu'alors, avouant que j'avois donné le mien de mon chef. Quoyque l'explication de l'Enigme, ne dist pas assés, neantmoins persuadé alors non seulement du savoir,

especially since they expressly inform me that His Majesty has taken note of the affair. I have responded that Hanover, small as it is, does not concede to London, large as it is, either in affection for the king, or in geometry, or even in philosophy. And if I have some leisure, I am determined stand up to Mr. Newton and all of his followers; for I also do not lack assistants. His philosophy seems to make God soul of the world and to give him organs and imperfections; his supporters disapprove of my calling God *Intelligentiam Supramundanam*. That is the opposite of my *Theodicy*. And as for geometry, we will see by whose means we will best deal with difficult problems, like the one Mr. [Johann] Bernoulli* proposed a long time before this dispute and which has been renewed on this occasion.[5] It's a kind of touchstone.

I have responded to the letter of Mr. Newton, and I have sent my response through the hands of a friend in Paris [Nicolas Rémond*], so that some connoisseurs who are there may peruse it.[6] As Mr. Newton is the aggressor, it is he who ought to be blamed. I cannot be indifferent when it is a matter of preserving my reputation. If it were a matter of which one privately knew the thing first (for it cannot be denied that I first made it known), I would not trouble myself about it, nor even if the question were which of us is the most skillful in the subject with which it deals; but his followers have dared to assert that I swindled my invention from him, and my friends think they have an inkling that it is rather he who has profited in that from my discoveries. The just means of making this acrimony cease is by imposing silence on prejudicial accusations, unless they have been justified before some competent and impartial judges. Otherwise I will be drawn into some extensive details that will occupy me more than I should want; but that is not my fault. Your Excellency will be a good judge of what is required and will be able to contribute the means to it.

I am entirely,

sir, of Your Excellency, etc.

P.S.

I am very grateful to Your Excellency because he appears to disapprove of the cavils that certain

Englishmen have made against me. I want to believe that the people who got mixed up in it,[7] who have informed the king of my proceedings with Mr. Newton, and who have sent his challenge to me, have done it from a zeal for the truth. And as they have gone so far as accusing me of dirty tricks, I could not refrain from defending myself and showing from the appearances that it is rather necessary to look at the other side and that it is for me to complain.

people have raised against me. But can I refrain from responding when they attack not only my science but also my good faith and my reputation? In 1676, in a letter written to the secretary of the Royal Society of England, I revealed that I had discovered a new mathematical calculus. I published it only in 1684, and it made quite

mais aussi de la candeur de M. Newton j'eus l'honnesteté de dire, et de faire dire à mes amis que je croyois que M. Newton avoit eu de son chef une invention approchante de la mienne. Les choses en demeurerent là mais apres 27 ans de ma possession, quelques personnes envieuses de la réputation d'autruy, voyant le grand usage de l'invention, dont le monde estoit redevable à moy, puisqu'en effect je l'avois publié, quoyque apres 8 ans d'attente, pendant que M. Newton avoit gardé in petto ce qu'il pouvoit avoir eu; ils chercherent un pretexte pour me faire querelle, et ils le trouverent dans certaines paroles d'un journal Latin de Leipzig, qu'ils supposerent avoir eté mises là avec mon consentement, et qu'ils expliquerent comme si j'accusois M. Newton d'avoir forgé son calcul sur le mien. Soit que M. Newton ait eté abusé par des suggestions malignes, soit qu'il ait eté bien aise d'avoir ce pretexte de s'attribuer l'invention, en m'excluant, ses adherens publierent un livre contre moy à Londres l'an 1712, plein de fausses interpretations de vieilles lettres, par les quelles ils m'accusoient comme par forme de retorsion, que c'estoit plus tost moy qui avois pris mon invention de M. Newton; et on eût grand soin d'envoyer ce libelle en france, en Italie, et ailleurs.

J'estois alors à Vienne, j'appris la publication du livre, mais asseuré qu'il devoit contenir des faussetés malignes, je ne daignay point de le faire venir par la poste, mais j'écrivis à Monsieur Bernoulli, l'homme de l'Europe qui a peutetre le mieux reussi dans la connoissance et dans l'usage de ce calcul, et qui etoit tout à fait neutre, de m'en mander son sentiment. Monsieur Bernoulli m'écrivit une lettre, datée de Bâle le 7 juin 1713 où il disoit qu'il paroissoit vraisemblable, que M. Newton avoit fabriqué son Calcul apres avoir vû le mien, par ce qu'il avoit eu plusieurs fois occasion dans ses ouvrages, d'employer ce calcul, sans qu'il en paroisse aucune trace; et même qu'il avoit fait des fautes qui paroissoient incompatibles avec une veritable intelligence de ce calcul. Un de mes amis publia cette lettre avec des reflexions. Et comme j'avois assés d'autres occupations, je ne voulus point entrer d'avantage là dedans. D'autant que M. Newton n'avoit point parlé luy même. Ainsi je crus qu'il suffisoit d'avoir opposé aux criailleries de ses adherens le jugement d'une personne de la science et de l'impartialité de M. Bernoulli.

Mais enfin on a trouvé le moyen de me faire parler, en donnant connoissance de l'affaire au Roy, et en m'envoyant en même temps un Cartel de M. Newton. J'y ay repondu par une lettre qui n'est pas trop longue, mais apparemment cela ira plus loin, et il faudra entrer dans un grand detail, s'il est permis à M. Newton et à ses adherens de continuer de noircir ma reputation. Je suis obligé indispensablement de me defendre et d'user de represailles, quoyque je souhaiterois d'employer mon temps plus utilement. Il pretend dans sa lettre que je suis l'aggresseur, que je l'ay accusé d'avoir usé de mauvaise foy, et que c'est à moy de prouver cette accusation. Je souhaite qu'on examine cette question preallable qui de nous deux est l'aggresseur, car il est fort aisé de la vuider. Il ne se fonde que dans les paroles du journal de Leipzig du janvier de l'an 1705 que voicy: Calculi Differentialis ejusque reciproci summatorii elementa ab inventore D. Godefrido Guilielmo Leibnitio in his Actis sunt tradita etc. biß methodo substituit. Commer[c]e. p. 108

a splash among connoisseurs and was soon introduced everywhere and usefully applied to a hundred difficult issues. Mr. Newton published a book in 1686[8] in which he indicated that he had presented something of this nature a long time ago in a riddle, but that he only explained it then,[9] acknowledging that I had presented mine of my own doing. Although the explanation of the riddle did not say enough, nevertheless, persuaded at the time not only of the knowledge, but also of the candor of Mr. Newton, I had the honesty to say, and to have my friends say, that I believed that Mr. Newton had of his own doing an invention much the same as mine. There things remained; but after 27 years of my possession, some individuals—envious of the reputation of others, seeing the wide use of the invention for which the world was indebted to me, since I had in fact published it, although after 8 years of delay, while Mr. Newton had kept secret what he may have had—sought a pretext to quarrel with me, and they found it in certain words from a Latin journal of Leipzig [*Acta Eruditorum*], which they supposed had been put there with my consent, and which they interpreted as if I accused Mr. Newton of having fabricated his calculus on the basis of mine. Whether Mr. Newton had been deceived by some malicious suggestions, or had been very happy to have this pretext to attribute to himself the invention, by excluding me, his followers published a book against me in London in 1712 [the *Commercium Epistolicum**], full of false interpretations of old letters, by which they accused me, as by a form of retaliation, that it was rather I who had taken my invention from Mr. Newton; and they took great care to send this libel to France, to Italy, and elsewhere.

I was then in Vienna. I learned of the publication of the book, but assured that it had to contain some malicious falsities, I did not deign to have it come by mail; but I wrote to Mr. Bernoulli, perhaps the most accomplished man in Europe in the knowledge and use of this calculus, and who was quite neutral, to ask his opinion of it. Mr. Bernoulli wrote me a letter, dated from Basil 7 June 1713, in which he said that it seemed likely that Mr. Newton had fabricated his calculus after having seen mine, because several times he had had occasion to employ this calculus in his works without any trace of it appearing, and even because he had made some errors that appeared incompatible with a true understanding of this calculus. One of my friends published this letter with some comments.[10] And as I had enough other occupations, I did not want to enter into it further, especially as Mr. Newton had not spoken himself. So I believed that it was enough to have put in opposition to the wrangling of his followers the judgement of a person of the skill and impartiality of Mr. Bernoulli.

But finally they found a way to make me speak, by making the affair known to the king and by sending me a challenge from Mr. Newton[11] at the same time. I have responded with a letter which is not too long,[12] but apparently that will go further, and it will be necessary to go into great detail if Mr. Newton and his followers are allowed to continue to blacken my reputation. I am indispensably forced to defend myself and retaliate, although I would hope to employ my time more usefully.

508   114. LEIBNIZ TO VON BOTHMER

Il n'y a pas un mot là dedans, qui ne soit vray à la rigueur; et il n'y a pas un mot qui dise que M. Newton a fabriqué son calcul sur le mien: mais on l'en a voulu tirer par une glosse marginale dans le livre fait contre moy p. 108, car lors que le journal de Leipzig [dit][14] pro differentiis Leibnitianis D. Newtonus adhibet semperque adhibuit fluxiones, l'auteur de la glosse l'explique ainsi: sensus verborum est quod Newtonus fluxiones differentiis Leibnitianis substituit. Mais ce substituit, est une interpretation maligne du glossateur et ne peut point s'accorder avec semper adhibuit, qui paroist avoir eté mis là tout expres pour marquer que déja avant la publication de mon calcul M. N. s'estoit servi des fluxions. Au lieu qu'on dit substituit en parlant du pere Fabry, qui étoit venu apres Cavalieri et en avoit changé les expressions; en quoy on a marqué la difference; en disant que M. Newton a tousjours employé sa methode, au lieu que le P. Fabry n'a forgé la sienne qu'à l'imitation d'un autre.

Ainsi on ne peut rien tirer de derogeant pour M. Newton de ces paroles qu'en les empoisonnant. Et si l'on les avoit trouvé obscures, on auroit pu demander une explication, et les journalistes auroient pris plaisir sans doute de redire ce qu'on avoit dit plusieurs fois ailleurs, qu'on croyoit que M. N. y étoit parvenu de son chef. Mais au lieu de se servir d'une telle voye, on a voulu chercher querelle de sorte que M. Newton se trouve l'aggresseur, et par consequent c'est luy qui a l'incumbence de prouver son accusation. Cependant il reconnoist qu'il s'est abusé, et laisse tomber sa pretendue retorsion. On peut en demeurer là, mais s'il s'opiniatre de continuer son accusation, il est juste qu'on impose silence là dessus, à luy et à ses adherans, jusqu'à ce qu'ils prouvent leur accusations devant des connoisseurs impartiaux. C'est la justice que j'ay droit de demander et je ne voy que ce moyen qui me puisse sauver le temps qu'autrement je seray obligé d'employer malgré moy pour soutenir cette querelle. Apres cela je laisse juger à V. E. si je ne me tiens entierement aux formes de la raison etc.[18]

He claims in his letter that I am the aggressor, that I accused him of acting in bad faith, and that it is up to me to prove this accusation. I want this preliminary question to be examined, which of us is the aggressor, for it is very easy to settle. It is based only on these words from the journal of Leipzig of January 1705: *Calculi Differentialis ejusque reciproci summatorii elementa ab inventore D. Godefrido Guilielmo Leibnitio in his Actis sunt tradita* etc. up to *methodo substituit.*[13] *Commercium* p. 108

There is not a word in there that is not strictly true, and there is not a word that says that Mr. Newton fabricated his calculus based on mine. But they have wanted to infer it by means of a marginal gloss in the book made against me p. 108. For where the journal of Leipzig says[14] *pro differentiis Leibnitianis D. Newtonus adhibet semperque adhibuit fluxiones,*[15] the author of the gloss explains it thus: *sensus verborum est quod Newtonus fluxiones differentiis Leibnitianis substituit.*[16] *Commercium* p. 108. But this *substituit* is a malicious interpretation by the commentator and is not at all consistent with *semper adhibuit*, which appeared to have been placed there expressly to indicate that Mr. Newton had already made use of fluxions before the publication of my calculus. *Substituit* is rather said in speaking about Father Fabri, who had come after Cavalieri and had modified his terminology; in this way the difference has been indicated by saying that Mr. Newton has always employed his method, whereas Father Fabri fabricated his own only in imitation of another.[17]

So nothing derogating to Mr. Newton can be inferred from these words except by poisoning them. And if they had been found obscure, an explanation could have been requested, and journalists would no doubt have taken pleasure in repeating what had been said elsewhere many times, that it is believed that Mr. Newton had achieved it on his own account. But instead of employing such an approach, they wanted to look for a fight, so that Mr. Newton is the aggressor, and consequently it is he who has the burden of proving his accusation. However he recognized that he was deceived and abandoned his intended retaliation. It may be left at that; but if he insists on continuing his accusation, it is just that silence about it be imposed on him and his followers until they prove their accusations before impartial connoisseurs. It is the justice that I have a right to demand, and this is the only way I see that can save me the time that I otherwise shall be forced to employ against my will to maintain this fight. After that, I leave it to Your Excellency to decide whether I stick to the rules of reason etc.[18]

---

[1] Forschunsbibliothek Gotha A 448–449, Bl. 30v–31r. Draft: 2.5 folio sides in Leibniz's hand. Only the P.S. has previously been published (in Des Maizeaux 1720, vol. 2, pp. 42–7 (excerpt); Dutens III 461–3 (excerpt)). For Bothmer's reply, see his letter to Leibniz of 5 May 1716 (NS) (document 116).

[2] I have dated this draft letter based on the fact that it begins below, and on the same folio page as, the end of Leibniz's draft letter to Caroline dated 28 April 1716 (see document 113). This dating is confirmed by the fact that in his reply, Bothmer refers to Leibniz's 'letter of 28th April' (see document 116, p. 519).

510   114. LEIBNIZ TO VON BOTHMER

114. LEIBNIZ TO VON BOTHMER 511

[3] That is, Leibniz's work on the history of the House of Braunschweig-Lüneburg, his *Annales imperii occidentis Brunsvicenses*.

[4] The 'esteemed individuals of our court' actually refers to a single individual, namely, the Abbé [Antonio Schinella] Conti*. See Conti's letter to Leibniz of 26 March 1716 (NS) (document 104).

[5] Leibniz is referring to a problem that Bernoulli formulated in the May 1700 issue of the *Acta Eruditroum*. On this problem, and Bernoulli's reformulation of it, see NC VI 322–4.

[6] For Leibniz's response to Newton, see his letter to Conti of 9 April 1716 (document 108).

[7] Again, 'the people who got involved with it' actually refers to a single individual, namely, the Abbé Conti. See Conti's letter to Leibniz of 26 March 1716 (NS) (document 104).

[8] That is, Newton's *Philosophiæ Naturalis Principia Mathematica*.

[9] In his letter of 24 October 1676 (OS) for Leibniz, Newton included an anagram encoding a reference to his method of fluxions and fluents; he later decoded the cipher in the Scholium to Book 2, Proposition 7 Lemma 2, of the first edition of the *Principia*, for the translation of which see Leibniz's letter to Conti of 9 April 1716 (document 108), p. 485 note 8.

[10] Leibniz is referring to the so-called *Charta Volans* (see NC VI 15–21 and note 3 to document 117a, pp. 125, 127), which was actually composed by Leibniz himself and not by a friend as Leibniz says here.

[11] See Newton's letter to Conti of 17 March 1716 (NS) (document 101g.).

[12] See Leibniz's letter to Conti of 9 April 1716 (document 108).

[13] This is a quotation from the anonymous review by Leibniz of the two mathematical treatises that Newton appended to the first edition of his *Opticks* (1704), namely, *Tractatus de Quadratura Curvarum* and *Enumeratio Linearum Tertii Ordinis*. The complete quotation, save for a short parenthetical comment about l'Hôpital's premature death, is found in the version of Leibniz's letter published by Des Maizeaux, as follows:

> *Calculi differentialis ejusque reciproci summatorii Elementa ab inventore D. Godefrido Guilielmo Leibnitio in his Actis sunt tradita, variique usus, tum ab ipso, tum à D. D. fratribus Bernoullis, tum & D. Marchione Hospitalio sunt ostensi. Pro differentiis igitur Leibnitianis D. Newtonus adhibit, semperque adhibuit Fluxiones, quæ sunt quam proxime ut fluentium augmenta æqualibus temporis particulis quam minimis genita; iisque tum in suis Principiis Naturæ Mathematicis, tum in aliis postea editis eleganter est usus; quemadmodum & Honoratus Fabrius in sua Synopsi Geometrica, motuum progressus Cavallerianæ methodo substituit.* [Des Maizeaux 1720, vol. 2, pp. 45–6; for the original, see the *Acta Eruditorum* for January 1705, pp. 34–5.]

That is,

> The elements of the differential, and of its inverse, the summatory [i.e., integral] calculus, have been delivered in these *Acta* by the inventor Mr. Gottfried Wilhelm Leibniz, and various applications have been presented, first by himself, then by Messrs. the brothers Bernoulli, and then by the Marquis de l'Hôpital. So instead of the Leibnizian differences, Mr. Newton employs, and has always employed, fluxions, which are very nearly the same as the increments of the fluents generated in the very least equal portions of time; and he has employed them elegantly, not only in his Mathematical Principles of Nature, but also in other things published thereafter, just as Honoré Fabri, in his *Synopsis geometrica*, substituted the increase of motions for Cavalieri's method [of indivisibles].

[14] In the draft of this letter, 'dit' was inadvertently omitted, but it is included in the version published by Des Maizeaux (see Des Maizeaux 1720, vol. 2, p. 46), which I follow here.

[15] That is, 'instead of the Leibnizian differences, Mr. Newton employs, and has always employed, fluxions' (*Acta Eruditorum* for January 1705, p. 35).

[16] That is, 'The sense of the words is that Newton substituted fluxions for the Leibnizian differences.'

[17] For more information about the relationship between Fabri and Cavalieri, as well a quotation of Newton's response to Leibniz's explanation of what was said in his anonymous review in the *Acta Eruditorum*, see note 6 to Leibniz's letter to Conti of 9 April 1716 (document 108, p. 485).

[18] The last four sentences are omitted in the versions published by Des Maizeaux and Dutens.

Caroline of Brandenburg-Ansbach,
Princess of Wales, to Leibniz

St James le $\frac{5}{24}$ d'avril 1716

J'ay receu toute[s] vos lettres Monsieur, mais les grandes dificuldé[3] que j'ay trouvez a antandre[4] parler nos Eveque sur le chapitr[5] de la reunion m'ont laissez dans l'insertidute[6] de vous reponder, jus qu'as ceque je l'ais eut[7] mis vn peu dans vn autre chemain.[8] L'archevéque, ne vois[10] point d'autre manier que d'introtuire[11] le service d'icy et faire passere[12] quelque Evéque pour ordonner les ministre aude la mere.[13] pour les point essansielle elle sont requse et lon sans contante icy.[14] Vous voiyé que sa ne consssisté que sur le seromoniel.[15] Je crois qu'a nous autre l'uderrien il nous passerais L'ostié[16] enfin Monsieur sy jamais vous faisiée vn voiagé[17] icy vous desterminerié plut que toute[18] les lettres du monde. mais d'ou vien[t] que vous me soupsonié de nestre pas lamême[19] pour vous. Je crois que d[']estre ferme pour les amis e[s]t vn des point[s] de notre devoir, et j'an apelle au Roy.[20] Doctteur chlerck n'an rien imprimé de ce qui ces passez antre[21] vous et luy, et don vous aurais antantu parler[23] sont des lettres que luy et vn Eclésyatique Ecossois ont écrit[24] il y a quelque tems. L'abée conty apris lapeñe de pertre quelque vn des papié[25] que vous avez bien voulu que je luy du confier,[26] il me promest[27] de les retrouver. ces ce qui manpeché ceste poste de vous anvoiyer la reponce dernier de chlercke.[28] samdy passez j'eu dé puis 6 jus-qu'a dis heur, L'abée conty et chlerck avec moy.[29] Je vous ayée souhaité beaucoup pour me soudenir;[30] et leur savoir, et la manier de raisoner claire de chlerck m'a pres-que fait vne converdy pour levidé.[31] J'ay veu la lettre que le chevailié nuthon vous a anvoiyé par conty.[32] il prestande que tous-cequ'il ya[33] mis sont des choses de faite.[34] J'atan avec empassiance votre reponce.[35] conty au moin ander nous ne trouvez au qu'vn savoir anfrance,[36] et dit que le tout consite andis pute[37] de religion. il vous conde[38] pour le plus grand home et Sr Jaisack nuwthon et trouvez[39] infiniment du savoir icy.[40] Je suis audesespoire[41] de voir que des persoñe dun sy[42] grand savoir que vous, et nuwthon ne soié pas reconsillié.[43] le publique profiderais[44] infiniment sy on le pouvoit[45] faire. Mais les grands homes ressamble ansela au femes qui ne c'este jamais[46] leur amans qu'avec le dernier chacrin[47] et mortification[48] mortelle et c'est ou vous estte logé[49] Méssieurs pour vos opinion[s]. J'ay dit au Roy et luy monterais aujour-dehuis[50] votre lettre ce qui est contre l'anvoiyé[51] de modene. Je crois que sy vous connessié le home, vous dire[52] avec la duchesse de choresbury, che pestia[54] et elle le dit toujours quand elle apersoit[55] son aimable pressance.[56] Permesté[57] moy de vous dire que tous les assistant ansamble[58] ne vous vauderon[59] pas. Ensy[60] Monsieur vous dire come tourno[61] dans vne de nos opera[s] de L[']Eveque de spica pas-ta soll d'is forcar touta la tera.[62,63] anfin je vous prirais de faire vne boñe pais, et a dacher ensamble afaire panser le monde plus justé par votre matématique et le randre mellieur par votre Philosophié,[64] au lieu de vous

115. Caroline* of Brandenburg-Ansbach, Princess of Wales, to Leibniz[1]

St James $\frac{5}{24}$ April 1716[2]

I have received all your letters, sir, but the great difficulties[3] that I have found in hearing[4] our bishops speak on the subject[5] of the reunion have left me in uncertainty[6] about responding to you until I had put it[7] a bit on a different path.[8] The archbishop[9] doesn't see[10] any other way than to introduce[11] the [church] service from here and send[12] some bishop to ordain ministers on the continent.[13] As regards the essential points, they are required, and people are content with them here.[14] You understand that that holds good only with regard to the ceremonial.[15] I believe that he would give us Lutherans the host.[16] Finally, sir, if you were ever to travel[17] here you would ascertain more than all[18] the letters in the world. But how is it that you suspect me of not being the same[19] for you? I believe that being steadfast for friends is one of the points of our duty, and I appeal to the king [George I, Georg Ludwig* of Braunschweig-Lüneburg] on account of it.[20] Doctor [Samuel] Clarke* has published nothing of what has passed between[21] you and him,[22] and what you probably heard about[23] are some letters that he and a Scottish clergyman wrote[24] some time ago. The Abbé Conti has taken the trouble to lose some of the papers[25] that you wanted me to entrust to him;[26] he promises[27] to find them again. This is what prevented me from sending you the last response of Clarke with this post.[28] Last Saturday I had the Abbé Conti and Clarke with me from six until ten o'clock.[29] I very much wanted you to support me;[30] their knowledge and Clarke's clear manner of reasoning nearly made me a convert to the void.[31] I have seen the letter that Chevalier Newton sent you through Conti.[32] He claims that everything he put in there[33] are matters of fact.[34] I impatiently await your response.[35] Conti, at least between us, does not find any knowledge in France[36] and says that the whole thing consists in dispute[37] about religion. He considers[38] you the greatest man, and Sir Isaac Newton is thought to be[39] infinitely knowledgeable here.[40] I am grieved[41] to see that persons of such[42] great knowledge as you and Newton are not reconciled.[43] The public would profit[44] immeasurably if it could[45] be done. But great men are in that like women, who never relinquish[46] their lovers but with the utmost chagrin[47] and extreme mortification,[48] and that is where you are lodged,[49] gentlemen, on account of your opinions. I spoke to the king and showed him your letter today,[50] which is in opposition to the envoy[51] from Modena. I believe that if you knew the man, you would say[52] with the Duchesse of Shrewsbury,[53] 'What a beast,'[54] and she always says it whenever she catches sight of[55] his amiable presence.[56] Permit[57] me to tell you that all the assistants together[58] will not be equal to[59] you. So[60] you will say, sir, like Turno[61] in one of our operas by the Bishop of Spiga [Agostino Steffani*], *basta sol di sforzar tutta la terra.*[62,63] Finally, I would ask that you to make a good

quereller. Je dis san an tere et vous doñe laboñ nouvelle[65] que nous avons anporté[66] le bille 7[tannial] dans lachamber pasce.[67,68] Je ne scest[69] pas de combien mais c'est du moin[s] de 100.[70] Sy vous autre Mes les matematissien, faisiez panser plus justé tout le monde serais de même santiment.[71] le santiment de vous estimer beaucoup sera toujours seluy[72] de

Caroline

Je suis bien aisez[73] quand vous alle[z] voir mon fils et je vous prie de le faire leplus souvant[74] que vous pourais.[75] apre[s] demain nous verons les experiment[76] du chevalié nuwthon. le Roy adonnez vne chamber a desagailiers[77] Je vous y souhaite coñe ausy pour samdy,[78] ou le chevalié nuwthon, l'abée conty, et chlerck seron[t] avec moy.

115. CAROLINE OF BRANDENBURG-ANSBACH TO LEIBNIZ 515

peace and to endeavor together to make people think more precisely with your mathematics and to make them better with your philosophy,[64] instead of quarreling. I speak without concealing any of it and give you the good news[65] that we have carried[66] the septennial bill in the House of Commons.[67,68] I don't know[69] by how many, but it is at least by 100.[70] If you made other mathematicians think more accurately, everyone would be of the same sentiment.[71] The sentiment of esteeming you very much will always be that[72] of

Caroline

I am very glad[73] when you go to see my son [Friedrich Ludwig* of Braunschweig-Lüneburg], and I ask you to do it as often[74] as you can.[75] The day after tomorrow we will see the experiments[76] of Chevalier Newton. The king has provided a room for [John Theophilus] Desaguliers*.[77] I wish for you there, as well as for Saturday,[78] when Chevalier Newton, the Abbé Conti, and Clarke will be with me.

[1] LBr. F 4 Bl. 54r–57r. Letter as sent: 6.1 quarto sides in Caroline's hand. Previously published in Klopp XI 90–2; Schüller 1991, p. 244 (excerpt in German translation); Robinet 1991, p. 66 (excerpt); HGA 193–4 (excerpt in English translation). This is Caroline's response to Leibniz's letter of 28 April 1716 (document 113). For Leibniz's reply, see his letter to Caroline of 12 May 1716 (document 117a).

[2] That is, 5 May (NS)/24 April (OS) 1716.

[3] Reading 'grandes difficultés' for 'grande dificuldé'.

[4] Reading 'j'ai trouvées à entendre' for 'j'ay trouvez a antandre'.

[5] Reading 'Evêques sur le chapitre' for 'Eveque sur le chapitr'.

[6] Reading 'laissée dans l'incertitude' for 'laissez dans l'insertidute'.

[7] Reading 'répondre, jusqu'à ce que je l'eusse' for 'reponder, jus qu'as ceque je l'ais eut'.

[8] Reading 'chemin' for 'chemain'.

[9] Presumably, the Archbishop of Canterbury, William Wake*.

[10] Reading 'voit' for 'vois'. Klopp mistranscribes 'vois' as 'croit' (see Klopp XI 90).

[11] Reading 'manière que introduire' for 'manier que d'introtuire'.

[12] Reading 'passer' for 'passere'.

[13] Reading 'ministres au-delà de la mer' for 'ministre aude la mere'.

[14] Reading 'Pour les points essentiels ils sont réquis et l'on s'en contente ici' for 'Pour les point essansielle elle sont requse et lon sans contante icy'. Klopp mistranscribes the sentence as 'Pour les points essentiels l'on consent icy' (see Klopp XI 90).

[15] Reading 'Vous voyez que ça ne consiste que sur le cérémoniel' for 'Vous voiyé que sa ne conssisté que sur le seromoniel'.

[16] That is, offer the Lutherans communion; reading 'autres luthériens il nous passerait l'hostie' for 'autre l'uderrien il nous passerais L'ostié'. This entire sentence is omitted by Klopp (see Klopp XI 90).

[17] Reading 'vous faisiez un voyage' for 'vous faisiée vn voiagé'.

[18] Reading 'détermineriez plus que toutes' for 'desterminerié plut que toute'.

[19] Reading 'soupçonnez de n'être la même' for 'soupsonié de nestre lamême'.

[20] Reading 'j'en appelle au Roy' for 'j'an apelle au Roy'.

[21] Reading 'n'a rien imprimé de ce qui s'est passé entre' for 'n'an rien imprimé de ce qui ces passez antre'.

[22] On Leibniz's suspicion that Clarke has published something about their correspondence, see his letter to Caroline of 28 April 1716 (document 113), pp. 501 and 503 note 5.

[23] Reading 'ce dont vous aurez entendu parler' for 'don vous aurais antantu parler'.

[24] Reading 'écrites' for 'écrit'.

[25] Reading 'a pris la peine de perdre quelques-uns des papiers' for 'apris lapeñe de pertre quelque vn des papié'.

[26] Reading 'que je lui confie' for 'que je luy du confier'. Klopp mistranscribes the latter as 'que je luy puisse confier' (see Klopp XI 91). Clarke's Third Reply was apparently among the papers that Conti had misplaced.

516   115. CAROLINE OF BRANDENBURG-ANSBACH TO LEIBNIZ

115. CAROLINE OF BRANDENBURG-ANSBACH TO LEIBNIZ 517

[27] Reading 'promet' for 'promest'.

[28] Reading 'C'est ce qui m'a empêchée cette poste de vous envoyer la réponse dernière de Clarke' for 'ces ce qui manpeché ceste poste de vous anvoiyer la reponce dernier de chlercke'.

[29] Reading 'Samedi passé j'eus depuis 6 jusqu'à dix heures l'Abbé Conti et Clarke avec moi' for 'Samdy passez j'eu dé puis 6 jus-qu'a dis heur, L'abée conty et chlerck avec moy'.

[30] Reading 'ai souhaité beaucoup pour me soutenir' for 'ayée souhaité beaucoup pour me soudenir'. Klopp mistranscribes 'ayée souhaité' as 'aurois souhaité' (see Klopp XI 91).

[31] Reading 'presque fait une convertie pour le vide' for 'pres-que fait vne converdy pour levidé'. This is mistranscribed by Klopp as 'presque fait me convertir pour le vuide' (see Klopp XI 91).

[32] Reading 'envoyée par Conti' for 'anvoiyé par conty'. The reference is to Newton's letter to Conti of 17 March 1716 (document 101g).

[33] Reading 'prétend que tout ce qu'il y a' for 'prestande que tous cequ'il ya'.

[34] Reading 'fait' for 'faite'.

[35] Reading 'J'attends avec impatience votre réponse' for 'J'atan avec empassiance votre reponce'. Klopp mistranscribes 'empassiance' as 'empressement' (see Klopp XI 91).

[36] Reading 'Conti au moins entre nous ne trouve aucun savoir en France' for 'Conty au moin ander nous ne trouvez au qu'vn savoir anfrance'.

[37] Reading 'consiste en dispute' for 'consite andis pute'.

[38] Reading 'compte' for 'conde'.

[39] Reading 'est trouvé' for 'et trouvez'.

[40] Klopp omits the previous two sentences (see Klopp XI 91).

[41] Reading 'au désespoir' for 'audesespoire'.

[42] Reading 'personnes d'un si' for 'persoñe dun sy'.

[43] Reading 'ne soient pas réconciliés' for 'ne soié pas reconsillié'.

[44] Reading 'public profiterais' for 'publique profiderais'.

[45] Klopp mistranscribes 'pouvoit' as 'pourroit' (see Klopp XI 91).

[46] Reading 'ressemblent en cela aux femmes qui ne cèdent jamais' for 'ressamble ansela au feñes qui ne c'este jamais'.

[47] Reading 'dernière chagrin' for 'dernier chacrin'.

[48] Klopp mistranscribes 'mortification' as 'colère' (see Klopp XI 91).

[49] Reading 'estes logés' for 'estte logé'.

[50] Reading 'montrais aujourd'hui' for 'monterais aujour-dehuis'. Klopp mistranscribes 'monterais' as 'montreray' (see Klopp XI 91).

[51] Reading 'l'envoyé' for 'l'anvoiyé'.

[52] Reading 'connaissiez le homme, vous diriez' for 'connessié le hoñe, vous dire'.

[53] That is, Duchess Adelhida Paleotti Talbot (1660–1726), wife of Charles Talbot, first duke of Shrewsbury. She was Caroline's Lady of the Bedchamber.

[54] Reading 'bestia' for 'pestia'.

[55] Reading 'aperçoit' for 'apersoit'.

[56] Reading 'présence' for 'pressance'.

[57] Reading 'permettez' for 'permesté'.

[58] Reading 'assistants ensembles' for 'assistant ansamble'.

[59] Reading 'vaudrons' for 'vauderon'.

[60] Reading 'Ainsi' for 'ensy'.

[61] Reading 'direz comme Turno' for 'dire coñe tourno'.

[62] Reading 'basta sol di sforzare tutta la terra' for 'pas-ta soll d'is forcar touta la tera': 'He alone is enough to subjugate the entire land'. Caroline is referring to a line spoken by Turno (Turnus) in Agostino Steffani's opera, *I trionfi del fato* (1695), which was written while he was Kapellmeister at the Hanoverian court of Ernst August (the libretto was written by Ortensio Mauro). The line is spoken by Turno at the end of the first speech of act 3, scene 3. In the brief preceding scene, Turno had proposed an alliance of mutual aid with Iarba (Iarbas), which the latter scornfully rejected. Iarba exits after his aria ('Tu rompesti, disciogliesti i sacri nodi'), leaving Turno alone on the stage. Turno then gives vent to astonishment and rage. He does not care what Iarba decides to do: 'I alone', he asserts, 'am enough to subjugate the entire land' (*Io sol basto a sforzare tutta la terra*). I am very grateful to Colin Timms of the University of Birmingham (England) for finding this line in his copy of the libretto of *I trionfi* and for explaining the context of the scene in which it occurs.

[63] Klopp omits the last two sentences without notice (see Klopp XI 91).

Johann Caspar von Bothmer to Leibniz

$$\text{à Londres ce } \frac{24^{\text{me}} \text{ Avril}}{5^{\text{me}} \text{ May}} \ 1716$$

Monsieur

J'apprens[3] avec beaucoup de regret par l'honneur de vostre lettre du 28eme Avril qu'on vous a envoyé une sorte de provocation de la part de Mr Nuton, je suis persuadé que le Roy scaura mauvais grés à ceux qui l'ont fait, puisque cela vous chagrine et vous detourne des occupations que vous vous donnés pour son service, pour l'utilité du public, et pour vostre propre gloire qui certe[s] sera bien plus grande et plus eternisée par vostre histoire que par une dispute sur une matiere ou parmis[5] mille personnes à peine un seul comprent[6] quelque chose. vostre silence loin de vous estre prejudiciable marquera un genereux mepris de la part d'une personne qui a comme vous des occupations plus illustres. Le Roy luy méme et ses plus grands Ministres en usent de cette maniere lor[s]qu'on publie par l'impression mème des injures contre eux.

[64] Reading 'Enfin je vous prierais de faire une bonne paix, et de tâcher ensemble à faire penser le monde plus juste par votre mathématique et le rendre meilleur par votre philosophie' for 'anfin je vous prirais de faire vne boñe pais, et a dacher ensamble afaire panser le monde plus justé par votre matématique et le randre mellieur par votre philosophié'.

[65] Reading 'Je dis sans en taire et vous donne la bonne nouvelle' for 'Je dis san an tere et vous doñe laboñnouvelle'.

[66] Reading 'emporté' for 'anporté'.

[67] Reading 'la chambre basse' for 'lachamber pasce'.

[68] Klopp simply replaces this entire sentence with 'je dis l'un et l'autre' (see Klopp XI 91).

[69] Reading 'sais' for 'scest'.

[70] Klopp omits this entire sentence without notice (see Klopp XI 91). Caroline is referring to the Septennial Act, which was passed by the House of Commons on 26 April 1716 (OS). The bill increased the maximum length of a parliament, and hence the maximum period between general elections, from three to seven years. The bill was favoured by the members of the royal family and their Whig allies because it had the effect of keeping the Whig party in power for a longer period of time (the Whigs had won the general election of 1715). The vote recorded was 264 'Tellers for the Yeas' and 121 'Tellers for the Noes', which accords with Caroline's guess that the bill passed by at least 100 votes (see JHC XVIII 432, under the heading 'Septennial Parliaments'). Caroline's letter is dated 24 April 1716 (OS), which suggests that she started the letter on that day and finished it after learning of the passage of the Septennial Act two days later.

[71] Reading 'Si vous autres Mes. les mathématiciens faisiez penser plus juste tout le monde serait de même sentiment' for 'Sy vous autre Mes les matematissien, faisiez panser plus justé tout le monde serais de même santiment'. Klopp transcribed the sentence as 'Si vous autres mathématiciens faisiez penser plus juste tout le monde serait de même sentiment', thus omitting 'Mes les' (see Klopp XI 91).

[72] Reading 'celui' for 'seluy'.

[73] Reading 'aise' for 'aisez'.

[74] Reading 'le plus souvent' for 'leplus souvant'.

[75] Reading 'pourrez' for 'pourais'.

[76] Reading 'verrons les experimens' for 'verons les experiment'.

[77] Reading 'Le Roy a donné une chambre à Desaguliers' for 'Le Roy adonnez vne chamber a desagailiers'. Klopp mistranscribes the sentence as 'Le Roy a donné un chambre pour cela' (see Klopp XI 92).

[78] Reading 'comme aussi pour Samedi' for 'coñe ausy pour samdy'.

116. Johann Caspar von Bothmer* to Leibniz[1]

in London $\frac{24 \text{ April}}{5 \text{ May}}$ 1716[2]

Sir

I learn[3] with great regret by the honour of your letter of 28 April [document 114] that you were sent a kind of provocation from Mr. Newton. I am persuaded that the king [George I, Georg Ludwig* of Braunschweig-Lüneburg] will be displeased with those who have done it, since that upsets you and diverts you from occupations to which you devote yourself for his service, for the benefit of the public, and for your own glory, which will most certainly be much greater and more immortalized by your history[4] than by a dispute concerning a matter about which, among[5] a thousand persons, scarcely a single one understands[6] anything. Your silence, far from being prejudicial to you, will bespeak a noble contempt on the part of a person who has, like you, some more illustrious occupations. The king himself, and his greatest ministers, make us of this behavior when even some insults against them are published in print.

Je ne doute pas au reste que l'ordre pour vous paier[7] vos arrèrages n'aye esté donné desia,[8] je suis bien aise que vous avés satisfaction la des[s]us aussi bien que de la cour de Modene, estant avec tout le zele possible

Monsieur
        Vostre

                        tres humble et tres
                        obeissant serviteur
                        Bothmer

Leibniz to Caroline of Brandenburg-Ansbach, Princess of Wales

Hanover ce 12 de May 1716   A Madame la princesse de Galles
Madame

Je demande pardon à V. A. R. si j'ay craint quelque refroidissement. C'est une marque combien ses bontés me sont precieuses. La maniere d'agir de l'Abbé Conti, a contribué à mes soubçons. Elle est un peu irreguliere à mon egard, et je le luy ay fait sentir par une reponse aussi seche que sa lettre, mais cela n'importe gueres. Il ne paroist pas avoir des principes fixes, et ressemble au Cameleon qui prend (dit on) la couleur des choses qu'il touche. Quand il repassera en France, on le fera retourner du vuide au plein. Quand on verra ma reponse à la lettre de M. Newton, on trouvera que les fondemens de ses pretensions contre moy, sont des faits imaginaires; et ce qu'on peut alleguer contre luy, n'est que trop reel. Puisqu'on m'attaque de gayeté de coeur et d'une mauvaise maniere, peut on trouver mauvais que je me defende, et que je fasse un peu sentir leur tort à ces gens la? Le monde hors de l'Angleterre n'est gueres pour eux. M. Newton n'effacera pas ce que M. Bernoulli luy a opposé, qu'il a taché inutilement de gagner. Quand ils cesseront de m'imputer des mauvais tours pour s'attribuer leur prerogative imaginare je les laisseray en repos, et dissimuleray ce qu'on leur impute. Plus ils entreront en dispute avec moy, plus ils decouvriront leur foible. Ils seroient demeurés plus philosophes, s'ils s'etoient tûs. <u>Si tacuisses, philosophus mansisses.</u>[4] Ils ont fait entrer la philosophie dans la dispute. A la

To conclude, I do not doubt that the order to pay[7] you your arrearages has already been given.[8] I am very glad that you have satisfaction on that point, as well as from the court of Modena, being with all possible enthusiasm,

sir

your

very humble and very
obedient servant
Bothmer

---

[1] LBr. 97 Bl. 142r–142v. Letter as sent: two quarto sides in Bothmer's hand. Previously published in Klopp XI 92 (excerpt).

[2] That is, 24 April 1716 OS and 5 May 1716 NS.

[3] Reading 'apprends' for 'apprens'.

[4] Bothmer is here referring to Leibniz's work on the history of the House of Braunschweig-Lüneburg, his so-called *Annales imperii occidentis Brunsvicenses**.

[5] Reading 'parmi' for 'parmis'.

[6] Reading 'comprend' for 'comprent'.

[7] Reading 'payer' for 'paier'.

[8] Reading 'déjà' for 'desia'.

117a. Leibniz to Caroline* of Brandenburg-Ansbach, Princess of Wales[1]

Hanover 12 May 1716   To Madame the Princess of Wales

Madame

I beg pardon of Your Royal Highness if I have feared some coolness. It is a sign of how precious her kindnesses are to me. The behavior of the Abbé Conti has contributed to my suspicions. It is a bit irregular toward to me, and I made him aware of it with a response as harsh as his letter,[2] but that scarcely matters. He does not appear to have any fixed principles and resembles the chameleon, which is said to take the colour of the things that it touches. When he returns to France, he will return from the void to the plenum. When my response to the letter of Mr. Newton is seen, it will be found that the bases of his claims against me are imaginary facts, and what can be alleged against him is only too real. Since I am attacked out of sheer wantonness and in a malicious way, can it be considered wrong that I defend myself and make these people feel a bit of their injustice? The world outside of England is scarcely on their side. Mr. Newton will not erase what Mr. [Johann]Bernoulli*, whom he has tried vainly to win over, has said against him.[3] When they cease imputing dirty tricks to me in order to claim their imaginary prerogative, I will leave them alone and conceal what is imputed to them. The more they enter into dispute with me, the more they will discover their weakness. They would have remained more philosophical if they had been silent. *If you had been silent, you would have remained a philosopher.*[4]

bonne heure, ils m'obligent par là de faire sentir le foible de la leur, dont sans cela je ne me serois point soucié. J'aurois poursuivi mes meditations sans attaquer celles d'autruy. Mr Newton s'est laissé persuader par des gens malins qu'on l'avoit maltraité dans les Actes de Leipzig. C'est ce qui l'a mis en feu, à ce qu'il a temoigné à quelques uns, et cependant cela se trouve tout a fait faux et mal entendu. Si la connoissance de sa meprise est capable de le faire rentrer en luy même, et de penser à la reconciliation, j'en seray[6] content. Mais s'il persiste neantmoins dans son opiniastreté à la bonne heure tant pis pour luy, puisqu'il s'attribue luy même à toute force ce que personne [n']avoit voulu dire de luy. Cependant je suis bien aise que le Roy a voulu voir les experiences de M. Newton. Cela servira à encourager les Anglois pour tourner l'esprit aux choses plus solides que leur disputes ordinaires.[7]

Si j'osois appliquer une phrase peu serieuse, à une matiere, qui l'est infiniment, je dirois que ce personnage que V. A. Royale a consulté a pris le Roman par la queue[8]. Faut il commencer par le ceremoniel pendant qu'on est en scission sur[9] des choses plus importantes. Il s'agit de traiter entre Brandenbourg et Bronsvic, et que les Anglois y soyent les mediateurs, voilà le plan le plus naturel. Les predecesseurs Morton, Davenant, Hall grands hommes dans leur temps, qui ont fait des ouvrages expres sur la matiere, ont raisonné tout autrement que cet ami. Il faut qu'il n'ait pas bien compris ce qu'il vouloit; ou (entre nous) il est à craindre qu'il n'ait gueres de zele. Son successeur n'y entrerat-il pas mieux? Jamais les conjonctures ont esté plus favorables, et c'est peché de les negliger. Combien ces grands hommes d'autres fois auroient il[s][12] souhaité de voir des conjonctures si favorable[s], dont leur successeur[s] savent si peu profiter? Viel Propheten und Konige wolten sehen das ihr sehet, und habens nicht gesehen.[13]

On dit que dans un imprimé M. Clarke a touché mon opinion de l'espace à la bonne heure. Si l'Abbé Conti ne retrouve point le dernier papier, j'en enverray une copie. Puisqu'on a preché le vuide à V. A. Royale, je mets mon sentiment la dessus sur un papier à part. Car cette lettre ce semble n'est pas pour étre veue ailleurs.

Madame la Duchesse d'orleans me fait l'honneur de me dire que V. A. Royale luy écrit toutes les semaines deux lettres bien considerables. Oserois je demander si c'est en françois ou en Allemand? V. A. Royale en ecrit bien d'autres encore. Apres cela, il faut que je m'etonne qu'Elle a trouvé encore quelque temps pour moy. Cela me console de ce que V. A. Royale a paru un peu chancelante non pas dans sa bonne volonté à mon egard, mais peut etre dans sa bonne opinion de moy et de mes opinions, sur tout depuis qu'il semble que la version de la Theodicée demeure en arriere.

Je suis avec devotion etc.

117A. LEIBNIZ TO CAROLINE OF BRANDENBURG-ANSBACH 523

They introduced philosophy into the dispute. Well and good. In doing so they force me to make them aware of the weakness of theirs, about which I would not otherwise have been concerned. I would have pursued my thoughts without attacking those of others. Mr. Newton has allowed himself to be persuaded by some malicious people that he had been mistreated in the *Acta Eruditorum* of Leipzig.[5] This is what has inflamed him, according to what he has confided to some, and yet it is entirely false and mistaken. If the recognition of his error is able to bring him back to his senses and bring him to think about reconciliation, I will be[6] satisfied with it. But if he nevertheless persists in his obstinacy, well and good, so much the worse for him, since he attributes to himself at all costs what no one had wanted to say about him. Nevertheless, I am very glad that the king [George I, Georg Ludwig* of Braunschweig-Lüneburg] wanted to see the experiments of Mr. Newton. That will serve to encourage the English to turn their attention to things more substantial than their usual disputes.[7]

If I dared apply a not very serious adage to a matter that is exceedingly so, I would say that this person that Your Royal Highness has consulted has taken the romance by the tail.[8] Must we begin with the ceremonial while people are in schism over[9] more important matters? It is a matter of negotiating between Brandenburg and Braunschweig, and let the English be the mediators in it; that is the most natural plan.[10] The predecessors, Morton, Davenant, Hall, great men in their time who have produced some works expressly about this matter,[11] have argued completely otherwise than this friend [of yours, William Wake*, Archbishop of Canterbury]. He must not have entirely understood what he wanted; or (between us) it is to be feared that he has scarcely any zeal. Won't his successor enter into it more agreeably? Never have circumstances been more favourable, and it is a sin to neglect them. These great men of the past, how much would they[12] have wanted to see such favourable circumstances, from which their successors know how to profit so little? *Many prophets and kings desired to see what you see and have not seen it.*[13]

It is said that in a printed paper Mr. [Samuel] Clarke* has touched on my view about space.[14] Well and good. If the Abbé Conti does not recover the last paper, I will send a copy of it. Since the void has been preached to Your Royal Highness, I am putting my view about it in a separate paper [document 117b]. For this letter, it appears, is not intended to be seen elsewhere.

Madame the Duchess of Orléans [Elisabeth Charlotte* of the Palatinate] has done me the honour of telling me that Your Royal Highness writes two substantial letters to her every week. Dare I ask whether it is in French or in German? Your Royal Highness writes many others as well. After that I have to be amazed that she has still found some time for me. That consoles me about the fact that Your Royal Highness has seemed a bit wavering, not in her good will toward me, but perhaps in her good opinion of me and of my views, above all since it seems that the translation of the *Theodicy* remains in arrears.

I am with devotion etc.

117A. LEIBNIZ TO CAROLINE OF BRANDENBURG-ANSBACH 525

[1] LBr. F 4 Bl. 60r. Draft: 1 folio side in Leibniz's hand. Previously published in Klopp XI 100–2; Schüller 1991, pp. 245–6 (excerpt in German translation). This is Leibniz's response to Caroline's letter of 5 May 1716 (document 115). For Caroline's response, see her letter to Leibniz of 26 May 1716 (document 122). For the P. S. that Leibniz added to this letter on the topic of atoms and the void, see document 117b.

[2] See Leibniz's letter to Conti of 9 April 1716 (document 108).

[3] Johann Bernoulli* (1667–1748) was a prominent Swiss mathematician. He and his older brother J were instrumental in developing and promulgating Leibniz's version of the calculus. Johann took Leibniz's side in the priority dispute with Newton over the discovery of the calculus, and he became his most ardent and able defender. In referring to what Bernoulli had said against Newton, Leibniz was almost certainly referring to what Bernoulli had said in a letter to Leibniz of 7 June 1713. Bernoulli was prompted to write the letter when his nephew Nikolaus brought him a copy of the *Commercium Epistolicum** from Paris. The *Commercium Epistolicum*, of course, was Newton's own account of the priority dispute with Leibniz, which had been officially approved, published (along with extracts from letters and other documents relevant to the dispute), and distributed gratis (in January–February 1713) among the learned in Europe by the Royal Society of London, of which Newton was then president. Not surprisingly, it came down roundly on the side of Newton, concluding that he was 'the first inventor' of the calculus and that Leibniz had at first concealed, and later denied, his knowledge of the prior achievements of Newton (see Hall 1980, pp. 178–9). In his letter, Bernoulli summed up the contents of the pamphlet: 'you are at once accused before a tribunal consisting, as it seems, of the participants and witnesses themselves, as if charged with plagiary, then documents against you are produced, sentence is passed; you lose the case, you are condemned' (NC VI 3). Bernoulli went on to summarize the main points of the dispute up to that point, mentioning in particular the letter that John Keill* sent to the Royal Society, in which he defended his claim, made in a paper published in the *Philosophical Transactions* for 1708 (published in 1710), that Newton had clearly discovered the calculus before Leibniz and that this calculus 'was afterwards published by Mr Leibniz in the *Acta Eruditorum* [in 1684] having changed the name and the symbolism' (as quoted in Hall 1980, p. 145). Based on, among other things, a misinterpretation (due ultimately to Bernoulli's nephew, Nikolaus) of the source of an error that Newton had made in his argument for Proposition 10 of Book II of the first edition of the *Principia*, Bernoulli was led, in turn, to accuse Newton of plagiarism, telling Leibniz that 'it is clear that the true way of differentiating differentials was not known to Newton until long after it was familiar to us' (NC VI 5; and see Hall 1980, pp. 194–9). But he then added that 'I do indeed beg you to use what I now write properly and not to involve me with Newton and his people, for I am reluctant to be involved in these disputes or to appear ungrateful to Newton who has heaped testimonies of his goodwill upon me' (ibid.). Leibniz, for his part, decided to prepare and distribute a leaflet, dated 29 July 1713 and known as the *Charta Volans* ('flying paper'), in which, writing in the third person, he attacked the *Commercium Epistolicum*. He quoted from Bernoulli's letter, describing it as asserting 'the judgment of a leading mathematician most skilled in these matters and free from bias', and then added:

> From these words it will be gathered that when Newton took to himself the honour due to another of the analytical discovery or differential calculus first discovered by Leibniz in numbers and then transferred (after having contrived the analysis of infinitesimals) to Geometry, because Newton was content with the fame of advancing [geometry] synthetically or directly by infinitely small quantities (or as they were formerly but less correctly called, the indivisibles of geometry), he was too much influenced by flatterers ignorant of the earlier course of events and by a desire for renown; having undeservedly obtained a partial share in this, through the kindness of a stranger, he longed to have deserved the whole—a sign of a mind neither fair nor honest. Of this [Robert] Hooke too has complained, in relation to the hypothesis of planets, and [John] Flamsteed* because of the use of [his] observations. [NC VI 18–19]

Although Leibniz did not mention Bernoulli by name in the original Latin version of the *Charta Volans*—thus honouring Bernoulli's request that Leibniz not 'involve me with Newton and his people'— Leibniz did let the cat out of the bag two years later in a letter he sent to Du Sauzet, the editor of weekly journal, *Nouvelles littéraires*, at the end of 1715. The letter was written in response to a brief review, published in the *Nouvelles littéraires* for 21 September 1715, of Newton's 'An Account of the Book Entitled *Commercium Epistolicum Collinii et aliorum, de analysi promota*', which Newton had published anonymously in the *Philosophical Transactions of the Royal Society of London* in the spring of 1715 (see document 56). Leibniz included with his letter a French translation of the extract from the letter by

117A. LEIBNIZ TO CAROLINE OF BRANDENBURG-ANSBACH   527

an 'eminent mathematician' that he had printed in Latin in the *Charta Volans*; but this time he wrote at the head of the extract, 'Lettre de M. Jean Bernoulli de Bâle, du 7 de Juin 1713'. So in his present letter to Caroline, Leibniz felt free to allude to 'what Mr. Bernoulli has said against' Newton.

⁴ This saying is generally thought to be based on the following short parable from Boethius' *Consolation of Philosophy*:

> You thought you were a philosopher, but let me tell you a story. There was a man who made such a claim, not from a dedication to truth and reason but out of vanity, as a way of enhancing his reputation. Somebody came along to taunt him and suggested that he was a fraud. And this critic said that he would believe the claim if the man could bear all the injuries fate heaped upon him in calm and in silence. Then he would admit that the fellow was a philosopher. Well, the other one adopted a patient manner and for months and even years bore up under the insults and injuries of life. And then he asked his challenger, 'Now do you admit that I am a philosopher?' To which the reply was, 'I would have, if you had kept silent.' [Boethius 2008, pp. 54–5]

⁵ In the *Acta Eruditorum* for January 1705 (pp. 30–6), Leibniz wrote an anonymous review of the two mathematical tracts that Newton had published along with the first edition of the *Opticks* in 1704— namely, *Enumeratio linearum tertii ordinis* and *De quadrature cuvarum*. In his letter to Leibniz of 7 June 1713, Bernoulli informed Leibniz of some of the contents of the recently distributed report of the Royal Society of London on the calculus priority dispute, the *Commercium Epistolicum*:

> They declare that the review of Newton's tracts *Enumeratio linearum tertii ordinis* and *De quadrature curvarum* published in the *Acta* [*Eruditorum*] of Leipzig for January 1705 is written in your style; moreover, they later on attribute it expressly to you, as its author. This review provides a particular excuse for complaint and provokes the gall of your accusers, inasmuch as they judge it to detract from Newton's inventions. And so Keill was stirred up by this to vindicate Newton's claim to his discoveries (in a letter printed in the *Philosophical Transactions*) and to show that the calculus of fluxions was invented before the differential calculus; indeed that the latter was adapted from the former (with a simple change of name and method of notation), and so having been thus stolen from Newton was published by you under a disguise in the *Acta Eruditorum*. [NC VI 3]

In his response of 17 June 1713, Leibniz falls just short of explicitly denying the truth that he was indeed the author of the review in the *Acta Eruditorum*:

> Your nephew writes to me that in the Leipzig review of which they complain the inventions of [Ehrenfried Walther von] Tschirnhaus are greatly praised. I do not clearly recollect, but if it is so you may readily judge that that review of Newton's book was not by me; for I could not promise, as you know, to think so well of Mr. Tschirnhaus. [ibid., p. 8]

⁶ Klopp mistranscribes 'seray' as 'serois' (see Klopp XI 101).

⁷ Klopp omits the last three sentences without notice (see Klopp XI 101).

⁸ A French saying meaning to marry before making love; or, the other way around, something said of a young woman who lives with a man as if he were her husband, but prior to being married to him. In either case: to put the cart before the horse.

⁹ Klopp mistranscribes 'sur' as 'par' (see Klopp XI 101).

¹⁰ The Electorate of Brandenburg was officially a Calvinist state, while that of Braunschweig (Hanover) was Lutheran. Leibniz thought that the English, representing Anglicanism, the third great branch of reformation Protestantism, could, with George I at its head, act as an honest broker between the Calvinists of Brandenburg and the Lutherans of Hanover.

¹¹ Thomas Morton (1564–1659) was Bishop of Chester from 1616 to 1618 and then of Durham from 1632 to 1646; Joseph Hall (1574–1656) was Bishop of Exeter from 1627–1641 and then of Norwich from 1641–1656; John Davenant (1572–1641) was Bishop of Salisbury from 1621 to 1641. All three were supporters of the Scottish Calvinist minister John Dury* (or Durie) (1596–1680), who crusaded for the reconciliation of the Calvinist and Lutheran churches. In 1641 he published his *Good Counsells for the Peace of Reformed Churches*, in which he published the bishops' reasons for believing that the Protestant churches could be reconciled (see Harris 1983, pp. 22–3).

¹² Klopp omits 'il' (see Klopp XI 101).

¹³ Luke 10:24.

¹⁴ For further information about this issue, see Leibniz's letter to Caroline of 28 April 1716 (document 113, pp. 501, 503 note 5).

Leibniz to Caroline of Brandenburg-Ansbach, Princess of Wales

cela doit etre joint a la lettre de[2] Madame la princesse de Galles écrite

P. S.   le 12 de may 1716

Tous ceux qui sont pour le vuide se laissent plus mener par l'imagination que par la raison. Quand j'étois jeune garçon je donnay aussi dans le vuide et dans les Atomes, mais la raison me ramena. L'imagination etoit riante; on borne là se[s] recherches, on fixe la meditation comme avec un clou; on croit avoir trouvé les premiers Elemens, un non plus ultra. Nous voudrions que la nature n'allât pas plus loin, et qu'elle fut finie comme notre esprit: mais c'est ne point connoistre la grandeur et la Majesté de l'Auteur des choses. Le moindre corpuscule est actuelle[me]nt subdivisé à infini et contient un monde de nouvelles creatures, dont l'univers manqueroit si ce corpuscule étoit un Atome, c'est à dire un corps tout d'une piece sans subdivision. Tout de même vouloir du vuide dans la nature, c'est attribuer à Dieu une production tres imparfaite; c'est violer le grand principe de la necessité d'une raison suffisante, que bien des gens ont eu dans la bouche, mais dont ils n'ont point connu la force; comme j'ay monstré dernierement, en faisant voir par ce principe, que l'espace n'est qu'un ordre des choses, comme le temps, et nullement un Estre absolu.

Sans parler de plusieurs autres raisons contre le vuide et les Atomes; en voicy celles que je prends de la perfection de Dieu, et de la raison suffisante. Je pose que toute perfection que Dieu a pû mettre dans les choses, sans deroger aux autres perfections qui y sont, y a eté mise. Or figurons nous un espace vuide,[4] Dieu y pouvoit mettre quelque matiere, sans deroger en rien à toutes les autres choses. Donc il y a mise.[6] Donc il n'y a point d'espace entierement vuide quelque petit qu'il soit. Donc tout est plein. La meme raisonnement prouve qu'il n'y a point de corpuscule, qui ne soit subdivisé.

Voicy encore l'autre raisonnement pris de la necessité d'une raison suffisante. Il n'est point possible[7] qu'il y ait un principe de determiner la proportion de la matiere ou du rempli au vuide, du vuide au plein. On dira peutetre que l'un doit etre egal à l'autre, mais comme la matiere est plus parfaite que le vuide, la raison veut qu'on observe la proportion geometrique, et qu'il y ait d'autant plus de plein qu'il merite d'etre preferé. Mais ainsi il n'y aura point de vuide du tout, car la perfection de la matiere est à celle du vuide, comme quelque chose à rien.

Il en est de même des Atomes, quelle raison peut on assigner de borner la nature dans le progrés de la subdivision? Fictions purement arbitraires et indignes de la vraye philosophie! Les raisons qu'on allegue pour le vuide ne sont que des sophismes.

117b. Leibniz to Caroline* of Brandenburg-Ansbach, Princess of Wales[1]

that is to be added to the letter written to[2] Madam the Princess of Wales

P. S.   12 May 1716

All those who are in favour of the void allow themselves to be led more by imagination than by reason. When I was a young boy, I also stumbled into the void and atoms, but reason brought me back. The imagination was pleasant; people confine their investigations there; they fix their thought as if with a nail; they believe they have found the first elements, a *non plus ultra*. We would have nature go no further and to be finite like our minds: but this is to fail to understand the grandeur and majesty of the author of things. The least corpuscle is actually subdivided to infinity and contains a world of new creatures, which the universe would lack if this corpuscle were an atom, that is to say, a body all of a piece without subdivision. Similarly, to admit a void in nature is to attribute to God a very imperfect production; it is to violate the great principle of the necessity of a sufficient reason, to which many people have given lip service, but whose force they have not understood at all, as I have recently demonstrated by showing that space is only an order of things, like time, and by no means an absolute being.

Without speaking of several other reasons against the void and atoms, here are those that I base on the perfection of God and sufficient reason. I postulate that every perfection that God[3] could have placed in things without derogating from the other perfections that are in them has been placed in them. Now let us imagine an empty space;[4] God[5] could place some matter there without derogating in any way from all the other things. Hence he placed some there.[6] Hence there is not any space entirely empty, however small it may be. Hence all is full. The same reasoning proves that there is no corpuscle which is not subdivided.

And here is the other argument, based on the necessity of a sufficient reason. It is not possible[7] that there be a principle for determining the proportion of matter, or plenum, to the void, of the void to the plenum. It will perhaps be said that one must be equal to the other, but since matter is more perfect than the void, reason determines that geometrical proportion is observed and that there is as much more of the plenum in proportion as it merits being preferred. But then there will not be any void at all, for the perfection of matter is to that of the void as something to nothing.

It is the same with atoms. What reason can be given to limit nature in the progression of subdivision? Fictions purely arbitrary and unworthy of the true philosophy! The reasons that are alleged for the void are only sophisms.

Louis Bourguet to Leibniz

Monsieur

Dés que j'eu receu l'honneur de vôtre Lettre du 3. d'avril, je récrivis à Milan afin de Solliciter de nouveau l'ami, que s'il se pouvoit il envoyat les graines, et j'atendois impatienment sa reponce, lorsque je reçoi[s] encore vôtre seconde du 20ᵉ du même mois. Mais comme jusqu'à present, je ne voi[s] rien venir de sa part, je conclû[s] que le tems étant trop avancé, il n'aura point envoyé les graines comme je l'en avois prié. Il me deplait extrémement de n'avoir pû reuscir à Vous rendre ce petit service, quoique je suis persuadé que vous me rendrez justice en croyant qu'au moins ce n['] est pas ma faute si vous n'avez pas été contenté.

Je ne manquerai pas, Monsieur, de suivre vôtre sage conseil, en tachant de donner s'il se peut une forme logique à mes pensées sur les trois hypotheses proposées à l'égard de la constitution de la univers, quoyque j'y apperçoive bien des difficultez.

Quand j'ai dit, que le resultat des perfections des êtres qui composent l'univers étoit comparable à une suite ou series infinie de Nombres dont la somme est finie; j'ai entendu simplement chaque état de l'univers consideré à part dont la perfection est limitée, et non le resultat entier de la suite infinie de ces états, qui est semblable à ces suites de nombres infinies dont la somme surpasse toute quantité assignable. Je fondois cette idée sur l'état de chaque singulier qui est veritablement une Series dont la somme est limitée, et de qui les rapports sont aussi limitez, quoiqu'ils puissent augmenter en nombre et par consequent en degré de perfection.

Si le rectangle avoit lieu, comme il n'admet point de commencement, je ne voi[s] pas pourquoi les productions de la sagesse, ne seroient pas coeternelles avec elle, quoi que leur changement empeche qu'elles soient d'une necessité de même nature que l'existence de la sagesse. Car s'il est impossible dans ce cas, d'assigner aucun état primitif aux productions of la sagesse, qui ait été précéde immediatement d'un état

118. BOURGUET TO LEIBNIZ   531

[1] LBr. F 4 Bl. 61r. Draft: 1 folio side in Leibniz's hand. This was correctly published in Klopp XI 102–3 as a postscript to Leibniz's letter to Caroline of 12 May 1716 (document 117a above), but Samuel Clarke* published it as a P.S. to Leibniz's Fourth Paper (see Clarke 1717, pp. 115–19).

[2] Reading 'à' for 'de'.

[3] In the published version, Clarke inserts a footnote here: '*See Dr. Clarke's Third Reply, § 9; and his Fourth Reply, § 22*' (Clarke 1717, p. 117).

[4] In the published version of the French text, 'entierement' is inserted after 'espace' and Clarke's English translation inserts 'wholly' before 'empty'(see Clarke 1717, pp. 116 and 117).

[5] In the published version, Clarke inserts a footnote here: '*See Dr. Clarke's Third Reply, § 9; and his Fourth Reply, § 22*' (Clarke 1717, p. 117).

[6] In the published version this sentence reads: 'Donc il l'y a mise', and I follow that reading here.

[7] In the published version, Clarke inserts a footnote here: '*See Dr. Clarke's Third Reply, § 9. and his Fourth Reply, § 22*'.

118. Louis Bourguet* to Leibniz[1]

[15 May 1716]

Sir

As soon as I had received the honour of your letter of 3 April [document 107], I wrote again to Milan in order to appeal again to the friend, that if he were able he might send the [silkworm] eggs, and I was waiting impatiently for his response when I received in addition your second of the 20th of this month [document 112]. But as I see nothing coming from him so far, I conclude that since the time is too advanced, he will not be able to succeed in rendering you this small service, although I am persuaded that you will do me justice by believing that at least it is not my fault if you have not been satisfied.[2]

I will not fail, sir, to follow your wise counsel by trying to give, if it is possible, a logical form to my thoughts about the three hypotheses proposed concerning the constitution of the universe,[3] although I perceive many difficulties with it.

When I said that the result of the perfections of the beings which compose the universe was comparable to an infinite succession or series of numbers whose sum is finite, I simply meant each state of the universe whose perfection is limited considered separately and not the entire result of the infinite succession of those states, which is similar to those infinite successions of numbers whose sum surpasses every assignable quantity. I based this idea on the state of each individual, which is really a series whose sum is limited and whose relations are also limited, although they can increase in number and, consequently, in degree of perfection.

If the rectangle obtained, since it does not admit a beginning, I do not see why the productions of wisdom would not be coeternal with it, although their change prevents them being from a necessity of the same nature as the existence of wisdom. For it is impossible in this case to assign any primitive state to the productions of wisdom that has been immediately preceded by a state of pure possibility. It will follow that it [wisdom] precedes its productions only in order alone. So the

de pure possibilité; il s'ensuivra qu'elle ne précéde ses productions qu'en ordre seulement. Ainsi la difference ne consistera que dans une precision metaphysique; puisque quant à l'essence les choses seront coeternelles dans un ordre de précédence, et quant à leur existence actuelle elles seront également éternelles qu'un ordre de consequence.

Il y auroit bien des choses à dire sur l'augmentation numerique des perfections égales dans chaque état de l'Univers; puis que deux emportant plus qu'un, et trois plus que deux, et ainsi de suite, il s'ensuit que l'univers consideré dans la nombre infini d'états dont il est capable, va toûjours en augmentant de perfection, ce qui cependant semble contraire à l'hypothese.

Il est vrai Monsieur, qu'il faut prémierement bien s'assurer des observations, avant que d'en venir au Calcul. Je commence à douter si la lune tourne veritablement autour de son axe. Les observations que j'ai faites depuis peu me paroissent rendre la chose encore douteuse. Si jamais j'ai loisir, je ne manquerai pas de reiterer mes observations, et même de les faire avec plus d'exactitude qu'auparavant. Mais il faudroit deux observateurs, l'un dans nôtre hemisphere, et le second dans l'autre.

Je croi[s] que Monsr Flamstead a raison sur ce qu'il croit que Mr Newton n'a pas assez employé les observations, principalement sur les cometes, dont on ne sauroit encore bien determiner le Systeme sans craindre de se tromper. Et je ne trouve rien si ridicule que la pretention de Mr Cheyne qui se sert du cours des cometes expliqué suivant Mr Newton, pour infirmer la circulation harmonique des corps celestes, que vous avez si sagement établie.

C'est precisément faute de prendre garde à la Maxime fondamentale de votre beau System; que rien ne se fait sans des raisons qui le determinent; que non seulement Mr Clarck, mais que tous les autres philosophes se sont trompez, et embarrassez dans mille difficultez dont ils n'ont pû sortir. C'est même ce qui a donné lieu au sentiment de Spinosa et d'autres semblables opinions qui n'ont absolument rien de tant soit peu raisonnable.

L'Anglois qui a semblé entrevoir quelque chose de la substance est Mr Barkeley Ecossois si je ne me trompe. Mais il s'embarasse dans les causes occasionnelles.

Je suis faché Monsieur, que vous soyez engagé, apparemment par the authorité de Sa Majesté, à travailler à l'histoire. C'est un travail dont peut-être quelqu'autre s'acquiteroit fort bien, au lieu que je ne sache personne au monde, qui peut mieux que vous Monsieur, rendre un trés-grand service au genre humain, en achevant de mettre au jour vôtre excellent système, soutenu des mathematiques. En effet, il faut des siecles avant qu'il vienne quelqu'un de ces heureux genies, qui penetrent dans les sciences sublimes, et qui savent les rendre utiles et agreables aux hommes. Je souhaite de tout mon coeur, qu'il plaise à Dieu cet etre si bon et si charitable, qu'il lui plaise dis-je vous conserver encore long tems en vie en santé, et veuille enfin vous fournir quelque occasion menagée par sa sage providence, afin que vous acheviez ce que vous avez autre fois si bien commencé.

difference will consist only in a metaphysical abstraction, since with regard to essence things will be coeternal in an order of precedence, and with regard to their actual existence they will also be eternal in an order of consequence.

There would be many things to say about the numerical increase of equal perfections in each state of the universe; since two gains more than one, and three more than two, and so on, it follows that the universe, considered as the infinite number of states of which it is capable, always progresses by increasing perfection, which, however, seems contrary to the hypothesis [of the rectangle].

It is true, sir, that we must first be sure of the observations before coming to the calculation of them. I began to doubt whether the moon really turns around its axis. The observations I have recently made appear to me to make it still doubtful. If I ever have spare time, I will not fail to repeat my observations, and even to make them with more precision than before. But it would require two observers, one in our hemisphere and the second in the other.

I believe that Mr. [John] Flamsteed* is right about what he believes, that Mr. Newton does not employ observations enough, principally about comets, whose system could still not be entirely determined without fear of error. And I find nothing so ridiculous as the claim of Mr. [George] Cheyne*, who makes use of the course of the comets, explained in accordance with Mr. Newton, to invalidate the harmonic circulation of the celestial bodies that you have so wisely established.[4]

It is precisely the failure to realize the fundamental maxim of your beautiful system, that nothing happens without some reasons that determine it, that not only Mr. [Samuel] Clarke*, but all the other philosophers, have been mistaken and entangled in a thousand difficulties from which they are not able to emerge. It is also what has given rise to the view of Spinoza and other similar opinions, which possess absolutely nothing the least bit reasonable.

The Englishman who seemed to catch a glimpse of something about substance is Mr. [George] Berkeley, Scotsman if I am not mistaken.[5] But he entangles himself in occasional causes.

I am displeased, sir, that you are engaged, apparently on the authority of His Majesty [King George I, Georg Ludwig* of Braunschweig-Lüneburg], in working on the history.[6] It is a work that perhaps some other would carry out very well, whereas I do not know anyone in the world who can render a very important service to the human race better than you, sir, by bringing to light your excellent system, supported by mathematics. In fact, centuries will be needed before there are some of these fortunate geniuses who penetrate into the sublime sciences and know how to make them useful and pleasing to men.

I hope with all my heart that it may please God, this being so good and so charitable, that it may please him, I say, to preserve you a long time yet in life, in health, and finally may he afford you some opportunity, provided by his wise providence, so that you may complete what you began so well in the past.

[...] Cy enclos vous avez Monsieur, la reponce de l'ami de Milan, qui vous assurera qu'aumoins il n'a pas dependu de moi, si vous n'avez point été servi des graines. Je desire que vous me fassiez naitre quelque meilleure occasion pour vous témoigner ma soumission et (que) je suis toujour et avec un profond respect

Monsieur

Morges le 15: May 1716.   Votre tres-humble et tres obeissant
                                           serviteur
                                           Louis Bourguet

[...]

Caroline of Brandenburg-Ansbach,
Princess of Wales, to Leibniz

St James le $\frac{15}{4}$ May 1716

Je vous anvoye[3] Monsieur la reponce[4] du docteur chlerque, qui par bonheur a estté retrouvez.[6] vous m'obligerié beaucoup[7] sy vous voulié manvoyer vos lettre que vous m'avez écrit[8] sur cette matiere. L'abée de conty et sa tres vive Ecollier m'an ont pertu[9] quelques une. le Roy m['ja fait l'honneur de me montrer votre lettre a M^d de pelniz. J'ay veu celle que vous avez repondu a L'abée. mais est-il possible qu'un home de votre merité et savoir se trouble pour de t'elle chose,[12] et sy même vous ou le chevalié neuthon layée trouvez[13] en même tems, ou l'un vn peu apres lautres,[14] faut-il se déchirer les vn[s] les autre[s]. vous estte tout deu[15] les plus grand[s] homes de notre tems. san[s] disputé tanderez an[16] amitié, et que vos disputé conssister afaire reconnoistre au peuble qui son gouverne par le Roy,[17] le bonheur dont il jouisse, et sa ne peut esttre quand les faissan panser[18] juste par votre matematique. les ces tomper vos disputé serieuse,[19] et prouvez nous le plain[20], et que le chevalié et chlerque de leur coté prouvez[21] le vide. la comtesse de B. M^d P. et moy, nous assisteron[s]

119. CAROLINE OF BRANDENBURG-ANSBACH TO LEIBNIZ   535

[...] Here enclosed you have, sir, the response of the friend from Milan, which will assure you that at least it was not up to me whether you were supplied with silkworm eggs. I want you to create some better opportunity for me to show my submission to you and that I am always, and with deep respect,

sir

Morges 15 May 1716.　　　　　　　　　　your very humble and very obedient

servant

Louis Bourguet

[...]

¹ Niedersächsische Staats- und Universitätsbibliothek Göttingen Handschriften Philos. 138 Bl. 15–16. Letter as sent: four quarto sides in Bourguet's hand. Not previously published.

² For the context of the remarks in this paragraph, see Leibniz's letter to Bourguet of 24 February 1716 (document 98, p. 401), Bourguet's letters to Leibniz of 16 March 1716 (document 103, p. 445) and 31 March 1716 (document 106, p. 461), and Leibniz's letter to Bourguet of 3 April (document 107, p. 463).

³ On the nature of these three hypotheses, see Leibniz's letter of Bourguet of 5 August 1715 (document 77).

⁴ Bourguet is referring to what Cheyne argues in § XXV of Chapter I of his *Philosophical Principles of Natural Religion: Containing the Elements of Natural Philosophy and the Proofs for Natural Religion, Arising from them*, which was first published in 1705 and which appeared in an enlarged and corrected second edition as the first part of his *Philosophical Principles of Religion: Natural and Revealed* (1715).

⁵ Berkeley was, of course, an Irishman.

⁶ That would be Leibniz's history of the House of Braunschweig-Lüneburg, his so-called *Annales imperii occidentis Brunsvicenses**.

119. Caroline* of Brandenburg-Ansbach, Princess of Wales, to Leibniz[1]

Saint James $\frac{15}{4}$ May 1716[2]

I am sending[3] you, sir, the response[4] of Doctor [Samuel] Clarke*,[5] which has fortunately been recovered.[6] I would be very grateful[7] if you would send me the letters that you have written me[8] about this matter. The Abbé [Antonio Schinella] Conti* and his very lively student have lost[9] some of them for me. The king [George I, Georg Ludwig* of Braunschweig-Lüneburg] has done me the honour of showing me your letter to Mademoiselle [Henriette Charlotte von] Pöllnitz*.[10] I have seen your response to the Abbey.[11] But is it possible that a man of your merit and learning troubles himself about such things?[12] And even if you or Chevalier Newton found it[13] at the same time, or the one shortly after the other,[14] is it necessary to defame each other? You are[15] the greatest men of our time. Without dispute you will reach out in[16] friendship, and let your dispute consist in making known to the peoples who are governed by the king[17] the happiness which they enjoy, and that can only be by making them think[18] aright through your mathematics. Drop your

a vos disputé[s], et nous repressanderon an original[22] ce que nous voiyons[23] dans mollier par copie. demain nous ver[r]ons les experimens des couleur[s] et vne que j'ay veu pour le vidé m[']a pres-que convertié. c[']est votre a[f]faire Monsieur de me ramener dans le trois chemains,[25] et je ladans, par la reponce[26] que vous ferais au[27] M^r chlerck. vous me trouverais malquerais vos soupsons toujours lamême[28]

Caroline

119. CAROLINE OF BRANDENBURG-ANSBACH TO LEIBNIZ 537

serious disputes[19] and prove to us the plenum,[20] and let the chevalier and Clarke prove[21] the void on their side. The Countess of Bückeburg [Johanne Sophie*, Gräfin (Countess) zu Schaumburg-Lippe], Mademoiselle Pöllnitz, and I, we will be witnesses to your disputes and we will portray the original[22] of what we see[23] in Molière by imitation.[24] Tomorrow we will see the experiments about colours, and one that I have seen for the void has nearly converted me. It is up to you, sir, to bring me back into the right path,[25] and I am expecting it by the response[26] that you will make to[27] Mr. Clarke. Despite your suspicions, you will find me always the same[28]

Caroline

[1] LBr. F 4 Bl. 58r–59r. Letter as sent: 2.6 quarto sides in Caroline's hand. Previously published in Klopp XI 93; Schüller 1991, pp. 246–7 (excerpt in German translation).

[2] That is, 15 May 1716 (NS) / 4 May 1716 (OS).

[3] Reading 'envoie' for 'anvoye'.

[4] Reading 'réponse' for 'reponce'.

[5] That is, the Third Reply of Samuel Clarke* (document 120).

[6] Reading 'été retrouvée' for 'estté retrouvez'. In her letter to Leibniz of 5 May 1716, Caroline had reported that Abbé Conti (that is, Antonio Schinella Conti*) had lost some of the papers in the correspondence, apparently including Clarke's Third Reply (document 115, p. 513).

[7] Reading 'm'obligeriez beaucoup' for 'm'obligerié beaucoup'.

[8] Reading 'vouliez m'envoyer vos lettres que vous m'avez écrites' for 'voulié manvoyer vos lettres que vous m'avez écrit'.

[9] Reading 'perdu' for 'pertu'.

[10] I have been unable to locate the letter to which Caroline refers here.

[11] See Leibniz's letter to Conti of 9 April 1716 (document 108).

[12] Reading 'telles choses' for 't'elle chose'.

[13] Reading 'l'avez trouvé' for 'layée trouvez'.

[14] Reading 'l'un un peu après l'autre' for 'l'un vn peu apres lautres'. Klopp omits 'un peu' (see Klopp XI 93).

[15] Reading 'êtes tous deux' for 'estte tout deu'.

[16] Reading 'Sans dispute tendrez en' for 'San disputé tanderez an'. Klopp mistranscribes the latter as 'sans dispute vous serez en' (see Klopp XI 93).

[17] Reading 'votre dispute consiste à faire reconnaître aux peuples qui sont gouvernés par le Roy' for 'vos disputé conssister afaire reconnoistre au peuble qui son gouverne par le Roy'.

[18] Reading 'ils jouissent, et ça ne peut être qu'en les faisant penser' for 'il jouisse, et sa ne peut esttre quand les faissan panser'. Klopp mistranscribes the latter as 'ils jouissent, et cela ne peut qu'estre grand, les faisant penser' (see Klopp XI 93).

[19] Reading 'Laissez tomber vos disputes sérieuses' for 'les ces tomper vos disputé serieuse'.

[20] Reading 'plein' for 'plain'.

[21] Reading 'prouvent' for 'prouvez'.

[22] Reading 'représenterons en original' for 'repressanderon an original'.

[23] Klopp mistranscribes 'nous voiyons' as 'nos voisins' (see Klopp XI 93).

[24] Caroline is apparently comparing the Countess of Bückeburg, Mademoiselle Pölniz, and herself to the three leading characters in Molière's play, *Les Femmes Savantes*. The title refers to three women— Philaminte, Bélise (Philaminte's sister-in-law), and Armande (Philaminte's eldest daughter)—who are obsessed with learning and culture, and who hold court in their literary salon.

[25] Reading 'droit chemin' for 'trois chemains'.

[26] Reading 'l'attends pour la réponse' for 'ladans par la reponce'. Klopp mistranscribes 'par' as 'pour' (see Klopp XI 93).

[27] Reading 'ferez à' for 'ferais au'.

[28] Reading 'Vous me trouverez malgré vos soupçons toujours la même' for 'vous me trouverais malquerais vos soupsons toujours lamême'.

Clarke's Third Reply

Troisiéme Réplique de Mr. Clarke.

1. *Ce que l'on dit ici, ne regarde que la* Signification *de certains* Mots. *On peut admettre les Définitions, que l'on trouve ici ; mais cela n'empêchera pas qu'on ne puisse appliquer les Raisonnemens* Mathematiques *à des Sujets* Physiques & Metaphysiques.
   2. *Il est indubitable, que rien n'*existe, *sans qu'il y ait une* Raison suffisante *de son existence ; & que rien n'existe d'une certaine maniere plûtôt que d'une autre, sans qu'il y ait aussi une* Raison suffisante *de cette* maniere *d'exister. Mais à l'égard des choses qui sont indifférentes en elles mêmes, la* simple Volonté *est une* Raison suffisante *pour leur donner l'existence, ou pour les faire exister d'une certain maniere ; & cette Volonté n'a pas besoin d'être déterminée par une Cause étrangere. Voici des Exemples de ce que je viens de dire. Lors que Dieu a créé ou placé une particule de Matiere dans* un lieu *plûtôt que dans* un autre, *quoique* tous les lieux *soient semblables ; il n'en a eu aucune autre raison que sa* Volonté. *Et supposé que l'*Espace *ne fût rien* de réel, *mas seulement un* Simple Ordre des Corps ; *la* Volonté *de Dieu ne laisseroit pas d'être la seule* possible *raison pour laquelle trois Particules égales auroient été placées ou rangées dans l'ordre* a, b, c,[2] *plûtôt que dans un ordre contraire. On ne sçauroit donc tirer de cette* Indifference *des* Lieux *aucun* Argument, *qui prouve qu'il n'y a point d'*Espace réel. *Car les* differens Espaces *sont réellement* distincts l'un de l'autre, quoiqu'ils soient parfaitement Semblables. D'ailleurs, si l'on suppose que l'Espace n'est point* réel, *& qu'il n'est simplement que l'*Ordre & l'Arrangement des Corps, *il s'ensuivra une absurdité palpable. Car, selon cette idée ; si la Terre, le Soleil, & la Lune, avoient été placez où les Etoiles fixes les plus éloignées se trouvent à present, (pourvû qu'ils eussent été placez dans le même ordre & à la meme distance l'un d l'autre ;) non seulement c'eut été la* même chose, *comme le sçavant Auteur le dit trèsbien ; mais il s'ensuivroit aussi que la* Terre, le Soleil & la Lune, *seroient* en ce cas-là *dans le* même Lieu, *où ils sont presentement :* Ce qui est une Contradiction manifeste. *Les Anciens* ||[3] *n'ont point dit que tout* Espace destitué de Corps *étoit un* Espace Imaginaire : *Ils n'ont donné ce nom qu'à l'*Espace *qui est au delà du Monde. Et ils n'ont pas voulu dire par là, que cet* Espace n'est * pas réel ; *mais seulement que nous ignorons entierement* quelles fortes *de chose il y a dans cet* Espace. *J'ajoute que les* Auteurs, *qui ont quelquefois employé le mot d'*imaginaire *pour marquer que l'*Espace n'étoit pas réel, n'ont point prouvé ce qu'ils avançoient par le simple usage de ce Terme.
   3. *L'*Espace *n'est pas une* Substance, *un* Etre eternal & infini ; *mais une* Proprieté, *ou une* † *suite de l'existence d'un Etre infini & éternel. L'*Espace infini *est l'*Immensité :

|| On a fait ces Remarques à l'occasion d'un Endroit de la Lettre de Mr. *Leibnitz*, qui servoit d'Enveloppe au troisiéme Ecrit, qu'il envoya.

 * Le *Néant* n'a point de *Dimensions*, de *Grandeur*, ni de *Quantité* : il n'a aucune *Proprieté*.

 † Voïez ci-dessous la Note sur ma quatriéme Réplique, § 10.

120. Clarke's Third Reply[1]

Dr. CLARKE'S *Third Reply.*

1. This relates only to the *Signification* of *Words.* The Definitions here given, may well be allowed ; And yet *Mathematical* Reasonings may be applyed to *Physical* and *Metaphysical* Subjects.

2. Undoubtedly nothing *is,* without a *sufficient* Reason *why* it *is,* rather than *not* ; and *why* it is *Thus,* rather than *Otherwise.* But in things in their own Nature indifferent ; *mere Will,* without any thing External to influence it, is alone *That sufficient Reason.* As in the Instance of God's creating or placeing any particle of matter in *One* place rather than in *Another,* when *All* places are Originally alike. And the Case is the same, even though *Space* were nothing *real,* but only the *mere Order of Bodies* : For still it would be absolutely *indifferent,* and there could be *no other reason* but mere *Will,* why Three equal Particles should be placed or ranged in the Order *a, b, c,*[2] rather than in the *contrary* Order. And therefore no Argument can be drawn from this *Indifferency* of *All* places, to prove that *no Space is real.* For *different Spaces* are really *different* or *distinct* one from another, though they be perfectly *alike.* And there is This evident absurdity in supposing *Space* not to be *real,* but to be merely the *Order of Bodies* ; that, according to That Notion, if the Earth and Sun and Moon had been placed where the remotest fixt Stars now are, (provided they were placed in the same Order and Distance they now are *with regard one to another,*) it would not only have been, (as this Learned Author rightly says,) *la même chose,* the *same Thing in effect* ; which is very true : But it would also follow, that they would *Then* have been in the same *Place* too, as they are *Now* : Which is an express Contradiction. The ||[3] *Ancients* did not call *All Space which is void of Bodies,* but only *extramundane* Space, by the Name of *Imaginary* Space. The meaning of which, is not, that such Space *is* * *not real* ; but only that We are wholly ignorant *what* kinds of Things are *in that Space.* Those Writers, who by the Word, *imaginary,* meant at any time to *affirm* that Space was not real ; did not thereby *prove,* that it was not real.

3. *Space* is not a *Being,* an eternal and infinite *Being,* but a *Property,* or a † consequence of the Existence of a Being infinite and eternal. *Infinite Space,* is *Immensity* : But *Immensity* is *not God* : And therefore *Infinite Space,* is *not God.* Nor is there any

---

|| *This was occasioned by a Passage in the private Letter, wherein Mr.* Leibnitz's *Third Paper came inclosed.*

* *Of* Nothing, *there are no* Dimensions, *no* Magnitude, *no* Quantity, *no* Properties.

† See below, *the* Note *on my Fourth Reply,* § 10.

*Mais l'*Immensité *n'est pas* Dieu : *donc l'*Espace infini *n'est pas* Dieu. *Ce que l'on dit ici des* parties *de l'Espace, n'est point une difficulté. L'Espace infini est absolument &* essentiellement indivisible ; *& c'est une Contradiction dans les termes, que de supposer qu'il soit* divisé ; *car il faudroit qu'il y eut un Espace entre les parties que l'on* suppose divisées ; *ce qui est supposer que l'Espace est* || divisé *& non* divisé *en* même *temps. Quoique Dieu soit* Immense *ou* Present *par tout, sa Substance n'en est pourtant pas plus divisée en parties, que son Existence l'est par la Durée. La difficulté que l'on fait ici, vient uniquement de l'abus du mot de* Parties.

4. *Si l'Espace n'étoit que l'*Ordre *des choses qui coëxistent, il s'ensuivroit que si* Dieu faisoit mouvoir le Monde tout entier en ligne droite, *quelque degré de vitesse qu'il eut, il ne laisseroit pas d'être toûjours dans le* même lieu ; *& que rien ne recevroit aucun choc, quoique ce mouvement fur*[4] *arrêté subitement. Et si le* Temps *n'étoit qu'un* Ordre de Succession *dans les créatures ; il s'ensuivroit que si Dieu avoit créé le Monde quelques millions d'années plûtôt, il n'auroit pourtant pas eté créé plûtôt. De plus, l'Espace &le Temps sont des* Quantitez ; *ce qu'on ne peut dire de la* Situation *& de l'*Ordre.

5. *On prétend ici, que parce que l'Espace est* uniforme *ou parfaitement* Semblable, *& qu'aucune de ses parties ne differe de l'autre ; il s'ensuit que si les Corps qui ont été créez dans* un autre lieu, (*supposé qu'ils conservassent la même Situation entre eux,*) ils ne laisseroient pas d'avoir été créez dans le* même lieu. Mais c'est un Contradiction manifeste. Il est vrai que l'*Uniformité *de l'*Espace *prouve, que Dieu n'a pu avoir aucune raison* externe *pour créer les choses dans* un lieu *plûtôt que dans* un autre : *Mais cela* empêche-t-il *que sa* volonté *n'ait été une* raison suffisante *pour agir en* quelque lieu que ce soit, *puisque* tous les lieux *sont indifferens ou sembables, & qui'il y a une* bonne raison *pour agir en* quelque lieu ?

6. *Le même raisonnement, dont je me suis servi dans la section précédente, doit avoir lieu ici.*

7, *& 8. Lorsqu'il y a quelque difference dans la* Nature *des choses, la* Consideration *de cette Difference détermine toûjours un Agent Intelligent & très-sage. Mais lors que deux manieres d'agir sont également bonnes, comme dans les case dont on a parlé ci-dessus ; dire que* Dieu *ne sçauroit agir du tout, & que ce n'est point une* Imperfection *de ne pouvoir* Agir *dans un tel cas, parce que* Dieu *ne peut avoir aucune raison* externe *pour agir d'une certaine maniere plûtôt que d'une autre ; dire une telle chose, c'est insinuer que Dieu n'a pas* en lui même *un* Principe d'Action, *& qu'il est toûjours, pour ainsi dire,* machinalement *déterminé par les choses de dehors.*

9. *Je suppose que* la Quantité *déterminée de* Matiere, *qui est à present dans le* Monde, *est* la plus convenable *à l'*Etat present *des choses ; & qu'une* plus grande *(aussi bien qu'une* plus petite*) Quantité de Matiere, auroit été* moins convenable *à l'*Etat present *du* Monde ; *& que par conséquent elle n'auroit pas été un plus grand Objet de la bonté de Dieu.*

|| Voïez ci-dessus, § 4. de ma *Seconde* Réplique.

Difficulty in what is here alledged about Space having *Parts*. For Infinite Space is *One*, absolutely and essentially *indivisible* : And to suppose it *parted*, is a contradiction in Terms ; because there must be Space in the *Partition it self*; which is to suppose it ‖ *parted*, and yet *not parted* at the same time. The *Immensity* or *Omnipresence* of *God*, is no more a dividing of his Substance into *Parts* ; than his *Duration*, or continuance of existing, is a dividing of his existence into *Parts*. There is no difficulty here, but what arises from the *figurative* Abuse of the Word, *Parts*.

4. If *Space* was nothing but the *Order of Things coexisting* ; it would follow, that if God should remove in a streight Line the whole Material World Entire, with any swiftness whatsoever ; yet it would still always continue in the *same Place* : And that nothing would receive any Shock upon the most sudden stopping of that Motion. And if *Time* was nothing but the *Order of Succession* of created Things ; it would follow, that if God had created the World Millions of Ages sooner than he did, yet it would not have been created *at all the sooner*. Further : *Space* and *Time* are *Quantities* ; which *Situation* and *Order* are *not*.

5. The Argument in This Paragraph, is ; That because *Space* is *Uniform* or *Alike*, and *One Part* does not differ from *another* ; therefore the Bodies created in *One place*, if they had been created in *Another* place, (supposing them to keep the same Situation with regard to each other,) would still have been created in the *Same Place* as before : Which is a manifest Contradiction. The *Uniformity* of Space, does indeed prove, that there would be no (*External*) reason, why God should create things in *One* place rather than in *another* : But does That hinder his own *Will*, from being to it self a *sufficient reason* of Acting in *Any* place, when *All* Places are Indifferent or Alike, and there be *Good reason* to Act in *Some* place ?

6. The *Same Reasoning* takes place here, as in the foregoing.

7 and 8. Where there is any *Difference* in the *Nature of things*, there the Consideration of That Difference always determines an Intelligent and perfectly wise Agent. But when Two ways of Acting are equally and alike good, (as in the Instances before mentioned ;) to affirm in such case, that God *cannot Act at all*, or that 'tis no Perfection in him to be *able to Act*, because he can have no External Reason to move him to Act *one way* rather than *the other*, seems to be a denying God to have in himself any *Original* Principle or *Power* of *beginning* to act, but that he must needs[5] (as it were *Mechanically*) be always determined by things extrinsick.

9. I suppose, *That determinate Quantity* of *Matter*, which is *now* in the World, is the *most Convenient* for the *present Frame of Nature*, or the *Present State of Things* : And that a *Greater* (as well as a Less) Quantity Matter, would have made the *Present Frame* of the World *less Convenient* ; and consequently would not have been a greater Object for God to have exercised his Goodness upon.

‖ *See above*, § 4. *of my* Second Reply.

10. *Il ne s'agit pas de sçavoir ce que* Goclenius *entend par le mot de* Sensorium, *mais en quel sens Mr. le Chevalier* * Newton *s'est servi de ce mot dans son Livre. Si* Goclenius *croit que l'Oeil, l'Oreille, ou quelque autre Organe des Sens, est le* Sensorium, *il se trompe. Mais quand un Auteur employe un Terme d'Art, & qu'il déclare en quel sens il s'en sert ; à quoi bon rechercher de quelle maniere d'autres Ecrivains ont entendu ce même Terme ?* Scapula *traduit le mot, dont il s'agit ici,* Domicilium, *c'est à dire, le* Lieu où l'Ame reside.

11. *L'Ame d'un Aveugle ne voit point, parce que certaines obstructions empêchent les Images d'être portées au* Sensorium, *où elle est present. Nous ne sçavons pas com-memt l'Ame d'un homme qui voit, apperçoit les Images, auxquelles elle est presente : Mais nous sçavons qu'elle ne sçauroit apercevoir les choses, auxquelles elle n'est pas presente ; parce qu'un Etre ne sçauroit ni* agir, ni *recevoir des impressions, dans un lieu où il n'est pas.*

12. *Dieu* étant par tout, *est actuellement present à tout,* Essentiellement & † Substantiellement. *Il est vrai que la Presence de Dieu se manifeste par son* Operation ; *mais cette Operation seroit impossible sans la* presence actuelle *de Dieu. L'Ame n'est pas presente à chaque partie du Corps ; & par conséquent elle n'agit, & ne sçauroit agir pas elle même sur toutes les parties du Corps, mais seulement sur le Cerveau, ou sur certains Nerfs & sur les Esprits, qui agissent sur tout le Corps, en vertu des Lois du mouvement, que Dieu a établies.*

13, 14. *Quoique les* ‡ *Forces Actives, qui sont dans l'Univers,* diminuent, *& qu'elles ayent besoin d'une* nouvelle impression ; *ce n'est point un desordre, ni une imperfection dans l'Ouvrage de Dieu : Ce n'est qu'une suite de la nature des créatures, qui sont* dans la dépendance. *Cette dépendance n'est pas une chose, qui ait besoin d'être rectifiée. L'Exemple qu'on allegue d'un* homme qui fait une Machine, *n'a aucun rapport à la matiere dont il s'agit ici ; parce que les Forces, en vertu des quelles cette Machine continue de se mouvoir, sont tout-à-fait indépendantes de l'Ouvrier.*

15. *On peut admettre les mots d'*Intelligentia supramundana, *de la maniere dont l'Auteur les explique ici : Mais sans cette explication, ils pourroient aisément faire naitre une fausse idée, comme si Dieu n'étoit pas* réellement & substantiellement present par tout.

---

* Voïez la Note sur § 3. de ma *Prémiere Replique.*

† *Deus ominpræsens est, &c.* C'est-à-dire : *Dieu est present par tout, non seulement* virtuellement, *mais encore* Substantiellement : *Car la* Force, [virtus] *ne sçauroit subsister sans une* Substance. Newtoni Principia, Scholium generale sub finem.

‡ Le mot de *Force Active* ne signifie ici que le *Mouvement,* & l'*Impetus* ou la *Force impulsive* & *relative des Corps, qui nait de leur mouvement ; & qui lui est proportionnée. Car c'est le Passage suivant, qui a donné lieu à tout ce qu'on dit sur ce sujet dans cette Dispute. Apparet motum & nasci posse & perire,* &c. C'est-a-dire. *Il est évident que le Mouvement peut augmenter & diminuer. Mais la Tenacité des Corps Fluides, l'Attrition de leurs parties, & la foiblesse de la Force Elastique dans les Corps Solides, sont que le Mouvement tend toûjours beaucoup plus à diminuer qu'à augmenter. _____ Puis donc que tous les differens mouvemens, qui sont dans le monde,* diminuent *continuellement ; il est absolument necessaire d'avoir recours à quelques Principes Actifs, pour conserver & pour renouveller ces mouvemens.* Newtoni Optice, Quæst. ult. pag. 341.343.

10. The Question is not, what *Goclenius*, but what Sir *Isaac Newton* means by the word *Sensorium*, when the Debate is about the Sense of * Sir *Isaac Newton's*, and not about the Sense of *Goclenius's* Book. If *Goclenius* takes the *Eye*, or *Ear*, or any other *Organ* of Sensation, to be the *Sensorium* ; he is certainly mistaken. But when any Writer *expressly explains* what he means by any Term of Art ; of What Use is it, in this case, to enquire in what different Senses perhaps some *other* Writers have sometimes used the same Word ? *Scapula* explains it by *domicilium*, the *place* where the Mind resides.

11. The Soul of a Blind Man does for This reason not see, because no Images are conveyed (there being some Obstruction in the way) to the *Sensorium* where the Soul is present. *How* the Soul of a Seeing Man, sees the Images to which it is *present*, we know not : But we are sure it cannot perceive what it is *not present* to ; because nothing can Act, or be Acted upon, where it Is not.

12. *God*, being *Omnipresent*, is really *present* to every thing, *Essentially* and † *Substantially*. His Presence *manifests* it self indeed by its *Operation*, but it could not operate if it was not *There*. The *Soul* is not Omnipresent to every part of the Body, and therefore does not and cannot it self actually Operate upon every part of the Body, but only upon the Brain, or certain Nerves and Spirits, which, by Laws and Communications of God's appointing, influence the whole Body.

13. *and* 14. The ‡ *Active Forces*, which are in the Universe, *diminishing themselves* so as to stand in need of *new impressions* ; is no inconvenience, no disorder, no imperfection in the Workmanship of the Universe ; but is the consequence of the Nature of *dependent* Things. Which Dependency of Things, is not a matter that wants to be rectified. The Case of a *Humane* Workman making a Machine, is quite another thing : Because the *Powers* or *Forces* by which the Machine continues to move, are altogether *independent* on the Artificer.

15. The Phrase, *Intelligentia supramundana*, may well be allowed, as it is here explained : But *without* this explication, the expression is very apt to lead to a wrong Notion, as if God was not *really* and *substantially* present every where.

---

* *See the* Note on § 3. *in my* First Reply.

† Deus Omnipræsens est, non per *virtutem* solam, sed etiam per *Substantiam* : Nam virtus sine Substantiâ subsistere non poest. i. e. *God is Omnipresent, not only virtually, but substantially : For*, Powers *cannot subsist without a* Substance. *Newtoni* Principia, Scholium generale sub finem.

‡ Note : *The word*, Active Force, *signifies here nothing but* Motion, *and the* Impetus *or* relative impulsive Force *of Bodies, arising from and being proportional to their Motion. For, the* Occasion *of what has passed upon This Head, was the* following *Passage*. Apparet Motum & nasci posse & perire. Verùm, per tenacitatem corporum fluidorum, partiumq; suarum Attritum, visq; elasticæ in corporibus solidis imbecillitatem ; multò magis in eam semper partem vergit natura rerum, ut pereat Motus, quàm ut nascatur. _____ Quoniam igitur varij illi Motus, qui in Mundo conspiciuntur, perpetuò decrescunt universi ; necesse est prorsus, quo ij conservari & recrescere possint, ut ad *actuosa* aliqua Principia recurramus. i. e. *Tis evident, that Motion can in the Whole both increase and diminish. But because of the Tenacity of Fluid Bodies, and the Attrition of their Parts, and the Weakness of elastick Force in Solid Bodies* ; Motion is, *in the Nature of things, always much more apt to* diminish, *than to* increase. _____ *Since therefore all the various Motions that are in the World, are perpetually* decreasing ; *'tis absolutely necessary, in order to preserve and renew those Motions, that we have recourse to some* Active Principles. Newtoni Optice, Quæst. ult. pag. 341, 343.

544 121. BERNOULLI TO LEIBNIZ

16. *Je réponds aux Questions que l'on propose ici : Que Dieu agit toûjours de la maniere* la plus réguliere & la plus parfaite : *Qu'il n'y a aucun* desordre *dans son Ouvrage* ; & que les changemens *qu'il fait dans l'Etat present de la Nature, ne sont pas plus* extraordinaires, *que le soin qu'il a de conserver cet Etat : Que lors que les choses sont en elles mêmes absolument égales &* indifferentes, *la Volonté de Dieu peut se déterminer librement sur le choix, sans qu'aucune cause étrangere la fasse agir;* & *que le pouvoir que Dieu a d'agir de cette maniere, est une véritable Perfection. Enfin, je réponds que l'Espace ne dépend point de l'*Ordre *ou de la* Situation, *ou de l'*Existence *des Corps.*

17. *A l'égard des Miracles ; Il ne s'agit pas de sçavoir ce que les* Théologiens *ou les* Philosophes *disent communément sur cette matiere, mais sur* quelles raisons *ils appuyent leurs sentimens. Si un* Miracle *est toûjours* une Action, qui surpasse la puissance de toutes les Creatures ; *il s'ensuivra que si un homme marche sur l'eau,* & *si le mouvement du Soleil (ou de la Terre) est arrêté, ce ne sera point un Miracle, puisque ces deux choses se peuvent faire sans l'intervention d'une Puissance* infinie. *Si un Corps se meut autour d'une Centre dans le Vuide,* & *si ce mouvement est une chose* ordinaire, *comme celui des Planetes autour du Soleil ; ce ne sera point un* Miracle, *soit que Dieu lui même produise ce mouvement immédiatement, ou qu'il soit produit par quelque Créature. Mais si ce mouvement autour d'un Centre est* rare & extraordinaire, *comme seroit celui d'un* Corps pesant *suspendu dans l'air ; ce sera* également un Miracle, *soit que Dieu même produise ce mouvement, ou qu'il soit produit par une Créature invisible. Enfin si tout ce qui n'est pas l'effet des Forces naturelles des Corps,* & *qu'on ne sçauroit expliquer par ces Forces, est un* Miracle ; *il s'ensuivra que tous les mouvemens des Animaux sont des* Miracles. *Ce qui semble prouver démonstrativement, que le sçavant Auteur a une fausse idée de la nature du* Miracle.

Johann Bernoulli to Leibniz

Vir Amplissime atque Celeberrime
Fautor Honoratissime

Basil. a.d. 20. Mai
1716.

Bene se habet, quod Newtonus ipse tandem in arenam descenderit pugnaturus sub proprio suo nomine et seposita larva: Credo enim Newtonum semper fuisse

16. To the Questions here proposed, the Answer is : *That* God does always act in the most *regular* and *perfect* manner : *That* there are no *Disorders* in the Workmanship of God ; and *that* there is nothing more extraordinary in the *Alterations* he is pleased to make in the Frame of things, than in his *continuation* of it : *That* in things in their own nature absolutely Equal and Indifferent, the Will of God can freely choose and determine it self, *without any External Cause* to impell it ; and *that* 'tis a *Perfection* in God, to be *able* so to do. *That* Space, does not at all depend on the *Order* or *Situation* or *Existence* of Bodies.[6] And as to the Notion of *Miracles,*

17. The Question is not, *what* it is that *Divines* or *Philosophers* usually allow or not allow ; but *what Reasons* Men alledge for their Opinions. If a *Miracle* be That only, which *surpasses the Power of all Created Beings* ; then for a Man to walk on the Water, or for the Motion of the Sun or the Earth to be stopped, is *no Miracle* ; since none of these things require *infinite* Power to effect them. For a Body to move in a Circle round a Center *in Vacuo* ; if it be *usual* (as the *Planets* moving about the *Sun,*) 'tis *no Miracle*, whether it be effected immediately by *God himself,* or mediately by any *Created Power* : But if it be *unusual,* (as, for a *heavy Body* to be suspended, and move so in the *Air,*) tis equally a *Miracle*, whether it be effected immediately by *God himself,* or mediately by any invisible *Created Power.* Lastly ; if whatever arises not from, and is not explicable by, the Natural Powers of Body, be a *Miracle* ; then *Every animal-motion* whatsoever, is a *Miracle*. Which seems demonstrably to show, that this Learned Author's Notion of a *Miracle* is erroneous.

[1] English and French translation are from Clarke's edition of the correspondence (Clarke 1717, pp. 73–91). LBr. 160 Bl. 23r–28r is the original in Clarke's hand. There is also a copy in a secretary's hand (LH 1, 20 Bl. 393r–395r). This is Clarke's reply to Leibniz's Third Paper (document 100); it was enclosed with Caroline's letter to Leibniz of 15 May 1716 (document 119). All footnotes are Clarke's; endnotes are mine. Clarke's references to the Appendix of his 1717 edition of the correspondence have been omitted.

[2] Clarke's original letter has '1, 2, 3' instead of 'a, b, c' (see LBr. 160 Bl.23r).

[3] The letter that Clarke refers to in this footnote is Leibniz's letter to Caroline of 25 February 1716. However, that letter as a whole is missing; all that now exists is an extract that Leibniz made from it (document 99), and unfortunately the passage that Clarke says occasioned his remarks does not appear in the extract. But see Leibniz's letter to Remond of 27 March 1716, document 105, p. 643.

[4] Reading 'fut arrêté subitement' for 'fur arrêté subitement'.

[5] Originally 'neds'; corrected in the Errata of the 1717 edition of the Correspondence.

[6] Clarke's original letter has 'the *Existence* or *Order* or *Situation* of Bodies' rather than 'the *Order* or *Situation* or *Existence* of Bodies' (see LBr. 160 Bl. 28r).

121. Johann Bernoulli* to Leibniz (excerpt)[1]

Greatest and Most Celebrated Man
   Most Honourable Supporter

Basil 20 May
1716

It is good that Newton himself has finally come down into the arena in order to fight under his own name, the mask having been set aside. For I believe that

Tuum Antagonistam sub nomine et persona Keilii qui nil nisi calamum suum præbuerit. Quicquid sit spero nunc veritatem Historicam melius detectum iri, siquidem Newtonus pro suo quem habere suppono et confido candore, res gestas fideliter enarrabit, eorumque quæ à Te producentur veritatem publice agnoscet. [...]

Miror quomodo Newtonus scire potuerit me Auctorem esse Epistolæ illius quam inseri curâsti chartæ illi contra Newtonum publicatæ, cum tamen nemo mortalium sciverit me eam[3] scripsisse nisi Tu ad quem scripta est et ego à quo scripta est: Fortassis autem expressio ista par un Mathematicien ou pretendu mathematicien alium habet sensum quam putas, potest enim etiam ita sumi, quasi Newtonus crediderit Epistolam istam esse suppositiam et tanquam à Mathematico quodam conficto exaratam, revera tamen ab ipso Auctore chartæ inventam et intrusam; quod si rem ita sumas, videbis par un pretendu mathematicien intelligendum esse mathematicum confictum et nunquam existentem.

Vellem Arnoldus locum indicasset in Transactionibus ubi Keilius dicet me quoque ignorare Calculum differentialem; interim parum me moveret, quod Keilius ex ira furiosus contra me deblaterat, etsi crederem verum esse quod Arnoldus retulit; sed cum nec ex Gallia, nec aliunde simile quid audiversim, Arnoldus forte deceptus est eo quod intellexerit Keilium alicubi dicere me usum Serierum convergentium Newtoni non satis intelligere. Aliàs enim Keilius si me dicere vellet calculi differentialis ignarum sibi ipsimet turpiter contradiceret, quippe qui in Diario Gallico Hagiensi ubi contra chartam illam, de qua supra, disputans ad me provocat tanquam ad judicem idoneum et calculi differentialis callentissimum, [...]; præterea alia in me cumulat elogia, quæ omnia ejus sunt naturæ, ut me necessario calculi differentialis peritissimum crediderit, adeo ut vel calumniator vel mente captus censendus esset, si nunc contrarium diceret.

[...]

Vale et Fave Amplit. T. Devotissimo JBernoulli

Newton has always been your antagonist under the name and person of [John] Keill*, who has furnished nothing but his own pen. Whatever it may be, I hope now that the historical truth will be more clearly revealed, if only Newton will, by virtue of the candor that I suppose and trust he has, faithfully explain in detail what has taken place and publicly acknowledge the truth of those things that will be brought forward by you. [...]

I wonder how Newton could have known that I was the author of that letter that you took the trouble to insert in that paper published against Newton,[2] when no one yet knew that I wrote it,[3] except you, to whom it was written, and I, by whom it was written. Perhaps, however, the very expression, *by a mathematician or pretended mathematician*, has a sense other than you suppose. For it can also be taken in this way, as if Newton believed that that letter was forged and written, so to speak, by a kind of fabricated mathematician, yet actually invented and put forth by the author of the paper himself; and if you take the matter in this way, you will see that *by a pretended mathematician* is to be understood *a fabricated and never existing mathematician*.

I wish that [John] Arnold[4] had indicated the place in the *Transactions*[5] where Keill says that I am also ignorant of the differential calculus. Meanwhile, what Keill babbles against me, raging from anger, does not particularly disturb me, even if I believed that what Arnold reported was true; but since I have heard nothing similar from France or elsewhere, Arnold is deceived there, because he has understood that Keill says somewhere that I did not sufficiently understand Newton's use of converging series. For otherwise, Keill, if he meant to say that I am ignorant of the differential calculus, shamefully contradicts himself. For in fact it was he who, in the French Journal of the Hague [*Journal Littéraire de la Haye*], when disputing against the above-mentioned paper, challenges me as if I were a fit judge and highly skilled in the differential calculus [...]. Besides, he heaps other compliments on me, all of which are of a nature that he must have believed me highly skilled in the differential calculus, so much so that he must be considered either a slanderer or insane, if he would now say otherwise.

Farewell and be well disposed toward Your Eminence's most devoted J[ohann]Bernoulli

---

[1] Staats-und Universitätsbibliothek Göttingen Handschriften Philos. 138 Bl. 11–12. Four quarto sides in Bernoulli's hand. There is also copy of the letter in a secretary's hand (Universitätsbibliothek Basel L I a 18 Bl. 226–227). Previously published in GM III-2 960–2 (excerpt) and NC VI 337–41 (excerpt with English translation). This is Bernoulli's response to Leibniz's letter of 13 April 1716 (document 110). For Leibniz's response, see his letter of 7 June 1716 (document 127).

[2] That is, the *Charta Volans* (see NC VI 15–21 and note 3 to Leibniz's letter to Caroline of 12 May 1716, document 117a, pp. 525, 527).

[3] Gerhardt (GM III-2 961) and NC VI 338 mistranscribe 'eam' as 'illam'.

[4] See note 7 to Leibniz's letter to Bernoulli of 13 April 1716 (document 110, p. 495).

[5] That is, the *Philosophical Transactions* of the Royal Society, but see NC VI 276n14.

Caroline of Brandenburg-Ansbach, Princess of Wales, to Leibniz

St James le $\frac{26}{15}$ de May, 1716

vous avez raison de me demander parton[3] Monsieur de m'avoir supsone[4] de n'estre pas la même pour vous, et votre merité m['']y obligerois[5] toujours. labée conty acreu de racomoder[6] les plus grands hom̂e[s] de notre tems, et du passez,[7] et je crain de l['']avenir. c'es[t] ce qui luy a fait vous anvoiyer[8] la lettre de chevallié nuthon. mais tout piqué que vous me paroiset esttre[9] contre luy, permeté moy,[10] que je vous dise, que c'est hom̂e a vne veritable anvie de recherger laverité et se conformé le plus qu'il luy samble ala raison.[11] Je vous prié damploiyer[12] votre tems plus udillement[13] que de disputer, ansamble,[14] et le moin[s] qu'on an parlerá le mieux sa vodera.[15] Je suis dans les experiment[s], et suis de plus anplus charmé des coulleurs.[16] Je ne puis man-pecher destre,[17] un peu prevenu, pour le vidé mais je crois que l'on ne se compran[18] pas, puis que ceque ces Mes icy apelle ainsy,[19] ne doit pas sinifier[20] rien, mais vne chose, qui n'est pas matiere. Je suis ridiculle de vous le vouloir expliquer. vous aurais veu[21] par ma dernier[e] lettre ou il y avoit la eponce de M^r chlerque ce qu'il dit la deceu.[22] revenon[s] a la grande a[f]faire. Je crain[s] que le Roy crois[23] tous ces accom[m]odement[s] de religion inudille et il dit avec la st$^{[e]}$ Ecriture 𝕰in jeder soll seines glaubens leben. pour Mes nos Eveque[s], il[25] crois lachose[26] pour precse inpraticable,[27] amoin qu'il veuille anvoiyer vn minider de la parolle[28] de Dieu et le faire Eveque pour consaqueré les autres confrere.[29] Je m['']eston̂e[30] Monsieur que vous dité[31] que lon comance par les seremony.[32] nesce pas[33] toujours le chemain que lon pran.[34] J'ay les livers[35] de Halle qui sont extremet bom̂e et quelque vne recread-ive.[36] Je vous ayée desja dit[37] dans vne de mes lettre[s], ce qui regardé docteur chler-que, et je vous anverais[39] avec laposte qui vien ce pety liver.[40] Madame me fais leplaisir de m'écrire ces lettres son ranplié de tans d'agrement, qu'on ne sans pas lapen̂e de luy reponder.[41] Je scerais ravié sy mes inportunidée aurais peu[42] faire quelque chose sur L'Esprit du Roy, pour vous faire avoir vne sy justé demande. Je revien[s] a votre dernier[e] lettre avec laquelle vous m'avez anvoiyé vn papié contre levidé je lais dom̂e au Roy, afin qu'il n'an laissez jamais dans votre pource.[44] L'abée conty la asteur.[45,46] Je ne suis nullement charmé du Zar,[47] et il me samble que ces maniere[48] avec la noblesse de Mecklenbourg n'est pas usidée[49] dans notre chere partrié. Je douté que S.M. amènera au qu'vn hom̂e pour convercer agreablement[50] sy ce n'est le duc de Richement, qui pour toute etudé a vne boudellé de double any.[51] lomenié ne suivera pas[52] le Roy, et tout honest hom̂e[53] qu'il est il n'est gere agreable.[54] voila vne grande lettre qui vous marquera, que j'ay toujours du tems pour me souvenir de mes amié.[55]

Caroline

122. Caroline* of Brandenburg-Ansbach, Princess of Wales, to Leibniz[1]

Saint James $\frac{26}{15}$ May, 1716[2]

You are right to beg my pardon,[3] sir, for having suspected[4] me of not being the same for you; your merit would always obligate me to it.[5] The Abbé Conti believed he was reconciling[6] the greatest men of our time, and of the past,[7] and, I fear, of the future. It is what made him send[8] you the letter of Sir Isaac Newton. But as roused against him as you appeared to me to be,[9] permit me[10] to tell you that this man has a true desire to seek the truth and conforms himself the more reasonable it appears to him.[11] I ask you to employ[12] your time more usefully[13] than in disputing with each other,[14] and the less it is spoken about, the better.[15] I am in on the experiments, and I am more and more charmed by colours.[16] I cannot help being[17] a bit biased in favour of the void, but I believe we do not understand each other,[18] since what these gentlemen here call the void[19] is not supposed to mean[20] anything but a thing that is not matter. I am ridiculous to try to explain it to you. You must have seen[21] from my last letter, in which there was the response of Mr. [Samuel] Clarke*, what he says about it.[22] Let us return to the grand affair. I fear that the king [George I, Georg Ludwig* of Braunschweig-Lüneburg] believes[23] all these accommodations of religion are useless, and he says with Holy Scripture, 'Each should live by his faith.'[24] As for our bishops, he[25] believes the matter[26] to be nearly unworkable,[27] unless he chooses to send a minister of the word[28] of God and make him a bishop to consecrate the other members.[29] I am astonished,[30] sir, that you say[31] that we begin with the ceremonies.[32] Isn't that[33] always the path that is taken?[34] I have the books[35] of [Joseph] Hall, which are very good, and some are entertaining.[36] I have already told you[37] about the situation concerning Doctor Clarke in one of my letters,[38] and I will send[39] you that little book with the next post.[40] Madame [Elisabeth Charlotte*, Duchess of Orléans] has obliged me by writing to me; these letters are full of so much charm that it is not a bother to respond to her.[41] I would be delighted if my persistent requests would have[42] affected the thinking of the king, in order to secure for you such a fair request.[43] I return to your last letter, with which you sent me a paper against the void; I have given it to the king so that he never leaves any [void] in your purse.[44] The Abbé Conti has it now.[45,46] I am not at all charmed by the czar,[47] and it seems to me that his manners[48] with the nobility of Mecklenburg are not usual[49] in our beloved fatherland. I doubt that His Majesty will bring any man for pleasant conversation[50] if it is not the Duke of Richmond [Charles Lennox (1672–1723)], who has a bottle of double anise for every study.[51] The almoner [William Nicolson*] will not accompany[52] the king, and however respectable[53] he may be, he is scarcely pleasant.[54] There now, a long letter that will show you that I always have time to remember my friends.[55]

Caroline

Je vous prié d'aller souvant[56] voir mon fils. Votre convercassion luy sera udille.[57] mandé moy come vous le drouvez.[58]

122. CAROLINE OF BRANDENBURG-ANSBACH TO LEIBNIZ 551

Please go see my son [Friedrich Ludwig* of Braunschweig-Lüneburg] often.[56] Your conversation will be beneficial for him.[57] Let me know how he is.[58]

[1] LBr. F 4 Bl. 62r–64r. Letter as sent: five quarto sides in Caroline's hand. Previously published in Klopp XI 112–13; Schüller 1991, p. 247 (excerpt in German translation); HGA 194–5 (excerpt in English translation). This is Caroline's reply to Leibniz's letter of 12 May 1716 (documents 117a and 117b above). For Leibniz's response, see his letter to Caroline of 2 June 1716 (document 124).

[2] That is, 26 May 1716 (NS), 15 May 1716 (OS).

[3] Reading 'pardon' for 'parton'.

[4] Reading 'soupçonnée' for 'supsone'.

[5] Reading 'obligerait' for 'obligerois'.

[6] Reading 'L'Abby Conti a cru de raccommoder' for 'labée conty acreu de racomoder'.

[7] Reading 'passé' for 'passez'.

[8] Reading 'envoyer' for 'anvoiyer'.

[9] Reading 'me paraissez être' for 'me paroiset esttre'.

[10] Reading 'permettez-moi' for 'permeté moy'.

[11] Reading 'cet homme a une véritable envie de rechercher la vérité et se conforme le plus qu'il lui semble à la raison' for 'c'est home a vne veritable anvie de recherger laverité et se conformé le plus qu'il luy samble ala raison'.

[12] Reading 'd'employer' for 'damploiyer'.

[13] Reading 'utilement' for 'udillement'.

[14] Reading 'ensemble' for 'ansamble'.

[15] Reading 'ça vaudra' for 'sa vodera'. Klopp mistranscribes 'sa vodera' as 'cela se fera' (see Klopp XI 112).

[16] Reading 'en plus charmée des couleurs' for 'anplus charmé des coulleurs'.

[17] Reading 'm'empêcher d'être' for 'manpécher destre'.

[18] Reading 'comprend' for 'compran'.

[19] Reading 'ce que ces Mess. ici appellent ainsi' for 'ceque ces Mes icy apelle ainsy'.

[20] Reading 'signifier' for 'sinifier'.

[21] Reading 'aurez vu' for 'aurais veu'.

[22] Reading 'là-dessus' for 'la deceu'.

[23] Reading 'croie' for 'crois'.

[24] See Habakuk 2:4.

[25] Here Caroline switches to the singular, 'il', perhaps to indicate that the Archbishop of Canterbury, William Wake*, was the spokesperson for the bishops. It is also to William Wake that Caroline refers in the same context in her letter to Leibniz of 5 May 1716 (document 115, p. 513).

[26] Reading 'Pour Mess. nos Eveques, il croit la chose' for 'pour Mes nos Eveque, il crois lachose'.

[27] I follow Klopp in reading 'presque impracticable' for 'precse inpracticable' (see Klopp XI 112); but I note that 'precse' is an extremely odd spelling for 'presque' even by Caroline's standards. Thus, for example, in her letter to Leibniz of 7 June 1714 (document 15, p. 52), she wrote 'pres-que' for 'presque'; and in her letter of 12 February 1715 (document 64, p. 212), she wrote 'persqué' for 'presque'. So to say the least, writing 'precse' for 'presque' is quite unusual for Caroline.

[28] Reading 'à moins qu'il veuille envoyer un ministre de la parole' for 'amoin qu'il veuille anvoiyer vn minider de la parolle'.

[29] Reading 'consacrer autres confrères' for 'consaqueré autres confrere'.

[30] Reading 'Je m'étonne' for 'Je mestoñe'.

[31] Reading 'dites' for 'dité'.

[32] Reading 'l'on commence par les cérémonies' for 'lon comance par les seremony'.

[33] Reading 'N'est ce pas' for 'nesce pas'.

[34] Reading 'chemin que l'on prend' For 'chemain que lon pran'.

[35] Reading 'livres' for 'livers'.

[36] Reading 'extrêmement bons et quelques-uns récréatifs' for 'extrement boñe et quelque vne recreadive'.

[37] Reading 'ai déjà dit' for 'ayée des à dit'.

[38] On the point concerning Clarke, see Caroline's letter to Leibniz of 5 May 1716 (document 115, p. 513).

552 122. CAROLINE OF BRANDENBURG-ANSBACH TO LEIBNIZ

122. CAROLINE OF BRANDENBURG-ANSBACH TO LEIBNIZ   553

[39] Reading 'enverrai' for 'anverais'.

[40] Reading 'la poste qui vient ce petit livre' for 'laposte qui vien ce pety liver'.

[41] Reading 'fait le plaisir de m'écrire ces lettres sont remplies de tant d'agrément, qu'on ne sent la peine de lui répondre' for 'fais leplaisir de m'écrire ces lettres son ranplié de tans d'agrement, qu'on ne sans pas lapeñe de luy reponder'.

[42] Reading 'serais ravie si mes importunités auraient pu' for 'scerais ravié sy mes inportunidée aurais peu'.

[43] Here Caroline is apparently referring to her requests that the king pay Leibniz his arrearages. On the topic of Leibniz's arrearages, see Leibniz's letter to Caroline of November 1715, document 85, and Caroline's letter to Leibniz of 6 December 1715, document 89.

[44] Reading 'envoyé un papier contre le vide. Je l'ai donné au Roy, afin qu'il n'en laisse jamais dans votre bourse' for 'anvoiyé vn papié contre levidé je lais doñe au Roy, afin qu'il n'an laissez jamais dans votre pource'.

[45] Reading 'L'abbé Conti l'a à cette heure' for 'L'abée conty la asteur'. Klopp omits this sentence without notice (Klopp XI 113).

[46] The meaning of the last four sentences is not entirely clear, but Caroline seems to be joking, using a complicated play on words. In the first of the four sentences, Caroline is apparently referring to Leibniz's ongoing request for his arrearages. In his previous letter to Caroline (see documents 117a and 117b above), as she recalls in the second of the four sentences, Leibniz had included a short P.S. against the void. Thus in the third sentence, Caroline says she gave Leibniz's paper on the void to the king so that he would never leave a void in Leibniz's purse by withholding his pay—that is, so that he would make good on Leibniz's arrearages. (The joke that takes the void to represent an empty purse was one that Leibniz liked enough to allude to it in his letter to Henriette Charlotte von Pöllnitz of 30 June 1716, document 130, p. 605.) It is not clear how to interpret the fourth sentence. In his previous letter to Caroline, Leibniz had joked that the Abbey Conti was like a chameleon, who was against the void when he was in Paris but who then changed his colours to embrace the void when he arrived in England (document 117a, p. 521). So in the fourth sentence, Caroline may mean to be suggesting that the Abbé Conti now has the void, taking 'l'a' to refer the void. In that case, she would seem to be picking up on Leibniz's joking remarks about the chameleon Abbé Conti, who she then jokingly suggests has (that is, embraces) the void at the present moment. On the other hand, taking 'l'a' to be referring to Leibniz's paper on the void rather than the void itself, Caroline would simply be informing Leibniz that his paper on the void is now in the possession of Conti. In any event, Klopp simply replaced the third sentence, without notice, with 'Je l'ay donné au Roy, afin qu'il ne laisse jamais de penser à vous', and then simply omitted the fourth sentence altogether, again without notice (see Klopp XI 113).

[47] Reading 'charmée du Czar' for 'charmé du Zar'. The reference is to Czar Peter I the Great* of Russia.

[48] Reading 'ses manières' for 'ces manieres'.

[49] Reading 'ne sont pas usitées' for 'n'est pas usidée'.

[50] Reading 'aucun homme pour converser agréablement' for 'au qu'vn hoñe pour convercer agreablement'.

[51] Reading 'étude a une bouteille de double anis' for 'etudé a vne boudellé de double any'.

[52] Reading 'L'Aumônier ne suivra pas' for 'lomenié ne suivera pas'.

[53] Reading 'honnête homme' for 'honest hoñe'.

[54] Reading 'guère agréable' for 'gere agreable'. The entry for Nicolson in the thirteenth edition of the Encyclopædia Britannica seems to confirm Caroline's judgment about his lack of sociability: 'Nicolson is remembered by the impulsiveness of his temperament, which led him into a good deal of strife as a bishop' (HC XIX 664).

[55] Reading 'amis' for 'amié'.

[56] Reading 'prie d'aller souvent' for 'prié d'aller souvant'.

[57] Reading 'conversation lui sera utile' for 'convercassion luy sera udille'.

[58] Reading 'Mandez-moi comment vous le trouvez' for 'mandé moy coñe vous le drouvez'.

Johann Caspar von Bothmer to Leibniz

à Londres ce $\frac{18}{29}$ me May1716

Monsieur

J'ay esté bien aise d'apprendre par l'honneur de vostre lettre du 15me de ce mois que vous avés esté satisfait de vos arrérages. vous le serés aussi de vos frais pour copier, Mr Schilden recevant ordre par cette poste de vous paier le compte que vous en avés donné, je me feray toujours un fort grand plaisir de vous servir touttes les fois que vous me jugeres propre à quelque chose.

Je vous ren[d]s beaucoup de graces de l'information que vous m'avés donné par vostre P.S. de l'estat de vostre different[4] avec M^r le Chevailler Nuton. c'est dommage que deux personnes d'un scavoir si excellent doivent se quereller pour rien estant d'accord dans leurs sentiments. il est evident parce que vous me faites l'honneur de me dire que vostre querelle n'a qu'un malentendu pour origine, de sorte qu'il auroit esté aise de l'appaiser si des amis se fussent appliqués d[']abord à vous espiquer[5] ensemble.[6] le public y auroit gaigné considerablement puisque vous auirés employé tous deux pour son service le tems qu'on vous fait perdre en vaines disputes. J'ay informé le Roy du contenu de vostre P.S. pour luy faire voir que vous n'avés pas offensé Mr Nuton, et que ce que vous proposés est raisonnable. je m'en prevaudray aussi ailleurs aux occasions, pour tacher d'assoupir vostre querelle et de vous mettre d'accord. si j'y pouvois réussir je croirois avoir rendu un service considerable au public. je vous supplie de continuer en attendant vostre assiduité à travailler à vostre histoire.

On ne scait pas encor qui sera du voyage du Roy en Allemagne s'il se fait. l'Eveque de Lincoln est fort scavant, mais c'est celuy de Carlyle qui est le grand aumonier du Roy. je suis avec tout le zele possible

Monsieur   Vostre   tres humble et tres
                                                                                obeissant serviteur
                                                                                Bothmer

123. Johann Caspar von Bothmer* to Leibniz[1]

in London $\frac{18}{29}$ May 1716[2]

Sir

I was very glad to learn by the honour of your letter of the 15th of this month that you have been satisfied with your arrearages. You will also be paid the expenses you are owed for copying, Mr. Schilden receiving order by this poste to pay you the account you have given of them. I will always be very happy to serve you any time you consider me suitable for something.

I thank you very much for the information that you have given me by means of your P.S.[3] about the state of your dispute[4] with Chevalier Newton. It is a shame that two persons of such excellent learning must quarrel for nothing, as they are in agreement in their opinions. It is evident because you do me the honour of telling me that your quarrel originates only from a misunderstanding, so that it would have been easy to dispel if some friends had applied themselves from the outset to explain[5] to you in tandem.[6] The public would have gained considerably by it, since both of you would have employed for its service the time that you were made to lose in vain disputes. I have informed the king [George I, Georg Ludwig* of Braunschweig-Lüneburg] about the content of your P.S. in order to show him that you have not offended Mr. Newton and that what you propose is reasonable. I will also avail myself of it elsewhere, should the occasions arise, to try to calm your quarrel and reconcile you. If I could succeed in this, I would believe that I had rendered a considerable service to the public. I beseech you to continue in the meantime your assiduity in working on your history.[7]

It is not yet known who will journey with king to Germany, if it happens. The Bishop of London [John Robinson (1650–1723)] is very learned, but it is the Bishop of Carlisle [William Nicolson*] who is the grand almoner of the king. I am with all possible enthusiasm

sir   your   very humble and very
                                               obedient servant
                                               Bothmer

---

[1] LBr. 97 Bl. 143r–144v. Draft: four quarto sides in Bothmer's hand. Previously published in Klopp XI 114 (excerpt) and by Eduard Bodemann in *Zeitschrift des Historischen Vereins für Niedersachsen*, 1890, pp. 166–7.

[2] That is, 29 May 1716 (NS), 18 May 1716 (OS).

[3] That is, the P.S. to Leibniz's letter to Bothmer of 28 April 1716 (document 114).

[4] Reading 'différend' for 'different'.

[5] Reading 'expliquer' for 'espiquer'.

[6] Klopp mistranscribes 'se fussent' as 's'y fussent' and omits 'à vous espiquer ensemble' (see Klopp XI 114).

[7] That is, Leibniz's history of the House of Braunschweig-Lüneburg, the *Annales imperii occidentis Brunsvicenses**.

Leibniz to Caroline of Brandenburg-Ansbach, Princess of Wales

Madame

Hanover ce 2 de juin 1716

Je remercie V. A. R. de la bonté qu'elle a de vouloir revoir mes papiers perdus, et je les feray copier de nouveau. Je joins icy une reponse à la derniere pièce de M. Clark. Lui et ses semblables ne comprennent pas encore bien ce grand principe que rien n'arrive sans qu'il y ait une raison suffisante pour cela; et ce qui suit que Dieu même[3] ne sauroit choisir sans qu'il y ait une raison de son choix. C'est l'erreur de l'indifference vague ou du decret absolument absolu, refutée dans la Theodicée. Cette erreur encore est la source du vuide et des Atomes.

Il me semble qu'il n'y a rien dans ma reponse à M. l'Abbé Conti, qui marque un esprit troublé. Il n'y a rien aussi qui dechire M. Newton. Mais comme il m'attaque je me defends,[4] et mes expressions sont assés honnestes. A quoy sert il de m'exhorter à la paix, quand on m'envoye des cartels?

J'ay peur que nous disputerons aussi inutilement sur le vuide que sur autres choses. Je n'ay pas assés de temps de reste, pour le perdre en amusemens. Il y a des choses plus importantes à faire. Je ne crois pas qu'il y ait aucun espace sans matiere. Les experiences qu'on appelle du vuide, n'excluent qu'une matiere grossiere, qu'on tire de la cavité du verre par le poids[5] du vif argent avec Torricelli, et par la pompe avec M. Guerike. Car les rayons de lumiere, qui ne sont point sans quelque matiere subtile passent à travers du verre. Je n'aurois point touché cette question du vuide, si je n'avois trouvé que l'opinion du vuide deroge aux perfections de Dieu, comme presque toutes les autres opinions de philosophie qui sont contraires aux miennes. Car les miennes sont presque toutes liées avec le grand principe de la supreme raison et perfection de Dieu. Ainsi je ne crains point que V. A. Royale quitte aisement ce qu'elle en aura eu le loisir de bien entendre: sa penetration, et son zele pour la gloire de Dieu m'en sont garants. | M. Clarke ne dit plus rien pour l'opinion de M. Newton qui rend les ouvrages de Dieu aussi imparfaits que ceux de nos ouvriers. Peut étre est il disposé à la quitter: en ce cas nous aurions gagné quelque chose. Mais si nous ne gagnons rien à la longue, la dispute cessera. |

En suppliant V.A. Royale de communiquer à M. l'Abbé Conti mes conferences avec M. Clarc, mon but avoit eté que par son moyen elles fussent communiqué[e]s à d'autres amis, mais puisque M. l'Abbé en a perdu une partie, je fais copier le tout de nouveau; et je crois qu'il seroit bon d'en faire part à d'autres, à fin que ces papiers ne se perdent plus si facilement.

Je ne suis nullement piqué contre M. l'Abbé Conti de ce qu'il m'a envoyé la lettre de M. Newton: au contraire cette lettre m'a fait plaisir, et m'a donné de l'esperance de desabuser celuy qui l'a écrite. Mais j'ay eté surpris de la lettre que l'Abbé y[7] avoit jointe du sien.[6] Il y change entierement langage. Il paroist avoir oublié tout ce qu'il

124. Leibniz to Caroline* of Brandenburg-Ansbach, Princess of Wales[1]

Madame

Hanover 2 June 1716

I thank Your Royal Highness for her kindness in wanting to recover my lost papers, and I will have them copied again. I enclose here a response to the last paper of Mr. [Samuel] Clarke*.[2] He and his fellows do not yet properly understand this great principle, that nothing happens without a sufficient reason for it, and that which follows, that God himself[3] could not choose without there being a reason for his choice. It is the error of vague indifference, or of the absolutely absolute decree, refuted in the *Theodicy*. That error is again the source of [the ideas of] the void and atoms.

It seems to me that there is nothing in my response to the Abbé [Antonio Schinella] Conti* that indicates a disturbed mind. There is also nothing that defames Mr. Newton. But as he attacks me, I defend myself,[4] and my words are fair enough. What is the point of urging me to make peace when I am sent challenges?

I am afraid that we will dispute as futilely about the void as about other things. I do not have enough time remaining to waste it in amusements. There are more important things to do. I do not believe that there is any space without matter. The experiments that they cite concerning the void exclude only a gross matter, which they draw from the cavity of the glass by the weight[5] of the mercury, in the case of [Evangelista] Torricelli*, and by the pump, in the case of Mr. [Otto von] Guericke*. For the rays of light, which are not devoid of some subtle matter, pass through the glass. I would not have touched upon this matter of the void if I had not found that the notion of the void derogates from the perfections of God, as do nearly all the other philosophical views that are contrary to mine. For mine are nearly all bound up with the great principle of the supreme reason and perfection of God. So I do not fear that Your Royal Highness will easily abandon what she will have had the leisure to understand thoroughly: her penetration and her zeal for the glory of God are my sureties. | Mr. Clarke says nothing in favour of the view of Mr. Newton that renders the works of God as imperfect as those of our workmen. Perhaps he is disposed to abandon it. In that case we would gain something. But if at length we gain nothing, the dispute will end. |

By imploring Your Royal Highness to communicate my exchanges with Mr. Clarke to the Abbé Conti, my purpose had been that they might be communicated by him to some other friends. But since the Abbé has lost some of them, I am having all of them copied again, and I believe that it would be a good idea to share them with others, so that these papers may not be lost so easily.

I am not at all roused against the Abbé Conti by the fact that he sent me the letter of Mr. Newton. On the contrary, that letter pleased me and gave me some hope of

558   124. LEIBNIZ TO CAROLINE OF BRANDENBURG-ANSBACH

m'avoit écrit, et tout ce que je luy avois écrit aussi, il n'avoit meme point menagé mon nom dans une certaine matiere comme je l'en avois prié par ma lettre, et il prenoit la peine de m'exhorter de repondre à la lettre qu'il m'envoyoit, comme si j'avois besoin d'une telle exhortation. Ainsi je ne pouvois point manquer de répondre sechement à une lettre aussi seche que la sienne; mais il n'y a rien qui le doive offencer. Il est le maitre d'estimer et de favoriser qui bon luy semble, | sans qu'on ait sujet de s'en plaindre |.

Si V. A. S. elle même avoit moins d'estime pour mes sentimens qu'auparavant, j'en serois faché, mais je n'aurois aucun sujet de m'en plaindre. Suffit qu'elle me garde la bonté, et Elle en a donné des preuves grandes et reelles. Ce que je dois juger de[8] la continuation de son estime se peut faire connoistre par ce qui se rapporte à la traduction de la Theodicée.

On a receu icy un lettre de Swerin d'un ministre du Czar qui demande 150 chevaux de Vorspan, et qu'on luy envoye une garde a pirmont. Elle ne marque point le temps. On a envoyé une estafette à M. Fabrice pour le savoir precisement. Je voudrois que le Czar et le Roy de Dannemarc imitassent dans le Meclenbourg et dans le Holstein, ce que le Roy fait dans le pays de Breme, mais ils imitent davantage ce que le Roy fait en pologne. Le Comte Mersch fera[11] des remontrances au Czar, mais il faudra que le Roy de la G. B. et le Roy de prusse y joignent les leurs.

Voicy un ouvrage posthume du Baron de la Hontan. Il se mêloit d'écrire sur les affaires, et un peu avant que de mourir il a envoyé a Leipzig ce petit discours contre une lettre imprimée opposée au manifeste du Roy. Et ce discours qu'on[13] nous a eté apporté de la foire je prends la liberté de envoyer à V. A. Royale. L'auteur fait voir son zele pour la gloire du Roy. Mais il ne paroist pas qu'il soit entré fort avant dans les affaires.

Je suis etc.

P.S.

J'admire combien les choses peuvent etre prises de travers. (1) Il est seur que la scission qui est entre les Protestans, qui fait que les uns condamnent les autres, s'excluent de la communion, et se regardent comme de differente religion est une chose tres pernicieuse. (2) Il est seur aussi que jamais on a vû des conjonctures plus favorables pour lever cette scission. (3) D'où il s'ensuit qu'une personne qui considere bien ces faits, qui a un veritable zele, et qui a de l'autorité en même temps doit penser fortement à lever ou à diminuer une chose si deplorable. Mais est ce venir au fait que de parler des differens sur la discipline Ecclesiastique? Car puisque les Reformés d'Angleterre et hors de l'Angleterre ne se condamnent point sur ces differens et ne s'excluent point de la communion mutuelle, cela n'a donc rien de commun avec l'affaire dont il s'agit. Et n'est ce pas aussi un travers que de dire d[']y objecter[16] pour s'excuser d'y penser serieusement, que chacun doit vivre de sa foy? C'est justement pour cela qu'on doit lever ces exclusions de la communion et ces condamnations parce que la difference des sentimens n'est pas assez grande pour la surmonter. Si ce que je viens de dire n'est pas assés clair, il ne servira de rien de le vouloir éclaircir. J'ay fait mon devoir. Et la conscience du chacun reglera le sien.

124. LEIBNIZ TO CAROLINE OF BRANDENBURG-ANSBACH 559

disabusing the one who wrote it. But I was taken aback by his own letter,[6] which the Abbé had included with it.[7] He completely changes his tune in it. He appears to have forgotten everything that he has written me and everything that I have written to him as well. He had not even been careful of my name in a certain matter as I had requested in my letter, and he took the trouble to exhort me to respond to the letter that he sent me, as if I needed such an exhortation. So I could not fail to respond harshly to a letter as harsh as his; but there is nothing which ought to offend him. He is in control of esteeming and favouring who appears good to him | without someone having reason to complain about it |.

If Your Serene Highness herself had less esteem for my views than before, I would be displeased by it, but I would not have any reason to complain about it. It is enough that she preserves her kindness for me, and she has given great and real proofs of it. What I ought to believe about[8] the continuation of her esteem can become known by what happens in relation to the translation of the *Theodicy*.

A letter from Schwerin has been received here from a minister of the czar [Peter the Great* of Russia] who requests one hundred fifty extra horse teams and that a guard be sent to him at Pyrmont*. It does not state the time. A courier has been sent to Mr. [Weipart Ludwig von] Fabrice[9] to find out precisely. I would have the czar and the King of Denmark [Frederick IV of Denmark and Norway (1671–1730)] imitate in Mecklenburg and in Holstein what the king [George I, Georg Ludwig* of Braunschweig-Lüneburg] does in the country of Bremen*, but they imitate more what the king does in Poland.[10] Count Mersch will raise[11] objections to the czar, but the King of Great Britain and the King of Prussia [Friedrich Wilhelm I*] will have to add theirs to them.

Here is a posthumous work of Baron Lahontan [Louis-Armand de Lom d'Arce, Baron de Lahontan*]. He got involved in writing about [public] affairs, and shortly before his death he sent to Leipzig this small discourse against a published letter opposed to the manifesto of the king.[12] And this discourse, which[13] was brought to us from the market, I take the liberty of sending to Your Royal Highness.[14] The author shows his zeal for the glory of the king, but it does not appear that he entered very deeply into the matters.

I am etc.

P. S.

I wonder at how many things can be taken amiss. (1) It is certain that the schism that separates the Protestants, and that makes them condemn each other, exclude each other from communion, and regard each other as from a different religion, is a very pernicious thing. (2) It is also certain that we have never seen circumstances more favourable for removing this schism. (3) From which it follows that a person who considers the facts thoroughly, who has a genuine zeal, and who has, at the same time, some authority, ought to think seriously about removing or diminishing something so deplorable. But is it to the point to talk about differences concerning the ecclesiastical discipline? For that has nothing to do with the matter in

124. LEIBNIZ TO CAROLINE OF BRANDENBURG-ANSBACH 561

question, since the Reformed of England and outside of England do not condemn each other on account of these differences and do not exclude each other from mutual communion.[15] And isn't it also an oddity to say, to object to it,[16] in order to excuse oneself from thinking seriously about the matter, that each should live by his faith?[17] It is precisely for that reason that one ought to remove these exclusions from communion and these condemnations, because the difference of opinions is not great enough to overcome the faith. If what I have just said is not clear enough, it will be of no use to try to clarify it. I have done my duty, and the conscience of each will determine his own.

[1] LBr. 160 Bl. 79r–79v. Draft: 1.5 folio sides in Leibniz's hand. Previously published: GP VII 378–81; Schüller 1991, pp. 247–50 (excerpt in German translation); Robinet 1991 pp. 78–80 (excerpt); HGA 195–6 (excerpt in English translation). The beginning of the draft is found at the bottom of the last page of the draft of Leibniz's fourth paper for Clarke. There is also a fair copy of this letter in Leibniz's hand, but it includes only the first two paragraphs and the first sentence of the third paragraph (LBr. F 4 Bl. 99r, .5 octavo sides). The letter is Leibniz's response to Caroline's letter to Leibniz of 26 May 1716 (document 122). For Caroline's response to the present letter see her letter to Leibniz of 26 June 1716 (document 128).

[2] That is, Leibniz's Fourth Paper (document 125a) in response to the Third Reply of Clarke (document 120).

[3] The fair copy has 'd'où il suit que Dieu luy même' instead of 'et ce qui suit que Dieu même' (see LBr. F 4 Bl. 99r). Gerhardt omits 'et' (see GP VII 379).

[4] The fair copy has 'Il m'attaque, et me defends' instead of 'Mais comme il m'attaque je me defends' (see LBr. F 4 Bl. 99r).

[5] Gerhardt mistranscribes 'poids' as 'puits' (see GP VII 379).

[6] Reading 'de la sienne' for 'du sien'.

[7] G VII 379 and Robinet 1991, p. 79 omit 'y'.

[8] Gerhardt omits 'Ce que je dois juger de' (see GP VII 380).

[9] Weipart Ludwig von Fabrice (1640–1724) was a German diplomat and statesman in the service of the Hanoverian court. From 1710 he was president of the highest court of appeal in the Electorate of Hanover.

[10] The King of Poland at the time was August II the Strong (1670–1733). August sought to rule as an absolute monarch, despite the opposition of the nobility.

[11] Gerhardt mistranscribes 'fera' as 'fait' (see GP VII 380).

[12] That is, the war manifesto of 4/15 October 1715 against Sweden, issued by King George I of Great Britain in his capacity as Elector of Hanover.

[13] GP VII 380 omits 'qu'on'.

[14] Shortly after George I declared war on Sweden on 4/15 October 1715, in part to secure his right to the duchies of Bremen* and Verden*, there was published a *Lettre d'un particulière opposée au Manifeste de Sa Majesté de la Grande-Bretagne, comme Électeur de Brunswic, contre Suede*, in response to which Leibniz wrote and anonymously published a short tract entitled *Réponse à la Lettre d'un particulière opposée au Manifeste de Sa Majesté de la Grande-Bretagne, comme Électeur de Brunswic, contre Suede*. On 4 May 1716, just two weeks after Lahontan's death on 21 April, Leibniz wrote to the printer and bookseller Forster of Leipzig, suggesting, in light of the numerous and confusing printing errors that infected the original, that a new edition of the *Réponse* be prepared and urging that 'it would be best that the name of H. Baron de la Hontan be placed on the title as author, for since he is dead, it can do him no harm' (Niedersächsische Landesbibliothek, Hanover, ms. XXXII, 1739, f. 6v; translation from the German based on the transcription in OB 1154n16). A second, corrected edition soon appeared under Lahontan's name—*Réponse du Baron de la Hontan à la Lettre d'un particulier opposée au Manifeste de Sa Majesté de la Grande-Bretagne, comme Électeur de Brunswic, contre Suede*—and, 'voulant consolider la supercherie, Leibniz écrit à la princesse de Galles Caroline' (OB 238), passing along to her a 'petit discours' that 'nous a eté apporté de la foire'.

[15] When Leibniz speaks of 'the Reformed of England' here, he apparently means the Anglican church; and by the Reformed 'outside of England', he apparently means the Reformed (Calvinist)

Leibniz's Fourth Paper

Quatriéme Ecrit de Mr. LEIBNITZ,

ou

Réponse au Troisiéme Ecrit Anglois.

1. *Dans les choses* indifferentes *absolument, il n'y a point de choix, & par consequent point d'élection ny volonté ; puisque le choix doit avoir quelque* raison *ou principe.*

2. *Une* simple volonté *sans aucun motif,* (a mere Will,) *est une fiction non seulement contraire à la perfection de Dieu, mais encore chimerique & contradictoire, incompatible avec la Definition de la* volonté, & *assez refutée dans la* Theodicée.[2]

3. *Il est* indifferent *de ranger trois corps égaux & en tout semblables, en quel ordre qu'on voudra ; & par consequent ils* ne seront jamais rangés, *par celuy qui ne fait rien qu'avec sagesse. Mais aussi étant l'Auteur des choses,* il n'en produira point, & *par consequent* il n'y en a point *dans la Nature.*

4. *Il n'y a point* deux Individus indiscernables. *Un Gentilhomme d'esprit de mes amis, en parlant avec moy en presence de Madame l'Electrice dans le jardin de* Herrenhausen, *crut qu'il trouveroit bien deux feuilles entierement semblables.* Madame l'Electrice *l'en defia, & il courut long temps en vain pour en chercher. Deux gouttes d'eau, ou de lait, regardées par le Microscope, se trouveront discernables. C'est un argument contre les* Atomes, *qui ne sont pas moins combattus que le* Vuide *par les Principes de la veritable Metaphysique.*

5. *Ces grands Principes de la* Raison suffisante & de l'Identité des indiscernables, *changent l'état de la Metaphysique ; qui devient réelle & demonstrative par leur moyen : Au lieu qu'autres fois elle ne consistoit presque qu'en termes Vuides.*

6. *Poser* deux *choses* indiscernables, est poser la même chose *sous* deux noms. *Ainsi l'hypothese, que l'Univers auroit eu d'abord une* autre *position du* Temps & du Lieu *que celle qui est arrivée effectivement ; & que pourtant toutes le parties de l'Univers auroient eu la même position entre elles, que celle qu'elles ont receüe en effect ; est une fiction* impossible.[5]

churches on the continent, and especially those in Brandenburg. This reading is supported by what Leibniz wrote to Caroline in his letter to her of mid-January, namely, that the 'Anglican church maintains that it does not have a religion different from that of the Reformed churches of the country of Brandenburg, since in any case neither adheres to the Synod of Dordrecht' (document 97, p. 387).

[16] GP VII has 'que dire' instead of 'que de dire d'y objecter'.

[17] Leibniz asks this in response to what Caroline reported in her letter to Leibniz of 26 May 1716, namely, that the King 'says with Holy Scripture, "Each should live by his faith"' (document 122, p. 549).

125a. Leibniz's Fourth Paper[1]

Mr. LEIBNITZ'S *Fourth Paper.*
BEING
An Answer to Dr. CLARKE'S *Third Reply*

1. In things *absolutely indifferent*, there is no [Foundation for] Choice ; and consequently no Election, nor Will ; since Choice must be founded on some *Reason*, or Principle.

2. *A mere Will* without any Motive, is a Fiction, not only contrary to God's Perfection, but also chimerical and contradictory ; inconsistent with the Definition of the *Will*, and sufficiently confuted in my *Theodicæa*.[2]

3. Tis a thing *indifferent*, to place three Bodies, equal and perfectly alike, in any order whatsoever ; and consequently they will *never be placed in Any order*, by Him who does nothing without Wisdom. But then, He being the Author of things, no such things will be *produced by him* at all ; and consequently there *are no such things* in Nature.

4. There is no such things as Two Individuals *indiscernible* from each other. An Ingenious Gentleman of my Acquaintance, discoursing with me, in the presence of Her *Electoral Highness the Princess* Sophia,[3] in the Garden of *Herrenhausen* ;[4] thought he could find two Leaves perfectly alike. The Princess defied him to do it, and he ran all over the Garden a long time to look for some ; but it was to no purpose. Two Drops of Water, or Milk, viewed with a Microscope, will appear distinguishable from each other. This is an Argument against *Atoms* ; which are confuted, as well as a *Vacuum*, by the Principles of true Metaphysicks.

5. Those great Principles of a *sufficient Reason*, and of the *Identity of Indiscernibles*, change the State of Metaphysicks. That Science becomes real and demonstrative by means of these Principles ; whereas before, it did generally consist in empty words.

6. To suppose *two* things *indiscernible*, is to suppose the *same thing* under *two Names*. And therefore to suppose that the Universe could have had at first *another* position of *Time* and *Place*, than that which it actually had ; and yet that all the Parts of the Universe should have had the same Situation among themselves, as that which they actually had ; such a Supposition, I say, is an impossible *fiction*.[5]

7. *La même raison qui fait que l'Espace* hors du monde *est* imaginaire, *prouve que* tout espace vuide *est une chose* imaginaire ; *car ils ne different que du grand au petit.*

8. *Si l'*Espace *est une* proprieté *ou un attribut, il doit être la* proprieté *de quelque* Substance. *L'Espace vuide* borné, *que ses patrons supposent entre deux Corps, de* quelle Substance *sera-t-il la proprietè ou l'Affection?*[6]

9. *Si l'*Espace infini *est l'immensité ; l'Espace* fini *sera l'opposé de l'immensité, c'est à dire, la* mensurabilité, *ou l'*Etendue bornèe. *Or l'Etendue doit etre l'affection d'un Etendu. Mais si cet Espace est vuide, il sera un* attribut sans sujet, *une Etendue d'aucun Etendu. C'est pourquoy, en faisant de l'Espace une* proprieté, *l'on tombe dans mon sentiment qui le fait un Ordre des choses & non pas quelque chose d'absolu.*

10. *Si l'*Espace *est une* realité absolu ; *bien loin d'etre une* proprieté *ou accidentalité opposée à la Substance, il sera* plus Subsistant *que les* Substances. *Dieu ne le sauroit detruire, ny méme changer en rien. Il est non seulement immense dans le tout, mais encore* Immuable *&* Eternal *en chaque partie. Il y aura une infinité[7] de choses* Eternelles hors de Dieu.

11. *Dire que l'Espace* infini *est* sans parties, *c'est dire que l'Espaces* finis *ne le composent point ; & que l'Espace* infini *pourroit subsister, quand tous les Espaces finis seroient reduits à rien. Ce seroit comme si l'on disoit dans la Supposition* Cartesienne *d'un Univers corporel étendu sans bornes, que cet Univers pourroit subsister, quand tous les Corps qui le composent, seroient reduits à rien.*

12. *On attribue des* parties *à l'Espace, p.* 19. 3ᵉᵐᵉ Edition *de la* Defense de l'Argument contre M. Dodwell ; *& on les fait inseparables* l'une de l'autre. *Mais p.* 30, *de la* Seconde Defense, *on en fait des* parties improprement dites : *Cela se peut entendre dans un bon sens.*[8]

13. *De dire que Dieu fasse* avancer *tout l'Univers, en ligne droite ou autre, sans y rien changer autrement, c'est encore une Supposition* Chimerique. *Car* deux états indiscernables *sont* le même état, *& par consequent c'est un changement qui ne change rien. De plus, il n'y a ny* rime *ny* raison. *Or Dieu ne fait rien sans* raison ; *& il est* impossible *qu'il y en ait icy. Outre que ce servit* agendo nihil agere, *comme je viens de dire, à cause de l'indiscernabilité.*

14. *Ce sont* Idola Tribûs, *Chimeres toutes pures, & Imaginations superficielles. Tout cela n'est fondé, que sur la Supposition que l'Espace imaginaire est* réel.

15. *C'est une fiction semblable, c'est à dire* impossible, *de supposer que Dieu ait* créé le Monde *quelques Millions d'années* plustost. *Ceux qui donnent dans ces sortes de Fictions, ne sauroient répondre à ceux qui argumenteroient pour l'Eternité du Monde. Car Dieu ne faisant rien sans raison, & point de raison n'estant assignable pourquoy il n'ait point créé le monde plustost ; il s'ensuivra, ou qu'il n'ait rien crée du tout, ou qu'il ait produit le monde avant tout temps assignable, c'est à dire que le monde soit* Eternal. *Mais quand on montre que le commencement, quel qu'il soit, est tousjours* la même chose, *la question pourquoy il n'en a pas été autrement, cesse.*

7. The same reason, which shows that *extramundane* Space is *imaginary*, proves that *All empty Space* is an *imaginary* thing; for they differ only as greater and less.

8. If *Space* is a *property* or Attribute, it must be the Property of some *Substance*. But *what Substance* will That *Bounded* empty Space be an Affection or Property of, which the Persons I am arguing with, suppose to be between Two Bodies ?[6]

9. If *infinite Space* is *Immensity, finite Space* will be the Opposite to Immensity, that is, 'twill be *Mensurability,* or *limited Extension.* Now Extension must be the Affection of some thing extended. But if That Space be empty, it will be an Attribute *without a Subject,* an Extension without any thing extended. Wherefore by making Space a *Property,* the Author falls in with My Opinion, which makes it an Order of things, and not any thing absolute.

10. If Space is an absolute *reality* ; far from being a *Property* or an Accident opposed to Substance, it will have a *greater reality* than *Substances* themselves. God cannot destroy it, nor even change it in any respect. It will be not only immense in the whole, but also *Immutable* and *Eternal* in every part. There will be an infinite number[7] of Eternal things *besides God.*

11. To say that *infinite Space* has no *parts,* is to say that it does not consist of *finite* Spaces ; and that Infinite Space might subsist, though all finite Spaces should be reduced to nothing. It would be, as if one should say, in the *Cartesian* Supposition of a material extended unlimited World, that such a World might subsist, though all the Bodies of which it consists, should be reduced to nothing.

12. The Author ascribes *Parts* to Space, *p.* 19. *Of the 3ᵈ Edition* of his *Defense of the Argument against Mr. Dodwell* ; and makes them *inseparable* one from another. But, *p.* 30. *Of his Second Defense,* he says they are *parts improperly so called :* Which may be understood in a good sense.[8]

13. To say that God can cause the whole Universe to *move forward* in a Right Line, or in any other Line, without making otherwise any Alteration in it ; is another *Chimerical* Supposition. For, *two States indiscernible* from each other, are the *same* State ; and consequently, 'tis a change without any change. Besides, there is neither *Rhime* nor *Reason* in it. But God does nothing without *Reason* ; And tis *impossible* there should be any here. Besides, it would be *agendo nihil agere,* as I have just now said, because of the Indiscernibility.

14. These are *Idola Tribûs,* mere Chimeras, and superficial Imaginations. All this is only grounded upon the Supposition, that imaginary Space is real.

15. It is a like fiction, (that is) an *impossible* one, to suppose that God might have created the World some Millions of Years sooner. They who run into such kind of Fictions, can give no answer to one that should argue for the *Eternity* of the World. For since God does nothing without Reason, and no Reason can be given why he did not create the World sooner ; it will follow, either that he has created nothing at all, or that he created the World before any assignable time, that is, that the World is *Eternal.* But when once it has been shown, that the Beginning, *whenever* it was, is always the *same thing* ; the Question, Why it was not otherwise ordered, becomes needless and insignificant.

16. *Si* l'Espace *& le* Temps *estoient quelque chose d'absolu, c'est à dire, s'ils estoient autre chose que certains* Ordres *des choses ; ce que je dis, seroit* Contradiction. *Mais cela n'étant point, l'Hypothese est contradictoire, c'est une Fiction* impossible.

17. *Et c'est comme dans la* Geometrie, *où l'on prouve quelque fois par la Supposition même, qu'une Figure* soit *plus grande, qu'en effect elle n'est point plus grande. C'est une* Contradiction ; *mais elle est dans l'Hypothese, laquelle pour cela même se trouve faussse.*

18. *L'uniformité de l'Espace fait qu'il n'y a aucune* Raison *ny* Interne *ny* Externe, *pour en discerner les parties, & pour y choisir. Car cette Raison* Externe *de discerner, ne sauroit étre fondée que dans l'*Interne ; *autrement c'est discerner l'indiscernable, ou c'est choisir sans discerner. La volonté sans Raison, seroit le* Hazard *des* Epicuriens. *Un Dieu qui agiroit par une telle volonté, seroit un Dieu de nom. La source de ces erreurs est, qu'on n'a point de soin d'éviter ce qui déroge aux Perfections Divines.*

19. *Lors que* deux *choses incompatibles sont* également bonnes, *& que tant en elles que par leur combinaison avec d'autres, l'une n'a point d'avantage sur l'autre ;* Dieu n'en *produira aucune.*

20. *Dieu n'est jamais determiné par les choses* externes, *mais tousjours par ce qui* est *en luy, c'est à dire par ses connoissances, avant qu'il y ait aucune chose hors de luy.*

21. *Il n'y a point de raison* possible, *qui* puisse limiter *la quantité de la matiere. Ainsi cette limitation ne sauroit avoir lieu.*

22. *Et supposé cette limitation arbitraire, on pourroit tousjours adjourter quelque chose sans deroger à la* Perfection *des choses qui sont deja : Et par consequent il faudra tousjours y adjouter quelque chose, pour agir suivant le Principe de la Perfection des operations Divines.*

23. *Ainsi on ne sauroit dire que la presente quantité de la matiere est la plus convenable pour leur presente Constitution. Et quand méme cela seroit, il s'ensuivroit que cette presente Constitution des choses ne seroit point la plus convenable absolument, si elle empeche d'employer plus de matiere ; il vaudroit donc en choisir une autre, capable de quelque chose de plus.*

24. *Je serois bien aise de voir le passage d'un Philosophe, qui prenne* Sensorium *autrement que* Goclenius.

25. *Si* Scapula *dit que* Sensorium *est la* place *où l'entendement reside, il entendra l'*Organe *de la sensation interne. Ainsi il ne s'éloignera point de* Goclenius.

26. Sensorium *a tousjours été l'*Organe *de la sensation. La glande pineale seroit selon* des Cartes, *le* Sensorium *dans le sens qu'on rapporte de* Scapula.

16. If *Space* and *Time* were any thing absolute, that is, if they were any thing else, besides certain *Orders* of things ; then indeed my assertion would be a *Contradiction*. But since it is not so, the Hypothesis [*that Space and Time are any thing absolute*] is contradictory, that is, 'tis an *impossible* Fiction.

17. And the Case is the same as in *Geometry* ; where by the very Supposition that a Figure *is* greater than it really is, we sometimes prove that it *is not* greater. This indeed is a *Contradiction* ; but it lies in the Hypothesis, which appears to be false for that very reason.

18. Space being *uniform*, there can be neither any *External* nor *Internal* Reason, by which to distinguish its parts, and to make any choice among them. For, any *External* Reason to discern between them, can only be grounded upon some *Internal* one. Otherwise we should discern what is indiscernible, or chuse without discerning. A Will without Reason, would be the *Chance* of the *Epicureans*. A God, who should act by such a Will, would be a God only in Name. The cause of these Errors proceeds from want of care to avoid what derogates from the Divine Perfections.

19. When *two* things which cannot Both be together, are *equally good* ; and neither in themselves, nor by their combination with other things, has the one any advantage over the other ; God will produce *Neither of them*.

20. God is never determined by *external* things, but always by what is *in himself* ; that is, by his Knowledge of things, before any thing exists *without* himself.

21. There is no *possible* Reason, that *can limit* the quantity of Matter ; and therefore such limitation can have no place.

22. And supposing an arbitrary Limitation of the Quantity of Matter, something might always be added to it without derogating from the Perfection of those things which do already exist ; and consequently something *must* always be added, in order to act according to the Principle of the Perfection of the divine Operations.

23. And therefore it cannot be said, that the present quantity of Matter is the fittest for the present Constitution of Things. And supposing it were, it would follow that this present Constitution of things would not be the fittest absolutely, if it hinders God from using more Matter. It were therefore better to chuse another constitution of things, capable of something more.

24. I should be glad to see a passage of any Philosopher, who takes *Sensorium* in any other Sense than *Goclenius* does.

25. If *Scapula* says that *Sensorium* is the *place* in which the Understanding resides, he means by it the *Organ* of internal Sensation. And therefore he does not differ from *Goclenius*.

26. *Sensorium* has always signified the *Organ* of Sensation. The *Glandula pinealis* would be, according to *Cartesius*, the *Sensorium*, in the above-mentioned sense of *Scapula*.

27. *Il n'y a gueres d'Expression moins convenable sur ce sujet, que celle qui donne à Dieu un* Sensorium. *Il semble qu'elle le fait l'Ame du Monde. Et on aura bien de la peine à donner à l'usage que* M. Newton *fait de ce mot, un sens qui le puisse justifier.*

28. *Quoy qu'il s'agisse du sens de* M. Newton, *& non pas de celuy de* Goclenius, *on ne me doit point blamer d'avoir allegué le Dictionnaire Philosophique de cet auteur; parceque le but des Dictionnaires est de marquer l'usage des termes.*

29.[9] *Dieu s'apperçoit des choses en luy même. L'Espace est le lieu des* choses, *& non pas le lieu des* Idées de Dieu : A *moins qu'on ne considere l'Espace comme quelque chose qui fasse l'Union de Dieu & des choses, à l'imitation de l'Union de l'Ame & du Corps qu'on s'imagine; ce qui rendroit encore Dieu l'Ame du Monde.*

30. *Aussi a-t-on tort dans la Comparaison qu'on fait de la connoissance & de l'Operation de Dieu avec celle des ames. Les ames connoissent les choses, parce que Dieu a mis en elles un* Principe Representatif *de ce qui est hors d'elles. Mais Dieu connoist les choses, parce qu'il les* produit *continuellement.*

31. *Les ames n'operent sur les choses selon moy, que parceque des Corps s'accommodent à leur desirs en vertu de l'harmonie que Dieu y a* préétablie.

32. *Mais ceux qui s'imaginent que les ames peuvent donner une Force nouvelle au Corps, & que Dieu en fait autant dans le monde pour redresser les defauts de sa machine; approchent trop Dieu de l'ame, en donnant trop à l'ame & trop peu à Dieu.*

33. *Car il n'y a que Dieu qui puisse donner à la nature de* nouvelles Forces, *mais il ne le fait que* surnaturellement. *S'il avoit besoin de le faire dans le cours* naturel, *il auroit fait un ouvrage tres imparfait. Il ressembleroit dans le monde à ce que le vulgaire attribue à l'Ame dans le Corps.*

34. *En voulant soutenir cette Opinion vulgaire de l'influence de l'Ame sur le Corps, par l'Example de Dieu operant hors de lui; on fait encore que Dieu ressembleroit trop à l'Ame du Monde. Cette affectation encore de blâmer mon Expression d'Intelligentia Supramundana, y semble pancher aussi.*

35. *Les images dont l'Ame est affectée immediatement, sont en elle même; mais elles repondent à celles du Corps. La presence de l'ame est imparfaite,[10] & ne peut être expliquée que par cette correspondance. Mais celle de Dieu est parfaite, & se manifeste par son Operation.*

36. *L'on suppose mal contre moy, que la presence de l'Ame est liée avec son* influence *sur le Corps; puis qu'on sait que je rejette cette* influence.

37. *Il est aussi inexplicable que l'Ame soit* diffuse *par le Cerveau, que de faire qu'elle soit diffuse par le Corps tout entier: La difference n'est que du plus au moins.*

125A. LEIBNIZ'S FOURTH PAPER   569

27. There is hardly any Expression less proper upon this Subject, than that which makes God to have a *Sensorium*. It seems to make God the *Soul of the World*. And it will be a hard matter to put a justifiable sense upon this Word, according to the Use Sir *Isaac Newton* makes of it.

28. Though the question be about the Sense put upon that Word by Sir *Isaac Newton*, and not by *Goclenius*; yet I am not to blame for quoting the Philosophical Dictionary of that Author, because the design of Dictionaries is to shew the use of Words.

29.[9] God perceives things in himself. Space is the Place of *things*, and not the Place of God's *Ideas*: Unless we look upon Space as something that makes an Union between God and Things, in imitation of the imagined Union between the Soul and the Body; which would still make God the *Soul of the World*.

30. And indeed the Author is much in the wrong, when he compares *God's* Knowledge and Operation, with the Knowledge and Operation of *Souls*. The *Soul* knows things, because God has put into it a *Principle Representative* of *Things without*. But *God* knows things, because he produces them continually.

31. The Soul does not *act* upon things, according to my Opinion, any otherwise than because the Body adapts it self to the Desires of the Soul, by virtue of the *Harmony*, which God has *pre-established* between them.

32. But They who fancy that the Soul can give a *new Force* to the Body; and that God does the same in the World, in order to mend the Imperfections of his Machine; make God too much like the Soul by ascribing too much to the Soul, and too little to God.

33. For none but God can give a *new Force* to Nature; And *he* does it only *supernaturally*. If there was need for him to do it in the *natural* course of things; he would have made a very imperfect Work. At That rate, *He* would be with respect to the *World*, what the *Soul*, in the vulgar notion, is with respect to the Body.

34. Those who undertake to defend the vulgar Opinion concerning the Soul's *influence* over the Body, by instancing in God's operating on things External; make God still too much like a Soul of the World. To which I add, that the Author's affecting to find Fault with the Words, *Intelligentia Supramundana*, seems also to incline that way.

35. The Images, with which the Soul is immediately affected, are within it self; but they correspond to those of the Body. The presence of the Soul is imperfect, and can only be explained by That Correspondence. But the presence of God is perfect, and manifested by his Operation.

36. The Author wrongly supposes against me, that the presence of the Soul is connected with its *influence* over the Body; for he knows, I reject That *influence*.

37. The Soul's being *diffused through the Brain*, is no less inexplicable than its being diffused through the whole Body. The Difference is only in *more* and *less*.

38. *Ceux qui s'imaginent que les* Forces actives *se* diminuent *d'elles mêmes dans le Monde, ne connoissent pas bien les principales loix de la nature, & la beauté des ouvrages de Dieu.*

39. *Comment prouveront ils, que ce* defaut *est une suite de la dependance des choses ?*

40. *Ce defaut de nos Machines, qui fait qu'elles ont besoin d'être redressées, vient de cela même, qu'elles ne sont pas assez dependantes de l'Ouvrier. Ainsi la dependance de Dieu qui est dans la Nature, bien loin d'être cause de ce* defaut, *est plustost cause que ce defaut n'y est point, parcequ'elle est si dependante d'un Ouvrier trop parfait pour faire un Ouvrage qui ait besoin d'être redressé. Il est vray que chaque Machine particuliere de la nature, est en quelque façon sujette à être detracquée ; mais non pas l'*Univers *tout entier, qui* ne sauroit diminuer en Perfection.

41. *On dit que l'*Espace *ne depend point de la* Situation des Corps. Je *repons qu'il est vray qu'il ne depend point d'une* telle ou telle *Situation des Corps ; mais il est cet* Ordre *qui fait que les* Corps *sont* Situables, *& par lequel ils ont une Situation entre eux en existant ensemble, comme le* temps *est cet* Ordre *par rapport à leur position successive. Mais s'il n'y avoit point de Creatures, l'*Espace *& le Temps ne seroient que dans les Idées de Dieu.*

42. *Il semble qu'on avoue icy que l'idée qu'on se fait du Miracle n'est pas celle qu'en ont* communement *les Theologiens & les Philosophes. Il me suffit donc, que mes Adversaires sont obligés de recourir à ce qu'on appelle* Miracle *dans l'usage* receu.[11]

43. *J'ay peur qu'en voulant changer le* sens receu *du Miracle, on ne tombe dans un sentiment incommode. La nature du Miracle ne consiste nullement dans l'*usualité *& inusualité ; autrement les* Monstres *seroient des Miracles.*

44. *Il y a des* Miracles *d'une* sorte inferieure, *qu'un Ange peut produire ; car il peut, par Exemple, faire qu'un homme aille sur l'eau sans enfoncer. Mais il y a des Miracles reservés à Dieu, & qui surpassent toutes les Forces naturelles ; tel est celuy de créer ou d'annihiler.*

45. *Il est surnaturel aussi, que les Corps s'attirent de loin sans aucun Moyen ; & qu'un Corps aille en rond, sans s'écarter par la tangente, quoyque rien ne l'empêchât de s'écarter ainsi. Car ces effects ne sont point explicables par les natures des choses.*

46. *Pourquoy la Motion des animaux ne seroit elle point explicable par les Forces* naturalles *? Il est vray que le* commencement *des animaux est aussi inexplicable par leur Moyen, que le commencement du Monde.*[12]

125A. LEIBNIZ'S FOURTH PAPER   571

38. They who fancy that * *active Force* lessens of it self in the World, do not well understand the principal Laws of Nature, and the beauty of the Works of God. *See above, the Note, on § 13, of Dr. Clarke's Third Reply*

39. How will they be able to prove, that this *Defect* is a consequence of the dependence of things ?

40. The imperfection of our Machines, which is the reason why they want to be mended, proceeds from this very thing, that they do not sufficiently depend upon the Workman. And therefore the dependence of Nature upon God, far from being the cause of such an imperfection, is rather the reason why there is no such imperfection in Nature, because it depends so much upon an Artist, who is too perfect to make a work that wants to be mended. 'Tis true that every particular Machine of Nature, is, in some measure, liable to be disordered ; but not the whole *Universe*, which *cannot diminish in Perfection*.

41. The Author contends, that *Space* does not depend upon the *Situation* of *Bodies*. I answer : 'Tis true, it does not depend upon *such* and *such* a situation of Bodies ; but it is *That Order*, which renders Bodies capable of being situated, and by which they have a Situation among themselves when they *exist together*; as *Time* is *That Order*, with respect to their *Successive* position. But if there were no Creatures, Space and Time would be only in the ideas of God.

42. The Author seems to acknowledge here, that his Notion of a Miracle is not the same with that which Divines and Philosophers *usually* have. It is therefore sufficient for my purpose, that my Adversaries are obliged to have recourse to what is *commonly called* a Miracle.[11]

43. I am afraid the Author, by altering the Sense *commonly put* upon the Word *Miracle*, will fall into an inconvenient Opinion. The nature of a Miracle does not at all consist in *Usualness* or *Unusualness* ; For then *Monsters* would be *Miracles*.

44. There are *Miracles* of an *inferior* sort, which an *Angel* can Work. He can, for instance, make a Man Walk upon the Water without sinking. But there are Miracles, which none but God can work ; they exceeding all natural Powers. Of which kind, are *Creating* and *Annihilating*.

45. 'Tis also a supernatural thing, that Bodies should *attract* one another at a distance, without any intermediate Means ; and that a Body should move round, without receding in the Tangent, though nothing hinder it from so receding. For these Effects cannot be explained by the Nature of things.

46. Why should it be impossible to explain the Motion of Animals by *Natural* Forces ? Tho' indeed, the *Beginning* of Animals is no less inexplicable by natural Forces, than the Beginning of the World.[12]

Leibniz's Proposed Additions to his Fourth Paper

Je pourrois faire quelques additions
à la 3me reponse:
Apres le nombre 8 on pourroit adjouter:

Cela se peut garder
pour une autre reponse

Si l'espace est une affection, nous avons des affections ou accidens, qui passent de sujet en sujet, chose qu'on m'admet[4] point dans la saine philosophie. Jusqu'icy on a cru que l'affection peut quitter son sujet en perissant; lors que le sujet est change; mais on n'a pas cru qu'elle puisse quitter son sujet et passer sur un autre sujet et encor moins qu'un sujet puisse quitter et laisser là son affection pour aller en chercher une autre déja existente auparavant; et que l'affection de laissée puisse prendre une autre sujet. Mais tout cela arrive si les espaces sont des realites absolues, et en même temps des affections.

125B. LEIBNIZ'S PROPOSED ADDITIONS TO HIS FOURTH PAPER   573

[1] The original French and the English translation are from Clarke's edition of the correspondence (Clarke 1717, pp. 92–115). LBr. 160 Bl. 78r–79v is the original draft (2.5 folio sides in Leibniz's hand). LBr. 160 Bl. 29r–29v/31r–33v (eight folio sides) and LH 1, 20 Bl. 396r–399r (6.5 folio sides) are fair copies in secretaries' hands. Leibniz enclosed this paper with his letter to Caroline of 2 June 1716 (document 124). It answers Clarke's Third Reply (document 120). Clarke's references to the Appendix of his 1717 edition of the correspondence have been omitted. Square brackets in the text and what they contain are Clarke's.

[2] In the original draft, Leibniz had here added, and then crossed out, the following sentence: 'Outre qu'elle est contraire à la perfection de Dieu' ('Besides, it is contrary to the perfection of God'). See LBr. 160 Bl.77r.

[3] That is, the late Dowager Electress, Sophie* of the Palatinate.

[4] Herrenhausen* castle was the summer palace of the dukes, and later electors, of Hanover.

[5] In the original draft, Leibniz added, and then crossed out, the following sentence: 'Mais cela se doit entendre de toutes les choses ensemble' ('But that must be understood about all things at the same time'). See LBr. 160 Bl. 77r.

[6] For an addition that Leibniz proposed to make to this section, see document 125b, pp. 573, 575.

[7] Since Leibniz denied that there were infinite numbers, Clarke's translation of 'un infinité' as 'an infinite number' is not entirely apropos. In his letter to Bartholomew Des Bosses of 11 March 1706, for example, Leibniz wrote that 'accurately speaking, instead of an infinite number, we ought to say that there are more than any number can express' (LDB 33; translation modified).

[8] For an addition that Leibniz proposed to make to sections 11 and 12, see document 125b, p. 575.

[9] In the draft, Leibniz first wrote, and then crossed out, '(29) Sensorium repond au Grec αἰσθητέριον qui est un instrument, un organe et non pas simplement une place'; that is, '(29) Sensorium answers to the Greek αἰσθητέριον, which is an instrument, an organ, and not simply a place' (see LBr. 160, Bl. 79r).

[10] Both the fair copies of the original draft have 'La presence de l'ame dans le corps est imparfaite', rather than 'La presence de l'ame est imparfaite' (see LBr. 160 Bl. 33r and LH 1, 20 Bl. 398r).

[11] In both the fair copies of the original draft, the last sentence of this paragraph ends with a comma and adds 'et qu'on tache d'eviter en philosophant' ('and which one tries to avoid in philosophizing'). See LBr. 160 Bl. 33v and LH 1, 20 Bl. 398r.

[12] At the end of the version of this paper that he published (see Clarke 1717, pp. 115–19), Clarke added the P.S. on atoms and the void that Leibniz had enclosed in his letter to Caroline of 12 May 1716 (see document 117b).

125b. Leibniz's Proposed Additions to his Fourth Paper[1]

[c.2 June 1716]
This can be saved
for another response.

I could make some additions
to the *third response*[2]
After *number 8*[3] one could add:

If space is an affection, we have some affections or accidents that pass from subject to subject, something that is not admitted[4] in sound philosophy. Up to now it has been thought that the affection can leave its subject by perishing, when the subject is changed; but it has not been thought that it can leave its subject and pass into another subject, and still less that a subject can depart and leave behind its affection in order to go and get another, preexisting [affection] and that the abandoned affection can lay hold of another subject. But all that happens if the spaces are absolute realities and, at the same time, affections.

Le corps quittant l'espace qu'il occupoit, et allant se mettre dans l'espace qu'un autre vient de quitter, voila une separation du sujet et de l'affection sans que l'affection perisse et même l'exemple d'une affection ou accidentalité qui peut exister non seulement sans son sujet, mais meme avant que son sujet existe, et apres qu'il sera peri. C'est aussi donner dans l'opinion des transsubstantiateurs qui font subsister les accidens ou affections sans sujet. Et c'est enfin detruire la difference entres les accidens et les substances.

Selon moy l'espace et le temps ne sont que des choses ideales comme tous les etres relatifs, qui ne sont autre chose que les termes incomplexes qui font les verites ou complexes comme sont par exemple les proportions. Quand je dis A est à B comme 2 à 1, je puis changer ce complexe en incomplexe en disant le rapport entre A et B, comme entre 2 et 1 est vray. Ainsi les étres relatifs se reduisent en effect aux verités.

Cela fait voir comment la proportion entre A et B n'est point un etre absolu, mais une chose ideale: autrement nous aurions un Accident qui auroit une jambe dans le sujet A, et l'autre dans le sujet B, et seroit en deux sujets en meme temps. Aussi les affections relatives, ne sont elles que des resultats des absolues, et ne terminent point une action à part. Ceux qui changent les relations en realites, qui soyent quelque autre chose que des verités; multiplient les etres mal a propos, et s'embarassent sans aucun besoin.

Il est tres visible dans le temps qu'il ne sauroit etre une realité absolue. Car puisqu'il n'a jamais ses parties ensemble on ne peut jamais dire qu'il existe. Or la grande Analogie entre l'Espace et le Temps, fait bien connoistre que si le Temps n'est qu'un ordre, l'Espace n'en sera pas autre chose.

On peut adjouter au nombre 11 et 12 de la 3me reponse que l'espace et le temps ont des parties quoy que l'une de ces parties soit inseparable de l'autre. L'Heure est une partie du jour la capacité de la chopine est une partie de la capacité de la pinte. La place du soleil est une partie de la place du système solaire. Mais on ne sauroit separer les heures ou les transposer, ny les espaces. Dieu ne peut rien sur elles. La Raison? C'est que ce ne sont que les incomplexes des verités eternelles, conçus en forme d'estres absolus par les manieres de nos expressions.

Mais si c'estoient des realités existentes absolues Dieu y pourroit faire du changement. Le temps et l'espace appartiennent aux essences et non aux existences, comme les nombres ou autres idealités. Et comme Dieu ne peut point faire que le nombre Ternaire ne soit point entre le binaire et la quaternaire, parceque ce seroit une absurdité; il ne peut point faire non plus qu'une heure comme celle ou nous sommes, soit levée d'entre l'heure precedente et suivante et reduite à rien ou placée ailleurs. Il en est de même du lieu ou de l'espace.

125B. LEIBNIZ'S PROPOSED ADDITIONS TO HIS FOURTH PAPER 575

The body leaving the space that it occupied and going into the space that another just left, there you have a separation of the subject and the affection without the affection perishing, and even an example of an affection or accident that can exist not only without its subject, but even before its subject exists and after it perishes. This is also to fall into the opinion of the transubstantialists, who make accidents or affections subsist without a subject. And this is finally to destroy the difference between accidents and substances.

In my opinion, space and time are only ideal things, like all relative beings, which are nothing but the simple terms that make truths or complexes, as are, for example, proportions. When I say A is to B as 2 to 1, I can change this complex into a simple by saying the relation between A and B, as between 2 and 1, is true. Thus relative beings actually reduce to truths.

This shows how the proportion between A and B is not an absolute being, but an ideal thing: otherwise we would have an accident that would have one leg in the subject A and the other in the subject B, and it would be in two subjects at the same time. Also, relative affections are only results of absolutes and do not complete a separate action. Those who change relations into realities, which are something other than truths, multiply beings inappropriately and needlessly entangle themselves.

It is very evident that time could not be an absolute reality. For because it never has its parts together, it cannot be said to exist. But the great analogy between space and time clearly shows that if time is only an order, space will not be anything different.

To numbers 11 and 12 of the third response[5] it can be added that space and time have parts, although one of these parts is inseparable from the other. An hour is a part of a day, the capacity of a half-liter is a part of the capacity of a pint. The place of the sun is a part of the place of the solar system. But hours could not be separated or transposed, nor spaces. God cannot do anything about them. The reason? It is because they are only the simples of eternal truths, conceived in the form of absolute beings by our manner of speaking.

But if these were existing absolute realities, God could cause some change in them. Time and space pertain to essences and not to existing things, like numbers or other ideal things. And as God cannot make the third number not be between the second and the fourth, because it would be an absurdity, he can no more make an hour, like the one in which we are, be removed from between the preceding hour and the following hour and reduced to nothing or placed elsewhere. The same is true of place or space.

---

[1] LBr. 160 Bl 30r–30v. 1.7 folio sides in Leibniz's hand. Not previously published.
[2] That is, Leibniz's Fourth Paper, which is his third response to Clarke.
[3] That is, section 8 of Leibniz's Fourth Paper.
[4] Reading 'n'admet' for 'm'admet'.
[5] That is, sections 11 and 12 of Leibniz's Fourth Paper.

Leibniz to John Arnold

Monsieur

Quoyque Vous soyés à Exon, je m'imagine que Vos nouvelles occupations, que je Vous souhaite heureuses, ne Vous empecheront point d'entretenir quelque correspondence avec Vos amis. Ainsi je Vous envoye, Monsieur, le petit papier cy joint, pour être communiqué à Votre ami à Cambridge, qui Vous avoit communiqué un extrait d'un Manuscrit. Puisqu'il y a de l'apparence que ce Manuscrit est venu d'Allemagne, il seroit bon d'apprendre ce qu'il contient outre les pieces dont on Vous a fait part.

Monsieur l'Abbé Conti m'ayant envoyé une lettre que M. Newton luy avoit écrite, à dessein de m'être communiquée; j'y ay répondu par une autre lettre à cet Abbé, mais que j'ay envoyée à M. Remond à Paris, avec une copie de celle de M. Newton, à fin qu'on en fut informée en France, ou l'on est moins partial. Comme j'apprends que M. Conti a receu ma réponse de M. Remond; nous verrons ce que M. Newton répliquera.

Ma dispute avec M. Clarke continue. Vous m'avés marqué, Monsieur, qu'il en étoit touché quelque chose dans un imprimé. Je serois bien aise d'en avoir plus d'information. M. Clarke a accusé mon expression, que Dieu est intelligentia supramundana pretendant que je l'excluois du gouvernement du monde, ce qui est une chicane manifeste. J'ay trouvé à redire à mon tour au sensorium de Dieu de M. Newton, je desapprouve aussi que ces Messieurs font du Monde une machine qui se detraque et s'arreste d'elle même comme une mauvaise montre, et que Dieu a besoin de la redresser de temps en temps extraordinairement. Je monstre aussi que par la supposition d'un Espace reel sans les corps, ils établissent une infinité d'êtres coëternals à Dieu, et sur les quels Dieu ne peut [faire] rien, et qu'ils contre viennent à la grande maxime, que rien n'arrive sans qu'il y en ait une raison suffisante. Enfin je monstre que leur philosophie est pleine de miracles c'est à dire d'actions qu'il est impossible d'expliquer par les natures et les forces des creatures, et qu'il paroist par leur réponse que leur idée du miracle est mauvais, et sera desapprouvée des Theologiens, comme si la difference entre le miraculeux et le naturel avoit lieu seulement dans nôtre opinion et non pas dans la verité, et par rapport à Dieu. Et que les miracles étoient seulement des actions moins usitées de Dieu au lieu que les miracles (au moins les principaux) sont ceux qui surpassent les forces des creatures; Comme seroit par exemple creer et annihiler. Voila un petit abregé de nôtre dispute. Il me semble que selon ces Messieurs là Dieu devient imparfait, et resemble trop à l'ame du Monde des anciens Philosophes. Puisqu'il a besoin d'un sensorium, puisqu'il habite dans une machine aussi imparfaite, que nostre corps; qu'il entretient sa machine par la force qu'il luy impresse de temps en temps comme le

126. Leibniz to John Arnold[1]

[5 June 1716]

Sir

Although you are at Exeter, I imagine that your new occupations, which I hope are successful for you, will not prevent you from maintaining some correspondence with your friends. So I am sending you, sir, the enclosed small paper to be communicated to your friend at Cambridge, who had communicated an extract of a manuscript to you. Since it appears that this manuscript came from Germany, it would be worth learning what it contains besides the parts that have been shared with you.

L'Abbé [Antonio Schinella] Conti* having sent me a letter that Mr. Newton had written to him,[2] in order to be communicated to me, I responded with another letter to this Abbé,[3] but which I sent to Mr. [Nicolas] Rémond* in Paris, with a copy of Mr. Newton's, so that they were informed about it in France, where they are less partial. Since I hear that Mr. Conti has received my response from Mr. Rémond, we will see what Mr. Newton will reply.

My dispute with Mr. [Samuel] Clarke* continues. You have indicated to me, sir, that he has touched on something about it in a printed document. I would be very glad to have further information about it.[4] Mr. Clarke has faulted my expression that God is *intelligentia supramundana*, alleging that I exclude him from the government of the world, which is an obvious cavil. I have, in turn, found fault with Mr. Newton's *sensorium* of God. I also take exception to these gentlemen making the world a machine that becomes disordered and stops by itself, like a faulty watch, and that God needs to adjust it extraordinarily from time to time. I also show that by the assumption of a real space without bodies, they create an infinity of beings coeternal with God, and about which God can do nothing, and that they violate the great principle that nothing happens without there being a sufficient reason for it. Finally, I show that their philosophy is full of miracles, that is to say, of actions that are impossible to explain by the natures and forces of creatures; and it appears from their response that their idea of a miracle is faulty and will be disapproved by theologians, as if the difference between the miraculous and the natural obtains only in our opinion and not in truth and in relation to God, and that miracles were only actions less utilized by God rather than that miracles (at least the principal ones) are those that surpass the forces of creatures, as would be, for example, creating and annihilating. There you have a summary of our dispute. It seems to me that according to those gentlemen, God becomes imperfect and resembles too much the world soul of the ancient philosophers, since he needs a *sensorium*, and since he inhabits a machine as imperfect as our bodies, since he maintains his machine by the force

vulgaire s'imagine que l'ame fait dans le corps. En un mot la Philosophie de ces Messieurs me paroist un peu degenerante et peu digne de la grandeur et la sagesse de l'auteur de choses. Je suis avec Zele,

Monsieur,

Hanover ce 5. de

Juin, 1716

A Monsieur

Arnold

Docteur en

Medecine

    à Exon[5]

vôtre tres-humble et

tres-obeissant serviteur

Leibniz

Leibniz to Johann Bernoulli

Vir Noblissime & Celeberrime
Fautor Honoratissime

[...]

Serram etiam Philosophicam nunc cum Newtono vel quod eodem redit cum ejus Hyperaspita Clarkio Regis Eleemosynario me reciprocare fortasse jam intellexeris. Scis, Keilium et præfatorem novæ editionis Principiorum Newtoni etiam Philosophiam meam pungere voluisse. Itaque scripseram ego forte Serenissimæ Principi Regiæ Walliæ, pro excellenti ingenio suo harum rerum non incuriosæ, degenerare nonnihil apud Anglos Philosophiam vel potius Theologiam Naturalem. Lockium et similes dubitare de immaterialitate Animæ, Newtonum Deo tribuere sensorium, quasi spatio tanquam organo sensationis opus habeat; inde alicui in mentem venire posse, quasi non sit nisi Anima mundi secundum veteres Stoicos. Eundem autorem Dei sapientiæ et perfectionibus derogare, dum velit mundum esse machinam non minus imperfectam quam horologia nostrorum artificum, quæ sæpe retendi debent, aut alias corrigi; ita machinam mundi secundum Newtonum et asseclas correctione quadam extraordinaria subinde indigere, quod

that he impresses on it from time to time, as the vulgar imagine that the soul does in the body. In a word, the philosophy of these gentlemen seems to me a bit degenerate and little worthy of the grandeur and wisdom of the author of things. I am enthusiastically,

sir,

Hanover 5
June, 1716

To Mr.
Arnold
Doctor of
Medicine
at Exeter[5]

your very humble and
very obedient servant
Leibniz

[1] LBr. 160 Bl. 97r–98v. Fair copy: four quarto sides in a secretary's hand. Previously published in Schüller 1991, pp. 250–1 (excerpt in German translation).
[2] See Newton's letter to Conti of 17 March 1716 (document 101g).
[3] That is, Leibniz's letter to Conti of 9 April 1716 (document 108).
[4] On this matter, see Leibniz's letter to Caroline of 28 April 1716 (document 113, pp. 501 and 503 note 5).
[5] This address, beginning 'A Monsieur' and ending 'à Exon', appears to be in Leibniz's hand.

127. Leibniz to Johann Bernoulli* (excerpt)[1]

Most Noble and Celebrated Sir
Most Honourable Patron

[7 June 1716]

[…]

Perhaps you have *already gathered* that I am now drawing a philosophical saw back and forth with Newton, or what comes to the same thing, with his defender [Samuel] Clarke*, the king's almoner [i.e., almoner of King George I, Georg Ludwig* of Braunschweig-Lüneburg]. You know that [John] Keill* and the preface of the new edition of Newton's *Principles* [written by Roger Cotes*] have endeavored to oppose even my philosophy. Therefore, I had casually written to the Most Serene Royal Princess of Wales [Caroline* of Brandenburg-Ansbach],[2] who due to her own excellent intellect is not unconcerned with these matters, that philosophy, or rather natural theology, is degenerating somewhat among the English; that [John] Locke* and others like him are in doubt about the immateriality of the soul; that Newton attributes a sensorium to God, as if he has need of space as a kind of organ of sensation, whence somebody might imagine that he is, as it were, nothing but the soul of the world, in accordance

580   127. LEIBNIZ TO BERNOULLI

parum sit dignum Deo autore. Mea sententia Deum omnia tam sapienter ab initio constituisse, ut correctione non sit opus quae imprudentiam arguat. Serenissima Princeps Walliæ excerpta hujus Epistolæ Clarkio communicavit. Is scriptum contra <u>Anglico sermone</u> ipsi dedit, quod Illa ad me misit; <u>respondi</u>, replicavit; duplicavi, triplicavit; Ego novissime quadruplicavi, seu ad tertium ejus scriptum respondi. Inter alia improbat formulam a me in Theodicæa usurpatam, quod Deus sit <u>intelligentia supramundana</u>, tanquam a me a mundi gubernatione excludatur. Ego quæsivi, an ergo velit Deum nihil, aliud esse quam intelligentiam mundanam, seu animam mundi? Male excusat doctrinam Newtonianam de spontanea virium activarum diminutione et tandem cessatione in mundo, nisi à Deo reparentur; ex quo intelligitur Newtonum ejusque asseclas veram scientiam rei dynamicæ nondum habere. Ex nostris enim Principiis semper servatur eadem quantitas virium. Male etiam excusat phrasin Newtonianam de spatio sensorio DEI. Et quia spatium hodie est Idolum Anglorum, ego ipsi ostendo, spatium non esse aliquid reale absolutum, non magis quam tempus, sed ordinem quendam generalem coëxistendi, uti tempus est ordo existendi successive. Itaque esse aliquid ideale, quod si creaturæ tollerentur, non futurum esset nisi in ideis Dei. Ostendo etiam secundum Newtonum crebris miraculis ad sustentandum naturæ cursum[3] opus esse; et ex Clarkii excusationibus deprehendo ipsum non habere bonam notionem miraculi. Ipsi enim miracula tantùm secundum nos à naturalibus differre videntur, tanquam minus usitata. Sed secundum Theologos et veritatem miracula (saltem ea quæ sunt superioris ordinis, velut creare, annihilare) transcendunt omnes naturæ creatæ vires. Itaque quidquid ex naturis rerum inexplicabile est, quemadmodum attractio generalis materiæ Newtoniana, aliaque ejus hujusmodi,[4] vel miraculorum est, vel absurdum. Fortasse nonnihil adhuc continuabitur nostra collatio, in qua absunt quæ offendere jure[5] possint, et videbo quo res sit evasura. Hujusmodi enim collationes mihi ludus jocusque sunt, quia in Philosophia:

Omnia præcepi atque animo mecum ante peregi.[6]

[…] Quod superest vale et fave
Dabam Hanoveræ 7 Juni 1716

Dedissimus
Godefridus Guilielmus Leibnitius[7]

with the ancient Stoics; that the same author derogates from the wisdom and perfections of God, as long as he is of the opinion that the world is a machine no less imperfect than the clocks of our craftsmen, which must often be rewound or otherwise corrected; that therefore the world machine, according to Newton and his followers, stands in need of some extraordinary correction from time to time, which is scarcely worthy of God the creator. In my opinion, God has arranged everything so wisely from the beginning that correction, which betrays a lack of foresight, is not needed. The Most Serene Princess of Wales shared excerpts of this letter with Clarke. He gave her a paper opposed to it in the *English language*, which she sent to me. *I responded*, and he replied; I responded a second time, and he replied a third time; I have most recently responded a fourth time, that is, I have responded to his third paper. Among other things, he disapproves of an expression employed in the *Theodicy*, that God is *intelligentia supramundana*, as if he is excluded by me from the government of the world. I have asked whether he is therefore of the opinion that God is nothing other than *intelligentia mundana*, that is, soul of the world. He offers a poor justification for the Newtonian doctrine concerning the spontaneous diminution of active forces and their eventual cessation in the world, unless they are restored by God, from which it is gathered that Newton and his followers do not yet have a true science of dynamics. For according to our principles, the same quantity of forces is always conserved. He even offers a poor justification for the Newtonian expression concerning the sensory space of God. And because space is now the idol of the English, I show him that space is not a real, absolute thing, any more than time, but a certain general order of coexisting, as time is the order of successive existing. Therefore, it is something ideal, since if created things were removed, it would not exist except in the ideas of God. And I even show that according to Newton, repeated miracles are needed to sustain the course[3] of nature; and from Clarke's excuses, I perceive that he himself does not have a sound notion of a miracle. For in his view miracles appear to differ from natural things only according to us, on the ground that they have been less usual; but according to theology and truth, miracles (at least those which are of a higher order, like creating or destroying) transcend all forces of created nature. Therefore, whatever is inexplicable by the natures of things, such as the Newtonian universal attraction of matter, and other things of this kind,[4] is either miraculous or absurd. Perhaps our confrontation, in which there is nothing that can justly[5] give offense, will still be continued a bit longer, and I shall see how the matter turns out. For confrontations of this sort, because they are in philosophy, are mere sport to me:

Caroline of Brandenburg-Ansbach, Princess of Wales, to Leibniz

$$S^t \text{ James le } \frac{26}{15} \text{ Juny } 1716$$

Je n'ay peu reponder[3] plus tost Monsieur avôtre[4] lettre du 2 de semois.[5] dockteur glerck, qui estois ala campanye[6] me m'araporté[7] plus tost la reponse. vous me permesterais malquerais[8] ce que j'ay trouvez[9] vn peu equer[10] dans votre lettre condre[11] moy, que je suis faché[e] de voir des geans[12] de votre merité se prouller pour lavanité[13] que vous deverié destruire par la bonté de vos raisonement;[14] qu'inporte que vous ou lechevalié neuthon ayée trouvez le calculle;[15] vous esttee les grand homes[16] de notre ciequel,[17] et tout deu[x] serviteur[s] d'vn Roy qui vous merité. vous voiyé[18] que latraduction de la deodisce, et asteur extremement dificille[19] et je me fladè de trouver quel vn, qui ne lagadera pas par satratiction.[20] L'archeveque lademere[21] mais il n'est pas an tout t'acord[22] avec vous. Je la relirais an pressance[23] de M^r conty, et le docteur clerck avec votre permission. Je ne crois pas mestre servié du terme[24] d'avoir trouvez[25] dans la lettre que vous avez écrit alabée conty,[26] que votre Esprit parut[27] troublé. Se scerais[29] marquer que le mien le feu[30] pour trouver ce desfau anvous.[31] J'ay plain le beauver abée,[32] qui crois estre metiateur, de resevoir des coup d'un home[33] qu'il estime tant;[34] je ne crois pas, Monsieur, que ces Mes[srs] on[t] jamais dit qu'il croioit que le vidé ne feu ramplié[35] de quelque chose qui ne feu pas matier.[36] voilà du moin cequi mansamble.[37] vous m'obligerais infiment de me renvoiyer le tressord que j'ay pertu.[38] tous ceque vous ecrivez lest ainsy[40] pour moy. J'ay

128. CAROLINE OF BRANDENBURG-ANSBACH TO LEIBNIZ   583

I have foreseen and thought over everything before with myself.[6]
[…] For the rest, farewell and be well disposed.
Delivered at Hanover 7 June 1716

Most devoted
Gottfried Wilhelm Leibniz[7]

---

[1] Universitätsbibliothek Basel L I a 19 Bl. 326–327. 3.5 quarto sides in a secretary's hand; sign-off lines in Leibniz's hand. There is also draft of the letter in Leibniz's hand (Niedersächsische Staats- und Universitätsbibliothek Göttingen Handschriften Philos. 138 Bl. 13–14). Previously published in GM III-2 962–4 (excerpt); NC VI 353–7 (excerpt, Latin with English translation); Schüller 1991, pp. 254–6 (excerpt in German translation); HGA 189 (excerpt in English translation). This is Leibniz's response to Bernoulli's letter of 20 May 1716 (document 121). For Bernoulli's response, see his letter to Leibniz of 14 July 1716 (document 133).

[2] See Leibniz's letter to Caroline from the end of November 1715 (document 85).

[3] GM-2 964 and NC VI 355 mistranscribe 'cursum' as 'censum'.

[4] GM III-2 964 and NC VI 355 mistranscribe 'ejus hujusmodi' as 'ejusmodi'.

[5] GM III-2 964 and NC VI 355 omit 'jure'.

[6] Vergil's Aeneid VI, 105.

[7] The last four sign-off lines are in Leibniz's hand.

---

128. Caroline* of Brandenburg-Ansbach, Princess of Wales, to Leibniz[1]

St James le $\frac{26}{15}$ June 1716[2]

I have not been able to respond[3] sooner, sir, to your[4] letter of the second of this month.[5] Doctor [Samuel] Clarke*, who was in the country,[6] did not bring me[7] the response back to me sooner. You will permit me, in spite of[8] what I found[9] a bit harsh[10] against[11] me in your letter, to be displeased to see persons[12] of your merit quarreling out of vanity,[13] which you should destroy with the excellence of your arguments.[14] What does it matter whether you or Chevalier Newton discovered the calculus?[15] You are the great men[16] of our century,[17] and both servants of a king [George I, Georg Ludwig* of Braunschweig-Lüneburg] who merits you. You understand[18] that the translation of the *Theodicy* is extremely difficult at the moment,[19] and I hope to find someone who will not corrupt it by his translation.[20] The archbishop [the Archbishop of Canterbury, William Wake*] admires it,[21] but he is not entirely in agreement[22] with you. With your permission I will reread it in the presence[23] of Mr.[Antonio Schinella] *Conti** and Doctor Clarke. I do not believe I used the expression[24] that I found[25] in the letter you wrote to the Abbé Conti[26] that your mind seemed[27] disturbed.[28] That would[29] indicate that my own mind was[30] disturbed for finding this fault in you.[31] I have pitied the poor Abbé,[32] who believes he is a mediator, for receiving blows from a man[33] whom he esteems so much.[34] I do not believe, sir, that these gentlemen have ever said that they

estte la semaine passez a grin wich, ché Flamsted,[41] qui ma resu dans son opservatoir, ou au lieu d'etoile j'ay eu laplus belle veu du monde.[42] il ma dapor demande[43] de vos nouvelles et ma dit dans vn langué plus naturelle que polié[44] que vous ettié vn si honest home[45] mais s^r yack nuthon vn grand fripon par cequ'il[46] luy avoit volé deus etoille.[47] Je n'ay peu manpecher[48] de rire. sa maison et saficure on laire de Merlain.[49] J'ay pansez[50] mille fois a M^d pelnit quelle aurais eu mille jolié idé sur la persoñe et demeur de flamestet.[51] Jespere qu'aleur qu'il est[52] le Zar aura quité pirmonth[53] pour aller acopenhagen.[54] rien n'areste le Roy que sa[55] icy et quoy que leplaisir[56] de faire ma cour À S. M. me soit extremement cher; sa santé me l[']est infiniment plus, et je ne latrouvee pas trop boñe.[57] les aux de pirmonth geriron c'este precieuse[58] santé. le beauver la hontan[59] avoit meilleur voulooir[60] que de force pour servir le Roy. ce qu'il dit sur le manifest,[61] n'est pas fort bien[62] raisoné, et on aurais peudire ase beauver home que le lon dit icy, a ceu qui ne parolle pas bien dans leur party,[63] souhaite beaucoup et n'anparlez jamais.[64] Madame m'a écrité qu[']elle croit que le Roy de prus[s]e fera vn tour aparis. elle et moy soñe de même santiment, que ladesmarché dans se pais pour se Roy sera Ridiculee.[65] tous vas[66] icy assez bien et je crois an confiance que se tems et proper[67] pour le voiagé[68] du Roy, qui abien de labondé[69] pour vous, et qui se faché quand on n'est andierement[70] de votre santiment. vous andez esttre glorieu.[71] Je me fladé qu'il yaura peut estre quelque choses bien tost icy pour vous raprocher de c'est ille.[72] faite regullierment votre cour au Roy, je vous an prié et ne parleé apersone de ceque je vous dit.[73] L'archeveque n'est pas icy. einsy,[74] je ne vous dirais[75] rien sur ceque[76] vous m'avez écrit sur lareunions[77] des Religions. Je chercherais avec ampressement les occasion a vous[78] marquer que je suis toujours lamême.[79]

Caroline

128. CAROLINE OF BRANDENBURG-ANSBACH TO LEIBNIZ   585

believed the void was full[35] of something that was not matter.[36] That at least is how it appears to me.[37] I would be very grateful to you for sending back to me the treasure that I have lost.[38,39] Everything you write is a treasure[40] for me. Last week I was in Greenwich, home of [John] Flamsteed*,[41] who received me in his observatory, where instead of stars, I had the most beautiful view of the world.[42] He first asked me[43] for news about you and told me, in language more natural than polite,[44] that you were such a decent man,[45] but Sir Isaac Newton a great rogue because he[46] had stolen two stars[47] from him. I was not able to keep[48] from laughing. His house and his appearance have the air of Merlin.[49] I have thought[50] a thousand times about Mademoiselle [Henriette Charlotte von] Pöllnitz*, who would have had a thousand fine ideas about the person and home of Flamsteed.[51] I hope that by now[52] the czar [Peter the Great* of Russia] has left Pyrmont*[53] to go to Copenhagen.[54] Nothing here detains the king [George I, Georg Ludwig* of Braunschweig-Lüneburg] but that;[55] and although the pleasure[56] of paying court to His Majesty is extremely dear to me, his health is infinitely more so, and I do not find it too good.[57] The waters of Pyrmont will cure this precious[58] health. The poor [Louis-Armand de Lom d'Arce, Baron] Lahontan*[59] was more willing[60] than able to serve the king. What he said about the manifesto[61] is not very well[62] reasoned, and one could say to this poor man what is said here to those who do not speak well within their party:[63] hope a lot and never speak of it.[64] Madame [Elisabeth Charlotte* of the Palatinate] has written me that she believes that the King of Prussia [Friedrich Wilhelm I*] will travel to Paris. She and I agree that the manners in that country will be ridiculous for this king.[65] Everything is going[66] well enough here, and I am confident that this time is right[67] for the voyage[68] of the king, who has a lot of favour[69] for you and who is upset when a person is not completely[70] in agreement with your opinion. You should be proud of it.[71] I hope that perhaps there will soon be something here to bring you closer this island.[72] Please pay your court regularly to the king and speak to no one about what I tell you.[73] The archbishop is not here, so[74] I will say[75] nothing about what[76] you have written me about the reunion[77] of the religions. I will eagerly seek opportunities to show you[78] that I am always the same.[79]

Caroline

---

[1] LBr. F 4, Bl. 66r–69r. Letter as sent: 6.5 quarto sides in Caroline's hand. Previously published in Klopp XI 114–16; Robinet 1991, p. 107 (excerpt); Schüller 1991, p. 256 (excerpt in German translation); HGA 196 (excerpt in English translation). This is Caroline's response to Leibniz's letter of 2 June 1716 (document 124), with which she enclosed Clarke's Fourth Reply (document 129). For Leibniz's response to this letter, see his letter to Caroline of 31 July 1716 (document 135). Arthur Michel de Boislisle mistakenly attributed this letter to Leibniz (see Boislisle 1898, p. 31 note 1).

[2] That is, 26 June 1716 (NS), 15 May 1716 (OS).

[3] Reading 'pu répondre' for 'peu reponder'.

[4] Reading 'à votre' for 'avôtre'.

[5] Reading 'ce mois' for 'semois'.

[6] Reading 'étais à la campagne' for 'estois ala campanye'.

586   128. CAROLINE OF BRANDENBURG-ANSBACH TO LEIBNIZ

128. CAROLINE OF BRANDENBURG-ANSBACH TO LEIBNIZ 587

[7] Reading 'ne m'a rapporté' for 'me m'araporté'.

[8] Reading 'permettrez malgré' for 'permesterais malquerais'.

[9] Reading 'trouvé' for 'trouvez'.

[10] Reading 'aigre' for 'equer'.

[11] Reading 'contre' for 'condre'.

[12] Reading 'gens' for 'geans'.

[13] Reading 'mérite se brouiller pour la vanité' for 'merité se prouller pour lavanité'.

[14] Reading 'devriez détruire par la bonté de vos raisonnements' for 'deverié destruire par la bonté de vos raisonement'.

[15] Reading 'qu'importe que vous ou le chevalier Newton ait trouvé le calcul?' for 'qu'inporte que vous ou lechevalié neuthon ayée trouvez le calculle?'

[16] Reading 'êtes les grands hommes' for 'esttee les grand homes'.

[17] Reading 'siècle' for 'ciequel'.

[18] Reading 'voyez' for 'voiyé'.

[19] Reading 'Théodicée est à cette heure extrêmement difficile' for 'deodisce et asteur extremement dificille'.

[20] Reading 'je me flatte de trouver quelqu'un qui ne la gâtera pas par sa traduction' for 'je me fladè de trouver quel vn qui ne lagadera pas par satratiction'. Klopp omits this independent clause (see Klopp XI 115).

[21] Reading 'L'archevêque l'admire' for 'L'archeveque lademere'.

[22] Reading 'en tout d'accord' for 'an tout t'acord'.

[23] Reading 'relirai en présence' for 'relirais an pressance'.

[24] Reading 'mètre servie du terme' for 'mestre servié du terme'.

[25] Reading 'trouvé' for 'trouvez'.

[26] Reading 'écrite à l'Abbé Conti' for 'écrit alabée conty'.

[27] Klopp mistranscribes 'parut' as 'paroist' (see Klopp XI 115).

[28] Caroline is referring to Leibniz's remark, in his letter to her of 2 June 1716, that 'Il me semble qu'il n'y a rien dans ma reponse à M. l'Abbé Conti, qui marque un esprit troublé' (document 124, p. 556). She points out here that she did not claim in her letter to Leibniz of 26 May 1716 that she believed Leibniz's mind was disturbed. Rather, in that letter she had only observed that Leibniz appeared to be 'roused' (piqué) against Conti (see document 122, p. 549).

[29] Reading 'Ce serait' for 'Se scerais'.

[30] Reading 'fut' for 'feu'.

[31] Reading 'défaut en vous' for 'desfau anvous'.

[32] Reading 'J'ai plaint le pauvre Abbé' for 'J'ay plain le beauver abée'. Klopp mistranscribes 'J'ay plain' as 'Je plains' (Klopp XI 115).

[33] Reading 'croit être médiateur de recevoir des coups d'un homme' for 'crois estre metiateur de resevoir des coup d'un home'.

[34] Klopp mistranscribes 'J'ay plain le beauver abée, qui crois estre metiateur, de resevoir des coup d'un home qu'il estime tant' as two sentences: 'Je plains le pauvre Abbé qui croit estre médiateur. Il croit de recevoir des coups d'un homme qu'il estime tant'. See Klopp XI 115.

[35] Reading 'qu'ils croient, que le vide ne fût rempli' for 'qu'il croioit, que le vidé ne feu ramplié'.

[36] Reading 'ne fût pas matière' for 'ne feu pas matier'.

[37] Reading 'Voilà du moins ce qui m'en semble' for 'voilà du moin cequi mansamble'.

[38] Reading 'm'obligerez infiniment de me renvoyer le trésor que j'ay perdu' for 'm'obligerais infiment de me renvoiyer le tressord que j'ay pertu'.

[39] Caroline here alludes to the fact, reported to Leibniz in her letter of 15 May 1716, that the Abbé Conti had lost some of the letters that Leibniz had written to her (document 119, p. 535). In his letter to Caroline of 2 June 1716, Leibniz told Caroline that 'since the Abbé has lost some of them, I have had all of them [that is, his papers for Clarke] copied again, and I believe that it would be a good idea to share them with others, so that these papers may not be lost so easily' (document 124, p. 557).

[40] Reading 'Tout ce que vous écrivez l'est ainsi' for 'Tous ceque vous ecrivez lest ainsy'.

[41] Reading 'été la semaine passée à Greenwich, chez Flamsteed' for 'estte la semaine passez a grin wich, ché Flamsted'.

588   128. CAROLINE OF BRANDENBURG-ANSBACH TO LEIBNIZ

128. CAROLINE OF BRANDENBURG-ANSBACH TO LEIBNIZ 589

[42] Reading 'm'a reçue dans son observatoire, où au lieu des étoiles j'ai eu la plus belle vue du monde' for 'ma resu dans son opservatoir, ou au lieu d'etoile j'ay eu laplus belle veu du monde'.

[43] Reading 'm'a d'abord demandé' for 'ma dapor demande'. Klopp mistranscribes 'dapor' as 'd'après' (see Klopp XI 115).

[44] Reading 'm'a dit dans une langue plus naturelle que polie' for 'ma dit dans vn langué plus naturelle que polié'. Klopp mistranscribes 'langué plus naturelle que polié' as 'langue naturelle', thus omitting both 'plus' and 'que polie' (see Klopp XI 115).

[45] Reading 'étiez un si honnête homme' for 'ettié vn si honest home'.

[46] Reading 'parce qu'il' for 'par cequ'il'.

[47] Reading 'deux étoiles' for 'deus etoille'.

[48] Reading 'pu m'empêcher' for 'peu manpecher'.

[49] Reading 'sa figure ont l'aire de Merlin' for 'saficure on laire de Merlain'.

[50] Reading 'pensé' for 'pansez'.

[51] Reading 'qu'elle aurait eu mille jolies idées sur la personne et demeure de Flamsteed' for 'quelle aurais eu mille jolié idé sur la persone et demeur de flamestet'.

[52] Reading 'J'espère qu'à l'heure qu'il est' for 'Jespere qu'aleur qu'il est'.

[53] Reading 'Czar aura quitté Pyrmont' for 'Zar aura quité pirmonth'.

[54] Reading 'à Copenhague' for 'acopenhagen'.

[55] Reading 'ça' for 'sa'.

[56] Reading 'quoique le plaisir' for 'quoy que leplaisir'.

[57] Reading 'la trouve pas trop bonne' for 'latrouvee pas trop bone'.

[58] Reading 'Les eaux de Pyrmont guériront cette précieuse' for 'les aux de pirmonth geriron c'este precieuse'.

[59] Reading 'Le pauvre Lahontan' for 'le beauver la hontan.'

[60] Reading 'vouloir' for 'voulooir'.

[61] Reading 'manifeste' for 'manifest'. Concerning the manifesto in question and Lahontan's defense of it, see Leibniz's letter to Caroline of 2 June 1716 (document 124, pp. 559, 561 notes 12 and 14).

[62] Klopp mistranscribes 'fort bien' as 'très-bien' (Klopp XI 116).

[63] Reading 'raisonné et on aurait pu dire à ce pauvre homme ce que l'on dit ici à ceux qui ne parlent pas bien dans leur parti' for 'raisoné et on aurais peudire ase beauver home que le lon dit icy a ceu qui ne parolle pas bien dans leur party'.

[64] Reading 'n'en parle jamais' for 'n'anparlez jamais'.

[65] Reading 'Elle et moi sommes de même sentiment que la démarche dans ce pays pour ce Roy sera ridicule' for 'elle et moy some de même santiment que ladesmarché dans se pais pour se Roy sera Ridiculee'.

[66] Reading 'Tout va' for 'Tous vas'.

[67] Reading 'ce temps est propre' for 'se tems et proper'.

[68] Reading 'voyage' for 'voiagé'.

[69] Reading 'a bien de la bonté' for 'abien de labondé'.

[70] Reading 'entièrement' for 'andierement'.

[71] Reading 'Vous en devez être glorieux' for 'vous andez esttre glorieu'.

[72] Reading 'flatte qu'il y aura peut-être quelque chose bientôt ici pour vous rapprocher de cette île' for 'fladé qu'il yaura peut estre quelque choses bien tost icy pour vous raprocher de c'est ille'.

[73] Reading 'Faites régulièrement votre cour au Roy, je vous en prie, et ne parlez à personne de ce que je vous dis' for 'faite regullierment votre cour au Roy, je vous an prié et ne parleé apersone de ceque je vous dit'.

[74] Reading 'Ainsi' for 'einsy'.

[75] Reading 'dirai' for 'dirais'.

[76] Reading 'ce que' for 'ceque'.

[77] Reading 'la réunion' for 'lareunions'.

[78] Reading 'chercherai avec empressement les occasions à vous' for 'chercherais avec ampressement les occasion a vous'.

[79] Reading 'la même' for 'lamême'.

Clarke's Fourth Reply

Quatriéme Réplique de Mr. CLARKE.

1, & 2. *La Doctrine que l'on trouve ici, conduit à la* Necessité & *à la* Fatalité, *en supposant que les* Motifs *ont le même rapport à la* Volonté d'un Agent Intelligent, *que* * *les* Poids *à une* Balance ; *de sorte que quand* deux choses *sont absolument indifferentes, un Agent Intelligent ne peut choisir* l'une ou l'autre, comme *une Balance ne peut se mouvoir lors que les Poids sont égaux des deux cotez. Mais voici en quoi consiste la Difference. Une* Balance *n'est pas un* Agent : *elle est tout-à-fait* Passive, & *les* Poids *agissent sur elle ; de sorte que quand les* Poids *sont égaux, il n'y a rien qui la puisse mouvoir. Mais les* Etres Intèlligens *sont des* Agents ; *ils ne sont point simplement* passifs, & *les* Motifs *n'agissent pas sur eux, comme les* Poids *agissent sur une* Balance : *Ils ont des* Forces Actives, & *ils* agissent, *quelque fois par de* puissans *Motifs, quelque fois par des Motifs* foibles, & *quelque fois lors que les choses sont* absolument indifferentes. *Dans ce dernier cas, il peut y avoir de* très-bonnes raisons pour agir, *quoique deux ou plusieurs* manieres d'agir *puissent être absolument* indifferentes. *Le sçavant* Auteur suppose toûjours le contraire, comme un Principe ; *mais il n'en donne* aucune Preuve *tirée de la* Nature des Choses, ou des Perfections de Dieu.

Voïez ci-dessus la Second Ecrit de Mr. Leibnitz, § 1.

3, & 4. *Si le raisonnement que l'on trouve ici, étoit bien fondé, il prouveroit que* Dieu *n'a créé aucune* Matiere, & même qu'il est *impossible qu'il en puisse créer. Car les* parties de Matiere, quelle qu'elle soit, *qui sont* parfaitement solides, *sont aussi parfaitement semblables, pourvû qu'elles ayent des* Figures & *des* Dimensions égales ; *ce que l'on peut toûjours supposer, comme une chose possible. Ces parties de Matiere pourroient donc occuper également bien un autre lieu que celui qu'elles occupent ;* & *par conséquent il étoit impossible, selon le* Raisonnement du sçavant Auteur, *que* Dieu *les plaçât où il les a actuellement placées, parce qu'il auroit pû avec la même facilité les placer à rebours. Il est vrai qu'on ne sçauroit voir* deux Feuilles, *ni peut-être* deux Goutes d'eau, *parfaitement semblables ; parce que ce sont des* Corps fort composez. *Mais il n'en est pas ainsi des parties de la* Matiere simple & solide. *Et même dans les* Composez, *il n'est pas impossible que* Dieu fasse deux Goutes d'eau *tout-à-fait semblables ;* & *nonobstant cette parfaite ressemblance, elles ne pourroient pas devenir* une seule & même Goute d'eau. *J'ajoute que le* Lieu de *l'*une de ces Goutes ne *seroit pas le* Lieu de l'*autre, quoique leur* Situation *fût une chose absolument indifferente. Le même* Raisonnement *a lieu aussi par rapport à la* prémiere Détermination du Mouvement *d'un certain coté, ou du coté* opposé.

5, & 6. *Quoique* deux choses *soient* parfaitement semblables, *elles ne cessent pas d'être* deux choses. *Les* parties du Temps *sont aussi* parfaitement semblables, *que* celles de l'Espace ; & *cependant* deux Instants *ne sont pas le* même Instant : *Ce ne sont* pas non plus *deux noms d'un seul & même* Instant. *Si* Dieu *n'avoit créé le* Monde *que dans ce moment, il n'auroit pas été créé dans le temps qu'il l'a été. Et si* Dieu *a donné,*

129. Clarke's Fourth Reply[1]

Dr. CLARKE'*s Fourth Reply.*

1, *and* 2. This Notion leads to universal *Necessity and Fate,* by supposing that *Motives* have same relation to the *Will of an Intelligent Agent, as* * *Weights* have to a *Balance* ; so that of *two* things absolutely indifferent, an intelligent Agent can no more choose *Either,* than a Balance can move it self when the Weights on both sides are Equal. But the Difference lies here. A *Balance* is no *Agent,* but is merely *Passive* and *acted upon* by the *Weights* ; so that, when the *Weights* are equal, there is *nothing* to *move* it. But *Intelligent Beings* are *Agents* ; not *passive,* in being *moved* by *Motives,* as a *Balance* is by *Weights* ; but they have *Active Powers* and do *move Themselves,* sometimes upon the View of *strong* Motives, sometimes upon *weak* ones, and sometimes where things are *absolutely indifferent.* In which *latter case,* there may be *very good reason* to *act,* though two or more *Ways* of acting may be absolutely *indifferent.* This learned Writer always *supposes* the contrary, as a *Principle* ; but gives no *Proof* of it, either from the *Nature of Things,* or the *Perfections of God.*

> * *See Above, Mr. Leibnitz's Second Paper,* § 1.

3, *and* 4. This Argument, if it was True, would prove that God neither *has cre-ated,* nor *can possibly create* any *Matter at all.* For the *perfectly solid parts* of *all* Matter, if you take them of equal Figure an Dimensions (which is always *possible* in Supposition,) are exactly alike ; and therefore it would be perfectly indifferent if they were transposed in Place ; and consequently it was *impossible* (according to this Learned Author's Argument,) for God to place them in those Places wherein he did actually place them at the Creation, because he might as easily have trans-posed their Situation. 'Tis very true, that *no two Leaves,* and perhaps *no two drops of Water* are exactly alike ; because they are *Bodies very much compounded.* But the case is very different in the parts of *simple solid Matter.* And even in *Compounds,* there is no impossibility for God to make *two drops of Water* exactly alike. And if he *should* make them *exactly alike,* yet they would never the more become *one and the same* drop of Water, because they were *alike.* Nor would the *Place* of the *One,* be the *Place* of the *Other* ; though it was absolutely indifferent, *which* was placed in *which place.* The same reasoning holds likewise concerning the original *determination* of *Motion,* this way or the contrary way.

5, *and* 6. *Two things,* by being *exactly alike,* do not cease to be *Two.* The parts of *Time,* are as exactly *like* to each other, as those of *Space* : Yet *two Points* of *Time,* are not the *same Point* of Time, nor are they *two Names of only the same Point of Time..* Had God created the World *but This Moment,* it would not have been created at the Time it was created. And if God *has made* (or *can* make) Matter *Finite* in

592   129. FOURTH REPLY OF CLARKE

(*ou s'il* peut *donner*) une Etendue bornée *à l'Univers, il s'ensuit que l'Univers doit être naturellement* capable de mouvement ; *Car ce qui est borné, ne peut être* immobile. *Il paroit donc par ce que je viens de dire, que ceux qui soûtiennent que Dieu ne pouvoit pas créer le Monde dans un autre* Temps, *ou dans un autre* Lieu ; *font la Matiere nécessairement infinie & éternelle, & reduisent tout à la* Necessité *& au* Destin.

7. *Si l'Univers a une Etendue bornée l'*Espace qui est au-delà du Monde, *n'est point* imaginaire, *mais* réel. *Les Espaces vuides dans le Monde même ne sont pas imaginaires. Quoi qu'il y ait des rayons de Lumiere, & peut-être quelque autre matiere en très-petite quantité, dans un* *²* Recipient ; *le* défaut de resistance *fait voir clairement, que la* plus grande partie *de cet Espace est destituée de Matiere. Car la* Subtilité *de la matiere ne peut être la cause du* défaut de Resistance. Le Mercure *est composé de parties, qui ne sont pas moins Subtiles & Fluides que celles de l'Eau ; & cependant il fait plus de* dix fois *autant de Resistance. Cette Resistance vient donc de la* Quantité, *& non de la* Grossiereté *de la Matiere.*

8. *L'Espace destitué de Corps, est une Proprieté d'une Substance immaterielle. L'Espace n'est pas* borné *par les Corps ; mais il existe également* dans *les Corps & hors des Corps. L'Espace n'est pas* renfermé *entre les Corps ; Mais les Corps, étant dans l'Espace immense, sont eux-mêmes bornez par leurs propres Dimensions.*

9. *L'*Espace vuide *n'est pas un* Attribut *sans Sujet ; car, par cet* Espace *nous n'entendons un* Espace *où il n'y a rien, mais un Espace* sans Corps. *Dieu est certainement present dans tout l'Espace vuide ; & peut-être qu'il y a aussi dans cet Espace plusieurs autres Substances, qui ne sont pas materielles, & qui par conséquent ne peuvent être* tangibles, *ni apperçues par aucun de nos sens.*

10. *L'*Espace *n'est pas une* Substance, *mais un* Attribut ; *& si c'est un Attribut d'un Etre nécessaire, il doit (comme tous les autres Attributs d'un Etre nécessaire) exister* plus nécessairement, *que les* Substances mêmes, *qui ne sont pas* nécessaires. *L'Espace est* immense, immuable, *& éternel ; & l'on doit dire la même chose de la* Durée. *Mais il ne s'ensuit pas de là, qu'il y ait rien d'éternel* hors de Dieu. *Car l'*Espace *& la* Durée *ne sont pas hors de Dieu : Ce sont* † *des* suites immédiates *& nécessaires de son* Existence, *sans lesquelles il ne seroit point* Eternel *& present par tout.*

---

* Un Passage de la Lettre de Mr. *Leibnitz,* qui servoit d'Envelope à son Ecrit, a donné lieu à ce que l'on dit ici.

† *Deus æternus est, &c. C'est-à dire :* Dieu est Eternel & Infini, il est Tout-puissant, & rien n'échape à sa connoissance ; je veux dire, que sa durée n'a ni commencement, ni fin ; & que sa Presence est immense, & n'a point des bornes : Qu'il régle toutes les choses qui existent, & qu'il connoit tout ce qu'il est possible de connoitre. Il n'est pas l'*Eternité* ou l'*Infinité ;* mais il est *Eternal* & *Infini.* Il n'est pas la *Durée,* ou l'*Espace* ; mail il *coninue d'exister,* & il *est present.* Il existe *toujours,* & il est present *par tout* ; & en existant toûjours & par tout, il constitue la *Durée* et l'*Espace,* l'Eternité & l'Infinité. Certainement, puisque chaque particule de l'Espace existe *toûjours,* & que chaque Moment indivisible de la Durée est *par tout,* on ne peut pas dire du Maitre & du Seigneur de toutes choses, qu'il n'existe *ni en aucun temps, ni en aucun lieu.* Il est present part tout, non seulement *Virtuellement,* mais encore *Substantiellement :* Car la *puissance* [virtus] ne sçauroit subsister sans une *Substance. Newtoni Principia, Schol. Generale sub finem.*

129. FOURTH REPLY OF CLARKE 593

Dimensions, the *material Universe* must consequently be in its Nature *Moveable* ; For nothing that is finite, is *immoveable*. To say therefore that God could not have altered the *Time* or *Place* of the existence of Matter, is making Matter to be necessarily Infinite and Eternal, and reducing all things to *Necessity* and *Fate*.

7. *Extra-mundane Space*, (if the material World be *Finite* in its Dimensions,) is not *imaginary*, but *real*. Nor are void Spaces *in* the World, merely imaginary. In an *2 *exhausted Receiver*, though Rays of Light, and perhaps some Other Matter, be There in an exceeding small Quantity ; yet the *want of Resistence* plainly shows, that the *greatest part* of That Space is void of Matter. For *Subtleness* or *Fineness* of Matter, cannot be the cause of *want of Resistence*. *Quicksilver* is as *subtle*, and consists of as *fine* parts and as *fluid*, as *Water* ; and yet makes more than *ten times* the resistence : Which resistence arises therefore from the *Quantity*, and not from the *Grossness* of the Matter.

8. *Space* void of Body, is the Property of an *incorporeal* Substance. Space is not *Bounded* by *Bodies*, but exists equally *within* and *without* Bodies. *Space* is not *inclosed between* Bodies ; but Bodies, existing in unbounded Space, are, *themselves only*, terminated by their own Dimensions.

9. Void Space, is not an *Attribute without a Subject* ; because, by *void Space*, we never mean *Space void of every thing*, but void of *Body* only. In All void *Space, God* is *certainly* present, and *possibly* many *other* Substances which are not Matter ; being neither *Tangible*, nor Objects of Any of *Our* Senses.

10. Space is not a *Substance*, but a *Property* ; And if it be a *Property* of That which is necessary, it will consequently (as all *other* Properties of That which is necessary must do,) exist *more necessarily*, (though it be not *itself* a Substance,) than those *Substances Themselves* which are *not necessary*. Space is *immense*, and *immutable*, and *eternal* ; and so also is *Duration*. Yet it does not at all from hence follow, that any thing is eternal *hors de Dieu*. For *Space* and *Duration* are not *hors de Dieu*, but † are *caused by*, and are *immediate and necessary Consequences of* His Existence. And *without* them, his *Eternity* and *Ubiquity* [or *Omnipresence*] would be taken away.

---

* *This was occasioned by a Passage in the Private Letter, wherein Mr. Leibnitz's Paper came inclosed.*

† Deus *Æternus* est & *Infinitus, Omnipotens & Omnisciens* ; id est, durat ab æterno in æternum, & adest ab infinito in infinitum ; omnia regit & omnia cognoscit, quæ fiunt aut sciri possunt. Non est *Æternitas* vel *Infinitas*, sed *Æternus & Infinitus* ; non est *Duratio* vel *Spatium*, sed *durat & adest*. Durat *Semper*, & Adest *Ubique* ; & existendo semper & ubique, *Durationem & Spatium*, æternitatem & infinitatem constituit. Cùm unaquæq; Spatij particula sit *semper*, & unumquodq; Durationis indivisibile momentum *Ubique* ; certè rerum omnium Fabricator ac Dominus, non erit *nunquam nusquam*. Omnipræsens est, non per *Virtutem* solam, sed etiam per *Substantiam* : Nam Virtus sine Substanciâ subsistere non potest. *i.e. God is* Eternal *and* Infinite, Omnipotent *and* Omniscient : *That is, he endures from Everlasting to Everlasting, and is present from Infinity to Infinity : He governs all things which are, and knows all things which are possible to be known. He is not* Eternity *or* Infinity, *but* Eternal *and* Infinite. *He is not* Duration, *or* Space ; *but he endures, and is* Present. *He endures* Always, *and is Present every* where ; *and, by existing always and every where, constitutes* Duration *and* Space, *Eternity and Infinity. Seeing every particle of Space is* Always, *and every indivisible Moment of Duration is* every where ; *surely it cannot be said of the Maker and Lord of all things, that he is* [at no Time, *and* in no Place,] Never *and* No-where. *He is* Omnipresent, *not only* Virtually, *but* Substantially : *For* Power *cannot subsist without a* Substance. Newtoni Prinipia, Schol. generale sub finem.

594   129. FOURTH REPLY OF CLARKE

11, & 12. *Les* Infinis *ne sont composez de* Finis, *que comme les* Finis *sont composez d'*Infinitesimes. *J'ai fait voir ci-dessus,* (§ 3. de ma 3 Réplique,) *en quel sens on peut dire que l'*Espace *a des parties, ou qu'il n'en a pas. Les* parties, *dans le sens que l'on donne à ce mot lors qu'on l'applique aux* Corps, *sont* separables, composées, desunies, indépendantes les unes des autres, & capables de mouvement. *Mais quoique l'Imagination puisse en quelque maniere concevoir des parties dans l'Espace infini ; cependant, comme ces parties, improprement ainsi dites, sont* essentiellement immobiles & inseparables *les unes des autres,* (*Voïez ci-dessus,* Réplique II, § 4. & Réplique III, § 3.) *il s'ensuit que cet Espace est* essentiellement *simple,* & absolument indivisible.

13. *Si le Monde a une Etendue* bornée, *il peut être* mis en mouvement *par la puissance de Dieu ; & par consequent l'Argument que je fonde sur cette* Mobilité, *est une preuve concluante. Quoique* deux Lieux *soient* parfaitement semblables, *ils ne sont pas* un seul & même Lieu. *Le* Mouvement *ou le* Repos *de l'Univers, n'est pas non plus le* même Etat ; *comme le* Mouvement *ou le* Repos *d'un* Vaisseau, *n'est pas le* même Etat, *parce qu'un homme renfermé dans la Cabane ne sçauroit s'appercevoir si le Vaisseau fait voile ou non, pendant que son mouvement est uniforme. Quoique cet homme ne s'apperçoive pas du mouvement du Vaisseau, ce mouvement ne laisse pas d'être un* Etat réel & different, *& il produit des* Effets réels & differens ; *& s'il étoit* arrêté tout d'un coup, *il auroit d'autres effets réels. Il en seroit de même d'un mouvement imperceptible de l'*Univers. *On n'a point répondu à cet* Argument ; *sur lequel Mr. le Chevalier* Newton *insiste beaucoup dans ses* Principes Mathematiques. *Aprez avoir consideré (dans sa* Definition 8.) *les* Proprietez, *les* Causes, *& les* Effets *du* Mouvement ; *cette consideration lui sert à faire voir la difference qu'il y a entre le* mouvement réel, *ou le transport d'un* Corps *qui passe d'une partie de l'Espace dans une autre ; & le* Mouvement rélatif, *qui n'est qu'un changement de l'*Ordre *ou de la* Situation *des* Corps *entre eux. C'est un* Argument Mathematique, *qui prouve par des* Effets réels, *qu'il peut y avoir un* mouvement réel, *où il n'y en a point de* rélatif ; *& qu'il peut y avoir un* mouvement rélatif, *où il n'y en a point de* réel : *C'est, dis-je, un* Argument Mathematique, *auquel on ne répond pas, quand on se contente d'assurer le contraire.*

14. *La* réalité de l'Espace *n'est pas une simple* Supposition : *Elle a été prouvée par les* Arguments *rapportez ci-dessus, auxquels on n'a point répondu. L'Auteur n'a pas répondu non plus à un autre* Argument, *sçavoir, que l'*Espace *& le* Temps *sont des* Quantitez ; *ce qu'on ne peut dire de la* Situation *& de l'*Ordre.

15. *Il n'étoit pas impossible que Dieu fît le Monde* plûtôt *ou plus tard, qu'il ne l'a fait. Il n'est pas impossible non plus, qu'il le détruise* plûtôt *ou plus tard, qu'il ne sera actuellement détruit. Quant à la doctrine de l'*Eternité du Monde ; *ceux qui supposent que la* Matiere *& l'*Espace *sont la même chose, doivent supposer que le Monde est non seulement* infini *& éternel, mais encore que son immensité & son éternité sont* nécessaires, *& même aussi nécessaires que l'*Espace *& la* Durée, *qui ne dépendent pas*

11, *and* 12. *Infinites* are composed of *Finites*, in no other sense, than as *Finites* are composed of *infinitesimals*. In what sense Space *has* or *has not Parts*, has been explained before, *Reply 3d*, § 3. *Parts*, in the *corporeal* Sense of the Word, are *separable, compounded, ununited, independent on, and moveable from, each other* : But infinite Space, though it may by Us be *partially apprehended*, that is, may in our Imagination be conceived as composed of *Parts* ; yet those *Parts* (*improperly* so called) being *essentially indiscerpible* and *immoveable* from each other, and not *partable* without an express Contradiction in Terms, [*See above, Reply* II, § 4. And *Reply* III, § 3 ;] *Space* consequently is in itself *essentially One*, and *absolutely indivisible.*

13. If the World be *Finite* in Dimensions, it is *moveable* by the Power of God ; and therefore my Argument drawn from that *moveableness*, is conclusive. Two *places*, though *exactly alike*, are not the *same place*. Nor is the *Motion* or *Rest* of the Universe, the *same State* ; any more than the *Motion* or *Rest* of a *Ship*, is the *same State*, because a Man shut up in the Cabbin cannot perceive whether the Ship sails or not, so long as it moves uniformly. The *Motion* of the *Ship*, though the Man perceives it not, is a *real different State*, and has *real different Effects* ; and, upon a *sudden stop*, it would have *Other real Effects* ; And so likewise would an indiscernable Motion of the *Universe*. To This Argument, no Answer has ever been given. It is largely insisted on by Sir *Isaac Newton* in his *Mathematical Principles*, (*Definit.* 8.) where, from the Consideration of the *Properties, Causes*, and *Effects* of Motion, he shows the difference between *real Motion*, or a Bodie's being carried from one part of Space to another ; and *relative Motion*, which is merely a change of the *Order* or *Situation* of Bodies with *respect to each other.* This Argument is a Mathematical one ; showing from *real Effects*, that there may be *real Motion* where there is *none relative* ; and *relative Motion*, where there is *none real* : And is not to be answered, by barely *asserting* the contrary.

14. The *reality of Space* is not a *Supposition*, but is *proved* by the fore-going Arguments, to which no Answer has been given. Nor is any Answer given to That other Argument, that *Space* and *Time* are *Quantities*, which *Situation* and *Order* are *not*.

15. It was no *impossibility* for God to make the World *sooner* or *later* than he did : Nor is it at all *impossible* for him to destroy it *sooner* or *later* than it shall actually be destroyed. As to the Notion of the *World's Eternity* ; They who suppose *Matter* and *Space* to be the same, *must* indeed suppose the World to be not only *Infinite* and *Eternal*, but *necessarily* so ; even as necessarily as *Space* and *Duration*,

596   129. FOURTH REPLY OF CLARKE

*Voïez
ci-dessus
la Note
sur § 10.

de la Volonté *de Dieu, mais de son* * Existence· *Au contraire, ceux qui croyent que* Dieu a créé la Matiere *en telle* quantité, *en tel* temps, & *en tels* Espaces *qu'il lui a plû, ne se trouvent embarassez d'aucune difficulté. Car la Sagesse de Dieu peut avoir eu de très-bonnes raisons pour créer* Ce Monde *dans un* certain temps : *elle peut avoir fait* d'autres choses *avant que* Ce Monde *fût créé ; & elle peut faire* d'autres choses *aprez que* Ce Monde *sera détruit.*

16, & 17. *J'ai prouvé ci-dessus, (Voïez ma Troisiéme Réplique § 4, & la 13, de cette Quatriéme Réplique,) que l'Espace & le Temps ne sont pas l'Ordre des choses, mais des* Quantitez *réelles ; ce qu'on ne peut dire de l'Ordre & de la Situation. Le sçavant Auteur n'a pas encore répondue à ces Preuves ; &, à moins qu'il n'y réponde, ce qu'il dit, est une* Contradiction, *comme il l'avoüé lui-même ici.*

18. *L'Uniformité de* toutes *les parties de l'Espace, ne prouve pas que Dieu ne puisse agir dans* aucune *partie de l'Espace, de la maniere qu'il le veut. Dieu peut avoir de* bonnes raisons *pour créer des* Etres finis *; & des Etres finis ne peuvent exister qu'en des* Lieux particuliers. *Et comme* tous les Lieux *sont originairement semblables, (quand même le* Lieux *ne seroit que la Situation des Corps ;) si Dieu place* un Cube de matiere *derriere* un autre Cube *egal de matiere, plûtôt qu'à rebours, ce choix n'est pas indigne des Perfections de Dieu, quoique* ces deux Situations *soient parfaitement semblables ; parce qu'il peut y avoir de* très-bonnes raisons *pour l'existence de* ces deux Cubes, & *qu'ils ne sçauroient exister que dans* l'une ou l'autre *de ces deux Situations également raisonnables. Le* hazard *d'Epicure n'est pas un* Choix, *mais une* Nécessité *aveugle.*

19. *Si l'Argument que l'on trouve ici, prouve quelque chose, il prouve, (comme je l'ai déja dit cit-dessus § 3.) que Dieu n'a créé, & même qu'il ne peut créer aucune* matiere ; *parce que la* Situation *des parties égales & similaires de la Matiere, étoit necessairement* indifferent *dés le commencement ; aussi bien que la prémiere* Détermination *de leur* mouvement, *d'un certain coté, ou du coté opposé.*

20. *Je ne comprends point ce que l'Auteur veut prouver ici, par rapport au sujet dont il s'agit.*

21. Dire que Dieu ne peut donner des bornes à la Quantité de la Matiere, *c'est avancer une chose d'une trop grande Importance, pour l'admettre* sans preuve. Et si *Dieu ne peut non plus donner des bornes à la* Durée de la Matiere, *il s'ensuivra que le Monde est infini & éternel* nécessairement & *indépendamment de Dieu.*

22, & 23. *Si l'Argument que l'on trouve ici, étoit bien fondé, il prouveroit que Dieu* ne sçauroit s'empêcher de faire *tout ce qu'il peut faire ; & par conséquent qu'il ne sçauroit* s'empêcher de rendre *toutes les Créatures infinies & éternelles. Mais, selon cette* Doctrine, Dieu ne seroit point le Gouverneur du Monde : *il seroit un* Agent *nécessaire ; c'est-à-dire qu'il ne seroit pas même un Agent, mais le* Destin, la Nature, & la Nécessité.

24. ———— 28. *On revient encore ici à l'usage du mot de* Sensorium, *quoique* Mr. Newton *se soit servi d'un Correctif, lors qu'il a employé ce mot. Il n'est pas nécessaire de rien ajouter à ce que j'ai dit sur cela. Voïez ma* Troisiéme Réplique, § 10. *la* Séconde, § 3. *la* Premiere § 3.

which depend not on the *Will*, but on the * *Existence* of God. But they who believe that God created Matter in what *Quantity*, and at what particular *Time*, and in what particular *Spaces* he *pleased*, are here under no difficulty. For the Wisdom of God may have *very good reasons* for creating *This World*, at *That particular Time* he did; and may have made *other kinds of things* Before this *material World* began, and may make *other kinds of things* After *This World* is destroyed.

* See above, the Note on § 10.

16. *and* 17. That *Space* and *Time* are not the *mere Order* of things, but real *Quantities*, (which Order and Situation are not;) has been proved *above*, (See *Third Reply*, § 4 ; and in *This Paper*, § 13,) and no Answer yet given to those Proofs. And till an Answer be given to those Proofs, this learned Author's assertion is (by *his own Confession* in this place) a *Contradiction*.

18. The *Uniformity* of *all* the parts of Space, is no Argument against God's acting in *Any* part, after what manner he pleases. God may have *good reasons* to create *finite* Beings, and Finite Beings can be but in *particular Places*. And, *all* places being originally alike, (even though *Place* were nothing else but the Situation of Bodies;) God's placing *one cube of matter* behind *another equal cube of matter*, rather than the *other* behind *That* ; is a *choice* no way unworthy of the Perfections of God, though *Both these Situations* be *perfectly equal* : Because there may be *very good reasons* why *Both the Cubes* should exist, and they cannot exist but in *one* or *other* of equally reasonable Situations. The *Epicurean Chance*, is not a *Choice* of *Will*, but a *blind Necessity* of Fate.

19. This Argument, (as I now observed, § 3,) if it proves any thing, proves that God neither *did* nor *can* create any *matter* at all; because the *Situation* of equal and similar parts of matter, could not but be originally *indifferent* : As was also the original *Determination* of their *Motions*, this way, or the contrary way.

20. What *This* tends to prove, with regard to the Argument before us ; I understand not.

21. That *God Cannot limit the Quantity of Matter*, is an Assertion of too great consequence, to be admitted without *Proof*. If he cannot limit the *Duration* of it neither, then the material World is both infinite and eternal *necessarily* and *independently upon God*.

22, *and* 23. This Argument, if it were good, would prove that Whatever God *can* do, he *cannot but do* ; *and* consequently that he *cannot but* make *every thing infinite*, and *every thing eternal*. Which is making him no *Governor* at all, but a *mere necessary Agent*, that is, indeed *no Agent at all*, but mere *Fate* and *Nature* and *Necessity*.

24. ———— 28. Concerning the Use of the word, *Sensory* ; (though Sir *Isaac Newton* says only, *as it were* the *Sensory* ;) enough has been said in my *Third Reply*, § 10 ; and *Second Reply*, § 3 ; and *First Reply*, § 3.

29. *L'*Espace *est le* Lieu *de* toutes les Choses *& de* toutes les Idées : *Comme la Durée est la* Durée *de* toutes les Choses, *& de* toutes les Idées. *J'ai fait voir ci-dessus* (Réplique II. § 12.) *que cette Doctrine ne tend point à faire Dieu l'*Ame du Monde. *Il n'y a point d'*Union *entre* Dieu *& le* Monde. *On pourroit dire avec plus de raison, que l'Esprit de l'homme est l'*Ame des Images des choses qu'il apperçoit, *qu'on ne peut dire que Dieu est l'*Ame *du Monde, dans lequel il est* present *par tout, &* sur lequel il agit *comme il veut, sans que le* Monde agisse sur lui. *Nonobstant cette Réponse qu'on a vû ci-dessus,* (Réplique II. § 12.) *l'Auteur ne laisse pas de répeter la même Objection plus d'une fois, comme si on n'y avoit point répondu.*

30. *Je n'entends point ce que l'Auteur veut dire par un* Principe répresentatif. *L'*Ame *apperçoit les choses, parce que les Images des choses lui sont portées par les Organes des Sens.* Dieu *apperçoit les choses, parce qu'il est present dans les Substances des choses mêmes. Il ne les apperçoit pas, en les* produisant continuellement ; (*car il* se repose de l'Ouvrage de la Création ;) *mais il les apperçoit, parce qu'il est* continu-ellement present *dans toutes les choses qu'il* a créés.

31. *Si l'Ame* n'agissoit point *sur le Corps ; & si le Corps, par un simple mouvement méchanique de la Matiere, se conformoit pourtant à la volonté de l'Ame dans une* varieté infinie *de mouvemens spontanées, ce seroit un* Miracle perpetuel. *L'*Harmonie préétablie *n'est qu'un mot, ou un terme d'Art ; & elle n'est d'aucun usage pour expliquer la cause d'un effet si miraculeux.*

32. *Supposer que dans le mouvement spontanée du Corps, l'Ame ne donne point un* nouveau mouvement *ou une* nouvelle Impresssion *à la Matiere, & que tous les mouvemens spontanées sont produits par une* impulsion méchanique de la Matiere ; *c'est reduire tout au Destin & à la Nécessité. Mais quand on dit que* Dieu agit *dans le Monde sur toutes les Créatures comme il le veut,* sans aucune Union, *&* sans qu'aucune chose agisse sur lui ; *cela fait voir évidemment la differ-ence qu'il y a entre un* Gouverneur *qui est* present par tout, *& une* Ame imag-inaire du Monde.

33. *Toute* Action *consiste à donner une* nouvelle Force *aux choses, sur lesquelles elle s'exerce. Sans cela, ce ne seroit pas une* Action réelle, *mais une simple* Passion, *comme dans toutes les* Loix méchaniques *du mouvement. D'où il s'ensuit que si la* communication d'une nouvelle Force *est* surnaturelle, toutes les actions de Dieu seront surnaturelles, *& il sera entierement exclu du Gouvernement du* Monde. *Il s'ensuit aussi de là, que toutes les* actions des hommes *sont* surnaturelles, *ou que l'*homme *est une pure* Machine, *comme une Horloge.*

34, *& 35. On a fait voir ci-dessus la difference qu'il y a entre la véritable Idée de* Dieu, *& celle d'une* Ame du Monde. *Voiez ma* Seconde Réplique, § 12 ; *& dans cette* Quatriéme Réplique, § 29 *& § 32.

36. *J'ai répondu ci-dessus, § 31. à ce que l'on trouve ici.*

29. *Space* is the *Place* of *All Things*, and of *All Ideas* : Just as *Duration* is the *Duration* of *All Things*, and of *All Ideas*. That This has no Tendency to make God *the Soul* of the World, *See above, Reply* II, § 12. There is no *Union* between *God* and the *World*. The *Mind of Man* might with greater propriety be stiled *The Soul of the Images of things which it perceives*, than *God* can be stiled the *Soul* of the *World*, to which he is *present* throughout, and *acts upon it* as he pleases, without being *acted upon by it*. Though this Answer was given before, (*Reply* II, § 12.) yet the same Objection is repeated again and again, without taking any Notice of the Answer.

30. What is meant by a[3] *representative Principle*, I understand not. The *Soul* discerns things, by having the *Images* of things conveyed to it through the Organs of Sense : *God* discerns things, by being present *to* and *in* the *Substances* of the Things themselves. Not by *producing them continually* ; (For he *rests* now from his work of *Creation* :) but by being *continually* omnipresent to every thing which he *created at the Beginning.*

31. That the Soul should *not operate* upon the Body ; and yet the Body, by mere mechanical impulse of Matter, conform itself to the Will of the Soul in all the *infinite variety* of spontaneous Animal-Motion ; is a *perpetual Miracle. Pre-established Harmony*, is a mere *Word* or Term of Art, and does nothing towards explaining the cause of so miraculous an effect.

32. To suppose that in spontaneous Animal-Motion, the Soul gives *no new Motion* or *Impression* to Matter ; but that all spontaneous Animal-Motion is performed by *mechanical impulse of Matter* ; is reducing all things to mere Fate and Necessity. God's *acting* in the World upon every thing, after what manner he pleases, *without* any *Union*, and *without* being *acted upon* by any thing ; shows plainly the difference between an *Omnipresent Governor*, and an imaginary *Soul of the World.*

33. Every *Action* is (in the nature of things) the giving of a *new Force* to the thing *acted upon*. Otherwise 'tis not really *Action*, but mere *passiveness* ; as in the case of all *mechanical and inanimate communications* of Motion. If therefore the *Giving a new Force*, be *supernatural* ; then *every action* of *God* is *supernatural*, and he is quite excluded from the Government of the *natural World* : And every *action of Man*, is either *supernatural*, or else *Man* is as mere a *Machine* as a Clock.

34, *and* 35. The *difference* between the true Notion of *God*, and that of a *Soul of the World*, has been before shown : *Reply* II, § 12. and in *This Paper*, § 29 *and* 32.

36. This has been answered just above, § 31.

600 129. FOURTH REPLY OF CLARKE

37. *L'Ame n'est pas* repandue dans le Cerveau ; *mais elle est presente dans le Lieu, qui est le* Sensorium.

38. *Ce que l'on dit ici, est une simple* Affirmation *sans* preuve. *Deux Corps, destituez d'*Elasticité, *se rencontrant avec des forces contraires & égales, perdent leur Mouvement. Et Mr. le Chevalier* Newton *a donné un Exemple Mathematique,* (pag. 341, *de l'Edition Latine de son* Optique,) *par lequel il paroit que le Mouvement* diminue & augmente *continuellement en* Quantité, *sans qu'il soit communiqué à d'autres Corps.*

39. *Le Sujet, dont on parle ici, n'est point un* défaut, *comme l'Auteur le suppose : C'est la* véritable *nature de la* Matiere inactive.

40. *Si l'Argument que l'on trouve ici, est bien fondé, il prouve que l'Univers doit* être infini ; *qu'il* a existé de toute éternité, & *qu'il ne sçauroit* cesser d'exister ; *que* Dieu a toûjours créé *autant d'*hommes, & *d'autres* Etres, *qu'il étoit* possible *qu'il en* créât ; & *qu'il les a créez pour les faire exister aussi* long temps, *qu'il lui étoit* possible.

41. *Je n'entends point ce que ces mots veulent dire :* Un Ordre, (*ou une Situation,*) qui rend les Corps situables. *Il me semble que cela veut dire, que la* Situation est la cause de la Situation. J'ai prouvé ci-dessus (Réplique III, § 2 & 4.) *que l'*Espace n'est pas l'Ordre des Corps : *Et j'ai fait voir dans cette* Quatriéme Réplique, § 13 & 14, *que l'Auteur n'a point répondu aux* Arguments que j'ai proposé. *Il n'est pas moins évident, que le* Temps n'est pas l'Ordre des chose qui succedent l'une à l'autre ; *puisque la* Quantité du Temps peut être plus grande *ou* plus petite, & *cependant* Cet Ordre ne laisse pas d'être le même. L'Ordre des choses qui succedent l'une à l'autre dans le Temps, n'est pas le Temps même : *Car elles peuvent succeder l'une à l'autre* plus vîte *ou* plus lentement *dans le même* Ordre de Succession, *mais non dans le même* Temps. *Supposé qu'il n'y eut point de Créatures, l'*Ubiquité *de* Dieu, & *la* Continuation de son Existence, *feroient* * *que l'*Espace & *la* Durée *seroient precisement les mêmes qu'*à present.

* Voïez ci-dessus la Note sur § 10.

42. *On appelle ici de la* Raison *à l'Opinion* vulgaire. *Mais comme l'Opinion vulgaire n'est pas la* Régle *de la* Vérité, *les Philosophes ne doivent point y avoir recours.*

43. *L'idée d'un Miracle* renferme *nécessairement l'idée d'une chose* rare & extraordinaire. *Car, d'ailleurs, il n'y a rien de* plus merveilleux, & *qui demande une* plus grande puissance, *que quelques unes des choses que nous appelons* naturelles ; *comme, par exemple, les Mouvemens des* Corps Celestes, *la* Géneration & *la* Formation des Planetes & des Animaux, &c. *Cependant ce ne sont pas des* Miracles, *parce que ce sont des choses* communes. *Il ne s'ensuit pourtant pas de là, que* tout ce qui est rare & extraordinaire, *soit un* Miracle. *Car plusieurs choses de cette nature, peuvent être des Effets irreguliers & moins communs, des Causes* ordinaires ; *come les* Eclipses, *les* Monstres, *la* Manie dans les hommes, & *une infinité d'autres choses que le Vulgaire appelle des* Prodiges.

129. FOURTH REPLY OF CLARKE   601

37. The Soul is not *diffused through the Brain* ; but is present to That particular Place, which is the *Sensorium*.

38. This is a bare *Assertion*, without *Proof.* Two Bodies, void of Elasticity, meeting each other with equal contrary Forces, Both lose their Motion. And Sir *Isaac Newton* has given a *Mathematical* Instance, (*page* 341 *of the Latin Edition of his Opticks*,) wherein *Motion* is continually *diminishing* and *increasing* in *Quantity*, without any communication thereof to other Bodies.[4]

39. This is no *Defect*, as is here supposed ; but 'tis the *just and proper* Nature of *inert Matter*.

40. This Argument (if it be good,) proves that the *Material* World *must* be *infinite*, and that it *must have been from eternity*, and *must continue to eternity* : And that God *must Always* have created as *many Men*, and as *many* of all other things, as 'twas *possible* for him to create ; and for as long a *time* also, as it was *possible* for him to do it.

41. What the meaning of these Words is ; *An Order*, (or Situation,) *which makes Bodies to be Situable* ; I understand not. It seems to me to amount to This, that *Situation* is the cause of *Situation*. That *Space* is not merely *the Order of Bodies*, has been shown before ; *Reply* III, § 2 *and* 4. And that no Answer has been given to the Arguments there offered, has been shown in *This Paper*, § 13 and 14. Also that *Time* is not merely the *Order of things succeeding each other*, is evident ; because the *Quantity* of Time may be *greater* or *less*, and yet *That Order* continue the *same*. The *Order of things succeeding each other in Time*, is not *Time itself* : For they may succeed each other *faster* or *slower* in the same *Order of Succession*, but not in the same *Time*. If *no Creatures* existed, yet the *Ubiquity* of God, and the *Continuance of his Existence*, would make * *Space* and *Duration* to be exactly the same as they are *Now*.

* See above,
the Note
on § 10.

42. This is appealing from *Reason* to *vulgar Opinion* ; which *Philosophers* should not do, because it is not the *Rule* of *Truth*.

43. *Unusualness* is *necessarily* included in the Notion of a *Miracle*. For otherwise there is nothing more *wonderful*, nor that requires *greater Power* to effect, than some of those things we call *natural*. Such as, the *Motions* of the *Heavenly-Bodies*, the *Generation* and *Formation* of *Plants and Animals*, &c. Yet these are for *This only reason* not *Miracles*, because they are *common*. Nevertheless, it does not follow, that every thing which is *unusual*, is *therefore* a Miracle. For it may be only the irregular and more *rare* effect of *usual* Causes : Of which kind are *Eclipses*, *Monstrous Births*, *Madness in Men*, and innumerable things which the Vulgar call *Prodigies*.

44. *On accorde ici ce que j'ai dit. On soûtient pourtant une chose contraire au* sentiment commun *des Théologiens, en supposant qu'un Ange peut faire des* Miracles.

45. *Il est vrai que si* un Corps *en* attiroit *un autre sans l'intervention d'aucun* moyen, ce ne seroit pas un Miracle, mais une *Contradiction ; car ce seroit suppose* qu'une chose agit où elle *n'est pas. Mais le Moyen par lequel deux Corps s'attirent l'un* l'autre, peut être *invisible & intangible, & d'une nature differente du* Méchanisme : *Ce qui n'empêche pas qu'une action réguliere & constante ne puisse être appellée* naturelle ; *puis qu'elle est beaucoup moins merveilleuse, que le* mouvement des Animaux, *qui ne passe pourtant pas pour un* Miracle.

46. *Si par le terme de* Forces naturelles, *on entend ici des Forces* Méchaniques ; *tous les* Animaux, *sans en excepter les* hommes, *seront de pures* Machines, *comme une* Horloge. *Mais si ce terme ne signifie pas des* Forces Méchaniques ; *la* Gravitation *peut être produite par des Forces* régulieres & naturelles, *quoi qu'elles ne soient pas* Méchaniques.

N.B. On a déjà repondu ci-dessus aux Arguments que Mr. *Leibnitz* a inferez dans une Addition à son Quatriéme Ecrit. La seule chose qu'il soit besoin d'observer ici, c'est que Mr. *Leibnitz* en soutenant l'impossibilité des *Atomes Phyiques*, (il ne s'agit pas entre nous des *Points Mathematiques*,) soutient une Absurdité manifeste. Car ou il y a des *parties parfaitement solides* dans la Matiere, ou il *n'y en a pas*. S'il y en a, & qu'en les subdivisant on y prenne de nouvelles particules, qui ayent toutes la même Figure & les mêmes Dimensions, (ce qui est toujours *possible*,) ces nouvelles particules seront des *Atomes Physiques parfaitement semblables*. Que s'il n'y a point des parties parfaitement solides dans la Matiere, il n'y a point de Matiere dans l'Univers. Car plus on Divise & Subdivise un Corps, pour arriver enfin à des parties parfaitement solides & sans pores, plus la Proportion que les Pores ont à la matiere solide de ce Corps, plus, dis-je, cette Proportion augmente. Si donc, en poussant la Division & la Subdivision à la infini, il est impossible d'arriver à des parties parfaitement solides & sans pores ; il s'en suivra que les Corps sont uniquement composez de pores, (le rapport de ceux-ci aux parties solides, augmentant sans cesse ;) & par consequent qu'il n'y a point de Matiere du tout : Ce qui est une Absurdité manifeste. Et le raisonnement sera le même, par rapport à la matiere dont les Especes particulieres des Corps sont composées, soit que l'on suppose que les pores sont vuides, ou qu'ils sont remplis d'une matiere etrangere.[6]

129. FOURTH REPLY OF CLARKE   603

44. This is a *Concession* of what I alleged. And yet 'tis *contrary* to the *common Opinion* of Divines, to suppose that an *Angel* can work a *Miracle*.

45. That *One Body* should *attract* another *without any* intermediate *Means*, is indeed not a *Miracle*, but a *Contradiction* : For 'tis supposing something to *act* where it *is not*. But the *Means* by which Two Bodies attract each other, may be *invisible* and *intangible*, and of a different nature from *mechanism* ; and yet, acting regularly and constantly, may well be called *natural* ; being much less wonderful than *Animal-motion*, which yet is *never* called a *Miracle*.

46. If the word, *natural Forces*, means here *Mechanical* ; then all *Animals*, and even *Men*, are as *mere Machines* as a *Clock*. But if the word does not mean, *mechanical Forces* ; then *Gravitation* may be effected by *regular* and *natural* Powers, though they be *not Mechanical*.

N.B. *The Arguments alleged in the Postscript to Mr.* Leibnitz's *Fourth Paper,*[5] *have been already answered in the foregoing Replies. All that needs here to be observed is, that his Notion concerning the Impossibility of* Physical Atomes, *(for the Question is not about* Mathematical Atomes,*) is a manifest Absurdity. For either there are, or there are not any perfectly solid particles of Matter. If there are any such ; then the parts of such perfectly solid particles, taken of equal Figure and Dimensions, (which is always possible in Supposition,) are* Physical Atoms *perfectly alike. But if there be No such perfectly solid particles, then there is no* Matter *at all in the Universe. For, the further the Division and Subdivision of the parts of any Body is carried, before you arrive at parts perfectly solid and without pores ; the greater is the Proportion of Pores to solid matter in That Body. If therefore, carrying on the Division in infinitum, you never arrive at parts perfectly solid and without Pores ; it will follow that All Bodies consist of Pores only, without any Matter at all : Which is a manifest Absurdity. And the Argument is the same with regard to the Matter of which any particular Species of Bodies is composed, whether its Pores be supposed empty, or always full of extraneous matter.*[6]

---

[1] The original English and French translation are from Clarke's edition of the correspondence (Clarke 1717, pp. 120–54). LBr. 160 Bl. 34r–43r is the original in Clarke's hand. This set includes only paragraphs 2–41; paragraphs 42–46 are missing. There is also a copy in a secretary's hand (LH 1, 20 Bl. 393r–395r). This is Clarke's reply to Leibniz's Fourth Paper (document 125a); it was enclosed with Caroline's letter to Leibniz of 26 June 1716 (document 128). All footnotes and marginal notes are Clarke's; endnotes are mine. Square brackets and what they contain are Clarke's. Clarke's references to the Appendix of his 1717 edition of the correspondence have been omitted.

[2] In this footnote, Clarke is referring to Leibniz's letter to Caroline of 2 June 1716, with which his Fourth Paper was sent. In that letter, Leibniz had written:

I am afraid that we will dispute as futilely about the void as about other things. I do not have enough time remaining to waste it in amusements. There are more important things to do. I do not believe that there is any space without matter. The experiments that they cite of the void exclude only a gross matter, which they draw from the cavity of the glass by the weight of the mercury, in the case of Torricelli, and by the pump, in the case of Mr. Guericke. For the rays of light, which are not devoid of some subtle matter, pass through the glass. I would not have touched upon this question of the vacuum if I had not found that the hypothesis of the vacuum derogates from the perfections of God, as do nearly all the other philosophical views that are contrary to mine. For mine are nearly

Leibniz to Henriette Charlotte von Pöllnitz

Mademoiselle

A Mademoiselle
de pelniz

Si la dispute entre M. Newton et moy avoit pû contribuer au divertissement du Roy je ne serois point faché d'y avoir perdu quelques heures. J'en serois encore plus aise, si le Roy estoit plus tot pour le plein que je defends, que pour le vuide de M. Newton, comme sa Mté vous a mandé. pourveu qu'elle ne l'entende dans un sens allegorique suivant le quel une bourse pleine seroit mieux qu'un bourse vuide. Il est vray que les richesses de la nature consistent dans la varieté des creatures, et comme dit le Tasse

Per variar natura e bella

Ainsi le vuide seroit à son egard une espace de pauvreté. L'espace est comme le temps quand on y laisse du vuide, il est mal employé. Si j'en disois d'avantage, j'employerois mal le votre et le mien; la page est pleine, et il n'y reste qu'autant qu'il en faut pour vous dire que je suis avec respect etc.

Mademoiselle

Hanover ce 30 de juin 1716

votre treshumble &
tres obéissant serviteur
Leibniz

all bound up with the great principle of the supreme reason and perfection of God. So I do not fear that Your Royal Highness will easily abandon what she will have had the leisure to understand thoroughly: her penetration and her zeal for the glory of God are my sureties. [document 124, p. 557]

³ The original omitted 'a'; corrected in the Errata of the 1717 edition of the Correspondence.

⁴ The example Clarke cites is from Query 31 of the second and subsequent English editions of the *Opticks* (see Newton 2014, p. 183). For a critical discussion, see Brown 1984, pp. 133 ff.

⁵ See document 117b.

⁶ This last sentence was added in the Errata of the 1717 edition of the Correspondence.

130. Leibniz to Henriette Charlotte von Pöllnitz*[1]

Mademoiselle

To Mademoiselle
Pölnitz
[Hanover, 30 June 1716]

If the dispute between Mr. Newton and me could have contributed to the entertainment of the king [George I, Georg Ludwig* of Braunschweig-Lüneburg], I would not be upset to have lost a few hours in it. I would be even more pleased about it if the king were in favour of the plenum that I defend rather than the void of Mr. Newton, as His Majesty has informed you, as long as he does not understand it in an allegoric sense, according to which a full purse would be better than an empty one.[2] It is true that the riches of nature consist in the variety of creatures, and as Tasso said

Per variar natura e bella[3]

So with regard to it, the void would be an impoverished space. Space is like time; when some void is left there, it is badly employed. If I said any more about it, I would employ yours and mine badly. The page is full, and there remains there only as much as is needed to tell you that I am with respect etc.

Mademoiselle

Hanover this 30ᵗʰ of June 1716

your very humble and
very obedient servant
Leibniz

¹ LBr. 735 Bl. 50r. Draft: one octavo side in Leibniz's hand. Not previously published.

² Here Leibniz repeats a joke that Caroline had made in her letter to him of 26 May (document 122, p. 549).

³ 'Through variety, nature is beautiful.' Although Leibniz attributes this line to Torquato Tasso (1544–1595), it seems to have originated in a stanza from a sonnet by Serafino dell'Aquila (aka Aquilano or Serafino dei Ciminelli) (1466–1500), Ciminelli 1894, p. 124:

Cosi va el mondo; ognun segue sua stella;
Ciascuno è in terra a qualche fin produtto
E per tal variar natura è bella.

Leibniz to Louis Bourguet (excerpt)

Hanover ce 2. Juillet 1716.

Monsieur

[...]

Il est trés seur que chaque estat de l'univers enveloppe l'infini; et même qui plus est, chaque portion de l'univers en eveloppe aussi, dont la raison est que chaque partie de la matiére est actuellement sous divisée & contient quelque varieté reglée; Autrement il y auroit dans la Nature quelque chaos, ou au moins quelque chose d'informe.

Mr Clark pour combattre ma maxime, que rien n'arrive sans une raison suffisante, et pour soûtenir que Dieu fait quelque chose par une mere volonté absolument sans aucune raison, a allegué que l'espace etant partout uniforme, il est indifférent à Dieu d'y placer les corps. J'ay répondu que cela même prouve, que l'espace n'est pas un etre absolu, mais un ordre, ou quelque chose de rélatif & qui ne seroit qu'ideal, si les corps n'y existoient point. Autrement il arriveroit quelque chose dont il n'y auroit aucune raison déterminante. Je dis encore là dessus, qu'il en est de l'espace come du tems; que le tems séparé des choses n'est pas un estre absolu, mais une chose ideale. Et que pour cette raison on ne peut point demander, pourquoi Dieu n'a pas crée le Monde mille ans plus tôt. Car le tems n'estant que ce rapport des successions; ce seroit la même chose, et la différence ne consiste que dans une fiction mal entenduë. Autrement il faudroit avouër que Dieu auroit fait quelque chose sans raison, ce qui estant une absurdité, il faudroit recourir à l'eternité du Monde.

Si le Rectangle[2] avoit lieu dans l'ordre des choses, il faudroit avouer que les productions de la sagesse divine seroient coëternelles avec elle, & que chaque substance auroit eté eternelle <u>à parte ante</u>, come je crois qu'elles le sont toutes <u>à parte post</u>.

[...]

J'ay fait ma Cour au Czar aux eaux de Pirmont et aussi icy, puisque Sa Majesté est demeurée deux nuits aprés son retour des eaux à une Maison de plaisance tout proche d'icy. Je ne saurois assés admirer la vivacité & le jugement de ce grand Prince. Il fait venir des habiles gens de tous côtés, & quand il leur parle, ils en sont tout etonnés, tant il leur parle à propos. Il s'informe de tous les arts mécaniques. Mais sa grande curiosité est pour tout ce qui a du rapport à la navigation; et par consequent il aime aussi l'Astronomie & la Géographie. J'espere que nous apprendrons par son moyen, si l'Asie est attachée à Amérique. Je suis avec Zele. etc.

131. Leibniz to Louis Bourguet* (excerpt)[1]

Hanover 2 July 1716

Sir

[...]

It is very certain that each state of the universe envelops infinity; and what is even more, each portion of the universe also envelops it, because each part of matter is actually subdivided and contains some ordered variety; otherwise, there would be in nature some chaos, or at least something formless.

To attack my maxim, that nothing happens without a sufficient reason, and to uphold God's doing something by a mere absolute will without reason, Mr. [Samuel] Clarke* has alleged that space, being everywhere uniform, is indifferent to God's placing bodies in it. I have responded that that itself proves that space is not an absolute being, but an order, or something relative, which would be only ideal if bodies did not exist. Otherwise, something would happen for which there would not be any determinate reason. On that head I said furthermore that what holds for space holds for time, that time separated from things is not an absolute being, but something ideal, and that for this reason it cannot be asked why God did not create the world a thousand years sooner. For since time is only this relation of successions, it would be the same thing, and the difference consists only in an ill-conceived fiction. Otherwise, it would have to be admitted that God would have done something without reason; and since that is absurd, it would be necessary to have recourse to the eternity of the world.

If the rectangle[2] obtained in the order of things, it would have to be admitted that the productions of the divine wisdom were coeternal with it and that each substance would have been eternal *à parte ante*, as I believe that they are all eternal *à parte post*.

[...]

I have paid my court to the Czar [Peter I the Great* of Russia] at the waters of Pyrmont*, and also here, since after his return from the waters, his Majesty stayed two nights at a country house very near here. I could not admire enough the vivacity and judgment of this great prince. He summons able persons from all sides, and when he speaks to them, he does it so aptly that they are thoroughly amazed. He inquires about all the mechanical arts, but his great curiosity is for everything having to do with navigation, and, consequently, he also loves astronomy and geography. I hope that we will learn through him whether Asia is attached to America. I am enthusiastically, etc.

---

[1] Bibliothèque Municipale de Rouen O 39 Bl. 331r–331v. Copy: 1.75 folio sides in a secretary's hand. Previously published in Dutens II-1 337–8; GP III 594–5; Erdmann 744–5; Schüller 1991, pp. 356–7 (excerpt in German translation). This is Leibniz's reply to Bourguet's letter of 15 May 1716 (document 118).

[2] For what Leibniz means by 'the rectangle', see his letter to Bourguet of 5 August 1715 (document 77 above, p. 261).

Johann Caspar von Bothmer to Leibniz

à Londres ce $\frac{29^{me} Juin}{10^{me} Juliet}$ 1716

Monsieur

[...]

J'ay fait voir vostre P. S. à des amis de Mr Nuton qui en ont paru fort contents, mais je ne scais pas encor ce qu'il en dit luy méme. J'ay fait connoistre en méme tems que ce n'est pas bien servir le Roy, que de vous detourner par des pareilles chicanes des ouvrages importants pour la gloire de sa famille qui vous occupent.

Je vous felicite M^r d'estre si fort avancé dans le dit ouvrage; j'espere que vous pourrés achever aussi bientost l'histoire de Henry le Saint, la presence du Roy vous donnera des occasions favorables pour en obtenir la gratification que vous en desires, je continuerois a vous y assister si j'eusse l'honneur de le suivre, comme il me laisse icy je suis obligé de ceder a mes amis l'avantage de vous y servir.

S. M. partira la semaine prochaine, et apportera à Mg^r son frere la jaretier[6] et le tiltre[7] de Duc de Yorck, j'espere que son petit fils aura l'ordre en méme tems. je suis avec tout la zele possible

Monsieur

Vostre

tres humble et tres

obeissant serviteur

Bothmer

132. Johann Caspar von Bothmer* to Leibniz (excerpt)[1]

in London $\frac{29^{me} Juin}{10^{me} Juliet}$ 1716[2]

Sir

[...]

I have shown your P.S.[3] to some of Mr. Newton's friends, who seemed very satisfied with it, but I do not yet know what he himself says about it. At the same time I have made it known that it does not serve the king [George I, Georg Ludwig* of Braunschweig-Lüneburg] well to divert you by such cavils from the important works for the glory of his family that occupy you.[4]

I congratulate you, sir, for being so far advanced in the said work; I hope that you will also soon be able to complete the history of Henry the Saint. The presence of the king will give you opportunities to obtain the extra pay that you desire from him. I would continue to assist you there if I had the honour of following him; since he leaves me here, I am obliged to cede to my friends the favour of serving you there.

His Majesty will leave[5] next week, and he will bring to his brother [Ernst August II* of Braunschweig-Lüneburg] the garter[6] and the title[7] of Duke of York . I hope his grandson [Friedrich Ludwig* of Braunschweig-Lüneburg] will have the order[8] at the same time. I am with all possible enthusiasm, sir

your

very humble and very

obedient servant

Bothmer

---

[1] LBr. 97 Bl. 145r–146v. Letter as sent: 3.5 quarto sides in Bothmer's hand. Previously published in Klopp XI 128 (excerpt).

[2] That is, 29 June OS and 10 July NS.

[3] That is, the P.S. that Leibniz appended to his letter to Bothmer of 28 April 1716 (document 114).

[4] The reference is to Leibniz's work on the history of the house of Braunschweig-Lüneburg, his *Annales imperii occidentis Brunsvicenses*.

[5] That is, on his return trip to his electorate in Germany.

[6] Reading 'jarretière' for 'jaretier'.

[7] Reading 'titre' for 'tiltre'.

[8] That is, the Order of the Garter, into which Friedrich Ludwig entered in 1718 when he was created a Knight of the Garter.

Johann Bernoulli to Leibniz

Vir Amplissime atque Celeberrime
Fautor Honoratissime

[...]

De disceptatione philosophica quæ Tibi est cum Clarkio nihil ante intellexeram: Ex iis quæ refers video, nihil tam absurdum proferri posse à Newtono, quod inter Anglos non inveniat Patronos ac Defensores suos; hi non disputant ut veritatem tueantur, sed quia de Nationis gloria agi putant quando vident Magistrum suum in cujus verba jurarunt in discrimine causæ suæ sive bonæ sive malæ (hoc non attendunt) versari: Hinc dubito, utrum hoc tantum sis ab ipsis consecuturus, ut agnoscant, Newtonum errare posse, aut omnino aliqua in re errasse: Mihi quoque dudum absona visa est ejus doctrina de spontanea virium diminutione et tandem cessation in mundo, siquidem per se clarissimum mihi apparet, nullam vim destrui quæ non simul effectum edat sibi æquivalentem, quia nihil tendit ad sui annihila-tionem; effectus autem nihil est aliud quam vis ipsa efficienti substituta, ita ut ean-dem virium quantitatem servari necesse sit. Dicit Newtonus alicubi in Princip. phil. mat. Vortices coelestes Cartesii ideo admitti non posse, quia ob partium sua-rum attritionem et frictionem tandem à motu cessarent; sed jam sibi ipsi con-tradicit, si enim secundum ipsum jactura virium in mundo reparari à Deo, et tota machina mundana subinde quasi retendi debet: annon et idem Cartesius in vorti-cum suorum defensionem reponere posset, quod nempe si vel maxime per attritio-nem partium in motu retardarentur, Deus tamen decrementum motus resarcire possit, eos quandoque per novam impulsionem ad pristinam celeritatem incitando.

[...] Quod superset vale ac fave

Amplit. T.

Basileæ a. d. 14. Julii
1716.

Devotissimo JBernoulli

P. S. [...]

133. Johann Bernoulli* to Leibniz (excerpt)[1]

Most Esteemed and Celebrated Sir
Most Honourable Supporter

[14 July 1716]

[...]

I had previously known nothing about your philosophical dispute with [Samuel] Clarke*. From those things you report, I see that nothing so absurd can be proposed by Newton that it does not meet with its advocates and defenders among the English. These don't argue in order to defend the truth, but because they believe that the glory of the nation is at stake when they see their master, to whose words they have sworn allegiance, is in danger of his cause, whether good or bad (this they do not consider). Hence I doubt whether you are going to seek to attain this much from them, that they acknowledge that Newton can err, or has erred in any matter at all. His doctrine of the spontaneous diminution and eventual cessation of forces in the world has long seemed unsuitable to me as well, since it appears most clear to me in itself that no force is destroyed that does not simultaneously bring about an effect equivalent to itself, because nothing tends to its own annihilation; however, the effect is nothing but force itself substituted for the efficient force in such a way that the same quantity of forces must be conserved. Somewhere in the *Principles of Natural Philosophy*, Newton says that the celestial vortices of Descartes cannot be admitted for that reason, because, by reason of the attrition and friction of their parts, they would eventually cease to move.[2] But now he contradicts himself. For if according to him the loss of force in the world must be restored by God, and the whole world-machine must be, as it were, rewound from time to time, might not Descartes likewise respond in defense of his vortices that certainly, if they were greatly slowed by the attrition of their parts, God could still restore the loss of motion at some time or other by accelerating them to their original speed by a new impulse?

[...] For the rest, farewell and be well disposed

toward Your Eminence's

Basil a. d. 14 July
1716

most devoted J[ohann]Bernoulli

P. S. [...]

---

[1] LBr. 57, Bl. 245r–246v. Letter as sent: four quarto sides in Bernoulli's hand. Previously published in GM III-2 965–7; NC VI 359–62 (excerpt with English translation); Schüller 1991, pp. 258–9 (excerpt in German translation). This is Bernoulli's response to Leibniz's letter of 7 June 1716 (document 127).

[2] Bernoulli may have in mind Newton's discussion of vortices in Proposition 52, Theorem 40 and its corollaries in Book II of the *Principia* (see Newton 1999, pp. 781–6).

Pierre Des Maizeaux to Philip Heinrich Zollmann

Ce 14 Juillet. [1715]

Sur ce que vous me dîtes, Monsieur, il y a quelques jours, que Son Altesse Royale, Madame la Princesse, souhaiteroit qu'on traduisit en Anglois la Theodicée de M^r. Leibniz, afin que ceux qui n'entendent pas le François puissent profiter d'un ouvrage où l'on deffend[2] la Religion avec autant d'esprit que de solidité; j'ai cherché & trouvé un Traducteur: j'ai meme trouvé un Libraire prêt à faire les fraix[3] de l'Impression; il demande seulement qu'on lui permette de marquer dans le Titre, que cette Traduction a été faite par ordre de Son Altesse Royale. On se flate en meme tems, que Son Altesse, voudra bien souffrir que le Traducteur prenne la liberté de lui dedier cette Traduction.

Je n'ai rien de nouveau à vous dire sur la question que vous m'avez faite, si je voudrois me charger du soin de revoir cette Traduction & la comparer avec l'original, en cas qu'on le jugeât necessaire. Je vous ai deja fait connoitre que la Revision d'un ouvrage comme celui-là, si excellent en lui-meme, & honoré de la protection de Son Altesse Royale, me seroit trop glorieuse, pour n'etre pas ravi de l'entreprendre. Il me suffira de savoir qu'on souhaite que j'y travaille, pour y donner toute l'attention dont je puis etre capable. Je renverrai plutot encore pour quelque tems à finir la vie de M^r. Bayle.

Je suis, Monsieur, Votre tres humble & tres obeissant

serviteur, Des Maizeaux.

Mr Zollman.

Leibniz to Caroline of Brandenburg-Ansbach, Princess of Wales

Hanover ce vendredi 31 juillet
1716

Madame

J'avois esperé, de pouvoir joindre à cette lettre que je me donne l'honneur d'ecrire à V. A. Royale la reponse au quatrieme papier de M. Clarke: mais ayant fait une course à Bronsvic, et jusqu'à Zeiz, avant l'arrivée du Roy pour depecher certaines petites affaires qui me regardent; j'ay eté obligé de differer cette reponse. Mais je n'ay point voulu diffrer de marquer à V. A. Royale combien je suis sensible à la continuation de ses bonnes graces. J'espere qu'Elle ne trouvera point mauvais que je me

134. Pierre Des Maizeaux* to Philipp Heinrich Zollmann*[1]

14 July [1716]

Concerning what you told me a few days ago, sir, that Her Royal Highness, Madame the Princess [Caroline* of Brandenburg-Ansbach, Princess of Wales, Princess of Wales], would like the *Theodicy* of Mr. Leibniz to be translated into English, so that those who do not understand French can profit from a work in which religion is defended[2] with as much wit as soundness. I have sought and found a translator; I have even found a bookseller ready to cover the cost[3] of the printing. He only asks that he be permitted to note in the title that this translation has been made by order of Her Royal Highness. At the same time he hopes that Her Highness will be willing to allow the translator to take the liberty of dedicating this translation to her.

I have nothing new to tell you concerning the question that you have asked me, whether I would like to take care of reviewing this translation and comparing it with the original, in case that was considered necessary. I have already made it known to you that the review of a work like this one, so excellent in itself, and honoured with the protection of Her Royal Highness, would be too glorious for me not to be delighted to undertake it. It will be enough for me to know that you desire me to work on it in order to give it all the attention of which I am capable. I would rather still delay for a while to finish the biography of Mr. [Pierre] Bayle*.
I am, sir, your very humble and very obedient
        servant, Des Maizeaux.
Mr. Zollman.

[1] LBr. F 4 Bl. 70. Letter as sent: one quarto side in Des Maizeaux's hand. Not previously published.
[2] Reading 'défend' for 'deffend'.
[3] Reading 'frais' for 'fraix'.

135. Leibniz to Caroline* of Brandenburg-Ansbach, Princess of Wales[1]

Hanover Friday 31 July
1716

Madame

I had hoped to be able to enclose the response to the fourth paper of Mr. [Samuel] Clarke* with this letter that I give myself the honour of writing to Your Royal Highness; but having made a trip, before the arrival of the king [George I, Georg Ludwig* of Braunschweig-Lüneburg], to Braunschweig, as far as Zeitz, in order to dispatch certain minor personal matters, I was forced to defer this response. But I did not want to defer mentioning to Your Royal Highness how much I appreciate

justifie | de je ne say quoi | des apparences recentes, d'une animosité et passion contre M. Newton. Si V. A. Royale avoit vu avec quelle grossiereté ses adherens m'ont attaqué (ce qu'il n'ignoroit pas) Elle auroit loué ma moderation. Je n'ay pas daigné de repondre à de telles gens qui n'en gardent aucune. Mais quand M. Newton a voulu paroistre luy même, j'y ay repondu comme il faut, et j'espere que ma reponse aura contenté ceux qui l'auront voulu examiner, et cela non seulement du coté de la justice de ma cause, mais encore par rapport aux manieres. Je ne pouvois endurer des expressions qui attaquoient ma bonne foy, et il falloit les repousser avec force, mais je crois qu'on remarquera assés, que je l'ay fait sans emotion.

Pour ce qui est de ma Theodicée elle sera applaudie des Anglois, à mesure que V. A. Royale en sera contente. | M. l'Archeveque y paroissoit en avoir des sentimens favorables, quand V. A. Royale temoignoit d'en avoir | On en remarquera les bons endroits apres vous, Madame, et les foibles de même. Car il n'y a point de livre qui n'en aye de l'une et de l'autre sorte. Vous estes un juge competent, Madame, et comme l'Abbé Conti et le docteur Clarc la liront devant vous, c'est à dire l'accuseront devant votre tribunal; il seroit à souhaiter pour moy que j'eusse aussi un Avocat alors qui fut porté a defendre ma cause. Je n'en saurois nommer aucun | en Angleterre | à Londres. Si ce n'est peutestre M. des Maiseaux ou M. Coste, quoyque peutetre ils ne soyent que neutres tout au plus. Je ne crois pas de n'avoir rien dit dont M. l'Abbé conti ait droit de se plaindre. Je ne me suis point plaint de luy, quoyque j'aye remarqué qu'il avoit cessé d'etre neutre. Car les jugemens et les volontés sont libres.

Comme M. des Maiseaux m'avoit demandé une copie de ce qui a esté echangé entre M. Clarke & moy je l'ay envoyé à un ami de M. des Maiseaux nommé Monsieur Zollman, qui est gouverneur du jeune Comte de Bothmar, et l'ay prié de s'informer de ce qui manquoit à V. A. Royale, ou qui avoit eté perdu, afin de le faire suppléer de cette copie entiere.

Graces à Dieu le Roy est arrivé en bonne santé Dimanche au soir. Sa Mté n'a voulu aucunes demonstrations exterieures pour signaler sa joyeuse entrée. Il est allé demeurer dans le chateau en ville mais on croit qu'au retour de pirmont ou il va demain, il pourra aller loger à Herrenhausen. J'ay eu l'honneur de diner avec sa Mté le lendemain, et elle m'a parue gaye; jusqu'à me reprocher, que je le paroissois un peu moins qu'autres fois. Tout le monde trouve que sa Mté est bien, et on est ravi de voir que les bruits contraires ont eté faux. La joye de son arrivée a esté universelle. Il sembloit que le soleil estoit revenu. Aussi paroist il que le beau temps a voulu attendre son voyage. Il y a encor peu d'estrangers icy, mais on en attend une foule au retour de Sa Mté de pirmont; j'y iray peutetre aussi pour quelques jours afin de mieux faire ma Cour. Je suis ravi que Monseigneur le prince a maintenant un Grand et beau champ pour exercer ses grands talens, pour charmer les Anglois de plus au plus, et pour se faire admirer en Europe—personne prenant plus de part à sa satisfaction que V. A. Royale, je l'en felicite. Ce que V. A. Royale raconte de

the continuation of her good graces. I hope that she will not find it amiss that I acquit myself | of I know not what | of recent appearances of an animosity and passion against Mr. Newton. If Your Royal Highness had seen with what crudeness his followers have attacked me (of which he was not unaware), she would have commended my moderation. I have not deigned to respond to such people, who do not observe any of it. But when Mr. Newton himself chose to make an appearance, I responded to him properly, and I hope that my response has satisfied those who have chosen to examine it, not only as regards the justice of my cause, but also in relation to conduct. I could not endure any statements that attacked my good faith, and it was necessary to respond forcefully; but I believe that people will note well enough that I have done so without emotion.

As for my *Theodicy*, it will be applauded by the English to the extent that Your Royal Highness will be satisfied with it. | The Archbishop [of Canterbury, William Wake*] there appeared to have some favourable opinions of it when your Royal Highness testified to having some. | Its good points will be noted following you, madame, and likewise the weak ones. For there is not any book that does not have some of each. You are a competent judge, madame, and as Abbé [Antonio Schinella] Conti* and Doctor Clarke will read it before you, that is to say, indict it before your tribunal, it would also be desirable for me to have an advocate at that time who was inclined to defend my cause. I could not nominate anyone | in England | in London for it, unless, perhaps, Mr. [Pierre] des Maizeaux* or Mr. [Pierre] Coste*, although perhaps they are at best only neutral. I do not believe I have said anything about which Abbé Conti has a right to complain. I have not complained about him, although I have noticed that he has ceased being neutral. For judgments and wills are free.

Since Mr. des Maizeaux has requested a copy of what has been exchanged between Mr. Clarke and me, I have sent it to a friend of Mr. des Maizeaux named Mr. [Philipp Heinrich (Henry)] Zollman*, who is governor of the young Count Bothmer,[2] and have bid him to find out what Your Royal Highness lacked, or what had been lost,[3] in order to have it made good by this complete copy.

Thank God the king arrived in good health Sunday evening.[4] His Majesty did not want any outward demonstrations to signal his joyous entry. He went to stay in the palace in town, but it is believed that on his return from Pyrmont*, where he is going tomorrow, he will be able to put up at Herrenhausen*. I had the honour of dining with His Majesty the day after [his arrival], and he seemed cheerful, to the point of reproaching me for appearing somewhat less so than in the past. Everyone finds that His Majesty is well, and we are delighted to see that the rumors to the contrary were false. The joy concerning his arrival has been universal. It seemed that the sun had returned. It also seemed that the good weather chose to await his journey. There are still few foreigners here, but we expect a crowd of them on the return of His Majesty from Pyrmont. I will perhaps go there as well for a few days in

M. Flamstead est plaisant. Il passe maintenant pour le meilleur observateur de l'Europe. Il a voulu publier des observations celestes faites depuis de plus de 30 ans. Ce seroit une espece de tresor; et il est a souhaiter que cet ouvrage paroisse. Comme ces observations sont importantes pour la navigation, feu M. le prince George, estant High Amiral of England voulut en favoriser l'impression mais la mort de ce prince a interrompu ce dessein tres noble. Je souhaiterois que Mon^sgr le prince de Galles le voulut faire reprendre ce qui se pourroit par le moyen du college de l'Amirauté. Ce seroit obliger toute l'Europe curieuse, & animer les Anglois, à quitter les pamphlets, pour s'attacher davantage au solide des sciences utiles ce qui arrivera quand on verra que la Cour, et particulierement M^sgr le prince les favoriseroit.

Le Roy de prusse s'est contenté d'une petite promenade vers Francfort. Nous avons eu icy le Czar chez qui j'ay fait un peu ma Cour. Il a emporté les globes que Mad. l'Electrice luy avoit destinés. Il a fait une experience sur son pope ou aumonier en faveur des eaux de pirmont. Comme il a fait boire ces eaux a toute sa suite, il a voulu aussi que tous se fissent saigner comme luy. Le sang du pope se trouva le pire de tout. Quand on eut fini de boire les eaux le Czar voulut qu'on tirat encore du sang au pretre pour voir s'il estoit amendé. Et cela se trouva en effect très notablement. Il n'a pas fort menagé en cela la santé de son aumonier, mais l'experience n'est pas a mepriser par rapport a la santé publique, car elle confirme l'utilite de ces eaux. Et un habile Medecin a qui j'en ay parlé ne croit pas que la seule bonne diete observee peut etre pendant les eaux aye pû faire si promtement un effect si considerable. Je suis etc.

135. LEIBNIZ TO CAROLINE OF BRANDENBURG-ANSBACH   617

order to better pay my court. I am delighted that the prince [Georg August* of Braunschweig-Lüneburg, Prince of Wales] now has a great and fine opportunity to exercise his great talents to charm the English more and more, and to make himself admired in Europe—no one participating more in his satisfaction than Your Royal Highness; I congratulate her for it. What Your Royal Highness recounts concerning Mr. [John] Flamsteed* is amusing. He is now considered the best European observer. He wanted to publish some celestial observations made for more than thirty years. This would be a kind of treasure, and it is desirable that this work see the light of day. As these observations are important for navigation, the late Prince George, being High Admiral of England,[5] intended to promote its printing, but the death of this prince interrupted this very noble project.[6] I wish the Prince of Wales wanted it taken up again, which could be by means of the college of the admiralty. This would gratify the whole of curious Europe and stimulate the English to lay aside the pamphlets in order to apply themselves more to the firm ground of the practical sciences, which will happen when they see that the court, and particularly the prince, will promote them.

The King of Prussia [Friedrich Wilhelm I*] contented himself with a short excursion to Frankfurt. Here we have had the czar [Peter I the Great* of Russia], to whom I have paid a little of my court. He has taken away the globes that Madam the Electress [late Electress of Braunschweig-Lüneburg, Sophie* of the Palatinate] had intended for him. He conducted an experiment on his priest or almoner in favour of the waters of Pyrmont. As he had all of his procession drink those waters, he also wanted everyone to be bled like him. The blood of the priest proved to be the worst of all. When they had finished drinking the waters, the czar wanted some blood drawn again from the priest in order to see if it was improved, and it was in fact very notably improved. In that he did not take much care of his almoner's health, but the experiment should not be disregarded in relation to the public health, for it confirms the benefit of those waters. And an able physician, to whom I have spoken about it, does not believe that the good diet by itself, observed perhaps during the waters, could have so quickly produced an effect so considerable. I am etc.

---

[1] LBr. F 4 Bl. 71r–71v. Draft: two quarto sides in Leibniz's hand. Previously published in Klopp XI 128–30 (excerpt) and Schüller 1991, pp. 257–8 (excerpt in German translation). This is Leibniz's response to Caroline's letter of 26 June 1716 (document 128).

[2] That is, the son of Johann Casper von Bothmer*.

[3] Concerning this, see Caroline's letters to Leibniz of 15 May 1716 (document 119, p. 535) and 26 June 1716 (document 128, p. 585), as well as Leibniz's letter to Caroline of 2 June 1716 (document 124, p. 557).

[4] The date of this letter thus sets 26 July as the date of George I's arrival in Hanover. This was the first of George I's five trips to Hanover after he became king of England, and the only such trip that he made during Leibniz's lifetime. In the spring of 1727 he set out for Hanover for a sixth time, but made it only as far as Osnabrück, where he died on 22 June.

[5] Here Leibniz refers to Prince George of Denmark (1653–1708), the late husband of Queen Anne, who was Lord High Admiral from 1702 until his death in 1708.

[6] Leibniz's brief description of the events surrounding the proposed printing of Flamsteed's observations omits some of a darker and more interesting aspect, namely those involving a bitter feud between

618   135. LEIBNIZ TO CAROLINE OF BRANDENBURG-ANSBACH

135. LEIBNIZ TO CAROLINE OF BRANDENBURG-ANSBACH 619

Flamsteed and Newton—a feud that Leibniz had referenced in his *Charta Volans* (1713) as evidence of Newton's mind being 'neither fair nor honest' (see note 3 of Leibniz's letter to Caroline of 12 May 1716 (document 117a, p. 525); see also the references to Flamsteed in Leibniz's letters to Bourguet (documents 107, p. 467, and 112, p. 499) and in Bourguet's letter to Leibniz of 15 May 1716 (document 118, p. 533), as well as in Caroline's letter to Leibniz of 26 June 1716, where she informed Leibniz that Flamsteed had told her that Leibniz was 'such a decent man, but Sir Isaac Newton was a great rogue because he had stolen two stars from him' (document 128, p. 585). Flamsteed had been reluctant to publish his lunar observations prematurely, before they could be verified. But in 1694 Newton was anxious to get his hands on Flamsteed's lunar observations in order to improve the lunar theory that he had presented in the first edition of the *Philosophiae Naturalis Principia Mathematica* (1687); and so, on 1 September of that year (OS), Newton paid a visit to Flamsteed at the Royal Observatory in Greenwich for the purpose of obtaining the data he desired. Flamsteed later wrote of this in one of a number of diary manuscripts that were published in 1835 under the title, *History of his own Life and Labors*:

> 1694, Saturday September 1st. Mr. Newton came to visit me. Esteeming him an obliged friend, I showed him about 150 places of the moon [...] On his earnest request I lent them to him, and allowed him to take copies of them (as I did not doubt but that by their help he would be able to correct the lunar theory) [...] (Bailey 1835, p. 61).

But Flamsteed did this on two conditions. First, because the observations in question 'were got with the help of a small catalogue of fixed stars from observations taken with the sextant', and thus 'their places were not so correct as they ought to be', Flamsteed required that Newton 'should not impart or communicate them to anybody without my consent', while promising to provide Newton and the public with corrected data once he was able to 'calculate the moon's places anew' (ibid., p. 62). Secondly, he required that Newton 'should not in the first instance impart the result of what he derived from them to anybody but myself: for, since I saved all the labor of calculating the moon's place both from the observations and tables, it was not just that he should give the result of my pains (the correction of the theory I had furnished with numbers) to any other but myself' (ibid.). Flamsteed reported that Newton consented to these conditions, but then added:

> Nevertheless he imparted what he derived from them, both to [the Scottish mathematician and Savilian Professor of Astronomy at Oxford] Dr. [David] Gregory [1659–1708] and [the English mathematician and astronomer] Mr. [Edmund] Hal[l]ey, *contra datam fidem*. The first of these conditions I was not much concerned whether he kept or not: but he has, I believe, kept it. The latter (which was the most material) he has forgot or broke [...] [ibid.]

Flamsteed then remarked that Newton continued to pester him 'for new observations of the moon: whilst some of his creatures in town cried up his success in correcting the lunar theory; but said not one word of his debt to the Royal Observatory' (ibid.). Letters continued to be exchanged between Flamsteed and Newton during the remaining months of 1694, and Flamsteed reported that 'I imparted to him about 100 more of the moon's places [...].' And in the following year

> [...] frequent letters passed between me and Mr. Newton, who ceased not to importune me [...] for more observations; and with that earnestness that looked as if he thought he had a right to command them; and had about 50 more imparted to him. But I did not think myself obliged to employ my pains to serve a person that was so inconsiderate as to presume he had a right to that which was only a courtesy. [...] I was therefore forced to leave off my correspondence with him at that time [...] [ibid., p. 63]

In an entry for '1695, or 1696', Flamsteed wrote:

> Sir Isaac Newton, being made an officer of the Mint [in March 1696], came to London. I sometimes visited there, or at his own house in Jermyn Street. We continued civil: but he was not so friendly as formerly [...] [ibid.]

Relations between the two men worsened substantially in 1699. In response to repeated requests from John Wallis* for a letter describing his observations concerning the parallax of the pole star, Flamsteed sent Wallis a letter sometime in November of 1698 in which he happened to mention that he had supplied Newton with '150 places of the Moon' (NC IV 293, 295n8). Upon hearing of this from David Gregory, Newton sent a most bizarre letter to Flamsteed, dated January 6 1698/9 (16 January 1699 NS), in which he wrote:

> Upon hearing occasionally that you had sent a letter to Dr Wallis about ye Parallax of ye fixt stars to be printed & that you had mentioned me therein with respect to the Theory of ye Moon I was concerned to be publickly brought upon ye stage about what perhaps will never be fitted for ye publick &

620   135. LEIBNIZ TO CAROLINE OF BRANDENBURG-ANSBACH

135. LEIBNIZ TO CAROLINE OF BRANDENBURG-ANSBACH   621

thereby the world *put into expectation of what perhaps they are never like to have*. I do not love to be printed upon every occasion much less to be dunned & teezed by forreigners [sic] about Mathematical things or to be thought by our own people to be *trifling* away my time about them when I should be about ye Kings business [as Master of the Mint]. [NC IV 296]

Flamsteed responded moderately enough in a letter dated just three days after Newton's letter to him; it ended with the following remarks:

> I Look on pride as the worst of sins, Humility as the greatest of virtues, this makes me excuse small faults in all mankind and bear great injurys without resentment & resolve to maintain a reale friendship with ingenious men to assist them what Lies in my power without ye regard of any interest but that of doeing good by obliging them. [ibid., p. 303]

This effectively ended the correspondence between Newton and Flamsteed for several years.

By 1704 Newton had still not been able to complete his lunar theory for want of Flamsteed's observations, so on 11 April of that year he again made a pilgrimage to Greenwich to meet with Flamsteed, as Flamsteed himself again reported in his *History of his own Life and Labors*:

> 1704, Tuesday, April 11th. Mr. Newton came to the Observatory; dined with me; saw the volume of observations; so much of the catalogue as was then finished; with the charts of the constellations [...]; desired to have the recommending of them to the Prince [i.e., Prince George of Denmark, husband of Anne, Queen of Great Britain]. I knew his temper; that he would be my friend no further than to serve his own ends; and that he was spiteful, and swayed by those that were worse than himself. This made me refuse him. However, when he went away he promised he would recommend them; though he never intended me any good by it, but to get me under him, that I might be obliged to cry him up as E. H[alley] has done hitherto. [Bailey 1835, p. 66]

Newton did as promised and persuaded Prince George to back a project to publish Flamsteed's observations. Flamsteed duly produced an estimate for a three-volume catalogue, of about 1450 pages in all, saying that 'the first Part may be put into the Press immediately [...]' (NC IV 421). But not wanting to leave matters in Flamsteed's hands, Newton arranged to have a committee, headed by himself, put in charge of examining Flamsteed's papers and seeing to their publication. A letter was then sent to Prince George, under signature of members of the committee, approving the printing of 400 copies of Flamsteed's proposed catalogue at the estimated cost of £683 (see NC IV 436; see also Flamsteed's comments in Bailey 1835, p. 66).

Flamsteed was able to delay the project so that when Prince George died in 1708, the first volume of the catalogue remained unfinished, and Newton's committee lost its power over Flamsteed:

> Newton's response was to have himself, as President of the R[oyal]S[ociety], appointed in 1710 a 'constant Visitor' to the Greenwich Observatory, with access to all observations and the right to direct the work of the Astronomer Royal. Shortly afterwards Flamsteed heard that the Queen had commanded him to hand over all outstanding material and so allow the work to be finally completed. [Gjertsen 1986, p. 212]

The catalogue was eventually published under the title *Historia Coelestis* in 1712. But it was edited by Edmund Halley in a form that did not conform to Flamsteed's original proposal, which envisioned the publication of a number of historical astronomical catalogues in addition to his own. This reflected Newton's desire to complete and publish only Flamsteed's observations. In a revealing passage from a letter to his assistant, Abraham Sharp, of 22 December 1711 (1 February 1712 NS), Flamsteed reported

> [...] another contest with the President of the Royal Society, who had formed a plot to make my instruments theirs; and sent for me to a Committee, where only himself and two physicians (Dr. [Hans] Sloan*, and another as little skillful as himself) were present. [...] I complained then of my catalogue being printed by Raymer [i.e., Halley], without my knowledge, and that I was *robbed of the fruits of my labors*. At this he fired, and called me all the ill names, puppy, &c., that he could think of. All I returned was, I put him in mind of his passion, desired him to govern it, and keep his temper: this made him rage worse: and he told me how much I had received from the Government in 36 years I had served. I asked what he had done for the £500 per annum that he had received ever since he settled in London. This made him calmer: but finding him going to burst out again, I only told him my catalogue, half finished, was delivered into his hands, on his own request, sealed up. He could not deny it, but said Dr. Arbuthnott had procured the Queen's order for opening it. This, I am persuaded, was false; or it was got after it had been opened. I said nothing to him in return;

Leibniz to Robert Erskine (Areskin)

Hanover ce 3. D'Aoust 1716.

Monsieur

J'espere que votre voyage avec Sa Majesté, le Grand Czar des Russes, aura eté heureux et je prie Dieu qu'il continue de l'etre. [...] Ma dispute avec M. Clarke defenseur de M. Newton dure encore, mais j'espere qu'elle sera bientost finie. Car je luy envoye maintenant une réponse assés ample à son derniere écrit, la quelle

A Monsieur Areskin premier Medecin du Grand Czar des Russes président de la Faculté de Medecine par tout son Empire

éclaircit les choses a fonds;[5] ainsi je crois qu'apres cela, je n'auray plus grand chose à dire sans repetition, et s'il ne se rend point à la raison, je le laissera là comme invincible. Aussi tost que cela sera fait, j'envoyeray au <u>Acta Eruditorum</u> de Leipzig une petite relation[6] de nostre controverse en forme de lettre addressée à vous Monsieur ou je vous en informeray, et me serviray de l'occasion pour dire combien on doit estre redevable à vos soins pour le public, sous les auspices de nostre Grand Monarque.

[...]

Voicy, Monsieur, l'empreinte d'une Medaille d'une grandeur sans exemple, qui un Medailleur de ma connoissance avoit fait pour le Roy de la Grande Bretagne. Mais comme on l'a negligee, il en a rompu le coin. S'il m'avoit consulté avant que de la faire, il auroit peutetre omis les colifichets, qui l'ont fait mepriser. Je crois qu'il pourroit faire quelque chose de grand et de beau pour le czar, et qui jusqu'icy auroit eté sans exemple[8]; car sa Medaille pour le Roy de la Grand Bretagne doit estre comptée pour rien, non seulement parce que le coin en est rompu, mais aussi parce qu'on n'en a tiré qu'une seule medaille que le medailleur

but, with a little more spirit than I had hitherto showed, told them that God (who was seldom spoke of with due reference in that meeting) had hitherto prospered all my labors, and I doubted not would do so to a happy conclusion; took my leave and left them. Dr. Sloane had said nothing all this while; the other Doctor told me I was proud, and insulted the President, and ran into the same passion with the President. At my going out I called to Dr. Sloane, told him he had behaved himself civilly, and thanked him for it. I saw Raymer after, drank a dish of coffee with him, and told him, still calmly, of the villainy of his conduct, and called it *blockish*. [Bailey 1835, pp. 294–5]

After George I ascended the throne in 1714, Flamsteed received a degree of satisfaction when the court responded to his petition to have the remaining 300 copies of the *Historia coelestis* delivered to him from the printer. 'I brought them down to Greenwich', he later reported,

and, finding both Halley's corrupted edition of my catalogue, and abridgment of my observations, no less spoiled by him, I separated them from my observations; and, some few days after, I made a *Sacrifice of them to Heavenly Truth*: as I should do of all the rest of my editor's pains of the like nature, if the Author of Truth should hereafter put them into my power [...] [Bailey 1835, p. 101]

A final vindication came when a version of his three-volume catalogue, in the form he had envisioned in his original proposal, was published posthumously in 1725, edited by his wife Margaret, under the title *Historia Coelestis Britannica*.

136. Leibniz to Robert Erskine (Areskin)[1] (excerpt)[2]

Hanover 3 August 1716

Sir

I hope that your trip with His Majesty, the Great Czar of the Russians [Peter the Great*], has been successful, and I pray God that it continues to be so. [...] My dispute with Mr. [Samuel] Clarke*, defender of Mr. Newton, still goes on, but I hope that it will soon be finished. For I am now sending him a quite expansive response[3] to his last paper[4] that thoroughly[5] clarifies matters. So I believe that after that I will no longer have much to say without repetition, and if he does not yield to reason, I will leave it there as invincible. As soon as that is done, I will send to the *Acta Eruditorum* of Leipzig a small account[6] of our controversy in the form of a letter addressed to you, sir, in which I will inform you of it and use the occasion to say how much we ought to be indebted to your care for the public, under the auspices of our great monarch [King George I, Georg Ludwig* of Braunschweig-Lüneburg].

[...]

Here, sir, is the imprint of a medallion of unparalleled size, which a medalist of my acquaintance had made for the King of Great Britain.[7] But since it was slighted, he broke the die. If he had consulted me before making it, he would perhaps have omitted the garish embellishments, which caused it to be scorned. I believe that he could make something grand and beautiful for the czar, which heretofore would have been unparalleled; for his medallion for the King of Great Britain must be counted for nothing, not only because the die is broken, but also because only a

To Mr. Areskin, chief physician of the Grand Czar of the Russians and president of the faculty of medicine throughout his empire

a fondue par le depit. Il n'en reste que des formes gyps, dont il a tire cette colle de poisson.

Je vous supplie, Monsieur, de marquer ma devotion à la Mté du Grand Czar, et de dire que ma Machine Arithmetique avance à grands pas; et que je fais estat d'en monstrer quelque effect. Elle pourra servir un jour de present au Monarque de la chine ou un autre grand Roy avec une Ambassade qu'on auroit dessein de luy envoyer. [...] Au reste vous m'obligeres, Monsieur, en me donnant quelques fois de vos cheres nouvelles, et je seray toujours avec zele

Monsieur   votre tres humble & tres obeissant
                                                                    serviteur
                                                                    Leibniz

P. S.[9]

[...]

La colle de poisson n'ayant pas été séchée encore, et le tour que je dois faire à Pirmont, pour y trouver le Roy de la Grand Bretagne, ne me permettant pas de differer cette lettre; je vous enverray cette empreinte de la medaille à mon retour.

Johann Caspar von Bothmer to Leibniz

à Londres ce $\frac{31^{me}\,Juliet}{11^{me}\,Aoust}$ 1716

Monsieur

Je pren[d]s beaucoup de part au bon acceuil[3] que le Roy vous a fait comme à tout ce qui peut vous donner du contentement. vous pouvés estre persuadé que je m'estimerois fort heureux si je pouvois y contribuer quelque chose moy méme. je suis tres aise de voir que vous croyés que ma presence à Hannover auroit pu faciliter le

single medallion was cast from it, which the medalist has melted out of spite. There remain only some gypsum molds of it, from which he has cast this isinglass.

I beg you, sir, to mention my devotion to the Majesty of the Grand Czar and to say that my arithmetic machine[8] progresses rapidly and that I intend to show some result with it. It will be able serve one day as a gift for the monarch of China or another great king with an embassy that he would intend to send to him. [...] To conclude, you will oblige me by occasionally sharing your dear news with me, and I will always be enthusiastically,

sir, your very humble and very obedient
servant
Leibniz

P. S.[9]

[...]

Since the isinglass has not yet been dried, and the trip that I must make to Pyrmont* to meet there with the King of Great Britain does not permit me to defer this letter, I will send you this imprint of the medallion when I return.

---

[1] Robert Erskine (1677–1719) was a Scotsman and son of Charles Erskine, first baronet of Alva. He studied medicine in Edinburgh, Paris, and finally Utrecht, where he received his M.D. in 1700. He was made a Fellow of the Royal Society in 1703, under the name of 'Areskin', the name by which Leibniz addressed him. As Leibniz indicates in the address, he was the chief physician to Czar Peter the Great* and president of the Russian medical faculty. He accompanied the czar on his European tour in 1716, during which he met Leibniz.

[2] LBr. 15 Bl. 1r–1v. Draft: two quarto sides in Leibniz's hand. Previously published in JGHF 13–17 (excerpt). A similar, complete version, apparently based on the letter that was actually sent, was published in AAK 225–7 and Guerrier 1873, pp. 361–4. A short excerpt was also published in NC VI 358–9.

[3] That is, Leibniz's Fifth Paper (document 140b).

[4] That is, Clarke's Fourth Reply (document 129).

[5] Reading 'à fond' for 'a fonds'.

[6] In AAK and Guerrier 1873, 'relation' is followed by 'Latine' (see p. 225 and p. 362, respectively).

[7] On the matter of the great medallion, see Leibniz's letter to Caroline of 3 August 1715 (document 76, p. 253), Caroline's letter to Leibniz of 13 September 1715 (document 78, p. 265), and Leibniz's letter to Caroline of 21 October 1715 (document 80, p. 279).

[8] Concerning Leibniz's 'arithmetic machine', see his letter to Bonneval of November 1714 (document 45, p. 151) and note 5 to Conti's letter to Newton of 10 December 1716 (document 160, p. 807).

[9] The draft of this letter does not contain the P.S., so I have followed the P.S. from the version of the letter published in AAK and Guerrier 1873.

---

137. Johann Caspar von Bothmer* to Leibniz[1]

in London $\frac{31\,\text{July}}{11\,\text{August}}$ 1716[2]

Sir

I take a great deal of interest in the kind reception[3] that the king [George I, Georg Ludwig* of Braunschweig-Lüneburg] has given you, as in everything that can give you some satisfaction. You can be quite sure that I would consider myself very fortunate if I could contribute something to it myself. I am very glad to see that you

succés de vostre intention à l'egard du caractere d'Historiografe[4] du Roy en ce Royaume. c'est rendre justice à mon zele pour vostre service. j'en ay parlé desia[5] icy au Roy. je ne scais s'il s'en souvient encor. on pourra luy rafraichir la mémoire. je suis persuadé que Mr de Stanhop secondera volontier[s] votre intention et qu'il pourra le faire efficacement il est non seulement d'un naturel bienfaisant, mais il connoit et aime les sciences et ceux qui les possedent. je suis assuré que si d'ailleurs il ne vous connoissoit pas vous n'auriés qu'a luy montrer vostre histoire de la Se^{me} maison de Bronsvic pour le convaincre que personne merite à plus juste tiltre[7] que vous celuy d'historiografe de S.M. On celebrera demain l'anniversaire de son avenement à la couronne, de sorte que le voila dans la troisième année de son règne que Dieu fasse durer long tems. La jeune cour paroit fort contente à Hambtoncourt. Je suis avec tous le zele possible
Monsieur

Vostre

tres humble et tres
obeissant serviteur
Bothmer

Leibniz to Nicolas Rémond (excerpt)

Aux Eaux de Pirmont, à la Cour
du Roi de la Grande Bretagne,
ce 15 d'Août 1716.

Monsieur

[…] M. *Clarke*, ou plûtôt M. *Newton* dont M. *Clarke* soutient les dogmes, est en dispute avec moi sur la Philosophie; nous avons déja échangé plusieurs Ecrits, & Madame la Princesse de Galles a la bonté de souffrir que cela passe par ses mains. Le Roi m'a fait la grace de dire ici, que *l'Abbé Conti viendra un jour en Allemagne, pour me convertir.* Il faut voir. Je suis avec zèle, Monsieur, Votre &c.

believe that my presence in Hanover could have facilitated the success of your intention concerning the dignity of historiographer[4] of the king of this realm. It is to do justice to my zeal for your service. I have already[5] spoken to the king about it here. I do not know if he still recalls it. You will be able refresh his memory. I am convinced that Mr. [James] Stanhope* will gladly support your intention and that he will be able to do it effectively. He is not only of a beneficent nature, but he knows and loves the sciences and those who have mastered them. I am sure that if he did not know you in other respects, you would only have to show him your history of the most serene house of Braunschweig[6] to convince him that no one deserves more justifiably than you the title[7] of historiographer of His Majesty. Tomorrow we will celebrate the anniversary of his accession to the crown, so that here in the third year of his reign, may God sustain it for a long time. The young court appears very happy at Hampton Court. I am with all possible enthusiasm,
sir

your

very humble and very
obedient servant
Bothmer

[1] LBr. 97 Bl. 147r–148r. Letter as sent: 2.5 quarto sides in Bothmer's hand. Previously published in Doebner 1884, pp. 238–9, and Klopp XI 130–1.

[2] That is, 31 July 1716 OS and 11 August 1716 NS.

[3] Reading 'accueil' for 'acceuil'.

[4] Reading 'd'Historiographe' for 'd'Historiografe'.

[5] Reading 'déjà' for 'desia'.

[6] That is, Leibniz's *Annales imperii occidentis Brunsvicenses**.

[7] Reading 'titre' for 'tiltre'.

138. Leibniz to Nicolas Rémond* (excerpt)[1]

At the waters of Pyrmont*, at the court
of the King of Great Britain,
15 August 1716

Sir

[…] Mr. [Samuel] Clarke*, or rather Mr. Newton, whose dogmas Mr. Clarke supports, is in dispute with me about philosophy. We have already exchanged several papers, and Madame the Princess of Wales [Caroline* of Brandenburg-Ansbach] has the kindness to allow them to pass through her hands. The king [George I, Georg Ludwig* of Braunschweig-Lüneburg] has done me the favour of saying here that Abbé [Antonio Schinella] Conti* will come one day to Germany in order to convert me. We'll have to see. I am enthusiastically, sir,
your etc.

Leibniz to Caroline of Brandenburg-Ansbach, Princess of Wales

Madame   Hanover 18 Aoust 1716

J'ay eu l'honneur d'écrire à V. A. Royale avant mon voyage de Pirmont, ou j'ay fait ma cour aupres du Roy, Sa Mté y estant plus libre qu'icy. J'ay prevenu son retour de 2 ou 3 jours. Elle est attendue à Herrenhausen demain ou apres demain. La cure par la boisson des eaux est allée le mieux du monde, et le Roy a paru fort gay. A pirmont j'ay eté souvent en compagnie de M. le secretaire d'Etat Stanhope, qui a sans doute un tres grand merite, outre qu'il a des manieres tres polies et tres obligeantes. Il est venu à Pirmont un courrier de Madrid (qui a porté la nouvelle du renversement du Cardinal di Giudice;) un courrier du Cabinet du Roy de France, et un expres de Wolfenbutel qui nous a appris ce que l'Imperatrice et le prince de Beveren avoient écrit l'une à sa soeur, l'autre à son epouse, touchant la grande defaite des Turcs prés du Save, dont on aura déja mandé le detail à Mgr le prince Royal et par consequent à V. A. Royale, par le même courrier qui etoit venu de Madrid, et qui d'icy a passé en Angleterre. Cette grande victoire a la mine ou de nous procurer une promte paix avec les ottomans par l'aquisition de Belgrade et de Temesvar, ou de faire chasser les Turcs de l'Europe, si la guerre dure.

Ma reponse au quatrième papier de M. Clarke vient icy en partie, l'autre moitié viendra par la poste suivante. Cette reponse est tres ample, par ce que j'ay volulu expliquer les choses a fond, et voir par là, s'il y a esperance de faire entendre raison à M. Clarke. Car s'il se jette sur les repetitions, il n'y aura rien à faire avec luy, et il faudra tacher de finir honnêtement.

Fondé sur les expressions gracieuse de V. A. Royale, j'ay fait savoir à quelque ami, qu'on vous feroit plaisir, Madame, par la Traduction de la Theodicée en Anglois. Maintenant on me mande d'avoir trouvé un bon Traducteur, et un libraire qui en veut procurer l'impression; mais qu'on desire qu'il soit permis de dedier le livre à V. A. Royale, et de marquer sur le titre, que la Traduction a eté faite par son ordre. Il me paroist que de demander ce dernier point, et de vouloir mettre l'ordre de V. A. R. sur le titre ce seroit trop honnorer le livre, quand il seroit cent fois meilleur qu'il n'est. Mais je crois que V. A. Royale permettra bien qu'on le luy dedie, et qu'on marque dans la dedicace, que V. A. Royale a voulu que ce livre fut traduit, puisqu'en le disant on dira la verité, et cela sera d'un grand poids pour faire valoir une defense de la religion et de la solide pieté. J'espere d'apprendre sa volonté gracieuse là dessus.

[1] The draft and original of this letter have apparently been lost, so I have relied on the version published in Des Maizeaux 1720, vol. 2, pp. 352–4. Also previously published in Dutens V 32–3; GP III 675–6; Scuüller, 1991, p. 259 (excerpt in German translation); Robinet 1991, p. 120 (excerpt). For Rémond's response, see his letter to Leibniz of 2 October 1716 (document 150).

139. Leibniz to Caroline* of Brandenburg-Ansbach, Princess of Wales[1]

Madame   Hanover 18 August 1716

I had the honour of writing to Your Royal Highness before my trip to Pyrmont*, where I paid my court to the king [George I, Georg Ludwig* of Braunschweig-Lüneburg], since his Majesty was freer there than here. I have preceded his return by two or three days. He is expected at Herrenhausen* tomorrow or the day after tomorrow. The cure by drinking the waters could not have gone better, and the king appeared very cheerful. At Pyrmont I was often in the company of Secretary of State [James] Stanhope*, who doubtless has very great merit, besides having very polite and obliging manners. There arrived at Pyrmont a courier from Madrid (who brought news of the overthrow of Cardinal del Giudice[2]), a courier from the Cabinet of the King of France,[3] and a messenger from Wolfenbüttel who informed us of what the empress [Empress Elisabeth Christine* of Braunschweig-Wolfenbüttel] and the Prince of Bevern [Ferdinand Albrecht II*] had written—the one to her sister,[4] the other to his spouse[5]—concerning the great defeat of the Turks near Save,[6] the details of which must have already been sent to the royal prince [Georg August* of Braunschweig-Lüneburg, Prince of Wales], and consequently to Your Royal Highness, by the same courier who arrived from Madrid, and who from here went on to England. This great victory has the appearance of either procuring for us a prompt peace with the Ottomans by the acquisition of Belgrade and Temesvar*, or having the Turks chased from Europe if the war continues.

My response to the fourth paper of Mr.[Samuel] Clarke* arrives herewith in part; the other half will arrive by the following post. This response is very expansive because I wanted to explain matters thoroughly and see from that whether there is hope of making Mr. Clarke listen to reason. For if he falls into repetitions, there will be nothing to do with him, and it will be necessary to try to end civilly.

Based on the gracious words of Your Royal Highness, I have informed a certain friend [Pierre des Maizeaux*] that you would be pleased, madame, by the translation of the *Theodicy* into English. I am now informed that a good translator has been found, and a bookseller who wants to provide the printing;[7] but they want to be permitted to dedicate the book to Your Royal Highness and to indicate on the title page that the translation has been made by her order. It seems to me that to request this last point, to want the order of Your Royal Highness to be placed on the

Des dames venues d'Angleterre, je n'ay encor vu que Madame de Schulenbourg, devenue duchesse, qui a pris les eaux à Pirmont. Je verray peutetre demain Madame de Kielmanseck. Il y a quelques semaines que je n'ay point vû Mademoiselle de pelniz, qui s'est excusée de me voir à cause de certains bains qu'elle prenoit, à ce qu'elle me fit dire. Le Roy a plaisanté plus d'une fois sur ma dispute avec M. Newton. Je n'ay pas encore vû M. l'Eveque de Carlisle; mais le chapelain de Sa Mté m'est venu voir avant mon voyage de pirmont; et il m'a paru savant et honnête homme, quoy-que nous n'ayons pû parler ensemble qu'en Latin.

Je joins icy les copies de ce qu'on m'a mandé de Vienne, quoyque je ne doute point que V. A. Royale n'en ait de meilleures nouvelles; mais il se peut que les miennes contiennent quelque petite circonstance qui pourra servir d'eclaircisse-ment. Et je suis avec devotion

Madame de V. A. Royale etc.

P. S.

On m'a dit que M. le Comte de Bikebourg a demandé que Messieurs ses fils fissent un tour chez luy de Wolfenbutel; mais qu'on s'en est excusé.

139. LEIBNIZ TO CAROLINE OF BRANDENBURG-ANSBACH   631

title page, would be to honour the book too much, though it were a hundred times better than it is. But I believe that Your Royal Highness will indeed permit it to be dedicated to her and permit it be indicated in the dedication that Your Royal Highness wanted this book to translated, since that is the truth, and it will be of great import for advancing a defence of religion and sound piety. I hope to learn her gracious wishes on the matter.

Of the ladies that have arrived from England, I have seen only Madame [Melusine] Schulenburg*, now a duchess, who has taken the waters at Pyrmont. Perhaps I will see Madame de Kielmansegg [Sophie Charlotte Kielmansegg*] tomorrow. It has been some weeks since I have seen Mademoiselle [Henriette Charlotte von] Pöllnitz*, who excused herself from seeing me on account of certain baths she took, according to the word she sent me. The king has joked more than once about my dispute with Mr. Newton. I have not yet seen the Bishop of Carlisle,[8] but His Majesty's chaplain [Lancelot Blackburne*] came to see me before my trip to Pyrmont, and he seemed to me a learned and honourable man, although we were only able to speak together in Latin.

I enclose here the copies of what has been sent to me from Vienna, although I do not doubt that Your Royal Highness has some better news about it; but it could be that mine contains some small circumstance that will be able to serve as clarification. And I am with devotion,

madame, of Your Royal Highness etc.

P. S. I am told that the Count of Bückeburg [Friedrich Christian*, Graf (Count) zu Schaumburg-Lippe] asked that his sons take a stroll around Wolfenbüttel with him, but that they declined.

---

[1] LBr. F 4 Bl. 72r–72v. Draft in Leibniz's hand: two quarto sides. Previously published in Klopp XI 131–3 (excerpt) and in Schüller 1991, p. 260 (excerpt in German translation); HGA 196 (excerpt in English translation). For Caroline's response, see her letter to Leibniz of 1 September 1716 (document 142).

[2] Francesco del Giudice (1647–1725) was an Italian cardinal (elevated in 1690) who represented Spain at the papal court from 1696 to 1698. In 1711 he became inquisitor general of Spain. In 1714 he issued an edict condemning regalist writings, and specifically condemning a strongly regalist memorandum drawn up by Melchor de Macanaz (1660–1760), which also called for a limitation of papal authority in Spain. The document had been authorized by King Philippe [Felipe] V*, and Giudice's condemnation of it led Philippe to order Giudice's resignation. When Macanaz fell from power in 1715, Giudice regained his offices. But as a result of disagreements with the de facto Spanish prime minister, Giulio Alberoni, Giudice again fell from power in 1716, as Leibniz learned from the 'courier from Madrid'. In January of 1717, he left Spain bound for Rome, where he spent the rest of his life. (See Frey and Frey 1995, p. 186; Kamen 1969, pp. 389–90.)

[3] That is, Louis XV (1710–1774). At the time, Louis XV was only six years old, and France was actually being ruled by the Regent Phillipe II*, Duke of Orléans. Louis XV assumed ruling power when he reached his maturity in 1723.

[4] At the time, the sole surviving sister of Empress Elisabeth Christine was Antoinette Amalie of Braunschweig-Wolfenbüttel (1696–1762).

[5] The spouse of Ferdinand Albrecht II* was Antoinette Amalie of Braunschweig-Wolfenbüttel (1696–1762).

First Draft of Leibniz's Fifth Paper

Quartriéme Réponse

Cet écrit a ete changé et augmenté, avant que d'etre envoyé

Sur 1 et 2 du papier precedent

(1) Il est vray que les raisons font dans l'esprit du sage ce qui répond à ce que les poids font dans une balance. Des foibles motifs cèdent à de plus forts et l'indifferent n'y fait rien. On objecte que cette notion mene à la necessité et à la fatalité. Mais cette necessité n'est que morale et heureuse, quand on se determine pour le bien: la necessité brute, comme celle qui est dans la balance et la necessité morale qui est[3] dans le choix ont cela de commun qu'elles ont leurs raisons suffisantes cependant j'ay montré dans la Theodicée, que notre volonté ne suit point necessairement le jugement de l'entendement parce qu'elle peut suspendre la decision finale. Il est vray que cette suspension a encore des raisons suffisantes mais toutes ces raisons quoyque elles causent une certitude infaillible, ne produisent point une necessité absolue, etant inclinantes et non necessitantes. La certitude du choix futur d'une substance libre ne sauroit etre revoquée en doute. Autrement on niera la providence divine avec les Sociniens. Et la destinée certaine de toutes choses, venant de la providence qui choisit tousjours le meilleur, est <u>fatum christianum</u> qui ne deroge en rien à la liberté ny à la contingence, puisque le choix même que font des creatures libres entre dans les raisons du decret ou du choix de Dieu. Je l'ay assés montré dans la Theodicée, et j'y ay repondu aux objections ordinaires.

(2) On m'objecte encore que la balance est passive, au lieu que l'esprit est actif. Mais les agens ont besoin d'une raison suffisante de leur action, aussi bien que les patiens en ont besoin, pour leur passion. Si un air comprimé etoit enfermé dans un verre parfaitement rond et uniforme dont le centre fut dans celuy de la terre, il ne casseroit point ce verre quelque grande que pourroit etre la force elastique de cet air, parce qu'il n'y auroit nulle[4] raison de casser un endroit plus tot qu'un autre.

(3) Comment et pour quoy un etre intelligent, aussi bien que quelque autre agent que ce soit, se determineroit il quand tout est absolument indifferent?

140A. FIRST DRAFT OF LEIBNIZ'S FIFTH PAPER   633

[6] That is, the River Save, which flows through the countries of Slovenia, Croatia, and Serbia. Leibniz is referring to the Battle of Petrovaradin (5 August 1716), in which Prince Eugène of Savoy led the Austrian army to a decisive victory over the Turks. Petrovaradin is now a part of Novi Sad in Serbia.

[7] Des Maizeaux provided this information in a letter of 14 of July 1716 to Philip Heinrich (Henry) Zollman* (document 134).

[8] At the time of writing, this was William Nicolson*, who was also the Lord High Almoner. But in her letter to Leibniz of 26 May 1716, Caroline had told Leibniz that 'the Almoner [that is, Nicolson] will not accompany the king [to the Hanoverian electorate]' (document 122, p. 549), so it is unclear why Leibniz was expecting to see him there.

140a. First Draft of Leibniz's Fifth Paper[1]

Fourth Response[2]   This paper has been changed and enlarged, before
                                 being sent

To 1 and 2 of the preceding paper

(1) It is true that reasons in the mind of the sage do what corresponds to that which weights do in a balance. Weak motives give way to stronger, and those indifferent do nothing. It is objected that this notion leads to necessity and fatality. But this necessity is only moral and happy, when one is determined to the good. Brute necessity, like that which is in the balance, and moral necessity, which is[3] in choice, have this in common, that they have their sufficient reasons; however, I have shown in the *Theodicy* that our will does not necessarily follow the judgment of the understanding, because it can suspend the final decision. It is true that this suspension also has some sufficient reasons, but all these reasons, though they cause an infallible certitude, do not produce an absolute necessity, since they are inclining and not necessitating. The certitude of the future choice of a free substance cannot be called into question. Otherwise divine providence will be denied with the Socinians. And the certain destiny of all things, since it comes from the providence that always chooses the best, is *Christian fate*, which does not derogate in any way from liberty, nor from contingency, since the choice itself that makes some creatures free enters into the reasons of the decree or the choice of God. I have demonstrated this sufficiently in the *Theodicy*, and I have responded to the usual objections.

(2) It has also been objected to me that the balance is passive, while the mind is active. But agents need a sufficient reason for their action, as patients also have need of it for their passion. If compressed air were enclosed in a perfectly round and uniform glass, whose centre coincided with that of the earth, it could not break this glass however great the elastic force of this air might be, because there would be no[4] reason to break one spot rather than another.

(3) How and why would an intelligent being, or any other agent whatsoever, be determined when everything is absolutely indifferent?

634   140A. FIRST DRAFT OF LEIBNIZ'S FIFTH PAPER

(4) Vouloir cela n'est ce pas renverser le grand principe, que tout evenement a besoin d'une raison suffisante, et par consequent soutenir des choses deraisonnables, comme je le feray voir davantage sur la fin de cet écrit.

(5) On avoit accordé cy dessus ce grand principe, maintenant on s'y oppose, c'est ou ne l'avoir point entendu, ou se retracter ou se contredire.

(6) Soûtenir de telles choses n'est ce pas une absurdité pareille à celle de la declinaison des Atomes d'Epicure, dont on se moquoit avec justice, parce qu'ils se detournoient de leurs chemins sans aucune raison.

(7) Je crois que des personnes impartiales m'accorderont que d'avoir reduit son adversaire nier ce grand principe de la raison c'est le reduire ad absurdum.

(6) Veut on que je prouve ce grand principe? Il a luy meme sa raison, mais il faudroit aller trop avant pour le demontrer a priori. Icy il suffira que tout le monde s'en sert sans difficulté.

(7) Qu'il n'y a point d'exemple non contesté ou il manque.

(8) Que sans l'employer on ne sauroit même prouver l'existence de Dieu.

(5) | (8) | On me dit : | there may be very good raison to act, though two or more ways of acting may be absolutely indifferent | qu'il y peut avoir une bonne raison pour agir quoyque les voyes d'agir soyent absolument indifferentes. Mais si toutes les voyes sont indifferentes il est impossible qu'il y ait une raison suffisante pour faire agir. Car puisqu'il faut agir dans une des voyes, | il faut pour qu'il y ait une bonne raison pour agir, il y ait aussi une raison pour agir dans cette voye < car on ne sauroit depouiller l'action de ses circonstances > mais alors les voyes ne sont point indifferentes. | et que l'action ne sauroit etre depouillée de ses circonstances il faut qu'il y ait aussi une raison suffisante pour une des voyes, donc elles ne sont point indifferentes.

<u>Sur 3 et 4</u>

(6) | (9) | J'ay prouvé par le même principe du besoin de la raison suffisante que Dieu ne produit point deux portions de matiere parfaitement egales et semblables. On m'objecte qu'ainsi Dieu ne produira point de matiere du tout, parceque les parties de la matiere sont parfaitement solides, qu'on peut supposer | egales et semblables. Mais c'est s'imaginer avec le vulgaire, qu'il y a des atomes, ou portions de matiere parfaitement solides[5]. Selon mes demonstrations chaque[6] portion de matiere est actuellement subdivisée en parties differemment mües. | egales et semblables. Mais outre que cette supposition | d'une parfaite convenance de deux corps | de deux corps entierement egaux et semblables n'est point admise et fait une petition de principe. Cette autre supposition de parties de matiere entierement solides | dans la matiere | et tout d'une piece sans varieté, comme l'on conçoit les pretendus Atomes, est une imagination populaire mal fondée. Selon mes demonstrations chaque portion de matiere est actuellement subdivisée en parties differemment mués; et pas une ne ressenble entierement à l'autre.

140A. FIRST DRAFT OF LEIBNIZ'S FIFTH PAPER 635

(4) Won't granting that be to overthrow the great principle that all events have a sufficient reason and consequently to assert some unreasonable things, as I shall show further at the end of this paper?

(5) The author had above granted this great principle; now he opposes it. This is either to have not understood it, or to recant, or to contradict oneself.

(6) Isn't maintaining such things an absurdity, like that of the declination of the atoms of Epicurus, which was rightly mocked, because the atoms turn from their paths without any reason?

(7) I believe that impartial persons will grant me that to reduce one's adversary to denying that great principle of reason is to reduce him to absurdity.

(6) Does the author want me to prove that great principle? It does itself have its reason, but it would require going too far to demonstrate it a priori. Here it will suffice that everyone makes use of it without difficulty.

(7) That there is not any uncontested example where it fails.

(8) That without employing it, not even the existence of God could be proved.

(5) | (8) | I am told: | *there may be very good reason to act, though two or more ways of acting may be absolutely indifferent* | *that there may be a good reason for acting, although the ways of acting be absolutely indifferent.* But if all the ways are indifferent, it is impossible that there should be a *sufficient reason* to act. For since it is necessary to act in one of the ways, | there must be a good reason to act, as well as a reason to act in this way < for the action could not be stripped of its circumstances > but then the ways are not indifferent. | and since the action could not be stripped of its circumstances, there must also be a sufficient reason for one of the ways, so they are not indifferent.

To 3 and 4

(6) | (9) | By the same principle of the need for sufficient reason, I have proved that God does not produce two portions of matter perfectly equal and alike. It is objected that then God will not produce any matter at all, because the parts of matter are perfectly solid, which may be assumed to be | equal and alike. But this is to imagine with the vulgar that there are atoms, or perfectly solid[5] portions of matter. According to my demonstrations, every[6] portion of matter is actually subdivided into parts differently moved. | equal and alike. But besides that, this supposition | of a perfect agreement of two bodies | of two bodies entirely equal and alike is not admitted and commits a *petito principii.* This other supposition of parts of matter entirely solid | in matter | and all of a piece without variety, as the so-called atoms are conceived, is an ill-grounded popular fantasy. According to my demonstrations, each part of matter is actually subdivided into parts differently moved, and one does not entirely resemble another.

636 140A. FIRST DRAFT OF LEIBNIZ'S FIFTH PAPER

(7) | (10) | La sagesse de Dieu ne permet pas qu'il y ait deux portions[7] de matiere parfaitement egales et semblables car cela choque | les principes de la sagesse et la maxime de la raison suffisante | le grand principe du besoin de la raison suffisante. Le vulgaire s'imagine de telles choses parce qu'il a des notions incompletes.

Sur 5 et 6

(8) | (11) | Il est vray que si deux choses parfaitement indiscernables existoient elles seroient deux. Mais la supposition est fausse et contraire au grand principe de la raison. Les philosophes | de l'Ecole | vulgaires se sont trompés lors qu'ils ont crû qu'il y avoit | quelque part deux choses differentes <u>solo numero</u> | des choses differentes <u>solo numero</u> ou seulement parce qu'elles sont deux; et c'est de cette erreur que sont venu leur perplexites sur ce qu'ils appeloient le principe de l'individuation. La metaphysique a ete traitée jusqu'icy ordinairement en simple doctrine des termes sans discuter les choses memes.

(9)

| (12) | La philosophie superficielle fondée en imaginations et non en raisons (comme celle des Atomistes et Vacuistes) se forge des choses que les raisons superieures n'admettent point. J'espere que mes demonstrations feront changer de face a la philosophie, malgré les foibles contradictions telles qu'on m'oppose icy.

(10) Mais sans entrer dans ces raisons profondes dont j'en ay encore propres a être produites ailleurs, il y un grand prejugé contre l'existence des indiscernables, c'est qu'on n'en trouve jamais aucun exemple.

(11) On m'avoue qu'il n'y a point deux feuilles semblables, et l'on dit que <u>peut etre</u> (perhaps), il en est autant de deux gouttes d'eau. Mais on pourroit je crois l'avouer sans balancer, (without perhaps) senza forse comme disent les italiens.

(12) | (14) | Et selon toutes les apparences dans les choses insensibles, il en va à cet égard comme dans les sensibles, à proportion. C'est tout comme icy, suivant ce qui se disoit dans la comédie de l'Empereur de la Lune.[8]

(13) Les parties du temps et du lieu sont des choses ideales. Ainsi elles se ressemblent parfaitement prises en elles-mêmes comme deux unités abstraites. Mais il n'en est pas ainsi de deux uns concrets. Ainsi les instans du temps et les points de l'espace en eux mêmes ne sont que des idealités | et non pas des estre[s] absolus. Ils consistent en rapports. | abstraites; cependant je ne dis point que deux[9] instans sont un même instant comme il semble qu'on m'impute. Mais faute de connoissance on peut s'imaginer deux instans ou il n'y en a qu'un.

(14) | (13) | La fiction de l'univers materiel mû tout entier dans l'espace est deraisonnable et impracticable parce que ce mouvement seroit sans but et parce que ce seroit <u>agendo nihil agere</u> puisqu'on produiroit aucun changement observable par qui que ce soit. Outre qu'il n'y a point d'espace dans l'univers materiel. Ce sont des

140A. FIRST DRAFT OF LEIBNIZ'S FIFTH PAPER 637

| (10) | (7) The wisdom of God does not permit there to be two parts[7] of matter perfectly equal and alike, for that violates | the principles of wisdom and the maxim of sufficient reason | the great principle of the need for a sufficient reason. The vulgar imagine such things because they have incomplete notions.

To 5 and 6

(8) | (11) | It is true that if two perfectly indiscernible things existed, they would be two. But the supposition is false and contrary to the great principle of reason. The vulgar | Scholastic | philosophers were wrong when they believed that there were | somewhere two things differing *solo numero* | some things differing *solo numero*, or only because they are two; and it is from this error that their perplexities arose about what they called the principle of individuation. Up to now metaphysics has usually been dealt with in a mere doctrine of terms, without discussing things themselves.

(9)

| (12) | The superficial philosophy grounded in imaginations and not in reasons (like that of the atomists and vacuists) invent things that superior reasons do not admit. I hope my demonstrations will alter the face of philosophy, despite such weak objections as the author raises against me here.

(10) But without entering into those profound reasons of which I also have some, suitable to be produced elsewhere, there is a great presumption against the existence of indiscernibles, namely that no example of them has ever been found.

(11) The author grants me that there are not two leaves alike, and he says that it is perhaps the same with two drops of water. But I believe it could be granted it without hesitating, (without perhaps) senza forse, as the Italians say.

(12) | (14) | And to all appearances, it holds proportionally in this respect for insensible things as for sensible things. It is all as it is here, according to what was said in the farce, *The Emperor of the Moon*.[8]

(13) The parts of time and of place are ideal things. So they resemble each other perfectly taken in themselves as two abstract unities. But it is not so with two concrete ones. Thus the instants of time and the points of space in themselves are only abstract idealities; | and not some absolute beings. They consist in relations. | however I do not say that two[9] instants are the same instant, as it seems that the author imputes to me. But due to lack of understanding, a person can imagine two instants where there is only one.

(14) | 13 | The fiction of the entire material universe moved in space is unreasonable and impracticable, because this movement would be without purpose and because it would be *to act by doing nothing*, since no change observable by anyone would be produced. Besides, there is not any space in the material universe. These are imaginings of | popular | philosophers with incomplete notions, which make

imaginations des philosophes | populaires | à notions incompletes qui font de l'espace une réalité absolue. Les simples Mathematiciens qui ne suivent que le jeu de l'imagination sont capables de se forger de telles notions, mais elles sont detruites par des raisons superieures.

(15) | (14) | Des Cartes a soutenu que la matiere n'a point de borne et je ne crois pas qu'on l'ait refuté, et quand on le luy accorderoit il ne s'ensuit point qu'elle soit eternelle, ou sans commencement. Je n'accorde point que tout fini est muable. Une partie de l'espace est finie et n'est point muable. Un fini materiel est muable s'il fait partie d'un autre, afin qu'il puisse arriver un changement observable.

(1| 5 |6) Puisque l'espace | sans corps | est une chose ideale comme le temps suivant ce que j'ay demonstré par le principe du besoin de la raison suffisante, il faut bien que l'espace hors du monde soit imaginaire, comme les Scholastiques l'on reconnu en effect.

Sur 7

17

(| 16 |) Il ne s'ensuit point de ce que la matiere grossiere a esté tirée du recipient, qu'il ait du vuide la dedans.

(1| 7 |8) La Resistence ne vient pas tant de la quantité de matiere, que[10] de ce qu'elle ne peut point ceder facilement. Il y a plus de matiere pesante dans de l'eau que dans du bois de pareil volume et cependant du bois flottant et non pas l'eau resistera notablement au bateau. Si nous estimons matiere grosse celle qui a de la pesanteur, et fine celle qui n'en a point (car c'est une fiction de faire toute la matiere pesante) le vif argent aura plus de matiere grosse que de l'eau.

Sur 8

(19)| (18) | J'ay déja refuté l'etrange imagination que l'espace est une propriété de Dieu. S'il est une propriété de Dieu il entre dans son essence. Or l'espace a des parties donc dans l'essence de Dieu il y auroit des parties, et quand les espaces sont tantôt vuides, tantost remplies, l'essence de Dieu auroit des parties tantôt vuides tantôt remplies et par consequent sujettes a un changement perpetuel. Les corps remplissant l'espace rempliroient une partie de l'essence de Dieu, et y seroient commensurées. Dans la supposition du vuide il y aura une partie de l'essence divine renfermée dans le recipient. Quelles etranges expressions! Un Dieu a parties ressemblera fort au Dieu stoicien qui etoit l'univers tout entier consideré comme un animal Divin. Je ne comprends pas aussi pour quoy en soutenant le vuide l'on nie icy que l'espace est renfermé entre les corps. Si un recipient etoit veritablement vuide, il y auroit un espace vuide renfermé dans le recipient.[11]

space an absolute reality. Mere mathematicians who follow only the play of imagination are capable of inventing such notions, but they are destroyed by superior reasons.

(15) | (14) | Descartes has maintained that matter does not have any limit, and I don't believe that he has been refuted, and even if that were granted to him, it does not follow that it is eternal, or without beginning. I do not grant that every finite thing is moveable. A part of space is finite and it is not moveable. A finite material thing is moveable if it is part of another, so that an observable change can occur.

(1| 5 |6) Since space | without bodies | is an ideal thing like time, according to what I have demonstrated by the principle of the need for a sufficient reason, space outside the world must indeed be imaginary, as the Scholastics did in fact recognize.

To 7

17

(| 16 |) It does not follow from the fact that gross matter has been drawn from the receiver that there is a vacuum in it.

(1| 7 |8) The resistance does not come so much from the quantity of matter as[10] from the fact that it cannot yield easily; there is more heavy matter in water than in timber of equal volume, and yet floating timber, and not the water, will significantly resist the boat. If we calculate gross matter, which has some weight, and fine matter, which does not (for it is a fiction to make all matter heavy), the mercury will have more gross matter than water.

To 8

(19) | (18) | I have already refuted the strange figment that space is a property of God. If it is a property of God, it enters into his essence. Now space has parts, therefore in the essence of God there would be parts; and when the spaces are sometimes empty and sometimes full, the essence of God would have parts sometimes empty and sometimes full and consequently subject to perpetual change. By filling space, bodies would fill a part of the essence of God and they would be commensurate with it. On the supposition of the vacuum, a part of the divine essence will be contained within the receiver. What strange expressions! A god of parts will very much resemble the Stoic god, which was the entire universe regarded as a divine animal. I also do not understand why, in supporting the vacuum, the author here denies that space is contained between bodies. If a receiver were truly empty, there would be an empty space contained within the receiver.[11]

Sur 9

(20) | (19) | Si l'espace vuide de corps n'est pas vuide tout a fait, de quoy est-il donc plein? Y at-il peut étre des esprits etendus, qui s'y promenent et qui se penetrent comme les ombres de deux corps se penetrent sur la surface d'une muraille? N'est ce pas renverser les notions des choses, donner à Dieu des parties, donner de l'etendue aux esprits.

(2| 0 |1) Le seul principe du besoin de la raison suffisante, fait disparoitre tous ces spectres d'imagination. Les hommes se font aisement des fictions faute d'empolyer ce grand principe.

Sur 10

(2| 1 |2) Si l'espace est necessaire pour que Dieu soit omnipresent, on suppose donc que Dieu est dans chaque partie de l'espace. L'espace ne sera pas une propriete de Dieu, mais étre dans l'espace, et dans chaque partie de l'espace ce sera une proprieté de Dieu. Et par consequent l'espace sera independant de Dieu, et plus tôt l'ominpresence de Dieu dependra de l'espace. D'ailleurs si etre dans l'espace est une proprieté d'un etre; l'espace luy meme ne sauroit etre une propriété de cet etre. Ceux qui parlent si etrangement renversent toute la proprieté des expressions et parlent un langage qui ne sauroit étre entendu.

Si l'espace est la propriete de ce qui est dans l'espace nous aurons une plaisante philosophie, les accidens ou attributs passeront de sujet en sujet. Les sujets quitteront leurs accidens comme un habit, et les laisseront là afin que les autres s'en puissent revetir.[12] Apres cela comment distinguerat-on les accidens et les substances? C'est aussi une chose inouie chimerique[13] en philosophie, de dire que le sujet est dans ses propriétés. Jusqu'icy les propriétés ont eté dans leur sujet. Maintenant on veut que Dieu est dans l'espace sa propriété à ce qu'on pretend.

(22) Je n'accorde point que l'infini soit composé d'infinitesimales. Les quantités infinitesimales sont des idealités mathematiques, comme les racines imaginaires.

Sur 11 et 12[14]

(23) Pourquoy faut il que les parties d'un tout soyent tousjours separables par discerption ou puissent etre eloignées l'une de l'autre? C'est s'ecarter des notions receues sans aucun autre besoin que de celuy d'avoir des echappatoires en refusant des parties à une chose etendue, telle que l'espace, pour le pouvoir faire un attribut de Dieu. S'il y avoit du vuide dans le recipeint, cet espace vuide auroit des parties, et on pourroit les distinguer soit par quelque corps entre deux soit même par les lignes ou surfaces qu'on y peut concevoir, quoyqu'on ne pourroit point detacher et eloigner une partie de l'autre. Je n'admets les infinitésimales que comme on admet

140A. FIRST DRAFT OF LEIBNIZ'S FIFTH PAPER 641

To 9

(20) | (19) | If space devoid of bodies is not entirely void, of what then is it full? Are there perhaps extended minds that wander about there and that penetrate each other like the shadows of two bodies penetrate each other on the surface of a wall? Isn't this to overthrow the notions of things, to give God parts, to give extension to minds?

(21) The principle of the need for a sufficient reason alone causes all these specters of imagination to disappear. Men easily make fictions for themselves for lack of employing this great principle.

To 10

(2| 1 |2) If space is necessary for God to be omnipresent, it is then supposed that God is in each part of space. Space will not be a property of God, but to be in space and in each part of space will be a property of God. And consequently, space will be independent of God, and the omnipresence of God will rather depend on space. Moreover, if being in space is a property of a being, space itself cannot be a property of this being. Those who speak so strangely overthrow every propriety of speech and speak a language that cannot be understood.

If space is the property of what is in space, we will have an amusing philosophy; the accidents or attributes will pass from subject to subject. The subjects will lay aside their accidents like clothing, and they will leave them there so that others may clothe themselves with them.[12] After that, how will we distinguish accidents and substances? It is also an incredible chimerical[13] thing in philosophy to say that the subject is in its properties. Up till now properties have been in their subject. Now they want God to be in space, his property according to what they claim.

(22) I do not grant that the infinite is composed of infinitesimals. Infinitesimal quantities are mathematical idealities, like imaginary roots.

To 11 and 12[14]

(23) Why must the parts of a whole always be separable by discerption, or capable of being distant from each another? This deviates from received notions without any other need than to have some ways of escape from that by refusing parts to an extended thing, such as space, in order to be able to make it an attribute of God. If there were a void in the receiver, this void space would have parts, and they could be distinguished, either by some body between two, or even by the lines or surfaces that can be conceived there, although one part could not be detached and removed from another. I allow infinitesimals only in the way imaginary roots are allowed,

642 140A. FIRST DRAFT OF LEIBNIZ'S FIFTH PAPER

les racines imaginaires, et je ne crois point que les finis[15] en soyent composés. Cela soit dit en passant.

Sur 13

(24) Il est vray qu'un vaisseau peut fort bien être en mouvement, sans que celuy qui est dedans s'en apperçoive. Mais il n'y a point de mouvement ou personne | jusqu'à Dieu même | ne puisse s'appercevoir du changement s'il etoit à portée. C'est pouquoy des Cartes a fait entrer dans l'essence du mouvement le changement de la situation entre les corps et en cela il a eu raison. L'univers n'est point mobile car il n'y a point de place hors de l'univers. Deux places ne sont pas la même place. Mais aussi ils sont toujours differens, | si ce n'est qu'on les prenne abstraits en cas ils[16] ne sont que possibilités. | et discernables par les choses.

(25) M. Hugens avoit aussi été au commencement pour un mouvement absolu sans changement respectif, comme M. Newton. Mais il m'a avoué dans une de ses lettres, d'avoir changé de sentiment.

(26) Je ne trouve rien dans les principes de M. Newton defin. 8 qui prouve le contraire. | Il faudroit montrer comment il le prouve | Je ne trouve pas non plus la realité absolue de l'espace prouvée et j'ay demontré le contraire par le grand principe du besoin de la raison suffisante.

Sur 14

| (27) L'espace et le temps ont quantité. |

(27) Rien n'empeche les chose relatives d'avoir quantité. Les raisons ou proportions dans les mathematiques ont leur quantité, et se mesurent par les logarithmes; et cependant ce sont des relations. Ainsi quoyque le temps et l'espace consistent en rapports, ils ne laissent pas d'avoir de la quantité.

Sur 15

(28) Je l'ay deja dit, supposer que Dieu ait commencé de créer le monde plus tost, est supposer quelque chose de chimerique. C'est faire du temps une chose absolu independante de Dieu; au lieu que le temps ne cöexiste qu'aux créatures, et ne se conçoit que par l'ordre de leurs changements. Detruire ce qui existe déjà est autre chose, et une destruction plus tardive se peut discerner d'une destruction anterieure.

(29) L'eternité du monde seroit demonstrable, si le temps estoit une réalité absolue, comme j'ay montré; mais elle n'est point prouvée par la negation de l'espace absolu car l'espace étant relatif ne sauroit durer plus que les choses dont il fait le rapport. Je ne dis point que la matiere et l'espace soient la même chose. Ils different comme le temps et le mouvement; mais ils sont inseparables.

140A. FIRST DRAFT OF LEIBNIZ'S FIFTH PAPER   643

and I do not believe that finites[15] are composed of them. That may be said in passing.

To 13

(24) It is true that a ship may very well be in motion without the person in the ship being aware of it. But there is not any movement when no one | even God himself| could be aware of the change if he were within range. This is why Descartes introduced change of position among bodies into the essence of motion, and in that he was right. The universe is not moveable because there is not any place outside of the universe. Two places are not the same place. But they are also always different | except that they are taken to be abstract when they[16] are only possibilities. | and discernible by things.

(25) Mr. Huygens had initially also been in favour of an absolute motion without relative change, like Mr. Newton. But he admitted to me in one of his letters that he had changed his mind.[17]

(26) I find nothing in the principles of Mr. Newton, definition 8, that proves the contrary. | It would be necessary to show how he proves it | Neither do I find the absolute reality of space proved, and I have demonstrated the contrary by the great principle of the need for a sufficient reason.

To 14

| (27) Space and time have quantity. |

(27) Nothing prevents relative things from having quantity. Ratios or proportions in mathematics have their quantity, and they are measured by logarithms; and yet these are relations. So although time and space consist in relations, they do not cease having quantity.

To 15

(28) I have already said, to assume that God began to create the world sooner is to assume something chimerical. It is to make time something absolute, independent of God, whereas time coexists only with creatures and is only conceived through the order of their changes. To destroy what already exists is something else, and a later destruction can be distinguished from a previous one.

(29) The eternity of the world would be demonstrable if time were an absolute reality, as I have demonstrated. But it is not proved by the denial of absolute space, because space, being something relative, could not endure any longer than the things of which it is the relation. I do not say that matter and space are the same thing. They differ as time and movement do, but they are inseparable.

(30) On ne peut point dire qu'un temps et qu'un espace plaise à Dieu, plus qu'un autre pour y placer les choses; puisque les temps ou les espaces sont absolument indiscernables, par où donc l'un plairoit il plus tost que l'autre? Quand les temps ou les lieux plaisent, c'est par les choses qui y sont: et non pas avant que des choses y soyent.

(31) Je ne dis pas ordre ou situation, mais ordre de la situation. Il semble qu'on ne me veut point entendre.[18]

(32) Si le temps devient plus grand ou plus petit, l'ordre n'est point le meme comme on avance icy, car il y a plus ou moins de choses interposées.

(33) Comme le nombre abstrait est distingué de la multitude dans les choses, de même le temps abstrait différe de l'affection des choses qui s'appelle la durée, et qui consiste dans le rapport des successions.

(34) On avance aussi que si Dieu seul existoit, il y auroit temps et espace, comme a present. C'est ce que je n'accorde point. Je ne les admettrois que dans les idées comme les choses possibles. L'eternité et l'immensité de Dieu sont quelque chose de plus eminent que la durée et l'entendue des creatures. Ces attributs divins n'ont point besoin de choses hors de Dieu, telles que sont l'espace et le temps. J'ay déja refuté l'imagination qui veut que l'espace et le temps sont les proprietés de Dieu.

(35) Le sentiment commun des Theologiens ne doit pas être traité simplement en opinion vulgaire. Il faut des grandes raisons, pour oser y contrevenir, et je n'en vois icy aucune.

(31) On dit sur le 15 nombre que Dieu peut avoir eu de bonnes raisons pour commencer le monde materiel dans un tel temps, parce que ce temps n'etoit pas indifferent, supposé qu'il ait eu en luy auparavant des substances immaterielles anterieures aux materielles: Et en cela on commence à se mettre à la raison et l'on s'accommode au principe du besoin de la raison suffisante, le temps étant varié par les choses qui y existent. (32) Mais outre que j'ay des raisons pour ne point admettre des substances créées entierement destitutées de matiere; au lieu que la philosophie vulgaire admet aisement toutes sortes de fictions faute de notions completes.

(33) Outre cela[19] (dis je), il faut considerer qu'il reste tousjours la même question à l'égard l'univers qui comprend les creatures materielles et immaterielles ensemble; car s'il n'est point eternel, il est indifferent, (selon la manière de parler vulgaire) en quel temps on le fasse commencer. Ainsi (dans la verité) c'est tousjours la même question comment on luy puisse assigner un temps plus tôt qu'un autre, quand même on commence le monde par les substances immaterielles | avant les materielles | puisque les temps sans les choses sont indiscernables, et par consequent les temps sans les choses ne sont que des idées incompletes et abstraites, et quel temps pretendu qu'on luy assigne, au commencement de l'univers, c'est tousjours la même chose.

140A. FIRST DRAFT OF LEIBNIZ'S FIFTH PAPER   645

(30) It cannot be said that one time and one space *pleases God* more than another for placing things there; since times or spaces are absolutely indiscernible, how would one please more than the other? When times or places please, it is by the things that are there and not before any things are there.

(31) I do not say order or situation, but order of the situation. It seems that the author does not wish to understand me.[18]

(32) If time becomes greater or less, the order is not the same, as the author advances here; for there are more or less things interposed.

(33) As abstract number is distinguished from multitude in things, so abstract time differs from the affection of things that is called duration and that consists in the relation of successions.

(34) The author also advances that if God alone were to exist, there would be time and space as they are at present. This is what I do not grant. I would only admit them in ideas, as possible things. The eternity and immensity of God are things more eminent than the duration and extension of creatures. These divine attributes do not have need of things outside of God, such as space and time. I have already refuted the imagination that will have space and time to be properties of God.

(35) The common opinion of theologians ought not to be treated merely as *vulgar opinion*. Substantial reasons are required in order to dare contravene them, and I do not see any of them here.

(31) To number 15 the author says that God may have had some good reasons to create the material world at such a time because this time was not indifferent, assuming it previously had some immaterial substances in it, prior to the material ones. And in that he begins to set about being reasonable, and he accommodates himself to the principle of the need for a sufficient reason, since time is changed by the things that exist in it. (32) But besides, I have reasons for not accepting created substances completely devoid of matter, whereas the vulgar philosophy easily admits all sorts of fictions for lack of complete notions.

(33) Besides that[19] (say I), it is necessary to consider that the same question always remains as regards the universe that contains material and immaterial creatures together; for if it is not eternal, it is indifferent (according to the vulgar manner of speaking) at which time it is made to begin. So in truth, it is always the same question, how it is possible to assign a time sooner than another even if the world begins with immaterial substances | before the material ones |, since times without things are indiscernible, and consequently times without things are only incomplete ideas and abstract, and whichever supposed time is assigned to it at the beginning, it is always the same thing.

Sur 16 et 17

(34) Je ne sache aucune preuve apportée contre moy, ou je n'aye repondu.

(35) J'ay fait voir que la contradiction est dans l'hypothese du sentiment opposé, et ce seroit une iniquité manifeste d'en vouloir inferer que j'ay reconnu de la contradiction dans mon propre sentiment.

Sur 18

(36) Les parties de l'espace ne sont determinees et distinguees que par les choses qui y sont, et la diversité des choses dans l'espace determine Dieu a agir differemment sur les differentes parties de l'espace. Mais l'espace pris sans les choses n'est rien de determinant, et même n'est rien d'actuel.

(37) Si Dieu est resolu à placer un certain cube de matiere, il s'est aussi determiné sur la place de ce cube; mais c'est par rapport à d'autres portions de matiere, et non pas par rapport à l'espace detaché ou il y a rien determinant.

(38) Dire que Dieu a de bonnes raisons pour placer deux cubes de matiere egaux et en tout semblables en deux places differentes, quoyqu'il n'y ait aucune raison pour discerner les cubes et les espaces, c'est vouloir que Dieu discerne des indiscernibles, et qu'il ait de bonnes raisons, où il n'y en a aucunes ny bonnes ny mauvaises.

(39) J'avois comparé une volonté sans motif au hazard d'Epicure; on y oppose que le hazard d'Epicure est une necessité aveugle, et non pas un choix de la volonté. Je replique que le hazard d'Epicure n'est pas une necessite, mais quelque chose d'indifferent. Il est vray que le hazard est aveugle mais une volonté sans motif ne seroit pas moins aveugle, et ne seroit pas moins düe au simple hazard.

(40) On me dit que l'ame n'est pas dans le cerveau, mais dans le _sensorium_, mais supposé que ce _sensorium_ est un corps, (comme je crois qu'on l'entend) c'est tousjours la même difficulté, et la question revient toujours si l'ame est diffuse par ce corps, quelque grand ou quelque petit qu'il soit. Car il est tousjours etendu le plus ou moins de grandeur n'y fait rien. Pour moy je trouve plus assure de comparer les ames aux autres ce sont des Monades.

(41) Je n'accorde point que deux corps egaux mous concourans avec vitesses egales perdent de leur[s] forces: car quand les forces ne sont point conservees entierement dans les mouvemens des touts comme dans les elastiques, le dechet est dissipé dans leurs parties qui sont mise en mouvement intestin. Ce n'est pas perdre la force, mais c'est faire comme l'on fait en changeant la grosse monnoye en petite.

Sur 19

J'ay repondu à cecy num. 6 du present papier.

140A. FIRST DRAFT OF LEIBNIZ'S FIFTH PAPER 647

To 16 and 17

(34) I do not know any proof brought against me to which I have not responded.

(35) I have shown that the contradiction is in the hypothesis of the contrary view, and it would be a manifest injustice to want to infer from that, that I have recognized some contradiction in my own view.

To 18

(36) The parts of space are determined and distinguished only by the things that are in it, and the diversity of things in space determine God to act differently on different parts of space. But space taken without things is nothing determinant, and even nothing actual.

(37) If God is resolved to place a certain cube of matter, he is also determined upon the place of this cube; but it is by relation to other portions of matter, and not by relation to isolated space, where nothing is determinant.

(38) To say that God has good reasons to place two cubes of matter equal and similar in all respects in two different places, although there is not any reason for distinguishing the cubes and the spaces, is to require God to distinguish indiscernibles and have good reasons when there are not any, either good or bad.

(39) I compared a will without motive to the chance of Epicurus; the author objects that the chance of Epicurus is a blind necessity and not a choice of the will. I reply that the chance of Epicurus is not a necessity, but something indifferent. It is true that chance is blind, but a will without motive would not be less blind and would not be less owing to mere chance.

(40) I am told that the soul is not in the brain, but in the *sensorium*, but supposing that this *sensorium* is a body, as I believe the author intends, it is always the same difficulty, and the question always recurs, whether the soul is diffused through this body, however great or small it may be. For it is always extended, the greater or lesser size makes no difference. For my part, I find it more secure to compare souls to other things. They are monads.

(41) I do not agree that two equal soft bodies, colliding with equal speeds, lose their forces. For when the forces are not entirely conserved in the movements of the wholes, as in elastic bodies, the loss is dissipated in their parts, which are put in internal motion. This is not to lose force, but it is like changing big money into small.

To 19

I have responded to this, number 6 of the present paper.

648 140A. FIRST DRAFT OF LEIBNIZ'S FIFTH PAPER

<u>Sur 20</u>

On m'avoit objecté dans le 3me papier (n. 7. 8) que Dieu n'auroit point de principe d'agir en luy, s'il etoit determiné par les externes: a cela j'ay repondu que les idées des choses externes sont en luy, et qu'ainsi il est determiné par des raisons internes: c'est à dire par sa sagesse; maintenant on ne veut point entendre à propros de quoy je l'aye dit.

<u>Sur 21</u>

Je ne dis point que Dieu ne peut point limiter la quantité de matiere, mais je dis qu'il ne veut point le faire sans sujet. De la quantité à la durée, non valet consequentia.[20] Si la nature des choses dans le total est de croitre uniformement en perfection, l'universe des creatures doit avoir commencé. | Mais si l'univers gardoit la meme perfection totale il seroit plus raisonnable de la croire eternal. | Ainsi il se peut qu'il y ait une raison pour limiter la durée des choses, quand même il n'y en auroit point pour en limiter la quantité. Outre que le commencement des choses ne deroge point à l'infinité de leur durée; mais les bornes de l'univers derogeroient à l'infinité de son etendue. Ainsi il est plus raisonnable d'en poser un commencement, que d'en admettre des bornes.

Cependant ceux qui admettent l'eternité du monde, ou du moins que cette eternité du monde etoit possible, ne nient point pour cela, sa dependance de Dieu, comme on leur imputé icy sans fondement.

<u>Sur 22–23</u>

On m'objecte sans fondement que selon moy tout ce que Dieu peut faire, | il ne peut manquer de le faire | doit etre fait necessairement, comme si l'on ignoroit que j'ay refuté cela solidement dans la Theodicée. On confond la necessité morale, qui vient du choix du meilleur, avec la necessité absolue. On confond la volonté avec la toute puissance de Dieu. Dieu peut produire tout possible qui n'implique point contradiction, mais il veut produire le meilleur entre les possibles.

Dieu n'est point un agent necessaire en produisant les creatures puisqu'il agit par choix. Cependant ce qu'on adjoute icy est mal fondé, qu'un agent necessaire, n'est point un agent. On prononce souvent sans fondement.

<u>Sur 24–28</u>

On s'excuse de n'avoir point dit que l'espace est le sensorium de Dieu, mais il est <u>comme</u> son sensorium. Je crois que l'un est aussi peu intelligible et fondé que l'autre.

140A. FIRST DRAFT OF LEIBNIZ'S FIFTH PAPER

To 20

The author objected in the third paper (numbers 7 and 8) that God would not have any principle of acting in him if he were determined by external things. I responded that the ideas of external things are in him and that therefore he is determined by internal reasons, that is by his wisdom. Now the author does not want to understand what I have said.

To 21

I do not say that God cannot limit the quantity of matter, but that he does not will to do it without reason. From quantity to duration, *non valet consequentia*.[20] If the nature of things in the whole is to grow uniformly in perfection, the universe of creation must have come to be. | But if the universe kept the same total perfection, it would be more reasonable to believe that it is eternal. | So it is possible that there is a reason to limit the duration of things, even if there would not be any reason to limit its quantity. Besides, the beginning of things does not derogate from the infinity of their duration; but the limits of the universe would derogate from the infinity of its extension. So it is more reasonable to grant a beginning of it than to accept limits of it.

However, those who accept the eternity of the world, or at least that this eternity of the world was possible, do not on that account deny its dependence on God, as the author imputes to them here without basis.

To 22–23

The author objects without basis that according to me everything that God can do, | he cannot fail to do | must be done necessarily, as if he were not aware that I have soundly refuted that in the *Theodicy*. He confuses moral necessity, which comes from the choice of the best, with absolute necessity. He confuses will with the omnipotence of God. God can produce everything possible which does not imply a contradiction, but he will produce the best among possibles.

God is not a necessary agent in producing creatures since he acts by choice. However, what the author adds here is ill founded, that a necessary agent is not an agent. He often declares his opinion without basis.

To 24–28

The author declines having said that space is the sensorium of God, but it is *as if* his sensorium. I believe that the one is as little intelligible and well founded as the other.

Sur 29. L'Espace n'est pas la place de toutes choses. Car il n'est pas la place de Dieu; autrement ce seroit une chose coëternelle à Dieu et independante de luy. Je ne voy pas aussi comment on puisse dire que l'espace est la place des idées. Car les idées sont dans l'entendement. Il est fort étrange aussi de dire que l'esprit de l'homme est l'ame des images. Les images qui sont dans l'entendement sont dans l'esprit, mais s'il etoit l'ame des images elles seroient hors de luy. Je ne parle pas des images corporelles, car ce sont des corps.

[Sur 39][21]

(42) On ne prouvera jamais que le defaut du systeme des adversaires qui rend la machine du monde aussi imparfaite que celle d'un mauvais horloger soit une suite de l'inertie de la matiere. Cette inertie mise en avant par Kepler, fait seulement que les vistesses sont diminuées quand la matiere est augmentée; mais elle ne detruit point les forces.

Sur 39[22]

(43) Si le temps etoit quelque autre chose que ce qui fait le rapport des successions, s'il estoit quelque chose d'absolu; l'eternité du monde seroit veritablement demonstrée, comme j'ay montré: Mais ce la même prouve, que le temps n'est point quelque chose d'absolu.

Sur 41

(44) Je ne dis pas ordre ou situation, mais ordre de la situation ; ou plutost que je dis que l'espace (abstrait) est cet ordre selon lequel on conçoit les choses situables. C'est quelque chose d'ideal, tandis que les choses sont seulement conçues possibles. Il semble qu'on ne me veut point entendre.

(45) Quand le temps devient plus grand ou plus petit, l'ordere des successions n'est point le même comme on l'avance icy. Car il y a plus ou moins d'etats successifs interposés. Il n'y a point de vuide dans le temps ny dans le lieu.

(46) Comme le nombre abstrait est distingué de la multitude dans les choses; de même le temps abstrait differe de l'affection des choses qui s'appelle la durée et qui consiste dans le rapport de leur succession; et de même l'espace abstrait differe de l'entendue des choses.

(4| 6 |7) S'il n'y avoit point de creature, il n'y auroit point d'espace actuel. L'immensité de Dieu est independante de l'espace, comme son eternité est independante du temps. Ces verités ont eté assés reconnuës par les Theologiens et par les philosophes.

(48) Ainsi je n'admets point ce qu'on avance icy que si Dieu seul existoit, il y auroit temps et espace comme a present; car je ne les admettrois alors que dans les

140A. FIRST DRAFT OF LEIBNIZ'S FIFTH PAPER   651

To 29. Space is not the place of all things. For it is not the place of God; otherwise it would be a thing coeternal with God and independent of him. I also do not see how it can be said that space is the place of ideas. For ideas are in the understanding. It is also very strange to say that the mind of man is the soul of images. Images that are in the understanding are in the mind, but if it were the soul of images, they would be outside of it. I do not speak of corporeal images, for they are bodies.

[To 39][21]

(42) The author never proves that the defect of the opponents' system that makes the machine of the world as imperfect as that of a bad watchmaker is a result of the *inertia* of matter. This inertia, put forward by Kepler, causes only the speeds to be diminished when the matter is increased; but it does not destroy the forces.

To 39[22]

(43) If time were something other than what forms the relation of successions, if it were something absolute, the eternity of the world would be truly demonstrated, as I have shown. But this itself proves that time is not something absolute.

To 41

(44) I do not say *order or situation* but order of situation; or rather, I say that (abstract) space is this order according to which things capable of being situated are conceived. It is something ideal, while the things are only conceived possibles. It seems that the author does not want to understand me.

(45) When time becomes greater or smaller, the order of successions are not the same, as the author proposes here. For there are more or less successive states interposed. There is not any void in time or place.

(46) Just as abstract number is distinguished from the multitude of things, abstract time also differs from the affection of things called duration, which consists in the relation of their succession; and abstract space also differs from the extension of things.

(4| 6 |7) If there were no creature, there would be no actual space. The immensity of God is independent of space, as his eternity is independent of time. These truths have been sufficiently recognized by theologians and philosophers.

(48) Therefore I do not admit what the author proposes here, that if God alone existed, there would be time and space as they are at present; for in that case I would admit them only in ideas as possibilities.

idées comme des possibilités. (49) L'Eternité et l'immensité de Dieu sont quelque chose de plus eminent que la durée et l'etendüe des creatures. Ces attributs divins n'ont point besoin de choses hors de Dieu, telles que sont l'espace et le temps. Car j'ay déja refuté l'imagination que l'espace et le temps sont des attributs de Dieu.

Sur 42[23]

(50) Le sentiment commun des Theologiens ne doit pas être traité simplement en opinion vulgaire. Il faut de grandes raisons, pour oser y contrevenir, et je n'en vois icy.

[Sur 43]

(51) Si le miracle ne differe du naturel que dans l'apparence par rapport à nous, en sorte que nous appellions seulement miracle ce que nous observons rarement; il n'y aura point de difference interne solide entre le miracle et le naturel; et dans le fond des choses tout sera egalement naturel, ou tout sera egalement miraculeux.

(52) Les Theologiens auront ils raison de s'accommoder du premier, et les philosophes du second?

(53) Cela n'irat il pas encore à faire Dieu Ame du Monde? Car la creation sera detruite, il ne fera que gouverner sa machine, mais il ne la produira pas. Car la creation est un veritable miracle, differant reellement d'autres actions, et non seulement par rapport à nous; mais on me nie qu'il y en ait. Ainsi Dieu ne fera dans le monde que ce qu'on attribue à notre Ame dans son corps.

(53) Si toutes les operations de Dieu sont naturelles dans le fond, Dieu sera[24] partie de la nature, telle que devroit être l'ame du monde.

(54) Mais en saine philosophie et en bonne theologie, il faut distinguer ce qui est explicable par les natures et forces des creatures, de ce qui n'est explicable que par les forces de la substance infinie. Il faut mettre une distance infinie, entre les operations de Dieu qui produit les choses, et entre les operations des choses, qui suivent leurs loix, que Dieu y a mises, et qu'il les a rendu capables de suivre avec son assistance.

| 54 | (55) par là tombent les attractions proprement dites, et d'autres qualités occultes scholastiques qu'on nous debite sous le nom specieux de forces; et qui nous ramenent dans le royaume des tenebres, c'est inventa fruge glaudibus vesci[25].

(56) Du temps du Chevalier Boyle, et d'autres excellens hommes, qui fleurissoient en Angleterre sous Charles II. on n'auroit pas osé nous debiter des notions si creuses. Le Capital de M. Boyle estoit d'inculquer que tout se faisoit mechaniquement dans la physique.

(57) Mais c'est un malheur des hommes de se dégouster enfin de la raison même, et de s'ennuyer de la lumiere. Les chimeres commencent à revenir, et plaisent par ce qu'elles ont quelque chose de merveilleux.

140A. FIRST DRAFT OF LEIBNIZ'S FIFTH PAPER   653

(49) The eternity and immensity of God are something more eminent than the duration and the extension of creatures. These divine attributes do not have need of things outside of God, such as space and time. For I have already refuted the imagination that space and time are attributes of God.

To 42[23]

(50) The common view of theologians should not be treated merely *as vulgar opinion*. Substantial reasons are required to dare contravene them, and I do not see any of them here.

[To 43]

(51) If a miracle differs from the natural only in appearance and in relation to us, so that we call a miracle only what we rarely observe, there will be no internal, substantial difference between a miracle and the natural, and all things will ultimately be equally natural or equally miraculous.

(52) Do theologians have reason to agree with the first and philosophers with the second?

(53) Won't that again lead to making God soul of the world? For creation will be destroyed; he will govern his machine, but he will not produce it. For creation is a genuine miracle, really different from other actions, and not only in relation to us; but the author denies that there is any. Thus God will do in the world only what is attributed to our soul in the body.

(53) If all the operations of God are ultimately natural, God will be[24] part of nature, such as would be the soul of the world.

(54) But in sound philosophy and good theology, one must distinguish what is explicable by the natures and forces of creatures from what is explicable only by the forces of the infinite substance. An infinite distance must be placed between the operations of God, who produces things, and the operations of things that follow their laws, which God has placed in them and made them capable of following with his assistance.

| 54 | (55) With that, attractions properly so called fall, along with the other scholastic occult qualities that the author spouts to us under the specious name of forces, and which bring us back into the kingdom of darkness; it is 'to feed on acorns when grain has been found'.[25]

(56) At the time of Sir Robert Boyle* and other excellent men who flourished in England under Charles II, people would not have dared to spout to us such chimerical notions. The principal point of Mr. Boyle was to teach that everything was done mechanically in physics.

(57) But it is a misfortune for men to grow weary at last of reason and bored with the light. The chimeras are beginning to return, and they are pleasing because there is something wondrous about them.

654   140A. FIRST DRAFT OF LEIBNIZ'S FIFTH PAPER

(57) Il arrive dans le paÿs philosophique ce qui est arrivé dans le pays poëtique; on s'est lassé des Romans raisonnables, tels que la Clelie de Mlle Scudery ou l'Aramene du duc Antoine; et on est retourné depuis quelque temps aux Contes de Fées.

Sur 45

(58) On dit icy que l'attraction sans aucune <u>moyen</u> est une contradiction: fort bien.[28] Mais comment l'entend on donc, quand on veut que le soleil a travers d'un espace vuide attire la globe de la terre. Est ce Dieu, qui sert de <u>moyen</u>; et ce seroit un miracle, s'il y en a jamais eu, cela surpasseroit les forces des creatures.

(59) Ou sont ce peutetre quelques esprits immateriels, ou quelques rayons spirituels ou quelque accident sans substance, ou quelque autre je ne sçay quoy, qui fait ce <u>moyen</u> pretendu; choses dont il semble qu'on a encore bonne provision en tête sans s'assés expliquer.

(60) Ce moyen de communication est (dit-on) invisible, intangible; non-mechanique. On pourroit adjouter avec le même droit, inexplicable, non-intelligible, precaire, sans fondement, sans exemple.

(61) Mais dit on il est regulier, il est constant, et par consequent naturel. Mais il ne sauroit etre regulier sans etre raisonnable, il ne sauroit etre naturel sans etre explicable par les natures des creatures.

(6| 1 |2) Si ce moyen qui fait une veritable attraction est constant et en meme temps inexplicable par les forces des creatures, et s'il est veritable avec cela; il est un miracle perpetuel. Et s'il n'est pas miraculeux, il est faux, c'est une chose chimerique, une qualité occulte scholastique.

(6| 2 |3) Il seroit comme le cas d'un corps allant en rond sans s'ecarter par la tangente quoyque rien d'explicable l'empechât de le faire, exemple que j'ay déjà allegué au quel on n'a pas trouvé a propos de répondre, parce qu'il monstre trop clairement la difference entre le veritable naturel d'un coté, et entre la qualité occulte chimerique de l'école de l'autre coté.

Sur 44[29]

(6| 3 |4) Il n'y a point de Theologien que je sache, qui nie que les Angles[30] font des miracles, mais d'un ordre inferieur. Disputer là seroit une question de nom. Cet ange qui transportoit Habacuc par les airs, qui remuoit le Lac de Bethesda en faisoit un. Mais ce n'est pas un miracle de la grande sorte; il est explicable par les forces naturelles des anges, qui sont doués de corps plus efficaces que les notres. Je me suis déja expliqué la dessus; et je ne voy pas qu'on y oppose, ou puisse y opposer quelque chose de raisonnable.

140A. FIRST DRAFT OF LEIBNIZ'S FIFTH PAPER 655

(57) What has happened in the land of poetry is happening in the land of philosophy; people have grown weary of rational romances, such as Clélie by Mademoiselle Scudéry,[26] or *Aramène* by Duke Anton,[27] and for some time now they have returned to fairy tales.

To 45

(58) The author says here that attraction without any *means* is a contradiction. Very well.[28] But then how does he understand it when he will have the sun attract the globe of the earth across an empty space? Is it God who serves as the *means*? That would be a miracle, if any there have ever been; that would surpass the forces of creatures.

(59) These are perhaps some immaterial minds, or some spiritual rays, or some accident without substance, or some other thing I know not what that forms this supposed *means*—things of which it seems the author has still a good supply in his head without explaining himself sufficiently.

(60) This means of communication is (says he) invisible, intangible, non-mechanical. He could have added, with equal right, inexplicable, unintelligible, precarious, groundless, unexemplified.

(61) But, says he, it is regular, it is constant, and consequently natural. But it could not be regular without being reasonable, and it could not be natural without being explicable by the natures of creatures.

(6| 1 |2) If this means of causing a genuine attraction is constant and at the same time inexplicable by the forces of creatures, and if it is true along with that, it is a perpetual miracle. And if it is not miraculous, it is false, a chimerical thing, a scholastic occult quality.

(6| 2 |3) It would be like the case of a body going around without moving away along the tangent, even though nothing explicable impeded it from doing so—an example that I have already cited, to which the author has not found it fitting to respond, because it shows too clearly the difference between the true nature, on the one hand, and the chimerical occult quality of the school, on the other.

To 44[29]

(6| 3 |4) There is not any theologian I know who denies that angels[30] perform miracles, but of an inferior order. To dispute that would be a matter of a name. That angel who transported Habakkuk through the air,[31] who stirred the pool of Bethesda,[32] performed one of them. But this is not a miracle of the great kind; it is explicable by the natural forces of angels, who are endowed with bodies more efficacious than ours. I have already explained myself about that, and I do not see that the author opposes it there, or can oppose to it anything reasonable.

656 140A. FIRST DRAFT OF LEIBNIZ'S FIFTH PAPER

[Sur 45 et 46]

65

| (64) | Il n'y a rien dans la motion des animaux qui ne soit explicable par le pur mechanisme, ainsi il n'y a rien là de miraculeux que dans l'origine des animaux, dont le mechanisme,[33] est un organisme qui suppose une preformation divine, comme tout ce qui se fait dans l'univers.

(6| 5 |6) Tout ce qui se fait dans le corps de l'homme, et de tout animal, est aussi mecanique, que ce qui se fait dans une montre, la difference[34] est seulement telle que doit etre entre la machine d'une invention divine, et entre la production d'un ouvrier aussi borné que l'homme.

(67)

(| 67 |) Je finis par ce qu'on m'oppose au commencement de ce quatrieme écrit au quel je reponds maintenant. On y pretend dans le premier paragraphe, que je commets une petition de principe. Mais de quel principe je vous en prie? plût à Dieu qu'on n'eût jamais supposé de principes moins clairs.

(6| 7 |8) Ce principe est celuy du besoin d'une raison suffisante pour qu'un evenement arrive, qu'une chose existe, qu'une verité ait lieu. Est ce un principe qui ait besoin de prevuve?

(69) On me l'avoit même accordé, ou fait semblant de l'accorder, au second nombre du 3me papier, mais ou on ne l'a fait qu'en paroles, ou l'on se contredit, ou l'on se retracte.

(70)

| (68) | J'ose dire que sans ce grand principe on ne sauroit venir à la preuve de l'existence de Dieu, ny rendre raison | des loix du mouvement et des phenomenes de la nature | de plusieurs autres verités importantes.

(71) | (68)| Tout le monde ne s'en est il point servi en mille occasions? Il est vray qu'on l'a oublié en beaucoup d'autres: mais c'est justement l'origine des chimeres, comme par exemple d'un temps absolu reel, d'un espace absolu reel, du vuide des atomes, d'une attraction à la scholastique, de l'influence physique de l'ame sur le corps, et de mille autres fictions, tant celles qui sont restées de la fausse persuasion des anciens que celles qu'on a inventées depuis peu.

(72) | (69) | N'est ce pas a cause de la violation de ce grand principe que les anciens se sont déja moqués de la declinaison sans sujet des Atomes d'Epicure; et l'attraction a la scholastique, qu'on renouvelle aujourd'huy et dont on ne se moquoit pas moins il y a 30 ans, qu'at-elle de plus raisonnable.

(73) On veut que je ne l'ay point prouvé ny par la nature des choses, ny par les perfections divines. Mais la nature des choses doit contenir la raison de ce qui leur arrive; tout evenement à ses predispositions qui le distinguent.

(74) Et la perfection divine ne permet pas, que la volonté de Dieu agisse sans aucun motif conforme à sa sagesse.

140A. FIRST DRAFT OF LEIBNIZ'S FIFTH PAPER 657

[To 45 and 46]

(65)

| (64) | There is nothing in the motion of animals that is not explicable by pure mechanism, so there is nothing miraculous except in the origin of animals, whose mechanism[33] is an organism that presupposes a divine preformation, like everything that happens in the universe.

(6| 5 |6) Everything that happens in the body of man, and of every animal, is also mechanical, like what happens in a watch; the difference[34] is only such as must be between a machine of divine invention and the production of a workman as limited as man.

(67)

(| 67 |) I end with what the author sets against me at the beginning of this fourth paper, to which I now respond. In the first paragraph the author claims that I commit a *petitio principii*. But, pray you, of which principle,? Would to God that any less clear principles had ever been postulated.

(6| 7 |8) This principle is that of the need of a sufficient reason in order that an event happens, that a thing exists, that a truth holds. Is this a principle that needs proof?

(69) The author had even granted it, or pretended to grant it, in the second number of the third paper, but either he did it only in worlds, or he contradicts himself, or he recants.

(70)

| (68) | I dare say that without this great principle, it would not be possible to arrive at the proof of the existence of God, nor account for | the laws of motion and the phenomena of nature | many other important truths.

(71) | (68)| Hasn't everyone made use of it on a thousand occasions? It is true that it has been forgotten on many other occasions, but that is precisely the origin of chimeras, like, for instance, of a real absolute time, of a real absolute space, of a void with atoms, of a scholastic attraction, of the physical influence of the soul upon the body, and a thousand other fictions, both those that have remained from the false opinion of the ancients and those that have lately been invented.

(72) | 69 | Is it not on account of the violation of this great principle that the ancients already mocked the groundless declination of the atoms of Epicurus; and is the scholastic attraction, which is revived today, and which was no less mocked thirty years ago, any more reasonable?

(73) The author states that I have not proven it, either by the nature of things or by the divine perfections. But the nature of things must contain the reason for what happens to them; every event has its predispositions, which distinguish it.

(74) And the divine perfection does not permit the will of God to act without any motive conformed to his wisdom.

658   140A. FIRST DRAFT OF LEIBNIZ'S FIFTH PAPER

(73) | (70) | Me nier ce grand principe, c'est faire a peu prés comme Epicurus, qui étoit reduit à nier cet autre grand principe: que toute enontiation doit etre vraye ou fausse.

(74) Chrysippe s'amusoit a le prouver contre Epicure, mais je crois de n'avoir point besoin de l'imiter quoyque je puisse dire quelque chose là dessus, mais qui est trop profond pour convenir à cette presente contestation; et je crois que des personnes raisonnables et impartiales m'accorderont, que d'avoir reduit son adversaire à nier le mien, c'est l'avoir mené ad absurdum.

140A. FIRST DRAFT OF LEIBNIZ'S FIFTH PAPER   659

(73) | (70) | To deny me this great principle is to be almost like Epicurus, who was reduced to denying this other great principle, that all statements must be true or false.

(74) Chrysippus amused himself by proving it against Epicurus,[35] but I don't believe I need to imitate him; I am able say something about it, but it is too profound to be suitable for this present dispute, and I believe that reasonable and impartial persons will grant me that to have reduced an adversary to deny mine is to have led him *ad absurdum*.

---

[1] LBr. 160 Bl. 80r–83v. This is a relatively short first draft (eight folio sides in Leibniz's hand) of Leibniz's Fifth Paper. LBr. 160 Bl. 84r–95v is a greatly expanded second draft (twenty-four folio sides in Leibniz's hand). LBr. 160 Bl. 44r–52v/55r–72r (fifty-three folio sides) is a fair copy in a secretary's hand with changes in Leibniz's hand; LH 1, 20 Bl. 405r–420v (31.5 folio sides) is a fair copy in a secretary's hand with changes in Leibniz's hand. It answers Clarke's Fourth Reply (document 129). The version that was finally published in Clarke's 1717 edition of the correspondence is found in document 140b. This first draft was previously published in Robinet 1991, pp.122–82.

[2] That is, Leibniz's Fifth Paper, being his response to Clarke's Fourth Reply (document 129).

[3] Robinet 1991, p. 124, mistranscribes 'est' as 'paroist'.

[4] Robinet 1991, p. 128, mistranscribes 'nulle' as 'nul'.

[5] Robinet 1991, p. 131, mistranscribes 'solides' as 'vuides'.

[6] Robinet 1991, p. 131, mistranscribes 'chaque' as 'une'.

[7] Robinet 1991, p. 132, mistranscribes 'portions' as 'parties'.

[8] A farce written in 1687 by the English playwright Aphra Behn (1640–1689). It was published in 1688. Robinet 1991, p. 134, omits 'se disoit'.

[9] Robinet 1991, p. 135, mistakenly indicates that Leibniz had struck 'deux'.

[10] Robinet 1991, p. 137, mistranscribes 'que' as 'qui'.

[11] Robinet 1991, p. 140, omits the last three sentences.

[12] Robinet 1991, p. 147, mistranscribes 'les autres s'en puissent revetir' as 'cet autre s'en puise revitir' and omits the following sentence.

[13] Robinet 1991, p. 147, omits 'chimerique'.

[14] Robinet 1991, p. 147, omits this heading.

[15] Robinet 1991, p. 148, mistranscribes 'finis' as 'infinis'.

[16] Robinet 1991, p. 149, mistranscribes 'en cas ils' as 'en ce cas ils'.

[17] See the letter from Christiaan Huygens* to Leibniz of 24 August 1694 (SHS X 669–70).

[18] The material deleted here and in the following four paragraphs is moved to numbers 44–50 below.

[19] Robinet 1991, p. 155, mistranscribes 'Outre cela' as 'Au lieu de cela'.

[20] That is, 'a consequence from quantity to duration is not valid'.

[21] I have inserted this section heading since the manuscript shows no legible heading here. Paragraph 42 that follows addresses paragraph 39 of Clarke's Fourth Reply.

[22] Here Leibniz mistakenly wrote 'sur 39' instead of 'sur 40'. Robinet 1991, p. 170, mistakenly transcribes it as '40'.

[23] Robinet 1991, p. 173, omits this heading.

[24] Robinet 1991, p. 174, mistranscribes 'sera' as 'fera'.

[25] After Cicero, *Orator ad M. Brutum* 31: *Quae est autem in hominibus tanta perversitas, ut inventis frugibus glande vescantur?*

[26] That is, the French novelist Madeleine de Scudéry (1607–1701). Her lengthy novel *Clélie* was published in ten volumes between 1654 and 1660.

[27] That is, Anton Ulrich* of Braunschweig-Wolfenbüttel. His novel, *Die durchleuchtige Syrerinn Aramena*, was published in five volumes between 1669 and 1773.

[28] Robinet 1991, p. 177, mistakenly marks 'fort bien' as having been struck by Leibniz.

[29] Here Leibniz inverts 'Sur 44' and 'Sur 45'.

[30] Reading 'Anges' for 'Angles'.

[31] This story about Habakkuk is recounted in the apocrypha of the Book of Daniel 14:33–36.

[32] John 5:2.

Leibniz's Fifth Paper

Cinquiéme Ecrit de Mr. LEIBNITZ,

ou

Réponse au Quatriéme Ecrit Anglois.[2]

[Les differentes Leçons, imprimées à la Marge de l'Ecrit suivant, sont des changements faits de la *propre main* de Mr. *Leibnitz* dans une autre Copie de cet Ecrit, laquelle il envoya à un de ses amis en *Angleterre* peu de temps avant la mort.]

Sur § 1 & 2, du Papier precedent.

1. *Je répondray cette fois plus amplement, pour éclaircir les difficultés, & pour essayer si l'on est d'humeur à se payer de raison, & de donner des marques de l'amour de la verité, ou si l'on ne fera que chicaner sans rien éclaircir.*

2. *On s'efforce souvent à m'imputer la* necessité *& la* fatalité, *quoyque peut être personne n'ait mieux expliqué & plus à fond que j'ay fait dans la* Theodicée, *la veritable difference entre* Liberté, Contingence, Spontaneité, *d'un coté ; &* Necessité absolue, Hazard, Coaction, *de l'autre. Je ne sais pas encore si on le fait parce qu'on le veut, quoyque je puisse dire ; ou si ces imputations viennent de bonne foy, de ce qu'on n'a point encore pesé mes sentimens : J'experimenteray bien tôt ce que j'en dois juger, & je me regleray là dessus.*

3. *Il est vray que les* Raisons *font dans l'Esprit du Sage, & les* Motifs *dans quelque Esprit que ce soit, ce qui répond à l'effect que les* Poids *font dans une* Balance. *On objecte, que cette notion mene à la* Necessité *& à la* Fatalité. *Mais on le dit sans le prouver ; & sans prendre connoissance des* Explications *que j'ay données autres fois pour lever toutes les difficultés qu'on peut faire là dessus.*

4. *Il semble aussi, qu'on se joüe d'équivoque. Il y a des* Necessités, *qu'il faut admettre. Car il faut distinguer entre une* Necessité absoliie *& une* Necessité Hypothetique. *Il faut distinguer aussi entre une* Necessité *qui a lieu parceque l'opposé implique* Contradiction, *& laquelle est appellée* Logique, Metaphysique, *ou* Mathematique ; *& entre une* Necessité *qui est* Morale, *qui fait que le sage choisit le Meilleur, & que tout esprit suit l'Inclination la plus grande.*

5. *La* Necessité Hypothetique *est celle, que la* Supposition *ou* Hypothese *de la prévision & préordination de Dieu impose qux futurs contingens. Et il faut l'admettre si ce n'est qu'avec les* Sociniens *on refuse à Dieu la prescience des Contingens futurs, & la Providence qui regle & gouverne les choses en detail.*

33 Robinet 1991, p. 178, mistranscribes 'dont le mechanisme est' as 'dont la machine pure est'.

34 Robinet 1991, p. 179, inserts 'mais' before 'la différence', although in the manuscript Leibniz had struck 'mais'.

35 See Cicero, *De fato* X.

140b. Leibniz's Fifth Paper[1]

Mr. LEIBNITZ'S *Fifth Paper.*

BEING

An Answer to Dr. CLARKE'S *Fourth Reply.*[2]

To § 1 & 2, *of the foregoing Paper.*

1. I Shall at This Time make a *larger* Answer ; to clear the difficulties ; and to try whether the Author be willing to hearken to reason, and to show that he is a lover of truth ; or whether he will only cavil, without clearing any thing.

2. He often endeavours to impute to me *Necessity and Fatality* ; though perhaps no One has better and more fully explained, than I have done in my *Theodicæa*, the true difference between *Liberty, Contingency, Spontaneity*, on the one Side ; and absolute *Necessity, Chance, Coaction*, on the other. I know not yet, whether the Author does this, because he *will* do it, whatever I may say ; or whether he does it, (supposing him sincere in those imputations,) because he has *not yet* duly *considered* my Opinions. I shall soon find what I am to think of it, and I shall take my measures accordingly.

3. It is true, that *Reasons* in the *Mind* of a Wise Being, and *Motives* in Any Mind whatsoever, do that which answers to the effect produced by *Weights* in a *Balance*. The Author objects, that this Notion leads to *Necessity* and *Fatality*. But he says so, without proving it, and without taking notice of the explications I have formerly given, in order to remove the difficulties that may be raised upon that Head.

4. He seems also to play with *Equivocal* Terms. There are *Necessities*, which ought to be admitted. For we must distinguish between an *absolute* and an *Hypothetical Necessity*. We must also distinguish between a *Necessity*, which takes place because the Opposite implies Contradiction ; (which necessity is called *Logical, Metaphysical,* or *Mathematical* ;) and a *Necessity* which is *Moral*, whereby a Wise Being chuses the Best, and every Mind follows the strongest Inclination.

5. *Hypothetical Necessity* is that, which the Supposition or *Hypothesis* of God's *Foresight* and *Pre-ordination* lays upon *future Contingents*. And This must needs be admitted, unless we deny, as the *Socinians* do, God's *Foreknowledge of future Contingents*, and his *Providence* which regulates and governs every particular thing.

6. *Mais ny cette prescience ny cette Preordination ne derogent point à la* Liberté. *Car Dieu porté par la Supreme Raison à choisir, entre plusieurs suites des choses ou Mondes possibles, celuy où les Creatures libres prendroient telles ou telles Resolutions, quoyque non sans son concours ; a rendu, par là, leur évenement certain & determiné une fois pour toutes : sans deroger par là à la Liberté de ces Creatures : Ce simple decret du choix, ne changeant point, mais actualisant seulement leur Natures libres qu'il y voyoit dans ses Idees.*

7. *Et quant à la Necessité* Morale, *elle ne deroge point non plus à la* Liberté. *Car lors que le sage, &, sur tout, Dieu, (le sage souverain,) choisit le Meilleur, il n'en est pas moins libre ; au contraire, c'est la plus parfaite Liberté, de n'être point empeché d'agir le mieux. Et lors qu'un autre choisit selon le bien le plus apparent, & le plus inclinant ; il imite en cela la Liberté du sage à proportion de sa disposition. Et sans cela, le choix seroit un hazard aveugle.*

8. *Mais le bien, tant vray qu'apparent, en un mot le motif, incline sans necessiter ; C'est à dire, sans imposer un Necessité absolue. Car lors que Dieu (pour exemple) choisit le Meilleur ; ce qu'il ne choisit point, & qui est inferieur en Perfection, ne laisse pas d'être possible. Mais si ce que Dieu choisit, estoit absolument Necessaire, tout autre parti seroit impossible ; contre l'Hypothese : Car Dieu choisit parmy les possibles, c'est à dire parmy plusieurs partis, dont pas un n'implique Contradiction.*

9. *Mais de dire que Dieu ne peut choisir que le meilleur, & d'en vouloir inferer que ce qu'il ne choisit point, est impossible ; C'est confondre les termes ; la* Puissance, *& la* Volonté ; *la* Necessité Metaphysique, *& la* Necessité Morale ; *les* Essences, *& les* Existences. *Car ce qui est necessaire, l'est par son Essence, puisque l'opposé implique Contradiction ; mais le Contingent qui existe, doit son existence au principe du Meilleur,* Raison suffisante *des choses. Et c'est pour cela que je dis, que les Motifs inclinent sans necessiter ; & qu'il y a une certitude & infallibilité, mais non pas une* Necessité absolüe *dans les choses contingents. Joignez à cecy, ce qui se dira plus bas,* Nomb. 73 & 76.

10. *Et j'ay assez montré dans ma* Theodicée *que cette* Necessité Morale *est heureuse, conforme à la perfection Divine, conforme au grand principe des Existences, qui est celuy du besoin d'une* Raison suffisante ; *au lieu que la Necessité absolue & Metaphysique, depend de l'autre grand principe de nos raisonnemens, qui est celuy des Essences, c'est à dire celuy de l'Identité, ou de la Contradiction : Car ce qui est absolument Necessaire, est seul possible entre les partis, & son contraire implique Contradiction.*

11. *J'ay fait voir aussi, que notre* Volonté *ne* suit *pas tousjours precisement l'En*tendement practique, *parcequ'elle peut avoir ou trouver des raisons pour* suspendre *sa Resolution jusqu'à une discussion ulterieure.*

12. *M'imputer aprés cela une* Necessité absolue, *sans avoir rien à dire contre des Considerations que je viens d'apporter, & qui vont jusqu'au fond des choses, peut être au delà de ce qui se voit ailleurs ; ce sera une obstination déraisonnable.*

6. But neither That *Foreknowledge*, nor That *Pre-Ordination*, derogate from *Liberty*. For God, being moved by his Supreme Reason to chuse, among many Series of Things or Worlds possible, That, in which free Creatures should take such or such Resolutions, though not without his Concourse ; has thereby rendred every Event certain and determined once for all ; without derogating thereby from the Liberty of those Creatures : That simple decree of Choice, not at all changing, but only *actualizing* their free Natures, which he saw in his ideas.

7. As for *Moral* Necessity, This also does not derogate from *Liberty*. For when a Wise Being, and especially God, who has Supreme Wisdom, chuses what is Best, he is not the less free upon that account : On the contrary, it is the most perfect Liberty, not to be hindered from acting in the best manner. And when Any Other chuses according to the most apparent and most strongly inclining Good, he imitates therein the Liberty of a truly Wise Being, in proportion to his disposition. Without this, the Choice would be a blind Chance.

8. But Good, either true or apparent, in a word, the Motive, inclines without necessitating ; that is, without imposing an *absolute Necessity*. For when God (for Instance,) chuses the Best ; what he does not chuse, and is inferior in Perfection, is nevertheless possible. But if what he chuses, was absolutely necessary ; any other way would be impossible : Which is against the Hypothesis. For God chuses among Possibles, that is, among many ways, none of which implies a Contradiction.

9. But to say, that God can only chuse what is *Best* ; and to infer from thence, that what he does not chuse, is impossible ; this, I say, is confounding of Terms : 'Tis blending *Power* and *Will*, *Metaphysical Necessity* and *Moral Necessity*, *Essences* and *Existences*. For, what is *necessary*, is so by its Essence, since the Opposite implies a Contradiction ; But a Contingent which exists, owes its Existence to the *Principle of what is Best*, which is a *sufficient Reason* for the Existence of Things. And therefore I say that Motives incline without necessitating ; and that there is a Certainty and Infallibility, but not an absolute Necessity in contingent Things. Add to this, what will be said hereafter, *Numb. 73 and 76*.

10. And I have sufficiently shown in my *Theodicæa*, that this *Moral Necessity* is a good Thing, agreeable to the Divine Perfection ; agreeable to the great Principle or Ground of *Existences*, which is that of *the Want of a sufficient Reason* : Whereas *Absolute and Metaphysical Necessity*, depends upon the Other great Principle of our Reasonings, *viz.* that of *Essences* ; that is, the Principle of Identity or Contradiction : For, what is absolutely necessary, is the only possible Way, and its contrary implies a Contradiction.

11. I have also shown, that our *Will* does *not* always exactly *follow* the *Practical Understanding* ; because it may have or find *Reasons* to *suspend* its Resolution till a further Examination.

12. To impute to me after this, the Notion of an *absolute Necessity*, without having any thing to say against the *Reasons* which I have just now alledged, and which go to the Bottom of Things, perhaps beyond what is to be seen elsewhere ; This, I say, will be an unreasonable Obstinacy.

664   140B. LEIBNIZ'S FIFTH PAPER

13. *Pour ce qui est de la* Fatalité, *qu'on m'impute aussi, c'est encore une Equivoque. Il y a* fatum Mahometanum, fatum Stoicum, fatum Christianum. Le destin à la Turque, *veut que les Effets arriveroient quand on en éviteroit la cause ; comme s'il y avoit une Necessité absolue.* Le destin Stoicien *veut qu'on soit tranquille, parce qu'il faut avoir patience par force, puisqu'on ne sauroit regimber contre la suite des choses. Mais on convient qu'il y a* fatum Christianum, *une destinée certaine de toutes choses, reglée par la Preference & par la Providence de Dieu.* Fatum *est derivé de* fari, *c'est à dire,* prononcer, decerner *; & dans le bon sens, il signifie le decret de la Providence. Et ceux qui s'y sousmettent par la connoissance des Perfections Divines, dont l'amour de Dieu est une suite,* * *ne prennent pas seulement patience comme les Philosophes Payens, mais ils sont même contents de ce que Dieu ordonne, sachans qu'il fait tout pour le mieux, & non seulement pour le plus grand bien en general, mais encore pour le plus grand bien particulier de ceux qui l'aiment.*

14. *J'ay été obligé de m'étendre, pour detruire une bonne fois les imputations mal fondées, comme j'espere de pouvoir faire par ces Explications dans l'Esprit de Personnes équitables. Maintenant je viendray à une Objection qu'on me fait icy contre la comparaison des* Poids *d'une* Balance *avec les* Motifs *de la* Volonté. *On objecte que la* Balance *est purement passive, & poussée par les* Poids, *au lieu que les Agens intelligens & doués de volonté sont* actifs. *A cela je reponds, que le Principe du besoin d'une* Raison suffisante *est commun aux* Agens *& aux* Patiens : *Ils ont besoin d'une* Raison suffisante *de leur* Action, *aussi bien que de leur* Passion. *Non seulement la* Balance *n'agit pas, quand elle est poussée Egalement de part & d'autre ; mais les* Poids Egaux *aussi n'agissent point quand ils sont en Equilibre, en sorte que l'un ne peut descendre sans que l'autre monte autant.*

15. *Il faut encore considerer qu'à proprement parler, les Motifs n'agissent point sur l'Esprit comme les Poids sur la Balance ; mais c'est plûtôt l'Esprit qui agit en vertu des Motifs, qui sont ses Dispositions à agir. Ainsi vouloir, comme l'on veut icy, que l'Esprit prefere quelques fois les Motifs foibles aux plus forts, & même l'indifferent aux Motifs ; c'est separer l'*Esprit *des* Motifs, *comme s'ils étoient* hors de luy, *comme le Poids est distingué de la Balance ; & comme si* dans l'Esprit *il y avoit d'autres* Dispositions *pour agir que les* Motifs, *en vertu desquelles l'Esprit rejetteroit où accepteroit les* Motifs. *Au lieu que dans la verité* les Motifs comprennent *toutes les* Dispositions *que l'Esprit peut avoir pour agir volontairement ; Car ils ne comprennent pas seulement les* Raisons, *mais encore les* Inclinations *qui viennent des Passions ou d'autres impressions precedentes. Ainsi si l'Esprit preferoit l'Inclination foible à la forte, il agiroit contre soy même, & autrement qu'il est* disposé *d'agir. Ce qui fait voir que les Notions contraires icy aux miennes, sont superficielles, & se trouvent n'avoir rien de solide, quand elles sont bien considerées.*

---

* (Puisq ; il consiste dans le plaisir que donne cette connoisance,)

140B. LEIBNIZ'S FIFTH PAPER   665

13. As to the Notion of *Fatality*, which the Author lays also to my Charge ; this is another Ambiguity. There is a *Fatum Mahometanum*, a *Fatum Stoicum*, and a *Fatum Christianum*. The *Turkish Fate* will have an Effect to happen, even though its Cause should be avoided ; as if there was an *Absolute Necessity*. The *Stoical Fate* will have a Man to be quiet, because he must have Patience whether he will or not, since 'tis impossible to resist the Course of Things. But 'tis agreed, that there is *Fatum Christianum*, a *Certain Destiny* of every Thing, regulated by the Foreknowledge and Providence of God. *Fatum* is derived from *Fari* ; that is, *to Pronounce*, to *Decree* ; and in its right Sense, it signifies the Decree of Providence. And those who submit to it through a Knowledge of the Divine Perfections, whereof the Love of God is a Consequence {since it consists in the pleasure that this knowledge gives,} ; have not only Patience, like the Heathen Philosophers, but are also contented with what is ordained by God, knowing he does every thing for the best ; and not only for the greatest Good in general, but also for the greatest particular Good of those who love him.

14. I have been obliged to enlarge, in order to remove ill-grounded Imputations once for all ; as I hope I shall be able to do by these Explications, so as to satisfy equitable Persons. I shall now come to an *Objection* raised here, against my comparing the *Weights* of a *Balance* with the *Motives* of the *Will*. 'Tis objected, that a *Balance* is merely *Passive*, and mov'd by the Weights ; whereas Agents intelligent, and endowed with Will, are *Active*. To this I answer, that the *Principle of the Want of a sufficient Reason* is common both to *Agents* and *Patients* : They want a *sufficient Reason* of their *Action*, as well as of their *Passion*. A *Balance* does not only not act, when it is equally *pulled* on both Sides ; but the *equal Weights* likewise do not act when they are in an *Æquilibrium*, so that one of them cannot go down without the others rising up as much.

15. It must also be considered, that, properly speaking, Motives do not act upon the Mind, as Weights do upon a Balance ; but 'tis rather the Mind that acts by virtue of the Motives, which are *its Dispositions* to act. And therefore to pretend, as the Author does here, that the Mind prefers sometimes weak Motives to strong ones, and even that it prefers that which is *indifferent* before *Motives* : This, I say, is to *divide* the *Mind* from the *Motives*, as if they were *without* the *Mind*, as the Weight is distinct from the Balance ; and as if the *Mind* had, besides *Motives*, other *Dispositions* to act, by Virtue of which it could reject or accept the *Motives*. Whereas, in truth, the *Motives* comprehend *all the Dispositions*, which the Mind can have to act voluntarily ; for they *include* not only the *Reasons*, but also the *Inclinations* arising from Passions, or other preceding Impressions. Wherefore, if the Mind should prefer a weak *Inclination* to a strong one, it would act against it self, and otherwise than it is disposed to act. Which shows that the Author's Notions, contrary to mine, are superficial, and appear to have no Solidity in them, when they are well considered.

16. *De dire aussi que l'*Esprit peut avoir de bonnes Raisons pour agir, *quand il n'a* aucuns Motifs, *& quand les choses sont* absolument indifferentes, *comme on s'explique icy ; c'est une Contradiction manifeste. Car s'il a de bonnes Raisons pour le parti qu'il prend, les choses ne luy sont point indifferentes.*

17. *Et de dire qu'on agira quand on a des* Raisons *pour agir,* quand même les voyes d'agir seroient absolument indifferentes ; *c'est encore parler fort superficiellement, & d'une manière tres insoutenable. Car on n'a jamais une* Raison suffisante *pour* agir, *quand on n'a pas aussi une* Raison suffisante *pour agir* tellement ; *toute action estant individuelle, & non generale ny abstraite des ses Circonstances, & ayant besoin de quelque voye pour étre Effectuée. Donc quand il y a une* Raison suffisante *pour agir* tellement, *il y en a aussi pour agir par une telle* voye ; *& par consequent les voyes ne sont point* indifferentes. *Toutes les fois qu'on a des* Raisons suffisantes *pour une action singuliere, on en a pour ses requisits. Voyés encore ce qui se dira plus bas,* Nom. 66.

18. *Ces raisonnemens sautent aux yeux ; & il est bien estrange de m'imputer que j'avance mon principe du besoin d'une* Raison suffisante, *sans aucune preuve tirée ou de la Nature des choses, ou des perfections Divines. Car la* nature des choses *porte que tout évenement ait preallablement ses Conditions, Requisits, Dispositions convenables, dont l'existence en fait la Raison suffisante.*

19. *Et la* perfection de Dieu *demande que toutes ses actions soyent conformes à sa sagesse, & qu'on ne puisse point luy reprocher d'avoir agi sans Raison, ou méme d'avoir preferé une Raison plus foible à une Raison plus forte.*

20. *Mais je parleray plus amplement sur la fin de ce papier, de la solidité & de l'importance de ce grand Principe du* besoin d'une Raison suffisante *pour tout évenement ; dont le renversement renverseroit la meilleure partie de toute la Philosophie. Ainsi il est bien étrange qu'on veut icy qu'en cela je commets une* Petition de Principe ; *& il paroist bien qu'on veut soutenir des sentimens insoutenables, puisq'on est reduit à me refuser ce grand Principe, un des plus essentiels de la Raison.*

Sur § 3 & 4.

21. *Il faut avouer que ce grand Principe, quoyqu'il ait été reconnu, n'a pas été assez employé. Et c'est en bonne partie la Raison pourquoy jusqu'icy la* Philosophie premiere *a été si peu feconde, & si peu Demonstrative. J'en infere entre autres consequences, qu'il n'y a point dans la Nature deux Etres réels absolus indiscernables ; parceque s'il y en avoit, Dieu & la Nature agiroient sans Raison, en traitant l'un autrement que l'autre ; & qu'ainsi Dieu ne produit point deux portions de matiere parfaitement* égales *& semblables. On repond à cette Conclusion, sans en refuter la Raison ; & on y repond par une Objection bien foible. Cet* Argument (*dit on*) s'il

140B. LEIBNIZ'S FIFTH PAPER   667

16. To assert also, that the *Mind may have good Reasons to act*, when it has *no Motives*, and *when Things are absolutely indifferent*, as the Author explains himself here ; this, I say, is a manifest Contradiction. For if the Mind has *good Reasons* for taking the *Part* it takes, then the Things are not *indifferent* to the Mind.

17. And to affirm that the Mind will act, when it has *Reasons* to act, *even though the Ways of acting were absolutely indifferent* : This, I say, is to speak again very superficially, and in a manner that cannot be defended. For a Man never has a sufficient Reason to *act*, when he has not also a sufficient Reason to act *in a certain particular manner* ; every Action being Individual, and not general, nor abstract from its Circumstances, but always needing some particular way of being put in Execution. Wherefore, when there is a sufficient Reason to do any particular Thing, there is also a sufficient Reason to do it in a certain particular manner ; and consequently, several manners of doing it are not *indifferent*. As often as a Man has sufficient Reasons for a single Action, he has also sufficient Reasons for all its Requisites. See also what I shall say below, *Numb. 66.*

18. These Arguments are very obvious ; and 'tis very strange to charge me with advancing my Principle of *the Want of a sufficient Reason*, without any Proof drawn either from the Nature of Things, or from the Divine Perfections. For the *Nature of Things* requires, that every Event should have before-hand its proper Conditions, Requisites, and Dispositions, the Existence whereof makes the sufficient Reason of such Event.

19. And *God's Perfection* requires, that all his Actions should be agreeable to his Wisdom ; and that it may not be said of him, that he has acted without Reason ; or even that he has prefer'd a weaker Reason before a stronger.

20. But I shall speak more largely at the Conclusion of this Paper, concerning the Solidity and Importance of this great Principle, of the *want of a sufficient Reason* in order to every Event ; the overthrowing of which Principle would overthrow the best part of all Philosophy. 'Tis therefore very strange that the Author should say, I am herein guilty of a *Petitio Principii* ; and it plainly appears he is desirous to maintain indefensible Opinions, since he is reduced to deny That great Principle, which is one of the most essential Principles of Reason.

To § 3, and 4.

21. It must be confessed, that though this great Principe has been acknowledged, yet it has not been sufficiently made use of. Which is, in great measure, the Reason why the *Prima Philosophia* has not been hitherto so fruitful and demonstrative, as it should have been. I infer from that Principle, among other Consequences, that there are not in Nature *two* real, absolute Beings, *indiscernible* from each other ; because if there were, God and Nature would act without Reason, in ordering the one otherwise than the other ; and that therefore God does not produce *Two* Pieces

estoit bon, prouveroit, qu'il seroit impossible à Dieu de créer aucune matiere. Car les parties de la matiere parfaitement solides, estant prises égales & de la même Figure, (ce qui est une Supposition possible,) seroient exactement faites l'une comme l'autre. *Mais c'est une Petition de principe tres manifeste, de supposer cette parfaite convenance, qui selon moy ne sauroit étre admise. Cette Supposition de* deux indiscernables, *comme de deux portions de matiere qui conviennent parfaitement entre elles, paroist possible en termes abstraits ; mais elle n'est point compatible avec l'ordre des choses, ny avec la sagesse Divine, où rien n'est admis sans Raison. Le vulgaire s'imagine de telles choses, parce qu'il se contente de Notions incompletes. Et c'est un des defauts des* Atomistes.

22. *Outre que je n'admets point dans la matiere des portions parfaitement* solides, *ou qui soyent tout d'une piece, sans aucune varieté ou mouvement particulier dans leur parties, comme l'on conçoit les pretendus Atomes. Poser de tels Corps, est encore une Opinion populaire mal fondée. Selon mes demonstrations, chaque portion de matiere est* actuellement *sous-divisée en parties differemment mües, & pas une ne ressemble entierement à l'autre.*

23. *J'avois allegué, que dans les choses* sensibles *on n'en trouve jamais deux* indiscernables, *& que (par exemple) on ne trouvera point deux* feuilles *dans un jardin, ny deux gouttes d'eau parfaitement semblables. On l'admet à l'egard des feuilles, & peut etre (perhaps), à l'égard des gouttes d'eau. Mais on pouvoit l'admettre sans balancer, ou sans* perhaps, *(senza forse, diroit un Italien,) encore dans les gouttes d'eau.*

24. *Je crois que ces Observations generales qui se trouvent dans les choses* sensibles, *se trouvent encore à proportion dans les* insensibles. *Et qu'à cet egard on peut dire, comme disoit* Arlequin *dans* l'Empereur d' la Lune, *que c'est tout comme icy. Et c'est un grand prejugé contre les* indiscernables, *qu'on n'en trouve aucun exemple. Mais on s'oppose à cette consequence, parce que (dit on) les Corps* sensibles *sont* Composes, *au lieu qu'on soutient qu'il y a d'insensibles qui sont* Simples. *Je reponds encore, que je n'en accorde point. Il n'y a rien de* Simple *selon moy, que les veritables* Monades, *qui n'ont point de Parties ny d'Etendue. Les Corps Simples, et même les parfaitement similaires, sont une suite de la fausse Position du* Vuide *& des* Atomes, *ou d'ailleurs de la Philosophie paresseuse, qui ne pousse pas assez l'analyse des choses, & s'imagine de pouvoir parvenir aux premiers Elemens Corporels de la Nature, parceque cela contenteroit nostre Imagination.*

25. *Quand je nie qu'il y ait deux gouttes d'eau entierement semblables, ou deux autres Corps* indiscernables ; *Je ne dis point qu'il soit* impossible absolument *d'en poser, mais que c'est une chose contraire à la Sagesse Divine, & qui par consequent n'existe point.*

of Matter perfectly *equal* and *alike*. The Author answers this Conclusion, without confuting the Reason of it ; and he answers with a very weak Objection. *That Argument, says he, if it was good, would prove that it would be impossible for God to create any Matter at all. For, the perfectly solid Parts of Matter, if we take them of equal Figure and Dimensions (which is always possible in Supposition,) would be exactly alike.* But 'tis a manifest *Petitio Principii* to suppose *That perfect Likeness,* which, according to me, cannot be admitted. This Supposition of two *Indiscernibles,* such as two Pieces of Matter perfectly alike, seems indeed to be *possible* in abstract Terms ; but it is not consistent with the Order of Things, nor with the Divine Wisdom, by which nothing is admitted without Reason. The Vulgar fancy such Things, because they content themselves with incomplete Notions. And this is one of the Faults of the *Atomists.*

22. Besides ; I don't admit in Matter, Parts perfectly *Solid,* or that are the same throughout, without any Variety or particular *Motion* in their Parts, as the pretended Atoms are imagined to be. To suppose such Bodies, is another popular Opinion ill-grounded. According to my Demonstrations, every Part of Matter is *actually* subdivided into Parts differently *moved,* and no one of them is perfectly *like* another.

23. I said, that in *sensible* Things, *two,* that are *indiscernible* from each other, can never be found ; that (for Instance) two *Leaves* in a Garden ; or two *Drops* of Water, perfectly alike, are not to be found. The Author acknowledges it as to *Leaves,* and *perhaps* as to *Drops* of Water. But he might have admitted it, without any Hesitation, without a *perhaps,* (as an Italian would say, *Senza Forse,*) as to *Drops* of Water likewise.

24. I believe that these general Observations in Things *sensible,* hold also in proportion in Things *insensible* ; and that one may say, in this Respect, what *Harlequin* says in the *Emperor of the Moon* ;[3] *'Tis there, just as 'tis here.* And 'tis a great Objection against *Indiscernibles,* that no instance of them is to be found. But the Author opposes this Consequence, because (says he) *sensible* Bodies are *compounded* ; whereas he maintains there are *insensible* Bodies, which are *simple.* I answer again, that I don't admit *simple* Bodies. There is nothing *simple,* in my Opinion, but true *Monads,* which have neither parts nor extension. Simple Bodies, and even perfectly similar ones, are a consequence of the false Hypothesis of a *Vacuum* and of *Atoms,* or of *Lazy* Philosophy, which does not sufficiently carry on the *Analysis* of things, and fancies it can attain to the first material Elements of Nature, because our Imagination would be therewith satisfied.

25. When I deny that there are Two Drops of Water perfectly alike, or any two other Bodies *Indiscernible* from each other ; I don't say, 'tis absolutely *impossible* to suppose them ; but that 'tis a thing contrary to the divine *Wisdom,* and which consequently does not exist.

Sur § 5 & 6.

26. *J'avoue que si deux choses parfaitement* indiscernables *existoient, elles seroient* Deux. *Mais la Supposition est fausse, & contraire au grand Principe de la raison. Les Philosophes vulgaires se sont trompés lors qu'ils ont crû qu'il y avoit des choses differentes* solo numero, *ou seulement parce qu'elles sont* Deux ; *& c'est de cette erreur que sont venues leurs perplexités sur ce qu'ils appelloient le* principe d'individuation. *La Metaphysique a été traitée ordinairement en simple Doctrine des* Termes, *comme un Dictionnaire Philosophique, sans venir à la discussion des Choses. La Philosophie superficielle, comme celle des Atomistes & Vacuistes, se forge des choses que les raisons superieures n'admettent point. J'espere que mes Demonstrations feront changer de face à la Philosophie, malgré les foibles contradictions telles qu'on m'oppose icy.*

27. *Les Parties du Temps ou du Lieu, prises* en elles-mêmes, *sont des choses Ideales ; ainsi elles se ressemblent parfaitement, comme deux* Unités abstraites. *Mais il n'en est pas de même de deux* uns concrets, *ou de deux Temps* effectifs, *ou de deux Espaces* remplis, *c'est à dire veritablement* actuels.

28. *Je ne dis pas que* deux *points de l'Espace sont un* même *point, ny que* deux *Instans du temps sont un* même *Instant, comme il semble qu'on m'impute : Mais on peut s'imaginer, faute de connoissance, qu'il y a* Deux *Instans differens, où il n'y en a qu'*Un ; *Comme j'ay remarqué dans l'*Article 17 de la precedente Reponse, *que souvent en Geometrie on suppose* Deux, *pour representer l'erreur d'un contredisant, & on n'en trouve qu'*Un. *Si quel qu'un supposoit qu'une ligne droite coupe l'autre en* deux *points, il se trouvera au bout du compte, que ces* deux *points pretendus doivent coincider, & n'en sauroient faire qu'*Un.

29. *J'ay demontré que l'Espace n'est autre chose qu'un* ordre de l'Existence des *Choses, qui se remarque dans leur simultaneité. Ainsi la Fiction d'un Univers materiel* fini, *qui se promene tout entier dans un Espace vuide infini, ne sauroit étre admise. Elle est tout à fait deraisonnable &* impracticable. *Car outre qu'il n'y a point d'Espace réel hors de l'Univers materiel ; une telle Action seroit sans but, ce seroit travailler sans rien faire,* agendo nihil agere. *Il ne se produiroit aucun changement observable par qui que ce soit. Ce sont des Imaginations des* Philosophes à Notions incompletes, *qui se font l'Espace une realité absolue. Les Simples Mathematiciens, qui ne s'occupent que de jeux de l'Imagination, sont capables de se forger de telles Notions ; mais elles sont detruites par des Raisons Superieures.*

30. *Absolument parlant, il paroist que* Dieu peut *faire l'*Univers materiel *fini en* Extension ; *mais le contraire paroist plus conforme à sa Sagesse.*

31. *Je n'accorde point que tout* fini *est* mobile. *Selon l'Hypothese même des Adversaires, une* Partie de l'Espace, *quoyque* finie, *n'est point* mobile. *Il faut que ce qui est* mobile, *puisse changer de Situation par rapport à quelque autre chose, & qu'il puisse arriver un Etat nouveau discernable du premier : Autrement le changement est*

To § 5 and 6.

26. I own, that if two things perfectly *indiscernible* from each other did exist, they would be *Two* ; but That Supposition is false, and contrary to the Grand Principle of Reason. The vulgar Philosophers were mistaken, when they believed that there are things different *solo numero,* or only because they are *two* ; And from this error have arisen their perplexities about what they called the *Principle of Individuation.* Metaphysicks have generally been handled like a Science of mere *Words,* like a Philosophical Dictionary, without entering into the discussion of *Things.* Superficial Philosophy, such as is that of the *Atomists* and *Vacuists,* forges things, which superior Reasons do not admit. I hope My Demonstrations will change the Face of Philosophy, notwithstanding such weak Objections as the Author raises here against me.

27. The *Parts* of *Time* or *Place,* considered *in themselves,* are *ideal* things ; and therefore they perfectly resemble one another, like two *abstract Units.* But it is not so with two *concrete Ones,* or with two *real Times,* or two *Spaces filled up,* that is, truly *actual.*

28. I don't say that *two* Points of Space are *one and the same* point, nor that *two* Instants of Time *are one and the same* Instant, as the Author seems to charge me with saying. But a Man may fancy, for want of Knowledge, that there are two different Instants, where there is but one : In like manner as I observed in the 17th Paragraph of the foregoing Answer, that frequently in Geometry we suppose *Two,* in order to represent the error of a gainsayer, when there is really but *One.* If any man should suppose that a right Line cuts another in two Points ; it will be found after all, that those two pretended Points must co-incide, and make but *One* Point.

29. I have demonstrated, that *Space* is nothing else but an *Order* of the existence of things, observed as existing Together ; And therefore the Fiction of a material finite Universe, moving forward in an infinite empty Space, cannot be admitted. It is altogether unreasonable and *impracticable.* For, besides that there is *no real Space* out of the material Universe ; such an Action would be without any Design in it : It would be working without doing any thing, *agendo nihil agere.* There would happen *no Change,* which could be observed by Any Person whatsoever. These are Imaginations of *Philosophers who have incomplete notions,* who make Space an absolute Reality. Mere Mathematicians, who are only taken up with the Conceits of Imagination, are apt to force such Notions ; but they are destroyed by superior Reasons.

30. Absolutely speaking, it appears that God can make the material Universe *finite* in Extension ; but the contrary appears more agreeable to his Wisdom.

31. I don't grant, that *every Finite* is *moveable.* According to the Hypothesis of my Adversaries themselves, a *part* of *Space,* though *finite,* is not *moveable.* What is moveable, must be capable of changing its situation with respect to *something else,* and to be in a new state *discernible* from the first : Otherwise the Change is but

une *fiction. Ainsi il faut qu'un fini mobile fasse partie d'un autre, afin qu'il puisse arriver un* changement observable.

32. Des Cartes *a soutenu que la Matiere n'a point de bornes, & je ne crois pas qu'on l'ait suffisamment* refuté. *Et quand on le luy accorderoit, il ne s'ensuit point, que la Matiere seroit necessaire, ny qu'elle ait été de tout éternité ; puisque cette Diffusion de la Matiere sans Bornes, ne seroit qu'un effect du Choix de Dieu, qui l'auroit trouvé mieux ainsi.*

Sur § 7.

33. *Puisque l'Espace en soy est une chose ideale comme le Temps, il faut bien que l'Espace hors du Monde soit imaginaire, comme les Scholastiques mêmes l'ont bien reconnu. Il en est de même de l'Espace vuide dans le Monde ; que je crois encore être imaginaire, par les Raisons que j'ay produites.*

34. *On m'objecte le* vuide *inventé par M.* Guerike de Magdebourg, *qui se fait en pompant l'air d'un Recipient ; & on pretend qu'il y a veritablement du vuide parfait, ou de l'Espace sans Matiere, en partie au moins, dans ce Recipient. Les* Aristoteliciens *& les* Cartesiens, *qui n'admettent point le veritable vuide, ont repondu à cette Experience de M.* Guerike, *aussi bien qu'à celle de M.* Torricelli de Florence (*qui vuidoit l'air d'un tuyau de verre par le moyen du Mercure,) qu'il n'y a point de vuide du tout dans le tuyau ou dans le Recipient ; puisque le verre a des Pores subtils, à travers desquels les Rayons de la Lumiere, ceux de l'aimant, & autres matieres tres minces peuvent passer. Et je suis de leur Sentiment, trouvant qu'on peut comparer le Recipient à une caisse pleine de trous, qui seroit dans l'eau, dans laquelle il y auroit des Poissons, ou d'autres Corps grossiers, lesquels en étant ôtés, la place ne laisseroit pas d'être remplie par de l'eau : Il y a seulement cette difference, que l'eau, quoyqu'elle soit fluide & plus obeissante que ces Corps grossiers, est pourtant aussi pesante & aussi massive, ou même d'avantage ; au lieu que la Matiere qui entre dans le Recipient à la place de l'Air, est bien plus mince. Les nouveaux Partisans du vuide repondent à cette Instance, que ce n'est pas la grossiereté de la Matiere, mais simplement sa quantité, qui fait de la Resistence ; & par consequent qu'il y a necessairement plus de vuide, où il y a moins de resistence. On adjoute que la subtilité n'y fait rien, & que les parties du vif argent sont aussi subtiles & fines que celles de l'eau, & que neantmoins le vif argent resiste plus de dix fois d'avantage. A cela je replique, que ce n'est pas tant la quantité de la Matiere, que la difficulté qu'elle fait de ceder, qui fait la resistence. Par Exemple, le* bois flottant *contient moins de Matiere pesante que l'eau de pareil volume, & neantmoins il resiste plus au bateau que l'eau.*

35. *Et quant au* vif Argent, *il contient à la verité environ quatorze fois plus de Matiere pesante que l'eau, dans un pareil Volume ; mais il ne s'ensuit point qu'il contienne quatorze fois plus de Matiere absolument. Au contraire, l'eau en contient autant ; mais prenant ensemble tant sa propre Matiere qui est pesante, qu'une*

a Fiction. A *moveable Finite*, must therefore make part of another *Finite*, that any Change may happen which can be *observed*.

32. *Cartesius* maintains, that *Matter* is *unlimited*; and I *don't* think he has been sufficiently *confuted*. And though this be granted him, yet it does not follow that Matter would be *necessary*, nor that it would have existed from all *eternity*; since That unlimited diffusion of Matter, would only be an effect of God's *Choice*, judging That to be the better.

To § 7.

33. Since *Space* in it self is an *Ideal* thing, like *Time*; Space *out of the World* must needs be imaginary, as the *Schoolmen* themselves have acknowledged. The case is the same with empty Space *within* the World; which I take also to be imaginary, for the reasons before alledged.

34. The Author objects against me the *Vacuum* discovered by Mr. *Guerike*[4] of *Magdeburg*, which is made by pumping the Air out of a *Receiver*; And he pretends that there is truly a perfect *Vacuum*, or a Space without Matter, (at least in part,) in that *Receiver*. The *Aristotelians* and *Cartesians*, who do not admit a true *Vacuum*, have said in answer to that Experiment of Mr. *Guerike*, as well as to that of *Torricellius*[5] of *Florence*, (who emptied the Air out of a Glass-Tube by the help of Quick-Silver,) that there is no *Vacuum* at all in the Tube or in the Receiver; since Glass has small Pores, which the Beams of Light, the *Effluvia* of the Load-Stone, and other very thin fluids may go through. I am of their Opinion: And I think the Receiver may be compared to a Box full of Holes in the Water, having Fish or other gross Bodies shut up in it; which being taken out, their place would nevertheless be filled up with Water. There is only this difference; that though Water be fluid and more yielding than those gross Bodies, yet it is as heavy and massive, if not more, than they: Whereas the Matter which gets into the Receiver in the room of the Air, is much more subtile. The new Sticklers for a *Vacuum* allege in answer to this Instance, that it is not the *grossness* of Matter, but its mere *quantity*, that makes resistance; and consequently that there is of necessity *more Vacuum*, where there is *less Resistance*. They add, that the *subtleness* of Matter has nothing to do here; and that the particles of *Quick-Silver* are as subtle and fine as those of *Water*; and yet that *Quick-Silver* resists above *Ten times more*. To this I reply, that it is not so much the *quantity* of Matter, as its *difficulty of giving place*, that makes *resistance*. For instance; *floating Timber* contains *less* of heavy Matter, than an equal Bulk of *Water* does; and yet it makes *more resistance* to a Boat, than the *Water* does.

35. And as for *Quick-Silver*; 'tis true, it contains about Fourteen times more of *heavy* Matter, than an equal Bulk of *Water* does; but it does not follow, that it contains Fourteen times more Matter absolutely. On the contrary, *Water* contains as much Matter; if we include both its own Matter, which is heavy; and the extraneous Matter void of heaviness, which passes through its Pores. For, both *Quick-Sliver*

Matiere étrangere non pesante, qui passe travers de ses pores. Car tant le vif Argent que l'Eau, sont des Masses de Matiere pesante, percées à jour, à travers desquelles passe beaucoup de Matiere non pesante *, *comme est apparemment celle des Rayons de lumiere, & d'autres fluides insensibles ; tels que celuy sur tout, qui cause luy même la pesanteur des Corps grossiers, en s'écartant du centre où il les fait aller. Car c'est une étrange fiction que de faire toute la Matiere pesante, & même vers toute autre Matiere, comme si tout Corps attiroit également tout autre Corps selon les Masses & les Distances ; & cela par une* Attraction *proprement dite, qui ne soit point derivée d'une Impulsion occulte des Corps : Au lieu que la pesanteur des Corps sensibles vers le Centre de la terre, doit étre produite par le mouvement de quelque fluide. Et il en sera de même d'autres pesanteurs, comme de celles des Planetes vers le soleil, ou entre elles* †.

Sur § 8 & 9.

36. *Comme j'avois objecté que l'Espace pris pour quelque chose de réel & d'absolu sans les Corps, seroit une Chose éternelle, impassible, independante de Dieu ; on a taché d'éluder cette difficulté, en disant que l'Espace est une proprieté de Dieu. J'ay opposé à cela dans mon Papier precedent, que la proprieté de Dieu est l'immensité ; mais que l'Espace, qui est souvent commensuré avec les Corps, & l'immensité de Dieu, n'est pas la même chose.*

37. *J'ay encore objecté, si l'Espace est une proprieté, & si l'Espace* infini *est l'Immensité de Dieu, que l'Espace* fini *sera l'Etendue ou la mensurabilité de quelque chose finie. Ainsi l'Espace occupé par un Corps, sera l'Etendue de ce Corps : Chose absurde, puisqu'un Corps peut changer d'Espace, mais il ne peut point quitter son Etendue.*

38. *J'ay encore demandé, si l'Espace est une Proprieté, de quelle chose sera donc la Proprieté un Espace vuide* borné, *tel qu'on s'imagine dans le Recipient épuisé d'air ? il ne paroist point raisonnable de dire, que cet Espace vuide, rond ou quarré, soit une Proprieté de Dieu. Sera ce donc peut être la Proprieté de quelques Substances immaterielles, étendues, imaginaires, qu'on se figure (ce semble) dans les Espaces imaginaires ?*

39. *Si l'Espace est la Proprieté ou l'Affection de la Substance qui est dans l'Espace, le même Espace sera tantôt l'Affection d'un Corps, tantôt d'un autre Corps, tantost d'une Substance* immaterielle, *tantost peut étre de Dieu, quand il est vuide de toute autre Substance materielle ou immaterielle. Mais voilà une estrange Propieté ou Affection, qui passe de sujet en sujet. Les sujets quitteront ainsi leurs accidens comme*

---

* (Et qui ne resiste point sensiblement,)

† Un Corps n'est jamais mû naturellement, que par un autre Corps qui le pousse en le touchant ; & aprés cela il continue jusqu'à ce qu'il soit empeché par un autre Corps qui le touche. Toute autre Operation sur les Corps, est ou miraculeuse ou imaginaire.

and *Water*, are masses of heavy matter, full of Pores, through which there passes a great deal of Matter void of Heaviness {and which produces no sensible resistance} ; such as is probably that of the Rays of Light, and other insensible Fluids ; and especially that which is it self the Cause of the gravity of gross Bodies, by receding from the Center towards which it drives those Bodies. For, it is a strange Imagination to make all Matter gravitate, and That towards all other Matter, as if each Body did equally *attract* every other Body according to their Masses and distances ; and this by an *Attraction* properly so called, which is not derived from an occult impulse of Bodies : Whereas the gravity of sensible Bodies towards the Centre of the Earth, ought to be produced by the motion of some Fluid. And the case must be the same with other gravities, such as is that of the Planets towards the Sun, or towards each other. {A body is never moved naturally except by another body that pushes it while touching it ; and then it continues until it is hindered by another body that touches it. Any other operation on bodies is either miraculous or imaginary.}

To § 8, *and* 9.

36. I objected, that Space, taken for something real and absolute without Bodies, would be a thing eternal, impassible, and independent upon God. The Author endeavours to elude this Difficulty, by saying that Space is a property of God. In answer to this, I have said, in my foregoing Paper, that the Property of God is *Immensity* ; but that *Space* (which is often commensurate with Bodies,) and God's Immensity, are not the same thing.

37. I objected further, that if Space be a property, and *infinite Space* be the *Immensity* of *God* ; *finite Space* will be the *Extension* or *Mensurability* of something *finite*. And therefore the *Space* taken up by a *Body*, will be the *Extension of that Body*. Which is an absurdity ; since a Body can change *Space*, but cannot leave its *Extension*.

38. I asked also ; if Space is a *Property*, What thing will an empty *limited Space*, (such as that which my Adversary imagines in an exhausted Receiver,) be the Property of ? It does not appear reasonable to say, that this empty Space, either round or square, is a Property of God. Will it be then perhaps the Property of some immaterial, extended, imaginary Substances, which the Author seems to fancy in the imaginary Spaces ?

39. If Space is the Property or Affection of the Substance, which is in Space ; the *same Space* will be sometimes the *Affection* of *One Body*, sometimes of *another Body*, sometimes of an *immaterial* Substance, and sometimes perhaps of *God* himself, when it is void of all other Substance material or immaterial. But this is a strange *Property* or *Affection*, which *passes from one Subject to another*. Thus

un habit, à fin que d'autres sujets s'en puissent revestir. Aprés cela, comment distinguera t'on les Accidens & les Substances ?

40. Que si les Espaces bornés sont les Affections des Substances bornées qui y sont, & si l'Espace infini est la Proprieté de Dieu ; il faut (chose étrange) que la Proprieté de Dieu soit composée des Affections des Creatures ; car tous les Espaces pris ensemble composent l'Espace infini.

soit.   41. Que si l'on nie que l'Espace borné * est une Affection des choses bornées ; il ne sera pas raisonnable non plus, que l'Espace infini soit l'Affection ou la Proprieté d'une chose infinie. J'avois insinué toutes ces difficultés dans mon papier precedent. Mais il ne paroist point qu'on ait taché d'y satisfaire.

42. J'ay encore d'autres Raisons contre l'étrange Imagination que l'Espace est une Proprieté de Dieu. Si cela est, l'Espace entre dans l'essence de Dieu. Or l'Espace a des parties : donc il y auroit des parties dans l'essence de Dieu. Spectatum admissi.[6]

43. De plus, les Espaces sont tantost vuides, tantost remplis : donc il y aura dans l'essence de Dieu des parties tantôt vuides, tantôt remplies, & par consequent sujettes à un changement perpetuel. Les Corps remplissant l'Espace, rempliroient une partie de l'essence de Dieu, & y seroient commensurés, &, dans la Supposition du vuide, une partie de l'essence de Dieu sera dans le Recipient. Ce Dieu à parties, ressemblera fort au Dieu Stoicien, qui estoit l'Univers tout entier consideré comme un Animal divin.

44. Si l'Espace infini est l'immensité de Dieu, le Temps infini sera l'éternitè de Dieu : Il faudra donc dire que ce qui est dans l'Espace, est dans l'immensité de Dieu, &
est dans l'eternité de Dieu.   par consequent dans son Essence ; & que ce qui est dans le Temps, * est aussi dans l'essence de Dieu. Phrases etranges, & qui font bien connoistre qu'on abuse des termes.

45. En voicy encore une autre instance. L'immensité de Dieu, fait que Dieu est dans tous les Espaces. Mais si Dieu est dans l'Espace, comment peut on dire que l'Espace est en Dieu, ou qu'il est sa proprieté ? On a bien oui dire que la Proprieté soit dans le Sujet, mais on n'a jamais öui dire que le Sujet soit dans sa Proprieté. De même, Dieu existe en chaque Temps : Comment donc le temps est il dans Dieu ; & comment peut il étre une Proprieté de Dieu ? Ce sont des Alloglossies[7] perpetuelles.

46. Il paroist qu'on confond l'immensité ou l'étendue des choses, avec l'Espace selon lequel cette étendue est prise. L'Espace infini n'est pas l'immensité de Dieu, l'Espace fini n'est pas l'étendue des Corps ; comme le temps n'est point la durée. Les choses gardent leur étendue, mais elles ne gardent point toujours leur Espace. Chaque chose a sa propre étendue, sa propre durée ; mais elle n'a point son propre temps, & elle ne garde point son propre Espace.

47. Voicy comment les hommes viennent à se former la notion de l'Espace. Ils considerent que plusieurs choses existent à la fois, & ils y trouvent un certain ordre de coexistence, suivant lequel le rapport des uns & des autres est plus ou moins simple. C'est leur Situation ou distance. Lors qu'il arrive qu'un de ces coexistens

140B. LEIBNIZ'S FIFTH PAPER   677

Subjects will leave off their Accidents like Cloaths ; that Other Subjects may put them on. At this rate, how shall we distinguish Accidents and Substances ?

40. And if *limited Spaces* are the *Affections* of *limited Substances*, which are in them ; and *infinite Space* be a Property of *God* ; a Property of God must (which is very strange,) be made up of the Affections of Creatures ; For All finite Spaces, taken together, make up infinite Space.

41. But if the Author denies, that *limited Space* is an *Affection* of *limited Things* ; it will not be reasonable neither, that *infinite Space* should be the *Affection* or Property of an *infinite thing*. I have suggested all these difficulties in my foregoing Paper ; but it does not appear that the Author has endeavoured to answer them.

42. I have still other Reasons against this strange Imagination, that Space is a Property of God. If it be so, Space belongs to the *Essence* of God. But Space has *parts* : Therefore there would be *parts* in the *Essence* of God. *Spectatum admissi.*[6]

43. Moreover, Spaces are sometimes empty, and sometimes filled up. Therefore there will be in the Essence of God, Parts sometimes empty, and sometimes full, and consequently liable to a perpetual *Change*. Bodies, filling up Space, would fill up part of God's Essence, and would be commensurate with it ; and in the Supposition of a *Vacuum*, Part of God's Essence will be within the *Receiver*. Such a *God having Parts*, will very much resemble the *Stoicks* God, which was the whole Universe considered as a Divine Animal.

44. If infinite *Space* is God's *Immensity*, infinite *Time* will be God's *Eternity* ; and therefore we must say, that what is in Space, is in God's Immensity, and consequently in his Essence ; and that what is in Time, {is in the eternity of God} is also in the Essence of God. *Strange* Expressions ; which plainly show, that the Author makes a wrong use of Terms.

45. I shall give another Instance of This. God's Immensity makes him actually present in all Spaces. But now if God is *in* Space, how can it be said that Space is *in* God, or that it is a Property of God ? We have often heard, that a Property is in its Subject ; but we never heard, that a Subject is in its Property. In like manner, God exists *in* all Time. How then can Time be *in* God ; and how can it be a Property of God ? These are perpetual *Alloglossies.*[7]

46. It appears that the Author confounds Immensity, or the *Extension of Things*, with the *Space* according to which that Extension is taken. Infinite Space, is not the Immensity of God ; Finite Space, is not the Extension of Bodies : As Time is not their Duration. Things keep their Extension ; but they do not always keep their Space. Every Thing has its own Extension, its own Duration ; but it has not its own Time, and does not keep its own Space.

47. I will here show, *how* Men come to form to themselves the Notion of *Space*. They consider that many things exist at once, and they observe in them a certain *Order* of Co-Existence, according to which the relation of one thing to another is more or less simple. This Order, is their *Situation* or Distance. When it happens that one of those Co-existent Things changes its *Relation* to a Multitude of others, which do not change

678   140B. LEIBNIZ'S FIFTH PAPER

de ce rapport, change de rapport à une multitude d'autres, sans qu'ils en changent entre eux ; & qu'un nouveau venu acquiert le rapport tel que le premier avoit eu à d'autres ; on dit qu'il est venu à sa place, & on appelle ce changement un mouvement qui est dans celuy où est la cause immediate du changement. Et quand plusieurs, ou même tous, changeroient selon certains regles connues de direction & de vistesse ; on peut tousjours determiner le rapport de Situation que chacun acquiert à chacun ; & même celuy que chaque autre auroit, ou qu'il auroit à chaque autre, s'il n'avoit point changé, ou s'il avoit autrement changé. Et supposant ou feignant que parmy ces coexistens il y ait un nombre suffisant de quelques uns, qui n'ayent point eu de changement en eux ; on dira que ceux qui ont un rapport à ces existens fixes, tel que d'autres avoient auparavant à eux, ont eu la même place que ces derniers avoient eue. Et ce qui comprend toutes ces places, est appellé Espace. Ce qui fait voir que pour avoir l'idée de la place, & par consequent de l'Espace, il suffit de considerer ces rapports & les regles de leurs changemens, sans avoir besoin de se figurer icy aucune realité absolue hors des choses dont on considere la Situation. Et, pour donner une Espece de definition, Place est ce qu'on dit étre le même à A & B, quand le rapport de coexistence de B, avec C, E, F, G, &c. convient entierement avec le rapport de coexistence qu'A a eu avec les mêmes ; supposé qu'il n'y ait eu aucune cause de changement dans C, E, F, G, &c. On pourroit dire aussi, sans ecthese, que place est ce qui est le même en momens differens à des existens quoyque differens, quand leur rapports de coexistence avec certains existens, qui depuis un de ces momens à l'autre sont supposés fixes, conviennent entierement. Et existens fixes sont ceux dans lesquels il n'y a point eu cause du changement de l'ordre de coexistence avec d'autres ; ou (ce qui est le même) dans lesquels il n'y a point eu de mouvement. Enfin, Espace est ce qui resulte des places prises ensemble. Et il est bon icy de considerer la difference entre la Place, & entre le rapport de Situation qui est dans le Corps qui occupe la place. Car la place d'A & de B est la même ; au lieu que le rapport d'A aux corps fixes, n'est pas precisement & individuellement le même que le rapport que B (qui prendra sa place) aura aux

*ces rapports conviennent memes fixes ; & *ils conviennent seulement. Car deux sujets differens, comme A & B, ne sauroient avoir precisement la même affection individuelle ; un même accident individuel ne se pouvant point trouver en deux sujets, ny passer de sujet en sujet. Mais l'esprit non content de la convenance, cherche une identité, une chose qui soit veritablement la même, & la conçoit comme hors de ces sujets ; & c'est ce qu'on appelle icy place & Espace. Cependant cela ne sauroit être qu'ideal, contenant un certain ordre où l'esprit conçoit l'application des rapports : Comme l'esprit se peut figurer un ordre consistant en lignes Genealogiques, dont les grandeurs ne conisteroient que dans le nombe des Generations, où chaque Personne auroit sa place ; Et si l'on adjoutoit la fiction de la metempsychose ; & faisoit revenir les mêmes ames humanes, les Personnes y pourroient changer de place ; Celuy qui a été pere ou grand pere, pourroit devenir fils ou petit fils, &c. Et cependant ces places, lignes, & Espaces Genealogiques, quoy qu'elles exprimeroient des verités réelles, ne seroient que chose ideales. Je donneray

their Relation among themselves ; and that another thing, newly come, acquires the same Relation to the others, as the former had ; we then say, it is come into the *Place* of the former ; And this Change, we call a *Motion* in That Body, wherein is the immediate Cause of the Change. And though Many, or even All the Co-existent Things, should change according to certain known Rules of Direction and Swiftness ; yet one may always determine the Relation of Situation, which every Co-existent acquires with respect to every other Co-existent ; and even That Relation, which any other Co-existent would have to this, or which this would have to any other, if it had not changed, or if it had changed any otherwise. And supposing, or feigning, that among those Co-existents, there is a sufficient Number of them, which have undergone no Change ; then we may say, that Those which have such a *Relation* to those fixed Existents, as Others had to them before, have now the same *Place* which those others had. And That which comprehends *all those Places*, is called *Space*. Which shows, that in order to have an Idea of *Place*, and consequently of *Space*, it is sufficient to consider these *Relations*, and the Rules of their Changes, without needing to fancy any absolute Reality *out of* the Things whose Situation we consider. And, to give a kind of a Definition : *Place* is That, which we say is the same to A and, to B, when the *Relation* of the Co-existence of B, with $C, E, F, G, \&c.$ agrees perfectly with the Relation of the Co-existence, which A had with the same $C, E, F, G, \&c.$ supposing there has been no cause of Change in $C, E, F, G, \&c.$ It might be said also, without entering into any further Particularity, that *Place* is That, which is the Same in different moments to different existent Things, when their *Relations of Co-existence* with certain Other Existents, which are supposed to continue fixed from one of those Moments to the other, agree intirely together. And *fixed Existents* are those, in which there has been no cause of any Change of the *Order* of their Co-existence with others ; or (which is the same Thing,) in which there has been no *Motion*. Lastly, *Space* is That which results from *Places taken together*. And here it may not be amiss to consider the Difference between *Place*, and the *Relation of Situation*, which is in the Body that fills up the Place. For, the *Place* of A and B, is the *same* ; whereas the *Relation* of A to fixed Bodies, is not precisely and individually the *same*, as the Relation which B (that comes into its Place) will have to the same fixed Bodies ; But these Relations *agree* only. For, two different Subjects, as A and B, cannot have precisely the *same* individual Affection ; it being impossible, that the same individual Accident should be in two Subjects, or pass from one Subject to another. But the Mind not contented with an Agreement, looks for an Identity, for something that should be truly the same ; and conceives it as being extrinsick to the Subjects : And this is what we here call *Place* and *Space*. But this can only be an Ideal Thing ; containing a certain *Order*, wherein the Mind conceives the Application of Relations. In like manner, as the Mind can fancy to it self an *Order* made up of *Genealogical Lines*, whose Bigness would consist only in the Number of Generations, wherein every Person would have his Place : And if to this one should add the Fiction of a *Metempsychosis*, and bring in the *same* Human Souls again ; the

encore un exemple de l'usage de l'esprit de se former, à l'occasion des accidens qui sont dans les sujets, quelque chose qui leur reponde hors des sujets. La Raison ou Proportion entre deux lignes, L, & M, peut etre concüe de trois façons : Comme Raison du plus grand L, au moindre M ; comme Raison du moindre M, au plu grand L ; & enfin comme quelque chose d'abstrait des deux, c'est à dire comme la Raison entre L & M, sans considerer lequel est l'anterieur ou le posterieur, le sujet ou l'objet : Et c'est ainsi que les proportions sont considerées dans la Musique. Dans la premiere consideration, L le plus grand, est le sujet ; Dans la seconde, M le moindre, est le sujet de cet accident, que les Philosophes appellent relation ou rapport : Mais quel en sera le sujet dans le troisieme sens ? On ne sauroit dire que tous les deux, L & M ensemble, * sont le sujet d'un tel accident ; car ainsi nous aurions un accident en deux sujets, qui auroit une jambe dans l'un, & l'autre dans l'autre ; ce qui est contre la notion des accidens. Donc il faut dire, que ce rapport dans ce[8] troisieme sens, est bien hors des sujets ; mais que n'étant ny substance ny accident, cela doit étre une chose purement ideale, dont la consideration ne laisse pas d'étre utile. Au reste, j'ay fait icy à peu pres comme Euclide, qui ne pouvant pas bien faire entendre absolument ce que c'est que Raison prise dans le sens des Geometres, definit bien ce que c'est que mêmes Raisons. Et c'est ainsi que, pour expliquer ce que c'est que la Place, j'ay voulu definir ce que c'est que la même Place. Je remarque enfin, que les traces des mobiles, qu'ils laissent quelques fois dans les immobiles sur lesquels ils exercent leur mouvement ; ont donné à l'imagination des hommes l'occasion de se former cette idée, comme s'il restoit encore quelque trace lors même qu'il n'y a aucune chose immobile : Mais cela n'est qu'ideal, & porte seulement que s'il y avoit là quelque immobile, on l'y pourroit designer. Et c'est cette Analogie qui fait qu'on s'imagine des Places, des Traces, des Espaces, quoyque ces choses ne consistent que dans la verité des Rapports, & nullement dans quelque realité absolue.

* soient le &c.

48. *Au reste, si l'Espace vuide de corps (qu'on s'imagine) n'est pas vuide tout à fait, de quoy est il donc plein ? Y a-t-il peut étre des Esprits étendus, ou des Substances immaterielles capables de s'étendre & de se resserrer, qui s'y promenent, & qui se penetrent sans s'incommoder, comme les ombres de deux corps se penetrent sur la surface d'une muraille ? Je voy revenir les plaisantes Imaginations de feu M. Henry Morus (homme savant & bien intentionné d'ailleurs,) & de quelques autres, qui ont crû que ces Esprits se peuvent rendre impenetrables quand bon leur semble. Il y en a même eu, qui se sont imaginé que l'homme dans l'état d'integrité, avoit aussi le don de la penetration ; mais qu'il est devenu solide, opaque & impenetrable, par as cheute. N'est ce pas renverser les Notions des choses, donner à Dieu des parties, donner de l'étendue aux Esprits ? Le seul principe du* besoin *de la Raison suffisante, fait disparoitre tous ces spectres d'Imagination. Les Hommes se font aisement des fictions, faute de bien employer ce grand Principe.*

Persons in those Lines might change Place; he who was a Father or a Grand-Father, might become a Son, or a Grand-Son, &c. And yet those Genealogical *Places*, *Lines*, and *Spaces*, though they should express real Truths, would only be Ideal Things. I shall allege another Example, to show how the Mind uses, upon occasion of Accidents which are *in* Subjects, to fancy to it self something answerable to those Accidents, *out of* the Subjects. The *Ratio* or *Proportion* between two Lines *L* and *M*, may be conceived three several Ways; as a *Ratio* of the greater *L*, to the lesser *M*; as a *Ratio* of the lesser *M*, to the greater *L*; and lastly, as something abstracted from Both, that is, as the *Ratio* between *L* and *M*, without considering which is the Antecedent, or which the Consequent; which the Subject, and which the Object. And thus it is, that Proportions are considered in Musick. In the first way of considering them, *L* the greater; in the second, *M* the lesser, is the Subject of That Accident, which Philosophers call *Relation*. But, Which of them will be the Subject, in the Third way of considering them? It cannot be said that both of them, *L* and *M* together, are the Subject of such an Accident; for if so, we should have an Accident in two Subjects, with one Leg in one, and the other in the other; Which is contrary to the Notion of Accidents. Therefore we must say, that this Relation, in this Third way of considering it, is indeed *out of* the Subjects; but being neither Substance, nor an Accident, it must be a mere Ideal Thing, the consideration of which is nevertheless useful. To conclude : I have here done much like *Euclid*, who not being able to make his Readers well understand what *Ratio* is absolutely in the Sense of Geometricians; defines what are the *same Ratio's*. Thus, in like manner, in order to explain what *Place* is, I have been content to define what is the *same Place*. Lastly; I observe, that the Traces of moveable Bodies, which they leave sometimes upon the immoveable ones on which they are moved; have given Men occasion to form in their Imagination such an Idea, as if some Trace did still remain, even when there is Nothing unmoved. But this is a mere Ideal Thing, and imports only, that *if there was any unmoved thing there, the Trace might be marked out upon it.* And 'tis This Analogy, which makes Men fancy *Places*, *Traces* and *Spaces*; though those things consist only in the Truth of *Relations*, and not at all in any absolute Reality.

48. To conclude. If the Space (which the Author fancies) void of all Bodies, is not altogether empty; what is it then full of? Is it full of extended Spirits perhaps, or immaterial Substances, capable of extending and contracting themselves; which move therein, and penetrate each other without any Inconveniency, as the Shadows of two Bodies penetrate one another upon the Surface of a Wall? Methinks I see the revival of the *odd* Imaginations of Dr. *Henry More*[9] (otherwise a Learned and well-meaning Man,) and of some Others, who fancied that those Spirits can make themselves impenetrable whenever they please. Nay, some have fancied, that *Man*, in the State of Innocency, had also the Gift of Penetration; and that he became Solid, Opake, and Impenetrable by his Fall. Is it not overthrowing our Notions of Things, to make God have Parts, to make Spirits have Extension? The Principle of the *Want of a sufficient Reason* does alone drive away all these Spectres of Imagination. Men easily run into Fictions, for want of making a right Use of that great Principle.

682   140B. LEIBNIZ'S FIFTH PAPER

Sur § 10.

49. *On ne* * *sauroit dire que la* Duration *est éternelle, mais que les* choses *qui durent toujours, sont éternelles. Tout ce qui existe du Temps & de la Duration, perit continuellement : Et comment une chose pourroit elle exister éternellement, qui à parler exactement n'existe jamais ? Car comment pourroit exister une chose, dont jamais aucune partie n'existe ? Du Temps n'existent jamais que des instans, & l'instant n'est pas même une partie du temps. Quiconque considerera ces Observations, comprendra bien que le Temps ne sauroit être qu'une chose ideale ; & l'analogie du Temps & de l'Espace fera bien juger, que l'un est aussi ideal que l'autre.* †

50. *Si la realité de l'Espace & du Temps est necessaire pour l'immensité & l'éternité de Dieu ; s'il faut que Dieu soit dans des Espaces ; si étre dans l'Espace est une Proprieté de Dieu ; Dieu sera en quelque façon dependant du Temps & de l'Espace, & en aura besoin. Car l'échappatoire que l'Espace & le Temps* ‖ *sont des Proprietés de Dieu, est deja fermé.*

Sur § 11 & 12.

51. *Comme j'avois objecté que l'Espace ne sauroit étre en Dieu, parce que l'Espace a des* parties ; *on cherche un autre échappatoire en s'éloignant du sens receu des termes, & soûtenant que l'Espace n'a point de parties, parceque ses parties ne sont point separables, & ne sauroient étre eloignées les unes des autres par discerption. Mais il suffit que l'Espace ait des parties, soit que ces parties soyent separables ou non ; & on les peut assigner dans l'Espace, soit par les corps qui y sont, soit par les lignes ou surfaces qu'on y peut mener.*

Sur § 13.

52. *Pour prouver que l'Espace sans les corps, est quelque realité absolue ; on m'avoit objecté que l'Univers materiel fini, se pourroit promener dans l'Espace. J'ay repondue, qu'il ne paroist point* raisonnable *que l'Univers materiel soit* fini ; *Et quand on le supposeroit, il est deraisonnalbe qu'il ait de* mouvement *autrement qu'entant que ses parties changent de Situation entre elles ; parcequ'un tel mouvement ne produiroit aucun* changement observable, *& seroit sans but. Autre chose est quand ses Parties*

---

* *peut point dire qu'une certaine durée est eternelle ; mais on peut dire que les choses qui durent tousjours, sont eternelles, en gagnant tousjours une durée nouvelle.* Tout ce qui existe du Temps & de la Duration, *etant successif*, perit, &c.

† Cependant, si en disant que la Duration d'une chose est éternelle, on entend seulement que la chose dure éternellement ; je n'ay rien à y redire.

‖ sont en Dieu, & comme des proprietés de Dieu, est deja fermé. Pourroit on supporter l'Opinion qui soutiendroit que les Corps se promenent dans les parties de l'essence divine ?

140B. LEIBNIZ'S FIFTH PAPER   683

To § 10.

49. It cannot be said that {a certain} *Duration* is Eternal ; but {it can be said} that *Things*, which continue always, are Eternal, {by always gaining a new duration}. Whatever exists of Time and of Duration, {being successive,} perishes continually : And how can a thing exist Eternally, which, (to speak exactly,) does never exist at all ? For, how can a thing exist, whereof no Part does ever exist ? Nothing of Time does ever exist, but Instants ; and an Instant is not even it self a part of Time. Whoever considers these Observations, will easily apprehend that Time can only be an Ideal Thing. And the Analogy between Time and Space, will easily make it appear, that the one is as merely Ideal as the other. {However, if by saying that the duration of a thing is eternal, it is only meant that the thing endures eternally, I have nothing to say against it.}

50. If the reality of Space and Time, is necessary to the Immensity and Eternity of God ; if God must be in Space ; if being in Space, is a Property of God ; he will, in some measure, depend upon Time and Space, and stand in need of them. For I have already prevented That Subterfuge, that Space and Time are {in God and like} *Properties* of God. {Could the view that maintains that bodies wander about in the parts of the divine essence be tolerated ?}

To § 11, *and* 12.

51. I objected that Space cannot be in God, because it has *Parts.* Hereupon the Author seeks another Subterfuge, by departing from the received Sense of Words ; maintaining that Space has no parts, because its parts are not separable, and cannot be removed from one another by discerption. But 'tis sufficient that Space has parts, whether those parts be separable or not ; And they may be assigned in Space, either by the Bodies that are in it, or by Lines and Surfaces that may be drawn and described in it.

To § 13.

52. In order to prove that Space, without Bodies, is an absolute reality ; the Author objected, that a finite material Universe might *move forward* in Space. I answered, it does not appear *reasonable* that the material Universe should be *finite* ; and, though we should suppose it to be finite ; yet 'tis *unreasonable* it should have motion any otherwise, than as its parts change their Situation among themselves ; because such a motion would produce no *Change* that could be observed, and would be without Design. 'Tis another thing, when its parts change their Situation among themselves ; For then there is a *motion in Space* ; but it consists in the *order*

*consi-
stant dans
&c.*

changent de Situation entre Elles ; car alors on y reconnoist un mouvement dans l'Espace, mais * qui consiste dans l'ordre des rapports, qui sont changés. On replique maintenant, que la verité du mouvement est independante de l'Observation, & qu'un Vaisseau peut avancer, sans que celuy qui est dedans s'en apperçoive. Je repons que le mouvement est independant de l'Observation, mais qu'il n'est point independant de l'observabilité. Il n'y a point de mouvement, quand il n'y a point de changement observable. Et même quand il n'y a point de changement observable, il n'y a point de changement du tout. Le Contraire est fondé sur la supposition d'un Espace réel absolu, que j'ay refuté demonstrativement par le principe du besoin d'une raison suffisante des choses.

53. Je ne trouve rien dans la definition huitiéme des Principes Mathematiques de la Nature, ny dans le Scholie de cette Definition, qui prouve ou puisse prouver la réalité de l'Espace en soy. Cependant j'accorde qu'il y a de la difference entre un Mouvement absolu veritable d'un corps, & un simple changement relatif de sa Situation par rapport à un autre Corps. Car lors que la Cause immediate du changement est dans le Corps, il est veritablement en mouvement ; & alors la Situation des autres par rapport à luy, sera changée par consequence, quoyque la Cause de ce changement ne soit point en eux. Il est vray qu'à parler exactement, il n'y a point de Corps qui soit parfaitement & entierement en repos ; mais c'est de quoy on fait Abstraction, en considerant la chose Mathematiquement. Ainsi je n'ay rien laissé sans reponse, de tout ce qu'on allequé pour la réalité absolue de l'Espace. Et j'ay demonstré la fausseté de cette réalité, par un principe fondamental des plus raisonnables & des plus éprouvés, contre lequel on ne sauroit trouver aucune Exception ny Instance. Au reste, on peut juger par tout ce que je viens de dire, que je ne dois point admettre un Univers mobile, ny aucune Place hors de l'Univers materiel.

Sur § 14.

54. Je ne connois aucune Objection à laquelle je ne crois d'avoir repondu suffisamment. Et quant à cette Objection, que l'Espace & le Temps sont des Quantités, ou plustost des choses douées de quantité, & que la Situation & l'Ordre ne le sont point ; Je repons que l'Ordre a aussi sa quantité ; il y a ce qui precede & ce qui suit ; il y a distance ou intervalle. Les choses Relatives ont leur Quantité, aussi bien que les absolues. Par Exemple, les Raisons ou Proportions dans le Mathematiques, ont leur quantité, & se mesurent par les Logarithmes ; & cependant ce sont des Relations. Ainsi quoyque le Temps & l'Espace consistent en rapports, ils ne laissent pas d'avoir leur quantité.

Sur § 15.

55. Pour ce qui est de la Question, si Dieu a pû créer le monde plustost, il faut se bien entendre. Comme j'ay demontré que le Temps sans les Choses n'est autre chose qu'une simple possibilité idéale, il est manifeste que si quelqu'un disoit que ce même

of Relations which are changed. The Author replies now, that the reality of Motion does not indeed depend upon being *observed* ; and that a Ship may go forward, and yet a Man, who is in the Ship, may not perceive it. I answer, Motion does not indeed depend upon being *Observed* ; but it does depend upon being *possible to be Observed*. There is no *Motion*, when there is no *Change that can be Observed*. And when there is no *Change that can be Observed*, there is *no Change at all*. The contrary Opinion is grounded upon the Supposition of a real absolute Space, which I have demonstratively confuted by the Principle of the *want of a sufficient Reason* of things.

53. I find nothing in the *Eighth Definition of the Mathematical Principles of Nature*, nor in the *Scholium belonging to it*, that proves, or can prove, the reality of Space in it self. However, I grant there is a *difference* between *an absolute true motion of a Body*, and a *mere relative Change of its Situation with respect to another Body*. For when the immediate Cause of the Change is in the Body, That Body is truly in Motion ; and then the Situation of other Bodies, with respect to it, will be changed consequently, though the Cause of that Change be not in Them. 'Tis true that, exactly speaking, there is not any one Body, that is perfectly and intirely at Rest ; but we frame an abstract[10] Notion of Rest, by considering the thing Mathematically. Thus have I left nothing unanswered, of what has been alledged for the absolute reality of Space. And I have demonstrated the falsehood of that reality, by a fundamental Principle, one of the most certain both in Reason and Experience ; against which, no Exception or Instance can be alledged. Upon the whole, one may judge from what has been said, that I ought not to admit a *moveable Universe* ; nor any *Place* out of the material Universe.

To § 14.

54. I am not sensible of any objection, but what I think I have sufficiently answered. As for the objection that *Space* and *Time* are *Quantities*, or rather things *endowed with Quantity* ; and that *Situation* and *Order* are not so : I answer, that *Order* also has its Quantity ; There is in it, that which goes before, and that which follows ; There is Distance or Interval. *Relative* things have their *Quantity*, as well as *absolute* ones. For instance, *Ratios* or *Proportions* in Mathematicks, have their *Quantity*, and are *measured* by *Logarithms* ; and yet they are *Relations*. And therefore though *Time* and *Space* consist in *Relations*, yet they have their *Quantity*.

To § 15.

55. As to the Question, Whether God could have created the World *sooner* ; 'tis necessary here to understand each other rightly. Since I have demonstrated, that *Time*, without Things, is nothing else but a mere ideal Possibility ; 'tis manifest, if any one should say that this Same World, which has been actually created, might

monde qui a eté créé effectivement, * sans aucun autre changement ait pû étre créé plustost, *il ne dira* rien d'intelligible. Car il n'y a aucune marque ou différence, par laquelle il seroit possible de connoistre qu'il eût été créé plustost. Ainsi, comme je l'ay deja dit, supposer que Dieu ait créé le même monde plustost, est supposer quelque chose de chimerique. C'est faire du Temps une chose absolue independante de Dieu ; au lieu † que le Temps ne coëxiste qu'aux Creatures, & ne se conçoit que par l'ordre & la quantité *de leurs changemens.*

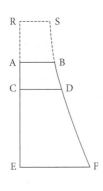

56. Mais absolument parlant, on peut concevoir *qu'un Univers ait commencé* plustost *qu'il n'a commencé effectivement.* Supposons que nostre Univers, ou quelque autre, soit respresenté par la Figue A F ; que *l'Ordonnée* A B, represente son premier estat ; & que les Ordonnées C D, E F, represent des Estats suivans. Je dis qu'on peut concevoir *qu'il ait commencé* plustost, *en concevant la Figure prolongée en arriere,* & *en y adjoutant* S R A B S. Car ainsi, les chose estant augmentées, le temps sera augmenté aussi. Mais si une telle Augmentation est raisonnable & conforme à la sagesse de Dieu, c'est une autre Question ; & il faut dire que non, autrement Dieu l'auroit faite. Ce seroit comme,

Humano capiti cervicem Pictor equinam
Jungere si velit.[11]

Il en est de même de la Destruction. Comme on pourroit concevoir quelque chose d'adjouté au commencement, on pourroit concevoir de même quelque chose de retranché vers la fin. Mais ce retranchement encore seroit deraisonnable.

57. C'est ainsi qu'il paroist comment on doit entendre que Dieu a créé les choses en quel temps *il luy a plû* ; car cela depend des choses *qu'il a resolu de créer.* Mais les choses étant resolues avec leurs rapports, il n'y a plus de choix sur le Temps *ny sur la* Place ; qui n'ont rien de réel en eux à part, & rien de determinant, ou même rien de discernable.

58. On ne peut donc point dire, comme l'on fait icy, que la sagesse de Dieu peut avoir de bonnes Raisons pour créer ce Monde (this World) dans un tel temps particulier ; ce temps particulier pris sans les choses, estant une fiction impossible ; & de bonnes Raisons d'un choix ne se pouvant point trouver là où tout est indiscernable.

59. Quand je parle de ce Monde, j'entends tout l'Univers des Creatures materielles & immaterielles prises ensemble, depuis le commencement des choses ; mais si l'on n'entendoit que le commencement du monde materiel, & supposoit avant luy des creatures immaterielles, on se mettroit un peu plus à la Raison en cela. Car le temps alors estant marqué par des Choses qui existeroient dejà, ne seroit plus indifferent ; & il y pourroit avoir du choix. Il est vray qu'on ne feroit que differer la difficulté. Car supposant que l'Univers entier des Creatures immaterielles & materielles ensemble a commencé, il n'y a plus de choix sur le temps où Dieu le voudroit mettre.

---

* ait, sans aucun autre changement, pû étre &c.
† que le temps doit coexister aux &c.

have been created *sooner*, without any other Change ; he would say *nothing that is intelligible*. For there is no mark or difference, whereby it would be possible to know, that this World was created *sooner*. And therefore, (as I have already said,) to suppose that God created the same World *sooner*, is supposing a Chimerical Thing. Tis making *Time* a thing absolute, independent upon God ; whereas *Time* does {must} only co-exist with Creatures, and is only conceived by the *Order* and *Quantity* of their Changes.

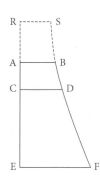

56. But yet, absolutely speaking, one *may conceive* that an Universe began *sooner*, than it actually did. Let us suppose our Universe, or any other, to be represented by the Figure *A F* ; and that the Ordinate *A B* represents its first State ; and the Ordinates *C D, E F*, its following States : I say, one *may conceive* that such a World began *sooner*, by conceiving the Figure prolonged backwards, and by adding to it *S R A B S*. For thus, *Things* being encreased, *Time* will be also encreased. But whether such an augmentation be *reasonable* and agreeable to God's Wisdom, is another Question, to which we answer in the Negative ; otherwise God *would* have made such an Augmentation. It would be like as

Humano capiti cervicem pictor equinam
Jungere si velit.[11]

The case is the same with respect to the *destruction* of the Universe. As one *might conceive* something added to the Beginning, so one *might also conceive* something taken off towards the End. But such a Retrenching from it, would be also *unreasonable*.

57. Thus it appears how we are to understand, that God created things at which *Time* he *pleased* ; For this depends upon the *Things*, which he resolved to create. But *Things* being once resolved upon, together with their *Relations* ; there remains no longer any choice about the *Time* and the *Place*, which of themselves have nothing in them real, nothing that can distinguish them, nothing that is at all discernible.

58. One cannot therefore say, as the Author does here, that the Wisdom of God may have *good reasons* to create this World at *such* or *such a particular Time* : That particular Time, considered without the *things*, being an *impossible* fiction ; and *good reasons* for a choice, being not to be found, where every thing is indiscernible.

59. When I speak of this *World*, I mean the whole *Universe* of material and immaterial Creatures taken together, from the beginning of Things. But if any one mean only the beginning of the *material* World, and suppose *immaterial* Creatures before it ; he would have somewhat more Reason for his Supposition. For *Time* then being *marked* by things that existed already, it would be no longer indifferent ; and there might be room for choice. And yet indeed, this would be only putting off the difficulty. For, supposing the whole Universe of immaterial and material Creatures together, to have a beginning ; there is no longer any Choice about the *Time*, in which God would place that Beginning.

688   140B. LEIBNIZ'S FIFTH PAPER

60. *Ainsi on ne doit point dire, comme l'on fait icy, que Dieu a creé les choses dans un* Espace, *ou dans un* Temps *particulier, qui* luy a plû. *Car tous les Temps, & tous les Espaces, en eux même, estant parfaitement uniformes & indiscernibles, l'un ne sauroit plaire plus que l'autre.*

61. *Je ne veux point m'arrester icy sur mon sentiment expliqué*[12] *ailleurs, qui porte qu'il n'y a point de Substances créées entierement destituées de Matiere. Car je tiens avec les Anciens & avec la Raison, que les Anges ou les Intelligences, & les Ames separées du corps grossier, ont toujours des Corps Subtils, quoyqu'elles mêmes soyent incorporelles. La Philosophie vulgaire admet aisement toute sorte de Fictions ; la mienne est plus severe.*

62. *Je ne dis point que la Matiere & l'Espace est la même chose ; je dis seulement qu'il n'y a point d'Espace, où il n'y a point de Matiere ; & que l'Espace en luy même n'est point une réalité absolue. L'Espace & la Matiere different comme le temps & le mouvement. Cependant ces choses, quoyque differentes, se trouvent* inseparables.

63. *Mais il ne s'ensuit nullement que la Matiere soit éternelle & necessaire, si non en supposant que l'*Espace *est éternel & necessaire ; Supposition mal fondée en toutes manieres.*

Sur § 16 & 17.

64. *Je crois d'avoir repondu à tout ; & j'ay repondu particulierement à cette Objection, qui pretend que l'Espace & le Temps ont une* Quantité, *& que l'Ordre n'en a point.* Voyés cydessus, n. 54.

65. *J'ay fait voir clairement, que la Contradiction est dans l'Hypothese du sentiment opposé, qui cherche une difference là où il n'y en a point. Et ce seroit une iniquité manifeste, d'en vouloir inferer, que j'ay reconnu de la Contradiction dans mon propre sentiment.*

Sur § 18.

66. *Il revient icy un raisonnement, que j'ay dejà detruit cydessus,* Nomb. 17. *On dit que Dieu peut avoir de* bonnes Raisons *pour placer deux Cubes parfaitement égaux & semblables : Et alors il faut bien (dit on) qu'il leur assigne leurs Places, quoyque tout soit parfaitement égal. Mais la chose ne doit point être detachée des ses Circonstances. Ce raisonnement consiste en Notions incompletes. Les Resolutions de Dieu, ne sont jamais abstraites & imparfaites ; comme si Dieu descernoit premierement à créer les deux Cubes & puis decernoit à part où les mettre. Les Hommes bornés comme ils sont, sont capables de proceder ainsi ; ils resoudront quelque chose, & puis ils se trouveront embarrassés sur les moyens, sur les voyes, sur les Places, sur les Circonstances. Dieu ne prend jamais une Resolution sur les Fins, sans en prendre en même temps sur les Moyens, & sur toutes les Circonstances. Et même j'ay montré dans la* Theodicée, *qu'à proprement parler, il n'y a qu'Un Seul Decret pour l'Univers tout entier, par lequel il est resolu de l'admettre de la possibilité à l'existence. Ainsi Dieu ne choisira point de Cube, sans choisir sa Place en même temps ; & il ne choisira jamais entre des* indiscernables.

140B. LEIBNIZ'S FIFTH PAPER   689

60. And therefore one must not say, as the Author does here, that God created things in what particular *Space*, and at what particular *Time* he *pleased*. For, All Time and All Spaces being in themselves perfectly uniform and indiscernible form each other, one of them cannot *please* more than another.

61. I shall not enlarge here upon my Opinion explained elsewhere, that there are no created Substances wholly destitute of Matter. For I hold with the Ancients, and according to Reason, that Angels or Intelligences, and Souls separated from a gross Body, have always subtil Bodies, though they themselves be incorporeal. The vulgar Philosophy easily admits all sorts of Fictions : Mine is more strict.

62. I don't say that Matter and Space are the same Thing. I only say, *there is no Space, where there is no Matter* ; and that Space in it self is not an absolute reality. Space and Matter differ, as Time and Motion. However, these things, though different, are *inseparable*.

63. But yet it does not at all follow, that Matter is eternal and necessary ; unless we suppose *Space* to be eternal and necessary : A Supposition ill grounded in all respects.

To § 16, and 17.

64. I think I have answered every thing ; And I have particularly replied to That Objection, that *Space* and *Time* have *Quantity*, and that *Order* has none. *See above, Numb.* 54.

65. I have clearly shown that the Contradiction lies in the Hypothesis of the opposite Opinion, which looks for a difference where there is none. And it would be a manifest Iniquity to infer from thence, that I have acknowledged a Contradiction in my own Opinion.

To § 18.

66. Here I find again an Argument, which I have overthrown above, *Numb.* 17. The Author says, God may have *good Reasons* to make two Cubes perfectly equal and alike : And then (says he) God must needs assign them their Places, though every other Respect be perfectly equal. But Things ought not to be separated from their Circumstances. This Argument consists in incomplete Notions. God's Resolutions are never abstract and imperfect : As if God decreed, first, to create two Cubes ; and then, made another decree where to place them. Men, being such limited Creatures as they are, may act in this manner. They may resolve upon a thing, and then find themselves perplexed about Means, Ways, Places, and Circumstances. But God never takes a Resolution about the Ends, without resolving at the same time about the Means, and all the Circumstances. Nay, I have shown in my *Theodicæa*, that, properly speaking, there is but One Decree for the whole Universe, whereby God resolved to bring it out of possibility into Existence. And therefore God will not chuse a Cube, without chusing its Place at the same time ; And he will *never chuse* among *Indiscernibles*.

690 140B. LEIBNIZ'S FIFTH PAPER

67. *Les parties de l'Espace ne sont determinées & distinguées que par les choses qui y sont : Et la diversité des choses dans l'Espace, determine Dieu à agir differement sur differentes parties de l'Espace. Mais l'Espace pris sans les choses, n'a rien de determinant, & même il n'est rien d'*actuel.

68. *Si Dieu est resolu de placer un certain Cube de matiere, il s'est aussi determiné sur la Place de ce Cube ; mais c'est par rapport à d'autres portions de matiere, & non pas par rapport à l'Espace detaché, où il n'y a rien de determinant.*

69. *Mais la sagesse ne permet pas qu'il place en même temps deux Cubes parfaitement égaux & semblables, parce qu'il n'y a pas moyen de trouver une Raison de leur assigner des places differentes. Il y auroit une* volonté sans motif.

70. *J'avois comparé une* volonté sans motif, (*telle que des raisonnements superficiels assignent à Dieu,) au* hazard d'Epicure. *On y oppose que le* hazard d'Epicure *est une necessité aveugle, & non pas un choix de volonté. Je replique que le* hazard d'Epicure *n'est pas une necessité, mais quelque chose d'indifferent.* Epicure *l'introduisoit exprés pour eviter la necessité. Il est vray que le hazard est aveugle ; mais une* volonté sans motif *ne seroit pas moins aveugle, & ne seroit pas moins due au* simple hazard.

Sur § 19.

71. *On repete icy ce qui a dejà été refuté cy dessus, Nomb. 21 ; que la matiere ne sauroit étre créé, si Dieu ne choisit point parmy les indiscernables. On auroit Raison, si la matiere consistoit en Atomes, en Corps similaires, ou autres fictions semblables de la Philosophie superficielle. Mais ce même grand principe, qui combat le choix entre les indiscernables, detruit aussi ces fictions mal bâties.*

Sur § 20.

72. *On m'avoit objecté dans le* 3me Papier, (*Nomb. 7 & 8.) que Dieu n'auroit point en luy un principe d'agir, s'il étoit determiné par les* * externes. *J'ay repondu que les idées des choses externes sont en luy ; & qu'ainsi il est determiné par des raisons internes, c'est à dire par sa sagesse. Maintenant on ne veut point entendre, à propos de quoy je l'aye dit.*

* choses externes ;

Sur § 21.

73. *On confond souvent dans les objections qu'on me fait, ce que Dieu ne* veut *point, avec ce qu'il ne* peut *point.* Voyés ci-dessus, Nomb. 9 †. *Par Exemple ;* Dieu peut *faire tout ce qui est possible, mais il ne* veut *faire que le Meilleur. Ainsi je ne dis point, comme on m'impute icy, que Dieu ne* peut *point donner des bornes à l'Etendue de la matiere, mais il y a de l'apparence qu'il ne le* veut *point, & qu'il a trouvé mieux de ne luy en point donner.*

† & plus bas, N° 76

67. The Parts of Space are not determined and distinguished, but by the Things which are in it : And the Diversity of Things in Space, determines God to act differently upon different Parts of Space. But Space without Things, has nothing whereby it may be distinguished ; and indeed not any thing *actual*.

68. If God is resolved to place a certain Cube of Matter at all, he is also resolved in what particular Place to put it. But 'tis with respect to Other Parts of Matter ; and not with respect to bare Space it self, in which there is nothing to distinguish it.

69. But Wisdom does not allow God to place at the same time *two Cubes perfectly equal and alike* ; because there is no way to find any *Reason* for assigning them different Places. At this Rate, there would be *a Will without a Motive*.

70. A *Will without Motive*, (such as superficial Reasoners suppose to be in God,) I compar'd to *Epicurus's Chance*. The Author answers ; *Epicurus's Chance* is a blind Necessity, and not a Choice of Will. I reply, that *Epicurus's Chance* is not a Necessity, but Something indifferent. *Epicurus* brought it in on purpose to avoid Necessity. 'Tis true, Chance is Blind ; but a *Will without Motive* would be no less Blind, and no less owing to mere Chance.

To § 19.

71. The Author repeats here, what has been already confuted above, *Numb.* 21 ; that Matter cannot be created, without God's chusing among Indiscernibles. He would be in the right, if Matter consisted of Atoms, similar Particles, or other the like Fictions of superficial Philosophy. But That great Principle, which proves there is no Choice among Indiscernibles, destroys also these ill-contrived Fictions.

To § 20.

72. The Author objected against me in his *Third Paper*, (*Numb.* 7, *and* 8 ;) that God would not have in himself a Principle of Acting, if he was determined by Things *External*. I answered, that the Ideas of External Things are in him ; and that therefore he is determined by Internal Reasons, that is, by his Wisdom. But the Author here will not understand, to what end I said it.

To § 21.

73. He frequently confounds, in his Objections against me, what God *will not* do with what he *cannot* do. *See above, Numb.* 9 {*and below, N° 76*}. For Example ; God *can* do every Thing that is possible, but he *will* do only what is best. And therefore I don't say, as the Author here will have it, that God *cannot* limit the Extension of Matter ; but 'tis likely he *will not* do it, and that he has thought it better to set no Bounds to Matter.

74. *De l'étendue à la durée, non valet consequentia. Quand l'étendue de la matiere n'auroit point de bornes, il ne s'ensuit point que sa durée n'en ait pas non plus ; pas même en arriere, c'est à dire qu'elle n'ait point eu de commencement. Si la nature des choses dans le total est de croitre uniformément en perfection, l'Univers des creatures doit avoir commencé. Ainsi il y aura des Raisons pour limiter la durée des choses, quand même il n'y en auroit point pour en limiter l'étendue. De plus, le commencement du Monde ne deroge point à l'infinité de sa durée à parte post, ou dans la suite ; mais les bornes de l'Universe derogeroient à l'infinité de son étendue. Ainsi il est plus raisonnable d'en poser un commencement, que d'en admettre des bornes ; à fin de conserver dans l'un & dans l'autre le caractere d'un Auteur infini.*

75. *Cependant ceux qui ont admis l'éternité du Monde, ou, du moins, comme ont fait des Theologiens celebres, la possibilité de l'éternité du Monde ; n'on point nié pour cela sa dependance de Dieu, comme on le leur impute icy sans fondement.*

Sur § 22 & 23.

76. *On m'objecte encore icy sans fondement, que, selon moy, tout ce que Dieu peut faire, doit étre fait necessairement. Comme si l'on ignoroit que j'ay refuté cela solidement dans la* Theodicée, *& que j'ay renversé l'opinion de ceux qui soutiennent qu'il n'y a rien de possible que ce qui arrive effectivement ; comme ont fait deja quelques anciens Philosophes, &, entre autres,* Diodore *chez* Ciceron. *On confond la necessité morale, qui vient du choix du meilleur, avec la necessité absolue ; on confond la volonté avec la puissance de Dieu. Il peut produire tout possible, ou ce qui n'implique point de contradiction ; mais il veut produire le meilleur entre les possibles.* Voyés ce qui a

* & Nº 74. été dit cy-dessus, Nº 9. *

77. *Dieu n'est donc point un Agent Necessaire en produisant les Creatures, puis qu'il agit par Choix. Cependant ce qu'on adjoute icy, est mal fondé, qu'un Agent Necessaire ne seroit point un Agent. On prononce souvent hardiment & sans fondement, en avançant* † *des theses qu'on ne sauroit prouver.*

† contre
moy des
theses

Sur § 24 ——— 28.

78. *On s'excuse de n'avoir point dit que l'Espace est le* sensorium *de Dieu, mais seulement comme* son sensorium. *Il semble que l'un est aussi peu convenable, & aussi peu intelligible que l'autre.*

Sur § 29.

79. *L'Espace n'est pas la place de toutes choses, car il n'est pas la place de Dieu ; autrement voilà une chose coëternelle à Dieu, & independante de luy, & même de laquelle il dependroit s'il a besoin de place.*

140B. LEIBNIZ'S FIFTH PAPER   693

74. From Extension to Duration, *non valet consequentia*. Though the *Extension* of Matter were unlimited, yet it would not follow that its *Duration* would be also unlimited ; nay, even *à parte ante*, it would not follow, that it had no Beginning. If it is the Nature of Things in the whole, to grow uniformly in Perfection ; the Universe of Creatures must have had a Beginning. And therefore, there will be Reasons to limit the *Duration* of Things, even though there were none to limit their Extension. Besides, the World's having a Beginning, does not derogate from the Infinity of its Duration *à parte post* ; but Bounds of the Universe would derogate from the Infinity of its Extension. And therefore it is more reasonable to admit a Beginning of the World, than to admit any Bounds of it ; that the Character of its infinite Author, may be in Both Respects preserved.

75. However, those who have admitted the *Eternity* of the World, or, at least, (as some famous Divines have done,) the *possibility* of its Eternity ; did not, for all that, deny its dependence upon God ; as the Author here lays to their Charge, without any Ground.

To § 22, 23.

76. He here further objects, without any Reason, that, according to my Opinion, whatever God *can* do, he *must needs* have done. As if he was ignorant, that I have solidly confuted this Notion in my *Theodicæa* ; and that I have overthrown the Opinion of those, who maintain that there is nothing possible but what really happens ; as some ancient Philosophers did, and among others *Diodorus* in *Cicero*.[13] The Author confounds *Moral Necessity*, which proceeds from the Choice of what is *Best*, with *Absolute Necessity* : He confounds the *Will* of God, with his *Power*. God *can* produce every Thing that is possible, or whatever does not imply a Contradiction ; but he *wills* only to produce what is the *Best* among Things possible. *See what has been said above, Numb.* 9 {& Nº 74}.

77. God is not therefore a *necessary Agent* in producing Creatures, since he acts with Choice. However, what the Author adds here, is ill-grounded, *viz.* that a *Necessary Agent* would not be an Agent at all. He frequently affirms Things boldly, and without any ground ; advancing {against me} Notions which cannot be proved.

To § 24 ———— 28.

78. The Author alledges, it was not affirmed that Space is God's *Sensorium*, but only *as it were* his *Sensorium*. The latter seems to be as improper, and as little intelligible, as the former.

To § 29.

79. *Space* is not the Place of all Things ; for it is not the Place of *God*. Otherwise there would be a thing co-eternal with God, and independent upon him ; nay, he himself would depend upon it, if he has need of *Place*.

80. *Je ne voy pas aussi comment on peut dire, que l'*Espace *est la* place des idées ; *car les* idées *sont dans l'*Entendement.

81. *Il est fort étrange aussi de dire que l'*Ame de l'Homme *est l'*Ame des images. *Les images qui sont dans l'Entendement, sont dans l'Esprit ; mais s'il étoit l'Ame des images, elles seroient hors de luy. Que si l'on entend des Images corporelles, comment veut on que nostre Esprit en soit l'Ame, puisque ce ne sont que des impressions passageres dans le Corps dont il est l'Ame ?*

82. *Si Dieu sent ce qui se passe dans le Monde, par le* moyen *d'un sensorium ; il semble que les choses agissent sur luy, & qu'ainsi il est comme on conçoit l'*Ame du Monde. *On m'impute de repeter les objections, sans prendre connoissance des reponses ; mais je ne voy point qu'on ait satisfait à cette difficulté ; on feroit mieux de* renoncer tout à fait *à ce* sensorium *pretendu.*

Sur § 30.

83. *On parle comme si l'on n'entendoit point comment selon moy l'*Ame *est un* principe representative, *c'est à dire, comme si l'on n'avoit jamais oüi parler de mon* harmonie préétablie[14].

84. *Je ne demeure point d'accorde des notions vulgaires, comme si les* Images des choses *étoient* transportées, (conveyed) *par les* Organes *jusqu'à l'*Ame. *Car il n'est point concevable par quelle ouverture, ou par quelle voiture, ce transport des images depuis l'Organe jusques dans l'Ame se peut faire. Cette notion de la Philosophie vulgaire, n'est point intelligible ; comme les nouveaux* Cartesiens *l'ont assez montré. L'on ne sauroit expliquer comment la Substance* immaterielle *est affectée par la* matiere : *& soutenir une chose non intelligible là dessus, c'est recourir à la notion Scholastique chimerique de je ne say quelles* Especes intentionelles *inexplicables, qui passent des* Organes dans l'Ame. Ces *Cartesiens* ont vû la difficulté, mais ils ne l'ont point resolue ; *ils ont eu recours à un concours* * *de Dieu, qui seroit miraculeux en effect : Mais je crois d'avoir donné la* veritable solution *de cet Enigme.*

85. *De dire que Dieu discerne les choses qui se passent, parce qu'il est* present aux Substances, & *non pas* † *par une* production continuelle, *c'est dire des choses non intelligibles. La simple* presence, *ou la proximité de coëxistence, ne suffit point pour entendre comment ce qui se passe dans un Etre, doit repondre à ce qui se passe dans un autre Etre.*

86. *Par aprés c'est donner justement dans la doctrine qui fait de Dieu l'*Ame du Monde, *puisqu'on le fait sentir les choses non pas par la dependance qu'elles ont de luy, c'est à dire par la* production continuelle *de ce qu'il y a de bon & de parfait en elles ; mais par une maniere de sentiment comme l'on s'imagine que* nostre Ame *sent ce qui se passe dans le Corps. C'est bien degrader la connoissance divine.*

---

   * de Dieu tout particulier,

   † par la dependance que la continuation de leur existence a de luy, & qu'on peut dire d'envelopper une production &c.

80. Nor do I see, how it can be said, that *Space* is the *Place of Ideas* ; for *Ideas* are in the *Understanding*.

81. 'Tis also very strange to say, that the *Soul of Man* is the *Soul of the Images* it perceives. The *Images*, which are in the Understanding, are in the Mind : But if the Mind was the *Soul of the Images*, they would then be extrinsick to it. And if the Author means *corporeal Images*, how then will he have a *human Mind* to be the *Soul of those Images*, they being only transient Impressions in a Body belonging to that Soul ?

82. If 'tis by *means* of a *Sensorium*, that God perceives what passes in the World ; it seems that Things act upon him ; and that therefore he is what we mean by *a Soul of the World*. The Author charges me with repeating Objections, without taking notice of the Answers ; but I don't see that he has answered this Difficulty. They had better *wholly lay aside* this pretended *Sensorium*.

To § 30.

83. The Author speaks, as if he did not understand, how, according to my Opinion, the *Soul* is a *Representative Principle*. Which is, as if he had never heard of my *Pre-established Harmony*.

84. I don't assent to the vulgar Notions, that the *Images of Things* are *conveyed* by the *Organs* [of Sense] to the *Soul*. For, it is not conceivable by what Passage, or by what Means of Conveyance, these Images can be carried from the Organ to the Soul. This Vulgar Notion in Philosophy is not intelligible, as the new *Cartesians* have sufficiently shown. It cannot be explained, how *Immaterial* Substance is affected by *Matter* : And to maintain an unintelligible Notion thereupon, is having recourse to the Scholastick Chimerical Notion of I know not what inexplicable *Species Intentionales*, passing from the Organs to the Soul. Those *Cartesians* saw the Difficulty ; but they could not explain it. They had recourse to a {special} Concourse of God, which would really be miraculous. But, I think, *I have given* the *true Solution* of that *Ænigma*.

85. To say that God perceives what passes in the World, because he is *present* to the Things, and not by {the dependence that the continuation of their existence has on him and that can be said to involve} a *continual Production* of them ; is saying something unintelligible. A mere *Presence* or Proximity of Co-existence, is not sufficient to make us understand, how that which passes in One Being, should answer to what passes in another.

86. Besides ; This is exactly falling into That Opinion, which makes God to be the *Soul of the World* ; seeing it supposes God to perceive Things, not by their dependence upon him, that is, by a *continual Production* of what is good and perfect in them ; but by a Kind of Perception, such as that by which Men fancy Our Soul perceives what passes in the Body. This is a degrading of God's Knowledge very much.

696   140B. LEIBNIZ'S FIFTH PAPER

87. *Dans la verité des choses, cette matiere de sentir est entierement chimerique, & n'a pas même lieu dans les Ames. Elles sentent ce qui se passe hors d'elles, par ce qui se passe en elles, repondant aux choses de dehors ; en vertu de l'*harmonie *que Dieu a préétablie, par la plus belle & la plus admirable de toutes ses productions ; qui fait que* chaque substance simple, *en vertu de sa nature, est, pour dire ainsi,* une concentration *& un* miroir vivant de tout l'Univers *suivant* son point de veue. *Ce qui est encore une des plus belles, & des plus incontestables Preuves de l'Existence de Dieu ; puisqu'il n'y a que Dieu, c'est à dire la cause commune, qui puisse faire cette harmonie des choses. Mais Dieu même ne peut sentir les choses par moyen par lequel il les fait sentir aux autres. Il les sent, parce qu'il est capable de produire ce moyen ; & il ne les feroit point sentir aux autres, s'il ne les produisoit luy même toutes* consentantes, *& s'il n'avoit ainsi en soy leur representation, non comme venant d'elles, mais parce qu'elles viennent de luy, & parcequ'il en est la cause efficiente & exemplaire. Il les sent parce qu'elles viennent de luy, s'il est permis de dire qu'il les sent ; ce qui ne se doit, qu'en depouillant le terme de son imperfection, qui semble signifier qu'elles agissent sur luy. Elles sont, & luy sont connues, parce qu'il les entend & veut ; & parce qu'il veut, est autant que ce qui existe. Ce qui paroist d'autant plus, parce qu'il les fait sentir les unes aux autres ; & qu'il les fait sentir mutuellement par la suite des Natures, qu'il leur a données une fois pour toutes, & qu'il ne fait qu'entretenir suivant les loix de chacune à part, lesquelles*[15] *bien que differentes aboutissement à une correspondence exacte des resultats. Ce qui passe toutes les Idées qu'on a eu vulgairement de la Perfection Divine & des Ouvrages de Dieu, & † l'éleve au plus haut degré ; comme M.* Bayle *a bien reconnu, quoy qu'il ait crû sans sujet que cela passe le possible.*

† les éleve

88. *Ce seroit bien abuser du Texte de la Sainte Ecriture, suivant lequel Dieu repose des ses Ouvrages ; que d'en inferer qu'il n'y a plus de* production *continuée. Il est vray qu'il n'y a point de Production de Substances simples nouvelles ; mais on auroit tort d'en inferer que Dieu n'est maintenant dans le Monde, que comme l'on conçoit que* l'Ame est dans le Corps, *en le* gouvernant seulement *par sa Presence, sans un concours necessaire pour lui faire continuer son Existence.*

Sur § 31.

89. *L'*Harmonie *ou* Correspondence *entre l'Ame & le* Corps, *n'est pas un* Miracle *perpetuel, mais l'Effect ou suite d'un Miracle primigene fait dans la Creation des choses, comme sont toutes les choses naturelles. Il est vray que c'est une* Merveille *perpetuelle, comme sont beaucoup de choses naturelles.*

90. *Le mot d'*Harmonie préétablie *est un Terme de l'Art, je l'avoue ; mais non pas un Terme qui n'explique rien ; puisqu'il est expliqué fort intelligiblement, & qu'on n'oppose rien qui marque qu'il y ait de la difficulté.*

140B. LEIBNIZ'S FIFTH PAPER 697

87. In Truth and Reality, this way of Perception is wholly Chimerical, and has no place even in *Human Souls*. They perceive what passes *without* them, by what passes *within* them, answering to the Things without ; in virtue of the *Harmony*, which God has pre-established by the most beautiful and the most admirable of all his Productions ; whereby *every simple Substance* is by its nature, (if one may so say,) a *concentration*, and a *living mirror* of the *whole Universe*, according to its *Point of view*. Which is likewise one of the most beautiful and most undeniable Proofs of the existence of God ; since none but God, *viz*. the universal Cause, can produce such a Harmony of things. But God himself cannot perceive things by the same Means whereby he makes other Beings perceive them. He perceives them, because he is able to produce That Means. And Other Beings would not be caused to perceive them, if he himself did not produce them all *harmonious*, and had not therefore in himself a representation of them ; Not as if that Representation came from the Things, but because the Things proceed from Him, and because he is the Efficient and Exemplary Cause of them. He perceives them, because they proceed from him ; if one may be allowed to say, that he *perceives* them : Which ought not to be said, unless we divest That Word of its imperfection ; for else it seems to signify, that things act upon him. They exist, and are known to him, because he understands and wills them ; and because what he wills, is the same[16] as what exists. Which appears so much the more, because he makes them to be perceived by one another ; and makes them perceive one another in consequence of the Natures which he has given them once for all, and which he Keeps up only, according to the laws of every one of them severally ; which, though different one from another, yet terminate in an exact correspondence of the Results of the whole. This surpasses all the Ideas, which Men have generally framed concerning the divine Perfections, and the works of God ; and raises [*our notion of*] them, to the highest degree ; as Mr. *Bayle*[17] has acknowledged, though he believed, without any ground, that it exceeded possibility.

88. To infer from That passage of Holy Scripture, wherein God is said to have rested from his Works, that there is no longer a *continual Production* of them ; would be to make a very ill use of that Text. 'Tis true, there is no production of *New* Simple Substances : But it would be wrong to infer from thence, that God is now in the World, only as the Soul is conceived to be in the Body, *governing it merely* by his presence, without any concourse being necessary to continue its Existence.

To § 31.

89. The *Harmony*, or Correspondence between the *Soul* and the *Body*, is not a perpetual *Miracle* ; but the effect or consequence of an original Miracle worked at the Creation of things ; as all natural things are. Though indeed it is a perpetual *Wonder*, as many natural things are.

90. The word, *Pre-established Harmony*, is a Term of Art, I confess ; but 'tis not a Term that explains nothing, since it is made out very intelligibly ; and the Author alledges nothing, that shows there is any difficulty in it.

91. *Comme la nature de* chaque Substance simple, Ame *ou* veritable Monade, *est telle que son état suivant est une Consequence de son état precedent ; voilà la cause de l'*Harmonie *toute trouvée. Car Dieu n'a qu'à faire que la* Substance simple *soit une fois & d'abord une* Representation de l'Univers *selon son* point de veue *: Puisque de cela seul il suit qu'elle le sera perpetuellement ; & que* toutes les Substances simples *auront tousjours une* Harmonie *entre elles, parcequ'elles* representent *tousjours le* même Univers.

Sur § 32.

92. *Il est vray que, selon moy, l'*Ame *ne trouble point les loix du* Corps, *ny le* Corps *celles de l'*Ame *; &* qu'ils s'accordent seulement *; l'un agissant librement, suivant les Regles des Causes finales ; & l'autre agissant machinalement, suivant les Loix des Causes efficientes. Mais cela ne deroge point à la Liberté de nos Ames, comme on le prend icy. Car tout Agent qui agit suivant les causes finales, est libre, quoyqu'il arrive qu'il s'accorde avec celuy qui n'agit que par des Causes efficientes sans connoissance, ou par* Machine *; parceque Dieu prevoyant ce que la cause libre feroit, a reglé d'abord sa* Machine *en sorte qu'elle ne puisse manquer de s'y accorder. Monsieur* Jaquelot *a fort bien resolu cette difficulté dans un de ses Livres contre M. Bayle ; & j'en y cite le Passage dans la* Theodicée, Part I. § 63. J'en parleray encore plus bas, Nomb. 124.

Sur § 33.

93. *Je n'admets point que toute* Action[19] *donne une* nouvelle force *à ce qui patit. Il arrive souvent dans le concours des Corps, que chacun garde sa force ; comme lors que deux corps durs égaux concourent directement. Alors la seule Direction est changée, sans qu'il y ait du changement dans la force ; chacun des Corps prenant la Direction de l'autre, & retournant avec la même* vitesse *qu'il avoit deja eue.*

94. *Cependant je n'ay garde de dire qu'il soit surnaturel de donner une nouvelle* force *à un Corps ; car je reconnois qu'un Corps reçoit souvent une nouvelle* force *d'un autre Corps, qui en perd autant de la sienne : Mais je dis seulement qu'il est surnaturel que tout l'Univers des Corps reçoive une nouvelle* force *; & ainsi qu'un corps gagne de la* Force, *sans que d'autres en perdent autant. C'est pourquoy je dis aussi, qu'il est insoutenable que l'*Ame *donne de la* Force *au* Corps *; car alors tout l'Univers des Corps recevroit une nouvelle* force.

95. *Le Dilemme qu'on fait icy, est mal fondé, que selon moy il faut ou que l'Homme agisse surnaturellement, ou que l'Homme soit une pure* Machine *comme un Montre. Car l'Homme n'agit point surnaturellement, & son Corps est veritablement* une Machine, *& n'agit que* machinalement *; mais son Ame ne laisse pas d'étre une cause libre.*

91. The nature of *every simple Substance, Soul,* or *true Monad,* being such that its following State is a consequence of the preceding one ; here now is the cause of the *Harmony* found out. For God needs only to make a *simple Substance* become *once* and from the beginning, a *representation of the Universe,* according to its *Point of view* ; Since from thence alone it follows, that it will be so *perpetually* ; and that *all simple Substances* will always have a *Harmony* among themselves, because they always *represent* the same *Universe.*

To § 32.

92. 'Tis true, that, according to Me, the *Soul* does not disturb the Laws of the *Body,* nor the *Body* those of the *Soul* ; and that the *Soul* and *Body* do *only agree* together ; the one acting freely, according to the rules of Final Causes ; and the other acting *mechanically,* according to the laws of Efficient Causes. But this does not derogate from the Liberty of our Souls ; as the Author here will have it. For, every Agent which acts according to Final Causes, is free, though it happens to agree with an Agent acting only by Efficient Causes without Knowledge, or *mechanically* ; because God, foreseeing what the free Cause would do, did from the beginning regulate the *Machine* in such manner, that it cannot fail to *agree* with that free Cause. Mr. *Jaquelot*[18] has very well resolved this difficulty, in one of his Books against Mr. *Bayle* ; and I have cited the Passage, in my *Theodicæa,* Part I. § 63. I shall speak of it again below, *Numb.* 124.

To § 33.

93. I don't admit, that every *action* gives a *new force* to the *Patient.* It frequently happens in the concourse of Bodies, that each of them preserves its *force* ; as when two equal hard Bodies meet directly. Then the Direction only is changed, without any change in the *Force* ; each of the Bodies receiving the Direction of the other, and going back with the same *swiftness* it came.

94. However, I am far from saying that it is *supernatural* to give a *new force* to a Body ; for I acknowledge that One Body does frequently receive a new *Force* from another, which loses as much of its own. But I say only, 'tis *Supernatural* that the whole *Universe of Bodies* should receive a *new force* ; and consequently that one body should acquire any new *force,* without the loss of as much in others. And therefore I say likewise, 'tis an indefensible opinion to suppose the *Soul* gives *force* to the *Body* ; for then the whole Universe of Bodies would receive a *new force.*

95. The Author's *Dilemma* here, is ill grounded; *viz.* that according to Me, either a Man must act Supernaturally, or be a mere *Machine,* like a Watch. For, Man does not act Supernaturally : And his Body is truely a *Machine,* acting only *mechanically* ; and yet his *Soul* is a free Cause.

Sur § 34 & 35.

96. *Je me remets aussi à ce qui a été ou sera dit dans ce present Papier,* Nomb. 82, 86, & 111 ; *touchant la comparaison entre* Dieu & l'Ame du Monde ; & *comment le sentiment qu'on oppose au mien, fait trop approcher l'un à l'autre.*

Sur § 36.

97. *Je me rapporte aussi à ce que je viens de dire touchant* l'Harmonie *entre l'*Ame & le Corps. Nomb. 89, & *Seqq* ;

Sur § 37.

98. *On me dit que l'Ame n'est pas dans le* Cerveau, *mais dans le* Sensorium, *sans dire ce que c'est que ce* Sensorium. *Mais supposé que ce* Sensorium *soit étendu, comme je crois qu'on l'entend ; c'est tousjours la même difficulte, & la* Question *revient si l'Ame est diffuse par tout cet Etendu, quelque grand ou quelque petit qu'il soit. Car le plus ou moins de grandeur, n'y fait rien.*

Sur § 38.

99. *Je n'entreprends pas icy d'établir ma* Dynamique, *ou ma Doctrine des* Forces : *Ce lieu n'y seroit point propre. Cependant je puis fort bien repondre à l'*Ojection *qu'on me fait icy. J'avois soutenu que les* Forces actives *se conservent dans le Monde. On m'objecte, que deux Corps* Mols *ou non-élastiques, concourant entre eux, perdent de leur force. Je reponds que non. Il est vray que les Touts la perdent par rapport à leur mouvement total ; mais les Parties la reçoivent, étant* * *agitées par la force du concours* [[ou du choc]][19]. *Les* Forces *ne sont point detruites, mais dissipées parmy les Parties menuës. Ce n'est pas les perdre, mais c'est faire comme font ceux qui changent la grosse Monnoye en petite. Je demeure cependant d'accord, que la quantité du mouvement ne demeure point la même ; & en cela j'approuve ce qui se dit, pag. 341 de l'*Optique *de M.* Newton, *qu'on cite icy. Mais j'ay montré ailleurs, qu'il y a de la difference entre la quantité du* mouvement & *la quantité de la force.*

* agitées interieurement

Sur § 39.

100. *On m'avoit soutenu que la* Force † *se diminuoit*[20] *naturellement dans l'Univers corporel, & que cela venoit de la dependance des Choses ; (3*me papier, *sur § 13 & 14.) J'avois demandé dans ma 3*me *reponse qu'on prouvât que ce defaut est une suite de la dependance des Choses. On esquive de satisfaire à ma demande, en se jettant sur un incident ; & en niant ce soit un defaut. Mais que ce soit un defaut ou non, il falloit prouver que c'est une suite de la dependance des Choses.*

† decroissoit

To § 34, *and* 35.

96. I here refer to what has been or shall be said in this Paper, *Numb.* 82, 86, *and* 111 ; concerning the comparison between *God* and a *Soul of the World* ; and how the opinion contrary to mine, brings the one of these too near to the other.

To § 36.

97. I here also refer to what I have before said, concerning the *Harmony* between the *Soul* and the *Body*, Numb. 89, *&c.*

To § 37.

98. The Author tells us, that the Soul is not in the Brain, but in the *Sensorium* ; without saying What that *Sensorium* is. But supposing That *Sensorium* to be extended, as I believe the Author understands it ; the same difficulty remains, and the Question returns, Whether the Soul be diffused through the whole Extension, be it great or small. For, more or less in bigness, is nothing to the purpose here.

To § 38.

99. I don't undertake here to establish my *Dynamics*, or my Doctrine of *Forces :* This would not be a proper Place for it. However, I can very well answer the Objection here brought against me. I have affirmed that * *Active Forces* are preserved in the World [*without diminution.*] The Author objects, that two *Soft* or Un-elastick Bodies meeting together, lose some of their *force*. I answer, No. 'Tis true, their *Wholes* lose it with respect to their Total Motion ; but their *Parts* receive it, being shaken {internally} by the force of the Concourse [[or of the impact]].[20] And therefore That loss of *Force*, is only in appearance. The *forces* are not destroyed, but scattered among the small parts. The Bodies do not *lose* their *forces* ; but the case here is the same, as when Men change great Money into small. However, I agree that the *quantity of Motion* does not remain the same ; And herein I approve what Sir *Isaac Newton* says, *page* 341 of his *Opticks*, which the Author here quotes. But I have shown elsewhere, that there is a difference between the quantity of *Motion*, and the quantity of *Force*.

> * *See above, the Note on* § 13, *of Dr. Clarke's Third Reply.*

To § 39.

100. The author maintained against me that Force does naturally *lessen*[21] in the material Universe ; and that This arises from the dependence of things, (*Third Reply*, § 13 *and* 14.) In my † *Third Answer*, I desired him to prove that this Imperfection is a consequence of the dependence of things. He avoids answering my demand ; by falling upon an Incident, and denying this to be an imperfection. But whether it be an imperfection, or not, he should have proved that 'tis a consequence of the dependence of things.

> † *Which is Mr. Leibnitz's Fourth Paper, in this Collection.*

702   140B. LEIBNIZ'S FIFTH PAPER

101. *Cependant il faut bien, que ce qui rendroit la Machine du Monde aussi imparfaite que celle d'une mauvais Horloger, soit un* defaut.

102. *On dit maintenant, que c'est une* faite *de l'*inertie *de la Matiere* ; *mais c'est ce qu'on ne prouvera pas non plus.* Cette inertie *mise en avant, & nommée par* Kepler, *& repetée par* Des Cartes *, & que j'ay employée dans la* Theodicée *pour donner une † Image de l'Imperfection naturelle des Creatures* ; *fait seulement que les vitesses sont diminuées quand les Matieres sont augmentées, mais c'est sans aucune* diminution des Forces.

Sur § 40.

103. *J'avois soutenu, que la dependance de la Machine du monde d'un Auteur Divin, est plustost cause que ce defaut n'y est point* ; *& que l'ouvrage n'a point besoin d'être redressé* ; *qu'il n'est point sujet à se detraquer* ; *& enfin, qu'il ne sauroit diminuer en Perfection. Je donne maintenant à deviner aux Gens, comment on en peut inferer contre moy, comme on fait icy, qu'il faut, si cela est, que le Monde materiel soit* infini *& éternel, sans aucun commencement* ; *& que Dieu doit tousjours avoir créé* autant *d'hommes & d'autres especes, qu'il est* possible *de créer.*

Sur § 41.

104. Je *ne dis point que l'Espace est un* Ordre ou Situation *qui rend les choses* situables ; *ce seroit parler galimatias. On n'a qu'à considerer mes propres paroles, & à les joindre à ce que je viens de dire cy dessus,* Nomb. 47 ; *pour montrer comment l'Esprit vient à former l'idée de l'Espace, sans qu'il faille qu'il y ait un être réel & absolu qui y reponde hors de l'Esprit & hors des rapports. Je ne dis donc point, que l'Espace est un* Ordre ou Situation, *mais un* Ordre des Situations, *ou selon lequel les Situations sont rangées* ; *& que l'Espace abstrait est cet* Ordre des Situations *conçues comme possibles. Ainsi c'est quelque chose d'idéal. Mais il semble qu'on ne me veut point entendre. J'ay repondu deja icy,* Nomb. 54, *à l'Objection qui pretend qu'un* Ordre *n'est point capable de* quantité.

105. *On objecte icy, que le Temps ne sauroit être un* Ordre des choses succes-sives, *parce que la* quantité *du* temps *peut devenir plus grande ou plus petite,* l'ordre des successions *demeurant le même. Je reponds que cela n'est point : Car si le* temps est *plus grand, il y aura plus d'états successifs pareils interposés* ; *& s'il est* plus petit, *il y en aura* moins ; *puisqu'il n'y a point de vuide ny de condensation ou penetration, pour ainsi dire, dans les* temps, *non plus que dans les* lieux.

---

*   dans ses Lettres,
†   Image, & en même temps un echantillon,

101. However ; That which would make the Machine of the World as imperfect, as that of an unskilful Watchmaker ; surely must needs be an imperfection.

102. The Author says now, that it is a Consequence of the *Inertia* of Matter. But This also, he will not prove. That *Inertia*, alledged here by *him*, mentioned by *Kepler*, repeated by *Cartesius* {in his letters}, and made use of by *Me* in my *Theodicæa*, in order to give a notion, {and at the same time an example,} of the natural imperfection of Creatures ; has no other effect, than to make the Velocities diminish, when the Quantities of Matter are encreased : But this is without any *diminution of the Forces.*

To § 40.

103. I maintained, that the dependence of the Machine of the World upon its divine Author, is rather a reason why there can be no such imperfection in it ; and that the Work of God does not want to be set right again ; that is not liable to be disordered ; and lastly, that it cannot lessen in Perfection. Let any one guess now, how the Author can hence infer against me, as he does, that, if this be the Case, then the material World must be *infinite* and *eternal*, without any beginning ; and that God must always have created *as many* Men and other Kinds of Creatures, as *can possibly* be created.

To § 41.

104. I don't say, that Space is an *Order* or *Situation*, which makes Things capable of being *situated* : This would be Nonsense. Any one needs only consider my own Words, and add them to what I said above, (*Numb.* 47.) in order to show how the Mind comes to form to it self an Idea of *Space*, and yet that there needs not be any real and absolute Being answering to that Idea, distinct from the Mind, and from all Relations. I don't say therefore, that *Space* is an *Order or Situation*, but an *Order of Situations* ; or [an Order] according to which, Situations are disposed ; And that *abstract Space* is *That Order of Situations*, when they are conceived as being possible. Space is therefore something [*merely*] Ideal. But, it seems, the Author will not understand me. I have already, in this Paper, (*Numb.* 54.) answered the Objection, that *Order* is not capable of *Quantity*.

105. The Author objects here, that *Time* cannot be an *Order of successive Things*, because the *Quantity of Time* may become *greater* or *less*, and yet the *Order of Successions* continue the *same*. I answer ; this is not so. For if the *Time* is *greater*, there will be *More* successive and like States interposed ; and if it be *less*, there will be *fewer* ; seeing there is no *Vacuum*, nor Condensation, or Penetration, (if I may so speak,) in *Times*, any more than in *Places.*

704   140B. LEIBNIZ'S FIFTH PAPER

* Je sou-
tiens que

106. * *Il est vray*[21] *que sans les Creatures, l'immensité & l'éternité de Dieu ne lais-seroient pas de subsister; mais sans aucune dependance ny des temps ny des lieux. S'il n'y avoit point de Creatures, il n'y auroit ny Temps ny Lieu, & par consequent point d'*Espace *actuel. L'immensité de Dieu est independante de l'*Espace, *comme l'éternité de Dieu est independante du Temps. Elles* † *portent que Dieu seroit present & coëxistant à toutes les choses qui existeroient. Ainsi je n'admets point ce qu'on avance icy, que si Dieu seul existoit, il y auroit Temps &* Espace, *comme à present. Au lieu qu'alors, à mon avis, ils ne seroient que dans les idées, comme des simples possibilités. L'immensité & l'éternité de Dieu sont quelque chose de plus éminent que la durée & l'étendue des Creatures ; non seulement par rapport à la* grandeur, *mais encore par rapport à la* nature *de la chose. Ces attributs Divins n'ont point besoin de choses hors de Dieu, comme sont les* lieux *&* temps *acutels. Ces verités on été assés reconnues par les* Theologiens *& par les* Philosophes.

Sur § 42.

107. *J'avois soutenu que l'operation de Dieu, par laquelle il redresseroit la machine du monde corporel, prête par sa nature (à ce qu'on pretend) à tomber dans le repos, seroit un* Miracle. *On a repondu, que ce ne seroit point une operation* Miraculeuse, *parce qu'elle seroit* ordinaire, *& doit arriver assés souvent. J'ay repliqué, que ce n'est pas l'*usuel *ou* non-usuel, *qui fait le* Miracle *proprement dit, ou de la plus grande espece, mais de* surpasser *les forces des creatures : Et que c'est le sentiment des* Theologiens *& des* Philosophes. *Et qu'ainsi on m'accorde au moins, que ce qu'on introduit, & que je desapprouve, est un Miracle de la plus grande Espece, suivant la* notion receue *; c'est à dire, qui* surpasse les forces créées *; & que c'est justement ce que tout le monde tâche d'eviter en Philosophie. On me repond maintenant, que c'est appeller de la* Raison *à l'opinion vulgaire. Mais je replique encore, que cette opinion vulgaire, suivant laquelle il faut éviter, en Philosophant, autant qu'il se peut, ce qui surpasse les natures des creatures, est tres-raisonnable. Autrement rien ne sera si aisé que de rendre raison de tout, en faisant survenir une Divinité. Deum ex machina, sans soucier des natures des choses.*

108. *D'ailleurs le sentiment commun des* Theologiens *ne doit pas être traité simplement en* opinion vulgaire. *Il faut de* grandes raisons *pour qu'on ose y contrevenir, & je n'en vois aucune icy.*

109. *Il semble qu'on s'écarte de sa propre notion, qui demandoit que le Miracle soit* rare *; en me reprochant (quoyque sans fondement,) sur § 31, que l'*harmonie *préétab-lie seroit un* Miracle *perpetuel ; si ce n'est qu'on ait voulu raisonner contre moy* ad hominem.

---

† portent seulement à l'egard de ces deux ordres des choses, que Dieu &c.

140B. LEIBNIZ'S FIFTH PAPER 705

106. 'Tis true,[22] the Immensity and Eternity of God would subsist, though there were no Creatures; but those Attributes would have no dependence either on *Times* or *Places*. If there were no Creatures, there would be neither *Time* nor *Place*, and consequently no actual *Space*. The Immensity of God is independent upon *Space*, as his Eternity is independent upon *Time*. These Attributes signify only, {regarding those two orders of things,} that God would be present and co-existent with all the Things that should exist. And therefore I don't admit what's here alledged, that if God existed alone, there would be *Time* and *Space* as there is now: Whereas then, in my Opinion, they would be only in the Ideas of God as mere Possibilities. The Immensity and Eternity of God, are things more *transcendent*, than the Duration and Extension of Creatures; not only with respect to the *Greatness*, but also to the *Nature* of the Things. Those Divine Attributes do not imply the Supposition of Things extrinsick to God, such as are actual *Places* and *Times*. These Truths have been sufficiently acknowledged by *Divines* and *Philosophers*.

To § 42.

107. I maintained that an Operation of God, by which he should mend the Machine of the material World, * tending in its Nature (as this Author pretends) to lose all its Motion, would be a *Miracle*. His Answer was; that it would not be a miraculous Operation, because it would be *usual*, and must frequently happen. I reply'd; that 'tis not *Usualness* or *Unusualness*, that makes a *Miracle* properly so called, or a Miracle of the highest Sort; but it's *surpassing the Powers of Creatures*; and this is the [*general*] Opinion of *Divines* and *Philosophers*: And that therefore the Author acknowledges *at least*, that the thing He introduces, and I disallow, is, according to the *received Notion*, a Miracle of the highest Sort, that is, one which surpasses all created Powers: And that this is the very Thing which all Men endeavour to avoid in Philosophy. He answers now, that this is appealing from *Reason* to *vulgar Opinion*. But I reply again, that this vulgar Opinion, according to which we ought in Philosophy to avoid, as much as possible, what surpasses the Natures of Creatures; is a very reasonable Opinion. Otherwise nothing will be easier than to account for Any thing by bringing in the Deity, *Deum ex Machina*, without minding the Natures of Things.

> * *See above, the Note on § 13, of Dr. Clark's Third Reply.*

108. Besides; the *common* Opinion of *Divines*, ought not to be looked upon merely as *vulgar Opinion*. A Man should have *weighty Reasons*, before he ventures to contradict it; and I see no such Reasons here.

109. The Author seems to depart from his own Notion, according to which a Miracle ought to be unusual; when, in § 31, he objects to me, (though without any Ground,) that the *pre-established Harmony* would be a perpetual *Miracle*. Here, I say, he seems to depart from his own Notion; unless he had a Mind to argue against me *ad Hominem*.

706   140B. LEIBNIZ'S FIFTH PAPER

Sur § 43.

110. *Si le* Miracle *ne differe du* naturel *que dans l'apparence & par rapport à* Nous, *en sorte que nous appellions seulement miracle ce que nous observons rarement, il n'y aura point de differnce* interne réelle *entre le* Miracle & le naturel *; &, dans le fond des chose, tout sera également naturel, ou tout sera également miraculeux. Les* Theologiens *auront ils raison de s'accommoder du premier, & les* Philosophes *du second ?*

111. *Cela n'irat-il pas encore à faire de* Dieu *l'Ame du Monde, si toutes ses operations sont* naturelles, *comme celles que l'Ame exerce dans le Corps ? Ainsi* Dieu *sera une partie de la* Nature.

112. *En bonne Philosophie, & en saine Theologie, il faut distinguer entre ce qui est explicable par les* Natures & Forces des Creatures, *& ce qui n'est explicable que par les forces de la* Substance Infinie. *Il faut mettre une distance infinie, entre l'operation de* Dieu *qui va au delà des* Forces des Natures *; & entre les operations des choses qui suivent les loix que* Dieu *leur a données, & qu'il les a rendu capables de suivre par leur* natures, *quoyqu'avec son assistance.*

113. *C'est par là que tombent les* Attractions *proprement dites, & autres operations inexplicables par les natures des creatures, qu'il faut faire effectuer par miracle, ou recourir aux absurdités, c'est à dire, aux* qualités occultes Scholastiques, *qu'on commence à nous debiter sous le specieux nom de* forces, *mais qui nous ramenent dans le royaume des tenebres. C'est,* inventa fruge, glandibus vesci.[24]

* de Monsieur Boyle,

114. *Du temps * du* Chevalier Boyle, *& d'autres excellens hommes qui fleurissoient en* Angleterre † *sous* Charles II, *on n'auroit pas osé nous debiter des notions si creuses. J'espere que ce beau temps reviendra sous un aussi bon gouvernement que celuy d'à present ||. Le capital de M.* Boyle *étoit d'inculquer que tout se faisoit* mechaniquement *dans la Physique. Mais c'est un malheur des hommes, de se degouter enfin de la raison même, & de s'ennuyer de la lumiere. Les chimeres commencent à revenir, & plaisent parce qu'elles ont quelque chose de merveilleux. Il arrive dans le Pays Philosophique ce qui est arrivé dans le pays Poëtique. On s'est lassé des Romans raisonnables, tels que la* Clelie Françoise,[26] *ou l'Aramene Allemande ;[27] & on est revenu depuis quelque temps aux* Contes des Fées.

115. *Quant aux* Mouvemens des corps celestes, *& plus encore quant à la* formation des plantes & des animaux *; il n'y a rien qui tienne du* Miracle, *excepté le commencement de ces choses. L'organisme des animaux est un* mechanisme *qui suppose une* Préformation Divine *: Ce qui en suit, est purement naturel, & tout à fait* mechanique.

116. Tout *ce qui se fait dans le* Corps de l'homme, *& de tout* animal, *est aussi* mechanique *que ce qui se fait dans une* Montre. *La difference est seulement telle*

---

† sous les commencemens de

|| & que les esprits un peu trop divertis par le malheur des temps, retourneront à mieux cultiver les connoissances solides. Le Capital &c.

To § 43.

110. If a *Miracle* differs from what is *Natural*, only in Appearance, and *with respect to Us*; so that we call That only a *Miracle*, which we seldom see; there will be no *internal real Difference*, between a *Miracle* and what is *natural*; and at the bottom, every thing will be either[23] equally *natural*, or equally *miraculous*. Will *Divines* like the former, or *Philosophers* the latter?

111. Will not this Doctrine, moreover, tend to make *God* the *Soul of the World*; if all his Operations are *natural*, like those of our Souls upon Bodies? And so *God* will be a part of *Nature*.

112. In good Philosophy, and sound Theology, we ought to distinguish between what is explicable by the *Natures* and *Powers* of *Creatures*, and what is explicable only by the *Powers* of the *Infinite Substance*. We ought to make an infinite Difference between the *Operation* of *God*, which goes beyond the Extent of *Natural Powers*; and the *Operations* of Things that follow the Law which God has given them, and which he has enabled them to follow *by their natural Powers*, though not without his Assistance.

113. This overthrows *Attractions*, properly so called, and other Operations inexplicable by the natural Powers of Creatures; which Kinds of Operations, the Assertors of them must suppose to be effected by *Miracles*;[24] or else have recourse to Absurdities, that is, to the *occult Qualities* of the Schools; which some Men begin to revive under the specious Name of *Forces*; but they bring us back again into the Kingdom of Darkness. This is, *inventa fruge, glandibus vesci*.[25]

114. In the time of Mr. *Boyle*,[26] and other excellent Men, who flourished in *England* under {the beginnings of} *Charles* the II^d, no Body would have ventured to publish such Chimerical Notions. I hope, That happy time will return under so good a Government as the present {and that minds, a bit too diverted by the misfortune of the times, will return to cultivating sound knowledge more readily}. Mr. *Boyle* made it his chief Business to inculcate, that every thing was done *mechanically* in natural Philosophy. But it is Men's Misfortune to grow, at last, out of Conceit with Reason it self, and to be weary of Light. *Chimæra*'s begin to appear again, and they are pleasing because they have something in them that is wonderful. What has happened in *Poetry*, happens also in the *Philosophical World*. People are grown weary of rational *Romances*, such as were the *French Clelia*,[27] or the *German Aramene*;[28] and they are become fond again of the *Tales of Fairies*.

115. As for the *Motions of the Celestial Bodies*, and even the *Formation* of *Plants* and *Animals*; there is nothing in them that looks like a *Miracle*, except their *Beginning*. The *Organism* of *Animals* is a *Mechanism*, which supposes a Divine *Preformation*. What follows upon it, is purely natural, and entirely *Mechanical*.

116. *Whatever* is performed in the *Body of Man*, and of every *Animal*, is no less *Mechanical*, than what is performed in a *Watch*. The Difference is only such, as

708   140B. LEIBNIZ'S FIFTH PAPER

qu'elle doit être entre une Machine d'une invention Divine, & entre la production d'un Ouvrier aussi borné que l'homme.

Sur § 44.

117. *Il n'y a point de difficulté chez les* Theologiens, *sur les* miracles des Anges. *Il ne s'agit que de l'usage du mot. On pourra dire que les* Anges *font des* miracles, *mais moins proprement dits, ou d'un ordre inferieur. Disputer là dessus seroit un question de nom. On pourra dire que cet Ange qui transportoit* Habacuc *par les airs, qui remuoit le Lac de* Bethesda, *faisoit un miracle. Mais ce n'estoit pas un miracle du premier rang ; car il est explicable par les forces naturelles des Anges superieures aux notres.*

Sur § 45.

118. *J'avois objecté, qu'un* Attraction *proprement dite, ou à la Scholastique, seroit une operation en distance,* sans moyen. *On repond icy qu'un* Attraction sans moyen *seroit une contradiction. Fort bien : mais comment l'entend on donc, quand on veut que le Soleil à travers d'un Espace vuide attire le globe de la Terre ? Est ce Dieu qui sert de moyen ? Mais ce seroit un* miracle, *s'il y en a jamais eu. Cela surpasseroit les forces des Creatures.*

119. *Ou sont-ce peut-être quelques substances immaterielles, ou quelques rayons spirituels, ou quelque accident sans substance, quelque Espece comme intentionnelle, ou quelque autre je ne say quoy, qui doit faire ce moyen pretendu ? choses dont il semble qu'on a encore bonne provision en tête, sans s'assés expliquer.*

120. *Ce moyen de communication est (dit on) invisible, intangible, non mechanique. On pouvoit adjouter avec le même droit, inexplicable, non intelligible, precaire, sans fondement, sans exemple.*

121. *Mais il est* regulier, *(dit on,) il est* constant, & *par consequent* naturel. *Je reponds, qu'il ne sauroit être regulier sans être raisonnable ; & qu'il ne sauroit être naturel, sans être explicable par les natures des creatures.*

122. *Si ce* moyen *qui fait une veritable* Attraction, *est constant, & en même temps inexplicable par les forces des creatures, & s'il est veritable avec cela ; c'est un* Miracle *perpetuel : Et s'il n'est pas miraculeux, il est faux. C'est une chose chimerique, une* qualité occulte Scholastique.

123. *Il seroit comme le cas d'un corps allant en rond sans s'écarter par la Tangente, quoyque rien d'explicable ne l'empechât de la faire. Exemple que j'ay dejà allegué, auquel on n'a pas trouvé à propos de repondre, parce qu'il montre trop clairement la difference entre le veritable* naturel *d'un coté, & entre la* qualité occulte *chimerique des Ecoles de l'autre côté.*

ought to be between a *Machine* of *Divine* Invention, and the Workmanship of such a limited Artist as *Man* is.

To § 44.

117. There is no Difficulty among Divines, about the *Miracles of Angels*. The Question is only about the use of that Word. It may be said that *Angels* work *Miracles* ; but less properly so called, or of an inferior Order. To dispute about this, would be a mere Question about a Word. It may be said that the *Angel*, who carried *Habakkuk* through the Air,[29] and he who troubled the Water of the Pool of *Bethesda*,[30] worked a *Miracle*. But it was not a Miracle of the highest Order ; for it may be explained by the natural Powers of Angels, which surpass those of Man.

To § 45.

118. I objected, that an *Attraction*, properly so called, or in the *Scholastic* Sense, would be an Operation at a Distance, without any *Means* intervening. The Author answers here, that an *Attraction* without any *Means* intervening, would be indeed a Contradiction. Very well ! But then what does he mean, when he will have the Sun to attract the Globe of the Earth through an empty Space ? Is it God himself that performs it ? But this would be a *Miracle*, if ever there was any. This would surely exceed the Powers of Creatures.

119. Or, are perhaps some immaterial Substances, or some spiritual Rays, or some Accident without a Substance, or some kind of *Species Intentionalis*, or some other *I know not what*, the *Means* by which this is pretended to be performed ? Of which sort of things, the Author seems to have still a good Stock in his Head, without explaining himself sufficiently.

120. *That Means* of communication (says he) is invisible, intangible, not Mechanical. He might as well have added, inexplicable, unintelligible, precarious, groundless, and unexampled.

121. But it is *regular*, (says the Author,) it is *constant*, and consequently *natural*. I answer ; it cannot be regular, without being reasonable ; nor natural, unless it can be explained by the Natures of Creatures.

122. If the *Means*, which causes an *Attraction* properly so called, be constant, and at the same time inexplicable by the Powers of Creatures, and yet be true ; it must be a perpetual *Miracle* : And if it is not miraculous, it is false. 'Tis a Chimerical Thing, a Scholastick *occult Quality*.

123. The Case would be the same, as in a Body going round without receding in the Tangent, though nothing that can be explained, hindered it from receding. Which is an Instance I have already alledged ; and the Author has not thought fit to answer it, because it shows too clearly the difference between what is truely *Natural* on the one side, and a *chimerical occult Quality* of the Schools on the other.

Sur § 46.

124. *Les forces naturelles des Corps, sont toutes soûmises aux* loix mecaniques ; *& les forces naturelles des Esprits, sont toutes soûmises aux loix morales. Les premieres suivent l'ordre des causes efficientes ; & les secondes suivent l'ordre des causes finales. Les premieres operent sans liberté, comme une Montre ; les secondes sont exercées avec liberté, quoyqu'elles s'accordent exactement avec cette espece de Montre, qu'une autre causes libre superieure a accommodée avec elles par avance. J'en ay deja parlé,* No. 92.

125. *Je finis par un point qu'on m'a opposé au commencement de ce quatriéme Papier, où j'ay dejà repondu cy-dessus,* Nomb. 18, 19, 20. *Mais je me suis reservé d'en dire encore d'avantage en concluant. On a prétendu d'abord que je commets une* Petition de Principe. *Mais de quel Principe, je vous en prie ? Plût à Dieu qu'on n'eut jamais supposé des Principes moins clairs. Ce Principe est celuy du* besoin d'une Raison suffisante, *pour qu'une chose existe, qu'un évenement arrive, qu'une verité ait lieu. Est ce un Principe qui a besoin de* preuve *? On me l'avoit même accordé, ou fait semblant de l'accorder, au* second Nombre du 3me papier : *Peut étre, parce qu'il auroit paru trop choquant de le nier. Mais ou on ne l'a fait qu'en paroles, ou l'on se contredit, ou l'on se retracte.*

126. *J'ose dire que sans ce grand Principe, on ne sauroit venir à la preuve de l'Existence de Dieu, ny rendre raison de plusieurs autres verités importantes.*

127. *Tout le monde ne s'en est il point servi en mille occasions ? Il est vray qu'on l'a oublié par negligence en beaucoup d'autres ; Mais c'est là justement l'origine des* Chimeres *; comme, par exemple, d'un* Temps *ou d'un* Espace *absolu réel, du* Vuide, *des* Atomes, *d'une* Attraction *à la* Scholastique, *de l'*Influence Physique * *de l'*Ame *sur le* Corps, *& de mille autres* Fictions, *tant de celles qui sont restées de la fausse persuasion des Anciens, que de celles qu'on a inventées depuis peu.*

* entre l' Ame & le Corps,

128. *N'est ce pas à cause de la violation de ce grand Principe, que les Anciens se sont deja moqués de la* Declinaison *sans sujet des Atomes d'*Epicure *? Et j'ose dire que l'*Attraction *à la* Scholastique *qu'on renouvelle aujourdhuy, & dont on ne se moquoit pas moins il y a 30 ans ou environ, n'a rien de plus raisonnable.*

129. *J'ay souvent defié les gens de m'apporter une* Instance *contre ce grand Principe, un* Exemple *non contesté, où il manque. Mais on ne l'a jamais fait, & on ne le fera jamais. Cependant il y a une infinité d'*Exemples, *où il* reussit dans tous les cas connus où il est employé. Ce qui doit faire juger raisonnablement, qu'il reussira encore dans les cas inconnus, ou qui ne deviendront connus que par son moyen ; suivant la Maxime de la Philosophie experimentale, qui procede à posteriori ; quand même il ne seroit point d'ailleurs justifié par la pure Raison, ou à priori.*

* reussit, ou plustôt il reussit dans tous

130. *Me nier ce grand Principe, c'est faire encore d'ailleurs comme* Epicure, *reduit à nier cet autre grand Principe, qui est celuy de la* Contradiction *; savoir, que toute*

To § 46.

124. All the natural forces of *Bodies*, are subject to *Mechanical Laws* ; and all the natural Powers of *Spirits*, are subject to *Moral Laws*. The former follow the Order of Efficient Causes ; and the latter follow the Order of Final Causes. The former operate without liberty, like a Watch ; the latter operate with liberty, though they exactly agree with That Machine, which Another Cause, Free and Superior, has adapted to them before-hand. I have already spoken of this, *above, Nº 92.*

125. I shall conclude with what the Author objected against me at the Beginning of this Fourth Reply: To which I have already given an Answer above, (*Numb.* 18, 19, 20.) But I deferred speaking more fully upon That Head, to the Conclusion of this Paper. He pretended, that I have been guilty of a *Petitio Principii.* But, of *What* Principle, I beseech you ? Would to God, less clear Principles had never been laid down. The Principle in Question, is the Principle of the *want of a sufficient Reason* ; in order to any thing's existing, in order to any Event's happening, in order to any truth's taking place. Is This a Principle, that wants to be *proved ?* The Author granted it, or pretended to grant it, *Numb.* 2, *of his Third Paper* ; Possibly, because the denial of it would have appeared too unreasonable. But either he has done it only in words, or he contradicts himself, or retracts his concession.

126. I dare say, that without this great Principle, one cannot prove the existence of God, nor account for many other important Truths.

127. Has not every body made use of This Principle, upon a thousand occasions ? 'Tis true, it has been neglected, out of carelessness, on many occasions : But That Neglect, has been the true cause of *Chimeras* ; such as are, (for instance,) an absolute real *Time* or *Space*, a *Vacuum, Atoms, Attraction* in the Scholastick sense, a *Physical Influence of the Soul over the Body* {*between the soul and the body*}, and a thousand other *fictions*, either derived from erroneous opinions of the Ancients, or lately invented by Modern Philosophers.

128. Was it not upon account of *Epicurus*'s violating this great Principle, that the Ancients derided his groundless *Declination* of Atoms ? And I dare say, the Scholastick *Attraction*, revived in our days and no less derided about thirty Years ago, is not at all more reasonable.

129. I have often defied People to alledge an Instance against that great Principle, to bring any one uncontested Example wherein it fails. But they have never done it, nor ever will. 'Tis certain, there is an infinite number of Instances, wherein it succeeds {or rather it succeeds} in all the Known Cases in which it has been made use of. From whence one may reasonably judge, that it will succeed also in Unknown Cases, or in such cases as can only by its means become known : According to the Method of Experimental Philosophy, which proceeds *a posteriori* ; though the Principle were not perhaps otherwise justified by bare Reason, or *a priori*.

130. To deny this great Principle, is likewise to do as *Epicurus* did ; who was reduced to deny That Other great Principle, *viz.* the *Principle of Contradiction* ;

Enonciation intelligible doit étre vraye, ou fausse. Chrysippe *s'amusoit à le prouver contre* Epicure *; mais je ne crois pas d'avoir besoin de l'imiter, quoyque j'aye deja dit cy dessus ce qui peut justifier le mien, & quoyque je puisse encore dire quelque chose là dessus, mais qui seroit peut étre trop profond pour convenir à cette presente contestation. Et je crois que des Personnes raisonnables & impartiales m'accorderont, que d'avoir reduit son Adversaire à nier ce Principe, c'est l'avoir mené* ad absurdum.

140B. LEIBNIZ'S FIFTH PAPER   713

which is, that every intelligible Enunciation must be either true, or false. *Chrysippus* undertook to prove That Principle against *Epicurus*;[31] but I think I need not imitate him. I have already said, what is sufficient to justify mine : And I might say something more upon it ; but perhaps it would be too abstruse for this present Dispute. And, I believe, reasonable and impartial Men will grant me, that having forced an Adversary to deny That Principle, is reducing him *ad absurdum*.

[1] The original French and the English translation are from Clarke's 1717 edition of the correspondence (Clarke 1717, pp. 154–278). LBr. 160 Bl. 80r–83v is a relatively short first draft (eight folio sides in Leibniz's hand, for which see document 140a.); LBr. 160 Bl. 84r–95v is a greatly expanded second draft (twenty-four folio sides in Leibniz's hand). LBr. 160 Bl. 44r–52v/55r–72r (fifty-three folio sides) is a fair copy in a secretary's hand with changes in Leibniz's hand; LH 1, 20 Bl. 405r–420v (31.5 folio sides) is a fair copy in a secretary's hand with changes in Leibniz's hand. It answers Clarke's Fourth Reply (document 129). Leibniz enclosed the present paper, in part, with his letter to Caroline of 18 August 1716. In that letter he told Caroline that the other half of this, his long, last paper, his response to Clarke's Fourth Reply, would be sent by the following post (document 139, p. 629). Footnotes and marginal notes are Clarke's; endnotes are mine. Single square brackets in the text and what they contain are Clarke's. Clarke's references to the Appendix of his 1717 edition of the correspondence have been omitted.

[2] The sentence in square brackets that heads the French version of Leibniz's Fifth Paper is Clarke's note in French, which I translate as follows: 'The variant readings printed in the margin of the following paper are changes made by Mr. Leibniz's own hand in a different copy of this paper that he sent to one of his friends in England shortly before his death.' (The friend in England referred to here is presumably Pierre Des Maizeaux*.) In his 1717 edition of the correspondence, Clarke did not supply English translations for the changes made by Leibniz that he printed in the left margins and at the bottom of pages as footnotes, so here I include my own translation of those changes within curly brackets at the appropriate locations within the English version of Leibniz's paper. All notes in the left margin of the French version of the paper and all footnotes are Clarke's notes of changes made by Leibniz; all notes in the right margin of the English version of the paper are Clarke's.

[3] The *Emperor of the Moon* was a farce written in 1687 by the English playwright Aphra Behn. It was published in 1688.

[4] That is Otto von Guericke*.

[5] That is, Evangelista Torricelli*.

[6] *Spectatum admissi risum teneatis amici?*: 'If you saw such a thing friends, could you restrain your laughter?' (Horace, *De Arte Poetica* I, 5).

[7] From the Greek ἀλλογλωσσια: 'use of a strange tongue, difference of tongue' (Liddell and Scott *Greek-English Lexicon*).

[8] Originally 'le'; corrected to 'ce' in the Errata of the 1717 edition.

[9] Henry More (1614–1687) was an English philosopher and one of the so-called Cambridge Platonists; he held that immaterial substances were extended in space.

[10] Originally 'abstarct'; corrected in the Errata of the 1717 edition.

[11] 'If a painter should wish to attach the neck of a horse to the head of a man' (Horace, *Ars Poetica* I, 1–2).

[12] Originally '*expliquée*'; corrected to 'expliqué' in the Errata of the 1717 edition.

[13] Diodorus Cronus (d. *c.*284 BCE) was a Greek philosopher who argued that nothing is possible which is not true and never will be. His view is discussed in Cicero's *De fato* VII.

[14] Originally 'préétablié'; corrected in the Errata of the 1717.

[15] Originally '*les quelles*'; corrected in the Errata of the 1717 edition.

[16] Originally there was a comma after 'same'; removed in the Errata of the 1717 edition.

[17] That is, Pierre Bayle*.

[18] That is the French Protestant theologian Isaac Jaquelot (1647–1708), who authored three books against Bayle's dictionary.

[19] Originally 'Act on'; corrected in the Errata of the 1717 edition.

[20] The double square brackets and the words within them were inserted by the editor; they were added by Leibniz in the secretary's copy at LBr. 160 Bl. 65v but were not added in Clarke's notes.

[21] In the marginal note to the French version of section 100, Clarke indicates that 'se diminuoit' should be changed to 'decroissoit', which reflects a change that Leibniz made to the secretary's copy at LBr. 160 Bl. 66r and which was included in the revised version that he sent to Des Maizeaux.

Leibniz to Pierre Des Maizeaux (excerpt)

Monsieur

Je dois vous remercier, de ce que vous prenés en main mes interests.[2] J'ay eu autres fois l'honneur de quelque commerce avec vous, tant du vivant de Monsieur Bayle, qu'apres son mort, quand vous m'avés demandé si j'avois quelques lettres de cet excellent homme qui meriteroient d'etre publiées. Mais je vous avois repondu, que celles que j'avois receues de luy avoient eté tres courtes, et n'avoient eté que des aveus de la reception de mes reponses à ses objections; où il avoit repliqué par apres dans ses ouvrages; excepté ma derniere reponse à la quelle je ne say s'il a repliqué. Car il ne s'en est rien trouvé dans ce qu'il a fait imprimer depuis. C'est pourquoy je vous avois envoyé cette derniere reponse, qui n'a pas encore paru en public; pour vous donner occasion de vous informer si M. Bayle y a repliqué: ce qui ne paroist point, puisque je n'en ay rien appris depuis.[4]

Mais pour venir à ce dont il s'agit presentement;[5] j'espere que vous aures receu ce qui s'est passé entre M. Clark et moy, jusqu'à son quatrieme papier inclusivement: au quel je reponds plus amplement qu'aux autres, pour éclaircir la chose a fond et pour m'approcher de la fin de la dispute. Madame la princesse de Galles recevra maintenant le reste de cette réponse; et je vous envoye aussi maintenant, Monsieur, la moitié de la copie; mais[7] vous en aurés l'autre moitié par la poste prochaine, l'un et l'autre vous doit venir par les mains de M. Zollman.[8] J'espere qu'il y a beaucoup de gens en Angleterre, qui ne seront pas de l'avis de M. Newton ou de M. Clark sur la philosophie et qui ne gouteront point les attractions proprement dites, ny le vuide, ny le sensorium de Dieu, ny cette imperfection de l'univers, qui oblige Dieu de le redresser de temps en temps, ny la necessité ou les sectateurs de Newton se trouvent de nier le grand principe du besoin d'une raison suffisante, par lequel je les bats en ruine.

141. LEIBNIZ TO DES MAIZEAUX   715

[22] In the marginal note to the French version of section 106, Clarke indicates that 'Il est vray' should be changed to 'Je soutiens', which reflects a change that Leibniz made to the secretary's copy at LBr. 160 Bl. 68r and which was included in the revised version that he sent to Des Maizeaux.

[23] Originally 'at the tom, every thing will be etiher'; corrected in the Errata of the 1717 edition.

[24] Originally no semi-colon after 'Miracle'; inserted in the Errata of the 1717 edition.

[25] That is, 'to feed on acorns when grain has been found'; after Cicero, *Orator ad M. Brutum* 31: *Quae est autem in hominibus tanta perversitas, ut inventis frugibus glande vescantur?*

[26] That is, Robert Boyle*.

[27] That is, the lengthy novel *Clélie* by the French novelist Madeleine de Scudéry (1607–1701). It was published in 10 volumes between 1654 and 1660.

[28] That is, the novel *Die durchleuchtige Syrerinn Aramena* by Anton Ulrich* of Braunschweig-Wolfenbüttel. The novel was published in five volumes between 1669 and 1773.

[29] This story about Habakkuk is recounted in the apocrypha of the Book of Daniel 14:33–36.

[30] See John 5:2.

[31] See Cicero, *De fato* X.

141. Leibniz to Pierre Des Maizeaux* (excerpt)[1]

[21 August 1716]

Sir

I must thank you for taking my interests in hand.[2] In the past I have had the honour of some correspondence with you, both while Mr. [Pierre] Bayle* was alive and after his death, when you asked if I had some letters from this excellent man that would merit being published. But I had responded that those that I had received from him had been very short and had only been acknowledgements of the receipt of my responses to his objections, to which he had later replied in his works, except my last response, to which I do not know if he replied. For there was nothing about it in what he had printed after that. That is why I had sent you that last response, which has not yet appeared in public,[3] to give you occasion to inquire if Mr. Bayle replied to it, which it seems he did not, since I have learned nothing about it since then.[4]

But to come to the present matter,[5] I hope that you have received what has passed between Mr. [Samuel] Clarke* and me, up to and including his fourth paper, to which I am responding more extensively than to the others in order to clarify the matter thoroughly and come to the end of the dispute. Madame the Princess of Wales [Caroline* of Brandenburg-Ansbach] will now receive the rest of this response,[6] and I am also now sending you, sir, half of the copy. But[7] you will have the other half of it by the next post; both are to reach you through the hands of Mr. [Philipp Heinrich] Zollman*[8] I hope that there are a lot of people in England who will not be of the opinion of Mr. Newton or Mr. Clarke about philosophy and who will not approve of the attractions properly so called, nor of the void, nor of the sensorium of God, nor of that imperfection of the universe that compels God to rectify it from time to time, nor of the necessity in which the followers of Newton

Pour ce qui est de la Traduction de la Theodicée, j'espère que Madame la Princesse de Galles permettra bien qu'on la luy dedie[9] et même qu'on marque dans la dedicace, ou dans quelque mot de preface qu'en la faisant on a voulu satisfaire a ce qu'Elle desiroit. J'attends ses sentimens là dessus.

Il sera peutétre bon de savoir qui en sera le Traducteur. Car vous savés, Monsieur, combien les Anglois sont delicats maintenant sur le style; et peutétre S. A. Royale voudroit en étre informee elle même de peur qu'on ne luy impute d'avoir mal choisi. Il est vray que pour moy, je me repose, Monsieur, sur votre choix, et sur votre surintendance, si vous voulés bien pousser votre bonté si loin.

Je pourrois peutétre aussi marquer quelques endroits ou je voudrois faire quelque petit changement. J'espere aussi qu'on aura un exemplaire complet; car j'en ay vû où il manquoit quelque chose aux additions. On le pourra juger par la liste des pieces même[10] additionnelles qui se trouve à la seconde page, immediatement avant la preface. Je souhaiterois de meriter votre soin obligeant, et je suis avec zele

Monsieur

votre tres humble et tres

obeissant serviteur

Hanover ce 21 d'Aoust
    1716

Leibniz

P. S.   Si vous en avés l'occasion, Monsieur, je vous supplie de faire mes complimens à M. Coste, que je remercie d'avoir fait publier mes petites remarques sur les ouvrages de Mylord Shaftesbury. Monsieur le Secretaire d'Etat Stanhope m'a marqué de les avoir vües: et son Excellence paroissoit de les avoir gouté[es].

141. LEIBNIZ TO DES MAIZEAUX   717

find themselves on account of denying the great principle of the need for a sufficient reason, by which I beat them into ruin.

As for the translation of the *Theodicy*, I hope that Madame the Princess of Wales
will indeed permit it[9] to be dedicated to her and even mentioned in the dedication,
or in some line of the preface, that by doing it we wished to fulfill what she desired.
I await her feelings about that.

It will perhaps be worth knowing who the translator will be. For you know,
sir, how fastidious the English are now about style; and perhaps Her Royal
Highness would want to be informed about it herself, for fear that she might be
charged with having chosen poorly. As for me, it is true that I rely, sir, upon your
choice and upon your superintendence, if you are willing to extend your kindness so far.

I could perhaps also indicate some places where I should want to make some
small change. I also hope that we will have a complete copy; for I have seen some in
which there was something missing in the additions. It will be possible to determine it by the list of pieces itself[10] additional that is found on the second page,
immediately before the preface.[11] I would wish to merit your kind attentions, and
I am enthusiastically

sir

> your very humble and very
> obedient servant

Hanover 21 August
    1716

> Leibniz

P. S. If you have the occasion, sir, I beseech you to pay my compliments to
Mr. [Pierre] Coste*, whom I thank for having had my brief remarks on the
works of Milord Shaftesbury published.[12] Secretary of State [James] Stanhope*
has told me of having seen them, and His Excellency appeared to have
enjoyed them.

---

[1] British Library, Add MS 4284 folio 210. Two quarto sides in Leibniz's hand. Previously published in:
Des Maizeaux 1720, vol. 2, pp. 355–8 (omits the P.S.); in Dutens V 38–9 (omits P.S.); Klopp XI 178–80;
GP VII 536–7 (omits P.S.); Schüller, 1991, p. 260–1 (excerpt in German translation); Robinet 1991,
p. 120–1 (excerpt).

[2] Des Maizeaux inserts a footnote at this point, which I translate as follows:

> A friend of Mr. Leibniz had written to him that Mr. Des Maizeaux tried to procure for him a good
> translator for the English version of his *Theodicy*, which Madame the Princess of Wales wished to
> be done. [Des Maizeaux 1720, vol. 2, p. 355n]

[3] This response was published shortly after Leibniz's death in *Histoire critique de la République des
Lettres*, vol. 11 (1716), pp. 78–115.

[4] Des Maizeaux 1720, vol. 2, p. 356, omits the last part of the sentence, beginning with 'ce qui ne
paroist'.

[5] Des Maizeaux 1720, vol. 2, p. 356, Dutens V 38, and GP VII 537 all omit this first part of the sentence.

[6] That is, Leibniz's Fifth Paper (document 140b).

Caroline of Brandenburg-Ansbach,
Princess of Wales, to Leibniz

Hamthancour le $\frac{31}{21}$ d'aut[2] 1716

J'ay receu par la poste passez deu[4] de vos lettres Monsieur avec lengluse[5] pour docteur chlerque; pour la lettre don vous me parlee[8] avant votre despart pour pirmonth je ne lais pas receu;[7] M^r chlerque n'est pas a londes, ensy j'aurais soin du papié[10] jusqu'a son retour. Je rand graces a dieu de la bon[11] santé du Roy, et j['']espere que le Repos et le plaisir de jouir de son aire natale, le remetera toutafait.[12] vous aurais trouvez sans toute beaucoup de plaisir destre dans la boñe companié[13] de M^r stanop. c'est vn hoñe savant sans le vouloir parroitre as ce que lon ma dit.[14] Je vous suis fort obligée des relassion[15] que vous m'avait anvoiyé[16] de la victoire du P. Eug[e]ne. lenfande de Portugalle[17] s[']y est trouvez,[18] et a tres bien peayée de sa persoñe.[19] J'ay veu vn hoñe qui madit qu'il traduire votre incomparable dodisée,[20] et qu'il me la destirais,[21] ce que j'ay accepté avec beaucoup de plaisir. Je crois que M^r chlerque y repondera.[22] Tans mieu,[23] puis que la verité ne peut estre assez epluché.[24]

142. CAROLINE OF BRANDENBURG-ANSBACH TO LEIBNIZ 719

[7] Klopp XI 179 omits 'mais'.

[8] Des Maizeaux 1720, vol. 2, p. 357 and GP VII 537 omit the last part of this sentence, beginning with 'l'un et l'autre'.

[9] Des Maizeaux 1720, vol. 2, p. 357, Dutens V 39, and GP VII 537 all have 'bien que le Traducteur ou le Libraire la lui dédient' instead of 'bien qu'on la luy dedie'.

[10] Klopp XI 180 omits 'même'.

[11] The reference is presumably to the second edition (1712) of Leibniz's *Theodicy*.

[12] Upon its publication in 1711, Coste sent a copy of Shaftesbury's *Characteristicks of Men, Manners, Opinion, Times* to Leibniz. Leibniz wrote his 'Remarques' in 1712, noting that

> These works are attributed to Milord Shaftesbury. Mr. Coste, who is among his friends, sent me a copy of it and has indicated that he would be very glad to see some reflections about it on my part. Thus I have put these few pages in writing. [GP III 423n]

Leibniz sent his 'Remarques' to Coste, who in turn sent them to Samuel Masson, the founder and editor of the *Histoire critique de la République des Lettres*, in which journal they were published in 1715 under the title 'Eloge critique des Oeuvres de Milord Shaftsbury, par Mr. Leibnits, Communiqué par Mr. Coste'. In his covering letter, Coste wrote:

> Here is a critical eulogy of the works of the late Earl of Shaftesbury, deceased in Naples the 15th of February 1713. Mr. Leibniz is its author. He did me the honour of sending it to me in 1713, and I first sent it to Milord Shaftesbury himself, who was very satisfied. If this piece appears to you worthy of being communicated to the public, please give it a place in your journal. Those who have already read the diverse works of which Mr. Leibniz judges with so much soundness may find in it some entirely new reasons that will confirm the view they have of these works; and those to whom they are quite unknown may be persuaded to read them by the favourable portrait created of them by Leibniz, one of the greatest geniuses of this century, whose judgement must be so much the more respected on this occasion because he himself has written with much aptness and profundity about the most important matters that have been discussed by Milord Shaftesbury. [*Histoire critique de la République des Lettres*, vol. 10 (1715), pp. 306-7]

142. Caroline* of Brandenburg-Ansbach, Princess of Wales, to Leibniz[1]

Hampton Court the $\frac{31}{21}$ August[2] 1716[3]

By the last post I received two[4] of your letters, Monsieur, with the enclosure[5] for Doctor Clarke;[6] I have not received the letter[7] about which you spoke to me[8] before your departure for Pyrmont*.[9] Mr. Clarke is not in London, so I will take care of the paper[10] until his return. I thank God for the good[11] health of the king [George I, Georg Ludwig* of Braunschweig-Lüneburg], and I hope that the rest and the pleasure of enjoying his native air will restore him entirely.[12] You must doubtless have found much pleasure being in the good company[13] of Mr. [James] Stanhope*. He is a wise man without desiring to appear so, according to what I have been told.[14] I am very grateful to you for the reports[15] that you sent me[16] about the victory of Prince Eugène* [of Savoy]. The Infante of Portugal[17] [Manuel de Bragança, Count of Ourém (1697–1736)] was there[18] and gave very well of himself.[19] I have seen a man who told me that he would translate your incomparable *Theodicy*[20] and would

J['] espere qu'on vera bien tost traduis se liver.[25] Je vousderais[26] de tout mon coeur que vos dispute[27] avec le chevalié neuthon feuse finy,[28] ou quelle n'usse jamais estté comancée.[29] J'ay peur que listoire[30] de la maison n'an patira.[32] flemstait m a promis vn papié pour monterer[33] que vous aviez la victoire sur le chevalié neuthon, mais y et tres lon a le produire,[35] et je crain que son grand ayeé ne le fassez aller a l'autre monde avant sa.[36] Je lie[37] avec plaisir les reponce[38] que vous m'avez adressé[39] pour M^r chlerque. Je ne scais ce qu'il y poura reponder.[40] C'est vn home d'une vivassidé[41] la plus grande et d'une Eloquance[42] selon moy qui e[s]t incomparable. J'espere que le Roy vous menera dans se peais,[43] et que j'aurais le plaisir de vous[44] and- antre parller ansamble.[45] Je vous dis ancore[46] qu'on me fera beaucoup d'honneur de me faire paraitre de quelque manier[e] qu'il vous plaira dans la desticassé de la deodisee.[47] le P. scerais ravié sy il[48] pour[r]oit faire paraitre dans lanplois[49] que ce Roy luy a confié qu'il merite se glorieux tire destre[51] le fils de le grand Roy. Je vous prié d'aller voir mon fils souvant.[52] Je vousderais le voir ausy[53] parfait dans son espece que vous avez le plaisir de voir votre deodisée.

Caroline

142. CAROLINE OF BRANDENBURG-ANSBACH TO LEIBNIZ 721

dedicate[21] it to me, which I have accepted with much pleasure. I believe that Mr. Clarke will respond[22] to it. So much the better,[23] since the truth cannot be examined thoroughly enough.[24] I hope that we will soon see this book translated.[25] I would[26] with all my heart that your dispute[27] with Chevalier Newton were finished[28] or that it had never begun.[29] I am afraid that the history[30] of the House[31] will suffer from it.[32] [John] Flamsteed* promised me a paper to show[33] that you would have the victory over Chevalier Newton,[34] but he is very long in producing it,[35] and I fear that his great age may cause him to pass to the other world before that.[36] I read[37] with pleasure the replies[38] that you have sent[39] to me for Mr. Clarke. I do not know what he will be able to say in response to them.[40] He is a man of the greatest vivacity[41] and of an eloquence[42] that is to me incomparable. I hope that the king will bring you to this country[43] and that I would have the pleasure of hearing you[44] speak together.[45] I tell you again[46] that it will do me great honor to have me appear in any way you please in the dedication of the *Theodicy*.[47] The prince [Georg August* of Braunschweig-Lüneburg, Prince of Wales] would be delighted if he[48] could demonstrate in the job[49] that the king has entrusted to him[50] that he merits this glorious title of being[51] the son of this great king. Please go to see my son [Friedrich Ludwig* of Braunschweig-Lüneburg] often.[52] I would see him as[53] perfect in his kind as you have the pleasure of seeing your *Theodicy*.

Caroline

[1] LBr. F 4 Bl. 75r–76v. Letter as sent: four quarto sides in Caroline's hand. Previously published in Klopp XI 181–2; Robinet 1991, p. 183 (excerpt); Schüller 1991, p. 262 (excerpt in German translation); HGA 196–7 (excerpt in English translation). This is Caroline's response to Leibniz's letter of 18 August 1716 (document 139).

[2] Reading 'Août' for 'aut'.

[3] That is 21 August 1716 (OS) and 1 September 1716 (NS). At the time of writing, the Gregorian calendar (NS) was eleven days in advance of the Julian calendar (OS), so Caroline was mistaken in writing 31 August rather than 1 September. For Leibniz's reply, see his letter to Caroline of 11 September 1716 (document 144).

[4] Reading 'J'ay reçu par la poste passée deux' for 'J'ay receu par la poste passez deu'.

[5] Reading 'l'incluse' for 'lengluse'.

[6] That is, Samuel Clarke*. One of the letters to which Caroline refers here is Leibniz's letter to her of 18 August 1716. For in that letter he writes that 'My response to the fourth paper of Mr. Clarke arrives herewith in part.' But he adds that 'the other half will arrive by the following post' (document 139, p. 629). It would appear that the second letter Caroline refers to here is the one in which Leibniz enclosed the second half of his Fifth Paper for Clarke. This second letter does not seem to have survived, and it may not have contained much more than the transmittal of the second half of Leibniz's Fifth Paper, a suggestion supported by the fact that in the present letter, Caroline seems to reply only to remarks contained in Leibniz's letter of 18 August 1716.

[7] Reading 'l'ai pas reçue' for 'l'ais pas receu'.

[8] Reading 'dont vous me parlez' for 'don vous me parlee'.

[9] The letter that Caroline says she did not receive is apparently Leibniz's letter to her of 31 July 1716, since in that letter Leibniz wrote that 'I will perhaps go there [i.e., to Pyrmont] as well for a few days in order to better pay my court [to King George I]' (document 135, pp. 615, 617). Moreover, he had begun his letter to Caroline of 18 August 1716, the letter to which Caroline is here responding, by saying that 'I had the honour of writing to Your Royal Highness before my trip to Pyrmont, where I paid my court to the king, since his Majesty was freer there than here' (document 139 above, p. 629).

[10] Reading 'à Londres, ainsi j'aurai soin du papier' for 'a londes, ensy aurais soin du papié'.

[11] Reading 'je rends grâces à Dieu de la bonne' for 'je rand graces a Dieu de la bon'.

142. CAROLINE OF BRANDENBURG-ANSBACH TO LEIBNIZ

142. CAROLINE OF BRANDENBURG-ANSBACH TO LEIBNIZ 723

[12] Reading 'remettra tout à fait' for 'remetera toutafait'.

[13] Reading 'aurez trouvé sans doute beaucoup de plaisir d'être dans la bonne compagnie' for 'aurais trouvez sans toute beaucoup de plaisir destre dans la boñe companié'.

[14] Reading 'paraître à ce que l'on m'a dit' for 'parroitre as ce que lon ma dit'.

[15] Reading 'relations' for 'relassion'. In his letter to Caroline of 18 August 1716, Leibniz mentioned 'the great defeat of the Turks near Save' in the battle of Petrovaradin; and at the end of the letter he added: 'I enclose here the copies of what has been sent to me from Vienna [about the battle of Petrovaradin], although I do not doubt that Your Royal Highness has better news about it; but it may be that mine contains some small circumstance that will be able to serve as a clarification'(document 139, p. 631).

[16] Reading 'm'avez envoyées' for 'm'avait anvoiyé'.

[17] Reading 'L'Infant de Portugal' for 'lenfande de Portugalle'. Manuel fought with Prince Eugène against the Turks at the Battle of Petrovaradin (5 August 1716) in present-day Serbia.

[18] Reading 'trouvé' for 'trouvez'.

[19] Reading 'très bien payé de sa personne' for 'tres bien peayée de sa persoñe'.

[20] Reading 'm'a dit qu'il traduirait votre incomparable Théodicée' for 'madit qu'il traduiré votre incomparable dodisie'.

[21] Reading 'dédierait' for 'destirait'.

[22] Reading 'répondra' for 'repondera'.

[23] Reading 'tant mieux' for 'tans mieu'.

[24] Reading 'épluchée' for 'epluché'.

[25] Reading 'verra bientôt traduit ce livre' for 'vera bien tost traduis se liver'.

[26] Reading 'voudrais' for 'vousderais'.

[27] Reading 'votre dispute' for 'vos dispute'.

[28] Reading 'fussent finies' for 'feuse finy'.

[29] Reading 'qu'elle n'eût jamais été commencée' for 'quelle n'usse jamais estté comancée'.

[30] Reading 'l'histoire' for 'listoire'.

[31] That is, the House of Braunschweig-Lüneburg, his history of which Leibniz entitled *Annales imperii occidentis Brunsvicenses**.

[32] Reading 'n'en pâtira' for 'n'an patira'.

[33] Reading 'm'a promis un papier pour montrer' for 'm a promis vn papié pour monterer'.

[34] Flamsteed's feud with Newton explains why he would be anxious to help Leibniz triumph over Newton. On this feud, see Leibniz's letter to Caroline of 31 July 1716 (document 135, p. 617 note 6).

[35] Reading 'il est très long à' for 'y et tres lon a'.

[36] Reading 'crains que son grand âge ne le fasse aller à l'autre monde avant ça' for 'crain que son grand ayeé ne le fassez aller a l'autre monde avant sa'.

[37] Reading 'lis' for 'lie'.

[38] Reading 'réponses' for 'reponce'.

[39] Reading 'adressées' for 'adressé'.

[40] Reading 'sais ce qu'il y pourra répondre' for 'scais ce qu'il y poura reponder'.

[41] Reading 'vivacité' for 'vivassidé'.

[42] Reading 'Eloquence' for 'Eloquance'.

[43] Reading 'ce pays' for 'se peais'.

[44] By 'vous' here Caroline would seem to mean Leibniz and Clarke, rather than Leibniz and the king.

[45] Reading 'entendre parler ensemble' for 'andantre parller ansamble'.

[46] Reading 'encore' for 'ancore'.

[47] Reading 'dédicace de la Théodicée' for 'desticassé de la deodisee'.

[48] Reading 'serait ravi s'il' for 'scerais ravié sy il'.

[49] Reading 'l'emploi' for 'lanplois'.

[50] Caroline is referring to the fact that Georg August was made Guardian and Lieutenant of the Realm in England while his father, King George I, was absent from England during his first visit to his German territories.

[51] Reading 'ce glorieux titre d'être' for 'se glorieux tire destre'.

[52] Reading 'souvent' for 'souvant'.

[53] Reading 'voudrais le voir aussi' for 'vousderais le voir ausy'.

Caroline of Brandenburg-Ansbach,
Princess of Wales, to Leibniz

hamthancour le $\frac{8}{28}$ d'aut 1716

Je vous suis tres obligée Monsieur de la relassion[3] de la patallé[4] des imperiau[x]. J'an ayeé regaleé[5] Madame, qui e[s]t toujours mal informé[e]. Je n'ay pas veu ancore[6] docteur chlerck. il est arivez depui her an ville, et je luy randerais vos papié la semaine qui vien.[7] M^d K et l'abée condy on prié la pen̄e de manperder beaucoup[8] je me fladée que vous reparerais c'estte perté.[9] labée est a oxfors, pour se consoller des cruaudée de son ambassadrise.[10] le peauver filosophie et toujours mal tredée andre les mains de lamour.[11] que dite vous de ceplascest[12] des Princes du sang an franes[13] contre les patar.[14] il y aurais vne belle cariere ala moralle la dessu, mais come dit la comedy quelle andor.[16] J'ay peure que lamiene ferais lemême efait[17] sur vous, et que vous renoncerais a écrire avne person̄e[18] qui vous estime tans[19] que

Caroline[20]

143. Caroline of Brandenburg-Ansbach, Princess of Wales, to Leibniz[1]

Hampton Court $\frac{8}{28}$ August 1716[2]

I am very grateful, sir, for the report[3] about the battle[4] of the imperial forces. I made a treat of it[5] for Madame [Elisabeth Charlotte*, Duchess of Orléans], who is always misinformed. I have not yet seen[6] Doctor [Samuel] Clarke*. He arrived in the city yesterday, and I will deliver your papers to him next week.[7] Madam [Sophie Charlotte von] Kielmansegg* and the Abbé [Antonio Schinella] Conti* have taken the trouble to lose a lot of them for me.[8] I hope that you will restore this loss.[9] The Abbé is in Oxford to console himself with the cruelty of his ambassadress.[10] The poor philosopher is always mistreated at the hands of love.[11] What do you think about that petition[12] of the Princes of the Blood in France[13] against the bastards?[14,15] There would be a fine career in morals on that subject, but as the comedy says, it sends one to sleep.[16] I fear that mine would have the same effect[17] upon you and that you would give up writing to a person[18] who esteems you as much[19] as

Caroline[20]

[1] LBr. F 4 Bl. 73r–73v. Letter as sent: 1.5 quarto sides in Caroline's hand. Previously published in Klopp XI 180 (excerpt); Schüller 1991, p. 261 (excerpt in German translation); and Robinet 1991, p. 183 (excerpt). For Leibniz's reply, see his letter to Caroline from the end of September to mid-October 1716 (document 149).

[2] That is, 28 August 1716 (OS) and 8 September (NS).

[3] Reading 'relation' for 'relassion'. In his letter to Caroline of 18 August 1716, Leibniz mentioned 'the great defeat of the Turks near Save' in the battle of Petrovaradin; and at the end of the letter he added: 'I enclose here the copies of what has been sent to me from Vienna [about the battle of Petrovaradin], although I do not doubt that Your Royal Highness has better news about it; but it may be that mine contains some small circumstance that will be able to serve as a clarification'(document 139, p. 631).

[4] Reading 'bataille' for 'patallé'.

[5] Reading 'J'en ai régalé' for 'J'an ayeé regaleé'.

[6] Reading 'vu encore' for 'veu ancore'.

[7] Reading 'Il est arrivé depuis hier en ville, et je lui rendrai vos papiers la semaine qui vient' for 'il est arivez depui her anville, et je luy randerais vos papié la semaine qui vien'.

[8] Reading 'ont pris la peine de m'en perdre beaucoup' for 'on prié la peñe de manperder beaucoup'.

[9] Reading 'Je me flatte que vous réparerez c'ette perte' for 'je me fladée que vous reparerais c'estte perté'.

[10] Reading 'L'Abbé est à Oxford, pour se consoler des cruautés de son ambassadrice' for 'labée est a oxfors, pour se consoller des cruaudée de son ambassadrise'.

[11] Reading 'Le pauvre philosophe est toujours mal traité entre les mains de l'amour' for 'le peauver filosophie et toujours mal tredée andre les mains de lamour'.

[12] Reading 'Que dites-vous de ce placet' for 'que dite vous de ceplascest'.

[13] Reading 'en France' for 'an franes'.

[14] Reading 'bâtards' for 'patar'.

[15] Caroline apparently refers to the petition of 22 August 1716 by those French princes who were legitimate descendants of the male royal line ('Princes of the Blood') against Louis XIV's bastard sons (by Madame de Montespan), Louis Auguste and Louis Alexandre. Louis XIV had legitimized both of them and had created Louis Auguste (1670-1736) the Duke of Maine (in 1673) and Louis Alexandre (1678-1737) the Count of Toulouse (in 1681). But in 1714, fearing that his direct line would die out, Louis XIV had taken the even more controversial step of raising Louis Auguste and Louis Alexandre to the rank of Princes of the Blood, thus making them eligible to succeed to the throne in the event of a

Leibniz to Caroline of Brandenburg-Ansbach, Princess of Wales

11 Sept. 1716
　　Madame　　　　　　　　　　　　　　　　A Madame la princesse
　　　　　　　　　　　　　　　　　　　　　　　de Galles[2]

Je suis de retour de Bronsvic dépuis quelques jours, ou j'ay fait un peu ma cour vers la fin de la foire; et je me suis donné l'honneur d'en écrire à Vôtre Altesse Royale, et de luy envoyer la relation de Mgr le Prince de Beveren, que Mgr le Duc Regent me donna luy même pour cet effect. J'ay été aussi quelques fois chez Madame la Princesse de Beveren soeur de l'Imperatrice; et je trouve cette Princesse aussi heureuse que sa soeur, à cela pres que son mari s'expose d'avantage maintenant: il est vray que l'Empereur ne l'a pas fait moins. On espere que Temesvar ne tiendra pas long temps; et quelques uns se flattent qu'on pourra encore assieger Belgrade. Mais si l'on avoit eu ce dessein, je crois qu'on auroit commencé par Belgrade. Cependant si Temesvar se rendoit bien tôt, et si la saison continuoit d'être favorable, peut-être pourroit on se resoudre encor au second siege, mais qui deviendra sans doute plus difficile par le delay.

Les nouvelles de Corfou sont assés variables. Les freres et soeurs ont eu grand sujet de craindre pour le General Schulenbourg. Cependant on croit maintenant que la ville tenoit encore bon, et qu'il avoit la mer libre pour recevoir du secours, et pour pouvoir sortir au besoin. On espere même qu'à l'arrivée des vaisseaux Espagnols et Portugais les Venitiens pourront étre en état d'attaquer avec succes la flotte Turque, et obliger les barbares de quitter l'isle. J'ay vû à Bronsvic un autre General Schulenbourg, qui est au service du Roy de Sicile, et qui paroissoit craindre pour Corfou: mais il y a de l'apparence que la porte Ottomanne ayant appris la grand defaite de Petervardein, rappellera les trouppes debarquées dans l'Isle de Corfu, pour les employer à mieux couvrir ses propres états menacés par les imperiaux.

Votre Altesse Royale aura sans doute esté informée des étranges deportemens du Marquis de Langallerie que j'ay connu à Berlin, ou il me parut assés raisonnable:

144. LEIBNIZ TO CAROLINE OF BRANDENBURG-ANSBACH   727

failure of legitimate heirs. But in 1717, under the regency of Philippe II*, Duke of Orléans (1674–1723), an edict in the name of the minor Louis XV rescinded the right of succession that Louis XIV had bestowed on his bastard sons. See Gerber 2012, pp. 84–5.

[16] Reading 'il y aurait une belle carrière à la morale là-dessus, mais comme dit la comédie qu'elle endort' for 'il y aurais vne belle cariere a la moralle la dessu, mais come dit la comedy quelle andor'.

[17] Reading 'peur que la mienne ferait le même effet' for 'peure que lamiene ferais lemême efait'.

[18] Reading 'à une personne' for 'avne persoñe'.

[19] Reading 'tant' for 'tans'.

[20] Klopp XI 180 simply replaces the last two sentences with 'Il n'y a personne qui vous estime tant que Caroline'.

144. Leibniz to Caroline* of Brandenburg-Ansbach, Princess of Wales[1]

11 September 1716
Madame

To Madame the Princess of Wales[2]

I returned some days ago from Braunschweig, where I paid a bit of my court towards the end of the fair, and I gave myself the honour of writing to Your Royal Highness about it and of sending her the report of the Prince of Bevern [Ferdinand Albrecht II*], which the regent duke himself gave me for this purpose. I have sometimes also been with the Princess of Bevern [Antoinette Amalie of Braunschweig-Wolfenbüttel (1696–1762)], sister of the empress [Elisabeth Christine* of Braunschweig-Wolfenbüttel], and I find this princess as happy as her sister, except that her husband is now more exposed.[3] It is true that the emperor [Emperor Karl VI*] has not made him less so. It is hoped that Temesvar* will not take a long time,[4] and some hope that they will yet be able to lay siege to Belgrade.[5] But if they had had this plan, I believe that they would have begun with Belgrade. However, if Temesvar surrendered soon, and if the weather continued to be favourable, perhaps they could yet resolve upon the second siege, but this will no doubt become more difficult with delay.

The news from Corfu is rather unsettled. The brothers and sisters have had good reason to fear for General [Johann Matthias, Count von] Schulenburg*. However it is now believed that the town still held its ground and that it had the open sea for receiving aid and for being able to leave if need be. It is even hoped that with the arrival of the Spanish and Portuguese ships, the Venetians will be in a position to attack successfully the Turkish fleet and compel the barbarians to leave the island. In Braunschweig I saw another General Schulenburg, who is in the service of the King of Sicily [Vittorio Amedeo Sebastiano*], and who seemed to fear for Corfu; but there is some likelihood that the Ottoman Porte,[6] having been learned of the great defeat at Petrovaradin,[7] will withdraw the troops disembarked on the Island of Corfu in order to use them to defend better its own estates, which are menaced by the imperial troops.

mais les malheurs luy ont tourné la téte. On m'ecrit de Vienne qu'ayant eté interrogé devant les Commissaires de l'Empereur, il a avoué d'abord son traité avec le Turc, mais il a adjouté qu'il n'y avoit point eu de guerre alors entre l'Empereur et les Ottomans, et qu'il avoit eu sujet de croire qu'il n'y en auroit point. Que depuis qu'il étoit sorti du service de France, il n'avoit jamais eu engagement avec des ennemis de Sa Majesté Imperiale; que son dessein avoit été de faire la guerre au Pape comme à un ennemi de Jesus Christ, de livrer le Pape aux Turcs, et la ville de Rome à l'Empereur. Que les Turcs luy avoient promis en echange un Royaume dans quelque Isle de la Mediterranée, et que l'echange d'un prêtre contre un Royaume n'auroit point été mauvais. Les Commissaires ont eu de la peine a s'empecher de rire. Quelques uns disent que le Pretendu Prince de Linange, qui est aussi arrivé à Vienne, est un fils naturel d'un Comte de Linange, d'autres pretendent qu'il est gentil-homme du Poitou et qu'aprés avoir fait mille fourberies en France, il est venu en Hollande, se disant premierement Prince deputé des pirates de Madagascar, qui tranchent de souverains dans cette grande Isle; et puis il a voulu faire le Messie ou du moins le precurseur du Messie des Juifs, et à trouvé[9] des fous qui luy ont donné de l'argent. On croit donc qu'il y a de la malice dans son fait, mais de la folie dans celuy du Marquis.

Le Roy a trouvé un successeur du Baron de la Hontan, mais d'une autre espece, c'est le Comte de Brandebourg. On dit qu'il est d'une bonne famille du Luxembourg, et que s'étant fait Capucin dans sa jeunesse, il est parvenu jusqu'a etre confesseur de la Reine Douariere d'Espagne. Il m'a raconté luy même, qu'étant ami du Comte de Melgar Amirante de Castille, qu'on voulu[t] attirer au service Bourbon sous pretexte de l'envoyer Ambassadeur en France, mais dans le dessein de le mettre en prison; il luy ecrivit une lettre pour l'en avertir; et que cette lettre estant tombée en fin entre les mains du parti du duc d'Anjou, il fut pris prisonnier et mené en France. Je me souviens que la gazette a parlé d'un Capucin mis en prison pour affaires d'état. Il est reste[12] dans la bastille jusqu'à la paix, et alors il a été relaché. Mais depuis étant desaccoutumé de la maniere de vivre Capucine, il a quitté la religion Romaine avec le Froc, et Madame de Kielmansek luy a obtenu une pension du Roy. Maintenant il est souvent à la Table de sa Majesté, et comme luy et l'Abbé Buquoy ont été compagnons de bastille, j'espere qu'ils s'accorderont mieux que l'Abbé et le Baron. S'il luy étoit permis depuis qu'il a quitte[15] le metier de rompre le s[c]eau de la confession, il nous pourroit dire si la Reine d'Espagne n'a pas été tentée d'epargner une grande guerre à l'Europa par un <u>peccadillo</u> comme quelques uns le voudroient peut-être appeler.

Je suis fort obligé à V. A. Royale de la permission qu'elle a donnée de luy dedier la traduction de la Theodicée, et de parler dans la dedicace de l'approbation qu'Elle a donnée à ce dessein. Je ne connois pas encor la personne qui là[17] entrepris, mais je souhaite qu'elle ecrive en bon style Anglois, qui puisse avoir l'approbation des connoissances:[18] Car les Anglois sont fort delicats, même par rapport au style, et ils ont raison: car cette delicatesse contribue beaucoup à faire exprimer nettement et

144. LEIBNIZ TO CAROLINE OF BRANDENBURG-ANSBACH 729

Your Royal Highness must doubtless have been informed of the strange misconduct of the Marquis de Langallerie [Phillipe de Gentils, Marquis de Langallerie*], with whom I was acquainted in Berlin, where he seemed pretty reasonable to me. But misfortunes have addled his brain. They write me from Vienna that when he was interrogated before the emperor's commissioners, he first confessed his treaty with the Turk; but he added there had not been any war at that time between the emperor and the Ottomans and that he had had reason to believe that there would not be any; that since he had left the service of France, he had never had engagement with any enemies of His Imperial Majesty [Emperor Karl VI]; that his plan had been to make war on the pope as on an enemy of Jesus Christ, to hand the pope over to the Turks and the city of Rome to the emperor; that the Turks had promised him in exchange a kingdom on some Mediterranean island, and that the exchange of a priest for a kingdom would not have been bad. The commissioners have had difficulty keeping themselves from laughing. Some say that the so-called Prince of Linange,[8] who has also arrived in Vienna, is an illegitimate son of a Count of Linange. Others claim that he is a gentleman from Poitou, and that after having made a thousand impostures in France, he arrived in Holland, saying at first that he was deputy prince of the pirates of Madagascar, who comport themselves as if they were sovereigns on that great island; after that he chose to personate the Messiah, or at least the harbinger of the Messiah, of the Jews, and found[9] some fools who gave him money. It is therefore believed that there is malice in his deed, but madness in that of the Marquis.

The king [George I, Georg Ludwig* of Braunschweig-Lüneburg] has found a successor to the Baron [Louis-Armand de Lom d'Arce] de Lahontan*, but of a different sort, namely the Count of Brandenburg.[10] It is said that he is from a good family of Luxemburg and that having become a Capuchin in his youth, he rose so far as to be the confessor of the Dowager Queen of Spain [Maria Anna of Neuburg].[11] He himself recounted to me that since he was a friend of the Count of Melgar, Admiral of Castile [Juan Tomás Enríquez de Cabrera (1647–1705)], whom they wanted to lure into the service of Bourbon on pretext of sending him to France as ambassador, but with the intent of putting him in prison, he wrote him a letter to warn him about it; and that since this letter finally fell into the hands of the party of the Duke of Anjou, he was taken prisoner and conveyed to France. I remember that the paper spoke of a Capuchin put in prison for affairs of state. He remained[12] in the Bastille until the peace,[13] and then he was released.

But after being disaccustomed to the Capuchin way of life, he abandoned the Roman religion along with the frock, and Madame [Sophie Charlotte, Freiin (Baroness) von] Kielmansegg* has obtained a pension for him from the king. Now he is often at the table of His Majesty, and since he and Abbé [Jean-Albert d'Archambaud, Comte de] Bucquoy* were Bastille companions, I hope that they will get along better than the Abbé and the Baron.[14] If he were permitted to break the seal of the confession now that he has abandoned[15] the vocation, he could tell us if

agreablement les pensées. Je ne saurois juger de l'elegance Angloise, mais il me semble que je puis juger au moins de la netteté des expressions. M. Clarke n'en manque pas asseurement, mais nous verrons bien tôt, si elle est accompagnée de sincerite, et s'il est homme à donner les mains à la verité: cela luy feroit plus d'honneur sans doute, que les detours, qu'il pourroit prendre pour s'en exemter. S'il continue à me disputer le grand principe que rien n'arrive sans qu'il y ait une raison suffisante pourquoy il arrive, et pourquoy ainsi plustôt qu'autrement, et s'il pretend encore que quelque chose peut arriver par un Mere Will of God, sans aucun motif; sentiment refuté parfaitement dans la Theodicée, et encore dans mon dernier ecrit; il faudra l'abandonner à son sens, ou plustost à son obstination. Car il est difficile que dans les fonds de l'ame il n'en soit touché: mais je crois que le public ne l'en tiendra point quitte. Cependant j'espere encore le meilleur; sur tout, puisque le tout s'agit sous le yeux de Vôtre Altesse Royale, qu'il n'est pas aisé de tromper. Au reste je suis avec devotion

Madame de Vôtre Altesse Royale

P.S. Les Anglois admirent Monseigneur le Duc de Cornouaille; ils souhaiteroient seulement qu'il eût aupres de luy quelque page ou valet Anglois choisi.

Hanover cet 11 de septembre
    1716[20]

les tres[21] soumis et tres obeissant
serviteur
Leibniz

144. LEIBNIZ TO CAROLINE OF BRANDENBURG-ANSBACH 731

the Queen of Spain was not tempted to spare Europe a great war by a *peccadillo*, as some would perhaps wish to call it.[16]

I am very grateful to Your Royal Highness for the permission that she has given to dedicate the translation of the *Theodicy* to her and to speak in the dedication of the approval that she has given to this project. I do not yet know the person who has undertaken it,[17] but I hope that he writes in good English style, which can gain the approval of the connoisseurs.[18] For the English are very fastidious, even in matters of style, and they are right: for this fastidiousness contributes a lot to making thoughts clearly and pleasantly expressed. I would not be able to judge of English elegance, but it seems to me that I am at least able to judge of clarity of expression. Mr. [Samuel] Clarke* certainly does not lack it, but we will soon see if it is accompanied by sincerity and if he is a man who yields to the truth. That would without doubt honour him more than the evasions that he might employ in order to exempt himself from it. If he continues to dispute the great principle *that nothing happens without there being a sufficient reason why it happens and why thus rather than otherwise*, and if he still claims that something can happen by a *Mere Will of God*, without any motive, a view completely refuted in the *Theodicy*, and again in my last paper,[19] it will be necessary to abandon him to his opinion, or rather to his obstinacy. For it is hard to believe that he is not moved by it in the depths of his soul; but I do not believe that the public will let him off the hook. However, I still hope for the best, above all because everything takes place under the eyes of Your Royal Highness, whom it is not easy to deceive. To conclude, I am with devotion,

Madam, of Your Royal Highness

P.S. The English admire the Duke of Cornwall [i.e., Georg August*of Braunschweig-Lüneburg, Prince of Wales]; they only wish that he had in his service some chosen English page or valet.

Hanover 11 September
1716[20]

the[21] very submissive and obedient
servant
Leibniz

---

[1] LBr. F 4 Bl. 82r–83r. Copy: three folio sides in a secretary's hand. Previously published in Kemble 536–9; Klopp XI 182–6; Schüller 1991, p. 263 (excerpt in German translation); HGA 197 (excerpt in English translation). This is Leibniz's reply to Caroline's letter of 1 September (document 142).

[2] This is in Leibniz's hand.

[3] Here Leibniz is presumably referring to the fact that Ferdinand Albrecht II* was then serving in the 1716 campaign of the Austro-Turkish War (1716–1718) under the command of Prince Eugene of Savoy*.

[4] Leibniz was hoping that it would not take long to take Temesvar, which Prince Eugène* of Savoy, leading the Austrian forces, did in fact capture in mid-October of 1716.

[5] The Austrian forces, led by Prince Eugène of Savoy, captured Belgrade in 1717.

[6] That is, the court of the Ottoman Empire.

Leibniz to Dowager Empress Wilhelmine Amalie of Braunschweig-Lüneburg

à la Majesté de l'Imperatrice Amalie

Hanover
20 Sept.
1716

Sacrée Majesté

Il n'y a pas long temps que Votre Majesté Imperiale m'a fait savoir de la part de l'Empereur, que ce grand Monarque étoit tout porté à la continuation des graces

145. LEIBNIZ TO WILHELMINE AMALIE OF BRAUNSCHWEIG-LÜNEBURG   733

[7] In the battle of Petrovaradin, the Austrian forces, under the command of Prince Eugène of Savoy, scored a decisive victory over the Turks on 5 August 1716.

[8] The reference is to a notorious impostor and grifter whose real name was apparently René Godefroy Louis Ernest Joseph Joumard*.

[9] Reading 'a trouvé' for 'à trouvé'.

[10] The identity of this person is somewhat of a mystery. In her biography of King George I, and speaking of George's 'English gentlemen of the bedchamber', Ragnhild Hatton writes that the 'fact that some of them combined their duties with administrative office and that others—like Charles Hamilton Douglas, Earl of Selkirk—were courtiers of long experience made them in their various ways useful to George, who liked conversation to focus on specific issues' (Hatton 1978, p. 141). In a footnote, she adds the following:

> Selkirk is mentioned by name as one of the *seigneurs* who attended George at Hampton Court (Görtz Archive: 121/6, Schulenburg's letter of 10 Sept. 1718). Two others mentioned as serving at the same time were the French Huguenot officer marquis de Miremont and a comte de Brandenbourg (whom I have not been able to identify but who, from his name, may have been an illegitimate member of the Hohenzollern family. [ibid., 342n109]

If the report that Leibniz was given about this man is to be believed, then we can know that he was not 'an illegitimate member of the Hohenzollern family', but rather that he was 'from a good family of Luxemburg'. Whether this, or any of the other specifics about this gentleman that Leibniz mentions, can be believed is an open question—in particular, the gentleman's claim to having been the confessor of the Dowager Queen of Spain, Maria Anna of Neuburg. Indeed, in Leibniz's next letter to Caroline, he reports that 'An eminent person from the Netherlands who sometimes writes to me denies that our Mr. Brandenburg was the confessor of the Dowager Queen of Spain' (document 149, p. 745).

[11] Maria Anna of Neuburg (1667–1740) was Queen of Spain from 1689 until the death of her husband, King Carlos II (1661–1700) of Spain, in November of 1700.

[12] Reading 'resté' for 'reste'.

[13] That is, when the War of the Spanish Succession* ended in 1714 with the Treaties of Utrecht* and Rastatt*.

[14] The 'Baron' being Lahontan.

[15] Reading 'quitté' for 'quitte'.

[16] While it may not be entirely clear what Leibniz intended by this remark, reasonable conjecture is possible. The War of the Spanish Succession* was touched off by the death of the childless, and undoubtedly impotent, King Carlos II of Spain on 1 November 1700. Carlos II had been married to his second wife, Maria Anna of Neuburg, since 1689; thus, since the War of the Spanish Succession had been triggered by the fact that Carlos II had died without heir, Leibniz was perhaps wondering whether Maria Anna had ever confessed to the Count of Brandenburg that she had been tempted to become pregnant by another man in order to provide an heir to the Spanish throne 'by a peccadillo', and hence avert the War of the Spanish Succession.

[17] Reading 'l'a' for 'là'.

[18] Reading 'connoisseurs' for 'connoissances'.

[19] That is, Leibniz's Fifth Paper, document 140b.

[20] This is in Leibniz's hand.

[21] Reading 'le' for 'les'.

145. Leibniz to Dowager Empress Wilhelmine Amalie* of Braunschweig-Lüneburg[1]

to the Majesty of the Empress Amalie

Hanover
20 September
Sacred Majesty   1716

It has been a long time since Your Imperial Majesty informed me on behalf of the emperor that this great monarch was quite inclined to the continuation of the

qu'il m'a accordées, et meme à la l'execution du projet qui les devoit augmenter d'une Societé des Sciences, où Sa Mté imp. et catholique m'avoit témoigne du panchant quand j'avois l'honneur de l'approcher a Vienne. Fondé la dessus je travaille fort à ferme[2] à depecher mon grand ouvrage de l'Histoire de l'Empire d'occident depuis le commencement de Charlemagne jusqu'a la fin de Henri le Saint qui est un intervalle de plus de deux siecles et demi, ou sera developpé la partie la plus obscure et la plus difficile de cette Histoire d'une maniere qui sera comme j'ose dire sans exemple en ce genre. Je me prepare aussi a pouvoir retourner à Vienne quand le Roy de la Grand Bretagne aura repassé la mer; Et pendant [que] je suis dans ces pensées on me mande tout d'un coup que mes gages établis par un decret de Sa Mté Imperiale doivent etre supprimés.

Si cela étoit fondé sur les besoins de la guerre je m'en consolerois par la necessité public qui ne feroit point de tort à ma reputation. Mais on me mande que la Cour imperiale veut augmenter les gages des conseillers actuels, au depens des titulaires et qu'on me veut comprendre sous le nombre des derniers malgré le decret de l'Empereur, malgré mes services actuels et malgré la double taxe tres grande qu'il m'a fallu payer pour etre Conseiller Actuel, et les depenses considerables ou j'ay eté assujettis[5], ce qui absorbe toute utilité de ce que j'ay tiré jusqu'icy des gages de Sa Mté Imperiale, sans parler de la perte de deux annees que j'ay employees à Vienne, et qui à l'âge que je suis me doivent etre d'un prix que je ne saurois estimer.

Et quant à mes services que presque dés ma jeunesse j'en ay rendu par mes travaux, lors que deja le Chancelier Hocher, les Comtes de Konigseck et de Cauniz, et d'autres grands Ministres se sont servis de mon zele, il est notoire par mon <u>Codex juris Gentium</u> que j'ay fait des decouvertes importantes et inconnues auparavant sur les droits de l'Empire, et Sa Mté Imperiale & Catholique se souvient peutetre et Sa Mté Imperiale sait[7] que j'ay deterré le premier <u>in forma</u> toute la disposition de Charles quint sur Florence, et que j'ay là dessus tout le proces verbal, par lequel on prouve incontestablement que Florence y est qualifiée ville ce qui contient la clef de tout, fait voir pourquoy ce pays n'est pas un fief mais un allodium de l'Empire et ne se trouve point à Vienne ny dans les Archives ny dans la Bibliotheque de Sa Mte Imperiale, ou j'ay rencontré un simple fragment de ces Acts, qui ne contient pas cette clause importante comme l'exemplaire entier que je possede. Lors aussi que j'etois à Vienne dernierement des Ministres de Sa Mté Imperiale m'ont employé à quelques travaux pour le service. Et ce Monarque même a bien voulu me charger de quelque chose. Mais quand il n'y auroit rien de tout cela; le grand ouvrage que je suis sur le point d'achever, d'une partie considerable de l'Histoire de l'Empire devroit ce semble passer pour un service reel puisqu'il est tres important pour les droits de l'Empire sans parler du projet que j'avois fait pour receuillir[8] ces droits à l'exemple de la France et d'autres nations. Et j'avois crû effectivement que la qualité de Conseiller Aulique actuel, et les gages qu'on m'avoit accordés ne seroient qu'un commencement de ce que je pourrois esperer de la genereuse et gratieuse disposition du Monarque que je me flattois d'avoir le bonheur de servir.

145. LEIBNIZ TO WILHELMINE AMALIE OF BRAUNSCHWEIG-LÜNEBURG 735

favours that he has accorded me and even to the execution of the project, which must increase them, of a Society of Sciences, to which His Imperial and Catholic Majesty [Emperor Karl VI*] had expressed his inclination when I had the honour of approaching him in Vienna. Based on that, I am working resolutely[2] to quickly dispatch my great work on the history of the Western Empire,[3] from the beginning of Charlemagne to the end of Henry the Saint, which is an interval of more than two and a half centuries, in which the most obscure and difficult part of this history will be developed in a manner that, as I dare say, will be without parallel in this genre. I am also preparing to be able to return to Vienna when the King of Great Britain [George I, Georg Ludwig of Braunschweig-Lüneburg] will have crossed over the sea again.[4] And while I am thinking about these things, I have suddenly been sent word that my wages, established by a decree of His Imperial Majesty, are to be cancelled.

If that were based on the needs of war, I would console myself with the public necessity of it, which would not harm my reputation. But I am informed that the imperial court wants to increase the wages of the current councilors at the expense of the titular councilors and that it wants to include me among the latter, despite the decree of the emperor, despite my current services, and despite the very large double tax that I had to pay for being a current councilor, and the considerable expenses to which I have been subjected,[5] which absorb all the profit from what I have so far drawn from the wages of His Imperial Majesty, not to mention the loss of two years that I have spent in Vienna, which at my age must be at a cost that I would not be able estimate.

And as regards my services, which I have provided by my labors almost since my youth, when Chancellor [Johann Paul Freiherr von] Hocher,[6] the Counts of Königseck and Kaunitz, and other great ministers already made use of my zeal; it is well known from my *Codex juris Gentium* that I have made some important and previously unknown discoveries about the rights of the Empire, and His Imperial and Catholic Majesty perhaps remembers and His Imperial Majesty knows[7] that I have unearthed the first-in-kind entire provision of Charles V regarding Florence, and that I have the entire official report about that, by which it is proved incontestably that Florence is there called an imperial city, which contains the key to everything, shows why this country is not a fief but an allodium of the empire; and [this report] is not found in Vienna, neither in the archives nor in the library of His Imperial Majesty, where I came across a simple fragment of these acts that does not contain this important clause, as does the complete copy that I possess. Then, too, when I was last in Vienna some ministers of His Imperial Majesty employed me at some labors for the service. And this monarch himself was pleased to charge me with something. But though there were nothing of all that, the great work that I am on the point of completing concerning a considerable part of the history of the empire ought, it seems, be considered a real service, since it is very important for the rights of the empire, not to mention the plan I had made to record[8] these rights

Mais si la nouvelle qu'on vient de me donner estoit veritable, ce seroit un coup qui me dérangeroit extremement, et outre la honte d'etre degrade pour ainsi dire que je n'aurois point essuyée, si je n'avois eté jamais receu; je suis retardé dans la course de mes bonnes intentions d'une manière fort sensible. Car fondé sur les declarations de Sa Mté verbales et par écrit, je commençois à enroller des gens d'une merite singulier, et qui n'auroient pas meme dem[an]dé de gage pour etre de la Societé Imperiale des Sciences, quand on viendroit à la fondation effective. Mais maintenant cette suppression feroit tomber tout mon credit.

Je me flatte encore que la nouvelle qu'on m'en a donnée, ne sera point fondée, ou du moins que ce reglement ou l'on m'aura voulu comprendre, aura ete fait sans qu'on en ait parlé particulierement [à] Sa Mté Imperiale sur ma personne: et cela me fait faire cette tentative pour apprendre ses sentimens et pour prevenir le tort qu'on me pourroit faire malgré luy. Mais si elle est inutile et si j'apprends que l'Empereur m'a condamné, je n'oserois l'importuner par des placets ou memoires, et apres[9] mes services, et à l'âge où je suis j'aurois honte de faire le solicitant. Mais mon zele n'en sera point diminué, quand même on m'oteroit les moyens d'exercer assés ce zele, et quand on m'obligeroit de changer de mesures apres le changement de mes esperances.

Comme Votre Majesté Imperiale a eu beaucoup de bonté pour un ancien serviteur [j']ay cru que je pouvois recourir à Sa protection sur un point qui regarde presque tout ce peu de vie qui me reste, et que je dois regler sur le resultat de cette affaire. Et je suis avec devotion

145. LEIBNIZ TO WILHELMINE AMALIE OF BRAUNSCHWEIG-LÜNEBURG   737

following the example of France and other nations. And I had indeed believed that the position of actual aulic councillor*, and the wages that had been accorded me, would be only a beginning of what I could hope for from the generous and gracious disposition of the monarch that I was proud to have the good fortune to serve.

But if the news that has just been given to me were true, it would be a blow that would greatly upset me; and beyond the disgrace of being degraded, so to speak, which I would not have suffered if I had never been received, I am hindered in the course of my good intentions in a very obvious way. For based on the spoken and written declarations of His Majesty, I began to enroll people of singular merit who would not have even asked for any pledge in order to be members of the Imperial Society of Sciences when the actual founding would be accomplished. But now this cancellation would undermine all my influence.

I still hope that the news that I have been given about it will not be justified, or at least that this settlement, in which they will have wanted to include me, must have been made without anyone having spoken about it specifically with His Imperial Majesty concerning me personally; it causes me to make this effort to understand his views and to prevent the harm that could be done to me despite him. But if it is futile, and if I learn that the emperor has condemned me, I would not dare importune him with petitions or memoranda, and after[9] my services, and at my age, I would be ashamed to play the supplicant. But my zeal will not be diminished on account of it, even if I would be deprived of the means of sufficiently exercising this zeal, and though I would be forced to change my arrangements after the change of my expectations.

As Your Imperial Majesty has shown much kindness for an old servant, I thought I could rely on her protection regarding a matter that concerns nearly all this small bit of life that remains to me and that I must conduct based on the outcome of this matter. And I am with devotion

---

[1] LBr. F 4 Bl. 21r–21v. Draft: 1.7 folio sides in Leibniz's hand. Previously published in Klopp XI 192–5.

[2] Reading 'fort et ferme' for 'fort à ferme'.

[3] That is, Leibniz's *Annales imperii occidentis Brunsvicenses**.

[4] That is, when the king will have returned to Great Britain. At the time of writing, George I was making his first return visit to his German estates since becoming king of England in August of 1714.

[5] Reading 'assujetti' for 'assujettis'.

[6] Johann Paul Freiherr von Hocher (1616–83) was an Austrian jurist and Court Chancellor (Hofkanzler) to Emperor Leopold I.

[7] It seems likely that Leibniz intended, but then forgot, to strike 'Sa Mté sait', since that was written on the next line of his text in normal position, whereas 'Sa Mté imperiale & Catholique se souvient peutetre' was added in the margin. It is also true that the latter expression is more polite and less pointed than the former, and Leibniz perhaps thought it wise to soften his original wording, which he then neglected to strike. In any event, Klopp simply omits 'Sa Mté sait' (Klopp XI 194).

[8] Reading 'recueillir' for 'receuillir'.

[9] Klopp mistranscribes 'apres' as 'autres' (Klopp XI 195).

Leibniz to Charlotte Elisabeth von Klenk

A Mlle de Klenk dame
de la lef d'or de impe
ratrice Amalie

Mademoiselle

Fondé sur les belles esperances que j'avois conçues des bonnes graces et des desseins de l'Empereur dont vous memes m'avés procuré des declarations, je travaillois fort et ferme, à achever mon ouvrage Historique, qui est presque fini, pour me disposer à retourner à Vienne l'année qui vient avec l'aide de Dieu: mais une nouvelle surprenante de la suppression de mes gages me met dans une grande incertitude. Je n'en veux parler ny écrire a aucun des Ministres, mais je recours aux bontés de notre incomparable Imperatrice, pour tacher de prevenir le mal, s'il est encore temps. Mais si l'affaire est faite et si elle est faite conformement aux intentions de l'Empereur; il faut que je prenne mes mesures là dessus le mieux que je pourray; car de faire le suppliant apres cela, me paroist indigne de moy. Ayés la bonté, Mademoiselle d'adjouter à toutes vos bontés pasees celle de me tirer de cet embarras, sans en parler à d'autres, qu'à l'imperatrice, il n'y a que M. Theobald Schottel à qui j'en aye écrit. Il est honneste homme et il menagera la chose. Je suis etc.

Leibniz to George Cheyne

Vir Clarissime

[...]

Mihi nunc cum Clarkio vestro vire docto et ingenioso concertatio est Epistolica; tuetur ille Newtoni philosophiam; ego mèam nixus magno axiomate, quod utramque in Theodicæa mea paginam facit nihil existere, evenire, locum inter veritates habere cujus ratio sufficiens cur sit potius quàm non sit, aut cur fit potius quàm aliter sic, reddi non possit. Hoc uno axiomate spatium reale, vacuum, atomi, difflantur ut folia vento! Et D. Clarkius eo redactus est; ut axioma neget, et aliquid mera Dei voluntate fieri posse putet, quo ratione nulla nitatur; quo uno mihi satis ad absurdum deductus videtur.

146. Leibniz to Charlotte Elisabeth von Klenk[*][1]

[20 September 1716]
To Mademoiselle Klenk Lady
of the Golden Key of Emp
ress Amalie

Based on the fine expectations that I had conceived from the good graces and plans of the emperor [Karl VI*], of which you yourself have procured for me some declarations, I worked resolutely to complete my historical work,[2] which is nearly finished, in order to prepare to return to Vienna next year with the help of God. But surprising news of the cancellation of my wages places me in great uncertainty. I do not want to speak or write about it to any of the ministers, but I am relying on the services of our incomparable [dowager] empress [Wilhelmine Amalie* of Braunschweig-Lüneburg] to try to prevent the harm, if there is still time. But if the matter is settled, and if it is settled in conformity with the intentions of the emperor, I must take measures about it as best I can; for to play the supplicant after that would seem unworthy of me. Have the kindness, mademoiselle, to add to all your former services that of extracting me from this embarrassment without speaking of it to any others but the empress. There is only Mr. Theobald Schöttel[3] to whom I have written about it. He is an honourable man, and he will manage the matter. I am etc.

[1] LBr. F 4 Bl. 21v. Draft: 0.3 folio sides in Leibniz's hand. Previously published in Klopp XI 191–2. The draft is undated, but it is found at the bottom of the last page of Leibniz's draft letter of 20 September 1716 to the Dowager Empress Wilhelmine Amalie* of Braunschweig-Lüneburg (document 145). For Klenk's response, see her letter to Leibniz of 30 September 1716 (document 148).
[2] That is, Leibniz's history of the House of Braunschweig-Lüneburg, the *Annales imperii occidentis Brunsvicenses**.
[3] Theobald Schöttel was the imperial chamberlain to Karl VI.

147. Leibniz to George Cheyne* (excerpt)[1]

[25 September 1716]

Honourable Sir
[…]

My dispute with your learned and ingenious man [Samuel] Clarke* is at present in the form of letters. He defends the Newtonian philosophy; I have defended mine with the great axiom, which is everywhere in my *Theodicy*, that nothing exists, happens, finds a place among truths, for which a sufficient reason why it is rather than not, or why it is this way rather than another, cannot be given. With this one axiom, real space, the vacuum, atoms are blown away like leaves in the wind! And Doctor Clarke is reduced by it, so that he denies the axiom and supposes that something can be done by *the mere will of God*, because it depends on no reason, by which alone it seems enough to me, since he has been led to absurdity.

740 148. VON KLENK TO LEIBNIZ

Quod meas mathematicas cum Newtono lites attinet, ego qui hominibus parum civiliter scribentibus respondendum non putavi contentus vacuo affectuum judicio egregiorum virorum; respondi tamen literis ipsius Newtoni ad nobilissimum virum Abbatem Contium nullis ostendique deceptum illum ab his qui plagii ad me accusatum vel connivere vel finxère, ut affectibus suis velificarentur: caeterum inania esse quibus tales candori meo notam inurere posse speraverunt. Vale. dabam Hanovero 25 Sept. 1716

Dn Cheyneo Medico et Mathematico Scoto   Londini

deditissimus
Godefridus Guilielmus Leibnitius

Charlotte Elisabeth von Klenk to Leibniz

de vienne le 30 de 7bre [1716]

Je suis si Persuadèz Monsieur que la nouvelle que l['] on vous a donnèz de la supression des gages dont vous jouissèz icy est absolument fausse, que J['] ay resolüe avec nostre amis Theobaldt d'empecher que Sa Maj. l['] imperatrice n'agisse en aucune façon Jusqu'á ce que nous voyons si le quartier que l['] on doit Payer en 15 Jours sera refusèz, alors l['] on pourroit demander l['] explication d'une pareille nouveautèz. oserois-je vous dire que vous avèz des Correspondants icy dont je crois les lumieres fort bornez et qui de toutes façons ne vous font point d'honneur[?] je crain mesme qu['] il[s] ne feroi[en]t pas un trop bon usage de la Confiance que vous pourièz avoir en eus par rapport a la mauvaise situation de leurs fortune[s], surtout Mr de Coswarin a qui l['] empereur ne donne plus d'audience et Mr Spetatzy. ce sont des aventuriers qui se font honneur a la veritèz de vostre amitièz mais qui s['] il est permis de parler si clairement ne la meritent pas. nostre amis qui est parfaitement hon[n]ete homme a Hesitèz a vous donner cet avis mais je ne Crois rien Hazarder a vous le mander esperant que vous n'en ferèz point d['] usage qui me pût estre dèsagreable et au bout du Compte ses[4] messieurs n'ont guerre l['] attention de qui que ce soit; si je n'estois pas autant de vos amies que je la suis je ne vous feroit point un detail qui ne convient guerre a mon Humeur; je donerèz vostre memoire a l['] imperatrice dès que j'en aurez l['] o[c]casion et je ne negligerèz[6] rien de ce qui pour[r]a estre utile a vos interests au[x] quelles je ne trouve pourtant que vostre presence qui puisse les mettre, entierement en bon estat; le siege de Temisvar traine en longueur et les Turcs font tous les efforts imaginable[s] pour le faire lever je

As far as my mathematical disputes with Newton are concerned, I, who have not thought that I should respond to men who write without sufficient civility, being satisfied with the objective judgment of eminent men, have nevertheless responded to a trifling letter of Newton himself to the most noble Abbé Conti;[2] and I have exposed that deception by some who have either connived or feigned to accuse me of plagiarism in order that they might direct their efforts toward their own ends and have shown that they are inanities with which such men have hoped to be able to impugn my integrity. Farewell. Delivered at Hanover 25 September 1716

To Master Cheyne, Scottish doctor and mathematician   most devoted
in London   Gottfried Wilhelm Leibniz

[1] LBr. 154 Bl. 2r. Draft: one quarto side in Leibniz's hand. Not previously published.
[2] That is, Antonio Schinella Conti*. Leibniz is referring to Newton's letter to Conti of 17 March 1716 (NS) (document 101g). For Leibniz's response to Newton's letter, see his letter to Conti of 9 April 1716 (document 108); Newton's letter was itself written as a response to the P.S. that Leibniz appended to his letter to Conti of 6 December 1715 (document 88b).

148. Charlotte Elisabeth von Klenk* to Leibniz[1]

from Vienna 30 September [1716]

I am so persuaded, sir, that the news that you have been given about the cancellation of the wages that you have here is absolutely false that I have resolved with our friend Theobald [i.e., the imperial chamberlain, Theobald [Schöttel] to prevent Her Majesty the Empress[2] from acting in any way until we see if the quarter wages that must be paid in fifteen days will be refused; then we could request the explanation of a similar innovation. Dare I tell you that you have some correspondents here whose intelligence I believe is very limited and who in any case do not do you any honour? I even fear that they would not make very good use of the confidence that you might have in them in relation to the poor status of their fortunes, above all Mr. [Count Joseph of] Corswarem, to whom the emperor [Karl VI*] no longer gives any audience, and Mr. [Giuseppe] Spedazzi.[3] They are adventurers who pride themselves on the verity of your friendship, but who, if it is permitted to speak so plainly, do not merit it. Our friend, who is a perfectly honourable man, has hesitated to give you this warning, but I do not believe I risk anything to inform you of it, trusting that you will not make any use of it that might be unpleasant for me; and after all, these[4] gentlemen scarcely have the attention of anyone. If I were not as much a friend to you as I am, I would not give you a detailed account, which scarcely suits my temperament; I will give your note to the empress[5] at the earliest opportunity, and I will neglect[6] nothing that may be beneficial to your interests, which I nevertheless think only your presence can put into an entirely good state. The siege of Temesvar* drags on, and the Turks make all imaginable efforts to

souhaite qu[']il[s] n[']y reussi[s]sent pas mais la saison est fort avancèz. Je suis plus
que personne

> Monsieur
> votre tres obeissante
> servante, C de Klenk

Leibniz to Caroline of Brandenburg-Ansbach,
Princess of Wales

Madame

Tout ce que j'apprends d'agreable touchant à V. A. Royale et Mon[sgr] le prince me
donne une sensible joye. Un nommé M. Clement, que j'ay connu secretaire de
l'Ambassade Angloise à Vienne, et que j'ay trouvé tres bien intentionné m'écrit en
ces termes: It is very remarkable to see, how much the courteous and affable behavior of their Royal Highnesses at Hampton court has gain'd upon the people of all the
country round; who dayly flock in multitudes to see them, and return extreemly satisfied with the liberties allow'd them to gratify their curiosity. On m'a dit que des
jacobites à qui on avoit fait la grace de leur parler, ont esté si charmés, qu'à leur
retour ils ont dechiré le pourtrait du pretendant. J'espere que dans peu V. A. Royale
donnera encor un coup mortel au mauvais parti. Apres cela vous n'auriés qu'à faire
un jour le tour des provinces dans la belle saison pour y etendre vos conquestes et
ramener les esprits. On dit déja que ceux d'oxford comm[enc]ent à faire poeni-
tence. Il ne leur sera point aisé de remedier aux maux qu'ils ont fait: mais ils pourront cesser à en faire, et se tourner même à faire des fruits dignes de leur penitence.

Votre jeune prince icy chasse de race[2] et fait aussi des conquestes comme pere et
mere. Tous les Anglois qui l'ont vû en partent charmés. Je monstray hier à
M. Dalrimple Ecossois un vieux diplome en original écrit en lettres d'or sur du
parch[emin] d'une couleur de pourpre, fait à Rome en l'an 972, c'est à dire il y a 744
ans, encore bien conservé, qui contient le douaire que l'empereur Otton. II. constitue à son Epouse. M. Dalrimple me raconta qu'on en avoit parlé en sa presence
chez le jeune prince, et quelq[u]'un de la compagnie ayant racconté la chose, sans
pouvoir nommer cette princesse, que le jeune prince en avoit d'abord suggeré le

149. LEIBNIZ TO CAROLINE OF BRANDENBURG-ANSBACH 743

overcome it. I hope they will not succeed in it, but the season is very much advanced. I am more than anyone

> sir
>
> your very obedient
> servant, C Klenk

[1] LBr. F 24 Bl. 26r–27r. Letter as sent: 2.5 quarto sides in Klenk's hand. Previously published in Klopp XI 195–6. This is Klenk's response to Leibniz's letter of 20 September 1716 (document 146).

[2] Klenk is presumably referring to her mistress, the Dowager Empress Wilhelmine Amalie* of Braunschweig-Lüneburg, rather than to the Reigning Empress Elisabeth Christine* of Braunschweig-Wolfenbüttel.

[3] Abbot Giuseppe Spedazzi was the imperial cryptanalyst and polymath; he corresponded with Leibniz between May 1713 and November 1716.

[4] Reading 'ces' for 'ses'.

[5] Klenk is again presumably referring to her mistress, the Dowager Empress Wilhelmine Amalie of Braunschweig-Lüneburg.

[6] Reading 'négligerai' for 'negligerèz'.

149. Leibniz to Caroline* of Brandenburg-Ansbach, Princess of Wales[1]

[End of September to mid–October 1716]

Madame

Everything pleasant that I learn concerning Your Royal Highness and the Prince gives me deep joy. A person named Mr. Clement, whom I knew as secretary of the English Ambassador at Vienna, and whom I found very well intentioned, wrote to me in these terms: 'It is very remarkable to see how much the courteous and affable behavior of their Royal Highnesses at Hampton Court has gain'd upon the people of all the country round; who dayly flock in multitudes to see them, and return extremely satisfied with the liberties allow'd them to gratify their curiosity.' I have been told that some Jacobites to whom you had done the favour of speaking were so charmed that on their return they tore up the portrait of the Pretender [James Francis Edward Stuart*]. I hope that soon Your Royal Highness will yet deliver a death blow to the bad party [i.e., the Tories]. After that you would only need to make some day the tour of the provinces in the summer months in order to extend your conquests and restore your spirits. It is said already that those from Oxford are beginning to do penance. It will not be easy for them to remedy the harms they have done, but they can stop doing them and turn themselves toward producing results worthy of their penance.

Your young prince [Friedrich Ludwig* of Braunschweig-Lüneburg] here is a chip off the old block[2] and also makes conquests like father and mother. All the English who have seen him leave charmed by him. Yesterday I showed Mr. Dalrymple, a Scotsman, an old document in original writing with letters of gold on crimson parchment, made in Rome in the year 972, that is to say, 744 years ago, still well preserved, which contains the dower that Emperor Otto II established for his wife.

nom, disant que c'estoit Theophanie princesse de Constantinople. Mais ses manieres obligeantes le font encor plus aimer, que son savoir ne le fait admirer. Il avoit dit à M. Da[l]rimple prest à partir, qu'il n'avoit eté qu'un moment icy et qu'il seroit bien aise de le voir davantage, et là dessus M. Dalrimple s'est arresté | encor quelques jours |. Quand M. Clement, dont j'ay parlé cy dessus, prit congé d'icy, le prince luy dit: je suis faché que nous ne pouvons pas bien converser ensemble, car M. Clement avoit de la peine à parler François. Il est effectivement facheux que cet aimable prince ne se peut pas encor bien exercer en Anglois comme il voudroit. J'espere qu'on y remediera.[3]

Les Armours[4] de M. l'Abbé Conti pourroient donner matiere a un Roman philosophique: quoyqu'il m'ait quitté pour M. Newton je ne laisse pas de le plaindre. Il est vray que je ne puis que louer l'Ambassadrice. Je ne croyois pas qu'il fut permis en Italie de faire cortege aux dames dans de telles circonstances. Si l'Ambassadeur ne s'en fache point, il faut qu'il croye que les philosophes sont sans consequence ou sans doute ceux de mon âge.

Toute notre Eglise Angloise part aujourdhuy dans la personne de M. Blackburn chapelain du Roy, doyen d'Exon car il s'en retourne.[5] Il a reputation de bien precher, et d'ailleurs il ne manque ny de savoir ny de zele. Je luy ay dit hier, quand il prenoit congé de moy, que j'esperois de luy ecrire bientost des lettres ou je retrancherois de son nom. Il m'entendoit. C'est que les Eveques ne signent et ne sont nommés que par leur nom de Bapteme sans le nom de famille. Et je luy souhaite un tel poste.

Le temps s'est un peu remis au beau, et j'espere que le Roy en profitera comme il faut; Sa Mté se portant bien. Si la Reine de prusse fut allé[e] avec au Ghoeur, apparemment le Roy son epoux seroit venu la quérir. Il y a encor des gens qui s'imaginent qu'il pourroit rendre une visite au Roy qui se trouve si proche de ses Etats: mais la chose paroist tres douteuse: et il y a des gens aupres de ce prince qui ne le pressent point de s'abboucher avec le Roy de la Grande Bretagne.

C'est une chose surprenante qu'au point de tenter la descente à scanie[8] on a changé de resolution, soit que le Czar est resolu de tourner ses forces contre les Turcs, soit qu'on ait pris ses mesures trop courtes.[9] Le Magistrat de Hambourg à la solicitation du Resident de sa Mté Czarienne a arreté un Seigneur, qu'on dit etre parent de Mazeppa. Mais le Ministre de Suede et meme l'Administrateur de Holstein le reclament, disant qu'il est au service du Roy de Suede.[12] On dit qu'il est riche, et a preté de l'argent au Roy de Suede.

Une personne considérable des pays bas qui m'écrit quelques fois nie que notre M. de Brandebourg ait eté confesseur de la Reine douairere d'Espagne. Ce n'est pas luy meme aussi qui me l'ait dit. Mais je ne voy rien qui le rende incroyable. Il est tousjours vray qu'il est d'un esprit aisé et qui donne du contentement au Roy. Je ne say s'il accompagnera Sa Mté en Angleterre. L'Abbé Bouquoy ne voudroit point le faire (dit il) quand il pourroit. Il se met quelques fois sur ses grands chevaux, et dame le pion à tout le monde.[14] Il se plaint que le Roy ne l'ecoute pas asses serieusement car il voudroit etre le Reformateur du genre humain, et croit que le Roy

149. LEIBNIZ TO CAROLINE OF BRANDENBURG-ANSBACH   745

Mr. Dalrymple told me that it was spoken of in his presence at the residence of the young prince, and, someone having recounted the matter without being able to name this princess, that the young prince had immediately suggested her name, saying that it was Theophanu, princess of Constantinople. But his obliging manners make him even more endearing than his knowledge makes him admirable. When Mr. Dalrymple was ready to leave, he [the young prince] told him that he had been here but a moment and that he [the young prince] would be very happy to see more of him, and thereupon Mr. Dalrymple remained | a few more days |. When Mr. Clement, of whom I spoke above, took his leave from here, the prince told him, 'I am sorry that we are not able to converse well together', because Mr. Clement had some difficulty speaking French. It is indeed regrettable that this amiable prince is not yet able to perform in English as he would wish. I hope that it will be remedied.[3]

The loves[4] of Abbé [Antonio Schinella] Conti* could provide material for a philosophical novel. Although he has left me for Mr. Newton, I feel sorry for him nevertheless. It is true that I can only praise the Ambassadress. I did not think that it was permitted in Italy to accompany ladies in any such circumstances. If the Ambassador is not offended by it, it must be that he believes that philosophers are without consequence, or doubtless those of my age.

Our entire English church left today in the person of Mr. [Lancelot] Blackburne*, chaplain of the king [George I, Georg Ludwig* of Braunschweig-Lüneburg], dean of Exon [Exeter], for he is going back.[5] He has a reputation for preaching well, and in fact he lacks neither knowledge nor zeal. Yesterday, when he took his leave of me, I told him that I hoped soon to write him some letters in which I would deduct from his name. He understood me: bishops only sign and are only named with their baptismal name, without the family name, and I wish him such a post.[6]

The weather is a bit nicer again, and I hope that the king will benefit from it properly, since His Majesty is well. If the Queen of Prussia [Sophie Dorothea of Braunschweig-Lüneburg][7] had gone along to Göhrde*, her husband the king [Friedrich Wilhelm I* of Prussia] would apparently have come to fetch her. There are still some people who imagine that he could visit the king, who is to be found so near to his estates; but the matter appears very doubtful, and there are people in service to this prince who do not press him to confer with the King of Great Britain.

It is astonishing that on the verge of attempting the descent on Scania,[8] some resolution has been changed: either the czar [Peter I the Great* of Russia] is resolved to turn his forces against the Turks or he has taken inadequate steps.[9] At the request of the Resident of Her Majesty the Czarina [Catherine I],[10] the magistrate of Hamburg has arrested a lord who is said to be a relative of [Ivan Stepanovych] Mazepa.[11] But the Swedish minister, and even the administrator of Holstein, claim him, saying that he is in the service of the King of Sweden [Karl XII of Sweden (1682–1718)].[12] It is said that he is rich and has loaned some money to the King of Sweden.

An eminent person from the Netherlands, who sometimes writes to me, denies that our Mr. Brandenburg was the confessor of the Dowager Queen of Spain [Maria Anna of Neuburg].[13] It is not he himself who told me, but I see nothing that renders it

pourroit seconder ses grands desseins, s'il en avoit envie. Il n'a pas laissé d'accompagner Sa Mté au Ghoeur.

Pour moy je travaille fort et ferme à mon Histoire qui m'occupera bien encore une bonne partie de l'année qui vient. Ainsi je n'espere point d'aller si tost en Angleterre; rien ne me pourroit donner plus d'envie d'y aller que les bontés de V. A. R., mais comme je ne l'espere point bien tost, je ne say si je pourrois l'esperer apres. Car il n'y a pas des grans[16] apres à esperer chez moy. Je verray comment M. Clark me repondra. S'il ne m'accorde pas entierement ce grand axiome receu | jus qu'à icy |, que rien n'arrive sans qu'il y ait une raison suffisante pourquoy il arrive plutot ainsi qu'autrement, je ne me pourray empecher de douter de sa sincerité, et s'il l'accorde à Dieu la philosophie de M. Newton.

Je suis etc.

149. LEIBNIZ TO CAROLINE OF BRANDENBURG-ANSBACH   747

unbelievable. It is true nevertheless that he has an easy disposition and gives the king some contentment. I do not know if he will accompany His Majesty to England. The Abbé [Jean-Albert d'Archambaud, Comte de] Bucquoy* would not want to do it (says he) even if he could. Sometimes he mounts his high horses and outwits everyone.[14] He complains that the king does not listen to him seriously enough; for he would like to be the reformer of humankind and believes that the king could support his great plans if he wanted to. He was not permitted to accompany His Majesty to Göhrde.

As for me, I am working resolutely on my history,[15] which will certainly still occupy me for a good part of the coming year. So I do not hope to go so soon to England. Nothing could tempt me to go there more than the kindnesses of Your Royal Highness, but as I do not hope to go there soon, I do not know if I could hope to go there later. For there is not much[16] later to hope for in me. I will see how Mr. [Samuel] Clarke* will respond to me. If he does not grant me entirely this great accepted | until now | axiom, that nothing happens without there being a sufficient reason why it happens thus rather than otherwise, I will not be able to refrain from doubting his sincerity; and if he does grant it, farewell the philosophy of Mr. Newton. I am etc.

[1] LBr. F 4 74r–74v. Draft: two quarto sides in Leibniz's hand. The letter is undated, but I think it can be dated to the weeks between 19 September and mid-October 1716. In the letter Leibniz makes reference to the decision of Czar Peter the Great* to abandon the descent on the Swedish province of Scania. The Czar made this decision on 19 September 1716 (NS) (see Hatton 1968, p. 424), so that date would establish the lower bound on the date of this letter. Furthermore, given the usual time it took for letters to pass between London and Hanover, the fact that Caroline's reply (document 158) is dated 4 November 1716 (NS) suggests that Leibniz's letter could not have been written much later than the middle of October 1716. It is Leibniz's response to Caroline's letter of 8 September 1716 (document 143) and is the last letter he wrote to Caroline before his death on 14 November 1716. Previously published in Klopp XI 186–90, and Schüller 1991, p. 262 (excerpt in German translation).

[2] Klopp XI 187 mistranscribes 'chasse de race' as 'chasse des rats'.

[3] Klopp XI 188 omits this sentence without notice.

[4] Klopp XI 188 mistranscribes 'Armours' as 'sermons'.

[5] Klopp XI 188 omits 'car il s'en retourner'.

[6] Leibniz's wish was soon granted. Blackburne was elevated to the bishopric of Exeter in 1717, after the death of the previous bishop, Ofspring Blackall, in late 1716.

[7] Sophie Dorothea of Braunschweig-Lüneburg was the daughter of the Elector Georg Ludwig* of Braunschweig-Lüneburg (later King George I of England) and his first cousin Sophie Dorothea* of Braunschweig-Lüneburg-Celle. She married Friedrich Wilhelm of Prussia in 1687. Friedrich Wilhelm (1688–1740) was the son of Georg Ludwig's sister, Sophie Charlotte* of Braunschweig-Lüneburg. Upon the death of his father (Friedrich I and III* of Prussia) in 1713, he became King Friedrich Wilhelm I of Prussia and Elector of Brandenburg.

[8] Klopp IX 188 omits 'à scanie' without notice. Scania is the southernmost traditional province of Sweden. It was supposed to be the target of a coordinated invasion involving English and Dutch ships and Russian and Danish ground forces. Czar Peter the Great of Russia abandoned the plan on 19 September 1716, arguing that the season was too far advanced for proceeding with the planned invasion. See Hatton 1968, p. 424.

[9] Klopp XI 188–9 mistranscribes this sentence as follows: 'C'est une chose surprenante qu'au point de tenter la descente on a changé, soit que le Czar est résolu de tourner ses forces contre les Turcs, soit qu'on ait pris ses mesures trop pour résolutions'.

[10] Catherine I (Marta Helena Skowronska, 1684–1727) was Peter I the Great's* second wife, whom he publicly married on 9 February 1712, after having fathered five of her children. She was rechristened Yekaterina (Catherine) Alekseyevna when she was received into the Russian Orthodox Church in 1705. After Peter's death in 1725, she ruled as Empress Catherine I of Russia, until her death in 1727.

Nicolas Rémond to Leibniz (excerpt)

Monsieur

[..]

mais ne me ferez vous nulle part de vostre dispute avec Monsieur Clark? c'est un homme dont je fais cas et j'ai veu dans les extraits que M. le Clerc a faits de ses ouvrages, des pensées qui m'ont plu. je voudrois bien estre instruit des points principaux de la controverse ou je ne doute point que vous ne conserviez la superiorité que vous avez sur tous les hommes.

je croiois que M. l'abbé Conti suivroit à Hanover Sa Majesté Britannique, et j'estoit bien assuré que dans les premieres conversations vous le convertiriez, mais il est demeuré en Angleterre, et j'apprends qu'actuellement il est à Oxford. on me mande qu'il se plaint de mon silence. je crois plustost qu'il se plaint de mes lettres.

[...]

je suis avec mon respect et mon admiration ordinaires

    Monsieur

Votre tres humble
et tres obeissant serviteur
Remond

a Paris ce 2 d'octobre 1716.

[11] Ivan Stepanovych Mazepa (1639–1709) was hetman of Ukrainian Cossacks from 1687–1708. In late October of 1708, Mazeppa deserted the forces of Czar Peter the Great* and joined sides with the Swedes in the Great Northern War (1700–1721). After hearing of this treachery, the czar proclaimed a new Ukrainian hetman. (See Hatton 1968, pp. 276–8.)

[12] Klopp XI 189 omits and modifies words in this sentence without notice, transcribing it as: 'Mais le Ministre de Suède le réclame, disant qu'il est au service du Roy of Suède'.

[13] Maria Anna of Neuburg (1667–1740) was Queen of Spain from 1689 until the death of her husband, Carlos II of Spain, in November of 1700. On Brandenburg and his supposed relation to the Dowager Queen, see Leibniz's letter to Caroline of 11 September 1716 (document 144, pp. 1029 & 1031).

[14] Klopp XI 189 mistranscribes 'dame le pion à tout le monde' as 'donne le pion à tout le monde'.

[15] That is, his history of the House of Braunschweig-Lüneburg, the *Annales imperii occidentis Brunsvicenses*.

[16] Here I follow Klopp XI 189 in reading 'pas grand' for 'pas des grans'.

150. Nicolas Rémond* to Leibniz (excerpt)[1]

[2 October 1716]

Sir

[…]

But will you not tell me anything about your dispute with Mr. [Samuel] Clarke*? This is a man I esteem, and I have seen some ideas that have pleased me in the extracts that Mr. Le Clerc[2] has made of his works. I should certainly like to be informed about the principal points of the controversy, in which I do not doubt that you only maintained the superiority that you have over all men.

I thought that Abbé [Antonio Schinella] Conti* would follow His British Majesty [George I, Georg Ludwig* of Braunschweig-Lüneburg] to Hanover, and I was very confident that in the first conversations you would convert him; but he has remained in England, and I understand that he is actually in Oxford. I have been informed that he complains of my silence; I rather believe that he complains of my letters.

[…]

I am with my usual respect and admiration

sir

Your very humble
and very obedient servant

in Paris 2 October 1716.   Rémond

[1] LBr. 768 Bl. 63r–64r, 54r. Letter as sent: three octavo sides in Rémond's hand. Previously published in GP III 676–7; Schüller 1991, p. 265 (excerpt in German translation); Robinet 1991, p. 185 (excerpt). This is Rémond's reply to Leibniz's letter of 15 August 1716 (document 138). For Leibniz's reply, see his letter to Rémond of 19 October 1716 (document 153).

[2] That is, Jean Le Clerc (1657–1736), a Swiss theologian who was born in Geneva and later became a professor of ecclesiastical history at Amsterdam. The reference is to Le Clerc's review of Clarke's works in Volume 25, Part II, Article 3 of his *Bibliotheque Choisie* (Amsterdam, 1713), pp. 279–437, parts of which were translated into English and published under the title, *An Abstract and Judgment of Dr. Clarke's Polemical or Controversial Writings* (London, 1713).

Caroline of Brandenburg-Ansbach, Princess of Wales, to Leibniz

hamthancour le $\frac{5}{25}$ Semp: 1716[2]

J['']espere que vous aurais receu[3] Monsieur, mes remerciment[4] de larelassion[5] que vous m'avez anvoiyée[6] du Prince de Beveren. Je luy trouvez[7] vn sy beau al[l]eman[d] que je l['']ay anvoiyé a[8] Madame. Je ne puis m['']anpecher[9] d'avoir pitié du beauver[10] Langallery. Je crois qu'une tete plus forté que la siene aurait eu de la peñe arescister aus impertinance de M[d] safeme.[11] Je souhaiterait lepeauver home dans les petité maison.[12] J'ay veu le pere Brandenbourg alahais il y a dues an.[14] il vous pourait dire beaucoup de nouvelles de Sa Reine puis-que se M[r] a estte anploiyée[16] dans les interique[17] de c'este[18] Princesse et de M[r] le Regeant de France. J'ay do[n]né au docteur chlerque vos papié[19] et il me fait vn recuelle de toute.[20] Je n'ay pas ancore veu la traduction de votre imcomparable liver.[21] J'ay receu come vn grand honneur que ladestication doit estre a moy.[22] la reponce[23] me sera ausy detié.[24] Je vousderais[25] que vous puisié estre an connessance[26] avec M[r] chlerque. Vous le couderié assurement.[27] Je desire plus ancore que les anglois d'avoir qu'elque vn[28] aupres de mon fils[29] à luy aprandre[30] l'Anglois.[31] Dieu m'est demoin[32] que [ce] n'est pas ma faute. Je me fladée[33] de vous voire icy avec le Roy, et vous me trouverais[34] toujours la meme.

Caroline

151. Caroline* of Brandenburg-Ansbach, Princess of Wales, to Leibniz[1]

Hampton Court $\frac{5}{25}$ September 1716[2]

I hope that you have received[3] my thanks[4], sir, for the report[5] of the Prince of Bevern [Ferdinand Albrecht II*] that you sent me.[6] I think[7] he is such a fine German that I have sent[8] it to Madame [Elisabeth Charlotte* of the Palatinate, Duchess of Orléans]. I can't help[9] pitying the poor[10] [Philippe de Gentils, Marquis de] Langallerie*. I believe that a stronger mind than his would have had trouble resisting the impertinences of his wife.[11] I would wish the poor man were in an insane asylum.[12] I saw Father Brandenburg[13] at The Hague two years ago.[14] He could tell you a lot of news about his queen,[15] since this gentleman has been employed[16] in the intrigues[17] of this[18] princess and the Regent of France [Philippe II*, Duke of Orléans]. I have given Doctor [Samuel] Clarke* your papers,[19] and he is making a collection of everything.[20] I have not yet seen the translation of your incomparable book.[21] I have accepted as a great honour that it is to be dedicated to me.[22] The response[23] [by Clarke] will also be dedicated[24] to me. I should[25] want you to be able to be acquainted[26] with Mr. Clarke. You would certainly like him.[27] I wish even more than the English to have someone[28] with my son[29] [Friedrich Ludwig* of Braunschweig-Lüneburg] to teach[30] him English.[31] God as my witness,[32] it is not my fault. I hope[33] to see you here with the king [George I, Georg Ludwig* of Braunschweig-Lüneburg], and you will find[34] me always the same

Caroline

---

[1] LBr. F 4 Bl. 84r–85r. Letter as sent: 2.5 quarto sides in Caroline's hand. Previously published in Klopp XI 197; Robinet 1991, p. 185 (excerpt); Schüller 1991, p. 264 (excerpt in German translation); HGA 197 (excerpt in English translation). This is Caroline's reply to Leibniz's letter of 11 September 1716 (document 144).

[2] That is, 25 September 1716 (OS) and 6 October (NS) 1716. At the time of writing the Gregorian calendar (NS) was eleven days in advance of the Julian calendar (OS), so Caroline was mistaken in writing $\frac{5}{25}$ instead of $\frac{6}{25}$. Klopp misdates the letter as $\frac{15}{26}$ Septembre (Klopp XI 197).

[3] Reading 'aurez reçu' for 'aurais receu'.

[4] Reading 'remercîments' for 'remerciment'.

[5] Reading 'la relation' for 'larelassion'.

[6] Reading 'envoyée' for 'anvoiyée'. Caroline sent her thanks for the report in her letter to Leibniz of 1 September 1716 (document 142). Leibniz had sent her the report of the Prince of Bevern with his letter to her of 18 August 1716 (document 139).

[7] Reading 'trouve' for 'trouvez'.

[8] Reading 'envoyé à' for 'anvoiyé a'.

[9] Reading 'empêcher' for 'anpecher'.

[10] Reading 'pauvre' for 'beauver'.

[11] Reading 'sienne aurait eu de la peine à résister aux impertinences de M^d sa femme' for 'siene aurait eu de la peine aus impertinance de M^d safeme'. Caroline is referring to Langallerie's second wife, Marguerite de Frère, whom Elisabeth Charlotte of the Palatinate, Duchess of Orléans, described as 'little worthy of' of Langallerie's passion, 'because her infidelity was notorious and most scandalous' (my translation of the French quoted in Boislisle 1898, p. 79).

Caroline of Brandenburg-Ansbach,
Princess of Wales, to Leibniz

Hamthancour le ⁸⁄₂₈ Semp: 1716[2]

quoy que je vous ayée[3] deja repondu à votre derniere lettre, Monsieur, je vous écris par com[m]ission pour M[r] chlerque, a qui j'ay parlee et lue avec luy vos papié.[4] il samble[5] que vous voulez les faire imprimer. il ma instanment prié[6] de vous persuader qu'an ca[7] que vous eussy [la] volonde[8] de les faire imprimer, vous vouliez faire mestre les papie[9] dans la langué dans laquelle il ont étte écrit,[10] et qu'il vous promestté[11] la même chose de son codé.[12] il il[13] a beaucoup de preud[14] icy pour les Eveque[s] qui ont restte[15] dans les inderes[16] de feu Roy Jaque. J'ay anvoiyé vn[17] petit phanphelet a[18] M[r] L'Eveque d'osnabruch qu'il aura je ne doute pas la bondé[19] de vous donner. J'ay estte extremement contan aujour-dehuis,[20] de landertien[21] du docteur chlerque qui ma refudée le chapiter de paille des manichien.[22] Je souhaite

[12] Reading 'souhaiterais le pauvre homme dans Les Petites Maisons' for 'souhaiterait lepeauver hoñe dans les petité maison'. 'Les Petites Maisons' was the name given to a psychiatric hospital that was created in 1557 and located in the rue de la Chaise in Paris. Its name was derived from the fact that the courtyard was surrounded with small houses used to house the inmates. Like 'Bedlam', a byname for the Bethlem Royal Hospital in London, 'petites maisons' came to refer to an insane asylum in general. See Saint-Victor 1809, pp. 658–9.

[13] Concerning this 'Father Brandenburg', see note 10 of Leibniz's letter to Caroline of 11 September 1716 (document 144, p. 733).

[14] Reading 'à La Haye il y a deux ans' for 'alahais il y a dues an'.

[15] That is, Maria Anna of Neuburg (1667–1740), Queen of Spain from 1689 until the death of her husband, Carlos II, in November of 1700.

[16] Reading 'ce M^r a été employé' for 'se M^r a estte anploiyée'.

[17] Reading 'intriques' for 'interique'.

[18] Reading 'cette' for 'c'este'.

[19] Reading 'papiers' for 'papié'.

[20] Reading 'un recueil de tout' for 'vn recuelle de toute'.

[21] Reading 'incomparable livre' for 'imcomparable liver'.

[22] Reading 'la dédicace doit être à moi' for 'ladestication doit estre a moy'.

[23] Reading 'réponse' for 'reponce'.

[24] Reading 'sera aussi dédiée' for 'sera ausy detié'.

[25] Reading 'voudrais' for 'vousderais'.

[26] Reading 'puissiez être en connaissance' for 'puisié estre an connessance'.

[27] Reading 'le goûteriez asseurément' for 'le couderié assurement'.

[28] Reading 'quelqu'un' for 'qu'elque un'.

[29] The words preceding 'fils' are illegible; I have followed Klopp's interpolation of 'de mon fils' (see Klopp XI 197).

[30] Reading 'apprendre' for 'aprandre'.

[31] The words following 'aprandre' are illegible; I have followed Klopp's interpolation of 'l'Anglois' (see Klopp XI 197).

[32] Reading 'témoin' for 'demoin'.

[33] Reading 'flatte' for 'fladée'.

[34] Reading 'trouverez' for 'trouverais'.

152. Caroline of Brandenburg-Ansbach, Princess of Wales, to Leibniz[1]

Hampton Court $\frac{8}{28}$ September 1716[2]

Although I have[3] already responded to your last letter, sir, I am writing you by commission on behalf of Mr. [Samuel] Clarke*, to whom I have spoken and with whom I have read your papers.[4] It seems[5] that you want to have them published. He urged me[6] to persuade you that in case[7] you intended[8] to have them published, that you would have the papers[9] printed in the language in which they were written,[10] and for his part[11] he promised[12] you the same thing. There is[13] a lot of talk[14] about the bishops who have remained[15] on the side[16] of the late King James. I have sent a[17] small pamphlet to[18] the Bishop of Osnabrück [Ernst August II* of Braunschweig-Lüneburg] that he will doubtless have the kindness[19] to give you. Today I was extremely pleased[20] with the conversation[21] with Doctor Clarke, who refuted

infiniment de vous voir ansamble,[23] et j'espere que vous me choisirais[24] quand vous vous derais[25] vous voir seulle aseulle[26] pour parler. Je scersais[27] toujours infiniment de vos amié.[28]

Caroline

le P. estté arrivez[29] hier au soir an tres bon̄e[30] santé de Porsmuth et fors contande[31] de la Reception qu'on luy a fait par tout.

152. CAROLINE OF BRANDENBURG-ANSBACH TO LEIBNIZ   755

[Pierre] Bayle's* chapter on Manicheans for me.[22] I very much wish to see your together,[23] and I hope that you will choose[24] me when you desire[25] to see each other to talk one-on-one.[26] I shall always forever be[27] your friend.[28]

Caroline

The prince [Georg August of Braunschweig-Lüneburg, Prince of Wales] arrived[29] last night in very good[30] health from Portsmouth and very pleased[31] with the reception that he received everywhere.

[1] LBr. F 4 Bl. 86r–87r. Letter as sent: 2.25 quarto sides in Caroline's hand. Previously published in Klopp XI 191 (excerpt); Schüller 1991, p. 264 (excerpt in German translation); HGA 197 (excerpt in English translation).

[2] That is, 28 September (OS) and 9 October (NS). At the time of writing, the Gregorian calendar (NS) was eleven days in advance of the Julian calendar (OS), so Caroline was mistaken in writing '$\frac{8}{28}$ semp' rather than '$\frac{9}{19}$ semp'. Klopp XI 191 misdates the letter as $\frac{8}{19}$ Septembre.

[3] Reading 'ai' for 'ayée'.

[4] Reading 'parlé et lu avec lui vos papiers' for 'parlee et lue avec luy vos papié'.

[5] Reading 'semble' for 'samble'.

[6] Reading 'm'a instamment priée' for 'ma instanment prié'.

[7] Reading 'qu'en cas' for 'qu'an ca'.

[8] Reading 'eussiez volonté' for 'eussy volonde'.

[9] Reading 'mettre les papiers' for 'mestre les papie'.

[10] Reading 'ils ont été écrits' for 'il ont étte écrit'.

[11] Reading 'côté' for 'codé'.

[12] Reading 'promettait' for 'promestté'.

[13] Reading 'Il y' for 'il il'.

[14] Reading 'bruit' for 'preud'.

[15] Reading 'sont restés' for 'ont restte'.

[16] Reading 'intérêts' for 'inderes'.

[17] Reading 'envoyé un' for 'anvoiyé vn'.

[18] Reding 'pamphlet à' for 'phanphelet a'.

[19] Reading 'bonté' for 'bondé'.

[20] Reading 'été extrêmement content aujourd'hui' for 'estte extremement contan aujour-dehuis'.

[21] Reading 'l'entretien' for 'landertien'.

[22] Reading 'm'a réfuté le chapitre de Bayle des Manichéens' for 'ma refadée le chapitre de paille des manichien'.

[23] Reading 'ensemble' for 'ansamble'.

[24] Reading 'choisirez' for 'choisirais'.

[25] Reading 'voudrez' for 'vous derais'.

[26] Reading 'seul à seul' for 'seulle aseulle'.

[27] Reading 'serai' for 'scerais'.

[28] Reading 'amies' for 'amié'.

[29] Reading 'est arrivé' for 'estté arrivez'.

[30] Reading 'en très bonne' for 'an tres boñe'.

[31] Reading 'fort content' for 'fors contande'.

Leibniz to Nicolas Rémond

Monsieur

[...]

Mons. Clarke et moy nous avons cet honneur que nostre dispute passe par les mains de Mad. la princesse de Galles. J'ay envoyé ma 4me reponse, et j'attends la sienne, sur laquelle je me regleray. Car dans la derniere je suis plus prolixe pour finir bien tost. Il a fait quasi semblant d'ignorer ma Theodicée, et m'a forcé à des repetitions. J'ay reduit l'estat de notre dispute à ce grand Axiome, que rien n'existe ou[4] n'arrive sans qu'il y ait une raison suffisante, pourquoy il en soit plustost ainsi qu'autrement. S'il continue de[5] me le nier, ou en sera sa sincerité? S'il me l'accorde, à Dieu le vuide, les Atomes, et toute la philosophie de M. Newton. Quand nous aurons fini, je ne manqueray pas de vous en faire part, et j'espere que Mad. la princesse de Galles m'en donnera la permission[6]. Je suis avec zele etc.

153. Leibniz to Nicolas Rémond* (excerpt)[1]

[19 October 1716]

Sir

[…]

Mr. [Samuel] Clarke* and I have this honour, that our dispute passes through the hands of Madame the Princess of Wales [Caroline* of Brandenburg-Ansbach]. I have sent my 4th response[2], and I await his, by which I will be guided.[3] For in my last response I am more expansive in order to end soon. He has pretended as if to be ignorant of my *Theodicy* and has forced me to repeat myself. I have reduced the state of our dispute to this great axiom, that nothing exists or[4] happens without there being a sufficient reason why it is so rather than otherwise. If he continues to[5] deny it, where will his sincerity be? If he grants it, farewell the void, atoms, and the entire philosophy of Mr. Newton. When we are finished, I will not fail to let you know about it, and I hope that Madame the Princess of Wales will give me permission to do it[6]. I am enthusiastically etc.

---

[1] LBr. 768 Bl. 64v, 63r. This is either an extract from, or an initial draft of, Leibniz's letter to Rémond of 19 October 1716, the first page of which is written on the reverse side of the last page of Rémond's letter to Leibniz of 2 October 1716 (LBr. 768 Bl. 64v), and the last lines of which are written above and below the body of the first page of Rémond's letter to Leibniz of 2 October 1716 (LBr. 768 Bl. 63r). Previously published in Schüller 1991, p. 265–6 (excerpt in German translation; Robinet 1991, pp. 185–6 (excerpt). The complete original manuscript that was sent to Rémond is now apparently lost, but it was published in Des Maizeaux 1720, vol. 2, pp. 359–61; in Dutens V 33–4; and in GP III 677–8.

[2] That is, Leibniz's Fifth Paper (see document 140b), which was his response to Clarke's Fourth Reply (document 129).

[3] Caroline transmitted Clarke's last response (document 157) in a letter to Leibniz of 29 October 1716 (NS) (document 156); but since Leibniz died just sixteen days later and could have received Caroline's letter no earlier than a week before his death, it is doubtful that he ever even read Clarke's last response.

[4] The extract at LBr 768 Bl. 63r omits 'n'existe ou', but it is included in Des Maizeaux 1720, vol. 2, p. 360, Dutens V 33, and GP III 678.

[5] Des Maizeaux 1720, vol. 2, p. 360, Dutens V 33, and GP III 678 all have 'à' instead of 'de'.

[6] The complete letter published by Des Maizeaux (p. 361) and Dutens (p. 34) has 'j'espere que ce sera avec la permission de Madame las Princess de Galles' rather than 'j'espere que Mad. la princesse de Galles m'en donnera la permission'. But the complete letter published by Gerhardt has the latter wording (see GP III 678), which is also found at LBr. 768 Bl. 63r.

Leibniz to Johann Bernoulli

Vir noblissime et celeberrime,
Fautor Honoratissime

[...]

Clarkium videor reduxisse ad absurdum. Coactus enim est mihi in effectu negare hanc propositionem: nihil existere, evenire, locum habere, cujus non detur sufficiens ratio, cur sit potius vel non sit, aut cur sic potius quàm aliter sit. Nam coactus est recurrere ad meram, ut vocat, Dei voluntatem nulla ratione, nullo motivo nixam, quod mihi absurdum, et Divinae Sapientiae pariter ac rerum naturæ contrarium videtur. Nam cum scias Anglos ex spatio facere aliquod absolutum ac reale, vacuum etiam admittere, ostendo, admissa absoluta realitate spatii, cum id ubique sit uniforme, impossibile esse dari rationem, cur res Deus in hac potius quàm alia parte spatii, aut hoc potius quàm inverso situ locet. Mihi verò spatium nihil aliud est quam ordo coëxistendi, adeoque sublatis rebus nullum est, et eodem manente rerum omnium situ, idem. Videtur et in aliis vadimonium deseruisse[2] Clarkius. Expecto adhuc responsionem ad novissimam meam scripturam, quæ videbo an replicationem à me mereatur. Omnia finito certamine edentur. Sed cum per manus eant Serenissimae principis Walliæ, ejus id venia fiet.

[...]

Quod superset vale et fave. Dabam Hanoveroæ 23 Octobr. 1716

deditissimus

G. G. Leibnitius

154. Leibniz to Johann Bernoulli* (excerpt)[1]

Most noble and celebrated sir,
Most Honourable Supporter

[23 October 1716]

[…]

I appear to have reduced [Samuel] Clarke* to absurdity. For I have in effect forced him to deny this proposition, that nothing exists, happens, or obtains for which there is not a sufficient reason why it is rather than not, or why it is so rather than otherwise. But now he has been forced to revert to what he calls the mere will of God with no reason, without motive, which to me is absurd, and it also seems contrary to divine wisdom and to the nature of things. For although you know the English make space something absolute and real, and even admit a void, I show that when the absolute reality of space has been granted, it is impossible to give a reason why God places a thing in this rather than another part of space, or in this rather than in the opposite position, since it is everywhere uniform. For me space is in fact nothing other than an order of coexisting, and is indeed nothing taken apart from things, and when the situation of all things remains the same, it is the same. And in other matters Clarke seems to have failed to show up.[2] I still await a response to my last paper;[3] I will see whether it merits a reply from me. Everything from the concluded dispute will be published. But since they pass through the hands of the Most Serene Princess of Wales [Caroline* of Brandenburg-Ansbach], it will be done with her permission.

[…]

For the rest, farewell and be well disposed. Delivered at Hanover 23 October 1716

most devoted

G. G. Leibniz

---

[1] Universitätsbibliothek Basel L I a 19 Bl. 330r–331v. 4 octavo sides in Leibniz's hand. Previously published in GM III-2 970–2 (excerpt); Schüller 1991, pp. 266–7 (excerpt in German translation); Robinet 1991, p. 186 (excerpt). For Bernoulli's reply, see his letter to Leibniz of 11 November 1716 (document 159).

[2] Literally, 'to have forfeited his bail'.

[3] That is, his Fifth Paper (document 140b).

Johann Caspar von Bothmer to Leibniz

à Hamptoncour ce $\frac{16}{27}$ Oct: 1716

Monsieur

Je vois avec beaucoup de plaisir par l'honneur de vostre lettre du 9me de ce mois l'assiduité avec la quelle vous continués à travailler à vostre illustre ouvrage. je ne doute pas, que M$^{rs:}$ de Bernstorf et de Stanhop ne s'emploient en revanche efficacement pour vous faire avoir au retour du Roy du Gohr la place vous souhaités icy d'Historiografe[4] de S.M. Tout le monde conviendra aisement que personne ne la merite à plus juste tiltre[5] que vous, non seulement par vos connoissances mais plus particulierement encor par l'ouvrage dont je viens de parler.

[...]

M$^{me:}$ La Princesse de Gales nous avoit allarmée[6] la semaine passée sur son accouchement s'estant effrayée d'une chute assés perilleuse que la Princesse Caroline fit devant Elle sans se faire pourtant aucun mal. S.A.R. est tout à fait remise à cette heure et se porte tres bien depuis 4 au 5 jours. On croit pourtant qu'elle pourra abbreger[7] son sejour icy de quelques jours, et partir pour Londres au commencement de la semaine prochaine au lieu que l'intention estoit de ne le faire qu'à la fin c'est à dire le 27me de ce mois. P. S. je crois que l'estat de sa santé reglera son depart. Tout le monde espere qu'elle aura un fils, je suis avec tout le zele possible Monsieur

Vostre

tres humble et tres
obeissant serviteur
Bothmer

155. Johann Caspar von Bothmer* to Leibniz (excerpt)[1]

at Hampton Court $\frac{16}{27}$ October 1716[2]

Sir

I observe with much pleasure, by the honour of your letter of the 9th of this month, the assiduity with which you continue to labor on your illustrious work.[3] I do not doubt that Messrs. [Andreas Gottlieb, Freiherr von] Bernstorff* and [James] Stanhope* are in return applying themselves effectively to deliver to you, on the return of the king [George I, Georg Ludwig* of Braunschweig-Lüneburg] from Göhrde*, the position you desire here of historiographer[4] of His Majesty. Everyone will readily agree that no one deserves a more just title[5] than you, not only for your knowledge, but more particularly still for the work about which I have just spoken.

[…]

Madame the Princess of Wales [Caroline* of Brandenburg-Ansbach] had alarmed[6] us last week concerning her delivery, being frightened by a fairly perilous forward fall that the Princess Caroline suffered, without, however, doing herself any harm. Her Royal Highness is now altogether recovered and has been doing very well for four or five days. However, we believe that she will be able to shorten[7] her stay here by a few days and depart for London at the beginning of next week,[8] whereas the intention was to do it only at the end, that is to say, the 27th of this month.[9] P. S. I believe that the state of her health will determine her departure. Everyone hopes that she will have a son.[10] I am with all possible enthusiasm

sir

your

very humble and very
obedient servant
Bothmer

---

[1] LBr. 97 Bl. 149r–150v. Letter as sent: 3.5 quarto sides in Bothmer's hand. Previously published in Doebner 1884, pp. 239–40, and Klopp XI 198 (excerpt).

[2] That is, 16 October 1716 (OS) and 27 October 1716 (NS).

[3] That is, Leibniz's history of the House of Braunschweig-Lüneburg, the *Annales imperii occidentis Brunsvicenses**.

[4] Reading 'd'Historiographe' for 'd'Historiografe'.

[5] Reading 'titre' for 'tiltre'.

[6] Reading 'alarmé' for 'allarmée'.

[7] Reading 'abréger' for 'abbreger'.

[8] That is, the week beginning November 2 (NS).

[9] Here Bothmer is using the old-style date of October 27th, by which style his letter is dated October 16th. So he is suggesting that the original intent was for Caroline to depart eleven days after the day he composed his letter, that is, on November 7th (NS).

[10] Despite these hopes, and whether or not the fall reported by Bothmer was a contributing factor, Caroline's pregnancy ended with the delivery of a stillborn son on 20 November, a day shy of a week after Leibniz's death on November 14th.

Caroline of Brandenburg-Ansbach, Princess of Wales, to Leibniz

Hampthoncour le $\frac{29}{18}$ 8ber, 1716

J'acompange de ces peu de ligné[3] Monsieur la reponce[4] du Docteur chlerck. Je souhaite que vous la trouviez du moin[s] agreable sy vous ne la trouvez, boñe.[5] J'ay fait connaissance, avec vn hoɱe[6] qui vous adimir[e] beaucoup, qui e[s]t l'archevêque de dublin docteur Kin. Je reponderais avos[8] lettres la poste, qui vien[t], et je scerais toujours[9] la même pour vous.

Caroline

Clarke's Fifth Reply

Cinquiéme Réplique de Mr. CLARKE.

Comme un Discours diffus n'est pas une marque d'un Esprit clair, ni un moyen propre à donner des idées claires aux Lectures ; Je tâcherai de repondre à ce cinquiéme Ecrit d'une manière distincte, & en aussi peu de mots qu'il me sera possible.

* § 3. *1, —— 20. Il n'y aucune* * *ressemblance entre une* Balance *mise en mouvement par des* Poids *ou par une* Impulsion, *& un* Esprit *qui se meut, ou qui agit, par la Consideration de certains* Motifs. *Voici en quoi consiste la Difference. La* Balance *est entierement passive, & par consequent sujette à une* nécessité absolue : *Au lieu que l'*Esprit *non seulement reçoit une Impression, mais encore agit ; ce qui fait l'*Essence † § 14. *de la* Liberté. *Supposer* † *que lors que differentes maniers d'agir paroissent également bonnes, elles ôtent entierement à l'*Esprit le *pouvoir d'agir, comme les* Poids *égaux empêchent* nécessairement *une* Balance *de se mouvoir ; c'est nier qu'un* Esprit *ait en lui-même un* principe d'Action ; *& confondre le* pouvoir d'agir, *avec l'*Impression *que les* Motifs *font sur l'*Esprit, *en quoi il est tout à fait* passif. Le Motif, *ou la chose que l'*Esprit considere, *& qu'il a* en vûë, *est quelque chose d'*Externe : *L'*Impression

156. Caroline of Brandenburg-Ansbach, Princess of Wales, to Leibniz[1]

Hampton Court the $\frac{29}{18}$ October 1716[2]

I send with these few lines,[3] sir, the response[4] of Doctor [Samuel] Clarke*. I hope you may find it at least pleasant, if not sound.[5] I have made the acquaintance of a man[6] who admires you a lot, who is the Archbishop of Dublin, Doctor [William] King.[7] I will respond to your[8] letters the next post, and I shall always be[9] the same for you.

Caroline

[1] LBr. F 4 Bl. 88r. Letter as sent: one quarto side in Caroline's hand. Previously published in Klopp XI 198; Schüller 1991, p. 267 (excerpt in German translation); Robinet 1991, p. 187 (excerpt); HGA 198 (excerpt in English translation).

[2] That is, 18 October 1716 (OS) and 29 October 1716 (NS).

[3] Reading 'J'accompagne de ce peu de lignes' for 'J'acompange de ces peu de ligné'.

[4] Reading 'réponse' for 'reponce'.

[5] Reading 'bonne' for 'boñe'.

[6] Reading 'un homme' for 'vn home'.

[7] William King (1650–1729) was the Archbishop of Dublin from 1703 to 1729. In 1702 he published *De Origine Mali*, which Leibniz critically discussed in an appendix to his *Theodicy* of 1710. Klopp XI 198 omits 'docteur Kin'.

[8] Reading 'répondrais à vos' for 'reponderais avos'.

[9] Reading 'serais toujours' for 'scerais toujours'.

157. Clarke's Fifth Reply[1]

Dr. CLARKE's *Fifth Reply.*

As *Multitudes of Words* are neither an Argument of *clear Ideas* in the *Writer*, nor a proper means of conveying *clear Notions* to the *Reader*; I shall endeavour to give a distinct Answer to this Fifth Paper, as *briefly* as I can.

1, —— 20. There is no * similitude between a *Balance* being *moved* by *Weights* or   * § 3.
Impulse, and a *Mind moving itself*, or *acting* upon the View of certain Motives. The Difference is, that the one is *entirely passive* ; which is being subject to *absolute Necessity* : The other not only is *acted upon*, but *acts* also ; which is the essence of *Liberty*. To † suppose that an *equal apparent Goodness in different Ways of acting*,   † § 14.
takes away from the Mind *all Power of Acting at all*, as an *equality of Weights* keeps a Balance *necessarily at Rest* ; is denying the Mind to have in itself a *Principle of Action* ; and is confounding the *Power of Acting*, with the *Impression made upon the Mind by the Motive*, wherein the Mind is purely *passive*. The *Motive*, or thing *considered* as in *View*, is something *extrinsick* to the Mind: The *impression* made upon the

que ce motif fait sur l'Esprit, est la qualité perceptive, *dans laquelle l'Esprit est* passif. *Faire quelque chose* aprez, *ou* en vertu *de cette Perception, est la* Faculté de se mouvoir de soi-même, *ou* d'agir. *Dans tous les* Agents animez, c'est la Spontaneité ; & *dans les* Agents intelligents, c'est proprement ce que nous appellons Liberté. L'erreur *où l'on tombe sur cette matiere, vient de ce qu'on ne* distingue *pas soigneusement ces*

* § 15. *deux choses ; de ce que l'on confond * le* motif *avec le* Principe d'action ; *de ce que l'on pretend que l'Esprit n'a point d'autre* Principe d'Action *que le* motif, *quoique l'Esprit soit tout à fait* Passif en recevant l'Impression du motif. *Cette Doctrine fait croire que l'Esprit n'est pas plus actif, que le seroit une* Balance, *si elle avoit d'ailleurs la* Faculté d'apercevoir *les choses : Ce que l'on ne peut dire sans reverser entierement l'idée de la Liberté. Une* Balance *poussée des deux cotez par une* force égale, *ou* pressée *des deux cotez par des* Poids égaux, *ne peut avoir* aucun mouvement. *Et supposé que cette* Balance *reçoive la* faculté d'apercevoir, *en sorte qu'elle* sçache *qu'il lui est* impossible *de se mouvoir, ou qu'elle se fasse illusion en s'imaginant qu'elle se meut elle même, quoi qu'elle n'ait qu'un* mouvement communiqué ; *elle se trouveroit précisément dans le même état, où le* sçavant *Auteur suppose que se trouve un* Agent libre, *dans tous les cas d'une* Indifference absolue. *Voici en quoi consiste la fausseté de l'Argument, dont il s'agit ici. La* Balance, *faute d'avoir en elle même un* Principe d'action, *ne peut se mouvoir lors que les* Poids *sont* égaux : *Mais un* Agent Libre, *lors qu'il se presente deux ou plusieurs maniere d'agir* également raisonnables & parfaitement semblables, *conserve encore en lui même le* pouvoir d'agir, *parce qu'il a la faculté de se mouvoir. De plus, cet Agent libre peut avoir de* très-bonnes & très-fortes Raisons, *pour ne pas* s'abstenir entierement d'agir ; *quoique peut être il n'y ait aucune Raison, qui puisse déterminer qu'une certaine* maniere d'agir vaut mieux qu'une autre. On ne

* § 16, 17, *peut donc soûtenir * que,* supposé *que deux differentes manieres de placer certaines*
18, 19; *particules de Matiere fussent* également bonnes & raisonnables, *Dieu ne pourroit*
& 69. absolument, ni conformément à sa sagesse, *les placer d'aucune de ces deux manieres, faute d'une* Raison suffisante *qui pût le déterminer à choisir l'une préferablement à l'autre ; on ne peut, dis-je, soûtenir une telle chose, sans faire Dieu un Etre purement* passif ; & par conséquent il ne seroit point Dieu, *ou le* Gouverneur du Monde. *Et quand on nie la possibilité de cette* Supposition, sçavoir, *qu'il peut y avoir deux parties égales de Matiere, dont la* Situation *peut être également bien transposée ; on n'en*

* § 20. sçauroit alleguer d'autre Raison, que cette * Petition de Principe, sçavoir, *qu'en ce cas là, ce que le sçavant Auteur dit d'une* Raison suffisante, *ne feroit pas bien fondé. Car*

† § 16, 17, *sans cela, comment peut-on dire qu'il est † impossible que Dieu puisse avoir de*
69, & 66. bonnes Raisons *pour créer* plusieurs *particules de Matiere* parfaitement semblables *en differens lieux de l'Univers ? Et en ce cas là, puisque les parties de l'Espace sont semblables, il est évident que si Dieu n'a point donné à ces parties de Matiere des Situations differentes dès le commencement, il n'a pû en avoir d'autre Raison que sa*

||§ 16, seule Volonté. *Cependant on ne peut pas dire avec raison, qu'une telle Volonté est* ||
& 69. *une* Volonté sans aucun motif ; *Car les* bonnes Raisons *que Dieu peut avoir de créer* plusieurs *particules de Matiere* parfaitement semblables, *doivent par conséquent lui servir de Motif pour choisir (ce qu'une* Balance *ne sçauroit faire) l'une de deux choses*

Mind by That Motive, is the *perceptive Quality*, in which the Mind is *passive :* The *Doing* of any thing, *upon* and *after*, or in consequence of, that perception; this is the *Power of Self-Motion*, or *Action* : Which in *All animate Agents*, is *Spontaneity* ; and, in *moral* Agents, is what we properly call *Liberty*. The not carefully *distinguishing* these things, but confounding * the *Motive* with the *Principle of Action*, and deny-   * § 15.
ing the Mind to have *any Principle of Action* besides the *Motive*, (when indeed *in receiving the impression of the Motive*, the Mind is *purely passive* ;) This, I say, is the Ground of the whole Error ; and leads Men to think that the Mind is *no more Active*, than a *Balance* would be with the Addition of a *Power of Perception* : Which is wholly taking away the very Notion of Liberty. A Balance *pushed* on Both sides with equal *force*, or *pressed* on Both sides with equal *Weights*, cannot *move at all :* And supposing the *Balance* indued with a Power of *Perception*, so as to be *sensible* of its own *incapacity to move* ; or so as to deceive itself with an imagination that it *moves itself*, when indeed it is *only moved* ; it would be exactly in the same state, wherein this learned Author supposes a *free Agent* to be in all cases of *absolute Indifference*. But the Fallacy plainly lies here : The *Balance*, for want of having *in itself* a *Principle* or *Power of Action*, cannot move at all when the Weights are *equal :* But a Free *Agent*, when there appear two, or more, *perfectly alike reasonable* ways of acting ; has still *within itself*, by virtue of its Self-Motive Principle, a *Power of acting :* And it may have very *strong and good Reasons*, not to *forbear acting at all* ; when yet there may be no possible reason to determine one particular *Way* of doing the thing, to be better than another. To affirm therefore, * that, *supposing* two different   * § 16,17,
ways of placing certain particles of Matter were *equally good and reasonable*, God   18, 19;
could neither *wisely* nor *possibly* place them in *either* of those ways, for want of a   *and* 69.
sufficient Weight to determine *which way* he should chuse ; is making God not an *Active*, but a *Passive* Being : Which is not to be *God*, or Governor, at all. And for denying the Possibility of the *Supposition*, that there *may* be two equal Parts of Matter, which may with equal fitness be transposed in situation ; no other reason can be alleged, but this || *petitio Principii*, that Then this Learned Writer's Notion of || § 20.
a *sufficient Reason* would not be well-grounded. For otherwise, *how* can any Man say, that 'tis † *impossible* for God to have *wise* and *good reasons* to create *many* parti-   † § 16, 17,
cles of Matter *exactly alike* in different Parts of the Universe ? In which case, the   69, *and* 66.
parts of Space being alike, 'tis evident there can be no reason, but *mere Will*, for not having originally *transposed* their Situations. And yet even *This* cannot be reason-ably said to be a * *Will without Motive* ; forasmuch as the *wise reasons* God may   *.§ 16
possibly have to create *many* particles of Matter *exactly alike*, must consequently be   *and* 69.
a *Motive* to him to take (what a *Balance* could not do,) *one* out of *two absolutely Indifferents* ; that is, to place them in *one* situation, when the *transposing* of them could not but have been *exactly alike good*.

766   157. FIFTH REPLY OF CLARKE

absolument indifferentes ; *c'est à dire, pour mettre ces particules dans un Certaine Situation, quoi qu'une Situation tout à fait contraire eut été également bonne.*

La Necessité, dans les Questions Philosophiques, signifie toûjours une Necessité absolue. La * Necessité † Hypothetique, & la Necessité Morale, *ne sont que des manieres de parler Figurées* ; & à la rigueur Philosophique, elles *ne sont point une* Necessité. *Il ne s'agit pas de sçavoir si une chose doit être, lors que l'on* suppose *qu'elle est, ou qu'elle sera :* C'est ce qu'on appelle une Necessité Hypothetique. *Il ne s'agit pas non plus de sçavoir, s'il est vrai qu'un* Etre bon, & *qui continue d'être* bon, *ne sçauroit faire le* mal *; ou si un Etre* sage, *qui continue d'être* sage, *ne sçauroit agit d'une maniere contraire à la sagesse ; ou si une persone qui aime la* vérité, & *qui continue d l'aimer, peut dire un* mensonge : *C'est ce que l'on appelle une* Necessité Morale. *Mais la véritable* & *la seule Question Philosophique touchant la* Liberté, *consiste à sçavoir, si la* Cause *ou le* Principe immédiat & physique de l'Action *est réellement dans celui que nous appellons l'*Agent ; *ou si c'est quelque* autre Raison suffisante, *qui est la* véritable cause *de l'Action, en agissant sur l'Agent,* & *en faisant qu'il ne soit pas un véritable* Agent, *mais un simple* Patient.

On peut remarquer ici en passant, que le sçavant Auteur *contredit sa* propre Hypothese, *lors qu'il dit que* * la Volonté ne suit pas *toûjours* exactement l'Entendement pratique, parce qu'elle peut quelquefois trouver des raisons pour suspendre sa resolution. Car *ces raisons-là ne sont-elles pas le dernier jugement de* l'Entendement pratique ?

21, —— 25. *S'il est* possible *que Dieu produise ou qu'il ait produit deux portions de Matiere* parfaitement semblables, *de sorte que le* changement *de leur Situation seroit une chose* indifferent ; *ce que le sçavant Auteur dit d'une Raison suffisante, ne prouve rien. En répondant à ceci, il ne dit pas (comme il le devroit dire,) qu'il est * impossible que Dieu fasse deux portions de Matiere tout-à-fait semblables ; mais que sa sagesse ne lui* permet pas *de le faire. Comment sçait-il cela ? Pourra-t-il prouver qu'il n'est pas possible que Dieu puisse avoir de* bonnes raisons *pour créer* plusieurs parties de Matiere *parfaitement semblables* en differents lieux de l'Univers ? La seule preuve qu'il allegue, est, qu'il n'y auroit aucune Raison Suffisante, qui pût déterminer la Volonté de Dieu à mettre une de ces Parties de Matiere dans une certaine Situation plûtôt que dans une autre. Mais si Dieu peut avoir* plusieurs bonnes raisons, (*on ne sçauroit prouver le contraire,) si Dieu, dis-je, peut avoir plusieurs* bonnes raisons *pour créer plusieurs parties de Matiere tout-a-fait semblables ; l'*indifference *de leur* Situation suffira-t-elle *pour en rendre la* Création impossible, *ou* contraire à sa Sagesse ? *Il me semble que c'est * formellement supposer ce qui est en Question. On n'a* point répondu à un autre Argument de la même Nature, que j'ai fondé sur l'*Indifference absolue *de la premiere* Determination particuliere *du* Mouvement *au commencement du Monde.*

§ 4, 5, 6, 7; 8, 9, 10, 11, 12, 13.

§ 11.

§ 20.

---

† Voyez mes Discours sur l'existence de Dieu, la vérité de la Religion naturelle &c. Part I. Pag. 106. quatriéme Edit.

* Voïez le Quatriéme Ecrit de Mr. *Leibnitz*, § 2, 3, 6, 13 & 15.

157. FIFTH REPLY OF CLARKE   767

Necessity, in Philosophical Questions, always signifies *absolute Necessity*. † †§ 4, 5, 6,
Hypothetical Necessity *, and *Moral Necessity*, are only *Figurative* Ways of 7; 8, 9, 10,
Speaking, and in Philosophical *strictness* of Truth, are *no Necessity* at all. The 11, 12, 13.
Question is not, whether a Thing *must* be, when it is *supposed* that it *is*, or that it
is *to be* ; (which is *Hypothetical* Necessity :) Neither is it the Question whether it
be True that a *good Being*, continuing to be *Good*, cannot *do Evil* ; or a *wise* Being,
continuing to be *Wise*, cannot act *unwisely* ; or a *veracious* Person, continuing to
be *veracious*, cannot tell a *Lie* ; (which is *moral* Necessity :) But the true and only
Question in Philosophy concerning *Liberty*, is, whether the *immediate Physical
Cause* or *Principle of Action* be indeed *in* Him whom we call the *Agent* ; or
whether it be some *other Reason sufficient*, which is the *real Cause* of the Action,
by operating upon the *Agent*, and making him to be, not indeed an *Agent*, but a
mere *Patient*.

It may here be observed, by the way ; that this learned Author *contradicts* his
own Hypothesis, when he says, that † *the Will does not always precisely follow the* †§ 11.
*practical Understanding, because it may sometimes find Reasons to suspend its
Resolution*. For are not *those very Reasons*, the last Judgment of the *practical
Understanding ?*

21 —— 25. If it is *possible* for God to *make* or to *have made* two Pieces of Matter
exactly alike, so that the *transposing* them in *Situation* would be perfectly *indifferent* ; this learned Author's Notion of a *sufficient Reason*, falls to the Ground. To this
he answers ; not, (as his Argument requires,) that 'tis * *impossible* for God to make * *See Mr.*
two Pieces exactly alike ; but, that 'tis *not Wise* for him to do so. But how does he Leibnitz's
know, it would not be *Wise* for God to do so ? Can he prove that it is *not possible* Paper, § 2,
God may have *Wise Reasons* for creating *Many* Parts of Matter *exactly alike* in dif- 3, 6,
ferent Parts of the Universe ? The only Argument he alledges, is, that then there 13, & 15.
would not be a *sufficient Reason* to determine the Will of God, *which Piece* should
be placed in *which Situation*. But if, for ought that any *otherwise* appears to the
contrary, God may possibly have *many wise Reasons* for creating *many* Pieces
exactly alike ; will the *Indifference alone* of the *Situation* of such Pieces, make it
impossible that he should create, or *impossible that it should be Wise in him to create*
them ? I humbly conceive, this is an † express *Begging of the Question*. To the like †§ 20.
Argument drawn by me from the *absolute Indifferency* of the original *particular
Determination of Motion*, no Answer has been returned.

---

* *See my Sermons at Mr. Boyle's Lecture*, Part I. Pag. 106. Edit 4.

768 157. FIFTH REPLY OF CLARKE

*§ 26.   26, —— 32. *Il semble qu'il ait ici* plusieurs *contradictions. On reconnoit* * que deux choses *tout-à-fait* semblables, *seroient véritablement* deux choses ; *& nonobstant cet aveu, on continue de dire qu'elles n'auroient pas le* principe d'Individuation : *& dans le* IV Ecrit, § 6, *on assure positivement, qu'elles ne seroient qu'une* même

†§ 26. chose sous deux noms. *Quoi que l'on reconnoisse* † *que ma supposition est possible,*

‖§ 27. *on ne veut pas me permettre de faire cette supposition. On avouë* ‖ *que les parties du* Temps *& de* l'Espace *sont parfaitement semblables* en elles-mêmes ; *mais on nie*

§ 28. cette ressemblance lors qu'il y a des Corps dans ces parties. On compare * les *differentes* parties de l'Espace qui coëxistent, *& les differentes* parties successives du Temps, *à une* Ligne droite, *qui coupe* une autre Ligne droite *en deux Points* coïnci-

†§ 29. dents, *qui ne sont qu'*un seul Point. *On soûtient que* † l'Espace *n'est que l'Ordre des*

‖§ 30. choses qui coëxistent ; *& cependant on avouë* ‖ *que le Monde materiel peut être* borné : *d'où il s'ensuit qu'il faut nécessairement qu'il y ait un* Espace vuide *au delà du*

§ 30, & Monde. On reconnoit * que Dieu pouvoit *donner des bornes à* l'Univers ; *& aprez*
8, & 73. *avoir fait cet aveu, on ne laisse pas de dire que cette supposition est non seulement*

†§ 29. ‖ IV *déraisonnable & sans But, mais encore une* † Fiction impossible ; *& l'on assure* ‖ *qu'il*
Ecrit, § 21. n'y a aucune raison possible, qui puisse limiter *la quantité de la Matiere. On soûtient*

†§ 29. † *que le* mouvement *de l'Univers tout entier, ne produiroit* aucun changement ; *& cependant on ne répond pas à ce que j'avois dit, qu'une* augmentation *ou une* cessation *subite du mouvement du Tout, causeroit un choc sensible à toutes les parties : Et il n'est pas moins évident, qu'un mouvement* circulaire *du Tout, produiroit une* Force Centrifuge *dans toutes les parties. J'ai dit que le Monde materiel doit être* mobile, *si le*

‖§ 31. Tout *est* borné : *On* ‖ *le nie, parce que les* parties de l'Espace *sont* immobiles, *dont le* Tout *est* infini *& existe nécessairement. On soûtient que le mouvement renferme*

§ 31. nécessairement un * changement Rélatif de Situation *dans un corps, par rapport à d'autres corps : Et cependant on ne fournit aucun moyen d'eviter cette conséquence absurde, sçavoir, que la* mobilité *d'un corps* dépend *de* l'existence *d'autres* Corps ; *& que si un corps existoit* seul, *il seroit* incapable de mouvement ; *ou que les parties d'un corps qui* circule, (*du Soleil, par exemple,*) *perdroient la* Force centrifuge *qui nait de leur mouvement circulaire, si toute la matiere exterieure, qui les environne,*

†§ 32. *étoit* annihilée. *Enfin, on soûtient que* † l'infinité *de la Matiere est l'effet de la* Volonté

‖ Ibid. de Dieu ; *& cependant on* ‖ approuve la doctrine *de Des Cartes, comme si elle étoit incontestable ; quoique tout le monde sçache que le seul fondement sur lequel ce Philosophe l'a établie, est* cette Supposition, *Que la Matiere étoit* nécessairement infinie, *puis que l'on ne sçauroit la supposer finie sans* contradiction. *Voici ses propres*

Epist. termes, Puto * implicare contradictionem, ut Mundus sit finitus. *Si cela est vrai,*
69, Partis Dieu *n'a jamais pu limiter la* Quantité de la Matiere ; *& par conséquent il n'en est*
primæ *point le* Créateur, *& il ne peut la* détruite.

    Il me semble que le sçavant Auteur n'est jamais *d'accord avec lui même, dans* tout

§ 29, 33, ce qu'il dit touchant la Matiere *& l'Espace. Car tantôt il combat le* Vuide, *ou* l'Espace
34, 35, destitué de Matiere, *comme s'il étoit* * absolument impossible, (*l'Espace & la Matiere*
62, 63
†§ 62. étant † inseparables ;) *& cependant il* reconnoit souvent, *que la* Quantité de la

‖§ 30, 32, Matiere *dans l'Univers* dépend de la ‖ Volonté de Dieu.
& 73.

157. FIFTH REPLY OF CLARKE 769

26, —— 32. In these Articles, there seem to be contained *many Contradictions*. It is allowed || that *Two Things* exactly *alike*, would really be *Two* ; and yet it is still alledged, that they would want the *Principle of Individuation* ; And in *Paper* 4th, § 6, it was expresly affirmed, that they would be only the *same Thing under two Names*. A * Supposition is allowed to be *possible*, and yet I must not be allowed to make the Supposition. The † Parts of *Time* and *Space* are allowed to be exactly alike in *Themselves*, but not so when *Bodies exist in them*. Different *co-existent Parts of Space*, and different *successive Parts of Time*, are * compared to a *strait* Line cutting *another strait Line* in *two coincident Points*, which are but *one Point only*. 'Tis affirmed, that † *Space* is nothing but the *Order of Things co-existing* ; and yet it is || confessed that the *material Universe* may *possibly* be *Finite* ; in which Case there must necessarily be an *empty* extra-mundane *Space*. 'Tis * allowed, that *God could* make the *material Universe Finite* : And yet the *supposing* it to be *possibly* Finite, is stiled not only a Supposition *unreasonable* and *void of Design*, but also an † *imprac- ticable Fiction* ; and 'tis affirmed, ||² *there can be no possible Reason which can limit the Quantity of Matter*. 'Tis affirmed, that the *Motion* of the material Universe would produce * *no Change at all* ; and yet no Answer is given to the Argument I alledged, that a sudden *Increase* or *Stoppage* of the Motion of the *Whole*, would give a sensible *Shock* to all the *Parts* : And 'tis as evident, that a *circular* Motion of the *Whole*, would produce a *vis centrifuga* in all the *Parts*. My Argument, that the material World must be *moveable*, if the *Whole* be *Finite* ; is * denied, because the Parts of Space are *immoveable*, of which the *Whole* is *Infinite* and *necessarily exist- ing*. It is affirmed, that Motion necessarily implies a † *Relative Change of Situation in one Body, with regard to other Bodies* : And yet no way is shown to avoid this absurd Consequence, that then the *Mobility* of *one Body* depends on the *Existence of other Bodies* ; and that any *single Body* existing *Alone*, would be *incapable of Motion* ; or that the Parts of a *circulating* Body, (suppose the Sun,) would lose the *vis centrifuga* arising from their circular Motion, if all the extrinsick Matter around them were annihilated. Lastly, 'tis affirmed that the || *Infinity of Matter* is an Effect of the *Will of God* ; And yet *Cartesius's* Notion is * approved as irrefragable ; the *only Foundation* of which, all Men know to have been *this Supposition*, that *Matter* was infinite *nec- essarily in the Nature of Things*, it being a *Contradiction* to suppose it Finite : His Words are, † *Puto implicare contradictionem, ut Mundus fit finitus*. Which if it be true, it never was in the Power of God to *determine* the *Quantity* of Matter ; and consequently he neither was the *Creator* of it, nor can *destroy* it.

And indeed there seems to run a *continual Inconsistency* through the *Whole* of what this Learned Author writes concerning *Matter* and *Space*. For *sometimes* he argues against a *Vacuum* (or *Space void of Matter*,) as if it was || *absolutely impossi- ble in the Nature of Things*, space and Matter being * *inseparable* : And yet fre- quently he allows the *Quantity of Matter* in the Universe, to depend upon the † *Will of God*.

|| § 26.

* § 26.
† § 27.

* § 28.

† § 29.

|| § 30.
* § 30,& 8, &73.

† § 29.

|| Fourth Paper, § 21.

* § 29.

* § 31.

† § 31.

|| § 32.
* Ibid.

† Epist. 69, Partis primæ

|| § 29, 33, 34, 35, 62, 63
* § 62.

† § 30, 32, & 73.

770   157. FIFTH REPLY OF CLARKE

33, —— 35. *Pour prouver qu'il y a du Vuide, j'ai ai dit que certains Espaces* ne font point de resistance. *Le sçavant Auteur répond que ces Espaces sont remplis d'une* † § 35. Matiere, *qui n'a point* † de Pesanteur. *Mais l'Argument n'étoit pas fondé sur la* Pesanteur : *Il étoit fondé sur la* Resistance, *qui doit être proportionnée à la* || Quantité de la Matiere, *soit que la Matiere ait de la* pesanteur, *ou qu'elle n'en ait pas*.

* § 34.   *Pour prévenir cette Réplique, l'Auteur dit que* * la Resistance *ne vient pas tant de la* Quantité de la Matiere, *que de la* difficulté qu'elle a à céder. *Mais cet Argument est tout-à-fait hors d'œuvre ; parce que la Question, dont il s'agit, ne regarde que les corps* fluides *qui ont peu de tenacité, ou qui n'en ont point du tout, comme l'*Eau *&* le Vif Argent, *dont les parties n'ont de la* peine à céder, *qu'à proportion*[3] *de la* Quantité de † Ibid. Matiere qu'elles contiennent. *L'Exemple que l'on tire du* † bois flotant, *qui contient* moins de matiere pesante *qu'un* égal Volume d'Eau, *& qui ne laisse pas de faire une* plus grande resistance ; *cet Exemple, dis-je, n'est rien moins que Philosophique. Car un* égal Volume d'eau *renfermée dans un Vaisseau, ou gelée & flotante, fait une* plus grande resistance *que le* bois flotant, *parce qu'alors la resistance est causée par le* Volume entier *de l'eau. Mais lors que l'eau se trouve en liberté & dans son état de flu-*idité, *la resistance n'est pas causée par* toute la masse *du Volume égal d'eau, mais* seulement par *une partie de cette masse ; de sorte qu'il n'est pas surprenant que dans* ce cas l'eau semble faire moins de resistance que le bois.

36, —— 48. *L'Auteur ne paroit pas raisonner serieusement dans cette partie de son* Ecrit. *Il se contente de donner un faux jour à l'idée de l'*Immensité *de Dieu, qui n'est pas une* Intelligentia supramundana, (semota à nostris rebus sejunctaque longè,) *&* || Acts *qui* || *n'est pas loin de chacun de nous ; car en lui nous avons la vie, le mouvement,* xvii. 27, 28. & l'être.

* § 36,37.   L'Espace occupé par un Corps *n'est pas* * l'Etendue de ce Corps ; *mais le* Corps étendu *existe dans cet Espace*.

† § 38.   *Il n'y a aucun Espace* † borné ; *mais notre Imagination considere dans l'Espace, qui n'a point de bornes, & qui n'en peut avoir, telle* partie *ou telle* quantité *qu'elle juge à propos d'y considerer.*

|| § 39.   L'Espace *n'est pas une* || Affection d'un *ou de plusieurs corps, ou d'aucun* Etre borné ; *& il ne* passe point d'un *Sujet à un autre ; mais il est toûjours & sans varia-*tion, *l'*Immensité d'un Etre Immense, *qui ne cesse jamais d'être le même.*

* § 40.   Les Espaces bornez *ne sont point des* * proprietez des Substances bornées. *Ils ne* sont que des parties *de l'*Espace infini, *dans lesquelles les Substances bornées existent.*

† § 41.   *Si la Matiere étoit* infinie, l'Espace infini *ne seroit pas plus une* † Proprieté *de ce* Corps infini, *que les Espaces finis sont des Proprietez des Corps finis : Mais en ce cas, la* Matiere infinie *seroit dans l'*Espace infini, *comme les Corps finis y sont presentement.*

|| § 42.   L'Immensité *n'est pas moins* || essentielle à Dieu, *que son* Eternité. Les * Parties de * Voïez l'Immensité *étant tout-a-fait differentes des Parties* materielles, separables, divisi-ci-dessus bles, & mobiles, *d'où nait la* corruptibilité ; *elles n'empêchent pas l'*Immensité *d'être*

dans ma 3
Replique,
§3;&quatri-
éme Re- || Sans cela, pourquoi seroit-il plus difficile de mettre la Terre en *mouvement* (même du coté où tend
plique, §11.   sa pesanteur,) que de faire mouvoir un *très-petit Globe ?*

157. FIFTH REPLY OF CLARKE   771

33, —— 35. To the Argument drawn against a *Plenum* of Matter, from the *Want of Resistence* in certain Spaces ; this Learned Author answers, that those Spaces are filled with a *Matter* which has no * *Gravity*. But the Argument was not drawn from *Gravity*, but from *Resistence* ; which must be proportionable to the to the * *Quantity of Matter*, whether the Matter had any *Gravity*, or *no*.   * § 35.

To obviate this Reply, he alleges that * *Resistence* does not arise so much from the Qu*antity of Matter*, as from its *Difficulty of giving Place*. But this Allegation is wholly wide of the Purpose ; because the Question related only to such *Fluid* Bodies which have little or no Tenacity, as *Water* and *Quicksilver*, whose Parts have no other *Difficulty of giving Place*, but what arises from the *Quantity of Matter they contain*. The instance of a † *floating Piece of Wood*, containing *less of heavy Matter* than an *equal Bulk of Water*, and yet making *greater Resistence*, is *wonderfully unphilosophical* : For an *equal Bulk of Water* shut up in a Vessel, or frozen into Ice, and floating, makes a *greater Resistence* than the *floating Wood* ; the Resistence Then arising from the *whole* Bulk of the Water : But when the Water is loose and at liberty in its State of *Fluidity*, the Resistence Then is made not by the *whole*, but by *part only*, of the equal Bulk of Water ; and then it is no wonder that it seems to make less Resistence than the *Wood*.   * § 34.   † Ibid.

36, — 48. These Paragraphs do not seem to contain serious *Arguments*, but only represent in an *ill Light* the Notion of the *Immensity* or *Omnipresence of God* ; who is not a mere *Intelligentia supramundana*, [Semota à nostris rebus sejunctaq; longè ;] *is not far from every one of us* ; *for in him we* (and all Things) *live and move and have our Being*.   Acts xvii. 27, 28

The *Space occupied by a Body*, is not the † *Extension of the Body* ; but the *extended Body* exists *in* that *Space*.   † § 36,37.

There is no such Thing in reality, as * *bounded Space* ; but only we in our Imagination *fix our Attention* upon what *Part* or *Quantity* we please, of that which it self is always and necessarily *unbounded*.   * § 38.

Space is not an † *Affection* of *one Body*, or of *another* Body, or of *any finite Being* ; nor *passes from Subject to Subject* ; but is always *invariably* the *Immensity* of *one only* and *always the same* Immensum.   † § 39.

Finite Spaces are not at all the || *Affections of Finite Substances* ; but they are only *those Parts* of Infinite Space, *in which* Finite Substances exist. || § 40.

If Matter was *infinite*, yet *infinite Space* would no more be an * *Affection* of that *infinite Body*, than *finite Spaces* are the *Affections* of *finite Bodies* ; but, in that Case, the *infinite Matter* would be, as finite Bodies now are, *in the infinite Space*.   * § 41.   † § 42.

Immensity, as well as Eternity, is † *essential* to God. The || *Parts of Immensity*, (being totally of a different kind from *corporeal, partable, separable, divisible, moveable* Parts, which are the ground of *Corruptibility* ;) do no more hinder *Immensity* || See above, in my Third Reply, § 3; and Fourth Reply, §11.

---

* *Otherwise, What makes the* Body *of the Earth more difficult to be* moved, *(even the same way that its* Gravity *tends,) than the* smallest Ball *?*

772 157. FIFTH REPLY OF CLARKE

essentiellement simple, *comme les* Parties *de la* Durée *n'empêchent pas que la même* Simplicité *ne soit essentielle à l'*Eternité.

† § 43.   *Dieu lui-même n'est sujet à aucun* † Changement, *par la diversité & les* changemens *des Choses, qui ont* la vie, le mouvement, & l'être en lui.

‖ § 44.   *Cette ‖ Doctrine, qui paroit si étrange à l'Auteur, est la Doctrine formelle de St.*
Act. xvii. Paul, *& la voix de la* Nature *& de la* Raison.
27, 28
* § 45.   *Dieu n'existe point* * dans *l'Espace, ni* dans *le Temps* ; *mais* son existence † *est* la
† Voïez Cause de l'Espace & du Temps. *Et lors que nous disons, conformément au Language*
ci-dessus *du Vulgaire, que Dieu existe* dans tout l'Espace & dans tout le Temps ; *nous voulons*
la Note sur *dire seulement qu'il est* par tout *& qu'il est* éternel, *c'est-a-dire, que l'*Espace infini &
ma IV le Temps *sont des* Suites *nécessaires de son Existence* ; *& non, que l'Espace & le Temps*
Réplique, *sont des Etres distincts de lui* ; DANS *lesquels il existe.*
§ 10.

* § 46.   *J'ai fait voir-ci-dessus, sur* § 40, * *que l' ‖* Espace borné *n'est pas l'*Etendue *des Corps. Et*
† Voïez *l'on n'a aussi qu'à comparer les deux Sections suivantes (47 & 48) avec ce que j'ai déja* † *dit.*
aussi   49, —— 51. *Il me semble que ce que l'on trouve ici, n'est qu'une* chicane *sur des*
ci-dessous *mots. Pour ce qui est de la question touchant les* parties *de l'Espace, voïez ci-dessus,*
sur la § 53, Réplique III, § 3 ; *&* Réplique IV, § 11.
& sur
la § 54.   52, & 53. *L'*Argument *dont je me suis servi ici pour faire voir que l'*Espace *est réellement indépendant des* Corps, *est fondé sur ce qu'il est* possible *que le Monde materiel soit* borné & mobile. *Le sçavant Auteur ne devoit donc pas se contenter de répliquer, qu'il ne croit pas que la* Sagesse de Dieu lui ait pû permettre de *donner des bornes à l'Universe, & de le rendre* capable de mouvement. *Il faut que l'Auteur soûtienne qu'il étoit* impossible *que Dieu fît un Monde* borné & mobile ; *ou, qu'il reconnoisse la force de mon Argument fondé sur ce qu'il est* possible *que le Monde soit* borné & mobile. *L'Auteur ne devoit pas non plus se contenter de* repeter *ce qu'il avoit* avancé, sçavoir, *que le* mouvement *d'un Monde borné ne seroit rien, & que, faute*

* § 52. *d'Autres Corps avec lesquels on pût le* comparere, il ne * *produiroit aucun changement sensible. Je dis que l'Auteur ne devoit pas se contenter de repeter cela, à moins qu'il ne fût en état de* refuter *ce que j'avois dit d'un* fort grand changement *qui arriveroit dans le cas proposé* ; *sçavoir, que* les Parties recevroient un choc sensible par une soudaine Augmentation du mouvement du Tout, ou par la Cessation de ce même mouvement. *On n'a pas entrepris de répondre à cela.*

‖ Voici, ce me semble, la principale raison *de la* confusion & des *contradictions*, que l'on trouve dans ce que la plûpart des Philosophes ont avancé sur la nature de l'Espace. Les hommes sont naturellement portez, faute d'attention, à négliger une distinction très-necessaire, & sans laquelle on ne peut raisonner clairement : Je veux dire qu'ils n'ont pas soin de distinguer, quoi qu'ils le dûssent toûjours faire, entre les Termes *Abstraits* & *Concrets*, comme sont l'*Immensité* & l'*Immense*. Ils négligent aussi de faire une distinction entre les *Idées* & les *Choses* ; comme sont l'*Idée* de l'Immensité, que nous avons *dans* notre Esprit ; & l'*Immensité réelle, qui existe actuellement hors de nous.*

Je crois que toutes les Notions qu'on a eu touchant la Nature de l'Espace, ou que l'on s'en peut former, se reduisent à celles-ci. L'Espace est un *pur néant*, ou il n'est qu'une *simple Idée*, ou *une simple Relation d'une chose à une autre*, ou bien il est la *Matiere*, ou quelque autre *Substance*, ou la *Proprieté d'une Substance*.

Il est évident que l'Espace n'est pas un *pur néant*. Car le néant n'a ni *Quantité*, ni *Dimensions*, ni *aucune Proprieté*. Ce Principe est le prémier Fondement de toute sorte de Science ; & il fait voir la seule difference qu'il y a entre ce qui *existe*, & ce qui *n'existe pas.*

from being essentially *One*, than the *Parts* of *Duration* hinder *Eternity* from being essentially *One*.

God himself suffers *no* * *Change* at all, by the *Variety* and *Changeableness* of Things which *live and move and have their Being in him*. * § 43.

This † *strange* Doctrine, is the express Assertion of * St. *Paul*, as well as the plain Voice of *Nature and Reason*. † § 44.
Acts
xvii. 27, 28.

God does not exist || *In* Space, and *In* Time ; but *His Existence* * *causes Space and Time*. And when, according to the *Analogy of vulgar Speech*, we say that he exists *in All Space* and *in All Time* ; the Words mean only that he is *Omnipresent* and *Eternal* ; that is, that *Boundless Space and Time* are necessary *Consequences* of his Existence ; and not, that Space and Time are Beings distinct from him, and *IN which* he exists. || § 45.
*See above,
the Note on
my Fourth
Reply,* § 10

† How || *Finite Space* is not the *extension of Bodies*, I have shown just above, on § 40. And the two following Paragraphs also (§ 47 *&* 48,) need only to be compared with what hath been *already* * said. † § 46.

49, —— 51. These seem to me, to be only a *quibbling* upon Words. Concerning the Question about *Space* having *Parts*, see *above* ; *Reply* 3, § 3 ; and *Reply* 4, § 11. * *See also
below, on
§ 53, &
on* § 54.

52, and 53. My Argument here, for the Notion of Space being really independent upon Body, is founded on the Possibility of the material Universe being finite and moveable : 'Tis not enough therefore for this Learned Writer to reply, that he thinks it would not have been wise and reasonable for God to have made the material Universe finite and moveable. He must either affirm, that 'twas impossible for God to make the material World finite and moveable ; or else he must of necessity allow the Strength of my Argument, drawn from the Possibility of the World's being finite and moveable. Neither is it sufficient barely to repeat his Assertion, that the Motion of a finite material Universe would be nothing, and (for want of other Bodies to compare it with) would † produce no discoverable Change : Unless he could disprove the Instance which I gave of a very great Change that would happen ; viz. that the Parts would be sensibly shocked by a sudden Acceleration, or stopping of the Motion of the Whole : To which Instance, he has not attempted to give any Answer. † § 52.

|| Note : *The principal Occasion or Reason of the* Confusion and Inconsistencies, *which appear in what most Writers have advanced concerning the Nature of* Space, *seems to be This : that (unless they attend carefully,) men are very apt to neglect That Necessary Distinction, (without which there can be no clear Reasoning,) which ought always to be made between* Abstracts *and* Concretes, *such as are* Immensitas *& * Immensum *; & also between* Ideas *and* Things, *such as are* The Notion *(which is* Within *our own Mind) of* Immensity, *and the* real Immensity *actually existing* Without us.

All the Conceptions (I think) that ever have been or can be framed concerning Space, *are these which follow. That it is either* absolutely Nothing, *or a* mere Idea, *or only a* Relation *of one thing to another, or that it is* Body, *or some other* Substance, *or else a* Property *of a Substance*.

That it is not absolutely Nothing, *is most evident. For of* Nothing *there is* No Quantity, No Dimensions, No Properties. *This Principle is the First Foundation of All Science whatsoever ; expressing the Only Difference between what* does, *and what* does not, *exist*.

774   157. FIFTH REPLY OF CLARKE

53. *Comme le sçavant Auteur est obligé de reconnoitre ici, qu'il y a de la* différence *entre le* mouvement absolu *&* le mouvement rélatif ; *il me semble qu'il s'ensuit de là nécessairement, que l'*Espace *est une chose tout-à-fait differente de la* Situation *ou de l'*Ordre *des Corps. C'est de quoi les* Lecteurs *pourront juger, en comparant ce que l'Auteur dit ici avec ce que l'on trouve dans les* Principes *de Mr. le* Chevalier Newton, lib. 1. defin. 8.

54. *J'avois dit que le* Temps *& l'*Espace *étoient des* QUANTITEZ ; *ce qu'on ne peut pas dire de la* Situation *& de l'*Ordre. *On réplique à cela, que l'*Ordre a sa Quantité ; *qu'*il y a dans l'Ordre quelque chose qui précéde, & quelque chose qui suit ; *qu'*il y a une Distance ou un Intervalle. *Je réponds, que ce qui précéde, & ce qui suit, constitue la* Situation *ou l'*Ordre ; *mais la* Distance, *l'*Intervalle, *ou la* Quantité *du* Temps *ou de l'*Espace, *dans lequel une chose suit une autre, est une chose tout-a-fait distincte de la* Situation *ou de l'*Ordre, *& elle ne constitue aucune* Quantité *de* Situation *ou d'*Ordre. *La* Situation *ou l'*Ordre *peuvent être les* mêmes, *lors que la* Quantité du Temps *ou de l'*Espace, *qui intervient, se trouve* fort differente. *Le sçavant Auteur*

|| § 54. *ajoute, que les* Raisons *& les* Proportions || *ont leur* Quantité ; *& que, par conséquent, le* Temps *& l'*Espace *peuvent aussi avoir leur* Quantité, *quoi qu'ils ne soient que des* Rélations. *Je réponds,* Prémierement, *que s'il étoit vrai que* quelques sortes de Relations, *(comme, par exemple, les* Raisons *ou les* Proportions,*) fussent des* Quantitez ; *il ne s'ensuivroit pourtant pas que la* Situation & l'Ordre, *qui sont des* Rélations *d'une* Nature tout-a-fait differente, *seroient aussi des* Quantitez. Secondement ; *les* Proportions *ne sont pas des* Quantitez, *mais les* Proportions *de* Quantitez. *Si elles étoient des* Quantitez, *elles seroient les* Quantitez *de* Quantitez ; *ce qui est absurde. J'ajoute que si elles étoient des* Quantitez, *elles augmenteroient toûjours par l'*Addition, *comme* toutes les autres Quantitez. *Mais l'Addition de la proportion de 1 à 1, à la Proportion de 1 à 1, ne fait pas plus que la Proportion de 1 à 1 : Et l'Addition de la Proportion de* $\frac{1}{2}$ *à 1, à la Proportion de 1 à 1, ne fait pas la*

Il est aussi évident que l'*Espace* n'est pas une *pure Idée.* Car il n'est pas possible de former une *Idée* de l'Espace, qui aille au delà du *Fini* ; & cependant la Raison nous enseigne que c'est une contradiction que l'*Espace lui-meme* ne soit pas actuellement *Infini.*

Il n'est pas moins certain que l'*Espace* n'est pas *une simple Rélation d'une chose à une autre,* qui resulte de leur *Situation,* ou de l'*Ordre* qu'elles ont *entre elles* : Puisque l'*Espace* est une *Quantité* ; ce qu'on ne peut pas dire des Rélations, telles que la *Situation* & l'*Ordre.* C'est ce que je fais voir amplement ci-dessous, sur § 54. J'ajoute que si le Monde materiel *est,* on *peut être,* borné ; il faut nécessairement qu'il y ait un Espace *actuel* ou *possible* au-delà de l'Univers. Voïez sur § 31, 52, & 73.

Il est très-évident, que l'*Espace* n'est pas la *Matiere.* Car, en ce cas, la *Matiere* seroit *nécessairement infinie* ; & il n'y auroit *aucun* Espace, *qui ne resistât au mouvement.* Ce qui est contraire à l'Experience. *Voïez ma quatrieme Réplique,* § 7 ; *& cinquieme Réplique,* § 33.[4]

Il n'est pas moins certain que l'Espace n'est *Aucune* sorte de *substance* ; puisque l'*Espace infini* est l'*Immensité,* & non pas l'*Immense* : *au lieu qu'une* Substance infinie *est* l'Immense, *& non pas* l'Immensité. Comme la *Durée* n'est pas une *Substance* ; parce qu'une *Durée infinie* est l'*Eternité,* & non un *Etre Eternel* : mais une *substance infinie* est un Etre *Eternel,* & non pas l'*Eternité.*

Il s'ensuit donc nécessairement de ce que l'on vient de dire, que l'*Espace* est une *Propriété,* de la même maniere que la *Durée.* L'*Immensité* est une Proprieté de l'Etre *Immense,* comme l'*Eternité* est une Proprieté de l'Etre *Eternel.*

157. FIFTH REPLY OF CLARKE   775

53. Whether this learned Author's being forced here to acknowledge the *difference* between *absolute real Motion* and *relative Motion*, does not necessarily infer that *Space* is really a quite different Thing from the *Situation* or *Order* of Bodies ; I leave to the Judgment of those who shall be pleased to compare what this learned Writer here alleges, with what Sir *Isaac Newton* has said in his *Principia, Lib.* 1, *Defin.* 8.

54. I had alleged that *Time* and *Space* were QUANTITIES, which *Situation* and *Order* were *not*. To this, it is replied ; that *Order has its Quantity* ; *there is that which goes before, and that which follows* ; *there is Distance or Interval.* I answer : *Going before,* and *following,* constitutes *Situation* or *Order* : But the *Distance, Interval,* or *Quantity* of *Time* or *Space,* wherein one Thing follows another, is entirely a distinct Thing from the *Situation* or *Order,* and does not constitute any *Quantity of Situation or Order* : The *Situation* or *Order* may be the *same* , when the *Quantity of Time* or *Space intervening* is *very different.* This Learned Author further replies, that *Ratio's* or *Proportions* † have their *Quantity* ; and therefore so may *Time* and *Space,* though they be nothing but *Relations.* I answer 1*st* ; If it had been true, that some *particular Sorts* of *Relations,* such as *Ratio's* or *Proportions,* were *Quantities* ; yet it would not have followed, that *Situation* and *Order,* which are Relations of a *quite different Kind,* would have been *Quantities* too. But 2*dly* ; *Proportions* are not *Quantities,* but the *Proportions of Quantities.* If they were *Quantities,* they would be *Quantities of Quantities* ; which is absurd. Also, if they were *Quantities,* they would (like *all other* Quantities) increase always by *Addition* : But the *Addition* of the Proportion of 1 to 1, to the Proportion of 1 to 1, makes still no more than the Proportion of 1 to 1 ; and

† § 54.

That it is not a mere Idea, *is likewise most manifest. For no* Idea *of Space, can possibly be framed larger than* Finite ; *and yet Reason demonstrates that 'tis a Contradiction for* Space itself *not to be actually* Infinite.

That it is not a bare Relation of one thing to another, *arising from their* Situation *or* Order among themselves, *is no less apparent : Because* Space *is a* Quantity, *which* Relation (*such as* Situation *and* Order) *are not* ; *As I have largely shown below, on* § 54. *Also because, if the material Universe* is, *or can possibly be,* Finite ; *there cannot but be,* actual *or possible,* Extramundane Space : See *on* § 31, 52, *and* 73.

That Space *is not* Body, *is also most clear. For then* Body *would be* necessarily infinite ; *and* No Space could be void of Resistence *to Motion. Which is contrary to Experience. See my Fourth Reply,* § 7 ; *& Fifth Reply,* § 33.[5]

That Space *is not* Any kind *of* Substance, *is no less plain. Because* infinite Space *is* Immensitas, *not* Immensum ; *whereas* infinite Substance *is* Immensum, *not* Immensitas. *Just as* Duration *is not a* Substance : *because* infinite Duration *is* æternitas, *not* æternum ; *but infinite Substance is* æternum, *not* æternitas.

It remains therefore, by Necessary Consequence, that Space *is a* Property, *in like manner as* Duration *is.* Immensitas *is to* Immensi ; *just as* Æternitas *is to* Æterni.

Proportion de $1\frac{1}{2}$ *à* 1, *mais seulement la Proportion de* $\frac{1}{2}$ *à* 1. *Ce que les Mathematiciens appellent quelquefois* avec peu d'exactitude *la* Quantité *de la* Proportion, n'est, à parler proprement, que la Quantité *de la* Grandeur Rélative *ou* Comparative d'une chose par rapport à une autre : Et la Proportion *n'est pas la* Grandeur comparative même, mais la Comparaison *ou le* Rapport d'une Grandeur à une autre. La Proportion de 6 à 1, par rapport à celle de 3 à 1, n'est pas une double Quantité de Proportion, mais la Proportion d'une double Quantité. Et en général, ce que l'on dit Avoir une plus grande ou plus petite Proportion, n'est pas, avoir une plus grande ou plus petite Quantité de proportion ou de rapport, mais, avoir la proportion ou le rapport d'une plus grande ou plus petite Quantité à une autre : Ce n'est pas une plus grande ou plus petite Quantité de Comparaison, mais la Comparaison d'une plus grande ou plus petite Quantité. L'Expression **** § 54.** Logarithmique d'une Proportion, n'est pas (comme le sçavant Auteur le dit) la Mesure, mais seulement l'Indice ou le Signe artificiel de la Proportion : Cet Indice ne designe pas une Quantité de la proportion ; il marque seulement combien de fois une Proportion est répétée ou compliquée. Le Logarithme de la Proportion d'Egalité, est 0 ; ce qui n'empêche pas que ce ne soit une Proportion aussi réelle qu'aucune autre : Et lors que le Logarithme est negatif, comme Ī; la proportion, dont il est le Signe ou l'Indice, ne laisse pas d'être affirmative. La Proportion doublée ou triplée, ne designe pas une double ou triple Quantité de Proportion ; elle marque seulement combien de fois la Proportion est répétée. Si l'on triple une fois quelque Grandeur ou quelque Quantité, cela produit une Grandeur ou une Quantité, laquelle par rapport à la prémiere a la proportion de 3 à 1. Si on la triple une seconde fois, cela produit (non pas une double Quantité de Proportion, mais) une Grandeur ou une Quantité, laquelle par rapport à la prémiere a la proportion (que l'on appelle doublée) de 9 à 1. Si on la triple une troisième fois, cela produit (non pas une triple Quantité de proportion, mais) une Grandeur ou une Quantité, laquelle par rapport à la prémiere a la proportion (que l'on appelle triplée) de 27 à 1 : Et ainsi du reste. Trosiémement, le Temps & l'Espace ne sont point du tout de la Nature des Proportions, mais de la Nature des Quantitez absolues, auxquelles les Proportions conviennent. Par exem-

* C'est-à-dire, comme je viens de le remarquer, elle n'est pas une plus grande Quantité *de* Proportion, *mais la* Proportion *d'une plus grande* Quantité comparative

ple ; la Proportion de 12 à 1, est une Proportion beaucoup plus grande ** que celle de 2 à 1 ; & cependant une seule & même Quantité peut avoir la proportion de 12 à 1 par rapport à une chose, & en même temps la proportion de 2 à 1 par rapport à une autre. C'est ainsi, que l'Espace d'un Jour a une beaucoup plus grande proportion à une Heure, qu'à la moitié d'un Jour ;*

& cependant, nonobstant ces deux Proportions, *il continue d'être la* même Quantité de Temps *sans aucune variation. Il est donc certain, que le* Temps [& l'Espace *aussi par la même raison]* n'est pas de la Nature des *Proportions, mais de la* Nature des Quantitez absolues & invariables, *qui ont des* Proportions differentes. Le Sentiment

† IV Ecrit, § 16. *du sçavant Auteur sera donc encore, de son* † *propre aveu, une* Contradiction ; *à moins qu'il ne fasse voir la fausseté de ce Raisonnement.*

the *Addition* of the Proportion of *half* to 1, to the Proportion of 1 to 1, does not make the Proportion of 1 *and a half* to 1, but the Proportion only of *half* to 1. That which Mathematicians sometimes *inaccurately* call the *Quantity* of *Proportion*, is (accurately and strictly speaking,) only the *Quantity* of the *Relative* or *Comparative Magnitude* of one Thing with regard to another : And *Proportion* is not the *comparative Magnitude* it self, but the *Comparison* or Relation *of the Magnitude* to Another. The Proportion of 6 to 1, with regard to that of 3 to 1, is not a *double Quantity of Proportion*, but the *Proportion of a double Quantity*. And in general, what they call *Bearing a greater or less Proportion*, is not *bearing a greater or less Quantity of Proportion or Relation*, but, *bearing the Proportion or Relation of a greater or less Quantity* to Another : 'Tis not a *greater or less Quantity of Comparison*, but the *Comparison of a greater or less Quantity*. The || *Logarithmick Expression* of a || § 54. Proportion, is not (as this learned Author stiles it) a *Measure*, but only an artificial *Index* or *Sign* of Proportion : 'Tis not the expressing a *Quantity* of Proportion, but barely a denoting the *Number of Times* that any Proportion is repeated or complicated. The Logarithm of the *Proportion of Equality*, is 0 ; and yet 'tis as *real* and as *much* a Proportion, as any other ; And when the Logarithm is *negative*, as $\bar{1}$; yet the Proportion, of which it is the Sign or Index, is it self *affirmative. Duplicate* or *Triplicate* Proportion, does not denote a double or triple *Quantity* of Proportion, but the *Number of Times* that the Proportion is repeated. The tripling of any Magnitude or Quantity *once*, produces a Magnitude or Quantity, which to the former bears the Proportion of 3 to 1. The tripling it a *second* time, produces (not a *double Quantity of Proportion*, but) a Magnitude or Quantity, which to the former bears the Proportion (called *duplicate*) of 9 to1. The tripling it a *third* time, produces (not a *triple Quantity of Proportion*, but) a Magnitude or Quantity, which to the former bears the Proportion (called *triplicate*) of 27 to 1 : And so on. 3*dly, Time* and *Space* are not of the Nature of *Proportions* at all, but of the Nature of *absolute Quantities* to which *Proportions belong*. As for Example : The Proportion of 12 to 1, is a much *greater Proportion*, (that is, as I now observed, not a greater *Quantity of Proportion*, but the *Proportion of a greater comparative Quantity*,) than that of 2 to 1 ; and yet one and the *same unvaried Quantity*, may to one Thing bear the Proportion of 12 to 1, and to another Thing at the same time the Proportion of 2 to 1. Thus the Space of a *Day*, bears a much greater Proportion to an *Hour*, than it does to *half a Day* ; and yet it remains, notwithstanding *Both the Proportions*, the *same unvaried Quantity of Time. Time* therefore, [and *Space* likewise by the same Argument,] is not of the Nature of a *Proportion*, but of an *absolute and unvaried Quantity, to which different Proportions belong*. Unless this Reasoning can be shown to be false, our Learned Author's Opinion still remains, by his * own *Confession*, a *Contradition*.

* *Fourth Paper*, § 16.

55, —— 63. *Il me semble que tout ce que l'on trouve ici, est une* Contradiction

|| § 56. *manifeste. Les Sçavans en pourront juger. On suppose formellement dans* || Un

* § 55, 57, endroit, *que Dieu auroit pu créer l'Univers* plûtôt *ou* plus tard. *Et* * Ailleurs *on dit*

58,—63. *que ces termes mêmes* (plûtôt & plus tard) *sont des terms* inintelligibles *& des* †

† IV Ecrit, *Suppositions impossibles. On trouve de semblables* Contradictions *dans ce que*

§ 15. *l'Auteur dit touchant l'*Espace *dans lequel la* Matiere *subsiste :* Voïez ci-dessus, sur

§ 26, — 32.

64, & 65. *Voïez ci-dessus*, § 54.

66, —— 70. *Voïez ci-dessus*, § 1, —— 20 ; & § 21, —— 25. *J'ajouterai seulement*

|| § 70. *ici, que l'Auteur, en* || comparant *la* Volonté de Dieu *au hazard d'*Epicure, *lors qu'en-*
tre plusieurs manieres d'agir également bonnes elle en choisit une, compare ensem-
ble deux choses, qui sont aussi differentes que deux choses le puissent être ; puis
*qu'*Epicure *ne reconnoissoit aucune* Volonté, *aucune* Intelligence, *aucun* Principe
actif dans la formation de l'Univers.

71. Voïez ci-dessus, § 21 —— 25.

72. Voïez ci-dessus, § 1 —— 20.

73 —— 75. *Quand on considere si l'*Espace *est* indépendant *de la* Matiere, *& si*
l'Univers peut être borné & mobile ; *(voïez ci-dessus*, § 1 —— 20, & § 26 — 32 ;) *il ne*

* § 73. *s'agit pas de la* Sagesse *ou de la* * Volonté de Dieu, *mais de la* Nature absolue &
nécessaire *des choses. Si l'*Univers PEUT *être* borné & mobile, *par la* Volonté de
Dieu ; *(ce que le sçavant Auteur est obligé d'*accorder *ici, quoi qu'il dise continuelle-*
ment que c'est une Supposition impossible *;) il s'ensuit évidemment que l'*Espace,
dans lequel ce mouvement se fait, est indépendant *de la* Matiere. *Mais si, au con-*

† IV Ecrit, *traire, l'*Univers † *ne* Peut *être* borné & mobile, *& si l'*Espace *ne* Peut *être* indépend-

§ 21 ; & V ant *de la* Matiere ; *il s'ensuit évidement, que* Dieu *ne* Peut *ni ne* Pouvoit *donner des*

Ecrit, § 29. *bornes à la* Matiere ; *& par conséquent l'*Univers *doit être, non seulement* sans

|| § 74. bornes, *mais encore* || éternel, *tant* à parte ante *qu'*à parte post, *nécessairement &*
indépendamment *de la* Volonté de Dieu. *Car l'*Opinion *de ceux qui soutiennent que*

* § 75. *le* Monde * *pourroit avoir existé de toute* Eternité, *par la* volonté de Dieu *qui exerçoit*
sa Puissance *éternelle ; cette* Opinion, *dis-je, n'a aucun rapport à la* Matiere *dont il*
s'agit ici.

76 & 77. *Voiez ci-dessus*, § 73 —— 75, & § 1 —— 20 ; & ci-dessous, § 103.

78. *On ne trouve ici aucune nouvelle* Objection. *J'ai fait voir amplement dans les*
Ecrits précédens, *que la* Comparaison *dont Mr. le Chevalier* Newton *s'est servi, & que*
l'on attaque ici, est juste & intelligible.

79, —— 82. *Tout ce que l'on objecte ici dans la* Section 79, *& dans l suivante, est*
une pure Chicane *sur* Mots. *L'*Existence de Dieu, *comme je l'ai déja dit plusieurs fois,*
est la Cause de l'Espace ; & Toutes les Autres choses *existent* dans cet Espace. *Il s'en-*

† § 80. *suit donc que l'*Espace *est aussi* † *le* Lieu des Idées ; *parce qu'il est le* Lieu *des*
Substances *mêmes, qui ont des* Idées *dans leur* Entendement.

J'avois dit, par voye de comparaison, *que le* Sentiment de l'Auteur *étoit aussi dérai-*

|| § 81. sonnable, *que si quelqu'un soûtenoit que* || l'Ame humaine *est l'*Ame des Images des
choses *qu'elle* apperçoit. *Le sçavant Auteur raisonne là dessus* en plaisantant, *comme*
si j'avois assuré que ce fût mon propre sentiment.

55, —— 63. All This, seems to me to be a plain *Contradiction* ; and I am willing to leave it to the Judgment of the Learned. In † one Paragraph, there is a plain and distinct Supposition, that the Universe *might* be created as much *sooner* or *later* as God pleased. In the || rest, the very Terms [*sooner* or *later*] are treated as *unintelligible* Terms and * *impossible* Suppositions. And the like, concerning the *Space* in which *Matter* subsists ; *See above, on* § 26 —— 32.

† § 56.

|| § 55, 57, 58,— 63.
* Fourth Paper, § 15.

64, and 65. *See above* upon § 54.

66, — 70, *See above, on* § 1, —— 20 ; *and on* § 21 —— 25. I shall here only add, that † *comparing* the *Will of God, when it chooses one out of many equally good ways of acting,* to *Epicurus's Chance,* who allowed *No Will, No Intelligence, No Active Principle at all* in the formation of the Universe ; is comparing together *Two things,* than which *No Two things* can possibly be more different.

† § 70.

71. *See above, on* § 21, —— 25.

72. *See above, on* § 1, —— 20.

73, —— 75. In the consideration whether *Space* be *independent* upon *Matter,* and whether the *material Universe Can be Finite and Moveable,* (*See above,* on § 1——20, *and on* 26, ——32 ;) the question is not concerning the *Wisdom* or * *Will* of *God,* but concerning the *absolute* and *necessary Nature* of *Things.* If the *Material Universe CAN possibly,* by the Will of God, be *Finite* and *Moveable* ; (which this learned Author here finds himself necessitated to *grant,* though he perpetually treats it as an *impossible* supposition ;) then *Space,* (in which That Motion is performed,) is manifestly *independent* upon *Matter.* But if, on the contrary, the *material Universe* † *Cannot* be *finite* and *moveable,* and *Space cannot* be *independent* upon *Matter* ; then (I say) it follows evidently, that God neither *Can* nor *ever Could* set Bounds to *Matter* ; and consequently the *material Universe* must be not only *boundless,* but || *eternal* also, both *a parte ante* and *a parte post, necessarily* and *independently on the Will of God.* For, the Opinion of those who contend, that the World * *might possibly* be Eternal, by the *Will* of God exercising his Eternal Power ; this has no Relation at all, to the Matter at present in Question.

* § 73.

† Fourth Paper, § 21, and Fifth Paper, § 29.

|| § 74.

* § 75.

76 and 77. *See above, on* § 73 —— 75 ; and on § 1 —— 20. And *below, on* § 103.

78. This Paragraph contains no new Objection. The Aptness and Intelligibleness of the *Similitude* made use of by Sir *Isaac Newton,* and here excepted against, has been abundantly explained in the foregoing Papers.

79, —— 82. All that is objected in the † *two former* of these Paragraphs, is a mere *quibbling* upon Words. The *Existence* of *God,* (as has often been already observed,) causes *Space* ; and *In* that Space, *All other Things* exist. It is therefore || the Place of *Ideas* likewise ; because it is the Place of the *Substances themselves,* in whose Understandings Ideas exist.

† § 79, 80.

|| § 80.

The Soul of Man being * *the Soul of the Images of the Things which it perceives,* was alledged by me, in way of *comparison,* as an *Instance* of a *ridiculous Notion :* And this learned Writer *pleasantly* argues against it, as if I had affirmed it to be my *own* Opinion.

* § 81.

780 157. FIFTH REPLY OF CLARKE

* § 82.   *Dieu apperçoit tout, non* * par le moyen d'un Organe, *mais parce qu'il est lui-même actuellement present par tout.* L'Espace universel *est donc le* Lieu *où il* apperçoit les Choses. *J'ai fait voir amplement ci-dessus ce que l'on doit entendre par le mot de* Sensorium, *& ce que c'est que l'*Ame du Monde. *C'est trop que de demander qu'on abandonne la* Consequence *d'un Argument, sans faire aucune nouvelle Objection contre les* Premisses.

83 —— 88 ; & 89 —— 91. *J'avouë que je n'entends point ce que l'Auteur dit, lors*

† § 83.   *qu'il avance, que* † l'Ame *est un* Principe representatif ; *que* || chaque Substance sim-
|| § 87.   ple *est par sa propre nature* une concentration & un miroir vivant de tout l'Univers ;
†§ 91.   *qu'elle* † est une Representation de l'Univers, selon son Point de vûë ; *& que* toutes les Substances Simples *auront toûjours une* Harmonie *entre elles, parce qu'elles representent toûjours le même* Univers.

* § 83, 87,   *Pour ce qui est de* * l'Harmonie préétablie, *en vertu de laquelle on prétend que les*
89, 90.   Affections *de l'Ame, & les* mouvemens méchaniques *du Corps, s'accordent sans aucune* influence *mutuelle ; voïez ci-dessous, sur* § 110 —— 116.

J'ai supposé que les Images *des choses sont portées par les Organes des Sens dans*
* § 84.   le Sensorium, *où l'Ame les apperçoit. On soûtient que c'est une chose* * inintelligible ; *mais on n'en donne aucune preuve.*

† § 84.   *Touchant cette Question, sçavoir, si* † une Substance immaterielle *agit sur une* Substance materielle, *ou si celle-ci agit sur l'autre ; voïez ci-dessous, § 110 —— 116.*

|| § 85.   *Dire que* Dieu || *apperçoit & connoit toutes choses, non par sa presence actuelle, mais parce qu'il les produit continuellement de nouveau ; ce sentiment, dis-je, est une pure Fiction des Scholastiques, sans aucun Fondement.*

* § 86, 87   *Pour ce qui est de l'Objection, qui porte que Dieu seroit* * l'Ame du Monde ; j'y ai
88, 82.   répondu amplement ci-dessus,* Réplique II, § 12 ; *& République* IV, § 32.

92. *L'Auteur suppose que tous les mouvemens de nos Corps sont* nécessaires, *&*
† § 92,   *produits* † par un simple impulsion méchanique *de la Matiere, tout à fait indépend-*
95, 116.   *ante de l'Ame : Mais je ne sçaurois m'empêcher de croire que cette Doctrine conduit à la* Nécessité *& au* Destin. *Elle tend à faire croire que les* hommes *ne sont que de* pures Machines, (*comme des* Cartes *s'étoit imaginé que les* Bêtes *n'avoient point d'*Ame ;) *en detruisant tous les* Argumens fondez sur les Phénomenes, *c'est-à-dire, sur les* Actions des hommes, *dont on se sert pour prouver qu'ils ont des* Ames, *& qu'ils ne sont pas des* Etres purement materiels. *Voïez ci-dessous, sur* § 110 —— 116.

93,——95. *J'avois dit que chaque* Action consiste à donner une *nouvelle* force *aux choses, qui* reçoivent quelque impression. *On répond à cela, que deux Corps durs & égaux, poussez l'un contre l'autre, réjaillissent avec la même* force ; *& que par conséquent leur* Action *reciproque ne donne point une* nouvelle *force. Il suffiroit de répliquer qu'aucun de ces deux Corps ne réjaillit avec sa* propre *force ; que chacun*
* Voïez la   *d'eux* * perd sa propre *force, & qu'il est repoussé avec une* nouvelle force *communi-*
§ 99. où   *quée par le* Ressort *de l'autre : Car si ces deux Corps n'ont point de* Ressort, *ils ne réjail-*
cette ma-   liront pas. *Mais il est certain que* toutes *les* Communications *de mouvement*
tiere est   purement méchaniques, *ne sont pas une* Action, *à parler proprement : Elles ne sont*
traitée plus   *qu'une simple* Passion, *tant dans les Corps qui* poussent, *que dans ceux qui sont*
ample-
ment.

157. FIFTH REPLY OF CLARKE 781

God perceives every Thing, not * *by means* of any *Organ*, but by being *himself*   * § 82.
actually present every where. This *every where* therefore, or *universal Space*, is
the *Place* of his *Perception*. The Notion of *Sensorium*, and of *the Soul of the
World*, has been abundantly explained *before*. 'Tis too much to desire to have the
Conclusion given up, without bringing any further Objection against the
Premises.

83, —— 88 ; *and* 89 —— 91. That † *the Soul* is a *Representative Principe* ; That   † § 83.
* *every simple Substance is by its Nature a Concentration and living Mirror of the*   * § 87.
whole Universe ; That * *it is a representation of the Universe, according to its Point of*   * § 91.
View ; and *that all simple Substances will always have a Harmony between themselves, because they always represent the same Universe* : All This, I acknowledge, I
understand not at all.

Concerning the || *Harmonia præstabilita*, by which the *Affections of the Soul*, and || § 83,
the *Mechanic Motions of the Body*, are affirmed to agree, without at all influencing   87, 89, 90.
each other ; *See below*, on § 110——116.

That the *Images of Things are conveyed by the Organs of Sense into the Sensory,
where the Soul perceives them* ; is affirmed, but not proved, to be an * *unintelligi-*   * § 84.
ble Notion.

Concerning || *immaterial Substance affecting, or being affected by, material* || § 84.
Substance ; See below, on § 110——116.

That God * *perceives and knows all Things, not by being Present to them, but by*   * § 85.
continually producing them anew ; is a mere Fiction of the Schoolmen, without
any Proof.

The Objection concerning God's being † *the Soul of the World*, has been abun-   † § 86, 87
dantly answered *above* ; *Reply II*, § 12 ; and *Reply IV*, § 32.   88, 82.

92. To suppose, that all the Motions of our Bodies are *necessary*, and caused
entirely || by *mere mechanical Impulses of Matter*, altogether independent on the || § 92, 95,
Soul ; is what (I cannot but think) tends to introduce *Necessity and Fate*. It tends to   *and* 116.
make *Men* be thought as *mere Machines*, as *Des Cartes* imagined *Beasts* to be ; by
taking away all Arguments drawn from *Phænomena*, that is, from the *Actions of
Men*, to prove that there *is* any *Soul*, or any thing more than *mere Matter* in Men at
all, *See below, on* § 110——116.

93——95. I alledged, that every *Action* is the giving of a *New Force* to Thing
acted upon. To this it is objected, that *two equal hard Bodies striking each other,
return with the same Force* ; and that therefore their *Action* upon each other, gives
no New Force. It might be sufficient to reply, that the Bodies do *Neither* of them
return with their *own* Force, but each of them * loses its *own* Force, and *each* returns   * *See more,*
with a *new Force* impressed by the others *Elasticity* : For if they are *not elastical*, they   on § 99.
return not *at all*. But indeed, *all mere mechanical* Communications of Motion, are
not properly *Action*, but mere *Passiveness*, both in the Bodies that *impell*, and that
are *impelled. Action*, is the beginning of a Motion where there was none before,

782   157. FIFTH REPLY OF CLARKE

poussez. *L'Action est le commencement d'un mouvement qui n'existoit point auparavant, produit par un Principe de* vie *ou d'*Activité : *Et si* Dieu *ou l'*Homme, *ou quelque* Agent vivant *ou* actif, agit *sur quelque partie du* Monde materiel ; *si tout n'est pas un* simple méchanisme ; *il faut qu'il y ait une* augmentation *& une* Diminution *continuelle de* toute la Quantité du mouvement qui est dans l'Univers. *Mais c'est ce que le sçavant Auteur* * *nie en plusieurs endroits.*

    * Tout ce que Mr. *Leibnitz* dit sur cette matiere, paroit rempli de confusion & de contradictions. Car le mot de *Force,* ou de *Force active,* signifie, dans la question dont il s'agit ici, l'*Impetus* ou la *Force impulsive & rélative* des *Corps en mouvement* : Voiez § 13 de mas Troisiéme Réplique. Mr. *Leibnitz* employe toûjours ce mot en ce sens : Comme lors qu'il dit, [§ 93, 94, 99, *& 107, de cette derniere Réponse,*] Que les Corps *ne changent point leur Force* aprez la *Réflexion,* parce qu'ils retournent *avec La même Vitesse* : Que quand un *Corps reçoit une nouvelle Force d'un autre Coprs, cet autre en perd autant de la sienne* : Qu'il *est impossible qu'un Corps reçoive une nouvelle Force, sans que les autres en perdent autant* : Que *l'Univers des Corps recevroit une nouvelle Force, si l'Ame donnoit de la Force au Corps* : Que les *Forces Actives continuent toûjours d'être les mêmes dans l'Univers, parce que la Force que les Corps sans ressort perdent dans leur Tout, est communiquée à leurs parties menuës, & dissipée parmi elles.* Or il paroit clairement tant par la Raison que par l'Experience, que cet *Impetus,* ou cette *Force active impulsive* & *rélative* des *Corps en mouvement,* est toûjours proportionnée à la *Quantité du Mouvement.* Donc, selon les Principes de Mr. *Leibnitz,* puisque cette *Force active* & *impulsive* est toûjours la même en Quantité, il faut *aussi* nécessairement que *la Quantité du Mouvement* soit toûjours la même dans l'Univers. Cependant il tombe en contradiction en reconnoissant ailleurs, [§ 99,] que la *Quantité du Mouvement* n'est *toûjours la même* : Et dans les *Acta Eruditorum, ad ann.* 1686. *pag.* 161, il tâche de *Prouver,* que la *Quantité du Mouvement* dans l'Univers *n'est pas toujours la même* ; il tâche, dis-je, de le *prouver* par cette même & seule Raison, que la Quantité de la *Force impulsive* est toûjours *la même.* Mais si cela étoit vrai, il s'ensuivroit au contraire, que la *Quantité du Mouvement seroit toûjours & nécessairement la même.* Ce qui a donné occasion à Mr. *Leibnitz* de se contredire sur cette matiere, c'est qu'il a supputé, par une méprise tout à fait indigne d'un Philosophe, la Quantité de la *Force impulsive* dans un *Corps qui monte,* par la Quantité de sa *Matiere* & de *l'Espace* qu'il décrit en montant, sans considere le *temps* que ce Corps employe à monter. *Suppono,* † dit-il, *tanta vi opus esse, &c.* C'est-à-dire : " Je " suppose que la même Force est réquisse pour élever le Corps *A* du poids d'Une Livre à la hauteur de quatre " aunes, que celle qui éleve le Corps *B* du poids de quatre Livres à la hauteur d'une aune. C'est de quoi les " *Cartesiens,* & les autres Philosophes &Mathematiciens de nôtre temps conviennent. Or il s'ensuit de là, " que le Corps *A* en tombant de la hauteur de quatre aunes, acquiert précisément la même Force, que le " Corps *B* en tombant de la hauteur d'Une aune ". Mais Mr. *Leibnitz* se trompe fort en faisant cette supposition. Ni les *Cartesiens,* ni les autres Philosophes ou Mathematiciens n'accordent jamais ce qu'il suppose, excepté dans les cas où les *Temps* que les Corps employent à monter ou à descendre, sont égaux entre eux. Si une *Pendule* décrit une Cycloïde, l'*Arc* de la Cycloïde décrite en montant, sera comme la *Force* avec laquelle le Corps suspendu commence à monter du plus bas point ; parce que les *temps* qu'il employe à monter, sont *égaux.* Et si des Corps égaux pesent sur le bras[6] d'une *Balance,* à differentes distances de l'Axe de la Balance ; les *Forces* des Corps seront en proportion comme les *Arcs* qu'ils décrivent en pesant, parce qu'ils les décrivent en même *temps.* Et si deux Globes égaux placez sur un Plan Horizontal, sont poussez par des *Forces* inégales, ils décriront en *temps égaux* des *Espaces* proportionnels aux Forces qui les poussent. Ou si des *Globes inégaux* sont poussez avec des *Forces égales,* ils décriront en *temps égaux* des *Espaces* reciproquement proportionnels à leurs Masses. Et dans tous ces cas, si des *Corps égaux* sont poussez par des *Forces inégales* ; les *Forces* imprimées, les *Vitesses* produites, & les *Espaces décrits en temps égaux,* seront proportionnels l'un à l'autre. Et si les Corps sont *inégaux,* la *Vitesse* des plus grands Corps sera d'autant *plus petite,* que les *Corps* sont *plus grands* ; Donc le *Mouvement* (qui resulte de la masse & de la vitesse prises ensemble) sera dans tous ces cas, & par conséquent dans tous les autres cas, proportionnel à la *Force* imprimée. [D'où il s'ensuit clairement, pour le dire en passant, que si la *même Force impulsive* subsiste toûjours dans le Monde, comme Mr. *Leibnitz* le prétend ; il faut qu'il y ait toûjours le *même Mouvement* dans le Monde, qui est *contraire à ce qu'il affirme.*]
    Mais Mr. *Leibnitz* confond les Cas où les *temps* sont *égaux,* avec les Cas où les *temps* sont *inégaux.* Il confond particulierement le Cas où des corps *montent* & *descendent aux extremitez des bras inégaux d'une Balance,* (*Acta Erudit. ad ann. 1685. pag. 162 ; & ad ann. 1690, pag. 234 ; & ad ann. 1691, pag. 439 ; & ad ann. 1695, pag. 155* ;) il confond, dis-je, ce Cas avec celui des corps qui *tombent en bas,* & que l'on *jette en haut,* sans faire attention à *l'inégalité du temps* Car un corps avec la même *Force* & la même

     † Acta Erudit. ad ann. 1686. pag 162.

157. FIFTH REPLY OF CLARKE   783

from a Principle of *Life* or *Activity* : And if *God* or *Man*, or *Any Living* or *Active Power*, ever *influences* any thing in the material World ; and every thing be not *mere absolute Mechanism* ; there must be a continual *Increase* and *Decrease* of the *whole Quantity of Motion in the Universe*. Which this learned Gentleman * frequently denies.

---

* *There appears a great Confusion and Inconsistency in Mr.* Leibnitz's *whole Notion of this Matter. For the Word,* Force, *and* Active Force, *signifies in the present Question, the* Impetus *or relative* Impulsive Force of Bodies in Motion : *See my* Third Reply, § 13. *Mr.* Leibnitz *constantly uses the Word in this Sense : As when he speaks* [§ 93, 94, 99, and 107, of this last Answer,] *of Bodies* not changing their Force *after Reflexion, because they return* with the same Swiftness : *Of* a Body's receiving a new Force from another Body, which loses as much of its own : *Of the impossibility, that* one Body should acquire any new Force, without the Loss of as much in Others : *Of the* new Force which the whole Universe would receive, if the Soul of Man communicated any Force to the Body : *And of* Active Forces continuing always the same in the Universe, because the Force which un-elastick Bodies lose in their Whole, is communicated to and dispersed among their small Parts. *Now this* Impetus, *or relative* Impulsive Active Force *of* Bodies in Motion, *is evidently both in Reason and Experience, always proportional to the* Quantity of Motion. *Therefore, according to Mr.* Leibnitz's *Principles, this* impulsive active Force *being always the same in Quantity, the* Quantity of Motion also *must of necessity be always the same in the Universe. Yet elsewhere, he inconsistently acknowledges,* [§ 99,] *that the* Quantity of Motion is Not always the same : *And in the* Acta Eruditorum, ad Ann. 1686, pag. 161, *he endeavours to Prove that the* Quantity of Motion *in the Universe is* Not always the same, *from that very Argument, and from that single Argument only, (of the Quantity of* Impulsive Force *being always the same,) which, if it was true, would necessarily infer on the contrary, that the* Quantity of Motion could not but be always the same. *The Reason of his Inconsistency in this Matter, was his computing, by a wonderfully unphilosophical Error, the Quantity of* Impulsive Force *in an* Ascending Body, *from the Quantity of its* Matter *and of the* Space *described by it in Ascending, without considering the* Time *of its ascending.* * " Suppono, *says he,* tantâ vi opus esse ad elevandum   * *Acta*
" corpus A unius librae usq; ad altitudinem quatuor ulnarum, quantâ opus est ad elevandum corpus B   *Erudit. ad*
" quatuor usq; ad altitudinem Unius Ulnae. Omnia hæc à *Cartesiens* pariter ac cæteris Philosophis &   *ann.* 1686.
" Mathematicis nostri temporis conceduntur. Hinc sequitur, corpus A delapsum ex altitudine quatuor   *pag* 162.
" ulnarum, præcise tantum acquisivisse virium, quantum B lapsum ex altitudine Unius Ulnæ". *That is :*
" [*I suppose the same Force is requisite to raise a Body* A *of one Pound Weight, to the Height of four Yards*;
" *which will raise the Body* B *of four Pounds Weight, to the Height of One Yard. This is* Granted *both by the*
"Cartesians, *and other Philosophers and Mathematicians of our Times. And from hence it follows, that the*
"*Body* A, *by falling from the Height of four Yards, acquires exactly the same Force, as the Body* B *by falling*
"*from the Height of One Yard*".] But *in this Supposition, Mr.* Leibnitz *is greatly mistaken. Neither the* Cartesians, *nor any other* Philosophers *or* Mathematicians *ever grant this, but in such Cases only, where the* Times *of Ascent and or Descent are equal. If a* Pendulum *oscillates in a* Cycloid *; the Arch of the* Cycloid *described in ascending, will be as the* Force *with which the pendulous Body begins to ascend from the lowest Point ; because the* Times *of ascending are equal. And if equal Bodies librate upon the Arm of a* Balance, *at various Distances from the Axis of the Balance ; the* Forces *of the Bodies will be in Proportion as the* Arches *described by them in librating, because they librate in the same Time. And if two equal* Globes *lying upon an Horizontal Plain, be impelled by unequal* Forces, *they will in* equal Times *describe* Spaces *proportional to the* Forces *impelling them. Or if* unequal Globes *be impelled with* equal Forces, *they will in* equal Times *describe* Spaces *reciprocally proportional to their Masses. And in all these Cases, if* equal Bodies *be impelled by* Unequal Forces, *the* Forces *impressed, the* Velocities *generated, and the* Spaces described *in equal Times, will be proportional to one another. And if the Bodies be* unequal, *the* Velocity *of the bigger Bodies will be so much* less, *as the Bodies are* bigger *; And therefore the* Motion *(arising from the* Mass *and* Velocity *together) will be in all these Cases, and in all other Cases consequently, proportional to the* Force *imprest.* [*From whence, by the way, it plainly follows, that if there be always the* same impulsive Force *in the World, as Mr.* Leibnitz *affirms ; there must be always* the same Motion *in the* World, *contrary to what he affirms.*]
But Mr. Leibnitz *confounds these Cases where the* Times *are* equal, *with the Cases where the* Times *are* unequal : *And chiefly That of* Bodies rising and falling at the Ends of the Unequal Arms of a Balance, [*Acta Erudit.* ad Ann. 1686, Pag. 162 ; & ad Ann. 1690, Pag. 234 ; & ad Ann. 1691, Pag. 439 ; & ad Ann. 1695, Pag. 155 ;] *is by him confounded with That of* Bodies falling downwards *and* thrown upwards,

784   157. FIFTH REPLY OF CLARKE

96, 97. Il se contente ici de renvoyer à ce qu'il a dit ailleurs. Je ferai aussi la même chose.

Vitesse, décrira un *plus grand Espace* dans un *temps plus long* : Il faut donc considerer le *temps* ; & l'on ne doit pas dire que les *Forces* sont proportionnelles aux *Espaces*, à moins que les *temps* ne soient *égaux*. Lors que les *temps* sont *inégaux*, les *Forces* des *Corps égaux* sont comme les *Espaces appliquez aux temps*. C'est en quoi les *Cartesiens* & les autres Philosophes & Mathematiciens s'accordent tous. Ils disent tous que les *Forces impulsives des Corps* sont proportionnelles à leurs *Mouvemens*, & ils mesurent leurs *Mouvemens* par leurs *masses* & leurs *Vitesses* prise ensemble, & leurs *Vitesses* par les *Espaces* qu'ils décrivent, *appliquez aux temps* dans lequels ils les décrivent. Si un Corps *jette en haut* monte, en *doublant* sa *Vitesse, quatre fois* plus haut dans un temps *double* ; sa *Force impulsive* sera augmentée, non pas à proportion de l'*Espace* qu'il décrit en montant, mais à proportion de *cet Espace applique au temps*, c'est-à-dire, à proportion de $\frac{4}{2}$ à $\frac{1}{1}$, ou de 2 à 1. Car si, dans *ce Cas*, la Force étoit augmentée à proportion de 4 à 1 ; & si le même corps, (ayant un mouvement d'Oscillation dans une Cycloïde,) avec la *même vitesse doublée*, ne décrit *qu'un Arc double*, & par consequent si sa *Force n'est que doublée* ; ce Corps, avec le *même* degré de *vitesse*, auroit *deux fois autant de Force* lors qu'il est *jetté en haut*, que lors qu'il est poussé horizontellement : Ce qui est une contradiction manifeste. La contradiction est la même quand on assure, que quoi qu'un Corps à l'extremité des bras inégaux d'une *Balance*, en *doublant sa vitesse*, n'acquiere qu'une *double Force impulsive*, cependant, si on le *jette en haut* avec la *même vitesse doublée*, il acquiert une *Force impulsive quadruple* ; je dis que ce sentiment renferme la même contradiction : Car des *Corps égaux* avec des *vitesses égales*, ne peuvent pas avoir des *Forces impulsives inégales*.

Galilée, en supposant que la Gravité est *uniforme*, a démontré le mouvement des Corps *projettez* dans les Milieux qui ne font point de resistance ; & tous les Mathematiciens conviennent de ses Propositions, sans en excepter Mr. *Leibnitz* lui-même. Or si l'on suppose que le *temps* qu'un corps employe à tomber, est divisé en parties égales ; puisque la Gravité est uniforme, & que par consequent elle agit également dans les parties égales du temps, il faut que par son action elle imprime & communique au corps qui tombe, des *Forces*, des *Vitesses*, & des *mouvemens* égaux, en *temps* égaux. Et par conséquent la *Force impulsive*, la *Vitesse*, & le *Mouvement* du corps qui tombe, augmenteront à proportion du *temps* de sa chute. Mais l'*Espace* décrit par le corps qui tombe, resulte *en partie* de la *Vitesse* du Corps, & *en partie* du *Temps* qu'il employe à tomber ; de sorte qu'il est en *raison composée* de la Vitesse & du Temps, ou comme le *Quarré* de l'un ou de l'autre ; & par conséquent comme le Quarré de la *Force impulsive*. Et par le même raisonnement on peut prouver, que lors qu'un Corps est *jetté en haut* avec une *Force* impulsive, la *Hauteur* à laquelle il montera, sera comme la *Quarré* de *cette Force* : Et que la *Force* réquise pour élever le Corps *B, du poids de quatre Livres*, à la hauteur d'*une aune*, élevera le Corps *A, du poids d'Une Livre*, (non pas à la hauteur de *quatre aunes*, comme Mr. *Leibnitz* le dit, mais) à la hauteur de *seize aunes*, en *quatre fois* le même temps. Car la Gravité du *poids de quatre Livres* dans *une* partie du *temps*, agit autant que la Gravité du *poids d'Une Livre* en *quatre parties du temps*.

Mais Mr. *Herman*, dans sa *Phoronomie*, pag. 113, soûtenant le parti de Mr. *Leibnitz* contre ceux qui disent que les *Forces* acquises par les corps qui tombent, sont proportionnelles aux *temps* qu'ils employent à tomber, ou aux *Vitesses* qu'ils acquierent ; Mr. *Herman*, dis-je, assure que cela est fondé sur une *fausse supposition*, sçavoir que les Corps *jettez en haut* reçoivent de la Gravité qui leur resiste, un *nombre égal d'impulsions en temps égaux*. C'est comme si Mr. *Herman* disoit, que la Gravité *n'est pas uniforme* ; &, par conséquent, c'est renverser la *Théorie de Galilée* touchant les corps *Projettez*, dont tous les Géometres conviennent. Je crois que Mr. *Herman* s'imagine que *plus* le mouvement des Corps a de *vitesse en montant, plus* les Corps reçoivent d'*impulsions* ; parce qu'ils *rencontrent* les particules [*imaginaires*] qui causent la Gravité. Ainsi le *poids* des corps sera *plus grand* lors qu'ils *montent*, & *plus petit* lors qu'ils *descendent*. Et cependant Mr. *Leibnitz* & Mr. *Herman* reconnoissent eux-mêmes, que la Gravité en *temps égaux* produit des *vitesses égales* dans les corps qui *descendent*, & qu'elle ôte des *vitesses égales* aux corps qui *montent* ; & par conséquent elle est *uniforme*. Ils reconnoissent qu'elle est *uniforme*, lors qu'elle agit sur les Corps pour produire la *Vitesse* ; & ils nient qu'elle soit *uniforme*, lors qu'elle agit sur eux pour produire la *Force impulsive* : De sorte qu'ils ne sont point d'accord avec eux-mêmes.

Si la *Force* qu'un Corps acquiert en tombant, est comme l'*Espace* qu'il décrit ; que l'on divise le *Temps* en parties *égales* ; & si dans la *premiere* partie du *temps* il acquiert *Une* partie de *Force* ; dans les *deux premieres* parties du *temps* il acquerra *quatre* parties de *Force* ; dans les *trois premieres* parties du *temps*, il acquerra *neuf* parties de *Force* ; & ainsi du reste. Et par conséquent, dans la seconde partie du *temps* il acquerra *trois* parties de *Force*, dans la *troisiéme* partie du *temps* il acquerra *cinq* parties de *Force*, dans la

157. FIFTH REPLY OF CLARKE   785

96 *and* 97. Here this learned Author refers only to what he has said elsewhere: And I also am willing to do the same.

without allowing for the Inequality of the Time. *For a Body with one and the same* Force, *and one and the same* Velocity, *will in a* longer Time *describe a* greater Space ; *and therefore the* Time *is to be considered ; and the* Forces *are not to be reckoned proportional to the* Spaces, *unless where the* Times *are equal. Where the* Times *are* unequal, *the* Forces *of equal* Bodies *are as the* Spaces applied to the Times. *And in This, the* Cartesians *and other* Philosophers and Mathematicians *agree ; all of them making the* impulsive Forces of Bodies *proportional to their* Motions, *and measuring their* Motions *by their* Masses and Velocities *together, and their* Velocities *by the* Spaces *which they describe,* applied to the Times *in which they describe them. If a Body* thrown upwards *does, by* doubling *its* Velocity, *ascend* four Times *higher in* twice the Time ; *its impulsive* Force *will be increased, not in the proportion of the* Space *described by its Ascent, but in the Proportion of* that Space *applied to the Time ; that is, in the Proportion of* $\frac{4}{2}$ *to* $\frac{1}{1}$ *or* 2 to 1. *For if, in this Case, the* Force *should be increased in the Proportion of* 4 to 1 ; *and, in oscillating in a* Cycloid, *the same Body, with the* same Velocity doubled, *describes* only a doubled Arch, *and its* Force *is therefore* only doubled ; *this Body, with* one and the same *Degree of* Velocity, *would have* twice as much Force *when* thrown upwards, *as when* thrown horizontally : *Which is a plain Contradiction. And there is the same Contradiction in affirming, that although a Body at the end of the unequal Arms of a* Balance, *by* doubling its Velocity, *acquires only a* double impulsive Force, *yet, by being* thrown upwards *with the* same doubled Velocity, *it acquires a* quadruple impulsive Force ; *in this Assertion, I say, there is the same Contradiction : For* equal Bodies *with* equal Velocities, *cannot have* unequal impulsive Forces.

Upon the Supposition of Gravity being Uniform, Galilæo *demonstrated the Motion of* Projectiles *in Mediums void of Resistence ; and his Propositions are allowed by all Mathematicians, not excepting Mr.* Leibnitz *himself. Now, supposing the* Time *of a falling Body to be divided into equal Parts ; since Gravity is uniform, and, by being so, acts equally in equal Parts of Time, it must by its Action impress and communicate to the falling Body,* equal impulsive Forces, Velocities, and Motions, *in* equal Times. *And therefore the* impulsive Force, *the* Velocity, *and the* Motion *of the falling Body, will increase in Proportion to the* Time *of falling. But the* Space *described by the falling Body, arises partly from the* Velocity *of the Body, and partly from the* Time *of its falling ; and so is in a* compound ratio *of them* Both, *or as the* Square *of either of them ; and consequently as the* Square *of the* impulsive Force. *And by the same way of arguing, it may be proved, that when a Body is* thrown upwards *with any* impulsive Force, *the* Height *to which it will ascend, will be as the* Square *of that* Force : *And that the* Force *requisite to make the Body* B, *of* four Pounds Weight, *rise up* one Yard, *will make the Body* A, *of* One Pound Weight, *rise up,* (not four Yards, *as Mr.* Leibnitz *represents, but*) sixteen Yards, *in* quadruple *the* Time. *For the Gravity of* four Pounds Weight *in* One *part of* Time, *acts as much as the Gravity of* one Pound Weight *in* Four Parts of Time.

But Mr. Herman[n]*, *in his* Phoronomia, Pag. 113, (*arguing for Mr.* Leibnitz *against Those who hold that the* Forces *acquired by* falling Bodies *are proportional to the* Times *of falling, or to the* Velocities *acquired,*) represents that this is founded upon a* False Supposition, *that Bodies* thrown upwards *receive from the Gravity which resists them, an* equal Number of Impulses *in* equal Times. *Which is as much as to say, that* Gravity *is* not uniform ; *and, by consequence, to overthrow the* Theory *of* Galilæo *concerning* Projectiles, *allowed by all Geometers. I suppose, he means that the* swifter *the* Motion of Bodies *is* upwards, *the more* numerous *are the* Impulses ; *because the Bodies* meet *the* [imaginary] *gravitating Particles. And thus the* Weight *of Bodies will be* greater *when they move* upwards, *and* less *when they move* downwards. *And yet Mr.* Leibnitz *and Mr.* Herman *themselves allow, that* Gravity *in* equal Times *generates equal* Velocities *in* descending Bodies, *and takes away* equal Velocities *in* ascending Bodies ; *and therefore is* Uniform. *In its action upon Bodies for generating* Velocity, *they allow it to be* uniform ; *in its action upon them for generating* impulsive Force, *they deny it to be* uniform : *And so are* inconsistent *with themselves.*

If the Force *acquired by a Body in falling, be as the* Space *described ; let the* Time *be divided into* equal parts ; *and if in the* first part *of* Time *it gain* One part *of* Force, *in the* two first parts *of* Time *it will gain* four parts *of* Force, *in the* three first parts *of* Time *it will gain* nine parts *of* Force, *and so on. And by consequence, in the* second part *of* Time *it will gain* three parts *of* Force, *in the* third part *of* Time *it will gain* five parts *of* Force, *in the* fourth part *of* Time *it will gain* seven parts *of* Force, *and so on. And therefore if the* Action of Gravity *for generating these Forces, be supposed, in the middle of the* first part *of* Time, *to be of* One *degree ; it will, in the* middle *of the* second, third, *and* fourth parts *of* Time, *be of* three, five, *and* seven degrees, *and so on : That is, it will be proportional to the* Time *and to the* Velocity *acquired : And by*

786 157. FIFTH REPLY OF CLARKE

98. *Si l'Ame est une* Substance, *qui remplit le* Sensorium, *ou le lieu* dans lequel elle apperçoit les Images des choses, qui y sont portées ; *il ne s'ensuit point de là qu'elle doit être composée de* Parties *semblables à celles de la* Matiere, (*Car les* Parties de la Matiere *sont des* Substances distinctes & *indépendantes l'une de l'autre ;) mais l'Ame* toute entiere voit, entend, & pense, *comme étant essentiellement* un seul Etre individuel.

* Voïez
ci-dessus
la Note,
§ 13 de
ma troi-
siéme Ré-
plique.
† Voïez
ci-dessus
la Note
sur § 93,
—95.

99. *Pour faire voir que les* * Forces actives *qui sont dans le Monde, c'est-à-dire, la* † Quantité du mouvement, *ou la* Force impulsive *communiquée aux Corps ; pour faire voir, dis-je, que ces Forces actives ne diminuent point naturellement, le sçavant Auteur soûtient, que deux Corps Mous & sans Ressort, se rencontrant avec des forces égales & contraires, perdent chacun* tout leur mouvement, *parce que ce mouvement est communiqué aux* petites parties *dont ils sont composez. Mais lors que deux Corps* tout-à-fait Durs & *sans Ressort perdent tout leur mouvement en se rencontrant, il s'agit de sçavoir que devient ce mouvement, ou cette force active & impulsive ? Il ne sçauroit être dispersé parmi les* parties de ces Corps, parce que ces parties ne sont sus-ceptibles d'aucun tremoussement, *faute de Ressort. Et si on nie que ces Corps doivent perdre leur mouvement* total ; *je réponds qu'en ce cas-là, il s'ensuivra que les Corps durs & Elastiques réjailliront avec une* double force, *sçavoir, avec la force qui resulte du Resort, & de plus avec toute la force directe & primitive, ou du moins avec une partie de cette force : ce qui est contraire à l'experience.*

Enfin, l'Auteur ayant consideré la Démonstration de Mr. Newton, que j'ai citée

* § 99. *ci-dessus, est obligé de* * reconnoitre, *que la* Quantité du mouvement *dans le* monde n'est pas toûjours la même ; & *il a recours à un autre subterfuge, en disant que le mouvement & la* force *ne sont pas toûjours les* mêmes *en* Quantité. *Mais ceci est aussi contraire à l'Experience. Car la* Force *dont il s'agit ici, n'est pas cette force de la*

---

quatriéme partie du *temps* il acquerra *sept* parties de *Force,* & ainsi du reste. Si l'on suppose donc que l'*Action de la Gravité* pour *produire ces Forces,* a *un* degré au milieu de la *premiere* partie du *temps* ; elle aura, au milieu de la *seconde,* de la *troisiéme,* & de la *quatriéme* parties du temps, *trois, cinq,* & *sept* degrez, & ainsi du reste ; c'est-à-dire, qu'elle sera proportionnelle au *temps* & à la *vitesse acquises* : &, par conséquent, au *commencement du temps* il n'y aura point de Gravité ; de sorte que, faute de Gravité, le Corps ne tombera pas. Et selon le même raisonnement, lors qu'un Corps est jetté *en haute,* sa Gravité diminuera à mesure que sa vitesse diminue, & elle cessera lors que le Corps cesse de monter ; & alors, faute de Gravité, le Corps demeurera dans l'air, & ne tombera plus. Tant il est vrai que le sentiment du sçavant Auteur sur ce Sujet, est rempli d'absurditez.

Pour décider cette Question d'une maniere *démonstrative* ; que l'on suspende *deux* Globes d'Acier par des *Rayons* égaux, ou des *Filets* d'une égale longueur ; en sorte que lors qu'ils sont suspendus, & qu'ils se touchent l'un l'autre, les *Rayons* ou les *Filets* soient Paralleles. Que l'*un* de ces Globes soit toûjours le même, & qu'il soit écarté de l'autre à la même distance dans toutes les Experiences suivantes. Que l'*autre* soit de telle grosseur que l'on voudra, & qu'il soit écarté du coté oppose à une distance reciproquement proportionnelle à son poids. Qu'on lâche *ces deux* Globes dans le même moment, en sorte qu'ils se puissent rencontrer dans le plus bas lieu de leur descente, où ils étoient suspendus avant que d'être écar-tez. Le *premier* Globe rebondira toûjours *de la même maniere,* c'est-à-dire, à la même hauteur. Donc la *Force* de l'*autre* est toûjours la même, lors que sa vitesse est reciproquement proportionnelle à son poids. Et par conséquent, si son poids continue d'être le même, sa Force sera proportionnelle à sa *vitesse.* Q. E. D.

157. FIFTH REPLY OF CLARKE   787

98. If the *Soul* be a *Substance* which fills the *Sensorium,* or *Place wherein it perceives the Images of Things conveyed to it* ; yet it does not thence follow, that it must consist of *corporeal Parts,* (for the *Parts* of *Body* are *distinct Substances* independent on each other ;) but the *Whole* Soul *sees,* and the *Whole hears,* and the *Whole thinks,* as being essentially *one Individual.*

99. In order to show that the * *Active Forces* in the World (meaning the † *Quantity of Motion* or *Impulsive Force* given to Bodies,) do not naturally diminish ; this Learned Writer urges, that two *soft* unelastick Bodies meeting together with equal and contrary Forces, do for *this only Reason* lose each of them the *Motion of their Whole,* because it is communicated and dispersed into a *Motion of their small Parts.* But the Question is ; when two *perfectly HARD* un-elastick Bodies lose their whole Motion by meeting together, what then becomes of the Motion or active impulsive Force ? It cannot be dispersed among the *Parts,* because the parts are capable of no tremulous Motion for want of elasticity. And if it be denied, that the Bodies would lose the Motion their *Wholes* ; I answer : Then it would follow, that *Elastick Hard* Bodies would reflect with a *double Force* ; viz. the force arising from the elasticity, and moreover all (or at least part of) the original direct force : Which is contrary to experience.

At length, (upon the *Demonstration* I cited from Sir *Isaac Newton,*[7]) he is obliged to * allow, that the *Quantity of Motion* in the World, is *not always the same* ; And goes to another refuge, that *Motion* and *Force* are not always the *same* in *Quantity.* But this also is contrary to experience. For the *Force* here spoken of is not the † *Vis inertiæ* of

> * *See above, the Note on my Third Reply,* § 13.
> † *See above, the Note on* § 93,—95.
>
> * § 99.

---

consequence, in the Beginning *of the Time it will be none at all ; and so the Body, for want of Gravity, will not fall down. And by the same way of arguing, when a Body is thrown* upwards, *its gravity will decrease as its velocity decreases, and cease when the Body ceases to ascend ; and then, for want of gravity, it will rest in the Air, and fall down no more. So full of* Absurdities *is the Notion of this Learned Author in this particular.*

To decide this question demonstratively ; *let two pendulous globes of hardned Steel, be suspended by equal radij or* Threads *of equal length : So that when they hang down and touch each other, the Radij or Threads may be parallel. Let* One *of the Globes be constantly the same, and be drawn aside from the Other to one and the same distance in All the subsequent Trials. Let the* Other *be of Any Bigness, and be drawn aside the contrary way to a Distance reciprocally proportional to its Weight. Let Both of them then be let go at one and the same Moment of Time, so that they may meet each other at the lowest place of their Descent, where they hung before they were drawn aside : And the first Globe will always rebound alike, from the Other. Wherefore the Force of the Other is always the same, when its Velocity is reciprocally proportional to its Weight. And by consequence, if its Weight remains the same, its Force will be proportional to its Velocity.* Q E. D.

† *The* Vis inertiæ *of Matter, is That* Passive Force, *by which it always continues of itself in the State 'tis in ; and never changes That State, but in proportion to a contrary Power acting upon it. 'Tis That Passive Force, not by which (as Mr.* Leibnitz *from Kepler understands it,) Matter resists* Motion ; *but by which it equally resists* Any Change *from the State 'tis in, either of* Rest *or* Motion *: So that the very same Force, which is requisite to given any certain* Velocity *to any certain* Quantity of Matter *at Rest, is always exactly requisite to reduce the same Quantity of Matter from the same degree of Velocity to a state of Rest again.*

157. FIFTH REPLY OF CLARKE

matiere, qu'on appelle * Vis inertiæ, *laquelle continue effectivement d'être toûjours la même, pendant que la* Quantité de la matiere *est la même ; mais la* Force *dont nous parlons ici, est la* Force active, impulsive, *&* rélative, *qui est* toûjours || *proportionnée à la* Quantité du mouvement *rélatif. C'est ce qui paroit constamment par l'Experience, à moins que l'on ne tombe dans quelque* erreur, *faute de bien* supputer *& de* déduire *la* Force contraire, *qui naît de la Resistance que les Fluides font aux Corps de quelque maniere que ceux-ci se puissent mouvoir, & de l'Action contraire & continuelle de la Gravitation sur les Corps jettez en haut.*

100 —— 102. *J'ai fait voir dans la derniere Section, que la* † Force active, *selon la Définition que j'en ai donnée,* diminue *continuellement & naturellement dans le Monde materiel. Il est évident que ce n'est pas un* défaut, *parce que ce n'est qu'une suite de l'*inactivité *de la Matiere. Car cette* inactivité *est non seulement la cause, comme l'Auteur le* remarque, *de la diminution de la* Vitesse *à mesure que la* Quantité de la Matiere *augmente ; (ce qui à la verité n'est point une* diminution de la Quantité du mouvement ; *) mais elle est aussi la cause pourquoi des Corps* solides, *parfaitement* Durs, *& sans* Ressort, *se rencontrant avec des forces égales & contraires, perdent* tout *leur* mouvement & toute *leur* Force active, *comme je l'ai montré ci-dessus ; & par conséquent ils ont* besoin de quelque *autre* Cause *pour recevoir un* nouveau *mouvement.*

103. *J'ai fait voir amplement dans mes Ecrits précedens, qu'il n'y a aucun défaut dans les choses dont on parle ici. Car pourquoi Dieu n'auroit-il pas eu la liberté de faire un Monde, qui continueroit dans l'état où il est presentement, aussi* long *temps ou aussi* peu *de temps qu'il le jugeroit à propos, & qui seroit en suite changé, & recevroit telle forme qu'il voudroit lui donner, par un changement* sage *& convenable, mais qui peut être seroit tout-à-fait au dessus des loix du* Méchanisme ? *L'Auteur* soûtient † *que* l'Univers ne peut diminuer en perfection ; *qu'il* n'y a aucune raison qui puisse † borner la Quantité de la Matiere ; *que* ‡ *les* Perfections de Dieu *l'obligent à produire* toûjours autant *de Matiere qu'il lui est possible ; & qu'un* Monde borné *est une* † Fiction

† IV Ecrit, § 40, 20, 21, 22 ; & V Ecrit, § 29.

---

* La Force de la Matiere, qu'on appelle *Vis inertiæ*, est cette *Force passive*, par laquelle la Matiere continue d'elle-même dans l'état où elle est, & ne sort jamais de cet état qu'à Proportion de la puissance contraire qui agit sur elle. C'est une Force passive, non pas par laquelle (comme Mr. *Leibnitz* l'entend aprez *Kepler,*) la Matiere resiste au *mouvement* ; mais par laquelle la Matiere resiste également à tout ce qui pourroit changer l'état où elle est, soit qu'elle se trouve en *repos*, ou en *mouvement* : De sorte que la même Force réquise pour donner une certaine *Vitesse* à une certain *Quantité de Matiere* qui est en *repos*, est aussi toûjours réquise pour faire perdre ce même degré de vitesse à la même degré de vitesse à la même Quantité de Matiere, & pour la reduire à l'état de repos où elle étoit auparavant. Cette *Vis inertiæ* est toûjours proportionnée à la *Quantité de la Matiere* ; & par conséquent elle est toûjours *la même sans aucune variation*, soit que la Matiere se trouve en *repos* ou en *mouvement* ; & elle ne passe jamais d'un Corps à un autre. Sans cette *Vis inertiæ*, la moindre Force mettroit en mouvement la Matiere qui est en repos, quelque grande qu'en fût la Quantité ; & cette même Quantité de Matiere étant en mouvement, quelque grande qu'en fût la vitesse, seroit arrêtée par la moindre force, sans aucun choc. De sorte qu'à parler proprement, *toute la Force* de la Matiere, soit qu'elle se trouve en *repos* ou en mouvement, toute son *Action* & sa *Ré-action*, toute son *Impulsion* & sa *Resistance*, n'est autre chose que cette *Vis inertiæ* en differentes Circonstances.

|| C'est-à-dire, proportionnée à la *Quantité de la Matiere* & à *la vitesse*, & non (comme Mr. *Leibnitz* l'assure, *Acta Erudit.* ad Ann. 1695, pag. 156,) à la *Quantité de la Matiere* & au *Quarré de la Vitesse*. Voïez ci-dessus la Note sur § 93——95.

† Voïez ci-dessus la Note sur § 93——95 ; & la III Réplique, § 13.

‡ Voïez ci-dessus l'Apostille de Mr. *Leibnitz* à la fin de son IV Ecrit.

Matter, (which continues indeed always the same, so long as the *Quantity of Matter* continues the same :) but the *Force* here meant, is relative *Active impulsive Force* ; which is *always* || proportional to the *Quantity of Relative Motion* ; As is constantly evident in Experience ; except where some *Error* has been committed, in not rightly *computing* and *subducting* the *contrary* or *impeding Force*, which arises from the Resistence of Fluids to Bodies moved *any way*, and from the continual contrary Action of Gravitation upon Bodies thrown *upwards*.

100 —— 102. That * *Active Force*, in the Sense above-defined, does naturally *diminish* continually in the material Universe ; hath been shown in the last Paragraph. That this is no *Defect*, is evident ; because 'tis only a Consequence of *Matter* being *lifeless*, *void of Motivity*, *unactive* and *inert*. For the *Inertia* of Matter, causeth, not only (as this learned Author observes,) that *Velocity* decreases in proportion as *Quantity of Matter* increases, (which is indeed no *decrease of the Quantity of Motion* ;) but also that *solid* and perfectly *hard Bodies*, void of Elasticity, meeting together with equal and contrary Forces, lose their *whole Motion* and *Active Force*, (as has been above shown,) and must depend upon some *other Cause* for *new Motion*.

103. That none of the things here referred to, are *Defects* ; I have largely shown in my former Papers. For *why* was not God at Liberty to make a World, that should continue in its present Form as *long* or as *short* a time as he thought fit, and should then be altered (by such Changes as may be *very wise* and *Fit*, and yet *Impossible* perhaps to be performed by *Mechanism*,) into whatever other Form he himself pleased ? Whether my Inference from this Learned Author's affirming † that *the Universe cannot diminish in Perfection*, that *there is no possible Reason which can* † *limit the Quantity of Matter*, that ‡ *God's Perfections* oblige him to produce always as *much* Matter as he can, and that a *Finite Material Universe* is an † *Impracticable Fiction* ; whether (I say) my *Inferring*, that (according to these Notions) the World *must needs* have been both *Infinite* and *Eternal*, be a *just Inference* or no, I am willing to leave to the Learned, who shall compare the Papers, to judge.

† Fourth Paper, § 40, 20, 21, 22 ; and Fifth Paper, § 29.

This Vis inertiæ *is always proportional to the* Quantity of Matter ; *and therefore continues* invariably the same, *in all possible States of Matter, whether at* Rest *or in* Motion ; *and is never transferred from One Body to another. Without this* Vis, *the Least Force would give Any Velocity to the Greatest Quantity of Matter at Rest ; and the Greatest Quantity of Matter in Any Velocity of Motion, would be stopped by the Least Force, without any the least shock at all. So that, properly and indeed,* All Force *in Matter either at* Rest *or in* Motion, *all its* Action *and* Reaction, *all* Impulse *and all* Resistence, *is nothing but this* Vis inertiæ *in different Circumstances.*

|| *That is* ; *proportional to the* Quantity of Matter and the Velocity : *not (as Mr.* Leibnitz *affirms,* Acta Erudit. ad Ann. 1695, pag. 156,) *to the* Quantity of Matter and the Square of the Velocity. *See above, the* Note *on* § 93,——95.

* *See above, the* Note *on* § 93 —— 95 ; & *Third Reply,* § 13.

‡ *See above, Mr.* Leibnitz's *Postscript to his Fourth Paper.*

impracticable. *J'ai inferé de cette doctrine, que le Monde doit être nécessairement* infini *& éternel. C'est aux Sçavans à juger si cette Consequence est bien fondée.*

|| § 104.   104, —— 106. *L'Auteur dit à present, que* || *l'Espace n'est pas un* Ordre *ou une* Situation, *mais un* Ordre de Situations. *Ce qui n'empêche pas que la même Objection ne subsiste toûjours, sçavoir, qu'un* Ordre de Situations *n'est pas une* Quantité, *comme l'Espace l'est. L'Auteur renvoye donc à la Section 54, où il croit avoir prouvé que l'*Ordre *est une* Quantité. *Et moi je renvoye à ce que j'ai dit sur cette Section dans ce dernier Ecrit ; où je crois avoir prouvé que l'*Ordre *n'est pas une* Quantité. *Ce que l'Auteur dit*

* § 105.   *aussi touchant le* * Temps, *renferme évidemment cette Absurdité : sçavoir, que le* Temps *n'est que l'*Ordre des chose successives ; *& que cependant il ne laisse pas d'être une* véritable Quantité *; parce qu'il est, non seulement l'ordre des chose successives, mais aussi la* Quantité *de la Durée qui intervient entre chacune des choses particulieres qui se succedent dans cet Ordre. Ce qui est une Contradiction manifeste.*

† § 106.   *Dire que* † *l'Immensité ne signifie pas un* Espace *sans bornes, & que l'Eternité ne signifie pas une* Durée *ou un* Temps *sans commencement & sans fin*[8], *c'est (ce me semble) soûtenir que les* mots *n'ont aucune signification. Au lieu de raisonner sur cet Article, l'Auteur nous renvoye à ce que certains* Théologiens *& Philosophes, (qui étoient de son sentiment,) ont pensé sur cette matiere. Mais ce n'est pas là de quoi il s'agit entre lui & moi.*

107 —— 109. *J'ai dit que parmi les choses possibles, il n'y en a aucune qui soit plus* miraculeuse *qu'une autre, par rapport à* Dieu *; & que par conséquent le* Miracle *ne consiste dans aucune* difficulté *qui se trouve dans la* Nature *d'une chose qui doit être* faite, *mais qu'il consiste simplement* en ce que Dieu le fait rarement. *Le mot de* Nature, *& ceux de* Forces de la Nature, *de* Cours de la Nature, *&c. sont des mots qui signifient simplement, qu'une chose arrive* ordinairement *ou* frequemment. *Lors qu'un* Corps humain reduit en poudre *est* ressuscité, *nous disons que c'est un* Miralce *; lors qu'un* corps humain est engendré de la manière ordinaire, *nous disons*[9] *que c'est une* chose naturelle *; & cette distinction est uniquement fondée sur ce que la* Puissance de Dieu *produit l'une de ces deux choses* ordinairement, *& l'autre* rarement. *Si le* soleil *(ou la* Terre*) est* arrêté soudainement, *nous disons que c'est un* Miracle *; & le* mouvement continuel du *soleil (ou de la* Terre*) nous paroit une chose naturelle : c'est uniquement parce que l'une de ces deux choses est* ordinaire, *& l'autre* extraordinaire. *Si les* hommes sortoient ordinairement du *Tombeau, comme le* Bled sort de la Semence, *nous dirions certainement que ce seroit aussi une* chose naturelle : *Et si le* soleil *(ou la* Terre*) étoit toûjours immobile, cela nous paroitroit* naturel *; & en ce cas-là nous regarderions le* mouvement du soleil *(ou de la* Terre,*) comme une* chose miraculeuse. *Le* sçavant

† § 108.   *Auteur ne dit rien contre ces Raison [ces* † grandes raisons, *comme il les appelle,] qui sont si* évidentes. *Il se contente de nous renvoyer encore aux* manieres de parler *ordinaires de certains* Philosophes *& de certains* Théologiens *; mais, comme je l'ai déjà remarqué ci-dessus, ce n'est pas là de quoi il s'agit entre l'Auteur & moi.*

110 —— 116. *Il est surprenant, que sur une matiere qui doit être décidée par la* || § 110.   Raison *& non par l'*Autorité, *on nous* || *renvoye encore à l'*Opinion *de certains* Philosophes *& Théologiens. Mais, pour ne pas insister sur cela ; que veut dire le* sça-
* § 110.   *vant* Auteur *par une* * difference réelle *& interne entre ce qui est* miraculeux, *& ce*

157. FIFTH REPLY OF CLARKE 791

104 —— 106. We are Now told, that † *Space* is not *an Order* or *Situation*, but an   † § 104.
Order of Situations. But still the Objection remains ; that an *Order of Situations* is
not *Quantity*, as *Space* is. He refers therefore to § 54, where he thinks he has proved
that *Order* is a *Quantity* : And I refer to what I have said *above* in this Paper, upon
that Section ; where I think I have proved, that it is *not a Quantity*. What he alledges
concerning ‖ *Time* likewise, amounts plainly to the following Absurdity : that *Time*   ‖ § 105.
is *only the Order of Things successive*, and yet is truly a *Quantity* ; because it is, *not
only* the *Order of Things successive*, but *also* the *Quantity* of Duration *intervening
between* each of the *Particulars succeeding in That Order*. Which is an express
Contradiction.

To say that * *Immensity* does not signify *Boundless Space*, and that *Eternity* does   * § 106.
not signify *Duration* or *Time without Beginning and End*, is (I think) affirming that
Words have no *meaning*. Instead of *reasoning* upon this Point, we are referred to
what certain *Divines* and *Philosophers* (that is, such as were of this Learned Author's
Opinion,) have *acknowledged* : Which is *not* the *Matter in Question*.

107——109. I affirmed, that, with regard to God, no one Possible thing is more
miraculous than another ; and that therefore a *Miracle* does not consist in any
Difficulty in the Nature of the Thing to be done, but merely in the *Unusualness of
God's doing it*. The Terms, *Nature*, and *Powers of Nature*, and *Course of Nature*, and
the like are nothing but *empty Words* ; and signify merely, that a thing *usually* or
frequently comes to pass. The *Raising a Human Body out of the Dust of the Earth*, we
call a *Miracle* ; the *Generation of a Human Body in the ordinary way*, we call *Natural* ;
for no other Reason, but because the *Power of God* effects one *usually*, the other
unusually. The sudden *stopping* of the *Sun* (or Earth,) we call a *Miracle* ; the continual *Motion* of the *Sun* (or Earth,) we call *Natural* ; for the very same Reason only, of
the one's being *usual*, the other *unusual*. Did Men *usually* arise out of the Grave, as
Corn grows out of Seed sown, we should certainly call *That* also *natural* : And did
the *Sun* (or *Earth*) constantly *stand still*, we should then think *That* to be *natural*,
and its *Motion at any time* would be *miraculous*. Against these *evident Reasons*, [*ces*
† *grandes Rasions*,] this learned Writer offers nothing at all ; but continues barely   † § 108.
to refer us to the Vulgar *Forms of Speaking* of certain *Philosophers* and *Divines* :
Which (as I before observed) is *not the Matter in Question*.

110 —— 116. It is here very surprizing, that, in a Point of *Reason* and not of
Authority, we are still *again* ‖ remitted to the *Opinions* of certain *Philosophers and*   ‖ § 110.
Divines. But, to omit This : What does this Learned Writer mean by a * *real Internal*   * § 110.
Difference between what is *miraculous*, and *not miraculous* ; or between * *Operations*   * § 111.
natural, and *not natural* ; absolutely, and with regard to *God* ? Does he think there
are *in God* two *different and really distinct Principles or Powers of Acting*, and that
one thing is more *difficult* to *God* than *another* ? If not : then either a *natural* and a
supernatural Action of God, are Terms whose Signification is *only relative* to *Us* ; we
calling an *usual* Effect of God's Power, *natural* ; and an *unusual* one, *supernatural* ;
the * *force of Nature* being, in truth, nothing but an *empty word* : Or else, by the *One*   * § 112.

792   157. FIFTH REPLY OF CLARKE

† § 111. *qui ne l'est pas ; ou entre* † des Operations naturelles & non naturelles, *absolument, & par rapport à Dieu ? Croit-il qu'il y ait* en Dieu *deux* Principes d'action differents & réellement distincts ? *Ou qu'une chose soit plus* difficile *à* Dieu *qu'une* autre ? *S'il ne le croit pas, il s'ensuit, ou que les mots d'*Action *de* Dieu naturelle *& surnaturelle, sont des Termes dont la Signification est* uniquement rélative aux hommes ; *parce que nous avons accoutumé de dire qu'un effet* ordinaire *de la puissance de Dieu est une chose* naturelle, *& qu'un effet* extraordinaire *de cette même puissance est une chose*

* § 112. surnaturelle ; *(ce qu'on appelle les* * Forces de la Nature, *n'étant véritablement qu'un* mot sans aucun sens :) Ou bien *il s'ensuit que par une* Action de Dieu surnaturelle, *il faut entendre ce que* Dieu *fait* lui-même immédiatement ; *& par une* Action de Dieu naturelle, *ce qu'il fait par l'*intervention *des Causes secondes. L'Auteur se déclare ouvertement dans cette partie de son Ecrit, contre la* premiere *de ces deux Distinctions ; & il rejette formellement la* seconde *dans la Section* 117, *où il reconnoit que les Anges peuvent faire de* véritables Miracles. *Cependant je ne crois pas que l'on puisse inventer une* troisiéme Distinction *sur la matiere dont il s'agit ici.*

‖ § 113.   *Il est tout-à-fait déraisonnable d'appeler* ‖ l'Attraction *un* Miracle, *& de dire que c'est un Terme qui ne doit point entrer dans la Philosophie ; quoique nous ayons si souvent déclaré* † *d'une maniere distincte & formelle, qu'en nous servant de ce Terme, nous ne prétendons pas exprimer la* Cause qui fait que les Corps tendent l'un vers l'autre, *mais seulement l'*Effet *de cette Cause, ou le* Phénomene *même, & les* Loix *ou* les Proportions selon lesquelles les Corps tendent l'un vers l'autre, *comme on les* découvre par l'Experience, quelle qu'en puisse être la Cause. *Il est encore plus déraisonnable de ne vouloir point admettre la* Gravitation *ou l'*Attraction *dans le sens que*

---

† *Quâ causâ efficiente hæ Attractiones peragantur, &c.* C'est-à-dire. " Je ne recherche point ici quelle
" est la Cause Efficiente de ces Attractions. Ce que j'appelle *Attraction,* est peut-être causé par quelque
" *impulsion,* ou *de quelque autre maniere* qui nous est inconnue. Je ne me sers du mot d'*Attraction* qu'en
" général, pour designer la Force par laquelle les corps tendent l'un vers l'autre, quelle que soit la Cause
" de certe Force. Car il faut que nous apprenions par les Phénomenes de la Nature, *quels Corps* s'attirement
" l'un l'autre, & *quelles* sont *les Loix & les Proprietez* de cette Attraction, avant qu'il soit convenable de
" rechercher *Quelle* est la *Cause efficiente* de l'Attraction " : *Et ailleurs :* " Je considere ces Principes, non
" comme les *Qualitez Occultes* que l'on supposeroit naitre des *Formes Specifiques* des choses ; mais
" comme des *Loix Universelles* de la Nature, selon lesquelles les choses mêmes ont été formées. Car il
" paroit par les Phénomenes de la Nature, qu'il y a actuellement de tels Principes, quoi qu'on ne puisse
" pas encore en expliquer les Causes. Soûtenir que chaque espece distincte des Choses, est douée de
" *Qualitez occultes Specifiques,* par le moyen desquelles les choses ont certains Forces Active ; soûtenir,
" dis-je, une telle Doctrine, c'est ne rien dire. Mais déduire des Phénomenes de la Nature, deux ou trois
" Principes généraux de mouvement ; & ensuite expliquer comment les Proprietez & les Actions de
" toutes les choses materielles suivent de ces Principes ; ce seroit faire un grand progrès dans la
" Philosophie, quoi que l'on ne connût pas encore les *Causes* de ces Principes. " *Et dans un autre endroit :*
" J'ai expliqué les Phénomenes des Cieux & de la Mer par la Force de la Gravité ; mais je n'en ai pas
" encore assigne la *Cause.* C'est une Force produite par quelque Cause, qui pénétre jusqu'aux Centres du
" Soleil & des Planetes, sans rien perdre de sa Force : Et elle n'agit pas proportionnellement aux *Surfaces*
" des Particules sur lesquelles elle agit, comme les Causes *Mechaniques* ont accoutumé de le faire, mais
" proportionnellement à la Quantité de la *Matiere solide :* Et son Action s'étend de tous cotez à des distances
" immenses, diminuant toûjours en Raison doublée des distances. _____ Mais je n'ai pas encore pû
" déduire des Phénomenes la *Cause* de ces proprietez de la Gravité : & je ne fais point d'*Hypotheses* ".
Newton. Optic. pag. 322 & 344. & Princip. Philosoph. Schol. Generale sub finem.

must be meant That which God does *immediately Himself*; and by the *Other*, that which he does *mediately* by the *instrumentality of second Causes*. The *former* of these Distinctions, is what this Learned Author is here professedly opposing: The *latter* is what he expressly disclaims, § 117, where he allows that *Angels* may work *True Miracles*. And yet, besides these *Two*, I think no *other* Distinction can possibly be imagined.

It is very unreasonable to call * *Attraction* a *Miracle*, and an unphilosophical * § 113. Term; after it has been so often distinctly † declared, that by That Term we do not mean to express the *Cause* of *Bodies tending towards each other*, but barely the *Effect*, or the *Phænomenon it self*, and the *Laws* or *Proportions of that Tendency* discovered by *Experience*; whatever *be* or *be not* the *Cause* of it. And it seems still *more*

---

† Quâ causâ efficiente hæ Attractiones peragantur, in id verò hic non inquiro. Quam ego *Attractionem* appello, fieri sanè potest ut ea efficiatur *Impulsu*, vel alio aliquo modo nobis ignoto. Hanc vocem *Attractionis* ita hic accipi velim, ut in universum solummodo vim aliquam significare intelligatur, quâ corpora ad se mutuo tendant; cuicunq; demùm causæ attribuenda sit illa vis. Nam ex phænomenis Naturæ illud nos prius edoctos oportet, quænam corpora se invicem Attrahant, & quænam sint Leges & Proprietates istius Attractionis; quàm in id inquirere par sit, quânam Efficiente Causâ peragatur Attractio. *Newtoni Optice, Qu. 23, pag.* 322. Atq; hæc quidem Principia considero, non ut *occultas Qualitates*, quæ ex *Specificis* rerum *Formis* oriri fingantur; sed ut *universales* Naturæ *Leges*, quibus res ipsæ sunt formatæ. Nam Principia quidem talia revera existere, ostendunt Phænomena Naturæ; licet ipsorum causæ quæ sint, nondum fuerit explicatum. Affirmare singulas rerum species, specificis præditas esse qualitatibus occultis, per quas eæ Vim certam in Agendo habeant; hoc utiq; est Nihil dicere. At ex phænomenis Naturæ, duo vel tria derivare generalia Motus Principia; & deinde explicare quemadmodum proprietates & actiones rerum corporearum omnium ex Principiis istis consequantur; id verò magnus esset factus in Philosophiâ progressus, etiamsi Principiorum istorum Causæ nondum essent cognitæ: *Id. ibid. Pag.* 344. Phænomena Cœlorum & maris nostri per Vim Gravitatis exposui, sed causam Gravitatis nondum assignavi. Oritur utique hæc Vis à causa aliqua, quæ penetrat ad usque centra Solis & Planetarum, sine virtutis diminutione; quæque agit non pro quantitate *Superficierum* particularum in quas agit, (ut solent causæ mechanicæ,) sed pro quantitate *materiæ solidæ*; & cuius actio in immensas distantias undique extenditur, decrescendo semper in duplicatâ ratione distantiarum. _____ Rationem verò harum Gravitatis proprietatum ex Phænomenis nondum potui deducere, & *Hypotheses* non fingo. *Principia Philos. Schol. generale sub finem.* i.e. *What the* efficient *Cause of these Attractions is, I do not here inquire. What I call* Attraction, *may possibly be caused by some* Impulse, *or some other way unknown to us. I use the Word* Attraction, *only in general, to signify the Force by which Bodies tend towards each other; whatever be the Cause of that Force. For we must first learn from the Phænomena of Nature, what Bodies attract each other, and what are the Laws and Properties of that Attraction, before 'tis proper to inquire what the efficient Cause of Attraction is. Again: I consider these Principles, not as occult Qualities, imagined to arise from the specifick Forms of Things; but as Universal Laws of Nature, according to which the Things themselves were formed. For, that such Principles do really exist, appears from the Phænomena of Nature; though, what the Causes of them are, be not yet explained. To affirm that every distinct Species of Things, is indued with specifick occult Qualities, by means whereof the Things have certain Active Forces; this indeed is saying Nothing. But to deduce from the Phænomena of Nature, two or three general Principles of Motion; and then to explain how the Properties and Actions of all corporeal Things follow from those Principles; This would be a great Progress in Philosophy, though the Causes of those Principles were not yet discovered. Again: I have explained the Phænomena of the Heavens and the Sea, by the Force of Gravity; but the Cause of Gravity I have not yet assigned. It is a Force arising from some Cause, which reaches to the very Centers of the Sun and Planets, without any diminution of its Force: And it acts, not proportionally to the Surfaces of the Particles it acts upon, as Mechanical Causes use to do; but proportionally to the Quantity of Solid Matter: And its Action reaches every way to immense Distances, decreasing always in a duplicate ratio of the Distances. But the Cause of these Properties of Gravity, I have not yet found deducible from Phænomena: And* Hypotheses *I make not.*

nous lui donnons, selon lequel elle est certainement un Phénomene de la Nature ; & de
prétendre en même temps que nous admettions un Hypothese aussi éstrange que l'est
celle de † l'Harmonie préétablie, selon laquelle l'Ame & le Corps d'un homme n'ont pas
plus d'influence l'un sur l'autre, que deux Horloges, qui vont également bien quelque
éloignées qu'elles soient l'une de l'autre, & sans qu'il y ait entre elles aucun action reciproque. Il est vrais que l'Auteur dit, que Dieu * prévoyant les inclinations de chaque Ame, a
formé dès le commencement la grande Machine de l'Univers d'une telle maniere, qu'en
vertu des simples Loix du Méchanisme, les Corps humains reçoivent des mouvemens
convenables, comme étant des parties de cette grande Machine. Mais est-il possible, que
de pareils mouvemens, & autant diversifiez que le sont ceux des Corps humains, soient
produits par un pur Méchanisme sans que la Volonté & l'Esprit agissent sur ces Corps ?
Est-il croyable, que lors qu'un homme forme une resolution, & qu'il sçait, un mois par
avance, ce qu'il fera un certain jour ou à une certain heure ; est-il croyable, dis-je, que
son Corps, en vertu d'un simple Méchanisme qui a été produit dans le Monde Materiel
dès le commencement de la Création, se conformera ponctuellement à toutes les resolutions de l'Esprit de cet homme au temps marqué ? Selon cette Hypothese, tous les
Raisonnemens Philosophiques, fondez sur les Phénomenes & sur les Experiences,
deviennent inutiles. Car, si l'Harmonie préétablie est véritable, un homme ne voit,
n'entend, & ne sent rien, & il ne meut point son Corps : Il s'imagine seulement voir,
entendre, sentir, & mouvoir son corps. Et si les hommes étoient persuadez que le Corps
humain n'est qu'une pure Machine, & que tous ses mouvemens qui paroissent volon-
taires, sont produits par les Loix nécessaires d'un Méchanisme materiel, sans aucune
influence ou operation de l'Ame sur le Corps ; ils conclurroient bientôt que cette
Machine est l'Homme tout entier, & que l'Ame Harmonique dans l'Hypothese d'un
Harmonie préetablie, n'est qu'une pure fiction & une vaine imagination. De plus :
Quelle dificulté évite-t-on par le moyen d'une si étrange Hypothese ? On n'évite que
celle-ci, sçavoir, qu'il n'est pas possible de concevoir comment une Substance immaterielle peut agir sur la Matiere. Mais Dieu n'est-il pas une Substance immaterielle ? Et
n'agit-il pas sur la Matiere ? D'ailleurs, est-il plus difficile de concevoir qu'une Substance
immaterielle agit sur la Matiere, que de concevoir que la Matiere agit sur la Matiere ?
N'est-il pas aussi aisé de concevoir que certains parties de Matiere peuvent être obligées
de suivre les mouvemens & les inclinations de l'Ame sans aucune impression corporelle,
que de concevoir que certaines portions de Matiere soient obligées de suivre leurs mouvemens reciproques à cause de l'Union ou Adhesion de leurs parties, qu'on ne sçauroit
expliquer par aucun Méchanisme ? Ou que les Rayons de la Lumiere soient réflechis
régulierement par une surface qu'ils * ne touchent jamais ? C'est de quoi Mr. le Chevalier
Newton nous a donné diverses Experiences oculaires dans son Optique.

Il n'est pas moins surprenant, que l'Auteur repete encore en termes formels, que †
depuis que le Monde a été créé, la continuation du mouvement des Corps celestes, la

---

* Voïez l'Optique de Mr. Newton, Edit. Lat. Pag. 224. Edit. Angloise Lib. 2. Pag. 65.

157. FIFTH REPLY OF CLARKE   795

unreasonable, not to admit *Gravitation* or *Attraction* in *This sense*, in which it is manifestly an *actual Phænomenon* of nature ; and yet at the same time to expect that there should be admitted so strange an *Hypothesis*, as the * *harmonia præsta-* *bilita* ; which is, that the *Soul* and *Body* of a Man have no more Influence upon each others Motions and Affections, than *two Clocks*, which, at the greatest *distance* from each other, *go alike*, without at all affecting each other. It is alleged indeed, that God, † foreseeing the *Inclinations* of every Man's *Soul*, so contrived at first the great *Machine* of the *material Universe*, as that, by the *mere necessary Laws of Mechanism, suitable* Motions should be excited in *Human Bodies*, as Parts of that great Machine. But is it *possible*, that such *Kinds* of *Motion*, and of such *variety*, as those in Human Bodies are ; should be performed by *mere Mechanism*, without any Influence of *Will and Mind* upon them ? Or is it *credible*, that when a Man has it in his Power to resolve and know *a Month before-hand*, what he will do upon such a particular Day or Hour to come ; is it *credible*, I say, that his *Body* shall by the mere Power of *Mechanism*, impressed originally upon the *material Universe* at its Creation, punctually conform it self to the Resolutions of the Man's *Mind* at the *Time appointed* ? According to *This* Hypothesis, *All Arguments* in Philosophy, taken from *Phænomena and Experiments*, are at an end. For, if the *Harmonia præstabilita* be true, a Man does not indeed *see*, nor *hear*, nor *feel* any thing, nor *moves his Body* ; but only *dreams* that he sees, and hears, and feels, and moves his Body. And if the World can once be perswaded, that a Man's Body is a *mere Machine* ; and that all his *seemingly voluntary* Motions are performed by the mere necessary Laws of *corporeal Mechanism*, without any *Influence*, or *Operation*, or *Action at all* of the *Soul* upon the Body ; they will soon conclude, that this *Machine* is the *whole Man* ; and that the *harmonical Soul*, in the Hypothesis of an *harmonia præstabilita*, is merely a *Fiction* and a *Dream*. Besides : *What Difficulty* is there *avoided*, by so strange an *Hypothesis* ? *This* only, that it cannot be conceived (it seems,) how *immaterial Substance* should *act* upon *Matter*. But is not *God* an *immaterial Substance* ? And does not *He* act upon *Matter* ? And *what greater Difficulty* is there in conceiving how an *immaterial Substance* should act upon Matter, than in conceiving how *Matter* acts upon Matter ? Is it not as easy to conceive, how certain Parts of Matter may be obliged to follow the Motions and Affections of the *Soul*, without corporeal Contact ; as that certain Portions of Matter should be obliged to follow *each others* Motions by the *adhæsion of Parts*, which *no Mechanism* can account for ? or that Rays of Light should reflect regularly from a Surface which they † *never touch ?* Of which, Sir *Isaac Newton* in his Opticks has given us several evident and ocular *Experiments*.

Nor is it less surprising, to find this Assertion again repeated in express Words, that, after the first Creation of Things, || *the continuation of the Motions of the*

margin notes:
* § 109 *and* 92, *and* 87, 89, 90.

† § 92.

|| § 115, 116.

---

† *See Sir* Isaac Newton's Opticks, *Latin Edition*, Pag. 224. *English Edition*, Book 2, Page 65.

formation des Plantes & des Animaux, & tous les mouvemens des Corps humains & de tous les autres Animaux, ne sont pas moins méchaniques que les mouvemens d'une Horloge. *Il me semble que ceux qui soûtiennent ce sentiment, devroient expliquer* en détail *par* quelles Loix de Méchanisme *les* Planetes & *les* Cometes *continuent de se mouvoir dans les* Orbes *où elles se meuvent, au travers d'un* Espace qui ne fait point de resistance ; *par* quelles Lois Méchaniques *les* Plantes & les Animaux *sont formez,* & *quelle est la cause des* mouvemens Spontanées *des* Animaux & des Hommes, *dont la varieté est presque infinie. Mais je suis fortement persuadé, qu'il n'est pas moins impossible d'expliquer toutes ces choses, qu'il le seroit de faire voir qu'une* Maison, *ou une* Ville, *a été bâtie par un* simple Méchanisme, *ou que le* Monde même *a été* formé *dès commencement sans aucune Cause* Intelligente & Active. *L'Auteur reconnoit formellement, que les choses ne pouvoient pas être* produites au commencement *par un* pur Méchanisme. *Aprez cet aveu, je ne sçaurois comprendre pourquoi il paroit si zélé à bannir Dieu du Gouvernement actuel du Monde,* & *à soûtenir que sa Providence ne consiste que dans un simple* Concours (*comme on l'appelle,*) *par lequel* toutes les Créatures *ne font que ce qu'elles feroient d'elles mêmes par un* simple Méchanisme. *Enfin, je ne sçaurois concevoir pourquoi l'Auteur s'imagine que Dieu est obligé, par sa* Nature *ou par sa* Sagesse, *de ne rien produire dans l'Univers, que ce qu'une* Machine corporelle peut *produire par de* simples Loix Méchaniques, *aprez qu'elle a été une fois mise en mouvement.*

117. *Ce que le sçavant Auteur avouë ici, qu'il y a du plus* & *du moins dans les* véritables Miracles, & *que les* Anges *peuvent faire de* tels Miracles ; *ceci, dis-je, est directement* * contraire *à ce qu'il a dit ci-devant de la* nature du Miracle *dans tous ces Ecrits.*

* Voïez ci-dessus le III E-crit de Mr *Leibnitz,* § 17.

118 —— 123. *Si nous disons que le* Soleil attire *la* Terre, *au travers d'un* Espace *vuide ; c'est à dire, que la* Terre & *le* Soleil *tendent l'un vers l'autre (quelle qu'en puisse être la cause,) avec une* Force qui est en proportion *directe de leur* Masses, *ou de leurs* Grandeurs & densitez prises ensemble, & *en* proportion *doublée inverse de leur* Distances ; & *que l'*Espace *qui est entre ces deux Corps, est* vuide, *c'est à dire, qu'il n'a rien qui resiste sensiblement au mouvement des Corps qui le traversent : tout cela n'est qu'un* Phénomene, *ou un* Fait actuel, *découvert par l'*Experience. *Il est sans doute*

|| § 118. *vrai que ce Phénomene n'est pas produit* || *sans moyen, c'est à dire, sans une* Cause *capable de produire un tel effet. Les* Philosophes *peuvent donc rechercher cette* Cause, & *tâcher de la découvrir, si cela leur est* possible, *soit qu'elle soit* méchanique *ou non* méchanique. *Mais s'ils ne peuvent pas découvrir cette* Cause ; *s'ensuit-il que l'*Effect *même, ou le* Phénomene découvert par l'Experience, (*car c'est-là* * tout ce que l'on veut dire par les mots d'*Attraction & *de* Gravitation,) *s'ensuit-il, dis-je, que ce* Phénomene soit moins certain & moins incontestable ? Une* Qualité évidente doit-elle être appellée* * occulte, parce que la* Cause *immédiate en est peut-être* occulte, *ou qu'elle n'est pas encore découverte ? Lors qu'un* Corps † *se meut dans un Circle, sans s'éloigner par la Tangente ; il y a certainement* quelque chose, qui l'en empêche : *Mais si dans quelques cas il n'est pas* possible || *d'expliquer méchaniquement la* Cause de

* Voïez ci-dessus la Note sur § 113.

* § 122.

† § 123.

|| § 123.

157. FIFTH REPLY OF CLARKE 797

heavenly Bodies, and the *Formation of Plants and Animals*, and *every Motion of the Bodies both of Men and all other Animals, is as mechanical as the Motions of a Clock*. Whoever entertains this Opinion, is (I think) obliged in reason to be able to explain *particularly*, by *what Laws of Mechanism* the *Planets* and *Comets* can continue to move in the *Orbs* they do, thro' *unresisting Spaces* ; and by *what mechanical Laws*, both *Plants and Animals* are formed ; and how the infinitely various *spontaneous Motions of Animals and Men*, are performed. Which, I am fully persuaded, is as impossible to make out, as it would be to show how a *House* or *City* could be *built*, or the *World it self* have been at first formed by *mere Mechanism*, without any *Intelligent* and *Active* Cause. That Things could not be *at first produced* by *Mechanism*, is expressly allowed : And, when this is once granted ; why, after That, so great Concern should be shown, to exclude God's *actual* Government of the World, and to allow his Providence to *act* no further than barely in *concurring* (as the Phrase is) to let *all Things* do only what they would do *of themselves* by *mere Mechanism* ; and why it should be thought that God is under any Obligation or Confinement either in *Nature* or *Wisdom*, never to bring about any thing in the Universe, but what is *possible* for a *corporeal Machine* to accomplish by *mere mechanick Laws*, after it is once set a going ; I can no way conceive.

117. This learned Author's allowing in this Place, that there is *greater* and *less* in *true Miracles*, and that *Angels* are capable of working some *true Miracles* ; is perfectly † contradictory to that Notion of the *Nature of a Miracle*, which he has all along pleaded for in these Papers.

† *See above, Mr Leibnitz's Third Paper,* § 17.

118 —— 123. That the Sun *attracts* the Earth, through the intermediate void Space ; that is, that the Earth and Sun *gravitate* towards each other, or *tend* (whatever be the Cause of that Tendency) towards each other, with a *Force* which is in a direct *proportion* of their *Masses*, or *Magnitudes and Densities together*, and in an inverse duplicate *proportion* of their *Distances* ; and that the Space betwixt them is *void*, that is, hath nothing in it which sensibly resists the Motion of Bodies passing transversly through : All This, is nothing but a *Phænomenon*, or *actual Matter of Fact*, found by *Experience*. That this Phænomenon is not produced || *sans moyen*, that is, without some *Cause* capable of producing such an Effect ; is undoubtedly true. Philosophers therefore may search after and discover That *Cause*, if they *can* ; be it *mechanical*, or *not mechanical*. But if they *cannot* discover the Cause ; is therefore the *Effect* it self, the *Phænomenon*, or the *Matter of Fact discovered by Experience*, (which is * all that is meant by the Words *Attraction* and *Gravitation*,) ever the less *True* ? Or is a *manifest Quality* to be called || *occult*, because the immediate efficient *Cause* of it (perhaps) is *occult*, or *not yet discovered* ? When a Body * moves in a Circle, without flying off in the Tangent ; 'tis certain there is something that *hinders* it : But if in some Cases it be not *mechanically* † *explicable*, or be not yet

|| § 118.

* *See above the Note, on* § 113.
|| § 122.
* § 123.

†* § 123.

798   157. FIFTH REPLY OF CLARKE

cet Effet, ou si elle n'a pas encore été découverte, *s'ensuit-il que le* Phénomene *soit faux ? Ce seroit une maniere de raisonner fort* singuliere.

124 —— 130. *Le* Phénomene *même, l'*Attraction, *la* Gravitation, *ou l'*effort *(quelque nom qu'on lui donne) par lequel les* Corps tendent l'un vers l'autre ; *& les* Loix, *ou les* Proportions, *de cette Force ; sont assez connues par les* Observations *& les* Experiences. *Si Mr.* Leibnitz, *ou quelque autre Philosophe, peut expliquer ces*

* § 124. *Phénomenes par* * *les* Loix du Méchanisme, *bien loin d'être contredit, tous les sça-vants l'en remercieront. En attendant, je ne sçaurois m'empêcher de dire que l'Auteur*

† § 128. *raisonne d'une maniere tout-à-fait extraordinaire, en* † *comparant la* Gravitation, *qui est un* Phénomene *ou un* Fait actuel, *avec la* Déclination des Atomes *selon la doctrine d'*Epicure ; *lequel ayant corrompu, dans le dessein d'introduire l'*Atheisme, *une Philosophie plus ancienne & peut être plus saine, s'avisa d'établir cette* Hypothese, *qui n'est qu'une pure* Fiction, *& qui d'ailleurs est* impossible *dans un Monde où l'on suppose qu'il n'y a aucune* Intelligence.

|| § 125, *Pour ce qui est du grand Principe d'une* || Raison suffisante, *toute ce que le sçavant*
&c. *Auteur ajoute ici touchant cette matiere, ne consiste qu'à* soûtenir *sa Conclusion, sans la prouver ; & par conséquent il n'est pas nécessaire d'y répondre. Je remarquerai seulement que cette Expression est* Equivoque ; *& qu'on peut l'entendre, comme si elle ne renfermoit que la* Nécessité, *ou comme si elle pouvoit aussi signifier une* Volonté &*

* § 125. un Choix. *Il est très-certain, & tout le monde convient, qu'en général* * *il y a une* Raison suffisante *de chaque chose. Mais il s'agit de sçavoir, si, dans certains cas, lors qu'il est* raisonnable *d'agir,* differentes manieres d'agir possibles *ne peuvent pas être*

† Voïez ci- également raisonnables ; *si, dans ces cas, la* † simple Volonté de Dieu *n'est pas une*
dessus sur Raison suffisante *pour agir d'*une certain manier *plûtôt que d'*une autre ; *& si, lors*
§ 1—20, *que les* raisons les plus fortes *se trouvent d'*un seul coté, *les* Agents intelligens &
& 21–25. libres *n'ont pas un* Principe d'action, *(en quoi je croi que l'Essence de la* Liberté *con-siste,) tout à fait* distinct *du Motif ou de la* Raison *que l'Agent a en vûë. Le sçavant*

|| § 20, & *Auteur nie tout cela : Et comme il* || *établit son Grand Principe d'une* Raison suffisante
125, &c. *dans un sens qui exclud tout ce que je viens de dire ; & qu'il demande qu'on lui accorde ce Principe dans ce sens-là, quoi qu'il n'ait pas entrepris de le prouver ; j'appelle cela une* Petition de Principe : *ce qui est tout à fait indigne d'un* Philosophe.

N. B. La mort de Mr. LEIBNITZ l'a empêché de répondre à ce dernier Ecrit.

----

157. FIFTH REPLY OF CLARKE   799

discovered, what *that something* is ; does it therefore follow, that the *Phænomenon it self* is false ? This is very *singular* Arguing indeed.

124 —— 130. The *Phænomenon* it self, the *Attraction, Gravitation*, or *Tendency of Bodies towards each other*, (or whatever other Name you please to call it by ;) and the *Laws*, or *Proportions*, of that Tendency, are now sufficiently known by *Observations* and *Experiments*. If This or any other learned Author can by || the *Laws of Mechanism* explain these Phænomena, he will not only not be contradicted, but will moreover have the abundant Thanks of the Learned World. But, in the mean time, to † compare *Gravitation*, (which is a *Phænomenon* or *actual Matter of Fact*,) with *Epicurus's Declination of Atoms*, (which, according to his corrupt and Atheistical Perversion of some more antient and perhaps better Philosophy, was an *Hypothesis* or *Fiction* only, and an *impossible one too* in a World where no *Intelligence* was supposed to be present ;) seems to be a very *extraordinary* Method of Reasoning. · || § 124. · † § 128.

As to the grand Principle of a * *sufficient Reason* ; all that this Learned Writer here adds concerning it, is only by way of *Affirming*, not *proving*, his Conclusion ; and therefore needs no Answer. I shall only observe, that the Phrase is of an *equivocal* Signification ; and may either be so understood, as to mean *Necessity only*, or so as to include likewise *Will* and *Choice*. That in general there || is a *sufficient Reason why* every Thing is, which *Is* ; is undoubtedly true, and agreed on all Hands. But the Question is, whether, in some Cases, when it may be highly *reasonable* to *act*, yet *different possible Ways of acting* may not possibly be *equally reasonable* ; and whether, in such Cases, the * *bare Will of God* be not *it self* a *sufficient Reason* for acting in *this* or the *other* particular *manner*; and whether in Cases where there are the *strongest possible Reasons* altogether on *One* Side, yet in all *Intelligent* and *Free Agents*, the *Principle of Action* (in which I think the Essence of *Liberty* consists,) be not a *distinct Thing* from the *Motive* or *Reason* which the Agent has in his View. All these are constantly denied by this Learned Writer. And his || laying down his grand Principle of a *sufficient Reason* in such a Sense as to exclude all these ; and expecting it should be *granted* him in that Sense, without *Proof* ; This is what I call his *Petitio Principii*, or *Begging of the Question* : Than which, nothing can be more unphilosophical. · * § 125, &c. · || § 125. · * See *above, on* § 1—20, & 21–25. · || § 20, & 125, &c.

N. B. *Mr.* Leibnitz *was prevented by* Death, *from returning any Answer to this last Paper.*

----

¹ The original English and French translation are from Clarke's edition of the correspondence (Clarke 1717, pp. 280–373). This is Clarke's reply to Leibniz's Fifth Paper (document 140b); it was enclosed with Caroline's letter to Leibniz of 29 October 1716 (document 156). Footnotes and marginal notes are Clarke's; endnotes are mine. Clarke's references to the Appendix of his 1717 edition of the correspondence have been omitted. All square brackets in the text and what they contain are due to Clarke.
² Here Clarke inserts '||' but in the marginal note he mistakenly (?) inserts '†'.

Caroline of Ansbach, Princess of Wales, to Leibniz

Hampthancour le $\frac{4}{24}$ 8ber 1716

Je scerais ravié Monsieur sy, l'on estté contande dans sepeais icy,[3] de la manier qu'on recevoit tous le monde,[4] et viques, come toris. Hampthancour,[5] et vne plasse ou tous ceu qui y viene doivez retourner contans.[6] Docteur Blackborren et arivez et ma lon tems parlee[7] de mon fils qu'il trouvez[8] assez bien Elevé mais il e[s]t extremement surpris qu'on neluy aprans pas langlois. ce n'est pas mafauté et je crain qu'on adantera[9] sy lontemps jus-as ceque letems sera passez pour aprander laprononciassion.[10] vn Eveque e[s]t fort malade einsy votre prophissié pourait sa complier, que lebon doiyen[11] devint Eveque. Je suis faché[e] de voir que vous ranvoiyée[12] pour sy lon tems votre voiagéi[13] pour icy. vous pourais travaller a l'histoire alonder come ahanovrer,[14] et, vos amis pourais[15] avoir le plaisir de jouir de votre convercassion.[16] Je repressandere[17] avec plaisir lecollegé de lasorboñe,[18] pour veu que j'eu leplaisir[19] de vous y andertenir, et esttre, quoy, que tres ingoran temoin de vos disputé[20] avec M^r chlerque. vous me trouverais come toujours lamême persoñe qui vous esttime[21] infiniment.

Caroline

[3] Originally '*propotion*'; corrected in the Errata of the 1717 edition.

[4] The sentence '*Voïez ma quatrieme Réplique*, § 7 ; & *cinquieme Réplique*, § 33' in the Errata of the 1717 edition.

[5] The sentence '*See my Fourth Reply*, § 7 ; & *Fifth Reply*, § 33' was inserted in the Errata of the 1717 edition.

[6] 'pesent sur le bras' was inserted in the Errata of the 1717 edition.

[7] See Clarke's Fourth Reply, document 129, p. 601 and p. 605 note 4.

[8] Originally just 'sans fin' not preceded by 'sans commencement'; corrected in the Errata of the 1717 edition.

[9] Originally '*disous*'; corrected in the Errata of the 1717 edition.

158. Caroline of Ansbach, Princess of Wales, to Leibniz[1]

Hampton Court $\frac{4}{24}$ October 1716[2]

I would be delighted, sir, if people in this country were satisfied[3] with the manner in which we received everyone,[4] both Whigs and Tories. Hampton Court[5] is a place where everyone who comes here ought to go back satisfied.[6] Doctor [Lancelot] Blackburne* arrived and talked with me for a long time[7] about my son, whom he finds[8] well enough mannered, but he is extremely surprised that they are not teaching him English. This is not my fault, and I fear that they will wait[9] so long, until the time for learning pronunciation will be over.[10] A bishop is very sick, so your prophecy, that the good dean becomes bishop, could be fulfilled.[11] I am displeased to see that you postpone[12] your trip[13] here for so long. You could work on the history in London as in Hanover,[14] and your friends could[15] have the pleasure of enjoying your conversation.[16] I would represent[17] with pleasure the College of Sorbonne,[18] provided that I had the pleasure[19] of speaking to you here, and of being, although very ignorant, witness to your disputes[20] with Mr. [Samuel] Clarke*. You will find me, as always, the same person who esteems you[21] infinitely.

Caroline

[1] LBr. F 4 Bl. 11r–11v. Letter as sent: two quarto sides in Caroline's hand. Previously published in Klopp XI 190; Schüller 1991, pp. 263–4 (excerpt in German translation); Robinet 1991, p. 185 (excerpt). Klopp, Schüller, and Robinet misdate the letter as 4/15 September 1716. This is Caroline's response to the last letter Leibniz wrote to her (document 149) before his death on 14 November 1716.

[2] That is, 24 October 1716 (OS) and 4 November 1716 (NS). Klopp misdates the letter as $\frac{1}{24}$ Septembre (Klopp XI 190).

[3] Reading 'si, l'on était content dans ce pays ici' for 'sy, l'on estté contande dans sepeais icy'.

[4] Reading 'tout le monde' for 'tous le monde'.

[5] Klopp XI 190 mistranscribes 'et viques, come toris. Hamp thancour', as 'et Whigs et Tories, à Hamptoncourt'; and he omits altogether the words that follow, namely, 'et vne plasse ou tous ceu qui y viene doivez retourner contant'.

[6] Reading 'Hampton Court est une place où tous ceux qui y viennent doivent retourner content' for 'hampthancour, et vne plasse ou tous ceu qui y viene doivez retourner contans'.

[7] Reading 'Docteur Blackburne est arrivé et m'a longtemps parlé' for 'Blackborren et arivez et ma lon tems parlée'.

[8] Reading 'trouve' for 'trouvez'.

[9] Klopp XI 190 mistranscribes 'adantera' as 'attende'.

[10] Reading 'ne lui apprend pas l'Anglais. Ce n'est pas ma faute, et je crains qu'on n'attendra si longtemps jusqu'à ce que le temps sera passé pour apprendre la prononciation' for 'neluy aprans pas langlois.

Johann Bernoulli to Leibniz

Vir Amplissime atque Celeberrime
Fautor Honoratissime

[...]

Theodicæam Tuam, opus sane elgantissimum, nondum vacavit perlegere totam, legi magna cum voluptate dissertationem de Conformitate Fidei cum Ratione, deprehendo solidissime scriptam mihique in plerisque, nec satis memini, an non in omnibus mirifice arridentem, inprimis vero placuere, quae contra Baylium Rationis inimicum disputas.

Clarkium, ut videtur, ad incitas redegisti, quando coactus est dicere, Dei voluntatem nulla ratione esse nixam, hoc enim pacto ex Deo fiet ens brutum et irrationale, quod ageret tantum caeco quodam impetu; nisi omnino cum Democrito et Epicuro recurrendum esset ad fortuitum atomorum concursum.

[...]

Cæterum Vale et fave

     Amplit. T. Devotiss. JBernoulli

Bas. a. d. XI. Nov. 1716.

ce n'est pas mafauté et je crain qu'on adantera sy lontemps jus-as ceque letems sera passez pour aprander laprononciassion.'

[11] Reading 'ainsi votre prophétie pourrait s'accomplir, que le bon doyen devient Eveque' for 'einsy votre prophissié pourait sa complier, que le bon doiyen devint Eveque'. For Leibniz's 'prophecy', see his letter to Caroline from the end of September 1716 (document 149, p. 745). The prophecy was indeed fulfilled in 1717: Blackburne was elevated to the bishopric of Exeter when the previous bishop, Ofspring Blackall, died shortly after Caroline wrote this letter.

[12] Reading 'renvoyez' for 'ranvoiyée'.

[13] Reading 'voyage' for 'voiagéi'.

[14] Reading 'pourriez travailler à l'histoire à Londres comme à Hanovre' for 'pourais travaller a l'histoire alonder côme ahanovrer'.

[15] Reading 'pourraient' for 'pourais'.

[16] Reading 'conversation' for 'convercassion'.

[17] Reading 'représenterais' for 'repressandere'.

[18] Reading 'le Collège de la Sorbonne' for 'lecollegé de lasorboñe'. Here Caroline is apparently alluding to the public theological disputations, held in the Hall of the Sorbonne, that the Theological Faculty of the College of Sorbonne required of candidates who sought membership in the college—the so-called Sorbonicae.

[19] Reading 'pourvu que j'eusse le plaisir' for 'pour veu que j'eu leplaisir'.

[20] Reading 'entretenir, et d'être, quoique très ignorante, témoin de vos disputes' for 'andertenir, et esttre, quoy que tres ingoran temoin de vos disputé'.

[21] Reading 'trouverez comme la même personne qui vous estime' for 'trouverais côme lamême persoñe' qui vous esttime'.

159. Johann Bernoulli* to Leibniz (excerpt)[1]

Most Esteemed and Celebrated Sir
  Most Honourable Supporter

[11 November 1716]

[…]

There has not yet been time to examine thoroughly your entire *Theodicy*, certainly a most elegant work. I have read with great pleasure the [*Preliminary*] *Dissertation on the Conformity of Faith with Reason;*[2] I discern a very solid work, and in most things (I do not quite remember whether or not in all), it has been extraordinarily pleasing to me, above all, what you contend against [Pierre] Bayle*, an enemy of *reason*, has certainly seemed right to me.

It seems you have checkmated [Samuel] Clarke* when he is forced to say that the will of God is based on no reason. For he will thereby make[3] of God a stupid and irrational being, who would act only by a kind of blind impulse, if it is true that he [Clarke] did not altogether have to have recourse, with Democritus and Epicurus, to the fortuitous collision of atoms.[4]

[…]

For the rest, farewell and be well disposed toward

Your Eminence's Most Devoted J[ohann]Bernoulli

Basil a. d. XI November 1716

Antonio Schinella Conti to Isaac Newton

Hanover 10 xbre 1716

Monsieur

Je vous demande pardon, si ie n'ay pas pû vous ecrire iusque a cette heure. Je suis tombè malade depuis que ie suis icy, et ie ne suis pas encore revenu de ma malade. Je n'ay vû ni le Roy ni la Cour, et ie suis obligè de garder la chambre depuis vingt jours.

M. Leibniz est mort; et la dispute est finie. Il y a laissè plusieurs lettres, et plusieurs manuscrits, qu'on imprimera avec des manuscrits d'autres scavants, une quelque Traitè de M. Des-cartes, qui n'est point paru jusque icy. Il y a des Dialoghes[2] sur les articles de La Teodicer, une i[n]struction au Prince Eugene sur les exercices milataires; une instruction au Czar pour faire fleurir les Arts et les Sciences dans son Païs; beaucoup des remarques sur la Langue Universelle, et sur l'etimologie des mots; Cõme ie espere que le Roy me donnera la permission de voir ces papiers, je remarquerai s'il y a quelque chose touchent votre dispute, mais peut-etre qu'on cachera ce qui ne fait point d'hoñeur a la mémoire de M. Leibniz. On a comencè a travailler sa Vie. M. Wolfius aura le soin d'ecrire tout ce qui appartient aux Mathematiques:

M. Leibniz a travaillè pendant toute sa vie a inventer des machines, qui n'ont point reussi. Il a voulu faire une espece de moulin a vent pour les mines, un Carosse, qui tire sans cheveaux:[3] un Carosse, qui se change en chaise a porteurs, et un charrette; iusque des Souliers a ressort; Il y a deux modelles de sa machine arithmetique, mais elle est tres composee, et on dit, qu'elle n'est alafin,[4] que la machine de Pascal multipliè.

Vous aurez vû l'insolente dissertation, qu'on a imprimè dans les Actes de Lipsic au mois de Juin. M. Bernoulli pretend a cette heure d'être l'inventeur de calcul integral; Je suis seur que la dissertation vous fera rire.

Je ne scay pas si M. l'Ambassadeur de Venise vous a priè de proposer a la Societè Royal M. le Marquis Orsi Senateur de Boulogne, et un de plus grand scavants que nous avons en Italie. Il est celebre en France par plusieurs livres, qu'il a ecrit et c'est

¹ LBr. 58 Bl. 14r–14v. Letter as sent: 1.2 quarto sides in Bernoulli's hand. Previously published in GM III-2 972–3; Schüller 1991, p. 268 (excerpt in German translation); Robinet 1991, pp. 186–7 (excerpt). This letter was composed just three days before Leibniz's death on 14 November; it almost certainly did not reach him in time to be read.

² That is, the *Preliminary Dissertation* of Leibniz's *Theodicy*.

³ Robinet 1991, p. 187 follows GM III-2 973 in mistranscribing 'fiet' as 'fierit'.

⁴ That is, if Clarke did not altogether have to have recourse to the fortuitous collision of atoms in order to affirm, as he did, that the principle of sufficient reason does not hold in all cases, since he affirmed that it did not hold in the case of God's will itself.

160. Antonio Schinella Conti* to Isaac Newton¹

Hanover 10 December 1716

Sir

I beg your pardon if I have not been able to write until now. I have fallen ill since I have been here, and I have not yet recovered from my illness. I have seen neither the king [George I, Georg Ludwig* of Braunschweig-Lüneburg] nor the court, and I have been forced to stay indoors for the last twenty days.

Mr. Leibniz is dead, and the dispute is finished. He has left behind left many letters and many manuscripts that will be published, along with some manuscripts of other scholars, some treatise of Descartes that has not previously been published. There are some dialogues² on the articles of the *Theodicy*, an instruction to Prince Eugène* [of Savoy] about military exercises, an instruction to the czar [Peter I the Great* of Russia] for promoting the arts and sciences in his country, a lot of remarks concerning the universal language and the etymology of words. As I hope that the king will give me permission to see these papers, I will make note if there is something concerning your dispute, but perhaps they will withhold what does not do honour to the memory of Mr. Leibniz. Work has begun on his biography. Mr. [Christian] Wolff* will take care of writing what pertains to mathematics.

Mr. Leibniz has worked his entire life to invent machines that have not been successful. He wanted to make a kind of windmill for mines, a coach that hauls without horses,³ a coach that transforms into a sedan chair and a cart, even shoes with springs. There are two models of his arithmetical machine, but it is very complicated, and it is said that in the end⁴ it is only Pascal's machine enhanced.⁵

You probably saw the insolent essay that has been published in the *Acts of Leipzig* [the *Acta Eruditorum*] for the month of June.⁶ Mr. [Johann] Bernoulli* now claims he is the inventor of the integral calculus. I am certain that the essay will make you laugh.

I do not know if the Ambassador of Venice has asked you to propose to the Royal Society the Marquis of Orsi [Giovanni Giuseppe],⁷ Senator from Bologna and one of the greatest scholars that we have in Italy. He is famous in France for

un Se[i]gneur, qui a beaucoup de merite, et de talent. On dit, qu'il a refusè autrefois d'etre Cardinal. Il s'est addressè a moy pour vous prier de cette grace, et ie le fais volontier[s], car ie connois le merite,[8] et le scavoir de M. le Marquis Orsi.

Si il y aura quelque chose de nouveau touchant l'affaire de M. Leibniz, ie vous en informerai avec tout l'exactitude. Il n'y a peut-etre une person[n]e plus interessè pour votre gloire, que moy. Je n'ay[9] l'obligation, et meme l'inclination. Je suis avec tout le zele, et en vous priant de faire mes compliments a Madame votre Niece;

Monsieur

> Votre tres-umble, et tres-obeissent
> serviteur
> Conti

160. CONTI TO NEWTON   807

many books that he has written, and he is a nobleman who has a lot of merit and talent. It is said that he previously refused to be a cardinal. He turned to me to ask you for this favour, and I do it gladly, for I know the merit[8] and the knowledge of Marquis Orsi.

If there is something new concerning the matter of Mr. Leibniz, I will inform you of it with complete accuracy. There is perhaps no one more interested in your glory than I. I have the obligation and even the inclination for it.[9] I am most enthusiastically, and I pray you give my compliments to your niece [Catherine Barton][10];

sir

Your very humble, and very obedient
servant

Conti

[1] King's College Library Cambridge, Keynes MS. 140. Previously published in Brewster 1855, vol. 2, pp. 434–5; NC VI 376–8.

[2] Reading 'Dialogues' for 'Dialoghes'.

[3] Reading 'chevaux' for 'cheveaux'.

[4] Reading 'à la fin' for 'alafin'.

[5] Blaise Pascal unveiled his calculator to the public in 1645. It could add and subtract two numbers directly and perform multiplication and division by means of repeated addition or subtraction. Leibniz also designed his calculator, the stepped reckoner, which, in his own words from a letter written to Alexandre Bonneval in November 1714 (document 45 above), 'is supposed to do multiplications and divisions of very large numbers by some turns of a wheel, without any supplementary additions and subtractions, without any need to seek the quotient by dividing, so that a great number may as soon be multiplied as a small one, because everything turns at once' (p. 151) Leibniz presented a model of his calculator to the Royal Society of London in February of 1673 and, on the basis of this invention, was elected that year a Fellow of the Royal Society. However, neither the model he presented to the Royal Society, nor the subsequent models that he would commission, were entirely functional. On this topic, see Jones 2018.

[6] Conti is referring to Bernoulli's essay, 'Epistola pro Eminente Mathematico', which was actually published in the *Acta Eruditorum* for July 1716, not June as Conti reports. See *Acta Eruditorum Anno 1716*, pp. 296–315.

[7] The Italian writer Giovanni Giuseppe, Marquis Orsi (1652–1733) had studied mathematics in his youth, but later became a poet and literary critic. He was elected to the Royal Society on 30 November 1716 (OS), that is, the day after the date of Conti's letter.

[8] NC VI 377 mistranscribes 'merite' as 'meure'. Brewster 1855, p. 435 mistranscribes 'merite' as 'mœurs'.

[9] Reading 'J'en ay' for 'Je n'ay'.

[10] Catherine Barton (1679–1739) was the daughter of Robert Barton and his second wife, Hannah Smith, who was Newton's half-sister.

808   161. A NOTE BY NEWTON CONCERNING HIS DISPUTE WITH LEIBNIZ

161. A Note by Isaac Newton Concerning his Dispute with Leibniz (excerpt)[1]

[After 10 December 1716]

[...]

About November or December 1715 Mr Leibnitz in a Letter to M^r l'Abbé [Antonio Schinella] Conti* wrote a large Postscript relating to these matters,[2] railling at the Commercium Epistolicum* as attaquing his candor by false interpretations & omitting what made for him or against Mr Newton, saying that his adversaries should not have the pleasure to see him return an answer to their slender reasonings, & endeavouring to run the dispute into a squabble about universal gravity, & occult qualities & miracles & Gods being not the soul of the world but intelligentia supramundana nor having need of a sensorium, & about atoms & the nature of space & time, & about solving of mathematical Problems. All which are[3] digressions prevarications & evasions serve to no other purpose than to avoid answering the Comercium Epistolicum. [by running the dispute into a squabble about other matters.][4] [...]

---

[1] Cambridge University Library Add 3968.9, f. 98r–98v. This is an excerpt from a private note that Newton wrote after the death of Leibniz, summarizing the history of their dispute. Previously published in Koyré and Cohen 1962, p. 77 (excerpt).

[2] For this postscript, see Leibniz's to Conti of 6 December 1715 (document 88b, p. 469 ff.).

[3] Newton here failed to delete 'are'.

[4] The square brackets here are Newton's.

1717–1718

162. Dedication and Advertisement to the Reader, Clarke's 1717 edition of the Correspondence

TO HER
ROYAL HIGHNESS,
THE
PRINCESS OF *WALES*.

M A D A M,

As the following Papers were at first written by your Command, and had afterwards the Honour of being severally transmitted through Your Royal Highnesses Hands : so the Principal Encouragement upon which they Now presume to appear in Publick, is the Permission they have of coming forth under the Protection of so Illustrious a Name.

The late Learned Mr. *Leibnitz* well understood, how great an Honour and Reputation it would be to him, to have his Arguments approved by a Person of Your Royal Highnesses Character. But the same steady Impartiality and unalterable Love of Truth, the same constant Readiness to hear and to submit to Reason, always so conspicuous, always shining forth so brightly in Your Royal Highnesses Conduct ; which justly made *Him* desirous to exert in these Papers his utmost Skill in defending his Opinions ; was at the same time an Equal Encouragement to such as thought him in an Error, to endeavour to prove that his Opinions could not be defended.

The Occasion of his giving your Royal Highness the Trouble of his *First* Letter,[1] he declares to be his having entertained some Suspicions, that the Foundations of *Natural Religion* were in danger of being hurt by Sir ISAAC NEWTON's Philosophy. It appeared to Me, on the contrary, a most certain and evident Truth, that from the earliest Antiquity to This Day, the Foundations of Natural Religion had never been so deeply and so firmly laid, as in the Mathematical and Experimental Philosophy of That Great Man. And Your Royal Highnesses singular Exactness in searching after Truth, and earnest Concern for every thing that is of real Consequence to Religion, could not permit those Suspicions, which had been suggested by a Gentleman of such eminent Note in the Learned World as Mr. *Leibnitz* was, to remain unanswered.

Christianity presupposes the Truth of *Natural Religion*. Whatsoever subverts Natural Religion, does consequently much more subvert Christianity : and whatsoever tends to confirm Natural Religion, is proportionably of Service to the True Interest of the Christian. Natural Philosophy therefore, so far as it affects Religion, by determining Questions concerning *Liberty* and *Fate*, concerning the *Extent* of the *Powers of Matter and Motion*, and the *Proofs from Phenomena* of *God's Continual Government of the World* ; is of very Great Importance. 'Tis of Singular

162. DEDICATION AND ADVERTISEMENT TO THE READER

162. DEDICATION AND ADVERTISEMENT TO THE READER   815

Use, rightly to understand, and carefully to distinguish from Hypotheses or mere Suppositions, the True and Certain Consequences of Experimental and Mathematical Philosophy ; Which do, with wonderful Strength and Advantage, to All Such as are capable of apprehending them, confirm, establish, and vindicate against all Objections, those *Great and Fundamental Truths of Natural Religion*, which the Wisdom of Providence has at the same time universally implanted, in some degree, in the Minds of Persons even of the Meanest Capacities, not qualified to examine Demonstrative Proofs.

'Tis with the highest Pleasure and Satisfaction, that the following Papers upon so important a Subject, are laid before a Princess, who, to an inimitable Sweetness of Temper, Candour and Affability towards All, has joined not only an Impartial Love of Truth, and a Desire of promoting Learning in general, but has Herself also attained to a Degree of Knowledge very Particular and Uncommon, even in matters of the nicest and most abstract Speculation : And whose Sacred and always Unshaken Regard to the Interest of sincere and uncorrupt Religion, made Her the Delight of all Good Protestants Abroad, and by a just Fame filled the Hearts of all true *Britons* at Home, with an Expectation beforehand, which, Great as it was, is fully answered by what they now see and are blessed with.

By the Protestant Succession in the Illustrious House of *HANOVER* having taken place, This Nation has Now, with the Blessing of God, a Certain Prospect, (if our Own Vices and Follies prevent not,) of seeing Government actually administered, according to the Design and End for which it was instituted by Providence, with no other View than that of the Publick Good, the general Welfare and Happiness of Mankind. We have a Prospect of seeing the True Liberty of a Brave and Loyal People, firmly secured, established, and regulated, by Laws equally advantageous both to the Crown and Subject : Of seeing Learning and Knowledge encouraged and promoted, in opposition to all kinds of Ignorance and Blindness : And, (which is the Glory of All,) of seeing the True Christian Temper and Spirit of Religion effectually prevail, both against Atheism and Infidelity on the one hand, which take off from Men All Obligations of doing what is Right ; and against Superstition and Bigottry on the other hand, which lay upon men the strongest Obligations to do the greatest Wrongs.

What Views and Expectations less than these, can a Nation reasonably entertain ; when it beholds a KING [George I, Georg Ludwig* of Braunschweig-Lüneburg] firmly settled upon the Throne of a wisely limited Monarchy, whose Will, when without Limitation, showed always a greater Love of Justice, than of Power ; and never took Pleasure in acting any otherwise, than according to the most perfect Laws of Reason and Equity? When it sees a Succession of the same Blessings continued, in a PRINCE [Georg August* of Braunschweig-Lüneburg, Prince of Wales], whose Noble Openness of Mind, and Generous Warmth of Zeal for the Preservation of the Protestant Religion, and the Laws and Liberties of these Kingdoms, make him every day more and more beloved, as he is more known? And when these glorious Hopes open still further into an unbounded Prospect in a

A VERTISSEMENT.

On prie les Lecteurs de remarquer :

1. *QUE les Ecrits suivans ont été imprimez conformément aux Originaux, sans ajourter, retrancher, ou changer un seul mot. On n'a ajouté que les* Notes marginales *&* l'Appendice.

2. *Que la Traduction est fort exacte, & qu'elle represente le véritable sens de* Mr. Leibnitz.

3. *Que les* Nombres *ou les Sections de chaque Ecrit de* Mr. *Clarke, se rapportent aux* Nombres *ou aux Sections de chaque Ecrit de* Mr. *Leibnitz, qui précede immédiatement.*

162. DEDICATION AND ADVERTISEMENT TO THE READER 817

numerous Royal Offspring? Through whom, that the Just and Equitable Temper of the Grandfather ; the Noble Zeal and Spirit of the Father ; the Affability, Goodness, and Judicious Exactness of the Mother ; may, with Glory to Themselves, and with the happiest Influences both upon These and Foreign Countries, descend to all succeeding Generations ; to the Establishment of Universal Peace, of Truth and Right amongst Men ; and to the entire rooting out That *Greatest Enemy* of Christian Religion, the *Spirit of Popery* both among *Romanists* and *Protestants* : And that Your *Royal Highness* may your Self long live, to continue a Blessing to these Nations, to see Truth and Virtue flourish in your own Days, and to be a Great Instrument, under the direction of Providence, in laying a Foundation for the Highest Happiness of the Publick in Times to come ; is the Prayer of,

MADAM,
Your ROYAL HIGNESSES
   most Humble and
    most Obedient Servant,
    SAM. CLARKE.

Advertisement to the R E A D E R.

The Reader will be pleased to observe,

1. THAT the following Letters are all printed exactly as they were written ; without adding, diminishing, or altering a *Word*. The *Marginal Notes* only, and the *Appendix*, being added.

2. That the Translation is made with Great Exactness, to prevent any Misrepresentation of Mr. *Leibnitz's* Sense.

3. That the *Numbers* or §'s in Each of Dr. *Clarke's* Papers, refer respectively to the *Numbers* or §'s of each of Mr. *Leibnitz's* Papers immediately fore-going.

---

[1] See documents 85 and 86.

818   163. CLARKE'S APPENDIX TO 1717 EDITION OF THE CORRESPONDENCE

Clarke's Appendix to his 1717 edition of the Correspondence

A P P E N D I C E,

O U

Recueil de Passages, tirez des Ouvrages imprimez de Mr. LEIBNITZ; *qui peuvent servir à éclaircir plusieurs Endroits des Ecrits précédens.*

N° 1.

[Cl.I.4, Lz.II.10, Lz.II.12, Cl.II.10, Lz.III.15][1]

DIEU selon nous est Intelligentia Extramundana, *comme* Martianus Capella *l'appelle ; ou plûtôt* Supramundana. Thedoicée, pag. 396.[2]

N° 2.

[Lz.I.4, Lz. II.1, Cl.II.9, Lz.V.87, Lz.V.91, Cl.V.83–91]

Il faut savoir qu'une spontaneïté *exacte nous est commune avec* toutes les substances simples; *& que dans la substance intelligente ou libre, elle devient un Empire sur ses actions.*—— *Naturellement* chaque substance simple *a de la* perception, *&c.* Theodicée pag. 479.[3]

Sed vis activa Actum quendam sive ἐντελέχειαν *continet, atque inter facultatem agendi actionemque ipsam media est, & conatum involvit, atque ita per se ipsam in* operationem fertur ; *nec auxiliis indiget, sed sola sublatione impedimenti. Quod Exemplis, Gravis suspensi funem sustinentem intendentis, aut Arcûs tensi, illustrari potest. Etsi enim gravitas aut vis elastica mechanicè explicari possint debeantque ex ætheris motu; ultima tamen* ratio motûs *in materia, est* vis in creatione impressa ; *quæ in unoquoque corpore inest, sed ipso conflictu corporum variè in natura limitatur & coercetur. Et hanc* agendi *virtutem omni substantiæ inesse aio, semperque aliquam ex ea actionem nasci ; adeoque nec ipsam substantiam Corpoream, (non magis quam spiritualem) ab* agendo *cessare unquam. Quod illi non satis percepisse videntur, qui Essentiam ejus in sola* extensione, *vel etiam* impenetrabilitate *collocaverunt, & corpus omnimodè quiescens concipere sibi sunt visi. Apparebit etiam ex nostris meditationibus, substantiam creatam ab alia substantia creata non ipsam* vim agendi, *sed* præexistentis jam nisûs sui, sive virtutis agendi, *limites tantummodo ac determinationem accipere.* Acta Erudit. Ann. 1694, pag. 112.[4]

Agere, *est character substantiarum.* Ibid. ad Ann. 1695. Pag. 145.[5]

Quæ [vis activa primitiva][6] *in omni substantiâ corporea per se inest ; cùm corpus omnimodè quiescens à rerum natura abhorrere arbiter.* Ibid. pag. 146.[7]

Ob formam, corpus omne *semper* agere. Ibid. pag. 147.[8]

163. Clarke's Appendix to his 1717 edition of the Correspondence

THE
APPENDIX.

BEING

A Collection of Passages out of Mr. L E I B N I T Z ' S *Printed Works, which may give some Light to many Parts of the fore-going Papers.*

N° 1.

[Cl.I.4, Lz.II.10, Lz.II.12, Cl.II.10, Lz.III.15][1]

God, according to My opinion, is an *Extramundane Intelligence,* as *Martianus Capella* stiles him ; or rather, a *Supramundane Intelligence. Theodicæa,* pag. 396.[2]

N° 2.

[Lz.I.4, Lz.II.1, Cl.II.9, Lz.V.87, Lz.V.91, Cl.V.83–91]

We must know, that a *Spontaneity* strictly speaking, is common to Us with *All simple Substances* ; and that This, in an Intelligent or Free Substance, amounts to a Dominion over its own Actions. —— Naturally, *every simple Substance* has *Perception,* &c. *Theodic. pag.* 479.[3]

But Active Force contains a certain Act or Efficacy, and is something of a middle nature between the Faculty of acting and Action itself : It involves a *Conatus* or Indeavour, and is of itself carried towards Action ; and stands in need of no Helps, but only that the Impediment be taken away. This may be illustrated by the Examples of a Heavy Body stretching the string it is hung by, and of a Bow bent. For though Gravity or Elasticity may and ought to be explained mechanically by the Motion of *Æther* ; yet the ultimate *Cause of Motion* in Matter, is a *Force impressed at the Creation* : Which is in *every part of matter,* but, according to the course of nature, is variously limited and restrained by Bodies striking against each other. And this *active Faculty* I affirm to be in *All Substance,* and that some action is always arising from it : So that not even *corporeal Substance,* any more than *Spiritual,* ever ceases *acting.* Which seems not to have been apprehended by Those, who have placed the Essence of Matter in *Extension* alone, or even in *Impenetrability* ; and fancied they could conceive a Body absolutely at Rest. It will appear also from what I have advanced, that One created Substance does not receive from Another the active Force it self, but only the Limits and Determination of the *Indeavour* or *Active Faculty* already pre-existing in it. *Acta Erud. Ann.* 1694, *Pag.* 112.[4]

To *Act,* is the Characteristick of Substances. *Ibid. ad Ann.* 1695, *Pag.* 145.[5]

Which *primitive active Power,* is of it self in *All corporeal Substance* : For, I think, a Body absolutely at Rest is inconsistent with the Nature of Things. *Ibid. Pag.* 146.[7]

Every *Part of Matter* is, by its *Form,* continually *Acting.* Ibid. Pag. 147.[8]

820   163. CLARKE'S APPENDIX TO 1717 EDITION OF THE CORRESPONDENCE

Potentiæ scilicet actricis *in formâ*, & *ignaviæ seu ad motum resistentiæ in materiâ.* Ibid. pag. 151.[9]

Etsi principium activum *materialibus notionibus superius & (ut sic dicam)* vitale, *ubique* in coporibus *admittam.* Ibid. pag. 153.[10]

Alibi à me explicatum est, etsi nondum fortasse satis perspectum omnibus ; ipsam *rerum* substantiam *in* agendi patiendique vi *consistere.* Ibid. ad Ann. 1698, Pag. 432.[11]

Ita ut non tantum omne quod agit, sit *Substantia singularis, sed etiam ut* omnis *singularis Substantiæ* agat *sine intermissione* ; corpore ipso *non excepto, in quo nulla unquam quies absoluta reperitur.* Ibid.[12]

Quod si vero menti nostræ vim insitam tribuimus, actiones immanentes producendi, vel, quod idem est, agendi immanenter ; *jam nihil prohibet, imò consentaneum est, aliis animabus vel* formis, *aut, si mavis,* naturis Substantiarum *eandem vim inesse* ; *Nisi quis* solas *in naturâ rerum nobis obviâ* Mentes *nostras* activas *esse* ; *aut omnem vim* agendi *immanenter, atque adeo vitaliter, ut sic dicam, eum intellectu esse conjunctam arbitretur : Quales certè Asseverationes neque ratione ulla confirmantur, nec nisi invitâ veritate propugnantur.* Ibid. Pag. 433.[13]

Hinc judicari potest, debere in corporea Substantia *reperiri entelechiam primam, tanquam* πρῶτον δεκτικὸν activitatis ; vim scilicet *motricem primitivam, quæ præter extensionem (seu id quod est merè Geometricum) & præter molem (seu id quod est mere materiale) superaddita, semper quidem* agit, *sed tamen variè ex corporum concursibus per conatus impetusve modificatur. Atque hoc ipsum* Substantiale principium *est, quod in viventibus* anima, *in aliis* forma Substantialis *appellatur.* Ibid. Pag. 434.[14]

Primam [materiam][15] *esse merè passivam, sed non esse completam Substantiam* ; *accedereque adeò debere* animam *vel* formam Animæ analogam, *sive* ἐντελέχειαν τὴν πρώτην, id est, nisum *quendam seu* vim agendi primitivam, *quæ ipsa est Lex insita, decreto divino impressa. A quâ sententiâ non puto abhorrere Virum celebrem & ingeniosum, qui nuper defendit,* Corpus *constare ex* Materia & Spirtu, *modò sumatur* Spiritus *non pro* re intelligente *(ut alias solet,) sed pro* Anima *vel* forma Animæ analoga ; *nec pro simplici* modificatione, *sed pro* constitutivo Substantiali perseverante, *quod* Monadis *nomine appellare soleo, in quo est velut* Perceptio & appetitus. *Ibid. Pag.* 435.[16]

Contrà potius arbitror, neque ordini neque pulchritudini rationive rerum esse consentaneum, ut vitale aliquid, *seu immanenter agens, sit in* exigua *tantum* parte materiæ ; *cùm ad majorem perfectionem pertineat, ut sit in* omni ; *neq; quicquam obstet, quo minus* ubiq; *sint* Animæ, *aut* analoga *saltem* Animabus ; *etsi* dominantes Animæ, *atque adeo* intelligentes, *quales sunt* humanæ *ubique esse non possint.* Ibid. Pag. 436.[17]

163. CLARKE'S APPENDIX TO 1717 EDITION OF THE CORRESPONDENCE 821

The *Active Power*, which is in the *Form* ; and the *inertia*, or repugnance to Motion, which is in the *Matter*. Ibid. Pag. 151.[9]

Though I admit every where in *Bodies*, a Principle superior to the [common] Notion of Matter ; a Principle *Active*, and (if I may so speak,) *Vital. Ibid. Pag.* 153.[10]

I have elsewhere explained, though it is a Thing perhaps not yet well understood by All ; that the *very Substance* of Things, *consists* in the Power of *Acting* and *being Acted upon.* Ibid. *ad Ann.* 1698. *Pag.* 432.[11]

So that, not only *every Thing which acts,* is a *single Substance* ; but also *every single Substance* does perpetually *act* : Not excepting even *Matter* it self ; in which there never is any Absolute Rest. *Ibid.*[12]

If we ascribe to *our own Minds* an intrinsick Power of producing immanent Actions, or (which is the same Thing) of Acting immanently : 'Tis no way unreasonable, nay 'tis very reasonable, to allow that there is the same Power in *other Souls* or *Forms,* or (if that be a better Expression,) in the *Natures* of *Substances.* Unless a Man will imagine, that, in the whole Extent of Nature within the compass of our Knowledge, *our own Minds* are the *only* Things endued with *Active Powers* ; or that All Power of *acting immanently* and *vitally* (if I may so speak,) is connected with Understanding. Which Kind of Assertions, certainly, are neither founded on any Reason ; nor can be maintained, but in opposition to Truth. *Ibid. Pag.* 433.[13]

Hence we may gather, that there must needs be in *corporeal Substance* an original Efficacy, or (as it were) prime Recipient of *Active Force :* That is, there must be in it a *primitive Motive Power :* Which being added over and above the Extension (or that which is merely geometrical,) and over and above the Bulk (or that which is merely material ;) *acts* indeed continually, but yet is variously modified by the *Conatus's* and *Impetus's* of Bodies striking against each other. And This is *That Substantial Principle,* which, in *Living Substances,* is stiled *Soul* ; in *Others,* the *Substantial Form.* Ibid. Pag. 434.[14]

The *materia prima* is indeed merely passive, but 'tis not a complete Substance. To make it complete Substance, there must be moreover a *Soul,* or a *Form analogous to Soul,* or *an original Efficacy,* that is, a certain *Indeavour,* or *Primitive Power of Acting* ; which is an innate Law, impressed by the Decree of God. Which Opinion I think is not different from that of an Eminent and Ingenious Gentleman, who has lately maintained, that *Body* consists of *Matter* and *Spirit* ; meaning by the word *Spirit,* not (as usually) an *intelligent thing,* but a *Soul* or *Form analogous to Soul* ; not a *simple Modification,* but a *substantial Permanent Constituent,* which I used to call a *Monad,* in which is, as it were, *Perception* and *Desire. Ibid. pag.* 435.[16]

On the contrary, I am rather of opinion, that 'tis neither agreeable to the Order, nor Beauty, nor Reason of things, that there should be a *Vital Principle* or *Power of acting immanently,* only in a *very small part of Matter* ; when it would be an argument of greater Perfection, for it to be in *All matter* ; and nothing hinders but that there may *Everywhere* be *Souls,* or at least *Something analogous to Souls* ; though *Souls indued with Dominion and Understanding,* such as are *Humane Souls,* cannot be Everywhere. Ibid. pag. 436.[17]

Cum id quod non agit, *quod vi* activa *caret, quod discriminibilitate, quod denique omni subsistendi ratione ac fundamento spoliatur*; substantia *esse nullo modo possit.* Ibid. Pag. 439.[18]

Voïez cy-dessous, No 11.

N° 3.

[Lz.II.1, Cl.VI.1–2, Lz.V.3, Lz.V.14]

Il [Monsieur Bayle][19] *fait voir assès amplement* (Rep. au Provincial, ch. 139, p. 748, seqq.) *qu'on peut comparer l'ame à une* Balance, *où les Raisons & les Inclinations tiennent lieu de poids ; & selon luy, on peut expliquer ce qui se passe dans nos resolutions, par l'Hypothese, que la volonté de l'Homme est comme une* Balance, *qui se tient en repos, quand les poids de ses deux bassins sont égaux ; & qui panche toûjours où d'un coté ou de l'autre, selon que l'un des bassins est plus chargé. Une nouvelle Raison fait un* poids *superieur ; une nouvelle Idée rayonne plus vivement que la vieille ; la crainte d'une grosse peine, l'emporte sur quelque plaisir ; quand deux passions se disputent le terrein, c'est toûjours la plus forte qui demeure la Maitresse, à moins que l'autre ne soit aidée par la Raison, ou par quelque autre passion combinée.* Theodicée, Pag. 514.[20]

L'on a d'autant plus de peine à se determiner, que les Raisons opposées approchent plus de l'égalité ; comme l'on voit que la Balance *se determine plus promtement, lors qu'il y a une grande difference entre les poids. Cependent ; comme bien souvent il y a plusieurs partis à prendre, on pourrait, au lieu de la* Balance, *comparer l'ame avec une force, qui fait effort en même tems de* plusieurs *cotés, mais qui n'agit que là où elle trouve le plus de facilité, ou le moins de resistance. Par Exemple, l'air étant comprimé trop fortement dans un Recipient de verre, le cassera pour sortir. Il fait effort sur chaque partie, mais il se jette enfin sur la plus foible. C'est ainsi que les* Inclinations *de l'ame vont sur tous les biens qui se presentent ; ce sont des volontés antecedentes ; mais la volonté consequente, qui en est le resultat, se determine vers ce qui touche le plus.* Thedoicée, Pag. 515.[21]

Voïez cy-dessous, No 4 & 9.

N° 4.

[Cl.II.1, Lz.III.5, Cl.III.7–8, Lz.IV.3, Lz.IV.19,
Cl.IV.1–2, Cl.IV.3–4, Cl.IV.19, Lz.V.69, Cl.V.1–20]

Il n'y a jamais d' indifference d'équilibre, *c'est à dire, où tout soit parfaitement égal de part & d'autre, sans qu'il y ait plus d'Inclination vers un côté.* Theodicée, Pag. 158.[22]

163. CLARKE'S APPENDIX TO 1717 EDITION OF THE CORRESPONDENCE 823

What doth not *act*, what wants *Active Power*, what is void of Discernibility, what wants the whole ground and foundation of Subsistence ; can no way be a *Substance*. *Ibid. pag.* 439.[18]

See below, Nº 11.

Nº 3.

[Lz.II.1, Cl.VI.1–2, Lz.V.3, Lz.V.14]

Mr. *Bayle* has shown at large (in his *Answer to a Provincial, ch.* 139, *p.* 748 *&c.*) that a Mans *Soul* may be compared to a *Balance*, wherein Reasons and Inclinations are in the place of Weights : And, according to Him, the manner of our forming our resolutions may be explained by This Hypothesis, that the *Will of Man* is like a *Balance*, which stands always unmoved when the Weights in Both Scales are equal, and always turns on one side or the other, in proportion as One Scale has more Weight in it than the Other. A *New Reason*, makes an Overpoise of *Weight*. A new Idea strikes the Mind more vigorously than a foregoing one. The Fear of a Great Pain, determines more strongly than the expectation of a Pleasure. When Two Passions contend against each other, the stronger always remains Master of the Field, unless the Other be assisted either by Reason or by some other passion conspiring with it. *Theodic. pag.* 514.[20]

A Man has always so much the more difficulty of determining himself, as the opposite Reasons draw nearer to an equality : Just as we see a *Balance* turn so much the more readily, as the Weights in each scale are more different from one another. However, since there are often more than two ways which a Man may take ; we may therefore, instead of This similitude of a *Balance*, compare the Soul to a *Force*, which has at one and the same time a *Tendency many ways*, but *acts on That part only* where it finds the Greatest Ease, or the Least Resistence. For example: Air strongly compressed in a Glass-Receiver, will break the Glass to get out. It presses upon every part, but at last makes its way where the Glass is weakest. Thus the *Inclinations of the Soul,* tend towards All apparent Goods ; And these are the antecedent Volitions : But the Consequent Volition, which is the last Result, determines itself towards That Good which affects us the most strongly. *Ibid. pag.* 515.[21]

See below, Nº 4 and 9.

Nº 4.

[Cl.II.1, Lz.III.5, Cl.III.7–8, Lz.IV.3, Lz.IV.19,
Cl.IV.1–2, Cl.IV.3–4, Cl.IV.19, Lz.V.69, Cl.V.1–20]

There is never any such thing as an *Indifference in æquilibrio* ; that is, such an one, where every circumstance is perfectly equal on Both sides, so that there is no inclination to one side rather than the other. *Theodicæa, pag.* 158.[22]

Il est vray, *si le cas* [de l'âne entre deux préz, également porté à l'un & à l'autre,][23] *étoit possible, qu'il faudroit dire qu'il se laisseroit* mourir de faim : *Mais dans le fond la Question est sur l'impossible, à moins que Dieu ne produise la chose exprés.* Ibid. Pag, 161.[24]

Voïez ci-dessus, N° 3 ; & ci-dessous, N° 9.

N° 5.

[Lz.II.4, Lz.II.5, Lz.IV.31, Cl.IV.31, Lz.V.83,
Lz.V.87, Lz.V.92, Cl.V.33–9, Cl.V.110–116]

—— *C'est une suite du Système de l'Harmonie préétablie, dont il est necessaire de donner quelque explication icy. Les Philosophes de l'Ecole croyoient, qu'il y avoit une* influence physique reciproque *entre le* corps *& l'ame : Mais depuis qu'on a bien consideré que la pensée & la masse étendue n'ont aucune liaison ensemble, & que ce sont des creatures qui different* toto genere *; plusieurs modernes ont reconnu, qu'il n'y a* aucune communication physique *entre l'ame & le* corps, *quoique la communication Metaphysique subsiste toujours, qui fait que l'ame & le corps composent un même suppost, ou ce qu'on appelle une personne. Cette communication physique, s'il y en avoit, feroit que l'ame changeroit le degré de la vitesse & la ligne de direction de quelques mouvemens qui sont dans le* corps *; & que, vice versa, le* corps *changeroit la suite des pensées qui sont dans l'ame. Mais on ne sauroit tirer cet effet d'aucune notion qu'on conçoive dans le corps, & dans l'ame ; quoique rien ne nous soit mieux connu que l'ame, puisqu'elle nous est intime, c'est à dire intime à elle même.* Theodicée, pag. 172.[25]

Je ne pouvois manquer de venir à ce système, qui porte que Dieu a créé l'ame d'abord de telle façon, qu'elle doit se produire & se representer par ordre ce qui se passe dans le corps ; & le corps aussi de telle façon, qu'il doit faire de soi même ce que l'ame ordonne. De sorte que les loix, qui lient les pensées de l'ame dans l'ordre des causes finales, & suivant l'évolution des perceptions, doivent produire des images qui se rencontrent *& s'accordent avec les impressions des corps sur nos organes ; & que les loix des mouvemens dans le* corps, *qui s'entresuivent dans l'ordre des causes efficientes, se* rencontrent *aussi & s'accordent tellement avec les pensées de l'ame, que le corps est porté à agir dans le tems que l'ame le veut.* Ibid. Pag. 176.[26]

Monsieur Jaquelot *a trés bien montré dans son Livre de la conformité de la Raison & de la Foy, que c'est comme si celui qui sait tout ce que j'ordonnerai à un valet le lendemain tout le long du jour, faisoit un* Automate *qui ressemblât parfaitement à ce* valet, *& qui executât demain à point nommé, tout ce que j'ordonnerois ; Ce qui ne m'empecheroit pas d'ordonner librement tout ce qui me plairoit, quoique l'action de l'Automate qui me serviroit, ne tiendroit rien du libre.* Ibid. pag. 176.[28]

Le vray moyen, par lequel Dieu fait que l'ame a des sentimens de ce qui se passe dans le corps, vient de la nature de l'ame, qui est representative des corps, *& faite en*

163. CLARKE'S APPENDIX TO 1717 EDITION OF THE CORRESPONDENCE   825

'Tis *True*, if the Case [*of the Ass standing between Two green Fields, and equally liking Both of them*][23] was possible, we *must say* he would suffer himself to be *starved to Death*. But at the bottom, the Case is impossible to happen ; unless God should order circumstances so on Purpose. *Ibid. Pag.* 161.[24]

See *above*, N° 3 ; and below, N° 9.

N° 5.

[Lz.II.4, Lz.II.5, Lz.IV.31, Cl.IV.31, Lz.V.83,
Lz.V.87, Lz.V.92, Cl.V.33–9, Cl.V.110–116]

This is a Consequence of my System of a *pre-established Harmony* ; which it may be necessary here to give some Account of. The Scholastick Philosophers were of Opinion, that the *Soul and Body mutually affected each other by a Natural Influence :* But since it has been well considered, that * *Thought* and *extended Substance* have no Connexion with each other, and are *Beings* that differ *toto genere* ; many modern Philosophers have acknowledged, that *there is no physical Communication* between the *Soul* and the *Body*, though *a Metaphysical Communication* there always is, by means of which the Soul and the Body make up *one Suppositum*, or what we call a *Person*. If there was any *physical Communication* between them, then the *Soul* could change the Degree of Swiftness, and the Line of Direction of certain Motions in the *Body* ; and, on the other side, the *Body* could cause a Change in the Series of Thoughts which are in the *Soul*. But now such an Effect as this, cannot be deduced from the Notion of any thing we can conceive in the Body and Soul ; though nothing be better known to us † than the Soul, because 'tis intimate to Us, that is, to itself. *Theodicæa, Pag.* 172.[25]

I cannot help coming into this Notion, that God created the *Soul* in such manner at first, as that it *produces within it self*, and *represents in it self* successively, what passes in the *Body* ; and that he has made the *Body also* in such a manner, as that it *must of it self* do what the Soul wills. So that the Laws which make the Thoughts of the Soul *follow each other* successively in the Order of final Causes, and in the Order of its Perceptions arising within it self ; *must* produce Images, which shall be *coincident*, and *go Hand in Hand* with the Impressions made by Bodies upon our Organs of Sense : And the Laws by which the Motions of the Body *follow each other* successively in the Order of efficient Causes, are likewise *coincident* and *go Hand in Hand* with the Thoughts of the Soul, in such manner as that these Laws of Motion make the Body act at *the same Time* that the Soul Wills. *Ibid. Pag.* 176.[26]

Mr. *Jaquelot*[27] has very well shown, in his Book concerning the *Agreement of Reason and Faith*, that this is just as if One who knew before-hand every particular

---

* The Thinking Substance, *he should have said : For* Thought, *or the* Act of Thinking, *is not a Substance.*

† Note. *As the* Eye *sees not* itself ; *and if a Man had never seen* Another's *Eye, nor the* Image *of his own in a* Glass, *he could never have had any Notion what an* Eye *is: So the* Soul *discerns not its* own Substance.

sorte par avance, que les representations, qui naîtront en elle les unes des autres *par une suite naturelle de pensées, répondent au changement des corps.* Ibid. Pag. 550.[29]

Voïez cy-dessus, N° 2 ; & cy-dessous N° 11.

N° 6.

[Lz.II.12]

Et de même, si Dieu vouloit que les organes des corps *humains se conformassent avec les volontés de l'*ame, *suivant le système des* causes occasionelles ; *cette loy ne s'executeroit aussi, que par des* miracles perpetuels. Theodicée, Pag. 383.[30]

Voiez cy-cessous, N° 8.

N° 7.

[Cl.V.99 Footnote]

Imò potius materiam resistere motui, *per quandam suam* inertiam naturalem, à Keplero *pluchrè sic denominatam ; ita ut non sit* indifferens ad motum & quietam, *uti vulgò rem æstimare solent ; sed ad* motum, *pro magnitudine suâ, vi tanto majore activâ indigeat.* Acta Erudit. Ad Ann. 1698. Pag. 434.[31]

Inertiam naturalem, oppositam motui. *Ibid.*[32]

Ignavia *quadam, ut sic dicam ; id est,* ad Motum repugnatione. Acta ad Ann. 1695, Pag. 147.[33]

Ignaviæ, *seu ad Motum resistentiæ, in materiâ.* Ibid. Pag. 151.[34]

Les Experiences aussi du choc des corps, jointes à la raison, font voir qu'il faut employer deux fois plus de force pour donner une même vitesse à un corps de la même matiere, mais deux fois plus grand : Ce qui ne seroit point necessaire, si la matiere étoit absolument indifferente au repos & au mouvement, *& si elle n'avoit pas cette* inertie naturelle, *dont nous venons de parler, qui lui donne une espece de* repugnance à être mûe. Theodicée. Pag. 142.[35]

163. CLARKE'S APPENDIX TO 1717 EDITION OF THE CORRESPONDENCE 827

thing that I should order my Footman to do to Morrow all the Day long, should make a *Machine* to resemble my Footman exactly, and punctually to perform all Day to Morrow every Thing I directed, Which would not at all hinder my freely ordering whatever I pleased, though the Actions of my *Machine-Footman* had no Liberty at all. *Ibid. Pag.* 176.[28]

The true Means by which God causes the Soul to have a Perception of what passes in the Body, is This ; that he has made the *Nature of the Soul* to be *Representative* of Bodies, and to be before-hand so constituted, as that the *Representations* which shall arise in it, one following another according to the natural Succession of Thoughts shall be *coincident with* such Change as happens in Bodies. *Ibid, Pag.* 550.[29]

See *above*, N⁰ 2; and *below*, N⁰ 11.

N⁰ 6.

[Lz.II.12]

In like manner, should it be the Will of God, that the Organs of human *Bodies* should move conformably to the Volitions of the *Soul*, considering those Volitions as *occasional Causes* ; such a Law could not be put in Execution, but by perpetual *Miracles. Theodicæa, Pag.* 383.[30]

See *below*, N⁰ 8.

N⁰ 7.

[Cl.V.99 Footnote]

Nay rather, Matter *resists Motion*, by a certain natural *Inertia*, very properly so stiled by *Kepler* : So that Matter is not *indifferent to Motion and Rest*, as is vulgarly supposed ; but needs a greater active Force, in proportion to the Magnitude of the Body, to put it in *Motion. Acta Erudit. ad Ann* 1698, *Pag.* 434.[31]

A Natural *Inertia*, repugnant to *Motion. Ibid.*[32]

A certain *Sluggishness*, if I may so speak, that is, a repugnancy to *Motion. Acta Erudit. ad Ann.* 1695, *Pag.* 147.[33]

A *Sluggishness*, or Resistence to *Motion*, in Matter. *Ibid. Pag.* 151.[34]

The *Experiments* of Bodies striking against each other, as well as *Reason*, show that twice as much Force is required to give the same Velocity * to a Body of the same Kind of Matter, double in Bigness. Which would not be needful if Matter was absolutely *indifferent to Rest and Motion*, and had not that natural *Inertia* I spoke of, which gives it a sort of Repugnancy to *Motion. Theodicæa*, Pag. 142.[35]

---

* Note. *The Author did not consider, that twice as much force is requisite* likewise *to stop the same Velocity in a Body of the same Kind of Matter, double in Bigness.*

*Il semble, en considerant l'*indifference de la matiere au mouvement & au repos, *que le plus grand corps en repos pourroit être emporté sans aucunce resistance par le moindre corps qui seroit en mouvement ; au quel cas il y auroit action sans reaction, & un effet plus grand que sa cause.* Ibid. Pag. 538.[36]

N° 8.

[Lz.III.17, Lz.V.113]

C'est pourquoy, si Dieu faisoit une loy generale, qui portât que les corps s'attiras-sent les uns les autres ; il n'en sauroit obtenir l'execution, que par des miracles *perpe-tuels.* Theodicée, Pag. 382.[37]

Voiez cy-dessus, N° 6.

N° 9.

[Lz.IV.3, Lz.IV.19, Cl.IV.3–4, Cl.IV.19]

On peut dire de même en matiere de parfaite sagesse, qui n'est pas moins reglée que les Mathematiques ; que s'il n'y avoit pas le Meilleur (Optimum) parmi tous les mondes possibles, Dieu n'en auroit produit aucun. Theodicée, pag. 116.[38]

Voiez cy-dessus, N° 4 & 3.

N° 10.

[Lz.IV.13, Cl.IV.13, Lz.V.29, Lz.V.52, Cl.V.26–32]

Si fingeremus duas sphæras concentricas perfectas, & perfectè tam inter se quàm in partibus suis similares, alteram alteri ita inclusam esse, ut nec minimus sit hiatus ; tunc, sive volvi inclusam, sive quiescere ponamus, ne Angelus quidem, ne quid amp-lius dicam, ullum poterit notare discrimen inter diversi temporis status, aut indicium habere discernendi utrum quiescat an volvatur inclusa sphæra, & quâ motûs lege. Acta Erudit. ad Ann. 1698, pag. 437.[39]

N° 11.

Lz.IV.30, Cl.IV.30, Lz.V.87, Lz.V.91, Cl.V.63–91]

J'y [dans le systeme de l'Harmonie préétablie][40] *fais voir, que naturellement* chaque substance simple *a de la* perception, *& que son individualité consiste dans la loy perpetuelle qui fait la suite des perceptions qui lui sont affectées, & qui naissent naturellement les unes des autres pour* representer *le* corps *qui lui est assigné, & par son moyen* l'Univers entier, *suivant* le point de veue *propre à cette substance simple, sans qu'elle ait besoin de recevoir aucune* influence physique *du* Corps : *Comme le*

163. CLARKE'S APPENDIX TO 1717 EDITION OF THE CORRESPONDENCE 829

It might be expected, supposing Matter *indifferent to Motion and Rest*, that the largest Body at Rest, might be carried away without any Resistence, by the least Body in Motion. In which Case, there would be Action without Reaction, and an Effect greater than its Cause. *Ibid. Pag.* 358.[36]

N° 8.

[Lz.III.17, Lz.V.113]
Wherefore if God made a general Law, that Bodies should Attract each other ; it could not be put in Execution, but by perpetual *Miracles. Theodicæa, Pag.* 382.[37]
See *above*, N° 6.

N° 9.

[Lz.IV.3, Lz.IV.19, Cl.IV.3–4, Cl.IV.19]
The same may be said concerning perfect Wisdom, (which is no less regular than Mathematicks ;) that if there was not a *Best* among all the Worlds that were possible to have been made, God would not have made *Any at all. Theodicæa, Pag.* 116.[38]
See *above*, N° 4, *and* 3.

N° 10.

[Lz.IV.13, Cl.IV.13, Lz.V.29, Lz.V.52, Cl.V.26–32]
If we imagine two perfect Spheres concentrical, and perfectly similar both in the Whole and in every Part, to be inclosed one in the other, so as that there shall not be the least Interstice between them ; then, whether the inclosed Sphere be supposed to revolve, or to continue at Rest ; an Angel himself (not to say more) could discover no difference between the State of these Globes at different Times, nor find Any Way of discerning whether the inclosed Globe continued at Rest, or turned about ; or with what Law of Motion it turned. *Acta Erudit. ad Ann.* 1698. *Pag.* 437.[39]

N° 11.

[Lz.IV.30, Cl.IV.30, Lz.V.87, Lz.V.91, Cl.V.63–91]
In my Doctrine of a *pre-established Harmony*, I show, that *every single Substance* is naturally indued with *Perception* ; and that its Individuality consists in that perpetual Law, which causes its appointed Succession of Perceptions, arising naturally in order one from another, so as to *represent* to it *its own Body*, and, by the same Means, the *Whole Universe*, according to the *Point of View* proper to that

163. CLARKE'S APPENDIX TO 1717 EDITION OF THE CORRESPONDENCE

Corps *aussi de son côté, s'accommode aux volontés de l'ame par* ses propres loix, *&* *par consequent ne lui obéït, qu'autant que* ces loix *le portent.* Theodicée, pag. 479.[41]

Aussi faut-il avouer, que chaque ame se represente l'Univers *suivant son point de* vûe, *& par un rapport qui luy est propre; mais une parfaite harmonie y subsiste toû- jours.* Ibid. Pag. 552.[42]

L'operation des Automates *spirituels, c'est à dire des Ames, n'est point mecanique ; mais elle contient éminemment ce qu'il y a de beau dans la Mecanique ; les mouve- mens, developpés dans les corps, y étant concentrés par la* representation, *comme dans un monde Ideal, qui exprime les loix du monde actuel & leurs suites ; avec cette difference du monde ideal parfait qui est en Dieu, que la plûplart des perceptions dans les autres ne sont que confuses. Car il faut savoir que* toute Substance simple *envel- oppe* l'Univers *par ses perceptions confuses ou sentimens, & que la suite des ces per- ceptions est reglée par la nature particuliere de cette substance ; mais d'une maniere qui exprime toûjours* toute la nature universelle : *& toute perception presente, tend à une perception nouvelle, comme tout mouvement qu'elle represente, tend à un autre mouvement. Mais il est impossible que l'ame puisse connoitre distinctement toute sa nature, & s'appercevoir comment ce nombre innombrable de petites perceptions entassées, ou plûtôt concentrées ensemble, s'y forme : Il faudroit pour cela qu'elle con- nût parfaitement tout l'Univers qui y est enveloppé, c'est à dire, qu'elle fût un Dieu.* Ibid. pag. 603.[43]

Voiez cy-dessus, N° 2 & 5.

N° 12.

[Cl.V.1–20, Cl.V.92, Cl.V.110–116]

L'enchainement *des causes liéées*[44] *les unes avec les autres, va loin. C'est pourquoi la raison que* M. Descartes *a alleguée, pour prouver l'independance de nos actions libres par un pretendu* sentiment vif interne, *n'a point de force. Nous ne pouvons pas sentir proprement nôtre independance ; & nous ne nous appercevons, pas tousjours des causes, souvent imperceptibles, dont nôtre resolution depend. C'est comme si l'éguille aimantée prenoit plaisir de se tourner vers le Nord ; car elle croiroit tourner independamment de quelque autre cause, ne s'appercevant pas des mouvemens insensibles de la matiere magnetique.* Theodicée pag. 162.[45]

Voiez cy-dessous, N° 13.

163. CLARKE'S APPENDIX TO 1717 EDITION OF THE CORRESPONDENCE 831

single Substance ; without its needing to receive any *physical Influence* from the *Body*. And the *Body* likewise, on *Its* Part, acts correspondently to the Volitions of the Soul, by its *own proper Laws* ; and consequently does not obey the Soul, any otherwise than as those Laws are correspondent. *Theodicæa. Pag.* 479.[41]

It must also be confessed, that every Soul *represents* to it self *the Universe*, according to its *Point of View*, and by a Relation *peculiar* to it : But there is always a perfect *Harmony* between them. *Ibid. Pag.* 552.[42]

The Operation of *Spiritual Machines*, that is, of Souls, is not mechanical ; but it contains eminently, whatever is excellent in Mechanism ; the Motions which appear actually in Bodies, being concentrated by *representation* in the Soul, as in an Ideal World, which represents the Laws of the Actual World, and the Series of their being put in Execution ; differing in This from the Perfect Ideal World which is in God, that most of the Perceptions in Human Souls are but confused. For we must know, that *every single Substance* includes *the Universe* in its indistinct Perceptions ; and that the Succession of these Perceptions is regulated by the particular Nature of the Substance ; but yet in a manner which always represents *Whole Universal Nature*. And every present Perception tends towards a new Perception ; as every Motion, which such Perception represents, tends towards a new Motion. But 'tis impossible the Soul should be able to understand distinctly its own whole Nature, and to apprehend how this numberless Number of little Perceptions, heaped up, or rather concentred together, are produced. In order to This, it would be requisite that the Soul understood perfectly the whole Universe, which is included within it ; that is, it must be a God. *Ibid. Pag.* 603.[43]

See *above*, N° 2 *and* 5.

N° 12.

[Cl.V.1–20, Cl.V.92, Cl.V.110–116]

The Chain of Causes connected[44] one with another, reaches very far. Wherefore the Reason alledged by *Des Cartes*, to prove by a pretended *vigorous inward Sense*, the independence of our Free Actions ; is altogether inconclusive. We cannot, strictly speaking, be *sensible of* our not depending on other Causes : For we cannot always *perceive* the Causes, (they being often *imperceptible*,) on which our Resolutions depend. 'Tis as if a Needle touched with a Loadstone, was *sensible of*, and *pleased with* its turning towards the *North*. For it would believe that it turned it self, independently on any other Cause ; not perceiving the insensible Motions of the Magnetick Matter. *Theodicæa, Pag.* 162.[45]

See *below*, N° 13.

N⁰ 13.

[Lz.V.92, Lz.V.116, Cl.V.92, Cl.V.110–116]

Une infinité *de* grands & de petits mouvemens internes & externes *concourent avec nous, dont le plus souvent l'on ne s'apperçoit pas ; & j'ai déja dit, que lors qu'on sort d'une chambre, il y a telles raisons qui nous determinent à mettre un tel pied devant, sans qu'on y reflechisse.* Theodicée pag. 158.[46]

Voiez cy-dessus, N⁰ 12.

163. CLARKE'S APPENDIX TO 1717 EDITION OF THE CORRESPONDENCE 833

N° 13.

[Lz.V.92, Lz.V.116, Cl.V.92, Cl.V.110–116]

An infinite Number of *Great and Small Motions Internal and External*, concur with us, which generally we are not sensible of. And I have already said, that, when a Man walks out of a Room, there are such reasons which determine him to set One Foot forward rather than the other, though he observes it not. *Theodicæa, Pag.* 158.[46]

See *above*, N° 12.

[1] I use 'Lz' or 'Cl', followed by a Roman numeral and an Arabic numeral, to refer, respectively, to a specific paper and section by Leibniz or Clarke in their correspondence. Thus 'Lz.I.1–4' would refer to the first four sections of Leibniz's First Paper, and 'Cl.II.1' would refer to the first section of Clarke's Second Reply. The paragraphs indicate those to which Clarke attached notes in his 1717 edition of the Correspondence referring to this section of his appendix. Footnotes are Clarke's.

[2] *Théodicée* § 217, GP VI 248/H 264.

[3] *Théodicée* § 291, GP VI 289/H 304.

[4] *De Prima Philosophiae Emendatione et de Notione substantiae* (GP VI 469–70/L 433).

[5] *Specimen Dynamicum* (GM VI 235 /AG 118).

[6] Clarke added 'vis activa primitiva' within square brackets.

[7] *Specimen Dynamicum* (GM VI 236/AG 119).

[8] *Speciment Dynamicum* (GM VI 237/AG 120).

[9] *Speciment Dynamicum* (GM VI 241/AG 124).

[10] *Speciment Dynamicum* (GM VI 242/AG 125).

[11] *De Ipsa Natura* § 8 (GP IV 508/AG 159).

[12] *De Ipsa Natura* § 9 (GP IV 509/AG 160).

[13] *De Ipsa Natura* § 10 (GP IV 510/AG 161).

[14] *De Ipsa Natura* § 11 (GP IV 511/AG 162).

[15] Clarke added 'materiam' within square brackets.

[16] *De Ipsa Natura* § 12 (GP IV 512/AG 162–3).

[17] *De Ipsa Natura* § 12 (GP IV 512/AG 163).

[18] *De Ipsa Natura* § 15 (GP IV 515/AG 165–6).

[19] Clarke added 'Monsieur Bayle' within square brackets.

[20] *Théodicée* § 324, GP VI 308/H 321–2.

[21] *Théodicée* § 324–5, GP VI 309/H 322.

[22] *Théodicée* § 46, GP VI 129/H 148–9.

[23] Clarke here added the square brackets and what they contain to replace '*de l'âne de Buridan*'.

[24] *Théodicée* § 49, GP VI 129/H 150.

[25] *Théodicée* § 59, GP VI 135/H 155.

[26] *Théodicée* § 62, GP VI 137/H 157.

[27] See p. 713 note 17.

[28] *Théodicée* § 63, GP VI 137/H 157.

[29] *Théodicée* § 355, GP VI 326/H 339.

[30] *Théodicée* § 207, GP VI 241/H 257.

[31] *De Ipsa Natura* § 11 (GP IV 510/AG 161).

[32] *De Ipsa Natura* § 11 (GP IV 511/AG 161).

[33] *Specimen Dynamicum* (GM VI 237/AG 120).

[34] *Specimen Dynamicum* (GM VI 241/AG 124).

[35] *Théodicée* § 30, GP VI 120/H 140–1.

[36] *Théodicée* § 347, GP VI 320/H 333.

[37] *Théodicée* § 207, GP VI 241/H 257.

[38] *Théodicée* § 8, GP VI 107/H 128.

[39] *De Ipsa Natura* § 13 (GP IV 513–14/AG 164).

[40] Clarke added 'dans le systeme de l'Harmonie préétablie' within square brackets.

[41] *Théodicée* § 291, G VI 289–90/H 304).

834   164. NEWTON TO DES MAIZEAUX

[42] *Théodicée* § 357, G VI 327/H 339.
[43] *Théodicée* § 403, G VI 356–7/H 365.
[44] Reading 'liées' for 'liéées'.
[45] *Théodicée* § 49–50, G VI 130/H 150–1.
[46] *Théodicée* § 46, G VI 128/H 149.

164. Isaac Newton to Pierre Des Maizeaux* (excerpt)[1]

[*c.* August 1718]

S^r

You know that when M^r l'Abbé [Antonio Schinella] Conti* had received a Letter from Mr Leibnitz with a large Postscript[2] against me full of accusations foreign to the Question, & the Postscript was shewed to the King [George I, Georg Ludwig* of Braunschweig-Lüneburg], & I was pressed for an answer to be also shewed to his Majesty, & the same was afterwards sent to Mr Leibnitz: he sent it with his Answer to Paris declining to make good his charge & pretending that I was the Aggressor, & saying that he sent those Letters to Paris that he might have neutral & intelligent witnesses of what passed Between us. I looked upon this an indirect practise & forbore writing an Answer in the form of a Letter to be sent to him, & only wrote some Observations upon his Letter[3] to satisfy my friends here that it was easy to have answered him had I thought fit to let him go on with his politicks. As soon as I heard that he was dead I caused the Letters and Observations to be printed least they should at any time come abroad imperfectly in France. You are now upon a design of reprinting them with some other Letters written at the same time, whose Originals have been left in your hands for that purpose by M^r l'Abbé Conti for making that Controversy complete & I see no necessity of adding any thing more to what has been said, especially now Mr Leibnitz is dead.

[...]

---

[1] University Library Cambridge Add. 3968(27), ff. 401r–403r. This same excerpt was published in NC VI 458n1. This is from one of the drafts that Newton composed in response to Des Maizeaux's request for comments on the proofs for volume 2 of the first edition of Des Maizeaux's *Recueil* (Des Maizeaux 1720).

[2] That is, Leibniz's letter to Conti of 6 December 1715 (document 88b).

[3] See Newton's letter to Conti of 17 March 1716 (NS) (document 101g), as well as earlier drafts of that letter (documents 101a–f).

836   165. NEWTON TO DES MAIZEAUX

165. Isaac Newton to Pierre Des Maizeaux* (excerpt)[1]

[c.August 1718]

Sr

I have viewed the printed papers you left in my hands. The Remarks [that follow][2] are only upon the Letter of Mr Leibnitz to Mr. l'Abbé [Antonio Schinella] Conti* dated 9 April 1716.[3] The Letters to the Comtesse of Kilmansegger [Sophie Charlotte von Kielmansegg*], & the Postscript of a Letter to Compt Bothmar[4] are without an Answer, & I do not see that they need any. None of his Letters were writ to me, & I had not answered any of them had not Mr l'Abbé Conti pressed me to write an Answer to the Postscript of a Letter to him[5] that both might be shewed to the King [George I, Georg Ludwig* of Braunschweig-Lüneburg]. But when I understood that Mr Leibnitz sent all the Letters open to Paris, & his Answer came hither from thence, I declined writing any more Letters, & only wrote the Remarks upon that Answer[6] to satisfy my friends here that what he writ was easy to have been answered if it had come hither directly. The Commercium Epistolicum*, notwit[h]standing any thing which has hitherto been said against it, remains in full force, & while that remains unshaken there is no need of writing any further about those matters.
[...]

---

[1] University Library Cambridge Add. 3968(27), ff. 393r–395r. Previously published in NC VI 454–7. This is from one of the drafts that Newton composed in response to Des Maizeaux's request for comments on the proofs for volume 2 of the first edition of Des Maizeaux's *Recueil* (Des Maizeaux 1720).

[2] In this excerpt, I omit Newton's remarks on Leibniz's letter to Conti of 9 April (document 108).

[3] See document 108. In this letter, Leibniz responded to Newton's letter to Conti of 17 March 1716 (NS) (document 101g).

[4] That is, Johann Caspar Bothmer*. For the postscript in question, see Leibniz's letter to Bothmer of 28 April 1716 (document 114).

[5] That is, the postscript to Leibniz's letter to Conti of 6 December 1715 (document 88b).

[6] That is, the remarks in his letter to Conti of 17 March 1716 (NS) (document 101g).

Starred References

Act of Settlement (1701). Through the Act of Settlement (1701), the English Parliament decided to amend the law of succession to the British throne in favour of the Protestant House of Stuart. In default of heirs from William III of Orange—who had ruled alone in England after the death of Mary in 1694—or Queen Anne, the Act declared that the English crown should devolve upon 'the most excellent princess Sophia, Electress and duchess-dowager of Hanover', granddaughter of James I, and 'the heirs of her body, being Protestant'. Queen Anne died on 1 (12 NS) August 1714; but since the Dowager Electress Sophie* of the Palatinate had died a little more than two months earlier, on 8 June 1714, the British crown fell to Sophie's eldest son, Georg Ludwig* of Braunschweig-Lüneburg, who became King George I.

Addison, Joseph (1672–1719), English essayist poet, playwright, and politician. In 1705, while serving as under-secretary of state, Addison accompanied Charles Montagu (1661–1715), 1st Earl of Halifax, on a diplomatic mission to Hanover. He was elected MP for the borough of Lostwithiel in 1708 and in 1710 he was elected MP for Malmesbury in Wiltshire, a post he held until his death. In 1708 he was appointed secretary to the Lord Lieutenant of Ireland, Thomas Wharton (1648–1715). His most famous work was his play *Cato, A Tragedy* (1712).

Amalie Wilhelmine (Braunschweig preferred form); see below, Wilhelmine Amalie (Austrian preferred form).

Annales imperii occidentis Brunsvicenses (*The Braunschweig Annals of the Western Empire*) was the name that Leibniz eventually came to employ for his history of the House of Braunschweig-Lüneburg. Leibniz had first suggested writing a brief account of the recent history of the House in 1680, shortly after being confirmed in the service of the new Duke of Braunschweig-Lüneburg-Calenberg (Hanover), Ernst August* (Aiton, 1985, p. 101). In 1685 he began pursuing in earnest the more ambitious project of tracing the history of the House back as far as 600 CE (ibid., p. 137), and he eventually came to embed the history of the House of Braunschweig-Lüneburg within a broader context that included the history of the Holy Roman Empire—whence the name *Annales imperii occidentis Brunsvicenses*. Until the end of his life, work on the history of the House of Braunschweig-Lüneburg became a continuing, and often burdensome duty for Leibniz. It became especially burdensome under his last employer at Hanover, the Elector Georg Ludwig* of Braunschweig-Lüneburg, who became King George I of England in August of 1714. Georg Ludwig had become increasingly irritated by Leibniz's long absences from Hanover and what he perceived as Leibniz's neglect of the history project—and this despite the fact that Leibniz had already published, under the title *Scriptores rerum Brunsvicensium*, three large volumes (1707, 1710, and 1711) of medieval writings related to the history of the Guelfs (or Welfs) and of Lower Saxony (Antognazza 2009, p. 464). In the end, Leibniz had decided to begin his *Annals* with the birth of Charlemagne and the rise of the Holy Roman Empire and to end it with the death (in 1024) of the first emperor of Braunschweig descent, Heinrich II. At the time of his death in November of 1716, Leibniz had brought his *Annales* to within two decades of its proposed

840   STARRED REFERENCES

ending with the year 1024. The nearly completed *Annales* were eventually published in three volumes (1843–1846) by Georg Heinrich Pertz (Antognazza 2009, pp. 329, 531).

Anton Ulrich (1633–1714) was Duke of Braunschweig-Wolfenbüttel, jointly with his brother from 1685 to 1702, and solely from 1704 to 1714. The duchy of Braunschweig-Wolfenbüttel was the senior branch of the Guelf (or Welf) House of Braunschweig, with the two duchies of Braunschweig-Lüneburg—namely the duchy of Braunschweig-Lüneburg-Calenberg (Hanover) and the duchy of Braunschweig-Lüneburg-Celle—forming the junior branch. Leibniz served both branches: he was librarian and counselor to a succession of dukes of Hanover, from 1676 until his death in 1716, and in 1691 he had also become director of the magnificent library in Wolfenbüttel that had been founded by Anton Ulrich's father, Duke August (1579–1666).

Arenberg, Léopold Philippe Charles Joseph, Duc d' (1690–1754), 4th Duke of Arenberg and an Austrian military officer; he eventually became a field marshal and the commander-in-chief of the imperial forces in the Austrian Netherlands.

Aulic Council. The Aulic Council was a personal council of the Holy Roman Emperor that functioned primarily as the organ through which the emperor exercised his judicial powers; its composition and powers were established by the Peace of Westphalia*. In addition to a president, a vice-president, and the vice-chancellor of the empire, it included some eighteen other members, one table of which consisted of nobles and the other of doctors of civil law, all nominated and paid by the emperor. Six members were required to be Protestants.

Bacon, Francis (1561–1626) was created Baron Verulam (1618), and 1st Viscount St Alban (1621). He was Lord Chancellor of England (1617–1621) under King James I and is perhaps best known for his *Novum Organum* (1620), in which he developed an empirical and experimental methodology for scientific investigation.

Barcelona, Siege of (1713–14), which began on 25 July 1713, was a battle that took place at the end of the War of Spanish Succession*. The allies in the war against France, which included Austria, Great Britain, Holland, Portugal, Denmark, and the Duchy of Savoy, evacuated from Spain and abandoned Barcelona once the Treaty of Utrecht* was signed in 1713. But the Catalans continued the fight and Barcelona was only subdued on 11 September 1714, after the nearly fourteen-month siege, by French and Spanish troops under the command of James FitzJames* 1st Duke of Berwick (1687).

Barrow, Isaac (1630–1677) was an English mathematician and theologian who held the Lucasian Chair in Mathematics at Cambridge University from 1663 to 1669. He was an early contributor to the development of the calculus; among other things, he devised a new method for determining tangents and formulated a geometrical proof of what came to be called the fundamental theorem of the calculus, showing that integration and differentiation are inverse operations. When he resigned the Lucasian Chair in 1669, he was instrumental in having Newton succeed him in that post.

Bayle, Pierre (1647–1706) was a French Huguenot émigré, Professor of History and Philosophy at Rotterdam. A significant philosophical and literary figure, Bayle was the founder and editor of the *Nouvelles de la République des Lettres*, a review of recent books that often contained references to Leibniz's works. But Bayle is most noted for his encyclopedic work, *Dictionaire Historique et Critique*, first published in 1696; in footnote H of the *Dictionary*'s article 'Rorarius,' Bayle included extended comments on Leibniz's *Système nouveau de la nature et de la communication des substances, aussi bien que de l'union qu'il y a entre l'âme et le corps* (published in the *Journal des savants* in July 1695), especially on his

STARRED REFERENCES   841

notion of the pre-established harmony. Leibniz responded to Bayle's comments in private notes, as well as in two articles, the first of which (*Lettre de M. Leibniz à l'auteur, contenant un éclaircissement des difficultés que Monsieur Bayle a trouvées dans le système nouveau de l'union de l'âme et du corps*) was published in the *Histoire des ouvrages des savants* for July 1698. Bayle commented on this article in the second edition of the *Dictionary* (1702) in the new note L that he added to the article 'Rorarius'; Leibniz replied to these new comments in an article published in *Histoire critique de la République des lettres* for 1716 (*Réponse de M. Leibniz aux reflexions contenues dans la seconde édition du Dictionnaire Critique de M. Bayle, article Rorarius, sur le système d l'harmonie préétablie*). (For background and texts on Leibniz and Bayle in connection with Leibniz's *Système nouveau*, see Woolhouse and Francks 1997, Chapter 5.) In his *Theodicy*, Leibniz also addressed Bayle's skeptical arguments against theodicy.

Benedicte Henriette of the Palatinate (1652–1730) was the daughter of Edward, Count Palatine of Simmern and his wife Anna Gonzaga. In 1668 she married Duke Johann Friedrich* of Braunschweig-Lüneburg. Her youngest daughter was Wilhelmine Amalie*, who married Holy Roman Emperor Joseph I in 1699.

Bernstorff, Andreas Gottlieb, Freiherr von (1649–1726) was Baron Bernstorff in the nobility of the Holy Roman Empire. He succeeded his father-in-law as chancellor of the Duchy of Lüneburg-Celle in 1677. He remained in the service of Duke Georg Wilhelm* of Celle until the latter's death in 1705, at which time he entered the service of Georg Wilhelm's nephew, Elector Georg Ludwig* of Braunschweig-Lüneburg (later George I of England), who had inherited Celle. He accompanied George I to England in 1714 and became his chief Hanoverian minister.

Bernoulli, Johann (1667–1748) was a Swiss mathematician and physicist. He corresponded frequently with Leibniz and was one of the most important promoters of Leibniz's differential calculus, to the development of which both he and his brother Jacob (1655–1705) were significant contributors.

Blackburne, Lancelot (1658–1743). Blackburne was awarded a canonry at Exeter Cathedral in 1691 and elevated to subdean of Exeter on 9 January 1695. When the Dean of Exeter, William Wake*, was elevated to the bishopric of Lincoln in 1705, Blackburne was appointed his successor as dean. Later, as Archbishop of Canterbury, Wake appointed Blackburne to accompany George I (Georg Ludwig* of Braunschweig-Lüneburg) as the king's chaplain on his visit to Hanover in 1716. It was on this trip that Blackburne met Leibniz and Caroline's eldest son, Friedrich Ludwig* (1707–1751), who, by order of his grandfather George I, had been left behind to be educated in Hanover when the rest of the royal family moved to England.

Bonneval, Claude Aléxandre, Comte de (1675–1747) was a French soldier of fortune who fought with the French army during the War of the Spanish Succession*. In 1704, while under the command of the Duke of Vandôme, he incurred the enmity of the French controller general Michel Chamillart in a dispute concerning Bonneval's disbursal of funds for military purposes. This led him to leave French service for fear of punishment, and he eventually entered the service of Austria in 1706 under the command of Prince Eugène* of Savoy, who brevetted him a major general (Wilding 1937, pp. 75–8; Hauc 2009, p. 30). He went on to distinguish himself in campaigns against France. In 1714 he joined Prince Eugène in the negotiations to end hostilities between France and Austria that resulted in the Treaty of Rasttat*, and upon his return to Vienna, Emperor Karl VI* elevated him to the rank of lieutenant general. In the war against the Ottomans, he again distinguished himself, especially at

842 STARRED REFERENCES

the battle of Petrovaradin (August 5, 1716), where he received a lance wound to the abdomen (Wilding 1937, pp. 79–80). The charges against him having been dropped in France, Bonneval returned to Paris in 1717, where he married a daughter of the Marquis de Biron. But within a week, Bonneval abandoned his wife—never to see her again—and returned to Vienna, where he was raised to the rank of general. Shortly thereafter he joined Prince Eugène in the successful siege of Belgrade against the Turks (Wilding 1937, p. 81). In 1725 Bonneval was sentenced to a year in prison as the result of a serious quarrel he had with Prince Eugène's Vice Governor of the Austrian Netherlands. After his release in February 1726, Bonneval spent three years in Venice, and eventually passed from there to Sarajevo, Bosnia. He was detained in Sarajevo by the Ottoman authorities and, in order to avoid being turned over to the Austrian authorities, he converted to Islam in 1730. Shortly thereafter he was made a pasha in the Turkish army and appointed commander of the artillery, at which time he adopted the name 'Humbaraci Ahmet Paşa' (Wilding 1937, pp. 96–9; Hauc 2009, p. 33).

Bothmer, Johann Caspar von (1656–1732). Bothmer entered the service of Duke Georg Wilhelm* of Lüneburg-Celle in 1677. After the death of Georg Wilhelm in 1705, his nephew, the Elector Georg Ludwig* of Braunschweig-Lüneburg, inherited the duchy of Lüneburg-Celle, and Bothmer continued his service as plenipotentiary at The Hague; but beginning in 1711 he spent increasing amounts of time in London. When Georg Ludwig became King of Great Britain in 1714, Bothmer remained in London as an adviser, and he, along with George I's other Hanoverian ministers, Andreas Gottlieb von Bernstorff* and John Robethon*, formed a group that came to be known as the 'Hanoverian junto'.

Boyle, Robert (1627–1691). A notable seventeenth-century natural philosopher in chemistry and physics, perhaps best known for his formulation of his gas law, according to which the pressure and volume of a gas are in inverse relation when the temperature of the gas is held constant. Boyle was born in Ireland but moved to Oxford in England in 1654. In 1663 Charles II named him a member of the council for the newly formed Royal Society of London. In 1680 he was elected president of the society, but he refused the office due to a religious objection to the taking of oaths. Boyle was an ardent defender of the mechanical philosophy.

Bourguet, Louis (1678–1742). Bourguet was a merchant and scholar living in Venice. He engaged in an important and lengthy correspondence with Leibniz beginning in 1709. In 1731 he became Professor of Philosophy and Mathematics at Neuchâtel. He published *Lettres philosophiques sur la formation des sels et des crystaux et sur la génération et le mechanisme organique des plantes et des animaux* (Amsterdam: François L'Honoré, 1729) and, with Pierre Cartier, *Traité des petrifications* (Paris: Briasson, 1742).

Bremen and Verden. Under the terms of the Peace of Westphalia* (specifically, the Treaty of Osnabrück (1648)), the prince-bishoprics of Bremen and Verden were secularized and ceded to the King of Sweden as the Duke of Bremen and the Duke of Verden. (The ruling monarch of Sweden at the time was Queen Christina, who thus became styled the Duchess of Bremen and the Princess of Verden.) They were occupied by Denmark from 1712 to 1715. To gain the support of George I of Great Britain (Georg Ludwig* of Braunschweig-Lüneburg) (in his capacity as Elector of Hanover) in the Great Northern War against Sweden, the allies (Denmark, Prussia, and Russia) agreed that Bremen* and Verden* would be sold to Hanover by Denmark. Frederick IV, King of Denmark and Norway, handed Bremen and Verden over to George I on 15 October 1715 (NS), and on the same day George I declared war on Sweden. By the Treaty of Stockholm (1619) between Hanover and Sweden, Sweden officially ceded

STARRED REFERENCES   843

Bremen and Verden to Hanover, for which Sweden was financially compensated. (See Hatton 1968, pp. 383–412; Hatton 1978, pp. 180–92.)

Bucquoy, Jean-Albert d'Archambaud, Comte de (*c*.1650–1740), was born in the French province of Champagne. He initially entered into military service, but later joined the Trappist order. He was eventually sent away by the Abbé de Rancé because his health was being adversely affected by the extreme disciplines to which he subjected himself. After two years in Paris living the life of a mendicant, Bucquoi moved to Rouen, where he maintained a free school for the poor under the name of Le Mort. He later returned to Paris and endeavoured to found a new order, taking the habit and title of Abbé. Discouraged by his inability to perform miracles, he reentered military service, but he was imprisoned at For-l'Évêque prison in Paris for making some rash political remarks. He escaped but was recaptured in 1707 and put in the Bastille, from which he again escaped in 1709. He entered Switzerland, where he tried to regain his confiscated property, and from there he went to Holland, where he recommended that the Allies transform France into a republic. In 1711, General Johann Matthias von Schulenburg* conducted him to Hanover, where the Elector Georg Ludwig* of Braunschweig-Lüneburg (later King George I of Great Britain) eventually granted him a pension. Georg Ludwig enjoyed Bucquoi's conversation, and Bucquoi was often a guest at his table. Bucquoi died in Hanover in 1740. See the article 'Buquoi, Buquoit ou Bucquoy (Jean-Albert d'Archambaud, comte de)' in FXF III 23–4; for Bucquoi's arrival in Hanover with General Schulenburg, see the Electress Sophie's letter to Leibniz of 31 August 1711 in Klopp IX 345–6.

Caroline of Brandenburg-Ansbach (Margravine Wilhelmine Charlotte Karoline of Brandenburg-Ansbach) (1683–1737) was the daughter of Johann Friedrich (1654–1686), the Margrave of Brandenburg-Ansbach, and his second wife, Eleonore Erdmuthe Louise of Saxe-Eisenach (1662–1696). Within two years of her birth, Caroline's father died of smallpox. Seven years later, the husband of Sophie Charlotte*, Elector Friedrich III* of Brandenburg (1657–1713) (later King Friedrich I of Prussia), arranged a marriage between Caroline's mother and Elector Johann Georg IV of Saxony (1668–1694), with whom Friedrich I wished to establish an alliance. But Georg was a brutal man who shunned Eleonore and her children in favour of his mistress. In 1694 Johann Georg and his mistress died of smallpox within two weeks of each other, and two years later Caroline's mother herself was dead. Consequently, Caroline at the age of thirteen and her brother Wilhelm Friedrich* at the age of eleven were left nearly alone in the world. They returned to Ansbach where their stepbrother Georg Friedrich II (1678–1703) was margrave. At this point Sophie Charlotte and Friedrich I offered to become Caroline's guardians and hence began Caroline's association with Sophie Charlotte and the court in Berlin (see R. L. Arkell, *Caroline of Ansbach: George the Second's Queen*, pp. 6–7). In 1703 a proposal of marriage for Caroline was sent on behalf of Archduke Karl of Austria, the future Emperor Karl VI*, to the Berlin court of the Electress of Brandenburg and Queen of Prussia, Sophie Charlotte. In the autumn of the following year, Father Orban, the Jesuit confessor of the then Elector Palatine Johann Wilhelm, Karl's uncle on his mother's side, arrived at Sophie Charlotte's palace at Lützenburg with the intention of converting Caroline to Catholicism in order to pave the way for her marriage to Archduke Karl. In the end, Caroline would not convert, and Leibniz, who had attended the sessions between Caroline and Orban, was commissioned to compose a letter to the elector Palatine to report Caroline's decision (for which see Klopp IX 108–9). Caroline then left Lützenburg to seek refuge in Ansbach with her brother, Wilhelm Friedrich, who was now the margrave. But even there she continued to receive letters from Father Orban, the elector Palatine, and others within the emperor's party to pressure her to reconsider, but she would not. In 1705 she married Georg August*, the son of Elector Georg

844   STARRED REFERENCES

Ludwig* of Braunschweig-Lüneburg, and thus she became the electoral princess at the court in Hanover, where she established a close friendship with Leibniz. After the death of Queen Anne on 12 August 1714, Georg Ludwig acceded to the throne of Great Britain, and he and Georg August, now the Prince of Wales, departed for England on 13 September. Caroline, who was still in Hanover when Leibniz arrived from Vienna on 14 September, requested that he stay with her at the summer palace at Herrenhausen* until her departure for England, which occurred a month later on 12 October 1715. Toward the end of November of the following year, Leibniz sent Caroline the letter that was responsible for igniting his correspondence with Samuel Clarke* (see document 85)—a correspondence that finally terminated, nearly a year later, with Leibniz's death on 14 November 1716.

Chamberlayne, John (1666–1723), a translator and literary editor, educated at Trinity College, Oxford, and Leyden University in Holland. He was a courtier at the courts of Queen Anne and George I (Georg Ludwig* of Braunschweig-Lüneburg) and was elected to the Royal Society in 1702. In 1714, with eminent goodwill, he made a failed attempt to reconcile Newton and Leibniz in their priority dispute over the discovery of the calculus. In the postscript to the dedication of his translation of selections from Fontenelle's *Eloges académiques*, Chamberlayne wrote:

> My Lord, I think my self bound to mention, by way of Postscript, a kind of Negative Injustice and Affront which the Ingenious Historian of the Transactions of the *Academy* [that is, Fontenelle] has put upon our Nation, and more immediately upon the *Royal Society*. Your Lordship will observe in the Lives of the Marquis *de L'Hopital*, and Messieurs [Vincenzo] *Vivani*, [Domenico] *Guglielmini*, and [Johann] *Bernoulli**, Four of the greatest *Mathematicians* of *Europe*, and all Members of the [Royal] *Academy* [of Sciences in Paris], that there is an Account given of the *Differential Calculation*, and the Invention thereof, which I think is every where ascribed to the late Mons. *Leibnitz*, a Privy-Counsellor and Historiographer of his Majesty, as Elector of *Brunswick-Luneburg*, and one of the most Learned Men of our Age; at least it is no where attributed to our own Countryman Sir *Isaac Newton*, the First Mathematician in the World. Now it is notorious that the Writers of the *Acta Leipsiensia* [i.e., the *Acta Eruditorum* of Leipzig] make Mons. *Leibnitz* the Author of the said Differential Calculation; but it is not less known to your Lordship, that Dr. [John] *Keill**, in the *Commercium Epistolicum**, has done our *British Philosopher* justice; and has fully proved that which Mr. *L.* did in some manner acknowledge to me (when I attempted to reconcile those two Great Men) that Sir *I. N.* might be the first Inventer, but that he himself had luckily fallen about the same Time upon the same Notions.
>
> [Fontenelle 1717, Postscript to Chamberlayne's dedication]

Charlottenburg was the name given to the settlement around Lützenburg castle shortly after the death of the then Queen of Prussia Sophie Charlotte* in February of 1705. Likewise, Lützenburg castle itself, which Sophie Charlotte's husband, the then Elector Friedrich* III of Brandenburg (later King Friedrich I of Prussia), had had constructed for her as a summer residence on the outskirts of Berlin, came to be known as Charlottenburg Schloss after her death.

Cheyne, George (1671/2–1743) was a Scottish physician, natural philosopher, and mathematician who received his MD in 1701 from King's College, Aberdeen. He practised medicine in London and Bath and published several books and papers on medical topics, as well as an unremarkable book on the calculus, *Fluxionum methodus inversa* (1703). After

STARRED REFERENCES 845

becoming morbidly obese (reaching a peak in the 1720s of 448 pounds) from a diet of rich food and drink, he became an enthusiastic promoter of vegetarianism and physical exercise. His primary work in natural philosophy and natural religion was *Philosophical Principles of Natural Religion: Containing the Elements of Natural Philosophy and the Proofs for Natural Religion, arising from them*, first published in 1705. A second edition, corrected and enlarged, appeared in 1715 as the first part of his *Philosophical Principles of Religion: Natural and Revealed*; the second part was entitled *The Nature and Kinds of Infinites; their Arithmetick and Uses; together with the Philosophick Principles of Revealed Religion*. He was a stout defender of Newtonian science and became a Fellow of the Royal Society in 1702 and of the Edinburgh College of Physicians in 1724.

Churchill, Sarah, Duchess of Marlborough (1660–1744). Sarah Churchill (née Jennings) married the English soldier and statesman John Churchill in the winter of 1667/68. She was an intimate and influential friend of Princess, and later, Queen Anne of Great Britain. When Anne became queen in 1702, she created John Churchill the Duke of Marlborough, as well as bestowing on him the Order of the Garter and making him Captain-General of the army. Sarah, for her part, was created Mistress of the Robes, Groom of the Stole, and Keeper of the Privy Purse. But by 1711 she had fallen out of favour with the queen, and she and her husband were eventually dismissed from court. They both returned to favour when Georg Ludwig* of Braunschweig-Lüneburg ascended the English throne in 1714 as George I.

Clarke, Samuel (1675–1729). Clarke was an English philosopher, theologian and ordained Anglican clergyman. After matriculating at Caius College Cambridge in 1691, he became interested in Newton's natural philosophy, which he studied independently at a time when Newton's views were still not widely known, even at his own university. In the disputation for his bachelor's degree in 1695, Clarke defended a proposition from Newton's *Principia*. At the request of his tutor at Caius College Cambridge, Clarke produced a Latin translation of Jacques Rohault's *Traité de physique*, a popular textbook of Cartesian physics that was still being used at Cambridge. In his translation, which was published in 1697, Clarke added a series of notes designed to correct Rohault's Cartesian physics in the light of Newtonian mechanics. Passing through three editions in the course of thirteen years, Clarke's translation, along with his ever-expanding notes on Newtonian mechanics, became the primary source through which Cambridge undergraduates became acquainted with Newtonian natural philosophy. As a result of his interest in Newton's work, Clarke became friends with the Newtonian popularizer William Whiston, who succeeded Newton as Lucasian Professor of Mathematics at Cambridge in 1702. At the time of their meeting in 1697, Whiston was chaplain to Bishop John Moore of Norwich, a position that Whiston passed on to Clarke. Subsequently Moore made Clarke the rector of Drayton, near Norwich. Clarke's reputation as a preeminent theologian and metaphysician was secured with the appearance of his Boyle lectures, delivered in 1704 and 1705, respectively, on the *Being and Attributers of God* and on *Evidences of Natural and Revealed Religion*. In 1706 he cemented his relationship with Newton by producing a Latin translation of the latter's *Opticks*. That same year he wrote a refutation of Henry Dodwell's view that the soul is mortal by nature and can attain immortality only through baptism. This led to an exchange with Anthony Collins, a materialist follower of John Locke* who defended the view that consciousness is an emergent property of material systems. It was also in 1706 that he was made rector of St Benet's, Paul's Wharf, as well as a chaplain of Queen Anne, who later established him as rector of St James's, Westminster in 1709. In 1712 he published a controversial book on *The Scripture Doctrine of the Trinity* that resulted in his being accused of Arianism—the theological doctrine that Christ is divine but created. A formal complaint about the work was made by the Lower

846   STARRED REFERENCES

House of Convocation, and Clarke responded by composing an apologetic preface. After he then promised the Upper House of Convocation that he would not write or preach on the subject any longer, the matter was dropped. Clarke's philosophical correspondence with Leibniz began at the end of 1715, ultimately ending with Leibniz's death on 14 November 1716. But Leibniz had already transmitted the first half of his fifth and final paper for Clarke in a letter of 18 August 1716 to the Princess of Wales Caroline* (document 139), with the second half being sent shortly thereafter; and Clarke had composed a response that Caroline transmitted to Leibniz in her letter to him of 29 October 1716 (document 156). But Caroline's letter arrived too late for a response from Hanover; for Leibniz died there just sixteen days after the letter bearing Clarke's fifth and final response had been dispatched. In 1717 Clarke published the entire correspondence, including his response to Leibniz's final letter; he dedicated the work to the Princess of Wales Caroline, who had mediated the exchange between himself and Leibniz.

Collins, John (1625–1683) was an English accountant and a largely self-educated mathematician who dedicated much of his life to collecting and disseminating news of mathematical works and discoveries to his circle of correspondents, which included, among others, Newton, James Gregory*, and, by way of Henry Oldenburg*, Leibniz as well. He was also active in soliciting and promoting the publication of mathematical texts.

Commercium Epistolicum was the official report of the Royal Society on the priority dispute between Newton and Leibniz; it was issued by a committee handpicked by Newton, who was then president of the Society. In events leading up to the formation of the committee, Leibniz had written to Hans Sloane*, the secretary of the Society, on 4 March 1711, complaining of a charge that John Keill* had made in his *Episotola ad Clarissimum Virum Edmundum Halleium Geometriae Professorem Savilianum, De legibus virium centripetarum.* Toward the end of this paper, which, although published in the *Philosophical Transactions* for 1708, did not appear until 1710, Keill clearly insinuated that Leibniz had plagiarized the calculus from Newton:

> All these things follow from the now most highly celebrated arithmetic of fluxions, which without any doubt Mr. Newton first invented, as will be easily established by anyone reading his letters published by Wallis. Nevertheless the same arithmetic was later published by Mr. Leibniz in *Acta Eruditorum* with a different name and form of notation.
>
> [*Philosophical Transactions* 26 (1708), p. 185]

Keill composed a reply to Leibniz's letter that he sent to Leibniz by way of Sloane. Leibniz responded on 18 December 1711 in a second letter to Sloane, appealing to Sloane's 'sense of justice, [to determine] whether or not such empty and unjust braying should not be suppressed, of which I believe even Newton himself would disapprove, being a distinguished person who is thoroughly acquainted with past events; and I am confident that he will freely give evidence of his opinion on this [issue]' (NC V, 208). But Newton's committee, established to adjudicate the dispute between Leibniz and Keill, was bound to disappoint Leibniz's hopes; it issued its report on 24 April 1712 (5 May 1712 NS), concluding that 'we reckon Mr Newton the first Inventor; and are of the opinion that Mr Keill in asserting the same has been noways injurious to Mr Leibniz' (NC V xxvi). The report was published early in 1713.

Conti, Antonio Schinella (1677–1749), known as Abbé Conti. Conti was born in Padua in 1677, the son of the Venetian nobleman Pio Conti and his wife Lucrezia Nani. In 1699 he entered the religious Order of the Oratorians in Venice, at the church officially named Santa

STARRED REFERENCES   847

Maria della Consolazione (but popularly known as Santa Maria della Fava). In an autobiographical sketch that was published posthumously along with other of his writings in 1756, Conti reported that he was in Luigi Pavini's bookstore in Venice one evening in 1706 when he overheard one of the gathered scholars discussing the virtues of Cartesian philosophy: 'His discourse,' Conti gushed, 'made such a profound impression on my mind so impatient for the truth, that I sought Abbot Fardella, who was then in Venice, and I spoke with him about Descartes* with such fervor of spirit that he instantly agreed to explain to me the metaphysical meditations of this same philosopher' (as quoted and translated in Messbarger 2002, pp. 52–3). Thus inspired, Conti left the Order of the Oratorians in 1708 and moved to Padua in order to pursue studies in philosophy, science, and mathematics. Under the direction of Michelangelo Fardella, then a professor of astronomy and philosophy at the University of Padua, Conti read Descartes' *Meditationes de Prima Philosophia* and *Principa Philosophiae*, as well as *Nicolas Malebranche's *De la recherche de la vérité*. Having been previously acquainted with Leibniz's first published work on the differential calculus, *Nova methodus pro maximis et minimis*, which had appeared in the *Acta eruditorum* in 1684, Conti was able to deepen his understanding of the Leibnizian infinitesimal calculus under the tutelage of the Swiss mathematician Jacob Hermann*, who, due in part to Leibniz's influence with Fardella, had been appointed chair of mathematics at the University of Padua in 1707. Beginning in 1710, Conti also collaborated with the naturalist/biologist Antonio Vallisnieri. In 1712, with Vallisnieri's encouragement, Conti published a scathing review of Francesco Maria Nigrisoli's book, *Conisderazioni intorno alla generazione de' viventi e particolarmente de' mostri* (*Considerations concerning the Generation of Living Things and particularly Monsters*), in the *Giornale de' Letterati*. Conti championed mechanistic approaches to the explanation of natural phenomena in opposition to Nigrisoli's theologically driven natural philosophy, which appealed to final causes and Cudworth's theory of plastic forces (Ferrone 1995, pp. 99–100).

Conti departed from Italy in 1713, bound for Paris, where he hoped to engage directly with the French philosophers. He met several times with Malebranche, but he grew increasingly skeptical of Malebranche's brand of theological rationalism and increasingly interested in Newtonian experimental philosophy. In 1715 he was thus inspired to depart Paris, bound this time for England. But while still in France, Conti had written a long and flattering letter to Leibniz; and once Conti had arrived in England, Leibniz began to explore the possibility of enlisting him as an ally in his war against the Newtonians, through the good offices of Princess Caroline*. In a letter written in mid-to-late December 1715, Leibniz recommended Conti to Caroline in the following terms:

> There is now a noble Venetian in England named Abbé Conti who applies himself earnestly to the investigation of fine things. When he was in France, he testified to being very much on my side, and he wrote me a nice letter in which, among other things, he makes known that he has marked well the beauty of the system I establish, above all in relation to souls. I do not know whether my antagonists from London will have since won him over a bit. He will be right to be accommodating in order to profit better from their conversation. However, I hope that the Abbé Conti will preserve some place for me. I would like him to have the honor of being known by Your Royal Highness, and I have since advised him to try to obtain it, if he has not yet done so.
>
> [document 91, p. 347]

In her reply of 10 January 1716, Caroline was already writing to Leibniz of her newly-established alliance with Conti, and of their intention, no doubt well intended, to mediate the dispute between Leibniz and Newton:

848   STARRED REFERENCES

I do not know if you will consent to it, but Abbé Conti and I have set ourselves up as mediators, and it would be a pity if two men as great as you and he [i.e., Newton] were divided by misunderstandings. I thank you for the acquaintance of the Abbé, who is, so they say, very learned. This is something about which I am not able to judge, but I think that he is witty and that he has a great respect for you.

[document 95, p. 373]

As time went on, Leibniz came to regret his introduction of Conti, suspecting him of changing his allegiances after arriving in England and of colluding with the Newtonians. See Leibniz's letters to Caroline of 12 May 1716 (document 117a, p. 521), of 2 June 1716 (document 124, pp. 557, 559), and from the end of September to mid-October 1716 (document 149, p. 745).

Coste, Pierre (1668–1747). Coste was a Huguenot refugee who fled France after Louis IV revoked the Edict of Nantes in 1685. He settled first in Amsterdam, but in 1697 he was hired as a tutor for the son of Francis Masham and Lady Damaris Cudworth Masham*. He stayed with the family in their home at Oates in Suffolk, England. During his time there he translated Locke's *Essay Concerning Human Understanding* into French. Later, with the help of Desaguliers* and apparently at the urging of Princess Caroline, he published the first French translation of Newton's *Opticks* in 1720 (see Gjertsen 1986, p. 140).

Cotes, Roger (1682–1716) was an English mathematician and the first Plumian Professor of Astronomy and Experimental Philosophy at Trinity College, Cambridge. He served as the editor of the second edition of Newton's *Principia* (1713) and prepared the preface for that edition.

Count of Bückeburg. See Friedrich Christian*, Graf (Count) zu Schaumburg-Lippe
Countess of Bückeburg. See Johanna Sophie*, Gräfin (Countess) zu Schaumburg-Lippe.

Cowper, Countess Mary (1685–1724). In 1706 Mary Cowper (née Mary Clavering) married William Cowper, who had, in October of the previous year, been appointed Lord Keeper of the Great Seal of Great Britain. In November of the following year, William succeeded to his father's baronetcy of Ratlingcourt, and in December he was raised to the peerage as Baron Cowper of Wingham, Kent. In 1707 he was appointed the first Lord High Chancellor of Great Britain, a position he resigned in 1710. When Queen Anne died in 1714, George I (Georg Ludwig* of Braunschweig-Lüneburg) appointed him one of the Lords Justice responsible for governing in the interregnum, and shortly thereafter, he was reappointed Lord High Chancellor. Shortly after the succession of George I, Mary herself was appointed a Lady of the Bedchamber to Caroline* of Brandenburg-Ansbach, Princess of Wales. This was probably the result of Mary's deliberate attempt to gain the friendship and trust of Caroline, as she writes at the beginning of her diary:

I believe it will be necessary, in the first Place, to recollect what passed in order to my coming into the *Court*: and to give a better Light in that Matter, I must tell that for four Years past I had kept a constant Correspondence with the *Princess* now my Mistress; I had received many, and those the kindest, Letters from her. Upon the Death of the *Queen* [i.e. Queen Anne], after she had done me the Honour to answer my Letter of Congratulation, I wrote another Letter to offer her my Service, and to express the perfect Resignation I had to whatever she would think fit to do, were it to choose or refuse me. This Letter she answered, telling me she was entirely at the *Prince's* Disposal, and so could give me no Promise; but that she did not doubt the *Prince's* Willingness to

express his Friendship to me on all Occasions. By the whole Letter I took it for granted that she had so many Importunities upon that Subject, that she could not take me into her Service, and therefore I resolved not to add to the Number of her Tormentors, and never mentioned the Thing any more. I was the more confirmed in my Opinion when I saw myself treated with such Marks of Distinction, and at the same Time two new Ladies made, and I had hear Nothing; but I knew that the Necessity of Affairs often forces Princes to do many Things against their Inclinations, and I daily received so many distinguishing Marks of the *Princess's* Favour that I had great Reason to be satisfied. Things stood in this Manner till the Coronation, which was *October* 20, 1714 [31 October, NS].

I went thither with Lady *Bristol*, who had still a greater Mind to be a Lady of the Bedchamber than I had; she told me I was to be one, but durst not then tell me she had heard it from the *Princess* herself.

[Cowper 1865, pp. 1–3]

In March 1718, William Cowper was created Earl Cowper and, as a result, Mary acquired the title of Countess Mary Cowper.

Cudworth, Ralph (1617–88) was an English Anglican clergyman and philosopher; he was a member of the group of Platonist philosophers and Christian theologians at Cambridge University known as the Cambridge Platonists. Perhaps his most important philosophical work, and the only one published during his lifetime, was *The True Intellectual System of the Universe* (1678). There he developed his distinctive theory of 'Plastic Nature', which he employed to explain movement and change, as well as life and the union of the soul and the body, that he thought could not be explained mechanically.

Desaguliers, John Theophilus (1683–1744) was the son of a Huguenot minister. He was just two years of age when his father fled with him to England to escape persecution after Louis XIV revoked the Edict of Nantes in 1685. He was educated at Christ Church, Oxford, and became a fellow of the Royal Society in 1714. He succeeded Francis Hauksbee as 'Curator and Operator of Experiments' for the Society, and in that capacity he often assisted Newton with his experiments. See Gjertsen 1986, pp. 168–9.

Descartes, René (1596–1650), one of the most important and influential philosophers of the seventeenth century. He wrote widely on metaphysics, mathematics, and natural philosophy. In metaphysics he is perhaps best known for his doctrine of mind-body dualism, according to which minds and bodies constitute distinct substances with distinct principal, or essential, attributes—the principal attribute of mind being thought and that of body being extension. Leibniz was a fierce critic of Descartes and took particular exception to the idea that extension could be an essential property of a genuine substance.

Des Maizeaux, Pierre (1672/3–1745). Des Maizeaux was a Huguenot who fled France with his family after Louis XIV revoked the Edict of Nantes in 1685. He settled in England in 1699, and in 1720 he published a two-volume work entitled *Recueil de divers pieces sur la philosophie*. The first volume was a reprinting of the Leibniz-Clarke correspondence, while the second volume included correspondence connected with the priority dispute between Leibniz and Newton over the discovery of the calculus. He is perhaps most noted as the translator and biographer of Pierre Bayle*.

De Nomis, Benedictus Andreas Caspar de, Marchese della Banditella-Pelusi (b.?, d. 1725?). Nomis was a relative of Agostino Steffani*, through whose agency he was brought to the court of Hanover in 1695. He married Sophie Eleonore von Bothmer-Lauenbrück in

850 STARRED REFERENCES

1712. He was a chamberlain at the court in Hanover until 1716/17 and was then on pension until 1723/1724, at which time he transferred to the court of the Elector of Cologne.

Dury, John (1596–1680). Dury was a Scottish Calvinist minister much involved in the attempt to unite the Calvinist and Lutheran churches. In 1638 he wrote *A Summary Discourse Concerning the work of Peace Ecclesiasticall, How it may concurre with the aim of a civill Confederation amongst Protestants*, which was published by Cambridge University in 1641 and which called on Protestants of all countries to unite. In England his work was supported by Thomas Morton (1564–1659), Bishop of Chester and later of Durham, Joseph Hall (1574–1641), Bishop of Exeter and later of Norwich, and John Davenant (1572–1641), Bishop of Salisbury. At Dury's request, Morton, Hall, and Davenant prepared Latin treatises on the subject of Protestant reunion that Dury published in 1634 under the title *De pacis ecclesiasticae rationibus inter evangelicos usurpandis*. In order to promote the cause of reunion, Dury wished to distribute the treatises on the continent, which he did when he attended a Convention of the Protestant Estates in Frankfort in the spring of 1634 (Batten 1944, pp. 53–5). A second edition of this work was published in Amsterdam in 1636 under the title *De pace ecclesiastica inter evangelicos procuranda sentential quattuour*, to which Dury had added another treatise written 'ab ecclesiae in Gallia pastoribus,' as well as a syllabus of writings promoting ecclesiastical peace. A third edition was published in London in 1638, which was subsequently translated and published (1641) in English at Oxford under the title *Good Counsels for the Peace of Reformed Churches*. This English edition included a treatise entitled 'Opinion of James Ussher, Archbishop of Armagh, with some other bishops of Ireland' (Batten 1944, p. 53n). Between 1635 and 1641, Dury travelled extensively on the continent to promote the cause of Protestant reunion. When he returned to England in 1641, he turned his attention to reconciling the English and Scottish churches. He became an earnest advocate of educational reform as a road to ecclesiastical peace (see Batten 1944, chapter VI; Rae 1998).

Eléonore Desmiers d'Olbreuse (1639–1722). Eléonore was a French Huguenot who, in 1665, entered into a 'marriage of conscience' with Duke Georg Wilhelm* of Celle, after the latter had signed an agreement with his youngest brother Ernst August* of Braunschweig-Lüneburg–who at the time held the non-hereditary position of prince-bishop of Osnabrück—that no male child from his union with Eléonore could inherit the duchy of Celle. This agreement amended an earlier agreement between the two brothers, signed in 1658, in which Georg Wilhelm had agreed never to marry legally, as a way of increasing the chances that Ernst August would inherit one of the two duchies of Braunschweig-Lüneburg that had been bequeathed in their father's will. This earlier agreement had been made in order to persuade Sophie* of the Palatinate and her brother, the Elector Palatine Karl I. Ludwig*, to release Georg Wilhelm from a marriage contract he had signed with Sophie in 1656 and allow Ernst August to stand in his stead for Sophie's hand. In 1666, Eléonore gave birth to a baby girl christened Sophie Dorothea*, and nine years later, despite his agreement with Ernst August, Georg Wilhelm married Eléonore. Eventually, Ernst August and Sophie encouraged the marriage of their eldest son, Georg Ludwig* of Braunschweig-Lüneburg (later George I of England) with his first cousin, Sophie Dorothea of Braunschweig-Lüneburg-Celle, a marriage that took place in 1682, three years after Ernst August had inherited the duchy of Lüneburg-Calenberg (Hanover) from his older brother, and employer of Leibniz, Duke Johann Friedrich*. In 1683 Sophie Dorothea gave birth to a son, Georg August* of Braunschweig-Lüneburg (later George II of England), and in 1687 to a daughter, also named Sophie Dorothea. Georg Ludwig divorced his wife in 1694, as a result of her affair with Philipp Christoph von Königsmarck; Georg Ludwig never married again. See Hatton 1978, pp. 20–42, 48–64.

STARRED REFERENCES 851

Elisabeth Charlotte of the Palatinate (1652–1722), Duchess of Orléans, was the daughter of the Elector Palatine Karl I. Ludwig*, who was a brother of Sophie* of the Palatinate. In 1671 she married Philippe I* (1640–1701), Duke of Orléans, younger brother of Louis XIV of France. Her only son was Duke Philippe II* of Orléans (1674–1723), who was the Regent in France after Louis XIV's death on 1 September 1715, until Louis XV attained his majority in February 1723. Elisabeth Charlotte eventually entered into a correspondence with Leibniz in September 1715; and though she never met Leibniz, she became his ardent friend and admirer (see Brown 2004b, pp. 98–100). On 13 November 1717, a day short of the first anniversary of Leibniz's death, Bernard Fontenelle, secretary of the French Académie Royale des Sciences, read before that body a eulogy for Leibniz based upon a biographical sketch that Elisabeth Charlotte had obtained for that purpose from Leibniz's secretary, Johann Georg Eckhart (see Aiton 1985, p. 350).

Elisabeth Christine of Braunschweig-Wolfenbüttel (1691–1750). Elisabeth Christine was the granddaughter of Duke Anton Ulrich* of Braunschweig-Wolfenbüttel, who in 1708, through negotiations with the Empress Wilhelmine Amalie*, arranged her marriage to the future emperor, Karl VI*.

Ernst August of Braunschweig-Lüneburg (1629–1698) was the youngest of four sons born to Duke Georg of Braunschweig-Lüneburg-Calenberg (1582–1641), and Anna Eleonor of Hesse-Darmstadt (1601–1659). He married Sophie* of the Palatinate in 1658. In 1641 his eldest brother Christian Ludwig (1622–1665) inherited Braunschweig-Lüneburg-Calenberg from his father Georg, and in 1648 Christian Ludwig also inherited the principality of Lüneburg from his uncle, Duke Friedrich of Lüneburg-Celle (1571–1648). Christian Ludwig decided thereupon to rule in Lüneburg-Celle and to relinquish the smaller principality of Calenberg-Göttingen to his younger brother, Georg Wilhelm*. As the youngest of four brothers, Ernst August had, at the time of his marriage to Sophie, only remote prospects for advancement. But as events transpired, he became, successively, the Prince-Bishop of Osnabrück (1662), Duke of Braunschweig-Lüneburg-Calenberg (Hanover) (1679), and the first Elector of Braunschweig-Lüneburg (1692). When he succeeded his elder brother, Duke Johann Friedrich*, as the Duke of Braunschweig-Lüneburg-Calenberg, Ernst August continued to employ Leibniz as librarian and counsellor, the positions that Leibniz had held under Johann Friedrich, who had been Leibniz's first employer at the court in Hanover. In 1692 Emperor Leopold I appointed Ernst August the first Elector of Braunschweig-Lüneburg (Hanover), although the Braunschweig-Lüneburg electorate was not officially recognized until 1708, when it was confirmed by the electoral college of the Imperial Diet.

Ernst August II of Braunschweig-Lüneburg (1674–1728) was the youngest son of Sophie* of the Palatinate and Ernst August* of Braunschweig-Lüneburg. In 1715 he became the Prince-Bishop of Osnabrück, an office that his father had occupied from 1662 to 1698. In 1716 he was created Duke of York and Albany and Earl of Ulster by his brother George I of England (Georg Ludwig* of Braunschweig-Lüneburg).

Eugène, Prince of Savoy (1663–1736). Eugenio-François di Savoia was born in Paris to Savoyard parents and grew up around the French court of King Louis XIV. When Louis XIV rejected him for service in the French army, Prince Eugène moved to Austria to serve the Imperial Habsburg court, becoming field marshal and president of the Imperial War Council. Leibniz's 'Principles of Nature and Grace, Based on Reason' was written in response to Prince Eugène's request for a written summary of Leibniz's philosophy, which Leibniz presented to the prince at the end of August 1714 (see Antognazza 2009, pp. 498–9).

852   STARRED REFERENCES

Falaiseau, Pierre de (1649–1726). Falaiseau was a Huguenot refugee and diplomat. Formerly a Prussian diplomat, he acted as a Hanoverian agent in London in the years 1705–7. As the personal representative in London of the [Dowager] Electress [of Braunschweig-Lüneburg] Sophie* of the Palatinate, he worked as an intermediary between the Whigs in London, on the one hand, and, on the other, Sophie and Leibniz in Hanover, who were hoping to obtain an invitation from Queen Anne or the Parliament for Sophie to reside in England with a pension and a household. See Gregg 2001, p. 209.

Fatio de Duillier, Nicolas (1664–1753) was a Swiss-born mathematician and natural philosopher who met with many prominent scientists of the day while touring Europe. He spent much of his adult life in England and Holland and was elected a fellow of the Royal Society in May of 1688. In June of the following year he met Newton at the Royal Society, and the two became close friends until a break in their relationship in May of 1693. He became involved in the dispute between Newton and Leibniz over the discovery of the calculus, and in his book *Lineæ brevissimi descensus investigatio geometrica duplex* (1699), Fatio fairly asserted that Newton was first inventor of the calculus, but then slyly and unfairly insinuated that Leibniz had plagiarized Newton's work:

> [. . .] I recognize that Newton was the first and by many years the most senior inventor of the calculus, being driven thereto by the factual evidence on this point; as to whether Leibniz, its second inventor, borrowed anything from him, I prefer to let those judge who have seen Newton's letters and other manuscript papers, not myself. Neither the silence of the more modest Newton nor the eager zeal of Leibniz in ubiquitously attributing the invention of this calculus to himself will impose on any who have perused those documents which I myself have examined.
>
> [For the original Latin and this translation, see NC V 98]

Ferdinand Albrecht II (1680–1735), Prince of Braunschweig-Wolfenbüttel-Bevern. He became Duke of Braunschweig-Wolfenbüttel in March of 1735 and died six months later. He fought in the War of the Spanish Succession* on the side of the Emperor Leopold I. In the Austro-Turkish war he fought under Field Marshal Prince Eugène* of Savoy and participated in the battles of Belgrade and Petrovaradin.

FitzJames, James (1670–1734), 1st Duke of Berwick (1687), illegitimate son of King James II of England by Arabella Churchill, sister of John Churchill, 1st Duke of Marlborough. He was an Anglo-French military leader and general in the pay of Louis XIV of France. He served with distinction in the War of Spanish Succession* and led the French and Spanish troops in the Siege of Barcelona* (1713–1714), the last great battle of that war.

Flamsteed, John (1646–1719) was an English astronomer and the first Astronomer Royal. A royal warrant was issued by King Charles II in June of 1675 providing for the founding of the Royal Greenwich Observatory, and Flamsteed laid the foundation stone of the observatory in August of that year. He was elected a Fellow of the Royal Society in 1677.

Fludd, Robert (1574–1637) was an English Paracelsian physician, occultist, cabalist and Rosicrucian apologist. In his *Philosophica Mosaica* (1638) he argued that the true philosophy is to be found in the Scriptures, especially in the Pentateuch of the Old Testament.

Friedrich I and III of Prussia (1657–1713). In 1688 he became, as Friedrich III, the Elector of Brandenburg, and in that same year he took Sophie Charlotte*, the daughter of Electress Sophie* of the Palatinate, as his second wife. He subsequently became the first King of Prussia, as Friedrich I, in 1701.

STARRED REFERENCES   853

Friedrich Christian, Graf (Count) zu Schaumburg-Lippe (1655–1728). In 1691 he married Johanne Sophie* of Hohenlohe-Langenburg. Schaumburg-Lippe was a small state in Germany in the present state of Lower Saxony. Its capital was at Bückeburg, and Friedrich Christian and Johanne Sophie were often called, respectively, the Count and Countess of Bückeburg. They were divorced in 1725 by papal dispensation.

Friedrich Ludwig of Braunschweig-Lüneburg (1707–1751) was the eldest son of Caroline* of Ansbach and Georg August* of Braunschweig-Lüneburg. By order of his grandfather, Georg Ludwig* of Braunschweig-Lüneburg (George I), he was left behind to be educated in Hanover when the rest of the royal family moved to England. He was not permitted to rejoin his family in England until 1728, after his father, Georg August of Braunschweig-Lüneburg (George II), had ascended the throne in June of 1727. He was created a Knight of the Garter in 1718 and created Duke of Gloucester, Duke of Edinburgh, Marquess of Ely, Earl of Eltham, Viscount Launceston, and Baron Snowdon in 1726. He became Prince of Wales on 8 January 1729 (NS), but he never became king in Great Britain because he predeceased his father by some nine years. Friedrich Ludwig's eldest son (George William Frederick, 1738–1820) by his wife Augusta of Saxe-Gotha, daughter of Duke Friedrich II of Saxe-Gotha, became King George III on 25 October 1760—the 'King George' of the American Revolution.

Friedrich Wilhelm I (1688–1740) was the son of Friedrich I and III* of Prussia and Sophie Charlotte* of Braunschweig-Lüneburg, Queen of Prussia and daughter of the Electress of Braunschweig-Lüneburg, Sophie* of the Palatinate. Upon the death of his father in 1713, Friedrich Wilhelm became King in Prussia and Elector of Brandenburg.

Gassendi, Pierre (1592–1655) was a French philosopher, astronomer, and prominent advocate of Epicurean atomism, which he sought to reconcile with Christian doctrine.

Georg August of Braunschweig-Lüneburg (1683–1760) was the only son of Georg Ludwig* of Braunschweig-Lüneburg by his marriage to his cousin, Sophie Dorothea of Braunschweig-Lüneburg-Celle; Georg August married Caroline* of Brandenburg-Ansbach in 1705. When his father became George I of England in 1714, he became the Prince of Wales, and, after Georg Ludwig's death in 1727, he ascended the throne of Great Britain as George II.

Georg Ludwig of Braunschweig-Lüneburg (1660–1727) was the eldest son of Sophie* of the Palatinate and Ernst August* of Braunschweig-Lüneburg. Though initially lacking realistic prospects for advancement, Ernst August became, successively, the Prince-Bishop of Osnabrück (1662), Duke of Braunschweig-Lüneburg-Calenberg (at Hanover) (1679), and the first elector of Braunschweig-Lüneburg (1692). When Ernst August died in January 1698, Georg Ludwig succeeded him as the Elector of Braunschweig-Lüneburg and continued to employ the services of Leibniz, who had previously served his father and his father's brother Johann Friedrich* at the court in Hanover. When Ernst August's brother, Duke Georg Wilhelm* of Braunschweig-Lüneburg-Celle, died in 1705, the latter duchy was united with the duchy of Braunschweig-Lüneburg-Calenberg in the Electorate of Braunschweig-Lüneburg (Hanover). Because she was Protestant and the granddaughter James I of England, the Parliament in England passed the Act of Settlement* (1701), which settled the succession to the English throne on 'the most excellent princess Sophia, Electress and duchess-dowager of Hanover and the heirs of her body, being Protestant'. But the Dowager Electress Sophie of the Palatinate died on 8 June 1714, so when Queen Anne of England died on 12 August 1714, it was Georg Ludwig who acceded to the English throne as George I.

Georg Wilhelm of Braunschweig-Lüneburg (1624–1705) was the second son born to Georg (1582–1641), Duke of Braunschweig-Lüneburg-Calenberg, and Anna Eleonor of

854   STARRED REFERENCES

Hesse-Darmstadt (1601–1659). Although Georg Wilhelm had originally been betrothed to Sophie* of the Palatinate, he changed his mind, and in 1658 he struck a bargain with Sophie, Sophie's brother, Karl I. Ludwig*, and his youngest brother Ernst August* to have Sophie marry Ernst August in his stead. In return for this, Georg Wilhelm pledged not to marry in order to increase Ernst August's chances of inheriting one of the two principalities of Lüneburg (Celle) and Calenberg, which were then under the rule, respectively, of the elder brothers Christian Ludwig (1571–1648) and Johann Friedrich* (Hatton 1978, pp. 21–2). When his eldest brother Duke Christian Ludwig of Braunschweig-Lüneburg-Celle died in 1665, Georg Wilhelm inherited the principality of Lüneburg (Celle) and relinquished the principality of Calenberg (Hanover) to Johann Friedrich. But despite his pledge not to marry, he first entered into a 'marriage of conscience' with Eléonore Demeris d'Olbreuse* in 1665, and then a legal marriage in 1675, after having fathered a daughter with her in 1666. Ernst August believed that this daughter, Sophie Dorothea* of Braunschweig-Lüneburg-Celle, now threatened the prospects of his own family and decided that his eldest son, Georg Ludwig* of Braunschweig-Lüneburg, should be married to Sophie Dorothea as a means of protecting his inheritance rights (ibid., pp. 30–3). The two were indeed married in 1682, but then divorced in 1694 as a result of Sophie Dorothea's affair with Philipp Christoph von Königsmarck (see the entry for Sophie Dorothea below).

Ghoeur. See Göhrde.

Göhrde. Göhrde was the hunting lodge of the Dukes of Celle, and later of Georg Ludwig*, Elector of Braunschweig-Lüneburg (Hanover) and King George I of Great Britain. It was located in the forests of Göhrde, about seventy miles north-east of Hanover.

Görtz, Friedrich Wilhelm (1647–1728) entered the service of Elector Georg Ludwig* of Braunschweig-Lüneburg in 1695 as minister and Oberhofmarschall (chief major-domo). A diplomat and financial administrator, he was Kammerpräsident (President of the Chamber) and chief minister in Hanover after 1714. When Georg Ludwig became King of England, Görtz accompanied him to London in September of 1714 and remained there several months before returning to Hanover.

Gregory, James (1638–1675) was a Scottish mathematician and astronomer. Elected a Fellow of the Royal Society in 1668, he was appointed Professor of Mathematics at the University of St Andrews in 1669 and later, in 1674, at the University of Edinburgh.

Guericke, Otto von (1602–1686), German scientist who demonstrated the existence of a vacuum by an experiment with two hollow copper hemispheres, from which, after having been sealed together, he used the air pump he had invented to evacuate the air and then proceeded to demonstrate that they could not be pulled apart even by teams of horses.

Harley, Robert (1661–1724). From 1701 to 1705, Harley served as Speaker of the House of Commons under King William III. In 1711 he was created Earl of Oxford by Queen Anne, whom he served as Secretary of State from 1704 to 1708, as Chancellor of the Exchequer from 1710 to 1711, and as Lord High Treasurer from 1711 to 1714. As Speaker of the House, he oversaw the passage of the Act of Settlement* of 1701.

Hartsoeker, Nicolaas (1656–1725) was a Dutch mathematician and physicist and was the inventor of the screw-barrel simple microscope. He developed an atomic theory in his *Essai de dioptrique* (1694) and later published several works in physics: *Principes de la physique* (1696), *Conjectures physiques* (1706), *Suite des conjectures physiques* (1708) and *Eclaircissements sur les conjectures physiques* (1710).

STARRED REFERENCES 855

Hermann, Jakob (1678–1733), Swiss mathematician whose treatise on theoretical mechanics, *Phoronomia, sive de Viribus et Motibus corporum solidorum et fluidorum libri duo,* was published in 1716.

Herrenhausen. Herrenhausen castle was the summer palace of the dukes, and later electors, of Hanover. It was established by Leibniz's first employer in Hanover, Johann Friedrich* of Braunschweig-Lüneburg, Duke of Calenberg-Göttingen (Hanover). The Elector Ernst August* of Braunschweig-Lüneburg died there and his son Georg Ludwig* of Braunschweig-Lüneburg (later George I of England) was born there. Primarily due to the efforts of Ernst August's wife, the Duchess (later Electress) Sophie* of the Palatinate, a magnificent baroque garden was laid out there between 1696 and 1714, under the direction of the French landscape gardener Martin Charbonnier.

Hobbes, Thomas (1588–1679), English philosopher and mathematician who was an early influence on Leibniz, especially concerning the psychology of human motivation. His *Leviathan* (1651) was a masterpiece in political theory; his *De copore* (1655) was a widely ranging book dealing with logic, mathematics, and natural philosophy.

Huygens, Christiaan (1629–1695), the great Dutch mathematician and physicist, renowned for his work in optics and mechanics, as well as for his inventions (most especially for his invention of the pendulum clock). While Leibniz was in Paris on a diplomatic mission, Huygens tutored him in mathematics, in which the brilliant student soon outpaced even his brilliant tutor.

Imperial Society of Sciences. In an audience with Emperor Karl VI* in mid-January 1713, Leibniz offered his plan for establishing a Society of Sciences in Vienna. Within a few months he had drafted for the emperor a charter for the proposed society (see Klopp 1868, pp. 236–40 and FC VII 373–82), and on 14 August 1713 the emperor issued an official proclamation naming Leibniz as its president (see Klopp 1869, pp. 241–2). Leibniz wrote numerous memos and letters concerning plans for organizing and funding the society, not only for the emperor, but also for the Empress Dowager Amalie* (see, for example, document 74), for Court Chancellor Count Philipp Ludwig Wenzel von Sinzendorf*, for the President of the Imperial War Council, Prince Eugène* of Savoy, among many others. Despite Leibniz's efforts, the proposed society never saw light of day in Leibniz's lifetime, and the project was abandoned after his death in November of 1716. Although several attempts were made to revive the project during the forty-year reign (1740–1780) of Maria Theresa (1717–1780) (see Feil 1861), it was not until 1847 that the Österreichischen Akademie der Wissenschaften in Vienna was finally established.

Jablonski, Daniel Ernst (1660–1741). Jablonski was a German theologian known for his efforts to reconcile Lutheran and Calvinist Protestants, working toward that end in concert with Leibniz. In 1691 the Elector of Brandenburg, Friedrich III* appointed him court chaplain at Königsberg, and in 1693 he was appointed court chaplain at Berlin. In 1699 he was consecrated a bishop of the Moravian Church. He became president of the Berlin Academy of Sciences in 1733.

Johann Friedrich of Braunschweig-Lüneburg (1625–1679) was the third of four sons born to Georg, Duke of Braunschweig-Lüneburg-Calenberg (1582–1641), and Anna Eleonor of Hesse-Darmstadt (1601–1659). Of the four brothers, Johann Friedrich was the only one to convert to Catholicism. When his eldest brother Duke Christian Ludwig of Braunschweig-Lüneburg-Celle died in 1665, Johann Friedrich's elder brother, Georg Wilhelm* of Braunschweig-Lüneburg, inherited the principality of Lüneburg (Celle) and relinquished

856 STARRED REFERENCES

the principality of Calenberg (Hanover) to Johann Friedrich. In 1668, Johann Friedrich married Benedicte Henriette* of the Palatinate Simmern. They had three daughters, the youngest of which, Wilhelmine Amalie*, married Archduke Joseph (1678–1711) in 1699; she became Holy Roman Empress when Joseph was elected Emperor in 1705. In 1676, Johann Friedrich retained the services of Leibniz as counselor and librarian, and Leibniz subsequently served the court in Hanover under two of Johann Friedrich's successors— under Johann Friedrich's youngest brother Ernst August*, from 1679 to 1698, and then under Ernst August's son Georg Ludwig*, from 1698 until Leibniz's death in November 1716.

Johanne Sophie, Gräfin (Countess) zu Schaumburg-Lippe (1673–1743), usually called Sophie, née Johanne Sophie of Hohenlohe-Langenburg, became Gräfin zu Schaumburg-Lippe by her marriage to Friedrich Christian* (1655–1728) in 1691. Schaumburg-Lippe was a small state in Germany in the present state of Lower Saxony. Its capital was at Bückeburg, and Friedrich Christian and Johanne Sophie were often called, respectively, the Count and Countess of Bückeburg. Johanne Sophie went to England in 1714 as a lady-in-waiting for the Princess of Wales Caroline*, but returned to Germany when her elder son, Albrecht Wolfgang (1699–1748), succeeded his father as Graf (Count) zu Schaumburg-Lippe in June of 1728. Johanne Sophie had been divorced from Friedrich Christian in 1725 by papal dispensation.

Jones, William (1675–1749) was a Welsh mathematician who was elected a Fellow of the Royal Society in 1711 and later served as its vice president. In 1711 he published a major collection of Isaac Newton's mathematical papers under the title *Analysis per quantitatum series*.

Joumard, René Godefroy Louis Ernest Joseph. See the entry for Langallerie below.

Karl I. Ludwig, Elector Palatine (1617–1680), was the second son of Elector Palatine Friedrich V (1596–1632) and Elizabeth Stuart (1596–1662), who was the eldest daughter of James I of England. He was thus the sister of Sophie* of the Palatinate. In 1648, by the terms of the Treaty of Westphalia*, Karl Ludwig regained at least a part of the Palatinate (the Rhenish Palatinate, along with an electoral vote) that his father (the so-called Winter King) had lost in 1620 as a result of his conflict with Habsburg forces over the Kingdom of Bohemia, which Protestant factions had called him to rule in 1619.

Karl VI, Holy Roman Emperor (1685–1740). Karl was the younger brother of Emperor Joseph I, and thus the brother-in-law of Wilhelmine Amalie*, daughter of Leibniz's first employer in Hanover, Duke Johann Friedrich*. In 1700, upon the death of Carlos II of Spain, Karl declared himself King of Spain as Karl III, which precipitated the War of the Spanish Succession*. In 1703 a proposal of marriage for Caroline of Ansbach was sent on behalf of Karl to the Berlin court of the Electress of Brandenburg and Queen of Prussia, Sophie Charlotte* of Braunschweig-Lüneburg, where Caroline had been taken in after the death of her mother in 1696. In the autumn of the following year, Father Orban, the Jesuit confessor of the then Elector Palatine, Johann Wilhelm, Karl's uncle on his mother's side, arrived at Sophie Charlotte's palace at Lützenburg with the intention of converting Caroline to Catholicism in order to pave the way for her marriage to Archduke Karl. In the end, Caroline would not convert, and Leibniz, who had attended the sessions between Caroline and Orban, was commissioned to compose a letter to the elector Palatine to report Caroline's decision. Caroline then left Lützenburg to seek refuge in Ansbach with her brother, Wilhelm Friedrich*, who was the Margrave of Brandenburg-Ansbach. But even there she continued to receive letters from Father Orban, the Elector Palatine, and others within the emperor's party to pressure her to reconsider, but she would not. Eventually, in 1708, as the result of

STARRED REFERENCES 857

negotiations between Wilhelmine Amalie* and Duke Anton Ulrich* of Braunschweig-Wolfenbüttel, Karl married Anton Ulrich's granddaughter, Elisabeth Christine*. She had agreed to convert to Catholicism as a requisite of the marriage, and Anton Ulrich himself converted in the following year. After the death of his brother Joseph I in 1711, Karl succeeded to the imperial throne as Emperor Karl VI and became, as Karl III, the Archduke of Austria and the King of Hungary.

Keill, John (1671–1721) was a Scottish mathematician, born in Edinburgh, who became a pupil of the Scottish mathematician, David Gregory, whom he accompanied to Oxford in 1694. There he gave lectures on Newtonian physics that were published in 1701 under the title *Introductio ad veram physicam*. Newton, whom Keill probably met through Gregory, later supported Keill for Gregory's old chair as Savillian Professor of Astronomy at Oxford, to which he was consequently elected in 1712. As Derek Gjertsen has noted, Keill became

> Newton's man, ever willing to do his bidding. In the dispute with Leibniz over the invention of the calculus, Keill was Newton's first line of defence and attack. Unwilling as ever to engage his critics directly, Newton chose the pen and name of Keill to defend his own position and to attack his enemies.
>
> [Gjertsen 1986, p. 284]

In the *Philosophical Transactions* of the Royal Society for 1708, which, however, did not appear until 1710, Keill published a paper entitled *Epistola ad Clarissimum Virum Edmundum Halleium Geometriae Professorem Savilianum, De legibus virium centripetarum*; toward the end of the work, he clearly insinuated that Leibniz had plagiarized the calculus from Newton:

> All these things follow from the now most highly celebrated arithmetic of fluxions, which without any doubt Mr. Newton first invented, as will be easily established by anyone reading his letters published by Wallis. Nevertheless the same arithmetic was later published by Mr. Leibniz in *Acta Eruditorum* with a different name and form of notation.
>
> [*Philosophical Transactions* 26 (1708), p. 185]

Leibniz responded to Keill's charge by lodging a complaint in letter of 4 March 1711 to the Secretary of the Royal Society, Hans Sloane*. Keill responded in a paper that he sent to Sloane for Leibniz in May 1711. This prompted a second reply from Leibniz, written to Sloane on 29 December 1711, in which he complained of Keill's 'empty and unjust braying' (NC V, 208). This eventually led to the formation of a committee of the Royal Society, whose not disinterested president at the time was Isaac Newton, to examine the dispute between Keill and Leibniz. The committee issued a report on 24 April (5 May NS) 1712, drafted by Newton himself, that fairly concluded that Newton was the first discoverer of the calculus, but unjustly found Leibniz guilty of concealing his knowledge of the prior achievements of Newton. At the beginning of 1713, this report was published with documentation under the title, *Commercium epistolicum D. Johannis Collins, et aliorum de analysi promota*. In his letter to John Chamberlayne of 21 April 1714, Leibniz recounts the history of the dispute with Keill as far as the publication of the *Commercium epistolicum**, complaining that the committee issuing the report has 'delivered a verdict in the matter, only *one party having been heard*, in a manner whose nullity is obvious' (document 7, p. 31). In the years following the publication of the report, Keill continued to stir the pot by publishing criticisms of Leibniz and goading Newton on to continue the fight, even long after Leibniz's death.

858   STARRED REFERENCES

Ker, John (1673–1726). Ker was a Scottish spy, born in Ayrshire. His original name was Crawford, which he changed to 'Ker' after having married the younger daughter of Robert Ker of Kersland, Ayrshire, and having purchased the Ker family estates from his wife's elder sister. He later wrote of his exploits, real or imagined, in a book published in 1726, at which time he was languishing in a debtor's prison, with the self-important title, *The Memoirs of John Ker, of Kersland in North Britain Esq; Containing his Secret Transactions and Negotiations in Scotland, England, and the Courts of Vienna, Hanover, and other Foreign Parts*. He claims to have 'employed Spies and Agents over all the Country, to inform [him] of every thing that passed among the Jacobites, at their Clubs and private Meetings,' information that he then passed along to officials in the British government (Ker 1726, Part I, p. 48). He records that he travelled to Vienna at the beginning of January 1714 in the hopes of persuading the Holy Roman Emperor Karl VI* to reject peace proposals with France and thus weaken French efforts to undermine the success of the expected succession of 'the Illustrious House of Hanover to the British throne' (ibid., pp. 74ff.). He writes that the day after arriving in Vienna, he 'visited the famous *Monsieur de Leibnitz*, and told him my story: he answered, That he would wait upon *Monsieur de Emmesen*, the Emperor's private Secretary, and let him know my Arrival, and get us together; by which Means the Affair would come directly before the Emperor himself, who he believed would not lay it before his Council, in the ordinary way, but would treat with me by his Cabinet Secretary' (ibid., pp. 77–8). Ker reports that he was ultimately unsuccessful in his efforts with the emperor, and then added that he 'employed [his] spare Hours at *Vienna*, in sending to the Electress *Sophia* [i.e. Sophie* of the Palatinate], all the Light I got, and what Information I could procure of the *British* Affairs' (ibid., p. 83). He also reported that 'Monsieur *de Leibnitz*, shewed me a Letter, dated 1 June 1714, wherein *she desired me to come to* Hanover, *that she might have the Pleasure to see the Person, who had been so Zealous to serve her*' (ibid.). Ker did, in fact, arrive in Hanover in July 1714, shortly after the death of the dowager electress on 8 June 1714. But the night before he left Vienna bound for Hanover, Ker writes that

> Monsieur de Leibnitz did me the Favour to Sup with me, and gave me a Letter to her Royal Highness, now Princess of *Wales*, one to Baron *Bernstorf**, and some others, to the *Hanoverian* Ministers, he delivered to my Interpreter. We sat some Hours together, and then he took his Leave with real Marks of sincere Affection and Respect.
>
> [ibid., p. 88]

Ker was still in Hanover when news arrived of Queen Anne's death on 12 August 1714. He wrote to Leibniz forthwith, urging him '*to make haste to* Hanover; *for, by reason of your universal Knowledge, particularly of the* British *Affairs, your long Experience, and great Reputation with the King, you are justly entituled* [sic], *more than any Man in the World, to be his chief Counsellor before he goes to* England, *whose Manners and Language he is but too much a stranger to*' (ibid., p. 94). He followed Georg Ludwig* of Braunschweig-Lüneburg, now King George I of Great Britain, to Holland and then on to England. He eventually returned to Hanover in November 1716, while King George was there on a visit from England. He arrived, as he told it in a now well-known passage,

> on the very Day the late Famous Monsieur *De Leibnitz* died, which plunged me into so much Sorrow and Grief, that I cannot express it. I shall not pretend to give the Character of this incomparable Senator, for more able Pens have already made Encomiums upon this truly great Man, whose Meritorious Fame must continue while Learning or the World endures; and therefore, I shall add no more, than to declare, in

STARRED REFERENCES 859

Gratitude to his Memory, that he was so much concerned with Hardships I suffered, that without my Knowledge he ordered a Debt of two hundred and thirty Pounds, which I had contracted in *Germany*, to be discharged out of his own pocket.

I must confess, it afforded me Matter of strange Reflexion, when I perceived the llitle [sic] Regard that was paid to his Ashes by the *Hanoverians*; for he was buried in a few Days after his Decease, more like a Robber than, what he really was, the Ornament of his Country.

[ibid., pp. 117–18]

Kielmansegg, Sophie Charlotte, Freiin (Baroness) von (1675–1725). Sophie Charlotte von Kielmansegg was the half-sister of the Elector Georg Ludwig* of Braunschweig-Lüneburg and the daughter of his father, Ernst August*, and his father's mistress, Klara Elisabeth von Meysenburg. In 1673 Klara married Franz Ernst, Baron of Platen-Hallermund. When Sophie Charlotte was born in 1675, she was accepted into Ernst August's family, although Ernst August's wife, Sophie* of the Palatinate, was much aggrieved by the relationship between her husband and Klara. Sophie Charlotte became a baroness by her marriage in 1701 to Freiherr (Baron) Johann Adolf von Kielmansegg, who later became George I's Hanoverian Vice-Master of the Horse. In 1721 Sophie Charlotte was created Countess of Leinster in the Irish peerage and in 1722 Countess of Darlington in the British peerage. Her coat of arms, as Countess of Darlington, included that of the house of Braunschweig-Lüneburg, but with a bend sinister. (See Hatton 1978, pp. 23–4, 402, 412.)

Klenk (Klencke), Charlotte Elisabeth von (1685–1748). Mademoiselle Klenk was Lady of the Golden Key (First Lady-In-Waiting) to the Dowager Empress Wilhelmine Amalie* and was a fast friend of Leibniz and an important contact for him at the imperial court in Vienna.

Lahontan, Louis-Armand de Lom d'Arce, Baron de (1666–1715). Lahontan was born in the village of Lahontan in the province of Béarn in southern France. He was a French soldier and writer who explored parts of what are now Canada and the northern United States. He travelled to Quebec in 1683 as a marine lieutenant, later exploring as far as the Great Lakes and on towards the Mississippi valley. He became interested in Native American culture and followed hunting bands of Algonquins in an endeavour to master their language; he also participated in the French campaign against the Iroquois Indians. In 1687 he was named a *Lieutenant réformé* in Canada and given command of Fort Saint Joseph (at the site of what is now Niles, Michigan). He was subsequently promoted to *Capitaine réformé* in 1691, and finally, in 1693, was named *garde marine* and *Lieutenant de Roy*. Later, having been charged with insubordination by Brouillan, then governor of the colony of Plaisance in Newfoundland, Lahontan fled New France and arrived in Portugal at the beginning of 1694, never to return to the New World. In 1703, he published a two-volume work containing extensive accounts of his travels in the New World and his encounters with native Americans (*Nouveaux Voyages de Mr. le Baron de Lahontan, dans l'Amérique septentrionale, qui contiennent une rélation des différens Peuples qui y habitant; la nature de leur Gouvernement; leur Commerce, leurs Coutumes, leur Religion, & leur maniére de faire le Guerre*)—a popular work, republished in several editions and translated into English and German. In 1707 Lahontan was residing at the court in Berlin, travelling thence to the court in Hanover, where he remained a courtesan without official position until his death in 1716. Leibniz met Lahontan at the court in Hanover in the year 1710–1711, as we know from his letters to Bierling (see OB. 1148–52), and Leibniz apparently drew upon Lahontan's observations in citing the examples of the Iroquois and the Hurons against the supposition of Aristotle and Hobbes that government was a necessary requirement for human society (see GP III 424/R 196).

860 STARRED REFERENCES

Langallerie (Langalerie), Philippe de Gentils, Marquis de (1661–1717). Langallerie was the son of Henri-François de Gentils, who was styled the Marquis de Langallerie, although Arthur Michel de Boislisle has noted that 'On ne trouve pas trace d'érection de ce marquisat' (Boislisle 1898, p. 16n2). Langallerie rose to the rank of lieutenant general in the French army, with whom he fought during the War of the Spanish Succession*. But while serving in the Italian campaigns he had a falling out with his general, the Duke of Vendôme, and like his fellow officer Claude Aléxandre Bonneval*, he also had a falling out with Michel Chamillart, the controller general of France. As a result, he deserted the French army in 1706 and left for Vienna to serve Emperor Joseph I; and at Langallerie's urging, Bonneval did so as well. When they arrived in Vienna, Langallerie received a commission as major general and Bonneval a commission as colonel in the cavalry. Langallerie eventually rose to become general of the cavalry, but he soon fell into disfavour with the great military leader and president of the Imperial War Council, Prince Eugène* of Savoy, and left imperial service toward the end of 1707. In August of 1709 Langallerie married his second wife, a Protestant daughter of the Baron de Gratens named Marguerite de Frère, who pressed Langallerie to renounce his Catholic faith; she finally prevailed, and Langallerie publicly abjured Catholicism and embraced Calvinism on 19 July 1711. Shortly thereafter he published a manifesto in which he presented forty grounds for rejecting the Catholic faith in favour of the reformed religion; he produced a new edition of this manifesto at the end of August 1712. In the spring of 1713, he received a title of lieutenant general, with pension and land, from the Landgrave Karl I von Hessen-Kassel. At this time he was becoming increasingly fanatical in his religious beliefs, and he finally left his wife, children, and the court of Kassel in August of 1714, bound for Holland, where he sought to rally the Protestant communities in support of his plans for campaigns against France and Rome and to rally the Jewish communities in support of his plans for the reestablishment of the kingdom of Jerusalem. In Amsterdam he met a fellow antipapist, a notorious impostor and grifter of French origin, the falsely self-styled Comte, sometimes Landgrave, de Linange, whose real name was apparently René Godefroy Louis Ernest Joseph Joumard (see Boislisle 1898, p. 54, and Heldmann 1901, p. 337). On 8 October 1715, Langallerie and the faux Linange entered into a pact to overthrow the pope and the Inquisition, founding a theocratic movement they christened the 'Théocratie du verbe incarné', of which they proclaimed themselves, respectively, the 'grand maréchal général' and the 'grand amiral généralissime' (Boislisle 1898, p. 60). At The Hague, in December of 1715 (see ibid., p. 63 note 1), the two men entered into an agreement with a certain Osman-bacha, a Turkish military commander and self-styled ambassador extraordinaire to the Ottoman Sultan Ahmed III. Langallerie and the faux Linange offered to ensure that the Ottoman became ruler of Rome, in return for which Osaman-bacha promised them, among other things, reception at Constantinople and accommodations 'worthy of their rank and merit', 'freedom of conscience' for them and their followers, six years of paid maintenance, the power to raise and prepare troops and vessels of war, and even to enlist Christian slaves in their service (ibid., p. 63). Furthermore:

> As soon as the Grand Seigneur is ruler of Rome, he swears and promises, by our holy prophet Mohammad, to give and transfer to said seigneurs, without division, certain Mediterranean islands and the provinces stipulated in their particular agreement and to transfer those to them with full sovereignty, and even to recognize them as kings so that their descendants and heirs will enjoy them in perpetuity and rule there independently of all force.
>
> [ibid.]

STARRED REFERENCES 861

When Langallerie went to Hamburg to have vessels prepared, the emperor had him arrested in Stade. He was then taken to Vienna to face an interrogation by military commissioners. Leibniz learned some of the details of this interrogation through his contacts in Vienna and passed them along to the Princess of Wales Caroline* in a letter of 11 September 1716:

> Your Royal Highness must doubtless have been informed of the strange misconduct of the Marquis de Langallerie, with whom I was acquainted in Berlin, where he seemed pretty reasonable to me. But misfortunes have addled his brain. They write me from Vienna that when he was interrogated before the emperor's commissioners, he first confessed his treaty with the Turk; but he added there had not been any war at that time between the emperor and the Ottomans and that he had had reason to believe that there would not be any; that since he had left the service of France, he had never had engagement with any enemies of His Imperial Majesty; that his plan had been to make war on the pope as on an enemy of Jesus Christ, to hand the pope over to the Turks and the city of Rome to the emperor; that the Turks had promised him in exchange a kingdom on some Mediterranean island, and that the exchange of a priest for a kingdom would not have been bad. The commissioners have had difficulty keeping themselves from laughing. Some say that the so-called Prince of Linange, who has also arrived in Vienna, is an illegitimate son of a Count of Linange. Others claim that he is a gentleman from Poitou, and that after having made a thousand impostures in France, he arrived in Holland, saying at first that he was deputy prince of the pirates of Madagascar, who comport themselves as if they were sovereigns on that great island; after that he chose to personate the Messiah, or at least the harbinger of the Messiah, of the Jews, and found some fools who gave him money. It is therefore believed that there is malice in his deed, but madness in that of the Marquis.
>
> [document 144, p. 729]

Langallerie was condemned to life imprisonment at the fortress of Győr in Hungary, but shortly before his death, he was taken back to Vienna, where he died on 18 September 1717 (Boislisle 1898, p. 78). For his part, the faux Comte de Linange was tried after Langallerie and condemned to life imprisonment for deception, forgery, blasphemy, and treason and sent to Špilberk Castle in southern Moravia, where he spent the remaining years of his life (ibid., p. 84). For more details about the adventures of Langallerie and the faux Comte de Linange, see ibid. and Montégut 1866).

Locke, John (1632–1704) was among the more important English philosophers of the seventeenth and eighteenth centuries. His most famous and influential work in political philosophy was the *Two Treatises of Government*, published anonymously in 1689; in metaphysics and epistemology it was his *Essay Concerning Human Understanding*, first published in 1690, but followed by several substantially revised editions. Leibniz completed a lengthy response to, and critique of, Locke's *Essay* in 1704, which he entitled *Nouveaux essais sur l'entendement humain*. But Leibniz withheld publication of the work because Locke had died that same year, and Leibniz felt it unfair to publish when Locke was incapable of responding.

Louise (Luise), Raugräfin zu Pfalz (Raugravine Palatine) (1661–1733) was the daughter of the Elector Palatine Karl I Ludwig* and Marie Luise von Degenfeld. Karl was himself the brother of the Electress Sophie* of the Palatinate, and Marie Luise was his second wife. His first wife was Charlotte of Hesse-Kassel, the mother, by Karl I Ludwig, of Elisabeth Charlotte*

862   STARRED REFERENCES

of the Palatinate. So Louise was the half-sister of Elisabeth Charlotte, and both were nieces of the Electress Sophie.

Malebranche, Nicolas (1638–1715), a major philosopher of the seventeenth century, who produced works on a wide range of subjects, including metaphysics, theology, ethics, and natural philosophy. His philosophy was largely a synthesis of the views of St Augustine and René Descartes* and is distinctive for its embrace of the occasionalist doctrine that God is the only real cause, a doctrine that Leibniz consistently and strongly rejected.

Masham, Lady Damaris Cudworth (1658–1708) was the daughter of Ralph Cudworth* and a correspondent, among others, of John Locke* and Leibniz. In 1691 Locke, of whom Masham had become a friend, came to live at Masham's house, where he resided until his death in 1704. Masham authored two books, *A Discourse Concerning the Love of God* (1696) and *Occasional Thoughts in Reference to a Vertuous or Christian Life* (1705), both of which were printed anonymously.

Maximilian Wilhelm of Braunschweig-Lüneburg (1666–1726) was the third surviving son of the Duchess (later Electress) of Braunschweig-Lüneburg, Sophie* of the Palatinate, and the Duke (later Elector) Ernst August* of Braunschweig-Lüneburg. He was a field general in the Imperial Army and the only one of Sophie's sons to convert to Catholicism.

Mersenne, Marin (1588–1648) was a Minim priest who, like Descartes*, was educated at the Jesuit College of La Flèche. He wrote on a wide variety of topics in theology, philosophy, mathematics, music theory, and acoustics. He translated Galileo's *Dialogo sopra i due massimi sistemi del mondo* and *Discoursi e Dimostrazioni Matematiche intorno a Due Nouove Scienze* into French, and he corresponded extensively with philosophers and scientists of his day, including Descartes.

Middleton, Charles (1650–1719), 2nd Earl of Middleton and Jacobite 1st Earl of Monmouth. He served, successively, as Secretary of State for Scotland and Secretary of State for the Northern Department under Charles II, and then as Secretary of State for the Southern Department under James II. After the deposition of James II, he was made Jacobite 1st Earl of Monmouth by James' son, James III (The Old Pretender, James Francis Edward Stuart*), whom he served as secretary of state in exile.

Molanus (van der Muelen), Gerhard Wolter (1633–1722) was a Lutheran theologian and abbot of Loccum Abbey who was known for his efforts to reconcile Lutheran and Calvinist Protestants, and who worked toward that end in concert with Leibniz.

Nicolson, William (1655–1727) was elected Bishop of Carlisle in 1702 and elected a Fellow of the Royal Society in 1705. He served as Lord High Almoner to George I (Georg Ludwig* of Braunschweig-Lüneburg) from 1716 to 1718. In 1718 he accepted an appointment as Bishop of Derry in the Church of Ireland.

Nomis, see De Nomis

Oeynhausen, Rabe Christoph von. Oeynhausen was the Oberjägermeister (Master of the Hunt) and Kammerherr (Gentleman of the Bedchamber) at Celle, in the Hanoverian Electorate. His wife was Sophie Juliane (1668–1755), born Freiin von der Schulenburg, a sister of George I's mistress, Ehrengard Melusine von Schulenburg* (known as Melusine von Schulenburg). The youngest of the three daughters that were born to Georg Ludwig* of Braunschweig-Lüneburg and Melusine, Margarethe Gertrud (b. 1701), was registered as the child of Oeynhausen and his wife Sophie Juliane. The other two daughters had been registered as the children of Magarethe Gertrud, another of Melusine's sisters. Although none of

STARRED REFERENCES 863

the three daughters of Georg Ludwig and Melusine were legitimized, they moved to England with Melusine when Georg Ludwig became King George I of England in 1714. (See Hatton 1978, pp. 52, 406.)

Oldenburg, Henry (*c.* 1618–1677) was a German expatriate who was appointed, along with John Wilkins, as a first secretary to the Royal Society of London, of which he was an inaugural member. He later became the founding editor of the *Philosophical Transactions*, official journal of the Royal Society of London. In those capacities he maintained an extensive correspondence with intellectuals throughout Europe and Great Britain, including Leibniz.

Peter I the Great. Pyotr Alekseyevich (1672–1725), Czar of Russia from 1682. Leibniz regarded Peter as an enlightened ruler and sought to engage him in plans to establish scientific institutions in Russia that would serve to improve the lives of the Russian peoples. In December 1708, at the request of the Russian envoy to Vienna, Johann Christoph Urbich (1653–1715), Leibniz prepared a memorandum for the czar on this topic, suggesting that the purpose of scientific studies was 'human happiness' (Gurrier 1873, part II, p. 95). On the occasion of the marriage of the daughter of Anton Ulrich* to the czar's son at Torgau, Leibniz was able to meet the czar for the first time in person—a meeting for which Leibniz had prepared a number of memoranda to present to the czar (see Gurrier 1873, part II, pp. 346–69). In the latter half of June 1716, Leibniz was able to meet personally with the czar again at Pyrmont*, where the czar had been relaxing while on his tour of Europe. In his letter to Caroline of 31 July 1716, Leibniz briefly described an interesting, if dubious, experiment that the czar conducted to establish the medical effectiveness of the waters of Pyrmont (see document 135, p. 617). In a letter to Bourguet of 2 July 1716, Leibniz reported that after leaving Pyrmont, the czar 'stayed two nights at a country house very near [Hanover]' and then proceeded to lavish him with praise:

> I could not admire enough the vivacity and judgment of this great prince. He summons able persons from all sides, and when he speaks to them, he does it so aptly that they are thoroughly amazed. He inquires about all the mechanical arts, but his great curiosity is for everything having to do with navigation, and, consequently, he also loves astronomy and geography. I hope that we will learn through him whether Asia is attached to America.
>
> [document 131, p. 607]

Philippe I, Duke of Orléans (1640–1701) was the younger son of Louis XIII of France and the younger brother of Louis XIV. In 1671 he took Elisabeth Charlotte* of the Palatinate as his second wife. Their only son was Philippe II*, Duke of Orléans, who served as Regent of France from 1715 to 1723.

Philippe II, Duke of Orléans (1674–1723), was the son of Louis XIV's younger brother, Philippe I*, and Elisabeth Charlotte* of the Palatinate. When Louis XIV died on 1 September 1715, his grandson, Louis XV, was only five years old, and Philippe II served as Regent of France until Louis XV reached his majority in 1723.

Philippe (Felipe) V of Spain (1683–1746) was the second son of Louis of France (1661–1711), who was himself the eldest son of Louis XIV. When the throne of Spain became vacant in 1700, Louis XIV agreed to permit his grandson, Philippe, then Duke of Anjou, to ascend the throne in Spain. Since Philippe was in the line of succession to the throne of France, the other European powers were concerned that the kingdoms of Spain and France might eventually be united under a single Bourbon monarch in the person of

864   STARRED REFERENCES

Philippe or one of his descendants, thus upsetting the balance of power in Europe. This formed the pretext for the so-called War of the Spanish Succession*. Philippe eventually renounced the French throne in 1712.

Pöllnitz, Henriette Charlotte von (1670–1722). Pöllnitz had been the lady of the chamber for Sophie Charlotte* of Braunschweig-Lüneburg (Hanover), Electress of Brandenburg and later first Queen of Prussia. When Sophie Charlotte died in 1705, Pöllnitz was taken into the household of Sophie Charlotte's mother, Sophie* of the Palatinate, the Dowager Electress of Braunschweig-Lüneburg. (See Biermann 1999, pp. 76–82.)

Pufendorf, Samuel (1632–94) was an important and influential German natural law theorist. In *Theodicy* 182, Leibniz criticized Pufendorf for rejecting the doctrine that there are some things that are just antecedently to the decrees of God and for thus embracing a voluntaristic account of moral truth (for which see Leibniz's letter to Bourguet of 24 February 1716, document 98, p. 405 note 9). He repeated this criticism, and added a number of others, in a letter written to Gerhard Wolter Molanus* in 1701—a letter that circulated anonymously in manuscript form until it was eventually printed, again anonymously, in 1709, under the title *Epistola Viri Excellentissimi ad Amicum, quâ monita quaedam ad principia Pufendorfiani Operis, De Officio Hominis & Civis, continentur*. Leibniz was later identified as the author of the letter by Jean Barbeyrac, who appended a French translation of the letter, along with a lengthy response, to the fourth edition of his French translation of Pufendorf's *De jure naturae et gentium* (Pufendorf 1718, pp. 429–95). For an English translation of the letter, see R 64–75.

Pyrmont, now known as Bad Pyrmont, is a spa resort in Lower Saxony located on the River Emmer, about 34 miles to the south-west of Hanover. It was frequented in the seventeenth and eighteenth centuries by royalty. The mineral waters at Pyrmont were thought to have medicinal value, and visitors would go there specifically for the purpose of drinking the waters for their supposed salutary effects. Bad Pyrmonter Mineralwasser is still bottled and sold in Germany.

Rastatt, Treaty of (7 March 1714). The Treaty of Rastatt was a peace treaty that ended hostilities between France and Austria in the War of the Spanish Succession*. France and Spain, on the one hand, and Great Britain and the Dutch Republic, on the other, had previously ended their hostilities in the same war by the Treaty of Utrecht*.

Rémond, Nicolas (1638–1725) was the chief counsellor to the Duke of Orléans in Paris and the brother of the mathematician Pierre Rémond de Montmort. He was an important source of information for Leibniz about affairs in Paris.

Roche, Michel de la (*c*.1680–1742). Michel de la Roche was a French Huguenot refugee and literary critic, living in London, who began editing the literary journal *Memoirs of Literature* in 1710.

Robethon, John (d. 1722). Robethon entered the service of the Elector Georg Ludwig* of Braunschweig-Lüneburg (later George I of England) in 1705. Robethon had previously been the private secretary of Georg Ludwig's uncle, Duke Georg Wilhelm* of Celle, who died in 1705. In 1709 Robethon was appointed 'conseiller privé des ambassades,' and he managed some correspondence, relating primarily to the politics of the Protestant succession, for the Dowager Electress Sophie* of the Palatinate, the Electoral Princess Caroline* of Brandenburg-Ansbach, and the Electoral Prince Georg August*. He accompanied George I to England, and because of his greater knowledge of British affairs, he came to be regarded as

STARRED REFERENCES 865

more influential than George's principal Hanoverian minister, Andreas Gottlieb von Bernstorff*.

Roberval, Gilles Personne de (1602–1675) was a French mathematician and chair of mathematics at the Royal College of France from 1633 until his death. In his *Le Système du Monde d'après Aristarque de Samos* (1644), he wrote in praise of Aristarchus's heliocentric system and maintained that there was a mutual attraction between all material particles.

Ryswick, Peace of (1697). The Peace of Ryswick was a series of treaties signed in September and October of 1697 in the Dutch city of Rijswijk. These treaties ended the Nine Years' War (1688–1697) between France and the Grand Alliance of England, Spain, the Dutch Republic, the Duchy of Savoy, Portugal, and the Holy Roman Empire, headed by Emperor Leopold I.

St John, Henry (1678–1751), 1st Viscount Bolingbroke, was a Tory politician and statesman who was returned to the House of Commons in 1701 and rapidly grew to prominence under the tutelage of then speaker, Robert Harley* (later Lord Oxford). When Queen Anne appointed Harley Secretary of State for the Northern Department in 1704, St John was appointed Secretary at War, an office he resigned in 1708. He was returned to office as Secretary of State in 1710, when Harley became Chancellor of the Exchequer, and served in that office until 1713, at which time he became Secretary of State of the Southern Department, after having been created Viscount Bolingbroke in 1712. By this time, the friendship between Bolingbroke and Harley—who had obtained the earldom of Oxford and become Lord High Treasurer in 1711—was over. Bolingbroke ultimately gained the greater confidence of Queen Anne, and on 27 July 1714 (OS), four days before the death of the queen, Oxford resigned his office. After the queen's death, Bolingbroke swore an oath of allegiance to the new king, George I (Georg Ludwig* of Braunschweig-Lüneburg), but it was too late for him to portray himself as a supporter of the new Hanoverian court. When he was asked to surrender his papers by the new Whig ministers, he fled to France in fear of his life at the beginning of April 1715. In September he was condemned *in absentia* by a parliamentary act of attainder, thus forfeiting his lands and his title in the peerage. His social rank was reduced to that of mere common labourer and he was thereafter referred to as St John the Labourer. In July of 1715, Bolingbroke accepted an earldom from the Pretender James Francis Edward Stuart* and agreed to become his secretary of state. On 25 May 1723 he was pardoned, but he did not recover either his estates, or his title, or his seat in the House of Lords. He returned to England in 1725. After a failure to revive his political fortunes in England, he eventually returned to France in 1735, but then returned to England for a final time in 1744. He died at Battersea on 12 December 1751.

Schulenburg, Ehrengard Melusine von der (1667–1743), Gräfin (Countess). She was a sister of Johann Matthias von der Schulenberg*. In 1690 she became a lady-in-waiting to the Duchess (later Electress) of Braunschweig-Lüneburg (Hanover), Sophie* of the Palatinate, and shortly thereafter the mistress of Sophie's son, Georg Ludwig* of Braunschweig-Lüneburg (later George I of England). Melusine and Georg Ludwig had three daughters together, the youngest of which, Margarethe Gertrud (b. 1701), was registered as the child of Georg Ludwig's master of the hunt, Rabe Christoph von Oeynhausen*, and his wife Sophie Juliane. The other two daughters had been registered as the children of Margarethe Gertrud, another of Melusine's sisters. Although none of the three daughters of Georg Ludwig and Melusine were legitimized, they moved to England with Melusine when Georg Ludwig became King of England in 1714. In 1716 Melusine was naturalized British and created Duchess of Munster in the Irish peerage and Duchess of Kendal in the English peerage in 1719 (see Hatton 1978, pp. 49, 52, 406).

866   STARRED REFERENCES

Schulenburg, Johann Matthias von der (1661–1747), Graf (Count), was an officer in Saxon service who later served in the Venetian army as field marshal, taking part in the successful defence of Corfu against the Ottoman siege of 1716. He was the brother of Melusine von der Schulenburg*, who was the mistress of Georg Ludwig* of Braunschweig-Lüneburg.

Seeländer, Nicolaus (1682–1744) was a medalist from Erfurt who, among other things, struck a very large medallion commemorating the coronation of George I (Georg Ludwig* of Braunschweig-Lüneburg). In a letter of 20 December to George I's minister Andreas Gottlieb von Bernstorff* (LBr 59, Bl. 152), Leibniz requested that Seeländer be granted a modest pension as engraver for the court in Hanover. In 1716 Leibniz employed Seeländer as engraver for the court library.

Sinzendorff, Philipp Ludwig Wenzel (Count) von (1671–1742) was made court chancellor to Emperor Joseph I in 1705. He continued in this office under the Emperor Karl VI*, who acceded to the imperial throne when his brother Joseph I died in 1711.

Sloane, Hans (1660–1753) was an Irish-born physician and naturalist. He was elected Fellow of the Royal Society in 1685 and became the secretary of the Royal Society in 1693. He was editor of the *Philosophical Transactions* of the Royal Society from 1695–1713, and he served as president of the Society until 1741, having succeeded Isaac Newton in that office in 1727.

Smalridge, George (1662–1719) was appointed Bishop of Bristol and Lord Almoner in March 1714. Smalridge was a committed Tory and hence was distressed by the death of Queen Anne on 12 August 1714 and the ascension of Georg Ludwig* of Braunschweig-Lüneburg to the British throne as George I of England. After the Jacobite uprising of 1715, he refused to sign the declaration against the Pretender James Francis Edward Stuart* and later published an account of his reasons for doing so. At the request of the Princess of Wales, Caroline* of Brandenburg-Ansbach, Smalridge sent his assessment of Leibniz's *Theodicy* in a letter to her of 15 March 1715 NS (document 65), a letter that Caroline then forwarded to Leibniz. Leibniz responded to Smalridge's criticism that the *Theodicy* was 'obscure' in a letter to Caroline of 29 March 1715 (document 67a), with which he enclosed separate paper of three folio sides rebutting Smalridge's assessment (document 67b).

Sophie of the Palatinate, Duchess (later Electress) of Braunschweig-Lüneburg (Hanover) (1630–1714), was the daughter of the Elector Palatine Friedrich V and Elizabeth Stuart, who was the eldest daughter of King James I of England. Because she was Protestant and a granddaughter of James I, she and 'the heirs of her body, being Protestant,' were declared successors to the throne in England by the Act of Settlement* (1701); this ultimately resulted in her eldest son, Georg Ludwig* of Braunschweig-Lüneburg, acceding to the throne of England as George I after the death of Queen Anne on August 1 (August 12 NS) 1714. In 1658 Sophie had married Prince Ernst August* of Braunschweig-Lüneburg, who at the time was without prospects of advancement, but who, through a series of improbable events, eventually became, successively, the Prince-Bishop of Osnabrück (1662), Duke of Braunschweig-Lüneburg-Calenberg (Hanover) (1679), and the first Elector of Braunschweig-Lüneburg (1692). When he inherited the duchy of Braunschweig-Lüneburg-Calenberg-Göttingen (Hanover) upon the death, in December 1679, of his elder brother, Johann Friedrich*, he also inherited the services of Leibniz, who had been the counsellor and librarian for Johann Friedrich. In time, Leibniz and Sophie became very close friends; and of all the members of the court at Hanover, the well-educated Sophie was the one who took the greatest interest in Leibniz's philosophical work. Later, Sophie's daughter, Sophie Charlotte*, would also become a close friend and disciple of Leibniz, as would Caroline* of Brandenburg-Ansbach

STARRED REFERENCES   867

after her marriage to Sophie's grandson, Georg August*, in 1705. Sophie fell ill while strolling in the Herrenhausen gardens with Caroline* of Brandenburg-Ansbach and Johanne Sophie* Gräfin (Countess) zu Schaumburg-Lippe; she died there, in their arms, on 8 June 1716. For a touching account of her death, see Johanne Sophie's letter to Raugravine Palatine Louise* of 12 July 1714 (document 21).

Sophie Charlotte of Braunschweig-Lüneburg, Electress of Brandenburg and Queen of Prussia (1668–1705), was the only daughter of the Electress Sophie* of the Palatinate and the Elector Ernst August* of Braunschweig-Lüneburg. In 1684 she married Friedrich of Brandenburg-Prussia, who became the elector Friedrich III* of Brandenburg-Prussia in 1688 and in 1701 the first King of Prussia, as Friedrich I and III*. Sophie Charlotte became (along with her lady of the chamber, Henriette Charlotte von Pöllnitz*) a devoted disciple of Leibniz, who visited her often at her court in Berlin and at her palace in Lützenburg. She died tragically, apparently of pneumonia, on 1 February 1705 at the age of thirty-six.

Sophie Dorothea of Braunschweig-Lüneburg-Celle (1666–1726) was the only child to survive her infancy of Eléonore Desmiers d'Olbreuse* and Duke Georg Wilhelm* of Braunschweig-Lüneburg. In 1682 she married her cousin, Georg Ludwig* of Braunschweig-Lüneburg, son of the Duchess (later Electress) Sophie* of the Palatinate and Duke (later Elector) Ernst August* of Braunschweig-Lüneburg. The marriage was encouraged by Sophie and Ernst August as a way of ensuring that the duchy of Braunschweig-Lüneburg-Celle would be united to Hanover upon the death of Ernst August's older brother, Duke Georg Wilhelm. The marriage ended in divorce in January of 1695, after Sophie Dorothea was discovered having an affair with Graf Philipp Christoph von Königsmarck, an officer in the Hanoverian army. As a result of the affair, Königsmarck was assassinated in 1694, and Sophie Dorothea was confined for life in the palace of Ahlden in the duchy of Celle and forbidden access to her children from her marriage to Georg Ludwig—a daughter, also named Sophie Dorothea, who became Queen of Prussia in 1713, and a son, Georg August*, who eventually married Caroline* of Brandenburg-Ansbach in 1705 and became King George II of Great Britain in 1727. See Hatton 1978, pp. 58–64.

Spanheim, Ezechiel, Freiherr (Baron) von (1629–1710), was a Swiss diplomat and scholar who, in 1656, became tutor to the son of the Elector Palatine Karl Ludwig* (1617–1680). In 1680 he became minister of state for Friedrich I and III* (1657–1713), Elector of Brandenburg and later first King of Prussia. He spent nine years in Paris as ambassador from Brandenburg and later studied a number of years in Berlin. He resumed his post as ambassador to France after the Peace of Ryswyk* in 1697. In 1702 the Elector Friedrich became first King of Prussia, at which point Spanheim became the first Prussian ambassador to England. See SMJ XI 35.

Spanish Succession, War of the. When the throne of Spain became vacant in 1700, Louis XIV agreed to permit his grandson, Philippe, then Duke of Anjou, to ascend the throne in Spain as Philippe (Felipe) V*. Since Philippe was in the line of succession to the throne of France, the other European powers were concerned that the kingdoms of Spain and France might eventually be united under a single Bourbon monarch in the person of Philippe or one of his descendants, thus upsetting the balance of power in Europe. This formed the pretext for the so-called War of the Spanish Succession (1701–1713/14), with France, Bavaria, and the Spanish loyal to Philippe, on the one side, and, on the other, Austria, Great Britain, Holland, Portugal, Denmark, the Duchy of Savoy and the Spanish loyal to the Habsburg claimant to the Spanish throne, Archduke Karl (later Holy Roman Emperor Karl VI*), who had declared himself King in Spain as Karl III. Hostilities between the allies (excluding Austria) and France were concluded with the Treaty of Utrecht* (1713). Although Philippe

868   STARRED REFERENCES

was allowed to remain king in Spain by the terms of this treaty, he was forced to renounce his and his descendants' claim to the throne of France, as well as forfeit significant portions of Spain's European empire, which were divided among the allies.

Spinoza, Baruch (1632–77), one of the most important and influential philosophers of the seventeenth century. In his most important work, the *Ethics* (published posthumously in 1677), Spinoza developed his most distinctive philosophical doctrine, namely, that God is the only genuine substance and that finite minds and bodies are only modes of God. According to his dual-aspect theory, finite minds and bodies are only different aspects (modes) of the same substance. Leibniz firmly rejected the idea that there was only one substance and argued that finite minds (monads) were genuine substances, distinct from, and created by, God.

Stanhope, James (1673–1721), Baron Stanhope of Elvaston and Viscount Stanhope (1717) and 1st Earl of Stanhope (1718) was a British statesman and army officer who served George I in many government positions during his reign. He served as Secretary of State for the Southern Department (1714–1716), as Secretary of State for the Northern Department (1716–1717) as First Lord of the Treasury (1717–18), and Chancellor of the Exchequer (1717–18).

States-General of the Republic of the Seven United Netherlands (Messieurs des États) was the general governing body of the seven provinces of the United Netherlands from 1579 to 1795. It was located in The Hague, with delegates from each of the seven provinces.

Steffani, Agostino (1653–1728) was an Italian ecclesiastic, diplomat, and musical composer. In 1668 he was appointed Kapellmeister at the Hanoverian court of Ernst August* of Braunschweig-Lüneburg. For the new opera house in Hanover that was opened in 1689, Steffani wrote eight operas. The scores of these operas are preserved at Buckingham Palace, along with five volumes of songs and three volumes of duets, all of which were brought to England by George I in 1714 (see HC XXV, 869–70). When Ernst August died in 1698, his son, Georg Ludwig* of Braunschweig-Lüneburg (later George I of England), became Elector of Braunschweig-Lüneburg. Colin Timms has pointed out that

> by the time Georg Ludwig succeeded to the electorate, Steffani had ceased to act as Kapellmeister and had been absent from Hanover for some years on diplomatic service. In 1693 he had been appointed Hanoverian 'envoy extraordinary' to the Bavarian court in Brussels, and from 1695 his responsibilities had been increased by the problem of the Spanish succession, which was becoming complex and urgent.
>
> [Timms 2003, p. 68]

In 1703 Steffani entered the service of the Elector Palatine, Johann Wilhelm, at his court in Düsseldorf. Johann Wilhelm lobbied the Vatican to elevate Steffani to the office of bishop. This eventually came to pass when Steffani was consecrated bishop of Spiga in January of 1707. As Timms notes, Spiga 'is identical with the modern Pegae, situated in the Hellespont under the metropolitan of Cyzicus. The diocese was thus 'in partibus infidelium' [. . .]' (ibid., p. 89). In his *Memoirs of the Life of Sig. Agostine Steffani, some time Master of the Electoral Chapel of Hanover, and afterwards Bishop of Spiga* (printed in London around 1750 and reprinted in *The Gentleman's Magazine* in 1761), John Hawkins noted that Steffani's appointment as bishop 'was only titular, for it does not appear that he ever went to reside in his diocese, or ever received any revenues from thence' (as quoted Timms 2003, p. 89).

STARRED REFERENCES   869

Stuart, James Francis Edward (1688–1766). James Frances Edward Stuart, Prince of Wales, was the son of James II of England, who was deposed in the Glorious Revolution of 1688. Known as The Old Pretender, James Francis Edward claimed the English, Scottish and Irish thrones, but as a Catholic he was excluded from the succession to the British throne by the Act of Settlement* of 1701. When his half-sister Queen Anne died in 1714, she was succeeded by Georg Ludwig* of Braunschweig-Lüneburg, eldest son of the Dowager Electress of Hanover, Sophie* of the Palatinate. However, James' followers, the so-called Jacobites, continued their efforts to claim the British throne, first for him and then later for his son, Charles Edward Stuart (1720–1788), who was known as The Young Pretender.

Temesvar (Timişoara in Romanian) is a city in the Banat region of western Romania. It was captured by the Ottomans in 1552 and remained in their hands until 1716, when it was captured by Prince Eugène* of Savoy in the 1716 campaign of the Austro-Turkish War (1716–1718).

Tenison, Thomas (1636–1715), Archbishop of Canterbury from 1695 to 1715.

Tillotson, John (1630–1694) was an Anglican priest who was Dean of Canterbury from 1672 to 1689, Dean of St Paul's from 1689 to 1691, and Archbishop of Canterbury from 1691 to 1694.

Torricelli, Evangelista (1608–1647), Italian physicist and mathematician, best known for his invention of the mercury barometer.

Tschirnhaus, Ehrenfried Walther von (1651–1708) was a German mathematician, philosopher, and physician. During his travels about Europe, he met Spinoza in The Hague, Leibniz in Paris, and Newton and Robert Boyle, among others, during his visit to England in 1675. He carried on a life-long correspondence with Leibniz.

Ursinus, Benjamin (1646–1720) was the Reformed (Calvinist) senior court chaplain of Friedrich I and III* of Prussia. He was made a bishop by Friedrich when the latter became King of Prussia in 1701. In 1702 Friedrich ordered Ursinus to convene a *Collegium Irenicum* in Berlin to attempt a unification of the Protestant churches. Daniel Ernst Jablonski* and the theologian Samuel Strimesius (1684–1744) represented the Reformed churches and Johann Joseph Winckler, Pietist deacon of the cathedral at Magdeburg, and Berlin provost Franz Julius Lütke (1650–1712) represented the Lutheran churches. But in his *Arcanum Regium*, which was published in Frankfort in 1703, Winckler defended a plan to make union compulsory through a declaration of the Prussian King, a proposal that led to violent disputes when the conference began. A second round of disputes erupted when Lütke printed a criticism of the way the *Collegium* had been organized. Shortly thereafter, as Leibniz reported in his letter to Caroline of *c.*14 January 1716, 'the negotiation was suspended in mutual silence' (document 97, p. 387).

Utrecht, Treaty of (1713). Established the Peace of Utrecht, which involved a number of individual peace treaties signed by the various participants in the War of the Spanish Succession*, specifically by representatives of Louis XIV of France and his grandson Philip (Felipe) V of Spain, on the one side, and representatives of Queen Anne of Great Britain, the Duke of Savoy, the King of Portugal, and the United Provinces of the Netherlands on the other. It resulted in, among other things, Louis XIV's grandson, Philippe, Duke of Anjou, being recognized as the lawful King of Spain, thus ending the attempt by Archduke Karl of Austria, later Holy Roman Emperor Karl VI*, to claim the kingdom of Spain for himself.

Verden. See **Bremen and Verden**.

870 STARRED REFERENCES

Vittorio Amedeo Sebastiano (1666–1732), Duke of Savoy (1675–1730); he was made King of Sicily in 1713 under the terms of the Treaty of Utrecht*. In 1720 he was forced to relinquish Sicily in exchange for the Kingdom of Sardinia, becoming King Victor Amadeus II of Sardinia.

Wake, William (1657–1737) was an Anglican priest who was Dean of Exeter from 1703 to 1705, Bishop of Lincoln from 1705 to 1716, and Archbishop of Canterbury from 1716 until his death in 1737.

Wallis, John (1616–1703) was an English cryptographer and perhaps the greatest English mathematician in the generation preceding Newton. His *Arithmetica Infinitorum* (1656) contributed to the development of the integral calculus and greatly influenced the work of Newton. Among other contributions to physics, Wallis developed collision rules for inelastic bodies in response to an essay contest proposed by the Royal Society of London in 1668.

Westphalia, Peace of. The Peace of Westphalia involved a series of settlements, signed in 1648, that brought an end of the Eighty Years' War between Spain and the Dutch and the German phase of the Thirty Years' War. The treaties were negotiated, beginning in 1644, in the Westphalian towns of Münster and Osnabrück.

Wilhelm Friedrich of Brandenburg-Ansbach (1686–1723), Margrave of Brandenburg-Ansbach (from 1723) and younger brother of Caroline* of Brandenburg-Ansbach.

Wilhelmine Amalie of Braunschweig-Lüneburg (1673–1742) was the youngest of the four daughters of Leibniz's first employer in Hanover, Duke Johann Friedrich* and his wife Benedicte Henriette*. In 1699 Wilhelmine Amalie married Holy Roman Emperor Joseph I, who died in 1711. Amalie was one of Leibniz's more important contacts in the court of Vienna, along with her First Lady-in-Waiting, Charlotte Elisabeth von Klenk*.

Winde, William (*c.* 1645–1722). Winde was an architect and soldier. Born in Holland to English parents, he was in England by 1660. After the Glorious Revolution, he became a noted architect of English country houses.

Wolff, Christian (1679–1754). Wolff was a philosopher and polymath, preeminent among the German scholars in the generation following Leibniz. He became professor of mathematics and natural philosophy at the University of Halle in 1706, a position from which he was ousted on the charge of fatalism and atheism. He was reinstated to his position at Halle in 1740. He was a friend and supporter of Leibniz who promulgated his own versions of many of Leibniz's views, although these versions often departed from the views of Leibniz himself.

Wotton, William (1666–1727) was an English theologian, classical scholar, and linguist. Leibniz had an occasional correspondence with him during the years 1702–4 and 1710–1711.

Wren, Christopher (1632–1723) was a brilliant English architect who designed 53 churches, including St Paul's Cathedral following the great London fire of 1666. He was also gifted in mathematics, astronomy, and physics. He served as president of the Royal Society of London from 1680–1682. He developed collision rules for elastic bodies in response to an essay contest proposed by the Royal Society of London in 1668.

Zendrini, Bernardino (1679–1747), an Italian mathematician, physician, astronomer, and engineer in the service of the Venetian Republic.

STARRED REFERENCES 871

Zollmann (Zollman), Philipp (Philip) Heinrich (Henry) (born before 1690, died 1748). Philipp Heinrich Zollmann immigrated to England in 1714 (where he used the anglicized spelling of his name) to serve as the governor of the children of Johann Caspar von Bothmer*. Before his death in November 1716, Leibniz was in regular correspondence with Zollman, to whom he had been introduced by the latter's father, Johann Zollmann. Philip Henry became an important contact for Leibniz in London, sending Leibniz news of the court and intellectual affairs in England. He also kept Leibniz abreast of new publications in England and procured books for him. In 1723 he was elected the Royal Society's First Assistant Secretary for Foreign Correspondence, a post he left shortly thereafter to serve as secretary to the ambassador to France, Horace Walpole, and subsequently as secretary to the ambassador to Sweden, Stephen Poyntz. He was eventually elected a fellow of the Royal Society in 1727. For more on Philip Henry Zollmann and his relation to Leibniz, see Massarella 1992.

Bibliography

Aiton, E. J. 1985. *Leibniz: A Biography*. Boston: Adam Hilger.

Alexander, H. G., ed. 1956, rpt. 1998. *The Leibniz-Clarke Correspondence*. Manchester, UK: Manchester University Press.

Amery, John S. 1880. 'John Lethbridge and his Diving Machine'. *Report and Transactions of the Devonshire Association for the Advancement of Science, Literature, and Art* 12, pp. 490–6.

Antognazza, Maria Rosa. 2009. *Leibniz: An Intellectual Biography*. New York: Cambridge University Press.

Antognazza, Maria Rosa, ed. 2018. *The Oxford Handbook of Leibniz*. New York: Oxford University Press.

Arkell, R. L. 1939. *Caroline of Ansbach: George the Second's Queen*. New York: Oxford University Press.

Bailey, Francis. 1835. *An Account of the Rv^d John Flamsteed, the first Astronomer Royal; compiled from his own Manuscripts, and other authentic documents, never before published. To which is added his British Catalogue of Stars, Corrected and Enlarged*. London.

Bailey, Francis. 1837. *Supplement to the Account of the Revd John Flamsteed, the First Astronomer Royal*. London.

Batten, J. Minton. 1944. *John Dury: Advocate of Christian Reunion*. Chicago: University of Chicago Press.

Bayle, Pierre. 1705. *Continuation des Pensées diverses, Ecrites à un Docteur de Sorbonne, à l'occasion de la Comete qui parut au mois de Decembre 1680*. Rotterdam: Reinier Leers.

Bertoloni Meli, Domenico 1999. 'Caroline, Leibniz, and Clarke'. *Journal of the History of Ideas* 60.3, pp. 469–86.

Biermann, Veronica. 1999. '"Ma Chére Pelnits" Henriette Charlotte von Pöllnitz (um 1670–1722), "Erstes Kammerfräulein" Sophie Charlottes'. In Herz, Vogtherr and Windt 1999, pp. 77–83.

Boethius. 2008. *The Consolation of Philosophy*. Translated by David R. Slavitt. Cambridge, MA: Harvard University Press.

Boileau-Despréaux, Nicolas. 1821. *Oeuvres de Boileau-Despréaux*. 4 vols. Paris: J. J. Blaise.

Boislisle, Arthur Michel de. 1898. *Les Aventures du Marquis de Langalerie (1661–1717)*. Nogent-le-Rotrou: Imprimerie Daupley-Gouverneur.

Boyer, Abel. 1722. *The History of the Life and Reign of Queen Anne*. London.

Brewster, David. 1855. *Memoirs of the Life, Writings, and Discoveries of Sir Isaac Newton*. Two volumes. Edinburgh: Thomas Constable and Co.

Brown, Beatrice Curtis, ed. 1968. *The Letters and Diplomatic Instructions of Queen Anne*. New York: Funk and Wagnalls.

Brown, Gregory. 1984. '"*Quod Ostendendum Susceperamus*": What Did Leibniz Undertake to Show in the *Brevis Demonstratio*?' In Heinkamp 1984, 122–37.

Brown, Gregory. 2004a. '"…et je serai tousjours la meme pour vous": Personal, Political, and Philosophical Dimensions of the Leibniz-Caroline Correspondance'. In Lodge 2004, pp. 262–92.

Brown, Gregory. 2004b. 'Leibniz's Endgame and the Ladies of the Courts'. *Journal of the History of Ideas* 65: 4, pp. 75–100.

874 BIBLIOGRAPHY

Brown, Gregory. 2016a. 'The *Theodicy* Translation Project and the Leibniz-Clarke Correspondence'. In Li 2016, pp. 51–67.

Brown, Gregory. 2016b. 'Did Samuel Clarke really Disavow Action at a Distance in His Correspondence with Leibniz? Newton, Clarke, and Bentley on Gravitation and Action at a Distance'. *Studies in History and Philosophy of Science* 60, pp. 38–47.

Brown, Gregory. 2016c. 'Leibniz on the Possibility of a Spatial Vacuum, the Connectedness Condition on Possible Worlds, and Miracles'. In Brown and Chiek 2016, pp. 201–26.

Brown, Gregory. 2020. 'The Correspondence with Clarke'. In Lodge and Strickland 2020, pp. 228–49.

Brown, Gregory and Yual Chiek, eds. 2016. *Leibniz on Compossibility and Possible Worlds*. Cham, Switzerland: Springer.

Cicero, Marcus Tullius. 1965. *The Letters to his Friends*. 3 vols. Translated by W. Glynn Williams. Cambridge, MA: Harvard University Press.

Ciminelli, Serafino dei. 1894. *Le rime di Serafino de'Ciminelli dall'Aquila*, vol. 1. Edited by Mario Menghini. Bologna: Presso Romagnoli-dall'Acqua.

Clarke, Samuel, ed. 1717. *A Collection of Papers, which passed between the late Learned Mr. Leibnitz, and Dr. Clarke, In the Years 1715 and 1716. Relating to the Principles of Natural Philosophy and Religion*. London: James Knapton.

Clarke, Samuel. 1738. *The Works of Samuel Clarke*. 4 vols. Ed. B. Hoadly. London: John and Paul Knapton.

Cowper, Mary. 1865. *Diary of Mary Countess Cowper, Lady of the Bedchamber to the Princess of Wales, 1714–1720*, 2nd edn. Edited by Spencer Cowper. London: John Murray.

De Risi, Vincenzo. 2007. *Geometry and Monadology: Leibniz's Analysis Situs and Philosophy of Space*. Basel: Birkhäuser.

De Risi, Vincenzo. 2018. 'Analysis Situs, the Foundations of Mathematics, and a Geometry of Space'. In Antognazza 2018, pp. 247–58.

Des Maizeaux, Pierre, ed. 1720. *Recueil de diverses Pièces, sur la Philosophie, la Religion Naturelle, l'Histoire, les Mathematiques, &c. Par Mrs. Leibniz, Clarke, Newton, & autres Autheurs célèbre*. 2 vols. Amsterdam: H. du Sauzet.

Doebner, R. 1881. 'Leibnizens Briefwechsel mit dem Minister von Bernstorf und andere Leibniz betreffende Briefe und Aktenstücke aus den Jahren 1705–1716. Mit einer Einleitung herausgegeben von Dr. Doebner'. *Zeitschrift des Historischen Vereins für Niedersachsen*, pp. 205–380.

Doebner, R. 1884. 'Nachträge zu Leibnizens Briefwechsel mit dem Minister von Bernstorff'. *Zeitschrift des Historischen Vereins für Niedersachsen*, pp. 206–41.

Echeverría, Javier, trans. and ed. 1989. *G. W. Leibniz: Filosofía para princesas*. Madrid: Alianza Editorial.

Feil, Joseph. 1861. 'Versuche zur Gründung einer Ackademie der Wissenschaften unter Maria Theresia'. *Jahrbuch für vaterländische Geschicte* 1, pp. 322–407.

Ferrone, Vincenzo. 1995. *The Intellectual Roots of the Italian Enlightenment*, translated by Sue Brotherton. Atlantic Highlands, NJ: Humanities Press International.

Fontenelle, Bernard Le Bovier de. 1717. *The Lives of the French, Italian, and German Philosophers, late Members of the Royal Academy of Sciences in Paris. Together with abstracts of some of the choicest pieces, communicated by them to that illustrious society. To which is added, the preface of the ingenious Monsieur Fontenelle, Secretary and Author of the History of the said Academy*. Translated by John Chamberlayne. London: W. Innys.

Frey, Linda and Marsha Frey. 1995. *The Treaties of the War of the Spanish Succession: An Historical and Critical Dictionary*. Westport, CT: Greenwood Press.

Garber, Daniel and Béatrice Longuenesse, eds. 2008. *Kant and the Early Moderns*. Princeton, NJ: Princeton University Press.

BIBLIOGRAPHY 875

Gerber, Matthew. 2012. *Bastards: Politics, Family, and Law in Early Modern France*. New York: Oxford University Press.

Gjertsen, Derek. 1986. *The Newton Handbook*. New York: Routledge & Kegan Paul.

Gregg, Edward. 2001. *Queen Anne*. New Haven, CT: Yale University Press.

Guerrier, Vladimir Ivanovic. 1873. *Leibniz in seinen Beziehungen zu Russland und Peter dem Grossen: eine geschichtliche Darstellung dieses Verhaltnisses nebst den darauf bezuglichen Briefen und Denkschriften*. St Petersburg and Leipzig: Der Kaiserlichen Akademie der Wissenschaften.

Guhrauer, Gottschalk Eduard. 1846. *Gottfried Wilhelm Freiherr von Leibnitz. Eine Biographie*. 2 vols. Breslau: Hirt. Reprint, Hildesheim: Olms, 1966.

Hall, A. Rupert. 1980. *Philosophers at War: The Quarrel between Newton and Leibniz*. New York: Cambridge University Press.

Harris, R. W. 1983. *Clarendon and the English Revolution*. Stanford, CA: Stanford University Press.

Harrison, Peter 1995. 'Newtonian Science, Miracles, and the Laws of Nature'. *Journal of the History of Ideas* 56.4, 531–53.

Hasluck, F. W. 1910. *Cyzicus*. Cambridge, UK: Cambridge University Press.

Hattendorf, John B. 2008. 'Savage, Richard, fourth Earl Rivers (c. 1654–1712)'. In *Oxford Dictionary of National Biography*. Retrieved 11 Jan. 2020, from https://www.oxforddnb.com/view/10.1093/ref:odnb/9780198614128.001.0001/odnb-9780198614128-e-24723.

Hatton, Ragnhild M. 1968. *Charles XII of Sweden*. New York: Weybright and Talley.

Hatton, Ragnhild M. 1978. *George I, Elector and King*. Cambridge, MA: Harvard University Press.

Hauc, Jean-Claude. 2009. *Aventuriers et libertins au siècle des Lumières*. Paris: Les Éditions de Paris.

Heinekamp, Albert, ed. 1984. *Leibniz Dynamica (Studia Leibnitiana Sonderheft* 13). Wiesbaden: Franz Steiner.

Heldmann, August. 1901. 'Zur Geschichte des Gerichts Viermünden und seiner Geschlechter. III. Das Geschlect von Dersch'. *Zeitschrift des Vereins für hessische Geschichte und Landeskunde* 24:2, pp. 159–360.

Herz, S., C. M. Vogtherr, and F. Windt, eds. 1999. *Sophie Charlotte und ihr Schloß: Ein Musenhof des Barock in Brandenburg-Preußen*. New York: Prestel.

Janiak, Andrew. 2015. *Newton*. Malden, MA: John Wiley & Sons.

Jauernig, Anja. 2008. 'Kant's Critique of the Leibnizian Philosophy: *Contra* Leibnizians, but *Pro* Leibniz'. In Garber and Longuenesse 2008, pp. 41–63.

Jones, Matthew L. 2018. 'Calculating Machine'. In Antognazza 2018, pp. 509–25.

Jordan, G. J. 1927. *The Reunion of the Churches: A Study of G. W. Leibnitz and his Great Attempt*. London: Constable & Co. Ltd.

Kamen, Henry. 1969. *The War of Succession in Spain 1700–1715*. Bloomington, IN: Indiana University Press.

Keill, John. 1708. 'Epistola ad Clarissimum Virum Edmundum Halleium Geometriae Professorem Savilianum, de Legibus Virium Centripetarum'. *Philosophical Transactions* 26, 174–88.

Ker, John. 1726. *The Memoirs of John Ker, of Kersland in North Britain Esq; containing His Secret Transactions and Negotiations in Scotland, England, the Courts of Vienna, Hanover, and other Foreign Parts*. London: Published by Himself.

Khamara, Edward. 2006. *Space, Time, and Theology in the Leibniz-Newton Controversy* Frankfurt: Ontos Verlag.

Klopp, Onno. 1869. 'Leibniz' Plan der Gründgung einer Societät der Wissenschaften in Wien'. *Archiv für österreichische Geschichte* 40, pp. 157–255.

876 BIBLIOGRAPHY

Koyré, Alexandre. 1965. *Newtonian Studies*. Chicago: Chicago University Press.

Koyré, Alexandre and I. Bernard Cohen. 1961. 'The Case of the Missing *Tanquam*: Leibniz, Newton & Clarke'. *Isis* 52:4, pp. 555–66.

Koyré, Alexandre and I. Bernard Cohen. 1962. 'Newton & the Leibniz-Clarke Correspondence'. *Archives Internationales d'Histoire des Sciences* 15, 63–126.

Laeven, H. 1990. *The 'Acta Eruditorum' under the Editorship of Otto Mencke (1644–1707): The History of An International Learned Journal Between 1682 and 1707*. Translated from the Dutch by Lynne Richards. Amsterdam and Maarssen: Academic Publishers Associated.

Li, Wenchao, ed. 2016. *Leibniz, Caroline und die Folgen der englischen Sukzession*. Stuttgart: Franz Steiner Verlag.

Lodge, Paul, ed. 2004. *Leibniz and His Correspondents*. New York: Cambridge University Press.

Lodge, Paul and Lloyd Strickland, eds. 2020. *Leibniz's Key Philosophical Writings*. Oxford: Oxford University Press.

Macpherson, James. 1775. *Original Papers; containing the Secret History of Great Britain from the Restoration to the Accession of the House of Hanover*. 2 vols. London: W. Strahan and T. Cadell.

Marthaler, Berard, Gregory F. LaNave, Jonathan Y. Tan, Richard E. McCarron, eds. 2003. *New Catholic Encyclopedia*. 15 vols. 2nd edn. Detroit, MI: Gale.

Massarella, Derek. 1992. 'Philip Henry Zollman, the Royal Society's First Assistant Secretary for Foreign Correspondence'. *Notes and Records of the Royal Society of London* 46:2, pp. 219–34.

Mathew, C. G. and Brian Harrison, eds. 2004. *Oxford Dictionary of National Biography*. New York: Oxford University Press.

Messbarger, Rebecca. 2002. *The Century of Women: Representations of Women in Eighteenth-Century Italian Public Discourse*. Toronto: University of Toronto Press.

Mieder, Wolfgang. 2002. *'Call A Spade A Spade': From Classical Phrase to Racial Slur, A Case Study*. New York: Peter Lang.

Montégut, Henry B. 1866. *Philippe de Gentils de Lajonchapt, Marquis de Langallerie, premier Baron de Saintonge, Lieutenant-Général des armées du roi, Feld-maréchal au service d'Autriche, etc., (1661–1717)*. Angoulême: Nadaud et CIE.

Murray, Michael J. 2002. 'Leibniz's Proposal for Theological Reconciliation among the Protestants'. *American Catholic Philosophical Quarterly*, pp. 623–646.

Newton, Isaac. 1959–77. *The Correspondence of Isaac Newton*. 7 vols. Eds H. Turnbull, J. F. Scott, A. Rupert Hall, and Laura Tilling. Cambridge: Cambridge University Press.

Newton, Isaac. 1999. *The Principia: Mathematical Principles of Natural Philosophy*. Translated by I. Bernard Cohen and Anne Whitman. Berkeley: University of California Press.

Newton, Isaac. 2014. *Philosophical Writings*, ed. Andrew Janiak. Cambridge: Cambridge University Press.

Pfizenmaier, Thomas C. 1997. 'Was Isaac Newton an Arian?' *Journal of the History of Ideas* 58.1, pp. 57–80.

Pufendorf, Samuel. 1695. *Jus feciale divinum sive de consensu et dissensu protestantium exercitatio posthuma*. Lubecae A.S.R.

Pufendorf, Samuel. 1712. *Le Droit de la Nature et des Gens*. 2 vols. Translated and edited by Jean Barbeyrac. Amsterdam: Pierre de Coup.

Pufendorf, Samuel. 1718. *Les devoirs de l'homme et du citoyen, tels qu'ils lui sont prescrits par la loi naturelle*. 2 vols. Translated and edited by Jean Barbeyrac. Amsterdam: Pierre de Coup.

Rae, Thomas H. H. 1998. *John Dury and the Royal Road to Piety*. New York: Peter Lang.

Raphson, Joseph. 1715. *Historia Fluxionum*. London. It should be noted, as A. Rupert Hall has, that '[. . .] probably in 1717 or 1718—Newton had the *History of Fluxions* reissued,

with the same title page and date as before but with errata noted on the opening pages and the last chapter (on the *Commercium Epistolicum*) added; to this he also appended the correspondence between Leibniz and the Abbé Conti with his own 'Observations' upon their letters' (Hall 1980, pp. 225–6).

Robertson, J. G. 1923. *Studies in the Genesis of Romantic Theory in the Eighteenth Century.* Cambridge, England: Cambridge University Press. Reprint, New York: Russell & Russell, 1962.

Robinet, André, ed. 1986. *Leibniz: Principes de la nature et de la grâce fondés en raison • Principes de la philosophie ou Monadologie.* 3rd edn. Paris: Presses Universitaires de France.

Robinet, André, ed. 1991. *Correspondance Leibniz-Clarke.* 2nd edn. Paris: Presses Universitaires de France.

Rodriguez-Pereyra, Gonzalo. 2014. *Leibniz's Principle of Identity of Indiscernibles.* New York: Oxford University Press.

Rouse, Ruth and Stephen Charles Neill, eds. 1954. *A History of the Ecumenical Movement.* Philadelphia: The Westminster Press.

Ryan, E. G. 2003. 'Januarius, St'. In Berard L. Marthaler, Gregory F. LaNave, Jonathan Y. Tan, Richard E. McCarron, eds, vol. 7, pp. 723–4.

Saint-Victor, Jacques Maximilien Benjamin Bins de. 1809. *Tableau historique et pittoresque Paris,* vol. 3. Paris: H. Nicolle.

Schüller, Volkmar, ed. 1991. *Der Leibniz-Clarke Briefwechsel.* Berlin: Akademie Verlag.

Schmidt, Martin. 1954. 'Ecumenical Activity on the Continent of Europe in the Seventeenth and Eighteenth Centuries'. In Rouse and Neil 1954, pp. 73–120.

Timms, Colin. 2003. *Polymath of the Baroque: Agostino Steffani and His Music.* New York: Oxford University Press.

Walpole, Robert. 1715. *A Report from the Committee of Secrecy, Appointed by Order of the House of Commons to Examine Several Books and Papers laid before the House, relating to the late Negotiations of Peace and Commerce, &c.* London: published by order of the House of Commons and printed for Jacob Tonson, Timothy Goodwin, Bernard Lintatt, and William Taylor.

Webster, Hutton. 1920. *Historical Source Book.* New York: D. C. Heath and Co.

Westfall, Richard 1980. *Never at Rest: A Biography of Isaac Newton.* New York: Cambridge University Press.

Wilding, Peter. 1937. *Adventurers in the Eighteenth Century.* New York: G. P. Putnam's Sons.

Woolhouse, R. S. and Richard Francks, trans. and eds. 1997. *Leibniz's 'New System' and Associated Contemporary Texts.* New York: Oxford University Press.

Name Index

Entries marked with an asterisk refer to items also found in the starred references

*Addison, Joseph (1672–1719) 281, 283n10, 283n12, 297, 311, 363
Alberoni, Giulio (1664–1752) 902n2
Alcibiades (c.450–404) BCE 155
Alexander the Great (356–323 BCE) 157
Anne (1665–1714), Queen of England, Ireland and Scotland (Great Britain after 1707) 1702–14 xxxviii, 53, 65n7, 67, 75–7, 81, 133
death of xxxviii, 93, 97
letter to Georg August, Electoral Prince of Braunschweig-Lüneburg 50–1
letter to Georg Ludwig, Elector of Braunschweig-Lüneburg 48–51
letter to Sophie of the Palatinate, Dowager Electress of Braunschweig-Lüneburg 48–9
Antognazza, Maria Rosa, liv, li note 25
Antoinette Amalie of Braunschweig-Wolfenbüttel (1696–1762), Duchess of Braunschweig-Wolftenbüttel (from 1735) 727
*Anton Ulrich (1633–1714), Duke of Braunschweig-Wolfenbüttel, sole ruling duke (from1704) l, 25n4, 71n10, 353n24, 655
Archimedes (ca. 287–ca. 212 BCE)
and Principle of Sufficient Reason 11, 355
Arenberg, Léopold Philippe Charles Joseph, Duc d' 97, 121, 135, 153
Areskin, Robert, see Erskine
Aristotle (384–322 BCE) 157, 355, 403n9, 429, 433, 435
Arminius, Jacobus, see Hermanszoon, Jakob
Arnold, John 493, 495n3, 503n3, 547
letter from Leibniz 576–9
August II the Strong (1670–1733), King of Poland (from 1694) 559/561n10
August III (1696–1763), King of Poland (from1733) 353n18
August Wilhelm (1662–1731), Duke of Braunschweig-Wolfenbüttel (from 1714) 151n6

Augustine of Hippo, Saint (354–430) 307, 309
Azzo II of Este (996–1097) 169

*Bacon, Francis (1561–1626) 327, 409, 459
Barbeyrac, Jean (1674–1744) 401/403n8/405n10, 451/453n7&n8, 465/467n9
*Barrow, Isaac (1630–1677) 423, 441, 455, 479
Barton, Catherine (1679–1739) 807
*Bayle, Pierre 15, 157, 325, 423, 425, 697, 699, 715, 755, 803
Beaune, Florimond de (1601–1652) 481
Becker, Andrew 279
diving machine 265n6, 279, 297, 309
Behn, Aphra (1640–1689) 659n8, 713n3
Berkeley, George (1685–1753) 461/463n5, 533
Bernoulli, Jacob (1655–1705) 241n6, 487n32, 525n3
*Bernoulli, Johann (1667–1748) lxviii, lxxix, 15, 241n6, 323, 417/419n3, 419/421n3, 421, 437/443n3, 471, 477, 481, 487n32, 505, 507, 511n5&n13, 521/525n3, 527n5, 805
letters from Leibniz 232–5, 318–21, 492–3, 578–83, 758–9
letters to Leibniz 544–7, 610–11, 802–5
*Bernstorff, Andreas Gottlieb von (1649–1726), chief Hanoverian minister in England for George I (Georg Ludwig of Braunschweig-Lüneburg) (1714) xxxvii, xxxix, xlvii, liv, lvi, lvii, 75, 95, 107, 305–7
letters from Leibniz 28–9, 96–7, 108–13, 142–5, 168–75, 186–7, 220–3
letters to Leibniz 24–7, 162–5, 164–5, 230–3
Berwick, Duke of, see James Fitzjames
*Blackburne, Lancelot (16581743), Dean of Exon (Exeter), Bishop of Exeter (1717), Archbishop of York (1724) 631, 745, 747n6, 801, 803n11
Boethius, Anicius Manlius Severinus (d. 524) 527n4
Boileau-Despréaux, Nicolas (1636–1711) 161n15, 299
Bolingbroke, see Henry St John

880 NAME INDEX

*Bonneval, Claude Aléxandre, Comte de
(1675–1747), French soldier of
fortune, imperial major general
(1706) and lieutenant general
(1714) xxxix, xliii, xlvi, l, 175
letter from Leibniz 120–3, 150–9
letter to Leibniz 134–7
Borelli, Giovanni Alfonso (1608–1679) 277
*Bothmer, Johann Caspar von (1656–1732),
minister to Georg Ludwig of
Braunschweig Lüneburg (later King
George I of England) xxxix–xli, xliii,
xlviii, lxix, lxxxiv, 75, 95
letter from Leibniz 502–9
letter from Philipp Ludwig Wenzel (Count)
von Sinzendorff 98–9
letters to Leibniz 518–21, 554–5, 608–9,
624–7, 760–1
Bourguet, Louis (1678–1742)
letters from Leibniz 254–63, 398–405, 462–7
letters to Leibniz 444–53, 460–3, 530–5
*Boyle, Robert (1627–691) xcix, 483, 633, 707
Bragança, Manuel de, Count of Ourém
(1697–1736) 719
Brandenburg, so-called Count of or
Father 729/733n10, 745, 751
Bückeburg, Countess of, see Johanne Sophie, Gräfin
(Countess) zu Schaumburg-Lippe
*Bucquoy, Jean-Albert d'Archambuad, Comte de
(ca. 1650–1740) 729, 747
Burnet, Gilbert (1643–1715), Bishop of Salisbury
(from 1689) 393n8
Burnett, Thomas of Kemney (1654–1729) xlviii
note 20, lxii, 363
Butler, James (1665–1745), 2nd Duke of Ormond
(from 1690) 373/375n15

Cabrera, Juan Tomás Enríquez de (1647–1705),
Count of Melgar 729
Calvin, John 2, 397n17, 403n9
Campbell, John (1680–1743), 2nd Duke of
Argyle 299
Carlos II (1661–1700), King of Spain
(1665–1700) 733n16
*Caroline of Brandenburg-Ansbach (b. 1683),
Electoral Princess of Braunschweig-
Lüneburg (1705–14), Princess of
Wales (1714–27), Queen of Great
Britain and Ireland (1727–37) xxxvi,
xxxix, xlii–xlvi, xliii–xlvii, lii–lxxxv,
57–58, 61, 71n10, 81–85, 95, 105, 107,
113–15, 121, 125, 135, 139, 149, 153,
187, 211, 213n2, 219n2, 231, 285, 325,
331, 353n24, 403, 451, 459, 465, 579,
613, 627, 715, 757, 759, 761, 1011n3

letter to Baroness Mary Cowper concerning
the death of Sophie of the Palatinate,
Dowager Electress of
Braunschweig-Lüneburg 86–9
letter from George Smalridge, Bishop of
Bristol 215–21
letters from Leibniz 44–7, 66–9, 72–7, 128–9,
174–7, 178–83, 200–3, 208–9, 224–5,
226–31, 236–41, 252–3, 278–83,
288–93, 302–15, 342–53, 406–9,
494–7, 500–3, 520–7, 556–63, 612–23,
628–33, 726–33, 742–49
letters to Leibniz 52–7, 184–5, 206–7, 212–13,
264–7, 296–303, 332–7, 372–9,
512–19, 534–7, 582–9, 718–23, 724–7,
750–3, 752–3, 762–3, 800–3
Carpenter, George (1657–1731), 1st Baron
Carpenter of Killaghy (from
1719) 299
Castagnéry, Pierre-Antoine de (1647?–1728),
Marquis de Châteauneuf 123
Castel, Charles-Irénée, abbé de Saint-Pierre
(1668–1743) 225
Catelan, Abbé François (fl. c.1700) 479
Catherine (Yekaterina) I (1684–1727), Empress
consort of Peter I the Great* (from
1712) and Empress Regnant of Russia
(from 1725) 745, 747n10
Cavalièri, Bonaventura Francesco
(1598–1647) 469, 475, 509, 511n13
*Chamberlayne, John (1669–1723) li–liii
letter from Leibniz 28–33
letters to Leibniz 27, 77–9, 91
letter from Newton 34–7
letter to Newton 37–9
Charles II of Spain, see Carlos II
Charles VI, Holy Roman Emperor, see Karl VI
*Cheyne, George (1673?–1743) 533
letter from Leibniz 738–41
Christian August of Saxe-Zeitz (1666–1725),
Cardinal Primate of Hungary 151
Christine Louise of Oettingen (1671–1747) 149
Chrysippus (c.280 bce–c.206 bce) 659, 713
Churchill, John (1650–1722) 135, 177n8
*Churchill, Sarah (1660–1744), Duchess of
Marlborough (1702) 121, 135
Cicero (106–43 bce) 161n13, 405, 693
*Clarke, Samuel xxxv–xxxvi, lii, lx, lxiii–lxxiv,
lxvi–lxxxv–cii, 161, 219n2, 259, 271,
297, 313, 325, 335, 345, 367, 373, 451,
459, 461, 495, 499, 501, 513, 515, 523,
533, 537, 549, 557, 577, 579, 581, 583,
607, 611, 615, 623, 629, 715, 721, 725,
731, 739, 747, 749, 751, 753, 757, 759,
801, 803

NAME INDEX 881

First Reply to Leibniz 338–43
Second Reply to Leibniz 378–85
Third Reply to Leibniz 538–45
Fourth Reply to Leibniz 590–605
Fifth Reply to Leibniz 762–801
Colbert, Jean-Babtiste (1665–1746), Marquis de Torcy 373
*Collins, John (1625–83) 323, 325, 417, 419, 423, 429, 437, 439, 471, 473, 475
Compton, Spencer (1674–1743), 1st Earl of Wilmington 283
*Conti, Antonio Schinella (1677–1749) lxix–lxxii, lxxvii–lxxviii, lxxx, lxxxv, 269, 319, 321, 331, 347, 373, 445, 459, 491, 493, 501, 503/511n4, 513, 515, 521, 535, 549, 557, 559, 577, 583, 615, 615, 627, 725, 741, 745, 749, 809, 835, 837
letters from Leibniz 322–31, 468–91
letters to Leibniz 274–7, 452–7
letters from Newton 417–19, 419–21, 421–29, 429–33, 433–5, 435–7, 437–43
letter to Newton 804–7
letters to Nicolas Rémond concerning Newton 268–74
Corneille, Pierre (1606–84) 299, 311
Cosimo III de' Medici (1642–1723) 171
*Coste, Pierre (1668–1747) lxxix, 239, 241, 615, 717, 719n12
*Cotes, Roger (1682–1716) 28n1, 469, 579
*Cowper Mary (1685–1724), Baroness (Countess Cowper, 1718) 219n2
letter from Johanne Sophie, Gräfin (Countess) zu Schaumburg-Lippe concerning the death of Sophie of the Palatinate, Dowager Electress of Braunschweig-Lüneburg 57–9
letter from Caroline, Electoral Princess of Braunschweig-Lüneburg, concerning the death of Sophie of the Palatinate, Dowager Electress of Braunschweig-Lüneburg 86–9
Cowper, William (1665–1723), Lord High Chancellor of Great Britain under Queen Anne (1707–10) and under Georg Ludwig of Braunschweig-Lüneburg (George I) (1714–18), created 1st Earl Cowper (1718) 89n2
Craggs, James the Younger (1686–1721) 95
Cresset, James (1655–1710) 393n8
Cromwell, Oliver (1599–1658) 393n8
Crousaz, Jean-Pierre de (1673–1750) 401/403n7, 451/453n6
Cudworth, Ralph (1618–88) 239

Dacier, Anne Le Fèvre (1647–1720) 309
Davenant, John (1572–1641) Bishop of Salisbury (1621–41) 523/527n11
Del Giudice, Francesco (1647–1725), cardinal (from 1690) 629
Democritus 329, 803
and materialism 355, 357
Desaguliers, John Theophilus (1683–1744) lxxii, 515
Des Bosses, Bartholomew (1668–1728) 7
*Descartes, René (1596–1650) 13, 201, 257, 259, 323, 463, 475, 479, 481, 567, 611, 639, 643, 673, 703, 769, 769, 781, 805, 831
*Des Maizeaux, Pierre (1673–1745) lxxix, 615, 629, 713n2
letter from Leibniz 714–19
letters from Newton 835, 837
letter to Philip Heinrich Zollmann 612–13
Desmarets, Samuel (1599–1673) 403n9
Diodorus Cronus (d. c.284 BCE) 693
Ditton, Humphry (1675–1715) 259
Dodwell, Henry (1641–1711) 345, 347, 565
*Dury, John (1596–1680) 389, 393n8, 527n11

Eckhart, Johann Georg 163, 223
*Eléonore Desmiers d'Olbreuse (1639–1722) Dowager Duchess of Braunschweig-Lüneburg-Celle 129n2, 131, 149, 179
letter from Leibniz 126–9
*Elisabeth Charlotte of the Palatinate (1652–1722), Duchess of Orléans (from 1671) 73, 281, 307, 343, 351n5, 373, 523, 549, 585, 725, 751, 751n11
*Elisabeth Christine of Braunschweig-Wolfenbüttel (1691–1750), Holy Roman Empress (from 1711) l, 25n4, 63, 71n10, 137, 149, 295, 353n24, 459, 629
Elisabeth Sophie Marie of Schleswig-Holstein-Senderburg-Norburg (1683–1767) 149
Epicurus (314–270 BCE) lxxxvii, 379, 635, 647, 657, 691, 711, 713, 779, 799, 803
and materialism 355, 357
Erasmus (1466–1536) 161n13
*Ernst August of Braunschweig-Lüneburg (1629–1698), Duke of Braunschweig-Lüneburg-Calenberg (Hanover) (1679, first Elector of Braunschweig-Lüneburg (Hanover) (1692) xxxvii, 223, 305, 311, 351, 353n23
*Ernst August II (1674–1728) of Braunschweig-Lüneburg, youngest son of Sophie of the Palatinate and Ernst August of Braunschweig-Lüneburg 95, 103, 105, 115, 293n8, 347, 609, 753

882 NAME INDEX

Erskine (Areskin), Robert (1677–1719)
  letter from Leibniz 622–5
*Eugène (Eugenio François di Savoia,
  1653–1736), Prince of Savoy-
  Carignan, Austrian Habsburg
  field-marshal and president of the
  Imperial War Council l, 41, 45, 53,
  69, 73, 97, 121, 135, 137, 155, 157, 167,
  175, 349, 719, 805

Fabri, Honoré (1608–88) 469/485n6, 509,
  511n13&n17
Fabrice, Weipart Ludwig von (1640–1724) 559
*Falaiseau, Pierre de (1649–1726) 281, 297, 363
*Fatio de Duillier, Nicolas (1664–1753) 35,
  35n4&n8, 441, 443n6
*Ferdinand Albrecht II (1680–1735), Prince of
  Braunschweig-Wolfenbütte-Bevernl,
  Duke of Braunschweig-Wolfenbüttel
  (from March 1735) 629, 727, 751
Fermat, Pierre (1607–1665) 479
Ferrari, Louis (1685–1733), count of 75
Fitton, Gerard (1663–1702), 3rd Earl of
  Macclesfield 129n3, 133
Fitzjames, James 113n9, 123
*Flamsteed, John 329, 467, 483, 499, 533, 585,
  617, 617n6, 721/723n34
*Fludd, Robert (1574–1637) 259, 275
Fontaine, Sir Andrew (1676–1753) 363
François Joseph de Lorraine (1670–5), Duke of
  Guise (from 1671) 349
*Friedrich I and III, Elector of Brandenburg
  (from 1688) and first King in Prussia
  (from 1701) 153, 287, 385, 393n8,
  497n4, 747n7
Friedrich IV (1671–1730), King of Denmark and
  Norway (from 1699) 559
*Friedrich Christian (1655–1728), Graf (Count)
  zu Schaumburg-Lippe (from
  1681) 631
Friedrich Karl von Schönborn (1674–1746) 97
*Friedrich Ludwig of Braunschweig-Lüneburg
  (1707–1751) 95, 203, 551, 609, 721,
  743, 751
*Friedrich Wilhelm I (1688–1740), King in
  Prussia (from 1713) 103, 143, 211,
  387, 495, 559, 585, 617, 745, 747n7

Galileo (1564–1642) 277, 784n
Gargan, Charles Nicolas (b.? d.?), secretary to
  Sophie of the Palatinate, Dowager
  Electress of Braunschweig-
  Lüneburg 73
*Gassendi, Pierre (1592–1655) 259
Gennaro, Saint 137, 139n9

*Georg August of Braunschweig-Lüneburg
  (1683–1760), Electoral Prince of
  Braunschweig-Lüneburg (Hanover)
  (from 1698), Prince of Wales
  (1714–27), Elector of Braunschweig-
  Lüneburg and King of Great Britain
  (from 1727) xxxviii, 25n4, 41, 41n3,
  45, 49, 53, 55n18, 59, 59n5, 61, 63,
  65n5, 67, 73, 89, 95, 133, 617, 721,
  731, 755
  letter from Leibniz 106–9
  letter from Queen Anne 51
*Georg Ludwig of Braunschweig-Lüneburg
  (1680–1727), Elector of
  Braunschweig-Lüneburg (Hanover)
  (from 1698), King George I of Great
  Britain (from 1714) xxxvii–xxxviii,
  xlvi, lix, lix, lxiii, lxxviii, lxxxiv, 25, 29,
  41n3, 53n4, 53, 59, 61, 63, 65n7, 67,
  75, 93, 95, 97, 99, 101, 109, 113n11,
  127, 133, 143, 149, 153, 163, 167, 171,
  179, 189, 189, 211, 213, 221, 231, 243,
  249, 265, 279, 285, 289, 291, 333, 385,
  387, 455, 495, 497, 519, 523, 549, 555,
  583, 585, 585, 605, 609, 615, 627, 719,
  835, 837
  letter from Queen Anne 48–51
*Georg Wilhelm of Braunschweig-Lüneburg
  (1624–1705), Duke of Celle (from
  1665) 127, 131
George (Jørgen) (1653–1708), Prince of
  Denmark and consort of Queen
  Anne 617
Giuseppe, Giovanni, Marquis Orsi
  (1652–1733) 805, 807, 807n7
Gregory, David (1659–1708) 619
*Gregory, James (1638–75) 423, 427, 439, 475
*Guericke, Otto von (1602–1686) 587, 603n2, 673
Gwynne, Rowland (1658–1726) 365

Habakkuk 655, 709
Hall, Joseph (1574–1656), Bishop of Exeter
  (1627–41), Bishop of Norwich
  (1641–56) 523/527n11, 549
Halley, Edmond (1656–1742) 483, 621
Harcourt, Simon (1661–1727), 1st Viscount
  Harcourt, Lord High Chancellor of
  Great Britain (1713–14) 43, 61, 65n7
*Harley, Robert (1661–1724), 1st Earl of Oxford
  (from 1711) 43, 47n3, 51n3, 55n16,
  65n7, 67, 93, 177n8, 287
Harley, Thomas (c.1667–1738), Tory MP
  (1698–1715) 43, 65n7
Harrach, Aloys Thomas Raimund, Count von
  (1669–1742) 251

NAME INDEX 883

*Hartsoeker, Nicolass (1656–1725) xxxvi, 17
  letter from Leibniz 4–15
Henri IV (1553–1610), King of France (from
  1589) 345
*Hermann, Jakob (1678–1733) 401, 405n11,
  451, 461, 499, 785n
Hermanszoon, Jakob (1560–1609) 395n9
*Herrenhausen xlii, lxiii, 61, 105, 121,
  149, 563
*Hobbes, Thomas (1588–1679) 155, 355, 467
Hocher, Johann Paul Freiherr von (1616–83),
  Court Chancellor to Emperor
  Leopold I 735
Homer (fl. 8th century BCE) 265, 279, 283, 297
Hooke, Robert (1635–1703) 483,
  489n4, 525n4
Horace (65 BCE–8 BCE) 483
Huldenberg, Daniel Erasmi von (1660–1733),
  Hanoverian ambassador to
  Vienna 25n4
Hutton, John (d. 1712) 365
*Huygens, Christiaan (1629–95) 255, 325, 327,
  475, 481, 643

Jablonski, Daniel Ernst (1660–1741) 385, 393n8,
  495, 497n4, 501
Januarius, *see* Gennaro, Saint
Jaquelot, Isaac (1647–1708) 15, 15n3, 699, 825
Jauernig, Anja lxxxix note 90
Jesus Christ lxiv, 3, 239, 287, 729
*Johann Friedrich (b. 1625, d. 1679); Duke of
  Braunschweig-Lüneburg-Calenberg
  (Hanover), 1665–79 25n4, 311
Johann Wilhelm (1658–1716), Elector
  Palatine 71n10
*Johanne Sophie, Gräfin (Countess) zu
  Schaumburg-Lippe
  (1673–1743) xxxviii, lvi, 61, 89, 265,
  299, 331, 537
  letters from Leibniz 186–9, 210–13, 284–9
  letter to Baroness (later Countess) Mary
    Cowper concerning the death of
    Sophie of the Palatinate, Dowager
    Electress of
    Braunschweig-Lüneburg 57–9
  letter to Louise, Raugravine Palatine
    concerning the death of Sophie of the
    Palatinate, Dowager Electress of
    Braunschweig-Lüneburg 78–87
*Jones, William (1675–1749) 455, 483
Joseph, Count of Corswarem 741
*Joumard, René Godefroy Louis Ernest Joseph,
  so-called Prince of Linange
  729/733n8
Jurieu, Pierre (1637–1713) 359

Karl I (1654–1730), Landgrave of Hesse-Cassel
  (from 1670) 211
Karl V (1500–58), Holy Roman Emperor (from
  1519) 181
*Karl VI (1685–1740), Holy Roman Emperor
  (from 1711) xxxvii, xxxix, 25n4, 67,
  71n10, 73, 99, 101, 103, 107, 111, 135,
  141, 221, 243, 245, 285, 291, 293, 305,
  349, 353n24, 727, 729, 735, 739, 741
Karl XII (1682–1718), King of Sweden (from
  1697) 211, 285, 363, 745
Karl Joseph of Lorraine (1680–1715),
  Archbishop-Elector of Trier (from
  1711) 347, 349, 351n15
Karl I Ludwig (1617–1680), Elector Palatine 155
*Keill, John (1671–1721) xxxv–xxxvi, li,
  lvii–lviii, lxxi, 29, 33n4, 35, 37n8,
  37n9, 79, 91, 407, 417, 419, 421, 423,
  425, 437, 455, 469, 481, 493, 525n3,
  527n5, 547, 579
  letter to John Chamberlayne rebuffing
    Leibniz's letter to John Chamberlayne
    of 21 April 1714 93
Kepler, Johannes (1571–1630) 651, 703,
  787n, 827
*Ker, John (1673–1726) 53, 67/69n2, 73, 173
Khamara, Edward lxxxvii note 87
*Kielmansegg (1675–1725), Sophie
  Charlotte, Freiin (Baroness)
  von 725, 729, 837
King, Gregory 363
King, William (1650–1729), Archbishop of
  Dublin (from 1703) lxxxiii, 763
Kinsky, Stephan Wilhem (1679–1749) 251
*Klenk (Klencke), Charlotte Elisabeth von
  (1685–1748), Lady of the Golden Key
  (First Lady-In-Waiting) to the
  Dowager Empress Wilhelmine
  Amalie xli, l, lxxxiii, 175
  letters from Leibniz 104–5, 146–51,
    242–3, 738–9
  letters to Leibniz 248–51, 292–5, 740–3
Klopp, Ono liv, lxxxiv
Königsmarck, Philip Christoph, Count von
  (1665–1694) 135n5

*Lahontan, Louis-Armand de Lom d'Arce, Baron
  de (1666–1715) 281, 559, 561n14,
  585, 729
Lamy, François (1636–1711) 15
*Langallerie, Philippe de Gentils, Marquis de
  (1661–1717) 729, 751
Le Clerc, Jean (1657–1736) 749
Leeuwenhoek, Antonie van
  (1632–1723) 255, 257

884 NAME INDEX

Leibniz
calculating machine 151, 625, 805, 807n5
First Paper for Clarke lxvi, 316–19
Second Paper for Clarke 354–61
Third Paper for Clarke 408–17
Fourth Paper for Clarke 562–73
Fifth Paper for Clarke 660–715
proposed additions to his Fourth
Paper 572–5
request for position of historiographer of
Great Britain liii–lvi, lviii, lx, lxxxiv,
171, 175, 183, 207, 209, 223, 225, 235,
237, 265, 627, 761
Lennox, Charles (1672–1723), 1st Duke of
Richmond (from 1675) 549
Leopold I, Holy Roman Emperor (1658–1705
(b. 1640) 41, 71n10
Léopold Clément Charles, hereditary prince of
Lorraine (1707–23) 75
Leopold Joseph Charles Dominque Agapet
Hyacinthe (1679–1729), Duke of
Lorraine (from 1690) 349/353n20
Léotaud, Vincent (1595–1672) 475/487n25
Lister, Martin (1639–1712) 483
*Locke, John (1632–1704) lvii, lxiii–lxiv, 5, 235,
239, 241, 265, 267n14, 279, 313, 316,
335, 339, 579
L'Hôpital, Guillaume François Antonie, Marquis
de (1661–1704) 511n13
Louis XIV (1638–1715), King of France
(1643–1715) 287/289n16,
291, 725n15
Louis Alexandre (1678–1737), Count of
Toulouse (1681) 725n15
Louis Auguste (1670–1736) Duke of Maine
(1673) 725n15
Louise (Luise) (1661–1733), Raugravine
Palatine,
letter from Johanne Sophie, Gräfin (Countess)
zu Schaumburg-Lippe concerning the
death of Sophie of the Palatinate,
Dowager Electress of
Braunschweig-Lüneburg 104–14
Ludwig Rudolf of Braunschweig-Wolfenbüttel
(1671–1735) 151n7
Lütke, Julius (1650–1712) 393n8

Macanaz, Melchor de (1670–1760) 631n2
*Malebranche, Nicolas (1638–1715) 225, 331,
357, 491
Manuel de Bragança, Infante Manuel, Count of
Ourém (1697–1736) 719
Maria Anna of Neuburg (1667–1740), Queen
consort of Spain (1689–1700) 729,
733n16, 745, 751/753n15

Maria Josepha (1697–1757), Queen consort of
Poland (from 1734) 349
Marie Amalie of Brandenburg-Schwedt
(16701739), Duchess of
Saxe-Zeitz 153
Marot, Clément (1496–1544) 269
Masham, Lady Damaris Cudworth 239
Maximillian II Emanuel (1662–1726), Elector of
Bavaria 153
Maximilian Wilhelm (1666–1726), Electoral
Prince of Braunschweig-
Lüneburg 103, 291, 347, 351n16
Mazepa, Ivan Stepanovych (1639–1709) 745
Mercator, Nicholas (ca.1620–1687) 475
*Mersenne, Marin (1588–1648 259
Middleton, Charles (1650–1719), 2nd Earl of
Middleton 75, 97
Moivre, Abraham de (1667–1754) lxxxv, 329
*Molanus (van der Muelen), Gerhard Wolter
(1633–1722) 385, 389, 393n8, 497
Molière (Jean-Baptiste Poquelin,
1622–73) 311, 537
Molyneux, William (1656–1698) 239
Montagu, Charles (1661–1715), 1st Earl of
Halifax 281/283n10, 297
Mordaunt, Charles (1658–1735), 3rd Earl of
Peterborough (from 1697) 363
More, Henry (1614–87) 197, 691, 713n9
Moritz Wilhelm (16641718), Duke of Saxe-
Zeitz 151, 159
Morton, Thomas (1564–1659), Bishop of Chester
(1616–18), Bishop of Durham
(1632–46) 522, 527n11
Murray, Anthony 363

Newton, Isaac (1643–1727) xxxv–xxxvi, xlviii,
l–liii, lv, lviii–lix, lxiv–lxvi, lxviii,
lxx–lxxiii, lxxv, lxxviii–lxxix,
lxxxiv–lxxxv, xcii–xcv, 5, 27, 29, 31,
33n4, 35n8, 77, 91, 201, 233, 237, 239,
269–277, 297, 313, 317–319,
323– 331, 335, 339, 347, 355–357, 361,
367, 373, 381, 401, 405n11, 407, 445,
451, 455, 459, 461, 467, 469–85, 491,
493, 499, 501, 503, 503–509, 513, 519,
521, 525n3, 533, 535, 543, 545–547,
549, 555, 557, 569, 577, 579–81, 583,
595, 597, 601, 605, 609, 611, 615.
617n6, 623, 627, 631, 643, 701, 715,
721, 739, 745, 747, 757, 775, 779, 786,
787, 795
letter from John Chamberlayne concerning
calculus dispute with Leibniz 37–9
letter from Antonio Schinella Conti 805–7
letter to Antonio Schinella Conti 417–43

letters to Des Maizeaus 835–7
letter to John Chamberlayne concerning
  calculus dispute with Leibniz 35–7
metaphysics narrow 327
unpublished draft letter to the editor of
  the *Memoirs of Literature*
  responding to Leibniz's letter
  to Hartsoeker 17–21
*Nicolson, William (1655–1727), Bishop of
  Carlisle (1702–18) 497, 549, 553n54,
  555, 631/633n8
Nigrisoli, Francesco Maria (1648–1727) 275,
  323, 485
*Nomis, Benedictus Andreas Caspar Baron de,
  Marchese della Banditella-Pelusi
  (b.? d. 1725?)
  letters to Leibniz 61–5, 93–7

Oeynhausen, Raben Christoph von 125,
  297, 343
Oldenburg, Henry (1615–1677) 427, 429, 439,
  455, 475, 477, 479
Orban, Ferdinand (1655–1732), Jesuit confessor
  of Elector Palatine Johann
  Wilhelm 71n10
Orsi, Giovanni Giuseppe 805, 807
Otto II (955–983), Holy Roman Emperor (from
  973) 743
Oxford, *see* Robert Harley*

Paget, Henry (ca. 1663–1743), 7th Baron Paget
  and 1st Earl of Uxbridge) 51
Pascal, Blaise (1623–62)
  calculating machine 805/807n5
Pell, John (1611–85) 475
*Peter I the Great (Pyotr Alekseyevich,
  1682–1725), Czar of Russia (from
  1682) 25n4, 141, 549/553n47, 559,
  585, 607, 617, 623, 745, 805, 827
*Philippe I, Duke of Orléans (1640–1701) 311
*Philippe II, Duke of Orléans (1674–1723) 285,
  289n16, 299, 373, 751
*Philippe V of Spain (1683–1746) 113n9, 285,
  289n16, 377n18, 631n2
Plato (429?–347 BCE) 155, 355, 405
*Pöllnitz, Henriette Charlotte von
  (1670–1722) lvii, 73, 105, 225, 237,
  253, 299, 535, 585, 631
  letter from Leibniz 604–5
  letter to Leibniz 234–5
Pope, Alexander (1688–1744) 265, 297, 309
Prior, Matthew 303n60, 311, 315n15, 363
*Pufendorf, Samuel (1632–94) 401, 403n9,
  405n10, 451, 465
Pythagoras (ca. 570–495 BCE) 355

Querini, Giacomo marchese de 331
Quinault, Philippe (1635–88) 311

Racine, Jean (1639–99) 299, 311
Ray, John (1627–1705) 483
Régnier, Mathurin (1573–1613) 299
*Rémond, Nicolas (1638–1725), chief counselor
  to the Duke of Orléans in Paris 277,
  319, 493, 501, 505, 577
  letters from Antonio Schinella Conti
  concerning Newton 269–75
  letters from Leibniz 206–209, 320–1, 330–3,
  456–9, 490–3, 626–9, 756–7
  letters to Leibniz 204–5, 230–1, 268–9,
  444–5, 748–9
Riccati, Jacopo Francesco (1676–1754) 461, 499
Rinaldo d'Este (1655–1737), Duke of Modena
  (from 1694) 503
*Roberval, Giles Personne de (1602–75) 11, 17,
  19, 21n2, 201, 258
  and attraction of bodies 11, 17
*Robethon, John (d. 1722), minister to Georg
  Ludwig of Braunschweig-Lüneburg
  (later King George I of England) 75
Robinson, John (1650–1723), Bishop of London
  (from 1714) 389, 555
*Roche, Michel de la (*c.* 1680–1742) lxi, lxii, 225,
  229, 331
Rodriguez-Pereyra, Gonzalo lxxxix, lxxxviii
  note 89, lxxxix note 90
Rolet, Charles 155/161n15
Rudbeck, Olaus (1630–1702) 281, 309
Rupert (1619–82), Count Palatine of the Rhine,
  Duke of Cumberland and Earl
  Holderness (from 1644) 483

*St John, Henry (1678–1751), 1st Viscount
  Bolingbroke (1712), minister under
  Queen Anne 47n3, 53, 55n16,
  297/303n58, 311/315n14
Savage, Richard, 4th Earl Rivers
  (1654–1712) 363/365n9
Schaftesbury, Anthony Ashley Cooper, 3rd of
  (1671–1713) 717, 719n12
Schlick, Leopold Anton Joseph (1663–1723),
  Count von 249
Schöttel, Theobald, imperial chaplain to Karl
  VI 1, 739, 741
*Schulenburg, Ehrengard Melusine von der
  (1667–1743) 631
*Schulenburg, Johann Matthias von der
  (1661–1747) xliv–xlvii, 65n1, 285,
  295, 727
  letters from Leibniz 124–5, 138–41, 166–9
  letters to Leibniz 146–7

886 NAME INDEX

Schütz, Georg Wilhelm Sinold (1683–1740),
    Hanoverian envoy to England
    (1710–14) 39, 41, 45, 61, 65n7
Scudéry, Madeleine de (1607–1701) 655
*Sebastiano, Vittorio Amedeo (1666–1732),
    Duke of Savoy (1675–1730, King of
    Sicily (1713–20) 109, 115, 119, 727
*Seeländer, Nicolaus 253, 265n4&n5, 279
Shaftesbury, Anthony Ashley Cooper, 3rd Earl
    of 239, 717, 719n13
Sharp, John (1645–1715), Archbishop of York
    (from 1691) 229
*Sinzendorff, Philipp Ludwig Wenzel (Count)
    von (1671–1742), court chancellor to
    Emperor Karl VI xxxix–xliii, xlviii, l,
    103, 115, 157, 251
    letter to Friedrich Wilhelm von Görtz 98–9
    letter to Johann Caspar von Bothmer 98–9
    letter from Leibniz 118–19
    letter to Leibniz 100–1
Skowronska, Marta Helena (1684–1727),
    Catherine I, Empress consort of
    Peter I the Great (1721–5) 745
*Sloane, Hans (1660–1753), editor of the
    Philosophical Transactions of the
    Royal Society (1695–1713) xxxv, 29,
    35n7&n8, 331, 483
Smalridge, George (1662–1719), Bishop of
    Bristol (from 1714) lxi, lxiii,
    225/324n2
    letter to Caroline of Brandenburg-Ansbach,
    Princess of Wales 215–21
    Leibniz's response to 226–31
*Spanheim, Ezechiel (1629–1710) 385, 393n8
Spedazzi, Giuseppe, imperial cryptanalyst 741
*Spinoza, Baruch (1632–77) 359, 463, 533
Stafford, *see* Wentworth
*Stanhope, James, (1673–1721), 1st Earl of
    Stanhope (1718) 627, 629, 717,
    719, 761
*Steffani, Agostino (1654–1728) lxx, 375, 513
Stepney, George (1663–1707) 311
Stillingfleet, Edward (1635–99), Bishop of
    Worcester (1689) lxiii, 5, 265,
    267n14, 279
Strickland, Lloyd lxii note 43
Strimesius, Johann Samuel
    (1684–1744) 393n8, 403n9
*Stuart, James Francis Edward, the Old
    Pretender (1688–1766) lxxxv note
    41n3, 47n3, 65n7, 67, 69, 75, 85, 95,
    113n11, 291, 299, 311, 363, 743
*Sophie of the Palatinate (1630–1714), Duchess
    of Braunschweig-Lüneburg-
    Calenberg (Hanover) (1679–92),

Electress of Braunschweig-Lüneburg
    (Hanover) (1692–8) xxxvii, xxxviii,
    41n3, 53, 61, 63, 65n7, 67, 73, 75, 103,
    127, 129, 131, 203n3, 375, 467n8, 563
    death of xxxviii, 57–9, 61–63, 73, 79–87,
    87–89, 303
    letter from Leibniz 38–43
    letter from Queen Anne 48–9
*Sophie Charlotte of Braunschweig-Lüneburg
    (1668–1705), Electress of
    Brandenburg (1688), first Queen of
    Prussia (1701) 203n3
Sophie Dorothea of Braunschweig-Lüneburg
    (1687–1757), Queen of Prussia
    and Electress of Brandenburg
    (from1713–31) 135n5, 745, 747n7
*Sophie Dorothea of Braunschweig-Lüneburg-
    Celle (1666–1726) 135n5, 747n7
Sutton, Robert (1662–1723), 2nd Baron
    Lexington (from 1668) 363
Swammerdam, Jan (1637–80) 259
Sydenham, Thomas (1624–1689) 483

Talbot, Adelhida Paleotti (1660–1726) Duchess
    of Shrewsbury (from 1705)
    513/517n53
Temple, Richard 1st Viscount Cobham, 165
*Tenison, Thomas (1616–1715), Archbishop of
    Canterbury (1695–1715) 145,
    389/397n15
Theophanu (ca. 955–991), Holy Roman Empress
    consort (973–83) 745
*Tillotson, John (1630–94), Archbishop of
    Canterbury (1691–94) 145, 217, 229,
    265, 373
*Torricelli, Evangelista (16081647) 277, 557,
    603n2, 673
Tschirnhaus, Ehrenfried Walther von
    (1651–1708) 479, 487n32, 537n5
Turrettini, François (1623–1687) 401

*Ursinus, Benjamin (1646–1720) 385,
    393n8, 497n4

Vallisneri, Antonio (1661–1730) 255, 257
Varignon, Pierre (1664–1722) 491
Villars, Claude Louis Hector, duc de
    (1653–1734) 225

*Wake, William (1657–1737), Bishop of Lincoln
    (1705–1716), Archbishop of
    Canterbury (from 1716) lxi,
    lxiii–lxiv, lxx, lxxviii, 297, 373,
    389/397n16, 513/515n9, 523, 583,
    585, 615

NAME INDEX 887

*Wallis, John (1616–1703) 323, 421, 423, 427, 429, 441, 481
Wentworth, Thomas (1672–1739), 1st Earl of Stafford 95
Westfall, Richard lxxvi
Whiston, William 329, 329n10
Whitworth, Charles (1675–1725) 79
*Wilhelm Friedrich 139, 149
*Wilhelmine Amalie of Braunschweig-Lüneburg (1673–1742), Holy Roman Empress (1705–11) xli, l, lix, lxxxiii, 25n4, 39, 45, 69, 71n10, 171, 175, 181, 243, 293, 307, 739, 741
   letters from Leibniz 100–3, 244–9, 732–7
William (1689–1700), Duke of Gloucester 133n4
William III, King of England, Ireland, and Scotland (1689–1702, b. 1650) 111, 127, 129n2, 131
Windischgrätz, Ernst Friedrich (Count) von (1670–1727), president of the Imperial Aulic Council xxv, xlii–xliii, xlviii, 247
   letter from Leibniz 112–17

Winckler, Johann Joseph (1670–1722), deacon of Magdeburg Cathedral (from 1698) 387, 393n7&n8
Wishart, James (1658–1723), admiral and British Commander-in-Chief of the Mediterranean 111, 123
Wolff, Christian (1679–1754) lvii–lviii, lxvi, lxviii, 487n10, 805
Woodward, John (1665–1728) 331, 483
Worsley, Henry (1672–1740) 363, 365n9
*Wotton, William (1666–1727) 27, 29, 171, 331, 483
*Wren, Christopher (1632–1723) 327, 483

*Zendrini, Bernardino (1679–1747) 263, 461, 499
Zenobia (d. c.275), Queen of the Palmyrene Empire 135
Zollmann (Zollman), Philipp (Philip) Heinrich (Henry) (b. before 1690, d. 1748) 615, 715
   letter from Des Maizeaux 612–613
Zwingli, Huldrych (1484–1531) 3, 397n17

Subject Index

Entries marked with an asterisk refer to items also found in the starred references

Act for the Naturalization of the Most Excellent
  Princess Sophia, Electress and
  Dowager of Hanover, and the Issue of
  her body (1705) 59n5, 83n5
*Act of Settlement (1701) xxxvii, liv, 111, 129,
  133, 173n11
*An Account of the Book entitled Commercium
  Epistolicum* 195–99
Anglican church/religion 143, 145, 173, 177,
  225, 287, 389, 391n1, 397n17, 561n13
animal(s)
  divine 639, 677
  generation/origin of 255, 257, 275, 323, 571,
    601, 657, 797
    presupposes divine preformation
      657, 707
  infertility of 447
  motion of 433, 437, 599, 603
    explained by natural forces 571, 657
    mechanical 599, 603, 657, 707, 797
    miraculous 545, 599
  seminal 371
Annales Imperii Occidentis Brunsvicenses,
  Leibniz's history of the House of
  Braunschweig-Lüneburg xxxvii, xlvi,
  xlix, lix, 29n2, 163/165n4, 169–171,
  181, 185, 207, 213, 223, 231–3, 245,
  291, 305, 349–51, 459, 499, 519, 609,
  627, 721, 735, 747
atoms xxxvi, lxxiii, lxxvi, c–cii, 7, 9, 11, 13, 319,
  325, 327, 425, 529, 557, 603, 637, 657,
  669, 691, 711, 739, 757, 799
  destroyed by the principle of sufficient reason/
    identity of indiscernibles 13, 563,
    657, 757
  hardness of 11, 13, 19, 669
    as an occult quality 11, 19
Augsburg Confession lxv, 3, 5, 145, 173, 177,
  239, 403n9

Barcelona, Siege of 111, 113n9, 123, 125, 141
Barrier Treaty 67/69n7, 141, 285
best, principle of the
  used by Samuel Clarke 461
body/matter 269, 273, 339, 355–7

acts mechanically, according to efficient
    causes 699
  and soul 197, 215, 269, 271, 319, 357, 569,
    599, 697, 699, 787, 795, 825, 829, 831
  cohesion of parts 7–9
  degrees of fluidity and tenacity 13
  divisible 271, 771
  duration of 19
  extension of 19, 677
  essence of 819
  gravitational (that which causes gravity, not
    heavy) 327, 675, 771
  gravity an essential property of 257–9
  infinitely divided 529, 607, 635, 669
  mobility of 19, 769
  prime 821
  quantity of
    not limited 413, 567, 597, 601, 639, 649,
      673, 693, 769, 789
    depends on will of God 769
  resistance of 593, 639, 673, 771, 789
  self-organizing 323
  subtle 323
  well-founded phenomenon 327
*Bremen 281, 285, 299, 311, 315n27, 559

calculating machine
  of Leibniz 151, 625, 805/807n5
  of Pascal 805/807n5
calculus dispute xxxv–xxxvi, xlviii, li–liii,
  lvii–lviii, lviii, lxvi, lxxviii, 27/29/31,
  35, 37–9, 77–9, 91–2, 237, 319, 361,
  367, 407–9, 417–43, 455, 469–89, 493,
  503, 503–11, 519, 521–3, 525n3, 555,
  557–9, 609, 615, 835–7
Cartesians 273, 325, 329, 357, 673, 695, 783n
cause
  efficient 199n, 255, 399, 447, 611, 699, 711,
    793n, 797
  final 255, 275, 385n, 399, 699, 711, 825
    agents act according to 699, 711
    consistent with freedom 699
  God as 697
  mechanical 699, 711
  of infertility 447

SUBJECT INDEX 889

Clélie 659n26
chance lxxxvii, 597, 647, 661, 691, 779
Charta Volans (1713) 417/419n4, 419/421n4,
  425/429n4, 437/443n4, 471/487n10,
  493/495n6, 507/511n10, 521/525n3,
  547n2, 619
coaction 661
comets 553, 797
Commercium Epistolicum xxxv–xxxvi, li–lii,
  31/33n7, 37n9, 91, 195, 271, 319, 323,
  361/365n3, 367/369n2, 417, 419, 423,
  425, 437, 439, 443, 455, 469, 471, 475,
  479, 481, 493, 507, 525n3&n5,
  809, 837
contingency 399, 445, 449, 661
contingents 399
  analysis goes to infinity 261
  certainty and infallibility in 663
  existence of owed to principle of the
    best 663
  future 661
contradiction/identity, principle of
  foundation of mathematics 355
  principle of essences 663

De Æquilibrio 355
De Æquiponderantibus 11
De origine Francorum 491
Dictionaire Historique et Critique 840
Die durchleuchtige Syrerinn Aramena
  659n27, 715n29
*Discours sur la théologie naturelle des
  Chinois* 459
Dordrecht, Synod of (1618–19) 387, 395n9
duration 541, 593, 595, 597, 599, 601, 645,
  649, 651, 677, 683, 693, 705, 773,
  775n, 791
dynamics lxxxvi, 235, 327, 355, 453, 461, 499,
  581, 701

Emperor of the Moon 637, 669
essences 447, 533, 663
  founded on necessity 261, 663
  time and space pertain to 575
Eucharist xlixn21, lxii, lxv, 3, 5, 239,
  393n8, 397n17
existence/existing things
  dependent on wisdom, fitness, and
    choice 465, 663
Evangelical 3, 145n3, 175n12, 287, 343, 345,
  393n5&n8, 397n17, 497n4
  belief that Christ's participation in the
    Eucharist is real 3
Evil
  moral 255

physical would not exist for rational creatures
  without moral evil 255
privative nature of 227
experiments lxxvi–lxxvii, 417, 419, 421, 425,
  427, 431, 433, 435, 439, 473, 515, 523,
  537, 549, 557, 617, 673, 795, 795,
  799, 827
crucial 327, 437
extension 19, 271, 345, 565, 649
  monads lack 669
  of creatures/bodies 645, 651, 653, 675, 677,
    705, 771, 773
  of God 463
  of souls/minds/spirits 503 641, 681, 701
  of universe/matter 671, 691, 693
  point the foundation of 261

Fatalism lxxxvi, 379, 413, 633, 661, 665, 781
  Fatum Christianum 665
  Fatum Mahometanum 665
  Fatum Stoicum 665
Force/power lxxxvi, xcviii–xcix, 197, 199nn2–4,
  235, 355, 599, 647, 653, 699, 701, 707,
  781, 787, 789, 819, 821, 823. 827
  and quantity of motion 701, 783n, 787, 789
  centrifugal 769
  conserved lxvi, 317, 647, 701, 787
  decreases/increases 401, 543, 571, 581, 601,
    611, 701, 783, 789
  elastic 327, 787, 819
  electrical 197, 327
  gravitational, *see* gravity/attraction
  magnetic 327
  mechanical xcix, 603

God 17–21
  argument for the existence of and principle of
    sufficient reason 355
  can/cannot act without reason lxxxvii, 411,
    415, 539, 541, 545, 557, 563, 567, 591,
    607, 647, 689, 691
  cause of the world 13, 449
  chooses the best 255, 259, 261, 461, 649, 663,
    665, 691, 693, 829
  conservation
    of world and creatures lxvii, xcvi, 325, 359,
      383, 415, 569, 695, 797
    of original forces 341
  corporeal 313, 317, 339
  does/does not limit the quantity of
    matter 567, 597, 601, 649, 673, 691,
      693, 769, 789
  duration of 541
  eternity of 399, 449, 645, 653, 683, 705, 771
    consists in necessity 399, 449

890 SUBJECT INDEX

God (*Continued*)
  identical with time 677, 683, 771, 772, 791
  independent of time 653, 705
  existence of
    causes space/time 773, 779
    not in space and time 773
  extended 319
  foresight/foreknowledge/
    pre-ordination of 383
  and future contingents 661
  does not derogate from liberty 663
  goodness of 217, 413, 431
  governance of the world xcvi, 341, 359, 367,
    383, 385, 577, 581, 597, 599, 797
  immensity of 539, 541, 645, 653, 675, 677,
    683, 705, 771
    identical with space, or not 409, 539,
      677, 771
    independent of space 645, 651, 705
  intelligentia supramundana 13, 197, 273, 325,
    341, 359, 361, 383, 413, 425, 431, 433,
    437, 505, 543, 569, 577, 581, 771,
    809, 819
  love of 665
  not determined by external things 567,
    649, 691
  of the Stoics 639, 677
  omnipresence/ubiquity of 273, 339, 381, 383,
    431, 541, 543, 593, 601, 641, 771, 773
  omnipotence of 649
  perception/knowledge of things
    by his immediate presence in space or
      rather by his operation 339, 357, 381,
      413, 569, 599, 695, 697, 781
  perfection of lxvii–lxviii, lxxiii, lxxvii,
    lxxxvi–lxxxvii, xc–xci, 335, 367, 373,
    529, 545, 557, 563, 567, 581, 591, 597,
    657, 665, 667, 697, 789
  permits evil 229
  power 313, 319, 327, 357, 359, 379, 381, 413,
    431, 451, 595, 663, 693
  presence and activity in the world xcv–xcvii,
    341, 383, 415, 425, 543, 569, 599
  providence of 359, 633, 661, 665, 797
  soul of the world xcv, 13, 197, 325, 345, 359,
    383, 425, 431, 433, 505, 569, 577, 579,
    599, 653, 695, 697, 701, 707, 781, 809
  spatial parts of 327, 639, 677, 683
  understanding of
    region of eternal truths 449
  will of 9, 199, 215, 379, 401, 413, 449, 465,
    539, 541, 545, 563, 567, 595, 649, 657,
    663, 693, 731, 739, 759, 765, 767, 769,
    769, 779, 799, 803
    morality depends on 401, 465

as sufficient reason lxxvii, lxxxi, lxxxvi,
  lxxxviii, 379, 539, 541, 591, 597, 731,
  739, 765, 767, 769, 799
wisdom of lxxxix, 217, 313, 319, 327, 357,
  359, 381, 383, 413, 431, 447, 449, 465,
  531, 581, 597, 637, 663, 667, 687, 691,
  759, 779, 829
*Görtz, Friedrich Wilhelm (1647–1728), chief
  minister in Hanover after 1714
  xxxix–xliii, xlviii, 95, 103, 111, 113,
  221, 225, 305
  letter from Leibniz 189–91
  letter from Philipp Ludwig Wenzel (Count)
    von Sinzendorff 98–101
grace 307, 459
  Jansenists and 307
  Jesuits and 309, 333
  miracles worked for the needs of 313, 319
gravity/attraction xxxvi, lxiv–lxv, 5, 17–19,
  195–197, 199n6&n7, 237, 257, 271,
  273, 319, 325, 327, 425, 429, 473,
  581, 653, 655, 675, 707, 709, 793,
  797, 799
  and immediate operation and presence in the
    Eucharist 5
  and planetary motion 13, 17–19, 195, 797
  and miracles xxxvi, xcvii–c, 11, 13, 17, 19,
    197, 319, 429, 571, 581, 603, 653, 655,
    793, 809, 829
  at a distance xxxvi
    a contradiction xcvii–c, 603, 655, 709
  cannot be explained by powers of
    creatures 709
  cause of 195, 199n6&n7, 273, 797, 819
  essential property of bodies 197
  mechanical/not mechanical 197, 273,
    797, 819
  occult quality xxxvi, 11, 19, 197, 325, 327,
    653, 655, 709, 797, 809
  primitive quality 11
Guarantee for the Protestant Succession to the
  Crown of England, Treaty of 67/69n8

harmonic circulation of celestial bodies 533
harmony, pre-established 13, 197, 273, 277, 313,
  319, 319, 359, 425, 427, 433, 435, 439,
  473, 569, 599, 697, 697, 699, 701, 705,
  781, 795, 825, 827, 829
  proof of God's existence 697
hypotheses 401, 417, 419, 421, 425, 427, 431,
  433, 435, 437, 439, 463

I trionfi del fato (1695) 517n62
identity/contradiction, principle of 663
infinitesimals 525n3, 595, 641

SUBJECT INDEX 891

Imperial Society of Sciences in Vienna xxxvii,
xliii, xlix, l lix. 25n4,119, 135, 157,
167, 243, 247, 251, 293, 735, 737
indiscernibles lxxxviii–lxxxix, 411, 563, 565,
567, 591, 637, 645, 647, 667, 669, 671,
687, 689, 691, 765, 767, 768
principle of identity of lxxxviii–lxxxix, 563
induction 417, 419, 421, 425, 431, 433, 439, 473
inertia 19, 227, 703, 789, 827
infinities
some larger than others 465
Iroquois 43n4

Jacobite uprising 285/289n12, 291, 311, 363
Jansenists
on nature of grace 307
Jesuits
in China 465

Le Système du Monde d'après Aristarque de Samos
(1644) 11, 17
liberty 663, 699, 763, 799
loadstone 13

materialism 339, 341, 355, 359
metaphysics 637
and materialism 355, 379
and mathematics 379, 409, 463, 539
miracles xcvii–c, 9, 11, 17–19, 21n1, 199, 313,
319, 327, 347, 361, 423–429, 433–435,
439, 545, 571, 577, 581, 653, 705, 707,
709, 791
and origin of plants and animals xcix, 707
and planetary motion xcix, 9, 11, 17–19, 601,
707, 709
angelic 571, 603, 655, 709, 709, 793, 797
exceed all powers of creatures xcvii, 415, 473,
545, 571, 577, 581, 653, 705, 707, 709
natural and rational vs. supernatural 11
relative to our conceptions of things xcvii,
383, 415, 577, 581, 653, 707, 791
unusual effects of God's power xcvii–xcviii,
545, 577, 581, 601, 705, 707, 791
wrought not for the needs of nature, but those
of grace lxvi, xcvii, 313, 319
monads/simple substances 259, 473, 647, 669,
699, 821
living mirrors of the universe 697, 699,
781, 831
primitive 259
without extension 669
without parts 669
motion
animal 197, 273
conspiring 7, 9, 197, 273, 319

perpetual 313, 317
principles of 341
real/absolute xci–xcii, 595, 643, 685, 775
relative xci–xcii, 595, 643. 685, 769, 775
motives 563, 591, 633, 647, 657, 661, 663, 665,
667, 691, 731, 759, 763, 765, 799

nature 329
laws of 199, 313, 317, 325
mechanical 799
must be capable of being carried out by the
natures of creatures 325
order of 259
plastic 277
posterior by 261
prior by 251
realm of efficient causes 255
necessary things
analysis of terminates in primitive
notions 261
necessity 379, 445, 449, 661, 663, 781,
absolute/metaphysical 633, 649, 661, 663,
665, 693, 763, 767
hypothetical 661, 767
moral 633, 649, 661, 663, 693, 767
does not derogate from liberty 663
Nova methodus pro maximis et minimis lviii note
37, 241n6, 847

Octavia 353n24

part
less than the whole 263
resolution into vs. into notions 263
Petrovaradin, battle of 633n6, 727
Philosophiæ Naturalis Principia Mathematica/
principles of philosophy lxxxvi, 355,
469, 475, 477, 579, 643, 685
and metaphysical principles 355, 379, 409
opposed to materialism 339, 379
same as those of materialism 355
philosophy 319, 581
conjectural/hypothetical 273, 319, 433
experimental 195, 273, 319, 431, 433, 1152–3
approved by Leibniz 327, 431
natural xxxvi, xlix, 7
Newton and Leibniz differ with respect
to 197, 271–3, 319
of Locke 265
of Newton 17, 237, 319, 813
requires the principle of sufficient
reason lxxxvi, 355
plants 255
generation/origin of 275, 601, 707, 797
perception of 259

892   SUBJECT INDEX

plenum lxxii, lxxxii, 521, 529, 537, 605, 771
possibles 449, 651
    God chooses among 649, 663
*Principes de la nature et de la grâce, fondés en
    raison* 137/139n8, 157/163n20
Protestant churches, reunion of lxxi, 385–91,
    495–7, 501, 513, 523, 549, 55961, 585
*Pyrmont 59, 63, 79, 89, 121, 559, 585, 607, 615,
    617, 625, 627, 629, 631, 719

quality
    occult xxxvi, xcix, 11, 13, 19, 21n1, 199, 325,
        327, 417, 423, 425, 429, 433, 435, 439,
        473, 653, 655, 675, 707, 709, 797, 809
    destroyed by principle of sufficient
        reason 13
    primitive 257

*Rastatt, Treaty of 95, 155, 291
reformed religion 3, 85, 97, 143, 145,
    173/175n13, 387, 393n7, 395n9,
    397n17, 403n9, 561, 561n15
relations 575
religion natural xxxvi, xlix, lxiii, lxvi, lxix,
    lxxxvi, 313, 317, 813
*Réponse de M. Leibniz aux reflexions contenues
    dans la seconde édition du
    Dictionnaire Critique de M. Bayle,
    article Rorarius, sur le système d
    l'harmonie préétablie* 841
Royal Society of London xxxv, xlviii, xlix, 29,
    35, 37n9, 77, 91, 271, 325, 361, 421,
    439, 455, 457n17, 473, 505,
    525n3, 807n5
*Ryswick, Peace of (1697) 127, 131, 395n8

sensorium lxvi, xciv–xcv, 233, 313, 317, 319,
    325, 327, 339, 357, 381, 413, 425, 431,
    433, 495, 543, 567, 569, 577, 579, 601,
    647, 649, 693, 695 701, 715, 781,
    787, 809
Septennial Act (1716) 515/519n70
silkworms 401, 445, 461, 463, 499, 531, 535
Socinians 3, 359, 633, 661
Sorbonne, college of 701
Souls/minds 201, 255, 269, 271, 335, 345, 347,
    355, 473, 599, 651, 695, 821, 823
    act freely according to final causes 699
    and body 197, 215, 269, 271, 319, 357,
        569, 599, 697, 699, 787, 795, 825,
        829, 831
    corporeal lxvi, 313, 317
    extended 545, 641, 681, 689
    immaterial 347, 355, 579
    immortal 345

indivisible 345, 357, 381
living representations of the universe 345,
    697, 829, 831
perception/knowledge of 357, 381, 413, 569,
    599, 695, 697, 829, 831
presence of 357, 381, 413, 569, 599
rational 347
space 271, 539, 605, 809
    absolute xcii, 409, 459, 565, 575, 577, 581,
        595, 639, 643, 657, 671, 675, 683,
        685, 759
    eternal 409, 539, 565, 593
    immense 593
    immutable 565
    infinite 409, 539, 569
    Leibniz's argument against based on
        principle of sufficient reason
        lxxxvii–xc, 409–411, 567, 577, 607,
        645, 647, 759
    Clarke's response based on mere will of
        God lxxxvi–lxxxvii, 539, 541, 597
    and God's immensity xcii, 409, 539, 541, 565,
        645, 675, 677, 683, 705, 771, 791
    and matter 595, 689, 771, 779, 919
    and quantity 541, 597, 643, 685, 689, 703,
        775–7, 789
    as consequence of God's existence xciii, 539,
        593, 597, 601, 645, 705, 773, 779
    as God xcii, 327, 409, 539
    as God's organ of perception (sensorium)
        xciv–xcv, 233, 313, 317, 339, 357, 381
        495, 579, 581, 649, 693
    as property/attribute 565, 575, 593, 641, 771
        of limited substances 677
        of God xcii–xciv, 271, 539, 593, 639, 641,
        641, 645, 675, 677, 683, 771
    dependent/independent upon matter 779
    extramundane 459, 539, 565, 593
    ideal 327, 575, 607, 639, 645, 673, 683, 691,
        703, 705
    imaginary 459, 539, 565, 567, 593, 639, 673
    indivisible 271, 541, 595
    necessary for God's omnipresence 641
    not a substance 235
    not actual without things 691
    origin of the idea of 677–81
    parts of xci, 409, 565, 595, 639, 641, 683, 769,
        771, 773
        ideal 637, 671, 691
        immovable 595, 639, 671, 769, 771
        inseparable 541, 565, 575, 595,
        683, 771
    pertains to essences, not existing things 575
    place of all things 599, 651, 693, 779
    place of ideas 599, 695, 779

relative/order of coexisting lxxxvii, 233–6,
327, 409, 425, 459, 539, 541, 571, 575,
581, 595, 597, 601, 607, 645, 671, 703,
759, 769, 775, 791
Clarke's argument against based on possible
motion of entire material world
xc–xcii, 541, 595, 769, 773
Leibniz's response based on identity of
indiscernibles and principle of
sufficient reason xc–xcii, 565, 637,
643, 671, 683–5, 689
*Spanish Succession, War of (1701–14) 43n4,
289n16, 733n16
spontaneity 661, 765, 819
*States-General of the Republic of the Seven
United Netherlands 67, 69n7, 75,
109, 141
substance 259, 327, 461
created essence of 819–821
not devoid of matter 413, 645, 689
perception of 413
perceptive 339–41n
spiritual 13
thinking 269, 339–41n
sufficient reason, principle of lxxxi, lxxxvi, 13,
355, 379, 409, 459, 529, 533, 539, 563,
635, 637, 641, 645, 657, 663, 665, 667,
669, 671, 681, 691, 711, 731, 739, 747,
757, 759, 765, 767, 799
and indiscernibles lxxxvii–lxxxix, 563, 635,
637, 643, 647, 667, 669, 671, 691,
765, 767
enables demonstration in metaphysics,
natural philosophy, natural
theology lxxxvi, 355, 563, 657
enables demonstration of the existence of
God lxxxvi, 355, 635, 657, 711
ground of existences 663
refutes absolute space 411, 634, 639, 657, 681,
711, 739, 759
refutes absolute time 411, 639, 657
refutes atoms 13, 529, 563, 657, 691, 711,
739, 757
refutes influence between soul and body
657, 711
refutes mere will/indifference lxxvii, 411, 563,
591, 635, 637, 657, 667, 731, 739, 759
refutes scholastic attraction 657, 711
refutes void 13, 529, 563, 657, 711, 739, 757
Système nouveau de la nature et de la
communication des substances 840

Temesvar 629, 727, 741
Theodicy, xxxvi, xxxix, lx–lxvii lxx, lxxvii–lxxxii,
53, 121, 135, 203, 215–221 255, 279,

297, 309, 313, 331, 333, 335, 355, 367,
373, 375, 391, 401, 403n9, 405n10,
459, 465, 501, 505, 523, 557, 559, 563,
581, 583, 613, 615, 629, 633, 649, 661,
663, 689, 693, 699, 703, 717, 719, 721,
731, 739, 757, 803, 805
Thirty-Nine Articles of Religion 145
time 261, 399, 447, 605, 645, 657, 683, 809
absolute lxxxvii
Leibniz's argument against based on
principle of sufficient reason lxxxviii,
411, 541, 657, 685–7
Clarke's response based on mere will
of God 541
and God's eternity 645, 677, 683, 705
and motion 689
and quantity 595, 643, 685, 689, 703, 791
as consequence of God's existence 593, 601,
645, 705
as property of God 645, 677, 683
consists in contingency 399, 449
ideal 575, 581, 607, 639, 645, 673, 683,
685, 705
instant of 399, 411, 447, 637, 683
first 259, 261
parts of 769
ideal 637, 671
inseparable 575
pertains to essences, not existing things 575
relative/order of existing of incompatible, or
successive, things lxxxviii, 235, 327,
409, 425, 459, 541, 571, 575, 581, 595,
601, 607, 643, 645, 687, 703, 791
Clarke's argument against 541
Tories liv, lvi, 39, 45, 145, 167, 173, 177, 179,
181, 185, 189, 209, 211, 389, 743, 801
twins
efficient cause of 399, 447
rarity of 399, 447

unity 399, 445, 463
divisible but not resolvable 261
fractions are parts of 261
foundation of numbers 259, 261
universe/world 201, 261, 685–7
actual 449
cannot diminish in perfection 571, 703, 789
could/could not have been created at a
different time 411, 541, 563, 591,
595–7, 643, 645, 685–9, 779
could/could not have been created
elsewhere lxxxvi, 411, 541, 563, 593,
645, 689, 759
divine animal 639, 677
duration of limited 649, 693

894   SUBJECT INDEX

universe/world (*Continued*)
  eternity of 565, 595, 601, 607, 643, 693, 779
    not inconsistent with dependence on
      God 649, 693
  finite/moveable 593, 637, 643, 685, 769, 773, 779
  imperfections of 15
  perfection of 399, 447, 465, 531–3
    always increases 259, 261, 533, 649, 693
    hypothesis of the hyperbola 261, 399, 451, 463
    hypothesis of the rectangle 261, 399, 451,
      463, 465, 531, 533, 607
    hypothesis of the triangle 261, 451, 463
    never truly infinite 447
    remains constant 649
    truly infinite 465
    possible 449, 649, 829
    requires/does not require mending lxvi,
      313, 317, 319, 327, 359, 367, 381–3,
      401, 413, 425, 431, 433–4, 437, 525,
      571, 577, 577–9, 581, 611, 703, 705, 715
    souls are living representations of 345, 697,
      829, 831
*Utrecht, Treaty of (1713) 47n3, 363

vacuum (void) xxxvi, lxxiii, lxxvi, lxxvii, lxxxii,
  c–cii, 13, 259, 271, 275, 319, 325, 327,
  355, 425, 529, 537, 549, 557, 593, 605,
  637, 639, 641, 671, 673, 675, 677, 759,
  769, 797
  destroyed by principle of sufficient reason 13,
    529, 563, 657, 711, 739, 757
  of forms 329
Verden 281, 287n9, 315n22, 561n14
vortices 17, 21n1, 433, 611

*Westphalia, Treaty of 291, 293n8, 351n15
Whigs lv, lvii–lviii, 75, 145, 167, 177,
  179, 181, 185, 209, 211,
  519n70, 801
will 823
  free, not inconsistent with pre-established
    harmony 15
  indifference of 11, 823
  mere/without motive lxxvii, lxxxi, lxxxvi,
    379, 411, 413, 539, 563, 647, 691,
    731, 739, 765
  Zenta, battle of 41